TOM SCOTT CADDEN

D0117395

WHAT A BUNCH OF CHARACTERS!

AN ENTERTAINING GUIDE
TO WHO PLAYED WHAT IN THE MOVIES

PRENTICE-HALL, INC.,
Englewood Cliffs, New Jersey 07632

Library of Congress Cataloging in Publication Data

Cadden, Tom Scott.
    What a bunch of characters!

    Bibliography: p.
    Includes index.
    1. Moving-picture actors and actresses — United States —
Dictionaries.   I. Title.
PN1993.45.C23 1984   791.43′028′0922   84-3272
ISBN 0-13-951914-9
ISBN 0-13-951906-8 (A Reward book : pbk.)

☆ Thanks to Loretta, Tom, Holly, and Tim for their help.

---

10 9 8 7 6 5 4 3 2 1

Editorial/production supervision
and book design by Eric Newman
Cover design by Hal Siegel
Cover illustration by Debi Hoeffner
Manufacturing buyer: Pat Mahoney

This book is available at a special discount when ordered in
bulk quantities. Contact Prentice-Hall, Inc., General
Publishing Division, Special Sales, Englewood Cliffs, N.J. 07632.

.

ISBN 0-13-951914-9

ISBN 0-13-951906-8 {A REWARD BOOK : PBK.}

Prentice-Hall International, Inc., *London*
Prentice-Hall of Australia Pty. Limited, *Sydney*
Prentice-Hall Canada Inc., *Toronto*
Prentice-Hall of India Private Limited, *New Delhi*
Prentice-Hall of Japan, Inc., *Tokyo*
Prentice-Hall of Southeast Asia Pte. Ltd., *Singapore*
Whitehall Books Limited, *Wellington, New Zealand*
Editora Prentice-Hall do Brasil Ltda., *Rio de Janeiro*

Contents

To the Reader

PREFACE

Remember the first movie you ever saw? Mine was *Wings*—the super saga of American pursuit pilots in World War I and winner of the first Academy Award for Best Picture (1927/1928).

Directed by William A. Wellman, produced by Lucien Hubbard for Paramount, written for the screen by Hope Loring and Louis D. Lighton, and based on an original story by John Monk Saunders, *Wings* thrilled millions of moviegoers with its spectacular and realistic combat scenes. Even now, I still remember the spine-tingling excitement that gripped me as I stared wide-eyed at those ripsnorting dogfights: daredevil gladiators in goggles and streaming white scarves, zooming through the war-torn heavens in their trusty Spads, dueling hordes of deadly Huns in their vaunted Fokkers!*

And there were the *characters:*

JOHN (JACK) "SPEED" POWELL: A small-town boy who enlists in the U.S. Army Air Service during WWI and becomes one of America's leading air aces. (Played by Charles "Buddy" Rogers.)

DAVID ARMSTRONG: Powell's flying buddy who escapes from behind enemy lines in a stolen German plane but, when he's mistaken for a German pilot, is shot down by Powell. (Played by Richard Arlen.)

MARY PRESTON: The "girl next door" who goes to France as a Red Cross ambulance driver. (Played by Clara Bow.)

CADET WHITE: A fatalistic young flying cadet who crashes to his death at a flight training field in the U.S. (Played by Gary Cooper.)

To these memorable characters, as well as to the myriad other make-believe movie characters created through the years, and to the talented people who brought them to the screen, this book is fondly dedicated.

---

*Many years later (in 1974), Buddy Rogers and Richard Arlen, the stars of the movie, graciously granted me an interview to discuss these memorable flying sequences and some of their other memories of the making of *Wings*. Although much of the basic flying in the movie was done by U.S. Army pilots and cadets, and the extremely risky daredevil stunt flying and crashes were performed by veteran civilian stunt pilots and barnstormers, Rogers and Arlen actually did some of their own flying in some of the scenes. Rogers, prior to *Wings*, had come to Paramount directly from the University of Kansas and had to learn how to fly while making the film. Arlen was already an experienced pilot, having gone to Canada during World War I to earn his wings in the Royal Flying Corps. Both William A. Wellman, the movie's director, and John Monk Saunders, who wrote the story, were also ex–World War I flyers.

Imagine you're a contestant on a TV show called *The Mammoth Movie Quiz.*

"Give me the name," says the M.C., "of the character Humphrey Bogart played in *The Treasure of the Sierra Madre.*"

"Kid stuff," you chortle. "Fred C. Dobbs."

"Fred C. Dobbs!" the M.C. shouts. "Absolutely correct! And now," he continues breathlessly, "the Jumbo Jackpot question! What famous he-man, early in his career, played the role of Ace Wilfong?"

"Ace Wilfong?" you babble. Quickly you're whisked off the stage while the Jumbo Jackpot goes down the tube. But it might have gone into your *pocket* if you had read this book! It tells you that Ace Wilfong—a villainous gangster in the 1931 movie *A Free Soul*—was played by Clark Gable.

Ace Wilfong is just one of the more than 2600 famous (and not-so-famous) movie characters you'll find listed in *What a Bunch of Characters!* For example, there's larcenous circus owner Larson E. Whipsnade. (Who else but W. C. Fields?) And zany private eye Wolf J. Flywheel. (It has to be Groucho Marx!) And mild-mannered bank clerk Wilbert Winkle. (It can't be tough guy Edward G. Robinson—or can it?)

There are colorful ladies, too. Like Goldie, the sexy carnival high-diver. (Who else but Jean Harlow?) And Tira, the voluptuous lady lion-tamer. (It's got to be Mae West!) And Trigger Hicks, the fiery Ozark mountain gal. (It couldn't be sophisticated Katharine Hepburn—or could it?)

Of course, *What a Bunch of Characters!* isn't only for quiz contestants; it's for movie fans young and old, students and teachers of the cinema, writers and editors, researchers, librarians, nostalgia and trivia buffs, onomatomaniacs (name enthusiasts), and anyone else who might find it informative and entertaining.

What a Bunch of Characters! is a handy reference guide to "which actors portrayed which characters"—a listing of more than 2600 different movie roles that have been played on the screen by 50 of Hollywood's most famous stars. For instance, there are 28 characters listed for Marilyn Monroe, 66 for Clark Gable, 74 for Humphrey Bogart, and close to 150 for John Wayne. With each character listed, you'll find:

- A brief description of the character.
- The name of the movie in which the character appeared.
- The year the film was released.
- The name of the studio/company that released the film.
- The name of the film's director.
- The name of the film's producer, when known. (In some films of the '20s and early '30s, the individual producer was not credited.) In addition—in most cases—the name of the production (or co-production) *company*, if different from that of the *releasing* studio/company, is shown in parentheses following the individual producer's name.
- The names of the film's screenplay/story writers.
- The names of a number of the other actors/actresses in the cast.

You'll also find listed the *real* names of the stars. Some are as intriguing as the characters' names, like Spangler Arlington Brugh (Robert Taylor), or Archibald Leach (Cary Grant), or Hedwig Kiesler (Hedy Lamarr). In addition, each star's date and place of birth are given, and, where applicable, the date and place of death.

Chances are you're already familiar with a number of the classic screen characters, such as Vivien Leigh's Scarlett O'Hara, Clark Gable's Rhett Butler, Humphrey Bogart's Rick, and Ingrid Bergman's Ilsa. And perhaps you're knowledgeable about a great many more. But with *What a Bunch of Characters!* as your guide, you can become an "expert" on *thousands* of movie characters. It not only gives you the names of the characters the 50 stars played, it also describes who each character is and what he or she does in the movie. *What a Bunch of Characters!* is loaded with the kind of information that can help you answer questions like these:

- Is it true that the devil-may-care Clark Gable once played the part of a strait-laced laundryman? (Answer can be found on page 113.)
- In what detective picture did the likeable, boyish James Stewart turn out to be the murderer? (Answer can be found on page 266.)
- In which films did Bette Davis play twin sisters? (Answers can be found on pages 69 and 71.)
- Who was the famous World War I spy that Greta Garbo portrayed? (Answer can be found on page 122.)

- Which of Paul Newman's roles have earned him his six Academy Award nominations as Best Actor? (Answers can be found on pages 210, 211, 212, and 214.)
- What well-known actor played characters who were known by the following nicknames: The Mug, Bugs, Turkey, Baby Face, Rocks, and Gloves? (Answers can be found on pages 11, 12, 13, and 15.)
- What shapely blonde played a musician called Sugar Kane? (Answer can be found on page 208.)
- What lively blonde played a fan dancer known as Alabam' Lee? (Answer can be found on page 201.)
- In which of Robert Redford's movies was he an escaped convict called "Bubber"? (Answer can be found on page 234.)
- What famous singer played the teen-age sister of a naïve Texas farm boy who, after he's discovered hurling muskmellons with uncanny accuracy across a two-acre field, becomes the star passer on a college football team? (Answer can be found on page 123.)
- Ronald Reagan played lots of "good guys" in the movies, but in what film was he the "bad guy"? (Answer can be found on page 234.)
- What rugged male star portrayed characters named John in at least 37 different movies but also played characters with such offbeat names as Dare, Wedge, Quirt, Taw, and Cord? (Answers can be found on pages 301, 305, 311, and 312.)

Whether you use *What a Bunch of Characters!* as a reference book or browse through it just for fun, it's sure to stir up nostalgic memories of the characters you've seen on the screen—characters who were good guys, characters who were bad guys; characters who were good dames, characters who were bad dames; characters you loved, characters you hated; characters who made you laugh, characters who made you cry.

As for characters and movies in this book that you *haven't* seen but would like to—who knows? You may get the chance. With today's rapidly expanding technological and marketing developments in video cassettes, cable and pay TV systems, satellite transmission, optical fibers, and digital recording, an increasing number of these films should become available—in one form or another—for viewing.

In the meantime, use and enjoy *What a Bunch of Characters!* Start turning the pages and discover who the many characters are and who played them. Once you've become aware of the many and varied roles the actors have played—doctors, nurses, teachers, students, kings, queens, dancers, singers, priests, killers, wardens, convicts, flyers, cabbies, cowboys, Indians, soldiers, sailors, G-men, gangsters, aquanauts, astronauts, reporters, novelists, boxers, golfers, vampires, zombies—you will readily see that these 50 famous stars have indeed brought to the screen a truly remarkable bunch of characters!

ABOUT THIS BOOK

When the idea for *What a Bunch of Characters!* first came to me, I determined that the book should cover a representative cross-section of famous actors and actresses—some from the past and some from the present—who have had noteworthy film careers and who have played a variety of interesting characters. I also determined, based on what I felt was the best size and format for the book, that the number of stars included should not exceed 50. Deciding *which* 50, however, was not as easy; there were so many deserving actors and actresses to choose from. Nevertheless, after considerable agonizing over whom to include and whom to leave out, I finally managed (on a partially but not totally objective basis) to narrow the list down to the 50 representative stars you'll find in the book. They range from a classic horror-film star who began his movie career as an extra in 1916 (Boris Karloff) to a handsome leading man whose first screen appearance was in 1962 (Robert Redford); from a sexy blonde bombshell of the 1930s (Jean Harlow) to another sexy blonde bombshell of the 1950s (Marilyn Monroe); from a teen-age rock idol who became a star (Elvis Presley) to an ex–coal miner who became a star (Charles Bronson); from an actress who has won four Oscars (Katharine Hepburn) to an actor who never won an Oscar—but won an election to the presidency of the United States (Ronald Reagan).

You may find that some of your favorites have not been included. I sincerely hope, however, that you will enjoy reading about those stars who *have* been included.

In gathering the multitude of facts that I needed in order to make the thousands and thousands of individual entries in *What a Bunch of Characters!*, I utilized numerous sources of information. At times, some of them differed over such matters as the correct spelling of a name, or the correct title or release date of a film, or the proper production/writing credits for a film, or the authentic *real name* or birthdate of a star. In some instances, it was extremely difficult to ascertain which source was right. If, as a result, any discrepancies, oversights, or errors have found their way into the book, I offer my apologies and ask for the reader's forbearance and understanding.

A few explanatory notes:

Characters/Films
Although the stars' lists of characters basically cover all the feature films in which the stars appeared, the following have been excluded: certain movies in which the actors were only extras, a few relatively obscure foreign-made films, and a handful of others in which only the actors' voices were used. With a few exceptions, movies made for TV have also been excluded.

The majority of movies in which the stars merely played cameo roles or made guest appearances as themselves are noted. In most instances, however, such notations are made at the end of the stars' character/film lists and give only the title of the film, the name of the releasing studio/company, and the year the film was released.

Italics
Immediately following the descriptions of characters are lists of other actors in the cast. In these lists, italics are used to indicate those performers who received higher billing in the credits than the actors who played the characters just described. Naturally, early in some stars' careers, their billing was sometimes well below those of several other members of the cast.

Foreign-made Films
Foreign-made films, with a few exceptions, are listed only by their English-language titles and not their foreign-language titles.

Academy Awards and Academy Award Nominations
Roles for which the stars received Academy Awards or Academy Award nominations are designated by appropriate footnotes.

Abbreviations

d	director
p	producer
sc	screenplay
b/o	based on
AA	Allied Artists
AFD	Associated Film Distribution
AIP	American-International Pictures
BV	Buena Vista
Col.	Columbia
FP-L	Famous Players–Lasky
FN	First National
Fox	Fox Picture Corporation
GN	Grand National Pictures
MGM	Metro-Goldwyn-Mayer
Mono.	Monogram
Nat. Gen.	National General
Para.	Paramount
Rank	J. Arthur Rank
Rep.	Republic
RKO	RKO Radio Pictures
20th-Fox	20th Century–Fox
Univ.	Universal Pictures; Universal-International
UA	United Artists
WB	Warner Brothers Pictures and First National Pictures

. . . Characters in fiction have one great advantage over the rest of us: their names (if their creators consider the matter well) always fit them.

Laurence M. Janifer, from his article
"The Game of the Name" in *The Writer*

Shakespeare wrote, "What's in a name?" But just imagine if Margaret Mitchell, instead of naming her two famous characters Scarlett O'Hara and Rhett Butler, had called them Myrtle Mertz and Clyde Snodgrass.

Tom Scott Cadden

☆ FRED ASTAIRE

Frederick Austerlitz

b: May 10, 1899, Omaha, Neb.

"If I'd forgotten myself with that girl, I'd remember it."

Jerry Travers (Fred Astaire)
talking about Dale Tremont (Ginger Rogers)
in *Top Hat,* 1935.

Dancing Lady (1933, MGM). *d:* Robert Z. Leonard; *p:* David O. Selznick; *sc:* Allen Rivkin and P. J. Wolfson—*b/o* a novel by James Warner Bellah.

FRED ASTAIRE (appeared as himself): Broadway song-and-dance man who does some dance numbers with an ex–burlesque dancer who rises to become the glamorous star of a big Broadway musical.

Joan Crawford, Clark Gable, Franchot Tone, May Robson, Winnie Lightner, Robert Benchley, Ted Healy, Moe Howard, Jerry Howard, Larry Fine, Art Jarrett, Grant Mitchell, Nelson Eddy, Sterling Holloway, Eunice Quedens (Eve Arden), Lynn Bari.

Flying Down to Rio (1933, RKO). *d:* Thornton Freeland; *p:* Louis Brock and Merian C. Cooper; *sc:* Cyril Hume, H. W. Hanemann, and Erwin Gelsey—*b/o* a story by Louis Brock, from a play by Anne Caldwell.

FRED AYRES: Accordion player and dancer with an American dance band that becomes a success when it flies to Rio de Janeiro to work at a large resort hotel.

Dolores Del Rio, Gene Raymond, Raul Roulien, Ginger Rogers, Blanche Frederici, Walter Walker, Etta Moten, Roy D'Arcy, Maurice Black, Paul Porcasi, Franklin Pangborn, Eric Blore, Luis Alberni, Clarence Muse, Betty Furness.

The Gay Divorcee (1934, RKO). *d:* Mark Sandrich; *p:* Pandro S. Berman; *sc:* George Marion Jr., Dorothy Yost, and Edward Kaufman—*b/o* the musical comedy *Gay Divorce* by Dwight Taylor.

GUY HOLDEN: Well-known American dancer who falls for a woman at a Brighton seaside resort, and she mistakenly thinks he's the professional corespondent hired by her lawyer to help provide grounds for her divorce.

Ginger Rogers, Alice Brady, Edward Everett Horton, Erik Rhodes, Eric Blore, Betty Grable, Charles Coleman, William Austin, Lillian Miles, Paul Porcasi, E. E. Clive.

Roberta (1935, RKO). *d:* William A. Seiter; *p:* Pandro S. Berman; *sc:* Jane Murfin and Sam Mintz (with additional dialogue by Glenn Tryon and Allan Scott)—*b/o* the novel *Gowns by Roberta* by Alice Duer Miller and the Broadway musical *Roberta* by Jerome Kern and Otto Harbach.

HUCKLEBERRY "HUCK" HAINES: American bandleader who falls for an old flame of his (who's posing as a Polish countess) when he comes to Paris with his pal—a former All-American halfback who has inherited the most fashionable dress salon in the city.

Irene Dunne, Ginger Rogers, Randolph Scott, Helen Westley, Victor Varconi, Claire Dodd, Luis Alberni, Torben Meyer, Adrian Rosley, Johnny "Candy" Candido, Gene Sheldon, Lucille Ball, Virginia Reid (Lynne Carver).

Top Hat (1935, RKO). *d:* Mark Sandrich; *p:* Pandro S. Berman; *sc:* Dwight Taylor and Allan Scott (adaptation by Karl Nolti)—*b/o* Alexander Farago and Laszlo Aladar's play *The Girl Who Dared.*

JERRY TRAVERS: Dancer who falls for a pretty young woman in London, pursues her to Venice, but is held at bay because she mistakenly thinks he's her best friend's husband.

Ginger Rogers, Edward Everett Horton, Helen Broderick, Erik Rhodes, Eric Blore, Lucille Ball, Leonard Mudie, Donald Meek, Edgar Norton.

Follow the Fleet (1936, RKO). *d:* Mark Sandrich; *p:* Pandro S. Berman; *sc:* Dwight Taylor—*b/o* the play *Shore Leave* by Hubert Osborne and Allan Scott.

"BAKE" BAKER: Song-and-dance man who, after he joins the Navy, becomes involved with a dime-a-dance singer and puts on a musical benefit show on board an old converted showboat.

Ginger Rogers, Randolph Scott, Harriet Hilliard, Astrid Allwyn, Harry Beresford, Addison (Jack) Randall, Russell Hicks, Brooks Benedict, Lucille Ball, Betty Grable, Tony Martin, Frank Jenks, Doris Lloyd.

Swing Time (1936, RKO). *d:* George Stevens; *p:* Pandro S. Berman; *sc:* Howard Lindsay and Allan Scott—*b/o* a story by Erwin Gelsey.

JOHN "LUCKY" GARNETT: Gambler-hoofer in New York who, though his romance with a pretty dancing teacher is complicated by his engagement to a woman back home, finally wins the teacher as they go on to become a top-notch dance team.

Ginger Rogers, Victor Moore, Helen Broderick, Eric Blore, Betty Furness, Georges Metaxa, Pierre Watkin, John Harrington, Edgar Dearing, Frank Jenks, Ralph Byrd.

Shall We Dance (1937, RKO). *p:* Pandro S. Berman; *sc:* Allan Scott and Ernest Pagano (adaptation by P. J. Wolfson)—*b/o* the story "Watch Your Step" by Lee Loeb and Harold Buchman.

PETER P. "PETE" PETERS (alias PETROV): Renowned ballet dancer who is mistakenly reported to be married to a famous musical-comedy star, whereupon they both have difficulty in convincing people it isn't so.

Ginger Rogers, Edward Everett Horton, Eric Blore, Jerome Cowan, Ketti Gallian, Harriet Hoctor, Ann Shoemaker, Ben Alexander, William Brisbane, Emma Young, Rolfe Sedan.

A Damsel in Distress (1937, RKO). *d:* George Stevens; *p:* Pandro S. Berman; *sc:* P. G. Wodehouse, Ernest Pagano, and S. K. Lauren—*b/o* a novel by P. G. Wodehouse and a play by P. G. Wodehouse and Ian Hay.

JERRY HALLIDAY: American dancing star in London who falls for an aristocratic young English woman who he mistakenly thinks is a chorus girl.

George Burns, Gracie Allen, Joan Fontaine, Reginald Gardiner, Ray Noble, Constance Collier, Montagu Love, Jan Duggan, Pearl Amatore.

Carefree (1938, RKO). *d:* Mark Sandrich; *p:* Pandro S. Berman; *sc:* Ernest Pagano and Allan Scott (adaptation by Dudley Nichols and Hagar Wilde)—*b/o* a story by Marian Ainslee and Guy Endore.

TONY FLAGG: Psychiatrist who, while he's treating a friend's radio-singer fiancée because she can't make up her mind to marry the friend, winds up falling for her himself.

Ginger Rogers, Ralph Bellamy, Luella Gear, Jack Carson, Clarence Kolb, Franklin Pangborn, Walter Kingsford, Kay Sutton, Hattie McDaniel, Richard Lane, James Finlayson.

The Story of Vernon and Irene Castle (1939, RKO). *d:* H. C. Potter; *p:* George Haight and Pandro S. Berman; *sc:* Richard Sherman (adaptation by Oscar Hammerstein II and Dorothy Yost)—*b/o* the books *My Husband* and *My Memories of Vernon Castle* by Irene Castle.

VERNON CASTLE: Male half of a world-famous husband-and-wife ballroom-dancing team who joins the British Royal Flying Corps in WWI, sees service in France, but is later killed in a plane crash while serving as a flying instructor in Texas.

Ginger Rogers, Edna May Oliver, Walter Brennan, Lew Fields, Etienne Girardot, Janet Beecher, Rolfe Sedan, Leonid Kinskey, Douglas Walton, Frances Mercer, Victor Varconi, Donald MacBride, Dick Elliott, Marjorie Bell (Marge Champion).

Broadway Melody of 1940 (1940, MGM). *d:* Norman Taurog; *p:* Jack Cummings; *sc:* Leon Gordon and George Oppenheimer—*b/o* a story by Jack McGowan and Dore Schary.

JOHNNY BRETT: Dancer who misses out on a big break when his male partner is mistakenly selected to co-star with a talented woman dancer in a Broadway musical but who finally gets his chance when the partner magnanimously feigns drunkenness so he can go on in his place.

Eleanor Powell, George Murphy, Frank Morgan, Ian Hunter, Florence Rice, Lynne Carver, Herman Bing, Jack Mulhall, Barbara Jo Allen (Vera Vague), Irving Bacon, Joseph Crehan, James Flavin, Joe Yule, Hal K. Dawson.

Second Chorus (1940, Para.). *d:* H. C. Potter; *p:* Boris Morros; *sc:* Elaine Ryan and Ian McClellan Hunter—*b/o* a story by Fred Cavett.

DANNY O'NEILL: One of a pair of collegiate jazz trumpet players who compete for a job with Artie Shaw's band, as well as for the affections of their pretty manager, who becomes Shaw's secretary.

Paulette Goddard, Artie Shaw, Charles Butterworth, Burgess Meredith, Frank Melton, Jimmy Conlin, Dan Brodie.

You'll Never Get Rich (1941, Col.). *d:* Sidney Lanfield; *p:* Samuel Bischoff; *sc:* Michael Fessier and Ernest Pagano.

ROBERT CURTIS: Broadway dance director who, when he is drafted by the Army, keeps winding up in the guardhouse but redeems himself by staging a big servicemen's revue.

Rita Hayworth, John Hubbard, Robert Benchley, Osa Massen, Frieda Inescort, Guinn "Big Boy" Williams, Donald MacBride, Marjorie Gateson, Ann Shoemaker, Martha Tilton, Frank Ferguson, Frank Sully.

Holiday Inn (1942, Para.). *d:* Mark Sandrich; *p:* Mark Sandrich; *sc:* Claude Binyon (adaptation by Elmer Rice)—*b/o* an original idea by Irving Berlin.

TED HANOVER: Song-and-dance man who, when his ex-partner turns an old Connecticut farmhouse into an inn open only on holidays, tries to woo away the ex-partner's star performer, a pretty singer and dancer.

Bing Crosby, Marjorie Reynolds, Virginia Dale, Walter Abel, Louise Beavers, John Gallaudet, James Bell, Irving Bacon, Leon Belasco, Harry Barris.

You Were Never Lovelier (1942, Col.). *d:* William A. Seiter; *p:* Louis F. Edelman; *sc:* Michael Fessier, Ernest Pagano, and Delmer Daves—*b/o* Carlos Olivari and Sixto Pondal Rios's story and screenplay *The Gay Señorita.*

ROBERT DAVIS: New York nightclub dancer who, when he goes to Buenos Aires to relax and play the horses, meets a beautiful woman who mistakenly thinks he's the one who's been writing her anonymous love notes.

Rita Hayworth, Adolphe Menjou, Leslie Brooks, Adele Mara, Isabel Elsom, Gus Schilling, Kathleen Howard, Larry Parks, Kirk Alyn, George Bunny, Xavier Cugat and his Orchestra.

The Sky's the Limit (1943, RKO). *d:* Edward H. Griffith; *p:* David Hempstead; *sc:* Frank Fenton and Lynn Root—*b/o* the story "A Handful of Heaven."

FRED ATWELL (alias FRED BURTON): Publicity-shy WWII Flying Tiger hero who skips a nationwide tour to head for New York, where—under an assumed name and dressed in civilian clothing—he falls for a pretty news photographer.

Joan Leslie, Robert Benchley, Robert Ryan, Elizabeth Patterson, Marjorie Gateson, Eric Blore, Clarence Kolb, Richard Davies, Paul Hurst, Ed McNamara, Olin Howlin, the Freddie Slack Orchestra.

Yolanda and the Thief (1945, MGM). *d:* Vincente Minnelli; *p:* Arthur Freed; *sc:* Irving Brecher—*b/o* a story by Jacques Thery and Ludwig Bemelmans.

JOHNNY RIGGS: American con man in South America who tries to convince a naïve heiress he plans to bilk that he is her "guardian angel" who has come down to earth.

Lucille Bremer, Frank Morgan, Mildred Natwick, Mary Nash, Leon Ames, Ludwig Stoessel, Remo Buffano, Francis Pierlot, Leon Belasco, Richard Visaroff.

Blue Skies (1946, Para.). *d:* Stuart Heisler; *p:* Sol C. Siegel; *sc:* Arthur Sheekman (adaptation by Allan Scott)—*b/o* an original idea by Irving Berlin.

JED POTTER: Dancing star who, over a period of years, competes with his ex-partner—a singing nightclub owner—for the hand of a pretty young woman they both love.

Bing Crosby, Joan Caulfield, Billy DeWolfe, Olga San Juan, Frank Faylen, Karolyn Grimes, Jack Norton, Joan Woodbury, John Gallaudet, Cliff Nazarro.

Easter Parade (1948, MGM). *d:* Charles Walters; *p:* Arthur Freed; *sc:* Sidney Sheldon, Frances Goodrich, and Albert Hackett.

DON HEWES: Famous song-and-dance man who, when he and his female partner break up, picks a small-time chorus girl as a replacement and makes a bet that he can make her into a star.

Judy Garland, Peter Lawford, Ann Miller, Jules Munshin, Clinton Sundberg, Jeni LeGon, Dick Simmons, Jimmy Dodd, Robert Emett O'Connor, Lola Albright, Joi Lansing.

The Barkleys of Broadway (1949, MGM). *d:* Charles Walters; *p:* Arthur Freed; *sc:* Betty Comden and Adolph Green.

JOSH BARKLEY: Male half of a bickering married musical-comedy team who leaves when the wife decides to become a dramatic actress, but who finally gets together with her again after they realize that they love and need each other.

Ginger Rogers, Oscar Levant, Billie Burke, Gale Robbins, Jacques Francois, George Zucco, Clinton Sundberg, Inez Cooper, Carol Brewster, Wilson Wood, Bess Flowers, Frank Ferguson, Hans Conried.

Three Little Words (1950, MGM). *d:* Richard Thorpe; *p:* Jack Cummings; *sc:* George Wells—*b/o* the lives of Bert Kalmar and Harry Ruby.

BERT KALMAR: New York vaudeville comedian and magician who befriends the piano player and would-be baseball player Harry Ruby in the 1920s, whereupon they rise to fame as a Tin Pan Alley songwriting team.

Red Skelton, Vera-Ellen, Arlene Dahl, Keenan Wynn, Gale Robbins, Gloria DeHaven, Phil Regan, Harry Shannon, Debbie Reynolds, Carleton Carpenter, Paul Harvey, Pierre Watkin, Harry Barris, Sid Saylor, Harry Ruby.

Let's Dance (1950, Para.). *d:* Norman Z. McLeod; *p:* Robert Fellows; *sc:* Allan Scott and Dane Lussier—*b/o* the story "Little Boy Blue" by Maurice Zolotow.

DON ELWOOD: New York nightclub dancer who, when he reunites with his former show-biz partner after five years of private life, helps her fight to win back her young son from her wealthy Back Bay society mother-in-law.

Betty Hutton, Roland Young, Ruth Warrick, Lucile Watson, Gregory Moffett, Barton MacLane, Sheppard Strudwick, Melville Cooper, Harold Huber, George Zucco, Milton DeLugg, James Burke.

Royal Wedding (1951, MGM). *d:* Stanley Donen; *p:* Arthur Freed; *sc:* Alan Jay Lerner.

TOM BOWEN: American musical-comedy star who, at the time of Princess Elizabeth's marriage to Prince Philip, takes a Broadway show to London, where he and his co-star sister both find romantic interests.

Jane Powell, Peter Lawford, Sarah Churchill, Keenan Wynn, Albert Sharpe, Viola Roache, James Finlayson, Jack Reilly, Kerry O'Day, Mae Clark.

The Belle of New York (1952, MGM). *d:* Charles Walters; *p:* Arthur Freed; *sc:* Robert O'Brien and Irving Elinson (adaptation by Chester Erskine)—*b/o* the stage musical by Hugh Morton and Gustave Kerker.

CHARLES HILL: Rich playboy in turn-of-the-century New York City who falls for a young girl who works and sings at a small sidewalk mission.

Vera-Ellen, Marjorie Main, Keenan Wynn, Alice Pearce, Clinton Sundberg, Gale Robbins, Lisa Ferraday, Henry Slate, Tom Dugan, Percy Helton, Dick Wessel.

The Band Wagon (1953, MGM). *d:* Vincente Minnelli; *p:* Arthur Freed; *sc:* Betty Comden and Adolph Green.

TONY HUNTER: Washed-up Hollywood movie star who, when he reluctantly agrees to take a chance in a Broadway musical under a temperamental stage director of serious drama, is surprised to find himself in a smash hit.

Cyd Charisse, Oscar Levant, Nanette Fabray, Jack Buchanan, James Mitchell, Robert Gist, Thurston Hall, LeRoy Daniels, Ava Gardner.

Daddy Long Legs (1955, 20th-Fox). *d:* Jean Negulesco; *p:* Samuel G. Engel; *sc:* Phoebe Ephron and Henry Ephron—*b/o* the novel and play by Jean Webster.

JERVIS PENDLETON: Millionaire bachelor who anonymously sponsors a young French orphan girl's college education in Massachusetts, then—when the girl grows up—finds that she loves him, and vice versa.

Leslie Caron, Terry Moore, Thelma Ritter, Fred Clark, Charlotte Austin, Larry Keating, Kelly Brown, Ralph Dumke, Damian O'Flynn, Janice Carroll, Ray Anthony Orchestra.

Funny Face (1957, Para.). *d:* Stanley Donen; *p:* Roger Edens; *sc:* Leonard Gershe—*b/o* his unproduced stage musical *Wedding Day*.

DICK AVERY: Fashion-magazine photographer who talks his editor into sending a shy, drab Greenwich Village bookstore clerk to Paris, where he turns her into a glamorous high-fashion model while falling in love with her.

Audrey Hepburn, Kay Thompson, Michel Auclair, Robert Fleming, Dovima, Virginia Gibson, Suzy Parker, Alex Gerry, Ruta Lee, Jean DeVal, Roger Edens.

Silk Stockings (1957, MGM). *d:* Rouben Mamoulian; *p:* Arthur Freed; *sc:* Leonard Gershe and Leonard Spigelgass—*b/o* the stage musical by George S. Kaufman, Leueen McGrath, and Abe Burrows, from the story "Ninotchka" by Melchior Lengyal and the screen version by Charles Brackett, Billy Wilder, Walter Reisch, and Ernst Lubitsch.

STEVEN "STEVE" CANFIELD: Hollywood movie producer making a film in Paris who thaws out a cold female Russian official who has been ordered to bring the film's Russian composer back to Russia.

Cyd Charisse, Janis Paige, Peter Lorre, Jules Munshin, George Tobias, Joseph Buloff, Wim Sonneveld, Barrie Chase, Tybee Afra.

On the Beach (1959, UA). *d:* Stanley Kramer; *p:* Stanley Kramer (Stanley Kramer); *sc:* John Paxton—*b/o* the novel by Nevil Shute.

JULIAN OSBORN: Alcoholic, race-car-driving scientist in Australia who is one of a group of survivors of a nuclear war who now face certain death from radioactivity.

Gregory Peck, Ava Gardner, Anthony Perkins, Donna Anderson, John Tate, Lola Brooks, Guy Dolman, John Mellon, Harp McGuire, Ken Wayne.

The Pleasure of His Company (1961, Para.). *d:* George Seaton; *p:* William Perlberg (Perlberg–Seaton); *sc:* Samuel Taylor—*b/o* a play by Cornelia Otis Skinner and Samuel Taylor.

BIDDEFORD "POGO" POOLE: Aging debonair playboy who returns to his ex-wife's San Francisco home and tries to break up the wedding of his about-to-be married daughter, while also attempting to romance his ex-wife and needle her new husband.

Debbie Reynolds, Lilli Palmer, Tab Hunter, Gary Merrill, Charlie Ruggles, Harold Fong, Elvia Allman, Edith Head.

The Notorious Landlady (1962, Col.). *d:* Richard Quine; *p:* Fred Kohlmar (Kohlmar–Quine); *sc:* Blake Edwards and Larry Gelbart—*b/o* the story "The Notorious Tenant" by Margery Sharp.

FRANKLIN ARMBRUSTER: Worldly American diplomat in London who, along with his young subordinate, gets involved in trying to prove the innocence of the subordinate's beautiful landlady, who is suspected of murdering her husband.

Kim Novak, Jack Lemmon, Lionel Jeffries, Estelle Winwood, Philippa Bevans, Maxwell Reed, Richard Peel, Scott Davey, Henry Daniell, John Uhler Lemmon II.

Finian's Rainbow (1968, WB–Seven Arts). *d:* Francis Ford Coppola; *p:* Joseph Landon; *sc:* E. Y. Harburg and Fred Saidy—*b/o* the stage musical by E. Y. Harburg and Fred Saidy.

FINIAN McLONERGAN: Old Irish wanderer who, when he takes his daughter and a pot of gold he's stolen to America, is followed by a leprechaun who is trying to get the gold back.

Petula Clark, Tommy Steele, Don Francks, Keenan Wynn, Al Freeman Jr., Barbara Hancock, Ronald Colby, Dolph Sweet, Roy Glenn.

Midas Run (1969, Cinerama). *d:* Alf Kjellin; *p:* Raymond Stross (Selmur); *sc:* James Buchanan and Ronald Austin—*b/o* a story by Berne Giler.

JOHN PEDLEY: British secret agent who earns knighthood and a reward when he solves the mystery of a $15 million gold bullion heist that he masterminded.

Anne Heywood, Richard Crenna, Roddy

McDowall, Sir Ralph Richardson, Cesar Romero, Adolfo Celi, Maurice Denham, Fred Astaire Jr.

The Towering Inferno (1974, 20th-Fox & WB). *d:* John Guillermin and Irwin Allen; *p:* Irwin Allen; *sc:* Stirling Silliphant—*b/o* the novels *The Tower* by Richard Martin Stern and *The Glass Inferno* by Thomas M. Scortia and Frank M. Robinson.

HARLEE CLAIBORNE*: Aging con artist who—along with the rich middle-aged woman he's out to bilk—is among the people trapped inside a 138-story glass-and-steel San Francisco skyscraper when it suffers a disastrous fire.

Paul Newman, Steve McQueen, William Holden, Faye Dunaway, Jennifer Jones, Susan Blakely, Richard Chamberlain, O. J. Simpson, Robert Vaughn, Robert Wagner, Susan Flannery, Don Gordon, Jack Collins, Dabney Coleman.

The Amazing Dobermans (1976, Golden). *d:* Byron Chudnow; *p:* David Chudnow; *sc:* Michael Kraike, William Goldstein, and Richard Chapman—*b/o* a story by Michael Kraike and William Goldstein.

DANIEL HUGHES: Bible-quoting ex-con artist whose five amazing Doberman pinschers help a treasury agent get the best of a gang of racketeers.

---

*Received an Academy Award nomination as Best Supporting Actor for this role.

James Franciscus, Barbara Eden, Jack Carter, Billy Barty, Parley Baer.

Un Taxi Mauve (The Purple Taxi) (1977, Parafrance). *d:* Yves Boisset; *p:* Peter Rawley and Hugo Lodrini; *sc:* Michel Deon and Yves Boisset—*b/o* the book by Michel Deon.

SCULLY: Aging leprechaun-like Irish doctor involved with a number of rich people who have come to Ireland, some to hide and others to die.

Charlotte Rampling, Philippe Noiret, Agostina Belli, Peter Ustinov, Edward Albert Jr., Mairin O'Sullivan, Jack Watson.

Ghost Story (1981, Univ.). *d:* John Irvin; *p:* Burt Weissbourd; *sc:* Lawrence D. Cohen—*b/o* the novel by Peter Straub.

RICKY HAWTHORNE: One of four elderly New England men who are haunted by a terrible act they committed 50 years before and by a mysterious woman (who can change herself into a skeleton) when she appears to seek revenge.

Melvyn Douglas, Douglas Fairbanks Jr., John Houseman, Craig Wasson, Alice Krige, Jacqueline Brookes, Patricia Neal, Mark Chamberlin, Tim Choate, Kurt Johnson, Ken Olin.

• In addition, Fred Astaire made cameo/guest appearances in the following feature films: *Ziegfeld Follies* (1946, MGM), *That's Entertainment* (1974, MGM/UA—on-screen co-narrator), and *That's Entertainment, Part 2* (1976, MGM/UA—on-screen co-narrator).

☆ INGRID BERGMAN

b: Aug. 29, 1915, Stockholm, Sweden
d: Aug. 29, 1982, London, England

"Play it, Sam. Play 'As Time Goes By.'"

> Ilsa Lund Lazlo (Ingrid Bergman) to Sam (Dooley Wilson) in *Casablanca*, 1942.

The Count of the Monk's Bridge (1934, Svenskfilmindustri). *d:* Edvin Adolphson and Sigurd Wallen; *sc:* Gosta Stevens—*b/o* the play *Greven fran Gamla Sta'n* by Arthur Fischer and Sigfried Fischer.

ELSA: Maid in a Stockholm hotel who becomes romantically involved with a young man who is part of a group of merrymakers out on the town.

Valdemar Dahlquist, Sigurd Wallen, Eric Abrahamson, Weyler Hildebrand, Artur Cederborg, Edvin Adolphson, Tollie Zellman, Julia Caesar.

Ocean Breakers (1935, Svenskfilmindustri). *d:* Ivar Johansson; *sc:* Ivar Johansson—*b/o* an idea by Henning Ohlssen.

KARIN INGMAN: Swedish fisherman's daughter who bears an illegitimate child but refuses to reveal that the local minister is the father.

Tore Svennberg, Sten Lindgren, Carl Strom, Bror Ohlsson, Knut Frankman, Carin Swenson, Weyler Hildebrand.

Swedenhielms (1935, Svenskfilmindustri). *d:* Gustaf Molander; *sc:* Stina Bergman—*b/o* the play by Hjalmar Bergman.

ASTRID: Wealthy young lady whose fiancé—the son of an impecunious scientist—hesitates to marry her because of her money.

Gosta Ekman, Karin Swanstrom, Bjorn Berglund, Hakan Westergren, Tutta Rolf, Sigurd Wallen, Nils Ericsson, Adele Soderblom.

Walpurgis Night (1935, Svenskfilmindustri). *d:* Gustaf Edgren; *sc:* Oscar Rydquist and Gustaf Edgren.

LENA BERGSTROM: Secretary whose love for her boss is complicated by the fact that he already has a wife.

Lars Hanson, Karin Carlsson, Victor Seastrom, Erik Berglund, Sture Lagerwall, Georg Rydeberg, Georg Blickingberg, Rickard Lund, Stig Jarrel.

On the Sunny Side (1936, Svenskfilmindustri). *d:* Gustaf Molander; *sc:* Oscar Hemberg and Gosta Stevens—*b/o* the play by Helge Krog.

EVA BERGH: City woman married to a shy and conservative country gentleman who worries that his wife may find life too dull with him.

Lars Hanson, Karin Swanstrom, Edvin Adolphson, Einar Axelson, Marianne Lofgren, Carl Browallius, Bullen Berglund, Eddie Figge.

Intermezzo (1936, Svenskfilmindustri). *d:* Gustaf Molander; *sc:* Gustaf Molander and Gosta Stevens—*b/o* a story by Gustaf Molander.

ANITA HOFFMAN: Talented music student and piano teacher who becomes the accompanist for a world-famous Swedish violinist, falls deeply in love with him, but finally gives him up unselfishly so that he'll return to his wife and children.

Gosta Ekman, Inga Tidblad, Hans Ekman, Britt Hagman, Erik Berglund, Hugo Bjorne, Emma Meissner, Anders Henrikson.

The Four Companions (1938, UFA). *d:* Carl Froelich; *sc:* Jochen Huth—*b/o* his play.

MARIANNE: Young art-school graduate who forms an advertising agency with three of her classmates but despite success decides to give up her career for marriage.

Sabine Peters, Ursula Herking, Carsta Lock, Hans Sohnker, Leo Slezak, Heinz Weizel, Willi Rose, Rudolf Klicks.

Dollar (1938, Svenskfilmindustri). *d:* Gustaf Molander; *sc:* Stina Bergman and Gustaf Molander—*b/o* the play by Hjalmar Bergman.

JULIA BALZAR: Actress who feels that her industrial-tycoon husband is neglecting her for his business, while he thinks she's having an affair with another man.

George Rydeberg, Kotti Chave, Tutta Rolf, Hakan Westergren, Birgit Tengroth, Elsa Burnett, Edvin Adolphson, Gosta Cederlund.

A Woman's Face (1938, Svenskfilmindustri). *d:* Gustaf Molander; *sc:* Gosta Stevens—*b/o* the play *Il Etait Une Fois* by François de Croisset.

ANNA HOLM: Embittered Swedish woman with a disfigured face who becomes the leader of a gang of blackmailers in Stockholm, but who is spiritually rejuvenated when her beauty is restored by a plastic surgeon.

Anders Henrikson, Erik Berglund, Magnus Kesster, Gosta Cederlund, Georg Rydeberg, Tore Svennberg, Goran Bernhard.

Only One Night (1939, Svenskfilmindustri). *d:* Gustaf Molander; *sc:* Gosta Stevens—*b/o* the story "En Eneste Natt" by Harold Tandrup.

EVA: Young upper-class woman whose wealthy, aristocratic guardian tries to arrange a marriage between her and his crude illegitimate son.

Edvin Adolphson, Aino Taube, Olof Sandborg, Erik Berglund, Marianne Lofgren, Magnus Kesster, Sophus Dahl, Tor Borong.

Intermezzo (1939, UA). *d:* Gregory Ratoff; *p:* David O. Selznick (Selznick International); *sc:* George O'Neil—*b/o* the original Swedish screenplay *Intermezzo* by Gustaf Molander and Gosta Stevens.

ANITA HOFFMAN: Talented music student and piano teacher who becomes the accompanist for a world-famous Swedish violinist, falls deeply in love with him, but finally gives him up unselfishly so that he'll return to his wife and children.

Leslie Howard, Edna Best, John Halliday, Cecil Kellaway, Enid Bennett, Ann Todd, Douglas Scott, Eleanor Wesselhoeft, Moira Flynn.

A Night in June (1940, Svenskfilmindustri). *d:* Per Lindberg; *sc:* Ragnar Hylten-Cavallius—*b/o* a story by Tora Nordstrom-Bonnier.

KERSTIN NORDBACK: Small-town Swedish girl who, after a scandalous and disastrous affair with a sailor, moves to Stockholm, changes her name, and finds true happiness with another young man.

Marianne Lofgren, Lill-Tollie Zellman, Marianne Aminoff, Olof Widgren, Gunnar Sjoberg, Gabriel Alw, Sigurd Wallen, Alf Kjellin.

Adam Had Four Sons (1941, Col.). *d:* Gregory Ratoff; *p:* Robert Sherwood; *sc:* William Hurlbutt and Michael Blankfort—*b/o* the novel *Legacy* by Charles Bonner.

EMILIE GALLATIN: French governess in America who, when a widower hires her to look after his four sons, finds herself falling in love with him.

Warner Baxter, Susan Hayward, Fay Wray, Richard Denning, Johnny Downs, Robert Shaw, Helen Westley, June Lockhart, Gilbert Emery, Renie Riano, Clarence Muse.

Rage in Heaven (1941, MGM). *d:* W. S. Van Dyke II; *p:* Gottfried Reinhardt; *sc:* Christopher Isherwood and Robert Thoeren—*b/o* the novel by James Hilton.

STELLA BERGEN: Faithful wife whose deranged English steel-mill-owner husband becomes insanely jealous and commits suicide so it looks as though her supposed lover murdered him.

Robert Montgomery, George Sanders, Lucile

Watson, Oscar Homolka, Philip Merivale, Aubrey Mather, Gilbert Emery, Ludwig Hart.

Dr. Jekyll and Mr. Hyde (1941, MGM). _d:_ Victor Fleming; _p:_ Victor Fleming; _sc:_ John Lee Mahin—_b/o_ the story by Robert Louis Stevenson.

IVY PETERSON: Seductive barmaid in 1880s London who is rescued from an assailant by Dr. Harry Jekyll but later—when Jekyll drinks a potion and is transformed into the evil Mr. Hyde—is murdered by Hyde.

Spencer Tracy, Lana Turner, Ian Hunter, Donald Crisp, Barton MacLane, C. Aubrey Smith, Sara Allgood, Peter Godfrey, William Tannen, Billy Bevan, Forrester Harvey, Lumsden Hare.

Casablanca (1942, WB). _d:_ Michael Curtiz; _p:_ Hal B. Wallis; _sc:_ Julius J. Epstein, Philip G. Epstein, and Howard Koch—_b/o_ the play _Everybody Comes to Rick's_ by Murray Burnett and Joan Alison.

ILSA LUND LASZLO: Refugee from occupied France who, while she and her anti-Nazi underground leader husband are trying to get passports out of Casablanca to Lisbon, runs into her old flame Rick, the owner of Rick's Café Americain—a WWII Casablanca hot spot for intrigue.

Humphrey Bogart, Paul Henreid, Claude Rains, Conrad Veidt, Sydney Greenstreet, Peter Lorre, S. Z. Sakall, Dooley Wilson, John Qualen, Leonid Kinsky, Helmut Dantine, Curt Bois, Marcel Dalio, Ludwig Stossel, Frank Puglia, Dan Seymour.

For Whom the Bell Tolls (1943, Para.). _d:_ Sam Wood; _p:_ Sam Wood; _sc:_ Dudley Nichols—_b/o_ the novel by Ernest Hemingway.

MARIA*: Spanish girl who, while serving with a band of peasant guerillas during the 1930s Spanish Civil War, falls in love with an idealistic American schoolteacher who is fighting for the Spanish loyalists.

Gary Cooper, Akim Tamiroff, Arturo de Cordova, Vladimir Sokoloff, Mikhail Rasumny, Fortunio Bonanova, Victor Varconi, Katina Paxinou, Joseph Calleia, Duncan Renaldo, George Coulouris, Frank Puglia, Pedro de Cordoba, Yakima Canutt, Yvonne De Carlo.

Gaslight (1944, MGM). _d:_ George Cukor; _p:_ Arthur Hornblow Jr.; _sc:_ John Van Druten, Walter Reisch, and John L. Balderston—_b/o_ the play _Angel Street_ by Patrick Hamilton.

PAULA ALQUIST†: Wife whose schizophrenic pianist husband gets her to move into her murdered aunt's house in Victorian London, then secretly tries to drive her insane to get rid of her so that he can search for the rubies the aunt hid before he murdered her.

Charles Boyer, Joseph Cotten, Dame May Whitty, Angela Lansbury, Barbara Everest, Emil Rameau, Halliwell Hobbes, Heather Thatcher, Lawrence Naismith.

The Bells of St. Mary's (1945, RKO). _d:_ Leo McCarey; _p:_ Leo McCarey (Rainbow); _sc:_ Dudley Nichols—_b/o_ a story by Leo McCarey.

SISTER BENEDICT*: Dedicated Mother Superior at a financially troubled church and parochial school who helps the affable new priest in charge talk a wealthy skinflint into donating money for a new building.

Bing Crosby, Henry Travers, Ruth Donnelly, Joan Carroll, Martha Sleeper, William Gargan, Rhys Williams, Una O'Connor, Matt McHugh, Dewey Robinson.

Spellbound (1945, UA). _d:_ Alfred Hitchcock; _p:_ David O. Selznick (Selznick International/Vanguard); _sc:_ Ben Hecht (adaptation by Angus MacPhail)—_b/o_ Francis Beeding's novel _The House of Doctor Edwards._

DR. CONSTANCE PETERSON: Psychiatrist who not only falls in love with the new head of a mental hospital but becomes his psychoanalyst when she discovers that he's an imposter, an amnesiac, and possibly a murderer.

Gregory Peck, Michael Chekhov, Jean Acker, Donald Curtis, Rhonda Fleming, Leo G. Carroll, Norman Lloyd, John Emery, Paul Harvey, Victor Kilian, Wallace Ford, Dave Willock, Bill Goodwin, Art Baker, Regis Toomey, Addison Richards.

Saratoga Trunk (1945, WB). _d:_ Sam Wood; _p:_ Hal B. Wallis; _sc:_ Casey Robinson—_b/o_ the novel by Edna Ferber.

CLIO DULAINE: Notorious Creole beauty—the illegitimate daughter of a Louisiana aristocrat—who, when she returns from exile in Paris to New Orleans to confront her father's snobbish family, joins up with a Texas cowboy-gambler involved in a fight among railroad owners over the Saratoga Trunk line.

Gary Cooper, Flora Robson, Jerry Austin, John Warburton, Florence Bates, Curt Bois, John Abbott, Marla Shelton, Minor Watson, Ruby Dandridge, William B. Davidson, Thurston Hall.

Notorious (1946, RKO). _d:_ Alfred Hitchcock; _p:_ Alfred Hitchcock; _sc:_ Ben Hecht—_b/o_ an original idea by Alfred Hitchcock.

ALICIA HUBERMAN: Notorious woman—recruited by the U.S. government—who, as part of a plan to trap a gang of Nazi spies in post-WWII Rio de Janeiro, marries one of the leaders, then has to be saved by the American intelligence officer she's fallen in love with.

---

*Received an Academy Award nomination as Best Actress for this role.
†Won the Academy Award as Best Actress for this role.

*Received an Academy Award nomination as Best Actress for this role.

Cary Grant, Claude Rains, Louis Calhern, Madame Konstantin, Reinhold Schunzel, Moroni Olsen, Wally Brown, Gavin Gordon, Antonio Moreno, Harry Hayden, Dink Trout.

Arch of Triumph (1948, UA). *d:* Lewis Milestone; *p:* David Lewis (Enterprise); *sc:* Lewis Milestone and Harry Brown—*b/o* the novel by Erich Maria Remarque.

JOAN MADOU: Drifter and nightclub entertainer in pre-WWII Paris who falls in love with an Austrian refugee doctor seeking revenge on a Gestapo agent who had persecuted him.

Charles Boyer, Charles Laughton, Louis Calhern, Roman Bohner, Stephen Bekassy, Curt Bois, J. Edward Bromberg, Michael Romanoff, Art Smith, Byron Foulger, William Conrad.

Joan of Arc (1948, RKO). *d:* Victor Fleming; *p:* Walter Wanger (Sierra); *sc:* Maxwell Anderson and Andrew Solt—*b/o* the play *Joan of Lorraine* by Maxwell Anderson.

JOAN OF ARC*: Famed peasant girl/saint in fifteenth-century France who leads the French armies against England but ends up being tried as a heretic by the English and condemned to burn at the stake.

Jose Ferrer, George Coulouris, Selena Royle, Jimmy Lydon, Robert Barrat, Francis L. Sullivan, Irene Rich, Gene Lockhart, Richard Ney, Leif Erickson, John Ireland, Ward Bond, J. Carrol Naish, Hurd Hatfield, Sheppard Strudwick, Jeff Corey, William Conrad.

Under Capricorn (1949, WB). *d:* Alfred Hitchcock; *p:* Sidney Bernstein and Alfred Hitchcock (Transatlantic); *sc:* James Bridie—*b/o* Hume Cronyn's adaptation of the play by John Colton and Margaret Linden and the novel by Helen Simpson.

LADY HENRIETTA CONSIDINE: Irish noblewoman in 1831 who marries an Irish groomsman, then—when he's deported to Australia after he's wrongly convicted of killing her brother—turns into an alcoholic, haunted by the fact that she's actually the one who murdered her brother.

Joseph Cotten, Michael Wilding, Margaret Leighton, Cecil Parker, Denis O'Dea, Jack Watling, Harcourt Williams, Bill Shine, Ronald Adam, Francis de Wolff.

Stromboli (1950, RKO). *d:* Roberto Rossellini; *p:* Roberto Rossellini (Roberto Rossellini); *sc:* Roberto Rossellini, Art Cohn, Renzo Cesana, Sergio Amidei, and G. P. Callegari.

KARIN: Czech refugee who escapes from an Italian displaced persons camp by marrying a

young Sicilian fisherman but—when he takes her to live on the lonely island of Stromboli—finds only more unhappiness.

Mario Vitale, Renzo Cesana, Mario Sponza.

Europa '51 (The Greatest Love) (1951, I.F.E.). *d:* Roberto Rossellini; *p:* Roberto Rossellini (Ponti–DeLaurentiis); *sc:* Roberto Rossellini, Sandro de Leo, Mario Pannunzio, Ivo Perilli, and Brunello Rondi—*b/o* a story by Roberto Rossellini.

IRENE GIRARD: American society woman in post-WWII Rome who, after her young son commits suicide and she's consumed with guilt, is finally placed in a mental institution by her impassive husband.

Alexander Knox, Ettore Giannini, Giulietta Masina, Teresa Pellati, Sandro Franchina, William Tubbs, Alfred Browne.

We, the Women (1953, Titanus). *d:* Alfredo Guarini, Gianni Francioli, Roberto Rossellini, Luigi Zampa, and Luchino Visconti; *p:* Alfredo Guarini; *sc:* Cesare Zavattini, Luigi Chiarini, Georgio Prosperi, and Suso Cecchi D'Amico.

Actress who grows some beautiful and prized roses, then engages in a battle of wits with a hungry chicken that tries to eat the roses.

Anna Magnani, Isa Miranda, Alida Valli, Emma Danieli, Anna Amendola.

Journey to Italy (1954, Titanus). *d:* Roberto Rossellini; *p:* Roberto Rossellini (Rossellini/Sveva-Junior); *sc:* Roberto Rossellini and Vitaliano Brancati.

KATHERINE JOYCE: London business executive's wife who is on the verge of divorce but discovers—when she and her husband inherit a house in Naples and go to live there—that their marriage is worth saving.

George Sanders, Paul Muller, Anna Proclemer, Maria Mauban, Leslie Daniels, Natalia Rai, Jackie Frost.

Joan at the Stake (1954, ENIC). *d:* Roberto Rossellini; *sc:* Roberto Rossellini—*b/o* the story and dialogue of Paul Claudel and on the oratorio of Paul Claudel and Arthur Honegger.

JOAN OF ARC: Famed peasant girl/saint in fifteenth-century France who leads the French armies against England but ends up being tried as a heretic by the English and condemned to burn at the stake.

Tullio Carminati, Giacinto Prantelli, Augusto Romani, Plinio Clabassi, Saturno Meletti, Agnese Dubbini, Pietro de Palma, Aldo Tenossi.

Fear (1955, Minerva Films). *d:* Roberto Rossellini; *sc:* Roberto Rossellini, Sergio Amidei, and Franz Graf Treuberg—*b/o* the novel *Der Angst* by Stefan Zweig.

*Received an Academy Award nomination as Best Actress for this role.

IRENE WAGNER: Wealthy factory owner's wife who is blackmailed by her lover's ex-girlfriend, then discovers that her husband actually instigated the blackmailing scheme.
Mathias Wiemann, Renate Mannhardt, Kurt Kreuger, Elise Aulinger.

Anastasia (1956, 20th-Fox). d: Anatole Litvak; p: Buddy Adler; sc: Arthur Laurents—b/o a play by Marcel Maurette as adapted by Guy Bolton.
"THE UNKNOWN"/ANASTASIA*: Amnesiac refugee in 1928 who is trained by an exiled White Russian general to pass herself off as the Grand Duchess Anastasia, reputed to have survived the 1918 execution of her father, Czar Nicholas II, and the rest of the Imperial Family.
Yul Brynner, Helen Hayes, Akim Tamiroff, Martita Hunt, Felix Aylmer, Sacha Piteoff, Ivan Desny, Natalie Schafer, Gregoire Gromoff, Karel Stepanek, Ina De La Haye, Katherine Kath, Olaf Pooley, Eric Pohlmann.

Paris Does Strange Things (1957, WB). d: Jean Renoir; p: Jean Renoir (Jean Renoir); sc: Jean Renoir.
ELENA: Flirtatious Polish princess in 1880s Paris who not only tries to control the lives and careers of the men around her but also becomes involved in a plot with a French general to take over the French government through a coup.
Mel Ferrer, Jean Marais, Juliette Greco, Marjane, George Higgins, J. Richard.

Indiscreet (1958, WB). d: Stanley Donen; p: Stanley Donen (Grandon); sc: Norman Krasna—b/o his play Kind Sir.
ANN KALMAN: World-famous European actress who, after falling for a handsome American diplomat/playboy who has told her he's married, is furious when she learns he's really single and that he only tells women he's married so he can play the field without becoming permanently attached.
Cary Grant, Cecil Parker, Phyllis Calvert, David Kossoff, Megs Jenkins, Oliver Johnston, Middleton Woods.

The Inn of the Sixth Happiness (1958, 20th-Fox). d: Mark Robson; p: Buddy Adler; sc: Isobel Lennart—b/o Alan Burgess's novel The Small Woman.
GLADYS AYLWARD: English servant girl who goes to China to become a missionary and, during the 1931 Japanese invasion, leads 100 orphan children on a dangerous trek through enemy territory to safety.
Curt Jurgens, Robert Donat, Michael David, Athene Seyler, Ronald Squire, Moultrie Kelsall,

Richard Wattis, Peter Chong, Teai Chin, Lian-Shin Yang, Burt Kwouk.

Goodbye Again (1961, UA). d: Anatole Litvak; p: Anatole Litvak (Mercury/Argus/Anatole Litvak); sc: Samuel Taylor—b/o the novel Aimez-Vous Brahms? by Françoise Sagan.
PAULA TESSIER: Fortyish Parisian interior decorator who has an affair with a twenty-five-year-old American law student but still craves her middle-aged playboy ex-lover.
Yves Montand, Anthony Perkins, Jessie Royce Landis, Jackie Lane, Pierre Dux, Jean Clarke, Peter Bull, Michele Mercier, Lee Patrick, Diahann Carroll.

The Visit (1964, 20th-Fox). d: Bernhard Wicki; p: Julian Derode; sc: Ben Barzman—b/o the play by Friedrich Duerrenmatt.
KARLA ZACHANASSIAN: Richest woman in the world, who returns to her European hometown and offers large sums of money to each of the townspeople if they will put her former lover to death.
Anthony Quinn, Irina Demick, Valentina Cortese, Ernest Schroeder, Paolo Stoppa, Hans-Christian Bleck, Romolo Valli, Claude Dauphin, Eduardo Ciannelli, Fausto Tozzi, Reno Palmer.

The Yellow Rolls-Royce (1965, MGM). d: Anthony Asquith; p: Anatole de Grunwald; sc: Terence Rattigan.
MRS. GERDA MILLETT: Wealthy American widow in early 1941 who, while en route from Trieste to Belgrade in her yellow-and-black town car, falls in love with a Yugoslav partisan who is fighting Nazi invaders.
Rex Harrison, Jeanne Moreau, Edmund Purdom, Moira Lister, Isa Miranda, Roland Culver, Shirley MacLaine, Alain Delon, George C. Scott, Art Carney, Omar Sharif, Joyce Grenfell, Wally Cox.

Stimulantia (1967, Omnia Film). d (Ingrid Bergman's segment only): Gustaf Molander; sc: (Ingrid Bergman's segment only): Gustaf Molander—b/o the short story "The Necklace" by Guy de Maupassant.
Government clerk's wife who borrows a beautiful diamond necklace from a wealthy friend and loses it, then—after scrimping for ten years to pay for a replacement—learns that the original was actually a worthless paste imitation.
(Ingrid Bergman's segment only): Gunnar Bjornstrand, Gunnel Brostrom.

Cactus Flower (1969, Col.). d: Gene Saks; p: M. J. Frankovich; sc: I. A. L. Diamond—from the play by Abe Burrows, b/o a French play by Pierre Barillet and Jean-Pierre Gredy.
STEPHANIE DICKINSON: Prim nurse who, after her dentist boss gets her to pose as his wife in

---

*Won the Academy Award as Best Actress for this role.

order to deceive his young mistress, blossoms when she and the dentist realize they love each other.

Walter Matthau, Goldie Hawn, Jack Weston, Rich Lenz, Vito Scotti, Irene Hervey, Eve Bruce, Irwin Charone, Matthew Saks.

A Walk in the Spring Rain (1970, Col.). *d:* Guy Green; *p:* Stirling Silliphant (Pingee); *sc:* Stirling Silliphant—*b/o* the novel by Rachel Maddux.

LIBBY MEREDITH: New York college professor's wife who, when she and her husband take a sabbatical in a Tennessee mountain community, has a tragic love affair with a local married backwoodsman.

Anthony Quinn, Fritz Weaver, Katherine Crawford, Tom Fielding, Virginia Gregg, Mitchell Silberman.

From the Mixed-Up Files of Mrs. Basil E. Frankweiler (1973, Cinema 5). *d:* Fielder Cook; *p:* Charles G. Mortimer Jr. (Westfall); *sc:* Blanche Hanalis—*b/o* the novel by E. L. Konigsburg.

MRS. FRANKWEILER: Wealthy recluse who is sought out by a twelve-year-old girl and her ten-year-old brother to help them authenticate the origins of a Metropolitan Museum of Art statue that's thought to have been sculpted by Michelangelo.

Sally Prager, Johnny Doran, George Rose, Richard Mulligan, Georgann Johnson, Madeline Kahn.

Murder on the Orient Express (1974, Para.). *d:* Sidney Lumet; *p:* John Brabourne and Richard Goodwin (EMI/GW Films); *sc:* Paul Dehn—*b/o* the novel by Agatha Christie.

GRETA OHLSSON*: Passenger on the Istanbul-to-Calais Orient Express in the 1930s who is one of several persons suspected by the famous Belgian sleuth Hercule Poirot of murdering a fellow passenger.

Albert Finney, Lauren Bacall, Martin Balsam, Jacqueline Bisset, Jean-Pierre Cassel, Sean

Connery, John Gielgud, Wendy Hiller, Anthony Perkins, Vanessa Redgrave, Rachel Roberts, Richard Widmark, Michael York, George Coulouris.

A Matter of Time (1976, AIP). *d:* Vincente Minnelli; *p:* Jack H. Skirball and J. Edmund Grainger; *sc:* John Gay—*b/o* the novel *Film of Memory* by Maurice Druon.

THE CONTESSA: Batty old contessa—once the toast of Europe but now living in poverty in a run-down hotel—who teaches a young chambermaid in pre-WWI Rome how to love life.

Liza Minnelli, Charles Boyer, Spiros Andros, Tina Aumont, Anna Proclemer, Gabriele Ferzeti, Orso Maria Guerrini, Fernando Rey, Isabella Rossellini.

Autumn Sonata (1978, New World Pictures). *d:* Ingmar Bergman; *p:* Ingmar Bergman (Martin Starger/GMBH/Personafilm); *sc:* Ingmar Bergman.

CHARLOTTE*: Self-oriented famous concert pianist whose love–hate relationship with her resentful middle-aged daughter resurfaces when they get together for the first time in seven years.

Liv Ullmann, Lena Nyman, Halvar Bjork, Georg Lokkeberg, Knut Wigert, Eva Von Hanno, Erland Josephson, Linn Ullmann, Arne Bang-Hansen.

A Woman Called Golda (1982, Para. [Made for TV]). *d:* Alan Gibson; *p:* Gene Corman and Marilyn Bennett (Harve Bennett Prod.); *sc:* Harold Gast.

GOLDA MEIR[†]: Russian-born, Milwaukee-raised woman who goes to Palestine in 1921, becomes a leader in the fight to create the state of Israel, and—after serving in various political capacities—serves as prime minister of Israel from 1969 to 1974.

Judy Davis, Leonard Nimoy, Robert Loggia, Anne Jackson, Jack Thompson, Yossie Graber, Ned Beatty, Bruce Boa, Barry Foster.

---

*Received an Academy Award nomination as Best Actress for this role.
[†]Won an Emmy Award as Outstanding Lead Actress in a Drama Special for this role.

---

*Won the Academy Award as Best Supporting Actress for this role.

Humphrey DeForest Bogart

b: Jan. 23, 1899, New York, N.Y.
d: Jan. 14, 1957, Los Angeles, Cal.

"When you're slapped, you'll take it and like it."

> Sam Spade (Humphrey Bogart) to Wilmer (Elisha Cook Jr.) in *The Maltese Falcon,* 1941.

A Devil with Women (1930, Fox). *d:* Irving Cummings; *p:* George Middleton; *sc:* Dudley Nichols and Henry M. Johnson—*b/o* the novel *Dust and Sun* by Clements Ripley.

TOM STANDISH: Rich playboy who tags along with a tough soldier of fortune as they track down a notorious bandit in a Central American banana republic.

Victor McLaglen, Mona Maris, Luana Alcaniz, Michael Vavitch, Soledad Jiminez, Mona Rico, John St. Polis, Robert Edeson.

Up the River (1930, Fox). *d:* John Ford; *p:* William Collier Sr.; *sc:* Maurine Watkins.

STEVE: Young ex-convict who, when his future happiness with his ex-convict girlfriend is jeopardized by a blackmailer, gets help from a pair of friends who escape from prison to save him.

Spencer Tracy, Claire Luce, Warren Hymer, Joan Marie Lawes, William Collier Sr., George MacFarlane, Robert E. O'Connor, Gaylord Pendleton, Goodee Montgomery, Noel Francis.

Body and Soul (1931, Fox). *d:* Alfred Santell; *sc:* Jules Furthman, from the play *Squadrons* by A. E. Thomas—*b/o* the story "Big Eyes and Little Mouth" by Elliott White Springs.

JIM WATSON: Philandering newlywed American flyer in a WWI British Royal Flying Corps squadron who is killed while attacking a German observation balloon.

Charles Farrell, Elissa Landi, Myrna Loy, Donald Dillaway, Pat Somerset, Ian MacLaren, Dennis D'Auburn, Douglas Dray, Harold Kinney, Bruce Warren.

Bad Sister (1931, Univ.). *d:* Hobart Henley; *p:* Carl Laemmle Jr.; *sc:* Raymond L. Schrock, Tom Reed, and Edwin H. Knopf—*b/o* Booth Tarkington's story "The Flirt."

VALENTINE CORLISS: City slicker who comes to a small town in Indiana, dupes the spoiled daughter of a wealthy industrialist, and fleeces the local citizens with a phony scheme to build a factory.

Conrad Nagel, Sidney Fox, Bette Davis, ZaSu Pitts, Slim Summerville, Charles Winninger, Emma Dunn, Bert Roach, David Durand.

Women of All Nations (1931, Fox). *d:* Raoul Walsh; *sc:* Barry Connors—*b/o* characters created by Maxwell Anderson and Laurence Stallings in their play *What Price Glory?*

STONE: Enlisted man who serves in the peacetime U.S. Marine Corps along with Sergeant Flagg and Sergeant Quirt, two legendary womenchasing non-coms.

Victor McLaglen, Edmund Lowe, Gretta Nissen, El Brendel, Fifi Dorsay, Bela Lugosi, Joyce Compton, Ruth Warren.

A Holy Terror (1931, Fox). *d:* Irving Cummings; *p:* Edmund Grainger; *sc:* Ralph Block, Alfred A. Cohn, and Myron Fagan—*b/o* the novel *Trailin'* by Max Brand.

STEVE NASH: Bad-guy ranch foreman who clashes with a wealthy polo-playing Easterner who has come out West to track down his father's murderer.

George O'Brien, Sally Eilers, Rita LaRoy, James Kirkwood, Stanley Fields, Robert Warwick, Richard Tucker, Earl Pingree.

Love Affair (1932, Col.). *d:* Thornton Freeland; *sc:* Jo Swerling and Dorothy Howell—*b/o* the *College Humor* magazine story by Ursula Parrott.

JIM LEONARD: Aviator-engineer who falls for a rich young heiress when she hires him to teach her to fly.

Dorothy Mackaill, Jack Kennedy, Barbara Leonard, Astrid Allwyn, Halliwell Hobbes, Hale Hamilton.

Big City Blues (1932, WB). *d:* Mervyn LeRoy; *sc:* Ward Morehouse and Lillie Hayward—*b/o* the play *New York Town* by Ward Morehouse.

ADKINS: One of several murder suspects in the killing of a young woman at a New York hotelroom party.

Joan Blondell, Eric Linden, Inez Courtney, Evalyn Knapp, Guy Kibbee, Lyle Talbot, Walter Catlett, Grant Mitchell, Thomas Jackson, Ned Sparks, Tom Dugan.

Three on a Match (1932, WB). *d:* Mervyn LeRoy; *p:* Sam Bischoff; *sc:* Lucien Hubbard, Kubec Glasmon, and John Bright—*b/o* a story by Kubec Glasmon and John Bright.

"THE MUG": Hoodlum hired by a crooked gambler to kidnap a young boy so the gambler can pay off his debts with the ransom money.

Joan Blondell, Warren William, Ann Dvorak, Bette Davis, Lyle Talbot, Patricia Ellis, Grant Mitchell,

Glenda Farrell, Frankie Darro, Clara Blandick, Dawn O'Day (Anne Shirley), Allen Jenkins, Edward Arnold.

Midnight (1934, Univ.). *d:* Chester Erskine; *p:* Chester Erskine (All-Star); *sc:* Chester Erskine—*b/o* the play by Paul and Claire Sifton.

GARBONI: Gangster who has an affair with a respectable young woman but, when he spurns her, ends up getting shot by her with his own gun.

Sidney Fox, O. P. Heggie, Henry Hull, Margaret Wycherly, Lynne Overman, Katherine Wilson, Richard Whorf, Granville Bates, Cora Witherspoon, Henry O'Neill.

The Petrified Forest (1936, WB). *d:* Archie Mayo; *p:* Henry Blanke; *sc:* Charles Kenyon and Delmer Daves—*b/o* the play by Robert E. Sherwood.

DUKE MANTEE: Merciless killer who holes up with his gang at a desert gas station–café in Arizona's Petrified Forest and holds a group of people captive.

Leslie Howard, Bette Davis, Genevieve Tobin, Dick Foran, Joseph Sawyer, Porter Hall, Charley Grapewin, Paul Harvey, Eddie Acuff, Adrian Morris.

Bullets or Ballots (1936, WB). *d:* William Keighley; *p:* Louis F. Edelman; *sc:* Seton I. Miller—*b/o* a story by Martin Mooney and Seton I. Miller.

NICK "BUGS" FENNER: Double-crossing gangster who bumps off the head of the mob, then faces a showdown with a rival gangster who is really an undercover cop.

Edward G. Robinson, Joan Blondell, Barton MacLane, Frank McHugh, Richard Purcell, George E. Stone, Louise Beavers, Joseph Crehan, Henry O'Neill, Henry Kolker, Herbert Rawlinson, Frank Faylen.

Two Against the World (1936, WB). *d:* William McGann; *p:* Bryan Foy; *sc:* Michel Jacoby—*b/o* the play *Five Star Final* by Louis Weitzenkorn.

SHERRY SCOTT: Crusading radio-station manager who, after one of the station's muckraking news stories causes two suicides, fights to clean up the profit-motivated program policies of the station's owner.

Beverly Roberts, Helen MacKellar, Henry O'Neill, Virginia Brissac, Robert Middlemass, Harry Hayden, Claire Dodd, Hobart Cavanaugh, Douglas Wood, Frank Orth, Paula Stone, Howard Hickman.

China Clipper (1936, WB). *d:* Ray Enright; *p:* Sam Bischoff; *sc:* Frank "Spig" Wead.

HAP STUART: Wisecracking ace flyer who pilots the China Clipper airplane on its first successful transpacific flight to China.

Pat O'Brien, Beverly Roberts, Ross Alexander, Marie Wilson, Henry B. Walthall, Wayne Morris, Anne Nagel, Marjorie Weaver, Milburn Stone.

Isle of Fury (1936, WB). *d:* Frank McDonald; *p:* Bryan Foy; *sc:* Robert Andrews and William Jacobs—*b/o* W. Somerset Maugham's novel *The Narrow Corner.*

VAL STEVENS: Fugitive from justice who, after he's happily married and leading a reformed life on a South Seas island, is tracked down by a detective.

Margaret Lindsay, Donald Woods, Paul Graetz, Gordon Hart, E. E. Clive, George Regas, Sidney Bracy.

Black Legion (1937, WB). *d:* Archie Mayo; *p:* Robert Lord; *sc:* Abem Finkel and William Wister Haines—*b/o* a story by Robert Lord.

FRANK TAYLOR: Hard-working factory worker who, when he loses a promotion to a foreign-born fellow worker, becomes bitter and joins a hooded Ku Klux Klan–type gang for revenge.

Dick Foran, Erin O'Brien-Moore, Ann Sheridan, Robert Barrat, Joseph Sawyer, Addison Richards, Eddie Acuff, Paul Harvey, Samuel S. Hinds, John Litel, Dickie Jones, Henry Brandon, Charles Halton, Harry Hayden.

The Great O'Malley (1937, WB). *d:* William Dieterle; *p:* Harry Joe Brown; *sc:* Milton Krims and Tom Reed—*b/o* Gerald Beaumont's story "The Making of O'Malley."

JOHN PHILLIPS: Family man who, after he's sent to prison for committing a robbery in order to provide for his wife and crippled daughter, escapes and tries to kill a policeman he blames for his misfortune.

Pat O'Brien, Sybil Jason, Ann Sheridan, Frieda Inescort, Donald Crisp, Henry O'Neill, Craig Reynolds, Hobart Cavanaugh, Mary Gordon, Frank Reicher.

Marked Woman (1937, WB). *d:* Lloyd Bacon; *p:* Louis F. Edelman; *sc:* Robert Rossen and Abem Finkel (with additional dialogue by Seton I. Miller).

DAVID GRAHAM: Racket-busting D.A. who is out to get a New York vice czar who's been exploiting and terrorizing a group of nightclub "hostesses."

Bette Davis, Eduardo Ciannelli, Jane Bryan, Lola Lane, Isabel Jewell, Mayo Methot, Ben Welden, Henry O'Neill, Allen Jenkins, John Litel, Raymond Hatton, William B. Davidson, Frank Faylen, Jack Norton, Kenneth Harlan.

Kid Galahad (1937, WB). *d:* Michael Curtiz; *p:* Samuel Bischoff; *sc:* Seton I. Miller—*b/o* the novel by Francis Wallace.

TURKEY MORGAN: Heavyweight champion's crooked fight manager who clashes with a rival manager whose fighter—a naïve ex-bellboy—K.O.s the champion.

Edward G. Robinson, Bette Davis, Wayne Morris, Jane Bryan, Harry Carey, Ben Welden, Joseph Crehan, Veda Ann Borg, Frank Faylen, Joyce Compton, Horace MacMahon, John Shelton.

San Quentin (1937, WB). *d:* Lloyd Bacon; *p:* Samuel Bischoff; *sc:* Peter Milne and Humphrey Cobb—*b/o* a story by Robert Tasker and John Bright.

JOE "RED" KENNEDY: San Quentin convict who gives a hard time to the prison-yard captain, who loves the convict's sister.

Pat O'Brien, Ann Sheridan, Barton MacLane, Joseph Sawyer, Veda Ann Borg, Joseph King, Gordon Oliver, Garry Owen, Marc Lawrence, Emmett Vogan, William Pawley, Ernie Adams.

Dead End (1937, UA). *d:* William Wyler; *p:* Samuel Goldwyn (Samuel Goldwyn); *sc:* Lillian Hellman—*b/o* the play by Sidney Kingsley.

BABY FACE MARTIN: Notorious gangster who returns to the street where he grew up—in New York's East Side tenement district—and is bitterly disillusioned when he finds that his mother hates him and that his childhood sweetheart has become a prostitute.

Sylvia Sidney, Joel McCrea, Wendy Barrie, Claire Trevor, Allen Jenkins, Marjorie Main, Billy Halop, Huntz Hall, Bobby Jordan, Leo Gorcey, Gabriel Dell, Bernard Punsley, Minor Watson, James Burke, Ward Bond.

Stand-In (1937, UA). *d:* Tay Garnett; *p:* Walter Wanger (Walter Wanger); *sc:* Gene Towne and Graham Baker—*b/o* the *Saturday Evening Post* serial by Clarence Buddington Kelland.

DOUGLAS QUINTAIN: Hard-drinking Hollywood producer who helps an efficiency expert save a financially ailing film studio by re-editing a jungle movie that's a "bomb."

Leslie Howard, Joan Blondell, Alan Mowbray, Marla Shelton, C. Henry Gordon, Jack Carson, Tully Marshall, J. C. Nugent, William V. Mong.

Swing Your Lady (1938, WB). *d:* Ray Enright; *p:* Samuel Bischoff; *sc:* Joseph Schrank and Maurice Leo—*b/o* the play by Kenyon Nicholson and Charles Robinson.

ED HATCH: Fast-buck promoter who takes a big dimwitted wrestler to the Ozarks and sets up a match with a village blacksmith—who happens to be a woman.

Frank McHugh, Louise Fazenda, Nat Pendleton, Penny Singleton, Allen Jenkins, The Weaver Brothers and Elviry (Leon Weaver, Frank Weaver, Elvira Weaver), Ronald Reagan, Daniel Boone Savage, Hugh O'Connell, Tommy Bupp, Sonny Bupp, Olin Howland.

Crime School (1938, WB). *d:* Lewis Seiler; *p:* Bryan Foy; *sc:* Crane Wilbur and Vincent Sherman—*b/o* a story by Crane Wilbur.

MARK BRADEN: Crusading law official who, when he discovers that the superintendent of a reform school is a sadist, takes over the job himself and wins the rebellious young inmates' trust and respect.

Gale Page, Billy Halop, Bobby Jordan, Huntz Hall, Leo Gorcey, Bernard Punsley, Gabriel Dell, Cy Kendall, Charles Trowbridge, Spencer Charters, Donald Briggs, Paul Porcasi, Ed Gargan.

Men Are Such Fools (1938, WB). *d:* Busby Berkeley; *p:* David Lewis; *sc:* Norman Reilly Raine and Horace Jackson—*b/o* the novel by Faith Baldwin.

HARRY GALLEON: Big-time radio contact man who is used by a female ad-agency account executive to make her ex–football-hero husband jealous.

Wayne Morris, Priscilla Lane, Hugh Herbert, Penny Singleton, Johnnie Davis, Mona Barrie, Gene Lockhart, Donald Briggs, Renie Riano, Claude Allister, Carole Landis.

The Amazing Dr. Clitterhouse (1938, WB). *d:* Anatole Litvak; *p:* Robert Lord; *sc:* John Wexley and John Huston—*b/o* the play by Barre Lyndon.

ROCKS VALENTINE: Leader of a gang of safecrackers who clashes with a psychologist who has joined the gang as a crook in order to gather material for a book he's writing about the criminal mind.

Edward G. Robinson, Claire Trevor, Allen Jenkins, Donald Crisp, Gale Page, Henry O'Neill, John Litel, Thurston Hall, Maxie Rosenbloom, Bert Hanlon, Curt Bois, Ward Bond, Vladimir Sokoloff, Irving Bacon.

Racket Busters (1938, WB). *d:* Lloyd Bacon; *p:* Samuel Bischoff; *sc:* Robert Rossen and Leonardo Bercovici.

PETE MARTIN: Powerful New York gang leader who runs into more resistance than he bargained for when he tries to take over Manhattan's trucking industry.

George Brent, Gloria Dickson, Allen Jenkins, Walter Abel, Henry O'Neill, Penny Singleton, Anthony Averill, Oscar O'Shea, Elliott Sullivan, Fay Helm.

Angels with Dirty Faces (1938, WB). *d:* Michael Curtiz; *p:* Samuel Bischoff; *sc:* John Wexley and Warren Duff—*b/o* a story by Rowland Brown.

JAMES FRAZIER: Racketeering lawyer and nightclub owner on New York's East Side who tangles with a rival gangster and the gangster's boyhood friend, a priest.

James Cagney, Pat O'Brien, Ann Sheridan, George

Bancroft, Billy Halop, Bobby Jordan, Leo Gorcey, Gabriel Dell, Huntz Hall, Bernard Punsley, Adrian Morris, William Tracy.

King of the Underworld (1939, WB). *d:* Lewis Seiler; *p:* Bryan Foy; *sc:* George Bricker and Vincent Sherman—*b/o* the *Liberty Magazine* serial *Dr. Socrates* by W. R. Burnett.

JOE GURNEY: Underworld big-shot who, after forcing a female doctor to treat him and other wounded mobsters, is outsmarted by her and captured when she temporarily blinds him with an eyedrop solution.

Kay Francis, James Stephenson, John Eldredge, Arthur Aylesworth, Jessie Busley, Harland Tucker, Charley Foy, Murray Alper, Joe Devlin, Elliott Sullivan, John Ridgely, Pierre Watkin, Charles Trowbridge.

The Oklahoma Kid (1939, WB). *d:* Lloyd Bacon; *p:* Samuel Bischoff; *sc:* Warren Duff, Robert Buckner, and Edward E. Paramore—*b/o* a story by Edward E. Paramore and Wally Klein.

WHIP McCORD: Vicious 1890s outlaw leader and saloon owner on the Cherokee Strip who, when he causes a local politician to be framed for murder and lynched, is hunted down by the politician's outlaw son, the Oklahoma Kid.

James Cagney, Rosemary Lane, Donald Crisp, Harvey Stephens, Hugh Sothern, Charles Middleton, Edward Pawley, Ward Bond, Trevor Bardette, John Miljan, Arthur Aylesworth, Irving Bacon, Joe Devlin, Wade Boteler.

Dark Victory (1939, WB). *d:* Edmund Goulding; *p:* Hal B. Wallis and David Lewis; *sc:* Casey Robinson—*b/o* the play by George Emerson Brewer Jr. and Bertram Bloch.

MICHAEL O'LEARY: Irish horse trainer whose overtures of love are rejected by his employer, a fast-living young heiress who recently learned that she has a malignant brain tumor.

Bette Davis, George Brent, Geraldine Fitzgerald, Ronald Reagan, Henry Travers, Cora Witherspoon, Dorothy Peterson, Virginia Brissac, Herbert Rawlinson, Leonard Mudie, Lottie Williams.

You Can't Get Away with Murder (1939, WB). *d:* Lewis Seiler; *p:* Samuel Bischoff; *sc:* Robert Buckner, Don Ryan, and Kenneth Gamet—*b/o* the play *Chalked Out* by Warden Lewis E. Lawes and Jonathan Finn.

FRANK WILSON: Mean, petty crook who leads a young man into a life of crime, commits a murder when they rob a pawnshop, and ends up in the electric chair at Sing Sing.

Billy Halop, Gale Page, John Litel, Henry Travers, Harvey Stephens, Harold Huber, Joseph Sawyer, Joseph Downing, George E. Stone, Joseph King, Joseph Crehan, John Ridgely, Herbert Rawlinson.

The Roaring Twenties (1939, WB). *d:* Raoul Walsh; *p:* Hal B. Wallis; *sc:* Jerry Wald, Richard Macaulay, and Robert Rossen—*b/o* a story by Mark Hellinger.

GEORGE HALLY: Ex–WWI doughboy who, after becoming a big-time New York bootlegger, becomes involved in a gang war in which he clashes with two ex–army buddies—one a rival gangster, the other a lawyer.

James Cagney, Priscilla Lane, Gladys George, Jeffrey Lynn, Frank McHugh, Paul Kelly, Elisabeth Risdon, Joseph Sawyer, Joseph Crehan, George Meeker, Abner Biberman, Bert Hanlon, Murray Alper, Dick Wessel, Raymond Bailey.

The Return of Doctor X (1939, WB). *d:* Vincent Sherman; *p:* Bryan Foy; *sc:* Lee Katz—*b/o* William J. Makin's story "The Doctor's Secret."

MARSHALL QUESNE (alias "DR. XAVIER"): Executed murderer brought back to life as a vampire who must prey on young girls for life-sustaining blood.

Wayne Morris, Rosemary Lane, Dennis Morgan, John Litel, Lya Lys, Huntz Hall, Charles Wilson, Howard Hickman, Olin Howland, Arthur Aylesworth, Creighton Hale, John Ridgely, Joseph Crehan, Glenn Langan, William Hopper.

Invisible Stripes (1939, WB). *d:* Lloyd Bacon; *p:* Hal B. Wallis; *sc:* Warren Duff—*b/o* a story by Jonathan Finn from the book by Warden Lewis E. Lawes.

CHUCK MARTIN: Ex-convict leader of a gang of bank robbers who, when he helps an ex-con friend try to keep his brother out of the rackets, runs afoul of the other gang members.

George Raft, Jane Bryan, William Holden, Flora Robson, Paul Kelly, Lee Patrick, Henry O'Neill, Frankie Thomas, Moroni Olsen, Marc Lawrence, Leo Gorcey, William Haade, Tully Marshall.

Virginia City (1940, WB). *d:* Michael Curtiz; *p:* Robert Fellows; *sc:* Robert Buckner.

JOHN MURRELL: Half-breed leader of a Nevada outlaw gang during the Civil War who is trying to lay his hands on a $5 million gold shipment earmarked for the Confederacy.

Errol Flynn, Miriam Hopkins, Randolph Scott, Frank McHugh, Alan Hale, Guinn "Big Boy" Williams, John Litel, Douglass Dumbrille, Moroni Olsen, Dickie Jones, Russell Simpson, Victor Kilian, Charles Middleton, Ward Bond, George Reeves.

It All Came True (1940, WB). *d:* Lewis Seiler; *p:* Hal B. Wallis; *sc:* Michael Fessier and Lawrence Kimble—*b/o* the story "Better Than Life" by Louis Bromfield.

CHIPS MAGUIRE (alias "MR. GRASSELLI"): Fugitive killer who, while hiding out in a boarding house full of amateur performers and old-time vaudevillians, helps them turn the place into a nightclub.

Ann Sheridan, Jeffrey Lynn, ZaSu Pitts, Una O'Connor, John Litel, Grant Mitchell, Felix Bressart, Charles Judels, Howard Hickman, Herbert Vigran.

Brother Orchid (1940, WB). *d:* Lloyd Bacon; *p:* Hal B. Wallis; *sc:* Earl Baldwin—*b/o* the *Collier's* magazine story by Richard Connell.

JACK BUCK: Racketeer who, when he discovers that his former mob leader has taken refuge in a monastery and learned to cultivate flowers, tries to muscle in on the monastery's flower-growing business.

Edward G. Robinson, Ann Sothern, Donald Crisp, Ralph Bellamy, Allen Jenkins, Charles D. Brown, Cecil Kellaway, Richard Lane, Paul Guilfoyle, John Ridgely, Tom Tyler, Dick Wessel, Granville Bates, Tim Ryan.

They Drive by Night (1940, WB). *d:* Raoul Walsh; *p:* Hal B. Wallis; *sc:* Jerry Wald and Richard Macaulay—*b/o* the novel *Long Haul* by A. I. Bezzerides.

PAUL FABRINI: Truck driver who loses an arm in an accident as he and his brother, also a truck driver, battle crooked owners in an effort to acquire their own trucking business.

George Raft, Ann Sheridan, Ida Lupino, Gale Page, Alan Hale, Roscoe Karns, John Litel, George Tobias, Henry O'Neill, Charles Halton, Paul Hurst, John Ridgely, Joyce Compton.

High Sierra (1941, WB). *d:* Raoul Walsh; *p:* Hal B. Wallis; *sc:* John Huston and W. R. Burnett—*b/o* the novel by W. R. Burnett.

ROY "MAD DOG" EARLE: Soft-hearted ex-con who robs a bank, becomes involved with a young crippled girl and a dance-hall hostess, and ends up trapped by police high atop a mountain in the California Sierras.

Ida Lupino, Alan Curtis, Arthur Kennedy, Joan Leslie, Henry Hull, Henry Travers, Jerome Cowan, Minna Gombell, Barton MacLane, Cornel Wilde, Donald MacBride, Paul Harvey, Isabel Jewell, Willie Best, Spencer Charters.

The Wagons Roll at Night (1941, WB). *d:* Ray Enright; *p:* Harlan Thompson; *sc:* Fred Niblo Jr. and Barry Trivers—*b/o* the novel *Kid Galahad* by Francis Wallace.

NICK COSTER: Owner of a traveling carnival who hires a young country-boy grocery clerk to be a lion-tamer but turns against him when the youth falls for the owner's sister.

Sylvia Sidney, Eddie Albert, Joan Leslie, Sig Rumann, Cliff Clark, Charley Foy, Frank Wilcox, John Ridgely, Clara Blandick, Aldrich Bowker, Garry Owen, Jack Mower, Frank Mayo.

The Maltese Falcon (1941, WB). *d:* John Huston;
p: Hal B. Wallis; *sc:* John Huston—*b/o* the novel by Dashiell Hammett.

SAM SPADE: Tough private eye who encounters a mysterious, beautiful woman and an assortment of other memorable characters as he tracks down his partner's killer and a priceless jeweled statuette of a falcon.

Mary Astor, Gladys George, Peter Lorre, Barton MacLane, Lee Patrick, Sydney Greenstreet, Ward Bond, Jerome Cowan, Elisha Cook Jr., James Burke, Murray Alper, John Hamilton, Emory Parnell, Walter Huston.

All Through the Night (1942, WB). *d:* Vincent Sherman; *p:* Jerry Wald; *sc:* Leonard Spigelgass and Edwin Gilbert—*b/o* a story by Leonard Q. Ross (Leo Rosten) and Leonard Spigelgass.

GLOVES DONAHUE: Wise cracking, big-shot Broadway gambler who enlists a gang of his colorful cronies to help battle a nest of WWII Nazi saboteurs in New York.

Conrad Veidt, Kaaren Verne, Jane Darwell, Frank McHugh, Peter Lorre, Judith Anderson, William Demarest, Jackie Gleason, Phil Silvers, Wallace Ford, Barton MacLane, Edward Brophy, Ludwig Stossel, James Burke, Ben Welden, Frank Sully.

The Big Shot (1942, WB). *d:* Lewis Seiler; *p:* Walter MacEwen; *sc:* Bertram Millhauser, Abem Finkel, and Daniel Fuchs.

DUKE BERNE: Ex–big shot and three-time loser who, when he's sent up again in a robbery frame-up, breaks out and gets the man responsible.

Irene Manning, Richard Travis, Susan Peters, Stanley Ridges, Minor Watson, Chick Chandler, Howard da Silva, Murray Alper, John Ridgely, John Hamilton, Virginia Brissac, Virginia Sale.

Across the Pacific (1942, WB). *d:* John Huston; *p:* Jerry Wald and Jack Saper; *sc:* Richard Macaulay—*b/o* the *Saturday Evening Post* serial "Aloha Means Goodbye" by Robert Carson.

RICK LELAND: WWII U.S. Army Intelligence officer who trails a pro-Japanese spy to Panama and breaks up an enemy plot to bomb the Panama Canal.

Mary Astor, Sydney Greenstreet, Charles Halton, Victor Sen Yung, Frank Wilcox, Lester Matthews, John Hamilton, Roland Drew, Monte Blue, Richard Loo, Keye Luke, Rudy Robles.

Casablanca (1942, WB). *d:* Michael Curtiz; *p:* Hal B. Wallis; *sc:* Julius J. Epstein, Philip G. Epstein, and Howard Koch—*b/o* the play *Everybody Comes to Rick's* by Murray Burnett and Joan Alison.

RICK BLAINE*: Former soldier of fortune who owns Rick's Café Americain, a hot spot for intrigue in WWII Casablanca where refugees from

---

*Received an Academy Award nomination as Best Actor for this role.

Nazi-occupied Europe—including Rick's old flame and her underground leader husband—try to get passports to Lisbon.

Ingrid Bergman, Paul Henreid, Claude Rains, Conrad Veidt, Sydney Greenstreet, Peter Lorre, S. Z. Sakall, Dooley Wilson, John Qualen, Leonid Kinsky, Helmut Dantine, Curt Bois, Marcel Dalio, Ludwig Stossel, Frank Puglia, Dan Seymour.

Action in the North Atlantic (1943, WB). *d:* Lloyd Bacon; *p:* Jerry Wald; *sc:* John Howard Lawson (with additional dialogue by A. I. Bezzerides and W. R. Burnett)—*b/o* the novel by Guy Gilpatric.

JOE ROSSI: U.S. merchant marine officer on a WWII Liberty ship that battles German subs and planes as it transports valuable cargo through the North Atlantic to Russia.

Raymond Massey, Alan Hale, Julie Bishop, Ruth Gordon, Sam Levene, Dane Clark, Peter Whitney, Minor Watson, J. M. Kerrigan, Kane Richmond, Chick Chandler, Don Douglas, Ray Montgomery, Glenn Strange, Ludwig Stossel, Dick Wessel, Frank Puglia, Iris Adrian, Irving Bacon, James Flavin.

Sahara (1943, Col). *d:* Zoltan Korda; *p:* Harry Joe Brown; *sc:* John Howard Lawson and Zoltan Korda (adaptation by James O'Hanlon)—from a story by Philip MacDonald—*b/o* an incident depicted in the Soviet film *The Thirteen*.

SGT. JOE GUNN: WWII American tank commander (attached to the British Eighth Army) who, when he and his crew are cut off by Nazis in the Libyan desert, picks up a group of assorted stragglers, finds a strategic water hole, and then has to fight off a thirst-crazed German battalion.

Bruce Bennett, J. Carrol Naish, Lloyd Bridges, Rex Ingram, Richard Nugent, Dan Duryea, Patrick O'Moore, Louis Mercier, Guy Kingsford, Kurt Krueger, Hans Schumm.

Passage to Marseille (1944, WB). *d:* Michael Curtiz; *p:* Hal B. Wallis; *sc:* Casey Robinson and Jack Moffitt—*b/o* the novel *Men without Country* by Charles Nordhoff and James Norman Hall.

MATRAC: French journalist who, because of his political views, is framed for murder and sent to Devil's Island, but who escapes and joins a WWII Free French bomber squadron.

Claude Rains, Michele Morgan, Philip Dorn, Sydney Greenstreet, Peter Lorre, George Tobias, Helmut Dantine, John Loder, Victor Francen, Vladimir Sokoloff, Eduardo Cianelli, Hans Conried, Monte Blue, Louis Mercier.

To Have and Have Not (1945, WB). *d:* Howard Hawks; *p:* Howard Hawks; *sc:* Jules Furthman and William Faulkner—*b/o* the novel by Ernest Hemingway.

HARRY MORGAN: Tough American skipper of a small fishing boat who is hired to smuggle a French underground leader and his wife into WWII Martinique.

Walter Brennan, Lauren Bacall, Dolores Moran, Hoagy Carmichael, Walter Molnar, Sheldon Leonard, Marcel Dalio, Walter Sande, Dan Seymour, Sir Lancelot.

Conflict (1945, WB). *d:* Curtis Bernhardt; *p:* William Jacobs; *sc:* Arthur T. Horman and Dwight Taylor—*b/o* a story by Robert Siodmak and Alfred Neumann.

RICHARD MASON: Unfaithful husband who murders his wife, then engages in a battle of wits with a shrewd psychiatrist who suspects the husband's guilt.

Alexis Smith, Sydney Greenstreet, Rose Hobart, Charles Drake, Grant Mitchell, Patrick O'Moore, Ann Shoemaker, Frank Wilcox, James Flavin.

The Big Sleep (1946, WB). *d:* Howard Hawks; *p:* Howard Hawks; *sc:* William Faulkner, Leigh Brackett, and Jules Furthman—*b/o* the novel by Raymond Chandler.

PHILIP MARLOWE: Tough private eye who, when he's hired by a wealthy man to get rid of a blackmailer, finds himself up to his neck in a complex assortment of murder, mayhem, and women.

Lauren Bacall, John Ridgely, Martha Vickers, Dorothy Malone, Regis Toomey, Bob Steele, Elisha Cook Jr., Louis Jean Heydt, James Flavin, Thomas Jackson, Theodore Von Eltz, Tom Fadden, Ben Welden, Trevor Bardette, Joseph Crehan.

Dead Reckoning (1947, Col.). *d:* John Cromwell; *p:* Sidney Biddell; *sc:* Oliver H.P. Garrett and Steve Fisher (adaptation by Allen Rivkin)—*b/o* a story by Gerald Adams and Sidney Biddell.

RIP MURDOCK: Ex–WWII paratrooper who becomes involved with a beautiful but treacherous woman when he sets out to track down the killer of his wartime paratrooper buddy.

Lizabeth Scott, Morris Carnovsky, William Prince, Charles Cane, Marvin Miller, Wallace Ford, James Bell, George Chandler, William Forrest, Ruby Dandridge.

The Two Mrs. Carrolls (1947, WB). *d:* Peter Godfrey; *p:* Mark Hellinger; *sc:* Thomas Job—*b/o* the play by Martin Vale.

GEOFFREY CARROLL: Psychopathic American artist living in London who likes to paint his wives as "Angels of Death" and then do them in with poisoned milk.

Barbara Stanwyck, Alexis Smith, Nigel Bruce, Isobel Elsom, Patrick O'Moore, Ann Carter, Colin Campbell, Peter Godfrey.

Dark Passage (1947, WB). *d:* Delmer Daves; *p:* Jerry Wald; *sc:* Delmer Daves—*b/o* the novel by David Goodis.

VINCENT PARRY: Husband who, after he's sent to San Quentin prison for the murder of his wife, escapes to San Francisco and undergoes plastic surgery as part of his plan to find his wife's real killer.

Lauren Bacall, Bruce Bennett, Agnes Moorehead, Tom D'Andrea, Clifton Young, Douglas Kennedy, Rory Mallinson, Houseley Stevenson.

The Treasure of the Sierra Madre (1948, WB). *d:* John Huston; *p:* Henry Blanke; *sc:* John Huston—*b/o* the novel by B. Traven.

FRED C. DOBBS: Greedy American bum in Mexico who teams up with two other down-on-their-luck drifters on a gold-hunting expedition in the Sierra Madre.

Walter Huston, Tim Holt, Bruce Bennett, Barton MacLane, Alfonso Bedoya, A. Soto Rangel, Margarito Luna, Bobby Blake, John Huston, Jack Holt.

Key Largo (1948, WB). *d:* John Huston; *p:* Jerry Wald; *sc:* Richard Brooks and John Huston—*b/o* the play by Maxwell Anderson.

FRANK McCLOUD: Disillusioned ex–WWII U.S. Army major who is one of a group of people held captive by a vicious gangster in an isolated hotel on a storm-swept Florida key.

Edward G. Robinson, Lauren Bacall, Lionel Barrymore, Claire Trevor, Thomas Gomez, Harry Lewis, John Rodney, Marc Lawrence, Dan Seymour, Monte Blue, William Haade, Jay Silverheels, Rodric Redwing.

Knock on Any Door (1949, Col.). *d:* Nicholas Ray; *p:* Robert Lord (Santana); *sc:* Daniel Taradash and John Monks Jr.—*b/o* the novel by Willard Motley.

ANDREW MORTON: Sincere defense attorney who mistakenly believes that his client—a young Chicago slum-bred hoodlum charged with murder—is an innocent victim of society and circumstantial evidence.

John Derek, George Macready, Allene Roberts, Susan Perry, Mickey Knox, Barry Kelley, Cara Williams, Jimmy Conlin, Sid Melton, Dewey Martin, Vince Barnett, Pierre Watkin, Argentina Brunetti, Dick Sinatra.

Tokyo Joe (1949, Col.). *d:* Stuart Heisler; *p:* Robert Lord (Santana); *sc:* Cyril Hume and Bertram Millhauser (adaptation by Walter Doniger)—*b/o* a story by Steve Fisher.

JOE BARRETT: Ex–WWII American flyer in post-war Japan who becomes involved in smuggling and blackmail in order to save his ex-wife and young daughter from Japanese criminals.

Alexander Knox, Florence Marly, Sessue Hayakawa, Jerome Courtland, Gordon Jones, Teru Shimada, Hideo Mori, Charles Meredith, Rhys Williams, Lora Lee Michael, Harold Goodwin, James Cardwell, Otto Han.

Chain Lightning (1950, WB). *d:* Stuart Heisler; *p:* Anthony Veiller; *sc:* Liam O'Brien and Vincent Evans—*b/o* a story by J. Redmond Prior.

MATT BRENNAN: Ex–WWII bomber pilot who is hired as a civilian test pilot and risks his life testing a newly designed jet with an experimental ejection cockpit.

Eleanor Parker, Raymond Massey, Richard Whorf, James Brown, Roy Roberts, Morris Ankrum, Fay Baker, Fred Sherman.

In a Lonely Place (1950, Col.). *d:* Nicholas Ray; *p:* Robert Lord (Santana); *sc:* Andrew Solt (adaptation by Edmund H. North)—*b/o* the novel by Dorothy B. Hughes.

DIXON STEELE: Violent-tempered Hollywood screenwriter who is one of the prime suspects in the murder of a hat-check girl.

Gloria Grahame, Frank Lovejoy, Carl Benton Reid, Art Smith, Jeff Donnell, Martha Stewart, Robert Warwick, Morris Ankrum, William Ching, Steven Geray, Hadda Brooks, Jack Reynolds, Ruth Warren, Lewis Howard.

The Enforcer (1951, WB). *d:* Bretaigne Windust; *p:* Milton Sperling (United States Pictures); *sc:* Martin Rackin.

MARTIN FERGUSON: Crusading assistant D.A. who is out to snare the head of the notorious hit-man organization known as Murder, Inc.

Zero Mostel, Ted De Corsia, Everett Sloan, Roy Roberts, Lawrence Tolan, King Donovan, Bob Steele, Don Beddoe, Jack Lambert, Patricia Joiner, Susan Cabot.

Sirocco (1951, Col.). *d:* Curtis Bernhardt; *p:* Robert Lord (Santana); *sc:* A. I. Bezzerides and Hans Jacoby—*b/o* the novel *Coup de Grâce* by Joseph Kessel.

HARRY SMITH: Mercenary gun-runner in 1925 French-occupied Damascus who plies his trade between the French and the Syrians, depending on which group offers him the most.

Marta Toren, Lee J. Cobb, Everett Sloane, Gerald Mohr, Zero Mostel, Nick Dennis, Onslow Stevens, Ludwig Donath, David Bond, Peter Ortiz, Jay Novello, Harry Guardino.

The African Queen (1951, UA). *d:* John Huston; *p:* S. P. Eagle (Sam Spiegel) (Horizon–Romulus); *sc:* James Agee and John Huston—*b/o* the novel by C. S. Forester.

CHARLIE ALLNUT*: Gin-soaked Canadian

---

*Won the Academy Award as Best Actor for this role.

riverboat captain of the *African Queen* who, along with a puritanical female missionary, heads down an African river to a lake where they plan to attack a WWI German gunboat.

Katharine Hepburn, Robert Morley, Peter Bull, Theodore Bikel, Walter Gotell, Gerald Onn, Peter Swanick, Richard Marner.

Deadline—U.S.A. (1952, 20th-Fox). *d:* Richard Brooks; *p:* Sol C. Siegel; *sc:* Richard Brooks.

ED HUTCHINSON: Big-city newspaper editor who, while fighting to keep the paper's owners from selling to a rival publisher, crusades against a crime czar.

Ethel Barrymore, Kim Hunter, Ed Begley, Warren Stevens, Paul Stewart, Martin Gabel, Joe De Santis, Jim Backus, Selmer Jackson, Parley Baer, John Douchette, Tom Powers, Philip Terry, Joseph Sawyer.

Battle Circus (1953, MGM). *d:* Richard Brooks; *p:* Pandro S. Berman; *sc:* Richard Brooks—*b/o* a story by Allen Rivkin and Laura Kerr.

MAJ. JED WEBBE: U.S. Army surgeon at a mobile field hospital behind the front lines in the Korean War who falls in love with a nurse.

June Allyson, Keenan Wynn, Robert Keith, William Campbell, Perry Sheehan, Jonathan Cott, Adele Longmire, Sarah Selby, Philip Ahn, Steve Forrest, Jeff Richards, Dick Simmons.

Beat the Devil (1954, UA). *d:* John Huston; *p:* Jack Clayton (Santana–Romulus); *sc:* John Huston and Truman Capote—*b/o* the novel by James Helvick.

BILLY DANNREUTHER: American fortune-hunter and front man for a quartet of international crooks scheming to buy some uranium-rich land in British East Africa.

Jennifer Jones, Gina Lollobrigida, Robert Morley, Peter Lorre, Edward Underdown, Ivor Barnard, Bernard Lee, Marco Tulli, Mario Perroni, Alex Pochet.

The Caine Mutiny (1954, Col.). *d:* Edward Dmytryk; *p:* Stanley Kramer (Stanley Kramer); *sc:* Stanley Roberts (with additional dialogue by Michael Blankfort)—*b/o* the novel by Herman Wouk.

CAPT. PHILIP FRANCIS QUEEG*: WWII Navy skipper of the destroyer *Caine* who, when he begins to crack under the strain of command and shows signs of paranoia, is relieved of command at sea by his executive officer—who is subsequently charged with mutiny.

Jose Ferrer, Van Johnson, Fred MacMurray, Robert Francis, May Wynn, Tom Tully, E. G.

---

*Received an Academy Award nomination as Best Actor for this role.

Marshall, Arthur Franz, Lee Marvin, Warner Anderson, Claude Akins, Jerry Paris, Steve Brodie, Todd Karns, Whit Bissell, James Best, James Edwards, Don Dubbins.

Sabrina (1954, Para.). *d:* Billy Wilder; *p:* Billy Wilder; *sc:* Billy Wilder, Samuel Taylor, and Ernest Lehman—*b/o* the play *Sabrina Fair* by Samuel Taylor.

LINUS LARRABEE: Rich, stuffy business tycoon who pretends to fall in love with the family chauffeur's daughter in order to break up her romance with his playboy younger brother.

Audrey Hepburn, William Holden, Walter Hampden, John Williams, Martha Hyer, Marcel Dalio, Nella Walker, Francis X. Bushman, Ellen Corby.

The Barefoot Contessa (1954, UA). *d:* Joseph L. Mankiewicz; *p:* Forrest E. Johnston (Figaro); *sc:* Joseph L. Mankiewicz.

HARRY DAWES: Has-been movie director who gets another chance when a coarse millionaire hires him to write and direct a film in Rome starring a beautiful cabaret dancer from Madrid.

Ava Gardner, Edmond O'Brien, Marius Goring, Valentina Cortessa, Rossano Brazzi, Elizabeth Sellars, Warren Stevens, Bessie Love, Bill Fraser, John Parrish, Jim Gerald.

We're No Angels (1955, Para.). *d:* Michael Curtiz; *p:* Pat Duggan; *sc:* Ranald MacDougall—*b/o* the play *La Cuisine des Anges* by Albert Husson.

JOSEPH: Forger-embezzler who—with two other convicts—escapes from Devil's Island, takes refuge with a French family in a dry goods store, and saves the family from a money-hungry relative plotting to take over the store.

Aldo Ray, Peter Ustinov, Joan Bennett, Basil Rathbone, Leo G. Carroll, John Baer, Gloria Talbott, Lea Penman, John Smith.

The Left Hand of God (1955, 20th-Fox). *d:* Edward Dmytryk; *p:* Buddy Adler; *sc:* Alfred Hayes—*b/o* the novel by William E. Barrett.

JIM CARMODY: WWII American flyer who, when he's forced down in China, is "drafted" by a renegade Chinese warlord but escapes and hides out by masquerading as a priest.

Gene Tierney, Lee J. Cobb, Agnes Moorehead, E. G. Marshall, Jean Porter, Carl Benton Reid, Victor Sen Yung, Philip Ahn, Benson Fong, Richard Cutting, Don Forbes, Noel Toy.

The Desperate Hours (1955, Para.). *d:* William Wyler; *p:* William Wyler; *sc:* Joseph Hayes—*b/o* his novel and play.

GLENN GRIFFIN: Ruthless leader of a trio of escaped convicts who break into a suburban household, where they terrorize and hold hostage a businessman, his wife, and their son and daughter.

Fredric March, Arthur Kennedy, Martha Scott, Dewey Martin, Gig Young, Robert Middleton, Alan Reed, Bert Freed, Ray Collins, Whit Bissell, Ray Teal, Don Haggerty, Pat Flaherty, Beverly Garland, Ann Doran.

The Harder They Fall (1956, Col.). *d:* Mark Robson; *p:* Philip Yordan; *sc:* Philip Yordan—*b/o* the novel by Budd Schulberg.

EDDIE WILLIS: Cynical sportswriter–turned–press agent who helps a crooked boxing promoter fix a series of fights and push a glass-jawed Argentine giant into a heavyweight championship bout.

Rod Steiger, Jan Sterling, Mike Lane, Max Baer, Jersey Joe Walcott, Edward Andrews, Harold J. Stone, Carlos Montalban, Nehemiah Persoff, Herbie Faye, Rusty Lane, Jack Albertson, Tommy Herman, Matt Murphy.

· In addition, Humphrey Bogart made cameo/guest appearances in the following feature films: *Thank Your Lucky Stars* (1943, WB), *Two Guys From Milwaukee* (1946, WB), *Always Together* (1948, WB), and *The Love Lottery* (1953, Rank).

☆ MARLON BRANDO

Marlon "Bud" Brando Jr.

b: April 3, 1924, Omaha, Neb.

"I coulda been a contender! I coulda been somebody! Instead of a bum, which is what I am!"

Terry Malloy (Marlon Brando) to
Charlie Malloy (Rod Steiger) in
On the Waterfront, 1954.

The Men (1950, UA). *d:* Fred Zinnemann; *p:* Stanley Kramer (Stanley Kramer); *sc:* Carl Foreman.

KEN: Young WWII American infantry lieutenant who, after he's hit by a sniper in Europe, winds up as a sullen, resentful paraplegic in a veteran's hospital but—with the help of others—learns to readjust to life.

Teresa Wright, Everett Sloane, Jack Webb, Richard Erdman, Arthur Jurado, Virginia Farmer, Dorothy Tree, Howard St. John, Nina Hunter, Cliff Clark, Ray Teal.

A Streetcar Named Desire (1951, WB). *d:* Elia Kazan; *p:* Charles K. Feldman; *sc:* Tennessee Williams (adaptation by Oscar Saul)—*b/o* his play.

STANLEY KOWALSKI*: Crude, brutal working man in a New Orleans tenement district who constantly taunts his neurotic sister-in-law, then finally rapes her and drives her over the brink into madness.

Vivien Leigh, Kim Hunter, Karl Malden, Rudy Bond, Nick Dennis, Peg Hillias, Wright King, Richard Garrick, Anne Dere, Edna Thomas.

Viva Zapata! (1952, 20th-Fox). *d:* Elia Kazan; *p:* Darryl F. Zanuck; *sc:* John Steinbeck.

EMILIANO ZAPATA*: Mexican peon-turned-revolutionary in the early 1920s who rises to power and becomes president of Mexico but, after deserting the office, is betrayed by a friend and is ambushed and murdered by soldiers.

Jean Peters, Anthony Quinn, Joseph Wiseman, Arnold Moss, Alan Reed, Margo, Harold Gordon, Lou Gilbert, Mildred Dunnock, Frank Silvera, Frank DeKova, Ross Bagdasarian, Abner Biberman, Phil Van Zandt.

Julius Caesar (1953, MGM). *d:* Joseph L. Mankiewicz; *p:* John Houseman; *sc:* Adapted by Joseph L. Mankiewicz from the play by William Shakespeare.

MARC ANTONY*: Soldier and loyal friend of Julius Caesar in 44 B.C. Rome who, after Caesar is assassinated, takes control of the city—along with Octavius Caesar—and purges it of suspected enemies.

James Mason, John Gielgud, Louis Calhern, Edmond O'Brien, Greer Garson, Deborah Kerr, George Macready, Michael Pate, Alan Napier, John Hoyt, Tom Powers, Ian Wolfe, Douglas Dumbrille, Rhys Williams, Michael Ansara, Edmund Purdom.

The Wild One (1953, Col.). *d:* Laslo Benedek; *p:* Stanley Kramer (Stanley Kramer); *sc:* John Paxton—*b/o The Cyclists' Raid* by Frank Rooney.

JOHNNY: Tough, leather-jacketed leader of a motorcycle gang that invades, vandalizes, and terrorizes a small California town before finally being run out.

*Received an Academy Award nomination as Best Actor for this role.

*Received an Academy Award nomination as Best Actor for this role.

Mary Murphy, Robert Keith, Lee Marvin, Jay C. Flippen, Ray Teal, Will Wright, Robert Osterloh, Robert Bice, Yvonne Doughty, Gil Stratton Jr., Darren Dublin, Jerry Paris, Alvy Moore.

On the Waterfront (1954, Col.). *d:* Elia Kazan; *p:* Sam Spiegel (Sam Spiegel); *sc:* Budd Schulberg—*b/o* articles by Malcolm Johnson.

TERRY MALLOY*: Young New York ex-fighter and dock worker who, after his older brother is murdered, battles the brutal waterfront gang boss responsible and breaks the stranglehold of labor-union racketeers.

Karl Malden, Lee J. Cobb, Rod Steiger, Pat Henning, Eva Marie Saint, Leif Erickson, James Westerfield, Tony Galento, John Hamilton, Rudy Bond, Mike O'Dowd, Marty Balsam, Fred Gwynne.

Desiree (1954, 20th-Fox). *d:* Henry Koster; *p:* Julian Blaustein; *sc:* Daniel Taradash—*b/o* the novel by Annemarie Selinko.

NAPOLEON BONAPARTE: Eighteenth-century Corsican in the French Army who falls in love with a silk merchant's daughter (Desiree), then—even though she marries his brother—becomes involved with her at various times while he becomes a famous military general and emperor of France.

Jean Simmons, Merle Oberon, Michael Rennie, Cameron Mitchell, Elizabeth Sellars, Cathleen Nesbitt, Isobel Elsom, John Hoyt, Alan Napier, Richard Deacon, Carolyn Jones, Nicolas Koster, Sam Gilman, Lester Matthews.

Guys and Dolls (1955, MGM). *d:* Joseph L. Mankiewicz; *p:* Samuel Goldwyn (Samuel Goldwyn); *sc:* Joseph L. Mankiewicz—from the musical play by Jo Swerling, Abe Burrows, and Frank Loesser—*b/o* Damon Runyon's story "The Idyll of Miss Sarah Brown."

SKY MASTERSON: Sharp Broadway gambler who bets a gambler friend that he can persuade a pretty Salvation Army missionary to fly to Havana with him for dinner—and wins.

Jean Simmons, Frank Sinatra, Vivian Blaine, Robert Keith, Stubby Kaye, B. S. Pully, Johnny Silver, Sheldon Leonard, George E. Stone, Regis Toomey, Veda Ann Borg, Joe McTurk.

The Teahouse of the August Moon (1956, MGM). *d:* Daniel Mann; *p:* Jack Cummings; *sc:* John Patrick—*b/o* the play by John Patrick from the book by Vern J. Sneider.

SAKINI: Young Army captain's congenial Okinawan interpreter who subtly outfoxes the U.S. Army when it attempts the post-WWII Americanization of an Okinawan village.

Glenn Ford, Machiko Kyo, Eddie Albert, Paul

Ford, Jun Negami, Nijiko Kiyokawa, Mitsuko Sawamura, Harry Morgan, Frank Tokunaga.

Sayonara (1957, WB). *d:* Joshua Logan; *p:* William Goetz (Goetz Pictures–Pennebaker); *sc:* Paul Osborn—*b/o* the novel by James Michener.

MAJ. LLOYD GRUVER*: American jet ace on recuperative duty in Tokyo during the Korean War who, when he falls in love with a beautiful Japanese dancing star and wants to marry her, is thwarted both by U.S. military regulations and Japanese customs.

Patricia Owens, Red Buttons, Ricardo Montalban, Martha Scott, James Garner, Miiko Taka, Miyoshi Umeki, Kent Smith, Douglas Watson, Reiko Kuba, Soo Yong.

The Young Lions (1958, 20th-Fox). *d:* Edward Dmytryk; *p:* Al Lichtman; *sc:* Edward Anhalt—*b/o* the novel by Irwin Shaw.

CHRISTIAN DIESTL: Young German ski instructor who, after becoming a Nazi and a dedicated WWII lieutenant in the German Army, grows disillusioned and ends up loathing the depravity of Nazism before being killed by American G.I.s.

Montgomery Clift, Dean Martin, Hope Lange, Barbara Rush, May Britt, Maximilian Schell, Dora Doll, Lee Van Cleef, Parley Baer, Arthur Franz, Hal Baylor, Herbert Rudley, John Alderson, L. Q. Jones.

One-Eyed Jacks (1960, Para.). *d:* Marlon Brando; *p:* Frank P. Rosenberg (Pennebaker); *sc:* Guy Trosper and Calder Willingham—*b/o* Charles Neider's novel *The Authentic Death of Hendry Jones.*

RIO: Outlaw in the 1880s who, after serving five years in prison because his partner betrayed him, escapes to seek revenge in Monterey, California—where his partner is now the town sheriff.

Karl Malden, Pina Pellicer, Katy Jurado, Ben Johnson, Slim Pickens, Timothy Carey, Elisha Cook, Rudolph Acosta, Ray Teal, John Dierkes, Hank Worden, Nina Martinez.

The Fugitive Kind (1961, UA). *d:* Sidney Lumet; *p:* Martin Jurow and Richard A. Shepherd (Jurow–Shepherd–Pennebaker); *sc:* Tennessee Williams and Meade Roberts—*b/o* the play *Orpheus Descending* by Tennessee Williams.

VAL XAVIER: Guitar-playing drifter from New Orleans who arrives in a Mississippi town and runs into trouble when he becomes involved with two women—one the middle-aged Italian-born wife of a man dying of cancer, the other an alcoholic nymphomaniac from a respectable family.

---

*Won the Academy Award as Best Actor for this role.

*Received an Academy Award nomination as Best Actor for this role.

Anna Magnani, Joanne Woodward, Maureen
Stapleton, Victor Jory, R. G. Armstrong, Emory
Richardson, Sally Gracie, Lucille Benson, John
Baragrey, Joe Brown Jr.

Mutiny on the Bounty (1962, MGM). *d:* Lewis
Milestone; *p:* Aaron Rosenberg (Arcola); *sc:*
Charles Lederer—*b/o* the novel by Charles
Nordhoff and James Norman Hall.

FLETCHER CHRISTIAN: Master's mate on the
British naval vessel H.M.S. *Bounty* who leads a
mutiny in 1789 against the tyrannical ship's
captain, William Bligh, sets Bligh adrift in a
small boat, then seeks refuge with the rest of the
mutineers on Pitcairn Island.

Trevor Howard, Richard Harris, Hugh Griffith,
Richard Haydn, Tarita, Percy Herbert, Duncan
Lamont, Gordon Jackson, Chips Rafferty, Noel
Purcell, Eddie Byrne, Frank Silvera.

The Ugly American (1962, Univ.). *d:* George
Englund; *p:* George Englund; *sc:* Stewart Stern—
b/o the novel by William J. Lederer and Eugene
Burdick.

HARRISON CARTER MacWHITE: Former
newspaper publisher whose arrival in a Southeast
Asian country as the newly appointed U.S.
Ambassador stirs up pro-Communist factions and
leads to personal and political disaster for him.

Eiji Okada, Sandra Church, Pat Hingle, Arthur
Hill, Jocelyn Brando, Kurrit Pramoj, Judson
Pratt, Reiko Sato, George Shibata, Philip Ober,
Pock Rock Ahn.

Bedtime Story (1964, Univ.). *d:* Ralph Levy; *p:*
Stanley Shapiro (Lankershim–Pennebaker); *sc:*
Stanley Shapiro and Paul Henning.

FREDDY BENSON: Wolfish U.S. Army corporal
who, while on the French Riviera, vies with
another smooth con man for the affections (and
money) of a supposedly rich visiting American
woman they've been told is a "soap queen"—but
who is actually only a working girl who has won a
beauty contest.

David Niven, Shirley Jones, Dody Goodman, Aram
Stephan, Parley Baer, Marie Windsor, Rebecca
Sand, Frances Robinson, Henry Slate, Norman
Alden, Francine York.

Morituri (1965, 20th-Fox). *d:* Bernard Wicki; *p:*
Aaron Rosenberg (Arcola–Colony); *sc:* Daniel
Taradash—*b/o* the novel by Werner Joerg
Luedecke.

ROBERT CRAIN: Wealthy German pacifist during
WWII who is blackmailed by British Intelligence
into posing as an SS agent aboard a German
cargo ship as part of a British plot to capture it.

Yul Brynner, Janet Margolin, Trevor Howard,
Martin Benrath, Hans Christian Blech, Wally
Cox, Rainer Penkert, William Redfield, Gary
Crosby, Carl Esmond, Robert Wilke.

The Chase (1966, Col.). *d:* Arthur Penn; *p:* Sam
Spiegel (Horizon); *sc:* Lillian Hellman—*b/o* the
novel and play by Horton Foote.

SHERIFF CALDER: Sheriff of a small Texas town
who tries in vain to prevent tragedy when a
convict escapes from prison, heads for the town,
and discovers that his wife is having an affair
with the wealthy town boss's son.

Jane Fonda, Robert Redford, E. G. Marshall,
Angie Dickinson, Janice Rule, Miriam Hopkins,
Martha Hyer, Robert Duvall, James Fox, Diana
Hyland, Henry Hull, Jocelyn Brando, Paul
Williams, Malcolm Atterbury, Nydia Westman,
Bruce Cabot.

The Appaloosa (1966, Univ.). *d:* Sidney J. Furie;
p: Alan Miller; *sc:* James Bridges and Roland
Kibbee—*b/o* a novel by Robert MacLeod.

MATT FLETCHER: American buffalo hunter in
the 1870s who pursues a Mexican bandit into
lawless Mexican territory to retrieve a valuable
appaloosa that the bandit has stolen from him.

Anjanette Comer, John Saxon, Emilio Fernandez,
Alex Montoya, Miriam Colon, Rafael Campos,
Frank Silvera, Larry D. Mann, Argentina
Brunetti.

A Countess from Hong Kong (1967, Univ.). *d:*
Charles Chaplin; *p:* Jerome Epstein; *sc:* Charles
Chaplin.

OGDEN MEARS: American millionaire diplomat
who, when he sails from Hong Kong on an ocean
liner, discovers a beautiful female Russian
stowaway in his stateroom—and faces
complications when his wife boards the ship at
Hawaii.

Sophia Loren, Sydney Chaplin, Tippi Hedren,
Patrick Cargill, Margaret Rutherford, Michael
Medwin, Oliver Johnston, John Paul, Bill Nagy,
Dilys Laye, Angela Pringle, Francis Dux, Charles
Chaplin.

Reflections in a Golden Eye (1967, WB–Seven
Arts). *d:* John Huston; *p:* Ray Stark (Huston–
Stark); *sc:* Chapman Mortimer and Gladys Hill—
b/o the novel by Carson McCullers.

MAJ. WELDON PENDERTON: Officer at a 1948
U.S. Army post in Georgia whose wife is having
an affair with another officer, and whose hidden
homosexuality is aroused when he becomes
obsessed with a young private who rides
horseback naked through the woods.

Elizabeth Taylor, Brian Keith, Julie Harris, Zorro
David, Gordon Mitchell, Irvin Dugan, Fay Sparks,
Robert Forster.

Candy (1968, Cinerama). *d:* Christian Marquand;
p: Robert Haggiag (Selmur/Dear/Corona); *sc:* Buck
Henry—*b/o* the novel by Terry Southern.

GRINDL: Indian guru, one of several weird and

oversexed male characters who seduce an amoral blonde teenager named Candy.

Ewa Aulin, Richard Burton, James Coburn, Walter Matthau, Charles Aznavour, John Huston, Elsa Martinelli, Ringo Starr, John Astin.

The Night of the Following Day (1969, Univ.). *d:* Hubert Cornfield; *p:* Hubert Cornfield (Gina); *sc:* Hubert Cornfield and Robert Phippeny—*b/o* Lionel White's novel *The Snatchers*.

BUD: Ringleader (posing as a limousine chauffeur) of an eccentric gang that kidnaps a young girl when she arrives in Paris to visit her father.

Richard Boone, Rita Moreno, Pamela Franklin, Jess Hahn, Gerard Buhr, Jacques Marin, Hughes Wanner.

Burn! (1970, UA). *d:* Gillo Pontecorvo; *p:* Alberto Grimaldi (Grimaldi/Produzioni Europee/Les Productions Artistes); *sc:* Franco Solinas and Giorgio Arlorio—*b/o* a story by Gillo Pontecorvo, Franco Solinas, and Giorgio Arlorio.

SIR WILLIAM WALKER: British government agent in the mid–nineteenth century who is sent to a small Caribbean island to instigate a slave uprising against Portuguese control so that the British can take charge of the island's sugar-cane industry.

Evaristo Marquez, Renato Salvatori, Norman Hill, Tom Lyons, Wanani, Joseph Persuad, Carlo Pammucci, Cecily Browne, Dana Ghia.

The Nightcomers (1972, Avco Embassy). *d:* Michael Winner; *p:* Michael Winner (Elliott Kastner–Jay Kanter–Alan Ladd Jr.–Scimitar); *sc:* Michael Hastings—*b/o* characters from *The Turn of the Screw* by Henry James.

PETER QUINT: Depraved Irish gardner/handyman who corrupts a young orphaned brother and sister but winds up—along with his proper Victorian housekeeper/governess/lover—being murdered by the children.

Stephanie Beacham, Thora Hird, Verna Harvey, Christopher Ellis, Harry Andrews, Anna Palk.

The Godfather (1972, Para.). *d:* Francis Ford Coppola; *p:* Albert S. Ruddy (Alfran); *sc:* Mario Puzo and Francis Ford Coppola—*b/o* the novel by Mario Puzo.

DON VITO CORLEONE*: Tough, aging Sicilian peasant who has risen to become the head of a powerful Mafia clan in the New York area, and whose youngest son—after the father dies of a heart attack—takes control of the clan.

Al Pacino, James Caan, Richard Castellano, Robert Duvall, Sterling Hayden, John Marley, Richard Conte, Diane Keaton, Al Lettieri, Abe

Vigoda, Talia Shire, John Cazale, Rudy Bond, Al Martino, Morgana King, Vito Scotti.

Last Tango in Paris (1972, UA). *d:* Bernardo Bertolucci; *p:* Alberto Grimaldi (Les Artistes Associes/PEA); *sc:* Bernardo Bertolucci and Franco Arcalli.

PAUL*: Confused, despairing middle-aged American in Paris who, shortly after his wife commits suicide, meets a young French woman while apartment-hunting and becomes involved in a three-day sexual encounter with her.

Maria Schneider, Darling Legitimus, Jean-Pierre Leaud, Catherine Sola, Mauro Marchetti, Dan Diament, Peter Schommer, Catherine Allegret, Maria Michi.

The Missouri Breaks (1976, UA). *d:* Arthur Penn; *p:* Elliott Kastner and Robert M. Sherman; *sc:* Thomas McGuane.

ROBERT E. LEE CLAYTON: Eccentric, sadistic gunman in 1880s Montana who is hired as a "regulator" by a rich cattle rancher to exterminate a gang of horse thieves.

Jack Nicholson, Randy Quaid, Kathleen Lloyd, Frederic Forrest, Harry Dean Stanton, John McLiam, John Ryan, Sam Gilman, Steve Franken, Richard Bradford, Luana Anders.

Superman (1978, WB). *d:* Richard Donner; *p:* Ilya Salkind and Pierre Spengler (Alexander Salkind); *sc:* Mario Puzo, David Newman, Leslie Newman, and Robert Benton—*b/o* a story by Mario Puzo. Creative consultant, Tom Mankiewicz. Based on the comic strip created by Jerry Siegel and Joe Shuster.

JOR-EL: Brilliant scientist on the planet Krypton who, just before the planet is destroyed, places his baby son (who will grow up to be Superman) inside a small rocket and launches it to land on Earth.

Gene Hackman, Christopher Reeve, Ned Beatty, Jackie Cooper, Glenn Ford, Trevor Howard, Margot Kidder, Jack O'Halloran, Valerie Perrine, Maria Schell, Terence Stamp, Phyllis Thaxter, Susannah York, Jeff East, Marc McClure, Sarah Douglas, Harry Andrews.

Apocalypse Now (1979, UA). *d:* Francis Ford Coppola; *p:* Francis Ford Coppola (Omni Zoetrope); *sc:* John Milius and Francis Ford Coppola—loosely *b/o* the novel *Heart of Darkness* by Joseph Conrad.

COLONEL WALTER E. KURTZ: Renegade Green Berets colonel during the Vietnam War who—after he has lost his sanity, taken refuge in the Cambodian jungles, and started waging his own wars, leading a group of ferocious Montagnard

---

*Won the Academy Award as Best Actor for this role.

*Received an Academy Award nomination as Best Actor for this role.

tribesmen—is targeted for execution by a U.S. Army Special Services officer.

Robert Duvall, Martin Sheen, Frederic Forrest, Albert Hall, Sam Bottoms, Larry Fishburne, Dennis Hopper, G. D. Spradlin, Harrison Ford.

The Formula (1980, UA). *d:* John G. Avildsen; *p:* Steve Shagan; *sc:* Steve Shagan—*b/o* his novel.

ADAM STEIFELL: One of a group of oil tycoons who, in order to further their own gain, stop at nothing in their efforts to suppress a secret formula for a cheap synthetic fuel.

George C. Scott, Marthe Keller, John Gielgud, G. D. Spradlin, Beatrice Straight, Richard Lynch, John Van Dreelen, Robin Clarke, Ike Eisenmann, Marshall Thompson.

☆ CHARLES BRONSON

Charles Dennis Bunchinsky

b: Nov. 3, 1921, Ehrenfeld, Pa.

"His gun made him older."

Det. Lou Torrey (Charles Bronson) when asked why he killed a seventeen-year-old fleeing suspect in The Stone Killer, 1973.

Charles Bronson made the first seventeen of the following films under the name Charles Buchinski, or sometimes Charles Buchinsky.

You're in the Navy Now (later called **U.S.S. Teakettle**) (1951, 20th-Fox). *d:* Henry Hathaway; *p:* Fred Kohlmar; *sc:* Richard Murphy—*b/o* an article in *The New Yorker* by John W. Hazard.

WASCYLEWSKI: Polish-American seaman, one of the crew of misfits aboard an experimental WWII patrol boat dubbed the U.S.S. *Teakettle* because it's powered by a steam turbine.

Gary Cooper, Jane Greer, Millard Mitchell, Eddie Albert, John McIntyre, Ray Collins, Harry Von Zell, Jack Webb, Richard Erdman, Harvey Lembeck, Henry Slate, Ed Begley, Jack Warden, Lee Marvin, Charles Smith.

The People Against O'Hara (1951, MGM). *d:* John Sturges; *p:* William H. Wright; *sc:* John Monks Jr.—*b/o* the novel by Eleazar Lipsky.

ANGELO KORVAC: One of the sons in a working-class family that is visited by a criminal lawyer investigating a murder case.

Spencer Tracy, Diana Lynn, Pat O'Brien, John Hodiak, James Arness, Eduardo Ciannelli, Richard Anderson, Jay C. Flippen, Regis Toomey, William Campbell, Ann Doran, Henry O'Neill, Arthur Shields, Emile Meyer, Frank Ferguson, Lee Phelps, Mae Clarke, Jack Kruschen.

The Mob (1951, Col.). *d:* Robert Parrish; *p:* Jerry Bresler; *sc:* William Bowers—*b/o* the *Collier's* magazine story "Waterfront" by Ferguson Findley.

JACK: One of several rugged characters encountered by an undercover detective posing as a dockworker and gunman in order to trap a waterfront mobster.

Broderick Crawford, Betty Buehler, Richard Kiley, Otto Hulett, Neville Brand, Ernest Borgnine, Ralph Dumke, John Marley, Frank de Kova, Jay Adler, Emile Meyer, Harry Lauter.

The Marrying Kind (1952, Col.). *d:* George Cukor; *p:* Bert Granet; *sc:* Ruth Gordon and Garson Kanin.

EDDIE: Post office fellow worker of a young man about to get a divorce.

Judy Holliday, Aldo Ray, Madge Kennedy, Sheila Bond, John Alexander, Phyllis Povah, Peggy Cass, Mickey Shaughnessy, Frank Ferguson, Gordon Jones, Nancy Kulp.

Red Skies of Montana (1952, 20th-Fox). *d:* Joseph M. Newman; *p:* Samuel G. Engel; *sc:* Harry Kleiner—*b/o* a story by Art Cohn.

NEFF: One of a courageous group of U.S. Forestry Service firefighters—known as "Smoke Jumpers"—in the forested mountains of Montana.

Richard Widmark, Constance Smith, Jeffrey Hunter, Richard Boone, Warren Stevens, James Griffith, Joe Sawyer, Richard Crenna, Larry Dobkin, Henry Kulky, Parley Baer.

My Six Convicts (1952, Col.). *d:* Hugo Fregonese; *p:* Stanley Kramer; *sc:* Michael Blankfort—*b/o* a story by Donald Powell Wilson.

JOCKO: Tough prisoner at a penitentiary where a sympathetic prison psychiatrist uses psychology to turn convicts into more useful citizens.

Millard Mitchell, Gilbert Roland, John Beal, Marshall Thompson, Alf Kjellin, Henry Morgan, Jay Adler, Regis Toomey, Carleton Young, John Marley, Byron Foulger, Jack Carr, Carol Savage, Fred Kelsey.

Diplomatic Courier (1952, 20th-Fox). *d:* Henry Hathaway; *p:* Casey Robinson; *sc:* Casey Robinson and Liam O'Brien—b/o the novel *Sinister Errand* by Peter Cheyney.

Billed as a "RUSSIAN": One of a pair of Soviet agents who board a European train and murder the American ambassador to Bucharest in order to prevent him from passing on a vital document to an American diplomatic courier.

Tyrone Power, Patricia Neal, Stephen McNally, Hildegarde Neff, Karl Malden, James Millican, Stefan Schnabel, Michael Ansara, Sig Arno, E. G. Marshall, Lee Marvin, Dabbs Greer, Carleton Young, Tom Powers.

Pat and Mike (1952, MGM). *d:* George Cukor; *p:* Lawrence Weingarten; *sc:* Ruth Gordon and Garson Kanin.

HANK TASLING: One of a pair of shady tough guys who get involved with a New York sports promoter and a champion female athlete.

Spencer Tracy, Katharine Hepburn, Aldo Ray, William Ching, Sammy White, George Mathews, Jim Backus, Chuck Connors, Carl Switzer, Frankie Darro, Mae Clarke, Tom Harmon, Babe Didrikson Zaharias, Gussie Moran, Don Budge, Alice Marble, Frank Parker.

Bloodhounds of Broadway (1952, 20th-Fox). *d:* Harmon Jones; *p:* George Jessel; *sc:* Sy Gomberg (adaptation by Albert Mannheimer)—b/o a story by Damon Runyon.

PITTSBURGH PHILO: Gangster who gets involved with a Broadway bookie and a backwoods orphan girl, while the girl and her pet bloodhounds become a hit act on Broadway.

Mitzi Gaynor, Scott Brady, Mitzi Green, Marguerite Chapman, Michael O'Shea, Wally Vernon, Henry Slate, George E. Stone, Edwin Max, Timothy Carey, Emile Meyer.

The Clown (1953, MGM). *d:* Robert Z. Leonard; *p:* William H. Wright; *sc:* Martin Rackin—b/o the 1931 movie *The Champ*, written by Leonard Praskins and Frances Marion.

EDDIE: Gambler who briefly gets involved in a crap game with a washed-up ex–Ziegfeld comedy star who has gambling and drinking problems but who, for the sake of his young son, tries to make a comeback.

Red Skelton, Tim Considine, Jane Greer, Loring Smith, Philip Ober, Fay Roope, Walter Reed, Don Beddoe, Steve Forrest, Ned Glass, Billy Barty, Sandra Gould.

House of Wax (1953, WB). *d:* Andre de Toth; *p:* Bryan Foy; *sc:* Crane Wilbur—b/o a story by Charles Belden.

IGOR: Deaf-mute who helps the demented owner of a wax museum by stealing bodies from the morgue to be used to create lifelike wax figures.

Vincent Price, Frank Lovejoy, Phyllis Kirk, Carolyn Jones, Paul Picerni, Roy Roberts, Angela Clarke, Paul Cavanagh, Dabbs Greer, Philip Tonge.

Miss Sadie Thompson (1953, Col.). *d:* Curtis Bernhardt; *p:* Jerry Wald (Beckworth); *sc:* Harry Kleiner—b/o the story "Miss Thompson" by W. Somerset Maugham and the play *Rain* by John Colton and Clemence Randolph.

EDWARDS: One of a group of tough post-WWII U.S. Marines stationed on a remote South Pacific island where a stranded shady lady becomes the center of attention.

Rita Hayworth, Jose Ferrer, Aldo Ray, Russell Collins, Diosa Costello, Harry Bellaver, Wilton Graff, Peggy Converse, Henry Slate, Peter Chong, Eduardo Cansino Jr.

Crime Wave (1953, WB). *d:* Andre de Toth; *p:* Bryan Foy; *sc:* Crane Wilbur (adaptation by Bernard Gordon and Richard Wormser)—b/o a story by John Hawkins and Ward Hawkins.

BEN HASTINGS: One of a pair of escaped San Quentin convicts who take a paroled ex-convict and his wife hostage in order to force the parolee to help rob a bank in Los Angeles's Chinatown.

Sterling Hayden, Gene Nelson, Phyllis Kirk, Ted de Corsia, Jay Novello, James Bell, Dub Taylor, Timothy Carey, Richard Benjamin, Fritz Feld.

Tennessee Champ (1953, MGM). *d:* Fred M. Wilcox; *p:* Sol Baer Fielding; *sc:* Art Cohn—b/o "The Lord in His Corner" and other stories by Eustace Cockrell.

SIXTY JUBEL: Tough-as-nails boxer who is one of the ring opponents faced by a young religiously oriented Tennessee fighter.

Shelley Winters, Keenan Wynn, Dewey Martin, Earl Holliman, Dave O'Brien, Yvette Dugay, Jack Kruschen, Johnny Indrisano, Alvin J. Gordon, William Newell.

Riding Shotgun (1954, WB). *d:* Andre de Toth; *p:* Ted Sherdeman; *sc:* Tom Blackburn—b/o a story by Kenneth Perkins.

PINTO: Member of a gang of stagecoach robbers whose nefarious career comes to an end during a gambling-casino gunfight.

Randolph Scott, Wayne Morris, Joan Weldon, Joe Sawyer, James Millican, James Bell, Fritz Feld, Victor Perrin, John Baer, Paul Picerni, Richard Benjamin, Dub Taylor.

Apache (1954, UA). *d:* Robert Aldrich; *p:* Harold Hecht (Hecht–Lancaster); *sc:* James R. Webb—b/o the novel *Bronco Apache* by Paul I. Wellman.

HONDO: Apache soldier with the U.S. Cavalry in the 1880s who is among the troops assigned to capture or kill an angry Apache leader who is waging war for his tribe's rights.

Burt Lancaster, Jean Peters, John McIntire, John

Dehner, Paul Guilfoyle, Ian MacDonald, Walter Sande, Morris Ankrum, Monte Blue.

Vera Cruz (1954, UA). *d:* Robert Aldrich; *p:* James Hill (Hecht–Lancaster); *sc:* Roland Kibbee and James R. Webb—*b/o* a story by Borden Chase.
PITTSBURGH: Tough gunslinger involved in a gold shipment through Mexico and a plot to overthrow Emperor Maximilian during the Mexican Revolution of 1866.
Gary Cooper, Burt Lancaster, Denise Darcel, Cesar Romero, George Macready, Ernest Borgnine, Henry Brandon, Morris Ankrum, Jack Lambert, Jack Elam, Charles Horvath, Juan Garcia.

Drum Beat (1954, WB). *d:* Delmer Daves; *p:* Alan Ladd (uncredited) (Jaguar); *sc:* Delmer Daves.
CAPTAIN JACK: Ruthless renegade Modoc Indian in 1869 Oregon who battles a peace commission appointed by President Ulysses S. Grant to negotiate a treaty with the Modoc tribe.
Alan Ladd, Audrey Dalton, Marisa Pavan, Robert Keith, Rodolfo Acosta, Warner Anderson, Elisha Cook Jr., Anthony Caruso, Hayden Rorke, Frank de Kova, Isabel Jewell, Frank Ferguson, Strother Martin.

Big House U.S.A. (1955, UA). *d:* Howard W. Koch; *p:* Aubrey Schenk (Bel-Air); *sc:* John C. Higgins.
BENNY KELLY: Rugged convict who, with four other cutthroats, breaks out of prison to get his hands on a fortune in hidden loot but is brutally done in by the leader of the gang.
Broderick Crawford, Ralph Meeker, Reed Hadley, Randy Farr, William Talman, Lon Chaney, Peter Votrian, Roy Roberts, Willis B. Bouchey.

Target Zero (1955, WB). *d:* Harmon Jones; *p:* David Weisbart; *sc:* Sam Rolfe—*b/o* a story by James Warner Bellah.
VINCE GASPARI: U.S. Army sergeant in the Korean War who, along with his lieutenant, leads a patrol from behind enemy lines as they battle their way to a strategic American mountain outpost.
Richard Conte, Peggie Castle, Richard Stapley, L. Q. Jones, Chuck Connors, Angela Loo, Strother Martin, Aaron Spelling.

Jubal (1956, Col.). *d:* Delmer Daves; *p:* William Fadiman; *sc:* Russell S. Hughes and Delmer Daves—*b/o* the novel *Jubal Troop* by Paul I. Wellman.
REB HAISLIPP: Ranch hand who, when his drifter cowboy friend is forced to kill their ranch owner boss in self-defense, helps save him from a lynching party.
Glenn Ford, Ernest Borgnine, Rod Steiger, Valerie French, Felicia Farr, Basil Ruysdael, Noah Beery

Jr., John Dierkes, Jack Elam, Robert Burton, Don C. Harvey.

Run of the Arrow (1957, Univ.). *d:* Samuel Fuller; *p:* Samuel Fuller (Globe/RKO); *sc:* Samuel Fuller.
BLUE BUFFALO: Sioux Indian chief who, when an ex–Confederate soldier is captured by the Sioux tribe, befriends him after the soldier has passed a grueling Indian test of endurance.
Rod Steiger, Sarita Montiel, Brian Keith, Ralph Meeker, Jay C. Flippen, Olive Carey, H. M. Wynant, Frank de Kova, Colonel Tim McCoy, Carleton Young.

Machine Gun Kelly (1958, AIP). *d:* Roger Corman; *p:* Roger Corman (El Monte); *sc:* R. Wright Campbell.
GEORGE "MACHINE GUN" KELLY: Vicious small-time hoodlum—with an affinity for machine guns—who graduates from petty robberies to become one of the 1930s' most famous and notorious public enemies.
Susan Cabot, Morey Amsterdam, Jack Lambert, Wally Campo, Bob Griffin, Barboura Morris, Mitzi McCall, Frank de Kova, Connie Gilchrist, Larry Thor.

Showdown at Boot Hill (1958, 20th-Fox). *d:* Gene Fowler Jr.; *p:* Harold E. Knox (Regal); *sc:* Louis Vittes.
LUKE WELSH: Hard-bitten bounty hunter who, after he tracks down and kills a wanted criminal, has trouble collecting the reward money because the hostile townspeople refuse to identify the victim.
Robert Hutton, John Carradine, Carole Mathews, Fintan Meyler, Thomas Brown Henry, William Stevens, George Pembroke, Argentina Brunetti.

Gang War (1958, 20th-Fox). *d:* Gene Fowler Jr.; *p:* Harold E. Knox (Regal); *sc:* Louis Vittes—*b/o* Ovid Demaris's novel *The Hoods Take Over.*
ALAN AVERY: Los Angeles high school teacher who, after witnessing a gangland killing and agreeing to identify the killers, is shattered by the subsequent murder of his wife and sets out for revenge.
Kent Taylor, Jennifer Holden, John Doucette, Gloria Henry, Barney Phillips, Ralph Manza, Jack Reynolds, Larry Gelbmann, Whit Bissell.

When Hell Broke Loose (1958, Para.). *d:* Kenneth G. Crane; *p:* Oscar Brodney and Sol Dolgin (Dolworth); *sc:* Oscar Brodney—*b/o* articles by Ib Melchoir.
STEVE BOLAND: Racketeer who, after joining the U.S. Army during WWII to avoid going to jail, reforms when he falls for a German woman and becomes involved in foiling a Nazi plot to assassinate General Eisenhower.

Violet Rensing, Richard Jaeckel, Arvid Nelson, Robert Easton, Bob Stevenson, Eddie Foy III, John Morley, Ed Penny.

Never So Few (1959, MGM). *d:* John Sturges; *p:* Edmund Grainger (Canterbury); *sc:* Millard Kaufman—*b/o* the novel by Tom T. Chamales.
JOHN DANFORTH: WWII U.S. Army sergeant who helps a daredevil American captain lead a band of Burmese guerillas as they battle not only the Japanese but Chinese bandits as well.
Frank Sinatra, Gina Lollobrigida, Peter Lawford, Steve McQueen, Richard Johnson, Paul Henreid, Brian Donlevy, Dean Jones, Philip Ahn, John Hoyt, Whit Bissell, Ross Elliott.

The Magnificent Seven (1960, UA). *d:* John Sturges; *p:* John Sturges (Mirisch); *sc:* William Roberts—*b/o* the Japanese film *The Seven Samurai* (1954).
BERNARDO O'REILLY: Irish-Mexican who is one of seven professional gunslingers hired by a group of Mexicans to stop the bandit raids that have plagued their village for years.
Yul Brynner, Eli Wallach, Steve McQueen, Horst Buchholz, Robert Vaughn, Brad Dexter, James Coburn, Vladimir Sokoloff, Whit Bissell, Bing Russell, Robert Wilke.

Master of the World (1961, AIP). *d:* William Witney; *p:* Samuel Z. Arkoff and James H. Nicholson; *sc:* Richard Matheson—*b/o* the novels *Master of the World* and *Robur, the Conqueror* by Jules Verne.
STROCK: Government agent in 1848 who, when a crazed inventor in a strange flying machine starts blowing up the armaments of all nations so there'll be world peace, manages to send the man and his machine to the bottom of the sea.
Vincent Price, Henry Hull, Mary Webster, David Frankham, Richard Harrison, Vito Scotti, Wally Campo, Steve Masino, Ken Terrell.

A Thunder of Drums (1961, MGM). *d:* Joseph M. Newman; *p:* Robert J. Enders; *sc:* James Warner Bellah.
TROOPER HANNA: Whiskey-drinking, woman-chasing trooper in the U.S. Cavalry who battles the Apaches in 1870s Arizona.
Richard Boone, George Hamilton, Luana Patten, Arthur O'Connell, Richard Chamberlain, Duane Eddy, James Douglas, Tammy Marihugh, Slim Pickens, Casey Tibbs.

X-15 (1962, UA). *d:* Richard D. Donner; *p:* Howard W. Koch, Henry Sanicola, and Tony Lazzarino (Essex); *sc:* Tony Lazzarino and James Warner Bellah—*b/o* a story by Tony Lazzarino.
LT. COL. LEE BRANDON: Courageous test pilot who, while doing research work on the X-15

missile project at California's Edwards Air Force Base, sets a world's speed record but is killed while saving a fellow pilot.
David McLean, Ralph Taeger, Brad Dexter, Kenneth Tobey, James Gregory, Mary Tyler Moore, Lisabeth Hush, Stanley Livingston, Patricia Owens.

Kid Galahad (1962, UA). *d:* Phil Karlson; *p:* David Weisbart (Mirisch); *sc:* William Fay—*b/o* a story by Francis Wallace.
LEW NYACK: Understanding boxing trainer and sparring partner who helps a young ex-G.I. become a champion prize fighter known as Kid Galahad.
Elvis Presley, Gig Young, Lola Albright, Joan Blackman, Ned Glass, Robert Emhardt, David Lewis, Michael Dante, Judson Pratt.

This Rugged Land (1962, BLC/Col. [Made for TV]). *d:* Arthur Hiller; *p:* William Sackheim (Wilrich); *sc:* Frank Nugent—*b/o* a story by Kathleen Hite.
PAUL MORENO: Ranch hand in the Southwest who is accused of murdering the foreman's daughter but is tried and found innocent.
Richard Egan, Terry Moore, Anne Seymour, Ryan O'Neal, Denver Pyle, Oliver McGowan, Warren Vanders.

The Great Escape (1963, UA). *d:* John Sturges; *p:* John Sturges (Mirisch–Alpha); *sc:* James Clavell and W. R. Burnett—*b/o* the book by Paul Brickhill.
DANNY VELINSKI: Polish-American POW in a WWII German prison camp who, though he suffers from claustrophobia, supervises the digging of three escape tunnels by Allied soldiers as part of a plan for a massive breakout.
Steve McQueen, James Garner, Richard Attenborough, James Donald, Donald Pleasance, James Coburn, David McCallum, Gordon Jackson, John Leyton, Angus Lennie, Nigel Stock.

4 for Texas (1963, WB). *d:* Robert Aldrich; *p:* Robert Aldrich (Sam Co.); *sc:* Teddi Sherman and Robert Aldrich.
MATSON: Outlaw leader in 1870s Texas who meets his demise when he and his crooked lawyer boss run afoul of two rival gamblers who have joined forces to fight them.
Frank Sinatra, Dean Martin, Anita Ekberg, Ursula Andress, Victor Buono, Nick Dennis, Richard Jaeckel, Mike Mazurki, Ellen Corby, Jack Elam, Jesslyn Fax, Fritz Feld, Percy Helton, Bob Steele, Grady Sutton, Dave Willock, Arthur Godfrey, The Three Stooges.

Guns of Diablo (1964, MGM). *d:* Boris Sagal; *p:* Boris Ingster; *sc:* Berne Giler—*b/o* Robert Lewis Taylor's novel *The Travels of Jaimie McPheeters*.

LINC MURDOCK: Tough wagonmaster in the West of the 1840s who, when he goes into a town for supplies, tangles with a revenge-bent gunman whose arm he once shattered, and who is now married to an old flame of his.

Susan Oliver, Kurt Russell, Jan Merlin, John Fiedler, Douglas Fowley, Rayford Barnes, Ron Hagerthy, Byron Foulger.

The Sandpiper (1965, MGM). *d:* Vincente Minnelli; *p:* Martin Ransohoff and John Calley (Filmways); *sc:* Dalton Trumbo and Michael Wilson (adaptation by Irene Kamp and Louis Kamp)—*b/o* a story by Martin Ransohoff.

COS ERICKSON: California hippie sculptor who, when a beautiful, liberated artist friend poses semi-nude for him, gets into a fight with the married clergyman who has fallen in love with her.

Elizabeth Taylor, Richard Burton, Eva Marie Saint, Robert Webber, James Edwards, Tom Drake, Doug Henderson, Morgan Mason.

Battle of the Bulge (1965, WB). *d:* Ken Annakin; *p:* Sidney Harmon, Milton Sperling, and Philip Yordan (United States Pictures); *sc:* Philip Yordan, Milton Sperling, and John Melson.

WOLENSKI: WWII U.S. Army infantry major in 1944 who, when the Germans break through Allied lines in Belgium's Ardennes sector, is killed while providing cover for retreating troops.

Henry Fonda, Robert Shaw, Robert Ryan, Dana Andrews, George Montgomery, Ty Hardin, Pier Angeli, Barbara Werle, Werner Peters, Hans Christian Blech, James MacArthur, Telly Savalas.

This Property Is Condemned (1966, Para.). *d:* Sydney Pollack; *p:* John Houseman (Seven Arts–Ray Stark); *sc:* Francis Ford Coppola, Fred Coe, and Edith Sommer—*b/o* a one-act play by Tennessee Williams.

J. J. NICHOLS: Lecherous boarder in a 1930s Mississippi town who, though the boarding-house owner is his girlfriend, winds up marrying her daughter—but is left in the lurch when she runs off to New Orleans to the man she really loves.

Natalie Wood, Robert Redford, Kate Reid, Mary Badham, Alan Baxter, Robert Blake, Dabney Coleman, Jon Provost, Quentin Sondergaard, Michael Steen, Bruce Watson.

The Dirty Dozen (1967, MGM). *d:* Robert Aldrich; *p:* Kenneth Hyman and Raymond Anzarut (M. K. H. Productions); *sc:* Nunnally Johnson and Lukas Heller—*b/o* the novel by E. M. Nathanson.

JOSEPH WLADISLAW: One of twelve WWII American soldier-convicts serving life sentences who are released in exchange for their participation in a suicide mission that calls for

them to parachute into German-occupied France and destroy a chateau full of Nazi brass.

Lee Marvin, Ernest Borgnine, Jim Brown, John Cassavetes, Richard Jaeckel, George Kennedy, Trini Lopez, Ralph Meeker, Robert Ryan, Telly Savalas, Donald Sutherland, Clint Walker, Robert Webber, Tom Busby, Thick Wilson, Dora Reisser.

Guns for San Sebastian (1967, MGM). *d:* Henri Verneuil; *p:* Jacques Bar (Cipra/Filmes/Ernesto Enriques); *sc:* (European version): Serge Ganz, Miguel Morayta, and Ennio de Concini; (English version): James R. Webb—*b/o* the novel *A Wall for San Sebastian* by William Barby Faherty.

TECLO: Half-breed in 1746 Mexico who leads raids against the peasants of a mountain village but meets his demise at the hands of a rebel gunman on the run who has stayed there to help the villagers.

Anthony Quinn, Anjanette Comer, Sam Jaffe, Silvia Pinal, Jorge Martinez De Hoyos, Jaime Fernandez, Rosa Furman, Leon Askin, Pedro Armendariz, Pancho Cordova.

Villa Rides (1968, Para.). *d:* Buzz Kulick; *p:* Ted Richmond; *sc:* Robert Towne and Sam Peckinpah—*b/o* the novel *Pancho Villa* by William Douglas Lansford.

FIERRO: Tough, ruthless lieutenant of Pancho Villa who fights alongside the famed Mexican rebel leader during the Mexican campaign in 1912.

Yul Brynner, Robert Mitchum, Grazia Buccella, Robert Viharo, Frank Wolff, Herbert Lom, Alexander Knox, Diana Lorys, Fernando Rey, John Ireland, Jill Ireland.

Farewell, Friend (1968, Greenwich/Medusa). *d:* Jean Herman; *p:* Serge Silberman; *sc:* Sebastien Japrisot.

FRANZ PROPP: American mercenary who, when he and a French doctor are discharged from the French Medical Corps at the end of the Algerian War, returns to Marseilles, where the two of them attempt a 200-million-franc robbery.

Alain Delon, Olga Georges-Picot, Brigitte Fossey, Bernard Fresson, Michel Barcet, Marianna Falk, Andre Dumas.

Once Upon a Time in the West (1969, Para.). *d:* Sergio Leone; *p:* Bino Cicogna and Fulvio Morsella (Rafran/San Marco); *sc:* Sergio Leone and Sergio Donati—*b/o* a story by Dario Argento, Bernardo Bertolucci, and Sergio Leone.

THE MAN (HARMONICA): Mysterious harmonica-playing stranger in 1870s Kansas who tracks down and kills a sadistic gunman who, years ago, forced him to play the harmonica while watching the torture and hanging of his older brother.

Henry Fonda, Claudia Cardinale, Jason Robards, Frank Wolff, Gabriele Ferzetti, Keenan Wynn, Paolo Stoppa, Marco Zuanelli, Lionel Stander, Jack Elam, Woody Strode.

Twinky (1969, Rank. [released in the U.S. by AIP in 1971 as *Lola*]). *d:* Richard Donner; *p:* Clive Sharp (World); *sc:* Norman Thaddeus Vane.

SCOTT WARDMAN: Dissolute thirty-eight-year-old American writer who marries a sixteen-year-old London schoolgirl but winds up getting a divorce because of lack of communication, meddlesome in-laws, and a twenty-two-year age gap.

Susan George, Michael Craig, Honor Blackman, Orson Bean, Paul Ford, Kay Medford, Jack Hawkins, Trevor Howard, Lionel Jeffries, Robert Morley.

Rider on the Rain (1970, Avco Embassy). *d:* Rene Clement; *p:* Serge Silberman (Greenwich/Medusa); *sc:* Sebastien Japrisot and Lorenzo Ventavoli.

COL. HARRY DOBBS: Tough U.S. Army colonel in southern France who, while searching for an insane military prisoner who has escaped with $60,000, gets caught up in a puzzling murder case involving a young French housewife.

Marlene Jobert, Annie Cordy, Jill Ireland, Gabriele Tinti, Jean Gaven, Marc Manza, Corinne Marchand, Jean Piat.

You Can't Win 'em All (1970, Col.). *d:* Peter Collinson; *p:* Gene Corman (S.R.O.); *sc:* Leo V. Gordon.

JOSH COREY: One of a pair of American soldiers of fortune—caught up in the Turkish Civil War of 1922—who form an uneasy alliance as they search for gold and vie for a sultry woman's affections.

Tony Curtis, Michele Mercier, Patrick Magee, Gregoire Aslan, Fikret Hakan, Salih Guney, Tony Bonner, Horst Jansen, Leo Gordon.

Violent City (1970, Fono Roma/Unidis/Universal France [released in the U.S. by International & EDP in 1974 as *The Family*]). *d:* Sergio Sollima; *p:* Arrigo Colombo and Giorgio Papi; *sc:* Sauro Scavolini, Gianfranco Calligarich, Lina Wertmuller, and Sergio Sollima—*b/o* a story by Dino Maiuri and Massimo De Rita.

JEFF: Ex-convict gunman in New Orleans who is out to get the man who betrayed him and stole his girlfriend.

Jill Ireland, Michel Constantin, Telly Savalas, Umberto Orsini, George Savalas, Ray Sanders, Benjamin Lev, Peter Dane.

Cold Sweat (1971, Les Films Corona/Fair Film [released in the U.S. in 1974 by Emerson Film]). *d:* Terence Young; *p:* Robert Dorfmann; *sc:* Shimon Wincelberg and Albert Simonin—*b/o* the novel *Ride the Nightmare* by Richard Matheson.

JOE MARTIN: Reformed criminal living in France who, when his wife and daughter are taken hostage by mobsters trying to force him into drug smuggling, outwits the crooks one by one.

Liv Ullmann, James Mason, Jill Ireland, Michel Constantin, Jean Topart, Yannick Delulle, Luigi Pistilli.

Someone Behind the Door (1971, GSF). *d:* Nicolas Gessner; *p:* Raymond Danon (Lira); *sc:* Jacques Robert, Marc Behm, Nicolas Gessner, and Lorenzo Ventavoli—*b/o* the novel by Jacques Robert.

THE STRANGER: Psychopathic amnesiac in an English hospital who is taken home by a neuropsychiatrist and brainwashed into murdering the French lover of the doctor's wife.

Anthony Perkins, Jill Ireland, Henri Garcin, Adriano Magestretti, Agathe Natason, Viviane Everly, Andre Penvern.

Red Sun (1971, Corona/Oceana/Balcazar [released in the U.S. in 1972 by Nat. Gen.]). *d:* Terence Young; *p:* Ted Richmond; *sc:* Laird Koenig, Denne Bart Petitclerc, William Roberts, and Lawrence Roman—*b/o* a story by Laird Koenig.

LINK: Rugged American in the late 1880s who, after a valuable jeweled Japanese sword is stolen by outlaws from a train crossing the Arizona desert, joins forces with a Samurai warrior to retrieve it.

Ursula Andress, Toshiro Mifune, Alain Delon, Capucine, Satoshi Nakamoura, Bart Barry, John Hamilton, Julio Pena.

Chato's Land (1972, UA). *d:* Michael Winner; *p:* Michael Winner (Scimitar); *sc:* Gerald Wilson.

PARDON CHATO: Stoic Apache half-breed in post–Civil War New Mexico who, after he kills a white sheriff in self-defense, eludes the posse pursuing him and picks off the members one by one.

Jack Palance, Richard Basehart, James Whitmore, Simon Oakland, Ralph Waite, Richard Jordan, Victor French, Roddy McMillan, Rudy Ugland, Raul Castro.

The Mechanic (1972, UA). *d:* Michael Winner; *p:* Robert Chartoff, Irwin Winkler, and Lewis John Carlino; *sc:* Lewis John Carlino.

ARTHUR BISHOP: Professional killer ("mechanic") who, after teaching a cocky young protégé how to be a syndicate hit man, discovers that the pupil has been assigned to kill the teacher.

Jan-Michael Vincent, Keenan Wynn, Jill Ireland, Linda Ridgeway, Frank de Kova, Lindsay H. Crosby, Takayuki Kubota, Patrick O'Moore, Kevin O'Neal.

The Valachi Papers (1972, Col.). *d:* Terence Young; *p:* Dino De Laurentiis (Euro France/De Laurentiis); *sc:* Stephen Geller—*b/o* the book by Peter Maas.

JOSEPH VALACHI: Brooklyn-born mobster who, while serving a life sentence in prison, is persuaded by an FBI man to turn informer and reveal names and facts about the Mafia before the McClellan U.S. Senate crime investigating committee.

Lino Ventura, Jill Ireland, Walter Chiari, Joseph Wiseman, Gerald S. O'Loughlin, Amedeo Nazzari, Angelo Infanti, Fausto Tozzi, Guido Leontini, Mario Pilar.

The Stone Killer (1973, Col.). *d:* Michael Winner; *p:* Dino De Laurentiis and Michael Winner (De Laurentiis); *sc:* Gerald Wilson—*b/o* the novel *A Complete State of Death* by John Gardner.

DET. LOU TORREY: Tough cop who sets out to stop a crazed underworld figure who is training Vietnam War veterans to stage a gangland massacre as revenge for the assassination of the mobster's Prohibition-era cronies in 1931.

Martin Balsam, David Sheiner, Norman Fell, Ralph Waite, Eddie Forestone, Walter Burke, David Moody, Charles Tyner, Stuart Margolin, John Ritter, Frank Campanella, Alfred Ryder.

Chino (1974, De Laurentiis/Coral/Universal Production France [released in the U.S. in 1977 by Intercontinental]). *d:* John Sturges; *p:* Alfredo De Laurentiis; *sc:* Dino Maiuri, Massimo De Rita, and Clair Huffaker—*b/o* Lee Hoffman's novel *The Valdez Horses.*

CHINO VALDEZ: Half-breed owner of a small stud farm in 1880s New Mexico who, when he falls in love with the sister of a wealthy ranch owner, is forced to fight the rancher and his henchmen.

Jill Ireland, Vincent Van Patten, Marcel Bozzuffi, Melissa Chimenti, Fausto Tozzi, Ettore Manni, Adolfo Thous.

Mr. Majestyk (1974, UA). *d:* Richard Fleischer; *p:* Walter Mirisch (Mirisch); *sc:* Elmore Leonard.

VINCE MAJESTYK: Struggling Colorado watermelon farmer who, while fighting the exploitation of migrant Chicano farm laborers by a crooked union, has to battle a vicious syndicate hit man for his life.

Al Lettieri, Linda Cristal, Lee Purcell, Paul Koslo, Taylor Lacher, Frank Maxwell, Alejandro Rey, Bert Santos.

Death Wish (1974, Para.). *d:* Michael Winner; *p:* Hal Landers, Bobby Roberts, and Michael Winner (De Laurentiis); *sc:* Wendell Mayes—*b/o* the novel by Brian Garfield.

PAUL KERSEY: Mild-mannered architect who, when his wife dies and his daughter becomes catatonic after being raped by three muggers, turns vigilante and gets revenge by methodically exterminating assorted criminals on the streets and in the subways of New York.

Hope Lange, Vincent Gardenia, Steven Keats, William Redfield, Stuart Margolin, Stephen Elliott, Kathleen Tolan, Jack Wallace, Jeff Goldblum.

Breakout (1975, Col.). *d:* Tom Gries; *p:* Robert Chartoff and Irwin Winkler; *sc:* Howard B. Kreitsek, Marc Norman, and Elliott Baker—*b/o* the novel *Ten-Second Jailbreak* by Warren Hinckle, William Turner, and Eliot Asinof.

NICK COLTON: Texas bush pilot who is hired by the wife of an innocent American—being held in a Mexican prison—to stage a daring breakout using a helicopter.

Robert Duvall, Jill Ireland, Randy Quaid, Sheree North, John Huston, Alejandro Rey, Paul Mantee, Roy Jenson, Alan Vint, Sidney Klute.

Hard Times (1975, Col.). *d:* Walter Hill; *p:* Lawrence Gordon; *sc:* Walter Hill, Bryan Gindorff, and Bruce Henstell—*b/o* a story by Bryan Gindorff and Bruce Henstell.

CHANEY: Depression-era drifter in 1930s New Orleans who turns to boxing in illegal bare-knuckle street fights that are set up by a small-time gambler/promoter who becomes his friend and manager.

James Coburn, Jill Ireland, Strother Martin, Maggie Blye, Michael McGuire, Robert Tessier, Nick Dimitri, Felice Orlandi, Bruce Glover, Edward Walsh, Naomi Stevens.

Breakheart Pass (1976, UA). *d:* Tom Gries; *p:* Elliott Kastner and Jerry Gershwin (Elliott Kastner); *sc:* Alistair MacLean—*b/o* his novel.

JOHN DEAKIN: Undercover agent in the 1870s who, while on the trail of gun runners, encounters a series of mysterious deaths among passengers traveling on a train through the snowbound mountains of Idaho.

Ben Johnson, Richard Crenna, Jill Ireland, Charles Durning, Ed Lauter, David Huddleston, Roy Jenson, Casey Tibbs, Archie Moore, Joe Kapp, Read Morgan, Rayford Barnes.

St. Ives (1976, WB). *d:* J. Lee Thompson; *p:* Pancho Kohner and Stanley Canter (Kohner–Beckerman–Canter); *sc:* Barry Beckerman—*b/o* Oliver Bleeck's novel *The Procane Chronicle.*

RAYMOND ST. IVES: Ex–crime reporter and would-be novelist in Los Angeles who, when he's hired by a wealthy recluse to retrieve some stolen ledgers, runs into treachery and a baffling murder case.

John Houseman, Jacqueline Bisset, Maximilian Schell, Harry Guardino, Harris Yulin, Dana

Elcar, Michael Lerner, Dick O'Neill, Elisha Cook, Jeff Goldblum, Joseph De Nicola.

From Noon Till Three (1976, UA). *d:* Frank D. Gilroy; *p:* M. J. (Mike) Frankovich and William Self (Frankovich–Self); *sc:* Frank D. Gilroy—*b/o* his novel.

GRAHAM DORSEY: Two-bit bank robber in the Old West who, after hiding out in a Victorian mansion and dallying with the widowed owner, is made into a legendary hero when the widow—thinking he's been killed—writes a fictional book about their romance.

Jill Ireland, Douglas V. Fowley, Stan Haze, Damon Douglas, Hector Morales, Bert Williams, William Lanteau, Sonny Jones, Hoke Howell, Don "Red" Barry.

Raid on Entebbe (1977, 20th-Fox and NBC-TV [Made for TV]). *d:* Irvin Kershner; *p:* Edgar J. Scherick and Daniel H. Blatt (Scherick Associates); *sc:* Barry Beckerman.

GEN. DAN SHOMRON: Israeli general who—on July 4, 1976, at Uganda's Entebbe Airport—leads the daring rescue by Israeli commandoes of 103 hostages from a French jetliner hijacked by four pro-Palestinian terrorists the week before.

Peter Finch, Yaphet Kotto, Jack Warden, Horst Buchholz, Eddie Constantine, Martin Balsam, John Saxon, Sylvia Sidney, Tige Andrews, Robert Loggia, David Opatoshu, James Woods, Harvey Lembeck, Billy Sands, Pearl Shear.

The White Buffalo (1977, UA). *d:* J. Lee Thompson; *p:* Pancho Kohner (Dino De Laurentiis); *sc:* Richard Sale—*b/o* his novel.

WILD BILL HICKOCK (alias JAMES OTIS): Legendary U.S. scout and frontier marshal—now officially retired—who returns to the West to track down a giant white buffalo that's been plaguing him in his dreams.

Jack Warden, Will Sampson, Kim Novak, Clint Walker, Stuart Whitman, Slim Pickens, John Carradine, Cara Williams, Douglas V. Fowley, Ed Lauter, Scott Walker.

Telefon (1977, UA). *d:* Don Siegal; *p:* James B. Harris (MGM); *sc:* Peter Hyams and Stirling Silliphant—*b/o* the novel by Walter Wager.

GRIGORI BORZOV: Hardboiled KGB agent in America whose mission is to stop a psychotic Stalinist from triggering hypnotized agents programmed to blow up U.S. military installations.

Lee Remick, Donald Pleasance, Tyne Daly, Alan Badel, Patrick Magee, Sheree North, Helen Page Camp, Jacqueline Scott, John Mitchum, Iggie Wolfington.

Love and Bullets (1979, AFD). *d:* Stuart Rosenberg; *p:* Sir Lew Grade and Pancho Kohner

(Sir Lew Grade); *sc:* Wendell Mayes and John Melson.

CHARLIE CONGERS: Phoenix plainclothes cop who, when he's sent by the FBI to Switzerland to bring back a Mafia leader's moll for questioning, falls in love with her.

Rod Steiger, Jill Ireland, Strother Martin, Bradford Dillman, Henry Silva, Paul Koslo, Sam Chew, Albert Salmi, Val Avery, Andy Romano, Robin Clarke.

Caboblanco (1980, Avco Embassy). *d:* J. Lee Thompson; *p:* Lance Hool and Paul A. Joseph (Cabo Prod.); *sc:* Milton Gelman—*b/o* a story by James Granby Hunter and Lance Hool.

GIFF HOYT: American adventurer/barkeeper in Peru who becomes involved in a 1949 search for a ship that was sunk during WWII off the coast of the small fishing village of Caboblanca.

Dominique Sanda, Jason Robards, Fernando Rey, Camilla Starv, Simon MacCorkindale, Gilbert Roland, Denny Miller, Clifton James.

Borderline (1980, AFD). *d:* Jerrold Freedman; *p:* James Nelson; *sc:* Steve Kline and Jerrold Freedman.

JEB MAYNARD: Dedicated officer in charge of a U.S. Border Patrol station near San Diego who, when one of his men and an innocent young Mexican immigrant are found shot dead, clashes with the FBI on how to handle the case and goes after the killer himself.

Bruno Kirby, Bert Remsen, Michael Lerner, Kenneth McMillan, Ed Harris, Enrique Castillo, A. Wilford Brimley, Panchito Gomez, Charles Cyphers.

Death Hunt (1981, 20th-Fox). *d:* Peter Hunt; *p:* Albert S. Ruddy, Raymond Chow, and Murray Shostak; *sc:* Michael Grais and Mark Victor.

ALBERT JOHNSON: Proud, reclusive 1930s Canadian trapper who is accused of murder—even though he killed in self-defense—and then is relentlessly pursued by a hard-nosed Canadian Mountie and vigilantes across the icy Northwest Territory.

Lee Marvin, Andrew Stevens, Carl Weathers, Ed Lauter, Scott Hylands, Angie Dickinson, Jon Cedar, Len Lesser, Dick Davalos.

Death Wish II (1982, Filmways). *d:* Michael Winner; *p:* Menahem Golan and Yoram Globus (Golan–Globus/Landers–Roberts); *sc:* David Englebach—*b/o* characters created by Brian Garfield.

PAUL KERSEY: Vengeful father who launches a one-man vigilante crusade against a Los Angeles street gang that raped and killed his daughter and his housekeeper.

Jill Ireland, Vincent Gardenia, J. D. Cannon,

Anthony Franciosa, Ben Frank, Robin Sherwood, Robert F. Lyons.

10 to Midnight (1983, Cannon). *d:* J. Lee Thompson; *p:* Pancho Kohner and Lance Hool (Y & M Prod.–City Films); *sc:* William Roberts.
LEO KESSLER: Hardboiled Los Angeles cop who is kicked off the force for cooking up phony evidence in an attempt to convict a crazed sex killer but remains determined to mete out justice on his own terms.
Lisa Eilbacher, Andrew Stevens, Gene Davis, Geoffrey Lewis, Robert Lyons, Wilford Brimley, Iva Lane, Shawn Schepps.

· In addition, Charles Bronson made a cameo/ guest appearance in the following feature film: *Ten North Frederick* (1958, 20th-Fox).

☆ JAMES CAGNEY

James Francis Cagney Jr.

b: July 17, 1899, New York, N.Y.

"Made it, Ma. Top of the world!"

> Cody Jarrett (James Cagney) just before he's blown to smithereens on top of a big oil tank during a shoot-out with the law in *White Heat*, 1949.

Sinner's Holiday (1930, WB). *d:* John G. Adolfi; *sc:* Harvey Thew and George Rosener—*b/o* the play *Penny Arcade* by Marie Baumer.
HARRY DELANO: Cowardly son of a penny-arcade owner who, after getting involved in rum-running and accidentally killing his boss, conspires with his mother to frame an innocent carnival barker for the murder.
Grant Withers, Evalyn Knapp, Joan Blondell, Lucille LaVerne, Noel Madison, Otto Hoffman, Warren Hymer, Purnell B. Pratt, Hank Mann.

Doorway to Hell (1930, WB). *d:* Archie Mayo; *sc:* George Rosener—*b/o* the story "A Handful of Clouds" by Rowland Brown.
STEVE MILEWAY: Bootlegging czar's right-hand man who takes over the operation when the boss gets married and tries to go straight.
Lewis (Lew) Ayres, Charles Judels, Dorothy Mathews, Leon Janney, Robert Elliott, Kenneth Thomson, Noel Madison, Dwight Frye, Richard Purcell.

Other Men's Women (1931, WB). *d:* William A. Wellman; *sc:* William K. Wells—*b/o* a story by Maude Fulton.
ED: Railroad workman who helps in the fight to save the railway when it's endangered by storms causing massive flooding.
Grant Withers, Mary Astor, Regis Toomey, Joan Blondell, Fred Kohler, J. Farrell MacDonald, Walter Long, Kewpie Morgan, Pat Hartigan.

The Millionaire (1931, WB). *d:* John G. Adolfi; *sc:* Julian Josephson and Maude T. Powell (with dialogue by Booth Tarkington)—*b/o* the story "Idle Hands" by Earl Derr Biggers.
SCHOFIELD: Brash young life-insurance salesman whose admonitions to a retired millionaire about the dangers of being inactive result in the millionaire's heading for California and becoming half-owner of a filling station.
George Arliss, Evalyn Knapp, David Manners, Bramwell Fletcher, Florence Arliss, Noah Beery, Ivan Simpson, Sam Hardy, J. Farrell MacDonald, Tully Marshall, J. C. Nugent.

The Public Enemy (1931, WB). *d:* William Wellman; *sc:* Kubec Glasmon and John Bright (with adaptation and dialogue by Harvey Thew)— *b/o* the story "Beer and Blood" by John Bright.
TOM POWERS: Cop's son who, after growing up in the slums as a petty thief, rises to become a notorious rum-runner on the South Side of Chicago during Prohibition but ends up with his bullet-riddled body being dumped on his mother's doorstep.
Edward Woods, Jean Harlow, Joan Blondell, Beryl Mercer, Donald Cook, Mae Clark, Leslie Fenton, Robert Emmett O'Connor, Frankie Darro, Purnell Pratt, Lee Phelps, Helen Parrish.

Smart Money (1931, WB). *d:* Alfred E. Green; *sc:* Kubec Glasmon, John Bright, Lucien Hubbard, and Joseph Jackson—*b/o* Lucien Hubbard and Joseph Jackson's story "The Idol."
JACK: Big-time gambler's pal who, when he tries to warn the gambler that his girlfriend is a stool pigeon, is slugged by the gambler and dies.
Edward G. Robinson, Evalyn Knapp, Ralf Harolde, Noel Francis, Maurice Black, Boris Karloff, Morgan Wallace, Billy House, Paul Porcasi, Polly Walters, Ben Taggert, John Larkin, Allan Lane, Charles Lane.

Blonde Crazy (1931, WB). *d:* Roy Del Ruth; *sc:* Kubec Glasmon and John Bright.

BERT HARRIS: Fast-talking bellhop–turned–con man who teams up with a wisecracking chambermaid to fleece petty crooks and big shots alike but who finally winds up behind bars.

Joan Blondell, Louis Calhern, Noel Francis, Guy Kibbee, Raymond Milland, Charles Lane, Maude Eburne, Nat Pendleton, Russell Hopton, Wade Boteler.

Taxi! (1932, WB). *d:* Roy Del Ruth; *sc:* Kubec Glasmon and John Bright—*b/o* Kenyon Nicholson's play *The Blind Spot*.

MATT NOLAN: Feisty New York cab driver involved in a taxicab war who, when his brother is killed by racketeers, goes after the man responsible.

Loretta Young, George E. Stone, Guy Kibbee, David Landau, Dorothy Burgess, Matt McHugh, Nat Pendleton, Berton Churchill, George Raft, Lee Phelps, Robert Emmett O'Connor.

The Crowd Roars (1932, WB). *d:* Howard Hawks; *sc:* Kubec Glasmon, John Bright, and Niven Busch—*b/o* a story by Howard Hawks and Seton I. Miller.

JOE GREER: Cocky, self-centered auto racing star who tries to keep his younger brother from becoming a driver, falls out with him over a girl, and then hits the skids when he causes the death of a pal in a race.

Joan Blondell, Ann Dvorak, Eric Linden, Guy Kibbee, Frank McHugh, William Arnold, Leo Nomis, Regis Toomey, Wilbur Shaw, Robert McWade, Ralph Dunn, John Conte.

Winner Take All (1932, WB). *d:* Roy Del Ruth; *sc:* Wilson Mizner and Robert Lord—*b/o* the magazine story "133 at 3" by Gerald Beaumont.

JIM KANE: Swell-headed prize fighter who throws away his career on women and booze, then—after making a comeback—finds himself torn between an unassuming small-town girl and a fickle New York society woman.

Marian Nixon, Virginia Bruce, Guy Kibbee, Clarence Muse, Dickie Moore, Allan Lane, Ralf Harolde, Alan Mowbray, Clarence Wilson, Selmer Jackson, Chris-Pin Martin, George Hayes, Lee Phelps.

Hard to Handle (1933, WB). *d:* Mervyn LeRoy; *sc:* Wilson Mizner and Robert Lord—*b/o* a story by Houston Branch.

LEFTY MERRILL: Fast-talking promoter who, in addition to pushing grapefruit diets and fat-reducing lotions, concocts a marathon dance and finds himself being pressured by the winner's mother to marry the girl.

Mary Brian, Ruth Donnelly, Allen Jenkins, Claire Dodd, Emma Dunn, Robert McWade, Matt McHugh, Bess Flowers, Berton Churchill, Harry

Holman, Douglass Dumbrille, Sterling Holloway, Charles Wilson.

Picture Snatcher (1933, WB). *d:* Lloyd Bacon; *sc:* Allen Rivkin and P. J. Wolfson (with additional dialogue by Ben Markson)—*b/o* a story by Danny Ahern.

DANNY KEAN: Ex-racketeer—just out of Sing Sing—who gets a job as a scandal photographer, steals a pass to an electrocution at Sing Sing, and takes an unauthorized picture of a notorious killer in the electric chair.

Ralph Bellamy, Patricia Ellis, Alice White, Ralf Harolde, Robert Emmett O'Connor, Robert Barrat, George Chandler, Sterling Holloway, Hobart Cavanaugh, Charles King, Milton Kibbee, Selmar Jackson, Cora Sue Collins.

The Mayor of Hell (1933, WB). *d:* Archie Mayo; *sc:* Edward Chodorov—*b/o* the story "Reform School" by Islin Auster.

PATSY GARGAN: Racketeer and ward-heeler who is appointed deputy inspector at a reform school, then turns legit as he kicks out the sadistic superintendent, takes his place, and wins the respect of the tough young prisoners.

Madge Evans, Allen Jenkins, Dudley Digges, Frankie Darro, Farina, Dorothy Peterson, Charles Wilson, Hobart Cavanaugh, Robert Barrat, Arthur Byron, Sheila Terry, Harold Huber, Edwin Maxwell, Sidney Miller, Adrian Morris, Snowflake.

Footlight Parade (1933, WB). *d:* Lloyd Bacon and Busby Berkeley; *p:* Robert Lord; *sc:* Manuel Seff and James Seymour.

CHESTER KENT: Enterprising musical comedy director who, when he tries to stage a comeback by producing spectacular musical numbers as prologues in movie theaters, discovers that someone is stealing his ideas as soon as he puts them in the shows.

Joan Blondell, Ruby Keeler, Dick Powell, Guy Kibbee, Ruth Donnelly, Claire Dodd, Hugh Herbert, Frank McHugh, Arthur Hohl, Herman Bing, Paul Porcasi, Dave O'Brien, George Chandler, Hobart Cavanaugh, John Garfield.

Lady Killer (1933, WB). *d:* Roy Del Ruth; *p:* Henry Blanke; *sc:* Ben Markson and Lillie Hayward—*b/o* Rosalind Keating Shaffer's novel *The Finger Man*.

DAN QUIGLEY: New York movie usher–turned–criminal who, after fleeing from police to Hollywood and becoming a movie star, is pressured by his old gang to help rob movie stars' homes.

Mae Clarke, Leslie Fenton, Margaret Lindsay, Henry O'Neill, Willard Robertson, Raymond Hatton, Russell Hopton, William Davidson, Marjorie Gateson, Douglass Dumbrille, George

Chandler, Edwin Maxwell, Dewey Robinson, Bud Flanagan (Dennis O'Keefe), Herman Bing.

Jimmy the Gent (1934, WB). *d:* Michael Curtiz; *p:* Robert Lord; *sc:* Bertram Milhauser—*b/o* a story by Laird Doyle and Ray Nazarro.

JIMMY CORRIGAN: Crook who supplies phony heirs for unclaimed estates but then, when his girlfriend leaves him and he wants her back, pretends he's going legit and becoming a gentleman.

Bette Davis, Alice White, Allen Jenkins, Arthur Hohl, Alan Dinehart, Philip Reed, Hobart Cavanaugh, Mayo Methot, Ralf Harolde, Joseph Sawyer, Joseph Crehan, Robert Warwick, Don Douglas, Bud Flanagan (Dennis O'Keefe).

He Was Her Man (1934, WB). *d:* Lloyd Bacon; *sc:* Tom Buckingham and Niven Busch—*b/o* the story "Without Honor" by Robert Lord.

FLICKER HAYES: Just-out-of-prison safecracker who gets involved in a love triangle with a former San Francisco prostitute and her fisherman fiancé but ends up being taken for a ride by his ex-gang.

Joan Blondell, Victor Jory, Frank Craven, Harold Huber, Russell Hopton, Ralf Harolde, Sarah Padden, J. M. (John) Qualen, Samuel S. Hinds, George Chandler.

Here Comes the Navy (1934, WB). *d:* Lloyd Bacon; *sc:* Ben Markson and Earl Baldwin—*b/o* a story by Ben Markson.

CHESTY O'CONNOR: Cocky sailor aboard the U.S.S. *Arizona* who—after alienating his fellow gobs, going AWOL, and getting court-martialed—redeems himself with a heroic attempt to land a dirigible and rescue endangered crew members.

Pat O'Brien, Gloria Stuart, Frank McHugh, Dorothy Tree, Robert Barrat, Willard Robertson, Guinn Williams, Maude Eburne, Joseph Crehan, Fred "Snowflake" Toone, Howard Hickman, Gordon (Bill) Elliott, Eddie Acuff.

The St. Louis Kid (1934, WB). *d:* Ray Enright; *p:* Samuel Bischoff; *sc:* Warren Duff and Seton I. Miller—*b/o* a story by Frederick Hazlitt Brennan.

EDDIE KENNEDY: Hardboiled truck driver on the St. Louis–Chicago milk delivery run who gets involved in a battle between crooked trucking company officials and striking dairy farmers.

Patricia Ellis, Allen Jenkins, Robert Barrat, Hobart Cavanaugh, Spencer Charters, Addison Richards, Arthur Aylesworth, Harry Woods, Russell Hicks, Mary Treen, Nan Grey, Virginia Grey, Charles Middleton, Wade Boteler.

Devil Dogs of the Air (1935, WB). *d:* Lloyd Bacon; *p:* Lou Edelman; *sc:* Malcom Stuart Boylan and Earl Baldwin—*b/o* the story "Air Devils" by John Monk Saunders.

TOMMY O'TOOLE: Wise-guy Brooklyn stunt flyer who joins the U.S. Marine Flying Corps and makes enemies of his fellow flyers because of his colossal conceit and irreverence toward Marine tradition but finally learns to respect the Corps.

Pat O'Brien, Margaret Lindsay, Frank McHugh, John Arledge, Robert Barrat, Russell Hicks, William B. Davidson, Ward Bond, Samuel S. Hinds, Selmer Jackson, Bud Flanagan (Dennis O'Keefe), Gordon (Bill) Elliott.

G-Men (1935, WB). *d:* William Keighley; *p:* Lou Edelman; *sc:* Seton I. Miller—*b/o* the story "Public Enemy No. 1" by Gregory Rogers.

JAMES "BRICK" DAVIS: Young lawyer who becomes a G-man to avenge the murder of his best pal and finds himself tracking down another old friend—the big-shot racketeer who raised him and paid for his education.

Ann Dvorak, Margaret Lindsay, Robert Armstrong, Barton MacLane, Lloyd Nolan, William Harrigan, Edward Pawley, Russell Hopton, Regis Toomey, Addison Richards, Harold Huber, Raymond Hatton, Monte Blue, Mary Treen, Edwin Maxwell, Ward Bond, Marc Lawrence.

The Irish in Us (1935, WB). *d:* Lloyd Bacon; *p:* Samuel Bischoff; *sc:* Earl Baldwin—*b/o* a story by Frank Orsatti.

DANNY O'HARA: New York fight manager who takes the place of his drunken fighter and wins not only the fight but also the girl over whom he's been feuding with his cop brother.

Pat O'Brien, Olivia de Havilland, Frank McHugh, Allen Jenkins, Mary Gordon, J. Farrell MacDonald, Thomas Jackson, Bess Flowers, Mushy Callahan, Edward Gargan.

A Midsummer Night's Dream (1935, WB). *d:* Max Reinhardt and William Dieterle; *p:* Jack L. Warner and Henry Blanke; *sc:* Charles Kenyon and Mary McCall Jr.—*b/o* the play by William Shakespeare.

BOTTOM: Dull-witted weaver who is maliciously endowed with an ass's head by Puck, boy servant of the fairy king Oberon; he becomes the temporary object of the fairy queen Titania's affections after she's given a love potion by the king as punishment for philandering.

Dick Powell, Joe E. Brown, Jean Muir, Hugh Herbert, Ian Hunter, Frank McHugh, Victor Jory, Olivia de Havilland, Ross Alexander, Grant Mitchell, Verree Teasdale, Anita Louise, Mickey Rooney, Otis Harlan, Arthur Treacher, Billy Barty.

Frisco Kid (1935, WB). *d:* Lloyd Bacon; *p:* Samuel Bischoff; *sc:* Warren Duff and Seton I. Miller.

BAT MORGAN: Tough sailor who, after battling his way to the top of San Francisco's Barbary

Coast, is almost hanged by vigilantes but is saved by a society girl from Nob Hill.

Margaret Lindsay, Ricardo Cortez, Lily Damita, Donald Woods, Barton MacLane, George E. Stone, Addison Richards, Robert McWade, Joseph Sawyer, Fred Kohler, John Wray, Charles Middleton, William Desmond.

Ceiling Zero (1935, WB). *d:* Howard Hawks; *p:* Harry Joe Brown (Cosmopolitan); *sc:* Frank Wead—*b/o* the play by Frank Wead.

DIZZY DAVIS: Irresponsible hot-shot airline pilot who clashes with his ground superintendent over a girl and indirectly causes the death of a flyer friend but then makes up for it by going on a suicide flight to test a newly invented de-icer.

Pat O'Brien, June Travis, Stuart Erwin, Henry Wadsworth, Isabel Jewell, Barton MacLane, Craig Reynolds, Addison Richards, Richard Purcell, Gordon (Bill) Elliott, Edward Gargan, Garry Owen, Carol Hughes, Frank Tomick, Paul Mantz, Jerry Jerome.

Great Guy (1936, GN). *d:* John G. Blystone; *p:* Douglas Maclean; *sc:* Henry McCarthy, Henry Johnson, James Edward Grant, and Harry Ruskin (with additional dialogue by Horace McCoy)—*b/o* "The Johnny Cave Stories" by James Edward Grant.

JOHNNY CAVE: Ex-prizefighter who joins the Bureau of Weights and Measures as a deputy inspector and fights a corrupt gang of short-weight chiselers who are defrauding shoppers.

Mae Clarke, James Burke, Edward Brophy, Henry Kolker, Bernadene Hayes, Edward J. McNamara, Joe Sawyer, Ed Gargan, Mary Gordon, Arthur Hoyt, Jack Pennick, Dennis O'Keefe, Robert Lowery, Bert Kalmar, Jr.

Something to Sing About (1937, GN). *d:* Victor Schertzinger; *p:* Zion Myers; *sc:* Austin Parker—*b/o* a story by Victor Schertzinger.

TERRY ROONEY: New York bandleader who goes to Hollywood and becomes a movie star but runs into difficulties with his wife because his contract calls for him to pretend he's a bachelor.

Evelyn Daw, William Frawley, Mona Barrie, Gene Lockhart, Harry Barris, Candy Candido, William B. Davidson, Richard Tucker, Dwight Frye, John Arthur, Philip Ahn, Kenneth Harlan, Herbert Rawlinson, Bo Peep Karlin.

Boy Meets Girl (1938, WB). *d:* Lloyd Bacon; *p:* George Abbott; *sc:* Bella Spewack and Sam Spewack—*b/o* their play.

ROBERT LAW: One of a pair of screwball Hollywood screenwriters who, as a gag, write a part into a horse opera for the unborn infant son of a studio commissary waitress; when the baby arrives, they actually make a star of him.

Pat O'Brien, Marie Wilson, Ralph Bellamy, Frank McHugh, Dick Foran, Ronald Reagan, Penny

Singleton, Bert Hanlon, James Stephenson, Pierre Watkin, John Ridgely, Carole Landis, Curt Bois, Hal K. Dawson, Clem Bevans.

Angels with Dirty Faces (1938, WB). *d:* Michael Curtiz; *p:* Samuel Bischoff; *sc:* John Wexley and Warren Duff—*b/o* a story by Rowland Brown.

ROCKY SULLIVAN*: Hardboiled Brooklyn racketeer—the idol of a gang of slum kids—who pretends, in answer to the pleas of the priest he grew up with, to turn yellow on his way to the electric chair, in order to destroy the boys' admiration.

Pat O'Brien, Humphrey Bogart, Ann Sheridan, George Bancroft, Billy Halop, Bobby Jordan, Leo Gorcey, Gabriel Dell, Huntz Hall, Bernard Punsley, Adrian Morris, William Tracy.

The Oklahoma Kid (1939, WB). *d:* Lloyd Bacon; *p:* Samuel Bischoff; *sc:* Warren Duff, Robert Buckner, and Edward E. Paramore—*b/o* a story by Edward E. Paramore and Wally Klein.

JIM KINKAID (alias "THE OKLAHOMA KID"): Desperado on the 1890s Cherokee Strip who, when his politician father is framed for murder and then lynched, hunts down the outlaw leader-saloon owner who was responsible.

Humphrey Bogart, Rosemary Lane, Donald Crisp, Harvey Stephens, Hugh Sothern, Charles Middleton, Edward Pawley, Ward Bond, Trevor Bardette, John Miljan, Arthur Aylesworth, Irving Bacon, Joe Devlin, Wade Boteler.

Each Dawn I Die (1939, WB). *d:* William Keighley; *p:* David Lewis; *sc:* Norman Reilly Raine, Warren Duff, and Charles Perry—*b/o* the novel by Jerome Odlum.

FRANK ROSS: Crusading reporter who, when he writes a story exposing a crooked district attorney, is framed for manslaughter and turns into a hardened convict while serving time in prison.

George Raft, Jane Bryan, George Bancroft, Maxie Rosenbloom, Stanley Ridges, Alan Baxter, Victor Jory, Edward Pawley, Emma Dunn, Paul Hurst, Louis Jean Heydt, Thurston Hall, John Ridgely, Selmer Jackson, James Flavin.

The Roaring Twenties (1939, WB). *d:* Raoul Walsh; *p:* Hal B. Wallis; *sc:* Jerry Wald, Richard Macaulay, and Robert Rossen—*b/o* a story by Mark Hellinger.

EDDIE BARTLETT: Ex-WWI doughboy who, after returning to New York and becoming a big-time bootlegger-racketeer, gets involved in a gang war in which he clashes with an ex–army buddy who is a rival racketeer.

Priscilla Lane, Humphrey Bogart, Gladys George, Jeffrey Lynn, Frank McHugh, Paul Kelly,

---

*Received an Academy Award nomination as Best Actor for this role.

Elisabeth Risdon, Joseph Sawyer, Joseph Crehan, George Meeker, Abner Biberman, Bert Hanlon, Murray Alper, Dick Wessel, Raymond Bailey.

The Fighting 69th (1940, WB). *d:* William Keighley; *p:* Hal B. Wallis; *sc:* Norman Reilly Raine, Fred Niblo Jr., and Dean Franklin.

PVT. JERRY PLUNKETT: Loud-mouth Irishman from Brooklyn who—when he joins the famed New York Irish "fighting 69th" regiment of the Rainbow Division in WWI—brags about his fighting ability, then turns yellow in the trenches, but redeems himself before he dies in battle.

Pat O'Brien, George Brent, Jeffrey Lynn, Alan Hale, Frank McHugh, Dennis Morgan, Dick Foran, William Lundigan, Guinn "Big Boy" Williams, Henry O'Neill, John Litel, Sammy Cohen, Harvey Stephens, DeWolfe (William) Hopper, Tom Dugan, George Reeves.

Torrid Zone (1940, WB). *d:* William Keighley; *p:* Mark Hellinger; *sc:* Richard Macaulay and Jerry Wald.

NICK BUTLER: Foreman of a banana plantation in Central America who gets involved with a hard-boiled torch singer and a manager's wife while stopping a local bandit from stirring up trouble.

Pat O'Brien, Ann Sheridan, Andy Devine, Helen Vinson, Jerome Cowan, George Tobias, George Reeves, Victor Kilian, Frank Puglia, John Ridgely, Grady Sutton, Paul Porcasi, Paul Hurst, Trevor Bardette.

City for Conquest (1941, WB). *d:* Anatole Litvak; *p:* Anatole Litvak; *sc:* John Wexley—*b/o* the novel by Aben Kandel.

DANNY KENNY: New York truck driver who becomes a top prizefighter, then—even though he's blinded in a fight and winds up selling newspapers on the street—finds inner peace knowing that he helped his younger brother become an acclaimed composer.

Ann Sheridan, Frank Craven, Donald Crisp, Arthur Kennedy, Frank McHugh, George Tobias, Jerome Cowan, Anthony Quinn, Lee Patrick, Joyce Compton, Thurston Hall, Ben Welden, John Arledge, Bob Steele.

The Strawberry Blonde (1941, WB). *d:* Raoul Walsh; *p:* Jack L. Warner and Hal B. Wallis; *sc:* Julius J. Epstein and Philip G. Epstein—*b/o* the play *One Sunday Afternoon* by James Hagan.

BIFF GRIMES: Turn-of-the-century Brooklyn dentist who, after years of bitterness because he once served an unjust prison term and because he's always felt he married the wrong girl, finally realizes he picked the right girl after all.

Olivia de Havilland, Rita Hayworth, Alan Hale, George Tobias, Jack Carson, Una O'Connor, George Reeves, Tim Ryan, Addison Richards, Suzanne Carnahan (Susan Peters), Dick Wessel,

Billy Newell, Herbert Anderson, Frank Orth, James Flavin.

The Bride Came C.O.D. (1941, WB). *d:* William Keighley; *p:* Hal B. Wallis and William Cagney; *sc:* Julius J. Epstein and Philip G. Epstein—*b/o* a story by Kenneth Earl and M. M. Musselman.

STEVE COLLINS: Charter air pilot who, when a runaway heiress tries to elope with a Hollywood bandleader, is hired by the girl's Texas oil tycoon father to deliver her, unmarried, to the family ranch.

Bette Davis, Stuart Erwin, Jack Carson, George Tobias, Eugene Pallette, Harry Davenport, William Frawley, Edward Brophy, Chick Chandler, Keith Douglas (Douglas Kennedy), Herbert Anderson, DeWolf (William) Hopper, William Justice (Richard Travis), John Ridgely.

Captains of the Clouds (1942, WB). *d:* Michael Curtiz; *p:* Hal B. Wallis and William Cagney; *sc:* Arthur T. Horman, Richard Macaulay, and Norman Reilly Raine—*b/o* a story by Arthur T. Horman and Roland Gillett.

BRIAN MacLEAN: Happy-go-lucky Canadian bush pilot who, after joining the WWII Royal Canadian Air Force, rebels at the strict training discipline but proves his worth under fire from the Nazis when he leads a squadron of new American bombers being ferried across the Atlantic to England.

Dennis Morgan, Brenda Marshall, Alan Hale, George Tobias, Reginald Gardiner, Air Marshal William A. (Billy) Bishop, Reginald Denny, Russell Arms, Paul Cavanagh, Clem Bevans, J. Farrell MacDonald, Benny Baker, Byron Barr (Gig Young).

Yankee Doodle Dandy (1942, WB). *d:* Michael Curtiz; *p:* Jack L. Warner and Hal B. Wallis; *sc:* Robert Buckner and Edmund Joseph—*b/o* a story by Robert Buckner.

GEORGE M. COHAN*: Celebrated American who, after a brilliant career as a vaudeville hoofer, dramatist, actor, singer, and songwriter, is decorated—for his stirring patriotic songs—by President Franklin D. Roosevelt.

Joan Leslie, Walter Huston, Richard Whorf, George Tobias, Irene Manning, Rosemary De Camp, Jeanne Cagney, S. Z. Sakall, George Barbier, Walter Catlett, Frances Langford, Minor Watson, Eddie Foy Jr., Spencer Charters.

Johnny Come Lately (1943, UA). *d:* William K. Howard; *p:* William Cagney (William Cagney); *sc:* John Van Druten—*b/o* the novel *McLeod's Folly* by Louis Bromfield.

TOM RICHARDS: Wandering newspaperman who, after he's jailed for vagrancy in a turn-of-the-century small town, is paroled to an elderly

---

*Won the Academy Award as Best Actor for this role.

woman publisher and helps her fight local politicians.

Grace George, Marjorie Main, Marjorie Lord, Hattie McDaniel, Bill Henry, Robert Barrat, George Cleveland, Margaret Hamilton, Lucien Littlefield, Irving Bacon, Tom Dugan, Clarence Muse, Arthur Hunnicutt, Victor Kilian.

Blood on the Sun (1945, UA). *d:* Frank Lloyd; *p:* William Cagney (William Cagney); *sc:* Lester Cole (with additional scenes by Nathaniel Curtis)—*b/o* a story by Garrett Fort.

NICK CONDON: American editor of a Tokyo newspaper in pre-WWII Japan who learns of the secret Tanaka Plan for world conquest, devised by Japanese militarists, and tries to get it out of Japan.

Sylvia Sidney, Wallace Ford, Rosemary De Camp, Robert Armstrong, John Emery, Frank Puglia, Jack Halloran, Philip Ahn, Marvin Miller, Rhys Williams, Porter Hall, James Bell, Hugh Beaumont.

13 Rue Madeleine (1946, 20th-Fox). *d:* Henry Hathaway; *p:* Louis de Rochemont; *sc:* John Monks Jr. and Sy Bartlett.

BOB SHARKEY: WWII American OSS agent posing as a Frenchman who, while on a mission to locate a Nazi rocket site in France, discovers that one of his fellow agents is really a German spy.

Annabella, Richard Conte, Frank Latimore, Walter Abel, Melville Cooper, Sam Jaffe, Everett G. (E. G.) Marshall, Blanche Yurka, Horace MacMahon, Red Buttons, Roland Winters, Karl Malden.

The Time of Your Life (1948, UA). *d:* H. C. Potter; *p:* William Cagney (William Cagney); *sc:* Nathaniel Curtis—*b/o* the play by William Saroyan.

JOE: Champagne-tippling armchair philosopher—one of several assorted characters who hang out in a San Francisco waterfront saloon where they talk about their dreams, their ambitions, and their lives.

William Bendix, Wayne Morris, Jeanne Cagney, Broderick Crawford, Ward Bond, James Barton, Paul Draper, Gale Page, James Lyon, Richard Erdman, Tom Powers, Natalie Schafer, Renie Riano.

White Heat (1949, WB). *d:* Raoul Walsh; *p:* Louis F. Edelman; *sc:* Ivan Goff and Ben Roberts—*b/o* a story by Virginia Kellogg.

CODY JARRETT: Paranoid killer with a mother fixation who, when his gang is infiltrated by an undercover Treasury agent, gets caught holding up the payroll office of a chemical plant and is blown sky-high atop a blazing oil tank.

Virginia Mayo, Edmond O'Brien, Margaret Wycherly, Steve Cochran, John Archer, Wally

Cassel, Mickey Knox, Fred Clark, Paul Guilfoyle, Ford Rainey, Robert Osterloh, Ian MacDonald, Ray Montgomery, Sid Melton, Lee Phelps.

The West Point Story (1950, WB). *d:* Roy Del Ruth; *p:* Louis F. Edelman; *sc:* John Monks Jr., Charles Hoffman, and Irving Wallace—*b/o* a story by Irving Wallace.

ELWIN BIXBY: Broadway musical director who is persuaded to become a plebe and stage the annual West Point show, as part of a plan to get the cadet writer of the show to leave the academy for a show-biz career.

Virginia Mayo, Doris Day, Gordon MacRae, Gene Nelson, Alan Hale Jr., Roland Winters, Jerome Cowan, Frank Ferguson, Jack Kelly, Glen Turnbull.

Kiss Tomorrow Goodbye (1950, WB). *d:* Gordon Douglas; *p:* William Cagney (William Cagney); *sc:* Harry Brown—*b/o* the novel by Horace McCoy.

RALPH COTTER: Violent criminal who breaks out of a chain gang and, before he gets his comeuppance, kills his partner, beats up the partner's sister, pulls some robberies, and blackmails a pair of crooked cops.

Barbara Payton, Ward Bond, Luther Adler, Steve Brodie, Rhys Williams, Barton MacLane, Frank Reicher, John Litel, Dan Riss, William Frawley, Kenneth Tobey, Neville Brand, William Cagney, King Donovan.

Come Fill the Cup (1951, WB). *d:* Gordon Douglas; *p:* Henry Blanke; *sc:* Ivan Goff and Ben Roberts—*b/o* a novel by Harlan Ware.

LEW MARSH: Ace newspaperman who, after he blows his career by drinking, cures himself with the help of a former lush, rises again to city editor, and is enlisted by his publisher to reform the publisher's drunken playboy nephew.

Phyllis Thaxter, Raymond Massey, James Gleason, Gig Young, Selena Royle, Larry Keating, Sheldon Leonard, William Bakewell, King Donovan, James Flavin.

What Price Glory? (1952, 20th-Fox). *d:* John Ford; *p:* Sol C. Siegel; *sc:* Phoebe Ephron and Henry Ephron—*b/o* the play by Maxwell Anderson and Laurence Stallings.

CAPTAIN FLAGG: Hard-drinking, two fisted U.S. Marine company commander in WWI France who, when he's not leading his young troops through the horrors of combat, feuds with Sergeant Quirt, his hardboiled top kick, over the village innkeeper's daughter.

Corinne Calvet, Dan Dailey, William Demarest, Robert Wagner, Marisa Pavan, James Gleason, Wally Vernon, Paul Fix, Henry Morgan, Bill Henry, Jack Pennick, Tom Tyler, Luis Alberni, Sean McClory.

A Lion Is in the Streets (1953, WB). *d:* Raoul Walsh; *p:* William Cagney (William Cagney); *sc:* Luther Davis—*b/o* the novel by Adria Locke Langley.

HANK MARTIN: Back-country peddler in the Deep South who, after rising to power as a Bible-thumping politician and friend of the poor, is elected governor but winds up being destroyed by his own ruthless ambition and corruption.

Barbara Hale, Anne Francis, Warner Anderson, John McIntyre, Jeanne Cagney, Lon Chaney Jr., Frank McHugh, Larry Keating, Onslow Stevens, James Millican, Sara Haden, Ellen Corby, Roland Winters.

Run for Cover (1955, Para.). *d:* Nicholas Ray; *p:* William H. Pine; *sc:* William C. Thomas—*b/o* a story by Harriet Frank Jr. and Irving Ravetch.

MATT DOW: Ex-con who, after he becomes the sheriff of a small Western town, finds that he and his young deputy—an embittered cripple—are on opposite sides in a fight between outlaws and Indians.

Viveca Lindfors, John Derek, Jean Hersholt, Grant Withers, Jack Lambert, Ernest Borgnine, Ray Teal, Irving Bacon, Trevor Bardette, John Miljan, Denver Pyle, Gus Schilling.

Love Me or Leave Me (1955, MGM). *d:* Charles Vidor; *p:* Joe Pasternak; *sc:* Daniel Fuchs and Isobel Lennart—*b/o* a story by Daniel Fuchs.

MARTIN "THE GIMP" SNYDER*: Cruel, clubfooted 1920s Chicago racketeer who, after pushing a Nebraska farm girl named Ruth Etting to the top as a famed torch singer, marries her, drives her to drink, and shoots her accompanist in a fit of jealousy.

Doris Day, Cameron Mitchell, Robert Keith, Tom Tully, Harry Bellaver, Richard Gaines, Peter Leeds, Claude Stroud, Henry Kulky, Jay Adler, Veda Ann Borg, James Drury.

Mister Roberts (1955, WB). *d:* John Ford and Mervyn LeRoy; *p:* Leland Hayward (Orange); *sc:* Frank Nugent and Joshua Logan—from the play by Joshua Logan and Thomas Heggen, *b/o* the novel by Thomas Heggen.

THE CAPTAIN: Tyrannical skipper of a WWII U.S. cargo ship in the Pacific who clashes with Mister Roberts, the well-liked exec officer, over the captain's harsh treatment of the crew, as well as the exec's efforts to get a transfer to a combat ship.

Henry Fonda, William Powell, Jack Lemmon, Betsy Palmer, Ward Bond, Phil Carey, Martin Milner, James Flavin, Jack Pennick, Ken Curtis, Nick Adams, Harry Carey Jr., William Henry, Perry Lopez, Robert Roark, Pat Wayne, Tiger Andrews.

The Seven Little Foys (1955, Para.). *d:* Melville Shavelson; *p:* Jack Rose; *sc:* Melville Shavelson and Jack Rose.

GEORGE M. COHAN: Famed song-and-dance man who briefly engages in repartee and an impromptu soft-shoe dance with the popular vaudeville performer Eddie Foy at a testimonial dinner for Foy at the Friars Club in New York.

Bob Hope, Milly Vitale, George Tobias, Angela Clarke, Billy Gray, Jimmy Baird, Lester Matthews, Milton Frome, King Donovan, Jimmy Conlin, Dabs Greer, Joe Flynn, Lewis Martin.

Tribute to a Bad Man (1956, MGM). *d:* Robert Wise; *p:* Sam Zimbalist; *sc:* Michael Blankfort—*b/o* a short story by Jack Schaefer.

JEREMY RODOCK: Hard-bitten rancher in 1875 Wyoming who protects his land by ruthless methods—such as hanging cattle rustlers—but finally learns, from a naïve Easterner and a saloon girl, to temper justice with mercy.

Don Dubbins, Stephen McNally, Irene Papas, Vic Morrow, James Griffith, Onslow Stevens, James Bell, Jeanette Nolan, Chubby Johnson, Royal Dano, Lee Van Cleef, Bud Osborne, Tom London, Buddy Roosevelt.

These Wilder Years (1956, MGM). *d:* Roy Rowland; *p:* Jules Schermer; *sc:* Frank Fenton—*b/o* a story by Ralph Wheelwright.

STEVE BRADFORD: Wealthy steel magnate who, when he sets out to find a son he illegitimately fathered twenty years earlier, runs into opposition from the adoption home's director, who placed the child with foster parents.

Barbara Stanwyck, Walter Pidgeon, Betty Lou Keim, Don Dubbins, Edward Andrews, Basil Ruysdael, Will Wright, Lewis Martin, Dorothy Adams, Dean Jones, Herb Vigran, Michael Landon, Russell Simpson.

Man of a Thousand Faces (1957, Univ.). *d:* Joseph Pevney; *p:* Robert Arthur; *sc:* R. Wright Campbell, Ivan Goff, and Ben Roberts—*b/o* a story by Ralph Wheelwright.

LON CHANEY: Son of deaf-mute parents who begins his show-business career as a vaudeville entertainer, goes on to become the silent screen's greatest horror-film star, but—at the peak of his career—dies of throat cancer.

Dorothy Malone, Jane Greer, Marjorie Rambeau, Jim Backus, Robert J. Evans, Celia Lovsky, Jeanne Cagney, Jack Albertson, Nolan Leary, Roger Smith, Clarence Kolb, Hank Mann, Snub Pollard.

Never Steal Anything Small (1958, Univ.). *d:* Charles Lederer; *p:* Aaron Rosenberg; *sc:* Charles

---

*Received an Academy Award nomination as Best Actor for this role.

Lederer—*b/o* the play *Devil's Hornpipe* by Maxwell Anderson and Rouben Mamoulian.

JAKE MacILLANEY: Crooked waterfront labor leader who uses every dirty trick in the book in his struggle to be elected head of the powerful longshoremen's union.

Shirley Jones, Roger Smith, Cara Williams, Nehemiah Persoff, Royal Dano, Anthony Caruso, Horace MacMahon, Jack Albertson, Robert J. Wilkie, Herbie Faye, Roland Winters, Jay Jostyn.

Shake Hands with the Devil (1959, UA). *d:* Michael Anderson; *p:* Michael Anderson (Pennebaker); *sc:* Ivon Goff and Ben Roberts (adaptation by Marian Thompson)—*b/o* the novel by Reardon Conner.

SEAN LENIHAN: Surgeon in Dublin who, as a secret leader of the IRA during the 1921 Irish Rebellion for "home rule," starts practicing violence as an end instead of a means.

Don Murray, Dana Wynter, Glynis Johns, Michael Redgrave, Sybil Thorndike, Cyril Cusack, John Breslin, Harry Brogan, Marianne Benet, Harry Corbett, Richard Harris, Niall MacGinnis, Noel Purcell.

The Gallant Hours (1960, UA). *d:* Robert Montgomery; *p:* Robert Montgomery (Cagney-Montgomery); *sc:* Beirne Lay Jr. and Frank D. Gilroy.

FLEET ADM. WILLIAM F. "BULL" HALSEY JR.: U.S. Fleet Admiral who becomes one of America's most famous WWII naval heroes as he battles the Japanese during the South Pacific campaign.

Dennis Weaver, Ward Costello, Richard Jaeckel, Les Tremayne, Robert Burton, Raymond Bailey, Carl Benton Reid, Walter Sande, Karl Swenson, Vaughan Taylor, Harry Landers, James T. Goto, Carleton Young, William Schallert, Selmer Jackson, Tyler McVey, James Cagney Jr., Robert Montgomery Jr.

One, Two, Three (1961, UA). *d:* Billy Wilder; *p:* Billy Wilder (Mirisch/Pyramid); *sc:* Billy Wilder and I. A. L. Diamond—*b/o* a one-act play by Ferenc Molnar.

C. P. MacNAMARA: Fast-talking American Coca-Cola executive in West Berlin who is aiming for a top London post but sees his plans go awry when his American boss's visiting daughter gets involved with an East Berlin beatnik.

Horst Buchholz, Pamela Tiffin, Arlene Francis, Lilo Pulver, Howard St. John, Hanns Lothar, Leon Askin, Peter Capell, Ralf Wolter, Red Buttons.

Ragtime (1981, Para.). *d:* Milos Forman; *p:* Dino De Laurentiis; *sc:* Michael Weller—*b/o* the novel by E. L. Doctorow.

POLICE COMMISSIONER RHEINLANDER WALDO: Tough, shrewd police commissioner in 1906 New York who, when a black ragtime piano player–turned–urban guerilla and his followers occupy the lavish J. P. Morgan Library, leads the siege to oust them.

Brad Dourif, Moses Gunn, Elizabeth McGovern, Kenneth McMillan, Pat O'Brien, Donald O'Connor, James Olson, Mandy Patinkin, Howard E. Rollins, Mary Steenburgen, Robert Joy, Norman Mailer, Bruce Boa, Hoolihan Burke.

• In addition, James Cagney made a cameo/guest appearance in the following feature film: *Starlift* (1951, WB).

☆ GARY COOPER

Frank James Cooper

b: May 7, 1901, Helena, Mont.
d: May 13, 1961, Los Angeles, Cal.

"If you want to call me that, smile."

The Virginian (Gary Cooper) to Walter Huston (Trampas) in *The Virginian*, 1929.

The Winning of Barbara Worth (1926, UA). *d:* Henry King; *p:* Samuel Goldwyn (Samuel Goldwyn); *sc:* Frances Marion (with titles by Rupert Hughes)—*b/o* the novel by Harold Bell Wright.

ABE LEE: Young engineer who, while working on a dam project in Colorado River country, competes with his engineer boss for the affections of a pretty young woman.

Ronald Colman, Vilma Banky, Charles Lane, Paul McAllister, E. J. Ratcliffe, Clyde Cooke, Erwin Connelly, Sam Blum, Edwin Brady.

It (1927, Para.). *d:* Clarence Badger; *p:* Clarence Badger and Elinor Glyn; *sc:* Hope Loring and Louis D. Lighton (adaptation by Elinor Glyn, titles by George Marion Jr.)—*b/o* the novel by Elinor Glyn.

Billed as "REPORTER": Newspaperman trying to get a story about a department-store salesgirl who has "it" (sex appeal).

Clara Bow, Antonio Moreno, William Austin, Jacqueline Gadson, Julia Swayne Gordon, Priscilla Bonner, Elinor Glyn, Lloyd Corrigan.

Children of Divorce (1927, Para.). *d:* Frank Lloyd; *p:* E. Lloyd Sheldon; *sc:* Hope Loring and Louis D. Lighton—*b/o* the novel by Owen McMahon Johnson.

TED LARRABEE: Young man from the social set who, after a wild party, is tricked into marrying a flapper instead of the woman he really loves.

Clara Bow, Esther Ralston, Einar Hanson, Norman Trevor, Hedda Hopper, Edward Martindel, Julia Swayne Gordon, Tom Ricketts, Albert Gran, Iris Stuart, Margaret Campbell.

Arizona Bound (1927, Para.). *d:* John Waters; *sc:* John Stone and Paul Gangelon (adaptation by Marion Jackson)—*b/o* a story by Richard Allen Gates.

Billed as "THE COWBOY": Young cowpoke who wanders into a small Western town and becomes the target of a lynch mob when he's falsely accused of robbing a stagecoach.

Betty Jewel, Jack Dougherty, Christian J. Frank, El Brendel, Charles Crockett, Joe Butterworth, Guy Oliver, Guinn "Big Boy" Williams.

Wings (1927, Para.). *d:* William A. Wellman; *p:* Lucien Hubbard; *sc:* Hope Loring and Louis D. Lighton (with titles by Julian Johnson)—*b/o* a story by John Monk Saunders.

CADET WHITE: Fatalistic young WWI American pilot who never makes it to France and combat with the rest of his pals because he's killed in a crash at a flight training field in the U.S.

Clara Bow, Charles "Buddy" Rogers, Richard Arlen, Jobyna Ralston, El Brendel, "Gunboat" Smith, Richard Tucker, Julia Swayne Gordon, Henry B. Walthall, George Irving, Hedda Hopper, Nigel de Brulier, Roscoe Karns, James Pierce, Carl von Haartman.

Nevada (1927, Para.). *d:* John Waters; *sc:* John Stone and L. G. Rigby (with titles by Jack Conway)—*b/o* the novel by Zane Grey.

NEVADA: Two-fisted, gun-toting cowboy who protects a girl and her brother from a gang of cattle rustlers secretly headed by a respected rancher.

Thelma Todd, William Powell, Philip Strange, Ernie S. Adams, Christian J. Frank, Ivan Christy, Guy Oliver.

The Last Outlaw (1927, Para.). *d:* Arthur Rosson; *sc:* John Stone and J. Walter Ruben—*b/o* a story by Richard Allen Gates.

SHERIFF BUDDY HALE: Western lawman who has problems with his girlfriend when he has to arrest her brother for murder.

Betty Jewel, Jack Luden, Herbert Prior, Jim Corey, Billy Butts, Flash the Wonder Horse.

Beau Sabreur (1928, Para.). *d:* John Waters; *p:* Milton E. Hoffman; *sc:* Tom J. Geraghty (with titles by Julian Johnson)—*b/o* the novel *Beau Geste* by Percival Christopher Wren.

MAJ. HENRI de BEAUJOLAIS: French Foreign Legion officer who is sent to a French garrison in the Sahara to negotiate a treaty with a villainous sheik and fend off an Arab uprising.

Evelyn Brent, Noah Beery, William Powell, Roscoe Karns, Mitchell Lewis, Arnold Kent, Raoul Paoli, Joan Standing, Frank Reicher, Oscar Smith.

The Legion of the Condemned (1928, Para.). *d:* William A. Wellman; *p:* William A. Wellman and E. Lloyd Sheldon; *sc:* John Monk Saunders and Jean de Limur (with titles by George Marion Jr.)—*b/o* a story by John Monk Saunders.

GALE PRICE: Young American pilot who joins a WWI French "suicide squadron" to forget a French woman he mistakenly believes is a German spy.

Fay Wray, Barry Norton, Lane Chandler, Francis McDonald, Albert Conti, Charlotte Bird, Voya George, E. H. Calvert, Toto Guette.

Doomsday (1928, Para.). *d:* Rowland V. Lee; *p:* Rowland V. Lee; *sc:* Donald W. Lee (adaptation by Doris Anderson, titles by Julian Johnson)—*b/o* the novel by Warwick Deeping.

ARNOLD FURZE: Young English farmer who, after he's jilted by his girlfriend when she marries an older man for money, takes her back after she has the marriage annulled and offers to be his housekeeper for six months to prove her worth.

Florence Vidor, Lawrence Grant, Charles A. Stevenson.

Half a Bride (1928, Para.). *d:* Gregory La Cava; *sc:* Doris Anderson and Percy Heath (with titles by Julian Johnson)—*b/o* the story "White Hands" by Arthur Stringer.

CAPTAIN EDMUNDS: Handsome young skipper of a yacht who finds himself marooned on a desert island in the Pacific with the spoiled, rich newlywed wife of a much older man.

Esther Ralston, William J. Worthington, Freeman Wood, Mary Doran, Guy Oliver, Ray Gallagher.

Lilac Time (1928, FN). *d:* George Fitzmaurice; *p:* George Fitzmaurice; *sc:* Carey Wilson (adaptation by Willis Goldbeck, titles by George Marion Jr.)—*b/o* the play by Jane Cowl and Jane Murfin, and the book by Guy Fowler.

CAPT. PHILIP BLYTHE: Aristocratic English WWI pilot in the Royal Flying Corps who falls in love with his squadron's mascot—a mischievous French peasant girl.

Colleen Moore, Eugenie Besserer, Burr McIntosh, Kathryn McGuire, Cleve Moore, Arthur Lake, Jack Stone, Dan Dowling, George Cooper, Edward Dillon, Paul Hurst, Philo McCullough.

The First Kiss (1928, Para.). *d:* Rowland V. Lee; *p:* Rowland V. Lee; *sc:* John Farrow (with titles by Tom Reed)—*b/o* the story "Four Brothers" by Tristram Tupper.

MULLIGAN TALBOT: Hard-working Chesapeake Bay fisherman who resorts to stealing money in order to finance his three shiftless brothers in their professions.

Fay Wray, Lane Chandler, Leslie Fenton, Paul Fix, Malcolm Williams, Monroe Owsley, George Nash.

The Shopworn Angel (1928, Para.). *d:* Richard Wallace; *p:* Louis D. Lighton; *sc:* Howard Estabrook and Albert Shelby LeVino (with titles by Tom Miranda)—*b/o* the story "Private Pettigrew's Girl" by Dana Burnet.

WILLIAM TYLER: Idealistic WWI doughboy from Texas who falls for a worldly New York show girl and changes her cynical outlook on life before he goes overseas and is killed in the trenches.

Nancy Carroll, Paul Lukas, Emmett King, Mildred Washington, Roscoe Karns, Bert Woodruff.

Wolf Song (1929, Para.). *d:* Victor Fleming; *p:* Victor Fleming; *sc:* John Farrow and Keene Thompson (with titles by Julian Johnson)—*b/o* the novel by Harvey Fergusson.

SAM LASH: Roving fur trapper who, after he kidnaps a fiery Mexican señorita, marries her, then deserts her, but finally returns to her.

Lupe Velez, Louis Wolheim, Constantine Romanoff, Michael Vavitch, Ann Brody, Russell (Russ) Columbo, Augustina Lopez, Leona Lane.

Betrayal (1929, Para.). *d:* Lewis Milestone; *p:* David O. Selznick; *sc:* Hans Kraly and Leo Birinsky (with titles by Julian Johnson)—*b/o* a story by Victor Schertzinger and Nicholas Soussanin.

ANDRE FREY: Moody young Viennese artist who covets the wife (his former sweetheart) of a middle-aged burgomaster of a small Alpine village but is killed in a toboggan crash.

Emil Jannings, Esther Ralston, Jada Welles, Douglas Haig, Bodil Rosing, Ann Brody, Paul Guertmann, Leone Lane.

The Virginian (1929, Para.). *d:* Victor Fleming; *p:* Louis D. Lighton; *sc:* Howard Estabrook—*b/o* the novel by Owen Wister and the play by Kirk LaShelle.

THE VIRGINIAN: Straight-shooting, Virginia-born foreman of a Wyoming ranch who falls for the local schoolmarm, has to hang his best friend for cattle rustling, and shoots it out at sundown with the town villain.

Walter Huston, Richard Arlen, Mary Brian, Chester Conklin, Eugene Pallette, Helen Ware, Charles Stevens, Jack Pennick, George Chandler, Willie Fung, Ernie S. Adams, Bob Kortman.

Only the Brave (1930, Para.). *d:* Frank Tuttle; *sc:* Edward E. Paramore Jr. (adaptation by Agnes Brand Leahy)—*b/o* a story by Keene Thompson.

CAPT. JAMES BRAYDON: Civil War Union cavalry officer who volunteers for spy duty and, as part of a plan to trick the Confederates, lets them capture him.

Mary Brian, Phillips Holmes, James Neill, Morgan Farley, Guy Oliver, John H. Elliot, E. H. Calvert, Virginia Bruce, Freeman S. Wood, William Bakewell.

The Texan (1930, Para.). *d:* John Cromwell; *p:* Hector Turnbull; *sc:* Daniel N. Rubin (adaptation by Oliver H.P. Garrett)—*b/o* the story "A Double-Dyed Deceiver" by O. Henry.

ENRIQUE (alias "QUICO," THE LLANO KID): A swaggering bandit in 1885 Texas who, as part of a plot to collect reward money, poses as the long-lost son of a wealthy aristocratic woman.

Fay Wray, Emma Dunn, Oscar Apfel, James Marcus, Donald Reed, Soledad Jiminez, Veda Buckland, Edwin J. Brady, Russell (Russ) Columbo.

Seven Days' Leave (1930, Para.). *d:* Richard Wallace; *p:* Louis D. Lighton; *sc:* John Farrow and Don Totheroh—*b/o* the play *The Old Lady Shows Her Medals* by Sir James M. Barrie.

KENNETH DOWEY: Young WWI Canadian soldier in the famous "Black Watch" regiment who, when he goes to London on leave, lets a lonely old scrubwoman pose as his proud mother.

Beryl Mercer, Daisy Belmore, Nora Cecil, Tempe Piggott, Arthur Hoyt, Arthur Metcalfe, Basil Radford, Larry Steers.

A Man From Wyoming (1930, Para.). *d:* Rowland V. Lee; *sc:* John V.A. Weaver and Albert Shelby LeVino—*b/o* a story by Joseph Moncure March and Lew Lipton.

JIM BAKER: WWI captain in the Engineer Corps who, after he is mistakenly reported killed in action, returns and finds his wife at a villa in Nice where she has become a hostess of wild parties to try to forget her devastation.

June Collyer, Regis Toomey, Morgan Farley, E. H. Calvert, Mary Foy, Emil Chautard, Ed Deering, William B. Davidson, Ben Hall.

The Spoilers (1930, Para.). *d:* Edward Carewe; *sc:* Bartlett Cormack and Agnes Brand Leahy—*b/o* the novel by Rex Beach.

ROY GLENISTER: Stalwart gold-mine owner whose battle with claim-jumping "spoilers" in the early 1900s Yukon culminates in a marathon fistfight with the number-one villain.

Kay Johnson, Betty Compson, William "Stage" Boyd, Harry Green, Slim Summerville, James Kirkwood, Lloyd Ingraham, Oscar Apfel, Knute Ericson.

Morocco (1930, Para.). *d:* Josef von Sternberg; *sc:* Jules Furthman—*b/o* the novel *Amy Jolly* by Benno Vigny.

TOM BROWN: Devil-may-care American in the French Foreign Legion who tames a gold-digging cabaret singer to the point where she finally trails him into the desert to become a "camp follower."

Marlene Dietrich, Adolphe Menjou, Ullrich Haupt, Juliette Compton, Francis McDonald, Albert Conti, Eve Southern, Paul Porcasi.

Fighting Caravans (1931, Para.). *d:* Otto Brower and David Brower; *sc:* Edward G. Paramore Jr., Keene Thompson, and Agnes Brand Leahy—*b/o* the novel by Zane Grey.

CLINT BELMET: Missouri scout who, while leading a wagon train westward through hostile Indian country, falls in love with a young French orphan girl.

Lily Damita, Ernest Torrence, Fred Kohler, Tully Marshall, Eugene Pallette, Roy Stewart, Syd Saylor, Charles Winninger, Jane Darwell, Irving Bacon, Iron Eyes Cody.

City Streets (1931, Para.). *d:* Rouben Mamoulian; *p:* E. Lloyd Sheldon; *sc:* Oliver H.P. Garrett (adaptation by Max Marcin)—*b/o* an original screen treatment by Dashiell Hammett.

THE KID: Young carnival worker who, when his girlfriend—a big-city racketeer's daughter—is railroaded to prison, joins the racketeers in hopes of getting her out.

Sylvia Sidney, Paul Lukas, William "Stage" Boyd, Guy Kibbee, Stanley Fields, Wynne Gibson, Betty Sinclair, Willard Robertson, Ethan Laidlaw, Bob Kortman, Bill Elliott, Bert Hanlon.

I Take This Woman (1931, Para.). *d:* Marion Gering and Slavko Vorkopich; *sc:* Vincent Lawrence—*b/o* the novel *Lost Ecstasy* by Mary Roberts Rinehart.

TOM McNAIR: Good-natured Wyoming ranch hand who, when the spoiled daughter of the absentee ranch owner comes out West, marries her, but then has trouble getting her to adjust to the rigors of ranch life.

Carole Lombard, Helen Ware, Lester Vail, Charles Trowbridge, Clara Blandick, Guy Oliver, Syd Saylor, Frank Darien, David Landau.

His Woman (1931, Para.). *d:* Edward Sloman; *sc:* Adelaide Heilbron and Melville Baker—*b/o* Dale Collins's novel *The Sentimentalist*.

CAPT. SAM WHALAN: Tramp-freighter captain who, when he rescues a foundling from a drifting boat, hires a dance-hall girl as a seagoing babysitter.

Claudette Colbert, Averill Harris, Richard Spiro, Douglass Dumbrille, Hamtree Harrington, Joan Blair, Joe Spurin Calleia, Harry Davenport, Barton MacLane, Donald McBride, Preston Foster.

Devil and the Deep (1932, Para.). *d:* Marion Gering; *sc:* Benn Levy—*b/o* a story by Harry Hervey.

LIEUTENANT SEMPTER: Navy officer on a British submarine based off the coast of North Africa who gets involved with the wife of his insanely jealous skipper.

Tallulah Bankhead, Charles Laughton, Cary Grant, Paul Porcasi, Juliette Compton, Henry Kolker, Arthur Hoyt, Kent Taylor, Lucien Littlefield, Dave O'Brien.

If I Had a Million (1932, Para.). *d:* Ernst Lubitsch, Norman Taurog, Stephen Roberts, Norman McLeod, James Cruze, William A. Seiter, and H. Bruce Humberstone; *p:* Louis D. Lighton; *sc:* Claude Binyon, Whitney Bolton, Malcolm Stuart Boylan, John Bright, Sidney Buchanan, Lester Cole, Isabel Dawn, Boyce DeGaw, Walter De Leon, Oliver H.P. Garrett, Harvey Gates, Grover Jones, Ernst Lubitsch, Lawton Macksill, Joseph L. Mankiewicz, William Slavens McNutt, Seton I. Miller, and Tiffany Thayer—*b/o* a story by Robert D. Andrews.

GALLAGHER: Rough 'n' ready U.S. Marine who gets a check for a million dollars from a wealthy eccentric but, thinking it's an April Fool's gag, gives it away.

George Raft, Wynne Gibson, Charles Laughton, Jack Oakie, Frances Dee, Charles Ruggles, Alison Skipworth, W. C. Fields, Mary Boland, Roscoe Karns, May Robson, Gene Raymond, Lucien Littlefield, Grant Mitchell, Joyce Compton, Irving Bacon, Dewey Robinson, Gail Patrick, Fred Kelsey, Willard Robertson, Kent Taylor, Jack Pennick, Berton Churchill.

A Farewell to Arms (1932, Para.). *d:* Frank Borzage; *sc:* Benjamin Glazer and Oliver H.P. Garrett—*b/o* the novel by Ernest Hemingway.

LT. FREDERIC HENRY: American ambulance driver with the Italian army during WWI who, when he's wounded in action on the Italian front, has an ill-fated love affair with an English nurse.

Helen Hayes, Adolphe Menjou, Mary Philips, Jack La Rue, Blanche Frederici, Henry Armetta, George Humbert, Gilbert Emery, Paul Porcasi.

Today We Live (1933, MGM). *d:* Howard Hawks; *p:* Howard Hawks; *sc:* Edith Fitzgerald and Dwight Taylor (with dialogue by William Faulkner)—*b/o* the story "Turnabout" by William Faulkner.

BOGARD: WWI American bomber pilot who falls in love with an aristocratic English girl, then volunteers for a suicide mission when he thinks she's been unfaithful.

Joan Crawford, Robert Young, Franchot Tone, Roscoe Karns, Louise Closser Hale, Rollo Lloyd, Hilda Vaughn.

One Sunday Afternoon (1933, Para.). *d:* Stephen

Roberts; *p:* Louis D. Lighton; *sc:* William Slavens McNutt and Grover Jones—*b/o* the stage play by James Hagan.

BIFF GRIMES: Turn-of-the-century dentist who—though he's bitter because he once served an unjust prison sentence, and because he's always felt he married the wrong girl—finally realizes he picked the right girl after all.

Fay Wray, Neil Hamilton, Frances Fuller, Roscoe Karns, Jane Darwell, Clara Blandick, Sam Hardy, Harry Schultz, James Burtis, A. S. Byron, Jack Clifford.

Design for Living (1933, Para.). *d:* Ernst Lubitsch; *p:* Ernst Lubitsch; *sc:* Ben Hecht—*b/o* the play by Noel Coward.

GEORGE CURTIS: American painter in Paris who, along with a playwright friend, moves in with a female artist when she suggests that the three of them live together—on a platonic basis—to enrich their careers.

Fredric March, Miriam Hopkins, Edward Everett Horton, Franklin Pangborn, Isabel Jewell, James Donlin, Vernon Steele, Jane Darwell, Wyndham Standing, Mary Gordon, Rolfe Sedan.

Alice in Wonderland (1933, Para.). *d:* Norman McLeod; *p:* Louis D. Lighton; *sc:* Joseph L. Mankiewicz and William Cameron Menzies—*b/o* the novels *Alice's Adventures in Wonderland* and *Alice Through the Looking-Glass* by Lewis Carroll.

THE WHITE KNIGHT: A gangly, bald-headed knight with a scraggly white mane, a bulbous nose, and a clanking suit of armor—one of the many colorful characters whom a young girl named Alice encounters when she is transported into a land of fantasy.

Charlotte Henry, Richard Arlen, Roscoe Ates, Billy Barty, Billy Bevan, Leon Errol, Louise Fazenda, W. C. Fields, Skeets Gallagher, Cary Grant, Raymond Hatton, Sterling Holloway, Edward Everett Horton, Roscoe Karns, Baby LeRoy, Lucien Littlefield, Mae Marsh, Polly Moran, Jack Oakie, Edna May Oliver, May Robson, Charlie Ruggles, Jackie Searl, Alison Skipworth, Ned Sparks, Ford Sterling, Jacqueline Wells (Julie Bishop).

Operator 13 (1933, MGM). *d:* Richard Boleslavsky; *p:* Lucien Hubbard (Cosmopolitan); *sc:* Harry Thew, Zelda Sears, and Eve Greene—*b/o* the story by Robert W. Chambers.

CAPT. JACK GAILLIARD: Civil War Confederate officer on General Jeb Stuart's staff who falls for "Operator 13"—a pretty actress–turned–Yankee spy.

Marion Davies, Jean Parker, Katharine Alexander, Ted Healy, Russell Hardie, Douglass Dumbrille, Willard Robertson, Fuzzy Knight, Sidney Toler, Robert McWade, Marjorie Gateson, Wade Boteler, Hattie McDaniel, The Four Mills Brothers, William Henry.

Now and Forever (1934, Para.). *d:* Henry Hathaway; *p:* Louis D. Lighton; *sc:* Vincent Lawrence and Sylvia Thalberg—*b/o* the story "Honor Bright" by Jack Kirkland and Melville Baker.

JERRY DAY: Jewel thief and con man who plans to sell his little daughter to a wealthy relative but is dissuaded by his girlfriend and partner in crime, who convinces him to go straight for the sake of the child.

Carole Lombard, Shirley Temple, Sir Guy Standing, Charlotte Granville, Gilbert Emery, Henry Kolker, Jameson Thomas, Harry Stubbs, Richard Loo, Akim Tamiroff, Buster Phelps, Rolfe Sedan.

The Wedding Night (1935, UA). *d:* King Vidor; *p:* Samuel Goldwyn (Samuel Goldwyn); *sc:* Edith Fitzgerald—*b/o* a story by Edwin Knopf.

TONY BARRETT: Married, once-popular New York author—searching for his lost inspiration—who moves to a Connecticut farm and becomes involved in a tragic love affair with a simple Polish farm girl.

Anna Sten, Ralph Bellamy, Helen Vinson, Sigfried Rumann, Esther Dale, Walter Brennan, Douglas Wood, George Meeker, Hedi Shope, Violet Axzelle.

The Lives of a Bengal Lancer (1935, Para.). *d:* Henry Hathaway; *p:* Louis D. Lighton; *sc:* Waldemar Young, John L. Balderston, and Achmed Abdullah (adaptation by Grover Jones and William Slavens McNutt)—*b/o* the novel by Major Francis Yeats-Brown.

LIEUTENANT McGREGOR: Veteran frontier fighter in a crack nineteenth-century British Army outfit in India who takes under his wing an inexperienced officer, the son of the regiment's ramrod colonel.

Franchot Tone, Richard Cromwell, Sir Guy Standing, C. Aubrey Smith, Monte Blue, Kathleen Burke, Douglass Dumbrille, Akim Tamiroff, Noble Johnson, J. Carroll Naish, Rollo Lloyd, Charles Stevens, Leonid Kinskey, James Bell.

Peter Ibbetson (1935, Para.). *d:* Henry Hathaway; *p:* Louis D. Lighton; *sc:* Vincent Lawrence and Waldemar Young (adaptation by Constance Collier, with additional scenes by John Meehan and Edwin Justus Mayer)—*b/o* the novel by George DuMaurier and the play by John Nathaniel Raphael.

PETER IBBETSON: London architect who, when he accidentally kills the husband of his childhood sweetheart, is sentenced to spend the rest of his life in a dungeon but is reunited with the sweetheart in his dreams and, finally, in heaven.

Ann Harding, John Halliday, Ida Lupino, Douglass Dumbrille, Virginia Weidler, Dickie Moore, Doris Lloyd, Christian Rub, Donald Meek, Gilbert Emery, Marcelle Corday, Colin Tapley.

Desire (1936, Para.). *d:* Frank Borzage; *p:* Ernst Lubitsch; *sc:* Edwin Justus Mayer, Waldemar Young, and Samuel Hoffenstein—*b/o* a play by Hans Szekely and R. A. Stemmle.

TOM BRADLEY: Young American automotive engineer on vacation who becomes an unwitting accomplice of a beautiful jewel thief when she plants a stolen pearl necklace on him at the Franco–Spanish border.

Marlene Dietrich, John Halliday, William Frawley, Ernest Cossart, Akim Tamiroff, Alan Mowbray, Zeffie Tilbury, Marc Lawrence, Gaston Glass, Robert O'Connor, Stanley Andrews.

Mr. Deeds Goes to Town (1936, Col.). *d:* Frank Capra; *p:* Frank Capra; *sc:* Robert Riskin—*b/o* the story "Opera Hat" by Clarence Budington Kelland.

LONGFELLOW DEEDS*: Naïve, tuba-playing poet from Mandrake Falls who inherits $20 million and goes to New York but—after being victimized by greedy opportunists and duped by the female reporter he loves—decides to give the money away to the poor and downtrodden.

Jean Arthur, George Bancroft, Lionel Stander, Douglass Dumbrille, Raymond Walburn, H. B. Warner, Warren Hymer, Muriel Evans, Ruth Donnelly, Spencer Charters, Emma Dunn, Mayo Methot, Irving Bacon, Walter Catlett, Edward Gargan, Paul Hurst, Franklin Pangborn, Bud Flanagan (Dennis O'Keefe).

The General Died at Dawn (1936, Para.). *d:* Lewis Milestone; *p:* William Le Baron; *sc:* Clifford Odets—*b/o* a novel by Charles G. Booth.

O'HARA: American soldier of fortune in China who falls for a beautiful blond spy while smuggling gold to help Chinese peasants resist a brutal warlord.

Madeleine Carroll, Akim Tamiroff, Dudley Digges, Porter Hall, William Frawley, J. M. Kerrigan, Philip Ahn, Leonid Kinskey, Willie Fung, Paul Harvey, Clifford Odets, John O'Hara, Sidney Skolsky, Lewis Milestone.

The Plainsman (1936, Para.). *d:* Cecil B. DeMille; *p:* Cecil B. DeMille; *sc:* Waldemar Young, Harold Lamb, and Lynn Riggs (adaptation by Jeanie McPherson)—*b/o* the stories "Wild Bill Hickok" by Frank J. Wilstach and "The Prince of Pistoleers" by Courtney Ryley Cooper and Grover Jones.

WILD BILL HICKOK (JAMES BUTLER HICKOK): Famed Old West lawman and scout who, with the help of Buffalo Bill and Calamity Jane, tracks down and kills an unscrupulous white man selling guns to the Indians but is later shot in the back by the man's cowardly accomplice.

---

*Received an Academy Award nomination as Best Actor for this role.

Jean Arthur, James Ellison, Charles Bickford, Porter Hall, John Miljan, Victor Varconi, Paul Harvey, Frank McGlynn Sr., Purnell Pratt, Anthony Quinn, George "Gabby" Hayes, Fuzzy Knight, Frank Albertson, Harry Woods, Francis Ford, Irving Bacon, Edwin Maxwell, Charlie Stevens, Bud Flanagan (Dennis O'Keefe).

Souls at Sea (1937, Para.). *d:* Henry Hathaway; *sc:* Grover Jones and Dale Van Every—*b/o* a story by Ted Lesser.

"NUGGIN" TAYLOR: Seaman in the 1840s who, when his ship sinks, takes command of an overcrowded lifeboat and has to force several occupants overboard so that the rest can survive.

George Raft, Frances Dee, Henry Wilcoxon, Harry Carey, Olympe Bradna, Robert Cummings, Porter Hall, George Zucco, Virginia Weidler, Joseph Schildkraut, Gilbert Emery, Lucien Littlefield, Paul Fix, Tully Marshall, Monte Blue.

The Adventures of Marco Polo (1938, UA). *d:* Archie Mayo; *p:* Samuel Goldwyn (Samuel Goldwyn); *sc:* Robert E. Sherwood—*b/o* a story by N. A. Pogson.

MARCO POLO: Venetian adventurer-explorer who travels to the court of Kublai Khan in thirteenth-century China and discovers Oriental treasures—including fireworks and a beautiful princess.

Sigrid Gurie, Basil Rathbone, Ernest Truex, Alan Hale, George Barbier, Binnie Barnes, Lana Turner, Stanley Fields, Harold Huber, H. B. Warner, Soo Yong, Henry Kolker, Hale Hamilton, Robert Greig, Ward Bond, Jason Robards.

Bluebeard's Eighth Wife (1938, Para.). *d:* Ernst Lubitsch; *p:* Ernst Lubitsch; *sc:* Charles Brackett and Billy Wilder (adaptation by Charlton Andrews)—*b/o* a play by Alfred Savoir.

MICHAEL BRANDON: American millionaire with seven ex-wives whose eighth—the daughter of an impoverished French aristocrat—marries him only for his money but, while trying to tame him, falls in love with him.

Claudette Colbert, Edward Everett Horton, David Niven, Elizabeth Patterson, Herman Bing, Warren Hymer, Franklin Pangborn, Rolfe Sedan, Lionel Pape, Charles Halton, Terry Ray (Ellen Drew), Leon Ames, Joseph Crehan.

The Cowboy and the Lady (1938, UA). *d:* H. C. Potter; *p:* Samuel Goldwyn (Samuel Goldwyn); *sc:* S. N. Behrman and Sonya Levien—*b/o* a story by Leo McCarey and Frank R. Adams.

STRETCH WILLOUGHBY: Shy rodeo cowpoke who—after going on a blind date with a young woman (who is posing as a Palm Beach housemaid) and later discovering she's really the daughter of a wealthy presidential candidate—marries her but then has trouble getting her to live on his Montana ranch.

Merle Oberon, Patsy Kelly, Walter Brennan, Fuzzy Knight, Mabel Todd, Henry Kolker, Harry Davenport, Emma Dunn, Berton Churchill, Arthur Hoyt, Ernie Adams.

Beau Geste (1939, Para.). *d:* William A. Wellman; *p:* William A. Wellman; *sc:* Robert Carson—*b/o* the novel by Percival Christopher Wren.
MICHAEL "BEAU" GESTE: The oldest of three gallant British brothers who, when he enlists in the French Foreign Legion after taking the blame for his aunt's theft of a valuable family jewel, is joined in the Legion by the other two brothers.
Ray Milland, Robert Preston, Brian Donlevy, Susan Hayward, J. Carrol Naish, Albert Dekker, Broderick Crawford, Charles Barton, James Stephenson, G. P. Huntley Jr., James Burke, Henry Brandon, Harold Huber, Donald O'Connor.

The Real Glory (1939, UA). *d:* Henry Hathaway; *p:* Samuel Goldwyn (Samuel Goldwyn); *sc:* Jo Swerling and Robert R. Presnell.
DR. BILL CANAVAN: Courageous U.S. Army doctor in the Philippines, just after the Spanish–American War, who helps put down a Moro uprising and a cholera outbreak.
Andrea Leeds, David Niven, Reginald Owen, Broderick Crawford, Kay Johnson, Charles Waldron, Russell Hicks, Vladimir Sokoloff, Rudy Robles, Henry Kolker, Luke Chan, Elmo Lincoln, Charles Stevens, Soledad Jiminez.

The Westerner (1940, UA). *d:* William Wyler; *p:* Samuel Goldwyn (Samuel Goldwyn); *sc:* Jo Swerling and Niven Busch—*b/o* a story by Stuart N. Lake.
COLE HARDIN: Cowboy drifter who, after being falsely accused of stealing a horse, escapes hanging by the infamous Judge Roy Bean of Texas when he convinces Bean that he can get him a lock of actress Lily Langtry's hair.
Walter Brennan, Doris Davenport, Fred Stone, Paul Hurst, Chill Wills, Charles Halton, Forrest Tucker, Tom Tyler, Arthur Aylesworth, Julian Rivero, Lillian Bond, Dana Andrews, Jack Pennick, Trevor Bardette, Blackjack Ward, Arthur "Art" Mix, Hank Bell.

North West Mounted Police (1940, Para.). *d:* Cecil B. DeMille; *p:* Cecil B. DeMille; *sc:* Alan LeMay, Jesse Lasky Jr., and C. Gardner Sullivan—*b/o* "Royal Canadian Mounted Police" by R. C. Fetherston-Haugh.
DUSTY RIVERS: Texas Ranger in 1885 Canada who, during a bloody Metis Indian uprising, competes with a Royal Canadian Mountie in tracking down a fugitive murderer—and for the heart of a beautiful frontier nurse.
Madeleine Carroll, Paulette Goddard, Preston Foster, Robert Preston, George Bancroft, Lynne Overman, Akim Tamiroff, Walter Hampden, Lon Chaney Jr., George E. Stone, Regis Toomey, Richard Denning, Robert Ryan, Ralph Byrd, Rod Cameron, Philip Terry, Kermit Maynard, Lane Chandler.

Meet John Doe (1940, WB). *d:* Frank Capra; *p:* Frank Capra; *sc:* Robert Riskin—*b/o* a story by Richard Connell and Robert Presnell.
LONG JOHN WILLOUGHBY (alias JOHN DOE): Down-and-out bush-league baseball pitcher who, as part of a phony political drive, is hired by a cynical female news columnist to impersonate a mythical "John Doe" who has written a letter threatening to jump off New York's highest building on Christmas Eve to protest world conditions.
Barbara Stanwyck, Edward Arnold, Walter Brennan, James Gleason, Spring Byington, Gene Lockhart, Rod La Rocque, Irving Bacon, Regis Toomey, Warren Hymer, Sterling Holloway, J. Farrell MacDonald, Andrew Tombes, Pierre Watkin, Garry Owen, Gene Morgan, Vernon Dent.

Sergeant York (1941, WB). *d:* Howard Hawks; *p:* Jesse L. Lasky and Hal B. Wallis; *sc:* Abem Finkel, Harry Chandlee, Howard Koch, and John Huston—*b/o* the diary of Sergeant York, edited by Tom Skeyhill.
ALVIN C. YORK*: Farmer from the mountains of Tennessee who starts out in WWI as a conscientious objector but, after changing his mind, winds up in the trenches and becomes America's most decorated doughboy.
Walter Brennan, Joan Leslie, George Tobias, Stanley Ridges, Margaret Wycherly, Ward Bond, Noah Beery Jr., June Lockhart, Clem Bevans, Howard da Silva, Charles Trowbridge, Harvey Stephens, David Bruce, Joseph Sawyer, Frank Wilcox, Frank Orth, Elisha Cook Jr., Byron Barr (Gig Young).

Ball of Fire (1941, RKO). *d:* Howard Hawks; *p:* Samuel Goldwyn (Samuel Goldwyn); *sc:* Charles Brackett and Billy Wilder—*b/o* the story "From A to Z" by Thomas Monroe and Billy Wilder.
PROF. BERTRAM POTTS: One of seven scholarly professors who, while they're researching slang for an encyclopedia, get mixed up with a heart-of-gold burlesque stripper hiding from the law.
Barbara Stanwyck, Oscar Homolka, Henry Travers, S. Z. Sakall, Tully Marshall, Leonid Kinskey, Richard Haydn, Aubrey Mather, Allen Jenkins, Dana Andrews, Dan Duryea, Charles Lane, Elisha Cook Jr., Addison Richards, Tim Ryan, Gene Krupa and his Orchestra.

The Pride of the Yankees (1942, RKO). *d:* Sam Wood; *p:* Samuel Goldwyn (Samuel Goldwyn); *sc:*

---

*Won the Academy Award as Best Actor for this role.

Jo Swerling and Herman J. Mankiewicz—*b/o* a story by Paul Gallico.

LOU GEHRIG*: American baseball hero of the 1920s and '30s who plays more than 2,000 consecutive games for the New York Yankees but is forced to retire when he becomes the victim of a rare, fatal neurological disease.

Teresa Wright, Walter Brennan, Dan Duryea, Babe Ruth, Elsa Janssen, Ludwig Stossel, Virginia Gilmore, Bill Dickey, Ernie Adams, Pierre Watkin, Bill Stern, Addison Richards, Frank Faylen, Bernard Zanville (Dane Clark), Tom Neal.

For Whom the Bell Tolls (1943, Para.). *d:* Sam Wood; *p:* Sam Wood; *sc:* Dudley Nichols—*b/o* the novel by Ernest Hemingway.

ROBERT JORDAN*: Idealistic American schoolteacher who joins a group of Loyalist guerilla fighters during the 1930s Spanish Civil War and falls in love with a Spanish refugee girl but loses his life while blowing up a strategic bridge.

Ingrid Bergman, Akim Tamiroff, Arturo de Cordova, Vladimir Sokoloff, Mikhail Rasumny, Fortunio Bonanova, Victor Varconi, Katina Paxinou, Joseph Calleia, Duncan Renaldo, George Coulouris, Frank Puglia, Pedro de Cordoba, Yakima Canutt, Yvonne De Carlo.

The Story of Dr. Wassell (1944, Para.). *d:* Cecil B. DeMille; *p:* Cecil B. DeMille; *sc:* Alan LeMay and Charles Bennett—*b/o* interviews with Commander Corydon M. Wassell and the story by James Hilton.

DR. CORYDON M. WASSELL: Heroic WWII U.S. Navy doctor from Arkansas who, when a group of U.S. Marines are wounded on the island of Java, saves them from the invading Japanese soldiers as he leads them through the Javanese jungles and gets them safely to Australia.

Laraine Day, Signe Hasso, Carol Thurston, Dennis O'Keefe, Carl Esmond, Stanley Ridges, Elliott Reid, Paul Kelly, James Millican, Philip Ahn, Doodles Weaver, Barbara Britton, Richard Loo, George Macready, Douglas Fowley, Yvonne De Carlo, Miles Mander, Harvey Stephens.

Casanova Brown (1944, RKO). *d:* Sam Wood; *p:* Nunnally Johnson (International/Christie); *sc:* Nunnally Johnson—*b/o* Floyd Dell and Thomas Mitchell's play *The Little Accident.*

CASANOVA BROWN: Timid college professor who has a brief whirlwind marriage that's annulled, then discovers—just when he's about to be married again—that he's a father.

Teresa Wright, Frank Morgan, Anita Louise, Patricia Collinge, Edmond Breon, Emory Parnell,

Mary Treen, Halliwell Hobbes, Byron Foulger, Grady Sutton, Florence Lake, Irving Bacon, James Burke, Snub Pollard.

Along Came Jones (1945, RKO). *d:* Stuart Heisler; *p:* Gary Cooper (International/Cinema Artists); *sc:* Nunnally Johnson—*b/o* a story by Alan LeMay.

MELODY JONES: Mild-mannered saddle tramp who, though he can't even handle a gun, is mistaken for a notorious outlaw and has to be saved by his straight-shooting girlfriend.

Loretta Young, William Demarest, Dan Duryea, Frank Sully, Russell Simpson, Willard Robertson, Don Costello, Ray Teal, Walter Sande, Lane Chandler, Erville Alderson, Ernie Adams, Chris-Pin Martin.

Saratoga Trunk (1945, WB). *d:* Sam Wood; *p:* Hal B. Wallis; *sc:* Casey Robinson—*b/o* the novel by Edna Ferber.

COL. CLINT MAROON: Texas cowboy-gambler who forms an alliance with a fortune-hunting Creole beauty in New Orleans and is hired by financiers to fight a rival group in order to save the Saratoga Trunk railroad line.

Ingrid Bergman, Flora Robson, Jerry Austin, John Warburton, Florence Bates, Curt Bois, John Abbott, Marla Shelton, Minor Watson, Ruby Dandridge, William B. Davidson, Thurston Hall.

Cloak and Dagger (1946, WB). *d:* Fritz Lang; *p:* Milton Sperling (United States Pictures); *sc:* Albert Maltz and Ring Lardner Jr.—*b/o* a story by Boris Ingster and John Larkin, and the book by Corey Ford and Alastair MacBain.

PROF. ALVAH JESPER: Mild-mannered physics professor who is drafted into the OSS during WWII to locate an atomic scientist being held captive in Italy by Nazis.

Lilli Palmer, Robert Alda, Vladimir Sokoloff, J. Edward Bromberg, Ludwig Stossel, Dan Seymour, Marc Lawrence, James Flavin, Don Turner, Ross Ford, Robert Coote, Douglas Walton, Frank Wilcox.

Unconquered (1947, Para.). *d:* Cecil B. DeMille; *p:* Cecil B. DeMille; *sc:* Charles Bennett, Frederic M. Frank, and Jesse Lasky Jr.—*b/o* the novel by Neil H. Swanson.

CAPT. CHRISTOPHER HOLDEN: Virginia militiaman who, in 1763, buys a beautiful English indentured slave and falls in love with her and helps put down an Indian uprising against Fort Pitt.

Paulette Goddard, Howard Da Silva, Boris Karloff, Cecil Kellaway, Ward Bond, Katherine De Mille, Henry Wilcoxon, Sir C. Aubrey Smith, Victor Varconi, Gavin Muir, Alan Napier, Robert Warwick, Chief Thundercloud, Virginia Grey,

---

*Received an Academy Award nomination as Best Actor for this role.

Porter Hall, Mike Mazurki, Marc Lawrence, Lloyd Bridges, Raymond Hatton.

Good Sam (1948, RKO). *d:* Leo McCarey; *p:* Leo McCarey (Rainbow); *sc:* Ken Englund—*b/o* a story by Leo McCarey and John Klorer.
SAM CLAYTON: Good samaritan store manager who, much to his wife's dismay, winds up as the fall guy every time he helps someone.
Ann Sheridan, Ray Collins, Edmund Lowe, Joan Lorring, Clinton Sundberg, Louise Beavers, Ruth Roman, Todd Karns, Irving Bacon, William Frawley, Tom Dugan, Ida Moore, Dick Wessell, Almira Sessions.

The Fountainhead (1948, WB). *d:* King Vidor; *p:* Henry Blanke; *sc:* Ayn Rand—*b/o* her novel.
HOWARD ROARK: Idealistic architect who blows up an unfinished public-housing project he designed after a number of changes in his original concept are made without his consent.
Patricia Neal, Raymond Massey, Kent Smith, Robert Douglas, Henry Hull, Ray Collins, Moroni Olsen, Jerome Cowan, Paul Harvey, Tristram Coffin, Thurston Hall, Jonathan Hale, Frank Wilcox, Douglas Kennedy, Selmer Jackson, John Doucette.

Task Force (1949, WB). *d:* Delmer Daves; *p:* Jerry Wald; *sc:* Delmer Daves.
JONATHAN L. SCOTT: Pioneer U.S. Navy flyer who begins his career in 1921 on the carrier *Langley,* subsequently serves on the U.S.S. *Saratoga,* and finally becomes skipper of a WWII carrier.
Jane Wyatt, Wayne Morris, Walter Brennan, Julie London, Bruce Bennett, Jack Holt, Stanley Ridges, John Ridgely, Richard Rober, Art Baker, Moroni Olsen, Ray Montgomery, Kenneth Tobey, John McGuire.

Bright Leaf (1950, WB). *d:* Michael Curtiz; *p:* Henry Blanke; *sc:* Ranald MacDougall—*b/o* the novel by Foster FitzSimons.
BRANT ROYLE: Nineteenth-century tenant farmer who, after being driven out by a tobacco tycoon, returns and wipes out the tycoon's business by building a successful cigarette empire (later destroyed by his vindictive wife).
Lauren Bacall, Patricia Neal, Jack Carson, Donald Crisp, Gladys George, Elizabeth Patterson, Jeff Corey, Taylor Holmes, Thurston Hall, William Walker, Cleo Moore, Nita Talbot, Chick Chandler.

Dallas (1950, WB). *d:* Stuart Heisler; *p:* Anthony Veiller; *sc:* John Twist.
BLAYDE "REB" HOLLISTER: Ex–Confederate colonel who comes to Dallas to shoot it out with three villainous brothers who plundered his land and murdered his family.

Ruth Roman, Steve Cochran, Raymond Massey, Barbara Payton, Leif Erickson, Antonio Moreno, Jerome Cowan, Reed Hadley, Will Wright, Monte Blue, Gene Evans, Tom Fadden, Buddy Roosevelt, Dewey Robinson.

You're in the Navy Now (originally called **U.S.S. Teakettle**) (1951, 20th-Fox). *d:* Henry Hathaway; *p:* Fred Kohlmar; *sc:* Richard Murphy—*b/o* an article in *The New Yorker* by John W. Hazard.
LT. JOHN HARKNESS: WWII Naval Reserve officer in command of a bunch of misfits on an experimental patrol boat dubbed the "U.S.S. *Teakettle*" because it's powered by a steam turbine.
Jane Greer, Millard Mitchell, Eddie Albert, John McIntyre, Ray Collins, Harry Von Zell, Jack Webb, Richard Erdman, Harvey Lembeck, Henry Slate, Ed Begley, Charles Buchinski (Charles Bronson), Jack Warden, Lee Marvin, Charles Smith.

It's a Big Country (1951, MGM). *d:* Richard Thorpe, John Sturges, Charles Vidor, Don Weis, Clarence Brown, William A. Wellman, and Don Hartman; *p:* Robert Sisk; *sc:* William Ludwig, Helen Deutsch, George Wells, Allen Rivkin, Dorothy Kingsley, Dore Schary, and Isobel Lennart—partly *b/o* stories by Edgar Brooke, Ray Chordes, Joseph Petracca, Lucille Schlossberg, Claudia Cranston, and John McNulty.
"TEXAS": Texas cowboy who delivers an amusing monologue in which he modestly maintains that the state of Texas isn't really "so big" or "so great"; but with tongue-in-cheek—and the help of newsreel shots depicting Texas's grandeur—he cleverly and deliberately proves just the opposite.
Ethel Barrymore, Keefe Brasselle, Nancy Davis, Van Johnson, Gene Kelly, Janet Leigh, Marjorie Main, Fredric March, George Murphy, William Powell, S. Z. Sakall, Lewis Stone, James Whitmore, Keenan Wynn, Leon Ames, Elisabeth Risdon, Ned Glass.

Distant Drums (1951, WB). *d:* Raoul Walsh; *p:* Milton Sperling (United States Pictures); *sc:* Niven Busch and Martin Rackin—*b/o* a story by Niven Busch.
CAPT. QUINCY WYATT: Veteran Indian fighter who leads a small force into the Florida Everglades to turn the tide in the savage nineteenth-century Indian Seminole War.
Mari Aldon, Richard Webb, Ray Teal, Arthur Hunnicutt, Robert Barrat, Clancy Cooper, Larry Carper, Dan White, Mel Archer, Sheb Woolley.

High Noon (1952, UA). *d:* Fred Zinnemann; *p:* Stanley Kramer (Stanley Kramer); *sc:* Carl Foreman—*b/o* John W. Cunningham's story "The Tin Star."

WILL KANE*: Dedicated sheriff who plans to retire and leave the town of Hadleyville on the morning of his wedding but refuses to run when he learns that a killer he sent to prison has been pardoned and is arriving on the noon train to join three henchmen and kill him.

Thomas Mitchell, Lloyd Bridges, Katy Jurado, Grace Kelly, Otto Kruger, Lon Chaney, Henry Morgan, Ian MacDonald, Harry Shannon, Lee Van Cleef, Bob Wilke, Sheb Woolley, Tom London, William Phillips, James Millican, Cliff Clark, Lucien Prival, Howland Chamberlin, Jack Elam.

Springfield Rifle (1952, WB). *d:* Andre de Toth; *p:* Louis F. Edelman; *sc:* Charles Marquis Warren and Frank Davis—*b/o* a story by Sloan Nibley.

MAJ. ALEX KEARNEY: Civil War Union Army officer who deliberately gets a dishonorable discharge so that he can infiltrate a renegade gang that's stealing government horses and selling them to the Confederates.

Phyllis Thaxter, David Brian, Paul Kelly, Philip Carey, Lon Chaney, James Millican, Martin Milner, Guinn "Big Boy" Williams, James Brown, Alan Hale Jr., Vince Barnett, Fess Parker, Poodles Hanneford, Ben Corbett.

Return to Paradise (1953, UA). *d:* Mark Robson; *p:* Theron Warth, Robert Wise, and Mark Robson (Aspen); *sc:* Charles Kaufman—*b/o* the book by James A. Michener.

MR. MORGAN: American beach bum who marries a native girl on a Polynesian island, leaves the island when she dies, but returns years later to find a half-caste daughter he left there.

Roberta Haynes, Barry Jones, Moira MacDonald, John Hudson, Hans Kruse, Mamea Mataumua, Ezra Williams, Terry Dunleavy, Howard Poulson.

Blowing Wild (1953, WB). *d:* Hugo Fregonese; *p:* Milton Sperling (United States Pictures); *sc:* Philip Yordan.

JEFF DAWSON: American wildcatter in the oilfields of Mexico who, while battling Mexican bandits, also has to fight off the psychotic wife of a jealous oil tycoon.

Barbara Stanwyck, Ruth Roman, Anthony Quinn, Ward Bond, Ian MacDonald, Richard Karlan, Juan Garcia.

Garden of Evil (1954, 20th-Fox). *d:* Henry Hathaway; *p:* Charles Brackett; *sc:* Frank Fenton—*b/o* a story by Fred Freiberger and William Tunberg.

HOOKER: One of a trio of American soldiers of fortune in 1850s Mexico who are hired by an American woman to lead her through hostile Indian country to rescue her husband, who has been trapped in a gold-mine cave-in.

Susan Hayward, Richard Widmark, Hugh Marlowe, Cameron Mitchell, Rita Moreno, Victor Manuel Mendoza, Fernando Wagner, Manuel Donde.

Vera Cruz (1954, UA). *d:* Robert Aldrich; *p:* James Hill (Hecht–Lancaster); *sc:* Roland Kibbee and James R. Webb—*b/o* a story by Borden Chase.

BENJAMIN TRANE: One of a duo of American soldiers of fortune during the Mexican Revolution of 1866 who are hired to escort a European countess from Mexico City to Vera Cruz, unaware that she's transporting gold for Emperor Maximilian's troops.

Burt Lancaster, Denise Darcel, Cesar Romero, George Macready, Ernest Borgnine, Henry Brandon, Charles Buchinsky (Charles Bronson), Morris Ankrum, Jack Lambert, Jack Elam, Charles Horvath, Juan Garcia.

The Court-Martial of Billy Mitchell (1955, WB). *d:* Otto Preminger; *p:* Milton Sperling (United States Pictures); *sc:* Milton Sperling and Emmet Lavery.

BILLY MITCHELL: Pioneer airman and visionary American general who predicts the Japanese attack on Pearl Harbor twenty years before it happens and is court-martialed when he argues with the military brass that the U.S. should bolster its air power.

Charles Bickford, Ralph Bellamy, Rod Steiger, Elizabeth Montgomery, Fred Clark, James Daly, Jack Lord, Peter Graves, Darren McGavin, Robert Simon, Charles Dingle, Will Wright, Ian Wolfe, Jack Perrin, Frank Wilcox, Phil Arnold, William Henry, Charles Chaplin Jr.

Friendly Persuasion (1956, AA). *d:* William Wyler; *p:* William Wyler (B–M); *sc:* Michael Wilson (uncredited)—*b/o* Jessamyn West's novel *The Friendly Persuasion.*

JESS BIRDWELL: Head of a Quaker family in southern Indiana during the Civil War who, when his son defies the family's pacifist religion and takes up arms against the South, comes to the realization that a man must be guided by his own conscience.

Dorothy McGuire, Marjorie Main, Anthony Perkins, Richard Eyer, Phyllis Love, Robert Middleton, Mark Richman, Walter Catlett, John Smith, Samantha (the family's goose), Russell Simpson, Charles Halton, William Schallert, Frank Jenks.

Love in the Afternoon (1957, AA). *d:* Billy Wilder; *p:* Billy Wilder; *sc:* Billy Wilder and I. A. L. Diamond—*b/o* the novel *Ariane* by Claude Anet.

FRANK FLANNAGAN: Middle-aged American playboy in Paris who, when the young daughter of

---

*Won the Academy Award as Best Actor for this role.

a French private detective comes to his apartment to warn him that a jealous husband is going to kill him, falls in love with her.

Audrey Hepburn, Maurice Chevalier, John McGiver, Lise Bourdin, Bonifas, Audrey Wilder, Olga Valery, Leila Croft, Valerie Croft, Charles Bouillard, Minerva Pious.

Ten North Frederick (1958, 20th-Fox). *d:* Philip Dunne; *p:* Charles Brackett; *sc:* Philip Dunne—*b/o* the novel by John O'Hara.

JOE CHAPIN: Middle-aged man with presidential aspirations who is destroyed by a grasping wife, an irresponsible daughter, and a hopeless love affair with the daughter's college roommate.

Diane Varsi, Suzy Parker, Geraldine Fitzgerald, Tom Tully, Ray Stricklyn, Philip Ober, John Emery, Stuart Whitman, Barbara Nichols, Joe McGuinn, Jess Kirkpatrick, Rachel Stephens, Joey Faye, Charles Bronson.

Man of the West (1958, UA). *d:* Anthony Mann; *p:* Walter M. Mirisch (Ashton); *sc:* Reginald Rose—*b/o* a novel by Will C. Brown.

LINK JONES: Reformed gunslinger who, in order to save some innocent people, pretends to rejoin the old gang that's headed by his sadistic uncle.

Julie London, Lee J. Cobb, Arthur O'Connell, Jack Lord, John Dehner, Royal Dano, Robert Wilke, Frank Ferguson, Emory Parnell, Tina Menard.

The Hanging Tree (1959, WB). *d:* Delmer Daves; *p:* Martin Jurow and Richard Shepherd (Baroda); *sc:* Wendell Mayes and Halstead Welles—*b/o* the novelette by Dorothy M. Johnson.

DOC JOSEPH FRAIL: Tough, poker-playing frontier doctor in a wild Montana mining camp who helps a temporarily blind young woman strike it rich, but is almost lynched by a gold-hungry, drunken mob after he kills a man who tries to harm her.

Maria Schell, Karl Malden, Ben Piazza, George C. Scott, Karl Swenson, Virginia Gregg, John Dierkes, King Donovan, Slim Talbot, Guy Wilkerson, Bud Osborne.

They Came to Cordura (1959, Col.). *d:* Robert Rossen; *p:* William Goetz (Goetz–Baroda); *sc:* Ivan Moffat and Robert Rossen—*b/o* the novel by Glendon Swarthout.

MAJ. THOMAS THORN: U.S. Army officer who, after being accused of cowardice during the 1916 Mexican expedition against Pancho Villa, is assigned the degrading job of "awards officer" and is ordered to find five men who deserve the Medal of Honor.

Rita Hayworth, Van Heflin, Tab Hunter, Richard Conte, Michael Callan, Dick York, Robert Keith, Carlos Romero, James Bannon, Edward Platt, Maurice Jara.

The Wreck of the Mary Deare (1959, MGM). *d:* Michael Anderson; *p:* Julian Blaustein (Blaustein–Baroda); *sc:* Eric Ambler—*b/o* the novel by Hammond Innes.

GIDEON PATCH: Sea captain who, after he's found dazed and alone on a floundering, burning freighter during a storm in the English Channel, is accused of deliberately trying to wreck the ship.

Charlton Heston, Michael Redgrave, Emlyn Williams, Cecil Parker, Alexander Knox, Virginia McKenna, Richard Harris, Ben Wright, Peter Illing, Ashley Cowan, Louis Mercier.

The Naked Edge (1961, UA). *d:* Michael Anderson; *p:* Walter Seltzer and George Glass (Pennebaker–Baroda); *sc:* Joseph Stefano—*b/o* the novel *First Train to Babylon* by Max Ehrlich.

GEORGE RADCLIFFE: American sales representative in England whose English wife begins to suspect that he's a murderer—and that she may be his next victim.

Deborah Kerr, Eric Portman, Diane Cilento, Hermione Gingold, Peter Cushing, Michael Wilding, Ronald Howard, Wilfrid Lawson, Helen Cherry, Joyce Carey.

• In addition, Gary Cooper made cameo/guest appearances in the following feature films: *Paramount on Parade* (1930, Para.), *Make Me a Star* (1932, Para.), *Hollywood Boulevard* (1936, Para.), *Variety Girl* (1947, Para.), *It's a Great Feeling* (1949, WB), *Starlift* (1951, WB), and *Alias Jesse James* (1959, UA).

☆ JOAN CRAWFORD

Lucille Fay LeSueur

b: March 23, 1908, San Antonio, Tex.
d: May 10, 1977, New York, N.Y.

"Get out, Veda. Get your things out of this house right now before I throw them into the street and you with them. Get out before I kill you."

Mildred Pierce (Joan Crawford) to Veda
Pierce (Ann Blyth) in Mildred Pierce, 1945.

Pretty Ladies (1925, MGM). *d:* Monta Bell; *sc:* Alice D.G. Miller—*b/o* the story by Adela Rogers St. Johns.

Billed (under the name of Lucille LeSueur) as "BOBBY": One of the showgirls in the Ziegfeld Follies.

ZaSu Pitts, Tom Moore, Ann Pennington, Lilyan Tashman, Bernard Randall, Helen D'Algy, Conrad Nagel, Norma Shearer, George K. Arthur, Roy D'Arcy.

Old Clothes (1925, MGM). *d:* Eddie Cline; *p:* Jack Coogan Sr.; *sc:* Willard Mack.

MARY RILEY: Destitute young girl who, when she gets a job in the office of a wealthy young Wall Streeter, falls in love with him but is thwarted by his snobbish mother.

Jackie Coogan, Max Davidson, Lillian Elliott, Alan Forrest, James Mason, Stanton Heck.

The Only Thing (1925, MGM). *d:* Jack Conway; *sc:* Elinor Glyn—*b/o* her novel.

LADY CATHERINE: A member of the court entourage in a mythical kingdom that is torn asunder by a revolution.

Eleanor Boardman, Conrad Nagel, Edward Connelly, Arthur Edmond Carew, Louis Payne, Vera Lewis, Ned Sparks.

Sally, Irene and Mary (1925, MGM). *d:* Edmund Goulding; *sc:* Edmund Goulding—*b/o* the musical play by Eddie Dowling and Cyrus Woods.

IRENE: Sentimental New York showgirl who, while on the rebound after being jilted by an unscrupulous Broadway lady-killer, is killed when a train hits her auto at a railroad crossing.

Constance Bennett, Sally O'Neil, William Haines, Douglas Gilmore, Ray Howard, Aggie Herrin, Kate Price, Lillian Elliott, Henry Kolker, Sam DeGrasse, Mae Cooper.

The Boob (1926, MGM). *d:* William A. Wellman; *sc:* Kenneth Clarke—*b/o* a story by George Scarborough and Annette Westbay.

JANE: Prohibition agent who joins forces with a scatterbrained farm boy in Wyoming to get the goods on a rum-runner.

Gertrude Olmstead, George K. Arthur, Charles Murray, Antonio D'Algy, Hank Mann, Babe London.

Tramp, Tramp, Tramp (1926, FN). *d:* Harry Edwards; *p:* Harry Langdon (Harry Langdon Corp.); *sc:* Frank Capra, Tim Whelan, Hal Conklin, J. Frank Holliday, Gerald Duffy, and Murray Roth.

BETTY: Young girl whose bumbling boyfriend is finally able to marry her when he wins $25,000 in a cross-country hiking contest.

Harry Langdon, Edwards Davis, Carlton Griffith, Alec B. Francis, Brooks Benedict, Tom Murray.

Paris (1926, MGM). *d:* Edmund Goulding; *sc:* Edmund Goulding.

"THE GIRL": Parisian girl who has an affair with a rich young American playboy but finally decides to stick with her sadistic apache lover.

Charles Ray, Douglas Gilmore, Michael Visaroff, Rose Dione, Jean Galeron.

The Taxi Dancer (1927, MGM). *d:* Harry Millarde; *sc:* A. P. Younger—*b/o* a story by Robert Terry Shannon.

JOSELYN POE: Virginia girl who heads for New York to be a dancer but winds up in a dime-a-dance emporium where she becomes involved with a wide variety of male admirers.

Owen Moore, Douglas Gilmore, Marc McDermott, William Orlamond, Gertrude Astor, Rockcliffe Fellowes, Claire McDowell, Bert Roach.

Winners of the Wilderness (1927, MGM). *d:* W. S. Van Dyke; *sc:* John Thomas Neville.

RENE CONTRECOEUR: French general's daughter in eighteenth-century colonial America who, during the French and Indian War, is captured by Chief Pontiac and his braves but is rescued by her lover, a dashing soldier-of-fortune colonel.

Tim McCoy, Edward Connelly, Frank Currier, Roy D'Arcy, Louise Lorraine, Edward Hearn, Will R. Walling, Tom O'Brien, Chief Big Tree, Lionel Belmore.

The Understanding Heart (1927, MGM). *d:* Jack Conway; *sc:* Edward T. Lowe Jr.—*b/o* the story by Peter B. Kyne.

MONICA DALE: Young girl who, while serving as a fire spotter for the Forest Rangers, gets involved not only with a forest fire but with a stalwart ranger.

Francis X. Bushman Jr., Rockcliffe Fellowes, Carmel Myers, Richard Carle, Harry Clark.

The Unknown (1927, MGM). *d:* Tod Browning; *sc:* Waldemar Young—*b/o* a story by Tod Browning.
ESTRELLITA: Young circus performer who is part of an act during which an armless man rings her with knives that he throws with his feet.
Lon Chaney, Norman Kerry, Nick de Ruiz, John George, Frank Lanning.

Twelve Miles Out (1927, MGM). *d:* Jack Conway; *sc:* Sada Cowan—*b/o* the play by William Anthony McGuire.
JANE: Young woman who is kidnapped by a handsome rum-runner and falls in love with him.
John Gilbert, Ernest Torrence, Betty Compson, Bert Roach, Eileen Percy, Edward Earle, Tom O'Brien, Harvey Clark.

Spring Fever (1927, MGM). *d:* Edward Sedgwick; *sc:* Albert Lewin and Frank Davies (with titles by Ralph Spence)—*b/o* the play by Vincent Lawrence.
ALLIE MONTE: Rich girl who marries a golf-playing "heir," then leaves him when she discovers that he's really only a poor shipping clerk—but reconciles with him when he wins $10,000 in a golf tournament.
William Haines, George K. Arthur, George Fawcett, Eileen Percy, Edward Earle, Bert Woodruff, Lee Moran.

West Point (1928, MGM). *d:* Edward Sedgwick; *sc:* Raymond L. Schrock (with titles by Joe Farnham).
BETTY CHANNING: Hotel owner's pretty daughter who is the sweetheart of a cocky, swell-headed West Point football star.
William Haines, William Bakewell, Neil Neely, Ralph Emerson, Edward Richardson, Baury Bradford Richardson, Leon Kellar, Major Raymond G. Moses, Major Philip B. Fleming.

Rose-Marie (1928, MGM). *d:* Lucien Hubbard; *sc:* Lucien Hubbard—*b/o* the operetta by Otto Harbach and Oscar Hammerstein II.
ROSE-MARIE: Fiery French Canadian mountain girl who, though a stalwart Royal Canadian Mounted Policeman is in love with her, falls for a fur trapper/adventurer who's wanted by the Mounties for a murder he didn't commit.
James Murray, House Peters, Creighton Hale, Gibson Gowland, Polly Moran, Lionel Belmore, William Orlamond, Gertrude Astor, Ralph Yearsley, Swen Hugo Borg, Harry Gribbon.

Across to Singapore (1928, MGM). *d:* William Nigh; *sc:* E. Richard Schayer—*b/o* the story by Ben Ames Williams.
PRISCILLA CROWNINSHIELD: New England girl in the clipper-ship era who, when she rejects a ship's captain, causes a feud between the captain and his younger seafaring brother, whom she really loves.
Ramon Novarro, Ernest Torrence, Frank Currier, Dan Wolheim, Duke Martin, Edward Connelly, James Mason.

The Law of the Range (1928, MGM). *d:* William Nigh; *sc:* E. Richard Schayer (with titles by Robert Hopkins)—*b/o* a story by Norman Houston.
BETTY DALLAS: Girl in the Old West whose rival suitors are a ranger and an outlaw who, unbeknownst to the ranger, is really his brother.
Tim McCoy, Rex Lease, Bodil Rosing, Tenen Holtz.

Four Walls (1928, MGM). *d:* William Nigh; *sc:* Alice D.G. Miller—*b/o* a story by Dana Burnet and George Abbot.
FRIEDA: New York moll who, when her gangster boyfriend reforms after a prison sentence, is jilted but finally wins him back.
John Gilbert, Vera Gordon, Carmel Myers, Robert Emmett O'Connor, Louis Natheaux, Jack Byron.

Our Dancing Daughters (1928, MGM). *d:* Harry Beaumont; *sc:* Josephine Lovett.
"DANGEROUS DIANA": Party-loving Roaring '20s flapper who loses her young millionaire boyfriend to a conniving rival but gets him back after the drunken wife falls to her death down a flight of stairs.
Johnny Mack Brown, Dorothy Sebastian, Anita Page, Nils Asther, Dorothy Cummings, Huntley Gordon, Evelyn Hall, Sam De Grasse, Edward Nugent, Eddie Quillan.

Dream of Love (1928, MGM). *d:* Fred Niblo; *sc:* Dorothy Farnum (with titles by Marion Ainslee and Ruth Cummings)—*b/o* the play *Adrienne Lecouvreur* by Eugene Scribe and Ernest Legouve.
ADRIENNE LECOUVREUR: European gypsy circus performer who has a brief clandestine love affair with a handsome prince, then, years later after she has become a famous actress, returns to his kingdom for a happy reunion.
Nils Asther, Aileen Pringle, Warner Oland, Carmel Myers, Harry Reinhardt, Harry Myers, Alphonse Martell, Fletcher Norton.

The Duke Steps Out (1929, MGM). *d:* James Cruze; *sc:* Raymond Schrock and Dale Van Every—*b/o* a story by Lucien Cary.
SUSIE: Pretty coed who falls for a mysterious student, then discovers he's really a millionaire's son as well as a professional boxer.
William Haines, Karl Dane, Tenen Holtz, Eddie Nugent, Jack Roper, Delmer Daves, Luke Cosgrove, Herbert Prior.

Our Modern Maidens (1929, MGM). *d:* Jack Conway; *p:* Hunt Stromberg; *sc:* Josephine Lovett (with titles by Ruth Cummings and Marion Ainslee).

BILLIE BROWN: Wealthy motor magnate's daughter who, shortly after she marries a young diplomat, discovers that both of them are really in love with others.

Rod LaRocque, Douglas Fairbanks Jr., Anita Page, Edward Nugent, Josephine Dunn, Albert Gran.

Untamed (1929, MGM). *d:* Jack Conway; *sc:* Sylvia Thalberg and Frank Butler (with titles by Lucile Newmark)—*b/o* a story by Charles E. Scoggins.

"BINGO": Uninhibited oil heiress who, when the penniless young engineer she loves won't marry her, talks him into it after she shoots him in the arm.

Robert Montgomery, Ernest Torrence, Holmes Herbert, John Miljan, Gwen Lee, Edward Nugent, Don Terry, Gertrude Astor, Lloyd Ingram, Grace Cunnard, Tom O'Brien, Wilson Benge.

Montana Moon (1930, MGM). *d:* Malcolm St. Clair; *sc:* Sylvia Thalberg and Frank Butler (with dialogue by Joe Farnham).

JOAN PRESCOTT: Rich Montana rancher's daughter who meets her match when she falls for and marries a handsome young cowboy from Texas.

Johnny Mack Brown, Dorothy Sebastian, Ricardo Cortez, Benny Rubin, Cliff Edwards, Karl Dane, Lloyd Ingraham.

Our Blushing Brides (1930, MGM). *d:* Harry Beaumont; *sc:* Bess Meredyth and John Howard Lawson (with additional dialogue by Edwin Justus Mayer)—*b/o* a story by Bess Meredyth.

JERRY: New York department-store model who at first rejects her boss's son's wolfish advances but has a change of heart when his intentions finally become honorable.

Robert Montgomery, Anita Page, Dorothy Sebastian, Raymond Hackett, John Miljan, Albert Conti, Edward Brophy, Hedda Hopper.

Paid (1930, MGM). *d:* Sam Wood; *sc:* Lucien Hubbard and Charles MacArthur—*b/o* the play *Within the Law* by Bayard Veiller.

MARY TURNER: Innocent girl unjustly sent to prison who, when she gets out, becomes a hardened con woman seeking revenge against the men who put her behind bars.

Robert Armstrong, Marie Prevost, Kent Douglass, Hale Hamilton, John Miljan, Purnell B. Pratt, Polly Moran, Robert Emmett O'Connor, Tyrell Davis, William Bakewell, George Cooper, Gwen Lee, Isabel Withers.

Dance, Fools, Dance (1931, MGM). *d:* Harry Beaumont; *sc:* Richard Schayer (with dialogue by Aurania Rouverol)—*b/o* a story by Aurania Rouverol.

BONNIE JORDAN: Young girl who, after her spoiled, formerly rich playboy brother joins a bootlegging gang, gains the confidence of the ruthless leader of the gang—until he discovers that she's a cub reporter secretly trying to pin a murder rap on him.

Lester Vail, Cliff Edwards, William Bakewell, Clark Gable, Earl Foxe, Purnell B. Pratt, Hale Hamilton, Natalie Moorhead, Joan Marsh, Russell Hopton.

Laughing Sinners (1931, MGM). *d:* Harry Beaumont; *sc:* Bess Meredyth (with dialogue by Martin Flavin)—*b/o* the play *Torch Song* by Kenyon Nicholson.

IVY STEVENS: Fallen entertainer who, when she tries to commit suicide after her unscrupulous lover deserts her, is saved by a Salvation Army worker who falls in love with her.

Neil Hamilton, Clark Gable, Marjorie Rambeau, Guy Kibbee, Cliff Edwards, Roscoe Karns, George Cooper, George F. Marion.

This Modern Age (1931, MGM). *d:* Nicholas Grinde; *sc:* Sylvia Thalberg and Frank Butler—*b/o* the story "Girls Together" by Mildred Cram.

VALENTINE WINTERS: Daughter who goes to Paris to visit her divorced mother—the mistress of a wealthy Frenchman—and falls for a rich Harvard man whose family disapproves of her.

Pauline Frederick, Neil Hamilton, Monroe Owsley, Hobart Bosworth, Emma Dunn, Albert Conti, Adrienne D'Ambricourt, Marcelle Corday.

Possessed (1931, MGM). *d:* Clarence Brown; *sc:* Lenore Coffee—*b/o* Edgar Selwyn's play *The Mirage.*

MARIAN: Small-town factory worker who goes to New York to seek riches, falls for a wealthy married lawyer, and—in order to avoid a divorce scandal that would hurt his political ambitions—becomes his secret mistress.

Clark Gable, Wallace Ford, Skeets Gallagher, Frank Conroy, Marjorie White, John Miljan, Clara Blandick.

Grand Hotel (1932, MGM). *d:* Edmund Goulding; *sc:* William A. Drake—*b/o* the novel and play by Vicki Baum.

FLAEMMCHEN: Berlin hotel stenographer who agrees to have an affair with an oafish industrialist but changes her outlook on life when she becomes genuinely attached to a bookkeeper with an incurable disease.

Greta Garbo, John Barrymore, Wallace Beery, Lionel Barrymore, Lewis Stone, Jean Hersholt, Robert McWade, Purnell B. Pratt, Tully Marshall, Frank Conroy, Edwin Maxwell.

Letty Lynton (1932, MGM). *d:* Clarence Brown; *sc:* John Meehan and Wanda Tuchock—*b/o* the novel by Marie Belloc Lowndes.

LETTY LYNTON: Rich New York socialite whose shipboard romance with a respectable Long Island man leads to their engagement, which is jeopardized when her blackmailing ex-lover shows up.

Robert Montgomery, Nils Asther, Lewis Stone, May Robson, Louise Closser Hale, Emma Dunn, Walter Walker, William Pawley.

Rain (1932, UA). *d:* Lewis Milestone; *sc:* Maxwell Anderson—*b/o* the play *Rain* by John Cotton and Clemence Randolph, adapted from the story "Miss Thompson" by W. Somerset Maugham.

SADIE THOMPSON: Cynical trollop stranded on the island of Pago Pago who falls for a U.S. Marine sergeant but also gets involved with a puritanical missionary who—while trying to convert her—sexually attacks her.

Walter Huston, William Gargan, Beulah Bondi, Matt Moore, Kendall Lee, Guy Kibbee, Walter Catlett, Ben Hendricks Jr., Fred Howard.

Today We Live (1933, MGM). *d:* Howard Hawks; *p:* Howard Hawks; *sc:* Edith Fitzgerald and Dwight Taylor (with dialogue by William Faulkner)—*b/o* the story "Turnabout" by William Faulkner.

DIANA BOYCE-SMITH: Aristocratic English playgirl during WWI whose brother and ex-boyfriend—both British naval officers—sacrifice themselves on a suicide mission in order to save the American aviator she loves.

Gary Cooper, Robert Young, Franchot Tone, Roscoe Karns, Louise Closser Hale, Rollo Lloyd, Hilda Vaughn.

Dancing Lady (1933, MGM). *d:* Robert Z. Leonard; *p:* David O. Selznick; *sc:* Allen Rivkin and P. J. Wolfson—*b/o* the novel by James Warner Bellah.

JANIE: Burlesque dancer who, when she gets the lead in a new Broadway musical, finds that she has to choose between two suitors—the show's rich playboy backer and the hardboiled stage manager.

Clark Gable, Franchot Tone, May Robson, Winnie Lightner, Fred Astaire, Robert Benchley, Ted Healy, Moe Howard, Jerry Howard, Larry Fine, Art Jarrett, Nelson Eddy, Sterling Holloway, Eunice Quedens (Eve Arden), Lynn Bari.

Sadie McKee (1934, MGM). *d:* Clarence Brown; *p:* Lawrence Weingarten; *sc:* John Meehan—*b/o* the story "Pretty Sadie McKee" by Vina Delmar.

SADIE McKEE: Small-town housemaid who, while becoming a successful New York nightclub entertainer, gets involved with three different romances—a smooth-talking playboy, an alcoholic millionaire, and her handsome ex-employer.

Gene Raymond, Franchot Tone, Edward Arnold, Esther Ralston, Jean Dixon, Leo Carrillo, Akim Tamiroff, Zelda Sears, Helen Ware, Leo G. Carroll, Gene Austin, Candy, Coco.

Chained (1934, MGM). *d:* Clarence Brown; *p:* Hunt Stromberg; *sc:* John Lee Mahin—*b/o* a story by Edgar Selwyn.

DIANE LOVERING: Ex–New York secretary who, though she falls for a wealthy Argentine rancher on an ocean cruise, marries her aging lover out of loyalty—but then winds up with the rancher when the husband unselfishly gives her up.

Clark Gable, Otto Kruger, Stuart Erwin, Una O'Connor, Marjorie Gateson, Akim Tamiroff, William Deggar.

Forsaking All Others (1934, MGM). *d:* W. S. Van Dyke; *p:* Bernard H. Hyman; *sc:* Joseph L. Mankiewicz—*b/o* the play by Edward Barry Roberts and Frank Morgan Cavett.

MARY: Young socialite who keeps getting engaged to a fickle childhood friend but finally realizes that another childhood friend of theirs—who has loyally stood by her for years—is the man she really loves.

Clark Gable, Robert Montgomery, Charles Butterworth, Billie Burke, Frances Drake, Rosalind Russell, Arthur Treacher, Ted Healy.

No More Ladies (1935, MGM). *d:* Edward H. Griffith and George Cukor; *p:* Irving Thalberg; *sc:* Donald Ogden Stewart and Horace Jackson—*b/o* the play by A. E. Thomas.

MARCIA: Society girl who marries a woman-chasing playboy, then—when he's unfaithful—tries to make him jealous by playing up to an ex-suitor.

Robert Montgomery, Charlie Ruggles, Franchot Tone, Edna May Oliver, Gail Patrick, Reginald Denny, Vivienne Osborne, Arthur Treacher.

I Live My Life (1935, MGM). *d:* W. S. Van Dyke; *p:* Bernard H. Hyman; *sc:* Joseph L. Mankiewicz—*b/o* the short story "Claustrophobia" by A. Carter Goodloe.

KAY: Flighty society girl who falls for a serious-minded working-class archaeologist, then has problems giving up her frivolous way of life.

Brian Aherne, Frank Morgan, Aline MacMahon, Eric Blore, Fred Keating, Jessie Ralph, Arthur Treacher, Hedda Hopper, Frank Conroy, Etienne Girardot, Edward Brophy, Sterling Holloway, Hilda Vaughn, Vince Barnett, Lionel Stander, Hale Hamilton.

The Gorgeous Hussy (1936, MGM). *d:* Clarence Brown; *p:* Joseph L. Mankiewicz; *sc:* Ainsworth

Morgan and Stephen Morehouse Avery—*b/o* the novel by Samuel Hopkins Adams.

PEGGY O'NEAL (EATON): Innkeeper's daughter and notorious Washington, D.C., belle who becomes a protégé and confidante of President Andrew Jackson, sacrificing her husband and friends and finally going into self-imposed exile.

Robert Taylor, Lionel Barrymore, Melvyn Douglas, James Stewart, Franchot Tone, Louis Calhern, Alison Skipworth, Beulah Bondi, Melville Cooper, Sidney Toler, Gene Lockhart, Clara Blandick, Frank Conroy, Nydia Westman, Louise Beavers, Charles Trowbridge, Willard Robertson, Bert Roach, Ward Bond.

Love on the Run (1936, MGM). *d:* W. S. Van Dyke; *p:* Joseph L. Mankiewicz; *sc:* John Lee Mahin, Manuel Seff, and Gladys Hurlbut—*b/o* the story by Alan Green and Julian Brodie.

SALLY PARKER: American heiress in Europe who, when she runs away from an unwanted wedding, becomes involved with a pair of rival American foreign correspondents and a ring of international spies.

Clark Gable, Franchot Tone, Reginald Owen, Mona Barrie, Ivan Lebedeff, Charles Judels, William Demarest.

The Last of Mrs. Cheyney (1937, MGM). *d:* Richard Boleslawski; *p:* Lawrence Weingarten; *sc:* Leon Gordon, Samson Raphaelson, and Monckton Hoffe—*b/o* the play by Frederick Lonsdale.

FAY CHEYNEY: Chic American jewel thief who, along with her suave gentleman partner (posing as a butler), plans to make a big heist at a British high-society weekend party in the countryside.

William Powell, Robert Montgomery, Frank Morgan, Jessie Ralph, Nigel Bruce, Benita Hume, Ralph Forbes, Aileen Pringle, Melville Cooper, Sara Haden, Lumsden Hare, Barnett Parker.

The Bride Wore Red (1937, MGM). *d:* Dorothy Arzner; *p:* Joseph L. Mankiewicz; *sc:* Tess Slesinger and Bradbury Foote—*b/o* Ferenc Molnar's play *The Girl from Trieste*.

ANNI: Cabaret singer in Trieste who, when a whimsical count gives her a two-week vacation at a Tyrolean resort, becomes involved with two handsome men—a wealthy aristocrat and the village postman.

Franchot Tone, Robert Young, Billie Burke, Reginald Owen, Lynne Carver, George Zucco, Mary Phillips, Paul Porcasi, Dickie Moore, Frank Puglia.

Mannequin (1938, MGM). *d:* Frank Borzage; *p:* Joseph L. Mankiewicz; *sc:* Lawrence Hazard—*b/o* a story by Katharine Brush.

JESSICA CASSIDY: Poor girl from New York's lower East Side who—after marrying a small-time crook—leaves him, gets a job modeling expensive clothes, and falls in love with a self-made millionaire shipping magnate.

Spencer Tracy, Alan Curtis, Ralph Morgan, Mary Phillips, Oscar O'Shea, Elizabeth Risdon, Leo Gorcey, George Chandler, Bert Roach, Marie Blake, Matt McHugh, Paul Fix, Helen Troy, Phillip Terry.

The Shining Hour (1938, MGM). *d:* Frank Borzage; *p:* Joseph L. Mankiewicz; *sc:* Jane Murfin and Ogden Nash—*b/o* the play by Keith Winter.

OLIVIA RILEY: New York showgirl who marries a gentleman farmer, then becomes romantically involved with the husband's younger married brother.

Margaret Sullavan, Robert Young, Melvyn Douglas, Fay Bainter, Allyn Joslyn, Hattie McDaniel, Oscar O'Shea, Frank Albertson, Harry Barris.

Ice Follies of 1939 (1939, MGM). *d:* Reinhold Schunzel; *p:* Harry Rapf; *sc:* Leonard Praskins, Florence Ryerson, and Edgar Allan Woolf—*b/o* a story by Leonard Praskins.

MARY McKAY: Ice skater who becomes a Hollywood movie star, then has marital problems because her Ice Follies–producer husband is based in New York, but who winds up happy when he becomes a Hollywood film producer and their careers become compatible.

James Stewart, Lew Ayres, Lewis Stone, Bess Ehrhardt, Lionel Stander, Charles D. Brown, Roy Shipstad, Eddie Shipstad, Oscar Johnson.

The Women (1939, MGM). *d:* George Cukor; *p:* Hunt Stromberg; *sc:* Anita Loos and Jane Murfin—*b/o* the play by Clare Boothe.

CRYSTAL ALLEN: Ambitious shopgirl who manages to steal a New York socialite's husband but winds up losing him back to his wife.

Norma Shearer, Rosalind Russell, Mary Boland, Paulette Goddard, Phyllis Povah, Joan Fontaine, Virginia Weidler, Lucile Watson, Florence Nash, Muriel Hutchinson, Esther Dale, Ann Morriss, Ruth Hussey, Mary Beth Hughes, Virginia Grey, Marjorie Main, Cora Witherspoon, Hedda Hopper.

Strange Cargo (1940, MGM). *d:* Frank Borzage; *p:* Joseph L. Mankiewicz; *p:* Lawrence Hazard (adaptation by Anita Loos)—*b/o* the book *Not Too Narrow, Not Too Deep* by Richard Sale.

JULIE: Hardboiled dance-hall girl who falls for a tough convict as she accompanies him and a group of other prisoners in a boat after they've escaped from the French penal colony on Devil's Island.

Clark Gable, Ian Hunter, Peter Lorre, Paul Lukas, Albert Dekker, J. Edward Bromberg, Eduardo Ciannelli, John Arledge, Victor Varconi.

Susan and God (1940, MGM). *d:* George Cukor; *p:* Hunt Stromberg; *sc:* Anita Loos—*b/o* the play by Rachel Crothers.

SUSAN: Selfish society woman who alienates her husband, daughter, and friends when she embraces a new religious movement, but who fails to practice what she overbearingly preaches.

Fredric March, Ruth Hussey, John Carroll, Rita Hayworth, Nigel Bruce, Bruce Cabot, Rita Quigley, Rose Hobart, Constance Collier, Gloria DeHaven, Richard Crane, Marjorie Main, Aldrich Bowker.

A Woman's Face (1941, MGM). *d:* George Cukor; *p:* Victor Saville; *sc:* Donald Ogden Stewart—*b/o* the play *Il Etait Une Fois* by Francis de Croisset.

ANNA HOLM: Embittered Swedish woman with a disfigured face who becomes the leader of a gang of blackmailers in Stockholm but is spiritually rejuvenated when her beauty is restored by a plastic surgeon.

Melvyn Douglas, Conrad Veidt, Osa Massen, Reginald Owen, Albert Bassermann, Marjorie Main, Donald Meek, Connie Gilchrist, Charles Quigley, George Zucco, Henry Kolker, Robert Warwick, Gilbert Emery, Henry Daniell, Sarah Padden, William Farnum.

When Ladies Meet (1941, MGM). *d:* Robert Z. Leonard; *p:* Robert Z. Leonard and Orville O. Dull; *sc:* S. K. Lauren and Anita Loos—*b/o* the play by Rachel Crothers.

MARY HOWARD: Successful novelist who falls in love with her married publisher but, after meeting his wife, changes her mind about trying to break up their marriage.

Robert Taylor, Greer Garson, Herbert Marshall, Spring Byington, Rafael Storm, Mona Barrie.

They All Kissed the Bride (1942, Col.). *d:* Alexander Hall; *p:* Edward Kaufman; *sc:* P. J. Wolfson—*b/o* a story by Gina Kaus and Andrew P. Solt.

MARGARET J. DREW: Hard-nosed career woman whose outlook on life changes when she falls for a crusading journalist assigned to expose working conditions in her company.

Melvyn Douglas, Roland Young, Billie Burke, Andrew Tombes, Allen Jenkins, Helen Parrish, Emory Parnell, Mary Treen, Nydia Westman, Ivan Simpson, Roger Clark, Gordon Jones, Edward Gargan.

Reunion in France (1942, MGM). *d:* Jules Dassin; *p:* Joseph L. Mankiewicz; *sc:* Jan Lustig, Marvin Borowsky, and Marc Connelly—*b/o* a story by Ladislas Bus-Fekete.

MICHELE DE LA BECQUE: Flighty Parisian dress designer during WWII who, when she finally realizes it's time to change her selfish philosophy

and resist France's Nazi invaders, agrees to help a downed American flyer escape the Gestapo.

John Wayne, Philip Dorn, Reginald Owen, Albert Bassermann, John Carradine, Ann Ayars, Moroni Olsen, J. Edward Bromberg, Henry Daniell, Howard Da Silva, Charles Arnt, Morris Ankrum, Ava Gardner.

Above Suspicion (1943, MGM). *d:* Richard Thorpe; *p:* Victor Saville; *sc:* Keith Winter, Melville Baker, and Patricia Coleman—*b/o* the novel by Helen MacInnes.

FRANCES MYLES: American bride on her honeymoon in pre-WWII Europe who, along with her Oxford professor husband, is recruited by the British secret service for a mission to Germany to get the plans for a new secret weapon.

Fred MacMurray, Conrad Veidt, Basil Rathbone, Reginald Owen, Cecil Cunningham, Richard Ainley, Ann Shoemaker, Sara Haden, Felix Bressart, Bruce Lester.

Mildred Pierce (1945, WB). *d:* Michael Curtiz; *p:* Jerry Wald; *sc:* Ranald MacDougall—*b/o* the novel by James M. Cain.

MILDRED PIERCE*: Ambitious housewife who, after leaving her husband and becoming a waitress, develops a successful chain of restaurants but has her heart broken by her vicious, ungrateful daughter.

Jack Carson, Zachary Scott, Eve Arden, Ann Blyth, Bruce Bennett, George Tobias, Lee Patrick, Moroni Olsen, Jo Ann Marlow, Barbara Brown.

Humoresque (1946, WB). *d:* Jean Negulesco; *p:* Jerry Wald; *sc:* Clifford Odets and Zachary Gold—*b/o* a story by Fannie Hurst.

HELEN WRIGHT: Neurotic married socialite who becomes hopelessly involved with an ambitious violinist when she becomes his patroness but finally ends it all by walking into the ocean.

John Garfield, Oscar Levant, J. Carroll Naish, Joan Chandler, Tom D'Andrea, Peggy Knudsen, Craig Stevens, Paul Cavanagh, John Abbott, Bobby Blake, Don McGuire, Fritz Leiber, Nestor Paiva.

Possessed (1947, WB). *d:* Curtis Bernhardt; *p:* Jerry Wald; *sc:* Silvia Richards and Ranald MacDougall—*b/o* the story "One Man's Secret!" by Rita Weiman.

LOUISE HOWELL†: Emotionally unstable nurse who marries her wealthy employer but still passionately loves a young engineer—whom she shoots and kills when he rebuffs her.

Van Heflin, Raymond Massey, Geraldine Brooks,

*Won the Academy Award as Best Actress for this role.
†Received an Academy Award nomination as Best Actress for this role.

Stanley Ridges, John Ridgely, Moroni Olsen, Erskine Sanford, Isabel Withers, Douglas Kennedy, Monte Blue, Don McGuire, Griff Barnett.

Daisy Kenyon (1947, 20th-Fox). *d:* Otto Preminger; *p:* Otto Preminger; *sc:* David Hertz—*b/o* a novel by Elizabeth Janeway.

DAISY KENYON: Chic New York fashion designer who marries a discharged WWII veteran and boat designer, then must decide whether or not to leave him when her former lover, a wealthy lawyer, finally gets a divorce so that he can marry her.

Henry Fonda, Dana Andrews, Ruth Warrick, Martha Stewart, Peggy Ann Garner, Connie Marshall, Nicholas Joy, Art Baker, Charles Meredith, Roy Roberts, Griff Barnett.

Flamingo Road (1949, WB). *d:* Michael Curtiz; *p:* Jerry Wald; *sc:* Robert Wilder—*b/o* the play by Robert Wilder and Sally Wilder.

LANE BELLAMY: Tough carnival dancer who, when she's stranded in a small Southern town, falls for the town deputy, marries a rising local politician, and accidentally kills the town's corrupt political boss.

Zachary Scott, Sidney Greenstreet, Gladys George, Virginia Huston, Fred Clark, Gertrude Michael, Alice White, David Brian.

The Damned Don't Cry (1950, WB). *d:* Vincent Sherman; *p:* Jerry Wald; *sc:* Harold Medford and Jerome Weidman—*b/o* a story by Gertrude Walker.

ETHEL WHITEHEAD: Housewife who leaves her laborer husband, then rises to wealth when she becomes the mistress of a crime boss, but finally reforms after suffering tragedy and disaster.

David Brian, Steve Cochran, Kent Smith, Hugh Sanders, Selena Royle, Morris Ankrum, Edith Evanson, Richard Egan, Sara Perry, Eddie Marr.

Harriet Craig (1950, Col.). *d:* Vincent Sherman; *p:* William Dozier; *sc:* Anne Froelick and James Gunn—*b/o* the play *Craig's Wife* by George Kelly.

HARRIET CRAIG: Ruthlessly ambitious middle-class housewife who selfishly loves her house and material possessions more than her easy-going husband, who finally walks out on her.

Wendell Corey, Lucile Watson, Allyn Joslyn, William Bishop, K. T. Stevens, Viola Roache, Raymond Greenleaf, Ellen Corby, Virginia Brissac, Douglas Wood, Charles Evans.

Goodbye My Fancy (1951, WB). *d:* Vincent Sherman; *p:* Henry Blanke; *sc:* Ivan Goff and Ben Roberts—*b/o* the play by Fay Kanin.

AGATHA REED: Congresswoman who returns to her alma mater—from which she was expelled twenty years before—in order to receive an honorary degree and to see her former love, now the college president.

Robert Young, Frank Lovejoy, Eve Arden, Janice Rule, Lurene Tuttle, Howard St. John, Viola Roache, Ellen Corby, Virginia Gibson, John Qualen.

This Woman Is Dangerous (1952, WB). *d:* Felix Feist; *p:* Robert Sisk; *sc:* Geoffrey Homes and George Worthing Yates—*b/o* a story by Bernard Girard.

BETH AUSTIN: Gangster and killer's mistress who, when she has an eye operation for failing eyesight, falls in love with her doctor.

Dennis Morgan, David Brian, Richard Webb, Mari Aldon, Philip Carey, Ian MacDonald, Katherine Warren, George Chandler, Sherry Jackson, Stuart Randall, Douglas Fowley.

Sudden Fear (1952, RKO). *d:* David Miller; *p:* Joseph Kaufman; *sc:* Lenore Coffee and Robert Smith—*b/o* the novel by Edna Sherry.

MYRA HUDSON*: Wealthy and famous playwright who marries a worthless actor, then learns that he and his mistress plan to kill her for her money.

Jack Palance, Gloria Grahame, Bruce Bennett, Virginia Huston, Touch Connors (Mike Connors).

Torch Song (1953, MGM). *d:* Charles Walters; *p:* Henry Berman and Sidney Franklin Jr.; *sc:* John Michael Hayes and Jan Lustig—*b/o* the story "Why Should I Cry?" by I. A. R. Wylie.

JENNY STEWART: Hardened, selfish musical-comedy star who finally reveals her tender side when she falls for a blind pianist who has secretly loved her for years.

Michael Wilding, Gig Young, Marjorie Rambeau, Henry Morgan, Dorothy Patrick, James Todd, Eugene Loring, Paul Guilfoyle, Benny Rubin, Peter Chong, Chris Warfield.

Johnny Guitar (1954, Rep.). *d:* Nicholas Ray; *p:* Herbert J. Yates; *sc:* Philip Yordan—*b/o* the novel by Roy Chanslor.

VIENNA: Gambling saloon owner in old Arizona who falls for a guitar-playing ex-gunman while clashing with a vicious female banker and hostile townspeople over some valuable property.

Sterling Hayden, Mercedes McCambridge, Scott Brady, Ward Bond, Ben Cooper, Ernest Borgnine, John Carradine, Royal Dano, Frank Ferguson, Paul Fix, Rhys Williams, Ian MacDonald.

Female on the Beach (1955, Univ.). *d:* Joseph Pevney; *p:* Albert Zugsmith; *sc:* Robert Hill and Richard Alan Simmons—*b/o* Robert Hill's play *The Besieged Heart.*

---

*Received an Academy Award nomination as Best Actress for this role.

LYNN MARKHAM: Wealthy widow who marries a handsome beach bum, then suspects that he intends to murder her.

Jeff Chandler, Jan Sterling, Cecil Kellaway, Natalie Schafer, Charles Drake, Judith Evelyn, Stuart Randall, Marjorie Bennett, Romo Vincent.

Queen Bee (1955, Col.). *d:* Ranald MacDougall; *p:* Jerry Wald; *sc:* Ranald MacDougall—*b/o* the novel by Edna Lee.

EVA PHILLIPS: Evil, dominating woman who drives her Georgia mill-owner husband to drink and destroys the lives of others while, like a queen bee, she "stings to death" any rivals who challenge her position.

Barry Sullivan, Betsy Palmer, John Ireland, Lucy Marlow, William Leslie, Fay Wray, Katherine Anderson, Tim Hovey, Willa Pearl Curtis, Bill Walker, Olan Soule.

Autumn Leaves (1956, Col.). *d:* Robert Aldrich; *p:* William Goetz (William Goetz Productions); *sc:* Jack Jevne, Lewis Meltzer, and Robert Blees.

MILLICENT WETHERBY: Middle-aged manuscript typist who marries a younger man who turns out to be mentally unbalanced and tries to murder her.

Cliff Robertson, Vera Miles, Lorne Greene, Ruth Donnelly, Sheppard Strudwick, Selmar Jackson, Maxine Cooper, Marjorie Bennett, Leonard Mudie.

The Story of Esther Costello (1957, Col.). *d:* David Miller; *p:* David Miller (Romulus); *sc:* Charles Kaufman—*b/o* the novel by Nicholas Monsarrat.

MARGARET LANDI: Wealthy American socialite in Iceland who helps rehabilitate a deaf-mute girl, sets up a charity fund in her name, then has to fight hucksters trying to exploit the girl.

Rossano Brazzi, Heather Sears, Lee Patterson, Ron Randell, Fay Compton, John Loder, Denis O'Dea, Sidney James, Bessie Love, Tony Quinn.

The Best of Everything (1959, 20th-Fox). *d:* Jean Negulesco; *p:* Jerry Wald; *sc:* Edith Sommer and Mann Rubin—*b/o* the novel by Rona Jaffe.

AMANDA FARROW: Embittered magazine editor in a New York publishing house who, after a disappointing affair with a married man, gives up her job to marry a widower with children—but then exits the marriage and returns to her old job.

Hope Lange, Stephen Boyd, Suzy Parker, Martha Hyer, Diane Baker, Brian Aherne, Robert Evans, Brett Halsey, Donald Harron, Sue Carson, Myrna Hansen, Louis Jourdan.

What Ever Happened To Baby Jane? (1962, WB). *d:* Robert Aldrich; *p:* Kenneth Hyman and Robert Aldrich (Seven Arts/Aldrich); *sc:* Lukas Heller —*b/o* the novel by Henry Farrell.

BLANCHE HUDSON: Crippled ex–movie queen—now living in a crumbling old Hollywood mansion—who is persecuted and held prisoner by her mentally unbalanced sister, who was once a famous child vaudeville star.

Bette Davis, Victor Buono, Marjorie Bennett, Maidie Norman, Anna Lee, Barbara Merrill, Julie Allred, Gina Gillespie, Dave Willock, Ann Barton.

The Caretakers (1963, UA). *d:* Hall Bartlett; *p:* Hall Bartlett (Hall Bartlett); *sc:* Henry F. Greenberg—*b/o* a story by Hall Bartlett and Jerry Paris—*b/o* a book by Daniel Telfer.

LUCRETIA TERRY: Aging, hardened head nurse at a West Coast mental hospital who clashes with a young doctor over how to best treat the patients.

Robert Stack, Polly Bergen, Janis Paige, Diane McBain, Van Williams, Constance Ford, Sharon Hugueny, Herbert Marshall, Robert Vaughn, Susan Oliver, Ellen Corby.

Strait Jacket (1964, Col.). *d:* William Castle; *p:* William Castle (William Castle); *sc:* Robert Bloch.

LUCY HARBIN: Woman who, after she's released from a mental hospital for the ax murder of her unfaithful husband twenty years earlier, becomes a prime suspect when more ax murders take place.

Diane Baker, Leif Erickson, Howard St. John, John Anthony Hayes, Rochelle Hudson, George Kennedy, Edith Atwater, Mitchell Cox, Vachel Cos.

I Saw What You Did (1965, Univ.). *d:* William Castle; *p:* William Castle (William Castle); *sc:* William McGivern—*b/o* the novel by Ursula Curtiss.

AMY NELSON: Shrewish woman who, when she discovers that her married lover is a murderer, tries to save two teen-age girls from being his next victims.

John Ireland, Leif Erickson, Sara Lane, Andi Garrett, Sharyl Locke, Patricia Breslin, John Archer, John Crawford, Joyce Meadows.

Berserk (1968, Col.). *d:* Jim O'Connolly; *p:* Herman Cohen (Herman Cohen); *sc:* Aben Kandel and Herman Cohen.

MONICA RIVERS: Shapely owner and ringmistress of a traveling English circus in which a series of brutal, mysterious murders take place.

Ty Hardin, Diana Dors, Michael Gough, Judy Geeson, Robert Hardy, Geoffrey Keen, Sydney Tafler, George Claydon, Ambrostine Phillpotts.

Trog (1970, WB). *d:* Freddie Francis; *p:* Herman Cohen (Herman Cohen); *sc:* Aben Kandel—*b/o* a story by Peter Bryan and John Gilling.

DR. BROCKTON: Anthropologist who unearths a troglodyte (an Ice Age "missing link" half-caveman, half-ape) and manages to domesticate him—until he's goaded by a villain into going on a rampage and is killed by the Army.

Michael Gough, Bernard Kay, David Griffin, Kim Braden, Joe Cornelius, John Hamill, Geoffrey Case, Thorley Walters.

• In addition, Joan Crawford made cameo/guest appearances in the following feature films: *Hollywood Revue of 1929* (1929, MGM), *Hollywood Canteen* (1944, WB), and *It's a Great Feeling* (1949, WB).

☆ BING CROSBY

Harry Lillis Crosby

b: May 2, 1903, Tacoma, Wash.
d: Oct. 14, 1977, Madrid, Spain

"You don't know what it's like to stand out there on that stage all alone, with the whole show on your shoulders. If I'm no good, the show's no good!"

Frank Elgin (Bing Crosby)
feeling the pressures of stardom in
The Country Girl, 1954.

The Big Broadcast (1932, Para.). *d:* Frank Tuttle; *sc:* George Marion Jr.—*b/o* the play *Wild Waves* by William Ford Manley.
BING HORNSBY: Easy-going, irresponsible radio crooner who loses his job but gets it back when a millionaire pal buys the station.
Stu Erwin, Leila Hyams, Sharon Lynne, George Burns, Gracie Allen, George Barbier, Spec O'Donnell, Kate Smith, The Mills Brothers, The Boswell Sisters, Vincent Lopez and his Orchestra, Cab Calloway and his Band, Arthur Tracy.

College Humor (1933, Para.). *d:* Wesley Ruggles; *sc:* Claude Binyon and Frank Butler—*b/o* a story by Dean Fales.
PROF. FREDERICK DANVERS: Drama history professor who is being chased by a pretty blond coed who is in turn being chased by the campus big-shot football star.
Jack Oakie, Mary Carlisle, Richard Arlen, Mary Kornmann, George Burns, Gracie Allen, Lona Andre, Joseph Sawyer.

Too Much Harmony (1933, Para.). *d:* Edward Sutherland; *sc:* Harry Ruskin—*b/o* a story by Joseph L. Mankiewicz.
EDDIE BRONSON: Handsome show-biz crooner who gets involved in backstage romances with two women—one "good," and one "bad."
Jack Oakie, Judith Allen, Skeets Gallagher, Harry Green, Lilyan Tashman, Ned Sparks, Kitty Kelly, Grace Bradley, Evelyn Oakie, Billy Bevan.

Going Hollywood (1933, Para.). *d:* Raoul Walsh; *sc:* Donald Ogden Stewart—*b/o* a story by Frances Marion.
BILL WILLIAMS: Famous crooner whose most avid fan—a lovesick schoolteacher—follows him to Hollywood, wins him away from a fiery movie actress, and becomes his leading lady.
Marion Davies, Fifi D'Orsay, Stuart Erwin, Patsy Kelly, Bobby Watson, Ned Sparks.

We're Not Dressing (1934, Para.). *d:* Norman Taurog; *p:* Benjamin Glazer; *sc:* Horace Jackson, George Marion Jr., and Francis Martin—from a story by Benjamin Glazer—*b/o* James M. Barrie's play *The Admirable Chrichton.*
STEVE JONES: Easy-going sailor on a spoiled heiress's yacht who, when the yacht sinks, winds up on a Pacific island with a bunch of wealthy passengers and is the only one resourceful enough to take charge and help them survive.
Carole Lombard, George Burns, Gracie Allen, Ethel Merman, Leon Errol, Raymond (Ray) Milland, Jay Henry, John Irwin, Charles Morris, Ben Hendricks, Ted Oliver.

She Loves Me Not (1934, Para.). *d:* Elliot Nugent; *p:* Benjamin Glazer; *sc:* Benjamin Glazer—*b/o* the play by Howard Lindsay, from the novel by Edward Hope.
PAUL LAWTON: One of a pair of Princeton University students who hide a pretty showgirl murder witness in their room after helping her disguise herself as a man.
Miriam Hopkins, Edward Nugent, Kitty Carlisle, Henry Stephenson, Lynne Overman, Warren Hymer, Judith Allen, George Barbier, Henry Kolker, Ralf Harolde, Matt McHugh.

Here Is My Heart (1934, Para.). *d:* Frank Tuttle; *p:* Louis D. Lighton; *sc:* Edwin Justus Mayer and Harlan Thompson—*b/o* Alfred Savoir's play *The Grand Duchess and the Waiter.*
J. PAUL JONES: Famous wealthy American crooner who, while visiting Monte Carlo, disguises himself as a waiter so he can be near a haughty princess he hopes to woo and win.

Kitty Carlisle, Roland Young, Alison Skipworth, Reginald Owen, Cecelia Parker, William Frawley, Marian Mansfield, Akim Tamiroff, Charles Arnt, Arthur Housman, Charles Wilson.

Mississippi (1935, Para.). *d:* Edward A. Sutherland; *p:* Arthur Hornblow Jr.; *sc:* Jack Cunningham and Francis Martin (adaptation by Herbert Fields and Claude Binyon)—*b/o* the play *Magnolia* by Booth Tarkington.

TOM GRAYSON: Peace-loving young Yankee in the Old South who accidentally acquires a phony reputation as a duelist, then—when he gets a job as a singer on a showboat—is exploited by the captain as "The Singing Killer."

W. C. Fields, Joan Bennett, Gail Patrick, Queenie Smith, Claude Gillingwater, John Miljan, Ed Pawley, Fred Kohler, John Larkin, Paul Hurst, King Baggott.

Two for Tonight (1935, Para.). *d:* Frank Tuttle; *sc:* George Marion Jr. and Jane Storm (with additional dialogue by Harry Ruskin)—*b/o* a play by Max Lief and J. O. Lief.

GILBERT GORDON: Talented young tunesmith who has to make good his mother's boast that he can write the book for a musical play in seven days.

Joan Bennett, Lynne Overman, Mary Boland, Thelma Todd, James Blakeley, Douglas Fowley, Ernest Cossart, Charles Lane, Charles Arnt.

Anything Goes (1936, Para.). *d:* Lewis Milestone; *p:* Benjamin Glazer; *sc: b/o* the play by P. G. Wodehouse and Guy Bolton, revised by Howard Lindsay and Russel Crouse.

BILLY CROCKER: Amiable young Wall Street businessman who accidentally winds up aboard an ocean liner and is smitten with one of the passengers—a runaway heiress being returned to England by a private detective.

Ethel Merman, Charles Ruggles, Ida Lupino, Arthur Treacher, Grace Bradley, Robert McWade, Margaret Dumont, Richard Carle, Matt Moore, Ed Gargan.

Rhythm on the Range (1936, Para.). *d:* Norman Taurog; *p:* Benjamin Glazer; *sc:* Walter DeLeon, Sidney Salkow, John C. Moffitt, and Francis Martin—*b/o* a story by Mervin J. Houser.

JEFF LARRABEE: Singing cowpoke and owner of a California dude ranch who meets up with a rich girl who has run away from New York to avoid marrying a man she doesn't love.

Frances Farmer, Bob Burns, Martha Raye, Samuel S. Hinds, Warren Hymer, Lucille Gleason, George E. Stone, James Burke, Clem Bevans, Leonid Kinskey, Emmett Vogan.

Pennies From Heaven (1936, Col.). *d:* Norman Z. McLeod; *p:* Emmanuel Cohen; *sc:* Jo Swerling—*b/o* *The Peacock's Feather* by Katherine Leslie Moore.

LARRY: Wandering minstrel who "adopts" a homeless young girl and her grandfather and, with their help, turns an old country mansion into a successful roadside restaurant.

Madge Evans, Edith Fellows, Donald Meek, Louis Armstrong, John Gallaudet, Tom Dugan, Nana Bryant, Charles Wilson, William Stack, Tom Ricketts.

Waikiki Wedding (1937, Para.). *d:* Frank Tuttle; *p:* Arthur Hornblow Jr.; *sc:* Frank Butler, Don Hartman, Walter DeLeon, and Francis Martin—*b/o* a story by Frank Butler and Don Hartman.

TONY MARVIN: Resourceful press agent for a pretty young girl who has been named the "Pineapple Queen" in a publicity scheme for a pineapple company on Hawaii.

Bob Burns, Shirley Ross, Martha Raye, George Barbier, Grady Sutton, Leif Erickson, Granville Bates, Anthony Quinn, Prince Leilani, Spencer Charters.

Double or Nothing (1937, Para.). *d:* Theodore Reed; *p:* Benjamin Glazer; *sc:* Charles Lederer, Erwin Gelsey, Duke Atterberry, and John C. Moffitt—*b/o* a story by M. Coates Webster.

LEFTY BOYLAN: An indigent singer—one of four down-and-out people who are each given a chance, through the will of an eccentric philanthropist, to inherit $1 million.

Martha Raye, Andy Devine, Mary Carlisle, William Frawley, Benny Baker, Samuel S. Hinds, William Henry, Fay Holden, Walter Kingsford, Gilbert Emery, John Gallaudet.

Doctor Rhythm (1938, Para.). *d:* Frank Tuttle; *p:* Emmanuel Cohen; *sc:* Jo Swerling and Richard Connell—*b/o* O. Henry's story "The Badge of Policeman O'Roon."

DR. BILL REMSEN: Affable medical doctor who fills in for a policeman pal as the bodyguard of a pretty young blonde, and then falls for her.

Beatrice Lillie, Mary Carlisle, Andy Devine, Rufe Davis, Laura Hope Crews, Fred Keating, Sterling Holloway, Franklin Pangborn, Emory Parnell, Louis Armstrong.

Sing You Sinners (1938, Para.). *d:* Wesley Ruggles; *p:* Wesley Ruggles; *sc:* Claude Binyon.

JOE BEEBE: Shiftless, happy-go-lucky thirty-five-year-old who, to the dismay of his mother and two brothers, can't seem to keep an honest job—but finally strikes it rich when he becomes the owner of a winning racehorse called Uncle Gus.

Fred MacMurray, Donald O'Connor, Elizabeth Patterson, Ellen Drew, John Gallaudet, Irving Bacon, William Haade, Tom Dugan.

Paris Honeymoon (1939, Para.). *d:* Frank Tuttle; *p:* Harlan Thompson; *sc:* Frank Butler and Don Hartman—*b/o* a story by Angela Sherwood.

LUCKY LAWTON: Amiable Texas tycoon who goes to France to marry a countess but instead falls for a beautiful peasant girl.

Franciska Gaal, Shirley Ross, Akim Tamiroff, Edward Everett Horton, Ben Blue, Gregory Gaye, Raymond Hatton, Victor Kilian.

East Side of Heaven (1939, Univ.). *d:* David Butler; *sc:* William Conselman—*b/o* a story by David Butler and Herbert Polesie.

DENNY MARTIN: Singing taxi driver who becomes the temporary guardian of a ten-month-old baby left with him by the mother when she kidnaps the infant from the father during a custody battle.

Joan Blondell, Irene Hervey, Mischa Auer, C. Aubrey Smith, Jerome Cowan, Baby Sandy, Robert Kent, Arthur Hoyt, Russell Hicks, J. Farrell MacDonald.

The Star Maker (1939, Para.). *d:* Roy Del Ruth; *p:* Charles R. Rogers; *sc:* Frank Butler, Don Hartman, and Art Caesar—*b/o* a story by Art Caesar and William Pierce—suggested by the career of Gus Edwards, pioneer showman.

LARRY EARL: Singer-songwriter who has little success until he forms a song-and-dance group made up of youngsters and turns them into a highly successful vaudeville act.

Linda Ware, Louise Campbell, Ned Sparks, Laura Hope Crews, Walter Damrosch, Janet Waldo, Thurston Hall, Billy Gilbert.

Road to Singapore (1940, Para.). *d:* Victor Schertzinger; *p:* Harlan Thompson; *sc:* Don Hartman and Frank Butler—*b/o* a story by Harry Hervey.

JOSH MALLON: Footloose son of a shipping magnate who, after he and his sidekick escape to a South Seas island to get away from work and women, immediately flips over a pretty girl in a sarong.

Dorothy Lamour, Bob Hope, Charles Coburn, Judith Barrett, Anthony Quinn, Jerry Colonna, Johnny Arthur, Pierre Watkin, Gaylord Pendleton, Miles Mander, John Kelly, Ed Gargan, Kitty Kelly.

If I Had My Way (1940, Univ.). *d:* David Butler; *p:* David Butler; *sc:* William Conselman and James V. Kern.

BUZZ BLACKWELL: Amiable steelworker who, when one of his co-workers is killed in an accident, accompanies the man's young orphaned daughter to New York to track down her great-uncle, an old ex–vaudeville performer.

Gloria Jean, Charles Winninger, El Brendel, Allyn Joslyn, Donald Woods, Claire Dodd, Moroni Olsen, Kathryn Adams, Nana Bryant.

Rhythm on the River (1940, Para.). *d:* Victor Schertzinger; *p:* William Le Baron; *sc:* Dwight

Taylor—*b/o* a story by Billy Wilder and Jacques Thery.

BOB SOMMERS: Young songwriter who, with his girlfriend, ghost writes songs for a once-famous egotistical composer who has lost his creative touch.

Mary Martin, Basil Rathbone, Oscar Levant, Oscar Shaw, Charlie Grapewin, William Frawley, Jean Cagney, Charles Lane, John Scott Trotter, Wingy Mannone, Pierre Watkin, Billy Benedict.

Road to Zanzibar (1941, Para.). *d:* Victor Schertzinger; *p:* Paul Jones; *sc:* Frank Butler and Don Hartman—*b/o* a story by Don Hartman and Sy Bartlett.

CHUCK REARDON: One of a duo of smooth-talking carnival hustlers who sell a phony diamond mine, then take it on the lam to Zanzibar, where two stranded American women talk them into taking them on an African Safari.

Bob Hope, Dorothy Lamour, Una Merkel, Eric Blore, Luis Alberni, Joan Marsh, Ethel Greer, Iris Adrian, Georges Renavent, Douglass Dumbrille, Lionel Royce, Leo Gorcey, Robert Middlemass, Norma Varden, Paul Porcasi.

Birth of the Blues (1941, Para.). *d:* Victor Schertzinger; *p:* B. G. De Sylva; *sc:* Harry Tugend and Walter De Leon—*b/o* a story by Harry Tugend.

JEFF LAMBERT: New Orleans clarinet player who discovers a talented trumpet player in jail and bails him out, then builds a Dixieland jazz band around him that becomes the hottest group on Bourbon Street.

Mary Martin, Brian Donlevy, Carolyn Lee, Eddie "Rochester" Anderson, Jack Teagarden, J. Carrol Naish, Cecil Kellaway, Warren Hymer, Horace MacMahon, Barbara Pepper, Harry Barris, Minor Watson.

Holiday Inn (1942, Para.). *d:* Mark Sandrich; *p:* Mark Sandrich; *sc:* Claude Binyon (adaptation by Elmer Rice)—*b/o* an original idea by Irving Berlin.

JIM HARDY: Nightclub singer who gets tired of working so hard, buys a Connecticut farmhouse, and converts it into a unique nightclub that's open only on holidays.

Fred Astaire, Marjorie Reynolds, Virginia Dale, Walter Abel, Louise Beavers, John Gallaudet, James Bell, Irving Bacon, Leon Belasco, Harry Barris.

Road to Morocco (1942, Para.). *d:* David Butler; *p:* Paul Jones; *sc:* Frank Butler and Don Hartman.

JEFF PETERS: One of two shipwrecked buddies who wind up in Morocco, where they encounter Arabian palaces, a captive princess, and talking camels.

Bob Hope, Dorothy Lamour, Anthony Quinn, Dona Drake, Mikhail Rasumny, Vladimir Sokoloff, George Givot, Andrew Tombes, Leon Belasco, Monte Blue, Louise La Planche, Yvonne De Carlo, Poppy Wilde, Dan Seymour, Richard Loo.

Dixie (1943, Para.). *d:* A. Edward Sutherland; *p:* Paul Jones; *sc:* Darrell Ware and Karl Tunberg (adaptation by Claude Binyon)—*b/o* a story by William Rankin.

DAN EMMETT: Struggling American songwriter in the Old South who, after leaving his Kentucky home to seek fame and fortune in New Orleans, finds success when he forms a minstrel troupe and his song "Dixie" becomes a hit.

Dorothy Lamour, Marjorie Reynolds, Billy De Wolfe, Lynne Overman, Eddie Foy Jr., Raymond Walburn, Grant Mitchell, Clara Blandick, Olin Howlin, Stanley Andrews, Norma Varden, James Burke, Harry Barris.

Going My Way (1944, Para.). *d:* Leo McCarey; *p:* Leo McCarey; *sc:* Frank Butler and Frank Cavett—*b/o* a story by Leo McCarey.

FATHER CHUCK O'MALLEY*: Down-to-earth young priest who, when he's assigned to a financially troubled parish to aid the aging priest who has been in charge for forty-five years, incurs the older man's resentment.

Rise Stevens, Barry Fitzgerald, Frank McHugh, Gene Lockhart, William Frawley, James Brown, Porter Hall, Fortunio Bonanova, Stanley Clements, Carl Switzer, Jack Norton.

Here Come the Waves (1944, Para.). *d:* Mark Sandrich; *p:* Mark Sandrich; *sc:* Allan Scott, Ken Englund, and Zion Myers.

JOHNNY CABOT: Famous singing idol who joins the U.S. Navy and, with a shipmate, gets mixed up with a couple of WAVES who are identical twins.

Betty Hutton, Sonny Tufts, Ann Doran, Gwen Crawford, Noel Neill, Mae Clark, Harry Barris, Oscar O'Shea, Mona Freeman, James Flavin, Yvonne De Carlo.

The Bells of St. Mary's (1945, RKO). *d:* Leo McCarey; *p:* Leo McCarey (Rainbow); *sc:* Dudley Nichols—*b/o* a story by Leo McCarey.

FATHER CHUCK O'MALLEY†: Affable priest who is sent to a financially troubled cathedral and parochial school to take charge and—with the help of the Mother Superior—to talk a wealthy tightwad into donating money for a new building.

Ingrid Bergman, Henry Travers, Ruth Donnelly, Joan Carroll, Martha Sleeper, William Gargan,

Rhys Williams, Una O'Connor, Matt McHugh, Dewey Robinson.

Road to Utopia (1945, Para.). *d:* Hal Walker; *p:* Paul Jones; *sc:* Norman Panama and Melvin Frank.

DUKE JOHNSON: One of a pair of shady song-and-dance men who steal the deed to a gold mine from two killers as they head for the Klondike to strike it rich.

Bob Hope, Dorothy Lamour, Douglas Dumbrille, Hillary Brooke, Jack La Rue, Robert Barrat, Nestor Paiva, Robert Benchley, Will Wright, Billy Benedict, Arthur Loft, Jim Thorpe.

Blue Skies (1946, Para.). *d:* Stuart Heisler; *p:* Sol C. Siegel; *sc:* Arthur Sheekman (adaptation by Allan Scott)—*b/o* an original idea by Irving Berlin.

JOHNNY ADAMS: Happy-go-lucky nightclub owner-singer who competes with his hoofer pal for the affections of a beautiful chorus girl but, after he wins her hand, encounters marital problems.

Fred Astaire, Joan Caulfield, Billy De Wolfe, Olga San Juan, Frank Faylen, Karolyn Grimes, Jack Norton, Joan Woodbury, John Gallaudet, Cliff Nazarro.

Welcome Stranger (1947, Para.). *d:* Elliot Nugent; *p:* Sol C. Siegel; *sc:* Arthur Sheekman—*b/o* a story by Frank Butler.

DR. JAMES PEARSON: Genial young doctor who, when he fills in for a vacationing older doctor in a small town, arouses the conservative elder man's resentment.

Joan Caulfield, Barry Fitzgerald, Wanda Hendrix, Frank Faylen, Elizabeth Patterson, Robert Shayne, Percy Kilbride, Charles Dingle, Don Beddoe, Thurston Hall, Milton Kibbee, Clarence Muse, Charles Middleton, Erville Alderson.

Road to Rio (1947, Para.). *d:* Norman Z. McLeod; *p:* Daniel Dare; *sc:* Edmund Beloin and Jack Rose.

SCAT SWEENEY: One of a duo of itinerant musicians who accidentally burn down a carnival, stow away on a boat to Rio de Janeiro, and save a beautiful señorita and her inheritance from her sinister aunt.

Bob Hope, Dorothy Lamour, Gale Sondergaard, Frank Faylen, Joseph Vitale, Frank Puglia, Nestor Paiva, Robert Barrat, Jerry Colonna, The Wiere Brothers, The Andrews Sisters, Charles Middleton, Ray Teal.

The Emperor Waltz (1948, Para.). *d:* Billy Wilder; *p:* Charles Brackett; *sc:* Charles Brackett and Billy Wilder.

VIRGIL SMITH: Smooth-talking American phonograph salesman in 1901 Austria who, while trying to sell a phono to the Emperor Franz Joseph, finds time to woo the emperor's niece.

---

*Won the Academy Award as Best Actor for this role.
†Received an Academy Award nomination as Best Actor for this role.

Joan Fontaine, Roland Culver, Richard Haydn, Lucile Watson, Sig Rumann, Harold Vermilyea, Julia Dean, Doris Dowling.

A Connecticut Yankee in King Arthur's Court (1949, Para.). *d:* Tay Garnett; *p:* Robert Fellows; *sc:* Edmund Beloin—*b/o* the novel by Mark Twain.

HANK MARTIN (alias SIR BOSS): New England blacksmith who is accidentally knocked unconscious and wakes up to find himself transported back to the time of King Arthur and the Knights of the Roundtable in Camelot.

Rhonda Fleming, William Bendix, Sir Cedric Hardwicke, Henry Wilcoxon, Murvyn Vye, Joseph Vitale, Richard Webb, Alan Napier, Virginia Field, Julia Faye.

Top o' the Morning (1949, Para.). *d:* David Miller; *p:* Robert L. Welch; *sc:* Edmund Beloin and Richard Breen.

JOE MULQUEEN: Easygoing American insurance investigator who journeys to the Emerald Isle to track down a thief who has stolen the Blarney Stone.

Ann Blyth, Barry Fitzgerald, Hume Cronyn, Eileen Crowe, Tudor Owen, Jimmy Hunt, John McIntire, John Eldredge, John Costello, Dick Ryan, Mary Field.

Riding High (1950, Para.). *d:* Frank Capra; *p:* Frank Capra; *sc:* Robert Riskin (with additional dialogue by Melville Shavelson and Jack Rose)—*b/o* a story by Mark Hellinger.

DAN BROOKS: Racehorse owner whose beloved horse, "Broadway Bill," finally wins a big race but dies when his heart bursts as he crosses the wire.

Colleen Gray, Charles Bickford, William Demarest, Frances Gifford, James Gleason, Raymond Walburn, Ward Bond, Clarence Muse, Percy Kilbride, Margaret Hamilton, Harry Davenport, Douglas Dumbrille, Gene Lockhart, Marjorie Lord, Frankie Darro, Irving Bacon, Charles Lane, Joe Frisco.

Mr. Music (1950, Para.). *d:* Richard Haydn; *p:* Robert L. Welch; *sc:* Arthur Sheekman—*b/o* the play by Samson Raphaelson.

PAUL MERRICK: Broadway songwriter who, because he'd rather be out playing golf or betting on the horses, has to be prodded by a college girl hired to keep him at the piano.

Nancy Olson, Charles Coburn, Robert Stack, Tom Ewell, Ruth Hussey, Ida Moore, Donald Woods, Claude Curdle, Gower Champion, Marge Champion, Groucho Marx, Peggy Lee, Dorothy Kirsten, The Merry Macs.

Here Comes the Groom (1951, Para.). *d:* Frank Capra; *p:* Frank Capra; *sc:* Virginia Van Upp, Liam O'Brien, and Myles Connolly—*b/o* a story by Robert Riskin and Liam O'Brien.

PETE GARVEY: Happy-go-lucky reporter who, when he needs a wife in order to keep two French war orphans, pursues a pretty girl already engaged to a rich but stuffy real estate man.

Jane Wyman, Alexis Smith, Franchot Tone, James Barton, Robert Keith, Connie Gilchrist, Walter Catlett, Alan Reed, Minna Gombell, Howard Freeman, H. B. Warner, Ian Wolfe, Ellen Corby, James Burke, Irving Bacon.

Just for You (1952, Para.). *d:* Elliot Nugent; *p:* Pat Duggan; *sc:* Robert Carson—*b/o* the novel *Famous* by Stephen Vincent Benet.

JORDAN BLAKE: Big-time Broadway producer who neglects his son and daughter for years while concentrating on his career, then—when he decides to devote more time to them and win their affection—has trouble communicating with them.

Jane Wyman, Ethel Barrymore, Robert Arthur, Natalie Wood, Cora Witherspoon, Regis Toomey, Ben Lessy, Art Smith, Willis Bouchey, Herbert Vigran.

Road to Bali (1952, Para.). *d:* Hal Walker; *p:* Harry Tugend; *sc:* Frank Butler, Hal Kanter, and William Morrow—*b/o* a story by Frank Butler and Harry Tugend.

GEORGE COCHRAN: One of two song-and-dance vaudevillians who wind up on the tropical island of Bali, where they meet a beautiful princess in a sarong, cannibals, wild animals, and a huge squid.

Bob Hope, Dorothy Lamour, Murvyn Vye, Peter Coe, Ralph Moody, Leon Askin, Michael Ansara, Carolyn Jones, Bob Crosby.

Little Boy Lost (1953, Para.). *d:* George Seaton; *p:* William Perlberg; *sc:* George Seaton—*b/o* the story by Marghanita Laski.

BILL WAINWRIGHT: American war correspondent who returns to France after WWII to find his young son who was born there during the war but whom he has never seen.

Claude Dauphin, Christian Fourcade, Gabrielle Dorziat, Nicole Maurey, Colette Dereal, Georgette Anys, Peter Baldwin.

White Christmas (1954, Para.). *d:* Michael Curtiz; *p:* Robert Emmett Dolan; *sc:* Norman Panama, Melvin Frank, and Norman Krasna.

BOB WALLACE: One of a pair of song-and-dance men who put on a big benefit show to save a financially troubled New England mountain resort that's owned by an old friend—their commanding officer during WWII.

Danny Kaye, Rosemary Clooney, Vera-Ellen, Dean Jagger, John Brascia, Mary Wickes, Grady Sutton, Sig Rumann, Percy Helton, Gavin Gordon.

The Country Girl (1954, Para.). *d:* George Seaton; *p:* William Perlberg and George Seaton; *sc:* George Seaton—*b/o* the play by Clifford Odets.

FRANK ELGIN*: Washed-up, self-pitying, alcoholic stage star who gives the false impression that his wife is at the root of his problems as he struggles to make a comeback through the persistent efforts of a brash young Broadway director.

Grace Kelly, William Holden, Anthony Ross, Gene Reynolds, Robert Kent, Ida Moore, Hal K. Dawson, Charles Tannen, Jon Provost.

Anything Goes (1956, Para.). *d:* Robert Lewis; *p:* Robert Emmett Dolan; *sc:* Sidney Sheldon—*b/o* the play by P. G. Wodehouse and Guy Bolton, revised by Russel Crouse and Howard Lindsay.

BILL BENSON: One of a pair of musical-comedy stars who, as they travel around the world in search of a leading lady for their new show, start feuding over which girl it will be.

Donald O'Connor, Mitzi Gaynor, Jeanmaire, Phil Harris, Kurt Kasznar, Walter Sande, Richard Erdman, Argentina Brunetti, Archer MacDonald, James Griffith.

High Society (1956, MGM). *d:* Charles Walters; *p:* Sol C. Siegel; *sc:* John Patrick—*b/o* Philip Barry's play *The Philadelphia Story*.

C. K. DEXTER-HAVEN: Wealthy ex-husband of a young society girl who sets out to stop her from marrying a pompous blueblood and win her back for himself.

Grace Kelly, Frank Sinatra, Celeste Holm, John Lund, Louis Calhern, Sidney Blackmer, Louis Armstrong, Margalo Gillmore, Lydia Reed, Gordon Richards, Richard Garrick, Hugh Boswell.

Man on Fire (1957, MGM). *d:* Ranald MacDougall; *p:* Sol C. Siegel; *sc:* Ranald MacDougall—*b/o* a story by Jack Jacobs and Malvin Wald.

EARL CARLETON: Middle-aged businessman who, when his wife divorces him to marry another man, refuses to let the wife see their young son and becomes embroiled in a bitter custody battle.

Inger Stevens, E. G. Marshall, Mary Fickett, Malcolm Brodrick, Richard Eastham, Anne Seymour, Dan Riss.

Say One for Me (1959, 20th-Fox). *d:* Frank Tashlin; *p:* Frank Tashlin (Bing Crosby); *sc:* Robert O'Brien.

FATHER CONROY: Down-to-earth priest in New York's show-business quarter who helps solve the romantic problems of a nightclub manager and a pretty student–turned–chorus girl.

Debbie Reynolds, Robert Wagner, Ray Walston, Les Tremayne, Frank McHugh, Joe Besser, Stella Stevens, Connie Gilchrist, Sebastian Cabot, Murray Alper, Richard Collier.

High Time (1960, 20th-Fox). *d:* Blake Edwards; *p:* Charles Brackett (Bing Crosby); *sc:* Tom Waldman and Frank Waldman—*b/o* a story by Garson Kanin.

HARVEY HOWARD: Well-to-do middle-aged widower who, despite his two grown children's opposition, enrolls in college to earn the degree he always wanted but never had a chance to get.

Fabian, Tuesday Weld, Nicole Maurey, Richard Beymer, Yvonne Craig, Jimmy Boyd, Kenneth MacKenna, Gavin MacLeod, Nina Shipman, Angus Duncan, Dick Crockett.

The Road to Hong Kong (1962, UA). *d:* Norman Panama; *p:* Melvin Frank (Melnor); *sc:* Norman Panama and Melvin Frank.

HARRY TURNER: One of two fast-talking vaudevillians—on the run in Hong Kong—who get involved with beautiful women, spies, and space ships.

Bob Hope, Joan Collins, Dorothy Lamour, Robert Morley, Walter Gotell, Roger Delgado, Felix Aylmer, Peter Madden. (Special guest stars: Frank Sinatra, Dean Martin, David Niven, Peter Sellers, Jerry Colonna.)

Robin and the 7 Hoods (1964, WB). *d:* Gordon Douglas; *p:* Frank Sinatra and Howard W. Koch (P–C Prod.); *sc:* David R. Schwartz.

ALLEN A. DALE: Mild-mannered orphanage worker who, when a gang of Chicago mobsters gives the orphanage $50,000, publicizes the head mobster as a sort of "Robin Hood" character.

Frank Sinatra, Dean Martin, Sammy Davis Jr., Peter Falk, Barbara Rush, Victor Buono, Hank Henry, Allen Jenkins, Jack La Rue, Phil Crosby, Phil Arnold, Hans Conried, Sig Rumann, Edward G. Robinson.

Stagecoach (1966, 20th-Fox). *d:* Gordon Douglas; *p:* Martin Rackin (Martin Rackin); *sc:* Joseph Landon—*b/o* the original screenplay by Dudley Nichols—from the short story "Stage to Lordsburg" by Ernest Haycox.

DOC BOONE: Alcoholic doctor—one of several colorful passengers making a dangerous stagecoach journey in the Old West through hostile Indian territory—who sobers up long enough to deliver an Army wife's baby.

Ann-Margret, Red Buttons, Alex Cord, Michael Connors, Bob Cummings, Van Heflin, Slim Pickens, Stefanie Powers, Keenan Wynn, Joseph Hoover.

Dr. Cook's Garden (1971, Para. [Made for TV]). *d:* Ted Post; *p:* Bob Markell; *sc:* Arthur Wallace—*b/o* a play by Ira Levin.

DR. COOK: Kindly, mild-mannered physician who is secretly killing off the sick and elderly of a small Vermont village in order to keep the town as "perfect" and as disease-free as possible.

---

*Received an Academy Award nomination as Best Actor for this role.

Frank Converse, Blythe Danner, Bethel Leslie, Abby Lewis, Barney Hughes.

• In addition, Bing Crosby made cameo/guest appearances in the following feature films: *King of Jazz* (1930, Univ.), *Reaching for the Moon* (1930, UA), *Confessions of a Co-ed* (1931, Para.), *The Big Broadcast of 1936* (1936, Para.), *My Favorite Blonde* (1942, Para.), *Star-Spangled Rhythm* (1942, Para.), *The Princess and the Pirate* (1944, Samuel Goldwyn), *Duffy's Tavern* (1945, Para.), *Out of This World* (1945, Para.—Bing's singing "voice-over" used for Eddie Bracken's character), *Variety Girl* (1947, Para.), *My Favorite Brunette* (1947, Para.), *The Greatest Show on Earth* (1952, Para.), *Son of Paleface* (1952, Para.), *Scared Stiff* (1953, Para.), *Alias Jesse James* (1959, UA), *Let's Make Love* (1960, 20th-Fox), *Pepe* (1960, Col.), *Cancel My Reservation* (1972, WB), and *That's Entertainment* (1974, MGM-UA—on-screen co-narrator).

☆ BETTE DAVIS

Ruth Elizabeth Davis

b: April 5, 1908, Lowell, Mass.

"What a dump!"

> Rosa Moline (Bette Davis) talking about her small-town Wisconsin home in *Beyond the Forest,* 1949.

Bad Sister (1931, Univ.). *d:* Hobart Henley; *p:* Carl Laemmle Jr.; *sc:* Raymond L. Schrock, Tom Reed, and Edwin H. Knopf—*b/o* the story "The Flirt" by Booth Tarkington.
LAURA MADISON: Small-town Indiana girl who is secretly in love with a young doctor, but he's in love with the girl's selfish, spoiled sister.
Conrad Nagel, Sidney Fox, ZaSu Pitts, Slim Summerville, Charles Winninger, Emma Dunn, Humphrey Bogart, Bert Roach, David Durand.

Seed (1931, Univ.). *d:* John M. Stahl; *p:* John M. Stahl; *sc:* Gladys Lehman—*b/o* the novel by Charles G. Norris.
MARGARET CARTER: Daughter whose publishing-house-clerk father becomes a successful novelist and divorces his wife to marry an ambitious woman who is a publishing executive.
John Boles, Genevieve Tobin, Lois Wilson, Raymond Hackett, Francis Dade, ZaSu Pitts, Richard Tucker, Dick Winslow, Helen Parrish, Dickie Moore.

Waterloo Bridge (1931, Univ.). *d:* James Whale; *p:* Carl Laemmle Jr.; *sc:* Benn W. Levy (with continuity and additional dialogue by Tom Reed)— *b/o* the play by Robert E. Sherwood.
JANET WETHERBY: Sister whose WWI Canadian soldier brother falls in love with an unemployed London chorus girl who, unbeknownst to the soldier, has been forced to become a prostitute.
Mae Clarke, Kent Douglass (Douglass Montgomery), Doris Lloyd, Ethel Griffies, Enid Bennett, Frederick Kerr, Rita Carlisle.

Way Back Home (1932, RKO). *d:* William A. Seiter; *p:* Pandro S. Berman; *sc:* Jane Murfin—*b/o* radio characters created by Phillips Lord.
MARY LUCY: Small-town girl in Maine who, along with a kindly preacher, helps save a runaway boy from his cruel, drunken father.
Phillips Lord, Effie Palmer, Mrs. Phillips Lord, Frank Albertson, Oscar Apfel, Stanley Fields, Dorothy Peterson, Frankie Darro.

The Menace (1932, Col.). *d:* Roy William Neil; *p:* Sam Nelson; *sc:* Dorothy Howell and Charles Logue (with dialogue by Roy Chanslor)—*b/o* Edgar Wallace's novel *The Feathered Serpent.*
PEGGY: Young English girl whose fiancé is framed by his stepmother for the murder of his father.
H. B. Warner, Walter Byron, Natalie Moorhead, William B. Davidson, Crauford Kent, Halliwell Hobbes, Charles Gerrard, Murray Kinnell.

Hell's House (1932, Capital Films Exchange). *d:* Howard Higgins; *p:* Benjamin F. Zeidman; *sc:* Paul Gangelin and B. Harrison Orkow—*b/o* a story by Howard Higgins.
PEGGY GARDNER: Young girl who becomes friendly with a bootlegger so he'll help free her boyfriend who—because of the bootlegger—has been unjustly sent to reform school.
Junior Durkin, Pat O'Brien, Junior Coughlan, Charley Grapewin, Emma Dunn, James Marcus, Morgan Wallace, Wallis Clark, Hooper Atchley.

The Man Who Played God (1932, WB). *d:* John Adolphi; *p:* Jack L. Warner; *sc:* Julian Josephson and Maude Howell—*b/o* a short story by Gouverneur Morris and the play *The Silent Voice* by Jules Eckert Goodman.
GRACE BLAIR: Young woman who, when her famous music-maestro fiancé goes deaf, is willing to sacrifice her happiness and stick by him, even though she has fallen in love with a younger man.
George Arliss, Violet Heming, Ivan Simpson, Louise

Closser Hale, Donald Cook, Paul Porcasi, Raymond Milland, Oscar Apfel, Hedda Hopper, Wade Boteler.

So Big (1932, WB). *d:* William A. Wellman; *p:* Jack L. Warner; *sc:* J. Grubb Alexander and Robert Lord—*b/o* the novel by Edna Ferber.
DALLAS O'MARA: Young artist who's in love with the son of a hard-working, idealistic farm woman who approves of the artist but is disappointed in the way the son has turned out.
Barbara Stanwyck, George Brent, Dickie Moore, Guy Kibbee, Hardie Albright, Robert Warwick, Alan Hale, Dorothy Peterson, Dawn O'Day (Anne Shirley), Dick Winslow, Elizabeth Patterson.

The Rich Are Always with Us (1932, WB). *d:* Alfred E. Green; *p:* Samuel Bischoff; *sc:* Austin Parker—*b/o* the novel by E. Pettit.
MALBRO: Flashy flapper who has designs on a famous newspaper correspondent who's in love with a New York society divorcée.
Ruth Chatterton, George Brent, Adrienne Dore, John Miljan, John Wray, Robert Warwick, Berton Churchill.

The Dark Horse (1932, WB). *d:* Alfred E. Green; *p:* Samuel Bischoff; *sc:* Joseph Jackson and Wilson Mizner—*b/o* a story by Melville Grossman, Joseph Jackson, and Courtenay Terrett.
KAY RUSSELL: Young political worker who helps a glib campaign manager she loves get a nincompoop dark-horse candidate elected governor.
Warren William, Guy Kibbee, Frank McHugh, Vivienne Osborne, Sam Hardy, Robert Warwick, Harry Holman, Charles Sellon, Robert Emmett O'Connor, Berton Churchill.

Cabin in the Cotton (1932, WB). *d:* Michael Curtiz; *p:* Jack L. Warner and Hal B. Wallis; *sc:* Paul Green—*b/o* the novel by Harry Harrison Kroll.
MADGE NORWOOD: Seductive Southern belle who almost ruins a sharecropper's son when he becomes a bookkeeper for her father, a wealthy, crooked cotton planter.
Richard Barthelmess, Dorothy Jordan, Henry B. Walthall, Berton Churchill, Hardie Albright, Tully Marshall, Clarence Muse, Russell Simpson, Dorothy Peterson, Snowflake.

Three on a Match (1932, WB). *d:* Mervyn LeRoy; *p:* Samuel Bischoff; *sc:* Lucien Hubbard—*b/o* a story by Kubec Glasmon and John Bright.
RUTH WESTCOTT: Stenographer—one of three women who, when they renew their childhood friendship, find themselves involved with gangsters, blackmail, kidnapping, and suicide.
Joan Blondell, Warren William, Ann Dvorak, Lyle Talbot, Humphrey Bogart, Patricia Ellis, Grant Mitchell, Glenda Farrell, Frankie Darro, Clara Blandick, Dawn O'Day (Anne Shirley), Allen Jenkins, Edward Arnold.

20,000 Years in Sing Sing (1933, WB). *d:* Michael Curtiz; *p:* Robert Lord; *sc:* Courtney Terrett, Robert Lord, Wilson Mizner, and Brown Holmes—*b/o* the book by Warden Lewis E. Lawes.
FAY: Gangster's girlfriend who, after she shoots another mobster to save her boyfriend's life, gets charged with murder but is saved when the boyfriend takes the blame and goes to the chair at Sing Sing.
Spencer Tracy, Lyle Talbot, Arthur Byron, Grant Mitchell, Warren Hymer, Louis Calhern, Sheila Terry, Spencer Charters, Nella Walker, Harold Huber, Arthur Hoyt, Clarence Wilson.

Parachute Jumper (1933, WB). *d:* Alfred E. Green; *p:* Jack L. Warner; *sc:* John Francis Larkin—*b/o* the story "Some Call It Love" by Rian James.
ALABAMA: Young Southern girl in New York whose boyfriend, an ex–Marine flyer, is duped by a racketeer into flying narcotics from Canada into the U.S.
Douglas Fairbanks Jr., Leo Carrillo, Frank McHugh, Claire Dodd, Sheila Terry, Harold Huber, Thomas Jackson, Pat O'Malley, Walter Miller.

The Working Man (1933, WB). *d:* John Adolphi; *p:* Jack L. Warner; *sc:* Maude T. Howell and Charles Kenyon—*b/o* Edgar Franklin's story "The Adopted Father."
JENNY HARTLAND: Spoiled daughter of a deceased shoe-company owner who, along with her equally spoiled brother, is taken under the wing of her father's long-time business rival.
George Arliss, Hardie Albright, Theodore Newton, Gordon Westcott, J. Farrell MacDonald, Charles Evans, Frederick Burton, Edward Van Sloan, Douglas Dumbrille.

Ex-Lady (1933, WB). *d:* Robert Florey; *p:* Lucien Hubbard; *sc:* David Boehm—*b/o* a story by Edith Fitzgerald and Robert Riskin.
HELEN BAUER: Liberated commercial artist who decides to live with her ad-writer boyfriend but concludes that marrying him is a better alternative.
Gene Raymond, Frank McHugh, Monroe Owsley, Claire Dodd, Kay Strozzi, Ferdinand Gottschalk, Alphonse Ethier, Bodil Rosing.

Bureau of Missing Persons (1933, WB). *d:* Roy Del Ruth; *p:* Henry Blanke; *sc:* Robert Presnell—*b/o* the book *Missing Men* by John H. Ayers and Carol Bird.
NORMA PHILLIPS: Young woman who, when she asks the Bureau of Missing Persons to find

her missing husband, is suspected of murdering him.

Lewis Stone, Pat O'Brien, Glenda Farrell, Allen Jenkins, Ruth Donnelly, Hugh Herbert, Alan Dinehart, Marjorie Gateson, Adrian Morris, Henry Kolker, George Chandler.

Fashions of 1934 (1934, WB). *d:* William Dieterle; *p:* Henry Blanke; *sc:* F. Hugh Herbert, Gene Markey, Kathryn Scola, and Carl Erickson—*b/o* a story by Harry Collins and Warren Duff.

LYNN MASON: Fashion designer–model who goes to Paris with her boss, a fashion con man who pirates dress designs, to make a killing at the Parisian fashion shows.

William Powell, Frank McHugh, Verree Teasdale, Reginald Owen, Henry O'Neill, Philip Reed, Hugh Herbert, Etienne Girardot, Spencer Charters, Jane Darwell, Arthur Treacher, Hobart Cavanaugh, Albert Conti.

The Big Shakedown (1934, WB). *d:* John Francis Dillon; *p:* Samuel Bischoff; *sc:* Niven Busch and Rian James—*b/o* a story by Sam Engels.

NORMA FRANK: Wife whose husband, a druggist-chemist, is duped into joining forces with a mobster in a counterfeit patent medicine racket.

Charles Farrell, Ricardo Cortez, Glenda Farrell, Allen Jenkins, Henry O'Neill, Robert Emmett O'Connor, John Wray, Adrian Morris, Dewey Robinson, Samuel S. Hinds, William B. Davidson.

Jimmy the Gent (1934, WB). *d:* Michael Curtiz; *p:* Robert Lord; *sc:* Bertram Milhauser—*b/o* a story by Laird Doyle and Ray Nazarro.

JOAN MARTIN: On-the-level girl whose racketeer boyfriend tries to win her back—after she breaks up with him—by pretending to go straight and becoming a refined gentleman.

James Cagney, Alice White, Allen Jenkins, Arthur Hohl, Alan Dinehart, Philip Reed, Hobart Cavanaugh, Mayo Methot, Ralf Harolde, Joseph Sawyer, Joseph Crehan, Robert Warwick, Don Douglas, Bud Flanagan (Dennis O'Keefe).

Fog over Frisco (1934, WB). *d:* William Dieterle; *p:* Robert Lord; *sc:* Robert N. Lee and Eugene Solow—*b/o* a story by George Dyer.

ARLENE BRADFORD: Reckless society girl who makes the fatal mistake of getting tangled up with a ruthless racketeer–nightclub owner and his gang.

Donald Woods, Margaret Lindsay, Lyle Talbot, Arthur Byron, Hugh Herbert, Douglas Dumbrille, Robert Barrat, Henry O'Neill, Irving Pichel, Alan Hale, William B. Davidson, George Chandler, William Demarest.

Of Human Bondage (1934, RKO). *d:* John Cromwell; *p:* Pandro S. Berman; *sc:* Lester Cohen—*b/o* the novel by W. Somerset Maugham.

MILDRED ROGERS: Slatternly English waitress who gets involved with a sensitive, club-footed medical student who's obsessed with her despite her contemptuous treatment of him.

Leslie Howard, Frances Dee, Kay Johnson, Reginald Denny, Alan Hale, Reginald Owen, Reginald Sheffield, Desmond Roberts.

Housewife (1934, WB). *d:* Alfred E. Green; *sc:* Manuel Seff and Lillie Hayward—*b/o* a story by Robert Lord and Lillie Hayward.

PATRICIA BERKELEY: Predatory ad-agency copywriter who tries to break up the marriage of an ad man who is an old flame of hers.

George Brent, Ann Dvorak, John Halliday, Ruth Donnelly, Hobart Cavanaugh, Robert Barrat, Phil Regan, Willard Robertson, William B. Davidson.

Bordertown (1935, WB). *d:* Archie Mayo; *p:* Robert Lord; *sc:* Laird Doyle and Wallace Smith (adaptation by Robert Lord)—*b/o* a novel by Carroll Graham.

MARIE ROARK: Unstable wife of the owner of a bordertown café who—after she throws herself at the café's bouncer (a disbarred Mexican lawyer) and is rejected—murders her husband and tells police that the bouncer was her accomplice.

Paul Muni, Margaret Lindsay, Robert Barrat, Soledad Jiminez, Eugene Pallette, William B. Davidson, Hobart Cavanaugh, Henry O'Neill, Oscar Apfel, Samuel S. Hinds, Chris-Pin Martin, Frank Puglia, Jack Norton.

The Girl from Tenth Avenue (1935, WB). *d:* Alfred E. Green; *p:* Robert Lord; *sc:* Charles Kenyon—*b/o* a play by Hubert Henry Davies.

MIRIAM BRADY: Young woman who marries a socially prominent attorney—who's on a drunken spree after being jilted—then has to fight to keep him from going back to his old flame.

Ian Hunter, Colin Clive, Alison Skipworth, John Eldredge, Philip Reed, Katherine Alexander, Helen Jerome Eddy, Mary Treen.

Front Page Woman (1935, WB). *d:* Michael Curtiz; *p:* Samuel Bischoff; *sc:* Roy Chanslor, Lillie Hayward, and Laird Doyle—*b/o* the story "Women Are Bum Newspapermen" by Richard Macauley.

ELLEN GARFIELD: Newspaper reporter who—while covering a murder story—tries to scoop her boyfriend, an ace reporter who believes that women are bum "newspapermen."

George Brent, June Martel, Dorothy Dare, Joseph Crehan, Winifred Shaw, Roscoe Karns, Joseph King, J. Farrell MacDonald, J. Carroll Naish, Selmer Jackson.

Special Agent (1935, WB). *d:* William Keighley; *p:* Martin Mooney (Cosmopolitan); *sc:* Laird Doyle and Abem Finkel—*b/o* an idea by Martin Mooney.

JULIE GARDNER: Bookkeeper for a crime syndicate who, when she falls in love with an IRS agent, helps him get evidence that will convict her racketeer boss.

George Brent, Ricardo Cortez, Jack LaRue, Henry O'Neill, Robert Strange, Joseph Crehan, J. Carroll Naish, Joseph Sawyer, William B. Davidson, Robert Barrat, Paul Guilfoyle, Irving Pichel, James Flavin, Douglas Wood, Lee Phelps.

Dangerous (1935, WB). *d:* Alfred E. Green; *p:* Harry Joe Brown; *sc:* Laird Doyle.

JOYCE HEATH*: Famous stage star who has hit the skids and become a drunken has-been but, with the help of a young architect who loves her, makes a comeback.

Franchot Tone, Margaret Lindsay, Alison Skipworth, John Eldredge, Dick Foran, Richard Carle, Pierre Watkin, William B. Davidson, Frank O'Connor, Edward Keane.

The Petrified Forest (1936, WB). *d:* Archie Mayo; *p:* Henry Blanke; *sc:* Charles Kenyon and Delmer Daves—*b/o* the play by Robert E. Sherwood.

GABRIELLE (GABBY) MAPLE: Waitress at a roadside café in the Arizona desert who, when she becomes one of several people held hostage by a brutal killer, finds love with an idealistic writer who sacrifices his life for her.

Leslie Howard, Genevieve Tobin, Dick Foran, Humphrey Bogart, Joseph Sawyer, Porter Hall, Charley Grapewin, Paul Harvey, Eddie Acuff, Adrian Morris.

The Golden Arrow (1936, WB). *d:* Alfred E. Green; *p:* Samuel Bischoff; *sc:* Charles Kenyon—*b/o* a play by Michael Arlen.

DAISY APPLEBY: Cafeteria cashier who, when she's hired for publicity purposes by a cosmetics firm to pose as a screwball heiress to a cosmetics fortune, winds up marrying a reporter covering her story.

George Brent, Eugene Pallette, Dick Foran, Carol Hughes, Craig Reynolds, Ivan Lebedeff, Eddie Acuff, E. E. Clive, G. P. Huntley Jr., Hobart Cavanaugh, Henry O'Neill, Bess Flowers, Mary Treen, Selmer Jackson.

Satan Met a Lady (1936, WB). *d:* William Dieterle; *p:* Henry Blanke; *sc:* Brown Holmes—*b/o* Dashiell Hammett's novel *The Maltese Falcon.*

VALERIE PURVIS: Conniving blonde who hires a ruthless private eye named Ted Shayne to help her track down a valuable art treasure—a ram's horn encrusted with priceless gems.

Warren William, Alison Skipworth, Arthur Treacher, Winifred Shaw, Marie Wilson, Porter Hall, Maynard Holmes, Olin Howland, Charles

---

*Won the Academy Award as Best Actress for this role.

Wilson, Joseph King, Barbara Blane, William B. Davidson.

Marked Woman (1937, WB). *d:* Lloyd Bacon; *p:* Louis F. Edelman; *sc:* Robert Rossen and Abem Finkel (with additional dialogue by Seton I. Miller).

MARY DWIGHT: Jaded hostess in a clip-joint nightclub who, when her younger sister is murdered by racketeers, helps the D.A. convict their leader—her boss.

Humphrey Bogart, Eduardo Ciannelli, Jane Bryan, Lola Lane, Isabel Jewell, Mayo Methot, Ben Welden, Henry O'Neill, Allen Jenkins, John Litel, Raymond Hatton, William B. Davidson, Frank Faylen, Jack Norton, Kenneth Harlan.

Kid Galahad (1937, WB). *d:* Michael Curtiz; *p:* Samuel Bischoff; *sc:* Seton I. Miller—*b/o* the novel by Francis Wallace.

FLUFF PHILLIPS: Prizefight promoter's mistress who falls for a naïve young bellhop-turned-fighter while the promoter is grooming him for the championship.

Edward G. Robinson, Humphrey Bogart, Wayne Morris, Jane Bryan, Harry Carey, Ben Welden, Joseph Crehan, Veda Ann Borg, Frank Faylen, Joyce Compton, Horace MacMahon, John Shelton.

That Certain Woman (1937, WB). *d:* Edmund Goulding; *p:* Hal B. Wallis; *sc:* Edmund Goulding—*b/o* his original screenplay *The Trespasser.*

MARY DONNELL: Gangster's widow—having trouble making a new life for herself—who becomes a secretary for a married attorney who secretly loves her, but then elopes with an irresponsible playboy.

Henry Fonda, Ian Hunter, Anita Louise, Donald Crisp, Katherine Alexander, Minor Watson, Ben Welden, Sidney Toler, Charles Trowbridge, Herbert Rawlinson, Frank Faylen, Willard Parker.

It's Love I'm After (1937, WB). *d:* Archie Mayo; *p:* Hal B. Wallis; *sc:* Casey Robinson—*b/o* a story by Maurice Hanline.

JOYCE ARDEN: Leading lady of the stage who, when her long-time fiancé/co-star is pursued by an ardent female fan, devises a scheme to rescue him and then lead him to the altar.

Leslie Howard, Olivia de Havilland, Patric Knowles, Eric Blore, George Barbier, Spring Byington, Bonita Granville, E. E. Clive, Veda Ann Borg, Irving Bacon.

Jezebel (1938, WB). *d:* William Wyler; *p:* Hal B. Wallis and Henry Blanke; *sc:* Clement Ripley, Abem Finkel, and John Huston—*b/o* the play by Owen Davis Sr.

JULIE MARSTON*: Scandalous New Orleans belle in the 1850s who, after her banker fiancé leaves her when she goes too far in trying to make him jealous, atones by unselfishly nursing him and others who become victims of a yellow-fever plague.

George Brent, Henry Fonda, Donald Crisp, Fay Bainter, Margaret Lindsay, Henry O'Neill, John Litel, Gordon Oliver, Spring Byington, Richard Cromwell, Irving Pichel, Eddie Anderson.

The Sisters (1938, WB). d: Anatole Litvak; p: Hal B. Wallis; sc: Milton Krims—b/o the novel by Myron Brinig.

LOUISE ELLIOTT: Montana girl who elopes with a handsome but unreliable newspaper reporter, then is deserted by him in San Francisco but reconciles with him after they both survive the 1906 earthquake.

Errol Flynn, Anita Louise, Ian Hunter, Donald Crisp, Beulah Bondi, Jane Bryan, Alan Hale, Dick Foran, Henry Travers, Patric Knowles, Lee Patrick, Laura Hope Crews, Harry Davenport, Paul Harvey, Mayo Methot, Irving Bacon, Stanley Fields, Susan Hayward.

Dark Victory (1939, WB). d: Edmund Goulding; p: Hal B. Wallis and David Lewis; sc: Casey Robinson—b/o the play by George Emerson Brewer Jr. and Bertram Bloch.

JUDITH TRAHERNE†: Spoiled Long Island society girl who, after she has a temporarily successful brain-tumor operation but then learns the tumor will recur, marries her brain surgeon and finds happiness in the few months she has left to live.

George Brent, Humphrey Bogart, Geraldine Fitzgerald, Ronald Reagan, Henry Travers, Cora Witherspoon, Dorothy Peterson, Virginia Brissac, Herbert Rawlinson, Leonard Mudie, Lottie Williams.

Juarez (1939, WB). d: William Dieterle; p: Hal B. Wallis and Henry Blanke; sc: John Huston, Aeneas MacKenzie, and Wolfgang Reinhardt—b/o the play *Juarez and Maximilian* by Franz Werfel and the book *The Phantom Crown* by Bertita Harding.

CARLOTTA: Empress of Mexico in the 1860s who, after she goes to France and futilely pleads with Napoleon to help her besieged husband, Emperor Maximilian, loses her sanity when Maximilian is executed by Mexicans supporting democratic leader Benito Juarez.

Paul Muni, Brian Aherne, Claude Rains, John Garfield, Donald Crisp, Joseph Calleia, Gale Sondergaard, Gilbert Roland, Henry O'Neill, Harry Davenport, Louis Calhern, Walter Kingsford, Montagu Love, John Miljan, Vladimir Sokoloff, Irving Pichel.

The Old Maid (1939, WB). d: Edmund Goulding; p: Hal B. Wallis and Henry Blanke; sc: Casey Robinson—b/o the play by Zoe Atkins—from the novel by Edith Wharton.

CHARLOTTE LOVELL: Self-sacrificing nineteenth-century unwed mother who, in order to ensure her daughter's happiness, lets her scheming cousin bring up the unsuspecting daughter as her own.

Miriam Hopkins, George Brent, Donald Crisp, Jane Bryan, Louise Fazenda, James Stephenson, Jerome Cowan, William Lundigan, DeWolf (William) Hopper.

The Private Lives of Elizabeth and Essex (1939, WB). d: Michael Curtiz; p: Robert Lord; sc: Norman Reilly Raine and Aeneas MacKenzie—b/o the play *Elizabeth the Queen* by Maxwell Anderson.

QUEEN ELIZABETH: Sixteenth-century ruler of England who, even though she loves the politically ambitious Earl of Essex, sends him to the chopping block for treason.

Errol Flynn, Olivia de Havilland, Donald Crisp, Alan Hale, Vincent Price, Henry Stephenson, Henry Daniell, James Stephenson, Nanette Fabares (Nanette Fabray), Ralph Forbes, Robert Warwick, Leo G. Carroll, John Sutton.

All This and Heaven Too (1940, WB). d: Anatole Litvak; p: Hal B. Wallis and David Lewis; sc: Casey Robinson—b/o the novel by Rachel Lyman Field.

HENRIETTE DELUZY DESPORTES: Children's governess in nineteenth-century France whose employer, a handsome married nobleman, falls in love with her—leading to scandal, murder, and suicide.

Charles Boyer, Jeffrey Lynn, Barbara O'Neill, Virginia Weidler, Helen Westley, Walter Hampden, Henry Daniell, Harry Davenport, George Coulouris, Montagu Love, Janet Beecher, June Lockhart, Ann Todd, Ian Keith.

The Letter (1940, WB). d: William Wyler; p: Hal B. Wallis and Robert Lord; sc: Howard Koch—b/o the play by W. Somerset Maugham.

LESLIE CROSBIE*: Malayan rubber plantation manager's unfaithful wife, who murders her lover, then pleads self-defense but is done in by a love letter she wrote and the lover's vengeful widow.

Herbert Marshall, James Stephenson, Frieda Inescort, Gale Sondergaard, Bruce Lester (David

---

*Won the Academy Award as Best Actress for this role.
†Received an Academy Award nomination as Best Actress for this role.

---

*Received an Academy Award nomination as Best Actress for this role.

Bruce), Cecil Kellaway, Doris Lloyd, (Victor) Sen Yung, Willie Fung, Otto Hahn.

The Great Lie (1941, WB). *d:* Edmund Goulding; *p:* Hal B. Wallis and Henry Blanke; *sc:* Lenore Coffee—*b/o* the novel *January Heights* by Polan Banks.

MAGGIE PATTERSON: Woman who marries a playboy aviator after his first marriage is annulled, then—when he's reported lost in a plane crash—discovers that the first wife is going to have his baby and so arranges to raise the child as her own.

George Brent, Mary Astor, Lucile Watson, Hattie McDaniel, Grant Mitchell, Jerome Cowan, Thurston Hall, Russell Hicks, Virginia Brissac, Charles Trowbridge, Olin Howland, J. Farrell MacDonald, Doris Lloyd, Addison Richards.

The Bride Came C.O.D. (1941, WB). *d:* William Keighley; *p:* Hal B. Wallis and William Cagney; *sc:* Julius J. Epstein and Philip G. Epstein—*b/o* a story by Kenneth Earl and M. M. Musselman.

JOAN WINFIELD: Runaway heiress who tries to elope with a Hollywood bandleader but is foiled when her Texas-oil-tycoon father hires a down-to-earth charter air pilot to kidnap and deliver her to the family ranch.

James Cagney, Stuart Erwin, Jack Carson, George Tobias, Eugene Pallette, Harry Davenport, William Frawley, Edward Brophy, Chick Chandler, Keith Douglas (Douglas Kennedy), Herbert Anderson, DeWolf (William) Hopper, William Justice (Richard Travis), John Ridgely.

The Little Foxes (1941, RKO). *d:* William Wyler; *p:* Samuel Goldwyn (Samuel Goldwyn); *sc:* Lillian Hellman—*b/o* her play.

REGINA GIDDENS*: Scheming, ruthless woman who presides over a greedy and corrupt Southern family but, though she finally gains money and power, ends up alone and unloved.

Herbert Marshall, Teresa Wright, Richard Carlson, Patricia Collinge, Dan Duryea, Charles Dingle, Carl Benton Reid, Russell Hicks, Lucien Littlefield, Virginia Brissac.

The Man Who Came to Dinner (1941, WB). *d:* William Keighley; *p:* Hal B. Wallis, Jerry Wald, and Jack Saper; *sc:* Julius J. Epstein and Philip G. Epstein—*b/o* the play by George S. Kaufman and Moss Hart.

MAGGIE CUTLER: Private secretary who accompanies her pompous, acerbic author boss to dinner at the home of a prominent family in Ohio—where the author slips on the ice and is forced to stay at the host's home, in a wheelchair, for the winter.

Ann Sheridan, Monty Woolley, Richard Travis, Jimmy Durante, Reginald Gardiner, Billie Burke, Elisabeth Fraser, Grant Mitchell, George Barbier, Mary Wickes, Russell Arms, Charles Drake, John Ridgely.

In This Our Life (1942, WB). *d:* John Huston; *p:* David Lewis; *sc:* Howard Koch—*b/o* the novel by Ellen Glasgow.

STANLEY TIMBERLAKE: Spoiled daughter of a Virginia family who steals and marries her sister's husband, then—when the husband commits suicide—sets out to get the man her sister is now in love with.

Olivia de Havilland, George Brent, Dennis Morgan, Charles Coburn, Frank Craven, Billie Burke, Hattie McDaniel, Lee Patrick, William B. Davidson, John Hamilton, Lee Phelps.

Now, Voyager (1942, WB). *d:* Irving Rapper; *p:* Hal B. Wallis; *sc:* Casey Robinson—*b/o* the novel by Olive Higgins Prouty.

CHARLOTTE VALE*: Repressed spinster who, after a psychiatrist helps her gain confidence and poise, goes on a South American cruise and falls in love with a handsome married man.

Paul Henreid, Claude Rains, Gladys Cooper, Bonita Granville, Ilka Chase, John Loder, Lee Patrick, Franklin Pangborn, Katharine Alexander, Mary Wickes, Frank Puglia, Charles Drake.

Watch on the Rhine (1943, WB). *d:* Herman Shumlin; *p:* Hal B. Wallis; *sc:* Dashiell Hammett—(with additional scenes and dialogue by Lillian Hellman)—*b/o* the play by Lillian Hellman.

SARA MULLER: American wife whose husband—a German anti-Nazi WWII underground leader—brings the family to Washington, D.C., for a visit and finds himself being pursued and harassed by Nazi agents in the U.S.

Paul Lukas, Geraldine Fitzgerald, Lucile Watson, Beulah Bondi, George Coulouris, Donald Woods, Henry Daniell, Clarence Muse, Anthony Caruso, Howard Hickman, Creighton Hale, Alan Hale Jr.

Old Acquaintance (1943, WB). *d:* Vincent Sherman; *p:* Henry Blanke; *sc:* John Van Druten and Lenore Coffee—*b/o* the play by John Van Druten.

KIT MARLOWE: Best-selling author whose visit to a girlhood friend in her home town results in the jealous friend's also becoming an author, starting a twenty-year personal and professional feud.

Miriam Hopkins, Gig Young, John Loder, Dolores Moran, Philip Reed, Roscoe Karns, Ann Revere, Esther Dale, Joseph Crehan, Pierre Watkin.

---

*Received an Academy Award nomination as Best Actress for this role.

*Received an Academy Award nomination as Best Actress for this role.

Mr. Skeffington (1944, WB). *d:* Vincent Sherman; *p:* Philip G. Epstein and Julius J. Epstein; *sc:* Philip G. Epstein and Julius J. Epstein—*b/o* the novel by "Elizabeth."

FANNY TRELLIS*: Vain, selfish 1900s WWI-era society girl who, after marrying an older stockbroker for money and then divorcing him, returns during WWII—when she's lost her beauty and youth and he's become blind—to unselfishly take care of him.

Claude Rains, Walter Abel, George Coulouris, Marjorie Riordan, Robert Shayne, Jerome Cowan, Dorothy Peterson, Peter Whitney, Halliwell Hobbes, Bunny Sunshine, Gigi Perreau, Dolores Gray, Walter Kingsford, Molly Lamont.

The Corn Is Green (1945, WB). *d:* Irving Rapper; *p:* Jack Chertok; *sc:* Casey Robinson and Frank Cavett—*b/o* the play by Emlyn Williams.

LILLY MOFFAT: Dedicated middle-aged English schoolteacher in a turn-of-the-century Welsh mining community who devotes herself to transforming a belligerent young miner into an honor student who goes on to Oxford.

John Dall, Joan Lorring, Nigel Bruce, Rosalind Ivan, Rhys Williams, Mildred Dunnock, Gwyneth Hughes, Arthur Shields, Billy Roy, Thomas Louden, Robert Regent.

A Stolen Life (1946, WB). *d:* Curtis Bernhardt; *p:* Bette Davis; *sc:* Catherine Turney (adaptation by Margaret Buell Wilder)—*b/o* the novel by Karel J. Benes.

(Dual role) KATE BOSWORTH: Artist who falls in love with a handsome lighthouse inspector on Martha's Vineyard, loses him to her vivacious twin sister, then—when the sister is killed in a sailing accident—assumes her identity so that she can have the husband.

PATRICIA BOSWORTH: Vivacious girl who steals her twin sister's beau and marries him but is killed in a boating accident.

Glenn Ford, Dane Clark, Walter Brennan, Charles Ruggles, Bruce Bennett, Peggy Knudsen, Esther Dale, Clara Blandick, Joan Winfield.

Deception (1946, WB). *d:* Irving Rapper; *p:* Henry Blanke; *sc:* John Collier and Joseph Than—*b/o* the play *Jealousy* by Louis Verneuil.

CHRISTINE RADCLIFFE: Music teacher/pianist—married to an accomplished cellist—who shoots her jealous ex-lover (a famous composer/conductor) when he threatens to reveal their former relationship and ruin her husband's career.

Paul Henreid, Claude Rains, John Abbott, Benson

Fong, Richard Walsh, Suzi Crandall, Richard Erdman, Ross Ford, Russell Arms, Bess Flowers.

Winter Meeting (1948, WB). *d:* Bretaigne Windust; *p:* Henry Blanke; *sc:* Catherine Turney—*b/o* the novel by Ethel Vance.

SUSAN GRIEVE: Neurotic spinster poetess who falls in love with an embittered young WWII Navy hero who, it turns out, intends to become a priest.

Janis Paige, James Davis (Jim Davis), John Hoyt, Florence Bates, Walter Baldwin, Ransom Sherman, Lois Austin, Robert Riordan.

June Bride (1948, WB). *d:* Bretaigne Windust; *p:* Henry Blanke; *sc:* Ranald MacDougall—*b/o* the play *Feature for June* by Eileen Tighe and Graeme Lorimer.

LINDA GILMAN: Editor of a women's magazine who, when she goes to Indiana to do a feature about a wedding in a typical middle-class home, vindictively assigns her old flame, a roving war correspondent, to be her reluctant assistant.

Robert Montgomery, Fay Bainter, Betty Lynn, Tom Tully, Barbara Bates, Jerome Cowan, Mary Wickes, James Burke, Ray Montgomery, George O'Hanlon, Sandra Gould, Debbie Reynolds.

Beyond the Forest (1949, WB). *d:* King Vidor; *p:* Henry Blanke; *sc:* Lenore Coffee—*b/o* the novel by Stuart Engstrand.

ROSA MOLINE: Small-town Wisconsin doctor's bored, neurotic wife who gets mixed up with a wealthy Chicago industrialist and ends up guilty of adultery, abortion, and murder.

Joseph Cotten, David Brian, Ruth Roman, Minor Watson, Dona Drake, Regis Toomey, Creighton Hale, Ann Doran, Sarah Selby, Frances Charles, Harry Tyler.

All About Eve (1950, 20th-Fox). *d:* Joseph L. Mankiewicz; *p:* Darryl F. Zanuck; *sc:* Joseph L. Mankiewicz—*b/o* Mary Orr's story "The Wisdom of Eve."

MARGO CHANNING*: Famous but aging stage star who, after hiring a young girl as her secretary-companion, discovers that she is a conniving would-be actress who'll do anything to take over the star's place in the theater.

Anne Baxter, George Sanders, Celeste Holm, Gary Merrill, Hugh Marlowe, Thelma Ritter, Marilyn Monroe, Gregory Ratoff, Barbara Bates, Walter Hampden, Randy Stuart, Claude Stroud, Bess Flowers.

Payment on Demand (1951, RKO). *d:* Curtis Bernhardt; *p:* Jack H. Skirball and Bruce

---

*Received an Academy Award nomination as Best Actress for this role.

*Received an Academy Award nomination as Best Actress for this role.

Manning; *sc:* Bruce Manning and Curtis Bernhardt.

JOYCE RAMSEY: Ambitious, social-climbing wife whose belief that her twenty-year marriage has been successful is shattered when her corporation-lawyer husband asks her for a divorce.

Barry Sullivan, Jane Cowl, Kent Taylor, Betty Lynn, John Sutton, Frances Dee, Peggie Castle, Otto Kruger, Walter Sande, Brett King, Richard Anderson, Natalie Schafer, Moroni Olsen.

Another Man's Poison (1952, UA). *d:* Irving Rapper; *p:* Douglas Fairbanks Jr. and Daniel M. Angel (Eros); *sc:* Val Guest—*b/o* the play *Deadlock* by Leslie Sands.

JANET FROBISHER: Mystery writer who, when her convict husband shows up at her home in the Yorkshire moors and tries to blackmail her, murders him—then finds herself contending with another escaped convict who's also out to blackmail her.

Gary Merrill, Emlyn Williams, Anthony Steele, Barbara Murray, Reginald Beckwith, Edna Morris.

Phone Call from a Stranger (1952, 20th-Fox). *d:* Jean Negulesco; *p:* Nunnally Johnson; *sc:* Nunnally Johnson—*b/o* a story by I. A. R. Wylie.

MARIE HOKE: Bedridden, paralyzed woman who, when she's visited by an air-crash survivor who breaks the sad news that her husband was killed in the crash, reminisces about the husband's unselfish devotion and kindness to her.

Shelley Winters, Gary Merrill, Michael Rennie, Keenan Wynn, Evelyn Varden, Warren Stevens, Beatrice Straight, Ted Donaldson, Craig Stevens, Helen Westcott, Hugh Beaumont, Thomas Jackson, Tom Powers, Nestor Paiva.

The Star (1952, 20th-Fox). *d:* Stuart Heisler; *p:* Bert E. Friedlob (Bert E. Friedlob); *sc:* Katherine Albert and Dale Eunson.

MARGARET ELLIOT*: Has-been Academy Award–winning movie star who hasn't worked in years but is obsessed with her past glory and with trying to make a comeback.

Sterling Hayden, Natalie Wood, Warner Anderson, Minor Watson, June Travis, Katherine Warren, Barbara Lawrence, David Alpert, Paul Frees.

The Virgin Queen (1955, 20th-Fox). *d:* Henry Koster; *p:* Charles Brackett; *sc:* Harry Brown and Mindret Lord.

QUEEN ELIZABETH: Sixteenth-century British queen who becomes infatuated with the fiery young Sir Walter Raleigh and appoints him

Captain of the Guard but then comes into conflict with him.

Richard Todd, Joan Collins, Jay Robinson, Herbert Marshall, Dan O'Herlihy, Robert Douglas, Romney Brent, Rod Taylor.

Storm Center (1956, Col.). *d:* Daniel Taradash; *p:* Julian Blaustein (Phoenix); *sc:* Daniel Taradash and Elick Moll.

ALICIA HULL: Librarian in a small New England town who clashes with local politicians when she refuses to remove a controversial book from the library.

Brian Keith, Kim Hunter, Paul Kelly, Kevin Coughlin, Joe Mantell, Sallie Brophy, Edward Platt, Kathryn Grant, Burt Mustin.

The Catered Affair (1956, MGM). *d:* Richard Brooks; *p:* Sam Zimbalist; *sc:* Gore Vidal—*b/o* the teleplay by Paddy Chayefsky.

AGNES HURLEY: Bronx taxicab driver's wife who, in order to give their daughter an expensive wedding reception, spends all the money the husband has been planning to use to buy his own cab.

Ernest Borgnine, Debbie Reynolds, Barry Fitzgerald, Rod Taylor, Robert Simon, Madge Kennedy, Dorothy Stickney, Ray Stricklyn, Jay Adler, Dan Tobin, Mae Clarke.

John Paul Jones (1959, WB). *d:* John Farrow; *p:* Samuel Bronston (Samuel Bronston); *sc:* John Farrow and Jesse Lasky, Jr.

EMPRESS CATHERINE: Eighteenth-century Russian ruler who arranges for the American naval hero John Paul Jones to come to Russia—ostensibly to take command of Russian ships in the Black Sea, but in reality for social activity.

Robert Stack, Marisa Pavan, Charles Coburn, Erin O'Brien, Bruce Cabot, Basil Sydney, Thomas Gomez, Eric Pohlmann, Frank Latimore, Ford Rainey, Macdonald Carey, Jean Pierre Aumont, David Farrar, Peter Cushing.

The Scapegoat (1959, MGM). *d:* Robert Hamer; *p:* Michael Balcon (Du Maurier Guinness); *sc:* Gore Vidal and Robert Hamer—*b/o* the novel by Daphne du Maurier.

COUNTESS de GUE: Bedridden, dope-addicted dowager whose son, a French nobleman, devises a bizarre scheme in which he murders his wife and implicates an English professor who is his exact double.

Alec Guinness, Nicole Maurey, Irene Worth, Pamela Brown, Annabel Bartlett, Geoffrey Keen, Noel Howlett, Peter Bull, Leslie French, Eddie Byrne, Peter Sallis.

Pocketful of Miracles (1961, UA). *d:* Frank Capra; *p:* Frank Capra (Franton); *sc:* Hal Kanter and Harry Tugend—*b/o* a screenplay by Robert

---

*Received an Academy Award nomination as Best Actress for this role.

Riskin and the story "Madame La Gimp" by Damon Runyon.

APPLE ANNIE: Gin-soaked Broadway apple peddler who, with the help of a big-hearted mobster, masquerades as a society matron when her daughter—believing that the mother is a socialite—brings her fiancé from Spain to meet her.

Glenn Ford, Hope Lange, Arthur O'Connell, Peter Falk, Thomas Mitchell, Edward Everett Horton, Mickey Shaughnessy, David Brian, Sheldon Leonard, Ann-Margret, Barton MacLane, John Litel, Jerome Cowan, Jay Novello, Frank Ferguson, Fritz Feld, Ellen Corby, Jack Elam, Mike Mazurki.

What Ever Happened to Baby Jane? (1962, WB). *d:* Robert Aldrich; *p:* Kenneth Hyman and Robert Aldrich (Seven Arts/Aldrich); *sc:* Lukas Heller—*b/o* the novel by Henry Farrell.

JANE HUDSON*: Demented, aging former child vaudeville star who enjoys mentally torturing her sister, a crippled former movie queen who lives with her in a decaying Hollywood mansion.

Joan Crawford, Victor Buono, Marjorie Bennett, Maidie Norman, Anna Lee, Barbara Merrill, Julie Allred, Gina Gillespie, Dave Willock, Ann Barton.

Dead Ringer (1964, WB). *d:* Paul Henreid; *p:* William H. Wright; *sc:* Albert Beich and Oscar Millard—*b/o* a story by Rian James.

(Dual role) EDITH PHILLIPS: Tavern owner who bitterly resents her rich look-alike twin sister, murders her, and takes over her home and jewels—but doesn't get away with it.

MARGARET (PHILLIPS) DE LORCA: Wealthy widow who is murdered by her bitter look-alike twin sister.

Karl Malden, Peter Lawford, Philip Carey, Jean Hagen, George Macready, Estelle Winwood, George Chandler, Monika Henreid, Bert Remsen, Ken Lynch.

The Empty Canvas (1964, Embassy Pictures). *d:* Damiano Damiani; *p:* Carlo Ponti (Joseph E. Levine); *sc:* Tonino Guerra, Ugo Liberatore, and Damiano Damiani—*b/o* a novel by Albert Moravia.

THE COUNTESS: Domineering American widow of an Italian nobleman whose son—an over-protected, frustrated would-be painter—becomes obsessed with a promiscuous model and suffers a nervous breakdown.

Horst Buchholz, Catherine Spaak, Daniela Rocca, Lea Padovani, Isa Miranda, Leonida Repaci, George Wilson.

---

*Received an Academy Award nomination as Best Actress for this role.

Where Love Has Gone (1964, Para.). *d:* Edward Dmytryk; *p:* Joseph E. Levine (Joseph E. Levine); *sc:* John Michael Hayes—*b/o* the novel by Harold Robbins.

MRS. GERALD HAYDEN: Domineering dowager whose daughter is a promiscuous, neurotic sculptress and whose granddaughter is charged with murdering one of the sculptress's lovers.

Susan Hayward, Michael (Mike) Connors, Joey Heatherton, Jane Greer, DeForest Kelley, George Macready, Anne Seymour, Willis Bouchey, Walter Reed, Ann Doran, Whit Bissell, Anthony Caruso.

Hush . . . Hush, Sweet Charlotte (1964, 20th-Fox). *d:* Robert Aldrich; *p:* Robert Aldrich (Associates/Aldrich); *sc:* Henry Farrell and Lukas Heller—*b/o* a story by Henry Farrell.

CHARLOTTE HOLLIS: Aging, demented recluse in a decaying house in the Louisiana bayous who is the victim of a plot by her conniving cousin and the cousin's former beau to drive her insane and gain control of the family fortune.

Olivia de Havilland, Joseph Cotten, Agnes Moorehead, Cecil Kellaway, Victor Buono, Mary Astor, Bruce Dern, George Kennedy, Dave Willock, Ellen Corby, Frank Ferguson, Lillian Randolph.

The Nanny (1965, 20th-Fox). *d:* Seth Holt; *p:* Jimmy Sangster (Seven Arts–Hammer); *sc:* Jimmy Sangster—*b/o* the novel by Evelyn Piper.

NANNY: English woman who is the nanny of a disturbed ten-year-old boy who claims that she drowned his baby sister two years ago and that now she's out to do him in.

Wendy Craig, Jill Bennett, James Villiers, William Dix, Pamela Franklin, Jack Watling, Alfred Burke, Angharad Aubrey.

The Anniversary (1968, 20th-Fox). *d:* Roy Ward Baker; *p:* Jimmy Sangster (Hammer); *sc:* Jimmy Sangster—*b/o* the play by Bill MacIlwraith.

MRS. TAGGART: Evil, one-eyed English widow (she wears an eyepatch) who gathers her three grown sons together on each anniversary of her hated husband's death and resorts to various dirty tricks to keep them under her domination.

Sheila Hancock, Jack Hedley, James Cossins, Christian Roberts, Elaine Taylor, Timothy Bateson.

Connecting Rooms (1970, London Screen). *d:* Franklin Gollings; *p:* Harry Field, Jack Smith, and Arthur S. Cooper; *sc:* Franklin Gollings—*b/o* Marion Hart's play *The Cellist.*

WANDA FLEMING: Cellist in England who is involved with a former schoolmaster and a rebellious young aspiring pop songwriter.

Michael Redgrave, Alexis Kanner, Kay Walsh, Gabrielle Drake, Leo Genn, Richard Wyler, Brian Wilde.

Bunny O'Hare (1971, AIP). *d:* Gerd Oswald; *p:* Gerd Oswald and Norman T. Herman; *sc:* Stanley Z. Cherry and Coslough Johnson.

BUNNY O'HARE: Little old lady who joins forces with an ex-convict plumber as they dress like hippies, rob banks, and ride a motorcycle to escape.

Ernest Borgnine, Jack Cassidy, Joan Delaney, Jay Robinson, Reva Rose, John Astin, Robert Foulk.

Madame Sin (1972, ITC Productions [Made for TV]). *d:* David Greene; *p:* Robert Wagner, Julius Wintle, and Lou Morheim; *sc:* David Greene and Barry Oringer.

MADAME SIN: Evil Oriental genius who kidnaps a former C.I.A. agent and forces him to help her gain control of a Polaris submarine.

Robert Wagner, Denholm Elliott, Gordon Jackson, Dudley Sutton, Catherine Schell, Paul Maxwell, Pik-Sen Lim, David Healey, Alan Dobie, Roy Kinnear.

Burnt Offerings (1976, UA). *d:* Dan Curtis; *p:* Dan Curtis and Robert Singer (PEA–Dan Curtis); *sc:* William F. Nolan and Dan Curtis—*b/o* the novel by Robert Marasco.

AUNT ELIZABETH: Elderly aunt of a family that, when it rents an old run-down mansion for the summer, suffers tragic consequences because of evil supernatural forces that control the house.

Karen Black, Oliver Reed, Burgess Meredith, Eileen Heckart, Lee Montgomery, Dub Taylor.

Return from Witch Mountain (1978, Buena Vista). *d:* John Hough; *p:* Ron Miller and Jerome Courtland (Walt Disney Prod.); *sc:* Malcolm Marmorstein—*b/o* characters created by Alexander Key.

LETHA: Wicked woman who, along with her greedy husband, captures and brainwashes a young boy from another planet so that they can use him in their nefarious plan to take over the whole world.

Christopher Lee, Kim Richards, Ike Eisenmann, Denver Pyle, Dick Bakalyan.

Death on the Nile (1978, Para.). *d:* John Guillermin; *p:* John Brabourne and Richard Goodwin (EMI); *sc:* Anthony Shaffer—*b/o* a novel by Agatha Christie.

MRS. VAN SCHUYLER: Greedy dowager with a taste for pearls—one of several passengers on a Nile River cruise whom the Belgian supersleuth Hercule Poirot suspects in the murder of an heiress on her honeymoon.

Peter Ustinov, Jane Birkin, Lois Chiles, Mia Farrow, Jon Finch, Olivia Hussey, I. S. Johar, George Kennedy, Angela Lansbury, Simon MacCorkindale, David Niven, Maggie Smith, Jack Warden, Harry Andrews, Sam Wanamaker.

The Dark Secret of Harvest Home (1978, Univ. [Made for TV]). *d:* Leo Penn; *p:* Jack Laird; *sc:* Jack Guss and Charles E. Israel (adaptation by James Miller and Jennifer Miller)—*b/o* the novel *Harvest Home* by Thomas Tryon.

WIDOW FORTUNE: Motherly midwife and homeopath in the seemingly idyllic New England farming village of Cornwall Coombe who, it turns out, is the chilling matriarch who presides over the villagers' ancient, bloodthirsty ritual of offering one of their young males as a human sacrifice every seven years in order to assure a bountiful corn crop.

David Ackroyd, Rosanna Arquette, Rene Auberjonois, John Calvin, Norman Lloyd, Joanna Miles, Michael O'Keefe, Laurie Prang.

Strangers: The Story of a Mother and Daughter (1979, Chris-Rose Productions [Made for TV]). *d:* Milton Katselas; *p:* Robert W. Christiansen and Rick Rosenberg; *sc:* Michael de Guzman.

LUCY MASON*: Lonely, embittered widow who, when her independent-minded daughter unexpectedly returns home after twenty years of absence, is resentful and unforgiving—until she learns that the daughter is dying.

Gena Rowlands, Ford Rainey, Donald Moffat, Whit Bissell, Royal Dano, Krishan Timberlake, Son Salo, John Zumino.

The Watcher in the Woods (1980, Buena Vista). *d:* John Hough; *p:* Ron Miller (Walt Disney Prod.); *sc:* Brian Cleens, Harry Soalding, and Rosemary Anne Sisson.

MRS. AYLWOOD: Crusty landlady of a strange old country house in England that—when an American family rents it—is haunted by the ghost of the landlady's young daughter, who mysteriously disappeared thirty years before.

Carroll Baker, David McCallum, Lynn-Holly Johnson, Kyle Richards, Ian Bannen, Richard Pasco.

• In addition, Bette Davis made cameo/guest appearances in the following feature films: *Thank Your Lucky Stars* (1943, WB) and *Hollywood Canteen* (1944, WB).

---

*Won an Emmy Award as Outstanding Lead Actress in a Drama Special for this role.

☆ MARLENE DIETRICH

Maria Magdalene Dietrich

b: Dec. 27, 1901, Berlin, Germany

"It took more than one man to change my name to Shanghai Lilly."

Shanghai Lilly (Marlene Dietrich) to Capt. Donald Harvey (Clive Brook) in *Shanghai Express*, 1932.

The Little Napoleon (1923, UFA). *d:* Georg Jacoby; *sc:* Robert Liebmann and Georg Jacoby.
KATHRIN: Maid to a baron's daughter who helps the daughter elude the advances of Jerome Bonaparte, Napoleon I's youngest brother, who has been named king of the newly created Kingdom of Westphalia in 1807.
Egon von Hagen, Paul Heidemann, Harry Liedtke, Jacob Tiedtke, Antonia Dietrich, Loni Nest, Alice Hechy.

Tragedy of Love (1923, UFA). *d:* Joe May; *p:* Joe May; *sc:* Leo Birinsk and Adolf Lantz.
LUCIE: A judge's mistress who is one of the spectators at the murder trial of a brutal French wrestler.
Emil Jannings, Erika Glassner, Mia May, Kurt Vespermann, Ida Wust, Arnold Korff, Charlotte Ander, Loni Nest.

Man by the Roadside (1923, Osmania). *d:* Wilhelm (William) Dieterle; *sc:* Wilhelm (William) Dieterle—*b/o* a short story by Leo Tolstoy.
Golden-braided peasant girl in a German village who is one of several people involved in a situation in which an old man suspected of murder is helped by a young man who is really an angel come to earth.
Alexander Granach, Wilhelm (William) Dieterle, Heinrich George, Wilhelm Volker, Wilhelm Diegelmann, Dr. Max Pohl, Ludwig Rex, Fritz Rasp.

The Leap into Life (1924, UFA). *d:* Dr. Johannes Guter; *p:* Oskar Messter; *sc:* Franz Schulz.
Pretty girl who futilely yearns for the affections of a handsome young scholar.
Xenia Desni, Walter Rilla, Paul Heidemann, Frida Richard, Kathe Haack, Olga Engl, Hans Brausewetter.

The Joyless Street (1925, Hirschal–Sofar [released in the U.S. in 1927 as **The Street of Sorrow**]). *d:* Georg Wilhelm Pabst; *sc:* Willi Haas—*b/o* the novel by Hugo Bettauer.
One of several women in line at a butcher's shop during the post-WWI depression in Vienna.

Jaro Furth, Werner Krauss, Asta Neilsen, Greta Garbo, Valeska Gert, Einar Hanson, Agnes Esterhazy, Loni Nest.

Manon Lescaut (1926, Universum). *d:* Arthur Robison; *sc:* Hans Kyser and Arthur Robison—*b/o L'Histoire de Manon Lescaut* by Abbe Prevost.
MICHELINE: Consort of a wealthy French Marquis who helps the dissolute nobleman in his various plots to woo a beautiful young girl away from her handsome young lover.
Lya De Putti, Vladimir Gaidarov, Eduard Rothauser, Fritz Greiner, Hubert von Meyerinck, Sigfried Arno.

A Modern du Barry (1926, UFA). *d:* Alexander Korda; *sc:* Robert Leibmann, Alexander Korda, and Paul Reboux—*b/o* the story "Eine du Barry von Heute" by Ludwig Biro.
Billed as "A COQUETTE": Attractive Parisian coquette who buys a gown at a stylish shop and leaves it for alterations, then is furious when she discovers the shop model wearing it in a fashionable nightclub.
Maria Corda, Alfred Abel, Friedrich Kayssler, Julius von Szoreghy, Jean Bradin, Hans Albers.

Madame Doesn't Want Children (1926, Deutsche Vereinsfilm). *d:* Alexander Korda; *p:* Karl Freund (Fox Europa); *sc:* Adolf Lantz and Bela Balazs—*b/o* the novel *Madame ne veut pas d'enfants* by Clement Vautel.
A "dress extra" in party scenes.
Maria Corda, Harry Liedtke, Maria Paudler, Trude Hesterberg, Dina Gralla, Camilla von Hollay, John Loder.

Heads Up, Charly! (1926, UFA). *d:* Dr. Willi Wolff; *sc:* Robert Liebmann and Dr. Willi Wolff—*b/o* a novel by Ludwig Wolff.
EDMEE MARCHAND: Young French woman whom men find charming.
Anton Pointner, Ellen Richter, Michael Bohnen, Max Gulsdorff, Margerie Quimby, Angelo Ferrari, Toni Tetzlaff.

The Imaginary Baron (1927, UFA). *d:* Dr. Willi Wolff; *sc:* Robert Liebmann and Dr. Willi Wolff—*b/o* the operetta by Pordes-Milo, Hermann Haller, and Walter Kollo.
SOPHIE: Young woman who plots to marry a rich baron but, when she discovers that he's really only an itinerant musician, disgustedly drops him.
Reinhold Schunzel, Henry Bender, Julia Serda, Teddy Bill, Colette Brettl, Albert Paulig, Trude Hesterberg.

His Greatest Bluff (1927, Sudfilm). *d:* Harry Piel; *sc:* Henrik Galeen.

YVETTE: French call girl who—along with her accomplice, a dwarf—becomes involved in stealing some jewels in Paris.

Harry Piel, Tony Tetzlaff, Lotte Lorring, Albert Pauling, Fritz Greiner, Charley Berger, Boris Michailow, Paul Walker, Kurt Gerron.

Café Electric (1927, Sascha). *d:* Gustav Ucicky; *p:* Karl Hartl; *sc:* Jacques Bachrach—*b/o* the play *Die Liebesborse* by Felix Fischer.

ERNI: Building contractor's daughter who becomes involved with a gigolo who frequents the Café Electric, a hangout for prostitutes and procurers.

Fritz Alberti, Anny Coty, Willi Forst, Nina Vanna, Igo Sym, Felix Fischer, Vera Salvotti.

Princess Olala (1928, Deutsches Lichtspiel). *d:* Robert Land; *sc:* Franz Schultz and Robert Land—*b/o* the operetta by Jean Gilbert, Rudolf Bernauer, and Rudolf Schanzer.

CHICHOTTE de GASTONE: Naughty Parisian lady who is nicknamed "Princess Olala" because she is famous for having taught a number of European princes how to make love.

Hermann Bottcher, Walter Rilla, Georg Alexander, Carmen Boni, Ila Meery, Hans Albers, Lya Christy.

I Kiss Your Hand, Madame (1929, Deutsches Lichtspiel). *d:* Robert Land; *sc:* Robert Land—*b/o* a story by Rolf E. Vanloo and Robert Land.

LAURENCE GERARD: Young Parisian divorcée who falls for a man she thinks is a count, then discovers he's working as a headwaiter.

Harry Liedtke, Pierre de Guingand, Karl Huszar-Puffy.

Three Loves (1929, Moviegraphs). *d:* Kurt Bernhardt; *sc:* Ladislas Vajda—*b/o* the novel by Max Brod.

STASHA: Sophisticated lady who, after becoming the mistress of her husband's murderer, falls in love with a young French engineer—but pays for it with her life.

Fritz Kortner, Frida Richard, Oskar Sima, Uno Henning, Bruno Ziener, Karl Ettlinger, Edith Edwards.

The Ship of Lost Souls (1929, Orplid–Metro). *d:* Maurice Tourneur; *p:* Max Glass (Glass–Wengeroff); *sc:* Maurice Tourneur—*b/o* the novel by Frenzos Kerzemen.

MISS ETHEL: Wealthy American aviatrix who, when she crashes while trying to break the European record across the Atlantic, is taken aboard a strange ship of "lost souls"—smugglers, pirates, escaped prisoners, and other criminals on the run from the law.

Fritz Kortner, Gaston Modot, Robin Irvine, Boris de Fast, Vladimir Sokoloff, Robert Garrison, Max Maximilian.

Dangers of the Engagement Period (1929, Hegewald). *d:* Fred Sauer; *sc:* Walter Wassermann and Walter Schlee.

EVELYNE: Young woman who, while on her way to marry a wealthy man she's never met, is seduced in a small Dutch town by an amorous baron who—it later turns out—is a friend of the husband-to-be.

Willi Forst, Lotte Loring, Elza Temary, Ernst Stahl-Nachbaur, Bruno Ziener, Oskar Sima.

The Blue Angel (1930, UFA). *d:* Josef von Sternberg; *p:* Erich Pommer (Erich Pommer/UFA); *sc:* Robert Liebmann (adaptation by Carl Zuckmayer and Karl Vollmoller)—*b/o* the novel *Professor Unrath* by Heinrich Mann.

LOLA-LOLA: Tawdry Berlin nightclub singer at the Blue Angel cabaret who, when a stuffy German professor falls blindly in love with her, marries him and causes his disastrous downfall.

Emil Jannings, Kurt Gerron, Rosa Veletti, Hans Albers, Reinhold Bernt, Eduard von Winterstein, Hans Roth, Karl Huszar-Puffy.

Morocco (1930, Para.). *d:* Josef von Sternberg; *sc:* Jules Furthman—*b/o* the novel *Amy Jolly* by Benno Vigny.

AMY JOLLY*: Cool, sexy cabaret singer in Morocco who, when she meets her match—a cynical, handsome American soldier in the French Foreign Legion—gives up her wealthy admirer and marches into the desert after the legionnaire to become a "camp follower."

Gary Cooper, Adolphe Menjou, Ullrich Haupt, Juliette Compton, Francis McDonald, Albert Conti, Eve Southern, Paul Porcasi.

Dishonored (1931, Para.). *d:* Josef von Sternberg; *sc:* Daniel H. Rubin—*b/o* a story by Josef von Sternberg.

"X-27": WWI officer's widow–turned–Viennese streetwalker who, when she's hired by the Austrian government to become a spy, falls in love with a Russian enemy agent, is charged with treason, and winds up in front of an Austrian firing squad.

Victor McLaglen, Lew Cody, Gustav von Seyffertitz, Warner Oland, Barry Norton, Davison Clark, Wilfred Lucas, Bill Powell, George Irving.

Shanghai Express (1932, Para.). *d:* Josef von Sternberg; *sc:* Jules Furthman—*b/o* a story by Harry Hervey.

---

*Received an Academy Award nomination as Best Actress for this role.

MADELINE (alias SHANGHAI LILY): Notorious adventuress who encounters her old flame, a British Army officer, on a Shanghai-bound train that is waylaid by Chinese bandits.

Clive Brook, Anna May Wong, Warner Oland, Eugene Pallette, Lawrence Grant, Louise Closser Hale, Gustav von Seyffertitz, Emile Chautard, Claude King, Willie Fung.

Blonde Venus (1932, Para.). *d:* Josef von Sternberg; *sc:* Jules Furthman and S. K. Lauren—*b/o* a story by Josef von Sternberg.

HELEN FARADAY: German café singer who marries an American research chemist, then—when the husband becomes seriously ill from radium poisoning—becomes the mistress of a wealthy playboy in order to get money to cure him.

Herbert Marshall, Cary Grant, Dickie Moore, Gene Morgan, Rita La Roy, Robert Emmett O'Connor, Sidney Toler, Dewey Robinson, Cecil Cunningham.

Song of Songs (1933, Para.). *d:* Rouben Mamoulian; *p:* Rouben Mamoulian; *sc:* Leo Birinski and Samuel Hoffenstein—*b/o* the novel by Hermann Sudermann and the play by Edward Sheldon.

LILY CZEPANEK: Innocent German peasant girl who goes to Berlin to live with her aunt, falls in love with a young sculptor, but then makes the mistake of marrying a lecherous baron.

Brian Aherne, Lionel Atwill, Alison Skipworth, Hardie Albright, Helen Freeman, Morgan Wallace, Hans Schumm.

The Scarlet Empress (1934, Para.). *d:* Josef von Sternberg; *sc:* Manuel Komroff—*b/o* a diary of Catherine the Great.

SOPHIA FREDERICA (CATHERINE II, also known as CATHERINE THE GREAT): German princess who is brought to Russia in the eighteenth century by the Empress Elizabeth to marry her half-witted son, the Grand Duke Peter, then—when Peter inherits the throne but is murdered—becomes the Empress of Russia.

John Lodge, Sam Jaffe, Louise Dresser, Maria Sieber, C. Aubrey Smith, Ruthelma Stevens, Olive Tell, Gavin Gordon, Erville Alderson, Jane Darwell, Edward Van Sloan, James Burke.

The Devil Is a Woman (1935, Para.). *d:* Josef von Sternberg; *sc:* John Dos Passos and S. K. Winston—*b/o* Pierre Louys's novel *The Woman and the Puppet.*

CONCHA PEREZ: Heartless Spanish beauty in 1890s Seville who ruins the lives of several male admirers, including an older man who was once a proud officer of the Spanish Civil Guard.

Lionel Atwill, Cesar Romero, Edward Everett Horton, Alison Skipworth, Don Alvaredo, Morgan Wallace, Tempe Pigott, Hank Mann, Edwin Maxwell.

Desire (1936, Para.). *d:* Frank Borzage; *p:* Ernst Lubitsch; *sc:* Edwin Justus Mayer, Waldemar Young, and Samuel Hoffenstein—*b/o* a play by Hans Szekely and R. A. Stemmle.

MADELEINE de BEAUPRE: Beautiful jewel thief who makes a young American engineer her unwitting accomplice when she plants a stolen pearl necklace on him at the Franco-Spanish border.

Gary Cooper, John Halliday, William Frawley, Ernest Cossart, Akim Tamiroff, Alan Mowbray, Zeffie Tilbury, Marc Lawrence, Gaston Glass, Robert O'Connor, Stanley Andrews.

The Garden of Allah (1936, UA). *d:* Richard Boleslawski; *p:* David O. Selznick (Selznick International); *sc:* W. P. Lipscomb and Lynn Riggs—*b/o* the novel by Robert Hichens.

DOMINI ENFILDEN: Sultry socialite who, after falling in love with a brooding young man in the Algerian desert and marrying him, discovers that he's a Trappist monk who has broken his vows and fled from the monastery.

Charles Boyer, Basil Rathbone, C. Aubrey Smith, Tilly Losch, Joseph Schildkraut, John Carradine, Alan Marshall, Lucile Watson, Henry Brandon, Helen Jerome Eddy, Pedro de Cordoba, Bonita Granville, Marcia Mae Jones, Ann Gillis.

Knight without Armour (1937, UA). *d:* Jacques Feyder; *p:* Alexander Korda (Alexander Korda–London); *sc:* Lajos Biro and Arthur Wimperis (adaptation by Frances Marion)—*b/o* the novel *Without Armour* by James Hilton.

COUNTESS ALEXANDRA: Widowed countess during the 1917 Russian Revolution who flees Russian revolutionaries with the help of a young British translator who has become a British Secret Service agent.

Robert Donat, Irene Vanburgh, Herbert Lomas, Austin Trevor, Basil Gill, David Tree, John Clements, Raymond Huntley.

Angel (1937, Para.). *d:* Ernst Lubitsch; *p:* Ernst Lubitsch; *sc:* Samson Raphaelson—*b/o* a play by Melchior Lengyel.

MARIA BARKER: English diplomat's wife who, when she feels neglected, secretly goes to Paris and becomes involved with a handsome young American, then meets him again when her unsuspecting husband introduces him as an old friend from WWI.

Herbert Marshall, Melvyn Douglas, Edward Everett Horton, Ernest Cossart, Laura Hope Crews, Herbert Mundin, Ivan Lebedeff, Dennie Moore, Lionel Pape, James Finlayson.

Destry Rides Again (1939, Univ.). *d:* George

Marshall; *p:* Joe Pasternak; *sc:* Felix Jackson, Henry Meyers, and Gertrude Purcell—*b/o* the novel by Max Brand.

FRENCHY: Fiesty, hardboiled dance-hall girl at the Last Chance Saloon who is finally tamed by the mild-mannered son of a famous lawman when he becomes deputy sheriff of the lawless town of Bottle Neck.

James Stewart, Charles Winninger, Mischa Auer, Brian Donlevy, Irene Hervey, Una Merkel, Allen Jenkins, Warren Hymer, Samuel S. Hinds, Jack Carson, Lillian Yarbo, Tom Fadden, Dickie Jones, Virginia Brissac, Joe King.

Seven Sinners (1940, Univ.). *d:* Tay Garnett; *p:* Joe Pasternak; *sc:* John Meehan and Harry Tugend—*b/o* a story by Ladislas Fodor and Lazlo Vadnay.

BIJOU BLANCHE: Often-deported torch singer in a South Seas gin joint called Tony's 7 Sinners who falls for a handsome young U.S. Navy Lieutenant and almost causes him to sacrifice his career.

John Wayne, Broderick Crawford, Mischa Auer, Albert Dekker, Billy Gilbert, Oscar Homolka, Anna Lee, Samuel S. Hinds, Reginald Denny, Vince Barnett, Herbert Rawlinson, James Craig, William Bakewell, Antonio Moreno, Russell Hicks.

The Flame of New Orleans (1941, Univ.). *d:* Rene Clair; *p:* Joe Pasternak; *sc:* Norman Krasna.

CLAIRE LEDEUX: European adventuress who passes herself off as a countess in 1841 New Orleans while scheming to marry a wealthy banker but winds up with an adventurous young seaman.

Bruce Cabot, Roland Young, Mischa Auer, Andy Devine, Frank Jenks, Eddie Quillan, Laura Hope Crews, Franklin Pangborn, Clarence Muse, Melville Cooper, Anne Revere, Gus Schilling, Bess Flowers, Reed Hadley, Dorothy Adams.

Manpower (1941, WB). *d:* Raoul Walsh; *p:* Mark Hellinger; *sc:* Richard Macaulay and Jerry Wald.

FAY DUVAL: Hostess-singer in a cheap Los Angeles clip joint who comes between two buddies who work for a power-and-light company and risk their lives repairing high-tension lines.

Edward G. Robinson, George Raft, Alan Hale, Frank McHugh, Eve Arden, Barton MacLane, Walter Catlett, Joyce Compton, Ward Bond, Cliff Clark, Ben Welden, Barbara Pepper, Faye Emerson.

The Lady Is Willing (1942, Col.). *d:* Mitchell Leisen; *p:* Mitchell Leisen; *sc:* James Edward Grant and Albert McCleery—*b/o* a story by James Edward Grant.

ELIZABETH MADDEN: Glamorous musical-comedy star who finds an abandoned baby and talks a handsome young pediatrician into

marrying her—on a platonic basis—so that she can legally adopt the child.

Fred MacMurray, Aline MacMahon, Stanley Ridges, Arline Judge, Sterling Holloway, Harry Shannon, Elisabeth Risdon, Charles Lane, Chester Clute, Neil Hamilton, Jimmy Conlin, Charles Halton.

The Spoilers (1942, Univ.). *d:* Ray Enright; *p:* Frank Lloyd; *sc:* Lawrence Hazard and Tom Reed—*b/o* the novel by Rex Beach.

CHERRY MALLOTTE: Lusty lady saloonkeeper in Nome, Alaska, during the gold rush who becomes involved with two Yukon adventurers whose fight over land rights culminates in a brawling marathon fistfight.

Randolph Scott, John Wayne, Margaret Lindsay, Harry Carey, Richard Barthelmess, George Cleveland, Samuel S. Hinds, Russell Simpson, William Farnum, Jack Norton, Charles Halton, Bud Osborne, Robert W. Service.

Pittsburgh (1942, Univ.). *d:* Lewis Seiler; *p:* Charles K. Feldman; *sc:* Kenneth Gamet and Tom Reed (with additional dialogue by John Twist)—*b/o* a story by George Owen and Tom Reed.

JOSIE WINTERS: Coal miner's daughter who, along with two roughneck coal miners who both love her, rises to social and financial prominence while Pittsburgh grows from a coal-mining town into a world center of coal and steel production.

Randolph Scott, John Wayne, Frank Craven, Louise Allbritton, Shemp Howard, Thomas Gomez, Samuel S. Hinds, Paul Fix, William Haade, Douglas Fowley, Hobart Cavanaugh, Wade Boteler.

Kismet (1944, MGM). *d:* William Dieterle; *p:* Everett Riskin; *sc:* John Meehan—*b/o* the play by Edward Knobloch. ———

JAMILLA: Queen of the castle of the Grand Vizier in Bagdad who carries on a clandestine affair with a roguish beggar-magician who is scheming to marry his daughter to a prince.

Ronald Colman, James Craig, Edward Arnold, Hugh Herbert, Florence Bates, Harry Davenport, Robert Warwick, Victor Kilian, Charles Middleton, Nestor Paiva, Cy Kendall, Dan Seymour.

Martin Roumagnac (1946, Alcina; released in the U.S. in 1948 by Lopert Films as ***The Room Upstairs***). *p:* Marc Pelletier; *sc:* Pierre Very—*b/o* the novel by Pierre-René Wolf.

BLANCHE FERRAND: Beautiful, sophisticated woman in a small French town whose engineer lover kills her in a rage when he discovers that she has a side-line occupation as a high-class prostitute.

Jean Gabin, Margo Lion, Marcel Herrand, Daniel

Gelin, Jean Darcante, Henri Poupon, Marcel Andre, Paulot, Charles Lemontier.

Golden Earrings (1947, Para.). *d:* Mitchell Leisen; *p:* Harry Tugend; *sc:* Abraham Polonsky, Frank Butler, and Helen Deutsch—*b/o* a novel by Yolanda Foldes.

LYDIA: Seductive Hungarian gypsy girl in the Black Forest who disguises a British Intelligence officer as a gypsy in order to help him smuggle a poison-gas formula out of pre-WWII Nazi Germany.

Ray Milland, Murvyn Vye, Bruce Lester, Dennis Hoey, Quentin Reynolds, Reinhold Schunzel, Ivan Triesault, Larry Simms, Robert Val, Gordon Arnold.

A Foreign Affair (1948, Para.). *d:* Billy Wilder; *p:* Charles Brackett; *sc:* Charles Brackett, Billy Wilder, and Richard L. Breen (adaptation by Robert Harari)—*b/o* a story by David Shaw.

ERIKA von SCHLUETOW: Alluring ex-Nazi nightclub singer in post-WWII Berlin who is the mistress of a U.S. Army captain but finds herself vying for his affections with a prim Iowa congresswoman who has come to Berlin to investigate the morale of U.S. troops in Germany.

Jean Arthur, John Lund, Millard Mitchell, Peter von Zerneck, Stanley Prager, Bill Murphy, Gordon Jones, Freddie Steele, Bobby Watson, Charles Meredith, Frederick Hollander.

Stage Fright (1950, WB). *d:* Alfred Hitchcock; *p:* Alfred Hitchcock; *sc:* Whitfield Cook (adaptation by Alma Reville, with additional dialogue by James Bridie)—*b/o* the novel *Man Running* by Selwyn Jepson.

CHARLOTTE INWOOD: Glamorous musical-comedy star in England who, after her young lover is accused of murdering the star's husband, finds herself being accused of the crime by the lover.

Jane Wyman, Michael Wilding, Richard Todd, Alistair Sim, Kay Walsh, Dame Sybil Thorndike, Joyce Grenfell, Patricia Hitchcock.

No Highway in the Sky (1951, 20th-Fox). *d:* Henry Koster; *p:* Louis D. Lighton; *sc:* R. C. Sherriff, Oscar Millard, and Alec Coppel—*b/o* the novel by Nevil Shute.

MONICA TEASDALE: Noted film actress who, while on a transatlantic flight aboard a new type of British commercial aircraft, sympathizes with and believes in an eccentric engineer who insists that the tail assembly is about to snap from metal fatigue.

James Stewart, Glynis Johns, Jack Hawkins, Ronald Squire, Janette Scott, Niall McGinnis, Elizabeth Allan, Kenneth More, David Hutcheson, Wilfrid Hyde-White.

Rancho Notorious (1952, RKO). *d:* Fritz Lang; *p:* Howard Welsch (Fidelity); *sc:* Daniel Taradash—*b/o* a story by Sylvia Richards.

ALTAR KEANE: Notorious dance-hall queen in 1870s Wyoming who—while operating a ranch called the Chuck-a-Luck, a refuge for outlaws and bandits—falls for a cowboy searching for his fiancée's killer.

Arthur Kennedy, Mel Ferrer, Lloyd Gough, Gloria Henry, William Frawley, Jack Elam, George Reeves, Frank Ferguson, Dan Seymour, John Doucette, Lane Chandler, Fuzzy Knight, Dick Wessell, William Haade.

Around the World in 80 Days (1956, UA). *d:* Michael Anderson; *p:* Michael Todd (Michael Todd Prod.); *sc:* James Poe, John Farrow, and S. J. Perelman—*b/o* the novel by Jules Verne.

Billed as "OWNER, BARBARY COAST SALOON": Dance-hall queen in a saloon in San Francisco—one of many colorful characters encountered by the English gentleman Phileas Fogg in 1872 while he is winning his bet that he can journey around the world in eighty days.

David Niven, Cantinflas, Robert Newton, Shirley MacLaine, Charles Boyer, Joe E. Brown, Ronald Colman, Noel Coward, Andy Devine, Fernandel, Sir John Gielgud, Sir Cedric Hardwicke, Buster Keaton, Peter Lorre, Col. Tim McCoy, John Mills, Robert Morley, George Raft, Cesar Romero, Frank Sinatra, Red Skelton.

The Monte Carlo Story (1957, UA). *d:* Samuel A. Taylor; *p:* Marcello Girosi (Titanus); *sc:* Samuel A. Taylor—*b/o* a story by Marcello Girosi and Dino Risi.

MARQUISE MARIA de CREVECOEUR: Compulsive gambler on the French Riviera who hopes to land a wealthy suitor but winds up with a handsome Italian nobleman who also needs cash because he, too, is a compulsive gambler.

Vittorio De Sica, Arthur O'Connell, Natalie Trundy, Jane Rose, Clelia Matania, Alberto Rabagliati, Mischa Auer, Truman Smith.

Witness for the Prosecution (1957, UA). *d:* Billy Wilder; *p:* Arthur Hornblow Jr. (Theme/Edward Small); *sc:* Billy Wilder and Harry Kurnitz (adaptation by Larry Marcus)—*b/o* the story and play by Agatha Christie.

CHRISTINE VOLE: Sultry, inscrutable woman who at first maintains that her husband—an opportunistic young man accused of murdering a wealthy widow—is innocent but then testifies, in a London court during the trial, that he told her he had murdered the widow.

Tyrone Power, Charles Laughton, Elsa Lanchester, John Williams, Henry Daniell, Ian Wolfe, Una O'Connor, Torin Thatcher, Francis Compton, Norma Varden, Philip Tonge, Ruta Lee, J. Pat O'Malley.

Touch of Evil (1958, Univ.). *d:* Orson Welles; *p:* Albert Zugsmith; *sc:* Orson Welles—*b/o* the novel *Badge of Evil* by Whit Masterson.

TANYA: Fortune-telling madam of a bordello in a Texas border town, as well as the mistress of a hulking, psychopathic cop who runs the town.

Charlton Heston, Janet Leigh, Orson Welles, Joseph Calleia, Akim Tamiroff, Ray Collins, Dennis Weaver, Zsa Zsa Gabor, Mercedes McCambridge, Joseph Cotten.

Judgment at Nuremberg (1961, UA). *d:* Stanley Kramer; *p:* Stanley Kramer (Roxlom); *sc:* Abby Mann—*b/o* the television play by Abby Mann.

MME. BERTHOLT: German general's aristocratic widow in whose home a U.S. judge lives when he's sent to post-WWII Germany to preside over the Nazi War Crimes Trials in an American court at Nuremberg.

Spencer Tracy, Burt Lancaster, Richard Widmark, Maximilian Schell, Judy Garland, Montgomery Clift, William Shatner, Edward Binns, Kenneth MacKenna, Werner Klemperer, Alan Baxter, Ray Teal, Virginia Christine, Karl Swenson, Sheila Bromley.

Just a Gigolo (1978, UA Classics). *d:* David Hemmings; *p:* Rolf Thiele (Leguan); *sc:* Joshua Sinclair.

BARONESS VON SEMERING: One of the women involved in the adventures of a young, aristocratic Prussian war veteran who becomes a gigolo in post-WWI Germany.

David Bowie, Sydne Rome, Kim Novak, David Hemmings, Maria Schell, Curt Jurgens, Erika Pluhar, Rudolf Schundler, Hilde Weissner, Werner Pochath, Bela Erny.

• In addition, Marlene Dietrich made cameo/guest appearances in the following feature films: *Follow the Boys* (1944, Univ.), *Jigsaw* (1949, UA), and *Paris When It Sizzles* (1964, Para.).

☆ KIRK DOUGLAS

Issur Danielovitch

b: Dec. 9, 1916, Amsterdam, N.Y.

"There are times when I am ashamed to be a member of the human race. This is one such occasion."

Colonel Dax (Kirk Douglas) commenting when WWI French soldiers are wrongly sentenced to death for cowardice in *Paths of Glory,* 1957.

The Strange Love of Martha Ivers (1946, Para.). *d:* Lewis Milestone; *p:* Hal B. Wallis (Hal B. Wallis Prod.); *sc:* Robert Rossen—*b/o* a story by Jack Patrick.

WALTER O'NEIL: Weak-kneed small-town D.A. who, along with his wife (a wealthy woman who as a child secretly murdered her aunt), is threatened with blackmail by a childhood friend.

Barbara Stanwyck, Van Heflin, Lizabeth Scott, Judith Anderson, Daryl Hickman, Ann Doran, Frank Orth, James Flavin, Mickey Kuhn, Chester D. Brown.

Out of the Past (1947, RKO). *d:* Jacques Tourneur; *p:* Warren Duff; *sc:* Geoffrey Homes—*b/o* the novel *Build My Gallows High* by Geoffrey Homes.

WHIT: Big-time criminal who, with his homicidal girlfriend, leads a former private detective–turned–gas station owner into a maze of murder and double-crosses.

Robert Mitchum, Jane Greer, Rhonda Fleming, Richard Webb, Steve Brodie, Virginia Huston, Paul Valentine, Dickie Moore, Ken Miles.

Mourning Becomes Electra (1947, RKO). *d:* Dudley Nichols; *p:* Dudley Nichols; *sc:* Dudley Nichols—*b/o* the play by Eugene O'Neill.

PETER NILES: Young Union Army officer in 1865 Massachusetts who has an ill-fated love affair with the daughter of an evil family that becomes involved in murder.

Rosalind Russell, Michael Redgrave, Raymond Massey, Katina Paxinou, Leo Genn, Nancy Coleman, Henry Hull, Sara Allgood, Thurston Hall, Walter Baldwin, Elizabeth Risdon, Jimmy Conlin, Emma Dunn, Clem Bevans.

I Walk Alone (1948, Para.). *d:* Byron Haskin; *p:* Hal B. Wallis (Hal B. Wallis Prod.); *sc:* Charles Schnee (adaptation by Robert Smith and John Bright)—*b/o* the play *Beggars Are Coming to Town* by Theodore Reeves.

NOLL TURNER: Unscrupulous nightclub owner–racketeer who, when his former Prohibition-era partner (who has taken a fourteen-year prison rap for him) is released, double-crosses him again.

Burt Lancaster, Lizabeth Scott, Wendell Corey, Kristine Miller, George Rigaud, Marc Lawrence, Mike Mazurki, Mickey Knox, Roger Neury.

The Walls of Jericho (1948, 20th-Fox). *d:* John M. Stahl; *p:* Lamar Trotti; *sc:* Lamar Trotti—*b/o* the novel by Paul Wellman.

TUCKER WEDGE: Newspaper publisher in 1908 Jericho, Kansas, who, at the urging of his conniving wife, starts a newspaper smear campaign against an old friend who's now the county prosecutor.

Cornel Wilde, Linda Darnell, Anne Baxter, Ann Dvorak, Marjorie Rambeau, Henry Hull, Colleen Townsend, Barton MacLane, William Tracy, Art Baker, Frank Ferguson, J. Farrell MacDonald, Will Wright.

My Dear Secretary (1948, UA). *d:* Charles Martin; *p:* Harry M. Popkin and Leo C. Popkin; *sc:* Charles Martin.

OWEN WATERBURY: Woman-chasing playboy writer who marries his secretary, then has marital problems when his novel is rejected by publishers but his wife writes a best-seller.

Laraine Day, Keenan Wynn, Helen Walker, Rudy Vallee, Florence Bates, Alan Mowbray, Grady Sutton, Irene Ryan, Gale Robbins, Virginia Hewitt, Russell Hicks.

A Letter to Three Wives (1948, 20th-Fox). *d:* Joseph L. Mankiewicz; *p:* Sol C. Siegel; *sc:* Joseph L. Mankiewicz (adaptation by Vera Caspary)—*b/o* the novel by John Klempner.

GEORGE PHIPPS: English-literature teacher whose wife, a radio soap-opera writer, is one of three wives who receive letters from the town flirt saying that she plans to run away with one of the wives' husbands—but doesn't reveal which one.

Jeanne Crain, Linda Darnell, Ann Sothern, Paul Douglas, Jeffrey Lynn, Connie Gilchrist, Florence Bates, Hobart Cavanaugh, Thelma Ritter, John Davidson, Carl Switzer.

Champion (1949, UA). *d:* Mark Robson; *p:* Stanley Kramer (Screen Plays Prod.); *sc:* Carl Foreman—*b/o* a story by Ring Lardner.

MIDGE KELLY*: Prizefighter who's a hero to the public—as he battles his way to the championship—but a vicious, selfish heel to those who really know him.

Marilyn Maxwell, Arthur Kennedy, Paul Stewart, Ruth Roman, Lola Albright, Luis Van Rooten, John Day, Harry Shannon.

Young Man with a Horn (1950, WB). *d:* Michael Curtiz; *p:* Jerry Wald; *sc:* Carl Foreman and Edmund H. North—*b/o* the novel by Dorothy Baker.

RICK MARTIN: Dedicated young jazz trumpet player in the Roaring '20s who rises to the top

---

*Received an Academy Award nomination as Best Actor for this role.

but, after a bad marriage to a selfish society girl, hits the skids.

Lauren Bacall, Doris Day, Hoagy Carmichael, Juano Hernandez, Jerome Cowan, Mary Beth Hughes, Nestor Paiva, Orley Lindgren, Walter Reed, Alex Gerry.

The Glass Menagerie (1950, WB). *d:* Irving Rapper; *p:* Jerry Wald and Charles K. Feldman; *sc:* Tennessee Williams and Peter Berneis—*b/o* the play by Tennessee Williams.

JIM O'CONNOR: Personable St. Louis warehouse worker who, when a fellow worker brings him home to dinner, helps the friend's crippled sister overcome her painful shyness and lack of self-confidence.

Jane Wyman, Gertrude Lawrence, Arthur Kennedy, Ralph Sanford, Ann Tyrrell, John Compton, Gertrude Graner, Sara Edwards, Louise Lorrimer, Cris Alcaide, Perdita Chandler.

Ace in the Hole (1951, Para.). *d:* Billy Wilder; *p:* Billy Wilder; *sc:* Billy Wilder, Lesser Samuels, and Walter Newman.

CHARLES TATUM: Conniving, down-on-his-luck reporter who, when a man is trapped in a cave near Albuquerque, delays the rescue efforts so that he can turn out a sensational story that will put him back in the big time.

Jan Sterling, Bob Arthur, Porter Hall, Frank Cady, Richard Benedict, Ray Teal, Lewis Martin, John Berkes, Frances Dominguez, Gene Evans, Harry Harvey, Bob Bumpas.

Along the Great Divide (1951, WB). *d:* Raoul Walsh; *p:* Anthony Veiller; *sc:* Walter Doniger and Lewis Meltzer—*b/o* a story by Walter Doniger.

LEN MERRICK: U.S. marshal who rescues from a lynch mob an old man accused of murder, then battles the elements and pursuers as he takes the prisoner across the Mojave Desert to stand trial.

Virginia Mayo, John Agar, Walter Brennan, Ray Teal, Hugh Sanders, Morris Ankrum, James Anderson, Charles Meredith.

Detective Story (1951, Para.). *d:* William Wyler; *p:* William Wyler (William Wyler); *sc:* Philip Yordan and Robert Wyler—*b/o* the play by Sidney Kingsley.

DET. JAMES McLEOD: Dedicated New York police detective with an almost psychopathic hatred of criminals—and particularly of a sleazy abortionist—who discovers that his own wife once had an abortion performed by this abortionist.

Eleanor Parker, William Bendix, Lee Grant, Bert Freed, Frank Faylen, Luis Van Rooten, Cathy O'Donnell, Horace McMahon, Warner Anderson, George Macready, Joseph Wiseman, Gladys George, Burt Mustin, Gerald Mohr.

The Big Trees (1952, WB). *d:* Felix Feist; *p:* Louis F. Edelman; *sc:* John Twist and James R. Webb—*b/o* a story by Kenneth Earl.

JIM FALLON: Unscrupulous lumberman in turn-of-the-century California who sets out to take over the giant redwood timberlands belonging to peaceful Quaker homesteaders but is finally won over to their side.

Eve Miller, Patrice Wymore, Edgar Buchanan, John Archer, Alan Hale Jr., Roy Roberts, Charles Meredith, Harry Cording, Ellen Corby.

The Big Sky (1952, RKO). *d:* Howard Hawks; *p:* Howard Hawks (Winchester); *sc:* Dudley Nichols—*b/o* the novel by A. B. Guthrie Jr.

DEAKINS: One of a pair of rugged Kentucky mountain men who head west in 1830 and join a fur-trading expedition on a keelboat going up the Missouri River into Blackfoot Indian country.

Dewey Martin, Elizabeth Threatt, Arthur Hunnicutt, Buddy Baer, Steven Geray, Hank Worden, Jim Davis, Booth Colman, Paul Frees, Frank de Kova.

The Bad and the Beautiful (1952, MGM). *d:* Vincente Minnelli; *p:* John Houseman; *sc:* Charles Schnee—*b/o* a story by George Bradshaw.

JONATHAN SHIELDS*: Hard-driving, ambitious movie producer who ruthlessly uses everyone—including his most successful director, screenwriter, and star—on the way to becoming one of Hollywood's top moviemakers.

Lana Turner, Walter Pidgeon, Dick Powell, Barry Sullivan, Gloria Grahame, Gilbert Roland, Leo G. Carroll, Vanessa Brown, Paul Stewart, Elaine Stewart, Sammy White, Kathleen Freeman, Robert Burton.

The Story of Three Loves (1953, MGM). *d:* Gotfried Reinhardt and Vincente Minnelli; *p:* Sidney Franklin; *sc:* John Collier, Jan Lustig, and George Froeschel—*b/o* stories by Arnold Phillips and Ladislas Vajda.

PIERRE NARVAL: Famous circus trapeze artist who retires when his female partner is killed while performing—but returns to the circus after he rescues a girl from suicide and trains her to be his new partner.

James Mason, Moira Shearer, Agnes Moorehead, Ethel Barrymore, Leslie Caron, Farley Granger, Ricky Nelson, Zsa Zsa Gabor, Pier Angeli, Richard Anderson.

The Juggler (1953, Col.). *d:* Edward Dmytryk; *p:* Stanley Kramer (Stanley Kramer); *sc:* Michael Blankfort—*b/o* his novel.

HANS MULLER: Once-famous German-Jewish juggler who, after surviving Nazi concentration camps (where his wife and children died), has trouble trying to build a new life in Israel.

Milly Vitale, Paul Stewart, Joey Walsh, Alf Kjellin, Beverly Washburn, Charles Lane, John Banner, Richard Benedict, Jay Adler, Shep Menkin.

Act of Love (1953, UA). *d:* Anatole Litvak; *p:* Anatole Litvak (Benagoss); *sc:* Irwin Shaw—*b/o* Alfred Hayes's novel *The Girl on the Via Flaminia*.

ROBERT TELLER: WWII American soldier in Paris whose love affair with a poor French girl tragically ends when she commits suicide because he's unable to get the required official permission to marry her.

Dany Robin, Barbara Laage, Robert Strauss, Gabrielle Dorziat, Gregoire Aslan, Martha Mercadier, Fernand Ledoux, Brigitte Bardot, George Mathews, Richard Benedict.

Ulysses (1954, Para.). *d:* Mario Camerini; *p:* Dino De Laurentiis, Carlo Ponti, and William Schorr (Lux); *sc:* Franco Brusati, Mario Camerini, Ennio de Concini, Hugh Gray, Ben Hecht, Ivo Perilli, and Irwin Shaw—*b/o* Homer's *Odyssey*.

ULYSSES: Mythological Greek king who, during his long odyssey back home from the Trojan War, encounters numerous obstacles—including the enchantress Circe, the murderous one-eyed Cyclops, and the sirens whose songs lure sailors to their death.

Silvano Mangano, Anthony Quinn, Rossana Podesta, Sylvie, Daniel Ivernel, Jacques Dumesnil.

20,000 Leagues Under the Sea (1954, Buena Vista). *d:* Richard Fleischer; *p:* Walt Disney (Walt Disney Prod.); *sc:* Earl Fenton—*b/o* the novel by Jules Verne.

NED LAND: Robust sailor-harpooner in the 1860s who, along with two scientists, becomes a prisoner aboard a futuristic cosmic-powered submarine called the *Nautilus* and commanded by the mysterious Captain Nemo.

James Mason, Paul Lukas, Peter Lorre, Robert J. Wilkie, Carleton Young, Ted de Corsia, Percy Helton, Ted Cooper, Edward Marr, Fred Graham, J. M. Kerrigan.

The Racers (1955, 20th-Fox). *d:* Henry Hathaway; *p:* Julian Blaustein; *sc:* Charles Kaufman—*b/o* the novel by Hans Reusch.

GINO: Ambitious Italian bus driver who turns to sports-car racing and, while experiencing numerous ups and downs competing on various famed European runways, becomes a champion.

Bella Darvi, Gilbert Roland, Cesar Romero, Lee J. Cobb, Katy Jurado, Charles Goldner, John Hudson, George Dolenz, Agnes Laury.

---

*Received an Academy Award nomination as Best Actor for this role.

Man without a Star (1955, Univ.). *d:* King Vidor; *p:* Aaron Rosenberg; *sc:* Borden Chase and D. D. Beauchamp—*b/o* the novel by Dee Linford.

DEMPSEY RAE: Wandering cowpoke who helps a ruthless female ranch owner fight neighboring ranchers in a barbed-wire range war, but—after he's beaten up by her henchmen—changes sides.

Jeanne Crain, Claire Trevor, William Campbell, Richard Boone, Jay C. Flippen, Myrna Hansen, Mara Corday, Sheb Wooley, George Wallace, Paul Birch, Roy Barcroft, William "Bill" Phillips.

The Indian Fighter (1955, UA). *d:* Andre de Toth; *p:* William Schorr (Bryna); *sc:* Frank Davis and Ben Hecht—*b/o* a story by Ben Kadish.

JOHNNY HAWKS: Veteran Indian fighter and Army scout in the 1870s who leads a wagon train bound for Oregon through territory where the Sioux Indians are on the rampage.

Elsa Martinelli, Walter Abel, Walter Matthau, Diana Douglas, Eduard Franz, Lon Chaney, Alan Hale, Elisha Cook, William Phipps, Ray Teal, Frank Cady, Hank Worden, Lane Chandler.

Lust for Life (1956, MGM). *d:* Vincente Minnelli; *p:* John Houseman; *sc:* Norman Corwin—*b/o* the novel by Irving Stone.

VINCENT VAN GOGH*: Young nineteenth-century Dutch evangelist who turns to painting but, after suffering from fits of depression and insanity, shoots himself at the age of thirty-seven.

Anthony Quinn, James Donald, Pamela Brown, Everett Sloan, Henry Daniell, Madge Kennedy, Lionel Jeffries, Laurence Naismith, Eric Pohlmann, William Phipps, Jay Adler.

Gunfight at the OK Corral (1957, Para.). *d:* John Sturges; *p:* Hal B. Wallis (Hal B. Wallis Prod.); *sc:* Leon Uris—*b/o* George Scullin's article "The Killer."

DOC HOLLIDAY: Aristocratic Virginian and ex-dentist who, after becoming a dissolute gambler, helps lawman Wyatt Earp wipe out the notorious Clanton gang in the famous gun battle at the OK Corral in Tombstone, Arizona, on October 26, 1881.

Burt Lancaster, Rhonda Fleming, Jo Van Fleet, John Ireland, Lyle Bettger, Frank Faylen, Earl Holliman, Ted De Corsia, Dennis Hopper, Whit Bissell, DeForest Kelley, Martin Milner, Kenneth Tobey, Lee Van Cleef, Jack Elam.

Top Secret Affair (1957, WB). *d:* H. C. Potter; *p:* Milton Sperling and Martin Rackin; *sc:* Roland Kibbee and Allan Scott—*b/o* characters from the novel *Melville Goodwin, U.S.A.* by John P. Marquand.

MAJ. GEN. MELVILLE GOODWIN: Tough U.S. Army general who, when he's nominated for an important diplomatic post, is opposed by a glamorous, powerful magazine publisher—until she falls in love with him.

Susan Hayward, Paul Stewart, Jim Backus, John Cromwell, Roland Winters, A. E. Gould-Porter, Michael Fox, Frank Gerstle, Charles Lane.

Paths of Glory (1957, UA). *d:* Stanley Kubrick; *p:* James B. Harris (Harris–Kubrick); *sc:* Stanley Kubrick, Calder Willingham, and Jim Thompson—*b/o* the novel by Humphrey Cobb.

COLONEL DAX: Tough but compassionate WWI French Army colonel who, after troops under his command at Verdun fail to take an impregnable German fortress called the Ant Hill, defends three scapegoat soldiers court-martialed for cowardice.

Ralph Meeker, Adolphe Menjou, George Macready, Wayne Morris, Richard Anderson, Joseph Turkel, Timothy Carey, Peter Capell, Susanne Christian, Bert Freed, Emile Meyer, John Stein.

The Vikings (1958, UA). *d:* Richard Fleischer; *p:* Jerry Bresler (Bryna); *sc:* Calder Willingham (adaptation by Dale Wasserman)—*b/o* Edison Marshall's novel *The Viking*.

EINAR: Warlike Viking prince who kidnaps a Welsh princess and holds her for ransom but is killed in a fight with a slave (actually the heir to the English throne) who helps the princess escape.

Tony Curtis, Ernest Borgnine, Janet Leigh, James Donald, Alexander Knox, Frank Thring, Maxine Audley, Eileen Way, Edric Connor, Dandy Nichols, Per Buchhij, Almut Berg.

Last Train from Gun Hill (1959, Para.). *d:* John Sturges; *p:* Hal B. Wallis (Hal B. Wallis/Bryna); *sc:* James Poe—*b/o* a story by Les Crutchfield.

MATT MORGAN: Marshal of a small Oklahoma town who, after his Indian wife is raped and murdered, discovers that one of the killers is the son of a powerful cattle baron who's an old friend.

Anthony Quinn, Carolyn Jones, Earl Holliman, Brad Dexter, Brian Hutton, Ziva Rodann, Bing Russell, Val Avery, Walter Sande, Lars Henderson.

The Devil's Disciple (1959, UA). *d:* Guy Hamilton; *p:* Harold Hecht (Hecht–Hill–Lancaster/Brynaprod); *sc:* John Dighton and Roland Kibbee—*b/o* the play by George Bernard Shaw.

RICHARD (DICK) DUDGEON: Roguish American in New England during the Revolutionary War who almost is hanged by the British General "Gentleman Johnny" Burgoyne when he lets the British mistakenly think that he's a wanted rebel pastor.

---

*Received an Academy Award nomination as Best Actor for this role.

Burt Lancaster, Laurence Olivier, Janette Scott, Eva Le Gallienne, Harry Andrews, Basil Sydney, George Rose, Neil McCallum, Mervyn Johns, David Horne.

Strangers When We Meet (1960, Col.). *d:* Richard Quine; *p:* Richard Quine (Bryna–Quine); *sc:* Evan Hunter—*b/o* his novel.
LARRY COE: Successful Beverly Hills architect who falls in love with a beautiful married neighbor, then is faced with choosing between her and his family and career.
Kim Novak, Ernie Kovacs, Barbara Rush, Walter Matthau, Virginia Bruce, Kent Smith, Helen Gallagher, John Bryant, Nancy Kovak, Paul Picerni, Bart Patton.

Spartacus (1960, Univ.). *d:* Stanley Kubrick; *p:* Edward Lewis and Kirk Douglas (Bryna); *sc:* Dalton Trumbo—*b/o* the novel by Howard Faust.
SPARTACUS: Thracian gladiator in 73 B.C. Rome who escapes from slavery and successfully leads an army of slaves against Roman legions but is finally crushed by the mighty Imperial Roman Army.
Laurence Olivier, Jean Simmons, Tony Curtis, Charles Laughton, Peter Ustinov, John Gavin, Nina Foch, Herbert Lom, John Ireland, John Dall, Charles McGraw, Joanna Barnes, Woody Strode, Paul Lambert, Nicholas Dennis, Robert J. Wilkie, John Hoyt.

The Last Sunset (1961, Univ.). *d:* Robert Aldrich; *p:* Eugene Frenke and Edward Lewis (Brynaprod); *sc:* Dalton Trumbo—*b/o* the novel *Sundown at Crazy Horse* by Howard Rigsby.
BRENDON O'MALLEY: Cowboy wanted for murder who, while on a cattle drive from Mexico to Texas, vies for the love of a girl with two other men—her drunken English husband and a lawman determined to bring the killer to justice.
Rock Hudson, Dorothy Malone, Joseph Cotten, Carol Lynley, Neville Brand, Regis Toomey, Rad Fulton, Adam Williams, Jack Elam, John Shay.

Town without Pity (1961, UA). *d:* Gottfried Reinhardt; *p:* Gottfried Reinhardt (Mirisch/Gloria); *sc:* Silvia Reinhardt and Georg Hurdalek—*b/o* Manfred Gregor's novel *The Verdict*.
MAJ. STEVE GARRETT: U.S. Army officer-lawyer who is assigned to defend four American G.I.s in Germany when they are accused of raping a young German girl.
Christine Kaufmann, E. G. Marshall, Robert Blake, Richard Jaeckel, Frank Sutton, Mal Sondock, Barbara Ruetting, Hans Nielsen, Ingrid Van Bergen.

Lonely Are the Brave (1962, Univ.). *d:* David Miller; *p:* Edward Lewis (Joel/Kirk Douglas); *sc:*

Dalton Trumbo—*b/o* the novel *Brave Cowboy* by Edward Abbey.
JACK BURNS: Rebellious loner cowboy in Arizona who lives by his own code of honor and refuses to conform to modern-day civilization but is finally beaten when he escapes from jail and is hunted down and killed by a posse.
Gena Rowlands, Walter Matthau, Michael Kane, Carroll O'Connor, William Schallert, Karl Swenson, George Kennedy, Dan Sheridan, William Mims, Bill Raisch, Lalo Rios.

Two Weeks in Another Town (1962, MGM). *d:* Vincente Minnelli; *p:* John Houseman; *sc:* Charles Schnee—*b/o* the novel by Irwin Shaw.
JACK ANDRUS: Ex-alcoholic, has-been movie actor who gets a chance for a comeback when the director of an in-trouble American film being shot in Rome becomes ill and asks the actor to take over the picture and try to save it.
Edward G. Robinson, Cyd Charisse, George Hamilton, Dahlia Lavi, Claire Trevor, James Gregory, Rosanna Schiaffino, George Macready, Mino Doro, Eric Von Stroheim Jr., Leslie Uggams.

The Hook (1963, MGM). *d:* George Seaton; *p:* William Perlberg (Perlberg–Seaton); *sc:* Henry Denker—*b/o* the novel *L'Hamecon* by Vahe Katcha.
SGT. P. J. BRISCOE: Tough Korean War Army sergeant—one of three American G.I.s escaping from Korea on a supply freighter who are ordered to execute a North Korean prisoner but can't bring themselves to do it.
Robert Walker Jr., Nick Adams, Enrique Magalona, Nehemiah Persoff, Mark Miller, John Bleifer.

For Love or Money (1963, Univ.). *d:* Michael Gordon; *p:* Robert Arthur; *sc:* Larry Marks and Michael Morris.
DEKE GENTRY: Playboy-type corporation lawyer who is hired by a wealthy widow to handle the estates of her three rebellious daughters—and, while he's at it, to find suitable husbands for them.
Mitzi Gaynor, Gig Young, Thelma Ritter, Leslie Parrish, Julie Newmar, William Bendix, Richard Sargent, William Windom, Elizabeth MacRae, Alvy Moore, Jose Gonzales Gonzales, Don McGowan, Billy Halop, Joey Faye.

The List of Adrian Messenger (1963, Univ.). *d:* John Huston; *p:* Edward Lewis (Joel); *sc:* Anthony Veiller—*b/o* the novel by Philip MacDonald.
GEORGE BROUGHAM: Member of an aristocratic British family and a master of bizarre disguises who turns out to be the mass murderer who has been methodically eliminating a long list of people in order to inherit an estate.

George C. Scott, Dana Wynter, Clive Brook, Gladys Cooper, Herbert Marshall, John Merivale, Marcel Dalio, John Huston, Bernard Fox, Tony Curtis, Burt Lancaster, Robert Mitchum, Frank Sinatra.

Seven Days in May (1964, Para.). *d:* John Frankenheimer; *p:* Edward Lewis (Seven Arts–Joel); *sc:* Rod Serling—*b/o* the novel by Fletcher Knebel and Charles W. Bailey II.

COL. MARTIN CASEY: U.S. Marine colonel who, when he discovers that his chief of staff is scheming to overthrow the government because the president has signed a nuclear disarmament treaty with Russia, helps prevent the coup from taking place.

Burt Lancaster, Fredric March, Ava Gardner, Edmond O'Brien, Martin Balsam, George Macready, Whit Bissell, Hugh Marlowe, Richard Anderson, Andrew Duggan, John Larkin, Malcolm Atterbury, John Houseman.

In Harm's Way (1965, Para.). *d:* Otto Preminger; *p:* Otto Preminger (Sigma); *sc:* Wendell Mayes—*b/o* the novel by James Bassett.

CMDR. PAUL EDDINGTON: Bitter, cuckolded WWII Navy officer in the Pacific who rapes a young nurse, then—filled with remorse—sacrifices himself flying a suicide mission against the Japanese.

John Wayne, Patricia Neal, Tom Tryon, Paula Prentiss, Brandon De Wilde, Jill Haworth, Dana Andrews, Stanley Holloway, Burgess Meredith, Franchot Tone, Henry Fonda, Patrick O'Neal, Carroll O'Connor, Slim Pickens, James Mitchum, George Kennedy, Bruce Cabot, Hugh O'Brian, Tod Andrews, Larry Hagman, Christopher George.

The Heroes of Telemark (1965, Col.). *d:* Anthony Mann; *p:* S. Benjamin Fisz (Benton); *sc:* Ivan Moffat and Ben Barzman—*b/o* the articles "Skis Against the Atom" by Knut Haukelid and "But for These Men" by John Drummond.

DR. ROLF PEDERSEN: Oslo University scientist who heads a group of WWII Norwegian resistance fighters to destroy a Nazi plant producing "heavy water"—an ingredient essential for developing an atomic bomb.

Richard Harris, Ulla Jacobsson, Michael Redgrave, David Weston, Anton Diffring, Eric Porter, Mervyn Johns, Jennifer Hilary, Barry Jones, Geoffrey Keen, Maurice Denham.

Cast a Giant Shadow (1966, UA). *d:* Melville Shavelson; *p:* Melville Shavelson and Michael Wayne (Mirisch/Llenroc/Batjac); *sc:* Melville Shavelson—*b/o* the biography of Col. David Marcus by Ted Berkman.

COL. DAVID "MICKEY" MARCUS: American colonel who is persuaded by the Israeli government in 1947 to train and command an army to defend the country from the Arabs after the British withdrawal from Palestine.

Yul Brynner, Senta Berger, Frank Sinatra, John Wayne, Angie Dickinson, Luther Adler, Stathis Giallelis, James Donald, Gordon Jackson, Haym Topol, Gary Merrill, Jeremy Kemp, Sean Barrett, Frank Latimore.

Is Paris Burning? (1966, Para.). *d:* René Clement; *p:* Paul Graetz (Transcontinental–Marianne); *sc:* Gore Vidal and Francis Coppola—*b/o* the book by Larry Collins and Dominique Lapierre.

GEN. GEORGE S. PATTON: Famed WWII American general who, when an envoy of the French underground forces in 1944 asks him to prevent the Nazis from burning Paris, sends him to an officer who helps set in motion the Allied liberation of the city.

Jean-Paul Belmondo, Charles Boyer, Leslie Caron, Jean-Pierre Cassel, George Chakiris, Alain Delon, Glenn Ford, Gert Frobe, E. G. Marshall, Yves Montand, Anthony Perkins, Simone Signoret, Robert Stack, Marie Versini, Skip Ward, Orson Welles.

The Way West (1967, UA). *d:* Andrew V. McLaglen; *p:* Harold Hecht (Harold Hecht); *sc:* Ben Madlow and Mitch Linderman—*b/o* the novel by A. B. Guthrie Jr.

SEN. WILLIAM J. TADLOCK: Obsessive, fanatical visionary in 1843 who leads a wagon train westward from Independence, Missouri, to Oregon, where he plans to build cities.

Robert Mitchum, Richard Widmark, Lola Albright, Sally Field, Stubby Kaye, William Lundigan, Roy Barcroft, Jack Elam, Patric Knowles, Ken Murray, Nick Cravat, Harry Carey Jr., Roy Glenn.

The War Wagon (1967, Univ.). *d:* Burt Kennedy; *p:* Marvin Schwartz (Batjac/Marvin Schwartz); *sc:* Clair Huffaker—*b/o* his novel *Badman.*

LOMAX: Two-fisted gunslinger who teams up with a rugged ex-con rancher and three confederates to ambush a half-million-dollar gold shipment being transported by a crooked mine owner in a special armored stagecoach called the War Wagon.

John Wayne, Howard Keel, Robert Walker, Keenan Wynn, Bruce Cabot, Gene Evans, Joanna Barnes, Bruce Dern, Sheb Wooley, Frank McGrath, Hal Needham.

A Lovely Way to Die (1968, Univ.). *d:* David Lowell Rich; *p:* Richard Lewis; *sc:* A. J. Russell.

JIM SCHUYLER: Former cop–turned–private eye who, when he's hired as a bodyguard for a beautiful young woman suspected of murdering her husband, falls in love with her and sets out to prove that she's innocent.

Sylva Koscina, Eli Wallach, Kenneth Haigh, Martyn Green, Sharon Farrell, Ruth White, Doris Roberts, Carey Nairnes, Meg Myles, Dana Elcar, Dolph Sweet, Conrad Bain.

The Brotherhood (1969, Para.). *d:* Martin Ritt; *p:* Kirk Douglas (Brotherhood Co.); *sc:* Lewis John Carlino.

FRANK GINETTA: Middle-aged, old-guard Mafia gangster who, after killing his younger brother's double-crossing father-in-law and fleeing to Sicily, is confronted by the brother, who's been ordered by the syndicate to execute him.

Alex Cord, Irene Papas, Luther Adler, Susan Strasberg, Murray Hamilton, Eduardo Ciannelli, Joe De Santis, Connie Scott, Val Avery, Alan Hewitt.

The Arrangement (1969, WB). *d:* Elia Kazan; *p:* Elia Kazan (Athena); *sc:* Elia Kazan—*b/o* his novel.

EDDIE ANDERSON: Madison Avenue ad exec who, after getting fed up with the rat race and unsuccessfully attempting suicide, reevaluates his emotionally unsatisfying life.

Faye Dunaway, Deborah Kerr, Richard Boone, Hume Cronyn, Michael Higgins, John Randolph Jones, Carol Rossen, Anne Hegira, William Hansen, Charles Drake, Harold Gould, E. J. Andre, Michael Murphy.

There Was a Crooked Man (1970, WB–Seven Arts). *d:* Joseph L. Mankiewicz; *p:* Joseph L. Mankiewicz; *sc:* David Newman and Robert Benton.

PARIS PITMAN JR.: Ruthless bandit-murderer in an 1833 Arizona prison who escapes but—at the moment he finds the $500,000 he has stashed away—is killed by a rattlesnake.

Henry Fonda, Hume Cronyn, Warren Oates, Burgess Meredith, John Randolph, Arthur O'Connell, Martin Gabel, Michael Blodgett, Alan Hale, Lee Grant, Bert Freed.

A Gunfight (1971, MGM). *d:* Lamont Johnson; *p:* Ronnie Lubin and Harold Jack Bloom (Harvest–Thoroughbred–Bryna); *sc:* Harold Jack Bloom.

WILL TENNERAY: One of a pair of weary veteran gunslingers who, for money, stage a gunfight in a bullring in a small Southwestern town where townspeople buy tickets and bet on who will win.

Johnny Cash, Jane Alexander, Raf Vallone, Karen Black, Eric Douglas, Philip Mead, John Wallwork, Dana Elcar, Robert J. Wilkie, Keith Carradine, Paul Lambert.

The Light at the Edge of the World (1971, Nat. Gen.). *d:* Kevin Billington; *p:* Kirk Douglas (Bryna/Jet/Triumfilm); *sc:* Tom Rowe—*b/o* the novel by Jules Verne.

DENTON: American drifter and keeper of a lighthouse near Cape Horn during the 1860s who battles a sadistic pirate captain when he tries to take over the lighthouse in a scheme to lure ships to their doom.

Yul Brynner, Samantha Eggar, Jean Claude Drouot, Fernando Rey, Renato Salvatori, Massimo Ranieri, Tito Garcia, Raul Castro.

Catch Me a Spy (1971, Rank). *d:* Dick Clement; *p:* Steven Pallos and Pierre Braunberger (Ludgate/Capitole/Bryna); *sc:* Dick Clement and Ian La Frenais—*b/o* the novel by George Marton and Tibor Meray.

ANDREJ: British agent posing as a Romanian waiter who, while smuggling Russian documents out of Romania into England, falls for the wife of a Russian spy.

Marlene Jobert, Trevor Howard, Tom Courtenay, Patrick Mower, Bernadette Lafont, Bernard Blier, Sacha Pitoeff, Richard Pearson, Garfield Morgan.

Scalawag (1973, Para.). *d:* Kirk Douglas; *p:* Anne Douglas (Bryna/Inex–Oceania); *sc:* Albert Maltz and Ben Barzman—*b/o* a story by Robert Louis Stevenson.

PEG: Roguish but good-hearted peg-legged pirate in 1840 Mexico who befriends a young boy as they try to get their hands on a hidden treasure.

Mark Lester, Neville Brand, George Eastman, Don Stroud, Lesley-Anne Down, Phil Brown.

Jacqueline Susann's Once Is Not Enough (1975, Para.). *d:* Guy Green; *p:* Howard W. Koch (Sujac/Aries); *sc:* Julius J. Epstein—*b/o* the novel by Jacqueline Susann.

MIKE WAYNE: Has-been Hollywood movie producer whose daughter—a nineteen-year-old with a father fixation—is corrupted by his circle of sexually promiscuous friends.

Alexis Smith, David Janssen, George Hamilton, Melina Mercouri, Gary Conway, Brenda Vaccaro, Deborah Raffin, Lillian Randolph.

Posse (1975, Para.). *d:* Kirk Douglas; *p:* Kirk Douglas (Bryna); *sc:* William Roberts and Christopher Knopf—*b/o* a story by Christopher Knopf.

HOWARD NIGHTINGALE: Ruthless, conniving U.S. Marshal in 1890s Texas who, when he tries to advance his campaign for the U.S. Senate by capturing a notorious outlaw, winds up being outfoxed by the wily badman.

Bruce Dern, Bo Hopkins, James Stacy, Luke Askew, David Canary, Alfonso Arau, Katharine Woodville, Mark Roberts, Beth Brickell.

The Chosen (1977, AIP). *d:* Alberto De Martino, *p:* Edmondo Amati (Samuel Z. Arkoff); *sc:* Sergio Donati, Alberto De Martino, and Michael Robson.

ROBERT CAINE: Nuclear-power executive who comes to the horrifying realization that his son is actually the Devil—whose mission is to destroy the world through nuclear power.

Simon Ward, Agostino Belli, Anthony Quayle, Virginia McKenna, Alexander Knox, Ivo Garrani, Adolfo Celli, Romolo Valli.

The Fury (1978, 20th-Fox). *d:* Brian De Palma; *p:* Ron Preissman (Frank Yablans); *sc:* John Farris—*b/o* his novel.

PETER SANZA: Man who, when his son with telekinetic powers is kidnaped by a super-secret government agency, tries desperately to save him from being used and possibly destroyed.

John Cassavetes, Carrie Snodgress, Amy Irving, Fiona Lewis, Andrew Stevens, Carol Rossen, Charles Durning, Joyce Easton, William Finley, J. Patrick McNamara, Bernie Kuby.

The Villain (1978, Col.). *d:* Hal Needham; *p:* Mort Engelberg; *sc:* Robert G. Kane.

CACTUS JACK: Inept Western outlaw (he reads dime Western novels to learn how to be a badman) who is hired to steal a safe full of money that a voluptuous young woman is transporting across Arizona's Monument Valley to her father.

Ann-Margret, Arnold Schwarzenegger, Paul Lynde, Foster Brooks, Ruth Buzzi, Jack Elam, Strother Martin, Robert Tessier.

Saturn 3 (1979, Associated Film). *d:* Stanley Donen; *p:* Stanley Donen (Lord Lew Grade/Elliott Kastner); *sc:* Martin Amis—*b/o* the story by John Barry.

ADAM: Futuristic space scientist who, besides his sexy female assistant (named Eve), is the sole inhabitant of one of Saturn's moons—until a villainous space pilot and his weird robot named Hector arrive.

Farrah Fawcett, Harvey Keitel, Douglas Lambert, Ed Bishop, Christopher Muncke.

Home Movies (1980, UA Classics). *d:* Brian De Palma; *p:* Brian De Palma, Jack Temchin, and Gil Adler; *sc:* Robert Harders, Gloria Norris, Kim Ambler, Dana Edelman, Stephen LeMay, and Charles Loventhal—*b/o* a story by Brian De Palma.

DR. TUTTLE: Egocentric college professor–film director who tries to help a teen-age boy—who's shooting an amateur film—find himself and not just wind up as "an extra in his own life."

Nancy Allen, Keith Gordon, Gerrit Graham, Vincent Gardenia, Mary Davenport.

The Final Countdown (1980, UA). *d:* Don Taylor; *p:* Peter Vincent Douglas; *sc:* David Ambrose, Gerry Davis, Thomas Hunter, and Peter Powell.

CAPT. MATTHEW YELLAND: Skipper of the nuclear-powered aircraft carrier *Nimitz* who—when the ship enters a time warp and winds up in the Pacific in December 1941—must decide whether to try to prevent the Japanese sneak attack on Pearl Harbor.

Martin Sheen, Katharine Ross, James Farentino, Ron O'Neal, Charles Durning, Victor Mohica, James C. Lawrence, Soon-Teck Oh, Alvin Ing, Mark Thomas, Dan Fitzgerald, Phil Philbin.

The Man from Snowy River (1983, 20th-Fox). *d:* George Miller; *p:* Geoff Burrowes (Michael Edgley/Cambridge); *sc:* John Dixon and Fred Cul Cullen—*b/o* the poem by A. B. ("Banjo") Paterson.

(Dual role) HARRISON: Wealthy rancher in Australia whose young daughter falls in love with an eighteen-year-old boy who—in order to lay claim to his late father's mountain home—proves himself a man by rounding up a pack of wild horses.

SPUR: Old, gimpy gold prospector in Australia (wounded years ago by his jealous rancher brother, Harrison) whose late partner's eighteen-year-old son falls in love with Harrison's daughter.

Jack Thompson, Tom Burlinson, Sigrid Thornton, Lorraine Bayly, Chris Haywood, Tony Bonner, Gus Mercurio, Terence Donovan, June Jago.

Eddie Macon's Run (1983, Univ.). *d:* Jeff Kanew; *p:* Louis A. Stroller (Martin Bregman Productions); *sc:* Jeff Kanew—*b/o* the novel by James McLendon.

CARL "BUSTER" MARZACK: Texas lawman who relentlessly pursues an escaped convict across 108 miles of Texas desert land as the convict tries to reach Mexico to join his wife and son.

John Schneider, Lee Purcell, Leah Ayres.

☆ CLINT EASTWOOD

Clinton Eastwood Jr.

b: May 31, 1930, San Francisco, Cal.

"Go ahead. Make my day."

Det. Dirty Harry Callahan (Clint Eastwood) urging an armed punk to make a play so he can blast him with his Magnum in Sudden Impact, 1983.

Revenge of the Creature (1955, Univ.). *d:* Jack Arnold; *p:* William Alland; *sc:* Martin Berkeley—*b/o* a story by William Alland.
Lab technician who misplaces some white mice.
John Agar, Lori Nelson, John Bromfield, Robert B. Williams, Nestor Paiva, Grandon Rhodes, Dave Willock.

Francis in the Navy (1955, Univ.). *d:* Arthur Lubin; *p:* Stanley Rubin; *sc:* Devery Freeman—*b/o* characters created by David Stern.
JONESY: One of the sailors who become involved with a talking mule named Francis who is mistakenly drafted into the Navy.
Donald O'Connor, Martha Hyer, Richard Erdman, Jim Backus, Myrna Hansen, Paul Burke, David Janssen, Martin Milner.

Lady Godiva (1955, Univ.). *d:* Arthur Lubin; *p:* Robert Arthur; *sc:* Oscar Brodney.
Billed as "FIRST SAXON": Saxon in medieval times who is involved in the battle between the Saxons and the Normans.
Maureen O'Hara, George Nader, Rex Reason, Victor McLaglen, Vic Morrow, Eduard Franz, Torin Thatcher.

Tarantula (1955, Univ.). *d:* Jack Arnold; *p:* William Alland; *sc:* Martin Berkeley—*b/o* a story by Jack Arnold and Robert M. Fresco.
Courageous U.S. Air Force pilot who leads a squadron of fighters in an attempt to napalm a gigantic tarantula that is terrorizing the countryside.
John Agar, Mara Corday, Leo G. Carroll, Nestor Paiva, Ross Elliott, Ed Rand.

Never Say Goodbye (1956, Univ.). *d:* Jerry Hopper; *p:* Albert J. Cohen; *sc:* Charles Hoffman—*b/o* the play *Come Prima Meglio Di Prima* by Luigi Pirandello.
WILL: Laboratory assistant whose doctor boss, along with the doctor's young daughter, reconciles with the wife the doctor walked out on years ago.
Rock Hudson, Cornell Borchers, George Sanders, Ray Collins, David Janssen, Shelley Fabares.

The First Traveling Saleslady (1956, RKO). *d:* Arthur Lubin; *p:* Arthur Lubin; *sc:* Stephen Longstreet and Devery Freeman.
JACK RICE: Young westerner in 1897 who falls for the blonde secretary of a New York corset designer who has come out West to make her fortune.
Ginger Rogers, Barry Nelson, Carol Channing, Brian Keith, James Arness, Robert Simon, Frank Wilcox, John Eldredge, Edward Cassidy, Bill Hale, Kate Drain Lawson.

Star in the Dust (1956, Univ.). *d:* Charles Hass; *p:* Albert Zugsmith; *sc:* Oscar Brodney—*b/o* the novel by Len Leighton.
Ranch hand involved in a sheriff's battle to bring in a professional killer who has murdered three farmers.
John Agar, Mamie Van Doren, Richard Boone, Lief Erickson, Colleen Gray, James Gleason, Henry Morgan.

Escapade in Japan (1957, RKO/Univ.). *d:* Arthur Lubin; *p:* Arthur Lubin; *sc:* Winston Miller.
DUMBO: U.S. serviceman in Tokyo who gives helpful advice to two boys—one American and one Japanese—as they search for the American boy's parents.
Teresa Wright, Cameron Mitchell, Jon Provost, Roger Nakagawa, Philip Ober.

Lafayette Escadrille (1958, WB). *d:* William A. Wellman; *p:* William A. Wellman; *sc:* A. S. Fleischman—*b/o* a story by William A. Wellman.
GEORGE MOSELEY: One of the American fighter pilots in the famed Lafayette Escadrille—the volunteer American air squadron that served in France in World War I.
Tab Hunter, Etchika Choureau, Bill Wellman Jr., Jody McCrae, Dennis Devine, Marcel Dalio, David Janssen, Paul Fix, Will Hutchins, Tom Laughlin, Brett Halsey, Henry Nakamura, Raymond Bailey.

Ambush at Cimarron Pass (1958, 20th-Fox). *d:* Jodie Copeland; *p:* Herbert E. Mendelson (Regal); *sc:* Richard G. Taylor and John K. Butler.
KEITH WILLIAMS: Ex–Confederate soldier who, when his rancher boss turns up with a group of Union soldiers to ward off an Apache attack, bitterly resents the Union officer in charge but later learns to respect him.
Scott Brady, Margia Dean, Baynes Barron, William Vaughan, Ken Mayer, John Manier, Keith Richards, John Merrick, Frank Grestle, Dirk London, Irving Bacon, Desmond Slattery.

A Fistful of Dollars (1964, UA). *d:* Sergio Leone; *p:* Arrigo Colombo and Giorgio Papi (Jolly/Constantin/Ocean); *sc:* Sergio Leone and Duccio Tessari—*b/o* the story *Yojimbo* by Akiro Kurosawa.

THE MAN WITH NO NAME: Cigar-smoking, gun-slinging stranger (with no name) who cleans up on two rival gangs that are battling for control of a Mexican border town and the money to be made from selling guns and liquor to the Mexicans and Indians.

Marianne Koch, John Wells, W. Lukschy, S. Rupp, Antonio Prieto, Jose Calvo, Margherita Lozano, Daniel Martin.

For a Few Dollars More (1965, UA). *d:* Sergio Leone; *p:* Alberto Grimaldi (PEA/Gonzales/Constantin); *sc:* Luciano Vincenzoni and Sergio Leone—*b/o* a story by Fulvio Morsella and Sergio Leone.

THE STRANGER: Steely-eyed, cigar-smoking bounty hunter in the post–Civil War Southwest who forms an uneasy alliance with an ex–Confederate colonel to hunt down the cutthroat bank robber who killed the colonel's sister.

Lee Van Cleef, Gian Maria Volonte, Rosemary Dexter, Mara Krup, Klaus Kinski, Mario Brega, Aldo Sambrel.

The Good, the Bad, and the Ugly (1966, UA). *d:* Sergio Leone; *p:* Alberto Grimaldi (PEA); *sc:* Age Scarpelli, Sergio Leone, and Luciano Vincenzoni.

THE STRANGER (BLONDY): Mysterious, cigar-smoking stranger who joins forces with a Mexican bandit and a sadistic bounty hunter to search for $200,000 in a cash box buried in an unmarked grave during the Civil War.

Eli Wallach, Lee Van Cleef, Aldo Giuffre, Mario Brega, Luigi Pistilli, Rada Rassimony, Enzio Petito.

The Witches (1967, UA). *d:* Vittorio De Sica (for Eastwood segment only); *p:* Dino De Laurentiis (Dino De Laurentiis); *sc:* Cesare Zavattini, Fabio Carpi, and Enzio Muzzi (for Eastwood segment only).

Billed as "HUSBAND": Dull, straight-laced banker whose bored Italian wife fantasizes that he has to compete for her affections with Flash Gordon, Batman, Diabolik, and Mandrake the Magician.

For Eastwood segment only: *Silvana Mangano,* Armando Bottin, Gianni Gori, Paolo Gozlino, Angelo Santi, Piero Torrisi.

Hang 'em High (1968, UA). *d:* Ted Post; *p:* Leonard Freeman (Malpaso/Leonard Freeman); *sc:* Leonard Freeman and Mel Goldberg.

JED COOPER: Cowboy who, when he's wrongly accused of murder, is lynched by vigilantes but manages to survive and seek revenge against the nine men responsible.

Inger Stevens, Ed Begley, Pat Hingle, Arlene Golonka, James MacArthur, Ruth White, Ben Johnson, Charles McGraw, Bruce Dern, Alan Hale Jr., Dennis Hopper, Bob Steele.

Coogan's Bluff (1968, Univ.). *d:* Don Siegel; *p:* Don Siegel; *sc:* Herman Miller, Dean Riesner, and Howard Rodman—*b/o* a story by Herman Miller.

WALT COOGAN: Arizona deputy sheriff who, after he's sent to New York City to extradite a wanted murderer, finds it necessary—when the prisoner escapes—to resort to some rough-and-ready Western tactics in order to recapture him.

Lee J. Cobb, Susan Clark, Tisha Sterling, Don Stroud, Betty Field, Tom Tully, Melodie Johnson, James Edwards, Rudy Diaz, David F. Doyle, Louis Zorich, James Gavin.

Where Eagles Dare (1969, MGM). *d:* Brian Hutton; *p:* Elliott Kastner (Winkast); *sc:* Alistair MacLean.

LT. MORRIS SCHAFFER: American Army lieutenant and right-hand man of a British officer in charge of a World War II commando squad that parachutes behind enemy lines to rescue an American general being held captive by the Nazis in a castle in the Bavarian Alps.

Richard Burton, Mary Ure, Michael Hordern, Patrick Wymark, Robert Beatty, Anton Diffring, Donald Houston, Ferdy Mayne, Neil McCarthy, Peter Barkworth, William Squire, Brook Williams, Ingrid Pitt.

Paint Your Wagon (1969, Para.). *d:* Joshua Logan; *p:* Alan Jay Lerner; *sc:* Alan Jay Lerner (adaptation by Paddy Chayefsky)—*b/o* the musical play by Alan Jay Lerner and Frederick Loewe.

"PARDNER": Soft-spoken prospector during the California gold rush who, when his grizzled partner buys a Mormon wife for $800, falls in love with her—whereupon the three of them live together.

Lee Marvin, Jean Seberg, Harve Presnell, Ray Walston, Tom Ligon, Alan Dexter, William O'Connell, Ben Baker, Alan Baxter, Paula Trueman, Robert Easton, Geoffrey Norman, H. B. Haggerty, Terry Jenkins, John Mitchum, Sue Casey.

Kelly's Heroes (1970, MGM). *d:* Brian G. Hutton; *p:* Irving Leonard (The Warriors/Avala); *sc:* Troy Kennedy Martin.

KELLY: Enterprising WWII U.S. Army private in France who, when he accidentally learns from a captured German general the location of $16 million in gold in a German-occupied town, organizes a motley group of G.I.s to steal it while they're on a three-day pass.

Telly Savalas, Don Rickles, Carroll O'Connor, Donald Sutherland, Gavin MacLeod, George Savalas, Hal Buckley, David Hurst, John Heller.

Two Mules for Sister Sara (1970, Univ.). *d:* Don Siegel; *p:* Martin Rackin (Malpaso); *sc:* Albert Maltz—*b/o* a story by Budd Boetticher.

HOGAN: American mercenary in Mexico who saves a nun from being raped, joins forces with her in helping Juarista guerillas fight the French, and finally discovers why she smokes cigars, drinks liquor, and uses four-letter words: she's a hooker.

Shirley MacLaine, Manolo Gabregas, Alberto Morin, Armando Silvestre, José Chavez, Pedro Galvan.

The Beguiled (1971, Univ.). *d:* Don Siegel; *p:* Don Siegel (Malpaso); *sc:* John B. Sherry and Grimes Grice—*b/o* the novel by Thomas Culliman.

JOHN McBURNEY: Wounded Civil War Union corporal who, after finding refuge at a Southern girls' school and making love to all the residents, is prevented from escaping when the jealous headmistress amputates his leg.

Geraldine Page, Elizabeth Hartman, Jo Ann Harris, Darleen Carr, Mae Mercer, Pamelyn Ferdin, Melody Thomas, Peggy Drier, Pattie Mattick.

Play Misty for Me (1971, Univ.). *d:* Clint Eastwood; *p:* Robert Daley (Malpaso); *sc:* Jo Heims and Dean Riesner.

DAVE GARVER: Late-night disc jockey on a California radio station who makes the mistake of entering into a casual affair with a sexy fan who turns out to be homicidally jealous.

Jessica Walter, Donna Mills, John Larch, Clarice Taylor, Irene Hervey, Jack Ging, James McEachin, Donald Siegel, Duke Everts.

Dirty Harry (1971, WB). *d:* Don Siegel; *p:* Don Siegel (Malpaso); *sc:* Harry Julian Fink, R. M. Fink, and Dean Reisner—*b/o* a story by Harry Julian Fink and R. M. Fink.

HARRY CALLAHAN (DIRTY HARRY): Hard-as-nails San Francisco police detective who, when a vicious sniper he's brought in is released for lack of evidence, bends a few rules as he sets out on his own to settle the score.

Harry Guardino, Reni Santoni, Andy Robinson, John Larch, John Mitchum, Mae Mercer, Lyn Edgington, Ruth Kobart, Woodrow Parfrey, Josef Sommer, William Paterson, James Nolan, John Vernon.

Joe Kidd (1972, Univ.). *d:* John Sturges; *p:* Sidney Beckerman (Malpaso); *sc:* Elmore Leonard.

JOE KIDD: Bounty hunter in turn-of-the-century New Mexico who, after he's hired by powerful American land barons to hunt down a Mexican-American guerilla leader, decides that he's on the wrong side and helps the guerillas battle the corrupt landowners.

Robert Duvall, John Saxon, Don Stroud, Stella Garcia, James Wainwright, Paul Koslo, Gregory Walcott, Lynne Marta.

High Plains Drifter (1973, Univ.). *d:* Clint Eastwood; *p:* Robert Daley (Malpaso); *sc:* Ernest Tidyman.

THE STRANGER: Drifter who, after he's hired by the citizens of the town of Lago to protect them from a gang of escaped convicts, shoots down the convicts, then disappears as mysteriously as he arrived.

Verna Bloom, Mariana Hill, Mitchell Ryan, Jack Ging, Stefan Gierasch, Ted Hartley, Billy Curtis, Geoffrey Lewis, Scott Walker, Walter Barnes.

Magnum Force (1973, WB). *d:* Ted Post; *p:* Robert Daley (Malpaso); *sc:* John Milius and Michael Cimino—*b/o* a story by John Milius (adapted from material by Harry Julian Fink and R. M. Fink).

HARRY CALLAHAN (DIRTY HARRY): Tough San Francisco police detective who, when he sets out to solve the murders of several gangsters, discovers that the killings are being done by a police hit squad meting out its own justice.

Hal Holbrook, Felton Perry, Mitchell Ryan, David Soul, Tim Matheson, Robert Urich, Kip Niven, Christine White, Adele Yoshioka.

Thunderbolt and Lightfoot (1974, UA). *d:* Michael Cimino; *p:* Robert Daley (Malpaso); *sc:* Michael Cimino.

JOHN "THUNDERBOLT" DOHERTY: Vietnam vet/bank robber who teams up with a young drifter and two ex-partners in crime to pull off a big heist using a Howitzer.

Jeff Bridges, Geoffrey Lewis, Catherine Bach, Gary Busey, George Kennedy, Jack Dodson, Gene Elman, Burton Gilliam, Roy Jenson, Claudia Lennear, Bill McKinney, Vic Tayback.

The Eiger Sanction (1975, Univ.). *d:* Clint Eastwood; *p:* Robert Daley, Richard D. Zanuck, and David Brown (Malpaso); *sc:* Hal Dresner, Warren B. Murphy, and Rod Whitaker—*b/o* the novel by Trevanian.

JONATHAN HEMLOCK: College art professor—formerly a paid assassin—who is persuaded by the head of a secret U.S. intelligence agency to undertake a mission in which he is to scale Eiger Mountain in Switzerland and kill an enemy spy there.

George Kennedy, Vonetta McGee, Jack Cassidy, Heidi Bruhi, Thayer David, Reiner Schene,

Michael Grimm, Jean-Pierre Bernard, Brenda Venus, Gregory Walcott.

The Outlaw Josey Wales (1976, WB). *d:* Clint Eastwood; *p:* Robert Daley (Malpaso); *sc:* Phil Kaufman and Sonia Chernus—*b/o* the book *Gone to Texas* by Forrest Carter.

JOSEY WALES: Farmer and ex–Confederate soldier who seeks revenge for the murder of his wife and son by renegade Union soldiers.

Chief Dan George, Sondra Locke, Bill McKinney, John Vernon, Paula Trueman, Sam Bottoms, Geraldine Keams, Woodrow Parfrey, Joyce Jameson, Sheb Wooley, Matt Clarke, John Verros, John Quade.

The Enforcer (1976, WB). *d:* James Fargo; *p:* Robert Daley (Malpaso); *sc:* Stirling Silliphant and Dean Reisner—*b/o* characters created by Harry Julian Fink and R. M. Fink.

HARRY CALLAHAN (DIRTY HARRY): Hardboiled San Francisco detective who at first resents a female rookie cop assigned as his partner, then falls in love with her but loses her when she's killed during a shootout with terrorists at the abandoned prison on Alcatraz.

Tyne Daly, Harry Guardino, Bradford Dillman, John Mitchum, DeVeren Brookwalter, John Crawford.

The Gauntlet (1977, WB). *d:* Clint Eastwood; *p:* Robert Daley (Malpaso); *sc:* Michael Butler and Dennis Shryack.

BEN SHOCKLEY: Down-and-out Phoenix police detective who, when he's assigned to escort a hooker from Las Vegas to testify in a sex scandal probe, is fingered by the mob, corrupt politicians, and his own Phoenix police force.

Sondra Locke, Pat Hingle, William Prince, Bill McKinney, Michael Cavanaugh.

Every Which Way but Loose (1978, WB). *d:* James Fargo; *p:* Robert Daley (Malpaso); *sc:* Jeremy Joe Kronsberg.

PHILO BEDDOE: Truck driver who travels around the country with an orangutan named Clyde and picks up money by challenging the toughest men in each town to bare-knuckle fights.

Sondra Locke, Geoffrey Lewis, Beverly D'Angelo, Ruth Gordon, Bill McKinney.

Escape from Alcatraz (1979, Para.). *d:* Don Siegel; *p:* Donald Siegel (Malpaso); *sc:* Richard Tuggle.

FRANK MORRIS: Convict who, after escaping from several prisons, is sent to the maximum-security prison at Alcatraz and, in 1962, proceeds with two other prisoners to pull off the only known escape in The Rock's history.

Patrick McGoohan, Roberts Blossom, Jack Thibeau, Fred Ward, Paul Benjamin, Larry Hankin, Bruce M. Fischer, Frank Ronzio, Donald Siegel.

Bronco Billy (1980, WB). *d:* Clint Eastwood; *p:* Dennis Hackin and Neal Dobrofsky (Malpaso); *sc:* Dennis Hackin.

BRONCO BILLY: Owner and star of a fly-by-night Wild West show who falls for a spoiled heiress when she is persuaded to join the show to serve as a target for his sharpshooting and knife-throwing act.

Sondra Locke, Geoffrey Lewis, Scatman Crothers, Bill McKinney, Sam Bottoms, Dan Vadis, Sierra Pecheur, Walter Barnes, Woodrow Parfrey, Hank Worden, William Prince.

Any Which Way You Can (1980, WB). *d:* Buddy Van Horn; *p:* Fritz Manes (Malpaso); *sc:* Stanford Sherman.

PHILO BEDDOE: Truck driver, owner of Clyde the orangutan, and bare-knuckle fighter who decides to quit fighting but changes his mind when the mob offers him a lucrative deal if he'll have one more fight with a former opponent of his.

Sondra Locke, Geoffrey Lewis, William Smith, Harry Guardino, Ruth Gordon, Michael Cavanaugh, Barry Corbin, Roy Jenson, Bill McKinney, Dan Vadis, Glen Campbell.

Firefox (1982, WB). *d:* Clint Eastwood; *p:* Clint Eastwood (Malpaso); *sc:* Alex Lasker and Wendell Wellman—*b/o* a novel by Craig Thomas.

MITCHELL GANT: U.S. Air Force pilot—a psychologically scarred veteran of the Vietnam War—who is recruited by British and American intelligence agencies to infiltrate Russia and steal the Soviet's revolutionary new fighter-bomber called the Firefox.

Freddie Jones, David Huffman, Warren Clarke, Ronald Lacey, Kenneth Colley.

Honkytonk Man (1982, WB). *d:* Clint Eastwood; *p:* Clint Eastwood (Malpaso); *sc:* Clancy Carlile—*b/o* his novel.

RED STOVALL: Hard-drinking, tubercular country-and-western singer/songwriter during the Depression era who sets out with his fourteen-year-old nephew in a big 1930s touring car from Oklahoma to Nashville, where he's been invited to audition for the Grand Ole Opry.

Kyle Eastwood, John McIntire, Alexa Kenin, Verna Bloom.

Sudden Impact (1983, WB). *d:* Clint Eastwood; p: Clint Eastwood (Malpaso); *sc:* Joseph C. Stinson—*b/o* a story by Earl B. Pierce.

HARRY CALLAHAN (DIRTY HARRY): Hard-nosed San Francisco detective who, while in the resort town of San Paulo, California, tracks down a vengeful murderess who is methodically eliminating, one by one, the six degenerates who raped her and her sister ten years earlier.

Sondra Locke, Pat Hingle, Bradford Dillman, Paul Drake, Audrie J. Neenan, Jack Thibeau.

☆ W. C. FIELDS

William Claude Dukenfield

b: Feb. 10, 1879, Philadelphia, Pa.
d: Dec. 25, 1946, Pasadena, Cal.

"You must come down with me after the show to the lumberyard and ride piggy-back on the buzz saw."

> Larson E. Whipsnade (W. C. Fields) to
> Charlie McCarthy in *You Can't Cheat an*
> *Honest Man,* 1939.

Janice Meredith (1924, MGM). *d:* E. Mason Hopper; *sc:* Lilly Hayward—*b/o* the novel by Paul Leicester.
Billed as "A BRITISH SERGEANT": Comic drunk British Army sergeant in America during the Revolutionary War.
Marion Davies, Harrison Ford, Maclyn Arbuckle, Joseph Kilgour, George Nash, Tyrone Power Sr., May Vokes, Olin Howland, Spencer Charters.

Sally of the Sawdust (1925, UA). *d:* D. W. Griffith; *sc:* Forrest Halsey—*b/o* the stage play *Poppy* by Dorothy Donnelly.
PROFESSOR EUSTACE McGARGLE: Good-natured crook, juggler, and sideshow faker who, after a young mother with the circus dies, becomes the guardian of her little girl and trains her to dance as a warm-up for his own act.
Carol Dempster, Alfred Lunt, Erville Alderson, Effie Shannon, Charles Hammond, Roy Applegate, Glenn Anders.

That Royle Girl (1926, Para.). *d:* D. W. Griffith; *p:* D. W. Griffith (FP-L); *sc:* Paul Schofield—*b/o* the story by Edwin Balmer.
Billed as "HER FATHER": Comical crook whose daughter falls for a jazz orchestra leader and becomes involved in a murder case.
Carol Dempster, James Kirkwood, Harrison Ford, Paul Everton, Kathleen Chambers, George Rigas, Florence Auer, Dorthea Love, Bobby Watson.

It's the Old Army Game (1926, FP-L). *d:* Edward Sutherland; *p:* Adolph Zukor and Jessie L. Lasky; *sc:* Thomas J. Geraghty—*b/o* the play by J. P. McEvoy.
ELMER PRETTYWILLIE: Trouble-prone village druggist who suddenly becomes rich from a bogus land deal.
Louise Brooks, Blanche Ring, William Gaxton, Mary Foy, Mickey Bennett.

So's Your Old Man (1926, FP-L). *d:* Gregory La Cava; *sc:* Howard Emmett—*b/o* the story "Mr. Bisbee's Princess" by Julian Street.
SAMUEL BISBEE: Bungling inventor in a small New Jersey town whose family, after he develops an unbreakable automobile glass and befriends a Spanish princess, is finally able to move up in society.
Alice Joyce, Charles Rogers, Kittins Reichert, Marcia Harris, Julia Ralph, Frank Montgomery, Jerry Sinclair.

The Potters (1927, Para.). *d:* Fred Newmeyer; *sc:* J. Clarkson Miller (adaptation by Sam Mintz and Ray Harris)—*b/o* the play by J. P. McEvoy.
PA POTTER: Gullible family man who finds himself in hot water when he invests his life's savings in some worthless oil stock without his wife's knowledge.
Mary Alden, Ivy Harris, Jack Egan, Skeets Gallagher, Joseph Smiley, Bradley Baker.

Running Wild (1927, Para.). *d:* Gregory La Cava; *sc:* Roy Briant—*b/o* a story by Gregory La Cava.
ELMER FINCH: Henpecked husband who is a doormat for the entire family until he's hypnotized and becomes a real "tiger."
Mary Brian, Claud Buchanan, Marie Shotwell, Barney Raskle, Frederick Burton, J. Moy Bennett, Frank Evans, Ed Roseman, Tom Madden, Rex the Horse.

Two Flaming Youths (1927, Para.). *d:* John Waters; *p:* John Waters; *sc:* Percy Heath and Donald Davis—*b/o* a story by Percy Heath.
GABBY GILFOIL: Financially strapped carnival showman who vies with a county sheriff for the affections and money of a wealthy woman who owns a hotel.
Chester Conklin, Mary Brian, Jack Luden, George Irving, Cissy Fitzgerald, Jimmie Quinn.

Tillie's Punctured Romance (1928, Para.). *d:* Edward Sutherland; *sc:* Monte Brice and Keene Thompson—*b/o* characters from an earlier film of the same title.
Billed as "THE RINGMASTER": Ringmaster of a circus that goes to France during WWI to entertain American troops.
Louise Fazenda, Chester Conklin, Mack Swain, Doris Hill, Grant Withers, Tom Kennedy, Babe London, Billy Platt.

Fools for Luck (1928, Para.). *d:* Charles F. Reisner; *sc:* J. Walter Ruben (with titles by George Marion).
RICHARD WHITEHEAD: Con man who sells what he believes to be dry oil wells to the richest man in town—only to find out later that there still is oil in them.
Chester Conklin, Sally Blane, Jack Luden, Mary

Alden, Arthur Housman, Robert Dudley, Martha Mattox.

Her Majesty Love (1931, WB). *d:* William Dieterle; *sc:* Robert Lord, Arthur Caesar, Henry Blanke, and Joseph Jackson—*b/o* a story by R. Berbrauer and R. Oesterreicher.

Billed as the heroine's "FATHER": Carnival juggler–turned–barber who is an embarrassment to his daughter and her fiancé's wealthy family.

Marilyn Miller, Ben Lyon, Ford Sterling, Leon Errol, Chester Conklin, Harry Stubbs, Maude Eburne, Harry Holman, Virginia Sale.

Million Dollar Legs (1932, Para.). *d:* Edward Cline; *sc:* Henry Myers and Nick Barrows—*b/o* a story by Joseph L. Mankiewicz.

Billed as "THE PRESIDENT": President of the mythical country of Klopstokia whose citizens are such super-athletes that Klopstokia decides to enter the Olympics being held in the United States.

Jack Oakie, Andy Clyde, Lyda Roberti, Susan Fleming, Ben Turpin, Hugh Herbert, George Barbier, Dickie Moore, Billy Gilbert, Vernon Dent, Irving Bacon, Sid Saylor.

If I Had a Million (1932, Para.). *d:* Ernst Lubitsch, Norman Taurog, Stephen Roberts, Norman McLeod, James Cruze, William A. Seiter, and H. Bruce Humberstone; *p:* Louis D. Lighton; *sc:* Claude Binyon, Whitney Bolton, Malcom Stuart Boylan, John Bright, Sidney Buchman, Lester Cole, Isabel Dawn, Boyce DeGaw, Walter DeLeon, Oliver H.P. Garrett, Harvey Gates, Grover Jones, Ernst Lubitsch, Lawton Mackaill, Joseph L. Mankiewicz, William Slavens McNutt, Seton I. Miller, and Tiffany Thayer—*b/o* a story by Robert D. Andrews.

ROLLO: Old-time ham actor—one of several people inheriting $1 million—who buys a bunch of old used cars and sets out to get even with all roadhogs by ramming them.

Gary Cooper, George Raft, Wynne Gibson, Charles Laughton, Jack Oakie, Frances Dee, Charlie Ruggles, Alison Skipworth, Mary Boland, Roscoe Karns, May Robson, Gene Raymond, Lucien Littlefield, Grant Mitchell, Joyce Compton, Irving Bacon, Dewey Robinson, Gail Patrick, Fred Kelsey, Willard Robertson, Kent Taylor, Jack Pennick, Berton Churchill.

International House (1933, Para.). *d:* Edward Sutherland; *sc:* Francis Martin and Walter De Leon—*b/o* a story by Lou Heifetz and Neil Brant.

PROFESSOR QUAIL: Screwball professor who, when he lands his aircraft at the International House hotel in China, becomes involved with a married woman, her jealous husband (a Chinese who has invented a television apparatus), and various other colorful characters.

Peggy Hopkins Joyce, Stuart Erwin, George Burns, Gracie Allen, Bela Lugosi, Franklin Pangborn, Sterling Holloway, Rudy Vallee, Baby Rose Marie, Colonel Stoopnagle and Budd, Cab Calloway and his Orchestra.

Tillie and Gus (1933, Para.). *d:* Francis Martin; *p:* Douglas MacLean; *sc:* Walter De Leon and Francis Martin—*b/o* a story by Rupert Hughes.

AUGUSTUS WINTERBOTTOM: Professional card shark who joins forces with his card-playing wife to prevent their neice from being swindled by a crooked lawyer.

Alison Skipworth, Baby LeRoy, Jacqueline Wells, Clifford Jones, Clarence Wilson, George Barbier, Barton MacLane, Edgar Kennedy.

Alice in Wonderland (1933, Para.). *d:* Norman McLeod; *p:* Louis D. Lighton; *sc:* Joseph L. Mankiewicz and William Cameron Menzies—*b/o* the novels *Alice's Adventure in Wonderland* and *Alice Through the Looking Glass* by Lewis Carroll.

HUMPTY DUMPTY: Egg-like nursery-rhyme character—one of the many colorful characters a young girl named Alice encounters when she is transported into a land of fantasy.

Charlotte Henry, Richard Arlen, Roscoe Ates, Billy Barty, Billy Bevan, Gary Cooper, Leon Errol, Louise Fazenda, Skeets Gallagher, Cary Grant, Raymond Hatton, Sterling Holloway, Edward Everett Horton, Roscoe Karns, Baby LeRoy, Lucien Littlefield, Mae Marsh, Polly Moran, Jack Oakie, Edna May Oliver, May Robson, Charlie Ruggles, Jackie Searle, Alison Skipworth, Ned Sparks, Ford Sterling, Jacqueline Wells (Julie Bishop).

Six of a Kind (1934, Para.). *d:* Leo McCarey; *sc:* Walter De Leon and Harry Ruskin—*b/o* a story by Keene Thompson and Douglas MacLean.

SHERIFF JOHN HOXLEY: Pool-playing sheriff of Nuggetville, Nevada, who arrests a visiting bank president he mistakenly thinks is an embezzler.

Charlie Ruggles, Mary Boland, George Burns, Gracie Allen, Alison Skipworth, Grace Bradley, James Burke, Walter Long, Lew Kelly, Irving Bacon.

You're Telling Me (1934, Para.). *d:* Earle Kenton; *sc:* Walter De Leon, Paul M. Jones, and J. P. McEvoy—*b/o* the story "Mr. Bisbee's Princess" by Julian Street.

SAM BISBEE: Screwball inventor and head of a family living on the wrong side of the tracks who, after a series of mishaps, sells a successful invention and moves up into society with the help of a princess he has befriended.

Joan Marsh, Larry "Buster" Crabbe, Adrienne Ames, Louise Carter, Kathleen Howard, James B. "Pop" Kenton, Robert McKenzie, George Irving, Vernon Dent.

The Old-Fashioned Way (1934, Para.). *d:* William Beaudine; *p:* William LeBaron; *sc:*

Garnett Weston and Jack Cunningham—*b/o* a story by Charles Bogle (W. C. Fields).

"THE GREAT McGONIGLE": Con-man head of a traveling troupe of thespians who, in order to elude various sheriffs who are pursuing him, keeps moving the troupe from town to town while they perform the old-time melodrama "The Drunkard."

Joe Morrison, Judith Allen, Jan Duggan, Nora Cecil, Baby LeRoy, Jack Mulhall, Joe Mills, Emma Ray, Richard Carle, Otis Harlan.

Mrs. Wiggs of the Cabbage Patch (1934, Para.). *d:* Norman Taurog; *p:* Douglas MacLean; *sc:* William Slavens McNutt and Jane Storm—*b/o* a story by Alice Hegan Rice and Anne Crawford Flexner.

MR. STUBBINS: A suitor who is nudged into matrimony by a fluttery neighbor of the "wrong side of the tracks" but optimistically happy Wiggs family.

Pauline Lord, ZaSu Pitts, Evalyn Venable, Kent Taylor, Charles Middleton, Donald Meed, Jimmy Butler, George Breakston, Edith Fellows, Virginia Weidler.

It's a Gift (1934, Para.). *d:* Norman McLeod; *p:* William LeBaron; *sc:* Jack Cunningham—*b/o* a story by Charles Bogle (W. C. Fields).

HAROLD BISSONETTE: Bumbling, henpecked proprietor of a small-town general store who, after he buys an orange grove through the mail, goes to California and discovers that the "orange grove" is a section of sunbaked desert land.

Jean Rouverol, Julian Madison, Kathleen Howard, Tom Bupp, Tammany Young, Baby LeRoy, Spencer Charters, James Burke.

David Copperfield (1935, MGM). *d:* George Cukor; *p:* David O. Selznick; *sc:* Howard Estabrook (adaptation by Hugh Walpole)—*b/o* the novel by Charles Dickens.

MR. WILKINS MICAWBER: Optimistic, flamboyant head of an English family who takes in a young lad (David Copperfield) as a boarder; he remains optimistic and flamboyant even when he's later sent to a debtor's prison.

Lionel Barrymore, Maureen O'Sullivan, Madge Evans, Edna May Oliver, Lewis Stone, Freddie Bartholomew, Frank Lawton, Elizabeth Allan, Roland Young, Basil Rathbone, Elsa Lanchester, Jessie Ralph, Una O'Connor, Herbert Mundin, Hugh Walpole.

Mississippi (1935, Para.). *d:* Edward Sutherland; *p:* Arthur Hornblow Jr.; *sc:* Jack Cunningham and Francis Martin (adaptation by Herbert Fields and Claude Binyon)—*b/o* the play *Magnolia* by Booth Tarkington.

COMMODORE JACKSON: Enterprising showboat captain who capitalizes on the phony dueling reputation of a passenger by hiring him and billing him as "the singing killer."

Bing Crosby, Joan Bennett, Gail Patrick, Queenie Smith, Claude Gillingwater, John Miljan, Ed Pawley, Fred Kohler, John Larkin, Paul Hurst, King Baggott.

The Man on the Flying Trapeze (1935, Para.). *d:* Clyde Bruckman; *p:* William LeBaron; *sc:* Ray Harris, Sam Hardy, Jack Cunningham, and Bobby Vernon—*b/o* a story by Charles Bogle (W. C. Fields) and Sam Hardy.

AMBROSE WOLFINGER: Browbeaten but good-natured head of a family who is pushed around by a shrewish second wife, a nagging mother-in-law, and a sponging brother-in-law—until he turns the tables on them all.

Mary Brian, Kathleen Howard, Grady Sutton, Vera Lewis, Lucien Littlefield, Lew Kelly, Walter Brennan, Arthur Aylesworth, David Clyde, James Flavin, Edward Gargan.

Poppy (1936, Para.). *d:* A. Edward Sutherland; *p:* William LeBaron; *sc:* Waldemar Young and Virginia Van Upp—*b/o* a play by Dorothy Donnelly.

PROFESSOR EUSTACE McGARGLE: Conniving patent-medicine salesman with a traveling carnival who tries to pass off his daughter—in love with a mayor's son—as a missing heiress.

Rochelle Hudson, Richard Cromwell, Granville Bates, Catherine Doucet, Lynne Overman, Maude Eburne, Bill Wolfe, Adrian Morris, Frank Sully, Dewey Robinson, Tom Kennedy.

The Big Broadcast of 1938 (1938, Para.). *d:* Mitchell Leisen; *p:* Harlan Thompson; *sc:* Walter De Leon, Francis Martin, and Ken Englund (adaptation by Howard Lindsay and Russel Crouse)—*b/o* a story by Frederick Hazlitt Brennan.

(Dual role) T. FROTHINGELL BELLOWS: Wealthy owner of the ocean super liner *Gigantic,* which is in a trans-Atlantic race with the super liner *Colossal.*

S. B. BELLOWS: T. Frothingell Bellows's brother, who is hired to sabotage the *Colossal* but mistakenly boards the *Gigantic* and tries to sabotage *it.*

Martha Raye, Dorothy Lamour, Shirley Ross, Lynne Overman, Bob Hope, Ben Blue, Leif Erikson, Grace Bardley, Rufe Davis, Russell Hicks, Tito Guizar, Shep Fields and his Orchestra.

You Can't Cheat an Honest Man (1939, Univ.). *d:* George Marshall; *p:* Lester Cowan; *sc:* George Marion Jr., Richard Mack, and Everett Freeman—*b/o* a story by Charles Bogle (W. C. Fields).

LARSON E. WHIPSNADE: Financially insolvent

circus owner who is constantly being pursued by the sheriff, and whose daughter plans to marry a wealthy young suitor to help solve the father's money problems.

Edgar Bergen, Charlie McCarthy, Mortimer Snerd, Constance Moore, Thurston Hall, John Arledge, Edward Brophy, Arthur Hohl, Eddie "Rochester" Anderson, Grady Sutton, Ivan Lebedeff.

My Little Chickadee (1940, Univ.). *d:* Edward Cline; *p:* Lester Cowan; *sc:* Mae West and W. C. Fields.

CUTHBERT J. TWILLIE: Card-cheating hair-oil salesman in the 1880s Wild West who becomes involved with a shady lady and a masked bandit.

Mae West, Joseph Calleia, Dick Foran, Margaret Hamilton, James Conlin, Gene Austin, Fuzzy Knight, Ruth Donnelly, Donald Meek, Jackie Searle, Billy Benedict, Hank Bell, Lane Chandler.

The Bank Dick (1940, Univ.). *d:* Edward Cline; *sc:* Mahatma Kane Jeeves (W. C. Fields).

EGBERT SOUSE: No-account citizen in a town called Lompoc who accidentally captures a bank robber and is rewarded with a job as a bank guard.

Cora Witherspoon, Una Merkel, Jessie Ralph, Franklin Pangborn, Shemp Howard, Richard Purcell, Grady Sutton, Russell Hicks, Pierre Watkin, Bill Wolfe, Jack Norton, Reed Hadley.

Never Give a Sucker an Even Break (1941, Univ.). *d:* Edward Cline; *sc:* John T. Neville and Prescott Chaplin—*b/o* a story by Otis Criblecoblis (W. C. Fields).

Billed as "THE GREAT MAN": Broken-down movie hack who acts out the plot of an outlandish movie he is trying to sell to a fussy producer at Esoteric Studios.

Gloria Jean, Anne Nagel, Franklin Pangborn, Mona Barrie, Leon Errol, Margaret Dumont, Charles Lang, Irving Bacon, Claude Allister, Dave Willock.

• In addition, W. C. Fields also made cameo/guest appearances in the following feature films: *Follow the Boys* (1944, Univ.), *Song of the Open Road* (1944, UA), and *Sensations of 1945* (1945, UA).

☆ ERROL FLYNN

Errol Leslie Flynn

b: June 20, 1909, Hobart, Tasmania, Austl.
d: Oct. 14, 1959, Vancouver, B.C., Canada

"Now for Australia and a crack at those Japs!"

Flight Lt. Terence Forbes (Errol Flynn)
after escaping from Nazi Germany during
WWII in *Desperate Journey*, 1942.

In the Wake of the Bounty (1933, Expeditionary Films [Australia]). *d:* Charles Chauvel; *p:* Charles Chauvel; *sc:* Charles Chauvel.

FLETCHER CHRISTIAN: Master's mate on the British naval ship H.M.S. *Bounty* who leads the crew in a mutiny in 1789 against the tyrannical Capt. William Bligh, sets Bligh adrift in a small boat, and then seeks refuge with the rest of the mutineers on Pitcairn Island.

Mayne Lynton, Victor Gourier, John Warwick, Patricia Penman.

Murder at Monte Carlo (1935, WB). *d:* Ralph Ince; *sc:* Michael Barringer—*b/o* a story by Tom Van Dycke.

DYTER: Newspaper reporter who goes to Monte Carlo to get a story on a new roulette system and finds himself trying to solve the murder of the system's inventor.

Eve Gray, Paul Graetz, Lawrence Hanray, Ellis Irving, Henry Victor, Brian Buchel, Molly Lamont, Gabriel Toyne.

The Case of the Curious Bride (1935, WB). *d:* Michael Curtiz; *p:* Harry Joe Brown; *sc:* Tom Reed (with additional dialogue by Brown Holmes)—*b/o* the novel by Erle Stanley Gardner.

GREGORY MOXLEY: Blackmailer whose ex-wife, when he tries to shake her down, goes to the famed lawyer-sleuth Perry Mason for help.

Warren William, Margaret Lindsay, Donald Woods, Claire Dodd, Allen Jenkins, Philip Reed, Barton MacLane, Winifred Shaw, Warren Hymer, Olin Howland, Thomas Jackson, Mayo Methot, Henry Kolker, Paul Hurst.

Don't Bet on Blondes (1935, WB). *d:* Robert Florey; *p:* Samuel Bischoff; *sc:* Isabel Dawn and Boyce DeGaw.

DAVID VAN DUSEN: Society playboy who vies with a big-time gambler for the affections of a wealthy Kentucky colonel's daughter—and loses.

Warren William, Guy Kibbee, Claire Dodd, William

Gargan, Vince Barnett, Hobart Cavanaugh, Spencer Charters, Walter Byron, Jack Norton, Mary Treen, Maude Eburne, Herman Bing.

Captain Blood (1935, WB). *d:* Michael Curtiz; *p:* Hal B. Wallis and Harry Joe Brown; *sc:* Casey Robinson—*b/o* the novel by Rafael Sabatini.

PETER BLOOD: Young seventeenth-century English doctor who, after he's convicted of treason for treating a wounded rebel, is sold into slavery in Jamaica but escapes and becomes a feared pirate captain.

Olivia de Havilland, Lionel Atwill, Basil Rathbone, Ross Alexander, Guy Kibbee, Henry Stephenson, Hobart Cavanaugh, Robert Barrat, Donald Meek, Jessie Ralph, Holmes Herbert, J. Carroll Naish, Pedro de Cordoba, E. E. Clive.

The Charge of the Light Brigade (1936, WB). *d:* Michael Curtiz; *p:* Hal B. Wallis and Samuel Bischoff; *sc:* Michel Jacoby and Rowland Leigh—*b/o* a story by Michel Jacoby.

MAJ. GEOFFREY VICKERS: Heroic British officer during the Crimean War who, in 1854, leads the 27th Lancers Light Brigade of about 700 men "into the Valley of Death" at Balaclava against a Russian force of more than 25,000.

Olivia de Havilland, Patric Knowles, Henry Stephenson, Nigel Bruce, Donald Crisp, David Niven, C. Henry Gordon, G. P. Huntley Jr., Robert Barrat, Spring Byington, E. E. Clive, J. Carroll Naish, Scotty Beckett, Lumsden Hare.

Green Light (1937, WB). *d:* Frank Borzage; *p:* Henry Blanke; *sc:* Milton Krims—*b/o* the novel by Lloyd C. Douglas.

DR. NEWELL PAIGE: Idealistic young surgeon who, after sacrificing his career by taking the blame for a patient's death caused by an older doctor, deliberately contracts spotted fever while developing a vaccine for it.

Anita Louise, Margaret Lindsay, Sir Cedric Hardwicke, Walter Abel, Henry O'Neill, Spring Byington, Erin O'Brien-Moore, Henry Kolker, Pierre Watkin, Granville Bates, Russell Simpson.

The Prince and the Pauper (1937, WB). *d:* William Keighley; *p:* Robert Lord; *sc:* Laird Doyle—*b/o* the novel by Mark Twain.

MILES HENDON: Sixteenth-century English soldier of fortune who befriends a young boy he believes to be a street urchin but then discovers he's really Prince Edward, who has changed places with a look-alike beggar.

Claude Rains, Henry Stephenson, Barton MacLane, Billy Mauch, Bobby Mauch, Alan Hale, Eric Portman, Lionel Pape, Halliwell Hobbes, Montagu Love, Fritz Leiber, Forrester Harvey, Robert Warwick, Holmes Herbert, Ian Wolfe.

Another Dawn (1937, WB). *d:* William Dieterle; *p:* Harry Joe Brown; *sc:* Laird Doyle.

CAPT. DENNY ROARK: Gentlemanly officer at a remote British Army outpost in the Sahara who falls in love with his C.O.'s wife.

Kay Francis, Ian Hunter, Frieda Inescort, Herbert Mundin, G. P. Huntley Jr., Billy Bevan, Clyde Cook, Richard Powell, Kenneth Hunter, Mary Forbes, Ben Welden.

The Perfect Specimen (1937, WB). *d:* Michael Curtiz; *p:* Harry Joe Brown; *sc:* Norman Reilly Raine, Lawrence Riley, Brewster Morse, and Fritz Falkenstein—*b/o* the *Cosmopolitan* magazine story by Samuel Hopkins Adams.

GERALD BERESFORD WICKS: Handsome, athletic heir of a wealthy family who, after never venturing off the estate while being raised by his grandmother to be the "perfect male specimen," is lured into the outside world by a female reporter.

Joan Blondell, Hugh Herbert, Edward Everett Horton, Dick Foran, Beverly Roberts, May Robson, Allen Jenkins, James Burke, Granville Bates, Harry Davenport, Spencer Charters.

The Adventures of Robin Hood (1938, WB). *d:* Michael Curtiz and William Keighley; *p:* Hal B. Wallis; *sc:* Norman Reilly Raine and Seton I. Miller—*b/o* Robin Hood legends.

SIR ROBIN OF LOCKSLEY (alias ROBIN HOOD): Legendary twelfth-century English outlaw who lives in Sherwood Forest with his band of "merry men," robs the rich to give to the poor, and fights to save the throne for Richard the Lion-Hearted.

Olivia de Havilland, Basil Rathbone, Claude Rains, Patric Knowles, Eugene Pallette, Alan Hale, Melville Cooper, Ian Hunter, Una O'Connor, Herbert Mundin, Montagu Love, Robert Warwick, Lester Matthews, Howard Hill.

Four's a Crowd (1938, WB). *d:* Michael Curtiz; *p:* David Lewis; *sc:* Casey Robinson and Sig Herzig—*b/o* a story by Wallace Sullivan.

ROBERT KENSINGTON LANSFORD: PR man who, when he's hired to improve an irascible millionaire's image, finds it advantageous to return to his old job as managing editor of a newspaper while romancing both the millionaire's daughter and a reporter.

Olivia de Havilland, Rosalind Russell, Patric Knowles, Walter Connolly, Hugh Herbert, Melville Cooper, Franklin Pangborn, Herman Bing, Margaret Hamilton, Joseph Crehan, Gloria Blondell, Carole Landis, Renie Riano, Charles Trowbridge, Spencer Charters.

The Sisters (1938, WB). *d:* Anatole Litvak; *p:* Hal B. Wallis; *sc:* Milton Krims—*b/o* the novel by Myron Brinig.

FRANK MEDLIN: Personable but unreliable newspaper reporter who elopes with a Montana girl to San Francisco, then deserts her, but—after they both survive the 1906 earthquake—reconciles with her.

Bette Davis, Anita Louise, Ian Hunter, Donald Crisp, Beulah Bondi, Jane Bryan, Alan Hale, Dick Foran, Henry Travers, Patric Knowles, Lee Patrick, Laura Hope Crews, Harry Davenport, Paul Harvey, Mayo Methot, Irving Bacon, Stanley Fields, Susan Hayward.

The Dawn Patrol (1938, WB). *d:* Edmund Goulding; *p:* Hal B. Wallis; *sc:* Seton I. Miller and Dan Totheroh—*b/o* the story "Flight Commander" by John Monk Saunders and Howard Hawks.

CAPTAIN COURTNEY: WWI British ace who inherits command of a Royal Flying Corps squadron in France, then agonizes over sending young pilots—including his best friend's younger brother—to their deaths.

Basil Rathbone, David Niven, Donald Crisp, Melville Cooper, Barry Fitzgerald, Carl Esmond, Peter Willes, Morton Lowry, Michael Brooke, James Burke, Stuart Hall, Herbert Evans, Sidney Bracy.

Dodge City (1939, WB). *d:* Michael Curtiz; *p:* Robert Lord; *sc:* Robert Buckner.

WADE HATTON: Irish soldier of fortune in the Old West who turns sheriff and brings law and order to the wide-open Kansas cattle town of Dodge City.

Olivia de Havilland, Ann Sheridan, Bruce Cabot, Frank McHugh, Alan Hale, John Litel, Henry Travers, Henry O'Neill, Victor Jory, William Lundigan, Guinn (Big Boy) Williams, Douglas Fowley, Ward Bond.

The Private Lives of Elizabeth and Essex (1939, WB). *d:* Michael Curtiz; *p:* Robert Lord; *sc:* Norman Reilly Raine and Aeneas MacKenzie—*b/o* the play *Elizabeth the Queen* by Maxwell Anderson.

EARL OF ESSEX: Youthful, power-hungry sixteenth-century English nobleman who has a love affair with the middle-aged Queen Elizabeth but—when he clashes with her over his ambition to become king—winds up losing his head.

Bette Davis, Olivia de Havilland, Donald Crisp, Alan Hale, Vincent Price, Henry Stephenson, Henry Daniell, James Stephenson, Nanette Fabares (Nanette Fabray), Ralph Forbes, Robert Warwick, Leo G. Carroll, John Sutton.

Virginia City (1940, WB). *d:* Michael Curtiz; *p:* Robert Fellows; *sc:* Robert Buckner.

KERRY BRADFORD: Union officer who escapes from a Confederate prison during the Civil War and goes to Virginia City to block a $5 million gold shipment slated for the Confederacy.

Miriam Hopkins, Randolph Scott, Humphrey Bogart, Frank McHugh, Alan Hale, Guinn (Big Boy) Williams, John Litel, Douglas Dumbrille, Moroni Olsen, Dickie Jones, Russell Simpson, Victor Kilian, Charles Middleton, Ward Bond, George Reeves.

The Sea Hawk (1940, WB). *d:* Michael Curtiz; *p:* Hal B. Wallis and Henry Blanke; *sc:* Howard Koch and Seton I. Miller—*b/o* the novel by Rafael Sabatini.

CAPT. GEOFFREY THORPE: Swashbuckling sixteenth-century English privateer who, with the encouragement of Queen Elizabeth, enriches England's treasury by plundering Spanish treasure ships and Spanish possessions in the Americas.

Brenda Marshall, Claude Rains, Donald Crisp, Flora Robson, Alan Hale, Henry Daniell, Una O'Connor, James Stephenson, Gilbert Roland, William Lundigan, Montagu Love, David Bruce, Fritz Leiber, Ian Keith, Jack La Rue, Herbert Anderson, Edgar Buchanan.

Santa Fe Trail (1940, WB). *d:* Michael Curtiz; *p:* Hal B. Wallis and Robert Fellows; *sc:* Robert Buckner.

JEB STUART: Young West Point graduate who, prior to the Civil War, is assigned to the Second U.S. Cavalry at Fort Leavenworth, Kansas—along with other West Point graduates—and later leads troops in the bloody 1859 battle against the radical abolitionist John Brown at Harpers Ferry, West Virginia.

Olivia de Havilland, Raymond Massey, Ronald Reagan, Alan Hale, William Lundigan, Van Heflin, Gene Reynolds, Henry O'Neill, Guinn (Big Boy) Williams, Alan Baxter, John Litel, Moroni Olsen, David Bruce, Hobart Cavanaugh, Joseph Sawyer, Ward Bond, Suzanne Carnahan (Susan Peters).

Footsteps in the Dark (1941, WB). *d:* Lloyd Bacon; *p:* Robert Lord; *sc:* Lester Cole and John Wexley—*b/o* the play *Blondie White* by Ladislas Fodor, Bernard Merivale, and Jeffrey Dell.

FRANCIS WARREN: Wealthy investment counselor who secretly plays amateur sleuth so he can dig up material for detective stories that he writes under a psuedonym.

Brenda Marshall, Ralph Bellamy, Alan Hale, Lee Patrick, Allen Jenkins, Lucile Watson, William Frawley, Roscoe Karns, Grant Mitchell, Jack La Rue, Turhan Bey, Frank Faylen, Garry Owen, Frank Wilcox, Harry Hayden.

Dive Bomber (1941, WB). *d:* Michael Curtiz; *p:* Hal B. Wallis; *sc:* Frank Wead and Robert Buckner—*b/o* a story by Frank Wead.

LT. DOUGLAS LEE: Flight surgeon in the 1941 U.S. Naval Air Corps who clashes with a flight instructor but—with his help—manages to develop a high-altitude pressure suit that will keep pilots from blacking out.

Fred MacMurray, Ralph Bellamy, Alexis Smith, Robert Armstrong, Regis Toomey, Allen Jenkins, Craig Stevens, Herbert Anderson, Moroni Olsen, Louis Jean Heydt, Addison Richards, Russell Hicks, Howard Hickman, Charles Drake, Gig Young, Alan Hale Jr.

They Died with Their Boots On (1942, WB). *d:* Raoul Walsh; *p:* Robert Fellows; *sc:* Wally Kline and Aeneas MacKenzie.

GEORGE ARMSTRONG CUSTER: U.S. Seventh Cavalry general who, along with approximately 225 men under his command, is killed by Sioux and Cheyenne Indians when he makes his famous "last stand" on June 25, 1876, near the Little Big Horn River.

Olivia de Havilland, Arthur Kennedy, Charley Grapewin, Gene Lockhart, Anthony Quinn, Stanley Ridges, John Litel, Walter Hampden, Sydney Greenstreet, Regis Toomey, Hattie McDaniel, Frank Wilcox, Joseph Sawyer, Minor Watson, Irving Bacon, Gig Young.

Desperate Journey (1942, WB). *d:* Raoul Walsh; *p:* Hal B. Wallis; *sc:* Arthur T. Horman.

FLIGHT LT. TERENCE FORBES: Australian commander of a WWII British RAF bomber who is shot down over Germany, then tries to make his way back to England as he and his surviving crew members are pursued by a relentless Nazi colonel and his men.

Ronald Reagan, Nancy Coleman, Raymond Massey, Alan Hale, Arthur Kennedy, Ronald Sinclair, Albert Basserman, Sig Rumann, Patrick O'Moore, Ilka Gruning, Elsa Basserman, Lester Matthews, Helmut Dantine, Hans Schumm, Douglas Walton.

Gentleman Jim (1942, WB). *d:* Raoul Walsh; *p:* Robert Buckner; *sc:* Vincent Lawrence and Horace McCoy—*b/o* James J. Corbett's autobiography.

JAMES J. CORBETT: Colorful, suave boxer who wins the world's heavyweight championship during the Gay '90s when he fights the mighty John L. Sullivan in a twenty-one-round bout in New Orleans.

Alexis Smith, Jack Carson, Alan Hale, John Loder, William Frawley, Minor Watson, Ward Bond, Rhys Williams, Arthur Shields, James Flavin, Pat Flaherty, Fred Kelsey, Charles Wilson, William B. Davidson, Mike Mazurki.

Edge of Darkness (1943, WB). *d:* Lewis Milestone; *p:* Henry Blanke; *sc:* Robert Rossen—*b/o* the novel by William Woods.

GUNNAR BROGGE: Patriotic Norwegian fisherman who is the ringleader of the underground movement in a Norwegian village occupied by WWII Nazis.

Ann Sheridan, Walter Huston, Nancy Coleman, Helmut Dantine, Judith Anderson, Ruth Gordon, John Beal, Morris Carnovsky, Charles Dingle, Art Smith, Tom Fadden, Henry Brandon, Frank Wilcox, Francis Pierlot, Monte Blue.

Northern Pursuit (1943, WB). *d:* Raoul Walsh; *p:* Jack Chertok; *sc:* Frank Gruber and Alvah Bessie—*b/o* the story "Five Thousand Trojan Horses" by Leslie T. White.

STEVE WAGNER: Royal Canadian Mounted Policeman who pretends to defect from the Mounties so that he can infiltrate and trap a group of Nazi saboteurs who have slipped into Canada.

Julie Bishop, Helmut Dantine, John Ridgely, Gene Lockhart, Tom Tully, Warren Douglas, Tom Fadden, Russell Hicks, Lester Matthews, John Forsythe, Charles Judels, James Millican, Robert Hutton.

Uncertain Glory (1944, WB). *d:* Raoul Walsh; *p:* Robert Buckner; *sc:* Laszlo Vadnay and Max Brand—*b/o* a story by Joe May and Laszlo Vadnay.

JEAN PICARD: French criminal during WWII who, in order to save 100 innocent French hostages held by the Nazis, pretends that he's a wanted saboteur and gives himself up for execution.

Paul Lukas, Jean Sullivan, Lucile Watson, Faye Emerson, James Flavin, Douglas Dumbrille, Sheldon Leonard, Francis Pierlot, Victor Kilian, Albert Van Antwerp, Art Smith, Pedro de Cordoba.

Objective, Burma! (1945, WB). *d:* Raoul Walsh; *p:* Jerry Wald; *sc:* Ranald MacDougall and Lester Cole—*b/o* a story by Alvah Bessie.

MAJOR NELSON: Officer in charge of WWII U.S. paratroopers who are dropped into the Burmese jungle to destroy a Japanese radar station, then are forced to hike 150 miles through enemy-infested territory to escape.

James Brown, William Prince, George Tobias, Henry Hull, Warner Anderson, Stephen Richards (Mark Stevens), Richard Erdman, Anthony Caruso, Hugh Beaumont, Rodd Redwing, Lester Matthews, Erville Anderson.

San Antonio (1945, WB). *d:* David Butler; *p:* Robert Buckner; *sc:* Alan LeMay and W. R. Burnett.

CLAY HARDIN: Cattleman in 1877 San Antonio who, while romancing a dance-hall singer, is determined to prove that her boss is the secret head of a gang of cattle thieves.

Alexis Smith, S. Z. Sakall, Victor Francen, Florence Bates, John Litel, Paul Kelly, Robert Shayne, Monte Blue, Robert Barrat, Pedro de Cordoba, Tom Tyler, Chris-Pin Martin, Charles

Stevens, Poodles Hanneford, Doodles Weaver, Howard Hill, Dan Seymour.

Never Say Goodbye (1946, WB). *d:* James V. Kern; *p:* William Jacobs; *sc:* I. A. L. Diamond and James V. Kern (adaptation by Lewis R. Foster)—*b/o* a story by Ben Barzman and Norma Barzman.
PHIL GAYLEY: Divorced man who, with the help of his seven-year-old daughter, tries to win back his ex-wife.
Eleanor Parker, Patti Brady, Lucile Watson, S. Z. Sakall, Forrest Tucker, Donald Woods, Peggy Knudsen, Tom D'Andrea, Hattie McDaniel, Arthur Shields, Tom Tyler, Monte Blue.

Cry Wolf (1947, WB). *d:* Peter Godfrey; *p:* Henry Blanke; *sc:* Catherine Turney—*b/o* the novel by Marjorie Carleton.
MARK CALDWELL: Mysterious scientist who, when his brother's widow shows up at the family estate to claim her inheritance, treats her coldly but is actually trying to shield her from a dark family secret.
Barbara Stanwyck, Geraldine Brooks, Richard Basehart, Jerome Cowan, John Ridgely, Patricia White, Rory Mallison, Paul Stanton, Barry Bernard, Lisa Golm, Creighton Hale.

Escape Me Never (1947, WB). *d:* Peter Godfrey; *p:* Henry Blanke; *sc:* Thames Williamson—*b/o* the novel *The Fool of the Family* and the play *Escape Me Never*, both by Margaret Kennedy.
SEBASTIAN DUBROK: Struggling turn-of-the-century composer who marries a young Italian woman with an illegitimate baby, but then becomes involved with a beautiful heiress who is his brother's fiancée.
Ida Lupino, Eleanor Parker, Gig Young, Isobel Elsom, Reginald Denny, Albert Basserman, Ludwig Stossel, Frank Puglia, Frank Reicher, Doris Lloyd, Anthony Caruso.

Silver River (1948, WB). *d:* Raoul Walsh; *p:* Owen Crump; *sc:* Stephen Longstreet and Harriet Frank Jr.—*b/o* an unpublished novel by Stephen Longstreet.
MIKE McCOMB: Civil War Union Army officer who is kicked out of the service, turns into an unscrupulous gambler in the West, and then rises to become a ruthless power in the silver-mining business.
Ann Sheridan, Thomas Mitchell, Bruce Bennett, Tom D'Andrea, Barton MacLane, Monte Blue, Jonathan Hale, Alan Bridge, Arthur Space, Art Baker, Joseph Crehan.

Adventures of Don Juan (1948, WB). *d:* Vincent Sherman; *p:* Jerry Wald; *sc:* George Oppenheimer and Harry Kurnitz—*b/o* a story by Herbert Dalmas.
DON JUAN de MARANA: Legendary seventeenth-century Spanish lover who not only strings along countless women, but even entices Queen Margaret while he's saving King Philip III from a political plot.
Viveca Lindfors, Robert Douglas, Alan Hale, Romney Brent, Ann Rutherford, Robert Warwick, Douglas Kennedy, Helen Westcott, Fortunio Bonanova, Aubrey Mather, Una O'Connor, Raymond Burr, G. P. Huntley Jr., David Bruce.

That Forsyte Woman (1949, MGM). *d:* Compton Bennett; *p:* Leon Gordon; *sc:* Jan Lustig, Ivan Tors, and James B. Williams (with additional dialogue by Arthur Wimperis)—*b/o* John Galsworthy's novel *The Man of Property* (Book One of *The Forsyte Saga*).
SOAMES FORSYTE: Pompous, stuffy English "pillar of society" in the Victorian era whose free-spirited, fickle wife leaves him and marries his black-sheep artist cousin.
Greer Garson, Walter Pidgeon, Robert Young, Janet Leigh, Harry Davenport, Aubrey Mather, Lumsden Hare, Halliwell Hobbes, Matt Moore, Marjorie Eaton, Richard Lupino, Billy Bevan.

Montana (1950, WB). *d:* Ray Enright; *p:* William Jacobs; *sc:* James R. Webb, Borden Chase, and Charles O'Neal—*b/o* a story by Ernest Haycox.
MORGAN LANE: Australian sheepherder who clashes with a wealthy female cattle rancher and other cattle barons over Montana grazing land.
Alexis Smith, S. Z. Sakall, Douglas Kennedy, James Brown, Ian MacDonald, Charles Irwin, Paul E. Burns, Tudor Owen, Lester Matthews, Lane Chandler, Monte Blue.

Rocky Mountain (1950, WB). *d:* William Keighley; *p:* William Jacobs; *sc:* Winston Miller and Alan LeMay—*b/o* a story by Alan LeMay.
LAFE BARSTOW: Civil War Confederate officer on a mission in California who finds it necessary to unite his men with a group of Yankees to fight off an Indian attack.
Patrice Wymore, Scott Forbes, Guinn (Big Boy) Williams, Dick Jones, Howard Petrie, Slim Pickens, Chubby Johnson, Buzz Henry, Sheb Wooley, Peter Coe, Yakima Canutt.

Kim (1951, MGM). *d:* Victor Saville; *p:* Leon Gordon; *sc:* Leon Gordon, Helen Deutsch, and Richard Schayer—*b/o* the novel by Rudyard Kipling.
MAHBUB ALI, THE RED BEARD: Afghan horse dealer who, while serving as a secret agent for the British in 1880s India, befriends Kim the orphaned son of a British soldier.
Dean Stockwell, Paul Lukas, Robert Douglas, Thomas Gomez, Cecil Kellaway, Arnold Moss, Reginald Owen, Hayden Rorke, Walter Kingsford, Frank Lackteen, Jeanette Nolan.

Adventures of Captain Fabian (1951, Rep.). *d:* William Marshall; *p:* William Marshall (Silver); *sc:* Errol Flynn—*b/o* the novel *Fabulous Ann Madlock* by Robert Shannon.

CAPT. MICHAEL FABIAN: Sea captain who returns to New Orleans to get revenge on a wealthy family that drove his father to bankruptcy and death.

Micheline Presle, Vincent Price, Agnes Moorehead, Victor Francen, Jim Gerald, Helena Manson, Howard Vernon, Roger Blin, Zanie Campan.

Mara Maru (1952, WB). *d:* Gordon Douglas; *p:* David Weisbart; *sc:* N. Richard Nash—*b/o* a story by Philip Yordan, Sidney Harmon, and Hollister Noble.

GREGORY MASON: Deep-sea diver who searches for a priceless diamond cross that was on a PT boat sunk in the China Sea during WWII.

Ruth Roman, Raymond Burr, Paul Picerni, Richard Webb, Dan Seymour, Georges Renavent, Robert Cabal, Henry Marco, Nestor Paiva, Howard Chuman, Michael Ross.

Against All Flags (1952, Univ.). *d:* George Sherman; *p:* Howard Christie; *sc:* Aeneas MacKenzie and Joseph Hoffman—*b/o* a story by Aeneas MacKenzie.

BRIAN HAWKE: Dauntless eighteenth-century British naval officer—disguised as a deserter—who infiltrates a Madagascar stronghold of pirates, one of whom is a pretty red-haired woman.

Maureen O'Hara, Anthony Quinn, Alice Kelley, Mildred Natwick, Robert Warwick, Phil Tully, Lester Matthews, Tudor Owen, James Craven, Michael Ross.

The Master of Ballantrae (1953, WB). *d:* William Keighley; *sc:* Herb Meadow (with additional dialogue by Harold Medford)—*b/o* the novel by Robert Louis Stevenson.

JAMIE DURRISDEER: The master of Ballantrae Castle in Scotland who goes off to fight for Bonnie Prince Charlie in the British insurrection of 1745, while his younger brother remains loyal to King George II.

Roger Livesey, Anthony Steel, Beatrice Campbell, Yvonne Furneaux, Felix Aylmer, Mervyn Johns, Ralph Truman, Francis de Wolff, Moultrie Kelsall.

Crossed Swords (1954, UA). *d:* Milton Krims; *p:* J. Barrett Mahon and Vottorio Vassarotti (Viva); *sc:* Milton Krims.

RENZO: Dashing Don Juan–type adventurer in medieval Italy who saves a beautiful girl and her father's dukedom from treasonous plotters.

Gina Lollobrigida, Cesare Danova, Nadia Gray,

Paola Mori, Roldano Lupi, Alberto Rabagliati, Silvio Bagolini, Mimo Billi.

Let's Make Up (1955, UA). *d:* Herbert Wilcox; *p:* Herbert Wilcox (Everest); *sc:* Harold Purcell—*b/o* Robert Nesbitt's play *The Glorious Days*.

JOHN BEAUMONT: English song-and-dance man who, after he helps his wife become a star, is forgotten by producers and the public but heads for Hollywood and winds up famous and rich.

Anna Neagle, David Farrar, Kathleen Harrison, Peter Graves, Helen Haye, Scott Sanders, Alma Taylor, Hetty King, Alan Gifford.

The Warriors (1955, AA). *d:* Henry Levin; *p:* Walter Mirisch; *sc:* Daniel B. Ullman.

PRINCE EDWARD: The "Black Prince" of England who stays in France after the Hundred Years' War to guard the conquered lands of his father, Edward III.

Joanne Dru, Peter Finch, Yvonne Furneaux, Patrick Holt, Michael Hordern, Moultrie Kelsall, Robert Urquhart, Vincent Winter, Noel Willman, Frances Rowe.

King's Rhapsody (1955, UA). *d:* Herbert Wilcox; *p:* Herbert Wilcox (Everest); *sc:* Pamela Bower and Christopher Hassall (with additional dialogue by A. P. Herbert)—*b/o* the musical play by Ivor Novello.

KING RICHARD: Exiled heir to the throne of the mythical kingdom of Laurentia who, when he leaves his mistress to return home and become king, is forced to marry a princess whom he doesn't care about but later learns to love.

Anna Neagle, Patrice Wymore, Martita Hunt, Finlay Currie, Francis de Wolff, Joan Benham, Reginald Tate, Miles Malleson, Edmund Hockridge.

Istanbul (1956, Univ.). *d:* Joseph Pevney; *p:* Albert J. Cohen; *sc:* Seton I. Miller, Barbara Gray, and Richard Alan Simmons—*b/o* a story by Seton I. Miller.

JAMES BRENNAN: American flyer and adventurer who, when he returns to Istanbul to recover a fortune in stolen diamonds, finds that his wife—whom he had thought was dead—has amnesia and is married to another man.

Cornell Borchers, John Bentley, Torin Thatcher, Leif Erickson, Peggy Knudsen, Nat King Cole, Werner Klemperer, Vladimir Sokoloff, Jan Arvan, Nico Minardos, Ted Hecht.

The Big Boodle (1957, UA). *d:* Richard Wilson; *p:* Lewis F. Blumberg (Monteflor); *sc:* Jo Eisinger—*b/o* the novel by Robert Sylvester.

NED SHERWOOD: Croupier in a Havana gambling casino who, when he's passed some counterfeit money by a banker's daughter and is mistakenly accused of being a member of a counterfeiting ring, searches the underworld for the bogus plates.

Pedro Armendariz, Rossana Rory, Gia Scala, Sandro Giglio, Jacques Aubuchon, Carlos Mas, Rogelio Hernandez, Velia Martinez, Aurora Pita.

The Sun Also Rises (1957, 20th-Fox). *d:* Henry King; *p:* Darryl F. Zanuck (Darryl F. Zanuck); *sc:* Peter Viertel—*b/o* the novel by Ernest Hemingway.

MIKE CAMPBELL: Boozy, happy-go-lucky member of a quintet of "lost generation" expatriates in 1920s Paris and Spain who, in reality, is a tragic, lonely man.

Tyrone Power, Ava Gardner, Mel Ferrer, Eddie Albert, Gregory Ratoff, Juliette Greco, Marcel Dalio, Henry Daniell, Danik Patisson, Robert Evans, Carlos Muzquiz, Rebecca Iturbi.

Too Much, Too Soon (1958, WB). *d:* Art Napoleon; *p:* Henry Blanke; *sc:* Art Napoleon and Jo Napoleon—*b/o* the book by Diana Barrymore and Gerold Frank.

JOHN BARRYMORE: Famed stage and movie actor with an alcohol problem whose actress daughter Diana also becomes an alcoholic as she goes through a tragic series of romances and marriages.

Dorothy Malone, Efrem Zimbalist Jr., Ray Danton, Neva Patterson, Murray Hamilton, Martin Milner, Robert Ellenstein, Kathleen Freeman, John Doucette, Jay Jostyn.

The Roots of Heaven (1958, 20th-Fox). *d:* John Huston; *p:* Darryl F. Zanuck (Darryl F. Zanuck); *sc:* Romain Gary and Patrick Leigh-Fermor—*b/o* the novel by Romain Gary.

MAJOR FORSYTHE: Disgraced, alcoholic former British Army officer who goes along with a group of adventurers, opportunists, and exploiters in French Equatorial Africa to help a zealous idealist save the African elephant from destruction by ivory hunters.

Juliette Greco, Trevor Howard, Eddie Albert, Orson Welles, Paul Lukas, Herbert Lom, Gregoire Aslan, Andre Luguet, Edric Connor, Pierre Dudan.

• In addition, Errol Flynn made cameo/guest appearances in the following feature films: *Thank Your Lucky Stars* (1943, WB) and *It's a Great Feeling* (1949, WB—played a "bit" as a character named Jeffrey Bushdinkel).

☆ HENRY FONDA

Henry Jaynes Fonda

b: May 16, 1905, Grand Island, Neb.
d: Aug. 12, 1982, Los Angeles, Cal.

"Wherever there's a fight so hungry people can eat, I'll be there. Wherever there's a cop beatin' up a guy, I'll be there."

Tom Joad (Henry Fonda) to Ma Joad (Jane Darwell) in *The Grapes of Wrath*, 1940.

The Farmer Takes a Wife (1935, Fox). *d:* Victor Fleming; *p:* Winfield Sheehan; *sc:* Edwin Burke—*b/o* the play by Frank B. Elser and Marc Connelly, and the novel *Rome Haul* by Walter D. Edmonds.

DAN HARROW: Conscientious young farmer in the 1800s who's working on the Erie Canal so he can make enough money to buy a farm and settle down with a wife.

Janet Gaynor, Charles Bickford, Slim Summerville, Andy Devine, Roger Imhof, Jane Withers, Margaret Hamilton, Siegfried Rumann, John Qualen, Kitty Kelly, Robert Gleckler.

Way Down East (1935, Fox). *d:* Henry King; *p:* Winfield Sheehan; *sc:* Howard Estabrook and William Hurlbut—*b/o* the play by Lottie Blair Parker.

DAVID BARTLETT: New England squire's son who falls in love with a young girl who's been accused of immorality after being tricked into a fake marriage and becoming an unwed mother.

Rochelle Hudson, Slim Summerville, Edward Trevor, Margaret Hamilton, Andy Devine, Russell Simpson, Spring Byington, Astrid Allwyn, Sara Haden, Clem Bevans, William Benedict.

I Dream Too Much (1935, RKO). *d:* John Cromwell; *p:* Pandro S. Berman; *sc:* James Gow and Edmund North—*b/o* a story by Elsie Finn and David G. Wittels.

JONATHAN: Young American composer whose marriage runs into trouble when his French wife becomes a successful opera singer.

Lily Pons, Eric Blore, Osgood Perkins, Lucien Littlefield, Esther Dale, Lucille Ball, Mischa Auer, Paul Porcasi, Scott Beckett.

The Trail of the Lonesome Pine (1936, Para.). *d:* Henry Hathaway; *p:* Walter Wanger; *sc:* Grover

Jones (adaptation by Harvey Threw and Horace McCoy)—*b/o* the novel by John Fox Jr.

DAVE TOLLIVER: Young Kentucky mountaineer whose family, the Tollivers, carries on a generations-old feud with another family, the Falins, while a railroad is being built on the feuders' land.

Fred MacMurray, Sylvia Sidney, Fred Stone, Beulah Bondi, Fuzzy Knight, Robert Barrat, Spanky McFarland, Nigel Bruce, Frank McGlynn Jr., Alan Baxter, Hank Bell, Richard Carle, Bud Geary, Bob Cortman.

The Moon's Our Home (1936, Para.). *d:* William A. Seiter; *p:* Walter Wanger; *sc:* Isabel Dawn and Boyce DeGaw (additional dialogue by Dorothy Parker and Alan Campbell)—*b/o* the novel by Faith Baldwin.

ANTHONY AMBERTON: New York novelist/explorer who meets a headstrong movie star and marries her on impulse, even though neither realizes who the other really is.

Margaret Sullavan, Charles Butterworth, Beulah Bondi, Margaret Hamilton, Henrietta Crosman, Dorothy Stickney, Lucien Littlefield, Walter Brennan, Spencer Charters.

Spendthrift (1936, Para.). *d:* Raoul Walsh; *p:* Walter Wanger; *sc:* Raoul Walsh and Bert Hanlon—*b/o* a story by Eric Hatch.

TOWNSEND MIDDLETON: Polo-playing millionaire playboy who finds himself without any cash because of his extravagant spending habits.

Pat Paterson, Mary Brian, June Brewster, George Barbier, Halliwell Hobbes, Spencer Charters, Richard Carle, J. M. Kerrigan, Edward Brophy.

Wings of the Morning (1937, 20th-Fox). *d:* Harold Schuster; *p:* Robert T. Kane; *sc:* Tom Geraghty—*b/o* stories by Donn Byrne.

KERRY: Canadian horse trainer in Ireland who, while training a horse to win the Derby at Epsom Downs, falls for the great-granddaughter of a gypsy princess.

Annabella, Leslie Banks, Stewart Rome, Irene Vanbrugh, Harry Tate, Helen Haye, Teddy Underdown, John McCormack.

You Only Live Once (1937, UA). *d:* Fritz Lang; *p:* Walter Wanger; *sc:* Gene Towne and Graham Baker.

EDDIE TAYLOR: Young ex-con who—after trying to go straight—lands back in prison for a murder he didn't commit, but then breaks out and tries to escape to Canada with his faithful wife.

Sylvia Sidney, Barton MacLane, Jean Dixon, William Gargan, Jerome Cowan, Chic Sale, Margaret Hamilton, Warren Hymer, Guinn Williams, John Wray, Jonathan Hale, Ward Bond, Wade Boteler.

Slim (1937, WB). *d:* Ray Enright; *p:* Hal B. Wallis; *sc:* William Wister Haines—*b/o* his novel.

SLIM: Naïve farm boy who, when he becomes a high-tension lineman, is taken under the wing of a tough veteran lineman but clashes with him over a girl.

Pat O'Brien, Margaret Lindsay, Stuart Erwin, J. Farrell MacDonald, John Litel, Dick Purcell, Joe Sawyer, Craig Reynolds, Jane Wyman, Dick Wessell, Walter Miller.

That Certain Woman (1937, WB). *d:* Edmund Goulding; *p:* Hal B. Wallis; *sc:* Edmund Goulding—*b/o* his original screenplay *The Trespasser.*

JACK MERRICK: Playboy who runs into marital problems when he marries a gangster's widow who's trying to make a better life for herself.

Bette Davis, Ian Hunter, Anita Louise, Donald Crisp, Katherine Alexander, Minor Watson, Ben Welden, Sidney Toler, Charles Trowbridge, Herbert Rawlinson, Frank Faylen, Willard Parker.

I Met My Love Again (1938, UA). *d:* Arthur Ripley and Joshua Logan; *p:* Walter Wanger; *sc:* David Hertz—*b/o* the novel *Summer Lightning* by Allene Corliss.

IVES TOWNER: Vermont college professor whose life is disrupted when his ex-love—who eloped ten years before with a romantic author—returns home as a widow.

Joan Bennett, Dame May Whitty, Alan Marshal, Louise Platt, Alan Baxter, Tim Holt, Dorothy Stickney, Florence Lake.

Jezebel (1938, WB). *d:* William Wyler; *p:* Hal B. Wallis and Henry Blanke; *sc:* Clement Ripley, Abem Finkel, and John Huston—*b/o* the play by Owen Davis Sr.

PRESTON DILLARD: Pre–Civil War New Orleans banker who, after breaking his engagement when his fiery Southern belle fiancée goes too far to make him jealous, becomes a victim of a yellow-fever plague.

Bette Davis, George Brent, Donald Crisp, Fay Bainter, Margaret Lindsay, Henry O'Neill, John Litel, Gordon Oliver, Spring Byington, Richard Cromwell, Irving Pichel, Eddie Anderson.

Blockade (1938, UA). *d:* William Dieterle; *p:* Walter Wanger; *sc:* John Howard Lawson.

MARCO: Peace-loving farmer who becomes a nationalist lieutenant during the Spanish Civil War and falls in love with a beautiful blonde Rebel spy.

Madeleine Carroll, Leo Carillo, John Halliday, Vladimir Sokoloff, Reginald Denny, Robert Warwick, William B. Davidson, Fred Kohler, Peter Godfrey, Katherine De Mille, Arthur Aylesworth.

Spawn of the North (1938, Para.). *d:* Henry Hathaway; *p:* Albert Lewin; *sc:* Jules Furthman—*b/o* the novel by Barrett Willoughby.

JIM KIMMERLEE: Salmon-cannery owner in Alaska who, after taking on his old pal as a partner, clashes with him when the friend joins Russian poachers who are trying to take over the salmon industry.

George Raft, Dorothy Lamour, Louise Platt, John Barrymore, Akim Tamiroff, Lynne Overman, Fuzzy Knight, Vladimir Sokoloff, Duncan Renaldo, Archie Twitchell, Wade Boteler, Henry Brandon, Monte Blue, Irving Bacon, Robert Middlemass, John Wray.

The Mad Miss Manton (1938, RKO). *d:* Leigh Jason; *p:* P. J. Wolfson; *sc:* Philip G. Epstein—*b/o* a story by Wilson Collinson.

PETER AMES: Newspaper columnist who becomes involved with a zany socialite-turned-sleuth and her debutante friends when they set out to solve a murder mystery.

Barbara Stanwyck, Sam Levene, Frances Mercer, Stanley Ridges, Whitney Bourne, Vicki Lester, Ann Evers, Hattie McDaniel, James Burke, Paul Guilfoyle, Penny Singleton, Miles Mander, John Qualen, Grady Sutton, Olin Howland.

Jesse James (1939, 20th-Fox). *d:* Henry King; *p:* Darryl F. Zanuck; *sc:* Nunnally Johnson—*b/o* historical material gathered by Rosalind Shaffer and Jo Frances James.

FRANK JAMES: Post–Civil War Missouri farm boy who, along with his brother, Jesse James, turns to robbing trains when railroad employees harass their family.

Tyrone Power, Nancy Kelly, Randolph Scott, Henry Hull, Slim Summerville, J. Edward Bromberg, Brian Donlevy, John Carradine, Donald Meek, Jane Darwell, John Russell, George Chandler, Charles Middleton, Lon Chaney Jr.

Let Us Live (1939, Col.). *d:* John Brahm; *p:* William Perlberg; *sc:* Anthony Veiller and Allen Rivkin—*b/o* a story by Joseph F. Dineen.

BRICK TENNANT: Innocent taxicab driver who is mistakenly identified as a murderer and is sentenced to die in the electric chair.

Maureen O'Sullivan, Ralph Bellamy, Alan Baxter, Stanley Ridges, Henry Kolker, Peter Lynn, George Douglas, Philip Trent, Martin Spellman, Charles Lane.

The Story of Alexander Graham Bell (1939, 20th-Fox). *d:* Irving Cummings; *p:* Kenneth Macgowan; *sc:* Lamar Trotti—*b/o* a story by Ray Harris.

THOMAS WATSON: Loyal assistant who works with Alexander Graham Bell in the 1870s as Bell struggles to invent the telephone.

Don Ameche, Loretta Young, Charles Coburn, Gene Lockhart, Spring Byington, Sally Blane, Polly Ann Young, Georgianna Young, Bobs Watson, Russell Hicks, Jonathan Hale, Harry Davenport, Elizabeth Patterson, Charles Trowbridge, Zeffie Tilbury.

Young Mr. Lincoln (1939, 20th-Fox). *d:* John Ford; *p:* Darryl F. Zanuck; *sc:* Lamar Trotti.

ABRAHAM LINCOLN: Struggling young lawyer in 1830s Illinois who stops a lynching and proves that a young man is innocent of murder.

Alice Brady, Marjorie Weaver, Arleen Whelan, Eddie Collins, Pauline Moore, Richard Cromwell, Donald Meek, Dorris Bowdon, Eddie Quillan, Spencer Charters, Ward Bond, Milburn Stone, Cliff Clark, Robert Lowery, Francis Ford, Fred Kohler, Russell Simpson, Edwin Maxwell, Charles Halton.

Drums Along the Mohawk (1939, 20th-Fox). *d:* John Ford; *p:* Darryl F. Zanuck; *sc:* Lamar Trotti and Sonya Levien—*b/o* the novel by Walter D. Edmonds.

GILBERT MARTIN: Hardy pioneer in colonial New York during the French and Indian War who, when the Indians destroy his family's Mohawk Valley cabin and burn his wheat, fights alongside his fellow colonists to hold the valley.

Claudette Colbert, Edna May Oliver, Eddie Collins, John Carradine, Jessie Ralph, Arthur Shields, Robert Lowery, Roger Imhof, Francis Ford, Ward Bond, Russell Simpson, Spencer Charters, Si Jenks, Arthur Aylesworth, Chief Big Tree, Clarence Wilson, Lionel Pape, Robert Grieg.

The Grapes of Wrath (1940, 20th-Fox). *d:* John Ford; *p:* Darryl F. Zanuck; *sc:* Nunnally Johnson—*b/o* the novel by John Steinbeck.

TOM JOAD*: Embittered, hard-nosed ex-convict who, after the Dust Bowl disaster during the 1930s Depression, makes the long trek from Oklahoma to California—along with his "Okie" family—to find a better life.

Jane Darwell, John Carradine, Charley Grapewin, Russell Simpson, Eddie Quillan, John Qualen, Zeffie Tilbury, Frank Sully, Darryl Hickman, Roger. Imhof, Grant Mitchell, John Arledge, Ward Bond, Arthur Aylesworth, Selmer Jackson, Charles Middleton, Paul Guilfoyle, Cliff Clark, Joseph Sawyer, Frank Faylen, Adrian Morris, Irving Bacon.

Lillian Russell (1940, 20th-Fox). *d:* Irving Cummings; *p:* Darryl F. Zanuck; *sc:* William Anthony McGuire.

ALEXANDER MOORE: One of the many male

---

*Received an Academy Award nomination as Best Actor for this role.

admirers of Lillian Russell, the famous Gay '90s American stage star.

Alice Faye, Don Ameche, Edward Arnold, Warren William, Leo Carillo, Helen Westley, Dorothy Peterson, Ernest Truex, Nigel Bruce, Claude Allister, Lynn Bari, Weber and Fields, Una O'Connor, Eddie Foy Jr., Elyse Knox, William Davidson, Hal K. Dawson, Charles Halton, Frank Sully, C. Cunningham.

The Return of Frank James (1940, 20th-Fox). *d:* Fritz Lang; *p:* Darryl F. Zanuck; *sc:* Sam Hellman.

FRANK JAMES: Famed outlaw Jesse James's older brother who avenges Jesse's murder by Bob Ford, then is acquitted when put on trial.

Gene Tierney, Jackie Cooper, Henry Hull, John Carradine, J. Edward Bromberg, Donald Meek, Eddie Collins, George Barbier, Lloyd Corrigan, Russell Hicks, Victor Kilian, George Chandler, Irving Bacon, Barbara Pepper, Stymie Beard, Frank Sully.

Chad Hanna (1940, 20th-Fox). *d:* Henry King; *p:* Nunnally Johnson; *sc:* Nunnally Johnson—*b/o* the novel *Red Wheels Rolling* by Walter D. Edmonds.

CHAD HANNA: Country boy who joins a small traveling circus in 1840s upstate New York after he becomes infatuated with the show's pretty bareback rider.

Dorothy Lamour, Linda Darnell, Guy Kibbee, Jane Darwell, John Carradine, Ted North, Roscoe Ates, Ben Carter, Frank Thomas, Olin Howland, Edward McWade, Sarah Padden, Tully Marshall, Almira Sessions, Virginia Brissac, Si Jenks, Victor Kilian, Louis Mason.

The Lady Eve (1941, Para.). *d:* Preston Sturges; *p:* Paul Jones; *sc:* Preston Sturges—*b/o* a story by Monckton Hoffe.

CHARLES PIKE: Naïve millionaire naturalist who, when he takes an ocean voyage, becomes the target of a glamorous gold digger and her card-shark father.

Barbara Stanwyck, Charles Coburn, Eugene Pallette, William Demarest, Eric Blore, Melville Cooper, Martha O'Driscoll, Janet Beecher, Robert Greig, Luis Alberni.

Wild Geese Calling (1941, 20th-Fox). *d:* John Brahm; *p:* Harry Joe Brown; *sc:* Horace McCoy—*b/o* a novel by Stewart Edward White.

JOHN MURDOCK: Oregon lumberjack who, while battling the elements and badmen of the 1890s Northwest woods, marries a honkytonk girl, then wrongly suspects her of infidelity but reconciles with her when she has his baby.

Joan Bennett, Warren William, Ona Munson, Barton MacLane, Russell Simpson, Iris Adrian, James C. Morton, Stanley Andrews, Robert Emmett Keane, Charles Middleton.

You Belong to Me (1941, Col.). *d:* Wesley Ruggles; *p:* Wesley Ruggles; *sc:* Claude Binyon—*b/o* a story by Dalton Trumbo.

PETER KIRK: Young millionaire playboy whose marriage to an attractive doctor hits a snag when he finds himself becoming jealous of her male patients.

Barbara Stanwyck, Edgar Buchanan, Roger Clark, Ruth Donnelly, Melville Cooper, Maude Eburne, Renie Riano, Mary Treen, Gordon Jones, Fritz Feld, Paul Harvey.

The Male Animal (1942, WB). *d:* Elliott Nugent; *p:* Hal B. Wallis; *sc:* Julius J. Epstein and Philip G. Epstein—*b/o* the play by James Thurber and Elliott Nugent.

TOMMY TURNER: Staid, bespectacled college professor who finally asserts his rights when his wife becomes attracted to a former football-hero friend from college days who visits them on the weekend of a big game.

Olivia de Havilland, Jack Carson, Joan Leslie, Eugene Pallette, Herbert Anderson, Ivan Simpson, Don DeFore, Hattie McDaniel, Frank Mayo, William B. Davidson.

Rings on Her Fingers (1942, 20th-Fox). *d:* Rouben Mamoulian; *p:* Milton Sperling; *sc:* Ken Englund—*b/o* a story by Robert Pirosh and Joseph Schrank.

JOHN WHEELER: Naïve young man who falls for a beautiful salesgirl who's in cahoots with a pair of swindlers out to fleece him.

Gene Tierney, Laird Cregar, John Shepperd, Spring Byington, Marjorie Gateson, Frank Orth, Henry Stephenson, Iris Adrian, Thurston Hall, Clara Blandick, Charles Wilson, George Lloyd.

The Magnificent Dope (1942, 20th-Fox). *d:* Walter Lang; *p:* William Perlberg; *sc:* George Seaton—*b/o* a story by Joseph Schrank.

TAD PAGE: Hick from the sticks who, after he's brought to New York by a "success" school as a publicity stunt to find America's most complete failure, winds up outwitting the city slickers.

Lynn Bari, Don Ameche, Edward Everett Horton, George Barbier, Frank Orth, Roseanne Murray, Kitty McHugh, Hobart Cavanaugh, Hal K. Dawson, Chick Chandler, William Davidson, Harry Hayden, Pierre Watkin.

Tales of Manhattan (1942, 20th-Fox). *d:* Julien Duvivier; *p:* Boris Morros and S. P. Eagle (Sam Spiegel); *original stories/sc:* Ben Hecht, Ferenc Molnar, Donald Ogden Stewart, Samuel Hoffenstein, Alan Campbell, Ladislas Fodor, Laslo Vadnay, Laszlo Gorog, Lamar Trotti, and Henry Blankfort.

GEORGE: One of the many New York characters involved in the history of a suit of tails as it is passed from owner to owner.

Charles Boyer, Rita Hayworth, Thomas Mitchell, *Ginger Rogers,* Cesar Romero, Gail Patrick, Charles Laughton, Elsa Lanchester, Edward G. Robinson, George Sanders, James Gleason, Paul Robeson, Ethel Waters, Eddie (Rochester) Anderson.

The Big Street (1942, RKO). *d:* Irving Reis; *p:* Damon Runyon; *sc:* Leonard Spigelgass—*b/o* the story "The Little Pinks" by Damon Runyon.

"LITTLE PINKS": Naïve Broadway busboy who idolizes a crippled nightclub singer who selfishly accepts his devotion and help without loving or even appreciating him in return.

Lucille Ball, Barton MacLane, Eugene Pallette, Agnes Moorehead, Sam Levene, Ray Collins, Marion Martin, William Orr, George Cleveland, Louise Beavers, Millard Mitchell, Harry Shannon.

The Immortal Sergeant (1943, 20th-Fox). *d:* John Stahl; *p:* Lamar Trotti; *sc:* Lamar Trotti—*b/o* a novel by John Brophy.

CPL. COLIN SPENCE: Former newspaperman/ novelist who, as a timid corporal in the WWII British Army in Libya, is transformed into a combat leader by a tough old battle-hardened sergeant.

Maureen O'Hara, Thomas Mitchell, Allyn Joslyn, Reginald Gardiner, Melville Cooper, Bramwell Fletcher, Morton Lowry, Donald Stuart, Heather Wilde, Italia De Nubila.

The Ox-Bow Incident (1943, 20th-Fox). *d:* William A. Wellman; *p:* Lamar Trotti; *sc:* Lamar Trotti—*b/o* the novel by Walter Van Tilburg Clark.

GIL CARTER: Itinerant cowpoke in 1885 who futilely tries to prevent a mob from lynching three men who have been tracked down at the Ox-Bow (a small valley in the mountains of Nevada) and wrongly accused of murdering a rancher.

Dana Andrews, Mary Beth Hughes, Anthony Quinn, William Eythe, Henry Morgan, Jane Darwell, Harry Davenport, Frank Conroy, Marc Lawrence, Paul Hurst, Victor Kilian, Chris-Pin Martin, Ted North, George Meeker, Margaret Hamilton, Francis Ford, George Lloyd.

My Darling Clementine (1946, 20th-Fox). *d:* John Ford; *p:* Samuel G. Engel; *sc:* Samuel G. Engel and Winston Miller—*b/o* a story by Sam Hellman from a book by Stuart N. Lake.

WYATT EARP: Famed Old West marshal who cleans up the town of Tombstone, Arizona, and, with his brothers and Doc Holliday, wipes out the infamous Clanton gang in the epic 1881 gunfight at the OK Corral.

Linda Darnell, Victor Mature, Walter Brennan, Tim Holt, Cathy Downs, Ward Bond, Alan Mowbray, John Ireland, Jane Darwell, Roy Roberts, Grant Withers, J. Farrell MacDonald, Russell Simpson, Francis Ford.

The Long Night (1947, RKO). *d:* Anatole Litvak; *p:* Robert Hakim and Raymond Hakim; *sc:* John Wexley—*b/o* a story by Jacques Viot.

JOE: Moody young man in a Pennsylvania mill town who, when his girlfriend is seduced by a carnival magician, shoots the magician and then barricades himself in his tenement room as the police close in.

Barbara Bel Geddes, Vincent Price, Ann Dvorak, Howard Freeman, Moroni Olsen, Elisha Cook Jr., Queenie Smith, Charles McGraw.

The Fugitive (1947, Argosy–RKO). *d:* John Ford; *p:* Merian C. Cooper and John Ford; *sc:* Dudley Nichols—*b/o* Graham Greene's novel *The Power and the Glory.*

"FUGITIVE": Revolutionary Latin American priest who, while on the run in a police state, is befriended and harbored by a man who later betrays him for silver.

Delores Del Rio, Pedro Armendariz, J. Carrol Naish, Leo Carillo, Ward Bond, Robert Armstrong, John Qualen, Fortunio Bonanova, Cris-Pin Martin.

Daisy Kenyon (1947, 20th-Fox). *d:* Otto Preminger; *p:* Otto Preminger; *sc:* David Hertz—*b/o* a novel by Elizabeth Janeway.

PETER LAPHAM: WWII veteran and boat designer who marries a chic New York dress designer, then is faced with losing her to her former lover, a wealthy lawyer who's finally gotten a divorce so that he can marry her.

Joan Crawford, Dana Andrews, Ruth Warrick, Martha Stewart, Peggy Ann Garner, Connie Marshall, Nicholas Joy, Art Baker, Charles Meredith, Roy Roberts, Griff Barnett.

On Our Merry Way (1948, UA). *d:* King Vidor and Leslie Fenton; *p:* Benedict Bogeaus and Burgess Meredith; *sc:* Laurence Stallings and Lou Breslow—*b/o* a story by Arch Oboler (original material for Fonda-Stewart sequence by John O'Hara).

LANK: One of a pair of musicians who try to make a fast buck by fixing an amateur music contest at a California beach resort so that the local mayor's son wins.

Burgess Meredith, Paulette Goddard, Fred MacMurray, Hugh Herbert, James Stewart, Dorothy Lamour, Victor Moore, William Demarest, Charles D. Brown, Tom Fadden, Paul Hurst, Carl "Alfalfa" Switzer.

Fort Apache (1948, RKO). *d:* John Ford; John Ford and Merian C. Cooper (Argosy); *sc:* Frank S. Nugent—*b/o* the *Saturday Evening Post* story "Massacre" by James Warner Bellah.

LT. COL. OWEN THURSDAY: Newly arrived U.S. Cavalry commander at Fort Apache, Arizona, who, despite the warning of his veteran captain, foolishly leads his outnumbered troops to slaughter in a battle against Apaches led by Cochise.

John Wayne, Shirley Temple, Pedro Armendariz, Ward Bond, Irene Rich, John Agar, George O'Brien, Anna Lee, Victor McLaglen, Dick Foran, Jack Pennick, Guy Kibbee, Grant Withers, Mae Marsh, Movita (Maria Castaneda), Mary Gordon, Francis Ford, Frank Ferguson.

Mister Roberts (1955, WB). *d:* John Ford and Mervyn LeRoy; *p:* Leland Hayward (Orange); *sc:* Frank Nugent and Joshua Logan—from the play by Joshua Logan and Thomas Heggen, *b/o* the novel by Thomas Heggen.

LT. DOUGLAS ROBERTS: Highly respected, well-liked executive officer on a WWII cargo ship in the Pacific who, despite opposition from his tyrannical captain, keeps trying to get transferred to a combat ship.

James Cagney, William Powell, Jack Lemmon, Betsy Palmer, Ward Bond, Phil Carey, Martin Milner, James Flavin, Jack Pennick, Ken Curtis, Nick Adams, Harry Carey Jr., William Henry, Perry Lopez, Robert Roark, Pat Wayne, Tiger Andrews.

War and Peace (1956, Para.). *d:* King Vidor; *p:* Dino De Laurentiis (A Ponti–De Laurentiis Production); *sc:* Bridget Boland, King Vidor, Robert Westerby, Mario Camerini, Ennio De Concini, and Ivo Perilli—*b/o* the novel by Leo Tolstoy.

PIERRE: Intellectual but bumbling Frenchman who becomes involved in Napoleon Bonaparte's invasion of Russia as he tries to learn why men fight wars and searches for the meaning of life.

Audrey Hepburn, Mel Ferrer, Vittorio Gassman, John Mills, Herbert Lom, Oscar Homolka, Anita Ekberg, Helmut Dantine, Barry Jones, Jeremy Brett, May Britt, Tullio Carminati, Wilfred Lawson.

The Wrong Man (1957, WB). *d:* Alfred Hitchcock; *p:* Herbert Coleman; *sc:* Maxwell Anderson and Angus MacPhail—*b/o* a story by Maxwell Anderson.

MANNY BALESTRERO: Jazz musician in New York's Stork Club who, after he's mistakenly identified as an armed bandit, is finally proved innocent—but not before the strain has caused his wife to have a mental breakdown.

Vera Miles, Anthony Quayle, Harold J. Stone, Charles Cooper, John Heldabrand, Esther Minciotti, Doreen Lang, Nehemiah Persoff.

The Tin Star (1957, Para.). *d:* Anthony Mann; *p:* William Perlberg and George Seaton (Perlberg–

Seaton); *sc:* Dudley Nichols—*b/o* a story by Barney Slater and Joel Kane.

MORG HICKMAN: Ex–sheriff–turned–bounty hunter who helps an inept young sheriff handle a tough town bully and his gang of outlaws.

Anthony Perkins, Betsy Palmer, Michel Ray, Neville Brand, John McIntire, Lee Van Cleef, James Bell, Howard Petrie, Russell Simpson, Hal K. Dawson, Mickey Finn.

12 Angry Men (1957, UA). *d:* Sidney Lumet; *p:* Henry Fonda and Reginald Rose; *sc:* Reginald Rose—*b/o* the TV play by Reginald Rose.

"JUROR NO. 8" (DAVID): Open-minded, conscientious member of a murder-trial jury who, when the other eleven jurors hastily vote to convict a boy accused of killing his father, finally manages to persuade them to vote "not guilty."

Lee J. Cobb, Ed Begley, E. G. Marshall, Jack Warden, Martin Balsam, John Fiedler, Jack Klugman, Edward Binns, Joseph Sweeney, George Voscovec, Robert Webber, Rudy Bond, James A. Kelly, Bill Nelson, John Savoca.

Stage Struck (1958, RKO). *d:* Sidney Lumet; *p:* Stuart Millar; *sc:* Ruth Goetz and Augustus Goetz—*b/o* the play *Morning Glory* by Zoe Akins.

LEWIS EASTON: Suave, worldly Broadway producer who becomes involved with a small-town stage-struck actress who has come to New York determined to become a big star.

Susan Strasberg, Joan Greenwood, Christopher Plummer, Herbert Marshall, Sally Gracie, Patricia Englund, Dan Ocko, Jack Weston, Pat Harrington, Frank Campanella, John Fiedler.

Warlock (1959, 20th-Fox). *d:* Edward Dmytryk; *p:* Edward Dmytryk; *sc:* Robert Alan Aurthur—*b/o* the novel by Oakley Hall.

CLAY BLAISDELL: Steel-nerved gunfighter who, after he's hired as an unofficial marshal by the citizens of Warlock to wipe out a gang of outlaws, finds that the townspeople have turned against him.

Richard Widmark, Anthony Quinn, Dorothy Malone, Dolores Michaels, Wallace Ford, Tom Drake, Richard Arlen, DeForest Kelley, Regis Toomey, Vaughn Taylor, Don Beddoe, Whit Bissell, Donald Barry, Frank Gorshin, Ian MacDonald, L. Q. Jones, Robert Osterloh, Joe Turkel, Ann Doran.

The Man Who Understood Women (1959, 20th-Fox). *d:* Nunnally Johnson; *p:* Nunnally Johnson; *sc:* Nunnally Johnson—*b/o* the novel *Colors of the Day* by Romain Gary.

WILLIE BAUCHE: Hollywood writer-director-producer who turns an ambitious young actress into a famous star, marries her, then never finds time for her—until she's attracted to a French soldier of fortune.

Leslie Caron, Cesare Danova, Myron McCormick, Marcel Dalio, Conrad Nagel, Edwin Jerome, Frank Cady.

Advise and Consent (1962, Col.). *d:* Otto Preminger; *p:* Otto Preminger (Carlyle/Alpha); *sc:* Wendell Mayes—*b/o* the novel by Allen Drury.

ROBERT LEFFINGWELL: Political liberal whose nomination by the president to be secretary of state causes a division in the Senate and results in the blackmail and suicide of a young senator.

Charles Laughton, Don Murray, Walter Pidgeon, Peter Lawford, Gene Tierney, Franchot Tone, Lew Ayres, Burgess Meredith, Eddie Hodges, Paul Ford, George Grizzard, Inga Swenson, Will Geer, Edward Andrews, Betty White, Malcolm Atterbury, Tiki Santos.

The Longest Day (1962, 20th-Fox). *d:* Ken Annakin, Andrew Martin, and Bernhard Wicki; *sc:* Cornelius Ryan (additional material by Romain Gary, James Jones, David Pursall, and Jack Seddon)—*b/o* the book by Cornelius Ryan.

GEN. THEODORE ROOSEVELT JR.: Eldest son of President Theodore Roosevelt who bravely leads elements of the U.S. 4th Infantry Division in the first wave to hit Utah Beach on D-Day, June 6, 1944.

John Wayne, Robert Mitchum, Robert Ryan, Rod Steiger, Robert Wagner, Richard Beymer, Mel Ferrer, Jeffrey Hunter, Paul Anka, Sal Mineo, Roddy McDowall, Stuart Whitman, Eddie Albert, Edmond O'Brien, Fabian, Red Buttons, Tom Tryon, Alexander Knox, Tommy Sands, Ray Danton, Steve Forrest, Richard Burton, Kenneth More, Peter Lawford, Richard Todd, Sean Connery, Curt Jurgens, Peter Van Eyck, Gert Froebe, Hans Christian Blech.

How the West Was Won (1963, MGM/Cinerama). *d:* Henry Hathaway, John Ford, and George Marshall; *p:* Bernard Smith; *sc:* James R. Webb—*b/o* the series *How the West Was Won* in *Life* magazine.

JETHRO STUART: Shaggy, grizzled buffalo hunter who is one of many colorful pioneers involved in the winning of the West in the 1800s.

Carroll Baker, Lee J. Cobb, Carolyn Jones, Karl Malden, Gregory Peck, George Peppard, Robert Preston, Debbie Reynolds, James Stewart, Eli Wallach, John Wayne, Richard Widmark, Walter Brennan, David Brian, Andy Devine, Raymond Massey, Agnes Moorehead, Henry (Harry) Morgan, Thelma Ritter, Mickey Shaughnessy, Russ Tamblyn.

Spencer's Mountain (1963, WB). *d:* Delmer Daves; *p:* Delmer Daves; *sc:* Delmer Daves—*b/o* the novel by Earl Hamner Jr.

CLAY SPENCER: Poor quarry worker in 1930s Wyoming who, despite various financial problems,

keeps promising to build another home for his wife and family of nine.

Maureen O'Hara, James MacArthur, Donald Crisp, Wally Cox, Mimsy Farmer, Virginia Gregg, Lillian Bronson, Whit Bissell, Hayden Rorke, Dub Taylor, Hope Summers, Barbara McNair, Buzz Henry.

The Best Man (1964, UA). *d:* Franklin Schaffner; *p:* Stuart Millar and Lawrence Turman; *sc:* Gore Vidal—*b/o* his play.

WILLIAM RUSSELL: Former secretary of state who becomes a liberal contender for the presidential nomination and, while at a political convention in Los Angeles, vies with a conservative candidate for the endorsement of the dying ex-president.

Cliff Robertson, Edie Adams, Margaret Leighton, Shelley Berman, Lee Tracy, Ann Sothern, Gene Raymond, Kevin McCarthy, Mahalia Jackson, Howard K. Smith, John Henry Faulk, Richard Arlen, Penny Singleton, Mary Lawrence, Blossom Rock.

Fail Safe (1964, Col.). *d:* Sidney Lumet; *p:* Max E. Youngstein; *sc:* Walter Bernstein—*b/o* the novel by Eugene Burdick and Harvey Wheeler.

THE PRESIDENT: President of the United States who, when an American Strategic Air Command plane accidentally drops a nuclear bomb on Moscow, tells the premier of the U.S.S.R. that the U.S. will compensate by dropping a bomb on New York.

Dan O'Herlihy, Walter Matthau, Frank Overton, Edward Binns, Fritz Weaver, Larry Hagman, William Hansen, Russell Hardie, Russell Collins, Hildy Parks, Dom DeLuise, Dana Elcar.

Sex and the Single Girl (1964, WB). *d:* Richard Quine; *p:* William T. Orr; *sc:* Joseph Heller and David R. Schwartz—from a story by Joseph Hoffman, *b/o* the book by Helen Gurley Brown.

FRANK: Male half of a battling married couple who are neighbors of a scandal-magazine editor who is involved with a female psychologist–sex researcher.

Natalie Wood, Tony Curtis, Lauren Bacall, Mel Ferrer, Fran Jeffries, Leslie Parrish, Edward Everett Horton, Larry Storch, Stubby Kaye, Howard St. John, Otto Kruger, Helen Kleeb, Count Basie and his Orchestra.

The Rounders (1965, MGM). *d:* Burt Kennedy; *p:* Richard E. Lyons; *sc:* Burt Kennedy—*b/o* a novel by Max Evans.

HOWDY LEWIS: One of a pair of aging itinerant bronco busters who, when they sign up with a tightwad rancher to break a string of horses, run up against an especially rambunctious roan.

Glenn Ford, Sue Ane Langdon, Hope Holiday, Chill Wills, Edgar Buchanan, Kathleen Freeman,

Joan Freeman, Denver Pyle, Barton MacLane, Doodles Weaver, Allegra Varron.

In Harm's Way (1965, Para.). *d:* Otto Preminger; *p:* Otto Preminger (Sigma); *sc:* Wendell Mayes—*b/o* the novel by James Bassett.

Billed as "CINCPAC II ADMIRAL": U.S. admiral who is in command of the Pacific Theater in WWII.

John Wayne, Kirk Douglas, Patricia Neal, Tom Tryon, Paula Prentiss, Brandon De Wilde, Jill Haworth, Dana Andrews, Stanley Holloway, Burgess Meredith, Franchot Tone, Patrick O'Neal, Carroll O'Connor, Slim Pickens, James Mitchum, George Kennedy, Bruce Cabot, Hugh O'Brian, Tod Andrews, Larry Hagman, Christopher George.

Battle of the Bulge (1965, WB). *d:* Ken Annakin; *p:* Sidney Harmon, Milton Sperling, and Philip Yordan (United States Pictures); *sc:* Philip Yordan, Milton Sperling, and John Nelson.

LT. COL. KILEY: WWII American lieutenant colonel in the Ardennes during the Battle of the Bulge in December, 1944, who helps outwit a crack Nazi Panzer commander.

Robert Shaw, Robert Ryan, Dana Andrews, George Montgomery, Ty Hardin, Pier Angeli, Barbara Werle, Charles Bronson, Werner Peters, Hans Christian Blech, James MacArthur, Telly Savalas.

A Big Hand for the Little Lady (1966, WB). *d:* Fielder Cook; *p:* Fielder Cook; *sc:* Sidney Carroll—*b/o* the TV play *Big Deal in Laredo* by Sidney Carroll.

MEREDITH: Compulsive gambler who, when he joins a high-stakes poker game in 1896 Laredo, apparently loses his life's savings but then, with the help of an accomplice (his wife), cleverly wins it all back—plus a nice profit.

Joanne Woodward, Jason Robards, Paul Ford, Charles Bickford, Burgess Meredith, Kevin McCarthy, Robert Middleton, John Qualen, Jim Boles, Virginia Gregg, Chester Conklin, Ned Glass, Mae Clarke, James Griffith.

The Dirty Game (1966, AIP). *d:* Terence Young, Christian-Jacque, and Carlo Lizzani; *p:* Richard Hellman (Franco-London/Echberg/Fair); *sc:* Jo Eisinger—*b/o* a screenplay by Jacques Remy, Christian-Jacque, Ennio de Concini, and Philippe Bouvard.

KOURLOV: Post-WWII Soviet intelligence officer who, when he breaks out of East Germany, is marked for assassination.

Robert Ryan, Vittorio Gassman, Annie Girardot, Bourvil, Robert Hossein, Peter Van Eyck, Maria Grazia Buccela.

Welcome to Hard Times (1967, MGM). *d:* Burt Kennedy; *p:* Max E. Youngstein and David Karr; *sc:* Burt Kennedy—*b/o* the novel by E. L. Doctorow.

WILL BLUE: Leading citizen of the tiny western town of Hard Times who refuses to stand up to a sadistic badman who terrorizes and practically destroys the town; but when the gunman returns, he shoots it out with him.

Janice Rule, Aldo Ray, Keenan Wynn, Janis Paige, John Anderson, Warren Oates, Fay Spain, Edgar Buchanan, Denver Pyle, Michael Shea, Arlene Golonka, Lon Chaney, Alan Baxter, Elisha Cook.

Stranger on the Run (1967, Univ.). *d:* Donald Siegel; *p:* Richard E. Lyons; *sc:* Dean Reisner—*b/o* a story by Reginald Rose.

THE STRANGER: Drifter in an 1885 New Mexico railroad town who, when he's falsely accused of murder, becomes the object of a manhunt in the desert by a gang of brutal railroad police.

Michael Parks, Anne Baxter, Dan Duryea, Sal Mineo.

Firecreek (1968, WB–Seven Arts). *d:* Vincent McEveety; *p:* Philip Leacock; *sc:* Calvin Clements.

LARKIN: Ruthless leader of a gang of outlaws who, when he and his men terrorize the western town of Firecreek, is finally stopped by a mild-mannered farmer who's also the town's part-time sheriff.

James Stewart, Inger Stevens, Gary Lockwood, Dean Jagger, Ed Begley, Jay C. Flippen, Jack Elam, James Best, Barbara Luna, John Qualen.

Yours, Mine and Ours (1968, UA). *d:* Melville Shavelson; *p:* Robert F. Blumofe (Desilu/Walden); *sc:* Melville Shavelson and Mort Lachman—*b/o* a story by Madelyn Davis and Bob Carroll Jr.

FRANK BEARDSLEY: Navy officer widower with ten children whose life takes some interesting new twists when he marries a widowed Navy nurse with eight children, and they all move into an old San Francisco house.

Lucille Ball, Van Johnson, Tom Bosley, Louise Troy, Ben Murphy, Jennifer Leak, Keven Burchett, Kimberly Beck, Mitchell Vogel.

Madigan (1968, Univ.). *d:* Don Siegel; *p:* Frank P. Rosenberg; *sc:* Henri Simoun and Abraham Polonsky—*b/o* Richard Dougherty's novel *The Commissioner.*

COMMISSIONER ANTHONY X. RUSSELL: Relentless, up-from-the-ranks New York police commissioner who, though he disapproves of the methods used by a maverick detective, feels sorrow and respect for him when the detective is killed while bringing in a vicious cop-killer.

Richard Widmark, Inger Stevens, Harry Guardino, James Whitmore, Susan Clark, Michael Dunn, Don Stroud, Sheree North, Warren Stevens,

Raymond St. Jacques, Bert Freed, Harry Bellaver, Virginia Gregg, Ray Montgomery, Conrad Bain.

The Boston Strangler (1968, 20th-Fox). *d:* Richard Fleischer; *p:* Robert Fryer; *sc:* Edward Anhalt—*b/o* the book by Gerold Frank.

JOHN S. BOTTOMLEY: Dedicated special representative of the Massachusetts attorney general who coordinates the manhunt for the notorious Boston Strangler who terrorizes the city for more than a year during the 1960s.

Tony Curtis, George Kennedy, Mike Kellin, Hurd Hatfield, Murray Hamilton, Jeff Corey, Sally Kellerman, William Marshall, George Voscovec, Richard X. Slattery, Alex Dreier, John Cameron Swayze, James Brolin, Dana Elcar.

Once Upon a Time in the West (1969, Para.). *d:* Sergio Leone; *p:* Bino Cigogna and Fulvio Morsella (Rafran/San Marco); *sc:* Sergio Leone and Sergio Donati—*b/o* a story by Dario Argento, Bernardo Bertolucci, and Sergio Leone.

FRANK: Sadistic gunman in 1870s Kansas who is tracked down and killed by a mysterious harmonica-playing stranger seeking revenge for the torture and murder of his brother many years before.

Claudia Cardinale, Jason Robards, Charles Bronson, Frank Wolff, Gabriele Ferzetti, Keenan Wynn, Paolo Stoppa, Marco Zuanelli, Lionel Stander, Jack Elam, Woody Strode.

Too Late the Hero (1970, Cinerama). *d:* Robert Aldrich; *p:* Robert Aldrich (Associates and Aldrich/Palomar); *sc:* Robert Aldrich and Lukas Heller—*b/o* a story by Robert Aldrich and Robert Sherman.

CAPT. JOHN G. NOLAN: WWII U.S. Army officer in the Pacific who is involved in planning a mission to destroy Japanese positions on a small island.

Michael Caine, Cliff Robertson, Ian Bannen, Harry Andrews, Denholm Elliott, Ronald Fraser, Lance Percival, Percy Herbert, Michael J. Parsons, Sean Macduff, Martin Horsey.

There Was a Crooked Man (1970, WB–Seven Arts). *d:* Joseph L. Mankiewicz; *p:* Joseph L. Mankiewicz; *sc:* David Newman and Robert Benton.

WOODWARD LOPEMAN: Ex-lawman-turned-warden of an 1833 Arizona prison who, when one of his prisoners escapes to lay his hands on $500,000 but is done in by a rattlesnake, grabs the loot himself and heads for Mexico.

Kirk Douglas, Hume Cronyn, Warren Oates, Burgess Meredith, John Randolph, Arthur O'Connell, Martin Gabel, Michael Blodgett, Alan Hale, Lee Grant, Bert Freed.

The Cheyenne Social Club (1970, Nat. Gen.). *d:* Gene Kelly; *p:* James Lee Barrett and Gene Kelly; *sc:* James Lee Barrett.

HARLEY SULLIVAN: Itinerant cowpoke in 1867 who, when his sidekick inherits the "Cheyenne Social Club," is delighted when they discover that it is a high-class bawdy house.

James Stewart, Shirley Jones, Jackie Joseph, Sue Ane Langdon, Robert Middleton, Sharon De Bord, Elaine Devry, Jackie Russell, Dabbs Greer, Richard Collier, Arch Johnson.

Sometimes a Great Notion (1971, Univ.). *d:* Paul Newman; *p:* John Foreman (Newman–Foreman); *sc:* John Gay—*b/o* the novel by Ken Kesey.

HENRY STAMPER: Patriarch of a rough-and-ready Oregon logging family that encounters devastating results when it defies a local strike by other loggers in the area.

Paul Newman, Lee Remick, Michael Sarrazin, Joe Maross, Richard Jaeckel, Sam Gilman, Cliff Potts, Jim Burk, Linda Lawson, Roy Poole.

The Serpent (also called **Night Flight from Moscow**) (1973, Avco Embassy). *d:* Henri Verneuil; *p:* Henri Verneuil (Les Films La Boetie); *sc:* Henri Verneuil and Gilles Perrault—*b/o* the novel *Le 13e Suicide* by Pierre Nord.

ALLAN DAVIES: American CIA director involved in an espionage operation in which a KGB colonel defects to the West and turns over a list of his fellow agents to the CIA and British Intelligence.

Yul Brynner, Dirk Bogarde, Phillippe Noiret, Farley Granger, Virna Lisi, Robert Alda, Marie Dubois, Elga Andersen.

Ash Wednesday (1973, Para.). *d:* Larry Peerce; *p:* Dominick Dunne (Sagittarius); *sc:* Jean-Claude Tramont.

MARK SAWYER: Husband whose fiftyish wife undergoes extensive cosmetic surgery in Europe in a desperate attempt to win back his love.

Elizabeth Taylor, Helmut Berger, Keith Baxter, Maurice Teynac, Margaret Blye, Monique Van Vooren, Kathy Van Lypps, Andrea Esterhazy, Jill Pratt.

My Name Is Nobody (1973, Univ.). *d:* Tonino Valerii; *p:* Claudio Mancini (Sergio Leone Prod.); *sc:* Ernesto Gastaldi—*b/o* a story by Fulvio Morsella and Ernesto Gastaldi, from an idea by Sergio Leone.

JACK BEAUREGARD: The Old West's greatest surviving gunfighter (in 1899) who tries to retire but is talked into teaming up with a young gun-slinging admirer for one last battle—a shoot-out against 150 members of the notorious Wild Bunch.

Terence Hill, Jean Martin, Piero Lulli, Leo Gordon, R. G. Armstrong, Neil Summers.

Last Days of Mussolini (1974, Para.). *d:* Carlo Lizzani; *p:* Enzo Peri (Aquila Cinematografica); *sc:* Carlo Lizzani and Fabio Pittorra.

CARDINAL SCHUSTER: Catholic church official in dictator Benito Mussolini's WWII Italy who acts as a mediator between partisan leaders of Milan to spare the city from further bloodshed and destruction.

Rod Steiger, Lisa Gastoni, Franco Nero, Lino Capolicchio.

Midway (1976, Univ.). *d:* Jack Smight; *p:* Walter Mirisch (Mirisch); *sc:* Donald S. Sanford.

ADM. CHESTER W. NIMITZ: Commander of U.S. forces in the Pacific during the historic fight with the Japanese in June 1942 known as the Battle of Midway.

Charlton Heston, Toshiro Mifune, Edward Albert, Robert Mitchum, James Shigeta, James Coburn, Glenn Ford, Hal Holbrook, Cliff Robertson, Ed Nelson, Robert Wagner, Robert Webber, Monte Markham, Kevin Dobson, Biff McGuire, Christopher George, Glenn Corbett, Dabney Coleman.

Rollercoaster (1977, Univ.). *d:* James Goldstone; *p:* Jennings Lang; *sc:* Richard Levinson and William Link—*b/o* a story by Sanford Sheldon, Richard Levinson, and William Link, suggested by a story by Tommy Cook.

SIMON DAVENPORT: Security expert who is one of a team of safety officials and law officers trying to catch a pyrotechnics expert and extortionist who's been sabotaging rollercoasters from coast to coast.

George Segal, Richard Widmark, Timothy Bottoms, Harry Guardino, Susan Strasberg, Helen Hunt, Dorothy Tristan, Michael Bell, Charlie Tuna, William Prince.

Tentacles (1977, AIP). *d:* Oliver Hellman; *p:* Enzo Doria (Esse Cinematografica); *sc:* Jerome Max, Tito Carpi, and Steve Carabatsos.

MR. WHITEHEAD: Industrialist whose marine tunneling company's use of illegal underwater radio waves causes a giant octopus off the California coast to go on a killing spree, until it's stopped by two trained killer whales.

John Huston, Shelley Winters, Bo Hopkins, Cesare Danova, Alan Boyd, Claude Akins.

The Great Smokey Roadblock (1977, Dimension). *d:* John Leone; *p:* Allan F. Bodoh (Mar Visto/Ingo Preminger); *sc:* John Leone.

ELEGANT JOHN: Veteran trucker—dying from cancer—who swipes back his repossessed eighteen-wheeler for one last fling and roars across the U.S., helped by six hookers who work for his old flame.

Eileen Brennan, Robert Englund, John Byner, Austin Pendleton, Susan Sarandon, Melanie Mayron, Marya Small, Leigh French, Valerie Curtin, Bibi Osterwald.

The Swarm (1978, WB). *d:* Irwin Allen; *p:* Irwin Allen; *sc:* Stirling Silliphant—*b/o* a novel by Arthur Herzog.

DR. KRIM: Distinguished immunologist who is brought in to help fight a gigantic swarm of African killer bees that attack an Air Force base and a nearby town.

Michael Caine, Katharine Ross, Richard Widmark, Richard Chamberlain, Olivia de Havilland, Ben Johnson, Lee Grant, Jose Ferrer, Patty Duke Astin, Slim Pickens, Bradford Dillman, Fred MacMurray.

Fedora (1978, UA). *d:* Billy Wilder; *p:* Billy Wilder (Geria/SFP); *sc:* Billy Wilder and I. A. L. Diamond—*b/o* a story "Fedora" from Thomas Tryon's book *Crowned Heads.*

Appears as HENRY FONDA, but in the supposed capacity as the Motion Picture Academy's president who has come to a remote Greek island to present an Oscar to Fedora—a legendary retired movie star living in seclusion.

William Holden, Marthe Keller, Jose Ferrer, Frances Sternhagen, Mario Adorf, Stephen Collins, Hans Jaray, Gottfried John, Hildegard Knef, Michael York, Panos Papadopulos, Elma Karlowa, Christoph Kunzer.

Meteor (1979, AIP). *d:* Ronald Neame; *p:* Arnold Orgolini and Theodore Parvin; *sc:* Stanley Mann and Edmund H. North—*b/o* a story by Edmund H. North.

THE PRESIDENT: President of the United States who, when a gigantic meteor hurtles toward Earth, reaches an agreement with the Russian premier to blow it apart with orbiting American and Russian missiles.

Sean Connery, Natalie Wood, Karl Malden, Brian Keith, Martin Landau, Trevor Howard, Richard Dysart, Joseph Campanella, Bo Brundin, Roger Robinson.

City on Fire (1979, Avco Embassy). *d:* Alvin Rakoff; *p:* Claude Heroux (Sandy Heroux–Astral–Belvue–Pathé); *sc:* Jack Hill, David P. Lewis, and Celine LaFreniere.

CHIEF ALBERT RISLEY: Big-city fire chief who, when a disgruntled ex–refinery worker sets a fire that engulfs the city, leads the fight to bring it under control.

Barry Newman, Susan Clark, Shelley Winters, Leslie Nielsen, James Franciscus, Ava Gardner, Jonathan Welsh, Richard Donat, Ken James, Donald Pilon, Terry Haig.

Wanda Nevada (1979, UA). *d:* Peter Fonda; *p:* Neal Dobrofsky and Dennis Hackin (Panda Film); *sc:* Dennis Hackin.

Billed as "OLD PROSPECTOR": Old prospector in the 1950s Southwest who briefly encounters a gambler and a young girl he's won in a poker game as they search for gold in the hills of the Grand Canyon.

Peter Fonda, Brooke Shields, Fiona Lewis, Luke Askew, Ted Markland, Severn Darden, Paul Fix, Larry Golden, John Denos, Bert Williams.

The Greatest Battle (1979, Dimension). *d:* Humphrey Longan; *p:* Louis Martin and Humphrey Longan.

GENERAL FOSTER: Allied general involved in the WWII Battle of Mareth in North Africa during 1943.

Helmut Berger, Samantha Eggar, Giuliano Gemma, John Huston, Stacy Keach.

On Golden Pond (1981, Univ.). *d:* Mark Rydell; *p:* Bruce Gilbert (ITC Films/IPC Films); *sc:* Ernest Thompson—*b/o* his play.

NORMAN THAYER JR.*: Retired professor who, with the help of his understanding wife of forty-eight years, tries to cope with old age and approaching death as he observes his eightieth birthday at their summer vacation cottage in New Hampshire.

Katharine Hepburn, Jane Fonda, Doug McKeon, Dabney Coleman, William Lanteau, Chris Rydell.

• In addition, Henry Fonda made a cameo/guest appearance in the following feature film: *Jigsaw* (1949, UA).

*Won the Academy Award as Best Actor for this role.

☆ JANE FONDA

Jane Seymour Fonda

b: Dec. 21, 1937, New York, N.Y.

". . . the whole world is like Central Casting. They got it all rigged before you ever show up."

Gloria Beatty (Jane Fonda) in *They Shoot Horses, Don't They?*, 1969

Tall Story (1960, WB). *d:* Joshua Logan; *p:* Joshua Logan; *sc:* J. J. Epstein—*b/o* the play by Howard Lindsay and Russel Crouse and Howard Nemerov's novel *The Homecoming Game.*

JUNE RYDER: Husband-hunting coed who snares a college basketball star who is tempted to take a bribe from gamblers trying to get him to throw a big game.

Anthony Perkins, Ray Walston, Marc Connelly, Anne Jackson, Murray Hamilton, Bob Wright, Bart Burns, Karl Lukas, Elizabeth Patterson, Tom Laughlin, Barbara Darrow.

Walk on the Wild Side (1962, Col.). *d:* Edward Dmytryk; *p:* Charles K. Feldman; *sc:* John Fante and Edmund Morris—*b/o* the novel by Nelson Algren.

KITTY TWIST: Prostitute in a 1930s New Orleans bordello whose unsuspecting ex-sweetheart, a poor farmer from Texas, comes to New Orleans to try to find her.

Laurence Harvey, Capucine, Anne Baxter, Barbara Stanwyck, Joanna Moore, Richard Rust, Karl Swenson, Donald Barry, Juanita Moore, John Anderson, Ken Lynch, Todd Armstrong.

The Chapman Report (1962, WB). *d:* George Cukor; *p:* Richard D. Zanuck (A Darryl F. Zanuck Prod.); *sc:* Wyatt Cooper and Don M. Mankiewicz (adaptation by Grant Stuart and Gene Allen)—*b/o* the novel by Irving Wallace.

KATHLEEN BARCLAY: Frigid young widow who becomes involved with a famous research psychologist when he conducts a scientific sex survey among a group of suburban-California women.

Efrem Zimbalist Jr., Shelley Winters, Claire Bloom, Glynis Johns, Ray Danton, Ty Hardin, Andrew Duggan, John Dehner, Cloris Leachman, Chad Everett, Henry Daniell, Jack Cassidy.

Period of Adjustment (1962, MGM). *d:* George Roy Hill; *p:* Lawrence Weingarten; *sc:* Isobel Lennart—*b/o* the play by Tennessee Williams.

ISABEL HAVERSTICK: Nervous Southern bride who, along with her jittery Korean War veteran husband, finds that they both have to go through a period of adjustment on their honeymoon.

Tony Franciosa, Jim Hutton, Lois Nettleton, John McGiver, Mabel Albertson, Jack Albertson.

In the Cool of the Day (1963, MGM). *d:* Robert Stevens; *p:* John Houseman; *sc:* Meade Roberts—*b/o* the novel by Susan Ertz.

CHRISTINE BONNER: Frail, consumptive wife of a New York publisher who, after she runs off to Greece with an English ex-colleague of her husband's, tragically dies.

Peter Finch, Angela Lansbury, Arthur Hill, Constance Cummings, Alexander Knox, Nigel Davenport, John LeMesurier, Alec McCowen, Valerie Taylor, Andreas Markos.

Sunday in New York (1964, MGM). *d:* Peter Tewksbury; *p:* Everett Freeman (Seven Arts); *sc:* Norman Krasna—*b/o* his play.

EILEEN TYLER: Pure young girl from Albany who, when she visits her airline-pilot brother in New York City, falls for a savvy young man and has the protective brother worried about what's going on.

Cliff Robertson, Rod Taylor, Robert Culp, Jo Morrow, Jim Backus, Peter Nero.

Joy House (1964, MGM). *d:* René Clement; *p:* Jacques Bar; *sc:* René Clement, Pascal Jardin, and Charles Williams—*b/o* the novel by Day Keene.

MELINDA: One of two American women living on the French Riviera who become involved with a handsome playboy on the run when he seeks refuge in their gloomy villa.

Alain Delon, Lola Albright, Carl Studer, Sorrell Booke, Andre Oumansky, Arthur Howard, Nick Del Negro, Jacques Bezard.

Circle of Love (1965, Continental–Walter Reade/Sterling). *d:* Roger Vadim; *p:* Robert Hakim and Raymond Hakim; *sc:* Jean Anouilh—*b/o* the play *La Ronde* by Arthur Schnitzler.

Billed as "THE MARRIED WOMAN": Wife who has a fling with a young student—one of a chain of sexual liaisons that take place in Sarajevo on June 28, 1914, the day Archduke Ferdinand is assassinated.

Marie Dubois, Claude Giraud, Anna Karina, Valerie Lagrange, Jean-Claude Brialy, Maurice Ronet, Catherine Spaak, Bernard Noel.

Cat Ballou (1965, Col.). *d:* Elliot Silverstein; *p:* Harold Hecht; *sc:* Walter Newman and Frank R. Pierson—*b/o* the novel by Roy Chanslor.

CATHERINE (CAT) BALLOU: Young schoolmarm in the 1890s West who, when her father is killed by a villainous gunman, becomes the leader of a motley gang of outlaws, including a drunken has-been gunfighter named Kid Shelleen.

Lee Marvin, Michael Callan, Dwayne Hickman, Nat King Cole, Stubby Kaye, Tom Nardini, John Marley, Reginald Denny, Jay C. Flippen, Arthur Hunnicutt, Bruce Cabot, Burt Austin, Paul Gilbert.

The Chase (1966, Col.). *d:* Arthur Penn; *p:* Sam Spiegel (Horizon); *sc:* Lillian Hellman—*b/o* the novel and play by Horton Foote.

ANNA REEVES: Sexy Texas girl whose affair with the son of the town's most influential citizen comes to an end when her wrongly imprisoned husband breaks out of the penitentiary and heads for home.

Marlon Brando, Robert Redford, E. G. Marshall, Angie Dickinson, Janice Rule, Miriam Hopkins, Martha Hyer, Robert Duvall, James Fox, Diana Hyland, Henry Hull, Jocelyn Brando, Paul

Williams, Malcolm Atterbury, Nydia Westman, Bruce Cabot.

Any Wednesday (1966, WB). *d:* Robert Ellis Miller; *p:* Julius J. Epstein; *sc:* Julius J. Epstein—*b/o* the play by Muriel Resnick.

ELLEN GORDON: New York executive's mistress who falls for the executive's young business associate when the young man is accidentally sent to use the apartment where the executive and the mistress get together every Wednesday.

Jason Robards, Dean Jones, Rosemary Murphy, Ann Prentiss, Jack Fletcher, Kelly Jean Peters, King Moody, Monty Margetts.

The Game Is Over (1966, Royal–Marceau). *d:* Roger Vadim; *p:* Roger Vadim; *sc:* Jean Cau, Roger Vadim, and Bernard Fretchman—*b/o* the novel *La Curée* by Emile Zola.

RENEE SACCARD: Pampered, selfish young wife of a middle-aged Parisian businessman who falls in love with her stepson but is driven mad when her husband tricks the stepson into betraying her.

Peter McEnery, Michel Piccoli, Tina Marquand, Jacques Monod, Simone Valere, Ham Chau Luong, Howard Vernon, Douglas Read.

Hurry Sundown (1967, Para.). *d:* Otto Preminger; *p:* Otto Preminger (Sigma); *sc:* Thomas C. Ryan and Horton Foote—*b/o* the novel by K. B. Gilden.

JULIE ANN WARREN: Sensual, decadent wife who helps her Georgia businessman husband in his ruthless attempts to buy up his cousin's farmlands—but leaves him when she learns that he was responsible for an injury their retarded son has suffered.

Michael Caine, John Philip Law, Diahann Carroll, Robert Hooks, Faye Dunaway, Burgess Meredith, Jim Backus, Robert Reed, Rex Ingram, George Kennedy, Frank Converse, Loring Smith, Luke Askew.

Barefoot in the Park (1967, Para.). *d:* Gene Saks; *p:* Hal Wallis (Hal B. Wallis Prod.); *sc:* Neil Simon—*b/o* his play.

CORIE BRATTER: Free-spirited young newlywed wife who runs into marital problems, as well as kooky neighbors, when she and her conservative lawyer husband move into a cold-water fifth-floor walk-up apartment in Greenwich Village.

Robert Redford, Charles Boyer, Mildred Natwick, Herbert Edelman, James Stone, Ted Hartley, Mabel Albertson, Fritz Feld.

Barbarella (1968, Para.). *d:* Roger Vadim; *p:* Dino De Laurentiis (Marianne/Dino De Laurentiis); *sc:* Terry Southern, Brian Degas, Claude Brule, Jean-Claude Forest, Roger Vadim, Clement Wood, Tudor Gates, and Villario Bonaceil—*b/o* the book by Jean-Claude Forest.

BARBARELLA: Sexy 41st-century astronaut

whose mission is to save the universe by preventing a positronic ray from falling into evil hands.

John Philip Law, Anita Pallenberg, Milo O'Shea, David Hemmings, Marcel Marceau, Ugo Tognazzi, Claude Dauphin.

Spirits of the Dead (1969, AIP). *d:* Federico Fellini, Louis Malle, and Roger Vadim; *p:* Marceau–Cocinor; *sc:* Federico Fellini, Louis Malle, Roger Vadim, Bernardino Zapponi, and Daniel Boulanger—*b/o* stories by Edgar Allan Poe.

FREDERIQUE: Medieval countess who has a love-hate relationship with a black stallion—who, it turns out, is really her dead lover.

Peter Fonda, Carla Marlier, Françoise Prevost, James Robertson Justice, Brigitte Bardot, Alain Delon, Terrence Stamp.

They Shoot Horses, Don't They? (1969, Cinerama). *d:* Sydney Pollack; *p:* Irving Winkler and Robert Chartoff (ABC/Palomar/Chartoff–Winkler–Pollack); *sc:* Robert E. Thompson—*b/o* the novel by Horace McCoy.

GLORIA BEATTY*: Embittered, self-destructive Texas girl whose entry in a 1930s dance marathon in Los Angeles with an aimless young partner leads to tragic consequences.

Michael Sarrazin, Susannah York, Gig Young, Red Buttons, Bonnie Bedelia, Michael Conrad, Bruce Dern, Al Lewis, Severn Darden, Madge Kennedy.

Klute (1971, WB). *d:* Alan Pakula; *p:* Alan Pakula; *sc:* Andy K. Lewis and Dave Lewis.

BREE DANIELS†: Sophisticated call girl who becomes involved with a small-town detective when he comes to New York to search for a missing friend.

Donald Sutherland, Charles Cioffi, Roy Scheider, Dorothy Tristan, Rita Gam, Vivian Nathan, Nathan George, Shirley Stoler, Jane White, Morris Strassberg, Jean Stapleton.

Steelyard Blues (1972, WB). *d:* Alan Myerson; *p:* Tony Bill, Michael Phillips, and Julia Phillips (S. B. Productions); *sc:* David S. Ward.

IRIS: Call girl who decides, along with her ex-con boyfriend and his misfit pals, to buck the establishment by swiping and repairing an old WWII airplane and flying it away.

Donald Sutherland, Peter Boyle, Garry Goodrow, Howard Hesseman, John Savage, Richard Schaal, Melvin Stewart, Morgan Upton, Roger Bowen, Nancy Fish.

Tout Va Bien (1972, New Yorker). *d:* Jean-Luc Godard and Jean-Pierre Gorin; *p:* Jean-Pierre Rassam; *sc:* Jean-Luc Godard and Jean-Pierre Gorin.

SUSAN DE WITT: American TV correspondent in Paris who, when she and her French filmmaker husband research a program on French workers, becomes involved in the takeover of a sausage factory by the workers.

Yves Montand, Vittorio Caprioli, Jean Pignol, Pierre Ondry, Illizabeth Chauvin, Eric Chartier, Yves Gabrielli.

A Doll's House (1973, World Film). *d:* Joseph Losey; *p:* Joseph Losey (Les Films de la Boétie); *sc:* David Mercer—*b/o* Michael Meyer's English translation of Henrik Ibsen's play.

NORA HELMER: Sheltered, doll-like Norwegian housewife who—after illegally getting money to save her sick husband's life, then working to pay the money back—realizes that she has learned how to make it on her own and leaves him so that she can lead a new life.

David Warner, Trevor Howard, Delphine Seyrig, Edward Fox, Anna Wing, Pierre Oudrey, Frode Lien, Tone Floor, Morten Floor, Ellen Holm.

The Blue Bird (1976, 20th-Fox). *d:* George Cukor; *p:* Edward Lewis and Paul Maslansky; *sc:* Hugh Whitemore and Alfred Hayes—*b/o* the play by Maurice Maeterlinck.

NIGHT: One of the many symbolic fairy-tale characters who become involved with Mytyl and Tyltyl, two Russian peasant children who are sent by the fairy Berylune to search for the Bluebird of Happiness but finally discover that it's in their own back yard.

Elizabeth Taylor, Ava Gardner, Ciçely Tyson, Robert Morley, Harry Andrews, Todd Lookinland, Patsy Kensit, Will Geer, Mona Washbourne, George Cole, Richard Pearson, Oleg Popov, Nadejda Pavlova.

Fun with Dick and Jane (1976, Col.). *d:* Ted Kotcheff; *p:* Peter Bart and Max Palevsky; *sc:* David Giler, Jerry Belson, and Mordecai Richler—*b/o* a story by Gerald Gaiser.

JANE HARPER: Aerospace executive's wife who, when her husband is fired and they go broke, joins him in committing armed robberies in order to pay their way.

George Segal, Ed McMahon, Dick Gautier, Allan Miller, Hank Garcia, John Dehner, Mary Jackson, Walter Brooke, Sean Frye, James Jeter, Maxine Stuart, Thalmus Rasulala.

Julia (1977, 20th-Fox). *d:* Fred Zinnemann; *p:* Richard Roth; *sc:* Alvin Sargent—*b/o* a story in the book *Pentimento* by Lillian Hellman.

LILLIAN HELLMAN*: Young American

---

*Received an Academy Award Nomination as Best Actress for this role.
†Won the Academy Award as Best Actress for this role.

*Received an Academy Award Nomination as Best Actress for this role.

JANE FONDA   **111**

playwright who is drawn by her dedicated childhood girlfriend (Julia) into involvement with the anti-Nazi resistance movement in 1930s Europe.

Vanessa Redgrave, Jason Robards, Maximilian Schell, Hal Holbrook, Rosemary Murphy, Meryl Streep, Lisa Pelikan, Susan Jones, Dora Doll, John Glover, Cathleen Nesbitt.

Coming Home (1978, UA). *d:* Hal Ashby; *p:* Jerome Hellman (IPC Films); *sc:* Waldo Salt and Robert C. Jones—*b/o* a story by Nancy Dowd, *b/o* an idea by Jane Fonda and Bruce Gilbert.

SALLY HYDE*: U.S. Marine captain's wife who, when she volunteers to work in a veterans' hospital while her husband is overseas, falls in love with an embittered paraplegic Vietnam War veteran.

Jon Voight, Bruce Dern, Robert Ginty, Penelope Milford, Robert Carradine, Willie Tyler, Cornelius H. Austin Jr., Tresa Hughes, Olivia Cole, Charles Cyphers.

Comes a Horseman (1978, UA). *d:* Alan J. Pakula; *p:* Gene Kirkwood and Dan Paulson (Chartoff–Winkler); *sc:* Dennis Lynton Clark.

ELLA CONNORS: Rancher in the 1940s West who joins up with a handsome young drifter in a fight to save her small ranch from a greedy cattle baron and a predatory oil company.

James Caan, Jason Robards, George Grizzard, Richard Farnsworth, Jim Davis, Mark Harmon, Macon McCalman, Basil Hoffman, James Kline, James Keach, Clifford A. Pellow.

California Suite (1978, Col.). *d:* Herbert Ross; *p:* Ray Stark (Rastar); *sc:* Neil Simon—*b/o* his play.

HANNAH WARREN: *Newsweek* editor staying at the Beverly Hills Hotel who engages in a tug-of-war with her ex-husband over their teen-age daughter.

Alan Alda, Michael Caine, Bill Cosby, Walter Matthau, Elaine May, Richard Pryor, Maggie Smith, Gloria Gifford, Sheila Frazier, Herbert Edelman.

The China Syndrome (1979, Col.). *d:* James Bridges; *p:* Michael Douglas (IPC Films); *sc:* Mike Gray, T. S. Cook, and James Bridges.

KIMBERLY WELLS†: Ambitious TV news reporter who exposes a plot by a California energy company to cover up a nuclear-power-plant accident that has resulted in a potentially disastrous radiation leak.

Jack Lemmon, Michael Douglas, Scott Brady, James Hampton, Peter Donat, Wilford Brimley, Richard Herd, Daniel Valdez, Stan Bohrman, Donald Hotton, Khalilah Ali.

The Electric Horseman (1979, Col./Univ.). *d:* Sydney Pollack; *p:* Ray Stark (Ray Stark/Wildwood); *sc:* Robert Garland—*b/o* a story by Paul Gaer, Robert Garland, and Shelly Burton.

HALLIE MARTIN: TV news reporter—after a big story—who pursues a hard-drinking ex-rodeo star who has kidnapped a once-great racehorse (that's being given tranquilizers) in order to return him to a remote valley and freedom.

Robert Redford, Valerie Perrine, Willie Nelson, John Saxon, Nicolas Coster, Allan Arbus, Wilford Brimley, Will Hare, Timothy Scott, James B. Sikking, Quinn Redeker, Tasha Zemrus.

9 to 5 (1980, 20th-Fox). *d:* Colin Higgins; *p:* Bruce Gilbert (IPC Films); *sc:* Colin Higgins and Patricia Resnick—*b/o* a story by Patricia Resnick.

JUDY BERNLY: One of a trio of liberated secretaries who get fed up coping with their sexist, patronizing boss and devise a strategy to get even.

Lily Tomlin, Dolly Parton, Dabney Coleman, Sterling Hayden, Elizabeth Wilson, Henry Jones, Lawrence Pressman, Marian Mercer, Ren Woods, Norma Donaldson, Peggy Pope.

Rollover (1981, Orion/WB). *d:* Alan J. Pakula; *p:* Bruce Gilbert (IPC Films); *sc:* David Shaber—*b/o* a story by David Shaber, Howard Kohn, and David Weir.

LEE WINTERS: Former film star who, when her tycoon husband is murdered, takes over his petrochemical company and becomes caught up in international financial warfare as she fights to save the business.

Kris Kristofferson, Hume Cronyn, Josef Sommer, Bob Gunton, Macon McCalman, Ron Frazier, Jodi Long, Crocker Nevin, Ira B. Wheeler, Norman Snow, Sally Sockwell.

On Golden Pond (1981, Univ.). *d:* Mark Rydell; *p:* Bruce Gilbert (ITC Films/IPC Films); *sc:* Ernest Thompson—*b/o* his play.

CHELSEA THAYER WAYNE*: Resentful, alienated daughter who finds that she still clashes with her eighty-year-old retired professor father when she joins her parents at their summer vacation cottage in New Hampshire.

Katharine Hepburn, Henry Fonda, Doug McKeon, Dabney Coleman, William Lanteau, Chris Rydell.

---

*Won the Academy Award as Best Actress for this role.
†Received an Academy Award Nomination as Best Actress for this role.

---

*Received an Academy Award Nomination as Best Supporting Actress for this role.

☆ CLARK GABLE

William Clark Gable

b: Feb. 1, 1901, Cadiz, Ohio
d: Nov. 16, 1960, Los Angeles, Cal.

"Frankly, my dear, I don't give a damn."

Rhett Butler (Clark Gable) to Scarlett
O'Hara (Vivien Leigh) in *Gone with the
Wind*, 1939.

The Painted Desert (1931, Pathe). *d:* Howard
Higgin; *sc:* Howard Higgin and Tom Buckingham.
BRETT: Tough young cowboy who vies with a
stalwart mining engineer for the affections of a
prospector's daughter and turns out to be the
villain who dynamited the engineer's mine.
*William Boyd, Helen Twelvetrees, William Farnum,
J. Farrell MacDonald*, Edward Hearn, Charles
Sellon, Wade Boteler, Richard Cramer.

The Easiest Way (1931, MGM). *d:* Jack Conway;
sc: Edith Ellis—*b/o* the play by Eugene Walter.
NICK: Hard-working, strait-laced laundry man
who objects when his wife wants to welcome her
disreputable younger sister into their home.
*Constance Bennett, Adolphe Menjou, Robert
Montgomery, Anita Page, Marjorie Rambeau,
J. Farrell MacDonald, Clara Blandick.*

Dance, Fools, Dance (1931, MGM). *d:* Harry
Beaumont; *sc:* Richard Schayer (with dialogue by
Aurania Rouverol)—*b/o* a story by Aurania
Rouverol.
JAKE LUVA: Ruthless bootlegger–gang leader
who—after a spoiled, formerly rich playboy joins
his gang—falls for the playboy's sister but then
discovers that she's a cub reporter secretly trying
to pin a murder rap on him.
*Joan Crawford, Lester Vail, Cliff Edwards,
William Bakewell*, Earl Foxe, Purnell B. Pratt,
Hale Hamilton, Natalie Moorhead, Joan Marsh,
Russell Hopton.

The Secret Six (1931, MGM). *d:* George Hill; *sc:*
Frances Marion.
CARL: One of two reporters hired by a secret
syndicate of six masked businessmen to get the
goods on a gang of Prohibition-era bootleggers
responsible for a series of killings.
*Wallace Beery, Lewis Stone, John Mack Brown,
Jean Harlow, Marjorie Rambeau, Paul Hurst,*
Ralph Bellamy, John Miljan, Frank McGlynn,
Theodore Von Eltz.

The Finger Points (1931, FN). *d:* John Francis
Dillon; *sc:* Robert Lord (with dialogue by John
Monk Saunders)—*b/o* a story by John Monk
Saunders and W. R. Burnett.
LOUIS BLANCO: Gangland czar who, when he
suspects that a big-time reporter taking payola
from him has pulled a double-cross, "points the
finger" at him to be rubbed out.
*Richard Barthelmess, Fay Wray, Regis Toomey,
Robert Elliott*, Oscar Apfel, Robert Gleckler, Noel
Madison, Mickey Bennett.

Laughing Sinners (1931, MGM). *d:* Harry
Beaumont; *sc:* Bess Meredyth (with dialogue by
Martin Flavin)—*b/o* the play *Torch Song* by
Kenyon Nicholson.
CARL LOOMIS: Salvation Army worker who,
after he saves a woman entertainer from
committing suicide because her unscrupulous
lover has deserted her, falls in love with her.
Joan Crawford, Neil Hamilton, Marjorie Rambeau,
Guy Kibbee, Cliff Edwards, Roscoe Karns, George
Cooper, George F. Marion.

A Free Soul (1931, MGM). *d:* Clarence Brown; *sc:*
John Meehan—*b/o* the novel by Adela Rogers St.
John.
ACE WILFONG: Brutal gambler-gangster who,
after a brilliant but alcoholic lawyer defends him
against a murder charge, has a sordid affair with
the lawyer's daughter.
Norma Shearer, Leslie Howard, Lionel Barrymore,
James Gleason, Lucy Beaumont.

Night Nurse (1931, WB). *d:* William A. Wellman;
sc: Oliver H.P. Garrett (with dialogue by Oliver
H.P. Garrett and Charles Kenyon)—*b/o* the novel
by Dora Macy.
NICK: Rough, conniving chauffeur who is in on a
plot to do away with a wealthy, alcoholic widow's
two little daughters in order to bilk her out of a
trust fund.
Barbara Stanwyck, Ben Lyon, Joan Blondell,
Charles Winninger, Vera Lewis, Edward Nugent,
Allan Lane.

Sporting Blood (1931, MGM). *d:* Charles Brabin;
sc: Willard Mack and Wanda Tuchock—*b/o* the
novel *Horseflesh* by Frederick Hazlitt Brennan.
TIP SCANLON: Shady gambling-joint proprietor
and racehorse owner who, after fixing a race so
his horse is supposed to win, gets into trouble
with mobsters who blow a bundle when the horse
loses.
Ernest Torrence, Madge Evans, Lew Cody, Marie
Prevost, Harry Holman, Halam Cooley, J. Farrell
MacDonald, John Larking, Eugene Jackson.

Susan Lenox: Her Fall and Rise (1931, MGM). *d:* Robert Z. Leonard; *sc:* Wanda Tuchock (with dialogue by Zelda Sears and Edith Fitzgerald)—*b/o* the novel by David Graham Phillips.

RODNEY SPENCER: Rugged engineer who, when he learns that the woman he loves has lost her virtue to another man, heads for the South American jungle to work on a construction project but forgives her when she follows him there.

Greta Garbo, Jean Hersholt, John Miljan, Alan Hale, Hale Hamilton, Russell Simpson, Cecil Cunningham, Theodore Von Eltz, Ian Keith.

Possessed (1931, MGM). *d:* Clarence Brown; *sc:* Lenore Coffee—*b/o* Edgar Selwyn's play *The Mirage*.

MARK WHITNEY: Wealthy young lawyer whose marriage to a box-factory worker causes problems when he runs for governor.

Joan Crawford, Wallace Ford, Skeets Gallagher, Frank Conroy, Marjorie White, John Miljan, Clara Blandick.

Hell Divers (1931, MGM). *d:* George Hill; *sc:* Harvey Gates and Malcolm Stuart Boylan—*b/o* a story by Lt. Cmdr. Frank Wead.

STEVE: Tough petty officer in the 1930s U.S. Naval Air Force who carries on a feud with a hardboiled, older petty officer but—after a plane crash—is saved by the older man's heroic actions.

Wallace Beery, Conrad Nagel, Dorothy Jordan, Marjorie Rambeau, Marie Prevost, Cliff Edwards, John Miljan, Landers Stevens, Reed Howes, Alan Roscoe.

Polly of the Circus (1932, MGM). *d:* Alfred Santell; *sc:* Carey Wilson (with dialogue by Laurence Johnson)—*b/o* the play by Margaret Mayo.

REV. JOHN HARTLEY: Warm-hearted, gentle minister who loses his church and congregation when he announces that he has secretly married a circus trapeze artist.

Marion Davies, C. Aubrey Smith, Raymond Hatton, David Landau, Ruth Selwyn, Maude Eburne, Guinn Williams, Ray Milland, Phillip Crane.

Red Dust (1932, MGM). *d:* Victor Fleming; *p:* Hunt Stromberg; *sc:* John Lee Mahin—*b/o* the play by Wilson Collison.

DENNIS CARSON: Rugged American in charge of a rubber plantation in Indochina who becomes involved with two women—one a good-hearted prostitute on the run from police, and the other the well-bred but unfaithful wife of an engineer who works for him.

Jean Harlow, Gene Raymond, Mary Astor, Donald Crisp, Tully Marshall, Forrester Harvey, Willie Fung.

Strange Interlude (1932, MGM). *d:* Robert Z. Leonard; *p:* Irving Thalberg; *sc:* Bess Meredyth and C. Gardner Sullivan—*b/o* the play by Eugene O'Neill.

DR. NED DARRELL: Physician who becomes the lover of the wife of one of his patients and has a son by her who the husband believes is his own.

Norma Shearer, Alexander Kirkland, Ralph Morgan, Robert Young, May Robson, Maureen O'Sullivan, Henry B. Walthall, Mary Alden, Tad Alexander.

No Man of Her Own (1932, Para). *d:* Wesley Ruggles; *sc:* Maurine Watkins and Milton H. Gropper—*b/o* a story by Edmund Goulding and Benjamin Glazer.

JERRY "BABE" STEWART: Big-time card shark who, while he's on the lam in a small Midwestern town, marries the local librarian and winds up being reformed by her.

Carole Lombard, Dorothy Mackaill, Grant Mitchell, George Barbier, Elizabeth Patterson, J. Farrell MacDonald, Tommy Conlon, Frank McGlynn Sr.

The White Sister (1933, MGM). *d:* Victor Fleming; *sc:* Donald Ogden Stewart—*b/o* the novel by F. Marion Crawford and Walter Hackett.

GIOVANNI SEVERA: WWI officer in the Italian Air Service who, after two years in an Austrian prison camp, escapes and finds that his Italian noblewoman lover—thinking he had been killed—has become a nun.

Helen Hayes, Lewis Stone, Louise Closser Hale, May Robson, Edward Arnold, Alan Edwards.

Hold Your Man (1933, MGM). *d:* Sam Wood; *p:* Sam Wood; *sc:* Anita Loos and Howard Emmett Rogers—*b/o* a story by Anita Loos.

EDDIE NUGENT: Slick con man who falls for a hardboiled but good-hearted blonde, then lets her take a prison rap for a crime he commits but finally turns himself in so that she can be released.

Jean Harlow, Stuart Erwin, Dorothy Burgess, Muriel Kirkland, Garry Owen, Paul Hurst, Barbara Barondess, Elizabeth Patterson, Inez Courtney.

Night Flight (1933, MGM). *d:* Clarence Brown; *sc:* Oliver H.P. Garrett—*b/o* the story by Antoine de Saint-Exupery.

JULES FABIAN: French air-mail pilot in South America who, while helping to pioneer dangerous night flights to speed up mail delivery, encounters a fierce storm on the Pantagonia route and loses his life when he bails out.

John Barrymore, Helen Hayes, Lionel Barrymore, Robert Montgomery, Myrna Loy, William Gargan, C. Henry Gordon, Leslie Fenton, Harry Beresford, Frank Conroy, Ralf Harolde.

Dancing Lady (1933, MGM). *d:* Robert Z. Leonard; *p:* David O. Selznick; *sc:* Allen Rivkin and P. J. Wolfson—*b/o* the novel by James Warner Bellah.

PATCH GALLAGHER: Ex-hoofer–turned–stage director who gives a burlesque dancer her big break when he hires her for a Broadway musical and she emerges a star.

Joan Crawford, Franchot Tone, May Robson, Winnie Lightner, Fred Astaire, Robert Benchley, Ted Healy, Moe Howard, Jerry Howard, Larry Fine, Art Jarrett, Nelson Eddy, Sterling Holloway, Eunice Quedens (Eve Arden), Lynn Bari.

It Happened One Night (1934, Col.). *d:* Frank Capra; *sc:* Robert Riskin—*b/o* the *Cosmopolitan* story "Night Bus" by Samuel Hopkins Adams.

PETER WARNE*: Jobless news reporter who, when he gets on a bus in Miami and recognizes a runaway heiress aboard, agrees to help her remain incognito and get to New York in return for an exclusive big story.

Claudette Colbert, Walter Connolly, Roscoe Karns, Jameson Thomas, Alan Hale, Ward Bond, Eddie Chandler, Arthur Hoyt, Charles C. Wilson, Harry Holman, Irving Bacon, James Burke, Joseph Crehan, Milton Kibbee, Mickey Daniels.

Men in White (1934, MGM). *d:* Richard Boleslavsky; *sc:* Waldemar Young—*b/o* the play by Sidney Kingsley.

DR. GEORGE FERGUSON: Ambitious young intern whose spoiled society fiancée resents his devotion to his medical career but finally learns to understand the importance of his work.

Myrna Loy, Jean Hersholt, Elizabeth Allan, Otto Kruger, C. Henry Gordon, Russell Hardie, Wallace Ford, Henry B. Walthall, Russell Hopton, Samuel S. Hinds, Frank Puglia, Leo Chalzel, Donald Douglas.

Manhattan Melodrama (1934, MGM). *d:* W. S. Van Dyke; *p:* David O. Selznick; *sc:* Oliver H.P. Garrett and Joseph L. Mankiewicz—*b/o* the story by Arthur Caesar.

BLACKIE GALLAGHER: Good-guy New York gangster who nobly goes to the electric chair knowing that his death will save the marriage between his ex-girlfriend and his boyhood pal, a D.A. who has become governor.

William Powell, Myrna Loy, Leo Carrillo, Nat Pendleton, George Sidney, Isabel Jewell, Muriel Evans, Thomas Jackson, Frank Conroy, Mickey Rooney.

Chained (1934, MGM). *d:* Clarence Brown; *p:* Hunt Stromberg; *sc:* John Lee Mahin—*b/o* a story by Edgar Selwyn.

---

*Won the Academy Award as Best Actor for this role.

MIKE BRADLEY: Wealthy Argentine rancher who, after falling for an ex–New York secretary on an ocean cruise, loses her when she marries her aging lover (out of loyalty) but then wins her back when the husband unselfishly gives her up.

Joan Crawford, Otto Kruger, Stuart Erwin, Una O'Connor, Marjorie Gateson, Akim Tamiroff, William Deggar.

Forsaking All Others (1934, MGM). *d:* W. S. Van Dyke; *p:* Bernard H. Hyman; *sc:* Joseph L. Mankiewicz—*b/o* the play by Edward Barry Roberts and Frank Morgan Cavett.

JEFF WILLIAMS: Likeable guy who returns to the United States from Spain to try to win the heart of his childhood playmate, even though she keeps getting engaged to a fickle friend of theirs.

Joan Crawford, Robert Montgomery, Charles Butterworth, Billie Burke, Frances Drake, Rosalind Russell, Arthur Treacher, Ted Healy.

After Office Hours (1935, MGM). *d:* Robert Z. Leonard; *p:* Bernard H. Hyman; *sc:* Herman J. Mankiewicz—*b/o* the story by Laurence Stallings and Dale Van Every.

JIM BRANCH: Opportunistic New York newspaper editor who hires a wealthy socialite as a cub reporter to get the inside scoop on a society divorce case, then—when it turns into a case of murder—enlists her in trapping the killer.

Constance Bennett, Stuart Erwin, Billie Burke, Harvey Stephens, Katherine Alexander, Hale Hamilton, Henry Travers, Henry Armetta.

Call of the Wild (1935, 20th-Fox). *d:* William Wellman; *p:* Darryl F. Zanuck; *sc:* Gene Fowler and Leonard Praskins—*b/o* the novel by Jack London.

JACK THORNTON: Adventurous gold prospector in the Klondike who, after saving an unmanageable St. Bernard from being killed by a cruel prospector, trains him to become a loyal and faithful sled dog.

Loretta Young, Jack Oakie, Reginald Owen, Frank Conroy, Katherine De Mille, Sidney Toler, James Burke, Charles Stevens, Herman Bing.

China Seas (1935, MGM). *d:* Tay Garnett; *p:* Albert Lewin; *sc:* Jules Furthman and James Keven McGuinness—*b/o* the novel by Crosbie Garstin.

CAPT. ALAN GASKELL: Two-fisted English skipper of a Hong Kong–bound tramp steamer in the China Seas who not only is caught between his tough but good-hearted ex-mistress and his sophisticated fiancée but also has to contend with a group of crooks and Malay pirates.

Jean Harlow, Wallace Beery, Lewis Stone, Rosalind Russell, Dudley Digges, C. Aubrey Smith, Robert Benchley, William Henry, Edward Brophy,

Donald Meek, Carol Ann Beery, Akim Tamiroff, Ivan Lebedeff, Soo Yong.

Mutiny on the Bounty (1935, MGM). *d:* Frank Lloyd; *p:* Irving Thalberg; *sc:* Talbot Jennings, Jules Furthman, and Carey Wilson—*b/o* the book by Charles Nordhoff and James Norman Hall.

FLETCHER CHRISTIAN*: Respected master's mate on the British naval vessel H.M.S. *Bounty* who leads a mutiny in 1789 against the tyrannical Captain William Bligh, sets Bligh adrift in a small boat, then seeks refuge with the rest of the mutineers on Pitcairn Island.

Charles Laughton, Franchot Tone, Herbert Mundin, Eddie Quillan, Dudley Digges, Henry Stephenson, Donald Crisp, Spring Byington, Movita, Mamo, Ian Wolfe, Stanley Fields.

Wife versus Secretary (1936, MGM). *d:* Clarence Brown; *p:* Hunt Stromberg; *sc:* Norman Krasna, Alice Duer Miller, and John Lee Mahin—*b/o* the novel by Faith Baldwin.

DAN SANFORD: Prosperous magazine publisher who, though he loves his wife, is suspected by her of having an affair with his attractive blond secretary.

Jean Harlow, Myrna Loy, May Robson, George Barbier, James Stewart, Hobart Cavanaugh, Gilbert Emery, Marjorie Gateson, Gloria Holden, Tom Dugan.

San Francisco (1936, MGM). *d:* W. S. Van Dyke; *p:* John Emerson and Bernard H. Hyman; *sc:* Anita Loos—*b/o* a story by Robert Hopkins.

BLACKIE NORTON: Ruthless owner of a Barbary Coast cabaret who hires a pretty young singer and selfishly exploits her—but then falls in love with her and changes his ways as they both survive the great 1906 San Francisco earthquake.

Jeanette MacDonald, Spencer Tracy, Jack Holt, Jessie Ralph, Ted Healy, Shirley Ross, Harold Huber, Al Shean, Kenneth Harlan, Roger Imhof, Russell Simpson, Bert Roach, Warren Hymer, Edgar Kennedy.

Cain and Mabel (1936, WB). *d:* Lloyd Bacon; *p:* Sam Bischoff (Cosmopolitan); *sc:* Laird Doyle—*b/o* a short story by H. C. Witwer.

LARRY CAIN: Champion prize fighter who agrees to stage a phony romance with a musical-comedy star for publicity purposes, but winds up falling for her.

Marion Davies, Allen Jenkins, Roscoe Karns, Walter Catlett, Hobart Cavanaugh, Ruth Donnelly, Pert Kelton, William Collier Sr., Sammy White, E. E. Clive, Joseph Crehan.

---

*Received an Academy Award nomination as Best Actor for this role.

Love on the Run (1936, MGM). *d:* W. S. Van Dyke; *p:* Joseph L. Mankiewicz; *sc:* John Lee Mahin, Manuel Seff, and Gladys Hurlbut—*b/o* the story by Alan Green and Julian Brodie.

MICHAEL ANTHONY: One of two rival American foreign correspondents in Europe who, while helping an American heiress avoid an unwanted wedding, uncover an international spy ring.

Joan Crawford, Franchot Tone, Reginald Owen, Mona Barrie, Ivan Lebedeff, Charles Judels, William Demarest.

Parnell (1937, MGM). *d:* John M. Stahl; *sc:* John Van Druten and S. N. Berhman—*b/o* the play by Elsie T. Schauffler.

CHARLES PARNELL: Famous nineteenth-century Irish patriot and member of British Parliament who, after he's named corespondent in a divorce suit, loses his political power and subsequently dies of a heart attack.

Myrna Loy, Edna May Oliver, Edmund Gwenn, Alan Marshal, Donald Crisp, Billie Burke, Berton Churchill, Donald Meek, Montagu Love, George Zucco.

Saratoga (1937, MGM). *d:* Jack Conway; *p:* Bernard H. Hyman; *sc:* Anita Loos and Robert Hopkins.

DUKE BRADLEY: Free-wheeling racetrack bookie who, when a spoiled young girl comes back from England to run her late father's racehorse stables, rubs her the wrong way at first but finally wins her love and respect.

Jean Harlow, Lionel Barrymore, Frank Morgan, Walter Pidgeon, Una Merkel, Cliff Edwards, George Zucco, Jonathan Hale, Hattie McDaniel, Frankie Darro, Henry Stone.

Test Pilot (1938, MGM). *d:* Victor Fleming; *p:* Louis D. Lighton; *sc:* Vincent Lawrence and Waldemar Young—*b/o* a story by Frank Wead.

JIM LANE: Famous daredevil test pilot who makes a forced landing in Kansas and marries a pretty farm girl, then runs into domestic problems when she has trouble adjusting to his wild ways and hazardous profession.

Myrna Loy, Spencer Tracy, Lionel Barrymore, Samuel S. Hinds, Marjorie Main, Ted Pearson, Gloria Holden, Louis J. Heydt, Virginia Grey, Priscilla Lawson, Claudia Coleman, Arthur Aylesworth.

Too Hot to Handle (1938, MGM). *d:* Jack Conway; *p:* Lawrence Weingarten; *sc:* Laurence Stallings and John Lee Mahin—*b/o* a story by Len Hammond.

CHRIS HUNTER: Ace newsreel cameraman who, in order to get a scoop, helps a famous female flier search for her missing brother in the Amazon jungle.

Myrna Loy, Walter Connolly, Walter Pidgeon, Leo Carrillo, Johnny Hines, Henry Kolker, Marjorie Main, Al Shean, Willie Fung.

Idiot's Delight (1939, MGM). *d:* Clarence Brown; *p:* Hunt Stromberg; *sc:* Robert Sherwood—*b/o* his play.

HARRY VAN: American song-and-dance man with an all-girl troupe who, when he's stranded at a Swiss hotel near the Italian border on the eve of a world war, runs across an old vaudeville flame masquerading as a Russian countess.

Norma Shearer, Edward Arnold, Charles Coburn, Joseph Schildkraut, Burgess Meredith, Laura Hope Crews, Skeets Gallagher, Fritz Feld.

Gone with the Wind (1939, MGM). *d:* Victor Fleming, Sam Wood, and George Cukor; *p:* David O. Selznick (Selznick International); *sc:* Sidney Howard—*b/o* the novel by Margaret Mitchell.

RHETT BUTLER*: Dashing but disreputable gambler during the Civil War who finally wins the beautiful, selfish Southern belle Scarlett O'Hara but in the end walks out on her.

Leslie Howard, Olivia de Havilland, Vivien Leigh, George Reeves, Hattie McDaniel, Thomas Mitchell, Barbara O'Neill, Victor Jory, Evelyn Keyes, Ann Rutherford, Butterfly McQueen, Howard Hickman, Laura Hope Crews, Harry Davenport, Jane Darwell, Eddie Anderson, Jackie Moran, Cliff Edwards, Ona Munson, Roscoe Ates, Eric Linden, John Arledge, Tom Tyler, William Bakewell, Paul Hurst, Isabel Jewell.

Strange Cargo (1940, MGM). *d:* Frank Borzage; *p:* Joseph L. Mankiewicz; *sc:* Lawrence Hazard (adaptation by Anita Loos)—*b/o* the book *Not Too Narrow, Not Too Deep* by Richard Sale.

VERNE: Tough leader of a group of convicts who escape from the French penal colony on Devil's Island and, along with a hardboiled dance-hall girl and a mystical Christ-like convict, make their getaway in a boat.

Joan Crawford, Ian Hunter, Peter Lorre, Paul Lukas, Albert Dekker, J. Edward Bromberg, Eduardo Ciannelli, John Arledge, Victor Varconi.

Boom Town (1940, MGM). *d:* Jack Conway; *p:* Sam Zimbalist; *sc:* John Lee Mahin—*b/o* a short story by James Edward Grant.

"BIG JOHN" McMASTERS: One of a pair of colorful oil wildcatters who become partners, argue and split, alternately make and lose fortunes, and finally become partners again.

Spencer Tracy, Claudette Colbert, Hedy Lamarr, Frank Morgan, Lionel Atwill, Chill Wills, Marion Martin, Minna Gombell, Joe Yule, Richard Lane,

George Lessey, Sara Haden, Frank Orth, Frank McGlynn Sr., Curt Bois.

Comrade X (1940, MGM). *d:* King Vidor; *p:* Gottfried Reinhardt; *sc:* Ben Hecht and Charles Lederer—*b/o* a story by Walter Reisch.

McKINLEY B. THOMPSON (alias COMRADE X): American foreign correspondent who is blackmailed into marrying an icy Communist streetcar conductor so that he can smuggle her out of Russia and take her to the United States.

Hedy Lamarr, Oscar Homolka, Felix Bressart, Eve Arden, Sig Rumann, Natasha Lytess, Vladimir Sokoloff, Edgar Barrier, George Renevant, Mikhail Rasumny.

They Met in Bombay (1941, MGM). *d:* Clarence Brown; *p:* Hunt Stromberg; *sc:* Edwin Justus Mayer, Anita Loos, and Leon Gordon—*b/o* the story by John Kafka.

GERALD MELDRICK: Suave jewel thief who falls for an equally smooth female jewel thief in India, then becomes a hero when he joins forces with British soldiers in a fight against Japanese troops.

Rosalind Russell, Peter Lorre, Jessie Ralph, Reginald Owen, Matthew Boulton, Eduardo Ciannelli, Luis Alberni, Rosina Galli, Jay Novello.

Honky Tonk (1941, MGM). *d:* Jack Conway; *p:* Pandro S. Berman; *sc:* Marguerite Roberts and John Sanford.

CANDY JOHNSON: Con man–gambler who gains control of a Western town but incurs the enmity of his fellow con man (a fake judge) when he marries the man's beautiful, refined daughter.

Lana Turner, Frank Morgan, Claire Trevor, Marjorie Main, Albert Dekker, Henry O'Neill, Chill Wills, Veda Ann Borg.

Somewhere I'll Find You (1942, MGM). *d:* Wesley Ruggles; *p:* Pandro S. Berman; *sc:* Marguerite Roberts (adaptation by Walter Reisch)—*b/o* a story by Charles Hoffman.

JOHNNY DAVIS: The older of two American war correspondent brothers who—just prior to the U.S. entry into WWII—break up over a pretty reporter but later encounter her in Indochina, where she's risking her life smuggling Chinese babies to safety.

Lana Turner, Robert Sterling, Patricia Dane, Reginald Owen, Lee Patrick, Charles Dingle, Rags Ragland, William Henry, Frank Faylen.

Adventure (1945, MGM). *d:* Victor Fleming; *p:* Sam Zimbalist; *sc:* Frederick Hazlitt Brennan and Vincent Lawrence (adaptation by Anthony Veiller and William H. Wright)—*b/o* the novel by Clyde Brion Davis.

HARRY PATTERSON: Roughneck merchant seaman who marries a prim librarian, deserts her

---

*Received an Academy Award nomination as Best Actor for this role.

to go back to sea, but finally returns and settles down when their baby is born.

Greer Garson, Joan Blondell, Thomas Mitchell, Tom Tully, John Qualen, Richard Hayden, Harry Davenport.

The Hucksters (1947, MGM). *d:* Jack Conway; *p:* Arthur Hornblow Jr.; *sc:* Luther Davis (adaptation by Edward Chodorov and George Wells)—*b/o* the novel by Frederic Wakeman.

VIC NORMAN: Opportunistic radio account executive with a Madison Avenue ad agency whose romance with an idealistic English widow gives him the integrity to refuse to be a yes-man to a despotic soap client and to renounce hucksterism.

Deborah Kerr, Sydney Greenstreet, Adolphe Menjou, Ava Gardner, Keenan Wynn, Edward Arnold, Frank Albertson, Douglas Fowley, Clinton Sundberg, Connie Gilchrist, Jimmy Conlin.

Homecoming (1948, MGM). *d:* Mervyn LeRoy; *p:* Sidney Franklin; *sc:* Paul Osborn (adaptation by Jan Lustig)—*b/o* the story by Sidney Kingsley.

ULYSSES JOHNSON: Self-centered, married New York society doctor who, after he goes overseas as a WWII major in the U.S. Army Medical Corps, learns to be more humane when a nurse he has fallen in love with is killed in action.

Lana Turner, Anne Baxter, John Hodiak, Ray Collins, Gladys Cooper, Cameron Mitchell, Marshall Thompson, Lurene Tuttle.

Command Decision (1948, MGM). *d:* Sam Wood; *p:* Sidney Franklin; *sc:* William R. Laidlaw and George Froeschel—*b/o* the play by William Wister Haines.

BRIG. GEN. K.C. "CASEY" DENNIS: Beleaguered WWII Army Air Forces general who, despite opposition from the top brass and politicians, is convinced that it's worth taking heavy U.S. daytime bomber losses in order to destroy vital German airplane factories.

Walter Pidgeon, Van Johnson, Brian Donlevy, Charles Bickford, John Hodiak, Edward Arnold, Marshall Thompson, Richard Quine, Cameron Mitchell, Clinton Sundberg, Ray Collins, Warner Anderson, John McIntire, Moroni Olsen, John Ridgely, James Millican.

Any Number Can Play (1949, MGM). *d:* Mervyn LeRoy; *p:* Arthur Freed; *sc:* Richard Brooks—*b/o* the book by Edward Harris Heth.

CHARLEY KING: Honest gambling-casino owner whose wife and seventeen-year-old son disapprove of his profession but finally realize that he's both honorable and worthy.

Alexis Smith, Wendell Corey, Audrey Totter, Frank Morgan, Mary Astor, Lewis Stone, Barry Sullivan, Marjorie Rambeau, Edgar Buchanan,

Leon Ames, Mickey Knox, Richard Rober, William Conrad, Darryl Hickman, Art Baker.

Key to the City (1950, MGM). *d:* George Sidney; *p:* Z. Wayne Griffin; *sc:* Robert Riley Crutcher—*b/o* the story by Albert Beich.

STEVE FISK: Ex-longshoreman–turned–mayor of a California city who, when he becomes involved in several escapades with a prim female mayor from Maine at a mayors' convention in San Francisco, falls in love with her.

Loretta Young, Frank Morgan, James Gleason, Marilyn Maxwell, Raymond Burr, Lewis Stone, Raymond Walburn, Pamela Britton, Zamah Cunningham, Clinton Sundberg, Marion Martin, Bert Freed, Emory Parnell, Clara Blandick.

To Please a Lady (1950, MGM). *d:* Clarence Brown; *p:* Clarence Brown; *sc:* Barre Lyndon and Marge Decker.

MIKE BRANNON: Rugged midget-car race driver who, after being barred from midget tracks as a result of an unfavorable column by a newspaperwoman denouncing his ruthless driving tactics, falls for the lady, buys a full-sized racing car, and enters the Memorial Day Classic at the Indianapolis Speedway.

Barbara Stanwyck, Adolphe Menjou, Will Geer, Roland Winters, Emory Parnell, Frank Jenks, Ted Husing.

Across the Wide Missouri (1951, MGM). *d:* William Wellman, *p:* Robert Sisk; *sc:* Talbot Jennings—*b/o* a story by Talbot Jennings and Frank Cavett.

FLINT MITCHELL: Two-fisted Kentucky fur trapper in the 1820s who, when he leads an expedition to beaver country in the Rockies, marries an Indian girl in the hope that it will help appease a warlike Blackfoot tribe guarding the territory.

Ricardo Montalban, John Hodiak, Adolphe Menjou, Maria Elena Marques, J. Carrol Naish, Jack Holt, Alan Napier, George Chandler, Douglas Fowley, Richard Anderson.

Lone Star (1952, MGM). *d:* Vincent Sherman; *p:* Z. Wayne Griffin; *sc:* Borden Chase and Howard Estabrook—*b/o* the magazine story by Borden Chase.

BURKE: Rugged Texas adventurer and cattle baron who is hired by President Andrew Jackson to persuade Sam Houston to change his mind about favoring a treaty of accord with Mexico and, instead, fight for U.S. annexation of the Republic of Texas.

Ava Gardner, Broderick Crawford, Lionel Barrymore, Beulah Bondi, Ed Begley, James Burke, William Farnum, Moroni Olsen, Russell Simpson, William Conrad, Harry Woods.

Never Let Me Go (1953, MGM). *d:* Delmer Daves; *p:* Clarence Brown; *sc:* Roland Millar and George Froeschel—*b/o* the novel *Came the Dawn* by Roger Bax.

PHILIP SUTHERLAND: American foreign correspondent in 1945 Moscow who, after he marries a beautiful Russian ballet dancer, is deported, then has to outwit the Communists in order to smuggle his wife out of the Soviet Union.

Gene Tierney, Richard Haydn, Bernard Miles, Belita, Kenneth More, Karel Stepanek, Theodore Bikel, Anna Valentina.

Mogambo (1953, MGM). *d:* John Ford; *p:* Sam Zimbalist; *sc:* John Lee Mahin—*b/o* the play *Red Dust* by Wilson Collison.

VIC MARSWELL: Famous hunter and safari leader in Kenya who becomes involved with two beautiful women—one a sexy American show girl, the other the wife of a British anthropologist.

Ava Gardner, Grace Kelly, Donald Sinden, Philip Stainton, Eric Pohlmann, Laurence Naismith, Dennis O'Dea.

Betrayed (1954, MGM). *d:* Gottfried Reinhardt; *sc:* Ronald Miller and George Froeschel.

COL. PIETER DEVENTER: WWII Dutch intelligence officer who, while serving with a Dutch underground group, discovers that the leader is a traitor secretly working for the Nazis.

Lana Turner, Victor Mature, Louis Calhern, Wilfrid Hyde-White, Ian Carmichael, Nora Swinburne, Roland Culver.

Soldier of Fortune (1955, 20th-Fox). *d:* Edward Dmytryk; *p:* Buddy Adler; *sc:* Ernest K. Gann—*b/o* the novel by Ernest K. Gann.

HANK LEE: American soldier of fortune and smuggler in Hong Kong who is hired by an American woman to find her photographer husband, who disappeared behind the bamboo curtain in Red China.

Susan Hayward, Michael Rennie, Gene Barry, Alex D'Arcy, Tom Tully, Anna Sten, Russell Collins, Leo Gordon, Richard Loo, Soo Yong, Jack Kruschen, Robert Burton, Victor Sen Yung.

The Tall Men (1955, 20th-Fox). *d:* Raoul Walsh; *p:* William A. Bacher and William B. Hawks; *sc:* Sydney Boehm and Frank Nugent—*b/o* the novel by Clay Fisher.

BEN ALLISON: Confederate Civil War veteran from Texas who, while acting as trail boss of a cattle drive from Texas to Montana, outmaneuvers hostile Indians, outwits his ruthless boss, and winds up with a pretty young woman.

Jane Russell, Robert Ryan, Cameron Mitchell, Juan Garcia, Harry Shannon, Emile Meyer, Will Wright, Russell Simpson, Mae Marsh, Tom Fadden.

The King and Four Queens (1956, UA). *d:* Raoul Walsh; *p:* David Hempstead (Russ–Field–Gabco); *sc:* Margaret Fitts and Richard Alan Simmons—*b/o* a story by Margaret Fitts.

DAN KEHOE: Western desperado who tries to outwit the wives of four dangerous gunmen and their gun-toting mother-in-law in a search for gold that's been stolen from a stagecoach and hidden on their ranch.

Eleanor Parker, Jo Van Fleet, Jean Willes, Barbara Nichols, Sara Shane, Roy Roberts, Jay C. Flippen, Arthur Shields.

Band of Angels (1957, WB). *d:* Raoul Walsh; *sc:* John Twist, Ivan Goff, and Ben Roberts—*b/o* the novel by Robert Penn Warren.

HAMISH BOND: Former slave trader–turned-gentleman in 1865 New Orleans who, when a Southern belle discovers that she has Negro ancestors and is put up for auction as a slave, buys her out of guilt and sympathy, then falls in love with her.

Yvonne de Carlo, Sidney Poitier, Efrem Zimbalist Jr., Patric Knowles, Rex Reason, Torin Thatcher, Andrea King, Ray Teal, Carolle Drake, Raymond Bailey, Juanita Moore, Roy Barcroft, Ann Doran, Bob Steele, William Schallert.

Run Silent, Run Deep (1958, UA). *d:* Robert Wise; *p:* Harold Hecht (Hecht–Hill–Lancaster); *sc:* John Gay—*b/o* the novel by Commander Edward L. Beach.

CMDR. "RICH" RICHARDSON: WWII submarine skipper who, after his sub is sunk by a Japanese destroyer, inherits an antagonistic executive officer and crew on a new sub but then wins their respect as the sub hunts down and sinks the destroyer.

Burt Lancaster, Jack Warden, Brad Dexter, Don Rickles, Nick Cravat, Joe Maross, Mary LaRoche, Eddie Foy III, Rudy Bond, H. M. Wynant, Ken Lynch.

Teacher's Pet (1958, Para.). *d:* George Seaton; *p:* William Perlberg (Perlberg–Seaton); *sc:* Fay and Michael Kanin.

JIM GANNON: Hardboiled newspaper editor who enrolls in a night-school journalism class to get next to the pretty woman who teaches it.

Doris Day, Gig Young, Mamie Van Doren, Nick Adams, Peter Baldwin, Marion Ross, Charles Lane, Jack Albertson, Harry Antrim.

But Not for Me (1959, Para.). *d:* Walter Lang; *p:* William Perlberg and George Seaton (Perlberg–Seaton); *sc:* John Michael Hayes—*b/o* the play *Accent on Youth* by Samuel Raphaelson.

RUSSELL WARD: Aging, washed-up Broadway producer who, when his young drama-student secretary falls in love with him, is rejuvenated at first but finally realizes that he really loves his mature, sophisticated ex-wife.

Carroll Baker, Lilli Palmer, Lee J. Cobb, Barry Coe, Thomas Gomez, Tom Duggan, Charles Land, Wendell Holmes.

It Started in Naples (1960, Para.). *d:* Melville Shavelson; *p:* Jack Rose; *sc:* Melville Shavelson, Jack Rose, and Suso Cecchi d'Amico—*b/o* the story by Michael Pertwee and Jack Davies.

MICHAEL HAMILTON: Philadelphia lawyer who, when he wants to take his nephew from Naples back to the United States, runs into objections from the boy's sexy Italian aunt—then winds up marrying her and staying in Italy.

Sophia Loren, Vittorio De Sica, Marietto, Paolo Carlini, Claudio Ermelli, Giovanni Filidoro.

The Misfits (1961, UA). *d:* John Huston; *p:* Frank E. Taylor (Seven Arts/John Huston); *sc:* Arthur Miller.

GAY LANGLAND: Rugged, independent, aging modern-day cowboy who goes on a roundup of small wild mustangs ("misfits") in the Nevada desert but turns them loose in response to the pleas of a young divorcée he's fallen in love with.

Marilyn Monroe, Montgomery Clift, Thelma Ritter, Eli Wallach, James Barton, Estelle Winwood, Kevin McCarthy, Dennis Shaw, Peggy Barton, Marietta Tree.

• In addition, Clark Gable made a cameo/guest appearance in the following film: *Callaway Went Thataway* (1951, MGM).

☆ GRETA GARBO

Greta Lovisa Gustafsson

b: Sept. 18, 1905, Stockholm, Sweden

"I want to be alone."

Grusinskaya (Greta Garbo) to Baron Felix von Geigern (John Barrymore) in *Grand Hotel,* 1932.

Peter the Tramp (1922, Erik A. Petschler). *d:* Erik A. Petschler; *p:* Erik A. Petschler; *sc:* Erik A. Petschler.

GRETA: A Swedish mayor's daughter who has a love affair with a woman-chasing Swedish soldier.

Erik A. Petschler, Helmer Larsson, Fredrik Olsson, Tyra Ryman, Gucken Cederborg.

The Story of Gosta Berling (1924, Svensk Filmindustri). *d:* Mauritz Stiller; *sc:* Mauritz Stiller and Ragnar Hylten-Cavallius—*b/o* the novel by Selma Lagerlof.

COUNTESS ELIZABETH DOHNA: Society woman in early nineteenth-century Sweden who helps redeem an alcoholic minister when he falls in love with her.

Lars Hanson, Ellen Cederstrom, Mona Martenson, Jenny Hasselquist, Karin Swanstrom, Gerda Lundequist.

The Joyless Street (1925, Hirschal–Sofar [released in the U.S. in 1927 as **The Street of Sorrow**]). *d:* George Wilhelm Pabst; *sc:* Willi Haas—*b/o* the novel by Hugo Bettauer.

GRETA RUMFORT: Eldest daughter of a post-WWI Vienna family made poor by the war who almost turns to prostitution but is saved by her father and an American Red Cross lieutenant.

Jaro Furth, Werner Krauss, Asta Neilsen, Valeska Gert, Einar Hanson, Agnes Esterhazy, Loni Nest, Marlene Dietrich.

The Torrent (1926, MGM). *d:* Monta Bell; *sc:* Dorothy Farnum (with titles by Katherine Hilliker and H. H. Caldwell)—*b/o* the novel by Vicente Blasco-Ibanez.

LEONORA MORENO: Young Spanish girl who wants to marry a Spanish aristocrat but, when the affair is broken up by the man's mother, becomes a famous prima donna instead.

Ricardo Cortez, Gertrude Olmstead, Edward Connelly, Lucien Littlefield, Martha Mattox, Lucy Beaumont, Tully Marshall, Mack Swain, Arthur Edmund Carew.

The Temptress (1926, MGM). *d:* Fred Niblo; *sc:* Dorothy Farnum (with titles by Marion Ainslee)—*b/o* the novel by Vicente Blasco-Ibanez.

ELENA FONTENOY: French marquis's wife who falls in love with an Argentine engineer, but—realizing she's no good for him—leaves him and winds up as a Parisian streetwalker.

Antonio Moreno, Marc McDermott, Lionel Barrymore, Armand Kaliz, Roy D'Arcy, Alys Murrell, Roy Coulson, Robert Anderson, Francis McDonald, Inez Gomez.

Flesh and the Devil (1927, MGM). *d:* Clarence Brown; *sc:* Benjamin F. Glazer (with titles by Marion Ainslee)—*b/o* Hermann Sudermann's novel *The Undying Past.*

FELICITAS VON RHADEN: Alluring Austrian beauty whose infidelity leads to a duel between her husband and his best friend—her lover.

John Gilbert, Lars Hanson, Barbara Kent, William Orlamund, George Fawcett, Eugenie Besserer, Marc MacDermott, Marcelle Corday.

Love (1927, MGM). *d:* Edmund Goulding; *sc:* Frances Marion (with titles by Marion Ainslee and Ruth Cummings)—*b/o* the novel *Anna Karenina* by Leo Tolstoy.

ANNA KARENINA: Wife of a wealthy aristocrat in czarist Russia who deserts her husband and young son to become the mistress of a handsome military officer.

John Gilbert, George Fawcett, Emily Fitzroy, Brandon Hurst, Philippe de Lacy.

The Divine Woman (1928, MGM). *d:* Victor Seastrom; *sc:* Dorothy Farnum (with titles by John Colton)—*b/o* the play *Starlight* by Gladys Unger.

MARIANNE: Young French farm girl who goes to Paris and becomes the mistress of one of her estranged mother's lovers when he promises to make her a big stage star.

Lars Hanson, Lowell Sherman, Polly Moran, Dorothy Cumming, John Mack Brown, Cesare Gravina, Paulette Duval, Jean de Briac.

The Mysterious Lady (1928, MGM). *d:* Fred Niblo; *sc:* Bess Meredyth (with titles by Marion Ainslee and Ruth Cummings)—*b/o* the novel *War in the Dark* by Ludwig Wolff.

TANIA: WWI Russian spy who steals important secret plans from an Austrian Army officer but falls in love with him.

Conrad Nagel, Gustav von Seyffertitz, Edward Connelly, Albert Pollet, Richard Alexander.

A Woman of Affairs (1929, MGM). *d:* Clarence Brown; *sc:* Bess Meredyth—*b/o* Michael Arlen's novel *The Green Hat*.

DIANA MERRICK: Reckless, aristocratic English woman who—when the man she married turns out to be a thief and commits suicide—sets out to pay back what he stole.

John Gilbert, Lewis Stone, John Mack Brown, Douglas Fairbanks Jr., Hobart Bosworth, Dorothy Sebastian.

Wild Orchids (1929, MGM). *d:* Sidney Franklin; *sc:* Willis Goldbeck (with continuity by Hans Kraly and Richard Schayer, and titles by Marion Ainslee)—*b/o* the story "Heat" by John Colton.

LILLIE STERLING: Young married woman who becomes involved in an affair with a Javanese prince when she and her husband are guests at the prince's palace.

Lewis Stone, Nils Asther.

The Single Standard (1929, MGM). *d:* John S. Robertson; *sc:* Josephine Lovett (with titles by Marion Ainslee)—*b/o* the novel by Adela Rogers St. John.

ARDEN STUART: San Francisco debutante who marries and has a child but almost loses both her husband and the child when she becomes involved with her sailor-turned-artist former lover.

Nils Asther, John Mack Brown, Dorothy Sebastian, Lane Chandler, Robert Castle, Mahlon Hamilton, Kathlyn Williams, Zeffie Tilbury.

The Kiss (1929, MGM). *d:* Jacques Feyder; *sc:* Hans Kraly—*b/o* a story by George M. Saville.

IRENE GUARRY: French silk merchant's wife who, when her jealous husband tries to kill a young man enamored of her, shoots the husband.

Conrad Nagel, Anders Randolf, Holmes Herbert, Lew Ayres, George Davis.

Anna Christie (1930, MGM). *d:* Clarence Brown; *sc:* Frances Marion—*b/o* the play by Eugene O'Neill.

ANNA CHRISTIE*: Bitter, cynical waterfront tramp with a past who comes to live on her father's fishing barge and falls in love with a rugged seaman.

Charles Bickford, George F. Marion, Marie Dressler, James T. Mack, Lee Phelps.

Romance (1930, MGM). *d:* Clarence Brown; *sc:* Bess Meredyth and Edwin Justus Mayer—*b/o* the play by Edward Sheldon.

RITA CAVALLINI*: Italian prima donna who is the mistress of a wealthy man but falls in love with a young clergyman.

Lewis Stone, Gavin Gordon, Elliott Nugent, Florence Lake, Clara Blandick, Henry Armetta, Mathilde Comont, Countess Rina De Liguoro.

Inspiration (1931, MGM). *d:* Clarence Brown; *sc:* Gene Markey.

YVONNE: Beautiful Parisian artist's model who falls in love with a young man studying for the consular service but—because of her sensational past—gives him up rather than ruin his career.

Robert Montgomery, Lewis Stone, Marjorie Rambeau, Beryl Mercer, John Miljan, Edwin Maxwell, Oscar Apfel, Joan Marsh, Zelda Sears, Karen Morley, Arthur Hoyt, Richard Tucker.

Susan Lenox: Her Fall and Rise (1931, MGM). *d:* Robert Z. Leonard; *sc:* Wanda Tuchock (with dialogue by Zelda Sears and Edith Fitzgerald)—*b/o* the novel by David Graham Phillips.

SUSAN LENOX: Farmer's daughter who has a brief love affair with a construction engineer,

---

*Received an Academy Award Nomination as Best Actress for this role.

then becomes a wealthy politician's mistress, but finally realizes that she really loves the engineer and follows him to a South American construction camp.

Clark Gable, Jean Hersholt, John Miljan, Alan Hale, Hale Hamilton, Russell Simpson, Cecil Cunningham, Theodore Von Eltz, Ian Keith.

Mata Hari (1932, MGM). *d:* George Fitzmaurice; *sc:* Benjamin Glazer and Leo Birinski (with dialogue by Doris Anderson and Gilbert Emery).

MATA HARI: Famed WWI spy for the Germans who poses as a dancer in Paris, wrecks men's lives to gain military secrets, and winds up in front of a firing squad.

Ramon Novarro, Lionel Barrymore, Lewis Stone, C. Henry Gordon, Karen Morley, Alec B. Francis, Edmund Breese, Helen Jerome Eddy, Frank Reicher.

Grand Hotel (1932, MGM). *d:* Edmund Goulding; *sc:* William A. Drake—*b/o* the novel and play by Vicki Baum.

GRUSINSKAYA: Famous but lonely ballet star who comes to stay at the plush Grand Hotel in Berlin and falls in love with an adventurer who is planning to steal her jewels.

John Barrymore, Joan Crawford, Wallace Beery, Lionel Barrymore, Lewis Stone, Jean Hersholt, Robert McWade, Purnell B. Pratt, Tully Marshall, Frank Conroy, Edwin Maxwell.

As You Desire Me (1932, MGM). *d:* George Fitzmaurice; *sc:* Gene Markey—*b/o* the play by Luigi Pirandello.

MARIA/ZARA: Exotic Budapest café singer suffering from amnesia who, when she's identified as the wife of a wealthy nobleman, returns to her husband but still can't remember him.

Melvyn Douglas, Erich von Stroheim, Owen Moore, Hedda Hopper, Rafaela Ottiano, Warburton Gamble, Albert Conti, Roland Varno.

Queen Christina (1933, MGM). *d:* Rouben Mamoulian; *p:* Walter Wanger; *sc:* H. M. Harwood and Salka Viertel (with dialogue by S. N. Behrman)—*b/o* a story by Salka Viertel and Margaret R. Levino.

QUEEN CHRISTINA: Seventeenth-century Swedish ruler who rejects the idea of an arranged political marriage, falls in love with a Spanish ambassador, and gives up her throne for him.

John Gilbert, Ian Keith, Lewis Stone, Elizabeth Young, C. Aubrey Smith, Reginald Owen, David Torrence, Gustav von Seyffertitz.

The Painted Veil (1934, MGM). *d:* Richard Boleslawski; *p:* Hunt Stromberg; *sc:* John Meehan, Salka Viertel, and Edith Fitzgerald—*b/o* the novel by W. Somerset Maugham.

KATRIN FANE: Beautiful woman who, when she goes to China with her doctor husband, has an affair with a diplomatic attaché but later redeems herself when she helps her husband fight a cholera epidemic.

Herbert Marshall, George Brent, Warner Oland, Jean Hersholt, Beulah Bondi, Katherine Alexander, Cecilia Parker, Soo Yong, Forrester Harvey.

Anna Karenina (1935, MGM). *d:* Clarence Brown; *p:* David O. Selznick; *sc:* Clemence Dane, Salka Viertel, and S. N. Behrman—*b/o* the novel by Leo Tolstoy.

ANNA KARENINA: Married woman in nineteenth-century Russia who deserts her wealthy husband and her young son to become the mistress of a dashing Russian military officer.

Fredric March, Freddie Bartholomew, Maureen O'Sullivan, May Robson, Basil Rathbone, Reginald Owen, Reginald Denny, Phoebe Foster, Gyles Isham, Buster Phelps, Joan Marsh, Cora Sue Collins.

Camille (1937, MGM). *d:* George Cukor; *p:* Irving Thalberg and Bernard Hyman; *sc:* Zoe Akins, Frances Marion, and James Hilton—*b/o* the novel and play *La Dame aux Camelias* by Alexandre Dumas.

MARGUERITE GAUTIER (alias CAMILLE)*: Beautiful, cynical nineteenth-century Parisian courtesan whose love affair with a boyish young Frenchman ends in tragedy when she's afflicted with a fatal illness.

Robert Taylor, Lionel Barrymore, Elizabeth Allan, Jessie Ralph, Henry Daniell, Lenore Ulric, Laura Hope Crews, Russell Hardie, E. E. Clive, Douglas Walton, Joan Brodel (Joan Leslie), Fritz Leiber Jr., Edwin Maxwell.

Conquest (1937, MGM). *d:* Clarence Brown; *p:* Bernard H. Hyman; *sc:* Samuel Hoffenstein, Salka Viertel, and S. N. Behrman—*b/o* the novel *Pani Walewska* by Waclaw Gasiorowski and a dramatization by Helen Jerome.

COUNTESS MARIE WALEWSKA: Married Polish countess in the early 1800s who, after she has an affair with Napoleon and is divorced by her husband, becomes Napoleon's mistress and bears him a son.

Charles Boyer, Reginald Owen, Alan Marshall, Henry Stephenson, Leif Erickson, Dame May Whitty, C. Henry Gordon, Vladimir Sokoloff, Maria Ouspenskaya, Scotty Beckett.

Ninotchka (1939, MGM). *d:* Ernst Lubitsch; *p:* Ernst Lubitsch; *sc:* Charles Brackett, Billy Wilder, and Walter Reisch—*b/o* a story by Melchior Lengyel.

NINOTCHKA*: Beautiful but icy Russian Communist emissary who comes to Paris to sell

---

*Received an Academy Award Nomination as Best Actress for this role.

some crown jewels and falls in love with an American man-about-town and the capitalistic way of life.

Melvyn Douglas, Ina Claire, Bela Lugosi, Sig Rumann, Felix Bressart, Alexander Granach, Gregory Gaye, Rolfe Sedan, Edwin Maxwell, Richard Carle.

Two-Faced Woman (1941, MGM). *d:* George Cukor; *p:* Gottfried Reinhardt; *sc:* S. N. Behrman, Salka Viertel, and George Oppenheimer—*b/o* the play by Ludwig Fulda.

KARIN: Down-to-earth ski instructor who marries a New York publisher, then, when she suspects that she may be losing him to his old flame, poses as her own more sophisticated twin sister to test his love.

Melvyn Douglas, Constance Bennett, Roland Young, Robert Sterling, Ruth Gordon, Francis Carson.

☆ JUDY GARLAND

Frances Ethel Gumm

b: June 10, 1922, Grand Rapids, Minn.
d: June 22, 1969, London, England

"If I ever go looking for my heart's desire again, I won't look any further than my own back yard, because if it isn't there, I never really lost it to begin with."

Dorothy Gale (Judy Garland) reflecting on her journey to the Land of Oz in *The Wizard of Oz*, 1939.

Pigskin Parade (1936, 20th-Fox). *d:* David Butler; *p:* Darryl F. Zanuck; *sc:* Harry Tugend, Jack Yellan, and William Conselman—*b/o* a story by Art Sheekman, Nat Perrin, and Mark Kelly.

SAIRY DODD: Teen-age Texas farm girl whose older brother is discovered hurling muskmellons with uncanny accuracy across a two-acre field and is signed up as the star passing quarterback of a jerkwater Texas college football team that's been mistakenly scheduled to play Yale.

Patsy Kelly, Jack Haley, The Yacht Club Boys, Stuart Erwin, Johnny Downs, Betty Grable, Arline Judge, Dixie Dunbar, Fred Kohler Jr., Grady Sutton, Elisha Cook Jr., Eddie Nugent, Pat Flaherty, Si Jenks.

Broadway Melody of 1938 (1937, MGM). *d:* Roy Del Ruth; *p:* Jack Cummings; *sc:* Jack McGowan—*b/o* a story by Jack McGowan and Sid Silvers.

BETTY CLAYTON: Boarding-house landlady's talented teen-age daughter who makes a hit singing and dancing in a handsome Broadway producer's big new musical.

Robert Taylor, Eleanor Powell, George Murphy, Binnie Barnes, Buddy Ebsen, Sophie Tucker, Charles Igor Gorin, Raymond Walburn, Robert Benchley, Willie Howard, Charley Grapewin, Robert Wildhack, Billy Gilbert, Barnett Parker, Helen Troy.

Thoroughbreds Don't Cry (1937, MGM). *d:* Alfred E. Green; *p:* Harry Rapf; *sc:* Lawrence Hazard—*b/o* a story by Eleanore Griffin and J. Walter Ruben.

CRICKET WEST: Boarding-house owner's niece who, along with the grandson of an English racehorse owner and a cocky young American jockey, is determined to make the grandfather's horse a winner.

Mickey Rooney, Sophie Tucker, C. Aubrey Smith, Ronald Sinclair, Forrester Harvey, Charles D. Brown, Frankie Darro, Henry Kolker, Helen Troy.

Everybody Sing (1938, MGM). *d:* Edwin L. Marin; *p:* Harry Rapf; *sc:* Florence Ryerson and Edgar Allan Woolf (with additional dialogue by James Gruen).

JUDY BELLAIRE: Fifteen-year-old daughter of an eccentric family of stage people (with a screwball maid and a singing chef) who put on a Broadway musical show to try to revive their waning fortunes.

Allan Jones, Fanny Brice, Reginald Owen, Billie Burke, Reginald Gardiner, Lynne Carver, Helen Troy, Monty Woolley, Henry Armetta.

Listen, Darling (1938, MGM). *d:* Edwin L. Marin; *p:* Jack Cummings; *sc:* Elaine Ryan and Anne Morrison Chapin—*b/o* a story by Katherine Brush.

PINKIE WINGATE: Teen-age girl who, with the help of her younger brother and her teen-age boyfriend, tries to steer her widowed mother from the "wrong man" into the arms of a "nice guy."

Freddie Bartholomew, Mary Astor, Walter Pidgeon, Alan Hale, Scotty Beckett, Barnett Parker, Gene Lockhart, Charley Grapewin.

Love Finds Andy Hardy (1938, MGM). *d:* George B. Seitz; *sc:* William Indwig—from the stories by Vivien R. Bretherton, *b/o* characters created by Aurania Rouverol.

BETSY BOOTH: Teen-age girl who visits the

small Midwestern town of Carvel and develops a crush on a teen-ager named Andy Hardy—who already has a crush on someone else.

Lewis Stone, Mickey Rooney, Cecilia Parker, Fay Holden, Ann Rutherford, Lana Turner, Marie Blake, Don Castle, Gene Reynolds, Mary Howard, George Breakston, Raymond Hatton.

The Wizard of Oz (1939, MGM). *d:* Victor Fleming; *p:* Mervyn LeRoy; *sc:* Noel Langley, Florence Ryerson, and Edgar Allan Woolf—*b/o* the book by L. Frank Baum.

DOROTHY GALE: Young Kansas farm girl who, after she's whisked away by a cyclone to the wonderful fantasy land of Oz, meets and accompanies the Scarecrow, the Tin Woodman, and the Cowardly Lion to the Emerald City to ask the mighty Wizard of Oz to help her get back home to Kansas.

Frank Morgan, Ray Bolger, Bert Lahr, Jack Haley, Billie Burke, Margaret Hamilton, Charley Grapewin, Clara Blandick, Toto.

Babes in Arms (1939, MGM). *d:* Busby Berkeley; *p:* Arthur Freed; *sc:* Jack McGowan and Kay Van Riper—*b/o* the musical by Richard Rodgers and Lorenz Hart.

PATSY BARTON: Young girl who, with her boyfriend, leads a group of Depression-era teen-age sons and daughters of retired vaudevillians in putting on a big musical revue to help the parents out of financial difficulties.

Mickey Rooney, Charles Winninger, Guy Kibbee, June Preisser, Betty Jaynes, Douglas MacPhail, Rand Brooks, John Sheffield, Henry Hull, Barnett Parker, Ann Shoemaker, Margaret Hamilton, Joseph Crehan.

Andy Hardy Meets Debutante (1940, MGM). *d:* George B. Seitz; *sc:* Annalee Whitmore and Thomas Seller—*b/o* characters created by Aurania Rouverol.

BETSY BOOTH: Faithful teen-age admirer of Andy Hardy who helps him straighten out his problems when he visits New York and becomes involved with a sophisticated debutante.

Lewis Stone, Mickey Rooney, Cecilia Parker, Fay Holden, Ann Rutherford, Diana Lewis, George Breakston, Sara Haden, Addison Richards, George Lessey, Gladys Blake, Cy Kendall.

Strike Up the Band (1940, MGM). *d:* Busby Berkeley; *p:* Arthur Freed; *sc:* John Monks Jr. and Fred Finklehoffe.

MARY HOLDEN: Singing, dancing girlfriend of a drum-playing teen-ager who transforms his high school band into a swing band that competes in orchestra leader Paul Whiteman's nationwide radio contest.

Mickey Rooney, Paul Whiteman, June Preisser, William Tracy, Larry Nunn, Ann Shoemaker,

Francis Pierlot, Virginia Brissac, George Lessey, Howard Hickman, Milton Kibbee, Helen Jerome Eddy.

Little Nellie Kelly (1940, MGM). *d:* Norman Taurog; *p:* Arthur Freed; *sc:* Jack McGowan—*b/o* the musical comedy by George M. Cohan.

(Dual role) NELLIE KELLY: Young Irish woman who marries the man she loves against the wishes of her father but dies while giving birth to their daughter.

LITTLE NELLIE KELLY: Daughter of Nellie Kelly who, when she grows up, tries to end the feud that has existed for years between her stubborn Irish cop father and her bitter maternal grandfather.

George Murphy, Charles Winninger, Douglas MacPhail, Arthur Shields, Rita Page, Forrester Harvey, James Burke, John Raitt.

Ziegfeld Girl (1941, MGM). *d:* Robert Z. Leonard; *p:* Pandro S. Berman; *sc:* Marguerite Roberts and Sonya Levien—*b/o* a story by William Anthony McGuire.

SUSAN GALLAGHER: One of three pretty women—she's a hard-working vaudeville singer and dancer—whose lives are changed when they become glamorous Ziegfeld Follies girls.

James Stewart, Hedy Lamarr, Lana Turner, Tony Martin, Jackie Cooper, Ian Hunter, Charles Winninger, Edward Everett Horton, Philip Dorn, Paul Kelly, Eve Arden, Dan Dailey Jr., Al Shean, Fay Holden, Felix Bressart, Rose Hobart.

Life Begins for Andy Hardy (1941, MGM). *d:* George B. Seitz; *sc:* Agnes Christine Johnston—*b/o* characters created by Aurania Rouverol.

BETSY BOOTH: Faithful teen-age admirer of Carvel High School graduate Andy Hardy who accompanies him to New York, where he plans to try to make good on his own for a month before deciding whether to go to college.

Lewis Stone, Mickey Rooney, Fay Holden, Ann Rutherford, Sara Haden, Patricia Dane, Ray McDonald.

Babes on Broadway (1941, MGM). *d:* Busby Berkeley; *p:* Arthur Freed; *sc:* Fred Finklehoffe and Elaine Ryan—*b/o* a story by Fred Finklehoffe.

PENNY MORRIS: Young girl who, after vainly trying to land a role on Broadway, finally decides—along with her boyfriend and their pals—that the only way to get a break is to produce their own show.

Mickey Rooney, Fay Bainter, Virginia Weidler, Ray McDonald, Richard Quine, Donald Meek, Alexander Woollcott, Louis Alberni, James Gleason, Emma Dunn, Cliff Clark.

For Me and My Gal (1942, MGM). *d:* Busby

Berkeley; *p:* Arthur Freed; *sc:* Richard Sherman, Fred Finklehoffe, and Sid Silvers—*b/o* a story by Howard Emmett Rogers.

JO HAYDEN: Vaudeville performer during WWI who has to choose between her two song-and-dance partners—one a fast-talking heel, the other a nice guy, faithfully standing by.

George Murphy, Gene Kelly, Marta Eggerth, Ben Blue, Horace McNally (Stephen McNally), Richard Quine, Lucille Norman, Keenan Wynn.

Presenting Lily Mars (1943, MGM). *d:* Norman Taurog; *p:* Joe Pasternak; *sc:* Richard Connell and Gladys Lehman—*b/o* a novel by Booth Tarkington.

LILY MARS: Stage-struck girl from a small Midwestern town who, when she falls in love with a New York producer who's visiting her mother, winds up marrying him and becoming a Broadway star.

Van Heflin, Fay Bainter, Richard Carlson, Spring Byington, Marta Eggerth, Connie Gilchrist, Leonid Kinskey, Ray McDonald, Tommy Dorsey and his Orchestra, Bob Crosby and his Orchestra.

Girl Crazy (1943, MGM). *d:* Norman Taurog; *p:* Arthur Freed; *sc:* Fred Finklehoffe—*b/o* a musical by Guy Bolton, Jack McGowan, George Gershwin, and Ira Gershwin.

GINGER GRAY: Southwestern college president's daughter who helps a New York playboy—sent to the school by his wealthy father to straighten him out—put on a big western jamboree show to save the school from going broke.

Mickey Rooney, Gil Stratton, Robert E. Strickland, Rags Ragland, June Allyson, Nancy Walker, Guy Kibbee, Frances Rafferty, Henry O'Neill, Howard Freeman, Tommy Dorsey and his Orchestra.

Meet Me in St. Louis (1944, MGM). *d:* Vincente Minnelli; *p:* Arthur Freed; *sc:* Irving Becher and Fred Finklehoffe—*b/o* a story by Sally Benson.

ESTHER SMITH: Middle daughter of a St. Louis family at the time of the 1903 World's Fair who, when the father announces that he's being transferred to New York, doesn't want to go because she has a crush on the boy next door.

Margaret O'Brien, Mary Astor, Lucille Bremer, Tom Drake, Marjorie Main, Leon Ames, Harry Davenport, June Lockhart, Joan Carroll, Hugh Marlowe, Chill Wills.

The Clock (1945, MGM). *d:* Vincente Minnelli; *p:* Arthur Freed; *sc:* Robert Nathan and Joseph Schrank—*b/o* a story by Paul Gallico and Pauline Gallico.

ALICE MAYBERRY: Lonely office worker who meets a young WWII soldier at New York's Pennsylvania Station, falls in love with him, and marries him—during the soldier's last forty-eight-hour furlough before he's shipped overseas.

Robert Walker, James Gleason, Keenan Wynn, Marshall Thompson, Lucille Gleason, Ruth Brady, Chester Clute, Dick Elliott, Ray Teal.

The Harvey Girls (1946, MGM). *d:* George Sidney; *p:* Arthur Freed and Roger Edens; *sc:* Edmund Beloin and Nathaniel Curtis—*b/o* a story by Samuel Hopkins Adams, Eleanore Griffin, and William Rankin.

SUSAN BRADLEY: One of a group of young women in the 1870s who go to the Wild West to become waitresses in Fred Harvey railroad station restaurants.

John Hodiak, Ray Bolger, Preston Foster, Virginia O'Brien, Angela Lansbury, Marjorie Main, Chill Wills, Kenny Baker, Selena Royle, Cyd Charisse, Jack Lambert, William "Bill" Phillips, Morris Ankrum, Ben Carter, Horace McNally (Stephen McNally), Ray Teal, Vernon Dent.

Till the Clouds Roll By (1946, MGM). *d:* Richard Whorf; *p:* Arthur Freed; *sc:* Myles Connolly and Jean Halloway (adaptation by George Wells)—*b/o* a story by Guy Bolton.

MARILYN MILLER: Famous singer and dancer of the 1920s who stars in some of composer Jerome Kern's musical Broadway shows.

Robert Walker, Lucille Bremer, Van Heflin, Paul Langton, Dorothy Patrick, Mary Nash, Harry Hayden, Rex Evans, Dinah Shore, Van Johnson, June Allyson, Angela Lansbury, Ray McDonald, Cyd Charisse, Gower Champion, Sally Forrest, Tony Martin, Kathryn Grayson, Frank Sinatra, Lena Horne.

The Pirate (1948, MGM). *d:* Vincente Minnelli; *p:* Arthur Freed; *sc:* Albert Hackett and Frances Goodrich—*b/o* a play by S. N. Behrman.

MANUELA: Lonely young lady in a West Indies port who, after she's swept off her feet by a handsome strolling thespian masquerading as a notorious Caribbean pirate called "Mack the Black Macoco," discovers that the corrupt mayor of the town is secretly the real pirate.

Gene Kelly, Walter Slezak, Gladys Cooper, Reginald Owen, George Zucco, The Nicholas Brothers, Lola Deem, Jean Dean, Marion Murray, Ben Lessy, Val Zetz, Cully Richards.

Easter Parade (1948, MGM). *d:* Charles Walters; *p:* Arthur Freed; *sc:* Sidney Sheldon, Frances Goodrich, and Albert Hackett.

HANNAH BROWN: Small-time chorus girl who is picked to become the partner of a famous male dancer who, while trying to forget his ex-partner, has made a bet that he can make the new girl into a star.

Fred Astaire, Peter Lawford, Ann Miller, Jules Munshin, Clinton Sundberg, Jeni LeGon, Dick Simmons, Jimmy Dodd, Robert Emmett O'Connor, Lola Albright, Joi Lansing.

In the Good Old Summertime (1949, MGM). *d:* Robert Z. Leonard; *p:* Joe Pasternak; *sc:* Samson Raphaelson—*b/o* a story by Mikolas Laszlo.

VERONICA FISHER: Salesgirl in a 1906 Chicago music store whose anonymous lonely-hearts correspondence is unknowingly carried on with a fellow worker whom she detests, and vice-versa.

Van Johnson, S. Z. "Cuddles" Sakall, Spring Byington, Buster Keaton, Clinton Sundburg, Marcia Van Dyke, Lillian Bronson.

Summer Stock (1950, MGM). *d:* Charles Walters; *p:* Joe Pasternak; *sc:* George Wells and Sy Gomberg—*b/o* a story by Sy Gomberg.

JANE FALBURY: Connecticut farm owner who, when her stage-struck sister invites a summer stock troupe to use her barn as a summer theater, resents the actors at first but ends up replacing her sister as the star of the show.

Gene Kelly, Eddie Bracken, Gloria DeHaven, Marjorie Main, Phil Silvers, Ray Collins, Carleton Carpenter, Nita Bieber, Hans Conried, Carole Haney, Erville Alderson, Bunny Waters, Almira Sessions, Eddie Dunn.

A Star Is Born (1954, WB). *d:* George Cukor; *p:* Sidney Luft (Transcona); *sc:* Moss Hart—*b/o* a screenplay by Dorothy Parker, Alan Campbell, and Robert Carson, and a story by William A. Wellman and Robert Carson.

ESTHER BLODGETT (alias VICKI LESTER)*: Band singer who, after she's helped by an aging movie idol to become a Hollywood star, marries him, then sticks by him as his own career slides and he ends up drowning himself.

James Mason, Jack Carson, Charles Bickford, Tommy Noonan, Amanda Blake, Irving Bacon, Hazel Shermet, James Brown, Lotus Robb, Dub Taylor, Louis Jean Heydt, Chick Chandler, Olin Howland, Mae Marsh, Grady Sutton, Richard Webb, Tristram Coffin, Frank Ferguson, Percy Helton.

Judgment at Nuremberg (1961, UA). *d:* Stanley Kramer; *p:* Stanley Kramer (Roxlom); *sc:* Abby Mann—*b/o* his TV play.

IRENE HOFFMAN†: Distraught German hausfrau who testifies against Nazi German war criminals during the post-WWII Nazi war crimes trials

---

*Received an Academy Award nomination as Best Actress for this role.
†Received an Academy Award nomination as Best Supporting Actress for this role.

presided over by an American judge in Nuremberg, Germany.

Spencer Tracy, Burt Lancaster, Richard Widmark, Marlene Dietrich, Maximilian Schell, Montgomery Clift, William Shatner, Edward Binns, Kenneth MacKenna, Werner Klemperer, Alan Baxter, Ray Teal, Virginia Christine, Karl Swenson, Sheila Bromley.

Gay Purr-ee (1962, WB). *d:* Abe Leviton; *p:* Henry G. Saperstein (UPA); *sc:* Dorothy Jones and Chuck Jones.

MEWSETTE: Judy does the *voice* of this animated sexy, fun-loving kitten who goes to the big city and meets up with an evil tabby.

Actors whose voices were used for other animated animal characters: Robert Goulet, Red Buttons, Hermione Gingold, Paul Frees, Morey Amsterdam, Mel Blanc, Julie Bennett, Joan Gardner.

A Child Is Waiting (1963, UA). *d:* John Cassavetes; *p:* Stanley Kramer (Stanley Kramer); *sc:* Abby Mann—*b/o* his TV play.

JEAN HANSEN: Spinster music teacher at a state institution for mentally retarded children who mistakenly believes—in opposition to the realistic philosophy of the head psychiatrist—that pampering and sheltering the children will solve their problems.

Burt Lancaster, Gena Rowlands, Steven Hill, Bruce Ritchey, Gloria McGehee, Paul Stewart, Barbara Pepper, John Morley, June Walker, Lawrence Tierney.

I Could Go On Singing (1963, UA). *d:* Ronald Neame; *p:* Stuart Millar and Lawrence Turman (Barbican); *sc:* Mayo Simon—*b/o* a story by Robert Dozier.

JENNY BOWMAN: American singing star who, when she returns to London to play the Palladium, looks up her ex-lover—now a prominent doctor—and tries to get custody of their illegitimate son, who is living with the father.

Dirk Bogarde, Jack Klugman, Gregory Phillips, Aline MacMahon, Pauline Jameson, Jeremy Burnham, Russell Waters, Gerald Sim, Leon Cortez.

• In addition, Judy Garland made cameo/guest appearances in the following feature films: *Thousands Cheer* (1943, MGM), *Ziegfeld Follies* (1946, MGM), and *Words and Music* (1948, MGM).

☆ CARY GRANT

Archibald Alexander Leach

b: Jan. 18, 1904, Bristol, England

"I'm more or less particular about whom my wife marries."

> Walter Burns (Cary Grant) about Bruce Baldwin (Ralph Bellamy), who is about to marry Burns's ex-wife, Hildy Johnson (Rosalind Russell), in *His Girl Friday,* 1940.

This Is the Night (1932, Para.). *d:* Frank Tuttle; *sc:* George Marion Jr.—*b/o* the play *Naughty Cinderella* by Avery Hopwood.
STEPAN (STEPHEN) MENDANICH: Famous Olympic javelin thrower who, after he finds his wife in the arms of a wealthy French bachelor, falls in love with a pretty Parisian movie extra.
Lily Damita, Charlie Ruggles, Roland Young, Thelma Todd, Irving Bacon, Claire Dodd, Davison Clark.

Sinners in the Sun (1932, Para.). *d:* Alexander Hall; *sc:* Vincent Lawrence, Waldemar Young, and Samuel Hoffenstein—*b/o* the story "The Beachcomber" by Mildred Cram.
RIDGEWAY: Ne'er-do-well playboy whose mistress, after traveling around the world gambling and drinking with him, commits suicide.
Carole Lombard, Chester Morris, Adrienne Ames, Alison Skipworth, Walter Byron, Reginald Barlow, Luke Cosgrove, Ida Lewis, Frances Moffett, Rita La Roy.

Merrily We Go to Hell (1932, Para.). *d:* Dorothy Arzner; *sc:* Edwin Justus Mayer—*b/o* the novel *I, Jerry, Take Thee, Joan* by Cleo Lucas.
CHARLES EXETER: Handsome actor who is the lead in a play written by a chic socialite's hard-drinking newspaperman husband.
Sylvia Sidney, Fredric March, Adrianne Allen, Skeets Gallagher, Florence Britton, Esther Howard, George Irving, Kent Taylor, Robert Greig.

Devil and the Deep (1932, Para.). *d:* Marion Gering; *sc:* Benn Levy—*b/o* a story by Harry Hervey.
LIEUTENANT JAECKEL: Young naval officer at a submarine base in North Africa who is one of several admirers of the wife of his jealous commanding officer.
Tallulah Bankhead, Gary Cooper, Charles Laughton, Paul Porcasi, Juliette Compton, Henry Kolker, Arthur Hoyt, Kent Taylor, Lucien Littlefield, Dave O'Brien.

Blonde Venus (1932, Para.). *d:* Josef von Sternberg; *sc:* Jules Furthman and S. K. Lauren—*b/o* a story by Josef von Sternberg.
NICK TOWNSEND: Wealthy playboy who takes as his mistress a young married woman who needs money from him to pay for her sick husband's medical treatments.
Marlene Dietrich, Herbert Marshall, Dickie Moore, Gene Morgan, Rita La Roy, Robert Emmett O'Connor, Sidney Toler, Dewey Robinson, Cecil Cunningham.

Hot Saturday (1932, Para.). *d:* William A. Seiter; *sc:* Seton I. Miller (adaptation by Josephine Lovett and Joseph Moncure March)—*b/o* the novel by Harvey Ferguson.
ROMER SHEFFIELD: Smooth playboy who causes a lot of local gossip and other problems when he becomes involved with a young small-town woman who's engaged to marry her childhood sweetheart.
Nancy Carroll, Randolph Scott, Edward Woods, Lillian Bond, William Collier Sr., Jane Darwell, Rita La Roy, Grady Sutton.

Madame Butterfly (1932, Para.). *d:* Marion Gering; *sc:* Josephine Lovett and Joseph Moncure March—*b/o* a story by John Luther Long and the play by David Belasco.
LT. B. F. PINKERTON: Young U.S. naval officer who marries a Japanese girl while on shore leave in Japan, sails back to America with the fleet, but then returns to Japan three years later—with an American wife.
Sylvia Sidney, Charlie Ruggles, Sandor Kallay, Irving Pichel, Helen Jerome Eddy, Edmund Breese, Sheila Terry, Judith Vasselli.

She Done Him Wrong (1933, Para.). *d:* Lowell Sherman; *p:* William LeBaron; *sc:* Harvey Thew and John Bright—*b/o* the play *Diamond Lil* by Mae West.
CAPTAIN CUMMINGS: Federal undercover agent who poses as a Salvation Army worker in the Gay '90s Bowery to get the goods on a shady lady saloon keeper—and winds up falling for her.
Mae West, Gilbert Roland, Noah Beery Sr., Rafaela Ottiano, David Landau, Rochelle Hudson, Owen Moore, Fuzzy Knight, Dewey Robinson, Tom Kennedy, Wade Boteler, Louise Beavers.

Woman Accused (1933, Para.). *d:* Paul Sloane; *sc:* Bayard Veiller—*b/o* a *Liberty* magazine serial written by Rupert Hughes, Vicki Baum, Zane Grey, Vina Delmar, Irvin S. Cobb, Gertrude Atherton, J. P. McEvoy, Ursula Parrott, Polen Banks, and Sophie Kerr.

JEFFREY BAXTER: Young lawyer who, when his fiancée is tried for killing her ex-lover, helps get her acquitted by thrashing a lying gangster with a blacksnake whip to make him tell the truth about the matter.

Nancy Carroll, John Halliday, Irving Pichel, Louis Calhern, Norma Mitchell, Jack La Rue, Harry Holman, Jay Belasco, Donald Stuart, Robert Quirk, Gaylord Pendleton.

The Eagle and the Hawk (1933, Para.). *d:* Stuart Walker; *sc:* Bogart Rogers and Seton I. Miller—*b/o* a story by John Monk Saunders.

HENRY CROCKER: Ruthless WWI aerial gunner in the British Royal Flying Corps who, though he and his ace American pilot are bitter enemies, nobly covers up the battle-weary pilot's suicide and makes it appear that he died a hero in aerial combat.

Fredric March, Jack Oakie, Carole Lombard, Sir Guy Standing, Forrester Harvey, Kenneth Howell, Layland Hodgson, Virginia Hammond, Crauford Kent, Douglas Scott, Robert Manning, Russell Scott.

Gambling Ship (1933, Para.). *d:* Louis Gasnier and Max Marcin; *sc:* Max Marcin and Seton I. Miller (adaptation by Claude Binyon)—*b/o* stories by Peter Ruric.

ACE CORBIN: Famous big-time gambler who takes over as the operator of a gambling ship off the coast of California and becomes involved in a gang war with a rival ship.

Benita Hume, Roscoe Karns, Glenda Farrell, Jack La Rue, Arthur Vinton, Charles Williams, Edwin Maxwell, Spencer Charters, Edward Gargan, Sid Saylor, Hooper Atchley, Gum Chung.

I'm No Angel (1933, Para.). *d:* Wesley Ruggles; *p:* William LeBaron; *sc:* Mae West (with continuity by Harlan Thompson and story suggestions by Lowell Brentano).

JACK CLAYTON: Rich, elusive playboy who, after getting slapped with a million-dollar breach-of-promise suit by a shapely circus lion tamer, finally ends up at the altar with her.

Mae West, Edward Arnold, Ralf Harolde, Russell Hopton, Gertrude Michael, Kent Taylor, Dorothy Peterson, Gregory Ratoff, Gertrude Howard, William Davidson, Irving Pichel, Nat Pendleton.

Alice in Wonderland (1933, Para.). *d:* Norman McLeod; *p:* Louis D. Lighton; *sc:* Joseph L. Mankiewicz and William Cameron Menzies—*b/o* the novels *Alice's Adventures in Wonderland* and *Alice Through the Looking Glass* by Lewis Carroll.

THE MOCK TURTLE: A mournful giant turtle that sings tearfully about "beautiful, beautiful soup"—one of the many colorful characters whom a young girl named Alice encounters when she is transported into a land of fantasy.

Charlotte Henry, Richard Arlen, Roscoe Ates, Billy Barty, Billy Bevan, Gary Cooper, Leon Errol, Louise Fazenda, W. C. Fields, Skeets Gallagher, Raymond Hatton, Sterling Holloway, Edward Everett Horton, Roscoe Karns, Baby LeRoy, Lucien Littlefield, Mae Marsh, Polly Moran, Jack Oakie, Edna May Oliver, May Robson, Charlie Ruggles, Jackie Searl, Alison Skipworth, Ned Sparks, Ford Sterling, Jacqueline Wells (Julie Bishop).

Thirty-Day Princess (1934, Para.). *d:* Marion Gering; *p:* B. P. Schulberg; *sc:* Preston Sturges and Frank Partos (adaptation by Sam Hellman and Edwin Justus Mayer)—*b/o* the novel by Clarence Buddington Kelland.

PORTER MADISON III: New York newspaper publisher who falls for a princess who is in the United States seeking a loan for her country, then discovers that she's really a show girl hired to impersonate the real princess, who has come down with the mumps.

Sylvia Sidney, Edward Arnold, Henry Stephenson, Vince Barnett, Edgar Norton, Ray Walker, Lucien Littlefield, Robert McWade, George Baxter, Marguerite Namara.

Born to Be Bad (1934, UA). *d:* Lowell Sherman; *p:* William Goetz and Raymond Griffith (Twentieth Century); *sc:* Ralph Graves (with continuity by Harrison Jacobs).

MALCOLM TREVOR: Respectable married trucking executive who adopts a small boy, then has to fight to keep him when the boy's loose-living unwed mother tries to blackmail the executive in an effort to get the boy back.

Loretta Young, Jackie Kelk, Henry Travers, Russell Hopton, Andrew Tombes, Howard Lang, Marion Burns, Paul Harvey, Matt Briggs, Geneva Mitchell, Etienne Girardot.

Kiss and Make Up (1934, Para.). *d:* Harlan Thompson; *p:* B. P. Schulberg; *sc:* Harlan Thompson and George Marion Jr.—*b/o* a story by Stephen Bekeffi.

DR. MAURICE LAMAR: Owner of a Paris beauty salon who remodels a client into a beautiful woman, marries her, but finds that beauty is only skin-deep and winds up with his plainer but nicer secretary.

Helen Mack, Genevieve Tobin, Edward Everett Horton, Lucien Littlefield, Mona Maris, Doris Lloyd, Toby Wing, Henry Armetta, Clara Lou (Ann) Sheridan, Jacqueline Wells (Julie Bishop).

Ladies Should Listen (1934, Para.). *d:* Frank Tuttle; *p:* Douglas MacLean; *sc:* Claude Binyon and Frank Butler (adaptation by Guy Bolton)—*b/o* a story by Alfred Savoir and Guy Bolton.

JULIAN DE LUSSAC: Eligible Parisian bachelor and successful businessman who, when he's pursued by two eager women, is saved by an eavesdropping telephone operator who is also smitten with him.

Frances Drake, Edward Everett Horton, Rosita Moreno, George Barbier, Nydia Westman, Charles Ray, Charles Arnt, Clara Lou (Ann) Sheridan.

Enter Madame (1935, Para.). *d:* Elliott Nugent; *p:* A. Benjamin Glaser; *sc:* Charles Brackett and Gladys Lehman—*b/o* a play by Gilda Varesi Archibald and Dorothea Donn-Byrne.

GERALD FITZGERALD: European opera star's husband who tires of taking a back seat to her career, returns to the States and takes up with another woman, but winds up with his wife again when she follows him to America.

Elissa Landi, Lynne Overman, Sharon Lynne, Michelette Burani, Paul Porcasi, Cecelia Parker, Frank Albertson, Diana Lewis.

Wings in the Dark (1935, Para.). *d:* James Flood; *p:* Arthur Hornblow Jr.; *sc:* Jack Kirkland and Frank Partos (adaptation by Dale Van Every and E. H. Robinson)—*b/o* a story by Nell Shipman and Philip D. Hurn.

KEN GORDON: Young flyer who, after he's blinded in an accident, manages to perfect a device for flying blind and uses it to save his stunt-pilot girlfriend when she's lost in a fog.

Myrna Loy, Roscoe Karns, Hobart Cavanaugh, Dean Jagger, Bert Hanlon, James Burtis, Russell Hopton, Samuel S. Hinds, Matt McHugh, Graham McNamee.

The Last Outpost (1935, Para.). *d:* Charles Barton and Louis Gasnier; *p:* E. Lloyd Sheldon; *sc:* Philip MacDonald (adaptation by Frank Partos and Charles Brackett)—*b/o* a story by F. Britten Austin.

MICHAEL ANDREWS: WWI British Army officer who, when he's wounded in Kurdistan and saved by a British intelligence agent, winds up in a Cairo hospital and falls in love with his nurse— the intelligence agent's wife.

Claude Rains, Gertrude Michael, Kathleen Burke, Colin Tapley, Akim Tamiroff, Billy Bevan, Georges Renevant, Margaret Swope, Harry Semels, Malay Clu, Jameson Thomas.

Sylvia Scarlett (1936, RKO). *d:* George Cukor; *p:* Pandro S. Berman; *sc:* Gladys Unger, John Collier, and Mortimer Offner—*b/o* Compton MacKenzie's novel *The Early Life and Adventures of Sylvia Scarlett*.

JIMMY MONKLEY: Raffish Cockney con man who joins a young girl (who's disguised as a boy) and her larcenous father when they take to the road in England as touring actors.

Katharine Hepburn, Brian Aherne, Edmund Gwenn, Natalie Paley, Dennie Moore, Harold Cheevers, Lionel Pape, Leonard Mudie, Gaston Glass, Bunny Beatty, E. E. Clive.

Big Brown Eyes (1936, Para.). *d:* Raoul Walsh; *p:* Walter Wanger; *sc:* Raoul Walsh and Bert Hanlon—*b/o* a story by James Edward Grant.

DANNY BARR: Two-fisted detective who—with the help of his girlfriend, a manicurist–turned– newspaper reporter—puts a gang of jewel thieves and murderers behind bars.

Joan Bennett, Walter Pidgeon, Lloyd Nolan, Alan Baxter, Marjorie Gateson, Isabel Jewell, Douglas Fowley, Joseph Sawyer, Edwin Maxwell, Francis McDonald.

Suzy (1936, MGM). *d:* George Fitzmaurice; *p:* Maurice Revnes; *sc:* Dorothy Parker, Alan Campbell, Horace Jackson, and Lenore Coffee— *b/o* the novel by Herbert Gorman.

ANDRE CHARVILLE: WWI French air ace who, after marrying an American showgirl in Paris, becomes involved with a glamorous German spy and is murdered—but is made to appear to have died a hero when his body is placed in his cracked-up plane.

Jean Harlow, Franchot Tone, Lewis Stone, Benita Hume, Reginald Mason, Inez Courtney, Christian Rub, George Spelvin, Una O'Connor, Charles Judels, Theodore Von Eltz, Stanley Morner (Dennis Morgan).

Wedding Present (1936, Para.). *d:* Richard Wallace; *p:* B. P. Schulberg; *sc:* Joseph Anthony— *b/o* a story by Paul Gallico.

CHARLIE: Happy-go-lucky newspaper editor who, after his reporter girlfriend jilts him and becomes engaged to a stuffy author, sets out to win her back.

Joan Bennett, George Bancroft, Conrad Nagel, Gene Lockhart, William Demarest, Inez Courtney, Edward Brophy, Purnell Pratt, George Meeker, Lois Wilson, Jack Mulhall.

When You're in Love (1937, Col.). *d:* Robert Riskin; *p:* Everett Riskin; *sc:* Robert Riskin—*b/o* a story by Ethel Hill and Cedric Worth.

JIMMY HUDSON: Itinerant American artist who is hired by an Australian opera singer—stranded in Mexico because of immigration problems—to temporarily marry her so that she can legally enter the United States.

Grace Moore, Aline MacMahon, Henry Stephenson, Thomas Mitchell, Catherine Doucet, Luis Alberni, Gerald Oliver Smith, Emma Dunn, Frank Puglia, Harry Holman, William Pawley.

Romance and Riches (1937, GN). *d:* Alfred Zeisler; *p:* Alfred Zeisler (Garrett-Klement Pictures); *sc:* John L. Balderston—*b/o* a story by E. Phillips Oppenheim.

ERNEST BLISS: Wealthy playboy who, after betting that he can earn his own living without using any of his fortune, works as an oven salesman, a grocer, and a chauffeur while finding love with a secretary.

Mary Brian, Peter Gawthorne, Henry Kendall, Leon M. Lion, John Turnbull, Arthur Hardy, Garry Marsh, Charles Farrell, Hal Gordon, Ralph Richardson.

Topper (1937, MGM). *d:* Norman Z. McLeod; *p:* Milton H. Bren (Hal Roach); *sc:* Jack Jerne, Eric Hatch, and Eddie Moran—*b/o* the novel by Thorne Smith.

GEORGE KERBY: Wealthy playboy who, along with his wife, is killed in a car wreck—whereupon they both return as ghosts to help "liberate" their friend Topper, a timid bank president with a boring career and a nagging wife.

Constance Bennett, Roland Young, Billie Burke, Alan Mowbray, Eugene Pallette, Arthur Lake, Hedda Hopper, Virginia Sale, Theodore Von Eltz, J. Farrell MacDonald, Elaine Shepard, George Humbert, Hoagy Carmichael.

Toast of New York (1937, RKO). *d:* Rowland V. Lee; *p:* Edward Small; *sc:* Dudley Nichols, John Twist, and Joel Sayre—*b/o The Book of Daniel Drew* by Bouck White and the book *Robber Barons* by Matthew Josephson.

NICK BOYD: Loyal business partner of Jim Fiske, the peddler who rose to become a colorful and famous nineteenth-century Wall Street tycoon.

Edward Arnold, Frances Farmer, Jack Oakie, Donald Meek, Thelma Leeds, Clarence Kolb, Billy Gilbert, George Irving, Frank M. Thomas, Russell Hicks, Oscar Apfel, Dewey Robinson, Stanley Fields, Joyce Compton.

The Awful Truth (1937, Col.). *d:* Leo McCarey; *p:* Everett Riskin; *sc:* Vina Delmar—*b/o* the play by Arthur Richmond.

JERRY WARRINER: Young husband who, when his wife divorces him and takes up with a rich yokel, becomes involved with a socialite but finally gets back together with his wife.

Irene Dunne, Ralph Bellamy, Alexander D'Arcy, Cecil Cunningham, Marguerite Churchill, Esther Dale, Joyce Compton, Robert Allen, Robert Warwick, Claude Allister, Edgar Dearing.

Bringing Up Baby (1938, RKO). *d:* Howard Hawks; *p:* Howard Hawks; *sc:* Dudley Nichols and Hagar Wilde—*b/o* a story by Hagar Wilde.

DAVID HUXLEY: Young, bespectacled paleontologist whose lifetime project—the reconstruction of a dinosaur skeleton—is disrupted by a screwball young heiress who owns a pet leopard named Baby.

Katharine Hepburn, Charlie Ruggles, May Robson, Walter Catlett, Barry Fitzgerald, Fritz Feld, George Irving, Tala Birrell, Asta (dog), Nissa (leopard), Ernest Cossart, Brooks Benedict, Jack Carson, Richard Lane, Ward Bond.

Holiday (1938, Col.). *d:* George Cukor; *p:* Everett Riskin; *sc:* Donald Ogden Stewart and Sidney Buchman—*b/o* the play by Philip Barry.

JOHNNY CASE: Happy-go-lucky young man who is engaged to marry a snobbish New York society girl but finally realizes that he loves her down-to-earth sister instead.

Katharine Hepburn, Doris Nolan, Lew Ayres, Edward Everett Horton, Henry Kolker, Binnie Barnes, Jean Dixon, Henry Daniell, Charles Trowbridge, Howard Hickman, Hilda Plowright, Bess Flowers, Frank Shannon, Matt McHugh, Luke Cosgrove.

Gunga Din (1939, RKO). *d:* George Stevens; *p:* Pandro S. Berman; *sc:* Joel Sayre and Fred Guiol—*b/o* a story by Ben Hecht and Charles MacArthur, suggested by the Rudyard Kipling poem.

SERGEANT CUTTER: Happy-go-lucky Cockney who's one of three hardboiled British soldiers in nineteenth-century India who foil a native uprising with the help of a loyal water boy named Gunga Din.

Victor McLaglen, Douglas Fairbanks Jr., Sam Jaffe, Eduardo Ciannelli, Joan Fontaine, Montague Love, Robert Coote, Abner Biberman, Lumsden Hare.

Only Angels Have Wings (1939, Col.). *d:* Howard Hawks; *p:* Howard Hawks; *sc:* Jules Furthman—*b/o* a story by Howard Hawks.

JEFF CARTER: Tough boss of a group of American flyers who make dangerous flights in rickety planes over the Andes for a fly-by-night South American mail and freight line.

Jean Arthur, Richard Barthelmess, Rita Hayworth, Thomas Mitchell, Allyn Joslyn, Sig Ruman, Victor Kilian, John Carroll, Donald Barry, Noah Beery Jr., Pat Flaherty, Candy Candido, James Millican, Vernon Dent.

In Name Only (1939, RKO). *d:* John Cromwell; *p:* George Haight and Pandro S. Berman; *sc:* Richard Sherman—*b/o* the novel *Memory of Love* by Bessie Brewer.

ALEC WALKER: Wealthy married man whose scheming, money-hungry wife refuses to divorce him when he falls in love with a young widowed commercial artist.

Carole Lombard, Kay Francis, Charles Coburn, Helen Vinson, Katharine Alexander, Jonathan Hale, Maurice Moscovich, Nella Walker, Peggy Ann Garner, Spencer Charters.

His Girl Friday (1940, Col.). *d:* Howard Hawks; *p:* Howard Hawks; *sc:* Charles Lederer—*b/o* Ben Hecht and Charles MacArthur's play *The Front Page.*

WALTER BURNS: Conniving Chicago newspaper editor who, when his ex-wife and star reporter decides to quit the paper and marry an insurance man, tricks her into staying on to cover a big murder story.

Rosalind Russell, Ralph Bellamy, Gene Lockhart, Porter Hall, Ernest Truex, Cliff Edwards, Clarence Kolb, Roscoe Karns, Frank Jenks, Regis Toomey, John Qualen, Helen Mack, Alma Kruger, Billy Gilbert, Edwin Maxwell, Pat Flaherty.

My Favorite Wife (1940, RKO). *d:* Garson Kanin; *p:* Leo McCarey; *sc:* Bella Spewack and Samuel Spewack—*b/o* a story by the Spewacks and Leo McCarey.

NICK ARDEN: Widower who remarries, then is dumbfounded by the return of his first wife, who—long presumed lost at sea—has been on a desert island for the past seven years with a handsome young scientist.

Irene Dunne, Randolph Scott, Gail Patrick, Ann Shoemaker, Scotty Beckett, Mary Lou Harrington, Donald MacBride, Hugh O'Connell, Granville Bates, Pedro de Cordoba, Victor Kilian, Chester Clute.

The Howards of Virginia (1940, Col.). *d:* Frank Lloyd; *p:* Frank Lloyd; *sc:* Sidney Buchman—*b/o* Elizabeth Page's novel *The Tree of Liberty.*

MATT HOWARD: Virginia backwoodsman and friend of Thomas Jefferson who marries an aristocratic Virginia girl, gets involved in politics, and joins the Colonial Army when the Revolutionary War breaks out.

Martha Scott, Sir Cedric Hardwicke, Alan Marshal, Richard Carlson, Paul Kelly, Irving Bacon, Elizabeth Risdon, Ann Revere, Richard Gaines, George Houston.

The Philadelphia Story (1940, MGM). *d:* George Cukor; *p:* Joseph L. Mankiewicz; *sc:* Donald Ogden Stewart—*b/o* the play by Philip Barry.

C. K. DEXTER HAVEN: Wealthy ex-husband of a Philadelphia society woman who sets out to stop her from marrying a pompous blueblood and win her back for himself.

Katharine Hepburn, James Stewart, Ruth Hussey, John Howard, Roland Young, John Halliday, Mary Nash, Virginia Weidler, Henry Daniell, Lionel Pape, Rex Evans, Hilda Plowright, Lee Phelps, Hillary Brooke.

Penny Serenade (1941, Col.). *d:* George Stevens; *p:* Fred Guiol; *sc:* Morrie Ryskind—*b/o* a story by Martha Cheavens.

ROGER ADAMS*: Newspaperman whose marriage to a music-store sales clerk manages to endure through the years, despite such tragedies as the loss of their unborn child and the death of their six-year-old adopted daughter.

---

*Received an Academy Award nomination as Best Actor for this role.

Irene Dunne, Beulah Bondi, Edgar Buchanan, Ann Doran, Eva Tee Kuneye, Leonard Wiley, Wallis Clark, Walter Soderling, Baby Biffle.

Suspicion (1941, RKO). *d:* Alfred Hitchcock; *sc:* Samson Raphaelson, Joan Harrison, and Alma Reville—*b/o* the novel *Before the Fact* by Francis Iles.

JOHNNIE AYSGARTH: Charming playboy whose shy newlywed English wife begins to suspect that he's a murderer, and that she's slated to be his next victim.

Joan Fontaine, Sir Cedric Hardwicke, Nigel Bruce, Dame May Whitty, Isabel Jeans, Heather Angel, Auriol Lee, Reginald Sheffield, Leo G. Carroll, Billy Bevan.

The Talk of the Town (1942, Col.). *d:* George Stevens; *p:* George Stevens; *sc:* Irwin Shaw and Sidney Buchman (adaptation by Dale Van Every)—*b/o* a story by Sidney Harmon.

LEOPOLD DILG: Soapbox radical in a small Massachusetts town who escapes from jail after a false murder charge, then hides out in the attic of a schoolteacher who persuades her boarder—a law-school dean and Supreme Court nominee—to defend the radical.

Jean Arthur, Ronald Colman, Edgar Buchanan, Glenda Farrell, Charles Dingle, Emma Dunn, Rex Ingram, Leonid Kinskey, Tom Tyler, Don Beddoe, Frank M. Thomas, Lloyd Bridges, Billy Benedict, Lee White, Dewey Robinson, Dan Seymour, Frank Sully, Clarence Muse.

Once Upon a Honeymoon (1942, RKO). *d:* Leo McCarey; *p:* Leo McCarey; *sc:* Sheridan Gibney—*b/o* a story by Leo McCarey.

PAT O'TOOLE: WWII American radio correspondent who, while trying to expose an Austrian baron as a Nazi agent, falls in love with the ex–American burlesque queen who has naïvely married the baron.

Ginger Rogers, Walter Slezak, Albert Dekker, Albert Basserman, Ferike Boros, Harry Shannon, John Banner, Hans Conried, George Irving, Fred Niblo, Bert Roach, Johnny Dime.

Mr. Lucky (1943, RKO). *d:* H. C. Potter; *p:* David Hempstead; *sc:* Milton Holmes and Adrian Scott—*b/o* the story "Bundles for Freedom" by Milton Holmes.

JOE ADAMS (alias JOE THE GREEK): Draft-dodging owner of a gambling ship during WWII who is out to bilk the women in a war-relief charity but has a change of heart when a sincere society woman falls for him.

Laraine Day, Charles Bickford, Gladys Cooper, Alan Carney, Henry Stephenson, Paul Stewart, Kay Johnson, Vladimir Sokoloff, Walter Kingsford, J. M. Kerrigan, Joseph Crehan, Hal K. Dawson, Emory Parnell, Florence Bates.

Destination Tokyo (1944, WB). *d:* Delmer Daves; *p:* Jerry Wald; *sc:* Delmer Daves and Albert Maltz—*b/o* a story by Steve Fisher.

CAPTAIN CASSIDY: Skipper of a WWII American submarine that sneaks into Tokyo Harbor to gather vital information in preparation for the American bombing of Tokyo by B-25s from the "Shangri-La" (code name for the aircraft carrier *Hornet*).

John Garfield, Alan Hale, John Ridgely, Dane Clark, Warner Anderson, William Prince, Robert Hutton, Peter Whitney, Tom Tully, Faye Emerson, Warren Douglas, John Forsythe, Whit Bissell, Maurice Murphy, Pierre Watkin, Cliff Clark, Kirby Grant, Lane Chandler, Paul Langton.

Once Upon a Time (1944, Col.). *d:* Alexander Hall; *p:* Louis Edelman; *sc:* Lewis Meltzer and Oscar Saul (adaptation by Irving Fineman)—*b/o* the radio play "My Client Curly" by Norman Corwin and Lucille Fletcher Hermann.

JERRY FLYNN: Glib, opportunistic Broadway producer who makes famous celebrities out of a young boy and his astonishing pet—a dancing caterpillar called Curly.

Janet Blair, James Gleason, Ted Donaldson, Howard Freeman, William Demarest, Art Baker, Paul Stanton, Mickey McGuire, John Abbott, Charles Arnt, Ian Wolfe.

None But the Lonely Heart (1944, RKO). *d:* Clifford Odets; *p:* David Hempstead; *sc:* Clifford Odets—*b/o* the novel by Richard Llewellyn.

ERNIE MOTT*: Embittered young Cockney in pre-WWII London's East End slums who, when he becomes appalled by the poverty surrounding him and his dying mother, joins a gang of thieves.

Ethel Barrymore, Jane Wyatt, June Duprez, Barry Fitzgerald, George Coulouris, Konstantin Shayne, Dan Duryea, Rosalind Ivan, Queenie Vassar, Joseph Vitale, Morton Lowry, Art Smith, Helen Thimig.

Arsenic and Old Lace (1944, WB). *d:* Frank Capra; *p:* Frank Capra; *sc:* Julius J. Epstein and Philip G. Epstein—*b/o* the play by Joseph Kesselring.

MORTIMER BREWSTER: Drama-critic nephew of two sweet elderly women who is thunderstruck when he discovers that they've been inviting lonely old men to their home and then poisoning them with elderberry wine.

Raymond Massey, Priscilla Lane, Josephine Hull, Jean Adair, Jack Carson, Edward Everett Horton, Peter Lorre, James Gleason, John Alexander, Grant Mitchell, Garry Owen, John Ridgely, Chester Clute, Charles Lane, Spencer Charters, Hank Mann, Lee Phelps.

---

*Received an Academy Award nomination as Best Actor for this role.

Night and Day (1946, WB). *d:* Michael Curtiz; *p:* Arthur Schwartz; *sc:* Charles Hoffman, Leo Townsend, and William Bowers (adaptation by Jack Moffit)—*b/o* the career of Cole Porter.

COLE PORTER: American composer who begins his career writing songs for school productions at Yale, serves with the French Foreign Legion during WWI, and returns to the United States to become one of America's most popular and famous songwriters.

Alexis Smith, Monty Woolley, Ginny Simms, Jane Wyman, Eve Arden, Victor Francen, Alan Hale, Dorothy Malone, Tom D'Andrea, Selena Royle, Donald Woods, Henry Stephenson, Paul Cavanagh, Sig Ruman, Clarence Muse, Herman Bing, Mary Martin.

Notorious (1946, RKO). *d:* Alfred Hitchcock; *p:* Alfred Hitchcock; *sc:* Ben Hecht—*b/o* an original idea by Alfred Hitchcock.

DEVLIN: American intelligence officer in post-WWII Rio de Janeiro who falls for his beautiful confederate, then has to rescue her from a gang of Nazi spies when—as part of a plan to trap them—she marries one of the leaders.

Ingrid Bergman, Claude Rains, Louis Calhern, Madame Konstantin, Reinhold Schunzel, Moroni Olsen, Wally Brown, Gavin Gordon, Antonio Moreno, Harry Hayden, Dink Trout.

The Bachelor and the Bobby Soxer (1947, RKO). *d:* Irving Reis; *p:* Dore Schary; *sc:* Sidney Sheldon.

DICK: Debonair playboy bachelor who, when a seventeen-year-old girl develops a crush on him, is ordered by the girl's older sister—a judge—to act as the teenager's escort so that her infatuation will wear off.

Myrna Loy, Shirley Temple, Rudy Vallee, Ray Collins, Harry Davenport, Johnny Sands, Don Beddoe, Lillian Randolph, Veda Ann Borg, Dan Tobin, Ransom Sherman, William Bakewell, Irving Bacon, Carol Hughes.

The Bishop's Wife (1947, RKO). *d:* Henry Koster; *p:* Samuel Goldwyn (Samuel Goldwyn); *sc:* Robert Sherwood and Leonardo Bercorici—*b/o* a novel by Robert Nathan.

DUDLEY: Suave guardian angel who comes to earth to help an overworked Episcopalian bishop whose preoccupation with raising money for a new cathedral has caused him to neglect his wife and to lose rapport with his congregation.

Loretta Young, David Niven, Monty Woolley, James Gleason, Gladys Cooper, Elsa Lanchester, Sara Haden, Regis Toomey, Erville Alderson, Almira Sessions, Isabel Jewell, Edgar Dearing.

Mr. Blandings Builds His Dream House (1948, RKO). *d:* H. C. Potter; *p:* Norman Panama and Melvin Frank; *sc:* Norman Panama and Melvin Frank—*b/o* the novel by Eric Hodgins.

JIM BLANDINGS: New York advertising executive who, after buying a 170-year-old Connecticut house, winds up tearing it down and then—after numerous frustrating and comical events—rebuilding it into his "dream house."

Myrna Loy, Melvyn Douglas, Reginald Denny, Sharyn Moffett, Connie Marshall, Louise Beavers, Ian Wolfe, Harry Shannon, Nestor Paiva, Jason Robards, Lurene Tuttle, Lex Barker, Emory Parnell, Will Wright, Cliff Clark, Charles Middleton, Hal K. Dawson.

Every Girl Should Be Married (1948, RKO). *d:* Don Hartman; *p:* Don Hartman and Dore Schary; *sc:* Stephen Morehouse Avery and Don Hartman—*b/o* a story by Eleanor Harris.

DR. MADISON BROWN: Bachelor pediatrician who is pursued by a pretty young department store sales clerk who's bent on getting him to the altar.

Franchot Tone, Diana Lynn, Betsy Drake, Alan Mowbray, Elizabeth Risdon, Richard Gaines, Harry Hayden, Chick Chandler, Leon Belasco, Anna Q. Nilsson.

I Was a Male War Bride (1949, 20th-Fox). *d:* Howard Hawks; *p:* Sol C. Siegel; *sc:* Charles Lederer, Leonard Spigelgass, and Hagar Wilde—*b/o* a novel by Henri Rochard.

CAPT. HENRI ROCHARD: French Army officer in occupied Germany who, in order to circumvent the red tape necessary for him to accompany his American WAC bride to the United States on a troop ship, disguises himself as a "war bride" WAC.

Ann Sheridan, William Neff, Eugene Gericke, Marion Marshall, Randy Stuart, Ken Tobey, Robert Stevenson, Alfred Linder, David McMahon, Harry Lauter.

Crisis (1950, MGM). *d:* Richard Brooks; *p:* Arthur Freed; *sc:* Richard Brooks—*b/o* George Tabori's short story "The Doubters."

DR. EUGENE FERGUSON: Famous brain surgeon who, while he and his wife are vacationing in a Latin American country on the verge of revolution, is kidnapped and forced to perform a delicate operation on the country's dictator.

Jose Ferrer, Paula Raymond, Signe Hasso, Ramon Navarro, Gilbert Roland, Leon Ames, Antonio Moreno, Teresa Celli, Vincente Gomez, Pedro de Cordoba, Soledad Jiminez, Alex Montoya.

People Will Talk (1951, 20th-Fox). *d:* Joseph L. Mankiewicz; *p:* Darryl F. Zanuck; *sc:* Joseph L. Mankiewicz—*b/o* the play *Dr. Praetorius* by Curt Goetz.

DR. NOAH PRAETORIUS: Unorthodox physician and teacher at a medical school who, when an unmarried pregnant student comes to him for treatment, falls in love with her and marries her.

Jeanne Crain, Findlay Currie, Hume Cronyn, Walter Slezak, Sidney Blackmer, Basil Ruysdael, Will Wright, Margaret Hamilton, Carleton Young, Larry Dobkin, Gail Bonney, Billy House, Parley Baer, Ray Montgomery.

Room for One More (1952, WB). *d:* Norman Taurog; *p:* Henry Blanke; *sc:* Jack Rose and Melville Shavelson—*b/o* the book by Anna Perrott Rose.

"POPPY" ROSE: Genial city engineer who feels neglected by his softhearted wife, who—even though she already has three children of her own—keeps taking stray animals and problem foster children into their home.

Betsy Drake, Lurene Tuttle, Randy Stuart, John Ridgely, Irving Bacon, Mary Lou Treen, Hayden Rorke, George Winslow, Gay Gordon, Larry Olson.

Monkey Business (1952, 20th-Fox). *d:* Howard Hawks; *p:* Sol C. Siegel; *sc:* Ben Hecht, I. A. L. Diamond, and Charles Lederer—*b/o* a story by Harry Segall.

PROF. BARNABY FULTON: Absent-minded research chemist who, along with his wife, accidentally drinks a "youth potion" he's developed—whereupon they both revert to acting like teen-agers.

Ginger Rogers, Charles Coburn, Marilyn Monroe, Hugh Marlowe, Robert Cornthwaite, Larry Keating, Esther Dale, George Winslow, Kathleen Freeman, Olan Soule, Harry Carey Jr., Jerry Paris, Roger Moore, Dabbs Greer.

Dream Wife (1953, MGM). *d:* Sidney Sheldon; *p:* Dore Schary; *sc:* Sidney Sheldon, Herbert Baker, and Alfred Lewis Levitt—*b/o* a story by Alfred Lewis Levitt.

CLEMSON READE: Debonair American bachelor who, because he believes that a wife's place is in the home, jilts his career-girl fiancée and becomes engaged to a Middle Eastern princess trained in the art of pleasing men.

Deborah Kerr, Walter Pidgeon, Betta St. John, Eduard Franz, Buddy Baer, Les Tremayne, Bruce Bennett, Richard Anderson, Dan Tobin, Movita, Gloria Holden, Steve Forrest.

To Catch a Thief (1955, Para.). *d:* Alfred Hitchcock; *p:* Alfred Hitchcock; *sc:* John Michael Hayes—*b/o* a novel by David Dodge.

JOHN ROBIE (alias "THE CAT"): Famous retired cat burglar on the French Riviera who, when he's suspected of a series of jewel robberies, sets out to catch the real jewel thief.

Grace Kelly, Jessie Royce Landis, John Williams, Charles Vanel, Brigitte Auber, Jean Martinelli, Georgette Anys, Wee Willie Davis, Don Megowan, Philip Van Zandt, Steven Geray, Louis Mercier.

The Pride and the Passion (1957, UA). *d:* Stanley Kramer; *p:* Stanley Kramer (Stanley

Kramer); *sc:* Edna Anhalt and Edward Anhalt—*b/o* C. S. Forester's novel *The Gun.*

CAPT. ANTHONY TRUMBULL: British naval officer during the Napoleonic campaign in Spain who joins forces with a Spanish guerrilla leader to transport a huge 6,000-pound cannon over rugged terrain in order to destroy a French-held fort.

Frank Sinatra, Sophia Loren, Theodore Bikel, John Wengraf, Jay Novello, Jose Nieto, Carlos Larranaga, Philip Van Zandt, Julian Ugarte.

An Affair to Remember (1957, 20th-Fox). *d:* Leo McCarey; *p:* Jerry Wald; *sc:* Delmer Daves and Leo McCarey—*b/o* a story by Leo McCarey and Mildred Cram.

NICKIE FERRANTE: Wealthy playboy who, after falling for an ex–nightclub singer on a transatlantic ocean liner, is disillusioned when she fails to keep a rendezvous months later—unaware that she has been seriously injured in an accident.

Deborah Kerr, Richard Denning, Neva Patterson, Cathleen Nesbitt, Robert Q. Lewis, Charles Watts, Fortunio Bonanova, Matt Moore, Louis Mercier, Jesslyn Fax, Walter Woolf King.

Kiss Them for Me (1957, 20th-Fox).*d:* Stanley Donen; *p:* Jerry Wald; *sc:* Julius Epstein—*b/o* the play *Kiss Them for Me* by Luther Davis and the novel *Shore Leave* by Frederic Wakeman.

COMMANDER CREWSON: One of a trio of WWII Navy flyers who spend an unofficial weekend leave in San Francisco living it up with wine, women, and song.

Jayne Mansfield, Suzy Parker, Leif Erickson, Ray Walston, Larry Blyden, Nathaniel Frey, Werner Klemperer, Jack Mullaney, Michael Ross, Harry Carey Jr., Frank Nelson.

Indiscreet (1958, WB). *d:* Stanley Donen; *p:* Stanley Donen (Grandon); *sc:* Norman Krasna—*b/o* his play *Kind Sir.*

PHILIP ADAMS: Marriage-shy American diplomat and playboy who, in order to play the field without becoming permanently attached, falsely tells women he's married—but runs into complications when he uses his system on a famous European actress.

Ingrid Bergman, Cecil Parker, Phyllis Calvert, David Kossoff, Megs Jenkins, Oliver Johnston, Middleton Woods.

Houseboat (1958, Para.). *d:* Melville Shavelson; *p:* Jack Rose; *sc:* Melville Shavelson and Jack Rose.

TOM TINSTON: Widowed Washington attorney—living on a houseboat—who hires a maid for his three children, not knowing that she's really the socially prominent daughter of a noted visiting Italian symphony conductor.

Sophia Loren, Martha Hyer, Harry Guardino, Eduardo Ciannelli, Murray Hamilton, Mimi

Gibson, Charles Herbert, Madge Kennedy, John Litel, Werner Klemperer, Kathleen Freeman.

North by Northwest (1959, MGM). *d:* Alfred Hitchcock; *p:* Alfred Hitchcock; *sc:* Ernest Lehman.

ROGER THORNHILL: Madison Avenue advertising executive who, when he's mistaken for a U.S. secret agent, becomes the target of enemy agents who finally face him in a showdown on the slippery precipices of the four presidential faces carved into Mount Rushmore.

Eva Marie Saint, James Mason, Jessie Royce Landis, Leo G. Carroll, Philip Ober, Josephine Hutchinson, Martin Landau, Edward Platt, Robert Ellenstein, Les Tremayne, Philip Coolidge, Patrick McVey, Edward Binns, Lawrence Dobkin, Harvey Stephens, Maudie Prickett, Olan Soule.

Operation Petticoat (1959, Univ.). *d:* Blake Edwards; *p:* Robert Arthur (Granart); *sc:* Stanley Shapiro and Maurice Richlin—*b/o* a story by Paul King and Joseph Stone.

LT. CMDR. M. T. SHERMAN: WWII American submarine skipper in the Pacific whose battered sub takes a group of nurses aboard and also is painted pink because of a supply shortage.

Tony Curtis, Joan O'Brien, Dina Merrill, Gene Evans, Arthur O'Connell, Richard Sargent, Virginia Gregg, Robert F. Simon, Robert Gist, Gavin MacLeod, Madlyn Rhue, Marion Ross, Frankie Darro, Tony Pastor Jr., Nicky Blair, Hal Baylor, Clarence E. Lung.

The Grass Is Greener (1961, Univ.). *d:* Stanley Donen; *p:* Stanley Donen (Grandon); *sc:* Hugh Williams and Margaret Williams—*b/o* their play.

VICTOR RHYALL: Financially strapped British earl whose life is complicated when he discovers, after opening his mansion to tourists, that his wife has fallen for one of them—an American oil tycoon.

Deborah Kerr, Robert Mitchum, Jean Simmons, Moray Watson.

That Touch of Mink (1962, Univ.). *d:* Delbert Mann; *p:* Stanley Shapiro and Martin Melcher (Granley/Arwin/Nob Hill); *sc:* Stanley Shapiro and Nate Monaster.

PHILIP SHAYNE: Suave, single business tycoon who falls for a beautiful, virtuous, unemployed secretary and offers to take her on a trip to Bermuda and Europe—on a strictly nonplatonic basis.

Doris Day, Gig Young, Audrey Meadows, Alan Hewitt, John Astin, Richard Sargent, Joey Faye, John Fiedler, Jack Livesey, Mickey Mantle, Roger Maris, Yogi Berra, Richard Deacon, Nelson Olmstead.

Charade (1963, Univ.). *d:* Stanley Donen; *p:* Stanley Donen (Stanley Donen); *sc:* Peter Stone—

b/o Peter Stone and Marc Behm's story "The Unsuspecting Wife."

PETER JOSHUA: Undercover C.I.A. agent who, when he becomes involved with a young Parisian woman whose husband has been murdered, helps protect her from a trio of sinister crooks trying to get their hands on a quarter of a million dollars her husband has hidden.

Audrey Hepburn, Walter Matthau, James Coburn, George Kennedy, Ned Glass, Jacques Marin, Paul Bonifas, Dominique Minot, Thomas Chelimsky.

Father Goose (1964, Univ.). *d:* Ralph Nelson; *p:* Robert Arthur (Granox); *sc:* Peter Stone and Frank Tarloff.—*b/o* the story "A Place of Dragons" by S. H. Barnett.

WALTER ECKLAND: Ex–American professor–turned–beach bum who, during WWII, is tricked by the Australian Navy into manning a strategic watching station on a Pacific island, as well as taking charge of seven refugee schoolgirls and their French schoolmistress.

Leslie Caron, Trevor Howard, Jack Good, Verina Greenlaw, Pip Sparke, Jennifer Berrington, Simon Scott, John Napier, Alex Finlayson, Ken Swofford.

Walk, Don't Run (1966, Col.). *d:* Charles Walters; *p:* Sol C. Siegel (Granley); *sc:* Sol Saks—*b/o* a story by Robert Russell and Frank Ross.

SIR WILLIAM RUTLAND: British industrialist in Tokyo during the 1964 Olympics who plays Cupid by bringing together an American athlete and a British Embassy secretary while the three of them—because of the housing shortage—are sharing the secretary's apartment.

Samantha Eggar, Jim Hutton, John Standing, Miiko Taka, Ted Hartley, Ben Astar, George Takei, Teru Shimada, Lois Kiuchi.

• In addition, Cary Grant made cameo/guest appearances in the following feature films: *Topper Takes a Trip* (1939, UA—a film clip of him as George Kerby in *Topper* was used as an intro) and *Without Reservations* (1946, RKO).

☆ JEAN HARLOW

Harlean Carpentier

b: March 3, 1911, Kansas City, Mo.
d: June 7, 1937, Los Angeles, Cal.

"Excuse me while I slip into something more comfortable."

Helen (Jean Harlow) to Monte Rutledge
(Ben Lyon) in *Hell's Angels,* 1930.

The Saturday Night Kid (1929, Para.). *d:* Edward Sutherland; *sc:* Lloyd Corrigan, Ethel Doherty, and Edward Paramore Jr.—*b/o* the play *Love 'em and Leave 'em* by George Abbott and John V.A. Weaver.

HAZEL: One of the sales clerks in Ginsberg's Department Store, where two co-worker sisters fall in love with the same floorwalker.
Clara Bow, James Hall, Jean Arthur, Charles Sellon, Ethel Wales, Frank Ross, Edna May Oliver, Hyman Mayer, Eddie Dunn, Leone Lane.

Hell's Angels (1930, UA). *d:* Howard Hughes; *p:* Howard Hughes (Caddo Co.); *sc:* Joseph Moncure March, Howard Estabrook, and Harry Behn—*b/o* a story by Marshall Neilan and Joseph Moncure March.

HELEN: Seductive English society playgirl who two-times a pair of American students (brothers) from Oxford University who have joined the British Royal Flying Corps as WWI fighter pilots.

Ben Lyon, James Hall, John Darrow, Lucien Prival, Frank Clarke, Roy Wilson, Douglas Gilmore, Jane Winton, Evelyn Hall, William B. Davidson, Wyndham Standing, Carl von Haartmen, Stephen Carr, F. Schumann-Heink.

The Secret Six (1931, MGM). *d:* George Hill; *sc:* Frances Marion.

ANNE: Chicago gangster's girlfriend who, after getting involved with two investigative reporters to throw them off the gangster's trail, turns against him when one of the reporters is murdered.

Wallace Beery, Lewis Stone, John Mack Brown, Marjorie Rambeau, Paul Hurst, Clark Gable, Ralph Bellamy, John Miljan, Frank McGlynn, Theodore Von Eltz.

The Iron Man (1931, Univ.). *d:* Todd Browning; *p:* Carl Laemmle Jr.; *sc:* Francis Edward Faragoh—*b/o* the novel by W. R. Burnett.

ROSE MASON: Treacherous wife whose faithful prize fighter husband finally gets wise to her two-timing, gold-digging ways and kicks her out.

Lew Ayres, Robert Armstrong, John Miljan, Eddie Dillon, Mike Donlin, Morrie Cohan, Mary Doran, Ned Sparks.

The Public Enemy (1931, WB). *d:* William A. Wellman; *sc:* Kubec Glasmon and John Bright (with adaptation and dialogue by Harvey Thew)—*b/o* the story "Beer and Blood" by John Bright.

GWEN ALLEN: Classy-looking blonde who becomes the new love interest of a cocky Prohibition-era gangster after he brushes off his mistress by shoving a grapefruit into her face.

James Cagney, Edward Woods, Joan Blondell, Beryl Mercer, Donald Cook, Mae Clarke, Leslie Fenton, Robert Emmett O'Connor, Frankie Darro, Purnell Pratt, Lee Phelps, Helen Parrish.

Goldie (1931, Fox). *d:* Benjamin Stoloff; *sc:* Gene Towne and Paul Perez.

GOLDIE: Sexy carnival high-diver whose affair with a naïve merchant seaman is broken up by the seaman's pal—who happens to know from first-hand experience that she's a gold digger.

Spencer Tracy, Warren Hymer, Jesse DeVorska, Leila Karnelly, Ivan Linow, Lina Basquette, Eleanor Hunt, Maria Alba, Eddie Kane.

Platinum Blonde (1931, Col.). *d:* Frank Capra; *sc:* Jo Swerling, Dorothy Howell, and Robert Riskin—*b/o* a story by Harry E. Chandler and Douglas W. Churchill.

ANNE SCHULYER: Snobbish platinum-blonde society girl who marries a wisecracking reporter but winds up losing him to the girl reporter he really loves.

Loretta Young, Robert Williams, Louise Closser Hale, Donald Dillaway, Reginald Owen, Walter Catlett, Edmund Breese, Halliwell Hobbes.

Three Wise Girls (1932, Col.). *d:* William Beaudine; *sc:* Agnes C. Johnson and Robert Riskin—*b/o* a story by Wilson Collison.

CASSIE BARNES: Small-town girl who becomes a New York model and gets involved with a wealthy young married man.

Mae Clarke, Walter Byron, Marie Prevost, Andy Devine, Natalie Moorhead, Lucy Beaumont, Robert Dudley, Walter Miller.

The Beast of the City (1932, MGM). *d:* Charles Brabin; *sc:* John Lee Mahin—*b/o* a story by W. R. Burnett.

DAISY: Racketeer's conniving girlfriend who, when the police chief's younger cop brother is assigned to keep an eye on her, uses her seductive charms to dupe him into taking part in a robbery.

Walter Huston, Wallace Ford, Jean Hersholt, Dorothy Peterson, Tully Marshall, John Miljan, Warner Richmond, J. Carrol Naish, Mickey Rooney, Julie Haydon.

Red-Headed Woman (1932, MGM). *d:* Jack Conway; *sc:* Anita Loos—*b/o* the novel by Katharine Brush.

LIL ANDREWS: Gold-digging secretary who, after causing her wealthy boss to divorce his first wife, marries him herself—but still finds time for hanky-panky with her chauffeur and a socially prominent business tycoon.

Chester Morris, Lewis Stone, Leila Hyams, Una Merkel, Henry Stephenson, May Robson, Charles Boyer, Harvey Clark.

Red Dust (1932, MGM). *d:* Victor Fleming; *p:* Hunt Stromberg; *sc:* John Lee Mahin—*b/o* the play by Wilson Collison.

VANTINE: Good-hearted tart—on the run from the police—who falls for the rugged head man at a rubber plantation in Indochina but discovers that he has eyes for the newlywed wife of his engineer.

Clark Gable, Gene Raymond, Mary Astor, Donald Crisp, Tully Marshall, Forrester Harvey, Willie Fung.

Hold Your Man (1933, MGM). *d:* Sam Wood; *p:* Sam Wood; *sc:* Anita Loos and Howard Emmett Rogers—*b/o* a story by Anita Loos.

RUBY ADAMS: Tough but soft-hearted blonde who is sent to prison for a crime her con-man boyfriend commits but then—when he gives himself up—is released and promises to wait for him.

Clark Gable, Stuart Erwin, Dorothy Burgess, Muriel Kirkland, Garry Owen, Barbara Barondess, Paul Hurst, Elizabeth Patterson, Inez Courtney.

Bombshell (1933, MGM). *d:* Victor Fleming; *p:* Hunt Stromberg; *sc:* Jules Furthman and John Lee Mahin—*b/o* a play by Caroline Francke and Mack Crane.

LOLA BURNS: Glamorous film star who gets fed up with her sexpot roles and wants to change her image but is thwarted by a conniving publicity man who loves her the way she is.

Lee Tracy, Frank Morgan, Franchot Tone, Pat O'Brien, Una Merkel, Ted Healy, Ivan Lebedeff, Isabel Jewell, Louise Beavers, C. Aubrey Smith.

Dinner at Eight (1934, MGM). *d:* George Cukor; *p:* David O. Selznick; *sc:* Frances Marion and Herman J. Mankiewicz—*b/o* the play by George S. Kaufman and Edna Ferber.

KITTY PACKARD: Hardboiled, scheming wife who—along with her oafish husband, a promoter—is a guest at a society dinner party where a financially troubled shipping magnate hopes to get some monetary help from the promoter.

Marie Dressler, John Barrymore, Wallace Beery, Lionel Barrymore, Lee Tracy, Edmund Lowe, Billie Burke, Madge Evans, Jean Hersholt, Karen Morley, Louise Closser Hale, Phillips Holmes, May Robson, Grant Mitchell.

The Girl from Missouri (1934, MGM). *d:* Jack Conway; *p:* Bernard H. Hyman; *sc:* Anita Loos and John Emerson.

EADIE: Missouri-born New York chorus girl who

is trying her best to snare a millionaire without sacrificing her virtue.

Lionel Barrymore, Franchot Tone, Lewis Stone, Patsy Kelly, Alan Mowbray, Clara Blandick, Hale Hamilton, Henry Kolker, Nat Pendleton.

Reckless (1935, MGM). *d:* Victor Fleming; *p:* David O. Selznick; *sc:* P. J. Wolfson—*b/o* a story by Oliver Jeffries.

MONA LESLIE: Glamorous musical star whose marriage to an irresponsible, drunken millionaire ends in disaster and scandal when the husband commits suicide.

William Powell, Franchot Tone, May Robson, Ted Healy, Nat Pendleton, Rosalind Russell, Henry Stephenson, Mickey Rooney, James Ellison, Man Mountain Dean, Farina, Allan Jones.

China Seas (1935, MGM). *d:* Tay Garnett; *p:* Albert Lewin; *sc:* Jules Furthman and James Keven McGuinness—*b/o* the novel by Crosbie Garstin.

DOLLY PORTLAND (alias "CHINA DOLL"): Discarded mistress of a sea captain who, while she's sailing on his ship from Hong Kong to Singapore, not only tries to break up his shipboard romance with an old flame but also gets involved in helping Malaysian pirates who are after the ship's cargo of gold.

Clark Gable, Wallace Beery, Lewis Stone, Rosalind Russell, Dudley Digges, C. Aubrey Smith, Robert Benchley, William Henry, Edward Brophy, Donald Meek, Carol Ann Beery, Akim Tamiroff, Ivan Lebedeff, Soo Yong.

Riffraff (1936, MGM). *d:* J. Walter Ruben; *p:* Irving Thalberg; *sc:* Frances Marion, H. W. Hanemann, and Anita Loos—*b/o* a story by Frances Marion.

HATTIE: California tuna fisherman's wife who runs afoul of the law and winds up behind bars, but then—after giving birth to their baby in prison—looks forward to the new life she'll have when she's released.

Spencer Tracy, Una Merkel, Joseph Calleia, Victor Kilian, Mickey Rooney, J. Farrell MacDonald, Roger Imhof, Juanita Quigley, Paul Hurst, Vince Barnett, Arthur Housman, Wade Boteler, George Givot.

Wife vs. Secretary (1936, MGM). *d:* Clarence Brown; *p:* Hunt Stromberg; *sc:* Norman Krasna, Alice Duer Miller, and John Lee Mahin—*b/o* the novel by Faith Baldwin.

WHITEY WILSON: Smart, attractive secretary who has problems with both her boyfriend and the wife of her handsome magazine-publisher boss when she's suspected of having an affair with the boss.

Clark Gable, Myrna Loy, May Robson, George Barbier, James Stewart, Hobart Cavanaugh, Gilbert Emery, Marjorie Gateson, Gloria Holden, Tom Dugan.

Suzy (1936, MGM). *d:* George Fitzmaurice; *p:* Maurice Revnes; *sc:* Dorothy Parker, Alan Campbell, Horace Jackson, and Lenore Coffee—*b/o* the novel by Herbert Gorman.

SUZY: American showgirl who, while in London and Paris during WWI, becomes involved with an Irish inventor-flyer, a famous French air ace, and a German spy ring.

Franchot Tone, Cary Grant, Lewis Stone, Benita Hume, Reginald Mason, Inez Courtney, Christian Rub, George Spelvin, Una O'Connor, Charles Judels, Theodore Von Eltz, Stanley Morner (Dennis Morgan).

Libeled Lady (1936, MGM). *d:* Jack Conway; *p:* Lawrence Weingarten; *sc:* Maurice Watkins, Howard Emmett Rogers, and George Oppenheimer—*b/o* a story by Wallace Sullivan.

GLADYS BENTON: Tough blonde whose conniving newspaper-editor fiancé talks her into marrying a slick lawyer as part of a blackmailing scheme to stop a hot-headed heiress from suing the paper for libel.

William Powell, Myrna Loy, Spencer Tracy, Walter Connolly, Charley Grapewin, Cora Witherspoon, E. E. Clive, Charles Trowbridge, Spencer Charters, George Chandler, William Benedict, Hal K. Dawson, William Newell.

Personal Property (1937, MGM). *d:* W. S. Van Dyke II; *p:* John W. Considine Jr.; *sc:* Hugh Mills and Ernest Vajda—*b/o* H. M. Harwood's play *The Man in Possession.*

CRYSTAL WETHERBY: Financially strapped American widow in England who hopes to marry a millionaire but instead falls for the bailiff sent to keep an eye on her house and furniture, which have been attached to pay her debts.

Robert Taylor, Reginald Owen, Una O'Connor, Henrietta Crosman, E. E. Clive, Cora Witherspoon, Marla Shelton, Forrester Harvey, Lionel Braham, Barnett Parker.

Saratoga (1937, MGM). *d:* Jack Conway; *p:* Bernard H. Hyman; *sc:* Anita Loos and Robert Hopkins.

CAROL LAYTON: Spoiled American girl who, when she comes back from England to run her late father's racehorse stables, meets and instantly dislikes a handsome racetrack bookie— but ends up falling in love with him.

Clark Gable, Lionel Barrymore, Frank Morgan, Walter Pidgeon, Una Merkel, Cliff Edwards, George Zucco, Jonathan Hale, Hattie McDaniel, Frankie Darro, Henry Stone.

☆ RITA HAYWORTH

Margarita Carmen Cansino

b: Oct. 17, 1918, New York, N.Y.

"If I'd been a ranch they would have called me the Bar *Nothing.*"

Gilda (Rita Hayworth) in *Gilda,* 1946.

Rita Hayworth made the first ten of the following films under her original stage name of Rita Cansino.

Under the Pampas Moon (1935, Fox). *d:* James Tinling; *p:* B. G. De Sylva; *sc:* Ernest Pascal and Bradley King (with additional dialogue by Henry Jackson)—*b/o* a story by Gordon Morris.
CARMEN: A waitress-dancer at an Argentine cantina in Buenos Aires who becomes involved with a gaucho who's searching for his stolen horse.
Warner Baxter, Ketti Gallian, J. Carrol Naish, John Miljan, Jack LaRue, George Irving, Veloz and Yolanda, Tito Guizar, Chris-Pin Martin, Paul Porcasi, Charles Stevens.

Charlie Chan in Egypt (1935, Fox). *d:* Louis King; *p:* Edward T. Lowe; *sc:* Robert Ellis and Helen Logan—*b/o* the character created by Earl Derr Biggers.
NAYDA: Pretty Egyptian girl who is one of several people involved with the famous Chinese sleuth Charlie Chan as he solves three murders and the disappearance of rare artifacts from an ancient Egyptian tomb.
Warner Oland, Pat Paterson, Thomas Beck, Frank Conroy, Nigel de Brulier, James Eagles, Paul Porcasi, Stepin Fetchit, George Irving.

Dante's Inferno (1935, Fox). *d:* Harry Lachman; *p:* Sol M. Wurtzel; *sc:* Philip Klein and Robert M. Yost—*b/o* a story by Cyrus Wood.
Billed as "SPECIALTY DANCER": Ballroom dancer who performs aboard a pleasure/gambling ship on its maiden voyage.
Spencer Tracy, Claire Trevor, Henry B. Walthall, Scotty Beckett, Alan Dinehart, Joe Brown, Nella Walker, Richard Tucker, Don Ameche, Warren Hymer, Willard Robertson, Barbara Pepper.

Paddy O'Day (1935, 20th-Fox). *d:* Lewis Seiler; *p:* Sol M. Wurtzel; *sc:* Lou Breslow and Edward Eliscu.
TAMARA PETROVITCH: Pretty Russian dancer in New York whose romance with her shy boyfriend is helped when a young Irish orphan girl plays Cupid.
Jane Withers, Pinky Tomlin, Jane Darwell, George Givot, Francis Ford, Vera Lewis, Russell Simpson,
Selmer Jackson, Tommy Bupp, Hal K. Dawson, Clarence Wilson.

Human Cargo (1936, 20th-Fox). *d:* Allan Dwan; *p:* Sol M. Wurtzel; *sc:* Jefferson Parker and Doris Malloy—*b/o* the novel *I Will Be Faithful* by Kathleen Shepard.
CARMEN ZORO: Illegal alien who is permanently silenced when she offers to testify and help a crusading D.A. break up the smuggling ring that's blackmailing her and other illegal aliens.
Claire Trevor, Brian Donlevy, Alan Dinehart, Ralph Morgan, Helen Troy, Morgan Wallace, Herman Bing, John McGuire, Ralf Harolde, Wade Boteler, Lee Phelps.

Meet Nero Wolfe (1936, Col.). *d:* Herbert Biberman; *p:* B. P. Schulberg; *sc:* Howard J. Green, Bruce Manning, and Joseph Anthony—*b/o* the novel *Fer de Lance* by Rex Stout.
MARIA MARINGOLA: Pretty young lady who asks the famous rotund sleuth Nero Wolfe to help her find her missing brother.
Edward Arnold, Joan Perry, Lionel Stander, Victor Jory, Nana Bryant, Dennie Moore, Russell Hardie, Walter Kingsford, John Qualen, Gene Morgan, Frank Conroy, William Benedict.

Rebellion (1936, Crescent). *d:* Lynn Shores; *p:* E. B. Derr; *sc:* John T. Neville.
PAULA CASTILLO: Young woman who becomes involved with a handsome U.S. Cavalry officer during the administration of President Zachary Taylor (1849-50).
Tom Keene, Duncan Renaldo, William Royle, Gino Corrado, Roger Gray, Robert McKenzie, Allen Cavan, Jack Ingram, Lita Cortez.

Trouble in Texas (1937, GN). *d:* R. N. Bradbury; *p:* Edward F. Finney; *sc:* Robert Emmett—*b/o* a story by Lindsley Parsons.
CARMEN: Undercover agent who, with the help of a straight-shooting rodeo star, investigates a series of mysterious hold-ups resulting in the theft of rodeo prize money.
Tex Ritter, Horace Murphy, Earl Dwire, Yakima Canutt, Charles King, Dick Palmer, Tom Cooper, Fox O'Callahan, Bob Crosby, Jack Smith.

Old Louisiana (1937, Crescent). *d:* Irvin V. Willat; *p:* E. B. Derr; *sc:* Mary Ireland—*b/o* a story by John Neville.
ANGELA GONZALES: Daughter of the Spanish governor of the Louisiana Territory during the days leading up to the United States' Louisiana Purchase from France under President Thomas Jefferson.

Tom Keene, Robert Fiske, Ray Bennett, Allan Cavan, Will Morgan, Budd Buster, Carlos DeValdez, Wally Albright, Ramsay Hill.

Hit the Saddle (1937, Rep.). *d:* Mack V. Wright; *p:* Nat Levine; *sc:* Oliver Drake—*b/o* a story by Oliver Drake and Maurice Geraghty, adapted from a novel by William Colt.
RITA: Fandango dancer who has a romance with one of a trio of hard-riding cowboys known as "The Three Mesquiteers."
Robert Livingstone, Ray Corrigan, Max Terhune, Yakima Canutt, J. P. MacGowan, Edward Cassidy, Sammy McKim, Harry Tenbrooke, Robert Smith.

Criminals of the Air (1937, Col.). *d:* Charles C. Coleman Jr.; *p:* Wallace MacDonald; *sc:* Owen Francis—*b/o* a story by Jack Cooper.
RITA: Sexy brunette dancer who serves as a smuggling gang's decoy in a below-the-border nightclub.
Rosalind Keith, Charles Quigley, John Gallaudet, Marc Lawrence, Patricia Farr, John Hamilton, Ralph Byrd, Russell Hicks, Frank Sully, Howard Hickman, Matty Kemp.

Girls Can Play (1937, Col.). *d:* Lambert Hillyer; *p:* Ralph Cohn; *sc:* Lambert Hillyer—*b/o* the story "Miss Casey at Bat" by Albert DeMond.
SUE COLLINS: Crooked druggist's girlfriend who plays on a girls' softball team as part of a scheme to promote an illegal liquor racket.
Jacqueline Wells (Julie Bishop), Charles Quigley, John Gallaudet, George McKay, Patricia Farr, Guinn "Big Boy" Williams, Joseph Crehan, James Flavin, Beatrice Blinn.

The Shadow (1937, Col.). *d:* Charles C. Coleman Jr.; *p:* Wallace MacDonald; *sc:* Arthur T. Horman—*b/o* a story by Milton Raison.
MARY GILLESPIE: Attractive manager of a small-time circus where a murderous maniac is on the loose.
Charles Quigley, Marc Lawrence, Arthur Loft, Dick Curtis, Vernon Dent, Marjorie Main, Dwight Frye, Bess Flowers, Ann Doran, Beatrice Blinn, Bud Jamison.

The Game That Kills (1937, Col.). *d:* D. Ross Lederman; *p:* Harry L. Decker; *sc:* Grace Neville and Fred Niblo Jr.—*b/o* a story by J. Benton Cheney.
BETTY HOLLAND: Pretty girlfriend of a handsome hockey player.
Charles Quigley, John Gallaudet, J. Farrell MacDonald, Arthur Loft, John Tyrell, Paul Fix, Dick Wessel, Dick Curtis, Edmund Cobb.

Paid to Dance (1937, Col.). *d:* Charles C. Coleman Jr.; *p:* Ralph Cohn; *sc:* Robert E. Kent—*b/o* a story by Leslie T. White.

BETTY MORGAN: Dance-hall hostess who helps an undercover policeman and policewoman bring to justice the racketeers who are exploiting the hostess.
Don Terry, Jacqueline Wells (Julie Bishop), Arthur Loft, Paul Stanton, Paul Fix, Louise Stanley, Ralph Byrd, Bess Flowers, Dick Curtis, Thurston Hall, John Gallaudet, Horace MacMahon, Ann Doran, Bud Jamison.

Who Killed Gail Preston? (1938, Col.). *d:* Leon Barsha; *p:* Ralph Cohn; *sc:* Robert E. Kent and Henry Taylor—*b/o* an original screen story, *Murder in Swingtime,* by Henry Taylor.
GAIL PRESTON: Glamorous nightclub singer who tries to blackmail her boss and winds up getting murdered.
Don Terry, Robert Paige, Wyn Cahoon, Gene Morgan, Marc Lawrence, Arthur Loft, John Gallaudet, Eddie Fetherston, James Millican, Dwight Frye, Vernon Dent, Jack Egan, Lee Shumway.

There's Always a Woman (1938, Col.). *d:* Alexander Hall; *p:* William Perlberg; *sc:* Gladys Lehman (and uncredited contributors: Joel Sayre, Philip Rapp, and Morrie Ryskind)—*b/o* the short story by Wilson Collison.
MARY: Pretty young woman in the D.A.'s office who serves as a confidante and "spy" for her boss's wife, a private eye.
Joan Blondell, Melvyn Douglas, Mary Astor, Frances Drake, Jerome Cowan, Robert Paige, Thurston Hall, Pierre Watkin, Walter Kingsford, Lester Matthews.

Convicted (1938, Col.). *d:* Leon Barsha; *p:* Kenneth J. Bishop (Central); *sc:* Edgar Edwards—*b/o* the story "Face Work" by Cornell Woolrich.
JERRY WHEELER: Young woman who faces danger when she poses as a singer in order to clear her brother of a murder charge.
Charles Quigley, Marc Lawrence, George McKay, Doreen MacGregor, Bill Irving, Eddie Laughton, Edgar Edwards, Don Douglas.

Juvenile Court (1938, Col.). *d:* D. Ross Lederman; *p:* Ralph Cohn; *sc:* Michael L. Simmons, Robert E. Kent, and Henry Taylor.
MARCIA ADAMS: Young woman who falls for a public defender while he tries to help her brother, the leader of a juvenile street gang in trouble with the law.
Paul Kelly, Frankie Darro, Hally Chester, Don Latorre, David Gorcey, Dick Selzer, Howard Hickman, Dick Curtis, Tom London, Edmund Cobb, Kane Richmond, Gloria Blondell, Bud Osborne.

The Renegade Ranger (1939, RKO). *d:* David Howard; *p:* Bert Gilroy; *sc:* Oliver Drake—*b/o* a story by Bennett Cohen.

JUDITH ALVAREZ: Courageous woman of the Old West who is falsely accused of murder after she organizes some homesteaders into a vigilante group that fights cattle rustlers and crooked politicians.

George O'Brien, Tim Holt, Ray Whitley, Lucio Villegas, William Royle, Neal Hart, Bob Kortman, Charles Stevens, Tom London.

Homicide Bureau (1939, Col.). *d:* Charles C. Coleman Jr.; *p:* Jack Frier; *sc:* Earle Snell.

J. G. BLISS: Police-laboratory expert who helps a brash detective and a crusading newsman break up a smuggling ring.

Bruce Cabot, Robert Paige, Marc Lawrence, Monroni Olsen, Gene Morgan, Eddie Fetherston, Stanley Andrews, Charles Trowbridge, Ann Doran, Dick Curtis.

The Lone Wolf Spy Hunt (1939, Col.). *d:* Peter Godfrey; *p:* Joseph Sistrom; *sc:* Jonathan Latimer—*b/o* Louis Joseph Vance's novel *The Lone Wolf's Daughter*.

KAREN: Sexy spy whose boss—a master spy who has stolen important government documents—is outwitted by the famed Lone Wolf (a gentleman thief whose real name is Michael Lanyard).

Warren William, Ida Lupino, Virginia Weidler, Ralph Morgan, Tom Dugan, Don Beddoe, Ben Welden, Irving Bacon, Dick Elliott, Jack Norton, Marc Lawrence, Dick Curtis, James Craig, Vernon Dent, James Millican.

Special Inspector (1939, Col.). *d:* Leon Barsha; *p:* Kenneth J. Bishop (Central); *sc:* Edgar Edwards.

PATRICIA LANE: Undercover agent who is out to expose a gang of highway hijackers who are victimizing truck drivers.

Charles Quigley, George McKay, Edgar Edwards, Eddie Laughton, Bob Rideout, Grant MacDonald, Bill Irving, Don Douglas.

Only Angels Have Wings (1939, Col.). *d:* Howard Hawks; *p:* Howard Hawks; *sc:* Jules Furthman—*b/o* a story by Howard Hawks.

JUDY MacPHERSON: Bride whose husband—a disgraced, washed-up pilot—is given a chance for a fresh start by her ex-flame, the boss of a fly-by-night mail and freight airline composed of a group of American flyers in South America.

Cary Grant, Jean Arthur, Richard Barthelmess, Thomas Mitchell, Allyn Joslyn, Sig Ruman, Victor Kilian, John Carroll, Donald Barry, Noah Beery Jr., Pat Flaherty, Candy Candido, James Millican, Vernon Dent.

Music in My Heart (1940, Col.). *d:* Joseph Santley; *p:* Irving Starr; *sc:* James Edward Grant—*b/o* the story "Passport to Happiness" by James Edward Grant.

PATRICIA O'MALLEY: Young woman who is about to enter into a marriage with a millionaire but changes her mind when she meets a handsome continental singer.

Tony Martin, Edith Fellows, Alan Mowbray, Eric Blore, George Tobias, Joseph Crehan, George Humbert, Don Beddoe, Andre Kostelanetz and his Orchestra.

Blondie on a Budget (1940, Col.). *d:* Frank R. Strayer; *p:* Robert Sparks; *sc:* Richard Flournoy—*b/o* a story by Charles Molyneaux Brown and the Chic Young cartoon characters.

JOAN FORRESTER: Attractive young woman who—when she comes to see her former sweetheart, an honest but bumbling family man named Dagwood Bumstead—causes his wife, Blondie, to become jealous.

Penny Singleton, Arthur Lake, Larry Simms, Danny Mummert, Don Beddoe, John Qualen, Irving Bacon, Thurston Hall, Emory Parnell, Willie Best, Hal K. Dawson, Dick Curtis, Gene Morgan.

Susan and God (1940, MGM). *d:* George Cukor; *p:* Hunt Stromberg; *sc:* Anita Loos—*b/o* the play by Rachel Crothers.

LEONORA STUBBS: Pretty wife who, when she and her older husband are weekend guests of a flighty Long Island society woman hooked on religion, becomes involved with a handsome young playboy.

Joan Crawford, Fredric March, Ruth Hussey, John Carroll, Nigel Bruce, Bruce Cabot, Rita Quigley, Rose Hobart, Constance Collier, Gloria DeHaven, Richard Crane, Marjorie Main, Aldrich Bowker.

The Lady in Question (1940, Col.). *d:* Charles Vidor; *p:* B. B. Kahane; *sc:* Lewis Meltzer—*b/o* the French screenplay *Gribouille* by H. G. Lustig and Marcel Archard.

NATALIE ROUGUIN: Young Parisian woman who, after she's acquitted in a murder trial and goes to work for a bicycle-shop owner who was on the jury, makes him jealous when she falls for his son.

Brian Aherne, Glenn Ford, Irene Rich, George Coulouris, Lloyd Corrigan, Evelyn Keyes, Edward Norris, Curt Bois, Frank Reicher, Sumner Getchell, Leon Belasco, Vernon Dent.

Angels over Broadway (1940, Col.). *d:* Ben Hecht and Douglas Fairbanks Jr.; *p:* Ben Hecht; *sc:* Ben Hecht.

NINA BARONA: Attractive woman who, on a rainy night in New York, becomes involved with a sharp con artist, a drunken has-been playwright, and an embezzling scheme.

Douglas Fairbanks Jr., Thomas Mitchell, John Qualen, George Watts, Ralph Theodore, Jack Roper, Constance Worth, Walter Baldwin, Jimmy

Conlin, Jerry Jerome, Harry Strang, Lee Phelps, Walter Sande.

The Strawberry Blonde (1941, WB). *d:* Raoul Walsh; *p:* Jack L. Warner and Hal B. Wallis; *sc:* Julius J. Epstein and Philip G. Epstein—*b/o* the play *One Sunday Afternoon* by James Hagan.

VIRGINIA BRUSH: Gold-digging strawberry blonde in Gay '90s New York who drastically affects the life of a young dentist when she rejects him and marries his egotistical pal.

James Cagney, Olivia de Havilland, Alan Hale, George Tobias, Jack Carson, Una O'Connor, George Reeves, Tim Ryan, Addison Richards, Suzanne Carnahan (Susan Peters), Dick Wessel, Billy Newell, Herbert Anderson, Frank Orth, James Flavin.

Affectionately Yours (1941, WB). *d:* Lloyd Bacon; *p:* Hal B. Wallis; *sc:* Edward Kaufman—*b/o* a story by Fanya Foss and Aleen Leslie.

IRENE MALCOLM: Glamorous newspaperwoman who is out to snare a foreign correspondent who's trying to woo back his ex-wife.

Merle Oberon, Dennis Morgan, Ralph Bellamy, George Tobias, James Gleason, Jerome Cowan, Renie Riano, Frank Wilcox, Pat Flaherty, Murray Alper, De Wolfe Hopper (William Hopper), Frank Faylen, Craig Stevens, Alexis Smith, Faye Emerson, Charles Drake.

Blood and Sand (1941, 20th-Fox). *d:* Rouben Mamoulian; *p:* Darryl F. Zanuck; *sc:* Jo Swerling—*b/o* the novel *Sangre y Arena* by Vicenté Blasco Ibañez.

DOÑA SOL: Beautiful but heartless Spanish socialite who causes a famous Spanish bullfighter's downfall when she comes between him and his faithful wife.

Tyrone Power, Linda Darnell, Nazimova, Anthony Quinn, J. Carrol Naish, John Carradine, Lynn Bari, Laird Cregar, George Reeves, Pedro de Cordoba, Fortunio Bonanova, Victor Kilian, Charles Stevens, Elena Verdugo, Monty Banks.

You'll Never Get Rich (1941, Col.). *d:* Sidney Lanfield; *p:* Samuel Bischoff; *sc:* Michael Fessier and Ernest Pagano.

SHEILA WINTHROP: Showgirl/dancer who becomes romantically involved with a Broadway dance director who, even though he has been drafted into WWII, still manages to put on his big show.

Fred Astaire, John Hubbard, Robert Benchley, Osa Massen, Frieda Inescort, Guinn "Big Boy" Williams, Donald MacBride, Marjorie Gateson, Ann Shoemaker, Martha Tilton, Frank Ferguson, Frank Sully.

My Gal Sal (1942, 20th-Fox). *d:* Irving Cummings; *p:* Robert Bassler; *sc:* Seton I. Miller, Darryl Ware, and Karl Tunberg—*b/o* the story "My Brother Paul" by Theodore Dreiser.

SALLY ELLIOTT: Broadway songstress in the Gay '90s who carries on a stormy romance with the young songwriter-singer Paul Dresser while helping him rise from a medicine show to Broadway musicals.

Victor Mature, John Sutton, Carole Landis, James Gleason, Phil Silvers, Walter Catlett, Frank Orth, Stanley Andrews, Curt Bois, Andrew Tombes, Charles Arnt, Hermes Pan, Robert Lowery, Ted North, Judy Ford (Terry Moore).

Tales of Manhattan (1942, 20th-Fox). *d:* Julien Duvivier; *p:* Boris Morros and S. P. Eagle (Sam Spiegel); *original stories/sc:* Ben Hecht, Ferenc Molnar, Donald Ogden Stewart, Samuel Hoffenstein, Alan Campbell, Ladislas Fodor, Laslo Vadnay, Laszlo Gorog, Lamar Trotti, and Henry Blankfort.

ETHEL HALLOWAY: Young woman whose husband "accidentally" shoots her lover, whereupon they both must figure out how they can dispose of the body.

Charles Boyer, Thomas Mitchell, Ginger Rogers, Henry Fonda, Cesar Romero, Gail Patrick, Charles Laughton, Elsa Lanchester, Edward G. Robinson, George Sanders, James Gleason, Paul Robeson, Ethel Waters, Rochester (Eddie Anderson).

You Were Never Lovelier (1942, Col.). *d:* William A. Seiter; *p:* Louis F. Edelman; *sc:* Michael Fessier, Ernest Pagano, and Delmer Daves—*b/o* Carlos Olivari and Sixto Pondal Rios's story and screenplay *The Gay Señorita.*

MARIA ACUÑA: Daughter whose father—an Argentine hotel tycoon—plays matchmaker as he tries to promote a romance between her and a New York song-and-dance man on vacation in Buenos Aires.

Fred Astaire, Adolphe Menjou, Leslie Brooks, Adele Mara, Isobel Elsom, Gus Schilling, Kathleen Howard, Larry Parks, Kirk Alyn, George Bunny, Xavier Cugat and his Orchestra.

Cover Girl (1944, Col.). *d:* Charles Vidor; *p:* Arthur Schwartz; *sc:* Virginia Van Upp, Marion Parsonnet, and Paul Gangelin—*b/o* an original screenplay by Erwin Gelsey.

RUSTY PARKER/MARIBELLE HICKS: Chorus girl named Maribelle Hicks who achieves fame and fortune when she becomes "Rusty Parker," a top magazine cover model, but then has trouble making up her mind about whom to marry.

Gene Kelly, Lee Bowman, Phil Silvers, Jinx Falkenburg, Eve Arden, Otto Kruger, Jess Barker, Anita Colby, Edward Brophy, Thurston Hall, Jack Norton, Eddie Dunn, Betty Brewer, Shelley Winters.

Tonight and Every Night (1945, Col.). *d:* Victor Saville; *p:* Victor Saville; *sc:* Lesser Samuels and Abe Finkel—*b/o* the play *Heart of a City* by Lesley Storm.

ROSALIND (ROZ) BRUCE: Singer-dancer in a WWII London music hall who—while performing in a nightly revue that never misses a performance, despite the London Blitz—falls for an RAF flyer.

Lee Bowman, Janet Blair, Marc Platt, Leslie Brooks, Florence Bates, Ernest Cossart, Dusty Anderson, Jim Bannon, Philip Merivale, Patrick O'Moore, Gavin Muir, Shelley Winters, Richard Haydn, Adele Jergens.

Gilda (1946, Col.). *d:* Charles Vidor; *p:* Virginia Van Upp; *sc:* Marion Parsonnet (adaptation by Jo Eisinger)—*b/o* a story by E. A. Ellington.

GILDA MUNDSON: Sultry wife of a Buenos Aires gambling-casino owner who, when her husband hires an American drifter as his assistant, discovers that the man is her old flame.

Glenn Ford, George Macready, Joseph Calleia, Steven Geray, Joseph Sawyer, Gerald Mohr, Robert Scott, Don Douglas, Lionel Royce, Ruth Roman, Eduardo Ciannelli.

Down to Earth (1947, Col.). *d:* Alexander Hall; *p:* Don Hartman; *sc:* Edward Blum and Don Hartman—*b/o* characters created in the play *Heaven Can Wait* by Harry Segall.

TERPSICHORE/KITTY PENDLETON: Greek Goddess of the Dance who comes down to earth posing as a mortal showgirl in order to make sure that a Broadway producer's new musical about the nine muses will be authentic and historically accurate.

Larry Parks, Marc Platt, Roland Culver, James Gleason, Edward Everett Horton, Adele Jergens, George Macready, William Frawley, William Haade, James Burke, Lucien Littlefield, Myron Healey, Cora Witherspoon.

The Lady from Shanghai (1948, Col.). *d:* Orson Welles; *p:* Orson Welles; *sc:* Orson Welles—*b/o* the novel *If I Should Die Before I Wake* by Sherwood King.

ELSA BANNISTER: Crippled lawyer's beautiful and homicidal wife who, when she becomes involved with an Irish seaman on a cruise, winds up in a gun battle with her husband in the Hall of Mirrors in an amusement park.

Orson Welles, Everett Sloane, Glenn Anders, Ted De Corsia, Gus Schilling, Harry Shannon, Wong Show Chong, Harry Strang, Phillip Morris, Milton Kibbee, Philip Van Zandt.

The Loves of Carmen (1948, Col.). *d:* Charles Vidor; *p:* Charles Vidor (Beckworth); *sc:* Helen Deutsch—*b/o* a story by Prosper Mérimee.

CARMEN: Hot-blooded Spanish gypsy in 1820s Seville who induces a dragoon corporal to desert the army, kill her husband, and become the leader of a gang of mountain-dwelling outlaws.

Glenn Ford, Ron Randell, Victor Jory, Luther Adler, Arnold Moss, Margaret Wycherly, Bernard Nedell, John Baragrey, Philip Van Zandt, Trevor Bardette, Francis Pierlot, Vernon Cansino, Jose Cansino.

Affair in Trinidad (1952, Col.). *d:* Vincent Sherman; *p:* Vincent Sherman (Beckworth); *sc:* Oscar Saul and James Gunn—*b/o* a story by Virginia Van Upp and Berne Giller.

CHRIS EMERY: American nightclub singer in Trinidad who, when she joins forces with her brother-in-law to track down her husband's murderer, runs up against an international spy ring.

Glenn Ford, Alexander Scourby, Valerie Bettis, Torin Thatcher, Howard Wendell, Karel Stepanek, George Voskovec, Steven Geray, Juanita Moore, Ralph Moody, Ross Elliott.

Salome (1953, Col.). *d:* William Dieterle; *p:* Buddy Adler (Beckworth); *sc:* Harry Kleiner—*b/o* a story by Harry Kleiner and Jesse L. Lasky Jr.

PRINCESS SALOME: Princess of Galilee who performs her famous dance of the seven veils for her lecherous step-father, King Herod, in a vain attempt to stop the beheading of John the Baptist.

Stewart Granger, Charles Laughton, Judith Anderson, Sir Cedric Hardwicke, Basil Sydney, Maurice Schwartz, Rex Reason, Arnold Moss, Robert Warwick, Michael Granger, Karl (Killer) Davis, Eduardo Cansino, Tristram Coffin, Lou Nova.

Miss Sadie Thompson (1953, Col.). *d:* Curtis Bernhardt; *p:* Jerry Wald (Beckworth); *sc:* Harry Kleiner—*b/o* the story "Miss Thompson" by W. Somerset Maugham and the play *Rain* by John Colton and Clemence Randolph.

SADIE THOMPSON: Bawdy shady lady who, when she's stranded on a remote South Pacific island where a group of post-WWII U.S. Marines are based, is briefly "converted" by a sanctimonious, hypocritical missionary—until she is sexually attacked by him.

Jose Ferrer, Aldo Ray, Russell Collins, Diosa Costello, Harry Bellaver, Wilton Graff, Peggy Converse, Henry Slate, Charles Buchinsky (Charles Bronson), Peter Chong, Eduardo Cansino Jr.

Fire Down Below (1957, Col.). *d:* Robert Parrish; *p:* Irving Allen and Albert R. Broccoli (Warwick); *sc:* Irwin Shaw—*b/o* the novel by Max Catto.

IRENA: Shady lady who causes problems between two partners in a Caribbean fishing and smuggling business while the three of them are on a boat trip between islands.

Robert Mitchum, Jack Lemmon, Herbert Lom, Bonar Colleano, Bernard Lee, Edric Connor, Peter Illing, Anthony Newley, Eric Pohlmann, "Stretch" Cox.

Pal Joey (1957, Col.). *d:* George Sidney; *p:* Fred Kohlmar (Essex–Sidney); *sc:* Dorothy Kingsley—*b/o* the musical play by John O'Hara, Richard Rodgers, and Lorenz Hart.

VERA SIMPSON: Wealthy, widowed ex-stripper who financially backs a fast-talking heel of a nightclub singer who hopes to build his own San Francisco nightclub.

Frank Sinatra, Kim Novak, Barbara Nichols, Bobby Sherwood, Hank Henry, Elizabeth Patterson, Frank Wilcox, Pierre Watkin, Frank Sully, John Hubbard, Hermes Pan, Gail Bonney.

Separate Tables (1958, UA). *d:* Delbert Mann; *p:* Harold Hecht (Hecht–Hill–Lancaster); *sc:* Terence Rattigan and John Gay—*b/o* the one-act plays *Table Number Seven* and *Table by the Window* by Terence Rattigan.

ANN SHANKLAND: Vain, selfish wife—one of several boarders at a British seaside guest house—who tries to win back her long-separated husband, whose mistress happens to be the proprietor of the guest house.

Deborah Kerr, David Niven, Wendy Hiller, Burt Lancaster, Gladys Cooper, Cathleen Nesbitt, Felix Aylmer, Rod Taylor, Audrey Dalton, Priscilla Morgan, May Hallatt, Hilda Plowright.

They Came to Cordura (1959, Col.). *d:* Robert Rossen; *p:* William Goetz (Goetz–Baroda); *sc:* Ivan Moffat and Robert Rossen—*b/o* the novel by Glendon Swarthout.

ADELAIDE GEARY: U.S. citizen who, after being arrested by the U.S. Army for consorting with the enemy during the 1916 expedition into Mexico against Pancho Villa, accompanies an officer once accused of cowardice and five motley Medal of Honor nominees on a grueling trek over rugged terrain to a military outpost at Cordura.

Gary Cooper, Van Heflin, Tab Hunter, Richard Conte, Michael Callan, Dick York, Robert Keith, Carlos Romero, James Bannon, Edward Platt, Maurice Jara.

The Story on Page One (1960, 20th-Fox). *d:* Clifford Odets; *p:* Jerry Wald (Company of Artists); *sc:* Clifford Odets.

JO MORRIS: Housewife who, when she and her lover are accused of murdering her cruel policeman husband, is defended in court by a down-on-his-luck shyster lawyer.

Anthony Franciosa, Gig Young, Mildred Dunnock, Hugh Griffith, Sanford Meisner, Robert Burton,

Alfred Ryder, Katherine Squire, Raymond Greenleaf, Myrna Fahey, Leo Penn, Biff Elliott, Jay Adler, Dan Riss, Joe Besser.

The Happy Thieves (1962, UA). *d:* George Marshall; *p:* James Hill and Rita Hayworth (Hillworth); *sc:* John Gay—*b/o* Richard Condon's novel *The Oldest Confession.*

EVE LEWIS: Sophisticated woman in Spain who, along with her gentleman-thief husband, is blackmailed into trying to steal a Goya painting from the famous Prado Museum.

Rex Harrison, Joseph Wiseman, Gregoire Aslan, Alida Valli, Virgilio Texera, Peter Illing, Brita Ekman (Britt Ekland), Karl-Heinz Schwerdtfeger, Yasmin Khan.

Circus World (1964, Para.). *d:* Henry Hathaway; *p:* Samuel Bronston (Bronston/Midway); *sc:* Ben Hecht, Julian Halevy, and James Edward Grant—*b/o* a story by Philip Yordan and Nicholas Ray.

LILI ALFREDO: Ex–circus trapeze performer in Europe who, after disappearing fifteen years before (when the husband she didn't love committed suicide), returns to the circus (owned by the man she really loved) and forms an aerial act with her daughter, whom she had left with him to raise.

John Wayne, Claudia Cardinale, Lloyd Nolan, Richard Conte, John Smith, Henri Dantes, Wanda Rotha, Kay Walsh, Margaret MacGrath, Katharine Kath, Moustache.

The Money Trap (1966, MGM). *d:* Burt Kennedy; *p:* Max E. Youngstein and David Karr (Youngstein); *sc:* Walter Bernstein—*b/o* the novel by Lionel White.

ROSALIE KENNY: Boozy, frowsy waitress who becomes involved with her old flame, an honest cop-turned-crook, and ends up being pushed off a building.

Glenn Ford, Elke Sommer, Joseph Cotten, Ricardo Montalban, Tom Reese, James Mitchum, Argentina Brunetti, Parley Baer, Ted De Corsia, Walter Reed, Stacy Harris.

The Poppy Is Also a Flower (1966, Comet Films [made for TV]). *d:* Terence Young; *p:* Evan Lloyd (Telsun–United Nations); *sc:* Jo Eisinger—*b/o* a story idea by Ian Fleming.

MONIQUE: Drug addict whose husband is the head of an international drug-smuggling ring.

Senta Berger, Stephen Boyd, Yul Brynner, Angie Dickinson, George Geret, Hugh Griffith, Jack Hawkins, Trevor Howard, Grace Kelly, Trini Lopez, E. G. Marshall, Marcello Mastroianni, Jean-Claude Pascal, Anthony Quayle, Gilbert Roland, Omar Sharif, Barry Sullivan, Eli Wallach.

The Rover (1967, Cinerama). *d:* Terence Young; *p:* Alfred Bini (Arco–Selmur); *sc:* Luciano

Vincenzoni and Jo Eisinger—*b/o* the novel by Joseph Conrad.

CATERINA: French woman whose neice—a beautiful but deranged young girl—becomes involved with an aging pirate and a young French naval officer during the bloody Napoleonic wars.

Anthony Quinn, Rosanna Schiaffino, Richard Johnson, Ivo Garranti, Mino Doro, Luciano Rossi, Mirko Valentin, Anthony Dawson, Franco Fantasia.

Sons of Satan (1969, WB–Seven Arts). *d:* Duccio Tessardi; *p:* Turi Vasile (Ultra Film–PECF–Rhein Main); *sc:* Ennio De Concini, Mario Di Nardo, and Duccio Tessardi—*b/o* a story by Mario Di Nardo.

MARTHA: Ex–Ziegfeld Follies beauty-turned-alcoholic whose two grown sons rob an Arizona jewelry store, but then both die when they doublecross each other.

Giuliano Gemma, Klaus Kinski, Margaret Lee, Serge Marquand, Claudine Auger, Umberto Raho, Hans Thorner, Karl Cik.

Road to Salina (1971, Avco Embassy). *d:* Georges Lautner; *p:* Robert Dorfmann and Yvon Guezel (Corona–Transinter–Fono Roma); *sc:* Georges Lautner, Pascal Jardin, and Jack Miller—*b/o* the novel by Maurice Cury.

MARA: Anguished mother who refuses to face the fact that her daughter murdered her own brother when the brother tried to break off his incestuous relationship with the girl.

Mimsy Farmer, Robert Walker Jr., Ed Begley, Bruce Pecheur, David Sachs, Sophie Hardy, Marc Porel, Ivano Staccioli, Albane Navizet.

The Naked Zoo (1971, Film Artists Int.). *d:* William Grefe; *p:* William Grefe; *sc:* Ray Preston and William Grefe—*b/o* a story by Ray Preston.

Wealthy woman whose affair with a drug-using writer-gigolo leads to the killing of her husband.

Fay Spain, Stephen Oliver, Ford Rainey, Fleurette Carter.

The Wrath of God (1972, MGM). *d:* Ralph Nelson; *p:* Peter Katz and William S. Gilmore Jr. (Rainbow/Cineman); *sc:* Ralph Nelson—*b/o* the novel by James Graham and excerpts from the story "Miss Criolla" by Ariel Ramirez.

SEÑORA DE LA PLATA: Long-suffering mother who, during a 1920s revolution in Central America, guns down her tyrannical, evil rebel son.

Robert Mitchum, Frank Langella, John Colicos, Victor Buono, Ken Hutchinson, Paula Pritchett, Gregory Sierra, Frank Ramirez, Enrique Lucero, Jorge Russel.

☆ KATHARINE HEPBURN

Katharine Houghton Hepburn

b: Nov. 8, 1907, Hartford, Conn.

"The calla lillies are in bloom again."

Terry Randall (Katharine Hepburn) delivering a line in a "play within a play" sequence in *Stage Door*, 1937.

A Bill of Divorcement (1932, RKO). *d:* George Cukor; *p:* David O. Selznick; *sc:* Howard Estabrook and Harry Wagstaff Gribble—*b/o* the play by Clemence Dane.

SYDNEY FAIRFIELD: Daughter who sacrifices her own happiness to look after her divorced father when he returns home from a mental hospital.

John Barrymore, Billie Burke, David Manners, Henry Stephenson, Paul Cavanagh, Elizabeth Patterson, Gayle Evers, Julie Haydon.

Christopher Strong (1933, RKO). *d:* Dorothy Arzner; *p:* Pandro S. Berman; *sc:* Zoe Akins—*b/o* the novel by Gilbert Frankau.

LADY CYNTHIA DARRINGTON: Daring British aviator who, after falling in love with a respectable married politician, discovers that she's pregnant and sacrifices her life for him by crashing her plane.

Colin Clive, Billie Burke, Helen Chandler, Ralph Forbes, Irene Browne, Jack La Rue, Desmond Roberts, Agostino Borgato, Margaret Lindsay, Donald Stewart, Zena Savina.

Morning Glory (1933, RKO). *d:* Lowell Sherman; *p:* Pandro S. Berman; *sc:* Howard J. Green—*b/o* the play by Zoe Akins.

EVA LOVELACE*: Stage-struck girl from a small town in Vermont who goes to New York and, while having an affair with a producer and falling in love with a playwright, struggles to become a great Broadway star.

Douglas Fairbanks Jr., Adolphe Menjou, Mary Duncan, C. Aubrey Smith, Don Alvarado, Fred Santley, Richard Carle, Tyler Brooke, Geneva Mitchell, Helen Ware, Theresa Harris.

---

*Won the Academy Award as Best Actress for this role.

Little Women (1933, RKO). *d:* George Cukor; *p:* Kenneth MacGowan; *sc:* Sarah Y. Mason and Victor Heerman—*b/o* the novel by Louisa May Alcott.

JO MARCH: Impulsive, headstrong young girl— one of four sisters growing up in Concord, Massachusetts, during the Civil War—who desperately wants to be a writer.

Joan Bennett, Paul Lukas, Edna May Oliver, Jean Parker, Frances Dee, Henry Stephenson, Douglass Montgomery, Spring Byington, Samuel S. Hinds, Nydia Westman, Harry Beresford, Olin Howland.

Spitfire (1934, RKO). *d:* John Cromwell; *p:* Pandro S. Berman; *sc:* Jane Murfin and Lula Vollmer— *b/o* the play *Trigger* by Lula Vollmer.

TRIGGER HICKS: Hot-tempered, simple mountain girl in the Ozarks who is driven from the community when she causes trouble because of her belief that prayers can heal the sick and raise the dead.

Robert Young, Ralph Bellamy, Martha Sleeper, Louis Mason, Sara Haden, Virginia Howell, Sidney Toler, High Ghere (Bob Burns), Therese Wittler, Jchn Beck.

The Little Minister (1934, RKO). *d:* Richard Wallace; *p:* Pandro S. Berman; *sc:* Jane Murfin, Sarah Y. Mason, and Victor Heerman (with additional scenes by Mortimer Offner and Jack Wagner)—*b/o* the novel and play by Sir James M. Barrie.

LADY BABBIE: Wayward ward of a nobleman in 1840 Scotland who, posing as a gypsy wench, falls in love with a strait-laced young pastor.

John Beal, Alan Hale, Donald Crisp, Lumsden Hare, Andy Clyde, Beryl Mercer, Dorothy Stickney, Mary Gordon, Frank Conroy, Reginald Denny, Leonard Carey, Harry Beresford.

Break of Hearts (1935, RKO). *d:* Philip Moeller; *p:* Pandro S. Berman; *sc:* Sarah Y. Mason, Victor Heerman, and Anthony Veiller—*b/o* a story by Lester Cohen.

CONSTANCE DANE: Struggling young composer whose brief but happy marriage to a famous conductor starts to crumble when he turns to alcohol and other women.

Charles Boyer, John Beal, Jean Hersholt, Sam Hardy, Inez Courtney, Ferdinand Gottschalk, Susan Fleming, Jean Howard, Jason Robards, Dick Elliott.

Alice Adams (1935, RKO). *d:* George Stevens; *p:* Pandro S. Berman; *sc:* Dorothy Yost and Mortimer Offner—*b/o* the novel by Booth Tarkington.

ALICE ADAMS*: Lonely, social-climbing small-

town girl whose efforts to impress her beau by putting on airs result in a fiasco.

Fred MacMurray, Fred Stone, Evelyn Venable, Frank Albertson, Ann Shoemaker, Charles Grapewin, Grady Sutton, Hedda Hopper, Jonathan Hale, Zeffie Tilbury, Hattie McDaniel.

Sylvia Scarlett (1936, RKO). *d:* George Cukor; *p:* Pandro S. Berman; *sc:* Gladys Unger, John Collier, and Mortimer Offner—*b/o* Compton MacKenzie's novel *The Early Life and Adventures of Sylvia Scarlett.*

SYLVIA SCARLETT: Young girl—disguised as a boy—who takes to the road in England with her larcenous father and a Cockney con man posing as touring actors.

Cary Grant, Brian Aherne, Edmund Gwenn, Natalie Paley, Dennie Moore, Harold Cheevers, Lionel Pape, Leonard Mudie, Gaston Glass, Bunny Beatty, E. E. Clive.

Mary of Scotland (1936, RKO). *d:* John Ford; *p:* Pandro S. Berman; *sc:* Dudley Nichols—*b/o* the play by Maxwell Anderson.

MARY STUART: Sixteenth-century Scottish queen who, when she refuses to renounce all Stuart claims to the English throne, is charged with treason and sentenced to death by Queen Elizabeth.

Fredric March, Florence Eldridge, Douglas Walton, John Carradine, Robert Barrat, Gavin Muir, Ian Keith, Moroni Olsen, Ralph Forbes, Alan Mowbray, Frieda Inescort, Donald Crisp, Anita Colby, Mary Gordon, Monte Blue, Doris Lloyd, Robert Warwick.

A Woman Rebels (1936, RKO). *d:* Mark Sandrich; *p:* Pandro S. Berman; *sc:* Anthony Veiller and Ernest Vajda—*b/o* the novel *Portrait of a Rebel* by Netta Syrett.

PAMELA THISTLEWAITE: Rebellious young woman in Victorian England who fights for women's rights, has an illegitimate baby, and becomes the crusading editor of a women's magazine.

Herbert Marshall, Elizabeth Allan, Donald Crisp, Doris Dudley, David Manners, Lucile Watson, Van Heflin, Eily Malyon, Margaret Seddon, Molly Lamont, Lionel Pape, Constance Lupino.

Quality Street (1937, RKO). *d:* George Stevens; *p:* Pandro S. Berman; *sc:* Mortimer Offner and Allan Scott—*b/o* the play by Sir James M. Barrie.

PHOEBE THROSSEL: English "old maid" who, when her beau returns from being away in the Napoleonic wars for ten years and doesn't recognize her, masquerades as her own flirtatious neice in a scheme to win him back.

Franchot Tone, Fay Bainter, Eric Blore, Cora Witherspoon, Estelle Winwood, Florence Lake,

---

*Received an Academy Award nomination as Best Actress for this role.

Bonita Granville, Sherwood Bailey, Joan Fontaine, William Bakewell.

Stage Door (1937, RKO). *d:* Gregory La Cava; *p:* Pandro S. Berman; *sc:* Morrie Ryskind and Anthony Veiller—*b/o* the play by Edna Ferber and George S. Kaufman.

TERRY RANDALL: Smug, self-confident rich woman who competes with the other residents of a New York theatrical boarding house for the lead in a Broadway play.

Ginger Rogers, Adolphe Menjou, Gail Patrick, Constance Collier, Andrea Leeds, Samuel S. Hinds, Lucille Ball, Pierre Watkin, Franklin Pangborn, Grady Sutton, Jack Carson, Frank Reicher, Eve Arden, Ann Miller, Katherine Alexander, Ralph Forbes, Theodore Von Eltz, Frances Gifford.

Bringing Up Baby (1938, RKO). *d:* Howard Hawks; *p:* Howard Hawks; *sc:* Dudley Nichols and Hagar Wilde—*b/o* a story by Hagar Wilde.

SUSAN VANCE: Madcap heiress who—along with her pet leopard, Baby—complicates the life of a shy paleontologist who's working on the reconstruction of a dinosaur skeleton.

Cary Grant, Charles Ruggles, May Robson, Walter Catlett, Barry Fitzgerald, Fritz Feld, George Irving, Tala Birell, Asta (dog), Nissa (leopard), Ernest Cossart, Brooks Benedict, Jack Carson, Richard Lane, Ward Bond.

Holiday (1938, Col.). *d:* George Cukor; *p:* Everett Riskin; *sc:* Donald Ogden Stewart and Sidney Buchman—*b/o* the play by Philip Barry.

LINDA SETON: Down-to-earth New York society woman who falls for the fiancé of her snobbish sister after realizing that he's more her type.

Cary Grant, Doris Nolan, Lew Ayres, Edward Everett Horton, Henry Kolker, Binnie Barnes, Jean Dixon, Henry Daniell, Charles Trowbridge, Howard Hickman, Hilda Plowright, Bess Flowers, Frank Shannon, Matt McHugh, Luke Cosgrave.

The Philadelphia Story (1940, MGM). *d:* George Cukor; *p:* Joseph L. Mankiewicz; *sc:* Donald Ogden Stewart—*b/o* the play by Philip Barry.

TRACY LORD*: Lofty Philadelphia society woman whose ex-husband shows up on the eve of her upcoming marriage to a stuffy blueblood and tries to win her back.

Cary Grant, James Stewart, Ruth Hussey, John Howard, Roland Young, John Halliday, Virginia Weidler, Mary Nash, Henry Daniell, Lionel Pape, Rex Evans, Hilda Plowright, Lee Phelps, Hillary Brooke.

Woman of the Year (1942, MGM). *d:* George Stevens; *p:* Joseph L. Mankiewicz; *sc:* Ring Lardner Jr. and Michael Kanin.

TESS HARDING*: Famous political columnist who marries an easy-going sportswriter but runs into domestic problems when she puts her career ahead of wifely duties.

Spencer Tracy, Fay Bainter, Reginald Owen, Minor Watson, William Bendix, Gladys Blake, Dan Tobin, Roscoe Karns, Ludwig Stossel, Sara Haden, Jimmy Conlin, Ben Lessy, Ray Teal, Joe Yule.

Keeper of the Flame (1942, MGM). *d:* George Cukor; *p:* Victor Saville; *sc:* Donald Ogden Stewart—*b/o* the novel by I. A. R. Wylie.

CHRISTINE FORREST: Widow of a recently deceased American national hero who, when a reporter visits her to write a laudatory article, is forced to reveal that the husband was secretly a traitorous Fascist.

Spencer Tracy, Richard Whorf, Margaret Wycherly, Donald Meek, Horace (Stephen) McNally, Audrey Christie, Frank Craven, Forrest Tucker, Percy Kilbride, Howard da Silva, Darryl Hickman, William Newell, Rex Evans, Blanche Yurka.

Dragon Seed (1944, MGM). *d:* Jack Conway and Harold S. Bucquet; *p:* Pandro S. Berman; *sc:* Marguerite Roberts and Jane Murfin—*b/o* the novel by Pearl Buck.

JADE: Idealistic Chinese peasant woman who convinces her farmer husband and his father and mother that they should help Chinese patriots fight Japanese invaders.

Walter Huston, Aline MacMahon, Akim Tamiroff, Turhan Bey, Hurd Hatfield, Frances Rafferty, Agnes Moorehead, Henry Travers, J. Carrol Naish, Abner Biberman, Leonard Mudie, Benson Fong, Philip Ahn, Frank Puglia, Jay Novello.

Without Love (1945, MGM). *d:* Harold S. Bucquet; *p:* Lawrence A. Weingarten; *sc:* Donald Ogden Stewart—*b/o* the play by Philip Barry.

JAMIE ROWAN: Attractive widow in WWII Washington, D.C., who, when she rents her home to a scientist so that he can conduct secret government experiments, enters into a platonic marriage with him—but fails to keep it platonic.

Spencer Tracy, Lucille Ball, Keenan Wynn, Carl Esmond, Patricia Morison, Felix Bressart, Gloria Grahame, George Chandler, Clancy Cooper, Charles Arnt, Eddie Acuff, Clarence Muse, Garry Owen, William Newell, James Flavin.

Undercurrent (1946, MGM). *d:* Vincente Minnelli; *p:* Pandro S. Berman; *sc:* Edward Chodorov—*b/o* a story by Thelma Strabel.

---

*Received an Academy Award nomination as Best Actress for this role.

*Received an Academy Award nomination as Best Actress for this role.

ANN HAMILTON: College professor's daughter who marries a handsome, mysterious industrialist, then—to her horror—slowly realizes that he's a psychopathic murderer.

Robert Taylor, Robert Mitchum, Edmund Gwenn, Marjorie Main, Jayne Meadows, Clinton Sundberg, Leigh Whipper, Dan Tobin, Charles Trowbridge, James Westerfield, Betty Blythe, Bess Flowers.

The Sea of Grass (1947, MGM). *d:* Elia Kazan; *p:* Pandro S. Berman; *sc:* Marguerite Roberts and Vincent Lawrence—*b/o* the novel by Conrad Richter.

LUTIE CAMERON: Wife who leaves her 1880s New Mexico cattle-baron husband because of his obsession with his land, then has an affair with his bitter lawyer enemy but finally returns to the husband.

Spencer Tracy, Melvyn Douglas, Phyllis Thaxter, Robert Walker, Edgar Buchanan, Harry Carey, William Phillips, James Bell, Robert Barrat, Charles Trowbridge, Russell Hicks, Robert Armstrong, Trevor Bardette, Morris Ankrum.

Song of Love (1947, MGM). *d:* Clarence Brown; *p:* Clarence Brown; *sc:* Ivan Tors, Irmgard Von Cube, Allen Vincent, and Robert Ardrey—*b/o* the play by Bernard Schubert and Mario Silva.

CLARA WIECK SCHUMANN: Brilliant pianist who marries the struggling nineteenth-century German composer Robert Schumann, gives up her career to care for him and their seven children, but—after her husband dies—returns to the stage to bring his music to the public.

Paul Henreid, Robert Walker, Henry Daniell, Leo G. Carroll, Else Janssen, Gigi Perreau, "Tinker" Furlong, Ludwig Stossel, Tala Birell, Henry Stephenson, Byron Foulger.

State of the Union (1948, MGM). *d:* Frank Capra; *p:* Frank Capra (Liberty Films); *sc:* Anthony Veiller and Myles Connolly—*b/o* the play by Howard Lindsay and Russel Crouse.

MARY MATTHEWS: Level-headed wife who, when her estranged businessman husband starts sacrificing his principles in order to win the Republican nomination for the presidency, steers him back onto the right track.

Spencer Tracy, Van Johnson, Angela Lansbury, Adolphe Menjou, Lewis Stone, Howard Smith, Raymond Walburn, Charles Dingle, Pierre Watkin, Margaret Hamilton, Irving Bacon, Carl Switzer, Tom Fadden, Charles Lane, Art Baker, Arthur O'Connell.

Adam's Rib (1949, MGM). *d:* George Cukor; *p:* Lawrence Weingarten; *sc:* Garson Kanin and Ruth Gordon.

AMANDA BONNER: Feminist lawyer who runs into marital problems with her D.A. husband when they wind up in court on opposing sides in the trial of a blonde who shot her two-timing husband.

Spencer Tracy, Judy Holliday, Tom Ewell, David Wayne, Jean Hagen, Hope Emerson, Clarence Kolb, Polly Moran, Will Wright, Marvin Kaplan, Ray Walker, Tommy Noonan, Anna Q. Nilsson.

The African Queen (1951, UA). *d:* John Huston; *p:* S. P. Eagle (Sam Spiegel) (Horizon–Romulus); *sc:* James Agee and John Huston—*b/o* the novel by C. S. Forester.

ROSE SAYER*: Old-maid English missionary in German East Africa during WWI who falls in love with the drunken Canadian riverboat captain of the *African Queen* as they head down the river to sink a German gunboat.

Humphrey Bogart, Robert Morley, Peter Bull, Theodore Bikel, Walter Gotell, Gerald Onn, Peter Swanick, Richard Marner.

Pat and Mike (1952, MGM). *d:* George Cukor; *p:* Lawrence Weingarten; *sc:* Ruth Gordon and Garson Kanin.

PAT PEMBERTON: College physical-education teacher who is signed up by a fast-talking sports promoter and, while becoming a top all-around pro athlete, falls in love with him.

Spencer Tracy, Aldo Ray, William Ching, Sammy White, George Mathews, Charles Buchinski (Charles Bronson), Jim Backus, Chuck Connors, Carl Switzer, Frankie Darro, Mae Clarke, Tom Harmon, Babe Didrikson Zaharias, Gussie Moran, Don Budge, Alice Marble, Frank Parker.

Summertime (1955, UA). *d:* David Lean; *p:* Ilya Lopert and Norman Spencer (Lopert); *sc:* David Lean and H. E. Bates—*b/o* Arthur Laurents's play *The Time of the Cuckoo*.

JANE HUDSON*: American spinster vacationing in Venice who falls hopelessly in love with a romantic Italian antique dealer who turns out to be married.

Rossano Brazzi, Isa Miranda, Darren McGavin, Mari Aldon, Jane Rose, MacDonald Parke, Gaitano Audiero, Andre Morell, Jeremy Spenser, Virginia Simeon.

The Rainmaker (1956, Para.). *d:* Joseph Anthony; *p:* Hal B. Wallis and Paul Nathan (Hal B. Wallis Prod.); *sc:* N. Richard Nash—*b/o* his play.

LIZZIE CURRY*: Repressed spinster on a drought-plagued farm in 1913 Kansas who is changed into a confident, loving woman by a smooth-talking con man who boasts that he can bring rain to the area for $100.

---

*Received an Academy Award nomination as Best Actress for this role.

Burt Lancaster, Wendell Corey, Lloyd Bridges, Earl Holliman, Cameron Prud'Homme, Wallace Ford, Yvonne Lime, Dottie Bee Baker, Dan White.

The Iron Petticoat (1956, MGM). *d:* Ralph Thomas; *p:* Betty E. Box (Benhar); *sc:* Ben Hecht— *b/o* a story by Harry Saltzman.

VINKA KOVELENKO: Flyer in the Russian Air Force who, when she lands her MIG at an American air base in Germany, falls in love with an American pilot who is assigned to try to convert her from communism to capitalism.

Bob Hope, James Robertson Justice, Robert Helpmann, David Kossoff, Alan Gifford, Paul Carpenter, Noelle Middleton, Nicholas Phipps, Sidney James, Tutte Lemkow.

Desk Set (1957, 20th-Fox). *d:* Walter Lang; *p:* Henry Ephron; *sc:* Phoebe Ephron and Henry Ephron—*b/o* William Marchant's play.

BUNNY WATSON: Brainy head of a TV network's reference library who clashes with an efficiency expert when she thinks he wants to replace her department with a giant computer he's invented.

Spencer Tracy, Gig Young, Joan Blondell, Dina Merrill, Sue Randall, Neva Patterson, Harry Ellerbe, Nicholas Joy, Diane Jergens, Merry Anders, Ida Moore, Rachel Stephens, Sammy Ogg.

Suddenly, Last Summer (1959, Col.). *d:* Joseph L. Mankiewicz; *p:* Sam Spiegel (Horizon); *sc:* Gore Vidal and Tennessee Williams—*b/o* the play by Tennessee Williams.

MRS. VIOLET VENABLE*: Dominating New Orleans matriarch who, in a desperate attempt to keep her neice from revealing the grisly details of the death of her homosexual son in North Africa, has the girl committed to an insane asylum.

Elizabeth Taylor, Montgomery Clift, Albert Dekker, Mercedes McCambridge, Gary Raymond, Mavis Villiers, Patricia Marmont, Joan Young, Maria Britneva.

Long Day's Journey into Night (1962, Embassy). *d:* Sidney Lumet; *p:* Ely Landau and Jack J. Dreyfus Jr.; *sc:* Eugene O'Neill—*b/o* his play.

MARY TYRONE*: Tragic, drug-addicted mother of a 1912 New England family whose miserly husband is a pompous actor, whose youngest son has tuberculosis, and whose oldest son is an alcoholic.

Ralph Richardson, Jason Robards Jr., Dean Stockwell, Jeanne Barr.

Guess Who's Coming to Dinner (1967, Col.). *d:* Stanley Kramer; *p:* Stanley Kramer (Stanley Kramer); *sc:* William Rose.

CHRISTINA DRAYTON*: Wealthy San Francisco art-gallery operator who, along with her crusading newspaper-editor husband, faces a test of her liberal beliefs when their daughter brings home a black doctor and announces that she plans to marry him.

Spencer Tracy, Sidney Poitier, Katharine Houghton, Cecil Kellaway, Roy E. Glenn Sr., Beah Richards, Isabel Sanford, Virginia Christine, Alexandra Hay, Grace Gaynor, Skip Martin.

The Lion in Winter (1968, Avco Embassy). *d:* Anthony Harvey; *p:* Martin Poll (Haworth); *sc:* James Goldman—*b/o* his play.

ELEANOR OF ACQUITAINE†: Strong-willed, estranged wife of King Henry II of England who, after being imprisoned by him for ten years in Salisbury Tower, is summoned by him in 1183 to Chinon Castle—along with their sons, Richard, Geoffrey, and John—to argue over which of the three will succeed to the throne when the king dies.

Peter O'Toole, Jane Merrow, John Castle, Timothy Dalton, Anthony Hopkins, Nigel Stock, Nigel Terry, Kenneth Griffith, O. Z. Whitehead.

The Madwoman of Chaillot (1969, WB–Seven Arts). *d:* Bryan Forbes; *p:* Ely Landau (Commonwealth United); *sc:* Edward Anhalt—*b/o* the play by Jean Giraudoux.

AURELIA, THE MADWOMAN OF CHAILLOT: Eccentric French countess who recruits some equally eccentric cronies to do away with the leaders of an international cartel plotting to turn Paris into a giant oil field.

Charles Boyer, Claude Dauphin, Edith Evans, John Gavin, Paul Henreid, Oscar Homolka, Margaret Leighton, Giulietta Masina, Nanette Newman, Richard Chamberlain, Yul Brynner, Donald Pleasance, Danny Kaye.

The Trojan Women (1971, Cinerama). *d:* Michael Cacoyannis; *p:* Michael Cacoyannis and Anis Nohra (Josef Shaftel); *sc:* Michael Cacoyannis—*b/o* the Greek tragedy by Euripides.

HECUBA: Queen of Troy during the Trojan War when the Greeks destroy Troy and force the Trojan women to become concubines.

Vanessa Redgrave, Genevieve Bujold, Irene Papas, Brian Blessed, Patrick Magee, Pauline Letts.

A Delicate Balance (1973, American Film Theater). *d:* Tony Richardson; *p:* Ely A. Landau; *sc:* Edward Albee—*b/o* his play.

AGNES: The wife in a bickering Connecticut family that experiences tension and fear when

---

*Received an Academy Award nomination as Best Actress for this role.

*Won the Academy Award as Best Actress for this role.
†Won the Academy Award as Best Actress for this role (tied with Barbra Streisand for her role in *Funny Girl*).

their best friends—an aging married couple—move into their home for an indefinite stay.

Paul Scofield, Lee Remick, Kate Reid, Joseph Cotten, Betsy Blair.

The Glass Menagerie (1973, Talent Asssociates/Norton–Simon [Made for TV]). *d:* Anthony Harvey; *p:* David Susskind; *sc:* Tennessee Williams—*b/o* his play.

AMANDA WINGFIELD*: Fading Southern-belle mother in 1930s St. Louis who futilely tries to instill confidence in her shy, unhappy crippled daughter—but gets some help from a personable gentleman caller.

Sam Waterston, Joanna Miles, Michael Moriarty.

Love Among the Ruins (1975, ABC Circle Films [Made for TV]). *d:* George Cukor; *p:* Allan Davis; *sc:* James Costigan.

JESSICA MEDLICOTT†: Aging actress in 1911 London who, when she's sued for breach of promise by a young man, is defended by a prestigious barrister who was once her lover.

Laurence Olivier, Colin Blakely, Richard Pearson, Joan Sims, Leigh Lawson, Gwen Nelson, Robert Harris.

Rooster Cogburn (1975, Univ.). *d:* Stuart Millar; *p:* Hal B. Wallis (Hal B. Wallis Prod.); *sc:* Martin Julien—*b/o* the ''Rooster Cogburn'' character created by Charles H. Portis in his novel *True Grit*.

EULA GOODNIGHT: Bible-thumping spinster in the Old West who teams up with a hard-drinking, one-eyed U.S. marshal in tracking down the gang of outlaws who murdered her minister father.

John Wayne, Anthony Zerbe, Richard Jordan, John McIntire, Strother Martin, Paul Koslo, Jack

Colvin, Jon Lormer, Richard Romancito, Lane Smith, Tommy Lee.

Olly Olly Oxen Free (1978, Sanrio). *d:* Richard A. Colla; *p:* Richard A. Colla (Rico–Lion); *sc:* Eugene Poinc—*b/o* a story by Maria L. de Ossio, Richard A. Colla, and Eugene Poinc.

MISS PUDD: Eccentric junk dealer who becomes involved in helping two young boys who dream of launching a huge hot-air balloon.

Kevin McKenzie, Dennis Dimster, Peter Kilman, Obie.

The Corn Is Green (1979, WB [Made for TV]). *d:* George Cukor; *p:* Neil Hartley; *sc:* Ivan Davis—*b/o* the play by Emlyn Williams.

LILLY MOFFAT*: Spinster English schoolteacher in a turn-of-the-century North Wales mining community who devotes herself to turning a belligerent young miner into an honor student who goes on to Oxford.

Ian Saynor, Bill Fraser, Patricia Hayes, Anna Massey, Artro Morris, Dorothea Phillips, Toyah Wilcox, Huw Richards.

On Golden Pond (1981, Univ.). *d:* Mark Rydell; *p:* Bruce Gilbert (ITC Films/IPC Films); *sc:* Ernest Thompson—*b/o* his play.

ETHEL THAYER†: Buoyant, understanding wife who tries to help her retired-professor husband of forty-eight years cope with old age and approaching death as they observe his eightieth birthday at their summer vacation cottage in New Hampshire.

Henry Fonda, Jane Fonda, Doug McKeon, Dabney Coleman, William Lanteau, Chris Rydell.

• In addition, Katharine Hepburn made a cameo/guest appearance in the following feature film: *Stage Door Canteen* (1943, UA).

---

*Received an Emmy Award nomination as Outstanding Lead Actress in a Drama Special for this role.
†Won an Emmy Award as Outstanding Lead Actress in a Drama Special for this role.

*Received an Emmy Award nomination as Outstanding Lead Actress in a Drama Special for this role.
†Won the Academy Award as Best Actress for this role.

☆ CHARLTON HESTON

b: Oct. 4, 1923, Evanston, Ill.

"Take your stinking paws off me, you damn dirty ape!"

> George Taylor (Charlton Heston) to an ape
> that has captured him in *Planet of the
> Apes,* 1968.

Dark City (1950, Para.). *d:* William Dieterle; *p:* Hal B. Wallis (Hal B. Wallis Prod.); *sc:* John Meredyth Lucas and Larry Marcus—*b/o* a story by Larry Marcus.

DANNY HALEY: WWII veteran–turned–gambler who, after taking part in a crooked poker game whose loser commits suicide, finds himself on the run from the man's revenge-seeking psychopathic brother.

Lizabeth Scott, Viveca Lindfors, Dean Jagger, Don DeFore, Jack Webb, Ed Begley, Henry Morgan, Mike Mazurki.

The Greatest Show on Earth (1952, Para.). *d:* Cecil B. DeMille; *p:* Cecil B. DeMille; *sc:* Fredric M. Frank, Barre Lyndon, and Theodore St. John—*b/o* a story by Fredric M. Frank, Theodore St. John, and Frank Cavett.

BRAD: Dedicated manager of the Ringling Brothers Circus who has no time for women or love, despite the fact that two of his female performers—an aerialist and the elephant girl—have fallen in love with him.

Betty Hutton, Cornel Wilde, Dorothy Lamour, Gloria Grahame, James Stewart, Lyle Betger, Henry Wilcoxon, Emmett Kelly, Lawrence Tierney, John Kellogg, John Ringling North, John Ridgely, Frank Wilcox, Julia Faye, Lane Chandler.

Ruby Gentry (1952, 20th-Fox). *d:* King Vidor; *p:* Joseph Bernhard and King Vidor; *sc:* Silvia Richards—*b/o* a story by Arthur Fitz-Richard.

BOAKE TACKMAN: Son of a fallen aristocratic family in the South who jilts his true love—a sexy girl from the swamplands—when he decides he needs to marry a rich society girl to regain wealth and position.

Jennifer Jones, Karl Malden, Tom Tully, Bernard Phillips, Josephine Hutchinson, James Anderson, Phyllis Avery, Frank Wilcox.

The Savage (1952, Para.). *d:* George Marshall; *p:* Mel Epstein; *sc:* Sydney Boehm—*b/o* the novel by L. L. Foreman.

WAR BONNET/JIM AHERN: White man in the Dakotas who, after having been raised by the Sioux tribe and called War Bonnet, finds himself forced to choose sides when fighting breaks out between the Indians and whites.

Susan Morrow, Peter Hanson, Joan Taylor, Richard Rober, Don Porter, Ted De Corsia, Ian MacDonald, Frank Richards.

The President's Lady (1953, 20th-Fox). *d:* Henry Levin; *p:* Sol C. Siegel; *sc:* John Patrick—*b/o* the novel by Irving Stone.

ANDREW JACKSON: Young Tennessee lawyer in the 1800s who marries a divorced woman, is wounded in a duel defending her honor, and—shortly after he's elected the seventh president of the United States—tragically loses her when she dies from an illness.

Susan Hayward, John McIntire, Fay Bainter, Carl Betz, Whitfield Connor, Ralph Dumke, Margaret Wycherly, Gladys Hurlbut.

Pony Express (1953, Para.). *d:* Jerry Hopper; *p:* Nat Holt; *sc:* Charles Marquis Warren—*b/o* a story by Frank Gruber.

BUFFALO BILL CODY: Famous nineteenth-century Westerner who teams up with the equally famous Wild Bill Hickock to set up Pony Express stations across California.

Rhonda Fleming, Jan Sterling, Forrest Tucker, Michael Moore, Porter Hall, Richard Shannon, Henry Brandon, Stuart Randall.

Arrowhead (1953, Para.). *d:* Charles Marquis Warren; *p:* Nat Holt; *sc:* Charles Marquis Warren—*b/o* the novel by W. R. Burnett.

ED BANNON: Rugged chief of scouts for the U.S. Cavalry in the post–Civil War Southwest who finally resolves the Army's fight with the Apache Indians by engaging in single hand-to-hand combat with a treacherous tribal chief.

Jack Palance, Katy Jurado, Brian Keith, Milburn Stone, Mary Sinclair, Richard Shannon, Lewis Martin, Frank de Kova.

Bad for Each Other (1953, Col.). *d:* Irving Rapper; *p:* William Fadiman; *sc:* Irving Wallace and Horace McCoy—*b/o* the novel by Horace McCoy.

DR. TOM OWEN: Ex–Korean War Army doctor who, after he returns to his Pennsylvania home town and rejects the poor miners for a society clientele, changes his philosophy when there's a mine disaster.

Lizabeth Scott, Dianne Foster, Mildred Dunnock, Arthur Franz, Ray Collins, Marjorie Rambeau, Lester Matthews, Rhys Williams.

The Naked Jungle (1953, Para.). *d:* Byron Haskin; *p:* George Pal; *sc:* Philip Yordan and Ranald MacDougall—*b/o* the story "Leiningen vs. the Ants" by Carl Stephenson.

CHRISTOPHER LEININGEN: South American planter who, with his beautiful mail-order bride, is besieged on his cocoa plantation by an advancing army of voracious red soldier ants.

Eleanor Parker, William Conrad, Abraham Sofaer, John Dierkes, Douglas Fowley, Romo Vincent, Leonard Strong, Norma Calderon.

Secret of the Incas (1954, Para.). *d:* Jerry Hopper; *p:* Mel Epstein; *sc:* Ranald MacDougall and Sydney Boehm.

HARRY STEELE: Soldier of fortune in South America who, when he arrives at the 400-year-old tomb of King Manca in search of a priceless Inca jewel, finds that an archaeological expedition is already there on the same mission.

Robert Young, Nicole Maurey, Yma Sumac, Thomas Mitchell, Glenda Farrell, Michael Pate, Leon Askin, William Henry, Kurt Katch, Marion Ross.

The Far Horizons (1955, Para.). *d:* Rudolph Mate; *p:* William H. Pine and William C. Thomas (Pine–Thomas); *sc:* Winston Miller and Edmund H. North—*b/o* the novel *Sacajawea of the Shoshones* by Della Gould Emmons.

WILLIAM CLARK: American explorer who—while he and his partner, Meriwether Lewis, make an historic 1803 trek westward through the Louisiana Purchase Territory—falls in love with their female Indian guide, Sacajawea.

Fred MacMurray, Donna Reed, Barbara Hale, William Demarest, Alan Reed, Larry Pennell, Herbert Heyes.

The Private War of Major Benson (1955, Univ.). *d:* Jerry Hopper; *p:* Howard Pine; *sc:* William Roberts and Richard Alan Simmons.

MAJ. BERNARD "BARNEY" BENSON: Hardboiled U.S. Army officer who, when he voices some outspoken and unauthorized opinions to *Newsweek* magazine, is chastised by the brass and assigned as commandant of a California boys' military school run by an order of nuns.

Julie Adams, William Demarest, Tim Considine, Tim Hovey, Sal Mineo, Nana Bryant, Milburn Stone, Mary Field, David Janssen, Don Haggerty, Edward C. Platt.

Lucy Gallant (1955, Para.). *d:* Robert Parrish; *p:* William H. Pine and William C. Thomas (Pine–Thomas); *sc:* John Lee Mahin and Winston Miller—*b/o* Margaret Cousins's novel *The Life of Lucy Gallant*.

CASEY COLE: Farmer who strikes it rich in a Texas oil boom town while he carries on an on-again–off-again romance with an ambitious girlfriend who builds the biggest fashion business in the state.

Jane Wyman, Claire Trevor, Thelma Ritter, William Demarest, Wallace Ford, Tom Helmore, Mary Field.

The Ten Commandments (1956, Para.). *d:* Cecil B. DeMille; *p:* Cecil B. DeMille; *sc:* Aeneas MacKenzie, Jesse L. Laskey Jr., Jack Gariss, and Fredric M. Frank—*b/o* the novels *Prince of Egypt* by Dorothy Clarke Wilson, *Pillar of Fire* by Rev. J. H. Ingraham, and *On Eagle's Wings* by Rev. G. E. Southton, in accordance with the Holy Scripture.

MOSES: Hebrew born during Biblical times in Egypt who—after being raised as an Egyptian—kills an Egyptian overseer and is banished by the Pharaoh but eventually returns as the prophesied Deliverer who leads the Israelites out of Egypt to the Promised Land.

Yul Brynner, Anne Baxter, Edward G. Robinson, Yvonne de Carlo, Debra Paget, John Derek, Sir Cedric Hardwicke, Nina Foch, Martha Scott, Judith Anderson, Vincent Price, John Carradine, H. B. Warner, Henry Wilcoxon, Woodrow Strode, Touch (Mike) Connors, Onslow Stevens, Clint Walker, Frankie Darro, Carl Switzer, Robert Vaughn.

Three Violent People (1956, Para.). *d:* Rudolph Mate; *p:* Hugh Brown; *sc:* James Edward Grant—*b/o* a story by Leonard Praskins and Barney Slater.

COLT SAUNDERS: Ex-Confederate captain in post–Civil War Texas who, as he battles land-grabbing carpetbaggers and clashes with his bitter one-armed brother, learns that his wife is a former prostitute.

Anne Baxter, Gilbert Roland, Tom Tryon, Bruce Bennett, Forrest Tucker, Elaine Stritch, Barton MacLane.

Touch of Evil (1958, Univ.). *d:* Orson Welles; *p:* Albert Zugsmith; *sc:* Orson Welles—*b/o* the novel *Badge of Evil* by Whit Masterson.

RAMON MIGUEL (MIKE) VARGAS: Mexican narcotics investigator who, while on his honeymoon, tangles with a corrupt American border-town police chief over a murder frameup.

Janet Leigh, Orson Welles, Joseph Calleia, Akim Tamiroff, Ray Collins, Dennis Weaver, Marlene Dietrich, Zsa Zsa Gabor, Mercedes McCambridge, Joseph Cotten.

The Big Country (1958, UA). *d:* William Wyler; *p:* William Wyler and Gregory Peck (Anthony/ Worldwide); *sc:* James R. Webb, Sy Bartlett, and Robert Wilder.

STEVE LEECH: Quick-tempered ranch foreman in the Old West who clashes with an ex–sea captain over a girl while getting involved in a feud between his stubborn boss and a neighboring family over water rights.

Gregory Peck, Jean Simmons, Carroll Baker, Burl Ives, Charles Bickford, Alfonso Bedoya, Chuck Connors, Buff Brady, Dorothy Adams, Chuck Hayward, Jim Burk.

The Buccaneer (1958, Para.). *d:* Anthony Quinn; *p:* Henry Wilcoxon for Cecil B. DeMille; *sc:* Jesse L. Lasky Jr. and Bernice Mosk.

ANDREW JACKSON: U.S. president who finds it necessary to rely on the French buccaneer Jean Lafitte to repel the British at the Battle of New Orleans during the War of 1812.

Yul Brynner, Claire Bloom, Charles Boyer, Inger Stevens, Henry Hull, E. G. Marshall, Lorne Greene, Douglas Dumbrille, Ted de Corsia, Robert F. Simon.

Ben-Hur (1959, MGM). *d:* William Wyler; *p:* Sam Zimbalist; *sc:* Karl Tunberg—*b/o* the novel by Lew Wallace.

JUDAH BEN-HUR*: Aristocratic Jew in Jerusalem who, after being sent to the Roman galleys as a slave, gains his freedom, returns to defeat his old Roman enemy in a chariot race, and—when Jesus is crucified—embraces Christianity.

Jack Hawkins, Stephen Boyd, Haya Harareet, Hugh Griffith, Martha Scott, Sam Jaffe, Cathy O'Donnell, Finlay Currie, Frank Thring, Terence Longden, Andre Morell, Ralph Truman.

Wreck of the Mary Deare (1959, MGM). *d:* Michael Anderson; *p:* Julian Blaustein (Goetz–Baroda); *sc:* Eric Ambler—*b/o* the novel by Hammond Innes.

JOHN SANDS: Salvage-boat skipper who helps the accused captain of a wrecked cargo ship expose an attempted insurance fraud and clear himself of negligence charges.

Gary Cooper, Michael Redgrave, Emlyn Williams, Cecil Parker, Alexander Knox, Virginia McKenna, Richard Harris, Ben Wright, Peter Illing, Ashley Cowan, Louis Mercier.

El Cid (1961, AA). *d:* Anthony Mann; *p:* Samuel Bronston (Samuel Bronston); *sc:* Philip Yordan and Fredric M. Frank.

RODRIGO DIAZ de BIVAR (EL CID): Heroic eleventh-century knight and Spanish national hero who, although once exiled by the king, returns to Spain as a champion of Christianity and drives out the Moors.

Sophia Loren, John Fraser, Raf Vallone, Genevieve Page, Gary Raymond, Herbert Lom, Hurd Hatfield, Massimo Serato, Andrew

Cruickshank, Michael Hordern, Douglas Wilmer, Frank Thring.

The Pigeon That Took Rome (1962, Para.). *d:* Melville Shavelson; *p:* Melville Shavelson; *sc:* Melville Shavelson—*b/o* Donald Downes's novel *The Easter Dinner.*

CAPT. PAUL MacDOUGALL: Tough WWII U.S. infantry officer who, when he's sent behind Nazi lines into occupied Rome, uses carrier pigeons to relay information back to Allied intelligence—and also finds time to romance a local beauty.

Elsa Martinelli, Harry Guardino, Brian Donlevy, Baccaloni, Marietto, Arthur Shields, Rudolph Anders.

Diamond Head (1962, Col.). *d:* Guy Green; *p:* Jerry Bresler; *sc:* Marguerite Roberts—*b/o* the novel by Peter Gilman.

RICHARD "KING" HOWLAND: Domineering, bigoted plantation owner in Hawaii who opposes the marriage of his sister to a full-blooded Hawaiian native, despite the fact that he himself has a Hawaiian native mistress.

Yvette Mimieux, George Chakiris, France Nuyen, James Darren, Aline MacMahon, Elizabeth Allen, Richard Loo, Philip Ahn, Harold Fong, Edward Mallory.

55 Days at Peking (1962, AA). *d:* Nicholas Ray; *p:* Samuel Bronston (Samuel Bronston); *sc:* Philip Yordan and Bernard Gordon.

MAJ. MATT LEWIS: Rugged U.S. Marine officer who leads the defense at Peking when the legations of eleven nations are besieged at the international diplomatic quarter during the 1900 Boxer Rebellion in China.

David Niven, Ava Gardner, Robert Helpmann, Flora Robson, Leo Genn, John Ireland, Paul Lukas, Harry Andrews, Elizabeth Sellars, Kurt Kasznar, Massimo Serrato, Jerome Thor, Nicholas Ray.

The Greatest Story Ever Told (1965, UA). *d:* George Stevens; *p:* George Stevens (George Stevens); *sc:* James Lee Barrett and George Stevens, in creative association with Carl Sandburg—*b/o* Books of the Old and New Testaments, other ancient writings, the book by Fulton Oursler, and writings by Henry Denker.

JOHN THE BAPTIST: Judean prophet sent by God to prepare people for the coming of Jesus the Messiah.

Max von Sydow, Dorothy McGuire, Robert Loggia, Robert Blake, Jamie Farr, David McCallum, Roddy McDowall, Sidney Poitier, Carroll Baker, Pat Boone, Van Heflin, Sal Mineo, Shelley Winters, Ed Wynn, John Wayne, Telly Savalas, Angela Lansbury Joseph Schildkraut, Jose Ferrer, Claude Rains, Richard Conte.

---

*Won the Academy Award as Best Actor for this role.

The Agony and the Ecstasy (1965, 20th-Fox). *d:* Carol Reed; *p:* Carol Reed (International Classics); *sc:* Philip Dunne—*b/o* the novel by Irving Stone.

MICHELANGELO: Famed fifteenth-century Italian sculptor/artist who, when he's persuaded by Pope Julius II to paint the ceiling of the Sistine Chapel, encounters artistic conflicts with the pontiff.

Rex Harrison, Diane Cilento, Harry Andrews, Alberto Lupo, Adolfo Celi, John Stacy, Fausto Tozzi, Maxine Audley.

Major Dundee (1965, Col.). *d:* Sam Peckinpah; *p:* Jerry Bresler; *sc:* Harry Julian Fink, Oscar Saul, and Sam Peckinpah.

MAJ. AMOS DUNDEE: Tough Union cavalry officer during the Civil War who, after Apaches stage a massacre at a New Mexico cavalry post, leads a motley bunch of misfits across the Mexican border in pursuit of the Indians.

Richard Harris, Jim Hutton, James Coburn, Senta Berger, Warren Oates, Ben Johnson, Michael Anderson Jr., Slim Pickens, Brock Peters, L. Q. Jones, Michael Pate.

The War Lord (1965, Univ.). *d:* Franklin J. Schaffner; *p:* Walter Seltzer (Court); *sc:* John Collier and Millard Kaufman—*b/o* Leslie Stevens's play *The Lovers*.

CHRYSAGON: Eleventh-century Norman knight who, after becoming ruler of a coastal village, has trouble when he demands his feudal tribute—the right to spend the first night with another man's bride.

Richard Boone, Rosemary Forsyth, Maurice Evans, Guy Stockwell, Niall MacGinnis, Henry Wilcoxon, James Farentino.

Khartoum (1966, UA). *d:* Basil Dearden; *p:* Julian Blaustein; *sc:* Robert Ardrey.

GEN. CHARLES "CHINESE" GORDON: Heroic British general who is defeated and killed in the 1880s when Arab tribesmen under the command of Mohammed Ahmed—a religious leader known as the Mahdi—lay siege to Khartoum in the Sudan.

Laurence Olivier, Richard Johnson, Ralph Richardson, Alexander Knox, Nigel Green, Zia Mohyeddin, Hugh Williams, Johnny Sekka, Michael Hordern.

Counterpoint (1967, Univ.). *d:* Ralph Nelson; *p:* Dick Berg; *sc:* James Lee and Joel Oliansky—*b/o* Alan Sillitoe's novel *The General*.

LIONEL EVANS: American symphony-orchestra conductor in WWII Europe who, along with his musicians, is captured by the Germans and forced by a Nazi general to put on a private concert.

Maximilian Schell, Kathryn Hays, Anton Diffring, Leslie Nielsen, Linden Chiles.

Will Penny (1967, Para.). *d:* Tom Gries; *p:* Fred Engel and Walter Seltzer; *sc:* Tom Gries.

WILL PENNY: Saddle-worn fifty-year-old cowpuncher who, when he meets and falls in love with a young widow, tries to keep out of trouble but winds up clashing with a family of villainous cutthroats.

Joan Hackett, Donald Pleasance, Lee Majors, Bruce Dern, Ben Johnson, Slim Pickens, Anthony Zerbe, Lydia Clarke Heston, Clifton James.

Planet of the Apes (1968, 20th-Fox). *d:* Franklin J. Schaffner; *p:* Arthur P. Jacobs and Mort Abrahams (Apjac); *sc:* Michael Wilson and Rod Serling—*b/o* the novel by Pierre Boulle.

GEORGE TAYLOR: American astronaut who, after he and his crew awaken from suspended animation during a long intergalactic journey, crash lands on a strange planet where apes are masters and human are slaves, then makes the horrifying discovery that it's Earth, 2000 years in the future.

Roddy McDowall, Kim Hunter, Maurice Evans, James Whitmore, James Daly, Linda Harrison, Robert Gunner, Woodrow Parfrey.

Number One (1968, UA). *d:* Tom Gries; *p:* Walter Seltzer; *sc:* David Moessinger.

RON "CAT" CATLAN: Veteran forty-year-old New Orleans Saints quarterback who, though age is catching up with him, stubbornly refuses to retire.

Jessica Walter, Bruce Dern, John Randolph, Diana Muldaur, Mike Henry, Kelly Williams, Richard Elkins, Ernie Barnes, Bobby Troup.

Beneath the Planet of the Apes (1969, 20th-Fox). *d:* Ted Post; *p:* Arthur P. Jacobs and Mort Abrahams (Apjac); *sc:* Paul Dehn and Mort Abrahams—*b/o* characters created by Pierre Boulle.

GEORGE TAYLOR: American astronaut who, after crash-landing on an ape-inhabited planet (which turns out to be Earth 2000 years in the future), is taken prisoner by mutant humans living in the underground ruins of New York City.

James Franciscus, Kim Hunter, Maurice Evans, Linda Harrison, Paul Richards, Victor Buono, James Gregory, Jeff Corey, Thomas Gomez, Tod Andrews.

The Hawaiians (1970, UA). *d:* Tom Gries; *p:* Walter Mirisch (Mirisch); *sc:* James R. Webb—*b/o* the second half of the novel *Hawaii* by James Michener.

WHIP HOXWORTH: Black sheep of a nineteenth-century family who encounters numerous conflicts and involvements as he rises to become the pineapple king of Hawaii.

Geraldine Chaplin, John Phillip Law, Tina Chen, Alec McCowen, Mako, Miko Mayana.

Julius Caesar (1970, AIP). *d:* Stuart Burge; *p:* Peter Snell (Commonwealth United); *sc:* Robert Furnival—*b/o* William Shakespeare's play.
MARC ANTONY: Roman political leader and general who, when Julius Caesar is assassinated in 44 B.C., rises to power by exposing and defeating the conspirators responsible for the killing.
Jason Robards, John Gielgud, Richard Johnson, Robert Vaughn, Richard Chamberlain, Diana Rigg, Christopher Lee, Jill Bennett, Alan Browning, Andrew Crawford.

The Omega Man (1971, WB). *d:* Boris Sagal; *p:* Walter Seltzer; *sc:* John William Corrington and Joyce H. Corrington—*b/o* the novel *I Am Legend* by Richard Matheson.
ROBERT NEVILLE: Only normal survivor of a plague—caused by germ warfare in the year 1977—who tries to stay alive in a desolated Los Angeles as he battles survivors who have turned into vampires.
Anthony Zerbe, Rosalind Cash, Paul Koslo, Eric Lanewille.

Skyjacked (1972, MGM). *d:* John Guillermin; *p:* Walter Seltzer; *sc:* Stanley R. Greenberg—*b/o* the novel *Hijacked* by David Harper.
CAPT. HANK O'HARA: Pilot of a Boeing 707 flying from Los Angeles to Minneapolis who, when the plane is hijacked by a deranged U.S. Army officer, is forced to fly to Moscow.
Yvette Mimieux, James Brolin, Claude Akins, Jeanne Crain, Susan Day, Roosevelt Grier, Mariette Hartley, Walter Pidgeon, Leslie Uggams.

Call of the Wild (1972, MGM). *d:* Ken Annakin; *p:* Harry Alan Towers (Massfilms/CCC/Izaro/ Oceania/UPF); *sc:* Peter Wellbeck (Harry Alan Towers), Wyn Wells, and Peter Yeldman—*b/o* the novel by Jack London.
JOHN THORNTON: Prospector during the early-1900s Klondike gold rush who befriends a loyal sled dog named Buck.
Michele Mercier, Raimund Harmstorf, George Eastman, Maria Rohm, Rik Battaglia.

Antony and Cleopatra (1972, AIP). *d:* Charlton Heston; *p:* Peter Snell (Transac/Izaro/Folio); *sc:* Charlton Heston—*b/o* William Shakespeare's play.
MARC ANTONY: Roman political leader and general who—after deserting his wife, Octavia, to live in Alexandria with Cleopatra, the queen of Egypt—is defeated at the Battle of Actium and commits suicide by falling on his own sword.
Hildegard Neil, Eric Porter, John Castle, Fernando Rey, Juan Luis Galiardo, Freddie Jones, Peter Arne, Roger Delgado.

Soylent Green (1973, MGM). *d:* Richard Fleischer; *p:* Walter Seltzer and Russell Thacher; *sc:* Stanley R. Greenberg—*b/o* the novel *Make Room! Make Room!* by Harry Harrison.
DETECTIVE THORN: Hardboiled police detective—living in polluted, overpopulated New York City in the year 2022—who investigates the murder of a big shot and discovers that "Soylent Green" (the people's principal food) is made of humans.
Leigh Taylor-Young, Chuck Connors, Joseph Cotten, Brock Peters, Paula Kelly, Edward G. Robinson, Stephen Young, Mike Henry, Whit Bissell, Jane Dulo, Dick Van Patten, Tim Herbert, Carlos Romero.

The Three Musketeers (1973, 20th-Fox). *d:* Richard Lester; *p:* Alexander Salkind (Film Trust); *sc:* George MacDonald Fraser—*b/o* the novel by Alexandre Dumas.
CARDINAL RICHELIEU: Seventeenth-century French cardinal and power behind the throne of King Louis XIII who, in order to gain more power, tries to expose a secret love affair between Queen Anne and England's Duke of Buckingham.
Michael York, Oliver Reed, Raquel Welch, Richard Chamberlain, Frank Finlay, Faye Dunaway, Christopher Lee, Geraldine Chaplin, Jean-Pierre Cassel, Simon Ward, Spike Milligan.

The Four Musketeers (1974, 20th-Fox). *d:* Richard Lester; *p:* Alexander Salkind and Michael Salkind (Film Trust/Este); *sc:* George MacDonald Fraser—*b/o* the novel by Alexandre Dumas.
CARDINAL RICHELIEU: French cardinal and power behind the throne of King Louis XIII in seventeenth-century France who, to gain more power, plots to reveal a secret love affair between Queen Anne and England's Duke of Buckingham.
Michael York, Oliver Reed, Richard Chamberlain, Frank Finlay, Raquel Welch, Faye Dunaway, Christopher Lee, Simon Ward, Geraldine Chaplin, Jean-Pierre Cassel, Roy Kinnear.

Airport 1975 (1974, Univ.). *d:* Jack Smight; *p:* Jennings Lang and William Frye; *sc:* Don Ingalls—inspired by the film *Airport* and *b/o* the novel by Arthur Hailey.
MURDOCK: Former jet pilot and airline troubleshooter who, when a 747 jet and its crew are disabled by a collision with a private aircraft, transfers from a helicopter to the cockpit of the 747 while the stewardess is maneuvering the plane.
Karen Black, George Kennedy, Efram Zimbalist Jr., Susan Clark, Helen Reddy, Linda Blair, Dana Andrews, Roy Thinnes, Sid Caesar, Myrna Loy, Ed Nelson, Nancy Olson, Larry Storch, Martha Scott, Jerry Stiller, Guy Stockwell, Gloria Swanson.

Earthquake (1974, Univ.). *d:* Mark Robson; *p:*

Jennings Lang and Mark Robson (Lang–Robson–Filmmakers); *sc:* George Fox and Mario Puzo.

STUART GRAFF: Construction executive who, while trapped in a flooded storm drain during a devastating earthquake, sacrifices his life when he tries in vain to rescue his wife.

Ava Gardner, George Kennedy, Lorne Green, Genevieve Bujold, Richard Roundtree, Marjoe Gortner, Victoria Principal, Walter Matuschanskayasky (Walter Matthau).

Midway (1976, Univ.). *d:* Jack Smight; *p:* Walter Mirisch (Mirisch); *sc:* Donald S. Sanford.

CAPT. MATT GARTH: WWII U.S. Navy pilot who loses his life when he single-handedly sinks a Japanese aircraft carrier in the Pacific during the June 1942 Battle of Midway.

Henry Fonda, Toshiro Mifune, Edward Albert, Robert Mitchum, James Shigeta, James Coburn, Glenn Ford, Hal Holbrook, Cliff Robertson, Ed Nelson, Robert Wagner, Robert Webber, Monte Markham, Kevin Dobson, Biff McGuire, Christopher George, Glenn Corbett, Dabney Coleman.

Two-Minute Warning (1976, Univ.). *d:* Larry Peerce; *p:* Edward S. Feldman (Filmways); *sc:* Edward Hume—*b/o* the novel by George La Fountaine.

CAPT. PETER HOLLY: Police captain whose job it is—along with a SWAT team—to track down a maniacal sniper who's killing fans during a championship football game in the Los Angeles Coliseum.

John Cassavetes, Beau Bridges, Martin Balsam, Jack Klugman, Gena Rowlands, David Janssen, Walter Pidgeon, Marilyn Hassett, Brock Peters, Mitchell Ryan, Merv Griffin, Howard Cossell, Frank Gifford.

The Last Hard Men (1976, 20th-Fox). *d:* Andrew V. McLaglen; *p:* William Belasco (Belasco–Seltzer–Thacher); *sc:* Guerdon Trueblood—*b/o* the novel *Gun Down* by Brian Garfield.

SAM BURGADE: Retired sheriff in early-1900s Arizona who, when his daughter is kidnapped by a half-breed Navajo, is lured into pursuing the outlaw—who has plans to slowly and brutally kill him.

James Coburn, Barbara Hershey, Jorge Rivero, Michael Parks, Christopher Mitchum.

Crossed Swords (1978, WB). *d:* Richard Fleischer; *p:* Pierre Spengler; *sc:* Berta Dominguez, Pierre Spengler, and George MacDonald Fraser—*b/o* Mark Twain's novel *The Prince and the Pauper.*

HENRY VIII: Sixteenth-century king of England whose son, young Prince Edward, secretly changes places with a ragged London beggar boy who is the prince's look-alike.

Oliver Reed, Raquel Welch, Mark Lester, Ernest Borgnine, George C. Scott, Rex Harrison, David Hemmings.

Gray Lady Down (1978, Univ.). *d:* David Greene; *p:* Walter Mirisch (Mirisch); *sc:* James Whittaker and Howard Sackler (adaptation by Frank P. Rosenberg)—*b/o* the novel *Event 1000* by David Lavallee.

CAPT. PAUL BLANCHARD: Skipper of the nuclear-powered U.S. Navy submarine *Neptune,* which—when it's rammed by a Norwegian freighter near Cape Cod—sinks to an ocean ledge 1400 feet below the surface, necessitating an urgent rescue attempt.

David Carradine, Stacy Keach, Ned Beatty, Stephen McHattie, Ronny Cox, Dorian Harewood, Rosemary Forsyth, Hilly Hicks, Charles Cioffi, William Jordon, Jack Rader, Christopher Reeve.

The Mountain Men (1980, Col.). *d:* Richard Lang; *p:* Martin Shafer and Andrew Scheinman; *sc:* Fraser Clarke Heston.

BILL TYLER: Grizzled Wyoming fur trapper who battles an Indian chief over a beautiful Indian girl he's fallen in love with.

Brian Keith, Victoria Racimo, Stephen Macht, John Glover, Seymour Cassel, David Ackroyd, Cal Bellini, Bill Lucking, Victor Jory, Tim Haldeman, Buckley Norris.

The Awakening (1980, Orion). *d:* Mike Newell; *p:* Robert Solo, Andrew Scheinman, and Martin Shafer; *sc:* Allan Scott, Chris Bryant, and Clive Exton—*b/o* Bram Stoker's novel *The Jewel of Seven Stars.*

MATTHEW CORBECK: Archaeologist who enters the secret tomb of the Egyptian Queen Kara and unleashes her evil spirit, which takes over the body of his newborn daughter.

Susannah York, Jill Townsend, Stephanie Zimbalist, Patrick Drury, Bruce Myers, Nadim Sawalha, Ian McDiarmid, Ahmed Osman, Miriam Margolyes, Chris Fairbanks.

Search for the Mother Lode . . . the Last Great Treasure! (1983, RKR Releasing). *d:* Charlton Heston; *p:* Fraser Heston (Agamemnon Films); *sc:* Fraser Heston.

(Dual role) SILAS McGEE: Evil old Scottish-born miner in the mountains of British Columbia who—obsessed with making a big gold strike—has been mining the same claim for nearly thirty years and who, when a Canadian bush pilot and his young female companion encroach upon his diggings, plots to do them in.

IAN McGEE: Mentally unbalanced, bagpipe-playing twin brother of Silas who mysteriously lurks about the mine and is killed by the bush-pilot, who mistakenly thinks that Ian is Silas.

Nick Mancuso, Kim Basinger, John Marley, Dale Wilson, Ricky Zantolas, Marie George.

☆ WILLIAM HOLDEN

William Franklin Beedle Jr.

b: April 17, 1918, O'Fallon, Ill.
found dead: Oct. 16, 1981, Santa Monica, Cal.

"If I ever run into any of you bums on a street corner, just let's pretend we never met before."

Sefton (William Holden) to his fellow POWs as he starts his escape from a WWII German prison camp in *Stalag 17*, 1953.

Golden Boy (1939, Col.). *d:* Rouben Mamoulian; *p:* William Perlberg; *sc:* Lewis Meltzer, Daniel Taradash, Sarah Y. Mason, and Victor Heerman—*b/o* the play by Clifford Odets.

JOE BONAPARTE: Sensitive young violin student who gives up a promising career in music to become a top prizefighter but is shattered when he breaks his hand and kills an opponent in the ring.

Barbara Stanwyck, Adolphe Menjou, Lee J. Cobb, Joseph Calleia, Sam Levene, Edward S. Brophy, Don Beddoe, Frank Jenks, Charles Halton, John Wray.

Invisible Stripes (1939, WB). *d:* Lloyd Bacon; *p:* Hal B. Wallis; *sc:* Warren Duff—*b/o* a story by Jonathan Finn, from the book by Warden Lewis E. Lawes.

TIM TAYLOR: Ex-convict's hot-headed younger brother who, in order to make money to get married, turns to crime but is steered back to the straight and narrow by the older brother.

George Raft, Jane Bryan, Humphrey Bogart, Flora Robson, Paul Kelly, Lee Patrick, Henry O'Neill, Frankie Thomas, Moroni Olsen, Marc Lawrence, Leo Gorcey, William Haade, Tully Marshall.

Our Town (1940, UA). *d:* Sam Wood; *p:* Sol Lesser (Principal Artists); *sc:* Thornton Wilder, Frank Craven, and Harry Chandler—*b/o* the Pulitzer Prize–winning play by Thornton Wilder.

GEORGE GIBBS: Doctor's son in the small turn-of-the-century town of Grover's Corners, New Hampshire, who falls in love with and marries the local newspaper editor's daughter but loses her when she dies.

Frank Craven, Martha Scott, Fay Bainter, Beulah Bondi, Thomas Mitchell, Guy Kibbee, Stuart Erwin, Doro Merande, Spencer Charters, Dix Davis.

Those Were the Days (1940, Para.). *d:* J. Theodore Reed; *p:* J. Theodore Reed; *sc:* Don Hartman—*b/o The Siwash Stories* by George Fitch.

P. J. "PETEY" SIMMONS: Brash mischief-making student at a small Midwestern college ("Old Siwash") in 1904 whose pranks are continually getting him into hot water.

Bonita Granville, Ezra Stone, Judith Barrett, Lucien Littlefield, Richard Denning, Phillip Terry, Douglas Kennedy, Gaylord Pendleton, Alan Ladd, James Dodd.

Arizona (1941, Col.). *d:* Wesley Ruggles; *p:* Wesley Ruggles; *sc:* Claude Binyon—*b/o* a story by Clarence Budington Kelland.

PETER MUNCIE: Itinerant Missouri cowboy who falls for a gun-slinging frontier woman in 1860s Tucson and helps her fight the villains who are sabotaging her wagon trains.

Jean Arthur, Warren William, Porter Hall, Paul Harvey, George Chandler, Byron Foulger, Regis Toomey, Edgar Buchanan, Syd Saylor, Wade Crosby, Addison Richards.

I Wanted Wings (1941, Para.).*d:* Mitchell Leisen; *p:* Arthur Hornblow Jr.; *sc:* Richard Maibaum, Lt. Beirne Lay Jr., and Sid Herzig—*b/o* a story by Eleanor Griffin and Frank Wead, from the book by Lt. Beirne Lay Jr.

AL LUDLOW: Sincere young garage mechanic who becomes a U.S. Army Air Corps cadet but ruins his career when he gets mixed up with a beautiful but conniving blonde.

Ray Milland, Wayne Morris, Brian Donlevy, Constance Moore, Veronica Lake, Harry Davenport, Edward Fielding, Richard Lane, Addison Richards, Hobart Cavanaugh, Richard Webb.

Texas (1941, Col.). *d:* George Marshall; *p:* Sam Bischoff; *sc:* Horace McCoy, Lewis Meltzer, and Michael Blankfort—*b/o* a story by Lewis Meltzer and Michael Blankfort.

DAN THOMAS: Confederate Army veteran in 1866 Texas who—when he becomes a cattle rustler—finds himself pitted against his ex–Army buddy, who works for a pretty cattle rancher.

Glenn Ford, Claire Trevor, George Bancroft, Edgar Buchanan, Don Beddoe, Andrew Tombes, Addison Richards, Joseph Crehan, Willard Robertson, Edward Cobb.

The Remarkable Andrew (1942, Para.). *d:* Stuart Heisler; *p:* Richard Blumenthal; *sc:* Dalton Trumbo—*b/o* his novel.

ANDREW LONG: Small-town courthouse clerk who, when he's framed by crooked politicians, is helped by the ghosts of Andrew Jackson and other assorted historical characters.

Ellen Drew, Brian Donlevy, Rod Cameron, Richard Webb, Porter Hall, Frances Gifford, Nydia Westman, Montagu Love, Jimmy Conlin, Spencer Charters, Tom Fadden, Minor Watson.

The Fleet's In (1942, Para.). *d:* Victor Schertzinger; *p:* Paul Jones; *sc:* Walter De Leon, Sid Silvers, and Ralph Spence—*b/o* a story by Monte Brice and J. Walter Rubin, and the play *Sailor Beware!* by Kenyon Nicholson and Charles Robinson.

CASEY KIRBY: Shy sailor on leave in San Francisco who mistakenly gets the reputation of being a Romeo and is pushed by his shipmates into a bet that he can kiss a glamorous but standoffish nightclub entertainer.

Dorothy Lamour, Eddie Bracken, Betty Hutton, Cass Daley, Gil Lamb, Leif Erickson, Betty Jane Rhodes, Jack Norton, Jimmy Dorsey and His Band.

Meet the Stewarts (1942, Col.). *d:* Alfred E. Green; *p:* Robert Sparks; *sc:* Karen DeWolf—*b/o* the Candy and Mike Stewart magazine stories by Elizabeth Dunn.

MICHAEL STEWART: Young white-collar worker who, when he marries a spoiled heiress, insists that they live on his salary—leading to a variety of marital problems.

Frances Dee, Grant Mitchell, Marjorie Gateson, Ann Revere, Ann Gillis, Margaret Hamilton, Don Beddoe, Mary Gordon, Edward Gargan, Tom Dugan.

Young and Willing (1943, UA). *d:* Edward H. Griffith; *p:* Edward H. Griffith (Para.); *sc:* Virginia Van Upp—*b/o* the play *Out of the Frying Pan* by Francis Swann.

NORMAN REESE: One of several struggling actors and actresses who share a large apartment in a Manhattan boarding house as they try to interest a big theatrical producer in a great play they've discovered.

Eddie Bracken, Robert Benchley, Susan Hayward, Martha O'Driscoll, Barbara Britton, James Brown, Paul Hurst, Olin Howlin, Billy Bevan.

Blaze of Noon (1947, Para.). *d:* John Farrow; *p:* Robert Fellows; *sc:* Frank Wead and Arthur Sheekman—*b/o* the novel by Ernest K. Gann.

COLIN McDONALD: Young 1920s flyer—one of four pioneer airmail-pilot brothers—who marries a nurse, then is torn between her fears about his risky occupation and his love of flying.

Anne Baxter, William Bendix, Sonny Tufts, Sterling Hayden, Howard da Silva, Johnny Sands, Jean Wallace, Lloyd Corrigan, Dick Hogan, Will Wright.

Dear Ruth (1947, Para.). *d:* William D. Russell; *p:*
Paul Jones; *sc:* Arthur Sheekman—*b/o* the play by Norman Krasna.

LT. WILLIAM SEACROFT: WWII Air Force bombardier who, when he makes a surprise visit to the home of a pretty young woman he's fallen in love with by correspondence, discovers that her young schoolgirl sister really wrote the letters.

Joan Caulfield, Edward Arnold, Mary Philips, Mona Freeman, Billy De Wolfe, Virginia Welles, Irving Bacon, Isabel Randolph.

Rachel and the Stranger (1948, RKO). *d:* Norman Foster; *p:* Richard H. Berger; *sc:* Waldo Salt—*b/o* the story "Rachel" by Howard Fast.

BIG DAVEY: Backwoods widower in the early 1800s Northwest who, when he buys a bondswoman for $22 to do his work and raise his son, at first ignores her but finally—when an itinerant hunter tries to take her away from him—realizes he loves her.

Loretta Young, Robert Mitchum, Gary Gray, Tom Tully, Sara Haden, Frank Ferguson, Walter Baldwin, Regina Wallace.

Apartment for Peggy (1948, 20th-Fox). *d:* George Seaton; *p:* William Perlberg; *sc:* George Seaton—*b/o* a story by Faith Baldwin.

JASON: Young WWII veteran struggling through college on the G.I. Bill who, with his bride, moves into an attic apartment in the home of a despondent retired professor.

Jeanne Crain, Edmund Gwenn, Gene Lockhart, Griff Barnett, Randy Stuart, Marion Marshall, Almira Sessions, Charles Lane, Ray Walker, Gene Nelson, Hal K. Dawson.

The Dark Past (1948, Col.). *d:* Rudolph Mate; *p:* Buddy Adler; *sc:* Philip MacDonald, Michael Blankfort, and Albert Duffy (adaptation by Malvin Wald and Oscar Saul)—*b/o* the play *Blind Alley* by James Warwick.

AL WALKER: Ruthless killer who, when he breaks out of prison and holds a psychiatrist and his family as hostages, is analyzed by the psychiatrist and learns what turned him into a criminal.

Nina Foch, Lee J. Cobb, Adele Jergens, Stephen Dunne, Lois Maxwell, Barry Kroeger, Steven Geray, Robert Osterloh, Ellen Corby.

The Man from Colorado (1949, Col.). *d:* Henry Levin; *p:* Jules Schermer; *sc:* Robert D. Andrews and Ben Maddow—*b/o* a story by Borden Chase.

CAPT. DEL STEWART: Ex–Union Army Civil War officer who, when he becomes a Colorado marshal, finds himself pitted against his former colonel, now a Federal judge who has turned into a sadistic psychopath.

Glenn Ford, Ellen Drew, Ray Collins, Edgar Buchanan, Jerome Courtland, James Millican,

Jim Bannon, William "Bill" Phillips, Denver Pyle, Ian MacDonald, Stanley Andrews, Myron Healey, Craig Reynolds.

Streets of Laredo (1949, Para.). *d:* Leslie Fenton; *p:* Robert Fellows; *sc:* Charles Marquis Warren—*b/o* a story by Louis Stevens and Elizabeth Hill.
JIM DAWKINS: Ex-outlaw who, after he and his sidekick join the Texas Rangers, is ordered to hunt down their old friend who has stayed on the wrong side of the law.
William Bendix, MacDonald Carey, Mona Freeman, Stanley Ridges, Alfonso Bedoya, Ray Teal, Clem Bevans, James Bell.

Miss Grant Takes Richmond (1949, Col.). *d:* Lloyd Bacon; *p:* S. Sylvan Simon; *sc:* Nat Perrin, Devery Freeman, and Frank Tashman—*b/o* a story by Devery Freeman.
DICK RICHMOND: Glib head of a bookie gang who—when he hires a wacky, not-too-bright secretary to innocently represent the gang's real estate office (a cover for their gambling business)—falls for her and goes legit.
Lucille Ball, Janis Carter, James Gleason, Gloria Henry, Frank McHugh, George Cleveland, Stephen Dunne, Will Wright, Roy Roberts, Charles Lane, Harry Harvey.

Dear Wife (1950, Para.). *d:* Richard Haydn; *p:* Richard Maibaum; *sc:* Arthur Sheekman and N. Richard Nash—*b/o* characters created by Norman Krasna.
BILL SEACROFT: Young husband whose teen-age sister-in-law maneuvers him into running for the state senate—which leads to problems with his father-in-law, who happens to be running for the same seat.
Joan Caulfield, Billy De Wolfe, Mona Freeman, Edward Arnold, Arleen Whelan, Mary Philips, Harry Von Zell, Elisabeth Fraser, Irving Bacon, Gordon Jones, Don Beddoe, Richard Haydn.

Father Is a Bachelor (1950, Col.). *d:* Norman Foster and Abby Berlin; *p:* S. Sylvan Simon; *sc:* Allen Leslie and James Edward Grant—*b/o* a story by James Edward Grant.
JOHNNY RUTLEDGE: Roustabout bachelor who becomes involved with a traveling medicine show, five young orphans, and the daughter of a local judge who's out to change his (Rutledge's) marital status.
Coleen Gray, Mary Jane Saunders, Charles Winninger, Stuart Erwin, Clinton Sundberg, Gary Gray, Sig Ruman, Billy Gray, Lloyd Corrigan, Arthur Space.

Sunset Boulevard (1950, Para.). *d:* Billy Wilder; *p:* Charles Brackett; *sc:* Charles Brackett, Billy Wilder, and D. M. Marshman Jr.—*b/o* the story "A Can of Beans" by Charles Brackett and Billy Wilder.

JOE GILLIS*: Young Hollywood hack screenwriter who meets with disaster when he moves into the Gothic mansion of an aging and demented has-been silent movie queen and becomes her kept lover.
Gloria Swanson, Erich von Stroheim, Nancy Olson, Fred Clark, Lloyd Gough, Jack Webb, Franklyn Farnum, Cecil B. DeMille, Hedda Hopper, Buster Keaton, Anna Q. Nilsson, H. B. Warner, Ray Evans, Jay Livingston.

Union Station (1950, Para.). *d:* Rudolph Mate; *p:* Jules Schermer; *sc:* Sydney Boehm—*b/o* a story by Thomas Walsh.
POLICE LT. WILLIAM CALHOUN: Chief of the railway police of a metropolitan terminal who, when the blind daughter of a wealthy man is kidnapped, heads a manhunt for the kidnappers in the bustling station where the payoff is to take place.
Nancy Olson, Barry Fitzgerald, Lyle Bettger, Jan Sterling, Allene Roberts, Herbert Heyes, Parley E. Baer, Harry Hayden.

Born Yesterday (1950, Col.). *d:* George Cukor; *p:* S. Sylvan Simon; *sc:* Albert Manheimer—*b/o* the play by Garson Kanin.
PAUL VERRALL: Scholarly young journalist in Washington, D.C., who is hired by a crooked junkyard tycoon to teach his dumb ex–chorus girl mistress how to talk and act like a "high-class dame."
Broderick Crawford, Judy Holliday, Howard St. John, Frank Otto, Larry Oliver, Barbara Brown, Grandon Rhodes, Claire Carleton.

Force of Arms (1951, WB). *d:* Michael Curtiz; *p:* Anthony Veiller; *sc:* Orin Jannings—*b/o* a story by Richard Tregaskis.
PETERSON: WWII American infantry sergeant on the Italian front who wins a battlefield commission, falls for and marries a WAC lieutenant, is wounded and reported missing in action, but finally is reconciled with her.
Nancy Olson, Frank Lovejoy, Gene Evans, Dick Wesson, Paul Picerni, Katherine Warren, Ross Ford, Slats Taylor, Ron Hagerthy, Bob Roark.

Submarine Command (1952, Para.). *d:* John Farrow; *p:* Joseph Sistrom; *sc:* Jonathan Latimer.
COMMANDER WHITE: U.S. submarine skipper in the Korean War who is filled with self-doubt about his questionable past performance under fire but ultimately turns out to be a hero.
Nancy Olson, William Bendix, Don Taylor, Arthur Franz, Darryl Hickman, Peggy Webber, Moroni Olsen, Jack Gregson, Jack Kelly, Don Dunning, Charles Meredith, Philip Van Zandt.

---

*Received an Academy Award nomination as Best Actor for this role.

Boots Malone (1952, Col.). *d:* William Dieterle; *p:* Milton Holmes; *sc:* Milton Holmes.

BOOTS MALONE: Shady jockey's agent who trains a rich teen-ager to be a jockey, then tells him he has to throw a big race or be killed by gamblers who have bet against him.

Johnny Stewart, Stanley Clements, Basil Ruysdael, Carl Benton Reid, Ralph Dumke, Ed Begley, Henry Morgan (Harry Morgan), Anna Lee, Anthony Caruso, Whit Bissell, Harry Shannon.

The Turning Point (1952, Para.). *d:* William Dieterle; *p:* Irving Asher; *sc:* Warren Duff—*b/o* a story by Horace McCoy.

JERRY McKIBBON: Crusading newspaper reporter who, while helping an old friend—the head of a state crime investigation committee—get the goods on the mob and discovers that the friend's cop father is mixed up with the crooks.

Edmond O'Brien, Alexis Smith, Tom Tully, Ed Begley, Don Dayton, Adele Longmire, Ray Teal, Ted De Corsia, Don Porter, Howard Freeman, Neville Brand.

Stalag 17 (1953, Para.). *d:* Billy Wilder; *p:* Billy Wilder; *sc:* Billy Wilder and Edwin Blum—*b/o* the play by Donald Bevan and Edmund Trczinski.

SEFTON*: Cocky, cynical American sergeant in a WWII Nazi prison camp who, after he is beaten up by the other prisoners in his barracks when they suspect him of being a German spy, determines to ferret out the real informer.

Don Taylor, Otto Preminger, Robert Strauss, Harvey Lembeck, Richard Erdman, Peter Graves, Neville Brand, Sig Ruman, Michael Moore, Peter Baldwin, Gil Stratton Jr., Edmund Trczinski, Ross Bagdasarian.

The Moon Is Blue (1953, UA). *d:* Otto Preminger; *p:* Otto Preminger and F. Hugh Herbert (Otto Preminger); *sc:* F. Hugh Herbert—*b/o* his play.

DONALD GRESHAM: Romance-minded young architect who competes with a middle-aged playboy for the affections of a savvy young woman determined to resist would-be wolves while holding out for a wedding ring.

David Niven, Maggie McNamara, Tom Tully, Dawn Addams, Fortunio Bonanova, Gregory Ratoff.

Forever Female (1953, Para.). *d:* Irving Rapper; *p:* Pat Duggan; *sc:* Julius J. Epstein and Philip G. Epstein—*b/o* the play *Rosalind* by James M. Barrie.

STANLEY KROWN: Supermarket clerk–turned–playwright who sells his play to a Broadway producer whose ex-wife insists on starring in it, even though she's far too old for the part.

---

*Won the Academy Award as Best Actor for this role.

Ginger Rogers, Paul Douglas, Pat Crowley, James Gleason, Jesse White, Marjorie Rambeau, George Reeves, King Donovan, Vic Perrin, Marion Ross, Almira Sessions, Hyacinthe Railla.

Escape from Fort Bravo (1954, MGM). *d:* John Sturges; *p:* Nicholas Nayfack; *sc:* Frank Fenton—*b/o* a story by Philip Rock and Michael Pate.

CAPTAIN ROPER: Civil War Union Army officer who, when his Confederate prisoners escape from a Yankee fort in Arizona, pursues and recaptures them but then has to fight off an Indian ambush.

Eleanor Parker, John Forsythe, William Demarest, William Campbell, John Lupton, Richard Anderson, Polly Bergen, Carl Benton Reid.

Executive Suite (1954, MGM). *d:* Robert Wise; *p:* John Houseman; *sc:* Ernest Lehman—*b/o* the novel by Cameron Hawley.

McDONALD WALLING: Idealistic young designer for a major furniture-manufacturing firm who becomes embroiled in a power struggle with several other company executives after his firm's president suddenly drops dead.

Fredric March, Barbara Stanwyck, June Allyson, Walter Pidgeon, Shelley Winters, Paul Douglas, Louis Calhern, Dean Jagger, Nina Foch, Tim Considine, William Phipps, Virginia Brissac, Harry Shannon.

Sabrina (1954, Para.). *d:* Billy Wilder; *p:* Billy Wilder; *sc:* Billy Wilder, Samuel Taylor, and Ernest Lehman—*b/o* the play *Sabrina Fair* by Samuel Taylor.

DAVID LARRABEE: Playboy son of a wealthy Long Island family who romances the pretty daughter of the family chauffeur but finally loses her to his stuffy older business-tycoon brother.

Humphrey Bogart, Audrey Hepburn, Walter Hampden, John Williams, Martha Hyer, Marcel Dalio, Nella Walker, Francis X. Bushman, Ellen Corby.

The Country Girl (1954, Para.). *d:* George Seaton; *p:* William Perlberg and George Seaton; *sc:* George Seaton—*b/o* the play by Clifford Odets.

BERNIE DODD: Broadway director who, while trying to help a has-been alcoholic singing star stage a comeback, falls in love with the singer's embittered wife.

Bing Crosby, Grace Kelly, Anthony Ross, Gene Reynolds, Robert Kent, Ida Moore, Hal K. Dawson, Charles Tannen, Jon Provost.

The Bridges at Toko-Ri (1955, Para.).*d:* Mark Robson; *p:* William Perlberg (Perlberg–Seaton); *sc:* Valentine Davies—*b/o* the novel by James A. Michener.

LT. HARRY BRUBAKER: Peace-loving Denver family man and lawyer who, when he's called back into service as a U.S. Navy jet pilot in the Korean War, is sent on a fatal mission to bomb strategic enemy bridges.

Fredric March, Grace Kelly, Mickey Rooney, Robert Strauss, Charles McGraw, Keiko Awaji, Earl Holliman, Richard Shannon, Willis B. Bouchey, Charles Tannen.

Love Is a Many-Splendored Thing (1955, 20th-Fox). *d:* Henry King; *p:* Buddy Adler; *sc:* John Patrick—*b/o* the novel *A Many-Splend′,ed Thing* by Han Suyin.

MARK ELLIOTT: Married American war correspondent in Hong Kong during the Korean War who has a passionate love affair with a glamorous Eurasian doctor.

Jennifer Jones, Torin Thatcher, Isobel Elsom, Murray Matheson, Ann Richards, Richard Loo, Soo Yong, Philip Ahn, Candace Lee, Kom Tong.

Picnic (1956, Col.). *d:* Joshua Logan; *p:* Fred Kohlmar; *sc:* Daniel Taradash—*b/o* the play by William Inge.

HAL CARTER: Smooth-talking drifter who arrives in the town of Salinson, Kansas, to look up an old schoolmate, arouses the ladies—young and old alike—and skips town with the schoolmate's girlfriend.

Rosalind Russell, Kim Novak, Betty Field, Susan Strasberg, Cliff Robertson, Arthur O'Connell, Verna Felton, Reta Shaw, Nick Adams, Raymond Bailey, Phyllis Newman, Don C. Harvey.

The Proud and the Profane (1956, Para.). *d:* George Seaton; *p:* William Perlberg; *sc:* George Seaton—*b/o* a novel by Lucy Herndon Crockett.

LT. COL. COLIN BLACK: Tough, ruthless WWII U.S. Marine officer who, though he has an alcoholic wife back in the States, falls in love with a widowed American Red Cross worker on the island of New Caledonia and impregnates her.

Deborah Kerr, Thelma Ritter, Dewey Martin, William Redfield, Ross Bagdasarian, Adam Williams, Marion Ross, Richard Shannon, Peter Hansen, Ward Wood, Jack Richardson, Robert Morse, Ray Stricklyn.

Toward the Unknown (1956, WB). *d:* Mervyn LeRoy; *p:* Mervyn LeRoy (Toluca); *sc:* Beirne Lay Jr.

MAJ. LINCOLN BOND: Post–Korean War Air Force test pilot who, while involved in X-2 experimental flights, competes with his commanding general over a woman and also has to deal with the stigma of having broken under Korean Communist brainwashing.

Lloyd Nolan, Virginia Leith, Charles McGraw, Murray Hamilton, Paul Fix, James Garner, L. Q. Jones, Karen Steele, Malcolm Atterbury, Bartlett Robinson, Ralph Moody.

The Bridge on the River Kwai (1957, Col.). *d:* David Lean; *p:* Sam Spiegel (Horizon); *sc:* Pierre Boulle—*b/o* his novel.

SHEARS: American sailor—posing as a commander in a WWII Japanese prison camp in Burma—who escapes but returns with a British raiding party to destroy the bridge the Japanese have forced British prisoners to build.

Alec Guinness, Jack Hawkins, Sessue Hayakawa, James Donald, Geoffrey Horne, Andre Morell, Peter Williams, John Boxer, Percy Herbert, Harold Goodwin, Ann Sears.

The Key (1958, Col.). *d:* Carol Reed; *p:* Carl Foreman (Highroad); *sc:* Carl Foreman—*b/o* the novel *Stella* by Jan de Hartog.

DAVID ROSS: American WWII tugboat skipper in the Canadian service who becomes one of a succession of sea captains receiving duplicate keys to the apartment of a woman who tries to give them happiness before they face possible death on hazardous missions.

Sophia Loren, Trevor Howard, Oscar Homolka, Kieron Moore, Bernard Lee, Beatrix Lehman, Noel Purcell, Bryan Forbes.

The Horse Soldiers (1959, UA). *d:* John Ford; *p:* John Lee Mahin and Martin Rackin (Mahin–Rackin/Mirisch); *sc:* John Lee Mahin and Martin Rackin—*b/o* the novel by Harold Sinclair.

MAJ. HANK KENDALL: Union Army Surgeon Major in 1863 whose different philosophy about war leads to a clash with the cavalry colonel in command as they infiltrate deep into Confederate territory to destroy a railroad supply center in Mississippi.

John Wayne, Constance Towers, Althea Gibson, Hoot Gibson, Anna Lee, Russell Simpson, Basil Ruysdael, Denver Pyle, Strother Martin, Hank Worden, Walter Reed, Jack Pennick.

The World of Suzie Wong (1960, Para.). *d:* Richard Quine; *p:* Ray Stark (Ray Stark Prod.); *sc:* John Patrick—*b/o* the novel by Richard Mason and the play by Paul Osborn.

ROBERT LOMAX: American architect who, when he takes a year's sabbatical in Hong Kong to try to become an artist, falls in love with his model—a Hong Kong prostitute.

Nancy Kwan, Sylvia Syms, Michael Wilding, Lawrence Naismith, Jacqueline Chan, Andy Ho, Bernard Cribbins, Yvonne Shima.

Satan Never Sleeps (1962, 20th-Fox). *d:* Leo McCarey; *p:* Leo McCarey; *sc:* Claude Binyon and Leo McCarey—*b/o* Pearl S. Buck's novel *The China Story.*

FATHER O'BANION: One of two American missionary priests in 1949 China who defy the Chinese communists when they invade the village where the priests are based.

Clifton Webb, France Nuyen, Athene Seyler, Martin Benson, Edith Sharpe, Robert Lee, Weaver Lee, Andy Ho, Anthony Chinn.

The Counterfeit Traitor (1962, Para.). *d:* George Seaton; *p:* William Perlberg (Perlberg–Seaton); *sc:* George Seaton—*b/o* the book by Alexander Klein.
ERIC ERICKSON: American-born Swedish citizen and oil importer who, when he's friendly with the Nazis and does business with them during WWII, is thought to be a traitor—but in reality is a spy for British intelligence.
Lilli Palmer, Hugh Griffith, Ernst Schroder, Eva Dahlbeck, Ulf Palme, Carl Raddatz, Helo Gutschwager, Erica Beer.

The Lion (1962, 20th-Fox). *d:* Jack Cardiff; *p:* Samuel G. Engel; *sc:* Irene Kamp and Louis Kamp—*b/o* the novel by Joseph Kessel.
ROBERT HAYWARD: American lawyer who, at the request of his ex-wife, visits her and her game-warden husband in Kenya because of concern over the lawyer and ex-wife's eleven-year-old daughter, whose best friend is a lion.
Trevor Howard, Capucine, Pamela Franklin, Makara Kwaiha Ramadhani, Zakee, Paul Oduor, Samuel Obiero Romboh, Christopher Agunda, Zamba the Lion.

Paris When It Sizzles (1964, Para.). *d:* Richard Quine; *p:* Richard Quine and George Axelrod; *sc:* George Axelrod—*b/o* a story by Julien Duvivier and Henri Jeanson.
RICHARD BENSON: American screenwriter who, when he's given forty-eight hours to finish a script for Noel Coward, hires a pretty secretary and—while acting out each scene with her—falls in love with her.
Audrey Hepburn, Gregoire Aslan, Noel Coward, Ramond Bussieres, Christian Duvallex.

The Seventh Dawn (1964, UA). *d:* Lewis Gilbert; *p:* Charles K. Feldman and Karl Tunberg (Holdean Prod.); *sc:* Karl Tunberg—*b/o* Michael Keon's novel *The Durian Tree.*
FERRIS: Rubber-plantation owner in 1953 Malaya who finds himself fighting terrorists headed by his best friend, a Malayan who helped him fight the Japanese in WWII.
Susannah York, Capucine, Tetsuro Tambo, Michael Goodlife, Allan Cuthbertson, Maurice Denham, Beulah Quo, Yap Mook Fui.

Alvarez Kelly (1966, Col.). *d:* Edward Dmytryk; *p:* Sol C. Siegel; *sc:* Franklin Coen and Elliott Arnold—*b/o* a story by Franklin Coen.
ALVAREZ KELLY: Mexican-American cattleman who sells a large herd of cattle to the Union Army during the Civil War, then is kidnapped by a Confederate colonel who forces him to help the Rebels try to steal the cattle for the South.

Richard Widmark, Janice Rule, Patrick O'Neal, Victoria Shaw, Roger C. Carmel, Richard Rust, Arthur Franz, Donald Barry, Duke Hobbie, Harry Carey Jr., Indus Arthur.

Casino Royale (1967, Col.). *d:* John Huston, Kenneth Hughes, Val Guest, Robert Parrish, and Joseph McGrath; *p:* Charles K. Feldman and Jerry Bresler (Famous Artists); *sc:* Wolf Mankowitz, John Law, and Michael Sayers—*b/o* the novel by Ian Fleming.
RANSOME: One of a group of international agents who ask the famous agent 007, James Bond, to come out of retirement and fight SMERSH's evil plans for eradicating most of the world's secret agents.
Peter Sellers, Ursula Andress, David Niven, Orson Welles, Joanna Pettet, Daliah Lavi, Woody Allen, Charles Boyer, John Huston, Kurt Kasznar, George Raft, Jean-Paul Belmondo, Jacky Bisset (Jacqueline Bisset).

The Devil's Brigade (1968, UA). *d:* Andrew V. McLaglen; *p:* David L. Wolper (Wolper Prod.); *sc:* William Roberts—*b/o* the book by Robert H. Adleman.
LT. COL. ROBERT T. FREDERICK: WWII American Army officer who trains a special commando force—to be used for combat in Norway and Italy—made up of misfit American G.I.s and crack Canadian commandos.
Cliff Robertson, Vince Edwards, Michael Rennie, Dana Andrews, Gretchen Wyler, Andrew Prine, Claude Akins, Carroll O'Connor, Richard Jaeckel, Paul Hornung, Gene Fullmer, Jeremy Slate, Richard Dawson, Harry Carey, Patric Knowles, James Craig.

The Wild Bunch (1969, WB–Seven Arts). *d:* Sam Peckinpah; *p:* Phil Feldman; *sc:* Walon Green and Sam Peckinpah—*b/o* a story by Walon Green and Roy N. Sickner.
PIKE BISHOP: Leader of a 1914 Texas gang of hardened, cynical outlaws who, after they're chased into Mexico by bounty hunters, are hired by a rebel Mexican general to rob an Army munitions train; they wind up in a bloody battle with the general when he and his bandits doublecross them.
Ernest Borgnine, Robert Ryan, Edmond O'Brien, Warren Oates, Jaime Sanchez, Ben Johnson, Strother Martin, L. Q. Jones, Pat Harrington, Bo Hopkins, Dub Taylor.

The Christmas Tree (1969, Walter Reade–Continental). *d:* Terence Young; *p:* Robert Dorfmann (Corona/Jupiter); *sc:* Terence Young—*b/o* the novel *L'Arbre de Noel* by Michel Bataille.
LAURENT: Millionaire French-American widower who, when his eleven-year-old son is accidentally contaminated by radiation and contracts

leukemia, devotes himself to making the boy's remaining few months as happy as possible.

Virna Lisi, Andre Bourvil, Brook Fuller, Madeleine Damien, Friedrich Ledebur, Mario Feliciani.

Wild Rovers (1971, MGM). *d:* Blake Edwards; *p:* Blake Edwards and Ken Wales (Geoffrey); *sc:* Blake Edwards.

ROSS BODINE: Middle-aged cowpoke in the 1880s who teams up with a younger cowhand to rob a bank, then is forced to hightail it to Mexico with a relentless posse in hot pursuit and finally—along with his cohort—is killed.

Ryan O'Neal, Karl Malden, Lynn Carlin, Tom Skerritt, Joe Don Baker, James Olson, Leora Dana, Moses Gunn, Victor French, Rachel Roberts, Alan Carney.

The Revengers (1972, Nat. Gen.). *d:* Daniel Mann; *p:* Martin Rackin (Martin Rackin Prod./Cinema Center); *sc:* Wendell Mayes—*b/o* a story by Steven W. Carabatsos.

JOHN BENEDICT: Civil War veteran–Colorado rancher who, when his wife and children are massacred by Comanches led by a white renegade, forms a posse of six condemned killers from a Mexican prison and sets out for revenge.

Susan Hayward, Ernest Borgnine, Woody Strode, Roger Hanin, Rene Koldehoffe, Jorge Luke, Arthur Hunnicutt, Larry Pennell, Scott Holden, James Daughton.

Breezy (1973, Univ.). *d:* Clint Eastwood (Univ./Malpaso); *p:* Robert Daley; *sc:* Jo Heims.

FRANK HARMON: World-weary, divorced fifty-year-old real estate agent in Los Angeles who gains a new lease on life when he has an affair with a seventeen-year-old "flower child."

Kay Lenz, Dennis Olivieri, Marj Dusay, Eugene Peterson, Joan Hotchkis, Roger C. Carmel, Shelley Morrison, Jamie Smith Jackson, Scott Holden.

Open Season (1974, Col.). *d:* Peter Collinson; *p:* George H. Brown and Jose S. Vicuna (Impala/Arpa); *sc:* David Osborn and Liz Charles Williams.

WOLKOWSKI: Vengeance-seeking father who—after his daughter has been kidnapped, tortured, raped, and then, along with her lover, hunted with guns like an animal—kills the three sadistic Vietnam War veterans who did it.

Peter Fonda, Cornelia Sharpe, John Phillip Law, Richard Lynch, Albert Mendoza.

The Towering Inferno (1974, 20th-Fox & WB). *d:* John Guillermin and Irwin Allen; *p:* Irwin Allen; *sc:* Stirling Silliphant—*b/o* the novels *The Tower* by Richard Martin Stern and *The Glass Inferno* by Thomas M. Scortia and Frank M. Robinson.

JAMES DUNCAN: Developer-builder of the world's tallest building—a 138-story glass-and-steel San Francisco skyscraper—which suffers a disastrous fire on the night of its opening.

Paul Newman, Steve McQueen, Faye Dunaway, Fred Astaire, Jennifer Jones, Susan Blakely, Richard Chamberlain, O. J. Simpson, Robert Vaughn, Robert Wagner, Susan Flannery, Don Gordon, Jack Collins, Dabney Coleman.

Network (1976, UA). *d:* Sidney Lumet; *p:* Howard Gottfried and Fred Caruso (MGM); *sc:* Paddy Chayefsky.

MAX SCHUMACHER*: TV network's news division chief who, while abandoning his wife to have an affair with a ruthless female programming executive, sticks by his mentally unbalanced anchorman colleague, who's being cynically exploited by management.

Faye Dunaway, Peter Finch, Robert Duvall, Wesley Addy, Ned Beatty, Arthur Burghardt, Darryl Hickman, William Prince, Sasha von Scherler, Beatrice Straight, Marlene Warfield.

Damien—Omen II (1978, 20th-Fox). *d:* Don Taylor; *p:* Harvey Bernhard; *sc:* Stanley Mann and Michael Hodges—*b/o* a story by Harvey Bernhard and on characters created by David Seltzer.

RICHARD THORN: Wealthy Chicagoan who gradually comes to the horrifying realization, after a number of grisly murders occur, that his thirteen-year-old nephew is really the demon child of the Devil.

Lee Grant, Jonathan Scott-Taylor, Robert Foxworth, Nicholas Pryor, Lew Ayres, Sylvia Sidney, Lance Hendriksen, Elizabeth Shepherd, Lucas Donat, Allan Arbus, Fritz Ford, Meshach Taylor, John J. Newcombe.

Fedora (1978, UA). *d:* Billy Wilder; *p:* Billy Wilder (Geria/SFP); *sc:* Billy Wilder and I. A. L. Diamond—*b/o* the story "Fedora" from Thomas Tryon's book *Crowned Heads*.

BARRY "DUTCH" DETWEILER: Down-and-out Hollywood film producer who, when he goes to a remote Greek island to try to lure a legendary retired movie star (now in her sixties) back into pictures, is startled to find her youth and beauty unchanged.

Marthe Keller, Jose Ferrer, Frances Sternhagen, Mario Adorf, Stephen Collins, Hans Jaray, Gottfried John, Henry Fonda, Hildegard Knef, Michael York, Panos Papadopulos, Elma Karlowa, Christoph Kunzer.

Ashanti (1979, Col.). *d:* Richard Fleischer; *p:* George-Alain Vuille (George-Alain Vuille); *sc:* Stephen Geller—*b/o* the novel *Ebano* by Alberto Vasquez-Figueroa.

---

*Received an Academy Award nomination as Best Actor for this role.

JIM SANDELL: Mercenary helicopter pilot who aids a World Health Organization white doctor in his pursuit of a modern-day Arabian slave trader who has kidnapped the doctor's beautiful black wife.

Michael Caine, Peter Ustinov, Beverly Johnson, Omar Sharif, Rex Harrison, Zia Mohyeddin, Tyrone Jackson, Johnny Sekka.

When Time Ran Out (1980, WB). *d:* James Goldstone; *p:* Irwin Allen; *sc:* Carl Foreman and Stirling Silliphant—*b/o* Gordon Thomas and Max Morgan Witts's novel *The Day the World Ended.*

SHELBY GILMORE: Wealthy owner of a plush Hawaii resort hotel who is one of a group of people trying to escape disaster when an island volcano erupts.

Paul Newman, Jacqueline Bisset, Edward Albert, Red Buttons, Barbara Carrera, Valentina Cortesa, Veronica Hamel, Alex Karras, Burgess Meredith, Ernest Borgnine, James Franciscus.

The Earthling (1981, Filmways). *d:* Peter Collinson; *p:* Stephen W. Sharmat, Elliot Schick, and John Strong; *sc:* Lanny Cotler.

PATRICK FOLEY: Cynical, terminally ill world traveler and loner who, when he returns to his birthplace in the Australian bush country,

encounters a young boy whose parents have been killed in an accident, takes him under his wing, and—before he dies—teaches the boy how to survive in the wilds so that he can safely find his way back to civilization.

Ricky Schroder, Jack Thompson, Olivia Hamnett, Jane Harders, Alwyn Kurts, Redmond Phillips, Walter Pym, Harry Neilson.

S.O.B. (1981, Para.). *d:* Blake Edwards; *p:* Blake Edwards and Tony Adams (Lorimar); *sc:* Blake Edwards.

TIM CULLEY: Amiable, hard-drinking Hollywood film director of a $30 million flop musical that becomes a hit after the film's producer (whose wife is the star) turns it into a soft-core porno extravaganza.

Julie Andrews, Marisa Berenson, Larry Hagman, Robert Loggia, Stuart Margolin, Richard Mulligan, Robert Preston, Craig Stevens, Loretta Swit, Robert Vaughn, Robert Webber, Shelley Winters, Benson Fong, Larry Storch, Virginia Gregg, Gene Nelson.

• In addition, William Holden made a cameo/guest appearance in the following feature film: *Variety Girl* (1947, Para.).

☆ BOB HOPE

Leslie Townes Hope

b: May 29, 1903, Eltham, London, England

"How did you get into that dress—with a spray gun?"

Hot Lips Barton (Bob Hope) to Lucia Maria de Andrade (Dorothy Lamour) in Road to Rio, 1947.

The Big Broadcast of 1938 (1938, Para.). *d:* Mitchell Leisen; *p:* Harlan Thompson; *sc:* Walter De Leon, Francis Martin, and Ken Englund (adaptation by Howard Lindsay and Russel Crouse)—*b/o* a story by Frederick Hazlitt Brennan.

BUZZ FIELDING: Radio announcer who, along with his three alimony-seeking ex-wives, is aboard an ocean liner that's competing in a transatlantic race.

W. C. Fields, Martha Raye, Dorothy Lamour, Shirley Ross, Lynne Overman, Ben Blue, Leif Erikson, Grace Bradley, Rufe Davis, Russell

Hicks, Tito Guizar, Shep Fields and His Orchestra.

College Swing (1938, Para.). *d:* Raoul Walsh; *p:* Lewis Gensler; *sc:* Walter De Leon and Francis Martin—*b/o* a story by Frederick Hazlitt Brennan (from an idea by Ted Lesser).

BUD BRADY: Brash manager of a group of vaudeville performers who are hired as teachers by a scatterbrained woman who has inherited a small-town college.

George Burns, Gracie Allen, Martha Raye, Edward Everett Horton, Ben Blue, Betty Grable, Jackie Coogan, John Payne, Robert Cummings, Skinnay Ennis, Slate Brothers, Jerry Colonna, Charles Trowbridge, Tully Marshall.

Give Me a Sailor (1938, Para.). *d:* Elliott Nugent; *p:* Jeff Lazarus; *sc:* Doris Anderson and Frank Butler—*b/o* a play by Anne Nichols.

JIM BREWSTER: Footloose Navy officer who, with a fellow officer, gets involved in romantic shenanigans with two sisters—one pretty, one plain.

Martha Raye, Betty Grable, Jack Whiting,

Clarence Kolb, J. C. Nugent, Bonnie Jean Churchill, Nana Bryant.

Thanks for the Memory (1938, Para.). *d:* George Archainbaud; *p:* Mel Shauer; *sc:* Lynn Starling—*b/o* a play by Albert Hackett and Francis Goodrich.

STEVE MERRICK: Writer whose newlywed wife goes back to work as a model to support him while he tries to turn out the Great American Novel.

Shirley Ross, Charles Butterworth, Otto Kruger, Hedda Hopper, Patricia Wilder, Roscoe Karns, Laura Hope Crews, William Collier Sr., Edward Gargan, Emma Dunn, Eddie Anderson, Jack Norton.

Never Say Die (1939, Para.). *d:* Elliott Nugent; *p:* Paul Jones; *sc:* Don Hartman, Frank Butler, and Preston Sturges—*b/o* a play by William H. Post.

JOHN KIDLEY: Millionaire hypochondriac who, when he's mistakenly told that he has less than a month to live, nobly marries a young woman so that she can inherit his fortune and then marry her real beau.

Martha Raye, Andy Devine, Alan Mowbray, Gale Sondergaard, Sig Rumann, Ernest Cossart, Paul Harvey, Frances Arms, Ivan Simpson, Monty Woolley, Foy Van Dolsen, Christian Rub.

Some Like It Hot (1939, Para.). *d:* George Archainbaud; *p:* William C. Thomas; *sc:* Lewis R. Foster and Wilkie C. Mahoney—*b/o* a play by Ben Hecht and Gene Fowler.

NICKY NELSON: Fast-talking barker and owner of a boardwalk amusement parlor who runs out of money and loses his girl-friend—but finds a way to recoup both.

Shirley Ross, Una Merkel, Gene Krupa, Rufe Davis, Frank Sully, Bernadene Hayes, Richard Denning, Clarence H. Wilson, Dudley Dickerson, Harry Barris, Edgar Dearing, Jack Smart.

The Cat and the Canary (1939, Para.). *d:* Elliott Nugent; *p:* Arthur Hornblow Jr.; *sc:* Walter De Leon and Lynn Starling—*b/o* a play by John Willard.

WALLIE CAMPBELL: Mystery-novel buff who, though he's scared stiff, manages to solve three murders that take place at a spooky old bayou mansion when prospective heirs to a fortune gather for the reading of the will.

Paulette Goddard, John Beal, Douglass Montgomery, Gale Sondergaard, Elizabeth Patterson, Nydia Westman, George Zucco, John Wray, George Regas.

Road to Singapore (1940, Para.). *d:* Victor Schertzinger; *p:* Harlan Thompson; *sc:* Don Hartman and Frank Butler—*b/o* a story by Harry Hervey.

ACE LANNIGAN: One of a duo of sea-going pals who, after they escape to an exotic South Seas island in order to elude two women bent on matrimony, immediately get involved with a beautiful native girl.

Bing Crosby, Dorothy Lamour, Charles Coburn, Judith Barrett, Anthony Quinn, Jerry Colonna, Johnny Arthur, Pierre Watkin, Gaylord Pendleton, Miles Mander, John Kelly, Ed Gargan, Kitty Kelly.

The Ghost Breakers (1940, Para.). *d:* George Marshall; *p:* Arthur Hornblow Jr.; *sc:* Walter De Leon—*b/o* a play by Paul Dickey and Charles Goddard.

LARRY LAWRENCE: Radio commentator who runs into ghosts, zombies, and buried treasure when he gets involved with a beautiful young woman who has inherited a haunted castle in Cuba.

Paulette Goddard, Richard Carlson, Paul Lukas, Anthony Quinn, Willie Best, Pedro De Cordoba, Virginia Brissac, Noble Johnson, Tom Dugan, Paul Fix, Lloyd Corrigan.

Road to Zanzibar (1941, Para.). *d:* Victor Schertzinger; *p:* Paul Jones; *sc:* Frank Butler and Don Hartman—*b/o* a story by Don Hartman and Sy Bartlett.

FEARLESS (HUBERT) FRAZIER: Gullible half of a duo of carnival hustlers who, after they sell a phony diamond mine, take it on the lam to darkest Africa and are conned by a pair of stranded American women into taking them along on a safari.

Bing Crosby, Dorothy Lamour, Una Merkel, Eric Blore, Luis Alberni, Joan Marsh, Ethel Greer, Iris Adrian, Georges Renavent, Douglass Dumbrille, Lionel Royce, Leo Gorcey, Robert Middlemass, Norma Varden, Paul Porcasi.

Caught in the Draft (1941, Para.). *d:* David Butler; *p:* B. G. DeSylva; *sc:* Harry Tugend (with additional dialogue by Wilkie C. Mahoney).

DON BOLTON: Draft-dodging movie star who, while trying to impress the pretty daughter of a U.S. Army colonel, accidentally enlists in the Army.

Dorothy Lamour, Lynne Overman, Eddie Bracken, Clarence Kolb, Paul Hurst, Ferike Boros, Phyllis Ruth, Irving Bacon, Arthur Loft, Edgar Dearing, Andrew Tombes.

Nothing But the Truth (1941, Para.). *d:* Elliott Nugent; *p:* Arthur Hornblow Jr.; *sc:* Don Hartman and Ken Englund—*b/o* a play by James Montgomery and a novel by Frederic S. Isham.

STEVE BENNET: Stockbroker who makes a $10,000 bet with three fellow stockbrokers that he can tell "nothing but the truth" for twenty-four hours.

Paulette Goddard, Edward Arnold, Leif Erikson, Glenn Anders, Helen Vinson, Grant Mitchell, Willie Best, Clarence Kolb, Rose Hobart, Leon Belasco, Dick Chandler.

Louisiana Purchase (1941, Para.). *d:* Irving Cummings; *p:* Harold Wilson; *sc:* Jerome Chodorov and Joseph Fields—*b/o* a story by B. G. DeSylva, from the musical by Morrie Ryskind.

JIM TAYLOR: Young state legislator who is forced by his crooked associates of the Louisiana Purchasing Co. to try to frame a U.S. senator planning to investigate the company.

Vera Zorina, Victor Moore, Irene Bordoni, Dona Drake, Raymond Walburn, Maxie Rosenbloom, Frank Albertson, Donald McBride, Andrew Tombes, Robert Warwick, Emory Parnell, Iris Meredith, Jack Norton, Barbara Britton, Jean Wallace, Louise La Planche.

My Favorite Blonde (1942, Para.). *d:* Sidney Lanfield; *p:* Paul Jones; *sc:* Don Hartman and Frank Butler—*b/o* a story by Melvin Frank and Norman Panama.

LARRY HAINES: Small-time variety-show performer who is pursued by Nazi agents when he agrees to help an attractive blonde British spy deliver secret instructions from the British government to an airplane factory in Los Angeles.

Madeleine Carroll, Gale Sondergaard, George Zucco, Victor Varconi, Lionel Royce, Crane Whitley, Otto Reichow, Charles Cain, Walter Kingsford, Erville Alderson.

Road to Morocco (1942, Para.). *d:* David Butler; *d:* Paul Jones; *sc:* Frank Butler and Don Hartman.

TURKEY (ORVILLE) JACKSON: One of two shipwrecked pals who wind up in Morocco, where they encounter Arab palaces, a captive princess, and talking camels.

Bing Crosby, Dorothy Lamour, Anthony Quinn, Dona Drake, Mikhail Rasumny, Vladimir Sokoloff, George Givot, Andrew Tombes, Leon Belasco, Monte Blue, Louise La Planche, Yvonne De Carlo, Poppy Wilde, Dan Seymour, Richard Loo.

They Got Me Covered (1943, RKO). *d:* David Butler; *p:* Samuel Goldwyn (Samuel Goldwyn Prod.); *sc:* Harry Kurnitz—*b/o* a story by Leonard Q. Ross and Leonard Spigelgass.

ROBERT KITTREDGE: Inept WWII American foreign correspondent in Moscow who, when he misses a big story (the German invasion of Russia), is called back to Washington and fired but wins his job back when he inadvertently breaks up an Axis spy ring.

Dorothy Lamour, Lenore Aubert, Otto Preminger, Eduardo Ciannelli, Marion Martin, Donald Meek, Philip Ahn, Donald McBride, Mary Treen, Florence Bates, Walter Catlett, John Abbott, Frank Sully.

Let's Face It (1943, Para.). *d:* Sidney Lanfield; *p:* Fred Kohlmar; *sc:* Harry Tugend—*b/o* the musical play by Dorothy Fields, Herbert Fields, and Cole Porter.

JERRY WALKER: One of a trio of G.I.s who, after they are hired to act as gigolos by three wives trying to get even with their unfaithful husbands, wind up in trouble when their own jealous girlfriends discover the scheme.

Betty Hutton, ZaSu Pitts, Phyllis Povah, Dave Willock, Eve Arden, Cully Richards, Marjorie Weaver, Dona Drake, Raymond Walburn, Andrew Tombes, Arthur Loft, Joe Sawyer.

The Princess and the Pirate (1944, RKO). *d:* David Butler; *p:* Don Hartman (Samuel Goldwyn Prod.); *sc:* Don Hartman, Melville Shavelson, and Everett Freeman (adaptation by Allen Boretz and Curtis Kenyon)—*b/o* a story by Sy Bartlett.

SYLVESTER THE GREAT: Hammy eighteenth-century English actor who, when he sails on a ship for America, is captured—along with a beautiful princess—by buccaneers on the Spanish Main.

Virginia Mayo, Walter Brennan, Walter Slezak, Victor McLaglen, Marc Kuznetzoff, Brandon Hurst, Tom Kennedy, Stanley Andrews, Robert Warwick.

Road to Utopia (1945, Para.). *d:* Hal Walker; *p:* Paul Jones; *sc:* Norman Panama and Melvin Frank.

CHESTER HOOTON: One of a pair of con men–vaudevillians who, when they head for the Klondike to strike it rich, steal the deed to a gold mine from two killers.

Bing Crosby, Dorothy Lamour, Douglas Dumbrille, Hillary Brooke, Jack La Rue, Robert Barrat, Nestor Paiva, Robert Benchley, Will Wright, Billy Benedict, Arthur Loft, Jim Thorpe.

Monsieur Beaucaire (1946, Para.). *d:* George Marshall; *p:* Paul Jones; *sc:* Melvin Frank and Norman Panama—*b/o* the novel by Booth Tarkington.

MONSIEUR BEAUCAIRE: Bumbling barber in the French court of Louis XV who gets into trouble, escapes the guillotine, and flees to the Spanish court—where he masquerades as a dashing count.

Joan Caulfield, Patric Knowles, Marjorie Reynolds, Cecil Kellaway, Joseph Schildkraut, Reginald Owen, Constance Collier, Hillary Brooke, Fortunio Bonanova, Leonid Kinskey, Howard Freeman.

My Favorite Brunette (1947, Para.). *d:* Elliott Nugent; *p:* Daniel Dare; *sc:* Edmund Beloin and Jack Rose.

RONNIE JACKSON: Baby photographer who turns detective to help a woman out of a jam, then finds himself framed for the murder of a government official.

Dorothy Lamour, Peter Lorre, Lon Chaney Jr., John Hoyt, Charles Dingle, Reginald Denny, Frank Puglia, Ann Doran, Willard Robertson, Jack La Rue.

Where There's Life (1947, Para.). *d:* Sidney Lanfield; *p:* Paul Jones; *sc:* Allen Boretz and Melville Shavelson—*b/o* a story by Melville Shavelson.

MICHAEL VALENTINE: New York disc jockey who doesn't know he's the legitimate heir to the throne of a small European country—until a delegation headed by a female general shows up to "escort" him there.

Signe Hasso, William Bendix, George Coulouris, Vera Marshe, George Zucco, Dennis Hoey, John Alexander, Victor Varconi, Joseph Vitale, Harry Von Zell.

Road to Rio (1947, Para.). *d:* Norman Z. McLeod; *p:* Daniel Dare; *sc:* Edmund Beloin and Jack Rose.

HOT LIPS BARTON: One of a pair of broke musicians who accidentally burn down a carnival, stow away on a liner to Rio de Janeiro, and save a pretty young woman and her money from her sinister aunt.

Bing Crosby, Dorothy Lamour, Gale Sondergaard, Frank Faylen, Joseph Vitale, Frank Puglia, Nestor Paiva, Robert Barrat, Jerry Colonna, The Wiere Brothers, The Andrews Sisters, Charles Middleton, Ray Teal.

The Paleface (1948, Para.). *d:* Norman Z. McLeod; *p:* Robert L. Welch; *sc:* Edmund Hartmann and Frank Tashlin.

PAINLESS POTTER: Inept correspondence-school dentist in the Wild West who becomes a reluctant hero when, with Calamity Jane's help, he captures villains who've been selling arms to the Indians.

Jane Russell, Robert Armstrong, Iris Adrian, Jack Searl, Joseph Vitale, Charles Trowbridge, Clem Bevans, Jeff York, Stanley Andrews, Wade Crosby, Chief Yowlachie, Iron Eyes Cody.

Sorrowful Jones (1949, Para.).*d:* Sidney Lanfield; *p:* Robert L. Welch; *sc:* Melville Shavelson, Edmund Hartmann, and Jack Rose—*b/o* the story by Damon Runyon.

SORROWFUL JONES: Racetrack bookie who, after taking a bet from a man who leaves his small daughter as collateral, becomes the child's foster father when the bettor is killed by gangsters.

Lucille Ball, William Demarest, Bruce Cabot, Thomas Gomez, Tom Pedi, Paul Lees, Housley Stevenson, Ben Weldon, Mary Jane Saunders.

The Great Lover (1949, Para.). *d:* Alexander

Hall; *p:* Edmund Beloin; *sc:* Edmund Beloin, Melville Shavelson, and Jack Rose.

FREDDIE HUNTER: Reporter and boy-scout leader who, while taking his troop to Europe on an ocean liner, becomes involved with a beautiful duchess and a card-playing murderer.

Rhonda Fleming, Roland Young, Roland Culver, Richard Lyon, Gary Gray, Jerry Hunter, Jackie Jackson, George Reeves, Jim Backus, Sig Arno.

Fancy Pants (1950, Para.). *d:* George Marshall; *p:* Robert Welch; *sc:* Edmund Hartmann and Robert O'Brien—*b/o* the novel *Ruggles of Red Gap* by Harry Leon Wilson.

HUMPHRY: English actor-turned-butler who is brought to a New Mexico cow town by a nouveau riche, social-climbing woman and is mistakenly taken for an earl by the townfolk.

Lucille Ball, Bruce Cabot, Jack Kirkwood, Lea Penman, Hugh French, Eric Blore, Joseph Vitale, John Anderson, Norma Varden, Virginia Kelley, Colin Keith-Johnston, Joe Wong.

The Lemon Drop Kid (1951, Para.). *d:* Sidney Lanfield; *p:* Robert L. Welch; *sc:* Edmund Hartmann and Robert O'Brien (adaptation by Edmund Beloin)—*b/o* a story by Damon Runyon.

THE LEMON DROP KID: Fast-talking racetrack tout who gets into hot water by giving out some bad tips and has to come up with $10,000 for the mob or else.

Marilyn Maxwell, Lloyd Nolan, Jane Darwell, Andrea King, Fred Clark, Jay C. Flippen, William Frawley, Harry Bellaver, Sid Melton, Ben Welden, Ida Moore, Francis Pierlot, Charles Cooley.

My Favorite Spy (1951, Para.). *d:* Norman Z. McLeod; *p:* Paul Jones; *sc:* Edmund Hartmann and Jack Sher (with additional dialogue by Hal Kanter)—*b/o* a story and adaptation by Edmund Beloin and Lou Breslow.

(Dual role) PEANUTS WHITE: Burlesque comic who, when government agents discover that he's a look-alike for the notorious spy Eric Augustine, is talked into impersonating Augustine on an important mission to Tangier.

ERIC AUGUSTINE: Suave, sophisticated, notorious European spy.

Hedy Lamarr, Francis L. Sullivan, Arnold Moss, Tonio Selwart, Stephen Chase, John Archer, Morris Ankrum, Marc Lawrence, Iris Adrian, Mike Mazurki, Luis Van Rooten, Ralph Smiley.

Son of Paleface (1952, Para.). *d:* Frank Tashlin; *p:* Robert Welch; *sc:* Frank Tashlin, Robert L. Welch, and Joseph Quillan.

JUNIOR POTTER: Tenderfoot Harvard-graduate son of the pioneer dentist and Indian fighter Painless Potter who, when he goes out West to claim his inheritance, becomes involved with a female bandit known as "The Torch."

Jane Russell, Roy Rogers, Bill Williams, Lloyd Corrigan, Paul E. Burns, Douglas Dumbrille, Harry Von Zell, Iron Eyes Cody, Wee Willie Davis, Charley Cooley.

Road to Bali (1952, Para.). *d:* Hal Walker; *p:* Harry Tugend; *sc:* Frank Butler, Hal Kanter, and William Morrow—*b/o* a story by Frank Butler and Harry Tugend.

HAROLD GRIDLEY: One of a duo of American vaudevillians who flee from some angry Australian fathers to a South Seas island, fall for a sarong-clad princess, and wind up as deep-sea divers hired by a potentate to recover sunken treasure.

Bing Crosby, Dorothy Lamour, Murvyn Vye, Peter Coe, Ralph Moody, Leon Askin, Michael Ansara, Carolyn Jones, Bob Crosby.

Off Limits (1953, Para.). *d:* George Marshall; *p:* Harry Tugend; *sc:* Hal Kanter and Jack Sher—*b/o* a story by Hal Kanter.

WALLY HOGAN: Prize-fight manager who enlists in the Army to stay with his drafted fighter but—when he's bilked out of his share of the fight profits—develops another G.I. into a champion boxer.

Mickey Rooney, Marilyn Maxwell, Eddie Mayehoff, Stanley Clements, Jack Dempsey, Marvin Miller, John Ridgely, Tom Harmon, Norman Leavitt, Art Aragon, Kim Spalding, Mike Mahoney.

Here Come the Girls (1953, Para.). *d:* Claude Binyon; *p:* Paul Jones; *sc:* Edmund Hartmann and Hal Kanter—*b/o* a story by Edmund Hartmann.

STANLEY SNODGRASS: Broadway chorus boy who thinks he's made it big when he's substituted for the leading man in a musical but is really being used as a clay pigeon—because "Jack the Slasher" plans to murder the lead.

Arlene Dahl, Rosemary Clooney, Tony Martin, Millard Mitchell, William Demarest, Fred Clark, Robert Strauss, Zamah Cunningham, Frank Orth, The Four Step Brothers, Hugh Sanders, Inesita.

Casanova's Big Night (1954, Para.). *d:* Norman Z. McLeod; *p:* Paul Jones; *sc:* Hal Kanter and Edmund Hartmann—*b/o* a story by Aubrey Wisberg.

PIPPO POPPOLINE: A tailor's assistant in eighteenth-century Venice who poses as the great lover Casanova and finds himself up to his neck in court intrigue.

Joan Fontaine, Audrey Dalton, Basil Rathbone, Vincent Price, Hugh Marlowe, Arnold Moss, John Carradine, John Hoyt, Hope Emerson, Robert Hutton, Lon Chaney, Raymond Burr, Frieda Inescort, Primo Carnera.

The Seven Little Foys (1955, Para.). *d:* Melville Shavelson; *p:* Jack Rose; *sc:* Melville Shavelson and Jack Rose.

EDDIE FOY: Popular American vaudeville star who, after his ballet-dancer wife dies, puts his seven children into his act and calls the group "The Singing and Dancing Foys."

Milly Vitale, George Tobias, Angela Clarke, Billy Gray, Jimmy Baird, James Cagney, Lester Matthews, Milton Frome, King Donovan, Jimmy Conlin, Dabs Greer, Joe Flynn, Lewis Martin.

That Certain Feeling (1956, Para.). *d:* Norman Panama and Melvin Frank; *p:* Norman Panama and Melvin Frank; *sc:* Norman Panama, Melvin Frank, I. A. L. Diamond, and William Altman—*b/o* a play by Jean Kerr and Eleanor Brooke.

FRANCIS X. DIGNAN: Unknown artist who is hired on the sly by his ex-wife's arrogant boss, a famous syndicated cartoonist, to "ghost" a popular comic strip.

Eva Marie Saint, George Sanders, Pearl Bailey, David Lewis, Al Capp, Jerry Mathers, Herbert Rudley, Florenz Ames.

The Iron Petticoat (1956, MGM). *d:* Ralph Thomas; *p:* Betty E. Box (Benhar); *sc:* Ben Hecht—*b/o* a story by Harry Saltzman.

MAJ. CHUCK LOCKWOOD: American Air Force pilot who—when a female Russian flyer lands her plane in the American zone of Germany—tries to convert her to democracy, falls for her, and foils Soviet attempts to liquidate them both.

Katharine Hepburn, James Robertson Justice, Robert Helpmann, David Kossoff, Alan Gifford, Paul Carpenter, Noelle Middleton, Nicholas Phipps, Sidney James, Tutte Lemkow.

Beau James (1957, Para.). *d:* Melville Shavelson; *p:* Jack Rose; *sc:* Jack Rose and Melville Shavelson—*b/o* the book by Gene Fowler.

JIMMY WALKER: Dapper mayor of 1920s New York City who runs into political trouble when he has an extra-marital affair with an actress and also is accused of questionable financial practices.

Vera Miles, Paul Douglas, Alexis Smith, Darren McGavin, Joe Mantell, Horace MacMahon, Richard Shannon, Willis Bouchey, Sid Melton, George Jessel, Walter Catlett.

Paris Holiday (1958, UA). *d:* Gerd Oswald; *p:* Bob Hope (Tolda); *sc:* Edmund Beloin and Dean Riesner—*b/o* a story by Bob Hope.

ROBERT LESLIE HUNTER: American actor who goes to Paris to buy a French screenplay but—along with a French comedian—becomes involved with a beautiful spy and a gang of counterfeiters.

Fernandel, Anita Ekberg, Martha Hyer, Preston Sturges, Andre Morell, Alan Gifford, Maurice Teynac, Ives Brainville, Jean Murat.

Alias Jesse James (1959, UA). *d:* Norman Z. McLeod; *p:* Jack Hope (Hope Enterprises); *sc:* William Bowers and Daniel D. Beauchamp—*b/o* a story by Robert St. Aubrey and Bert Lawrence.

MILFORD FARNSWORTH: Inept Coney Island insurance salesman who is mistaken for Jesse James when he's sent out West to cancel Jesse's life insurance policy because the notorious outlaw is considered such a poor risk.

Rhonda Fleming, Wendell Corey, Jim Davis, Gloria Talbott, Will Wright, Mary Young.

The Facts of Life (1960, UA). *d:* Melvin Frank; *p:* Norman Panama (HLP); *sc:* Norman Panama and Melvin Frank.

LARRY GILBERT: Discontented husband who arranges a tryst with the discontented wife of a friend, only to have the affair turn into a ludicrous fiasco.

Lucille Ball, Ruth Hussey, Don DeFore, Louis Nye, Philip Ober, Marianne Stewart, Peter Leeds, Hollis Irving, William Lanteau, Robert F. Simon, Louise Beavers, Mike Mazurki.

Bachelor in Paradise (1961, MGM). *d:* Jack Arnold; *p:* Ted Richmond; *sc:* Valentine Davies and Hal Kanter—*b/o* a story by Vera Caspary.

ADAM J. NILES: Bachelor writer of advice to the lovelorn who upsets a suburban community of married couples when he moves there incognito to write a book about its lifestyle.

Lana Turner, Janis Paige, Jim Hutton, Paula Prentiss, Don Porter, Virginia Grey, Agnes Moorehead, Florence Sundstrom, Clinton Sundberg, John McGiver, Alan Hewitt, Reta Shaw.

Road to Hong Kong (1962, UA). *d:* Norman Panama; *p:* Melvin Frank (Melnor); *sc:* Norman Panama and Melvin Frank.

CHESTER BABCOCK: One of two fast-talking vaudevillians on the run in Hong Kong who become involved with beautiful women, spies, and space ships.

Bing Crosby, Joan Collins, Dorothy Lamour, Robert Morley, Walter Gotell, Roger Delgado, Felix Aylmer, Peter Madden. (Special guest stars: Frank Sinatra, Dean Martin, David Niven, Peter Sellers, Jerry Colonna.)

Critic's Choice (1963, WB). *d:* Don Weis; *p:* Frank P. Rosenberg; *sc:* Jack Sher—*b/o* the play by Ira Levin.

PARKER BALLENTINE: Broadway drama critic who winds up in the doghouse with his wife when he shows up drunk at the opening of a play she has written and gives it a bad review.

Lucille Ball, Marilyn Maxwell, Rip Torn, Jessie Royce Landis, John Dehner, Jim Backus, Marie Windsor, Richard Deacon, Lurene Tuttle, Ernestine Wade, Stanley Adams, Jerome Cowan.

Call Me Bwana (1963, UA). *d:* Gordon Douglas; *p:* Harry Saltzman and Albert R. Broccoli (Rank/Eon); *sc:* Nate Monaster and Johanna Harwood.

MATT MERRIWETHER: Bogus explorer and author of fake African adventure books who is unwittingly sent by the U.S. government to the African jungles to find a lost space capsule before enemy agents can.

Anita Ekberg, Edie Adams, Lionel Jeffries, Arnold Palmer, Percy Herbert, Paul Carpenter, Bari Jonson, Orlando Martins, Al Mulock, Mai Ling.

A Global Affair (1964, MGM). *d:* Jack Arnold; *p:* Hall Bartlett (Seven Arts); *sc:* Arthur Marx, Bob Fisher, and Charles Lederer—*b/o* a story by Eugene Vale.

FRANK LARRIMORE: United Nations department head who, when an abandoned baby is left at the U.N., acts as temporary guardian while female representatives from various countries argue over who should get custody of the child.

Lilo Pulver, Michele Mercier, Elga Andersen, Yvonne De Carlo, Miiko Taka, Robert Sterling, Nehemiah Persoff, John McGiver, Jacques Bergerac, Mickey Shaughnessy.

I'll Take Sweden (1965, UA). *d:* Frederick De Cordova; *p:* Edward Small (Edward Small Prod.); *sc:* Nat Perrin, Bob Fisher, and Arthur Marx—*b/o* a story by Nat Perrin.

BOB HOLCOMB: Widowed oil-company executive who swings a transfer from the U.S. to Sweden to get his daughter away from a motorcycling boyfriend, only to have her fall for a suave playboy.

Tuesday Weld, Frankie Avalon, Dina Merrill, Jeremy Slate, Rosemarie Frankland, Walter Sande, John Qualen, Peter Bourne, Fay De Witt, Alice Frost, Roy Roberts.

Boy, Did I Get a Wrong Number! (1966, UA). *d:* George Marshall; *p:* Edward Small (Edward Small Prod.); *sc:* Burt Styler, Albert E. Lewin, and George Kennett—*b/o* a story by George Beck.

TOM MEADE: Small-town married real estate man who, along with his wacky maid, gets involved with a sexy French movie star who is hiding out during a contract dispute.

Elke Sommer, Phyllis Diller, Cesare Danova, Marjorie Lord, Kelly Thorsden, Benny Baker, Terry Burnham, Joyce Jameson, Harry Von Zell, Kevin Burchett, Keith Taylor, John Todd Roberts.

Eight on the Lam (1967, UA). *d:* George Marshall; *p:* Bill Lawrence (Hope Enterprises); *sc:* Albert E. Lewin, Burt Styler, Bob Fisher, and Arthur Marx—*b/o* a story by Bob Fisher and Arthur Marx.

HENRY DIMSDALE: Widowed bank teller who, when he finds $10,000 and is falsely accused of embezzling bank funds, takes it on the lam with his seven children until he can clear himself.

Phyllis Diller, Jonathan Winters, Shirley Eaton, Jill St. John, Stacey Maxwell, Kevin Brody, Robert Hope, Avis Hope, Debi Storm, Austin Willis, Peter Leeds.

The Private Navy of Sgt. O'Farrell (1968, UA). *d:* Frank Tashlin; *p:* John Beck (Naho); *sc:* Frank Tashlin—*b/o* a story by John L. Greene and Robert M. Fresco.

SERGEANT O'FARRELL: WWII Army non-com on a South Pacific island who, while trying to boost his men's morale by searching for a torpedoed cargo ship loaded with beer, manages to capture a Japanese submarine.

Phyllis Diller, Jeffrey Hunter, Gina Lollobrigida, Mylene Demongeot, John Myhers, Mako, Henry Wilcoxon, Dick Sargent, Christopher Dark, Michael Burns, William Wellman Jr., Robert Donner, Jack Grinnage, William Christopher, John Spina.

How to Commit Marriage (1971, Cinerama). *d:* Norman Panama; *p:* Bill Lawrence (Naho); *sc:* Ben Starr and Michael Kanin.

FRANK BENSON: Father who is dismayed when his daughter—after she learns that he and the mother are planning to divorce—reacts by moving in with her rock-musician boyfriend.

Jackie Gleason, Jane Wyman, Maureen Arthur, Leslie Nielsen, Tina Louise, Paul Stewart, Irwin Corey, Joanna Cameron, Tim Matthieson.

Cancel My Reservation (1972, WB). *d:* Paul Bogart; *p:* Bob Hope and Gordon Oliver (Naho); *sc:* Arthur Marx and Robert Fisher—*b/o* Louis L'Amour's novel *The Broken Gun*.

DAN BARTLETT: Co-host of a New York TV show who argues with his co-host wife over women's rights, goes to an Arizona ranch for a rest, and finds himself implicated in the murder of a young Indian woman.

Eva Marie Saint, Ralph Bellamy, Forrest Tucker, Keenan Wynn, Doodles Weaver, Betty Ann Carr, Chief Dan George, Anne Archer, Herb Vigran, Roy Rowan, Gordon Oliver, Paul Bogart, Buster Shaver.

• In addition, Bob Hope made cameo/guest appearances in the following feature films: *Star Spangled Rhythm* (1942, Para.), *Variety Girl* (1947, Para.), *The Greatest Show on Earth* (1952, Para.), *Scared Stiff* (1953, Para.), *The Five Pennies* (1959, Para.), *Not with My Wife You Don't* (1966, WB), *The Oscar* (1966, Embassy), and *The Muppet Movie* (1979, AFD).

☆ BORIS KARLOFF

William Henry Pratt

b: Nov. 23, 1887, London, England
d: Feb. 2, 1969, Midhurst, Sussex, England

"She hate me. Like others!"

The Monster (Boris Karloff) when The Bride (Elsa Lanchester) looks at him and screams in *The Bride of Frankenstein*, 1935.

His Majesty, the American (1919, UA). *d:* Joseph Henabery; *sc:* Joseph Henabery and Elton Banks.

Villainous member of a gang of spies.

Douglas Fairbanks, Lillian Langton, Frank Campeau, Sam Southern, Marjorie Daw.

The Prince and Betty (1919, Pathe). *d:* Robert Thornby; *sc: b/o* a story by P. G. Wodehouse.

One of the inhabitants of the mythical kingdom of Mervo.

William Desmond, Mary Thurman, Anita Kay, George Swann.

The Deadlier Sex (1920, Pathe). *d:* Robert Thornby; *sc: b/o* a story by Fred Myton.

JULES BORNEY: Murderous French-Canadian fur trapper who intimidates a pretty young woman.

Blanche Sweet, Mahlon Hamilton.

The Courage of Marge O'Doone (1920, Vitagraph). *d:* David Smith; *sc:* Robert North Bradbury—*b/o* the novel by James Oliver Curwood.

Dangerous northwoods trapper.

Pauline Starke, Jack Curtis, Niles Welch, William Dyer.

The Last of the Mohicans (1920, Associated Producers). *d:* Maurice Tourneur and Clarence Brown; *sc:* Robert Dillon—*b/o* the novel by James Fenimore Cooper.

Villainous Indian during the French-Indian War in colonial America.

Wallace Beery, Barbara Bedford, Albert Roscoe, Lillian Hall, Harry Lorraine.

Without Benefit of Clergy (1921, Pathe). *d:* James Young; *sc:* Randolph C. Lewis—*b/o* a story by Rudyard Kipling.

AHMED KAHN: Menacing villain in the mystic Far East.

Virginia Brown Faire, Percy Marmont, Thomas Holding, Evelyn Selbie, Otto Lederer, Nigel De Brulier, Philippe De Lacey.

Cheated Hearts (1921, Univ.). *d:* Hobart Henley; *p:* Carl Laemmle; *sc:* Wallace Clifton—*b/o* the novel *Barry Gordon* by William F. Payson.

NLI HAMED: Villainous Arabian bandit who is at odds with two courageous American brothers in Morocco.

Herbert Rawlinson, Warner Baxter, Marjorie Daw, Doris Pawn, Winter Hall, Murdock MacQuarrie, Anna Lehr, Hector Sarno.

The Cave Girl (1921, FN). *d:* Joseph J. Franz; *sc:* William Parker—*b/o* a play by Guy Bolton and George Middleton.

BAPTISTE: Wicked half-breed in the western wilderness who kidnaps a pretty young woman but is finally bested by her lover.

Teddie Gerard, Charles Meredith, Wilton Taylor, Eleanor Hancock, Lillian Tucker, Frank Coleman, Jake Abrahams, John Beck.

The Man from Downing Street (1922, Vitagraph). *d:* Edward Jose; *p:* Albert E. Smith; *sc:* Bradley J. Smollen—*b/o* a story by Clyde Westover, Lottie Horner, and Florine Williams.

MAHARAJAH JEHAN: Maharajah in India who is suspected by the British Secret Service of being involved in murder and treason.

Earle Williams, Charles Hill Mailes, Betsy Ross Clarke, Kathryn Adams, Herbert Prior, Eugenia Gilbert, James Butler, George Stanley.

The Infidel (1922, FN). *d:* James Young; *p:* B. P. Schulberg; *sc:* James Young—*b/o* a story by Charles A. Logue.

THE NABOB: Murderous ruler of the South Seas island of Menang who burns a village and slaughters some of the island's white settlers.

Katherine MacDonald, Robert Ellis, Joseph Dowling, Melbourne MacDowell, Oleta Otis, Loyola O'Connor.

The Altar Stairs (1922, Univ.). *d:* Lambert Hillyer; *p:* Carl Laemmle; *sc:* Doris Schroeder and George Hively—*b/o* a story by G. B. Lancaster.

HUGO: One of several characters involved in adventure and intrigue on a South Seas island.

Frank Mayo, Louise Lorraine, Lawrence Hughes, J. J. Lanoe, Dagmar Godowsky, Nick De Ruiz.

Omar the Tentmaker (1922, FN). *d:* James Young; *p:* Richard Walton Tully; *sc:* Richard

Walton Tully—*b/o* the play *Omar Khayyam, the Tentmaker* by Richard Walton Tully.

IMAM MOWAFFAK: Sympathetic ruler in the Middle East who is involved in the adventures of young Omar Khayyam.

Guy Bates Post, Virginia Brown Faire, Nigel De Brulier, Noah Beery, Rose Dione, Patsy Ruth Miller, Will Jim Hatton, Evelyn Selbie.

The Woman Conquers (1922, FN). *d:* Tom Forman; *p:* B. P. Schulberg; *sc: b/o* a story by Violet Clark.

RAOUL MARIS: French-Canadian woodsman involved in adventure and intrigue centered around the Hudson Bay area.

Katherine MacDonald, Bryant Washburn, Mitchell Lewis, June Elvidge, Clarissa Selwynne, Francis McDonald.

The Prisoner (1923, Univ.). *d:* Jack Conway; *sc:* Edward T. Lowe—*b/o* the novel *Castle Craneycrow* by George Barr McCutcheon.

PRINCE KAPOLSKI: Nobleman in a mythical European country where murder and duels crop up.

Herbert Rawlinson, Eileen Percy, George Cowl, June Elvidge, Lincoln Stedman, Bertram Grassby, Hayford Hobbs, Esther Ralston.

The Hellion (1924, Sunset). *d:* Bruce Mitchell; *sc:* Bruce Mitchell.

One of the members of an outlaw gang in the West.

Alline Goodwin, William Lester, J. B. Warner, Marin Sais.

Dynamite Dan (1924, Sunset). *d:* Bruce Mitchell; *p:* Anthony J. Xydias; *sc:* Bruce Mitchell.

TONY: Villainous character involved in the boxing game.

Kenneth MacDonald, Frank Rice, Eddie Harris, Diana Alden, Harry Woods, Jack Richardson.

Parisian Nights (1925, FBO). *d:* Alfred Santell; *p:* Gothic Pictures; *sc:* Fred Myton and Doty Hobart—*b/o* a story by Emile Forst.

PIERRE: Brutal Parisian apache who is involved in a gang war.

Elaine Hammerstein, Gaston Glass, Lou Tellegen, Renée Adorée, William J. Kelly.

Forbidden Cargo (1925, FBO). *d:* Tom Buckingham; *sc:* Fred Myton.

PIETRO CASTILLANO: Villainous first mate aboard a ship that illegally runs rum between the U.S. and the Bahamas and whose captain is a woman who falls for a Secret Service agent.

Evelyn Brent, Robert Ellis.

The Prairie Wife (1925, MGM). *d:* Hugo Ballin; *sc:* Hugo Ballin—*b/o* a story by Arthur Stringer.

DIEGO: Mexican half-breed who is involved in the adventures of a young couple who go West to homestead.

Dorothy Devore, Herbert Rawlinson, Gibson Gowland, Leslie Stuart, Frances Prim, Erich von Ritzau, Rupert Franklin.

Lady Robinhood (1925, FBO). *d:* Ralph Ince; *sc:* Fred Myton—*b/o* a story by Clifford Howard and Burke Jenkins.

CABRAZA: Menacing henchman of an evil governor who clashes with a female masked bandit who avenges injustice and aids the poor.

Evelyn Brent, Robert Ellis, William Humphrey, *D'Arcy Corrigan, Robert Cauterio.*

Never the Twain Shall Meet (1925, MGM). *d:* Maurice Tourneur; *sc:* Eugene Mullin—*b/o* a story by Peter B. Kyne.

Villain on a South Seas island who is involved in the adventures of a beautiful native girl, an American businessman, and an American reporter.

Anita Stewart, Bert Lytell, Huntly Gordon, George Siegmann, Lionel Belmore, Princess Marie de Bourbon, James Wang.

The Greater Glory (1926, FN). *d:* Curt Rehfeld; *sc:* June Mathis—*b/o* the novel *Viennese Medley* by Edith O'Shaughnessy.

Billed as "SCISSORS GRINDER": Character in WWI Vienna who is involved in the adventures of the daughter of a wealthy family that disowns her.

Conway Tearle, Anna Q. Nillson, May Allison, Ian Keith, Lucy Beaumont, Jean Hersholt, Nigel De Brulier, Hale Hamilton, Bess Flowers, Marcelle Corday.

Her Honor, the Governor (1926, FBO). *d:* Chet Withey; *sc:* Doris Anderson—*b/o* a story by Hyatt Daab and Weed Dickinson.

SNIPE COLLINS: Cocaine addict who kills a political boss's henchman in a fight and tries to pin it on the son of the woman who is governor of the state.

Pauline Frederick, Carroll Nye, Greta von Rue, Tom Santschi, Stanton Heck, Jack Richardson, Kathleen Kirkham.

The Bells (1926, Chadwick). *d:* James Young; *sc:* James Young—*b/o* Alexandre Chatrian and Emile Erckmann's play *The Polish Jew.*

THE MESMERIST: Mysterious side-show mesmerist who, using his hypnotic powers, breaks down a burgomaster guilty of killing a man for his gold.

Lionel Barrymore, Gustav von Seyffertitz, E. Alyn Warren, Lola Todd, Edward Phillips, Caroline Frances Cooke, Lorimer Johnson, Lucille La Verne.

Eagle of the Sea (1926, Para.). *d:* Frank Lloyd; *sc:* Julian Josephson—*b/o* the novel *Captain Sazarac* by Charles Tenney Jackson.

Pirate under the command of the buccaneer Jean Lafitte in New Orleans during the time of President Andrew Jackson.

Florence Vidor, Ricardo Cortez, Sam De Grasse, Andre Beranger, Guy Oliver, George Irving, James Marcus.

Flames (1926, Associated Exhibitors). *d:* Lewis Moomaw; *sc:* Alfred A. Cohn.

BLACKIE BLANCHETTE: Notorious bandit in Oregon who meets a fiery death in a cabin.

Eugene O'Brien, Virginia Valli, Jean Hersholt, Bryant Washburn, Cissy Fitzgerald, George Nichols.

The Golden Web (1926, Gotham). *d:* Walter Lang; *sc:* James Bell Smith—*b/o* the novel by E. Phillips Oppenheim.

DAVE SINCLAIR: Part owner of a South African mine who becomes involved in a crooked deal and is murdered.

Lillian Rich, Huntly Gordon, Jay Hunt, Lawford Davidson, Nora Hayden, Syd Crossley, Joe Moore.

Flaming Fury (1926, FBO). *d:* James Hogan; *sc:* Ewart Adamson—*b/o* the story "The Scourge of Fate" by Ewart Adamson.

GASPARD: Villainous French-Canadian in the northwoods who is killed by his equally villainous partner.

Charles Delaney, Betty May, Ranger (dog), Eddie Chandler.

Valencia (1926, MGM). *d:* Dimitri Buchowetzki; *sc:* Alice D.G. Miller—*b/o* a story by Dimitri Buchowetzki and Alice D.G. Miller.

Character "bit" in a drama about a sailor and a Spanish dancing girl in Barcelona.

Mae Murray, Lloyd Hughes, Roy D'Arcy, Max Barwyn, Michael Vavitch, Michael Visaroff.

Man in the Saddle (1926, Univ.). *d:* Clifford S. Smith; *p:* Carl Laemmle; *sc:* Charles A. Logue.

Villain briefly involved in a struggle between a gang of bandits and ranchers.

Hoot Gibson, Charles Mailes, Clark Comstock, Fay Wray, Sally Long, Emmett King.

Old Ironsides (1926, Para.). *d:* James Cruze; *sc:* Dorothy Arzner, Walter Woods, and Harry Carr—*b/o* a novel by Laurence Stallings.

Billed as "A SARACEN GUARD": Nineteenth-century Barbary pirate who's involved in a tale of the adventures of the U.S.S. frigate *Constitution* (*Old Ironsides*).

Esther Ralston, Wallace Beery, George Bancroft, Charles Farrell, Johnny Walker, Effie Ellsler, Fred Kohler.

Tarzan and the Golden Lion (1927, FBO). *d:* J. P. McGowan; *sc:* William E. Wing—*b/o* the novel by Edgar Rice Burroughs.

OWAZA: Chief of the Waziris, a tribe of African lion worshippers involved in the adventures of Tarzan the Ape Man.

James Pierce, Frederic Peters, Edna Murphy, Harold Goodwin, Liu Yu-Ching, Dorothy Dunbar, D'Arcy Corrigan, Jad-Bal-Ja (the golden lion).

Let It Rain (1927, Para.). *d:* Edward Cline; *sc:* Wade Boteler, George J. Crone, and Earle Snell.

Villain who is briefly involved in the adventures of a U.S. Marine sergeant who falls for a telephone operator and foils a mail robbery.

Douglas MacLean, Shirley Mason, Wade Boteler, Frank Campeau, James Bradbury Jr., Lincoln Stedman, Lee Shumway.

The Meddlin' Stranger (1927, Pathe). *d:* Richard Thorpe; *sc:* Christopher B. Booth.

Villainous cowboy card-cheater who kills a man but is brought to justice by a straight-shooting cowpoke.

Wally Wales, Nola Luxford, Charles K. French, Mabel Van Buren, James Marcus.

Princess from Hoboken (1927, Tiffany). *d:* Allan Dale; *sc:* Sonya Levien.

PAVEL: Character who's briefly involved in the adventures of a family of restaurant owners in Hoboken whose daughter poses as a Russian princess.

Edmund Burns, Blanche Mehaffey, Ethel Clayton, Lou Tellegen, Babe London, Aggie Herring.

The Phantom Buster (1927, Pathe). *d:* William Bertram; *sc:* Betty Burbridge—*b/o* a story by Walter J. Coburn.

RAMON: Member of a gang of crooks who are smuggling arms from the U.S. across the Mexican border.

Buddy Roosevelt, Alma Rayford, Charles Whitaker, John Junior, Walter Maly, Lawrence Underwood.

Soft Cushions (1927, Para.). *d:* Edward Cline; *sc:* Wade Boteler and Frederik Chapin—*b/o* a story by George Randolph Chester.

Billed as "THE CHIEF CONSPIRATOR": The main conspirator in an Arabian Nights adventure involving a young thief and a beautiful harem girl.

Douglas MacLean, Sue Carol, Richard Carle, Russell Powell, Frank Leigh, Wade Boteler, Nigel De Brulier, Albert Prisco, Fred Kelsey, Noble Johnson.

Two Arabian Knights (1927, UA). *d:* Lewis Milestone; *p:* Howard Hughes (Caddo Co.); *sc:* James O'Donohue (adaptation by Wallace Smith and Cyril Gardner)—*b/o* a story by Donald McGibney.

Billed as "PURSER": Purser on a Jaffa-bound Greek steamer that is carrying two WWI Yank soldiers who have escaped (disguised as Arabs) from the Germans.

William Boyd, Mary Astor, Louis Wolheim, Michael Vavitch, Ian Keith, DeWitt Jennings, Michael Visaroff.

The Love Mart (1927, FN). *d:* George Fitzmaurice; *sc:* Benjamin Glazer—*b/o* Edward Childs Carpenter's novel *The Code of Victor Jallot.*

FLEMING: Villain in a tale about a nineteenth-century New Orleans belle who's sold into slavery when she's accused of having Negro ancestry.

Billie Dove, Gilbert Roland, Noah Beery, Armand Kaliz, Emile Chautard, Mattie Peters.

Burning the Wind (1928, Univ). *d:* Henry MacRae and Herbert Blache; *sc:* George Plympton and Raymond Schrock—*b/o* the novel *A Daughter of the Dons* by William MacLeod Raine.

PUG DORAN: Bad-guy foreman of a ranch in New Mexico who kidnaps the sweetheart of a good-guy cowboy.

Hoot Gibson, Virginia Brown Faire, Cesare Gravina, Pee Wee Holmes, Robert Homans, George Grandee.

Little Wild Girl (1928, Trinity). *d:* Frank Mattison; *sc:* Cecil B. Hill—*b/o* a story by Putnam Hoover.

MAURICE KENT: Villain in a tale of the northwoods.

Lila Lee, Cullen Landis, Frank Merrill, Sheldon Lewis, Jimmy Aubrey, Bud Shaw, Arthur Hotaling, Cyclone (dog).

The Devil's Chaplain (1929, Rayart). *d:* Duke Worne; *sc:* Arthur Hoerl—*b/o* a story by George Bronson Howard.

BORIS: Character briefly involved in an international spy case that is cracked by a U.S. Secret Service agent.

Cornelius Keefe, Virginia Brown Faire, Joseph Swickard, Wheeler Oakman, Leland Carr, George McIntosh.

Two Sisters (1929, Rayart). *d:* Scott Pembroke; *sc:* Arthur Hoerl—*b/o* a story by Virginia T. Vandewater.

CECIL: Henchman of a female thief.

Viola Dana, Rex Lease, Claire Dubrey, Irving Bacon, Tom Lingham, Tom Curran.

The Phantom of the North (1929, Biltmore). *d:* Harry Webb; *sc:* George Hull and Carl Krusada—*b/o* a story by Flora E. Douglas.

JULES GREGG: Villain in the northwoods who is involved in stolen furs and murder.

Edith Roberts, Donald Keith, Kathleen Key, Joe Bonomo, Josef Swickard.

Anne Against the World (1929, Rayart). *d:* Duke Worne; *sc:* Arthur Hoerl—*b/o* a story by Victor Thorne.

Character in a show-business tale about a pretty musical-comedy star who falls for a handsome rich man.

Shirley Mason, Jack Mower, James Bradbury Jr., Isabel Keith, Belle Stoddard, Tom Curran.

Behind That Curtain (1929, Fox). *d:* Irving Cummings; *sc:* Sonya Levien and Clarke Silvernail—*b/o* the novel by Earl Derr Biggers.

Billed as "SUDANESE SERVANT": Explorer's faithful servant in a tale of mystery and murder.

Warner Baxter, Lois Moran, Gilbert Emery, Claude King, Philip Strange, Montague Shaw, Finch Smiles, E. L. Park.

The Unholy Night (1929, MGM). *d:* Lionel Barrymore; *sc:* Dorothy Farnum and Edwin Justus Mayer—*b/o* a story by Ben Hecht.

ABDOUL: Mysterious Hindu servant in a tale about murders that are solved by Scotland Yard.

Ernest Torrence, Dorothy Sebastian, Roland Young, Natalie Moorhead, Polly Moran, Sojin, George Cooper, Claude Fleming, John Miljan, Richard Tucker, John Loder.

The Bad One (1930, UA). *d:* George Fitzmaurice; *p:* John Considine Jr.; *sc:* Carey Wilson and Howard Emmett Rogers—*b/o* a story by John Farrow.

A sadistic guard in a prison colony where an American sailor has been sent for killing a man in a fight over a Marseilles café dancer.

Dolores Del Rio, Edmund Lowe, Don Alvarado, Blanche Frederici, Ulrich Haupt, Charles McNaughton, Henry Kolker, Tommy Dugan.

The Sea Bat (1930, MGM). *d:* Wesley Ruggles; *sc:* Bess Meredyth and John Howard Lawson—*b/o* a story by Dorothy Yost.

Billed as "CORSICAN": Evil half-breed Corsican in a tale of Caribbean sponge divers, murder, voodoo, and a giant sea bat.

Raquel Torres, Charles Bickford, Nils Asther, George F. Marion, John Miljan, Gibson Gowland, Edmund Breese, Mack Swain.

The Utah Kid (1930, Tiffany). *d:* Richard Thorpe; *sc:* Frank Howard Clark.

BAXTER: Western bandit involved in the adventures of a young outlaw who plans to reform when he marries a young school teacher.

Rex Lease, Dorothy Sebastian, Tom Santschi, Mary Carr, Walter Miller, Lafe McKee, Bud Osborne.

Mother's Cry (1930, FN). *d:* Hobart Henley; *p:* Robert North; *sc:* Leonore J. Coffee—*b/o* the novel by Helen Grace Carlisle.

Character "bit" as a murder victim in a drama about a widowed mother and the heartaches her grown children cause her.

Dorothy Peterson, Helen Chandler, David Manners, Edward Woods, Evalyn Knapp, Pat O'Malley, Sidney Blackmer.

The Criminal Code (1931, Col.). *d:* Howard Hawks; *p:* Harry Cohn; *sc:* Fred Niblo Jr. and Seton I. Miller—*b/o* the play by Martin Flavin.

NED GALLOWAY: Tough convict who kills a prison guard, then—when his young cellmate is accused of the crime—refuses to let him take the rap and pays for the murder with his own life.

Walter Huston, Phillips Holmes, Constance Cummings, Mary Doran, De Witt Jennings, John Sheehan.

Cracked Nuts (1931, RKO). *d:* Edward Cline; *sc:* Al Boasberg (with dialogue by Ralph Spence).

Billed as "REVOLUTIONIST": Revolutionary in El Dorania, a mythical country ruled by a zany king.

Bert Wheeler, Robert Woolsey, Edna May Oliver, Louis Calhern, Dorothy Lee, Leni Stengel, Stanley Fields.

Young Donovan's Kid (1931, RKO). *d:* Fred Niblo; *sc:* J. Walter Ruben—*b/o* the story "Big Brother" by Rex Beach.

COKEY JOE: Dope peddler who tries to corrupt a young orphaned boy who is being looked after by a gangster friend of the boy's late father.

Richard Dix, Marion Shilling, Jackie Cooper, Frank Sheridan.

Smart Money (1931, WB). *d:* Alfred E. Green; *sc:* Kubec Glasmon, John Bright, Lucien Hubbard, and Joseph Jackson—*b/o* Lucien Hubbard and Joseph Jackson's story "The Idol."

SPORT WILLIAMS: Crooked gambler who unsuccessfully tries to fleece a big-time gambler known as Nick the Barber.

Edward G. Robinson, James Cagney, Evalyn Knapp, Ralf Harolde, Noel Francis, Maurice Black, Morgan Wallace, Billy House, Paul Porcasi, Polly Walters, Ben Taggert, John Larkin, Allan Lane, Charles Lane.

The Public Defender (1931, RKO). *d:* J. Walter Ruben; *sc:* Bernard Schubert—*b/o* the novel by George Goodschild.

"THE PROFESSOR": Cultured accomplice of a young stockbroker who has become a sort of Robin Hood to protect the defenseless poor against crooked bank officials.

Richard Dix, Shirley Grey, Paul Hurst, Edmund Breese, Purnell Pratt, Ruth Weston.

I Like Your Nerve (1931, WB). *d:* William McGann; *sc:* Houston Branch—*b/o* a story by Roland Pertwee.

LUIGI: Butler who's briefly involved in the adventures of a devil-may-care Yank in Central America who saves a pretty young woman from an unwanted marriage.

Douglas Fairbanks Jr., Loretta Young, Edmund Breon, Henry Kolker, Claude Allister, Ivan Simpson, Paul Porcasi.

Pardon Us (1931, Roach–MGM). *d:* James Parrott; *sc:* H. M. Walker.

(Appeared in the French foreign-language version only.) Convict who menaces a pair of comic, bumbling fellow convicts imprisoned for brewing beer illegally.

Stanley Laurel, Oliver Hardy, June Marlowe, Guido Trento, James Finlayson, Walter Long.

Graft (1931, Univ.). *d:* Christy Cabanne; *sc:* Barry Barringer.

TERRY: Henchman who is hired by a crooked big-city politician to murder the district attorney and kidnap the crook's former mistress to keep her from talking.

Regis Toomey, Sue Carol, Dorothy Revier, George Irving, William Davidson, Richard Tucker, Willard Robertson, Harold Goodwin.

Five Star Final (1931, WB). *d:* Mervyn LeRoy; *sc:* Byron Morgan (adaptation by Robert Lord)—*b/o* the play by Louis Weitzenkorn.

T. VERNON ISOPOD: Unsavory expelled divinity student who is hired by an unscrupulous New York scandal sheet to dig up some dirt on a woman acquitted of murder twenty years earlier.

Edward G. Robinson, H. B. Warner, Marion Marsh, Anthony Bushell, Frances Starr, Ona Munson, George E. Stone, Oscar Apfel, Purnell Pratt, Aline MacMahon, Robert Elliott, Gladys Lloyd.

The Mad Genius (1931, WB). *d:* Michael Curtiz; *sc:* J. Grubb Alexander and Harvey Thew—*b/o* Martin Brown's play *The Idol.*

Billed as "FEDOR'S FATHER": Brutal father whose foster son is rescued from him by a half-mad puppeteer and then trained as a ballet dancer.

John Barrymore, Marian Marsh, Donald Cook, Carmel Meyers, Charles Butterworth, Luis Alberni, Frankie Darro, Mae Madison.

The Yellow Ticket (1931, Fox). *d:* Raoul Walsh; *sc:* Jules Furthman and Guy Bolton—*b/o* the play by Michael Morton.

Billed as "ORDERLY": Drunken orderly of the head of the czar's secret police in 1913 Russia who tries to force his attentions on a young Jewish girl.

Elissa Landi, Lionel Barrymore, Laurence Olivier, Walter Byron, Sarah Padden, Mischa Auer, Rita La Roy.

The Guilty Generation (1931, Col.). *d:* Rowland V. Lee; *sc:* Jack Cunningham—*b/o* the play by Jo Milward and J. Kirby Hawkes.

TONY RICCA: Gangster whose son falls in love with the daughter of a rival gangster while the two gangsters are fighting for control of the bootlegging racket.

Leo Carillo, Constance Cummings, Robert Young, Emma Dunn, Leslie Fenton, Ruth Warren, Murray Kinnell, Elliott Rothe.

Frankenstein (1931, Univ.). *d:* James Whale; *p:* Carl Laemmle Jr.; *sc:* Garrett Fort and Francis Faragoh (adaptation by John L. Balderston from the play by Peggy Webling)—*b/o* the novel by Mary Wollstonecraft Shelley.

THE MONSTER: Gruesome monster that is created from parts of dead bodies and brought to life in a nineteenth-century Bavarian village by an obsessed scientist, Dr. Henry Frankenstein.

Colin Clive, Mae Clarke, John Boles, Edward Van Sloan, Dwight Frye, Frederick Kerr, Lionel Belmore, Michael Mark, Marilyn Harris.

Tonight or Never (1931, UA). *d:* Mervyn LeRoy; *p:* Samuel Goldwyn (Samuel Goldwyn Prod.); *sc:* Ernest Vajda (adaptation by Frederick and Fanny Hatton)—*b/o* the play by Lili Hatvany.

Billed as "THE WAITER": Waiter who is briefly involved in the adventures of a prima donna who falls for a Venetian gigolo who's really an impresario for New York's Metropolitan Opera.

Gloria Swanson, Melvyn Douglas, Ferdinand Gottschalk, Robert Greig, Greta Mayer, Warburton Gamble, Alison Skipworth.

Behind the Mask (1932, Col.). *d:* John Francis Dillon; *sc:* Jo Swerling and Dorothy Howell—*b/o* the story *In the Secret Service* by Jo Swerling.

JIM HENDERSON: Ex–Sing Sing convict and a member of a dope ring that is infiltrated by a Secret Service agent.

Jack Holt, Constance Cummings, Claude King, Bertha Mann, Edward Van Sloan, Willard Robertson, Tommy Jackson.

Business and Pleasure (1932, Fox). *d:* David Butler; *sc:* William Conselman and Gene Towne—from Arthur Goodrich's play *The Plutocrat,* *b/o* the novel by Booth Tarkington.

Billed as "SHEIK": A bearded Arabian desert chieftan involved in tribal warfare that is ended by a canny American razor-blade manufacturer.

Will Rogers, Jetta Goudal, Joel McCrea, Dorothy Peterson, Peggy Ross, Cyril Ring, Jed Prouty, Oscar Apfel, Vernon Dent.

Scarface (1932, UA). *d:* Howard Hawks; *p:* Howard Hughes (Caddo Co.); *sc:* Ben Hecht, Seton I. Miller, John Lee Mahin, and W. R. Burnett.

GAFFNEY: Prohibition-era Chicago gangster who is murdered by a rival mobster in a bowling-alley massacre.

Paul Muni, Ann Dvorak, Karen Morley, Osgood Perkins, C. Henry Gordon, George Raft, Purnell Pratt, Vince Barnett, Inez Palange, Harry J. Vejar, Edwin Maxwell, Tully Marshall, Henry Armetta, Bert Starkey.

The Miracle Man (1932, Para.). *d:* Norman Z. McLeod; *sc:* Waldemar Young and Samuel Hoffenstein—*b/o* a story by Frank L. Packard and Robert H. Davis, and the play by George M. Cohan.

NIKKO: Shady owner of a tavern that serves as a base for a gang of big-city crooks operating a phony faith-healing racket.

Sylvia Sidney, Chester Morris, Irving Pichel, John Wray, Robert Coogan, Hobart Bosworth, Ned Sparks, Lloyd Hughes, Virginia Bruce, Lew Kelly, Jackie Searle.

Alias the Doctor (1932, WB). *d:* Michael Curtiz; *sc:* Houston Branch and Charles Kenyon—*b/o* a play by Emric Foeldes.

Billed as "AUTOPSY SURGEON": Pathologist in the tale of a medical student in Bavaria who takes the blame and goes to prison for the misdeeds of his foster brother.

Richard Barthelmess, Marian Marsh, Norman Foster, Lucille La Verne, Adrienne Dore, Oscar Apfel, Claire Dodd, Reginald Barlow, Arnold Lucy.

Night World (1932, Univ.). *d:* Hobart Henley; *sc:* Richard Schayer—*b/o* a story by P. J. Wolfson and Allen Rivkin.

"HAPPY" MacDONALD: Nightclub owner who is betrayed by his unfaithful wife and is murdered by the mob when he refuses to buy bootleg liquor from them.

Lew Ayres, Mae Clark, Dorothy Revier, Russell Hopton, Bert Roach, Dorothy Peterson, Florence Lake, Gene Morgan, Paisley Noon, Hedda Hopper, Greta Granstedt, Louise Beavers, Sammy Blum, Harry Woods, Eddie Phillips, George Raft, Robert Emmett O'Connor.

The Old Dark House (1932, Univ.). *d:* James Whale; *p:* Carl Laemmle Jr., *sc:* Benn W. Levy—*b/o* the novel by J. B. Priestley.

MORGAN: Brutish mute butler who is one of the weird characters three stranded travelers encounter when they seek shelter in a spooky old mansion in the Welsh mountains.

Melvyn Douglas, Charles Laughton, Gloria Stuart, Lilian Bond, Ernest Thesiger, Eva Moore, Raymond Massey, Brember Wills, John Dudgeon.

The Mask of Fu Manchu (1932, MGM). *d:* Charles Brabin; *sc:* Irene Kuhn, Edgar Allan Woolf, and John Willard—*b/o* the novel by Sax Rohmer.

DR. FU MANCHU: Evil Oriental who, as part of his plan to rule the world, resorts to torture and murder while he tries to gain possession of a priceless ceremonial mask and sword from the tomb of Genghis Kahn in the Gobi Desert.

Lewis Stone, Karen Morley, Charles Starrett, Myrna Loy, Jean Hersholt, Lawrence Grant, David Torrence, Ferdinand Gottschalk, Willie Fung.

The Mummy (1932, Univ.). *d:* Karl Freund; *p:* Carl Laemmle Jr.; *sc:* John L. Balderston—*b/o* a story by Nina Wilcox Putnam and Richard Schayer.

IM-HO-TEP (alias ARDETH BEY): An Egyptian high priest who, after being buried alive 3700 years earlier, comes back to life when his tomb is desecrated by British archaeologists.

Zita Johann, David Manners, Edward Van Sloan, Arthur Byron, Bramwell Fletcher, Noble Johnson, Leonard Mudie, Katheryn Byron, Eddie Kane.

The Ghoul (1933, Gaumont–British). *d:* T. Hayes Hunter; *p:* Kevin Francis; *sc:* Rupert Downing, Roland Pertwee, and John Hastings Turner—*b/o* the novel and play by Dr. Frank King and Leonard J. Hines.

PROFESSOR MORLANT: Egyptologist who dies and is buried with a valuable jewel strapped to his wrist in the belief that it will give him immortality but, when the jewel is stolen, rises from his tomb for revenge.

Cedric Hardwicke, Ernest Thesiger, Dorothy Hyson, Anthony Bushell, Kathleen Harrison, Harold Huth, D. A. Clarke-Smith, Ralph Richardson, Jack Raine.

The Lost Patrol (1934, RKO). *d:* John Ford; *p:* Cliff Reid; *sc:* Dudley Nichols and Garrett Fort—*b/o* the story "Patrol" by Philip MacDonald.

SANDERS: Religious fanatic who is a member of a patrol of WWI British soldiers who find themselves stranded in the Mesopotamian Desert and are picked off, one by one, by Arab snipers.

Victor McLaglen, Wallace Ford, Reginald Denny, J. M. Kerrigan, Billy Bevan, Alan Hale, Brandon Hurst, Douglas Walton, Sammy Stein, Neville Clark.

The House of Rothschild (1934, UA). *d:* Alfred Werker; *p:* Darryl F. Zanuck (20th Century); *sc:* Nunnally Johnson—*b/o* the play by George Hembert Westley.

BARON LEDRANTZ: Anti-Semitic Prussian ambassador who, at the time of the Napoleonic Wars, opposes the famous Rothschild banking family.

George Arliss, Loretta Young, Robert Young, C. Aubrey Smith, Arthur Byron, Helen Westley, Reginald Owen, Florence Arliss, Alan Mowbray,

Holmes Herbert, Paul Harvey, Ivan Simpson, Noel Madison.

The Black Cat (1934, Univ.). *d:* Edgar Ulmer; *p:* Carl Laemmle Jr.; *sc:* Peter Ruric—*b/o* the story by Edgar Allan Poe.

HJALMAR POELZIG: Ex-WWI Hungarian Army engineer and maniacal leader of a cult of devil-worshipers who holds a revenge-seeking doctor and a young newlywed couple prisoner in his castle.

Bela Lugosi, David Manners, Jacqueline Wells, Lucille Lund, Harry Cording, Henry Armetta, Albert Conti, Tony Marlo, Paul Weigel, Herman Bing, Luis Alberni, King Baggott, John Carradine.

The Bride of Frankenstein (1935, Univ.). *d:* James Whale; *p:* Carl Laemmle Jr.; *sc:* William Hurlbut and John L. Balderston—*b/o* characters created by Mary Wollstonecraft Shelley.

THE MONSTER: Dr. Henry Frankenstein's gruesome creation who is rejected by the strange-looking female monster that Dr. Frankenstein and his former teacher, Dr. Pretorius, create to be the Monster's mate.

Colin Clive, Valerie Hobson, Elsa Lanchester, Ernest Thesiger, O. P. Heggie, Dwight Frye, E. E. Clive, Una O'Connor, Douglas Walton, Gavin Gordon, Mary Gordon, Lucien Prival, John Carradine, Billy Barty, Joan Woodbury, Arthur S. Byron, Kansas DeForrest, Walter Brennan, Helen Parrish.

The Black Room (1935, Col.). *d:* Roy William Neill; *sc:* Henry Meyers and Arthur Strawn.

(Dual role) GREGOR De BERGHMAN: Brutally sadistic baron in nineteenth-century Czechoslovakia who murders his younger twin brother (Anton), assumes his identity, and takes control of the family castle and estate.

ANTON De BERGHMAN: Kindly, cultured twin brother who, after being murdered by his evil twin (Gregor), eerily fulfills an ancient curse which predicts that he will kill his twin in the castle's Black Room.

Marian Marsh, Robert Allen, Thurston Hall, Katherine De Mille, John Buckler, Henry Kolker, Colin Tapley, Torben Meyer, Egon Brecher, Edward Van Sloan.

The Raven (1935, Univ.). *d:* Louis Friedlander; *sc:* David Boehm—*b/o* the poem by Edgar Allen Poe.

EDMOND BATEMAN: Notorious gangster who, when his face is horribly mutilated by a mad doctor, is forced to perform torture and murder in return for the doctor's promise to restore his features to normal.

Bela Lugosi, Irene Ware, Lester Matthews, Samuel Hinds, Inez Courtney, Ian Wolfe, Spencer Charters, Maidel Turner, Arthur Hoyt, Walter Miller.

The Invisible Ray (1936, Univ.). *d:* Lambert Hillyer; *sc:* John Colton—*b/o* a story by Howard Higgin and Douglas Hodges.

DR. JANOS RUKH: Scientist who becomes contaminated by a super-radioactive element that makes him glow in the dark, causes his mind to deteriorate, and gives him the power to destroy any living thing by merely touching it.

Bela Lugosi, Frances Drake, Frank Lawton, Walter Kingsford, Beulah Bondi, Violet Kemble Cooper, Nydia Westman, Frank Reicher, Ernie Adams, Walter Miller.

The Walking Dead (1936, WB). *d:* Michael Curtiz; *sc:* Ewart Adamson, Peter Milne, Robert Andrews, and Lilli Hayward.

JOHN ELLMAN: Ex-con who, after he's falsely convicted of murder and executed in the electric chair, is brought back to life by a scientist and seeks out the racketeers who framed him.

Ricardo Cortez, Edmund Gwenn, Marguerite Churchill, Warren Hull, Barton MacLane, Henry O'Neill, Paul Harvey, Joseph Sawyer, Eddie Acuff, Addison Richards, Kenneth Harlan, Milt Kibbee, Bill Elliot.

The Man Who Lived Again (1936, Gaumont–British). *d:* Robert Stevenson; *sc:* L. DuGarde Peach, Sidney Gilliat, and John L. Balderston.

DR. LAURIENCE: Scientist in London who develops an apparatus that enables him to transfer the mind of one person into the body of another.

Anna Lee, John Loder, Frank Cellier, Donald Calthrop, Cecil Parker, Lynn Harding.

Juggernaut (1936, GN). *d:* Henry Edwards; *sc:* Cyril Campion, H. Fowler Mear, and H. Fraenkel—*b/o* a story by Alice Campbell.

DR. SARTORIUS: Evil French doctor in England who agrees to murder a greedy wife's rich old husband in return for £20,000 so that the doctor can continue his experiments for a cure for paralysis.

Joan Wyndham, Arthur Margetson, Mona Goya, Anthony Ireland, Morton Selten, Nina Boucicault, Gibb McLaughlin, J. H. Roberts, V. Rietti.

Charlie Chan at the Opera (1937, 20th-Fox). *d:* H. Bruce Humberstone; *sc:* W. Scott Darling and Charles S. Belden—*b/o* the Charlie Chan stories by Earl Derr Biggers.

GRAVELLE: Mental-asylum escapee—actually a famous opera baritone presumed to have been burned to death in a theater fire years earlier—who seeks revenge on his unfaithful wife and her lover.

Warner Oland, Keye Luke, Charlotte Henry, Thomas Beck, Margaret Irving, Gregory Gaye, Nedda Harrigan, Frank Conroy, Guy Usher, William Demarest, Maurice Cass, Tom McGuire.

Night Key (1937, Univ.). *d:* Lloyd Corrigan; *sc:* Tristram Tupper and John C. Moffit.

DAVE MALLORY: Investor who, when his plans for a burglar-alarm system are stolen by his former partner, is forced into helping crooks stage a wave of burglaries.

Jean Rogers, Warren Hull, Hobart Cavanaugh, Samuel Hinds, Alan Baxter, David Oliver, Edwin Maxwell, Ward Bond, Frank Reicher, Ethan Laidlaw.

West of Shanghai (1937, WB). *d:* John Farrow; *sc:* Crane Wilbur—*b/o* the play by Porter Emerson Browne.

GEN. WU YEN FANG: Renegade Chinese warlord who, after his army of cutthroat bandits takes a group of Americans and missionaries hostage, winds up in front of a government firing squad.

Beverly Roberts, Ricardo Cortez, Gordon Oliver, Sheila Bromley, Vladimir Sokoloff, Gordon Hart, Richard Loo, Douglas Wood, Luke Chan, Selmer Jackson, Eddie Lee.

The Invisible Menace (1938, WB). *d:* John Farrow; *sc:* Crane Wilbur—*b/o* the play by Ralph Spencer Zink.

JEVRIES: Ex-convict and civilian construction supervisor at an island U.S. Army military post who becomes the prime suspect in the murder of an Army officer.

Marie Wilson, Eddie Craven, Eddie Acuff, Regis Toomey, Henry Kolker, Cy Kendall, Charles Trowbridge, Frank Faylen, William Haade, John Ridgely.

Mr. Wong, Detective (1938, Mono.). *d:* William Nigh; *p:* Scott R. Dunlap; *sc:* Houston Branch—*b/o* stories by Hugh Wiley.

JAMES LEE WONG: Famous Chinese detective who sets out to solve the poison-gas murders of a chemical manufacturer and his two business partners.

Grant Withers, Maxine Jennings, Evelyn Brent, Lucien Prival, William Gould, John Hamilton, Tchin, Hooper Atchley.

Son of Frankenstein (1939, Univ.). *d:* Rowland V. Lee; *p:* Rowland V. Lee; *sc:* Willis Cooper—*b/o* characters created by Mary Wollstonecraft Shelley.

THE MONSTER: Dr. Henry Frankenstein's monster who, when he's revived by Henry's son (Baron Wolf von Frankenstein), falls under the influence of an evil, deformed shepherd-graverobber named Ygor and commits a series of murders.

Basil Rathbone, Bela Lugosi, Lionel Atwill, Josephine Hutchinson, Emma Dunn, Donnie Dunagan, Edgar Norton, Perry Ivins, Lorimer Johnson, Gustov von Seyffertitz, Ward Bond.

The Mystery of Mr. Wong (1939, Mono.). *d:* William Nigh; *sc:* W. Scott Darling—*b/o* stories by Hugh Wiley.

JAMES LEE WONG: Famous Chinese detective who solves a baffling case involving murder and the theft of the largest star sapphire in the world.

Grant Withers, Dorothy Tree, Lotus Long, Morgan Wallace, Holmes Herbert, Craig Reynolds, Ivan Lebedeff, Hooper Atchley, Lee Tong Foo, Chester Gan.

Mr. Wong in Chinatown (1939, Mono.). *d:* William Nigh; *sc:* W. Scott Darling—*b/o* stories by Hugh Wiley.

JAMES LEE WONG: Scholarly Chinese detective who, when a Chinese princess-client is killed by a poisoned dart, tracks down the murderer.

Grant Withers, Marjorie Reynolds, Peter George Lynn, William Royle, Huntly Gordon, James Flavin, Lotus Long, Richard Loo, Angelo Rosita.

The Man They Could Not Hang (1939, Col.). *d:* Nick Grinde; *sc:* Karl Brown—*b/o* a story by Leslie T. White and George W. Sayre.

DR. HENRYK SAVAARD: Scientist convicted of murder who, after being hanged, is brought back to life with a mechanical heart and sets out to murder the jurors who condemned him.

Lorna Gray, Robert Wilcox, Roger Pryor, Don Beddoe, Ann Doran, Joseph DeSteffani, Charles Trowbridge, Byron Foulger, Dick Curtis, James Craig, John Tyrrell.

Tower of London (1939, Univ.). *d:* Rowland V. Lee; *sc:* Robert N. Lee.

MORD: Bald-headed, club-footed torturer and executioner in fifteenth-century England who helps the power-hungry King Richard III commit various murders to gain the British throne.

Basil Rathbone, Barbara O'Neil, Ian Hunter, Vincent Price, Nan Grey, John Sutton, Leo G. Carroll, Miles Mander, Lionel Belmore, Rose Hobart, Ralph Forbes, Frances Robinson, Ernest Cossart, G. P. Huntley, John Rodion, Ronald Sinclair, Ernie Adams.

The Fatal Hour (1940, Mono.). *d:* William Nigh; *sc:* W. Scott Darling—*b/o* stories by Hugh Wiley.

JAMES LEE WONG: Erudite Chinese detective who sets out to solve a case involving diamond smugglers and four murders.

Grant Withers, Marjorie Reynolds, Charles Trowbridge, John Hamilton, Craig Reynolds, Jack Kennedy, Lita Cheveret, Frank Puglia, Stanford Jolley, Jason Robards Sr., Pauline Drake, Richard Loo, Tristram Coffin.

British Intelligence (1940, WB). *d:* Terry Morse; *sc:* Lee Katz—*b/o* the play *Three Faces East* by Anthony Paul Kelly.

SCHILLER (alias VALDAR): WWI German master spy who, while posing as a butler in the home of an important British war official, encounters a female German spy who's really a British agent.

Margaret Lindsay, Maris Wrixon, Bruce Lester, Leonard Mudie, Holmes Herbert, Winifred Harris, Lester Matthews, John Graham Spacy.

Black Friday (1940, Univ.). *d:* Arthur Lubin; *sc:* Curt Siodmak and Eric Taylor.

DR. ERNEST SOVAC: Brain surgeon who, in order to save his injured college-professor friend's life, transplants part of a notorious gangster's brain into that of the professor, with disastrous results.

Bela Lugosi, Stanley Ridges, Ann Nagel, Anne Gwynne, Virginia Brissac, Edmund MacDonald, Paul Fix, Murray Alper, Jack Mulhall.

The Man with Nine Lives (1940, Col.). *d:* Nick Grinde; *sc:* Karl Brown—*b/o* a story by Harold Shumate.

DR. LEON KRAVAAL: Scientist who, while seeking a cure for cancer by freezing bodies in suspended animation, is accidentally locked in his ice chamber but ten years later is discovered and thawed out.

Roger Pryor, Jo Ann Sayers, Stanley Brown, John Dilson, Hal Taliaferro, Byron Foulger, Charles Trowbridge, Ernie Adams.

Devil's Island (1940, WB). *d:* William Clemens; *sc:* Kenneth Gamet and Don Ryan—*b/o* a story by Anthony Coldewey and Raymond L. Schrock.

DR. CHARLES GAUDET: Noted French surgeon who, when he treats a wounded revolutionary, is unjustly sentenced to ten years in the French Guiana penal colony on Devil's Island.

Nedda Harrigan, James Stephenson, Adia Kuznetzoff, Rolla Gourvitch, Will Stanton, Edward Keane, Robert Warwick, Pedro de Cordoba, George Lloyd, Stuart Holmes.

Doomed to Die (1940, Mono.). *d:* William Nigh; *sc:* Ralph G. Bettinson and Michael Jacoby—*b/o* stories by Hugh Wiley.

JAMES LEE WONG: Famed Chinese detective who, when a ship containing more than a million dollars' worth of bonds is sunk and a shipping magnate is murdered, tracks down the killer.

Grant Withers, Marjorie Reynolds, Melvin Lang, Guy Usher, Catherine Craig, William Sterling, Henry Brandon, Wilbur Mack.

Before I Hang (1940, Col.). *d:* Nick Grinde; *sc:* Robert D. Andrews—*b/o* a story by Karl Brown and Robert D. Andrews.

DR. JOHN GARTH: Aging research scientist who develops a serum that transforms him into a younger man—but also turns him into a murderer.

Evelyn Keyes, Bruce Bennett, Edward Van Sloan, Ben Taggart, Pedro de Cordoba, Bertram Marburgh, Don Beddoe, Kenneth MacDonald.

The Ape (1940, Mono.). *d:* William Nigh; *sc:* Curt Siodmak and Richard Carroll—*b/o* the play by Adam Shirk.

DR. BERNARD ADRIAN: Demented doctor who disguises himself in an ape's hide and kills people in order to get human spinal fluid for his experimental polio serum.

Maris Wrixon, Gertrude Hoffman, Henry Hall, Gene O'Donnell, Jack Kennedy, I. Stanford Jolley, Selmer Jackson, Philo McCullough, George Cleveland.

You'll Find Out (1940, RKO). *d:* David Butler; *sc:* James V. Kern—*b/o* a story by David Butler and James V. Kern.

JUDGE MAINWARING: One of a sinister trio of guests at a gloomy mansion who are secretly plotting to murder a debutante to claim her inheritance.

Kay Kyser, Peter Lorre, Dennis O'Keefe, Bela Lugosi, Helen Parrish, Alma Kruger, Joseph Eggenton, Ginny Simms, Harry Babbitt, Ish Kabibble, Sully Mason.

The Devil Commands (1941, Col.). *d:* Edward Dmytryk; *sc:* Robert D. Andrews and Milton Gunzberg—*b/o* William Sloane's story "The Edge of Running Water."

DR. JULIAN BLAIR: Scientist who uses stolen dead bodies and a brainwave machine for experiments in which he obsessively tries to communicate with his dead wife.

Richard Fiske, Amanda Duff, Anne Revere, Ralph Penney, Dorothy Adams, Walter Baldwin, Kenneth MacDonald, Shirley Warde.

The Boogie Man Will Get You (1942, Col.). *d:* Lew Landers; *sc:* Edwin Blum—*b/o* a story by Hal Fimberg and Robert B. Hunt.

PROF. NATHANIEL BILLINGS: Mad scientist who conducts basement experiments on unsuspecting traveling salesmen in an effort to turn them into supermen who could help the U.S. win WWII.

Peter Lorre, Maxie Rosenbloom, Jeff Donnell, Larry Parks, Maude Eburne, Don Beddoe, George McKay, Frank Sully, Frank Puglia.

The Climax (1944, Univ.). *d:* George Waggner; *p:* George Waggner; *sc:* Curt Siodmak and Lynn Starling—*b/o* the play by Edward J. Locke.

DR. HOHNER: Demented Paris Opera House physician who once loved and murdered a famous opera singer, then tries ten years later to murder another singer who resembles the first one.

Susanna Foster, Turhan Bey, Gale Sondergaard, Thomas Gomez, June Vincent, George Dolenz, Ludwig Stossel, Jane Farrar, Lotte Stein, Scotty

Beckett, Maurice Costello, William Desmond, Stuart Holmes, Eddie Polo, Jack Richardson.

House of Frankenstein (1944, Univ.). *d:* Erle C. Kenton; *p:* Paul Malvern; *sc:* Edward T. Lowe—*b/o* a story by Curt Siodmak.
DR. GUSTAV NIEMANN: Crazed scientist who escapes from prison; brings back to life the Frankenstein Monster, The Wolf Man, and Dracula; and uses them to get revenge on his enemies.
Lon Chaney Jr., John Carradine, Lionel Atwill, George Zucco, Anne Gwynne, Peter Coe, Elena Verdugo, Glenn Strange, Sig Ruman, Philip Van Zandt, Frank Reicher.

The Bodysnatcher (1945, RKO). *d:* Robert Wise; *p:* Val Lewton; *sc:* Philip MacDonald and Carlos Keith—*b/o* the short story by Robert Louis Stevenson.
JOHN GRAY: Sinister coachman and grave robber in 1831 Edinburgh who provides cadavers for medical experiments by the head of a medical school.
Bela Lugosi, Henry Daniell, Edith Atwater, Russell Wade, Rita Corday, Sharyn Moffett, Donna Lee, Bill Williams, Robert Clarke, Jim Moran.

Isle of the Dead (1945, RKO). *d:* Mark Robson; *p:* Val Lewton; *sc:* Ardel Wray, Josef Mischel, and Val Lewton.
GENERAL PHERIDES: Greek general during the 1912 Balkan War who becomes involved with vampires and witchcraft while he and various other characters are stranded on an island infested with the plague.
Ellen Drew, Marc Cramer, Katherine Emery, Helene Thimig, Alan Napier, Jason Robards Sr., Ernst Dorian, Skelton Knaggs, Sherry Hall.

Bedlam (1946, RKO). *d:* Mark Robson; *p:* Val Lewton; *sc:* Mark Robson and Carlos Keith (suggested by William Hogarth's engraving *The Rake's Progress*).
MASTER GEORGE SIMS: Sadistic chief warden of a notorious eighteenth-century London insane asylum (called Bedlam) who winds up being done in by the inmates.
Anna Lee, Billy House, Richard Fraser, Glenn Vernon, Ian Wolfe, Jason Robards Sr, Leland Hodgson, Joan Newton, Elizabeth Russell, Skelton Knaggs, Robert Clarke.

The Secret Life of Walter Mitty (1947, RKO). *d:* Norman Z. McLeod; *p:* Samuel Goldwyn; *sc:* Ken Englund and Everett Freeman—*b/o* the short story by James Thurber.
DR. HOLLINGSHEAD: Phony psychiatrist and head of a gang of jewel thieves who is foiled by a timid pulp-magazine proofreader and his

girlfriend when the gang tries to steal some valuable jewels from the woman's uncle.
Danny Kaye, Virginia Mayo, Fay Bainter, Ann Rutherford, Thurston Hall, Gordon Jones, Florence Bates, Konstantine Shayne, Reginald Denny, Henry Corden, Doris Lloyd, Frank Reicher, Milton Parsons.

Lured (1947, UA). *d:* Douglas Sirk; *p:* James Nasser; *sc:* Leo Rosten—*b/o* a story by Jacques Companeez, Ernest Neuville, and Simon Gantillon.
CHARLES van DRUTEN: Mentally deranged dress designer in London who is one of Scotland Yard's prime suspects in the murder of a young woman.
George Sanders, Lucille Ball, Charles Coburn, Alan Mowbray, Sir Cedric Hardwicke, George Zucco, Joseph Calleia, Tanis Chandler.

Unconquered (1947, Para.). *d:* Cecil B. DeMille; *p:* Cecil B. DeMille; *sc:* Charles Bennett, Frederick M. Frank, and Jesse Lasky Jr.—*b/o* the novel by Neil H. Swanson.
CHIEF GUYASUTA: Indian chief who, under the direction of an unscrupulous white trader, leads a rebellion against Fort Pitt in 1763 colonial America.
Gary Cooper, Paulette Goddard, Howard Da Silva, Cecil Kellaway, Ward Bond, Katherine De Mille, Henry Wilcoxon, Sir C. Aubrey Smith, Victor Varconi, Virginia Grey, Porter Hall, Mike Mazurki, Gavin Muir, Alan Napier, Marc Lawrence, Robert Warwick, Lloyd Bridges, Raymond Hatton, Chief Thundercloud.

Dick Tracy Meets Gruesome (1947, RKO). *d:* John Rawlins; *sc:* Robertson White and Eric Taylor—*b/o* the cartoon strip *Dick Tracy* by Chester Gould.
GRUESOME: Ex-convict and bank robber who runs up against detective Dick Tracy when he tries to get control of a mysterious nerve gas that will paralyze people.
Ralph Byrd, Anne Gwynne, Edward Ashley, June Clayworth, Lyle Latell, Tony Barrett, Skelton Knaggs, Jim Nolan, Joseph Crehan, Milton Parsons, Lex Barker.

Tap Roots (1948, Univ.). *d:* George Marshall; *sc:* Alan LeMay—*b/o* the novel by James Street.
TISHOMINGO: Faithful seventy-year-old Choctaw Indian friend of a Mississippi anti-slavery family that tries to remain neutral during the Civil War.
Van Heflin, Susan Hayward, Julie London, Whitfield Connor, Ward Bond, Richard Long, Arthur Shields, Griff Barnett, Sondra Rogers, Ruby Dandridge, Russell Simpson.

Abbott and Costello Meet the Killer, Boris Karloff (1949, Univ.). *d:* Charles T. Barton; *p:* Robert Arthur; *sc:* Hugh Wedlock Jr., Howard

Snyder, and John Grant—*b/o* a story by Hugh Wedlock and Howard Snyder.

SWAMI TALPUR: Fake fortune teller and hypnotist from Brooklyn who tries to do away with a bumbling bellboy who, along with a hotel house detective, is playing amateur sleuth in a murder case.

Bud Abbott, Lou Costello, Lenore Aubert, Gar Moore, Donna Martell, Alan Mowbray, James Flavin, Roland Winters, Nicholas Joy, Percy Helton, Claire Dubrey.

The Strange Door (1951, Univ.). *d:* Joseph Pevney; *p:* Ted Richmond; *sc:* Jerry Sackheim—*b/o* Robert Louis Stevenson's story "The Sire de Maletroit's Door."

VOLTAN: Crazed nobleman's faithful servant in eighteenth-century France who is forced to destroy the nobleman in order to save some innocent prisoners from being killed.

Charles Laughton, Sally Forrest, Richard Stapley, Michael Pate, Paul Cavanagh, Alan Napier, William Cottrell, Morgan Farley, Edwin Parker, Charles Horvath.

The Black Castle (1952, Univ.). *d:* Nathan Juran; *sc:* Jerry Sackheim.

DR. MEISSEN: Physician to a murderous German count in an eighteenth-century Black Forest castle who is killed by the count when he tries to help the count's wife and her young English lover escape from the castle.

Richard Greene, Stephen McNally, Paula Corday, Lon Chaney Jr., John Hoyt, Michael Pate, Nancy Valentine, Tudor Owen, Henry Corden, Otto Waldis.

Abbott and Costello Meet Dr. Jekyll and Mr. Hyde (1953, Univ.). *d:* Charles Lamont; *p:* Howard Christie; *sc:* Lee Loeb and John Grant—*b/o* a story by Sidney Fields and Grant Garrett.

DR. HENRY JEKYLL/MR. HYDE: Respectable turn-of-the-century London physician who develops a serum that transforms him into a half-man–half-beast called Mr. Hyde, who terrorizes London before two bumbling American detectives help apprehend him.

Bud Abbott, Lou Costello, Helen Westcott, Craig Stevens, Reginald Denny, John Dierkes, Edwin Parker.

Monster of the Island (1953, Romana Films). *d:* Roberto Montero; *sc:* Roberto Montero and Alberto Vecchietti—*b/o* a story by Alberto Vecchietti.

DON GAETANO: Elderly philanthropist and founder of a children's nursery who turns out to be the secret head of a dope-smuggling ring on the island of Ischia.

Franco Marzi, Renata Vicario, Patrizia Remiddi, Iole Fierro, Carlo Duse, Germana Paolieri,

Giuseppe Chinnici, Giulio Battiferri, Clara Gamberini.

The Hindu (1953, UA). *d:* Frank Ferrin; *sc:* Frank Ferrin.

GENERAL POLLEGAR: Maharaja's military aide in India who becomes involved with a fearless young elephant trainer out to destroy an evil cult of fire worshippers.

Nino Marcel, Lou Krugman, Reginald Denny, Victory Jory, June Foray, Lisa Howard, Jay Novello, Peter Coe, Paul Marion, Vito Scotti, Lou Merrill, Larry Dobkin, Jeanne Bates.

Voodoo Island (1957, UA). *d:* Reginald LeBorg; *p:* Aubrey Schenck and Howard W. Koch; *sc:* Richard Landau.

PHILLIP KNIGHT: Professional exposer of hoaxes who, when he's hired by a hotel builder to investigate a potential resort hotel on a tropical island where voodoo is practiced, runs into man-eating plants and zombies.

Beverly Tyler, Murvyn Vye, Elisha Cook, Rhodes Reason, Jean Engstrom, Frederich Ledebur, Glenn Dixon.

The Haunted Strangler (1958, MGM). *d:* Robert Day; *sc:* Jan Read and John C. Cooper—*b/o* a story by Jan Read.

JAMES RANKIN: English novelist in 1880s London who, while researching the case of an innocent man hanged for murder twenty years earlier, discovers that he has had amnesia and that *he* was the lunatic who committed the murder.

Anthony Dawson, Jean Kent, Elizabeth Allan, Derek Birch, Dorothy Gordon, Diane Aubrey, Tim Turner, Vera Day, Max Brimmell.

Frankenstein 1970 (1958, AA). *d:* Howard Koch; *p:* Aubrey Schenck; *sc:* Richard Landau and George Worthing Yates—*b/o* a story by Aubrey Schenck and Charles A. Moses.

BARON VICTOR von FRANKENSTEIN: Disfigured German scientist who lets an American camera crew use his castle for a TV horror show in return for an atomic reactor—which he utilizes to recreate the legendary "Monster" originally conceived 140 years earlier by his grandfather Dr. Henry Frankenstein.

Tom Duggan, Jana Lund, Donald Barry, Charlotte Austin, Irwin Berke, Rudolph Anders, John Dennis, Norbert Schiller, Mike Lane.

The Raven (1963, AIP). *d:* Roger Corman; *p:* Roger Corman; *sc:* Richard Matheson—*b/o* the poem by Edgar Allan Poe.

DR. SCARABUS: Villainous sixteenth-century sorceror who engages in a power struggle with another potent magician whose wife he has stolen.

Vincent Price, Peter Lorre, Hazel Court, Olive Sturgess, Jack Nicholson, Connie Wallace, William Baskin, Aaron Saxon.

Corridors of Blood (1963, Altura). *d:* Robert Day; *p:* John Croydon (Amalgamated); *sc:* Jean Scott Rogers.

DR. THOMAS BOLTON: British surgeon in 1840 London who, while researching for an anasthetic that will prevent pain during operations, accidentally becomes a dope addict and gets involved with unsavory characters, blackmail, and violence.

Betta St. John, Francis Matthews, Francis De Wolff, Adrienne Corri, Frank Pettingell, Finlay Currie, Christopher Lee, Basil Dignam, Nigel Green.

The Terror (1963, AIP). *d:* Roger Corman; *p:* Roger Corman and Francis Ford Coppola (Filmgroup); *sc:* Leo Gordon and Jack Hill.

BARON von LEPPE: Madman owner of a Baltic coast castle in the 1800s who has been mourning the death of his wife for twenty years and is finally driven by a witch to commit suicide.

Jack Nicholson, Sandra Knight, Richard Miller, Dorothy Neumann, Jonathan Haze.

Comedy of Terrors (1963, AIP). *d:* Jacques Tourneur; *p:* Anthony Carras and Richard Matheson; *sc:* Richard Matheson.

AMOS HINCHLEY: Senile old founder of an 1890s New England funeral parlor whose son-in-law—a debt-ridden undertaker—tries to poison him but instead winds up being accidentally poisoned himself.

Vincent Price, Peter Lorre, Basil Rathbone, Joe E. Brown, Joyce Jameson, Beverly Hills, Paul Barsolow, Linda Rogers, Luree Nicholson, Buddy Mason, Rhubarb the Cat.

Black Sabbath (1964, AIP). *d:* Mario Bava; *sc:* Marcello Fondato, Alberto Bevilacqua, and Mario Bava—*b/o* stories by Anton Chekhov, Howard Snyder, and Alexei Tolstoy.

GORCA: East European peasant who, after killing a bandit thought to be a Wurdalak (a kind of vampire who lives on the blood of those it loves), becomes a Wurdalak himself and kills every member of his family, thus turning them into Wurdalaks too.

Jacqueline Pierreux, Milly Monti, Michele Mercier, Lidia Alfonsi, Susy Andersen, Mark Damon, Glauco Onorato, Rika Dialina, Massimo Righi.

Die, Monster, Die (1965, AIP). *d:* Daniel Haller; *sc:* Jerry Sohl—*b/o* H. P. Lovecraft's story "The Color Out of Space."

NAHUM WITLEY: Wheelchair-bound recluse in a remote English village who, when he uses a radioactive meteorite to create plant and insect mutations, contaminates himself and others, turning them into hideous monsters.

Nick Adams, Freda Jackson, Suzan Farmer, Terence DeMarney, Patrick Magee, Paul Farrell, George Moon, Gretchen Franklin, Sydney Bromley.

Ghost in the Invisible Bikini (1966, AIP). *d:* Don Weis; *sc:* Louis M. Heyward and Elwood Ullman.

HIRAM STOKLEY: Wealthy deceased old man who is told by a heavenly visitor that if he performs a good deed in the next twenty-four hours, he can enter Heaven with his long-dead sweetheart.

Tommy Kirk, Deborah Walley, Aron Kincaid, Quinn O'Hara, Jesse White, Harvey Lembeck, Nancy Sinatra, Basil Rathbone, Patsy Kelly, Susan Hart, Francis X. Bushman, Benny Rubin, Bobbi Shaw.

The Daydreamer (1966, Embassy). *d:* Jules Bass; *sc:* Arthur Rankin Jr.—*b/o* stories and characters created by Hans Christian Andersen.

"THE RAT": The *voice* of a villainous animated rat who is one of several fairy-tale characters that thirteen-year-old Hans Christian Andersen meets and later writes about.

On-camera actors: *Paul O'Keefe, Jack Gilford, Ray Bolger, Margaret Hamilton.* Actors whose voices were used for other animated characters: *Cyril Ritchard, Hayley Mills, Burl Ives, Tallulah Bankhead, Terry-Thomas, Victor Borge, Ed Wynn, Patty Duke,* Sessue Hayakawa, Robert Goulet.

The Venetian Affair (1967, MGM). *d:* Jerry Thorpe; *p:* Jerry Thorpe; *sc:* E. Jack Neuman—*b/o* the novel by Helen MacInnes.

DR. PIERRE VAUGIROUD: Mysterious political scientist in Venice who is used by Communist agents when they drug him in an attempt to get possession of an important document.

Robert Vaughn, Elke Sommer, Felicia Farr, Karl Boehm, Luciana Paluzzi, Roger C. Carmel, Edward Asner, Joe De Santis, Fabrizio Mioni, Bill Weiss.

The Sorcerers (1967, AA). *d:* Michael Reeves; *sc:* Michael Reeves.

PROFESSOR MONSERRAT: Ex–stage hypnotist whose power to control another person's brain ends in disaster for both him and his greedy wife.

Catherine Lacey, Ian Ogilvy, Elizabeth Ercy, Victor Henry, Susan George, Dani Sheridan, Ivor Dean, Bill Barnsley, Alf Joint.

Mad Monster Party (1967, Embassy). *d:* Jules Bass; *sc:* Len Korobkin and Harvey Kurtzman—*b/o* a story by Arthur Rankin Jr.

BARON VON FRANKENSTEIN: The *voice* of this animated character who brings together several famous animated puppet movie monsters to announce his retirement.

Actors whose voices were used for other animated characters: Ethel Ennis, Gale Garnett, Phyllis Diller, Alan Swift.

Targets (1968, Para.). *d:* Peter Bogdanovich; *p:* Peter Bogdanovich (Saticoy); *sc:* Peter Bogdanovich—*b/o* a story by Polly Platt and Peter Bogdanovich.

BYRON ORLOK: Elderly horror-film star who, while making a personal appearance at a drive-in theater, confronts and disarms a psychotic Vietnam veteran who's turned into a mass-murdering sniper.

Tim O'Kelly, Nancy Hsueh, James Brown, Sandy Baron, Arthur Peterson, Mary Jackson, Tanya Morgan, Peter Bogdanovich.

The following films were released after the death of Boris Karloff:

The Crimson Cult (1970, AIP). *d:* Vernon Sewell; *sc:* Mervyn Haisman and Henry Lincoln.

PROFESSOR MARSHE: Expert on black magic and witchcraft who fights an evil witch's ancient curse that was put on the people of an English village 300 years earlier.

Christopher Lee, Mark Eden, Barbara Steele, Michael Gough, Rupert Davies, Virginia Wetherell, Rosemarie Reede, Derek Tansey.

The Snake People (1971, Col.). *d:* Jack Hill and Juan Ibanez; *p:* Luis Vergara; *sc:* Jack Hill.

KARL VAN MOLDER: Respected land owner on the island of Coaibai who is the secret head (known as "Damballah") of an evil voodoo cult of snake worshippers.

Julissa, Carlos East, Rafael Bertrand, Santanon, Quinton Bulnes, Tongolele.

The Incredible Invasion (1971, Col.). *d:* Jack Hill and Juan Ibanez; *p:* Luis Vergara; *sc:* Karl Schanzer and Luis Vergara.

PROF. JOHN MAYER: Scientist whose body is taken over by an alien from outer space in order to gain control of a powerful potential military weapon the scientist has invented.

Enrique Guzman, Christa Linder, Maura Monti, Yerye Beirute, Tere Valez, Sergio Kleiner, Griselda Mejia, Tito Novarro.

Cauldron of Blood (1971, Cannon). *d:* Edward Mann; *sc:* John Melson and Edward Mann.

FRANZ BADULESCU: Blind sculptor who discovers that his skeletal models are actually the victims of his murdering wife.

Jean-Pierre Aumont, Viveca Lindfors, Rosenda Monteros, Milo Queseda, Dianik Zurakowska, Ruben Rojo.

· In addition, Boris Karloff made cameo/guest appearances in the following feature films: *The Cohens and Kellys in Hollywood* (1932, Univ.), *The Gift of Gab* (1934, Univ.), and *Bikini Beach* (1964, AIP).

· Boris Karloff also appeared in the following serials: *The Hope Diamond Mystery* (1921, Kosmik—as DAKAR, a Hindu servant), *Vultures of the Sea* (1928, Mascot), *The Fatal Warning* (1929, Mascot), *King of the Kongo* (1929, Mascot—as SCARFACE MACKLIN, leader of a gang), and *King of the Wild* (1931, Mascot).

☆ HEDY LAMARR

Hedwig Eva Maria Kiesler

b: Nov. 9, 1914, Vienna, Austria

"I am Tondelayo."

> Tondelayo (Hedy Lamarr)
> introducing herself in a sultry voice
> in *White Cargo*, 1942.

Hedy Lamarr made the following first five films under her original stage name of Hedy Kiesler:

Money on the Street (1930, Sascha). *d:* Georg Jacoby; *p:* Nikolaus Deutsch; *sc:* Rudolf Oesterreicher—*b/o* a play by Rudolf Bernauer and Rudolf Oesterreicher.

Billed as "YOUNG GIRL": Pretty young woman clad in a black evening gown who is one of the people seated at a table in a German nightclub.

Georg Alexander, Leopold Kramer, Rosa Albach-Retty, Lydia Pollmann, Hans Moser, Hugo Thimig, Hans Thimig, Franz Schafheitlin, Karl Ziegler, Ernst Arnold.

The Flower Woman of Lindenau (1931, Sascha–Felsom). *d:* Georg Jacoby; *sc:* Walter Wassermann, W. Schlee, and Felix Salten—*b/o* a play by Bruno Frank.

Billed as "BURDACH'S SECRETARY": Pretty secretary whose boss, a dedicated young German newspaperman, helps a poor old flower lady get back her impounded dog.

Hansi Niese, Renate Muller, Paul Otto, Harald Paulsen, Herbert Huebner, Grete Maren.

His Majesty, King Ballyhoo (1931, Sascha). *d:*
Karl Boese; *p:* Dr. Wilhelm Szekely; *sc:* Karl Noti
and Hans Wilhelm—*b/o* a play by F. Altenkirch.

KATHE BRANDT: Pretty young woman in a
small German village who is the sweetheart of an
ambitious bank clerk.

Heinz Ruhmann, Hans Moser, Ida Wust, Hans
Junkermann, Kurt Gerron, Paul Henckels.

The Trunks of Mr. O.F. (1932, Tobis). *d:* Alexis
Granowsky; *p:* Hans Conradi and Mark Asarow;
sc: Leo Lania and Alexis Granowsky—a story by
Hans Homberg.

HELENE: Mayor's daughter in a small German
town where thirteen trunks marked "O.F." lead to
a series of events resulting in a fantastic financial
boom and the town's becoming a city.

Alfred Abel, Peter Lorre, Harald Paulsen, Ludwig
Stoessel, Margo Lion, Ilse Korseck, Liska March.

Ecstasy (1933, Elekta). *d:* Gustav Machaty; *p:*
Franz Horky and Moriz Grunhut; *sc:* Gustav
Machaty, Franz Horky, Vitezslav Nezval, and
Jacques A. Koerpel.

EVA: Romantic young woman who, after she
marries a wealthy old man, has an affair with a
young engineer that results in her husband's
committing suicide.

Jaromir Rogoz, Aribert Mog, Leopold Kramer.

Algiers (1938, UA). *d:* John Cromwell; *p:* Walter
Wanger (Walter Wanger Prod.); *sc:* John Howard
Lawson and James M. Cain—*b/o* the book *Pepe le
Moko* by Detective Ashelbe.

GABY: Alluring, wealthy Parisian in Algiers
whose love affair with a handsome jewel thief
(Pepe Le Moko) ends in tragedy when Pepe risks
leaving the safety of the criminal-infested Casbah
to try to flee to Paris with her.

Charles Boyer, Sigrid Gurie, Joseph Calleia, Gene
Lockhart, Johnny Downs, Alan Hale, Joan
Woodbury, Robert Greig, Stanley Fields, Leonid
Kinsky, Walter Kingsford, Paul Harvey, Bert
Roach.

Lady of the Tropics (1939, MGM). *d:* Jack
Conway; *p:* Sam Zimbalist; *sc:* Ben Hecht.

MANON de VARGNES: Half-caste Eurasian girl
whose marriage to an American playboy in Saigon
ends tragically when she kills her former
influential Eurasian lover because he has
prevented her from leaving the country with her
husband.

Robert Taylor, Joseph Schildkraut, Gloria
Franklin, Ernest Cossart, Mary Taylor, Charles
Trowbridge, Frederick Worlock, Paul Porcasi,
Margaret Padula, Cecil Cunningham, Natalie
Moorhead.

I Take This Woman (1940, MGM). *d:* W. S. Van
Dyke; *p:* Bernard H. Hyman; *sc:* James Kevin
McGuinness—*b/o* a story by Charles MacArthur.

GEORGI GRAGORE: Beautiful fashion model
who, after she marries a dedicated doctor, at first
has trouble forgetting her married ex-lover but
finally realizes that she loves her husband.

Spencer Tracy, Verree Teasdale, Kent Taylor,
Laraine Day, Mona Barrie, Jack Carson, Paul
Cavanagh, Louis Calhern, Marjorie Main, Frances
Drake, George E. Stone, Willie Best, Don Castle,
Reed Hadley.

Boom Town (1940, MGM). *d:* Jack Conway; *p:*
Sam Zimbalist; *sc:* John Lee Mahin—*b/o* a short
story by James Edward Grant.

KAREN VANMEER: Sophisticated New York girl
who becomes the business confidante and mistress
of a two-fisted oil tycoon but finally bows out
when the oil man realizes that he still loves his
wife.

Clark Gable, Spencer Tracy, Claudette Colbert,
Frank Morgan, Lionel Atwill, Chill Wills, Marion
Martin, Minna Gombell, Joe Yule, Richard Lane,
George Lessey, Sara Haden, Frank Orth, Frank
McGlynn Sr., Curt Bois.

Comrade X (1940, MGM). *d:* King Vidor; *p:*
Gottfried Reinhardt; *sc:* Ben Hecht and Charles
Lederer—*b/o* a story by Walter Reisch.

THEODORE: Icy Communist streetcar conductor
whose father blackmails an American foreign
correspondent into marrying her in order to
smuggle her out of Russia to the United States.

Clark Gable, Oscar Homolka, Felix Bressart, Eve
Arden, Sig Rumann, Natasha Lytess, Vladimir
Sokoloff, Edgar Barrier, George Renevant,
Mikhail Rasumny.

Come Live with Me (1941, MGM). *d:* Clarence
Brown; *p:* Clarence Brown; *sc:* Patterson McNutt—
b/o a story by Virginia Van Upp.

JOHNNY JONES (JOHANNA JANNS): Wealthy
Austrian refugee who, after paying a financially
strapped young writer to marry her so that she
won't be deported from the U.S., winds up falling
in love with him.

James Stewart, Ian Hunter, Verree Teasdale,
Donald Meek, Barton MacLane, Edward Ashley,
King Baggot, Frank Orth, Frank Faylen, Horace
MacMahon.

Ziegfeld Girl (1941, MGM). *d:* Robert Z. Leonard;
p: Pandro S. Berman; *sc:* Marguerite Roberts and
Sonya Levien—*b/o* a story by William Anthony
McGuire.

SANDRA KOLTER: Beautiful wife of a struggling
violinist who, when she gets to be a famous
Ziegfeld girl, leaves the husband—but returns
when he becomes a successful concert violinist
and she realizes that she loves him.

James Stewart, Judy Garland, Lana Turner, Tony Martin, Jackie Cooper, Ian Hunter, Charles Winninger, Edward Everett Horton, Philip Dorn, Paul Kelly, Eve Arden, Dan Dailey Jr., Al Shean, Fay Holden, Felix Bressart, Rose Hobart.

H. M. Pulham, Esq. (1941, MGM). *d:* King Vidor; *p:* King Vidor; *sc:* King Vidor and Elizabeth Hill— *b/o* the novel by John P. Marquand.

MARVIN MYLES: Young Iowa woman in post-WWI New York who becomes a successful ad-agency copywriter and has a brief love affair with a bright young ad man; then some twenty years later she falls in love with him again, though he's now a stuffy, married Boston businessman.

Robert Young, Ruth Hussey, Charles Coburn, Van Heflin, Fay Holden, Bonita Granville, Douglas Wood, Charles Halton, Leif Erickson, Walter Kingsford, Byron Foulger, Grant Withers, Connie Gilchrist, Frank Faylen, Anne Revere, John Raitt.

Tortilla Flat (1942, MGM). *d:* Victor Fleming; *p:* Sam Zimbalist; *sc:* John Lee Mahin and Benjamin Glazer—*b/o* the novel by John Steinbeck.

DOLORES (SWEETS) RAMIREZ: Sultry, hard-working Portuguese cannery worker in a California fishing village who manages to hold her own with a group of indolent but good-hearted Mexican peasants, two of whom are vying for her affections.

Spencer Tracy, John Garfield, Frank Morgan, Akim Tamiroff, Sheldon Leonard, John Qualen, Donald Meek, Connie Gilchrist, Allen Jenkins, Henry O'Neill, Betty Wells, Harry Burns.

Crossroads (1942, MGM). *d:* Jack Conway; *p:* Edwin Knopf; *sc:* Gus Trosper—*b/o* a story by John Kafka and Howard Emmett Rogers.

LUCIENNE TALBOT: Loyal wife whose respected French diplomat husband is accused in court of being a former notorious criminal when it's revealed that he's been a victim of amnesia for many years.

William Powell, Claire Trevor, Basil Rathbone, Margaret Wycherly, Felix Bressart, Sig Rumann, H. B. Warner, Philip Merivale, Vladimir Sokoloff, Fritz Leiber, Frank Conroy.

White Cargo (1942, MGM). *d:* Richard Thorpe; *p:* Victor Saville; *sc:* Leon Gordon, from his stage play—*b/o* the novel *Hell's Playground* by Ida Vera Simonton.

TONDELAYO: Seductive, scheming native girl who, after she marries a young British rubber planter at an African plantation and causes his deterioration, tries to poison him but is forced to drink the poison herself.

Walter Pidgeon, Frank Morgan, Richard Carlson, Reginald Owen, Henry O'Neill, Bramwell Fletcher, Clyde Cook, Leigh Whipper, Oscar Polk, Darby Jones, Richard Ainley.

The Heavenly Body (1943, MGM). *d:* Alexander Hall; *p:* Arthur Hornblow Jr.; *sc:* Michael Arlen and Walter Reisch—*b/o* a story by Jacques Thery.

VICKY WHITLEY: Neglected wife who, when she turns to astrology and meets a dark, handsome stranger as predicted, finds her husband suddenly paying attention to her again.

William Powell, James Craig, Fay Bainter, Henry O'Neill, Spring Byington, Robert Sully, Morris Ankrum, Franco Corsaro, Connie Gilchrist, Arthur Space, Nicodemus.

The Conspirators (1944, WB). *d:* Jean Negulesco; *p:* Jack Chertok; *sc:* Vladimir Pozner and Leo Rosten (with additional dialogue by Jack Moffitt)—*b/o* a novel by Fredic Prokosch.

IRENE: Anti-Nazi spy in 1944 Lisbon who, while falling in love with a Dutch underground agent, discovers that her German husband (posing as an anti-Nazi) is a traitor to their cause.

Paul Henreid, Sydney Greenstreet, Peter Lorre, Victor Francen, Joseph Calleia, Vladimir Sokoloff, Eduardo Ciannelli, Steven Geray, Marcel Dalio, George Macready, Doris Lloyd, Monte Blue.

Experiment Perilous (1944, RKO). *d:* Jacques Tourneur; *p:* Robert Fellows; *sc:* Warren Duff— *b/o* a novel by Margaret Carpenter.

ALLIDA: Beautiful woman whose wealthy philanthropist husband tries to make her appear insane when, in fact, he is really the insane one and a murderer.

George Brent, Paul Lukas, Albert Dekker, Carl Esmond, Margaret Wycherly, Stephanie Bachelor, Julia Dean, Larry Wheat, Sam McDaniels.

Her Highness and the Bellboy (1945, MGM). *d:* Richard Thorpe; *p:* Joe Pasternak; *sc:* Richard Connell and Gladys Lehman.

PRINCESS VERONICA: Visiting ruler in New York who, after a bellboy mistakenly thinks he loves her but gives her up for his crippled sweetheart, follows suit and gives up her throne to marry an American reporter.

Robert Walker, June Allyson, Carl Esmond, Agnes Moorehead, "Rags" Ragland, Ludwig Stossel, George Cleveland, Warner Anderson, Ben Lessy, Edward Gargan, Gladys Blake, Jack Norton, Audrey Totter.

The Strange Woman (1946, UA). *d:* Edgar Ulmer; *p:* Jack Chertok (Hunt Stromberg Prod.); *sc:* Herb Meadows—*b/o* the novel by Ben Ames Williams.

JENNY HAGER: Selfish, conniving woman in 1820s Bangor, Maine, who, after marrying a wealthy merchant, persuades his son to kill him, then—after inheriting the husband's money— kicks out the son so that she can marry a handsome lumber-camp boss.

George Sanders, Louis Hayward, Gene Lockhart, Hillary Brooke, Rhys Williams, June Storey, Moroni Olsen, Olive Blakeney, Dennis Hoey, Ian Keith, Edward Biby, Katherine York.

Dishonored Lady (1947, UA). *d:* Robert Stevenson; *p:* Jack Chertok (Hunt Stromberg Prod.); *sc:* Edmund H. North—*b/o* a play by Edward Sheldon and Margaret Ayer Barnes.

MADELEINE DAMIEN: New York magazine editor who is accused of murdering an ex-lover but is cleared with the help of her scientist fiancé and her psychiatrist.

Dennis O'Keefe, John Loder, William Lundigan, Morris Carnovsky, Paul Cavanagh, Natalie Schafer, Douglas Dumbrille, Margaret Hamilton, Nicholas Joy.

Let's Live a Little (1948, Eagle–Lion). *d:* Richard Wallace; *p:* Eugene Frenke and Robert Cummings (United California); *sc:* Howard Irving Young, Edmund Hartmann, and Albert J. Cohen—*b/o* a story by Albert J. Cohen and Jack Harvey.

DR. J. O. LORING: Psychiatrist who, while treating a bundle-of-nerves advertising executive, becomes a bundle of nerves herself but finally ends up in his arms.

Robert Cummings, Anna Sten, Robert Shayne, Mary Treen, Harry Antrim, Hal K. Dawson, Billy Bevan, John Newland, Frank Sully, John Dehner, Frank Wilcox, Norma Varden, Lillian Randolph, Lucien Littlefield, Byron Foulger.

Samson and Delilah (1949, Para.). *d:* Cecil B. DeMille; *p:* Cecil B. DeMille; *sc:* Jesse Lasky Jr. and Frederick M. Frank (from original treatments by Harold Lamb and Vladimir Jabotinsky)—*b/o* the history of Samson and Delilah in the Holy Bible, Judges 13–16.

DELILAH: Philistine woman in 1100 B.C. who, after cutting super-strong Samson's hair (the source of his strength), delivers him to the Philistines for torture; but she repents and leads him to the columns that he shakes loose to bring down the temple on his enemies, Delilah, and himself.

Victor Mature, George Sanders, Angela Lansbury, Henry Wilcoxon, Fay Holden, Rusty (Russ) Tamblyn, William Farnum, Moroni Olsen, John Miljan, Arthur Q. Bryan, Frank Wilcox, Nils Asther, Karen Morley, George Reeves, Mike Mazurki, Frank Reicher, Tom Tyler.

A Lady without Passport (1950, MGM). *d:* Joseph H. Lewis; *p:* Samuel Marx; *sc:* Howard Dimsdale (adaptation by Cyril Hume)—*b/o* a story suggestion by Lawrence Taylor.

MARIANNE LORRESS: Beautiful refugee in Havana—one of a group of aliens slated to be smuggled into the U.S.—who falls in love with a U.S. undercover agent who's out to snare the smugglers.

John Hodiak, James Craig, George Macready, Steven Geray, Bruce Cowling, Nederick Young, Steven Hill, Robert Osterloh, Trevor Bardette, Mario Siletti.

Copper Canyon (1950, Para.). *d:* John Farrow; *p:* Mel Epstein; *sc:* Jonathan Latimer—*b/o* a story by Richard English.

LISA ROSELLE: Owner of a gambling saloon in post–Civil War Nevada who falls for a gunslinger who's helping Confederate veterans-turned-miners battle a gang of Northern crooks.

Ray Milland, Macdonald Carey, Mona Freeman, Harry Carey Jr., Frank Faylen, Hope Emerson, Taylor Holmes, Peggy Knudsen, James Burke, Percy Helton, Philip Van Zandt, Ian Wolfe.

My Favorite Spy (1951, Para.). *d:* Norman Z. McLeod; *p:* Paul Jones; *sc:* Edmund Hartmann and Jack Sher (with additional dialogue by Hal Kanter)—*b/o* a story and adaptation by Edmund Beloin and Lou Breslow.

LILY DALBRAY: International spy in Tangier (posing as a cabaret singer) who joins forces with an American burlesque comic (impersonating a notorious spy who is his double) to get hold of a vital piece of microfilm for the U.S. government.

Bob Hope, Francis L. Sullivan, Arnold Moss, Tonio Selwart, Stephen Chase, John Archer, Morris Ankrum, Marc Lawrence, Iris Adrian, Luis Van Rooten, Mike Mazurki, Ralph Smiley.

The Love of Three Queens (1954, Cino Del Duca–P.C.E.). *d:* Marc Allegret and Edgar Ulmer; *p:* Victor Pahlen; *sc:* Nino Novarese, Marc Allegret, and Salka Viertel (with additional dialogue by Aeneas Mackenzie and Hugh Gray)—*b/o* a story by Aeneas Mackenzie, Marc Allegret, and Vadim Plenianikoy.

HEDY WINDSOR: Beautiful socialite who, when she receives an invitation to a masked ball and must decide on a costume, selects three different famous women in history and imagines herself as each of them: Helen of Troy, Empress Josephine, and Genevieve de Brabant.

Gerard Oury, Massimo Serato, Robert Beatty, Cathy O'Donnell, Guido Celano, Enrico Glori, Seren Michelotti, Alba Arnova, Terence Morgan, Caesar Danova.

The Story of Mankind (1957, WB). *d:* Irwin Allen; *p:* Irwin Allen (Cambridge); *sc:* Irwin Allen and Charles Bennett—*b/o* the book by Hendrik van Loon.

JOAN OF ARC: Fifteenth-century French peasant girl who leads the French armies against the English and is burned at the stake as a heretic.

Ronald Colman, Groucho Marx, Harpo Marx, Chico Marx, Virginia Mayo, Agnes Moorehead, Vincent Price, Peter Lorre, Charles Coburn,

Cedric Hardwicke, Cesar Romero, John Carradine, Dennis Hopper, Marie Wilson, Helmut Dantine, Edward Everett Horton, Reginald Gardiner, Marie Windsor, Cathy O'Donnell, Francis X. Bushman, Jim Ameche, Franklin Pangborn, Henry Daniell, Tudor Owen.

The Female Animal (1957, Univ.). *d:* Harry Keller; *p:* Albert Zugsmith; *sc:* Robert Hill—*b/o* a story by Albert Zugsmith.

VANESSA WINDSOR: Aging Hollywood star who, after she's saved from death by a handsome young movie extra, takes him as a lover, then has to give him up when he falls in love with her adopted daughter.

Jane Powell, George Nader, Jan Sterling, Jerry Paris, Gregg Palmer, Mabel Albertson, James Gleason, Casey Adams, Ann Doran, Richard Cutting.

☆ BURT LANCASTER

Burton Stephen Lancaster

b: Nov. 2, 1913, New York, N.Y.

"You couldn't just play it smart, could you? All ya had to do was box. But no, not you, you hard-head!"

Sgt. Milton Warden (Burt Lancaster) lamenting the death of Robert E. Lee Prewitt (Montgomery Clift) in *From Here to Eternity*, 1953.

The Killers (1946, Univ.). *d:* Robert Siodmak; *p:* Mark Hellinger; *sc:* Anthony Veiller—*b/o* the short story by Ernest Hemingway.

SWEDE (PETE LUNN/OLE ANDERSON): Ex–prize fighter who, after he's gotten mixed up with mobsters and a double-crossing dame, waits resignedly in his small-town hotel room for two hitmen to find and kill him.

Ava Gardner, Edmond O'Brien, Albert Dekker, Sam Levene, Jack Lambert, Jeff Corey, Donald McBride, Vince Barnett, Virginia Christine, John Miljan, Charles McGraw, William Conrad.

Desert Fury (1947, Para.). *d:* Lewis Allen; *p:* Hal B. Wallis; *sc:* Robert Rossen—*b/o* a story by Ramona Stewart.

TOM HANSON: Young sheriff in the Southwest who clashes with a big-time gambler when they both fall for the headstrong daughter of a female owner of a gambling casino.

Lizabeth Scott, John Hodiak, Mary Astor, Wendell Corey, Kristine Miller, William Harrigan, James Flavin, Jane Novak.

Brute Force (1947, Univ.). *d:* Jules Dassin; *p:* Mark Hellinger; *sc:* Richard Brooks—*b/o* a story by Robert Patterson.

JOE COLLINS: Tough leader of a group of convicts who, goaded by a sadistic prison-guard captain, attempt a daring and bloody prison break.

Hume Cronyn, Charles Bickford, Sam Levene, Howard Duff, Art Smith, John Hoyt, Jeff Corey, Vince Barnett, Yvonne De Carlo, Ann Blyth, Ella Raines, Anita Colby, Whit Bissell, Sir Lancelot.

I Walk Alone (1948, Para.). *d:* Byron Haskin; *p:* Hal B. Wallis (Hal Wallis Prod.); *sc:* Charles Schnee (adaptation by Robert Smith and John Bright)—*b/o* the play *Beggars Are Coming to Town* by Theodore Reeves.

FRANKIE MADISON: Former Prohibition-era bootlegger who, when he's released after serving fourteen years in prison on a frame-up, is double-crossed again by his ex-partner, a conniving nightclub owner–racketeer.

Lizabeth Scott, Kirk Douglas, Wendell Corey, Kristine Miller, George Rigaud, Marc Lawrence, Mike Mazurki, Mickey Knox, Roger Neury.

All My Sons (1948, Univ.). *d:* Irving Reis; *p:* Chester Erskine; *sc:* Chester Erskine—*b/o* the play by Arthur Miller.

CHRIS KELLER: Upstanding son who is shattered when he discovers that his father, a wealthy airplane manufacturer, was a WWII war profiteer who knowingly sold defective parts to the U.S. Army Air Force, causing the deaths of several American pilots.

Edward G. Robinson, Mady Christians, Louisa Horton, Howard Duff, Frank Conroy, Lloyd Gough, Arlene Francis, Henry Morgan (Harry Morgan), Charles Meredith, Elizabeth Fraser, Herbert Vigran, Harry Harvey.

Sorry, Wrong Number (1948, Para.). *d:* Anatole Litvak; *p:* Anatole Litvak and Hal B. Wallis; *sc:* Lucille Fletcher—*b/o* her radio play.

HENRY STEVENSON: Husband who, because he needs money to pay his gambling debts, hires a killer to murder his wealthy bedridden wife—who accidentally overhears the murder being plotted on the telephone.

Barbara Stanwyck, Ann Richards, Wendell Corey,

Harold Vermilyea, Ed Begley, Leif Erickson, William Conrad, John Bromfield, Paul Fierro, Kristine Miller.

Kiss the Blood off My Hands (1948, Univ.). *d:* Norman Foster; *p:* Richard Vernon (Hecht–Norma); *sc:* Leonardo Bercovici (adaptation by Ben Maddow and Walter Bernstein, with additional dialogue by Hugh Gray)—*b/o* the novel by Gerald Butler.

BILL SAUNDERS: Ex-soldier who kills a London pub owner in a fight, then falls in love with a nurse when he hides out in her flat, but—after the nurse kills a blackmailer—is convinced that they both should give themselves up to the police.
Joan Fontaine, Robert Newton, Lewis L. Russell, Aminta Dyne, Grizelda Hervey, Jay Novello, Colin Keith-Johnston, Reginald Sheffield, Campbell Copelin.

Criss Cross (1949, Univ.). *d:* Robert Siodmak; *p:* Michael Kraike; *sc:* Daniel Fuchs—*b/o* a novel by Don Tracy.
STEVE THOMPSON: Honest armored-car guard who is coerced by his double-crossing ex-wife and her vicious gangster husband into helping rob his own money truck.
Yvonne De Carlo, Dan Duryea, Stephen McNally, Richard Long, Esy Morales, Percy Helton, Alan Napier, Griff Barnett, Meg Randall, John Doucette, Tony Curtis.

Rope of Sand (1949, Para.). *d:* William Dieterle; *p:* Hal B. Wallis; *sc:* Walter Doniger (with additional dialogue by John Paxton).
MIKE DAVIS: Former hunting guide who returns to a South African town and tangles with a sadistic police chief and a diamond-company executive as he tries to grab a fortune in stashed-away diamonds.
Paul Henreid, Claude Rains, Corinne Calvet, Peter Lorre, Sam Jaffe, John Bromfield, Mike Mazurki, Kenny Washington.

The Flame and the Arrow (1950, WB). *d:* Jacques Tourneur; *p:* Harold Hecht and Frank Ross (Norma–FR); *sc:* Waldo Salt.
DARDO: Colorful, swashbuckling rebel leader in medieval Italy who leads his people to victory in a fight against the tyrannical Hessian ruler of the city of Granezia.
Virginia Mayo, Robert Douglas, Aline MacMahon, Frank Allenby, Nick Cravat, Norman Lloyd, Victor Kilian, Francis Pierlot, Robin Hughes.

Mister 880 (1950, 20th-Fox). *d:* Edmund Goulding; *p:* Julian Blaustein; *sc:* Robert Riskin—*b/o* articles in the *New Yorker* by St. Clair McKelway.
STEVE BUCHANAN: Sympathetic U.S. Treasury agent who is assigned to track down a nice old gentleman who's been making a living by printing his own one-dollar bills.
Dorothy McGuire, Edmund Gwenn, Millard Mitchell, Minor Watson, Howard St. John, James Millican, Larry Keating, Kathleen Hughes, Hugh Sanders, Geraldine Wall.

Vengeance Valley (1951, MGM). *d:* Richard Thorpe; *p:* Nicholas Nayfack; *sc:* Irving Ravetch—*b/o* the novel by Luke Short.
OWEN DAYBRIGHT: Two-fisted ranch foreman who runs into trouble when he tries to keep his worthless foster brother's misdeeds from their cattle-baron father.
Robert Walker, Joanne Dru, Sally Forrest, John Ireland, Carleton Carpenter, Ray Collins, Ted de Corsia, Hugh O'Brian, Will Wright, Stanley Andrews.

Jim Thorpe—All American (1951, WB). *d:* Michael Curtiz; *p:* Everett Freeman; *sc:* Douglas Morrow and Everett Freeman (with additional dialogue by Frank Davis)—*b/o* a story by Douglas Morrow and Vincent X. Flaherty, and the biography by Russell J. Birdwell and Jim Thorpe.
JIM THORPE: Oklahoma Indian who becomes a famous All-American football star and all-around athlete but hits the skids after the medals he won in the 1912 Olympics are taken away from him for violating the rules of professionalism.
Charles Bickford, Steve Cochran, Phyllis Thaxter, Dick Wesson, Jack Big Head, Suni Warcloud, Al Mejia, Hubie Kerns, Nestor Paiva, Jimmy Moss, Billy Gray.

Ten Tall Men (1951, Col.). *d:* Willis Goldbeck; *p:* Harold Hecht (Norma Prod.); *sc:* Roland Kibbee and Frank Davis—*b/o* a story by James Warner Bellah and Willis Goldbeck.
SGT. MIKE KINCAID: Tough French Foreign Legion sergeant who, when he leads a patrol to prevent a Riff attack on Tarfa, captures a Riff princess and falls in love with her.
Jody Lawrance, Gilbert Roland, Kieron Moore, George Tobias, John Dehner, Nick Dennis, Mike Mazurki, Gerald Mohr, Ian MacDonald, Mari Blanchard, Robert Clary, Philip Van Zandt.

The Crimson Pirate (1952, WB). *d:* Robert Siodmak; *p:* Harold Hecht (Norma Prod.); *sc:* Roland Kibbee.
VALLO: Ex–circus acrobat in the eighteenth century who becomes a swashbuckling pirate and leads the oppressed people on a Caribbean island in a rebellion against a tyrant.
Nick Cravat, Eva Bartok, Torin Thatcher, James Hayter, Leslie Bradley, Margot Grahame, Noel Purcell, Frank Pettingill, Dagmar (Dana) Wynter, Christopher Lee.

Come Back, Little Sheba (1952, Para.). *d:* Daniel

Mann; *p:* Hal B. Wallis; *sc:* Ketti Frings—*b/o* the play by William Inge.

DOC DELANEY: Middle-aged, alcoholic ex-chiropractor who, when a pretty female student moves in as a boarder, realizes that the old emotional problems between him and his pathetic, slatternly wife still exist.

Shirley Booth, Terry Moore, Richard Jaeckel, Philip Ober, Edwin Max, Lisa Golm, Walter Kelley, Paul McVey.

South Sea Woman (1953, WB). *d:* Arthur Lubin; *p:* Sam Bischoff; *sc:* Edwin Blum—*b/o* a play by William M. Rankin.

SERGEANT O'HEARN: One of a pair of brawling U.S. Marine buddies in the Pacific who, besides fighting WWII, battle over a sexy blonde nightclub girl.

Virginia Mayo, Chuck Connors, Arthur Shields, Barry Kelley, Leon Askin, Veola Vonn, Robert Sweeney, Hayden Rorke, Raymond Greenleaf, Paul Burke, Henri Letondal.

From Here to Eternity (1953, Col.). *d:* Fred Zinnemann; *p:* Buddy Adler; *sc:* Daniel Taradash—*b/o* the novel by James Jones.

SGT. MILTON WARDEN*: Hardboiled regular Army top-kick at Schofield Barracks in 1941 Honolulu who becomes involved in an ill-fated affair with his no-good captain's wife just prior to the Japanese attack on Pearl Harbor.

Montgomery Clift, Deborah Kerr, Donna Reed, Frank Sinatra, Philip Ober, Mickey Shaughnessy, Harry Bellaver, Ernest Borgnine, Jack Warden, Merle Travis, Tim Ryan, Claude Akins, Robert Wilke, George Reeves, Don Dubbins, Willis Bouchey.

His Majesty O'Keefe (1954, WB). *d:* Byron Haskin; *p:* Harold Hecht; *sc:* Borden Chase and James Hill—*b/o* a novel by Lawrence Kingman and Gerald Green.

HIS MAJESTY O'KEEFE: Sea-faring soldier of fortune in the 1870s who, while teaching the natives on a tropical island how to cash in on their copra, tangles with a villainous South Seas pirate.

Joan Rice, Andre Morell, Abraham Sofaer, Archie Savage, Benson Fong, Tessa Prendergast, Charles Horvath, Philip Ahn, Guy Doleman, Grant Taylor, Alexander Archdale.

Apache (1954, UA). *d:* Robert Aldrich; *p:* Harold Hecht (Hecht–Lancaster); *sc:* James R. Webb—*b/o* the novel *Bronco Apache* by Paul I. Wellman.

MASSAI: Peace-seeking Apache Indian leader in the 1880s who, after he's wronged by the U.S. Cavalry, wages a bitter one-man war for his tribe's rights.

---

*Received an Academy Award nomination as Best Actor for this role.

Jean Peters, John McIntire, Charles Buchinsky (Bronson), John Dehner, Paul Guilfoyle, Ian MacDonald, Walter Sande, Morris Ankrum, Monte Blue.

Vera Cruz (1954, UA). *d:* Robert Aldrich; *p:* James Hill (Hecht–Lancaster); *sc:* Roland Kibbee and James R. Webb—*b/o* a story by Borden Chase.

JOE ERIN: One of a duo of American soldiers of fortune during the Mexican Revolution of 1866 who are hired to escort a European countess from Mexico City to Vera Cruz, unaware that she's transporting gold for Emperor Maximilian's troops.

Gary Cooper, Denise Darcel, Cesar Romero, George Macready, Ernest Borgnine, Henry Brandon, Charles Buchinsky (Bronson), Morris Ankrum, Jack Lambert, Jack Elam, Charles Horvath, Juan Garcia.

The Kentuckian (1955, UA). *d:* Burt Lancaster; *p:* Harold Hecht (Hecht–Lancaster); *sc:* A. B. Guthrie Jr.—*b/o* Felix Holt's novel *The Gabriel Horn*.

BIG ELI: Two-fisted backwoodsman in the 1820s who, along with his young son, fights his way across the Kentucky frontier to a new life in Texas.

Dianne Foster, Diana Lynn, John McIntire, Una Merkel, Walter Matthau, John Carradine, John Litel, Rhys Williams, Edward Norris, Clem Bevans, Lisa Ferraday.

The Rose Tattoo (1955, Para.). *d:* Daniel Mann; *p:* Hal B. Wallis (Hal Wallis Prod.); *sc:* Tennessee Williams (adaptation by Hal Kanter)—*b/o* the play by Tennessee Williams.

ALVARO MANGIACAVALLO: Brawny, dull-witted truck driver in a Gulf Coast city who makes an earthy Italian-American widow forget about remaining faithful to the memory of her late husband.

Anna Magnani, Marisa Pavan, Ben Cooper, Virginia Grey, Jo Van Fleet, Sandro Giglio, Mimi Aguglia, Florence Sundstrom, Rosa Rey.

Trapeze (1956, UA). *d:* Carol Reed; *p:* James Hill (Hecht–Lancaster); *sc:* James R. Webb (adaptation by Liam O'Brien)—*b/o* Max Catto's book *The Killing Frost*.

MIKE RIBBLE: Crippled ex–star trapeze artist with a Paris circus who, after making a successful comeback by forming a new act with an ambitious youngster and a shapely female, clashes with the young man over the woman.

Tony Curtis, Gina Lollobrigida, Katy Jurado, Thomas Gomez, Johnny Puleo, Minor Watson, Gerard Landry, Sidney James, Pierre Tabard, Michel Thomas.

The Rainmaker (1956, Para.). *d:* Joseph Anthony; *p:* Hal B. Wallis and Paul Nathan (Hal B. Wallis Prod.); *sc:* N. Richard Nash—*b/o* his play.

STARBUCK: Smooth-talking con man in 1913 who pops up at a drought-stricken Kansas farm, boasts that he can make it rain, and—while waiting for the rain to start—shows a repressed spinster the way to self-confidence and romance.

Katharine Hepburn, Wendell Corey, Lloyd Bridges, Earl Holliman, Cameron Prud'homme, Wallace Ford, Yvonne Lime, Dottie Bee Baker, Dan White.

Gunfight at the OK Corral (1957, Para.). *d:* John Sturges; *p:* Hal B. Wallis (Hal B. Wallis Prod.); *sc:* Leon Uris—*b/o* George Scullin's article "The Killer."

WYATT EARP: Famed lawman who, along with his brothers and Doc Holliday, wipes out the notorious Clanton gang in the celebrated shoot-out at the OK Corral in Tombstone, Arizona, on October 26, 1881.

Kirk Douglas, Rhonda Fleming, Jo Van Fleet, John Ireland, Lyle Bettger, Frank Faylen, Earl Holliman, Ted De Corsia, Dennis Hopper, Whit Bissell, DeForest Kelley, Martin Milner, Kenneth Tobey, Lee Van Cleef, Jack Elam.

Sweet Smell of Success (1957, UA). *d:* Alexander Mackendrick; *p:* James Hill (Norma/Curtleigh); *sc:* Clifford Odets and Ernest Lehman—*b/o* the novelette by Ernest Lehman.

J. J. HUNSECKER: Ruthless Broadway columnist who coerces a fawning press agent into framing a young jazz musician on drug charges in order to break up his romance with the columnist's sister.

Tony Curtis, Susan Harrison, Martin Milner, Sam Levene, Barbara Nichols, Jeff Donnell, Emile Meyer, Joe Frisco, David White, Lawrence Dobkin, Lurene Tuttle, Queenie Smith, Jay Adler, Lewis Charles.

Run Silent, Run Deep (1958, UA). *d:* Robert Wise; *p:* Harold Hecht (Hecht–Hill–Lancaster); *sc:* John Gay—*b/o* the novel by Commander Edward L. Beach.

LT. JIM BLEDSOE: Executive officer on a WWII U.S. submarine in Japanese waters who, along with the rest of the crew, resents the new sub commander but eventually grows to respect him as the sub hunts down a Japanese destroyer and sinks it.

Clark Gable, Jack Warden, Brad Dexter, Don Rickles, Nick Cravat, Joe Maross, Mary LaRoche, Eddie Foy III, Rudy Bond, H. M. Wynant, Ken Lynch.

Separate Tables (1958, UA). *d:* Delbert Mann; *p:* Harold Hecht (Hecht–Hill–Lancaster); *sc:* Terence Rattigan and John Gay—*b/o* the one-act plays *Table Number Seven* and *Table by the Window* by Terence Rattigan.

JOHN MALCOLM: Boarder at a British seaside guest house whose mistress is the proprietress,

and whose ex-wife turns up as a guest and begs him for another chance.

Rita Hayworth, Deborah Kerr, David Niven, Wendy Hiller, Gladys Cooper, Cathleen Nesbitt, Felix Aylmer, Rod Taylor, Audrey Dalton, Priscilla Morgan, May Hallatt, Hilda Plowright.

The Devil's Disciple (1959, UA). *d:* Guy Hamilton; *p:* Harold Hecht (Hecht–Hill–Lancaster/Brynaprod); *sc:* John Dighton and Roland Kibbee—*b/o* the play by George Bernard Shaw.

ANTHONY ANDERSON: New England pastor who, when he takes up arms against the British during the Revolutionary War, almost loses his wife to a devil-may-care fellow revolutionist but becomes a hero and wins her back.

Kirk Douglas, Laurence Olivier, Janette Scott, Eva LeGallienne, Harry Andrews, Basil Sydney, George Rose, Neil McCallum, Mervyn Johns, David Horne.

The Unforgiven (1960, UA). *d:* John Huston; *p:* James Hill (James/Hecht–Hill–Lancaster); *sc:* Ben Maddow—*b/o* a novel by Alan Le May.

BEN ZACHARY: Pre–Civil War Texan who feuds with savage Kiowa Indians when they try to take his foster sister, claiming that she was actually a Kiowa orphan at the time she was adopted by the whites.

Audrey Hepburn, Audie Murphy, John Saxon, Charles Bickford, Lillian Gish, Albert Salmi, Joseph Wiseman, June Walker, Kipp Hamilton, Carlos Rivas, Doug McClure.

Elmer Gantry (1960, UA). *d:* Richard Brooks; *p:* Bernard Smith; *sc:* Richard Brooks—*b/o* the novel by Sinclair Lewis.

ELMER GANTRY*: Opportunistic, itinerant salesman in the 1920s Midwest who, after he joins a female evangelist's traveling show, rises to become a powerful revivalist on his own—but in reality is a corrupt con man.

Jean Simmons, Arthur Kennedy, Shirley Jones, Dean Jagger, Patti Page, Edward Andrews, John McIntire, Joe Maross, Michael Whalen, Hugh Marlowe, Philip Ober, Wendell Holmes, Barry Kelley, Rex Ingram, John Qualen.

The Young Savages (1961, UA). *d:* John Frankenheimer; *p:* Harold Hecht and Pat Duggan (Contemporary); *sc:* Edward Anhalt and J. P. Miller—*b/o* the novel *A Matter of Conviction* by Evan Hunter.

HANK BELL: Idealistic, slum-born district attorney who battles street-gang hoodlums as he seeks justice in a case involving the murder of a Puerto Rican gang member on New York's East Side.

---

*Won the Academy Award as Best Actor for this role.

Dina Merrill, Shelley Winters, Edward Andrews, Vivian Nathan, Larry Gates, Telly Savalas, Pilar Seurat, Jody Fair, Roberta Shore, Milton Selzer, Robert Burton, Luis Arroyo.

Judgment at Nuremberg (1961, UA). *d:* Stanley Kramer; *p:* Stanley Kramer (Roxlom); *sc:* Abby Mann—*b/o* his TV play.
ERNEST JANNING: One of the ex-Nazi judges who is tried and found guilty during the post-WWII Nazi War Crimes Trials held by the Allies in Nuremberg, Germany, in 1948.
Spencer Tracy, Richard Widmark, Marlene Dietrich, Maximilian Schell, Judy Garland, Montgomery Clift, William Shatner, Edward Binns, Kenneth MacKenna, Warner Klemperer, Alan Baxter, Ray Teal, Virginia Christine, Karl Swenson, Sheila Bromley.

Birdman of Alcatraz (1962, UA). *d:* John Frankenheimer; *p:* Stuart Millar and Guy Trosper (Hecht-Lancaster); *sc:* Guy Trosper—*b/o* the book by Thomas E. Gaddis.
ROBERT STROUD*: Murderer who, while spending nearly sixty years in prison, educates himself to become a world-famous expert in the science of birds.
Karl Malden, Thelma Ritter, Betty Field, Neville Brand, Edmond O'Brien, Hugh Marlowe, Telly Savalas, Whit Bissell, Crahan Denton, Leo Penn, James Westerfield, Chris Robinson.

A Child Is Waiting (1963, UA). *d:* John Cassavetes; *p:* Stanley Kramer (Stanley Kramer Prod.); *sc:* Abby Mann—*b/o* his TV play.
DR. MATTHEW CLARK: Head psychiatrist at a state institution for mentally retarded children who disagrees with a female staff member over her mistaken belief that pampering and sheltering the children will solve the children's problems.
Judy Garland, Gena Rowlands, Steven Hill, Bruce Ritchey, Gloria McGehee, Paul Stewart, Barbara Pepper, John Morley, June Walker, Lawrence Tierney.

The List of Adrian Messenger (1963, Univ.). *d:* John Huston; *p:* Edward Lewis (Joel); *sc:* Anthony Veiller—*b/o* the novel by Philip MacDonald.
Played (in disguise) the part of a "ban the fox hunt" matron—one of several characters involved in the mysterious case of a series of murders that a retired British Intelligence officer and Scotland Yard are trying to solve.
George C. Scott, Dana Wynter, Clive Brook, Gladys Cooper, Herbert Marshall, John Merivale, Marcel Dalio, John Huston, Bernard Fox, Tony Curtis, Kirk Douglas, Robert Mitchum, Frank Sinatra.

The Leopard (1963, 20th-Fox). *d:* Luchino Visconti; *p:* Goffredo Lombardo (Titanus/SNPC/GPC); *sc:* Suso Cecchi D'Amico, Pasquale Festa Campanile, Massimo Franciosa, Enrico Medioli, and Luchino Visconti.
PRINCE DON FABRIZIO SALINA: Aging aristocrat in 1860s Sicily who, when Garibaldi and his red shirts invade, is devastated by the realization that the aristocracy must yield to the new order.
Alain Delon, Claudia Cardinale, Rina Morelli, Paolo Stoppa, Romolo Valli, Lucilla Morlacchi, Serge Reggiani, Ida Galli, Ottavia Piccolo, Leslie French.

Seven Days in May (1964, Para.). *d:* John Frankenheimer; *p:* Edward Lewis (Seven Arts–Joel); *sc:* Rod Serling—*b/o* the novel by Fletcher Knebel and Charles W. Bailey II.
GEN. JAMES M. SCOTT: Chairman of the Joint Chiefs of Staff who, when the president of the United States signs a nuclear disarmament treaty with Russia in 1974, secretly plots a military takeover of the government.
Kirk Douglas, Fredric March, Ava Gardner, Edmond O'Brien, Martin Balsam, George Macready, Whit Bissell, Hugh Marlowe, Richard Anderson, Andrew Duggan, John Larkin, Malcolm Atterbury, John Houseman.

The Train (1965, UA). *d:* John Frankenheimer; *p:* Jules Bricken (Ariane/Dear); *sc:* Franklin Coen and Frank Davis—*b/o* *Le Front de l'Art* by Rose Valland.
LABICHE: Patriotic WWII French railway official who leads the Resistance in a plan to waylay a train on which the Nazis are trying to ship France's valuable art treasures to Germany.
Paul Scofield, Jeanne Moreau, Michel Simon, Suzanne Flon, Wolfgang Preiss, Richard Munch, Albert Remy, Charles Millot, Donal O'Brien, Jean-Pierre Zola, Art Brauss.

The Hallelujah Trail (1965, UA). *d:* John Sturges; *p:* John Sturges (Mirisch/Kappa); *sc:* John Gay—*b/o* the novel by Bill Gulick.
THADDEUS GEARHART: U.S. Cavalry captain in 1867 who, when he's ordered to protect a wagonload of whiskey bound for Denver, finds himself in a donnybrook involving saloon owners, thirsty miners, Sioux Indians, and a band of militant temperance women.
Lee Remick, Jim Hutton, Pamela Tiffin, Donald Pleasance, Brian Keith, Martin Landau, John Anderson, Robert J. Wilke, Dub Taylor, Bill Williams, Bing Russell, Billy Benedict, Whit Bissell, John Dehner.

The Professionals (1966, Col.). *d:* Richard Brooks; *p:* Richard Brooks (Pax); *sc:* Richard Brooks—*b/o*

---

*Received an Academy Award nomination as Best Actor for this role.

the novel *A Mule for the Marquesa* by Frank O'Rourke.

DOLWORTH: Dynamite expert—one of four soldiers of fortune hired by a wealthy American rancher to rescue his young Mexican wife who, following the 1917 Mexican Revolution, has allegedly been kidnapped by a Mexican guerilla leader.

Lee Marvin, Robert Ryan, Jack Palance, Claudia Cardinale, Ralph Bellamy, Woody Strode, Joe De Santis, Marie Gomez, Carlos Romero, Vaughn Taylor.

The Scalphunters (1968, UA). *d:* Sydney Pollack; *p:* Jules Levy, Arthur Gardner, and Arnold Laven (Levy–Gardner–Laven/Roland Kibbee); *sc:* William Norton.

JOE BASS: Frontier fur trapper who teams up with an educated runaway slave to battle Indians and a band of scalp-hunting white renegades for some stolen furs.

Shelley Winters, Telly Savalas, Ossie Davis, Armando Silvestre, Dan Vadis, Dabney Coleman, Paul Picerni, Nick Cravat, Jack Williams, Agapito Roldan, John Epper.

The Swimmer (1968, Col.). *d:* Frank Perry; *p:* Frank Perry and Roger Lewis (Horizon); *sc:* Eleanor Perry—*b/o* a story by John Cheever.

NED MERRILL: Middle-aged ad man who, when he decides to swim home through the back-yard pools of his Connecticut suburbanite neighbors, is haunted by regrets from the past and fears of the future.

Janice Rule, Janet Landgard, Charles Drake, Tony Bickley, Marge Champion, John Garfield Jr., Kim Hunter, Bernie Hamilton, House Jameson, Jan Miner, Diana Muldaur, Joan Rivers, Cornelia Otis Skinner.

Castle Keep (1969, Col.). *d:* Sydney Pollack; *p:* Martin Ransohoff and John Calley (Filmways); *sc:* Daniel Taradash and David Rayfiel—*b/o* the novel by William Eastlake.

MAJ. ABRAHAM FALCONER: One-eyed WWII Army major who is killed by the attacking Germans when he and a small group of American infantrymen occupy an art-treasure-filled tenth-century castle in the Ardennes Forest.

Peter Falk, Patrick O'Neal, Jean-Pierre Aumont, Scott Wilson, Tony Bill, Michael Conrad, Bruce Dern, Al Freeman Jr., James Patterson, Astrid Heeren, Ernest Clark.

The Gypsy Moths (1969, MGM). *d:* John Frankenheimer; *p:* Hal Landers and Bobby Roberts; *sc:* William Hanley—*b/o* the novel by James Drought.

MIKE RETTIG: Barnstorming skydiver who—when he and his two buddies hit a small Kansas town—falls for a local housewife but is killed while trying to perform a dangerous stunt.

Deborah Kerr, Gene Hackman, Scott Wilson, William Windom, Bonnie Bedelia, Sheree North, Carl Reindel, Ford Rainey, John Napier.

Airport (1970, Univ.). *d:* George Seaton; *p:* Ross Hunter; *sc:* George Seaton—*b/o* the novel by Arthur Hailey.

MEL BAKERSFELD: Unhappily married manager of a Midwestern metropolitan airport who has to cope with his girlfriend, a paralyzing blizzard, and a Boeing 707 that has to be "talked down" after it's damaged by a mad bomber.

Dean Martin, Jean Seberg, Jacqueline Bisset, George Kennedy, Helen Hayes, Van Heflin, Maureen Stapleton, Barry Nelson, Dana Wynter, Lloyd Nolan, Barbara Hale, Gary Collins, Jesse Royce Landis, Larry Gates, Whit Bissell, Virgina Grey, Paul Picerni, Dick Winslow.

Valdez Is Coming (1971, UA). *d:* Edwin Sherin; *p:* Ira Steiner (Norlan–Ira Steiner); *sc:* Roland Kibbee and David Rayfiel—*b/o* the novel by Elmore Leonard.

BOB VALDEZ: Aging Mexican-American deputy sheriff who, after he's forced to kill an innocent fugitive in self-defense, tries to provide for the man's pregnant widow and finds himself clashing with a crooked land baron.

Susan Clark, Jon Cypher, Barton Heyman, Richard Jordan, Frank Silvera, Hector Elizondo, Roberta Haynes, Maria Montez, Jose Garcia, Concha Hombria, Per Barclay.

Lawman (1971, UA). *d:* Michael Winner; *p:* Michael Winner (Scimitar); *sc:* Gerald Wilson.

JERED MADDOX: Dedicated New Mexico marshal who—when he rides into a nearby town to arrest a cowman and his boys for the drunken, accidental killing of an old man—finds the townspeople hostile and is forced into a bloody shoot-out.

Robert Ryan, Lee J. Cobb, Sheree North, Joseph Wiseman, Robert Duvall, Albert Salmi, J. D. Cannon, John McGiver, Ralph Waite, Charles Tyner, John Hillerman, Robert Emhardt, Richard Bull.

Ulzana's Raid (1972, Univ.). *d:* Robert Aldrich; *p:* Carter De Haven; *sc:* Alan Sharp.

McINTOSH: Veteran Indian fighter who helps a green young U.S. Cavalry lieutenant and his troops battle a rampaging band of Indians led by a renegade Apache.

Bruce Davison, Jorge Luke, Richard Jaeckel, Joaquin Martinez, Lloyd Bochner, Karl Swenson, Douglass Watson, Dran Hamilton, Gladys Holland, Richard Bull.

Scorpio (1973, UA). *d:* Michael Winner; *p:* Walter

Mirisch (Scimitar/Mirisch); *sc:* David W. Rintels and Gerald Wilson—*b/o* a story by David W. Rintels.

CROSS: Veteran CIA agent who plays a deadly game of cat-and-mouse with Scorpio—a fellow agent who has been hired to kill him.

Alain Delon, Paul Scofield, John Colicos, Gayle Hunnicutt, J. D. Cannon, Joanne Linville, Melvin Stewart, Mary Maude, Jack Colvin, Burke Byrnes, William Smithers, Robert Emhardt.

Executive Action (1973, Nat. Gen.). *d:* David Miller; *p:* Edward Lewis, Dan Bessie, and Gary Horowitz (EA Enterprises and Wakefond/Orloff); *sc:* Dalton Trumbo—*b/o* a story by Donald Freed and Mark Lane.

FARRINGTON: One of a group of political conspirators—powerful members of the military-industrial complex—who hire three gunmen to kill President John F. Kennedy in Dallas on November 22, 1963. (This movie is based on the filmmakers' premise of what *could* have happened.)

Robert Ryan, Will Geer, Gilbert Green, John Anderson, Paul Carr, Colby Chester, Ed Lauter, Deanna Darrin, Lloyd Gough, James MacColl, Oscar Oncidi, Paul Sorenson.

The Midnight Man (1974, Univ.). *d:* Roland Kibbee and Burt Lancaster; *p:* Roland Kibbee and Burt Lancaster (Norlan); *sc:* Roland Kibbee and Burt Lancaster—*b/o* David Anthony's novel *The Midnight Lady and the Mourning Man.*

JIM: Former cop—on parole after killing his wife's lover—who becomes a security guard at a small Southern college and tracks down the murderer of a coed.

Susan Clark, Cameron Mitchell, Morgan Woodward, Harris Yulin, Robert Quarry, Joan Lorring, Lawrence Dobkin, Ed Lauter, Charles Tyner, Mills Watson, Quinn Redeker, Nick Cravat.

Conversation Piece (1975, New Line). *d:* Luchino Visconti; *p:* Giovanni Bertolucci (Rusconi/ Gaumont); *sc:* Suso Cecchi D'Amico, Enrico Medioli, and Luchino Visconti—*b/o* an idea by Enrico Medioli.

PROFESSOR: Aging American-born professor in Rome whose life changes disastrously when he leases the upstairs apartment in his home to a rich, pushy marquesa, her young German lover, her teen-age daughter, and the daughter's lover.

Silvana Mangano, Helmut Berger, Claudia Marsani, Stefano Patrizi, Elvira Cortese, Dominique Sanda, Claudia Cardinale.

Moses (1976, Avco Embassy). *d:* Gianfranco De Bosio; *p:* Vincenzo Labella (ITC/RAI); *sc:* Anthony Burgess, Vittorio Bonicelli, and Gianfranco De Bosio.

MOSES: Hebrew born during Biblical times in Egypt who falls out of favor with the Pharoah and is banished but returns as the prophesied Deliverer who leads the Israelites out of Egypt to the Promised Land.

Anthony Quayle, Ingrid Thulin, Irene Papas, Yousef Shiloah, Aharon Ipale, Marina Berti, Shmuel Rodensky, Mariangela Melato, Laurent Terzieff, William Lancaster.

1900 (1976, Para.). *d:* Bernardo Bertolucci; *p:* Alberto Grimaldi (P.E.A./Artistes Associes/ Artemis); *sc:* Bernardo Bertolucci, Franco Arcalli, and Giuseppe Bertolucci.

ALFREDO BERLINGHIERI: Aging patriarch of a well-to-do family of Italian land owners whose lives are changed by the rise of unionism and Mussolini's Fascists.

Romolo Valli, Anna-Maria Gherardi, Laura Betti, Robert De Niro, Paolo Pavesi, Dominique Sanda, Sterling Hayden, Donald Sutherland, Werner Bruhns, Alida Valli.

Buffalo Bill and the Indians, or Sitting Bull's History Lesson (1976, UA). *d:* Robert Altman; *p:* Robert Altman and David Susskind (Dino De Laurentiis); *sc:* Alan Rudolph and Robert Altman—*b/o* the play *Indians* by Arthur Kopit.

NED BUNTLINE: Dime novelist in the Old West—among the first to fictionalize the exploits of Buffalo Bill Cody—who is one of Bill's most amused fans when he puts on a Wild West show for tourists in the 1880s.

Paul Newman, Joel Grey, Kevin McCarthy, Harvey Keitel, Geraldine Chaplin, John Considine, Denver Pyle, Pat McCormick, Shelley Duvall.

The Cassandra Crossing (1977, Avco Embassy). *d:* George Pan Cosmatos; *p:* Carlo Ponti and Sir Lew Grade (AGF/CCC/International Cine); *sc:* Robert Katz, George Pan Cosmatos, and Tom Mankiewicz.

MACKENZIE: U.S. Army Intelligence chief in Geneva, Switzerland, who—when he learns that the Geneva-to-Stockholm Express (carrying 1000 passengers) has been exposed to deadly pneumonic plague germs—orders the train sealed and rerouted to the Polish border and a fatally flawed bridge crossing.

Sophia Loren, Richard Harris, Ava Gardner, Martin Sheen, Ingrid Thulin, Lee Strasberg, John Phillip Law, Ann Turkel, O. J. Simpson, Lionel Stander, Alida Valli.

Twilight's Last Gleaming (1977, AA). *d:* Robert Aldrich; *p:* Merv Adelson (Geria/Lorimar– Bavaria); *sc:* Ronald M. Cohen and Edward Huebsch—*b/o* the novel *Viper 3* by Walter Wager.

LAWRENCE DELL: Unstable ex–U.S. Air Force general who—after he escapes from Death Row with three other prisoners and seizes control of a

SAC missile silo—threatens to bomb Russia and start WWIII unless the U.S. admits some shocking facts concerning its former Vietnam War policy.

Richard Widmark, Charles Durning, Melvyn Douglas, Paul Winfield, Burt Young, Joseph Cotten, Roscoe Lee Browne, Richard Jaeckel, Vera Miles, Charles Aidman, Leif Erickson, Charles McGraw, Simon Scott, Bill Walker.

The Island of Dr. Moreau (1977, AIP). *d:* Don Taylor; *p:* John Temple-Smith and Skip Steloff; *sc:* John Herman Shaner and Al Ramrus—*b/o* the novel by H. G. Wells.

DR. MOREAU: Mad doctor on a remote South Seas island who—when a shipwrecked sailor discovers that the doctor has created a group of half-man, half-beast "humanimals"—feels compelled to make the sailor a victim, too.

Michael York, Nigel Davenport, Barbara Carrera, Richard Basehart, Nick Cravat, The Great John L., Bob Ozman, Fumio Demura, Gary Baxley, John Gillespie, David Cass.

Go Tell the Spartans (1978, Avco Embassy). *d:* Ted Post; *p:* Alan F. Bodoh and Mitchell Cannold (Mar Vista/Spartan); *sc:* Wendell Mayes—*b/o* the novel *Incident at Muc Wa* by Daniel Ford.

MAJ. ASA BARKER: Cynical commander of a group of American military "advisers" in 1964 Vietnam who, along with South Vietnamese mercenaries, battle the Viet Cong as they try to secure a garrison at Muc Wa.

Craig Wasson, Jonathan Goldsmith, Marc Singer, Joe Unger, Dennis Howard, David Clennon, Evan Kim, Hilly Hicks, Dolph Sweet, James Hong, Tad Horino, Phong Diep.

Zulu Dawn (1979, American Cinema). *d:* Douglas Hickox; *p:* Nate Kohn and James Faulkner (Samarkand); *sc:* Cy Endfield and Anthony Storey—*b/o* a story by Cy Endfield.

COLONEL DURNFORD: British Army officer in South Africa who is in command of British and Natal troops that are overwhelmed and massacred by spear-throwing Zulus at Isandhlwana on January 22, 1879.

Peter O'Toole, Simon Ward, John Mills, Nigel Davenport, Michael Jayston, Ronald Lacey, Denholm Elliott, Freddie Jones, Ronald Pickup, Donald Pickering, Peter Vaughn.

Cattle Annie and Little Britches (1980, Univ.). *d:* Lamont Johnson; *p:* Rupert Hitzig and Alan King; *sc:* David Eyre and Robert Ward—*b/o* the novel by Robert Ward.

BILL DOOLIN: Aging outlaw in 1893 whose fading Doolin-Dalton gang is rejuvenated by two teen-age girls from the East who join the bad men to help rob banks.

Scott Glenn, Redmond Gleeson, William Russ, Ken Call, John Savage, Buck Taylor, Michael Conrad, Amanda Plummer, Diane Lane, Chad Hastings, Tom Delaney, Rod Steiger, Steven Ford.

Atlantic City (1981, Para.). *d:* Louis Malle; *p:* Denis Heroux; *sc:* John Guare.

LOU*: Aging small-time gangster in the Boardwalk town who, along with an ambitious young female hustler, gets his big chance when he comes upon a cache of cocaine and starts dealing it.

Susan Sarandon, Kate Reid, Michel Piccoli, Hollis McLaren, Robert Joy, Al Waxman, Robert Goulet, Moses Znaimer, Angus MacInnes, Sean Sullivan, Louis Del Grande, Eleanor Beecroft.

La Pelle (The Skin) (1981, Gaumont). *d:* Liliana Cavani; *p:* Renzo Rossellini; (Opera Films Produzione/Gaumont); *sc:* Robert Katz and Liliana Cavani—*b/o* the memoirs of Curzio Malaparte.

GEN. MARK CLARK: Famed WWII general who is in command of the U.S. Fifth Army as its troops liberate Naples, Italy.

Marcello Mastroianni, Claudia Cardinale, Ken Marshall, Alexandra King, Carlo Giuffre.

Local Hero (1983, WB). *d:* Bill Forsyth; *p:* David Puttnam (Enigma/Goldcrest); *sc:* Bill Forsyth.

FELIX HAPPER: Eccentric Houston oil tycoon who, along with a young computer-whiz assistant, are smitten with a small village on the Scottish coast after they go there to sweet-talk the local citizens into selling drilling rights to their land.

Peter Riegert, Denis Lawson, Fulton Mackay, Peter Capaldi, Jenny Seagrove, Norman Chancer, Tam Dean Burn, Kenny Ireland.

The Osterman Weekend (1983, 20th-Fox). *d:* Sam Peckinpah; *p:* Peter S. Davis and William N. Panzer; *sc:* Alan Sharp (adaptation by Ian Masters)—*b/o* a novel by Robert Ludlow.

MAXWELL DANFORTH: Conniving CIA director who's involved in a CIA scheme to discredit a left-wing talk-show host by convincing him that three of his old college chums are KGB agents, then pressuring him into taking part in a plot to entrap them.

Rutger Hauer, John Hurt, Craig T. Nelson, Dennis Hopper.

• In addition, Burt Lancaster made cameo/guest appearances in the following feature films: *Variety Girl* (1947, Para.) and *Three Sailors and a Girl* (1953, WB).

---

*Received an Academy Award nomination as Best Actor for this role.

☆ JACK LEMMON

John Uhler Lemmon III

b: Feb. 8, 1925, Boston, Mass.

"Captain, it is I—Ensign Pulver—and I just threw your stinking palm tree overboard. Now, what's all this crud about no movie tonight?"

Ensign Frank Pulver (Jack Lemmon) to the Captain (James Cagney) in *Mister Roberts*, 1955.

It Should Happen to You (1954, Col.). *d:* George Cukor; *p:* Fred Kohlmar; *sc:* Garson Kanin.

PETE SHEPPARD: Young would-be documentary filmmaker whose romance has problems when his girlfriend—an unemployed model—rents a New York billboard, puts her name on it, and becomes famous.

Judy Holliday, Peter Lawford, Michael O'Shea, Connie Gilchrist, Vaughn Taylor, Heywood Hale Broun, Rex Evans, Whit Bissell, Melville Cooper, Constance Bennett, Ilka Chase, Wendy Barrie.

Phffft! (1954, Col.). *d:* Mark Robson; *p:* Fred Kohlmar; *sc:* George Axelrod.

ROBERT TRACY: Successful New York attorney who—when he and his soap-opera-writer wife become bored with marriage—gets a divorce, only to discover that they were both happier married.

Judy Holliday, Jack Carson, Kim Novak, Luella Gear, Donald Curtis, Merry Anders, Arny Freeman, Donald Randolph, Eddie Searles.

Three for the Show (1955, Col.). *d:* H. C. Potter; *p:* Jonie Taps; *sc:* Edward Hope and Leonard Stern—*b/o* a play by W. Somerset Maugham.

MARTY STEWART: Broadway composer who, after mistakenly being reported killed in action during the war, returns to find that his musical-comedy-star wife has married his best friend.

Betty Grable, Gower Champion, Marge Champion, Myron McCormick, Paul Harvey, Robert Bice.

Mister Roberts (1955, WB). *d:* John Ford and Mervyn LeRoy; *p:* Leland Hayward (Orange); *sc:* Frank Nugent and Joshua Logan, from the play by Joshua Logan and Thomas Heggen—*b/o* the novel by Thomas Heggen.

ENS. FRANK THURLOWE PULVER*: Girl-crazy, misfit laundry officer on a WWII cargo ship in the Pacific who tries to impress his executive officer and idol (Mister Roberts) while they and the rest of the crew battle boredom and a tyrannical captain.

Henry Fonda, James Cagney, William Powell, Betsy Palmer, Ward Bond, Phil Carey, Martin Milner, James Flavin, Jack Pennick, Ken Curtis, Nick Adams, Harry Carey Jr., William Henry, Perry Lopez, Robert Roark, Pat Wayne, Tiger Andrews.

My Sister Eileen (1955, Col.). *d:* Richard Quine; *p:* Fred Kohlmar; *sc:* Blake Edwards and Richard Quine, from the play by Joseph Fields and Jerome Chodorov—*b/o New Yorker* stories by Ruth McKenney.

BOB BAKER: Wolfish magazine editor interested in some stories written by the elder of two sisters from a small town in Ohio who have come to New York to find fame and fortune.

Betty Garrett, Janet Leigh, Bob Fosse, Richard York, Lucy Marlow, Tommy Rall, Kurt Kasznar, Horace McMahon, Queenie Smith.

You Can't Run Away from It (1956, Col.). *d:* Dick Powell; *p:* Dick Powell; *sc:* Claude Binyon and Robert Riskin, *b/o* the screenplay *It Happened One Night*—from a short story by Samuel Hopkins Adams.

PETER WARNE: Newspaper reporter who falls for a runaway heiress on a cross-country bus after he has agreed to help her reach her destination in return for an exclusive big story.

June Allyson, Charles Bickford, Paul Gilbert, Stubby Kaye, Jim Backus, Henny Youngman, Allyn Joslyn, Frank Sully, Dub Taylor, Walter Baldwin, Howard McNear, Elvia Allman, Jack Albertson.

Fire Down Below (1957, Col.). *d:* Robert Parrish; *p:* Irving Allen and Albert Broccoli (Warwick); *sc:* Irwin Shaw—*b/o* the novel by Max Catto.

TONY: One of a pair of partners in a Caribbean fishing-and-smuggling business who fall out over a shady lady aboard their boat during a voyage between islands.

Rita Hayworth, Robert Mitchum, Herbert Lom, Bonar Colleano, Bernard Lee, Edric Connor, Peter Illing, Anthony Newley, Eric Pohlmann, "Stretch" Cox.

Operation Mad Ball (1957, Col.). *d:* Richard Quine; *p:* Jed Harris (Jed Harris Prod.); *sc:* Jed Harris, Blake Edwards, and Arthur Carter—*b/o* the play by Arthur Carter.

PRIVATE HOGAN: Wheeler-dealer American G.I. based in France who masterminds a wild off-limits party for his outfit and a bevy of Army nurses.

Kathryn (Grant) Crosby, Ernie Kovacs, Arthur O'Connell, Mickey Rooney, Dick York, James

*Won the Academy Award as Best Supporting Actor for this role.

Darren, Roger Smith, William Leslie, Paul Picerni, Jeanne Manet.

Cowboy (1958, Col.). *d:* Delmer Daves; *p:* Julian Blaustein (Phoenix); *sc:* Edmund H. North—*b/o* the novel *My Reminiscences As a Cowboy* by Frank Harris.

FRANK HARRIS: Young Chicago hotel clerk who joins a cattle drive to Mexico as a green tenderfoot but—after clashing with his tough cattleman boss, battling the elements, and undergoing various other hardships—matures, by the end of the trail, into a rugged trail boss.

Glenn Ford, Anna Kashfi, Brian Donlevy, Dick York, Richard Jaeckel, James Westerfield, King Donovan, Vaughn Taylor.

Bell, Book and Candle (1958, Col.). *d:* Richard Quine; *p:* Julian Blaustein (Phoenix); *sc:* Daniel Taradash—*b/o* the play by John Van Druten.

NICKY HOLROYD: Wisecracking, modern-day warlock who, when his beautiful sister casts a love spell over a New York publisher who's doing a book on witchcraft, reveals to the publisher that the sister is a witch.

James Stewart, Kim Novak, Ernie Kovacs, Hermione Gingold, Elsa Lanchester, Janice Rule, Howard McNear, Gail Bonney, Wolfe Barzell, Monty Ash.

Some Like It Hot (1959, UA). *d:* Billy Wilder; *p:* Billy Wilder (Ashton/Mirisch); *sc:* Billy Wilder and I. A. L. Diamond—*b/o* a suggestion from a story by R. Thoeren and M. Logan.

JERRY/DAPHNE*: One of a pair of musicians who dress up as women and join an all-girl band to escape gangsters who know that the two witnessed the 1929 St. Valentine's Day massacre in Chicago.

Marilyn Monroe, Tony Curtis, George Raft, Pat O'Brien, Joe E. Brown, Nehemiah Persoff, Billy Gray, George E. Stone, Dave Barry, Mike Mazurki, Edward G. Robinson Jr., Tom Kennedy.

It Happened to Jane (1959, Col.). *d:* Richard Quine; *p:* Richard Quine (Arwin); *sc:* Norman Katkov—*b/o* a story by Max Wilk and Norman Katkov.

GEORGE DENHAM: Small-town lawyer in Maine who, when a pretty lobster-grower's lobster shipment is spoiled, helps her sue a penny-pinching railroad tycoon and become a national heroine.

Doris Day, Ernie Kovacs, Steve Forrest, Teddy Rooney, Parker Fennelly, Mary Wickes, Casey Adams.

The Apartment (1960, UA). *d:* Billy Wilder; *p:*

Billy Wilder (Mirisch); *sc:* Billy Wilder and I. A. L. Diamond.

C. C. "BUD" BAXTER*: Lonely, ambitious office clerk who furthers his career by lending his apartment to his philandering boss—but becomes emotionally involved with the boss's latest girlfriend, an attractive elevator operator.

Shirley MacLaine, Fred MacMurray, Ray Walston, Jack Kruschen, Edie Adams, Hope Holiday, Johnny Seven, Naomi Stevens, Joyce Jameson, Willard Waterman, David White, Hal Smith, Dorothy Abbott.

The Wackiest Ship in the Army (1961, Col.). *d:* Richard Murphy; *p:* Fred Kohlmar (Fred Kohlmar); *sc:* Richard Murphy (adaptation by Herbert Margolis and William Raynor)—*b/o* a story by Herbert Carlson.

LT. RIP CRANDALL: WWII Naval officer who is tricked by his superior into commanding an old U.S. sailing vessel with a bumbling crew whose mission is to secretly land a coast watcher on a Japanese-held island in the Pacific.

Ricky Nelson, John Lund, Chips Rafferty, Tom Tully, Patricia Driscoll, Joby Baker, Warren Berlinger, Mike Kellin, Richard Anderson, Alvy Moore.

The Notorious Landlady (1962, Col.). *d:* Richard Quine; *p:* Fred Kohlmar (Kohlmar–Quine); *sc:* Blake Edwards and Larry Gelbart—*b/o* Margery Sharp's story "The Notorious Tenant."

WILLIAM GRIDLEY: Young American diplomat in London who rents an apartment from a beautiful American woman suspected by Scotland Yard of murdering her missing British husband.

Kim Novak, Fred Astaire, Lionel Jeffries, Estelle Winwood, Philippa Bevans, Maxwell Reed, Richard Peel, Scott Davey, Henry Daniell, John Uhler Lemmon II.

Days of Wine and Roses (1962, WB). *d:* Blake Edwards; *p:* Martin Manulis (Martin Manulis–Salem); *sc:* J. P. Miller—*b/o* his TV play.

JOE CLAY*: Ambitious, hard-drinking PR man who introduces his young wife to social drinking but—after they both become alcoholics—seeks help, even though she won't.

Lee Remick, Charles Bickford, Jack Klugman, Alan Hewitt, Debbie Megowan, Katherine Squire, Maxine Stuart, Jack Albertson, Ken Lynch, Gail Bonney, Pat O'Malley.

Irma La Douce (1963, UA). *d:* Billy Wilder; *p:* Billy Wilder (Phalanx/Mirisch/Alperson); *sc:* Billy Wilder and I. A. L. Diamond—*b/o* the musical play by Marguerite Monnot, Alexander Breffort, Julian More, David Heneker, and Monty Norman.

---

*Received an Academy Award nomination as Best Actor for this role.

*Received an Academy Award nomination as Best Actor for this role.

NESTOR PATOU: Naïve French gendarme who falls for a French hooker, then resorts to posing as a British nobleman called Lord X in a scheme to keep her for himself.

Shirley MacLaine, Lou Jacobi, Herschel Bernardi, Bruce Yarnell, Hope Holiday, Joan Shawlee, Grace Lee Whitney, Tura Santana, Harriet Young.

Under the Yum-Yum Tree (1963, Col.). *d:* David Swift; *p:* Frederick Brisson (Sonnis–Swift); *sc:* Lawrence Roman and David Swift—*b/o* the play by Lawrence Roman.

HOGAN: Lecherous landlord who keeps trying to romance a pretty young coed who's sharing an apartment with her college-student fiancé.

Carol Lynley, Dean Jones, Edie Adams, Imogene Coca, Paul Lynde, Robert Lansing, Asa Maynor, Pamela Curran, Jane Wald.

Good Neighbor Sam (1964, Col.). *d:* David Swift; *p:* David Swift (David Swift Prod.); *sc:* James Fritzell, Everett Greenbaum, and David Swift—*b/o* the novel by Jack Finney.

SAM BISSELL: Clean-living New York ad man who's talked into pretending that he's married to a sexy neighbor—instead of to his real wife—as part of a plan for the neighbor to inherit $15 million.

Romy Schneider, Dorothy Provine, Edward G. Robinson, Michael Connors, Edward Andrews, Louis Nye, Robert Q. Lewis, Joyce Jameson, Anne Seymour, Charles Lane, Tris Coffin, Neil Hamilton, The Hi-Lo's, Bernie Kopell, Dave Ketchum.

How to Murder Your Wife (1965, UA). *d:* Richard Quine; *p:* George Axelrod (Jalem); *sc:* George Axelrod.

STANLEY FORD: Comic-strip cartoonist who, when he wakes up the morning after a wild bachelor party and discovers that he has married the luscious Italian girl who popped out of the cake, starts scheming to get rid of her.

Virna Lisi, Terry-Thomas, Eddie Mayehoff, Claire Trevor, Sidney Blackmer, Max Showalter, Jack Albertson, Alan Hewitt, Mary Wickes.

The Great Race (1965, WB). *d:* Blake Edwards; *p:* Martin Jurow (Patricia–Jalem–Reynard); *sc:* Blake Edwards and Arthur Ross.

(Dual role) PROFESSOR FATE: Dastardly villain who enters a turn-of-the-century auto race from New York to Paris and uses every dirty trick he can to try to foil the hero and win.

PRINCE HAPNIK: Endangered royal prince of the mythical country of Carpania.

Tony Curtis, Natalie Wood, Peter Falk, Keenan Wynn, Arthur O'Connell, Vivian Vance, Dorothy Provine, Larry Storch, Ross Martin, George

Macready, Marvin Kaplan, Hal Smith, Denver Pyle, Frank Kreig.

The Fortune Cookie (1966, UA). *d:* Billy Wilder; *p:* Billy Wilder (Phalanx–Jalem/Mirisch); *sc:* Billy Wilder and I. A. L. Diamond.

HARRY HINKLE: TV cameraman who, when he's accidentally knocked down by a pro football player while covering a game, is talked into exaggerating the injury by his shyster lawyer brother-in-law so that they can soak the insurance company.

Walter Matthau, Judi West, Ron Rich, Marge Redmond, Lurene Tuttle, Cliff Osmond, Noam Pitlik, Harry Holcombe, Les Tremayne, Archie Moore.

Luv (1967, Col.). *d:* Clive Donner; *p:* Martin Manulis (Jalem); *sc:* Elliott Baker—*b/o* the play by Murray Schisgal.

HARRY BERLIN: Suicidal derelict who is stopped from jumping off the Manhattan Bridge by an old college chum who takes him home to dinner, hoping that the derelict will fall for his wife so that the chum can marry his mistress.

Peter Falk, Elaine May, Nina Wayne, Eddie Mayehoff, Paul Hartman, Severn Darden.

The Odd Couple (1968, Para.). *d:* Gene Saks; *p:* Howard W. Koch; *sc:* Neil Simon—*b/o* his play.

FELIX UNGAR: About-to-be-divorced, hypochondriac TV newswriter with a mania for neatness who—after moving in with his sloppy, divorced sportswriter friend—finds that they really bug each other.

Walter Matthau, John Fiedler, Herb Edelman, David Sheiner, Larry Haines, Monica Evans, Carole Shelley, Iris Adrian, Heywood Hale Broun, John C. Becher.

The April Fools (1969, Nat. Gen.). *d:* Stuart Rosenberg; *p:* Gordon Carroll (Cinema Center/Jalem); *sc:* Hal Dresner.

HOWARD BRUBAKER: Mild-mannered, married Wall Street broker who meets his boss's beautiful wife at a cocktail party and—twenty-four hours later—runs away to Paris with her.

Catherine Deneuve, Peter Lawford, Sally Kellerman, Jack Weston, Myrna Loy, Charles Boyer, Harvey Korman, Melinda Dillon, Kenneth Mars, Janice Carroll, David Doyle.

The Out-of-Towners (1970, Para.). *d:* Arthur Hiller; *p:* Paul Nathan (Jalem); *sc:* Neil Simon.

GEORGE KELLERMAN: Harried executive from Dayton, Ohio, who, with his wife, flies to New York City for a job interview and encounters a multitude of big-city problems and hassles.

Sandy Dennis, Anne Meara, Sandy Baron, Ann Prentiss, Graham Jarvis, Billy Dee Williams, Ron Carey, Dolph Sweet, Johnny Brown.

The War Between Men and Women (1972, Nat. Gen.). *d:* Melville Shavelson; *p:* Danny Arnold (Cinema Center/Shavelson–Arnold); *sc:* Melville Shavelson and Danny Arnold—suggested by the writings and drawings of James Thurber.

PETER WILSON: New York writer-cartoonist who, despite his dislike for women and kids, marries a divorcée with three children and—after he discovers that he's going blind—learns to love them.

Barbara Harris, Jason Robards, Herb Edelman, Lisa Gerritsen, Moosie Drier, Lisa Eilbacher, Severn Darden.

Avanti! (1972, UA). *d:* Billy Wilder; *p:* Billy Wilder (Phalanx–Jalem/Mirisch); *sc:* Billy Wilder and I. A. L. Diamond—*b/o* the play by Samuel Taylor.

WENDELL ARMBRUSTER: Uptight businessman from Baltimore who falls for the daughter of his late father's English mistress when he journeys to Italy to claim the old man's body.

Juliet Mills, Clive Revill, Edward Andrews, Gianfranco Barra, Giselda Castrini.

Save the Tiger (1973, Para.). *d:* John G. Avildsen; *p:* Steve Shagan (Filmways–Jalem–Cirandinha); *sc:* Steve Shagan.

HARRY STONER*: Disillusioned, once-idealistic New York dress manufacturer who, when his business verges on bankruptcy, tries to convince his partner that they should hire an arsonist to set fire to their warehouse so that they can collect the insurance money.

Patricia Smith, Jack Gilford, Laurie Heineman, Norman Burton, Lara Parker, William Hansen, Harvey Jason, Thayer David, Ned Glass, Pearl Shear, Biff Elliott.

The Front Page (1974, Univ.). *d:* Billy Wilder; *p:* Paul Monash; *sc:* Billy Wilder and I. A. L. Diamond—*b/o* the play by Ben Hecht and Charles MacArthur.

HILDY JOHNSON: Ace reporter on the Chicago Examiner in the Roaring '20s who is all set to get married and join a Philadelphia ad agency but is conned by his conniving editor into staying and covering a big murder story.

Walter Matthau, Susan Sarandon, Austin Pendleton, Carol Burnett, Vincent Gardenia, David Wayne, Martin Gabel, Harold Gould, Allen Garfield, Charles Durning, Dick O'Neill, Herbert Edelman.

The Prisoner of Second Avenue (1975, WB). *d:* Melvin Frank; *p:* Melvin Frank; *sc:* Neil Simon—*b/o* his play.

MEL: Harried, middle-aged New York ad man who suddenly loses his job, nearly has a nervous breakdown, but then manages to pull through with the help of his wife.

Anne Bancroft, Gene Saks, Maxine Stuart, Elizabeth Wilson, Florence Stanley, Gene Blakely, Ivor Francis, Stack Pierce, Ed Peck, Sylvester Stallone.

The Entertainer (1976, NBC [made for TV]). *d:* Donald Wrye; *p:* Beryl Vertue and Marvin Hamlisch (Robert Stigwood Prod./Persky–Bright); *sc:* Elliott Baker—*b/o* the play by John Osborne.

ARCHIE RICE*: Vain, third-rate vaudevillian in a 1940s California burlesque house who desperately strives to be a star like his once-famous father.

Ray Bolger, Sada Thompson, Tyne Daly, Michael Cristofer, Annette O'Toole, Mitch Ryan, Allyn Ann McLerie, Rita O'Connor, Dick O'Neill, Leanna Johnson.

Alex and the Gypsy (1976, 20th-Fox). *d:* John Korty; *p:* Richard Shepherd; *sc:* Lawrence B. Marcus—*b/o* Stanley Elkin's novella *The Bailbondsman.*

ALEXANDER MAIN: Cynical California bail bondsman who becomes involved in a wild love affair with an attractive but headstrong gypsy who is accused of attempted murder.

Genevieve Bujold, James Woods, Robert Emhardt, Joseph X. Flaherty, Ramon Bieri, Gino Ardito, Todd Martin.

Airport '77 (1977, Univ.). *d:* Jerry Jameson; *p:* Jennings Lang and William Frye; *sc:* David Spector and Michael Scheff—inspired by the movie *Airport,* *b/o* the novel *Airport* by Arthur Hailey.

DON GALLAGHER: Captain of a 747 jet that—when it's hijacked while flying over the Bermuda Triangle with millions of dollars' worth of art treasures—crashes and sinks into 100 feet of water, forcing a daring rescue attempt.

Lee Grant, Brenda Vaccaro, George Kennedy, James Stewart, Joseph Cotten, Olivia de Havilland, Darren McGavin, Christopher Lee, Robert Foxworth, Robert Hooks, Monte Markham, James Booth.

The China Syndrome (1979, Col.). *d:* James Bridges; *p:* Michael Douglas (IPC Films); *sc:* Mike Gray, T. S. Cook, and James Bridges.

JACK GODELL†: Dedicated chief engineer at a California nuclear power plant who, when he discovers that his company is trying to cover up a potentially disastrous radiation leak, siezes the

---

*Received an Emmy Award nomination as Outstanding Lead Actor in a Drama Special for this role
†Received an Academy Award nomination as Best Actor for this role.

---

*Won the Academy Award as Best Actor for this role.

control room and threatens to shut down the plant.

Jane Fonda, Michael Douglas, Scott Brady, James Hampton, Peter Donat, Wilford Brimley, Richard Herd, Daniel Valdez, Stan Bohrman, Donald Hotton, Khalilah Ali.

Tribute (1980, 20th-Fox). *d:* Bob Clark; *p:* Joel B. Michaels and Garth H. Drabinsky; *sc:* Bernard Slade—*b/o* his play.
SCOTTIE TEMPLETON*: Clownish stage performer—dying of cancer—who tries to break down the barriers that exist between him and his young son, who can't forgive the father for deserting him when he was a kid.
Robby Benson, Lee Remick, Colleen Dewhurst, John Marley, Kim Cattrall, Gale Garnett, Teri Keane, Rummy Bishop, John Dee, Bob Windsor.

Buddy Buddy (1981, MGM/UA). *d:* Billy Wilder; *p:* Jay Weston; *sc:* Billy Wilder and I. A. L. Diamond—*b/o* the play and story by Francis Veber.
VICTOR CLOONEY: Hapless CBS network censor who, when his wife leaves him, checks into a California hotel to commit suicide but changes his mind after he mistakenly believes that he's found a new friend—a professional hit man.
Walter Matthau, Paula Prentiss, Klaus Kinski, Dana Elcar, Miles Chapin, Michael Ensign, Joan Shawlee, Fil Formicola, Bette Raya.

Missing (1982, Univ.). *d:* Costa-Gavras; *p:* Sean Daniel; *sc:* Costa-Gavras and Donald Stewart—*b/o* Thomas Hauser's book *The Execution of Charles Horman.*
ED HORMAN*: New York businessman who goes to Santiago, Chile, to help his daughter-in-law look for his freelance-writer son, who disappeared during the 1973 right-wing coup.
Sissy Spacek, John Shea, Melanie Mayron, Charles Cioffi, David Clennon, Richard Venture, Jerry Hardin, John Doolittle, Janice Rule, Ward Costello.

• In addition, Jack Lemmon made cameo/guest appearances in the following feature films: *Pepe* (1960, Col.) and *Kotch* (1971, ABC/Kotch Co.— played a bit part as a stranger on a bus).

---

*Received an Academy Award nomination as Best Actor for this role.

*Received an Academy Award nomination as Best Actor for this role.

☆ CAROLE LOMBARD

Jane Alice Peters

b: Oct. 6, 1908, Fort Wayne, Ind.
d: Jan. 16, 1942, near Las Vegas, Nev.

"Darling, if you had it all to do over again, would you marry me?"

> Ann Smith (Carole Lombard) posing a fateful question to David Smith (Robert Montgomery) in *Mr. and Mrs. Smith,* 1941.

A Perfect Crime (1921, Associated Producers). *d:* Allan Dwan; *sc:* Allan Dwan—*b/o* the *Saturday Evening Post* story by Carl Clausen.

Billed (under the name of Jane Peters) as "GRIGG'S SISTER": Twelve-year-old girl who is supported by her brother, a drab bank clerk who leads an after-hours double life posing as a debonair sportsman.

Monte Blue, Jacqueline Logan, Stanton Heck, Hardee Kirkland.

Marriage in Transit (1925, Fox). *d:* R. William Neill; *sc:* Dorothy Yost—*b/o* a story by Grace Livingston Hill Lutz.
CELIA HATHAWAY: Young woman who marries a secret government agent—a look-alike for her conspirator boyfriend—mistakenly believing that the agent is her real boyfriend.
Edmund Lowe, Adolph Milar, Frank Beal, Harvey Clarke, Fred Walton, Wade Boteler, Fred Butler, Byron Douglas.

Hearts and Spurs (1925, Fox). *d:* W. S. Van Dyke; *sc:* John Stone—*b/o* Jackson Gregory's novel *The Outlaw.*
SYBIL ESTABROOK: Young Eastern woman out West who falls for a straight-shooting cowboy as he helps save her brother from crooks.
Charles (Buck) Jones, William Davidson, Freeman Wood, Jean Lamott, J. Gordon Russell, Walt Robbins, Charles Eldridge.

Durand of the Badlands (1925, Fox). *d:* Lynn Reynolds; *sc: b/o* the novel by Maibelle Heikes.
ELLEN BOYD: Western banker's young daughter who is held captive in a mine shaft by outlaws but is rescued by a courageous cowboy.

Charles (Buck) Jones, Marion Nixon, Malcolm
Waite, Fred De Silva, Luke Cosgrove, Buck Black,
James Corrigan.

The Divine Sinner (1928, Rayart). *d:* Scott
Pembroke; *p:* Trem Carr; *sc:* Robert Anthony
Dillon.

MILLIE CLAUDERT: Young French woman in
Paris at the close of WWI.

*Vera Reynolds, Nigel De Brulier, Bernard Seigel,
Ernest Hilliard, John Peters,* Harry Northrup,
James Ford.

Power (1928, Pathe). *d:* Howard Higgin; *sc:* Tay
Garnett (with titles by John Krafft).

Billed as "ANOTHER DAME": One of several
good-looking women involved in the dame-chasing
shenanigans of two ironworkers on a dam project
in the West.

*William Boyd, Alan Hale, Jacqueline Logan, Jerry
Drew, Joan Bennett,* Pauline Curley.

Me, Gangster (1928, Fox). *d:* Raoul Walsh; *sc:*
Charles Francis Coe and Raoul Walsh—*b/o* the
Saturday Evening Post story by Charles Francis
Coe.

BLONDE ROSIE: Shapely New York blonde who
is involved with gangsters.

*June Collyer, Don Terry, Anders Randolf, Stella
Adams, Al Hill, Burr McIntosh, Joe Brown, Nigel
De Brulier, Gustav von Seyffertitz, Harry Cattle.*

Show Folks (1928, Pathe). *d:* Paul L. Stein; *sc:*
Jack Jungmeyer and George Dromgold (with titles
by John Krafft)—*b/o* a story by Phillip Dunning.

CLEO: Gold digger who walks out on her male
dancing partner just before a big show opens.

Eddie Quillan, Lina Basquette, Robert Armstrong,
Crauford Kent, Bessie Barriscale, Maurice Black.

Ned McCobb's Daughter (1928, Pathe). *d:*
William J. Cowen; *sc:* Beulah Marie Dix (with
titles by Edwin Justus Mayer)—*b/o* the play by
Sidney Howard.

JENNIE: Waitress who becomes involved with a
married bootlegger who kills a revenue agent.

*Irene Rich, Theodore Roberts, Robert Armstrong,
George Baeraud, Edward Hearn,* Louis Natheaux.

High Voltage (1929, Pathe). *d:* Howard Higgin;
sc: James Gleason and Kenyon Nicholson (with
dialogue by Elliott Clawson and James Gleason)—
b/o a story by Elliott Clawson.

BILLIE DAVIS: Sheriff's prisoner who is stranded,
along with other bus passengers, in the High
Sierras during a blizzard.

William Boyd, Owen Moore, Diane Ellis, Billy
Bevan, Phillips Smalley.

Big News (1929, Pathe). *d:* Gregory La Cava; *sc:*
Walter De Leon (with dialogue by Frank Reicher,

adaptation by Jack Jungmeyer)—*b/o* on the play
For Two Cents by George S. Brooks.

MARG BANKS: Newspaper reporter who—when
her wisecracking, alcohol-drinking reporter
husband is fired—threatens to leave him but
remains loyal when he gets his job back and
exposes the murdering head of a narcotics ring.

Robert Armstrong, Sam Hardy, Tom Kennedy,
Louis Payne, Wade Boteler, Cupid Ainesworth,
Charles Sellon, Warner Richmond.

The Racketeer (1930, Pathe). *d:* Howard Higgin;
p: Ralph Block; *sc:* Paul Gangelin (with dialogue
by A. A. Kline).

RHODA PHILBROOK: Young blonde who
promises a rich bootlegger she'll marry him if
he'll help the man she really loves in his career
as a concert violinist.

Robert Armstrong, Roland Drew, Jeanette Loff,
John Loder, Paul Hurst, Winter Hall, Al Hill, Kit
Guard, Bobbie Dunn, Hedda Hopper, Bud Fine.

The Arizona Kid (1930, Fox). *d:* Alfred Santell;
sc: Ralph Block and Joseph Wright—*b/o* a story
by Ralph Block.

VIRGINIA HOYT: Treacherous Eastern blonde in
Arizona who, along with her villainous husband,
plots to steal some gold from a Mexican bandit-
hero known as the Arizona Kid (who is really the
Cisco Kid).

Warner Baxter, Mona Maris, Theodore von Eltz,
Arthur Stone, Walter P. Lews, Jack Herrick,
Wilfred Lucas, Hank Mann.

Safety in Numbers (1930, Para.). *d:* Victor
Schertzinger; *sc:* Marion Dix—*b/o* a story by
George Marion Jr. and Percy Heath.

PAULINE: One of three New York chorus girls
who become involved with a handsome twenty-
year-old millionaire from San Francisco who
comes to the big city to be a songwriter.

*Charles "Buddy" Rogers, Kathryn Crawford,
Josephine Dunn,* Roscoe Karns, Francis
MacDonald, Virginia Bruce, Richard Tucker,
Louise Beavers.

Fast and Loose (1930, Para.). *d:* Fred Newmeyer;
sc: Doris Anderson and Jack Kirkland (with
additional dialogue by Preston Sturges)—*b/o*
David Gray's play *The Best People.*

ALICE O'NEIL: Show girl who, when her rich
young suitor's snobbish mother objects to her,
refuses to marry the son—whereupon the mother,
feeling insulted, begins to push the romance.

Miriam Hopkins, Frank Morgan, Charles Starrett,
Henry Wadsworth, Winifred Harris, Herbert Yost,
David Hutcheson, Ilka Chase.

It Pays to Advertise (1931, Para.). *d:* Frank
Tuttle; *sc:* Arthur Kober—*b/o* the play by Roi
Cooper Megrue and Walter Hackett.

MARY GRAYSON: Smart young secretary who helps a young man become a business rival of his father, a pompous soap manufacturer.

Norman Foster, Skeets Gallagher, Eugene Pallette, Lucien Littlefield, Helen Johnson, Louise Brooks, Tom Kennedy, Junior Coghlan.

Man of the World (1931, Para.). *d:* Richard Wallace and Edward Goodman; *sc:* Herman J. Mankiewicz.

MARY KENDALL: American debutante in Paris who falls in love with a suave con man planning to blackmail her.

William Powell, Wynne Gibson, Guy Kibbee, Lawrence Gray, Tom Ricketts, George Chandler, Tom Costello, Maud Truax.

Ladies' Man (1931, Para.). *d:* Lothar Mendes; *sc:* Herman J. Mankiewicz—*b/o* the story by Rupert Hughes.

RACHEL FENDLEY: Banker's daughter who falls in love with a debonair gigolo, even though she knows that he's been romancing her mother.

William Powell, Kay Francis, Gilbert Emery, Olive Tell, Martin Burton, John Holland, Frank Atkinson, Manda Turner Gordon.

Up Pops the Devil (1931, Para.). *d:* Edward Sutherland; *sc:* Arthur Kober and Eve Unsell—*b/o* the play by Albert Hackett and Francis Goodrich.

ANNE MERRICK: Young Greenwich Village author's wife who goes to work as a dancer to help support him while he writes his novel.

Richard Gallagher, Stuart Erwin, Lilyan Tashman, Norman Foster, Edward J. Nugent, Theodore von Eltz, Joyce Compton, Harry Beresford, Sleep N. Eat, Guy Oliver, Pat Moriarty, Effie Ellsler.

I Take This Woman (1931, Para.). *d:* Marion Gering and Slavko Vorkapich; *sc:* Vincent Lawrence—*b/o* the novel *Lost Ecstasy* by Mary Roberts Rinehart.

KAY DOWLING: Pampered young rich woman from New York who is sent out West to her father's ranch, marries a good-natured Wyoming cowhand, then finds ranch life more rugged than she bargained for.

Gary Cooper, Helen Ware, Lester Vail, Charles Trowbridge, Clara Blandick, Guy Oliver, Syd Saylor, Frank Darien, David Landau.

No One Man (1932, Para.). *d:* Lloyd Corrigan; *sc:* Sidney Buchman, Agnes Bran Leahy, and Percy Heath—*b/o* the novel by Rupert Hughes.

PENELOPE NEWBOLD: Spoiled, wealthy divorcée who, although attracted to an upstanding Viennese doctor, makes the mistake of choosing a worthless playboy as her second husband.

Ricardo Cortez, Paul Lukas, Juliette Compton, George Barbier, Virginia Hammond, Arthur Pierson, Francis Moffet, Irving Bacon.

Sinners in the Sun (1932, Para.). *d:* Alexander Hall; *sc:* Vincent Lawrence, Waldemar Young, and Samuel Hoffenstein—*b/o* Mildred Cram's story "The Beachcomber."

DORIS BLAKE: Ambitious fashion model who—after refusing to marry a poor auto mechanic she loves—becomes a wealthy married man's mistress, while the mechanic becomes a chauffeur and marries his millionairess boss.

Chester Morris, Adrienne Ames, Alison Skipworth, Walter Byron, Reginald Barlow, Cary Grant, Luke Cosgrove, Ida Lewis, Frances Moffett, Rita La Roy.

Virtue (1932, Col.). *d:* Edward Buzzell; *sc:* Robert Riskin—*b/o* a story by Ethel Hill.

MAE: New York streetwalker who—after reforming when a nice-guy taxi driver marries her—gets involved in a jam that makes her husband think she's reverted to her old ways.

Pat O'Brien, Ward Bond, Willard Robertson, Shirley Grey, Ed Le Saint, Jack La Rue, Mayo Methot.

No More Orchids (1932, Col.). *d:* Walter Lang; *sc:* Gertrude Purcell (adaptation by Keene Thompson)—*b/o* a story by Grace Perkins.

ANNE HOLT: Self-sacrificing daughter who plans to marry a rich prince to help her financially troubled father, even though she really loves a handsome but broke bachelor.

Walter Connolly, Louise Closser Hale, Lyle Talbot, Allen Vincent, Ruthelma Stevens, C. Aubrey Smith, William V. Mong, Harold Minjir.

No Man of Her Own (1932, Para.). *d:* Wesley Ruggles; *sc:* Maurine Watkins and Milton H. Gropper—*b/o* a story by Edmund Goulding and Benjamin Glazer.

CONNIE RANDALL: Small-town librarian who learns that the suave visitor she married—who she thinks is a Wall Street broker—is really a crooked New York card shark.

Clark Gable, Dorothy Mackaill, Grant Mitchell, George Barbier, Elizabeth Patterson, J. Farrell MacDonald, Tommy Conlon, Frank McGlynn Sr.

From Hell to Heaven (1933, Para.). *d:* Erle C. Kenton; *sc:* Percy Heath and Sidney Buchman—*b/o* the play by Lawrence Hazard.

COLLY TANNER: Divorcée in need of money who, when she meets up with an old flame who's a bookie, bets her virtue with him against $10,000 on a horse race.

Jack Oakie, Adrienne Ames, David Manners, Sidney Blackmer, Shirley Grey, Berton Churchill, Nydia Westman, Cecil Cunningham, Thomas Jackson, Rita La Roy, Clarence Muse.

Supernatural (1933, Para.). *d:* Victor Halperin; *sc:* Harvey Thew and Brian Marlow—*b/o* a story and adaptation by Garnett Weston.

ROMA COURTNEY: Young heiress whose body is taken over by the spirit of a dead murderess seeking revenge against a fake spiritualist who betrayed her to the police.

Randolph Scott, Vivienne Osborne, Alan Dinehart, H. B. Warner, Beryl Mercer, William Farnum, Willard Robertson, George Burr MacAnnon, Lyman Williams.

The Eagle and the Hawk (1933, Para.). *d:* Stuart Walker; *sc:* Bogart Rogers and Seton I. Miller—*b/o* a story by John Monk Saunders.

THE BEAUTIFUL LADY: Nameless beautiful blonde in WWI London who spends the night with a cynical, war-weary American ace on leave from the British Royal Flying Corps.

Fredric March, Cary Grant, Jack Oakie, Sir Guy Standing, Forrester Harvey, Kenneth Howell, Leland Hodgson, Virginia Hammond, Crauford Kent, Douglas Scott, Robert Manning, Russell Scott.

Brief Moment (1933, Col.). *d:* David Burton; *sc:* Brian Maslow and Edith Fitzgerald—*b/o* the play by S. N. Behrman.

ABBY FANE: Nightclub singer who, after she marries a carefree playboy who depends on his father's money, has trouble trying to get him to work for a living.

Gene Raymond, Monroe Owsley, Donald Cook, Arthur Hohl, Reginald Mason, Jameson Thomas, Irene Ware, Herbert Evans.

White Woman (1933, Para.). *d:* Stuart Walker; *sc:* Samuel Hoffenstein and Gladys Lehman—*b/o* a story by Norman Reilly Raine and Frank Butler.

JUDITH DENNING: Sexy cabaret singer in Malaya who—in order to keep from being deported—marries the cruel Cockney overseer of a rubber plantation but then falls for one of her husband's workers.

Charles Laughton, Charles Bickford, Kent Taylor, Percy Kilbride, Charles B. Middleton, James Bell, Claude King, Jimmie Dime, Marc Lawrence.

Bolero (1934, Para.). *d:* Wesley Ruggles; *sc:* Horace Jackson—*b/o* a story by Carey Wilson and Kubec Glasmon—from an idea by Ruth Ridenour.

HELEN HATHAWAY: Dancer in Paris who teams up with an ambitious male dancing partner on a "strictly business" basis but runs into problems when the partner becomes emotionally involved with her.

George Raft, William Frawley, Frances Drake, Sally Rand, Ray Milland, Gloria Shea, Gertrude Michael, Del Henderson, Paul Panzer, Gregory Golubeff.

We're Not Dressing (1934, Para.). *d:* Norman Taurog; *p:* Benjamin Glazer; *sc:* Horace Jackson, George Marion Jr., and Francis Martin—from a story by Benjamin Glazer—*b/o* James M. Barrie's play *The Admirable Chrichton.*

DORIS WORTHINGTON: Spoiled heiress who, when her yacht sinks, winds up on a Pacific island where she and the other wealthy survivors are forced to depend on a resourceful sailor in order to survive.

Bing Crosby, George Burns, Gracie Allen, Ethel Merman, Leon Errol, Raymond (Ray) Milland, Jay Henry, John Irwin, Charles Morris, Ben Hendricks, Ted Oliver.

Twentieth Century (1934, Col.). *d:* Howard Hawks; *sc:* Ben Hecht and Charles MacArthur—*b/o* their play, which was adapted from the play *Napoleon of Broadway* by Charles Bruce Milholland.

LILLY GARLAND (whose real name is MILDRED PLOTKA): Acclaimed actress who, while aboard the famous Twentieth Century Limited train en route to New York, is tricked by an egotistical producer—her former mentor and lover—into signing for the lead in his new play.

John Barrymore, Walter Connolly, Roscoe Karns, Charlie Levison, Etienne Girardot, Ralph Forbes, Billie Seward, Gigi Parrish, Edgar Kennedy, Ed Gargan, Snowflake, Herman Bing, Pat Flaherty, Charles Lane.

Now and Forever (1934, Para.). *d:* Henry Hathaway; *p:* Louis D. Lighton; *sc:* Vincent Lawrence and Sylvia Thalberg—*b/o* the story "Honor Bright" by Jack Kirkland and Melville Baker.

TONI CARSTAIRS: Girlfriend and partner-in-crime of an international jewel thief who finally convinces him that they should go straight for the sake of his little girl.

Gary Cooper, Shirley Temple, Sir Guy Standing, Charlotte Granville, Gilbert Emery, Henry Kolker, Jameson Thomas, Harry Stubbs, Richard Loo, Akim Tamiroff, Buster Phelps, Rolfe Sedan.

Lady by Choice (1934, Col.). *d:* David Burton; *p:* Robert North Production; *sc:* Jo Swerling—*b/o* a story by Dwight Taylor.

ALABAM' LEE: Mercenary fan dancer who, as a publicity stunt on Mother's Day, adopts a gin-soaked old woman from a retirement home as her "mother."

May Robson, Roger Pryor, Walter Connolly, Arthur Hohl, Raymond Walburn, James Burke, Henry Kolker, Lillian Harmer, Fred (Snowflake) Toones.

The Gay Bride (1934, MGM). *d:* Jack Conway; *p:* John W. Considine Jr.; *sc:* Bella Spewack and Samuel Spewack—*b/o* the *Saturday Evening Post* story "Repeal" by Charles Francis Coe.

MARY: Gold-digging show girl who becomes

involved with a series of gangsters but finally reforms and marries the office boy.

Chester Morris, ZaSu Pitts, Leo Carrillo, Nat Pendleton, Sam Hardy, Walter Walker.

Rumba (1935, Para.). d: Marion Gering; p: William LeBaron; sc: Howard J. Green (with additional dialogue by Harry Ruskin and Frank Partas)—b/o the story by Guy Endore and Seena Owen.

DIANA HARRISON: Wealthy society woman who falls for a smooth, ambitious male dancer whom she discovers in Cuba and takes to New York.

George Raft, Lynne Overman, Margo, Monroe Owsley, Iris Adrian, Samuel S. Hinds, Virginia Hammond, Gail Patrick, Soledad Jiminez, Paul Porcasi, Raymond McKee, Akim Tamiroff.

Hands Across the Table (1935, Para.). d: Mitchell Leisen; p: E. Lloyd Sheldon; sc: Norman Krasna, Vincent Lawrence, and Herbert Fields—b/o a story by Vina Delmar.

REGI ALLEN: Fortune-hunting manicurist who vows to marry for money but winds up with a penniless playboy.

Fred MacMurray, Ralph Bellamy, Astrid Allwyn, Ruth Donnelly, Marie Prevost, William Demarest, Edward Gargan, Harold Minjir, Marcelle Corday.

Love Before Breakfast (1936, Univ.). d: Walter Lang; p: Edmund Grainger; sc: Herbert Fields (with additional dialogue by Gertrude Princell)—b/o the novel *Spinster Dinner* by Faith Baldwin.

KAY COLBY: Beautiful young woman who has trouble choosing between a rich oil man and his handsome assistant, both of whom are in love with her.

Preston Foster, Janet Beecher, Cesar Romero, Don Briggs, Bert Roach, Richard Carle, Joyce Compton, John King, E. E. Clive, Forrester Harvey.

The Princess Comes Across (1936, Para.). d: William K. Howard; p: Arthur Hornblow Jr.; sc: Walter De Leon, Francis Martin, Frank Butler, and Don Hartman (adaptation by Philip MacDonald)—b/o the novel by Louis Lucien Rogers.

PRINCESS OLGA: Brooklyn show girl—posing as a Swedish princess—who sails on a transatlantic luxury liner, falls for a handsome bandleader, and becomes involved in a shipboard murder.

Fred MacMurray, Douglas Dumbrille, Alison Skipworth, William Frawley, Porter Hall, George Barbier, Lumsden Hare, Sig Ruman, Mischa Auer, Bennie Bartlett.

My Man Godfrey (1936, Univ.). d: Gregory La Cava; p: Gregory La Cava; sc: Morrie Ryskind and Eric Hatch—b/o the novel by Eric Hatch.

IRENE BULLOCK*: Scatterbrained society woman who hires a shanty bum as the family butler, falls in love with him, then discovers that he's really a well-to-do member of an old Boston family.

William Powell, Alice Brady, Gail Patrick, Jean Dixon, Eugene Pallette, Alan Mowbray, Mischa Auer, Robert Light, Pat Flaherty, Franklin Pangborn, Grady Sutton, Ed Gargan, James Flavin.

Swing High, Swing Low (1937, Para.). d: Mitchell Leisen; p: Arthur Hornblow Jr.; sc: Virginia Van Upp and Oscar Hammerstein II—b/o the play *Burlesque* by George Manker Watters and Arthur Hopkins.

MAGGIE KING: Show girl who—after meeting a trumpet player on board a ship—marries him in Panama, divorces him for neglecting her when he becomes a jazz hit in New York, but goes back to him when he hits the skids.

Fred MacMurray, Charles Butterworth, Jean Dixon, Dorothy Lamour, Harvey Stephens, Cecil Cunningham, Anthony Quinn, Bud Flanagan (Dennis O'Keefe), Charles Arnt, Franklin Pangborn, Charles Judels.

Nothing Sacred (1937, UA). d: William Wellman; p: David O. Selznick (Selznick International); sc: Ben Hecht—b/o the short story "Letter to the Editor" by James H. Street.

HAZEL FLAGG: Small-town young Vermont woman who is told that she has only six months to live, then—even though she has subsequently learned that the doctor's diagnosis was wrong—goes to New York and lets an unknowing reporter exploit her in a series of sensational news stories.

Fredric March, Charles Winninger, Walter Connolly, Sig Ruman, Frank Fay, Maxie Rosenbloom, Monte Wooley, Margaret Hamilton, Hattie McDaniel, Olin Howland, George Chandler.

True Confession (1937, Para.). d: Wesley Ruggles; p: Albert Lewin; sc: Claude Binyon—b/o the play *Mon Crime* by Louis Verneuil and Georges Berr.

HELEN BARTLETT: Secretary with a penchant for telling lies who confesses to a murder she didn't commit, then has trouble convincing her lawyer husband that she's really innocent.

Fred MacMurray, John Barrymore, Una Merkel, Porter Hall, Edgar Kennedy, Lynne Overman, Fritz Feld, Richard Carle, John T. Murray, Tom Dugan, Garry Owen, Toby Wing, Hattie MacDaniel.

Fools for Scandal (1938, WB). d: Mervyn Le Roy; p: Mervyn Le Roy; sc: Herbert Fields and Joseph Fields (with additional dialogue by Irving

---

*Received an Academy Award nomination as Best Actress for this role.

Beecher)—b/o the play *Return Engagement* by Nancy Hamilton, James Shute, and Rosemary Casey.

KAY WINTERS: Famous American film star who hires an impoverished French nobleman as a cook/butler and falls in love with him.

Fernand Gravet, Ralph Bellamy, Allen Jenkins, Isabel Jeans, Marie Wilson, Marcia Ralston, Tola Nesmith, Heather Thatcher, Tempe Piggott.

Made for Each Other (1939, UA). *d:* John Cromwell; *p:* David O. Selznick (Selznick International); *sc:* Jo Swerling.

JANE MASON: Young Boston woman who marries a young New York attorney, then runs into meddling in-laws, financial problems, illness, and other assorted matrimonial pitfalls.

James Stewart, Charles Coburn, Lucile Watson, Eddie Quillan, Alma Kruger, Ruth Weston, Donald Briggs, Harry Davenport, Esther Dale, Louise Beavers, Ward Bond, Olin Howland.

In Name Only (1939, RKO). *d:* John Cromwell; *p:* George Haight and Pandro S. Berman; *sc:* Richard Sherman—b/o the novel *Memory of Love* by Bessie Brewer.

JULIE EDEN: Young widowed commercial artist who falls in love with a wealthy married man whose scheming, money-hungry wife refuses to divorce him.

Cary Grant, Kay Francis, Charles Coburn, Helen Vinson, Katharine Alexander, Jonathan Hale, Maurice Moscovich, Nella Walker, Peggy Ann Garner, Spencer Charters.

Vigil in the Night (1940, RKO). *d:* George Stevens; *p:* George Stevens; *sc:* Fred Guidl, P. J. Wolfson, and Rowland Leigh—b/o the novel by A. J. Cronin.

ANNE LEE: Dedicated English nurse who takes the blame for the death of a child that resulted from the negligence of another nurse, her younger sister.

Brian Aherne, Anne Shirley, Julien Mitchell, Robert Coote, Brenda Forbes, Rita Page, Peter Cushing, Ethel Griffies, Doris Lloyd, Emily Fitzroy.

They Knew What They Wanted (1940, RKO). *d:* Garson Kanin; *p:* Erich Pommer; *sc:* Robert Ardrey—b/o the play by Sidney Howard.

AMY PETERS: Lonely waitress who carries on a correspondence with an aging Italian grape-grower in California and—though she's never seen him—accepts his proposal of marriage.

Charles Laughton, William Gargan, Harry Carey, Frank Fay, Joe Bernard, Janet Fox, Lee Tung-Foo, Karl Malden, Victor Kilian, Paul Lepers.

Mr. and Mrs. Smith (1941, RKO). *d:* Alfred Hitchcock; *p:* Harry E. Edington; *sc:* Norman Krasna.

ANN SMITH: Wife who—after she discovers that because of a technicality she and her husband aren't really legally married—locks him out of the bedroom when he fails to immediately ask her to marry him.

Robert Montgomery, Gene Raymond, Jack Carson, Philip Merivale, Lucile Watson, William Tracy, Charles Halton, Esther Dale, Emma Dunn, Betty Compson, Patricia Farr, Adele Pearce, Georgia Carroll, James Flavin.

To Be or Not to Be (1942, UA). *d:* Ernst Lubitsch; *p:* Ernst Lubitsch (Alexander Korda); *sc:* Edwin Justus Mayer—b/o a story by Ernst Lubitsch and Melchior Lengyel.

MARIA TURA: Polish actress who, with her Shakespearean-actor husband, belongs to a theater troupe that—in order to escape from WWII Warsaw—becomes involved in an underground plot and a masquerade of high Nazi officers (including Hitler).

Jack Benny, Robert Stack, Felix Bressart, Lionel Atwill, Stanley Ridges, Sig Ruman, Tom Dugan, Charles Halton, Henry Victor, Maude Eburne.

☆ GROUCHO MARX

Julius Henry Marx

b: Oct. 2, 1890, New York, N.Y.
d: Aug. 19, 1977, Los Angeles, Cal.

"If I hold you any closer, I'll be in back of you."

Dr. Hugo Z. Hackenbush (Groucho Marx)
to Flo Marlowe (Esther Muir) in *A Day at the Races*, 1937.

The Cocoanuts (1929, Para.). *d:* Robert Florey
and Joseph Santley; *p:* Walter Wanger; *sc:* Morrie
Ryskind—*b/o* the musical play by George S.
Kaufman and Morrie Ryskind (music and lyrics
by Irving Berlin).
MR. HAMMER: Broke, chiseling manager of a
Florida hotel who auctions off real estate on the
side as he tries to cash in on the 1920s property
boom.
Harpo Marx, Chico Marx, Zeppo Marx, Margaret
Dumont, Mary Eaton, Oscar Shaw, Kay Francis,
Cyril Ring, Basil Ruysdael, Sylvan Lee.

Animal Crackers (1930, Para.). *d:* Victor
Heerman; *sc:* Morrie Ryskind (continuity by
Pierre Collings)—*b/o* the musical play by George
S. Kaufman and Morrie Ryskind (music and lyrics
by Bert Kalmar and Harry Ruby).
CAPTAIN JEFFREY T. SPAULDING: Famous
African jungle explorer who is a guest of honor at
a Long Island society dowager's party where
thieves plan to steal a valuable painting.
Harpo Marx, Chico Marx, Zeppo Marx, Margaret
Dumont, Lillian Roth, Louis Sorin, Hal Thompson,
Margaret Irving, Kathryn Reece, Robert Greig,
Edward Metcalf.

Monkey Business (1931, Para.). *d:* Norman
McLeod; *sc:* S. J. Perelman and Will B. Johnstone
(with additional dialogue by Arthur Sheekman).
Billed as a "STOWAWAY": One of four kooky
stowaways on an ocean liner who crash a society
party and catch a gang of crooks.
Harpo Marx, Chico Marx, Zeppo Marx, Thelma
Todd, Rockcliffe Fellowes, Tom Kennedy, Ruth
Hall, Harry Woods, Ben Taggart, Otto Fries,
Evelyn Pierce, Maxine Castle.

Horse Feathers (1932, Para.). *d:* Norman
McLeod; *sc:* Bert Kalmar, Harry Ruby, S. J.
Perelman, and Will B. Johnstone.
PROFESSOR QUINCEY ADAMS WAGSTAFF:
Daffy, irreverent president of Huxley College who
recruits two strange characters he mistakenly
thinks are star football players and—in a wild
and woolly football game—manages to beat arch
rival Darwin U.

Harpo Marx, Chico Marx, Zeppo Marx, Thelma
Todd, David Landau, Robert Greig, James Pierce,
Nat Pendleton, Reginald Barlow, Florine
McKinney.

Duck Soup (1933, Para.). *d:* Leo McCarey; *sc:* Bert
Kalmar and Harry Ruby (with additional dialogue
by Arthur Sheekman and Nat Perrin).
RUFUS T. FIREFLY: Zany, incompetent president
of the republic of Freedonia, which wages a wacky
war against its scheming neighbor, the country of
Sylvania.
Harpo Marx, Chico Marx, Zeppo Marx, Margaret
Dumont, Louis Calhern, Raquel Torres, Edgar
Kennedy, Edmund Breese, William Worthington,
Edwin Maxwell, Leonid Kinsky, Verna Hillie,
Charles B. Middleton.

A Night at the Opera (1935, MGM). *d:* Sam
Wood; *p:* Irving G. Thalberg; *sc:* George S.
Kaufman and Morrie Ryskind (with additional
material by Al Boasberg)—*b/o* a story by James
Kevin McGuinness.
OTIS B. DRIFTWOOD: Fast-talking promoter who
unsuccessfully tries to sign up a famous opera
singer, then—with the help of two kooky
associates—sabotages one of the singer's
performances so that he can replace him with a
young tenor whose contract he owns.
Harpo Marx, Chico Marx, Margaret Dumont,
Siegfried Rumann, Kitty Carlisle, Allan Jones,
Walter Woolf King, Edward Keane, Robert
Emmett O'Connor, Lorraine Bridges.

A Day at the Races (1937, MGM). *d:* Sam Wood;
p: Max Siegel; *sc:* George Seaton, Robert Pirosh,
and George Oppenheimer—*b/o* a story by George
Seaton and Robert Pirosh.
DR. HUGO Z. HACKENBUSH: Wacky horse
doctor who poses as the personal physician of a
hypochondriac dowager while he and two zany
cronies help a young couple's horse win a
steeplechase.
Harpo Marx, Chico Marx, Margaret Dumont,
Siegfried Rumann, Allan Jones, Maureen
O'Sullivan, Douglas Dumbrille, Leonard Ceeley,
Esther Muir, Robert Middlemass.

Room Service (1938, RKO). *d:* William A. Seiter;
p: Pandro S. Berman; *sc:* Morrie Ryskind—*b/o* the
stage play by John Murray and Allen Boretz.
GORDON MILLER: Penniless stage producer who,
along with his two pals, resorts to various
schemes to keep from being kicked out of his
hotel while he tries to dig up a backer for his
show.
Harpo Marx, Chico Marx, Lucille Ball, Ann

Miller, Frank Albertson, Donald MacBride, Cliff Dunstan, Philip Loeb, Charles Halton.

At the Circus (1939, MGM). *d:* Edward Buzzell; *p:* Mervyn LeRoy; *sc:* Irving Brecker.

J. CHEEVER LOOPHOLE: Shyster lawyer who's hired to save a circus from going broke—and with the help of two incompetents, somehow manages to do it.

Harpo Marx, Chico Marx, Margaret Dumont, Florence Rice, Kenny Baker, Eve Arden, Nat Pendleton, Fritz Feld, James Burke, Jerry Marenghi, Barnett Parker.

Go West (1940, MGM). *d:* Edward Buzzell; *p:* Jack Cummings; *sc:* Irving Brecher.

S. QUENTIN QUALE: Con man from the East who heads for the Old West and, with the help of two zany sidekicks, gets the best of a villainous town boss.

Harpo Marx, Chico Marx, John Carroll, Diana Lewis, Robert Barrat, Walter Woolf King, June MacCloy, George Lessey, Mitchell Lewis, Tully Marshall, Lee Bowman, Clem Bevans, Joe Yule.

The Big Store (1941, MGM). *d:* Charles Reisner; *p:* Louis K. Sidney; *sc:* Sid Kuller, Hal Fimberg, and Ray Golden—*b/o* a story by Nat Perrin.

WOLF J. FLYWHEEL: Seedy private eye who, when he's hired by the wealthy female owner of a department store to pose as a floorwalker, manages—with the help of a pair of kooky associates—to snare the crooked manager.

Harpo Marx, Chico Marx, Margaret Dumont, Douglas Dumbrille, Tony Martin, Virginia Grey, William Tannen, Marion Martin, Virginia O'Brien, Henry Armetta, Paul Stanton, Russell Hicks, Bradley Page, Charles Holland.

A Night in Casablanca (1946, UA). *d:* Archie L. Mayo; *p:* David L. Loew; *sc:* Joseph Fields and Roland Kibbee (with additional material by Frank Tashlin).

RONALD KORNBLOW: Hotel manager in Casablanca who, along with his two wacky assistants, outwits some Nazi spies operating in North Africa.

Harpo Marx, Chico Marx, Sig Ruman, Lisette Verea, Charles Drake, Lois Collier, Dan Seymour, Lewis Russell, Frederick Gierman, Harro Mellor, David Hoffman, Hall Harvey.

Copacabana (1947, UA). *d:* Alfred E. Green; *p:* Sam Coslow; *sc:* Laslo Vadnay, Allen Boretz, and Howard Harris.

LIONEL Q. DEVEREAUX: Free-wheeling agent who runs into complications when he makes a wild deal for his only client to play two people at once in a nightclub show: a harem-veiled French singer and a peppery Latin vocalist.

Carmen Miranda, Steve Cochran, Gloria Jean, Andy Russell, Andrew Tombes, Louis Sobel, Earl Wilson, Abel Green.

Love Happy (1949, UA). *d:* David Miller; *p:* Lester Cowan (A Mary Pickford Presentation); *sc:* Frank Tashlin and Mac Benoff—*b/o* a story by Harpo Marx.

SAM GRUNION: Seedy private eye who, along with two kooky helpers, clashes with a gang of crooks as he tries to track down the valuable Romanoff royal diamond necklace.

Harpo Marx, Chico Marx, Vera-Ellen, Ilona Massey, Marion Hutton, Raymond Burr, Melville Cooper, Paul Valentine, Leon Belasco, Eric Blore, Bruce Gordon, Marilyn Monroe.

Double Dynamite (1951, RKO). *d:* Irving Cummings; *p:* Irving Cummings Jr.; *sc:* Melville Shavelson (with additional dialogue by Harry Crane)—from a story by Leo Rosten —*b/o* a character created by Mannie Manheim.

EMIL J. KEECH: Friendly, wisecracking waiter who tries to help vindicate a young bank-clerk friend mistakenly accused of embezzling funds.

Frank Sinatra, Jane Russell, Don McGuire, Howard Freeman, Nestor Paiva, Frank Orth, Harry Hayden, Joe Devlin, Lou Nova, Ida Moore, Hal K. Dawson, George Chandler.

A Girl in Every Port (1952, RKO). *d:* Chester Erskine; *p:* Irwin Allen and Irving Cummings Jr.; *sc:* Chester Erskine.

BENNY LINN: Wheeler-dealer sailor who, after he and his good-natured but dumb shipmate inherit a racehorse, foils a race-fixing scheme and winds up with his horse winning the big race.

Marie Wilson, William Bendix, Don Defore, Gene Lockhart, Hanley Stafford, Percy Helton, George E. Stone.

The Story of Mankind (1957, WB). *d:* Irwin Allen; *p:* Irwin Allen (Cambridge); *sc:* Irwin Allen and Charles Bennett—*b/o* the book by Hendrik Van Loon.

PETER MINUIT: Dutch colonial official in 1626 America who cons the Indians out of Manhattan Island for some pieces of cloth and baubles valued at 60 guilders (about $24).

Ronald Colman, Hedy Lamarr, Harpo Marx, Chico Marx, Virginia Mayo, Agnes Moorehead, Vincent Price, Peter Lorre, Charles Coburn, Cedric Hardwicke, Cesar Romero, John Carradine, Dennis Hopper, Marie Wilson, Helmut Dantine, Edward Everett Horton, Reginald Gardner, Marie Windsor, Cathy O'Donnell, Francis X. Bushman, Jim Ameche, Franklin Pangborn, Henry Daniell, Tudor Owen.

Skidoo (1969, Para.). *d:* Otto Preminger; *p:* Otto Preminger (Sigma); *sc:* Doran William Cannon.

"GOD": Big-shot syndicate boss who's briefly involved in a plot in which a retired hood has been hired to silence another mobster who's cooperating with a Senate investigating committee.

Jackie Gleason, Carol Channing, Frankie Avalon, Fred Clark, Michael Constantine, Frank Gorshin, John Phillip Law, Peter Lawford, Burgess

Meredith, George Raft, Cesar Romero, Mickey Rooney, Austin Pendleton.

• Groucho Marx also made cameo/guest appearances in the following movies: *Mr. Music* (1950, Para.) and *Will Success Spoil Rock Hunter?* (1957, 20th-Fox—as a gag "bit," GEORGE SCHMIDLAPP, the secret love of sex bomb Jayne Mansfield).

☆ MARILYN MONROE

Norma Jean Baker
also known as
Norma Jean Mortenson

b: June 1, 1926, Los Angeles, Cal.
d: Aug. 5, 1962, Los Angeles, Cal.

"I always say a kiss on the hand might feel very good, but a diamond tiara lasts forever."

Lorelei Lee (Marilyn Monroe) to Sir Francis Beekman (Charles Coburn) in *Gentlemen Prefer Blondes,* 1953.

Dangerous Years (1948, 20th-Fox). *d:* Arthur Pierson; *p:* Sol M. Wurtzel; *sc:* Arnold Belgard.

EVE: Pretty young waitress at a juke box joint where a young hoodlum and some teen-age friends hang out.

William Halop, Ann E. Todd, Jerome Cowan, Scotty Beckett, Darryl Hickman, Harry Shannon, Dickie Moore, Gil Stratton Jr.

Ladies of the Chorus (1948, Col.). *d:* Phil Karlson; *p:* Harry A. Romm; *sc:* Harry Sauber and Joseph Carol—*b/o* a story by Harry Sauber.

PEGGY MARTIN: Young burlesque chorus girl who, when she falls for a rich socialite, finds that her mother (also a burlesque dancer) objects.

Adele Jergens, Rand Brooks, Nana Bryant, Steven Geray, Bill Edwards, Dave Barry, Gladys Blake, Myron Healey, Robert Clarke, Emmett Vogan.

Love Happy (1949, UA). *d:* David Miller; *p:* Lester Cowan (A Mary Pickford Presentation); *sc:* Frank Tashlin and Mac Benoff—*b/o* a story by Harpo Marx.

Billed as "GRUNION'S CLIENT": Sexy would-be client who naïvely tells a private eye that "men keep following me."

Groucho Marx, Harpo Marx, Chico Marx, Vera-Ellen, Ilona Massey, Marion Hutton, Raymond Burr, Melville Cooper, Paul Valentine, Leon Belasco, Eric Blore, Bruce Gordon.

A Ticket to Tomahawk (1950, 20th-Fox). *d:* Richard Sale; *p:* Robert Bassler; *sc:* Mary Loos and Richard Sale.

CLARA: One of a troupe of show girls who are passengers on a train headed for Tomahawk, Colorado, in 1876.

Dan Dailey, Anne Baxter, Rory Calhoun, Walter Brennan, Connie Gilchrist, Arthur Hunnicutt, Will Wright, Victor Sen Yung, Raymond Greenleaf, Chief Thundercloud.

The Asphalt Jungle (1950, MGM). *d:* John Huston; *p:* Arthur Hornblow Jr.; *sc:* Ben Maddow and John Huston—*b/o* the novel by W. R. Burnett.

ANGELA PHINLAY: Beautiful blonde mistress who betrays her crooked lawyer boyfriend when he becomes involved in a jewel robbery and murder.

Sterling Hayden, Louis Calhern, Jean Hagan, Sam Jaffe, James Whitmore, John McIntire, Marc Lawrence, Barry Kelley, Anthony Caruso, Brad Dexter.

All About Eve (1950, 20th-Fox). *d:* Joseph L. Mankiewicz; *p:* Darryl F. Zanuck; *sc:* Joseph L. Mankiewicz—*b/o* Mary Orr's story "The Wisdom of Eve."

MISS CASWELL: Shapely aspiring young actress who is the "protegée" of a lecherous New York drama critic.

Bette Davis, Anne Baxter, George Sanders, Celeste Holm, Gary Merrill, Hugh Marlowe, Thelma Ritter, Gregory Ratoff, Barbara Bates, Walter Hampden.

The Fireball (1950, 20th-Fox). *d:* Tay Garnett; *p:* Bert Friedlob (Thor Prod.); *sc:* Tay Garnett and Horace McCoy.

POLLY: Mercenary young woman—one of several female admirers who get involved with a cocky roller-skating champion.

Mickey Rooney, Pat O'Brien, Beverly Tyler, Glenn Corbett, James Brown, Ralph Dumke, Milburne Stone.

Right Cross (1950, MGM). *d:* John Sturges; *p:* Armand Deutsch; *sc:* Charles Schnee.

(Unbilled appearance.) Beautiful woman in a nightclub at a table with a hard-drinking sports reporter.

June Allyson, Dick Powell, Ricardo Montalban, Lionel Barrymore, Teresa Celli, Barry Kelley, Marianne Stewart, John Gallaudett, Larry Keating, Ken Tobey.

Hometown Story (1951, MGM). *d:* Arthur Pierson; *p:* Arthur Pierson; *sc:* Arthur Pierson.

MISS MARTIN: Good-looking blonde secretary who works in a newspaper office.

Jeffrey Lynn, Donald Crisp, Marjorie Reynolds, Alan Hale Jr., Melinda Plowman, Glenn Tryon, Byron Foulger, Griff Barnett, Harry Harvey.

As Young as You Feel (1951, 20th-Fox). *d:* Harmon Jones; *p:* Lamar Trotti; *sc:* Lamar Trotti—*b/o* a story by Paddy Chayefsky.

HARRIET: Sexy secretary of the fat-headed president of a printing firm.

Monty Woolley, Thelma Ritter, David Wayne, Jean Peters, Constance Bennett, Allyn Joslyn, Albert Dekker, Clinton Sundberg, Minor Watson, Ludwig Stossel, Renie Riano, Wally Brown, Rusty Tamblyn, Roger Moore.

Love Nest (1951, 20th-Fox). *d:* Joseph Newman; *p:* Jules Buck; *sc:* I. A. L. Diamond—*b/o* a novel by Scott Corbett.

ROBERTA STEVENS: Curvacious ex-WAC who, when she moves into an apartment building owned by an ex-GI friend, causes friction between the GI and his jealous wife.

June Haver, William Lundigan, Frank Fay, Jack Paar, Leatrice Joy, Henry Kulky, Marie Blake, Joe Ploski, Faire Binney.

Let's Make It Legal (1951, 20th-Fox). *d:* Richard Sale; *p:* Robert Bassler; *sc:* F. Hugh Herbert and I. A. L. Diamond—*b/o* a story by Cyril Mockridge.

JOYCE: Beautiful, shapely blonde who tries to snare a handsome millionaire industrialist when he has problems with his wife.

Claudette Colbert, Macdonald Carey, Zachary Scott, Barbara Bates, Robert Wagner, Frank Cady, Carol Savage, Harry Harvey Sr.

Clash by Night (1952, RKO). *d:* Fritz Lang; *p:* Harriet Parsons (Wald–Krasna Prod.); *sc:* Alfred Hayes—*b/o* the play by Clifford Odets.

PEGGY: Sexy blonde worker in a West Coast fish cannery who becomes engaged to the brother of an older, adulterous woman friend.

Barbara Stanwyck, Paul Douglas, Robert Ryan, J. Carrol Naish, Keith Andes, Silvio Minciotti.

We're Not Married (1952, 20th-Fox). *d:* Edmund Goulding; *p:* Nunnally Johnson; *sc:* Nunnally Johnson (adaptation by Dwight Taylor)—*b/o* a story by Gina Kaus and Jay Dratler.

ANNABEL NORRIS: Curvy housewife who, after winning the title of "Mrs. Mississippi," discovers that through a mistake by a bumbling justice of the peace, she and her husband are one of five couples who were never legally married.

Ginger Rogers, Fred Allen, Victor Moore, David Wayne, Eve Arden, Paul Douglas, Eddie Bracken, Mitzi Gaynor, Louis Calhern, Zsa Zsa Gabor, James Gleason, Paul Stewart, Jane Darwell, Tom Powers, Alan Bridge, Ralph Dumke, Lee Marvin, Marjorie Weaver, Selma Jackson.

Don't Bother to Knock (1952, 20th-Fox). *d:* Roy Baker; *p:* Julian Blaustein; *sc:* Daniel Taradash—*b/o* the novel by Charlotte Armstrong.

NELL: Psychopathic young woman who takes a job as a baby sitter in a hotel, becomes involved with an airline pilot, and almost commits a murder.

Richard Widmark, Anne Bancroft, Donna Corcoran, Jeanne Cagney, Lurene Tuttle, Elisha Cook Jr., Jim Backus, Willis B. Bouchey, Don Beddoe, Gloria Blondell, Michael Ross.

Monkey Business (1952, 20th-Fox). *d:* Howard Hawks; *p:* Sol C. Siegel; *sc:* Ben Hecht, Charles Lederer, and I. A. L. Diamond—*b/o* a story by Harry Segall.

LOIS LAUREL: Dumb, beautiful secretary who becomes involved with an absent-minded research chemist when he drinks a "youth potion" and reverts to acting like a teen-ager.

Cary Grant, Ginger Rogers, Charles Coburn, Hugh Marlowe, Robert Cornthwaite, Larry Keating, Esther Dale, George Winslow, Kathleen Freeman, Olan Soule, Harry Carey Jr., Jerry Paris, Roger Moore, Dabbs Greer.

O. Henry's Full House (1952, 20th-Fox). *d:* Henry Koster; *p:* Andre Hakim; *sc:* Lamar Trotti—*b/o* short stories by O. Henry.

Billed as "STREETWALKER": Beautiful woman who, when accosted by a bum, turns out to be a streetwalker in search of business.

Charles Laughton, David Wayne, Thomas Browne Henry, Richard Karlan, Erno Verebes, Nico Lek, William Vedder, Billy Wayne.

Niagara (1953, 20th-Fox). *d:* Henry Hathaway; *p:* Charles Brackett; *sc:* Charles Brackett, Walter Reisch, and Richard Breen.

ROSE LOOMIS: Cheating wife who plots with her lover to kill her husband while they are on vacation at Niagara Falls.

Joseph Cotten, Jean Peters, Casey Adams, Denis O'Dea, Don Wilson, Lurene Tuttle, Russell Collins, Will Wright, Lester Matthews, Carleton Young, Sean McClory.

Gentlemen Prefer Blondes (1953, 20th-Fox). *d:* Howard Hawks; *p:* Sol C. Siegel; *sc:* Charles Lederer—*b/o* the musical comedy by Joseph Fields and Anita Loos.

LORELEI LEE: One of two show-biz beauties from Little Rock who are on the prowl for men and diamonds aboard the *Ile de France* and in Paris.

Jane Russell, Charles Coburn, Elliott Reid, Tommy Noonan, George Winslow, Taylor Holmes, Norma Varden, Steven Geray, Leo Mostovoy.

How to Marry a Millionaire (1953, 20th-Fox). *d:* Jean Negulesco; *p:* Nunnally Johnson; *sc:* Nunnally Johnson—*b/o* plays by Zoe Akins, Dale Eunson, and Katherine Albert.

POLA DEBEVOISE: Nearsighted member of a trio of beauteous models who rent an expensive New York penthouse apartment as part of their plan to trap millionaire husbands for themselves.

Betty Grable, Lauren Bacall, William Powell, David Wayne, Rory Calhoun, Cameron Mitchell, Alex D'Arcy, Fred Clark, George Dunn, Percy Helton.

River of No Return (1954, 20th-Fox). *d:* Otto Preminger; *p:* Stanley Rubin; *sc:* Frank Fenton—*b/o* a story by Louis Lantz.

KAY WESTON: Saloon singer in the Northwest during the 1870s who, when her no-good gambler husband deserts her, is helped by an ex-con and his young son.

Robert Mitchum, Rory Calhoun, Tommy Rettig, Murvyn Vye, Don Beddoe, Edmund Cobb, Will Wright, Jarma Lewis, Hal Baylor.

There's No Business Like Show Business (1954, 20th-Fox). *d:* Walter Lang; *p:* Sol C. Siegel; *sc:* Phoebe Ephron and Henry Ephron—*b/o* a story by Lamar Trotti.

VICKY: Hat-check girl who, while trying to become a successful nightclub singer, gets involved with a song-and-dance man and his show-business family.

Ethel Merman, Donald O'Connor, Dan Dailey, Johnnie Ray, Mitzi Gaynor, Richard Eastham, Hugh O'Brian, Frank McHugh, Rhys Williams, Lee Patrick, Lyle Talbot, Alvy Moore, Chick Chandler.

The Seven-Year Itch (1955, 20th-Fox). *d:* Billy Wilder; *p:* Charles K. Feldman and Billy Wilder; *sc:* Billy Wilder and George Axelrod—*b/o* the play by George Axelrod.

Billed as "THE GIRL": Voluptuous model who lives in the apartment above a man who daydreams about having love affairs when his wife goes away on a summer vacation.

Tom Ewell, Evelyn Keyes, Sonny Tufts, Robert Strauss, Oscar Homolka, Marguerite Chapman, Victor Moore, Donald MacBride, Carolyn Jones.

Bus Stop (1956, 20th-Fox). *d:* Joshua Logan; *p:* Buddy Adler; *sc:* George Axelrod—*b/o* the play by William Inge.

CHERIE: B-girl in a Phoenix clip joint who is pursued by a love-sick rodeo cowboy to a bus stop in the Arizona wilds.

Don Murray, Arthur O'Connell, Betty Field, Eileen Heckart, Hope Lange, Hans Conried, Casey Adams, Henry Slate.

The Prince and the Showgirl (1957, WB). *d:* Laurence Olivier; *p:* Laurence Olivier (Marilyn Monroe Prod./L.O.P. Ltd.); *sc:* Terence Rattigan—*b/o* a play by Terence Rattigan.

ELSIE MARINA: American show girl in London who is romanced by the Prince Regent of Carpathia during the 1911 coronation of George V.

Laurence Olivier, Sybil Thorndike, Richard Wattis, Jeremy Spenser, Esmond Knight, Paul Hardwick, Rosamund Greenwood, Harold Goodwin, Aubrey Dexter.

Some Like It Hot (1959, UA). *d:* Billy Wilder; *p:* Billy Wilder (Ashton/Mirisch); *sc:* Billy Wilder and I. A. L. Diamond—*b/o* a suggestion from a story by R. Thoeren and M. Logan.

SUGAR KANE (KOVALCHICK): Beautiful, dumb blonde ukelele player and vocalist in a 1920s all-girl band who gets mixed up with a pair of male musicians—masquerading as women—who are on the run from gangsters.

Tony Curtis, Jack Lemmon, George Raft, Pat O'Brien, Joe E. Brown, Nehemiah Persoff, Billy Gray, George Stone, Dave Barry, Mike Mazurki, Edward G. Robinson Jr., Tom Kennedy.

Let's Make Love (1960, 20th-Fox). *d:* George Cukor; *p:* Jerry Wald; *sc:* Norman Krasna (with additional material by Hal Kanter).

AMANDA DELL: Singer in an off-Broadway revue who falls for a cast member who is playing the role of a prominent billionaire—which, as she later learns, he really is.

Yves Montand, Tony Randall, Frankie Vaughan, Wilfred Hyde-White, David Burns, Michael David, Mara Lynn, Joe Besser, Bing Crosby, Milton Berle, Gene Kelly.

The Misfits (1961, UA). *d:* John Huston; *p:* Frank E. Taylor (Seven Arts/John Huston); *sc:* Arthur Miller.

ROSLYN TABOR: Tender-hearted divorcée who goes along with a trio of modern-day cowboys to round up a herd of wild horses but tries to stop the roundup when she learns that the horses are to be slaughtered and made into dog food. *Clark Gable,* Montgomery Clift, Thelma Ritter, Eli Wallach, James Barton, Estelle Winwood, Kevin McCarthy, Dennis Shaw, Peggy Barton, Marietta Tree.

• In addition, a posthumous documentary film entitled *Marilyn* (1963, 20th-Fox) was based on film clips from Marilyn Monroe's various movies. Included were some scenes from her last film (unfinished and never released), entitled *Something's Got to Give.*

☆ PAUL NEWMAN

b: Jan. 26, 1925, Cleveland, Ohio

"Wish you'd stop being so good to me, Captain."

Luke (Paul Newman) to the Captain (Strother Martin) in *Cool Hand Luke,* 1967.

The Silver Chalice (1954, WB). *d:* Victor Saville; *p:* Victor Saville; *sc:* Lester Samuels—*b/o* the novel by Thomas B. Costain.
BASIL: Talented young Greek sculptor who, after being sold into slavery in Nero's Rome by an evil uncle, is chosen to design a receptacle for the chalice from which Christ drank at the Last Supper.
Virginia Mayo, Pier Angeli, Jack Palance, Walter Hampden, Joseph Wiseman, Alexander Scourby, Lorne Greene, Herbert Rudley, E. G. Marshall, Natalie Wood, Robert Middleton, Ian Wolfe, Lawrence Dobkin, Albert Dekker.

Somebody Up There Likes Me (1956, MGM). *d:* Robert Wise; *p:* Charles Schnee; *sc:* Ernest Lehman—*b/o* the autobiography of Rocky Graziano, written with Rowland Barber.
ROCKY GRAZIANO: Small-time hood who fights his way up from the sidewalks of New York to become the middleweight boxing champion of the world.
Pier Angeli, Everett Sloane, Eileen Heckart, Sal Mineo, Harold J. Stone, Sammy White, Arch Johnson, Robert Loggia, Harry Wismer, Robert Easton, Ray Sticklyn, Frank Campanella.

The Rack (1956, MGM). *d:* Arnold Laven; *p:* Arthur M. Loew Jr.; *sc:* Stewart Stern—*b/o* the teleplay by Rod Serling.
CAPT. EDWARD W. HALL JR.: Young U.S. Army captain who faces a court-martial for collaboration with the enemy when he was tortured while a P.O.W. in the Korean War.
Wendell Corey, Walter Pidgeon, Edmond O'Brien, Anne Francis, Lee Marvin, Cloris Leachman, Robert Burton, Robert Simon, Trevor Bardette, James Best.

Until They Sail (1957, MGM). *d:* Robert Wise; *p:* Charles Schnee; *sc:* Robert Anderson—*b/o* a novel by James A. Michener.
CAPT. JACK HARDING: WWII U.S. Marine officer who falls in love with a New Zealand widow who is trying to be faithful to the memory of her husband.
Jean Simmons, Joan Fontaine, Piper Laurie, Charles Drake, Wally Cassell, Sandra Dee.

The Helen Morgan Story (1957, WB). *d:* Michael Curtiz; *p:* Martin Rackin; *sc:* Oscar Saul, Dean Riesner, Stephen Longstreet, and Nelson Gidding.
LARRY MADDUX: Prohibition-era gangster, bootlegger, and dyed-in-the-wool heel who uses and abuses a famous 1920s–'30s torch singer who's made the mistake of falling in love with him.
Ann Blyth, Richard Carlson, Gene Evans, Alan King, Cara Williams, Walter Woolf King, Ed Platt, Warren Douglas, Sammy White, Jimmy McHugh, Rudy Vallee, Walter Winchell.

The Long Hot Summer (1958, 20th-Fox). *d:* Martin Ritt; *p:* Jerry Wald; *sc:* Irving Ravetch and Harriet Frank Jr.—*b/o* two stories, "Barn Burning" and "The Spotted Horses," and a part of the novel *The Hamlet,* all by William Faulkner.
BEN QUICK: Wandering Mississippi handyman who goes to work as a sharecropper for a domineering Southern land owner and decides to marry the boss's spinsterish daughter.
Joanne Woodward, Anthony Franciosa, Orson Welles, Lee Remick, Angela Lansbury, Richard Anderson, Mabel Albertson, J. Pat O'Malley, William Walker, Byron Foulger.

The Left-Handed Gun (1958, WB). *d:* Arthur Penn; *p:* Fred Coe (Haroll); *sc:* Leslie Stevens—*b/o* Gore Vidal's teleplay *The Death of Billy the Kid.*
BILLY THE KID: Legendary young desperado in the 1880s who vows to hunt down a deputy sheriff and three other men after they murder a kindly rancher friend of his.
Lita Milan, Hurd Hatfield, James Congdon, James Best, John Dierkes, Wally Brown, Denver Pyle, Nestor Paiva, Jo Summers, Anne Barton.

Cat on a Hot Tin Roof (1958, MGM). *d:* Richard Brooks; *p:* Lawrence Weingarten (Avon); *sc:* Richard Brooks and James Poe—*b/o* the play by Tennessee Williams.

BRICK POLLITT*: Former football hero who is dominated by his rich Southern-plantation-owner father, and who has grown to like booze better than his beautiful wife.

Elizabeth Taylor, Burl Ives, Jack Carson, Judith Anderson, Madeleine Sherwood, Larry Gates, Vaughn Taylor, Patty Ann Gerrity, Rusty Stevens, Hugh Corcoran, Deborah Miller, Brian Corcoran, Vince Townsend Jr., Zelda Cleaver.

Rally 'Round the Flag, Boys! (1958, 20th-Fox). *d:* Leo McCarey; *p:* Leo McCarey; *sc:* Claude Binyon and Leo McCarey—*b/o* the novel by Max Shulman.

HARRY BANNERMAN: Connecticut suburbanite who becomes involved in various shenanigans when his wife leads a protest movement against a secret Army plan to set up a missile base in their community.

Joanne Woodward, Joan Collins, Jack Carson, Dwayne Hickman, Tuesday Weld, Gale Gordon, Stanley Livingston, Burt Mustin, Percy Helton, Richard Collier, Murvyn Vye.

The Young Philadelphians (1959, WB). *d:* Vincent Sherman; *sc:* James Gunn—*b/o* Richard Powell's novel *The Philadelphian.*

TONY LAWRENCE: Ambitious young Philadelphia lawyer who schemes his way to the top but finally proves his integrity by defending an ex–Army buddy in a murder trial.

Barbara Rush, Alexis Smith, Brian Keith, Diane Brewster, Billie Burke, John Williams, Robert Vaughn, Otto Kruger, Paul Picerni, Robert Douglas, Frank Conroy, Adam West, Richard Deacon.

From the Terrace (1960, 20th-Fox). *d:* Mark Robson; *p:* Mark Robson (Linebrook); *sc:* Ernest Lehman—*b/o* the novel by John O'Hara.

ALFRED EATON: Ruthless young Philadelphian who wheels and deals his way to success with a Wall Street investment house, only to realize the emptiness of both his career and his marriage to a wealthy heiress.

Joanne Woodward, Myrna Loy, Ina Balin, Leon Ames, Elizabeth Allen, Barbara Eden, George Grizzard, Patrick O'Neal, Felix Aylmer, Malcolm Atterbury, Raymond Bailey, Ted DeCorsia, Dorothy Adams, Blossom Rock.

Exodus (1960, UA). *d:* Otto Preminger; *p:* Otto Preminger (Carlyle/Alpha); *sc:* Dalton Trumbo—*b/o* the novel by Leon Uris.

ARI BEN CANAAN: Courageous officer and leader in the Palestine-based Hagannah, a Jewish underground group that protects Jewish refugees and fights for the establishment of an independent Israel in 1947.

Eva Marie Saint, Ralph Richardson, Peter Lawford, Lee J. Cobb, Sal Mineo, John Derek, Hugh Griffith, David Opatoshu, Jill Haworth, Gregory Ratoff, Felix Aylmer, Marius Goring, George Maharis.

The Hustler (1961, 20th-Fox). *d:* Robert Rossen; *p:* Robert Rossen; *sc:* Robert Rossen and Sidney Carroll—*b/o* the novel by Walter Tevis.

EDDIE FELSON*: Itinerant pool shark who hustles suckers, gets involved with a gangster who indirectly causes his girlfriend to commit suicide, and finally gets a crack at the pool champ, Minnesota Fats.

Jackie Gleason, Piper Laurie, George C. Scott, Myron McCormick, Murray Hamilton, Michael Constantine, Jake LaMotta, Vincent Gardenia, Donald Crabtree, Brendan Fay.

Paris Blues (1961, UA). *d:* Martin Ritt; *p:* Sam Shaw (Pennebaker); *sc:* Jack Sher, Irene Kamp, and Walter Bernstein (adaptation by Lulla Adler)—*b/o* a novel by Harold Flender.

RAM BOWEN: Ex-patriate American jazz musician in a Left Bank nightclub who falls for a vacationing young American woman in Paris, then has to choose between her and his ambition to be a composer.

Joanne Woodward, Sidney Poitier, Louis Armstrong, Diahann Carroll, Serge Reggiani, Barbara Laage, Andre Luguet, Moustache, Roger Blin, Niko.

Sweet Bird of Youth (1962, MGM). *d:* Richard Brooks; *p:* Pandro S. Berman (Roxbury); *sc:* Richard Brooks—*b/o* the play by Tennessee Williams.

CHANCE WAYNE: Hollywood beach boy and aspiring actor who returns, along with a neurotic has-been movie actress, to his Florida hometown and learns—the hard way—that a vicious political boss whose daughter he impregnated is out to get him.

Geraldine Page, Shirley Knight, Ed Begley, Rip Torn, Mildred Dunnock, Madeleine Sherwood, Philip Abbott, Corey Allen, Barry Cahill, Dub Taylor, Charles Arnt, Robert Burton.

Hemingway's Adventures of a Young Man (1962, 20th-Fox). *d:* Martin Ritt; *p:* Jerry Wald; *sc:* A. E. Hotchner—*b/o* stories by Ernest Hemingway.

---

*Received an Academy Award nomination as Best Actor for this role.

*Received an Academy Award nomination as Best Actor for this role.

THE BATTLER: Punchy fifty-five-year-old ex-boxer who is one of a variety of characters a young Wisconsin man meets in his travels when he leaves home in 1917 to see the world.

Richard Beymer, Diane Baker, Corrine Calvet, Fred Clark, Dan Dailey, James Dunn, Juano Hernandez, Arthur Kennedy, Ricardo Montalban, Susan Strasberg, Jessica Tandy, Eli Wallach, Edward Binns, Whit Bissell, Tullio Carminati, Simon Oakland, Michael J. Pollard.

Hud (1963, Para.). *d:* Martin Ritt; *p:* Martin Ritt and Irving Ravetch (Salem–Dover); *sc:* Irving Ravetch and Harriet Frank Jr.—*b/o* Larry McMurtry's novel *Horseman, Pass By.*

HUD BANNON*: Hard-drinking, woman-chasing rancher in the modern West who uses people, disregards the rights of others, and alienates his elderly father and his teen-age nephew, who idolizes him.

Melvyn Douglas, Patricia Neal, Brandon de Wilde, John Ashley, Whit Bissell, Val Avery, Sheldon Allman, Pitt Herbert, Curt Conway, George Petrie.

A New Kind of Love (1963, Para.). *d:* Melville Shavelson; *p:* Melville Shavelson (Llenroc); *sc:* Melville Shavelson.

STEVE SHERMAN: Woman-chasing American newspaper columnist who, when he's exiled to Paris for playing around with his publisher's wife, becomes involved with a visiting American fashion designer who can't stand him—and vice-versa.

Joanne Woodward, Thelma Ritter, Eva Gabor, George Tobias, Marvin Kaplan, Robert Clary, Robert Simon, Maurice Chevalier.

The Prize (1963, MGM). *d:* Mark Robson; *p:* Pandro S. Berman (Roxbury); *sc:* Ernest Lehman—*b/o* the novel by Irving Wallace.

ANDREW CRAIG: Hard-drinking, woman-chasing American writer who, when he goes to Stockholm to receive the Nobel Prize for Literature, stumbles across an Iron Curtain plot to kidnap the Physics prize winner.

Edward G. Robinson, Elke Sommer, Diane Baker, Micheline Presle, Gerard Oury, Sergie Fantoni, Kevin McCarthy, Leo G. Carroll, Don Dubbins, John Qualen, Karl Swenson, Lester Mathews, John Banner, Jerry Dunphy, Queenie Leonard.

What a Way to Go! (1964, 20th-Fox). *d:* J. Lee Thompson; *p:* Arthur P. Jacobs (APJAC/Orchard); *sc:* Betty Comden and Adolph Green—*b/o* a story by Gwen Davis.

LARRY FLINT: American taxi driver and would-be artist in Paris who, after he becomes the second of five husbands of an eccentric millionairess, invents a bizarre painting machine with disastrous results.

Shirley MacLaine, Robert Mitchum, Dean Martin, Gene Kelly, Bob Cummings, Dick Van Dyke, Reginald Gardiner, Margaret Dumont, Fifi D'Orsay, Wally Vernon, Lenny Kent.

The Outrage (1964, MGM). *d:* Martin Ritt; *p:* A. Ronald Lubin (Harvest/February/Ritt/Kayos); *sc:* Michael Kanin—*b/o* the Japanese film *Rashomon*; from stories by Ryunosuke Akutagawa and the play *Rashomon* by Fay Kanin and Michael Kanin.

JUAN CARRASCO: Violent Mexican bandit in the post–Civil War West who kidnaps a traveler and his wife, then rapes the wife and murders the husband.

Laurence Harvey, Claire Bloom, Edward G. Robinson, William Shatner, Howard da Silva, Albert Salmi, Thomas Chalmers, Paul Fix.

Lady L (1965, MGM). *d:* Peter Ustinov; *p:* Carlo Ponti (Concordia/Champion); *sc:* Peter Ustinov—*b/o* the novel by Romain Gary.

ARMAND: Robin Hood–like thief and bank robber in turn-of-the-century Paris who joins an underground revolutionary group and becomes a bomb-carrying anarchist.

Sophia Loren, David Niven, Claude Dauphin, Philippe Noiret, Michel Piccoli, Marcel Dalio, Cecil Parker, Peter Ustinov, Tanya Lopert.

Harper (1966, WB). *d:* Jack Smight; *p:* Jerry Gershwin and Elliott Kastner (Gershwin–Kastner); *sc:* William Goldman—*b/o* Ross MacDonald's novel *The Moving Target.*

LEW HARPER: Cool, hardboiled Los Angeles private eye who, when he's hired by a wealthy woman to find her missing husband, gets involved with an assortment of unsavory characters and an illegal-alien smuggling ring.

Lauren Bacall, Julie Harris, Arthur Hill, Janet Leigh, Pamela Tiffin, Robert Wagner, Robert Webber, Shelley Winters, Harold Gould, Strother Martin, Roy Jensen, China Lee.

Torn Curtain (1966, Univ.). *d:* Alfred Hitchcock; *p:* Alfred Hitchcock (Alfred Hitchcock Prod.); *sc:* Brian Moore.

PROF. MICHAEL ARMSTRONG: Eminent U.S. atomic scientist who, while pretending to be a defector to East Germany in order to track down a secret anti-missile formula, finds himself and his fiancée battling deadly Communist agents.

Julie Andrews, Lila Kedrova, Hansjoerg Felmy, Tamara Toumanova, Wolfgang Kieling, Gunter Strack, Ludwig Donath, David Opatoshu, Mort Mills.

Hombre (1967, 20th-Fox). *d:* Martin Ritt; *p:*

---

*Received an Academy Award nomination as Best Actor for this role.

Martin Ritt and Irving Ravetch (Hombre Prod.); *sc:* Irving Ravetch and Harriet Frank Jr.—*b/o* the novel by Elmore Leonard.

RUSSELL: White man raised by Apache Indians in the 1880s Arizona who, even though he's discriminated against by other passengers on a stagecoach, sacrifices his life to save them from outlaws.

Fredric March, Richard Boone, Diane Cilento, Cameron Mitchell, Barbara Rush, Peter Lazer, Margaret Blye, Martin Balsam, Frank Silvera.

Cool Hand Luke (1967, WB). *d:* Stuart Rosenberg; *p:* Gordon Carroll (Jalem); *sc:* Donn Pearce and Frank R. Pierson—*b/o* the novel by Donn Pearce.

LUKE JACKSON*: Cool, gutsy prisoner in a Southern chain gang who, while refusing to buckle under to authority, keeps escaping and being recaptured.

George Kennedy, J. D. Cannon, Lou Antonio, Robert Drivas, Strother Martin, Jo Van Fleet, Clifton James, Luke Askew, Dennis Hopper, Wayne Rogers, Charles Tyner, Ralph Waite, Anthony Zerbe, Joe Don Baker, Donn Pearce.

The Secret War of Harry Frigg (1968, Univ.). *d:* Jack Smight; *p:* Hal E. Chester (Albion); *sc:* Peter Stone and Frank Tarloff—*b/o* a story by Frank Tarloff.

PVT. HARRY FRIGG: Goldbrick American G.I. in WWII who, because of his knack for escaping from stockades, is made a general so that he can engineer the escape of five not-too-bright Allied generals captured by the Italians.

Sylva Koscina, Andrew Duggan, Tom Bosley, John Williams, Charles D. Gray, Vito Scotti, James Gregory, Norman Fell, Buck Henry, Richard X. Slattery, George Ives.

Winning (1969, Univ.). *d:* James Goldstone; *p:* John Foreman (Newman–Foreman); *sc:* Howard Rodman.

FRANK CAPUA: Victory-obsessed auto-racing driver who, after he marries a divorcée with a teen-age son, has problems with both them and his racing.

Joanne Woodward, Richard Thomas, Robert Wagner, David Sheiner, Clu Gulager, Barry Ford, Bob Quarry, Eileen Wesson, Toni Clayton, Bobby Unser.

Butch Cassidy and the Sundance Kid (1969, 20th-Fox). *d:* George Roy Hill; *p:* John Foreman and Paul Monash (Campanile); *sc:* William Goldman.

BUTCH CASSIDY: Famed nineteenth-century outlaw leader of a Wyoming gang (called the Wild Bunch or the Hole-in-the-Wall Gang) who teams up with the gun-slinging outlaw Sundance Kid to rob trains—first in the Old West, and then in Bolivia, where they are finally ambushed.

Robert Redford, Katharine Ross, Strother Martin, Henry Jones, Jeff Corey, Cloris Leachman, Ted Cassidy, Kenneth Mars, Don Keefer, Charles Dierkop, Nelson Olmstead, Sam Elliott.

WUSA (1970, Para.). *d:* Stuart Rosenberg; *p:* Paul Newman and John Foreman (Mirror/Coleytown/ Stuart Rosenberg); *sc:* Robert Stone—*b/o* the novel *A Hall of Mirrors* by Robert Stone.

RHEINHARDT: Alcoholic disc jockey and radio newscaster who becomes the star of a right-wing New Orleans radio station owned by a corrupt neo-Fascist.

Joanne Woodward, Anthony Perkins, Laurence Harvey, Pat Hingle, Cloris Leachman, Don Gordon, Moses Gunn, Bruce Cabot, Lou Gosset, Robert Quarry, Wayne Rogers.

Sometimes a Great Notion (1971, Univ.). *d:* Paul Newman; *p:* John Foreman (Newman–Foreman); *sc:* John Gay—*b/o* the novel by Ken Kesey.

HANK STAMPER: Oldest son of a rough-and-ready Oregon logging family that encounters devastating results when it defies a local strike by other loggers in the area.

Henry Fonda, Lee Remick, Michael Sarrazin, Joe Maross, Richard Jaeckel, Sam Gilman, Cliff Potts, Jim Burk, Linda Lawson, Roy Poole.

Pocket Money (1972, Nat. Gen.). *d:* Stuart Rosenberg; *p:* John Foreman (First Artists); *sc:* Terry Malick—*b/o* the novel *Jim Kane* by J. P. S. Brown.

JIM KANE: Good-natured, not-too-bright Texas cowpoke who, along with his shifty, not-too-bright sidekick, runs into difficulties after a crooked rodeo supplier cons him into going to Mexico to bring back some steers.

Lee Marvin, Strother Martin, Christine Belford, Kelly Jean Peters, Fred Graham, Wayne Rogers.

The Life and Times of Judge Roy Bean (1972, Nat. Gen.). *d:* John Huston; *p:* John Foreman (Famous Artists); *sc:* John Milius.

JUDGE ROY BEAN: Kentucky-born rapscallion who settles in 1880s Texas, calls himself a judge, and hangs outlaws and other passers-by who happen to have money or property he can confiscate.

Victoria Principal, Anthony Perkins, Tab Hunter, John Huston, Stacy Keach, Roddy McDowall, Jacqueline Bisset, Ned Beatty, Ava Gardner.

The Mackintosh Man (1973, WB). *d:* John Huston; *p:* John Foreman (Newman–Foreman/ John Huston); *sc:* Walter Hill—*b/o* Desmond Bagley's novel *The Freedom Trap*.

---

*Received an Academy Award nomination as Best Actor for this role.

REARDEN: British secret agent who poses as a diamond thief and is sent to jail as part of a plan to track down a master spy—who, it turns out, is an influential Member of Parliament.

James Mason, Dominique Sanda, Harry Andrews, Ian Bannen, Mickey Hordern, Nigel Patrick, Peter Vaughan, Roland Culver, Leo Genn.

The Sting (1973, Univ.). *d:* George Roy Hill; *p:* Tony Bill, Michael Phillips, and Julia Phillips (R. Zanuck/D. Brown); *sc:* David S. Ward.

HENRY GONDORFF: "Old pro" con man in 1930s Chicago who is persuaded by a younger con man to put the "Big Con" on an egotistical, ruthless New York racketeer who has murdered the younger man's friend.

Robert Redford, Robert Shaw, Charles Durning, Ray Walston, Sally Kirkland, Eileen Brennan, Robert Earl Jones, Harold Gould, John Heffernan, Dana Elcar, Jack Kehoe, Dimitra Arliss, Avon Long.

The Towering Inferno (1974, 20th-Fox & WB). *d:* John Guillermin and Irwin Allen; *p:* Irwin Allen; *sc:* Stirling Silliphant—*b/o* the novels *The Tower* by Richard Martin Stern and *The Glass Inferno* by Thomas M. Scortia and Frank M. Robinson.

DOUG ROBERTS: Architect of the world's tallest building—a 138-story glass-and-steel San Francisco skyscraper—which suffers a disastrous fire on the night of its opening.

Steve McQueen, William Holden, Faye Dunaway, Fred Astaire, Jennifer Jones, Susan Blakely, Richard Chamberlain, O. J. Simpson, Robert Vaughn, Robert Wagner, Susan Flannery, Don Gordon, Jack Collins, Dabney Coleman.

The Drowning Pool (1975, WB). *d:* Stuart Rosenberg; *p:* Lawrence Turman and David Foster (Coleytown); *sc:* Tracy Keenan Wynn, Lorenzo Semple Jr., and Walter Hill—*b/o* the novel by Ross MacDonald.

LEW HARPER: California private eye who goes to New Orleans in response to a plea by a former girlfriend—now a Southern society woman—to protect her from a blackmailer.

Joanne Woodward, Tony Franciosa, Murray Hamilton, Gail Strickland, Linda Hayes, Richard Jaeckel, Melanie Griffith.

Buffalo Bill and the Indians, or Sitting Bull's History Lesson (1976, UA). *d:* Robert Altman; *p:* Robert Altman and David Susskind (Dino De Laurentiis); *sc:* Alan Rudolph and Robert Altman—*b/o* the play *Indians* by Athur Kopit.

BUFFALO BILL (WILLIAM F. CODY): Aging frontier scout who, while presiding over Buffalo Bill's Wild West Show in 1885, has come to believe the legends created by dime novelist Ned Buntline and others about his heroic youth as an Indian fighter.

Joel Grey, Kevin McCarthy, Harvey Keitel, Burt Lancaster, Geraldine Chaplin, John Considine, Denver Pyle, Pat McCormick, Shelley Duvall.

Silent Movie (1976, 20th-Fox). *d:* Mel Brooks; *p:* Michael Hertzberg; *sc:* Mel Brooks, Ron Clark, Rudy De Luca, and Barry Levinson—*b/o* a story by Ron Clark.

(Appears as himself.) One of several top Hollywood stars whom a has-been Hollywood director tries to sign up to appear in a silent movie he plans to make.

Mel Brooks, Marty Feldman, Dom De Luise, Bernadette Peters, Sid Caesar, Harold Gould, Ron Carey, Fritz Feld, Harry Ritz, Charlie Callas, Henny Youngman, Anne Bancroft, James Caan, Marcel Marceau, Liza Minnelli, Burt Reynolds.

Slap Shot (1977, Univ.). *d:* George Roy Hill; *p:* Robert J. Wunsch and Stephen Friedman (Pan Arts); *sc:* Nancy Dowd.

REGGIE DUNLOP: Aging player-coach of a bush-league Massachusetts hockey team that keeps losing games—until he teaches the players how to play dirty.

Michael Ontkean, Lindsay Crouse, Jennifer Warren, Melinda Dillon, Strother Martin, Jerry Houser, Yvon Barrette, Steve Carlson, Jeff Carlson, Andrew Duncan, Emmett Walsh, Swoosie Kurtz.

Quintet (1979, 20th-Fox). *d:* Robert Altman; *p:* Robert Altman (Lion's Gate); *sc:* Frank Barhydt, Robert Altman, and Patricia Resnick—*b/o* a story by Robert Altman, Lionel Chetwynd, and Patricia Resnick.

ESSEX: Seal hunter who, when the world is dying after a great war, comes to a frozen, ice-covered city where the survivors spend their time playing "quintet"—a backgammon-like game in which the winners murder the losers.

Vittorio Gassman, Fernando Rey, Bibi Andersson, Brigitte Fossey, Nina Van Pallandt, David Langton, Tom Hill, Monique Mercure, Craig Richard Nelson.

When Time Ran Out (1980, WB). *d:* James Goldstone; *p:* Irwin Allen; *sc:* Carl Foreman and Stirling Silliphant—*b/o* Gordon Thomas and Max Morgan Witts's novel *The Day the World Ended.*

HANK ANDERSON: Oil driller in Hawaii who suspects that a volcano is about to erupt and—when it does—leads a group of people toward higher ground in order to escape disaster.

Jacqueline Bisset, William Holden, Edward Albert, Red Buttons, Barbara Carrera, Valentina Cortesa, Veronica Hamel, Alex Karras, Burgess Meredith, Ernest Borgnine, James Franciscus.

Fort Apache, the Bronx (1981, 20th-Fox/Time-Life). *d:* Daniel Petrie; *p:* David Susskind, Martin

Richards, Tom Fiorello, Mary Lou Johnson, and Gill Champion; *sc:* Heywood Gould—*b/o* the experiences of Thomas Mulhearn and Pete Tessitore.

MURPHY: Dedicated veteran cop—based at an embattled police station in the poverty-plagued, crime-infested South Bronx section of New York City—who agonizes over whether to reveal that a fellow cop has killed an innocent Puerto Rican teen-ager by throwing him off a roof.

Edward Asner, Ken Wahl, Danny Aiello, Rachel Ticotin, Pam Grier, Kathleen Beller, Tito Goya, Miguel Pinero, Lance William Guecia, Ronnie Clanton, Sully Boyar, Rik Colitti.

Absence of Malice (1981, Col.). *d:* Sydney Pollack; *p:* Sydney Pollack (Mirage); *sc:* Kurt Luedtke.

MICHAEL GALLAGHER*: Honest Miami liquor wholesaler who—when an ambitious female reporter writes an unfounded story suggesting that he's involved with his mobster uncle in the disappearance of a union leader—becomes outraged and takes action to get even.

Sally Field, Bob Balaban, Melinda Dillon, Luther Adler, Barry Primus, Josef Sommer, John Harkins, Don Hood, Wilford Brimley, Arnie Ross,

Shelley Spurlock, Rooney Kerwin, Oswaldo Calvo, Clardy Malugen.

The Verdict (1982, 20th-Fox). *d:* Sidney Lumet; *p:* Richard Zanuck and David Brown (Zanuck/Brown); *sc:* David Mamet—*b/o* the novel by Barry Reed.

FRANK GALVIN*: Down-and-out, boozing Boston lawyer who gets a chance to redeem himself when he's handed a negligence case against a hospital (run by the Archdiocese of Boston) in which a young woman went into a coma because she was given the wrong anaesthetic.

Charlotte Rampling, Jack Warden, James Mason, Milo O'Shea, Edward Binns, Julie Bovasso, Lindsay Crouse, Lewis Stadlen, Wesley Addy.

Harry & Son (1984, Orion). *d:* Paul Newman; *p:* Paul Newman and Ronald L. Buck; *sc:* Ronald L. Buck and Paul Newman—suggested by the novel *A Lost King* by Raymond DeCapite.

HARRY: Hard-nosed widowed construction worker who is at odds with his young son (a car-wash–worker, surfer, and would-be writer) but tries to reconcile with him.

Robby Benson, Ellen Barkin, Wilford Brimley, Ossie Davis, Joanne Woodward.

---

*Received an Academy Award nomination as Best Actor for this role.

*Received an Academy Award nomination as Best Actor for this role.

☆ SIDNEY POITIER

b: Feb. 20, 1924, Miami, Fla.

"Man! I'm a volcano! A giant surrounded by ants!"

Walter Lee Younger (Sidney Poitier) in *A Raisin in the Sun*, 1961.

No Way Out (1950, 20th-Fox). *d:* Joseph L. Mankiewicz; *p:* Darryl F. Zanuck; *sc:* Joseph L. Mankiewicz and Lesser Samuels.

LUTHER BROOKS: Young intern at a county hospital who, when a wounded hoodlum in his care dies, is targeted for revenge by the hoodlum's brother—a pathological Negro-hating, cop-hating bigot.

Richard Widmark, Linda Darnell, Stephen McNally, Mildred Joanne Smith, Harry Bellaver, Stanley Ridges, Dots Johnson, Ruby Dee, Ossie Davis, Maude Simmons, Ken Christy, Bert Freed, Ray Teal, Will Wright.

Cry the Beloved Country (1952, London Films/Lopert). *d:* Zoltan Korda; *p:* Zoltan Korda and Alan Paton; *sc:* Alan Paton—*b/o* his novel.

REVEREND MSIMANGU: Young South African clergyman who helps a back-country preacher find his missing sister-turned-prostitute and son-turned-thief in the slums of Johannesburg.

Canada Lee, Charles Carson, Joyce Carey, Geoffrey Keen, Vivien Clinton, Michael Goodliffe, Albertina Temba, Edric Connor, Charles McCrae, Lionel Ngakane, Bruce Anderson.

Red Ball Express (1952, Univ.). *d:* Budd Boetticher; *p:* Aaron Rosenberg; *sc:* John Michael Hayes—*b/o* a story by Marcel Klauber and Billy Grady Jr.

CORP. ANDREW ROBERTSON: U.S. Army corporal who feuds with his redneck first sergeant as their WWII trucking outfit—known as the "Red Ball Express"—pushes from the Normandy beachhead through German-held territory to resupply General Patton's stalled tanks at the front.

Jeff Chandler, Alex Nicol, Charles Drake, Judith Braun, Jacqueline Duval, John Hudson, Hugh O'Brian, Jack Kelly, Howard Petrie, Bubber Johnson, Arthur Space, Walter Reed.

Go, Man, Go! (1954, UA). *d:* James Wong Howe; *p:* Anton M. Leader (Sirod); *sc:* Arnold Becker.

INMAN JACKSON: Star center on the all-black Harlem Globetrotters basketball team (formed in the late 1920s) who sticks with the team's white manager/promoter through the ups and downs as the team rises from obscurity to national fame.

The Harlem Globetrotters, Dane Clark, Patricia Breslin, Edmon Ryan, Bram Nossen, Ruby Dee, Anatol Winogradoff, Slim Gaillard, Bill Stern.

The Blackboard Jungle (1955, MGM). *d:* Richard Brooks; *p:* Pandro S. Berman; *sc:* Richard Brooks—*b/o* the novel by Evan Hunter.

GREGORY MILLER: Rebellious student at a New York City high school who, after he and several hooligan classmates give a dedicated young male teacher a hard time, finally is won over when the teacher draws out the student's sensitivity and leadership ability.

Glenn Ford, Anne Francis, Louis Calhern, Margaret Hayes, John Hoyt, Richard Kiley, Emile Meyer, Basil Ruysdael, Warner Anderson, Vic Morrow, Paul Mazursky, Horace McMahon, Jameel Farah (Jamie Farr), Henny Backus, Richard Deacon.

Goodbye, My Lady (1956, WB). *d:* William A. Wellman; *p:* William A. Wellman (Batjac); *sc:* Sid Fleischman—*b/o* the novel by James Street.

GATES WATSON: Young Southern farmer who is a friend of a teen-age swamp boy who finds a rare and remarkable dog that sheds tears when sad and laughs instead of barks.

Walter Brennan, Phil Harris, Brandon de Wilde, William Hopper, Louise Beavers, George Cleveland, Joe Brooks.

Band of Angels (1957, WB). *d:* Raoul Walsh; *sc:* John Twist, Ivan Goff, and Ben Roberts—*b/o* the novel by Robert Penn Warren.

RAU-RU: Strong-willed slave who, after being raised and educated by a slave runner–turned–New Orleans plantation owner, joins the Union Army during the Civil War but still remains indebted to his former master.

Clark Gable, Yvonne De Carlo, Efrem Zimbalist Jr., Patric Knowles, Rex Reason, Torin Thatcher, Andrea King, Ray Teal, Carolle Drake, Raymond Bailey, Juanita Moore, Roy Barcroft, Ann Doran, Bob Steele, William Schallert.

Something of Value (1957, MGM). *d:* Richard Brooks; *p:* Pandro S. Berman; *sc:* Richard Brooks—*b/o* the novel by Robert C. Ruark.

KIMANI: Native youth in East Africa who, when he becomes a Mau Mau leader dedicated to driving the British out of Kenya, finds himself pitted against a British colonial farmer who was his closest childhood friend.

Rock Hudson, Dana Wynter, Wendy Hiller, Juano Hernandez, William Marshall, Robert Beatty, Walter Fitzgerald, Michael Pate, Ivan Dixon, Samadu Jackson, Frederick O'Neal, Lester Matthews.

Edge of the City (1957, MGM). *d:* Martin Ritt; *p:* David Susskind (Jonathan); *sc:* Robert Alan Aurthur—*b/o* on the TV play *A Man Is Ten Feet Tall* by Robert Alan Arthur.

TOMMY TYLER: Easy-going freightcar loader on New York's waterfront whose friendship with a white Army deserter/co-worker leads to his death in a brutal loading-hooks fight with a bigoted gang boss.

John Cassavetes, Jack Warden, Kathleen Maguire, Ruby Dee, Robert Simon, Ruth White, William A. Lee, Val Avery, Estelle Hemsley, Ralph Bell.

The Defiant Ones (1958, UA). *d:* Stanley Kramer; *p:* Stanley Kramer (Stanley Kramer/Lomitas–Curtleigh); *sc:* Nathan E. Douglas and Harold Jacob Smith.

NOAH CULLEN*: Convict in a Southern chain gang who, when he and a white convict escape while chained together at the wrists, finds that they both must overcome their racial hatred for each other in order to survive.

Tony Curtis, Cara Williams, Theodore Bikel, Charles McGraw, Lon Chaney Jr., King Donovan, Claude Akins, Lawrence Dobkin, Whit Bissell, Carl "Alfalfa" Switzer, Kevin Coughlin, Robert Hoy.

The Mark of the Hawk (1958, Univ.). *d:* Michael Audley; *p:* Lloyd Young (Lloyd Young/Film Prod. Int./World Horizons); *sc:* H. Kenn Carmichael—*b/o* a story by Lloyd Young.

OBAM: Ambitious young native legislator in colonial Africa who, though his terrorist brother tries to get him to embrace violence, sticks to peaceful means in seeking independence for his people.

Eartha Kitt, Juano Hernandez, John McIntire, Patrick Allen, Earl Cameron, Gerard Heinz, Clifton Macklin, Helen Horton, Lockwood West, N. C. Doo.

Virgin Island (1958, Films-Around-the-World). *d:* Pat Jackson; *p:* Leon Clore and Grahame Tharp (Countryman/British Lion); *sc:* Philip Rush and

---

*Received an Academy Award nomination as Best Actor for this role.

Pat Jackson—*b/o* the novel *Our Virgin Island* by Robb White.

MARCUS: Friendly West Indian fisherman who helps a young American writer and his English wife set up housekeeping on a small desert island in the Caribbean after the writer buys it for $85.00.

John Cassavetes, Virginia Maskell, Isabel Dean, Colin Gordon, Howard Marion Crawford, Edric Connor, Ruby Dee, Gladys Root, Arnold Bell, Alonzo Bozan.

Porgy and Bess (1959, Col.). *d:* Otto Preminger; *p:* Samuel Goldwyn (Samuel Goldwyn Prod.); *sc:* N. Richard Nash—*b/o* the musical play by George Gershwin, from the novel *Porgy* by DuBose Heyward and the play *Porgy* by DuBose Heyward and Dorothy Heyward.

PORGY: Big-hearted crippled beggar—living in the 1912 Charleston, South Carolina, waterfront ghetto called Catfish Row—who has a tragic love affair with a beautiful but loose-living woman by the name of Bess.

Dorothy Dandridge, Sammy Davis Jr., Pearl Bailey, Brock Peters, Leslie Scott, Diahann Carroll, Ruth Attaway, Clarence Muse, Ivan Dixon, Roy Glenn, William Walker, Claude Akins.

All the Young Men (1960, Col.). *d:* Hall Bartlett; *p:* Hall Bartlett (Bartlett/Jaguar); *sc:* Hall Bartlett.

SERGEANT TOWLER: U.S. Marine sergeant in the Korean War who, when his dying C.O. gives him command of a combat patrol, is forced to fight not only the enemy but the resentment and racial prejudice of his own men.

Alan Ladd, Ingemar Johansson, James Darren, Glenn Corbett, Mort Sahl, Ana St. Clair, Paul Richards, Paul Baxley, Michael Davis, Chris Seitz.

A Raisin in the Sun (1961, Col.). *d:* Daniel Petrie; *p:* David Susskind and Philip Rose (Paman–Doris); *sc:* Lorraine Hansberry—*b/o* her play.

WALTER LEE YOUNGER: Husband in a struggling South Side Chicago black family whose members finds themselves arguing over how to spend a $10,000 life-insurance payment they've received.

Claudia McNeil, Ruby Dee, Diana Sands, Ivan Dixon, John Fiedler, Louis Gossett, Stephen Perry, Joel Fluellen, Roy Glenn, Ray Stubbs, Louis Terkel.

Paris Blues (1961, UA). *d:* Martin Ritt; *p:* Sam Shaw (Pennebaker); *sc:* Jack Sher, Irene Kamp, and Walter Bernstein (adaptation by Lulla Adler)—*b/o* a novel by Harold Flender.

EDDIE COOK: One of a pair of American musicians working at a Left Bank jazz club in Paris who must make important personal and career decisions when they become involved with two pretty American tourists.

Paul Newman, Joanne Woodward, Louis Armstrong, Diahann Carroll, Serge Reggiani, Barbara Laage, Andre Luguet, Moustache, Roger Blin, Niko.

Pressure Point (1962, UA). *d:* Hubert Cornfield; *p:* Stanley Kramer (Stanley Kramer/Larcas); *sc:* Hubert Cornfield and S. Lee Pogostin—*b/o* Dr. Robert Lindner's book *The Fifty-Minute Hour.*

DOCTOR: Dedicated prison psychiatrist who struggles to deal with a vicious inmate who's a racist and a 1942 German-American Nazi Bund leader.

Bobby Darin, Peter Falk, Carl Benton Reid, Mary Munday, Barry Gordon, Howard Caine, Anne Barton, James Anderson, Yvette Vickers, Clegg Hoyt, Richard Bakalyan.

Lilies of the Field (1963, UA). *d:* Ralph Nelson; *p:* Ralph Nelson (Rainbow); *sc:* James Poe—*b/o* the novel by William E. Barrett.

HOMER SMITH*: Ex-G.I. jack-of-all-trades who, when he runs across five East German refugee nuns in the New Mexico desert, winds up building a chapel for them.

Lilia Skala, Lisa Mann, Iso Crino, Francesca Jarvis, Pamela Branch, Stanley Adams, Dan Frazer, Ralph Nelson.

The Long Ships (1964, Col.). *d:* Jack Cardiff; *p:* Irving Allen (Warwick/Avala); *sc:* Berkely Mather and Beverley Cross—*b/o* the novel by Frans Bengtsson.

EL MANSUH: Ruthless Moorish shiek who clashes with a Viking adventurer who's trying to retrieve the fabled Golden Bell of St. James, cast from gold looted from Saracens by Crusaders.

Richard Widmark, Russ Tamblyn, Rosanna Schiaffino, Oscar Homolka, Lionel Jeffries, Edward Judd, Beba Loncar, Clifton Evans, Colin Blakely, Gordon Jackson, Henry Oscar.

The Bedford Incident (1965, Col.). *d:* James B. Harris; *p:* James B. Harris and Richard Widmark (Bedford); *sc:* James Poe—*b/o* the novel by Mark Rascovich.

BEN MUNCEFORD: Dedicated correspondent-photographer—aboard the nuclear destroyer U.S.S. *Bedford* in the North Atlantic—whose quest for a story ends when the destroyer accidently fires an atomic weapon at a Russian sub—and the sub retaliates.

Richard Widmark, James MacArthur, Martin Balsam, Wally Cox, Eric Portman, Michael Kane, Colin Maitland, Michael Graham, Bill Edwards, Brian Davies, Donald Sutherland.

---

*Won the Academy Award as Best Actor for this role.

The Slender Thread (1965, Para.). *d:* Sydney Pollack; *p:* Stephen Alexander (Athene); *sc:* Stirling Silliphant—*b/o* the *Life* magazine article "Decision to Die" by Shana Alexander.

ALAN NEWELL: University of Washington student on volunteer duty at the Seattle Crisis Clinic who tries frantically to maintain a telephone conversation with a suicidal woman (who has swallowed a lethal dose of sleeping pills) while police try to locate her.

Anne Bancroft, Telly Savalas, Steven Hill, Indus Arthur, Greg Jarvis, Robert Hoy, John Benson, Paul Newlan, Edward Asner, Dabney Coleman, H. M. Wynant.

The Greatest Story Ever Told (1965, UA). *d:* George Stevens; *p:* George Stevens (George Stevens); *sc:* James Lee Barrett and George Stevens, in creative association with Carl Sandburg—*b/o Books of the Old and New Testaments*, other ancient writings, the book by Fulton Oursler, and writings by Henry Denker.

SIMON OF CYRENE: Bystander who helps Jesus arrange the wooden cross on his shoulder as he drags it through the streets of Bethlehem to the Crucifixion.

Max von Sydow, Dorothy McGuire, Robert Loggia, Charlton Heston, Robert Blake, Jamie Farr, David McCallum, Roddy McDowall, Carroll Baker, Pat Boone, Van Heflin, Sal Mineo, Shelley Winters, Ed Wynn, John Wayne, Telly Savalas, Angela Lansbury, Joseph Schildkraut, Jose Ferrer, Claude Rains, Richard Conte.

A Patch of Blue (1965, MGM). *d:* Guy Green; *p:* Pandro S. Berman; *sc:* Guy Green—*b/o* the novel *Be Ready with Bells and Drums* by Elizabeth Kata.

GORDON RALFE: Thoughtful young store clerk whose kind-hearted treatment of a poor eighteen-year-old white blind girl results in her falling in love with him, unaware that he's black.

Shelley Winters, Elizabeth Hartman, Wallace Ford, Ivan Dixon, Elizabeth Fraser, John Qualen, Kelly Flynn, Debi Storm, Renata Vanni, Dorothy Lovett.

Duel at Diablo (1966, UA). *d:* Ralph Nelson; *p:* Ralph Nelson and Fred Engel (Nelson/Engel/Cherokee); *sc:* Marvin H. Albert and Michael M. Grilikhes—*b/o* the novel *Apache Rising* by Marvin H. Albert.

TOLLER: Ex–U.S. Cavalry sergeant–turned–horse dealer who teams up with a frontier scout as they battle Apaches and track down the man who scalped the scout's Comanche wife.

James Garner, Bibi Andersson, Dennis Weaver, Bill Travers, William Redfield, John Hoyt, John Crawford, John Hubbard, Kevin Coughlin, Jay Ripley, Jeff Cooper, Alf Elson.

To Sir, with Love (1967, Col.). *d:* James Clavell; *p:* James Clavell; *sc:* James Clavell—*b/o* the novel by E. R. Braithwaite.

MARK THACKERAY: Unemployed West Indian engineer who, when he takes a temporary job as a teacher at a high school in London's tough East End, has trouble with the unruly white students at first but gradually manages to earn their respect.

Judy Geeson, Christian Roberts, Suzy Kendall, Faith Brook, Christopher Chittell, Geoffrey Balydon, Patricia Routledge, Adrienne Posta, Edward Burnham, Rita Webb.

In the Heat of the Night (1967, UA). *d:* Norman Jewison; *p:* Walter Mirisch (Jewison/Mirisch); *sc:* Stirling Silliphant—*b/o* the novel by John Ball.

VIRGIL TIBBS: Sharp homicide detective from Philadelphia who, while visiting his mother in a small Mississippi town, is reluctantly asked by the town's antagonistic, bigoted police chief to help him solve a murder case.

Rod Steiger, Warren Oates, Lee Grant, James Patterson, Quentin Dean, Larry Gates, William Schallert, Beah Richards, Scott Wilson, Jack Teter, Matt Clark, Anthony James, Khalil Bezaleel, Timothy Scott.

Guess Who's Coming to Dinner (1967, Col.). *d:* Stanley Kramer; *p:* Stanley Kramer (Stanley Kramer Prod.); *sc:* William Rose.

DR. JOHN PRENTICE: Successful doctor who, when he falls in love with and wants to marry the daughter of a socially prominent San Francisco white couple, runs into opposition from both her parents and his own.

Spencer Tracy, Katharine Hepburn, Katharine Houghton, Cecil Kellaway, Beah Richards, Roy E. Glenn Sr., Isabel Sanford, Virginia Christine, Alexandra Hay, Skip Martin.

For Love of Ivy (1968, Cinerama). *d:* Daniel Mann; *p:* Edgar J. Sherick and Jay Weston (Palomar); *sc:* Robert Alan Aurthur—*b/o* a story by Sidney Poitier.

JACK PARKS: Affable businessman (involved in illegal gambling) who is pressured by a well-to-do white family into wooing their black maid in hopes of keeping her from quitting her job to go to secretarial school.

Abbey Lincoln, Beau Bridges, Nan Martin, Lauri Peters, Carroll O'Connor, Leon Bibb, Hugh Hird, Lon Satton, Stanley Greene.

The Lost Man (1969, Univ.). *d:* Robert Alan Aurthur; *p:* Edward Muhl and Melville Tucker; *sc:* Robert Alan Aurthur—*b/o* the novel *Odd Man Out* by Frederick Laurence Green.

JASON HIGGS: Former U.S. Army lieutenant who, after becoming a black militant during the

1960s Black Revolutionary movement, is wounded when he pulls a payroll heist to help imprisoned "brothers" and has to hide from the police.

Joanna Shimkus, Al Freeman Jr., Michael Tolan, Leon Bibb, Richard Dysart, David Steinberg, Beverly Todd, Paul Winfield, Bernie Hamilton, Dolph Sweet, Virginia Capers, Maxine Stuart.

They Call Me Mister Tibbs! (1970, UA). *d:* Gordon Douglas; *p:* Herbert Hirschman (Mirisch); *sc:* Alan R. Trustman and James R. Webb—*b/o* a story by Alan R. Trustman—*b/o* the character created by John Ball.

LT. VIRGIL TIBBS: Detective in San Francisco who is torn between duty and friendship when he discovers that a prime suspect in the murder of a young woman is one of his closest friends—a crusading minister.

Martin Landau, Barbara McNair, Anthony Zerbe, Jeff Corey, David Sheiner, Juano Hernandez, Norma Crane, Edward Asner, Ted Gehring, Beverly Todd, Jerome Thor.

The Organization (1971, UA). *d:* Don Medford; *p:* Walter Mirisch (Mirisch); *sc:* James R. Webb—*b/o* the character created by John Ball.

LT. VIRGIL TIBBS: San Francisco police detective who risks his career when he joins forces with a vigilante gang of street people to help bust an international drug-smuggling ring.

Barbara McNair, Gerald S. O'Loughlin, Sheree North, Fred Bier, Allen Garfield, Bernie Hamilton, Graham Jarvis, Raul Julia, Ron O'Neal, Billy Green Bush, Demond Wilson, Ross Hagen.

Brother John (1971, Col.). *d:* James Goldstone; *p:* Joel Glickman (E & R Prod.); *sc:* Ernest Kinoy.

JOHN KANE: Mysterious man who, when he returns to his hometown in Alabama for his sister's funeral, is thought to be an outside labor agitator—until it's revealed that he's really a heavenly messenger.

Will Geer, Bradford Dillman, Beverly Todd, Ramon Bieri, Warren J. Kemmerling, Lincoln Kilpatrick, P. Jay Sidney, Richard Ward, Paul Winfield, Zara Cully, Michael Bell.

Buck and the Preacher (1972, Col.). *d:* Sidney Poitier; *p:* Joel Glickman (E & R Prod./Belafonte); *sc:* Ernest Kinoy—*b/o* a story by Ernest Kinoy and Drake Walker.

BUCK: Ex–Union cavalryman who, after becoming wagonmaster for a group of former slaves headed West to homestead, teams up with a bogus preacher–con man to stop night riders hired to drive the slaves back into the South for use as cheap labor.

Harry Belafonte, Ruby Dee, Cameron Mitchell, Denny Miller, Nita Talbot, James McEachin,

Clarence Muse, Julie Robinson, Enrique Lucero, John Kelly, Errol John, Ken Menard, Pamela Jones, Drake Walker.

A Warm December (1973, Nat. Gen.). *d:* Sidney Poitier; *p:* Melville Tucker (First Artists/Verdon); *sc:* Lawrence Roman.

MATT YOUNGER: Widowed Washington doctor who, while in London on vacation, falls in love with the niece of an African ambassador, then learns that she's dying of sickle-cell anemia.

Esther Anderson, Yvette Curtis, George Baker, Johnny Sekka, Earl Cameron, Hilary Crane, John Beardmore, Ann Smith, Stephanie Smith, Letta Mbulu.

Uptown Saturday Night (1974, WB). *d:* Sidney Poitier; *p:* Melville Tucker (First Artists/Verdon); *sc:* Richard Wesley.

STEVE JACKSON: Factory worker who, with his cab-driver buddy, encounters assorted zany characters as they try to get back a winning lottery ticket from the black underworld after it's taken from them during a hold-up at an after-hours gambling club.

Bill Cosby, Harry Belafonte, Flip Wilson, Richard Pryor, Rosalind Cash, Roscoe Lee Browne, Paula Kelly, Lee Chamberlin, Johnny Sekka, Lincoln Kilpatrick, Ketty Lester, Calvin Lockhart.

The Wilby Conspiracy (1975, UA). *d:* Ralph Nelson; *p:* Helmut Dantine and Martin Baum (Optimus and Baum/Dantine); *sc:* Rod Amateau and Harold Nebenzal—*b/o* the novel by Peter Driscoll.

SHACK TWALA: South African revolutionary who is pursued—along with a reluctant white British mining engineer—across the country from Cape Town to Johannesburg by a white racist South African policeman.

Michael Caine, Nicol Williamson, Prunella Gee, Persis Khambatta, Saeed Jaffrey, Ryk De Gooyer, Rutger Hauer, Patrick Allen, Brian Epsom, Helmut Dantine.

Let's Do It Again (1975, WB). *d:* Sidney Poitier; *p:* Melville Tucker (First Artists/Verdon); *sc:* Richard Wesley—*b/o* a story by Timothy March.

CLYDE WILLIAMS: Atlanta milkman who, when he and his factory-worker pal hypnotize a prize fighter to win a fight, bilks two big-time gamblers in New Orleans out of a bundle of cash to help build a new meeting hall for the two friends' fraternal lodge.

Bill Cosby, Jimmie Walker, Cavin Lockhart, John Amos, Denise Nicholas, Lee Chamberlin, Mel Stewart, Val Avery, Ossie Davis, Billy Eckstine, Morgan Roberts, Talya Ferro, Jayne Kennedy.

A Piece of the Action (1977, WB). *d:* Sidney Poitier; *p:* Melville Tucker (First Artists/Verdon);

sc: Charles Blackwell—b/o a story by Timothy March.

MANNY DURRELL: One of a pair of Chicago con men who—in order to avoid going to jail when a cop catches them pulling a heist—agree to help a pretty social worker steer some South Side ghetto kids onto the right path.

Bill Cosby, James Earl Jones, Denise Nicholas, Hope Clarke, Tracy Reed, Titos Vandis, Frances Foster, Jason Evers, Marc Lawrence, Wonderful Smith, Sherri Poitier, Cyril Poitier.

☆ TYRONE POWER

Tyrone Edmund Power III

b: May 5, 1914, Cincinnati, Ohio
d: Nov. 15, 1958, Madrid, Spain

"How do you get a guy to be a geek? Is that the only one? I mean, is a guy born that way?"

Stan Carlisle/"The Great Stanton" (Tyrone Power) referring to a sideshow freak in *Nightmare Alley*, 1947.

Tom Brown of Culver (1932, Univ.). d: William Wyler; p: Carl Laemmle Jr.; sc: Tom Buckingham (with additional dialogue by Clarence Marks)—b/o a story by George Green and Dale Van Every.
DONALD MacKENZIE: Stern, "by the book" upperclassman at Culver Military Academy in Indiana.
Tom Brown, H. B. Warner, Slim Summerville, Richard Cromwell, Ben Alexander, Sidney Toler, Russell Hopton, Andy Devine, Willard Robertson, Eugene Pallette, Dick Winslow.

Flirtation Walk (1934, WB). d: Frank Borzage; p: Frank Borzage; sc: Delmer Daves—b/o a story by Delmer Daves and Lou Edelman.
One of a number of West Point cadets who become involved in the staging of the Academy's annual musical show.
Dick Powell, Ruby Keeler, Pat O'Brien, Ross Alexander, John Arledge, John Eldredge, Henry O'Neill, Guinn "Big Boy" Williams, Gertrude Keeler, Dick Winslow, Paul Fix, Emmett Vogan.

Girls' Dormitory (1936, 20th-Fox). d: Irving Cummings; p: Darryl F. Zanuck; sc: Gene Markey—b/o a play by Ladislaus Fodor.
COUNT VALLAIS: Handsome young escort of a pretty French student at a girls' finishing school in the Tyrolean Alps.
Herbert Marshall, Ruth Chatterton, Simone Simon, Constance Collier, J. Edward Bromberg, Dixie Dunbar, John Qualen, Frank Reicher, Lynn Bari.

Ladies in Love (1936, 20th-Fox). d: Edward H. Griffith; p: B. G. DeSylva; sc: Melville Baker—b/o a play by Ladislaus Bus-Fekete.

KARL LANYI: Dashing young Hungarian count who has a romance with a pretty chorus girl but breaks off the affair and marries a Hungarian countess.
Janet Gaynor, Loretta Young, Constance Bennett, Simone Simon, Don Ameche, Paul Lukas, Alan Mowbray, Virginia Field, J. Edward Bromberg, Lynn Bari, Monty Woolley.

Lloyds of London (1936, 20th-Fox). d: Henry King; p: Darryl F. Zanuck; sc: Ernest Pascal and Walter Ferris—b/o a story by Curtis Kenyon.
JONATHAN BLAKE: Dedicated young eighteenth-century Englishman who rises to power in the famed Lloyds of London insurance underwriting house as his boyhood friend Horatio Nelson becomes one of England's greatest naval heroes.
Freddie Bartholomew, Madeleine Carroll, Sir Guy Standing, George Sanders, C. Aubrey Smith, Virginia Field, Montagu Love, Una O'Connor, J. M. Kerrigan, Douglas Scott, E. E. Clive, Miles Mender, Robert Greig.

Love Is News (1937, 20th-Fox). d: Tay Garnett; p: Earl Carroll and Harold Wilson; sc: Harry Tugend and Jack Yellen—b/o a story by William R. Lipman and Frederick Stephani.
STEVE LAYTON: Brash reporter who writes unflattering stories about a newspaper-hating heiress who carries on a feud with him but winds up marrying him.
Loretta Young, Don Ameche, Dudley Digges, George Sanders, Slim Summerville, Walter Catlett, Jane Darwell, Stepin Fetchit, Elisha Cook Jr., Frank Conroy, Edwin Maxwell, Jack Mulhall.

Cafe Metropole (1937, 20th-Fox). d: Edward H. Griffith; p: Nunnally Johnson; sc: Jacques Deval—b/o a story by Gregory Ratoff.
ALEXANDER BROWN (alias PRINCE ALEXIS PANAIEFF): Penniless Princeton playboy who poses as a Russian prince in order to charm an American heiress in Paris out of some money to pay a gambling debt.
Loretta Young, Adolphe Menjou, Gregory Ratoff, Charles Winninger, Helen Westley, Leonid

Kinsky, Hal K. Dawson, Paul Porcasi, Bill Robinson.

Thin Ice (1937, 20th-Fox). *d:* Sidney Lanfield; *p:* Raymond Griffith; *sc:* Boris Ingster and Milton Sperling—*b/o* the novel *Der Komet* by Attilla Orbok.

PRINCE RUDOLPH: Dashing prince who disguises himself as a reporter in order to get next to a pretty ice-skating instructor at an Alpine ski resort.

Sonja Henie, Arthur Treacher, Raymond Walburn, Joan Davis, Alan Hale, Sig Rumann, Melville Cooper, George Givot, Lon Chaney Jr., Frank Puglia.

Second Honeymoon (1937, 20th-Fox). *d:* Walter Lang; *p:* Raymond Griffith; *sc:* Kathryn Scola and Darrell Ware—*b/o* a *Redbook* magazine story by Philip Wylie.

RAOUL McLISH: Handsome, irresponsible playboy who sets out to win back his ex-wife from a stuffed-shirt business tycoon.

Loretta Young, Claire Trevor, Stuart Erwin, Marjorie Weaver, Lyle Talbot, J. Edward Bromberg, Paul Hurst, Mary Treen, Hal K. Dawson, Lon Chaney Jr., Robert Lowery, Fred Kelsey, Wade Boteler, Joseph King.

In Old Chicago (1938, 20th-Fox). *d:* Henry King; *p:* Darryl F. Zanuck; *sc:* Lamar Trotti and Sonya Levien—*b/o* the novel *We, the O'Learys* by Niven Busch.

DION O'LEARY: Gambler–saloon keeper and crooked politician who is one of the three sons of the O'Leary family whose legendary cow starts the great Chicago fire of 1871.

Alice Faye, Don Ameche, Alice Brady, Andy Devine, Brian Donlevy, Phyllis Brooks, Tom Brown, Sidney Blackmer, Berton Churchill, June Storey, Paul Hurst, Gene Reynolds, Bobs Watson, Billy Watson, Spencer Charters, Rondo Hatton.

Alexander's Ragtime Band (1938, 20th-Fox). *d:* Henry King; *p:* Darryl F. Zanuck; *sc:* Kathryn Scola and Lamar Trotti (adaptation by Richard Sherman).

ROGER GRANT (alias ALEXANDER): Wealthy Nob Hill aristocrat in 1911 San Francisco who chucks a career as a concert violinist to become the leader of a jazz band that eventually makes it to Carnegie Hall in 1938.

Alice Faye, Don Ameche, Ethel Merman, Jack Haley, Jean Hersholt, Helen Westley, John Carradine, Ruth Terry, Paul Hurst, Wally Vernon, Douglas Fowley, Chick Chandler, Eddie Collins, Dixie Dunbar, Grady Sutton, Lon Chaney Jr.

Marie Antoinette (1938, MGM). *d:* W. S. Van Dyke II; *p:* Hunt Stromberg; *sc:* Claudine West,

Donald Ogden Stewart, and Ernest Vajda—*b/o* a story by Stefan Zweig.

COUNT AXEL de FERSEN: Dashing Swedish lover of Queen Marie Antoinette who vainly tries to save her from the guillotine during the eighteenth-century French Revolution.

Norma Shearer, John Barrymore, Gladys George, Robert Morley, Anita Louise, Joseph Schildkraut, Henry Stephenson, Reginald Gardiner, Peter Bull, Albert Dekker, Joseph Calleia, Cora Witherspoon, Scotty Beckett, Henry Daniell.

Suez (1938, 20th-Fox). *d:* Allan Dwan; *p:* Darryl F. Zanuck; *sc:* Philip Dunne and Julien Josephson—*b/o* a story by Sam Duncan.

FERDINAND De LESSEPS: Famed nineteenth-century French diplomat and engineer who plans and supervises the building of the Suez Canal in Egypt.

Loretta Young, Annabella, Joseph Schildkraut, J. Edward Bromberg, Henry Stephenson, Leon Ames, Maurice Moscovich, Sig Rumann, Sidney Blackmer, Nigel Bruce, Miles Mander, George Zucco.

Jesse James (1939, 20th-Fox). *d:* Henry King; *p:* Darryl F. Zanuck; *sc:* Nunnally Johnson—*b/o* historical material gathered by Rosalind Shaffer and Jo Frances James.

JESSE JAMES: Missouri sodbuster who becomes a legendary outlaw as he and his brother Frank stage holdups and bank robberies in the post–Civil War Midwest.

Henry Fonda, Nancy Kelly, Randolph Scott, Henry Hull, Slim Summerville, J. Edward Bromberg, Brian Donlevy, John Carradine, Donald Meek, Jane Darwell, John Russell, George Chandler, Charles Middleton, Lon Chaney Jr.

Rose of Washington Square (1939, 20th-Fox). *d:* Gregory Ratoff; *p:* Darryl F. Zanuck; *sc:* Nunnally Johnson—*b/o* a story by John Larkin and Jerry Horwin.

BART CLINTON: Good-for-nothing heel and swindler who marries a 1920s Ziegfeld Follies star, but whose crooked ways finally land him in prison.

Alice Faye, Al Jolson, Willian Frawley, Joyce Compton, Hobart Cavanaugh, Moroni Olsen, Charles Wilson, Ben Welden, E. E. Clive, Louis Prima, James Flavin, Charles Lane, Chick Chandler, Edgar Dearing, Murray Alper.

Second Fiddle (1939, 20th-Fox). *d:* Sidney Lanfield; *p:* Darryl F. Zanuck; *sc:* Harry Tugend—*b/o* a story by George Bradshaw.

JIMMY SUTTON: Movie-studio publicity chief who, while helping a small-town Minnesota ice skater–school teacher become a Hollywood star, falls in love with her.

Sonja Henie, Rudy Vallee, Edna May Oliver, Mary Healy, Lyle Talbot, Alan Dinehart, Minna Gombell, Spencer Charters, George Chandler, Irving Bacon, Robert Lowery, Minerva Urecal, Purnell Pratt.

The Rains Came (1939, 20th-Fox). *d:* Clarence Brown; *p:* Darryl F. Zanuck; *sc:* Philip Dunne and Julien Josephson—*b/o* the novel by Louis Bromfield.

MAJOR RAMA SAFTI: American-educated Hindu surgeon in Ranchipur, India, whose ill-fated love affair with the socialite wife of a wealthy English industrialist comes to an end during the aftermath of a devastating earthquake, torrential rains, and a flood.

Myrna Loy, George Brent, Brenda Joyce, Maria Ouspenskaya, Nigel Bruce, Joseph Schildkraut, Jane Darwell, Marjorie Rambeau, Henry Travers, H. B. Warner, Laura Hope Crews, Harry Hayden, Abner Biberman.

Day-Time Wife (1939, 20th-Fox). *d:* Gregory Ratoff; *p:* Darryl F. Zanuck; *sc:* Art Arthur and Robert Harari—*b/o* a story by Rex Taylor.

KEN NORTON: Playboy executive of a roofing firm whose wife, when she learns that he's carrying on with his secretary, decides to get even by going to work as a secretary for a suave client of his.

Linda Darnell, Warren William, Binnie Barnes, Wendy Barrie, Joan Davis, Joan Valerie, Leonid Kinsky, Mildred Glover, Renie Riano, Robert Lowery.

Johnny Apollo (1940, 20th-Fox). *d:* John Cromwell; *p:* Harry Joe Brown; *sc:* Philip Dunne and Rowland Brown—*b/o* a story by Samuel G. Engel and Hal Long.

BOB CAIN (alias JOHNNY APOLLO): Smart college grad who, when his stockbroker father is sent to prison for embezzlement, becomes disillusioned and bitterly turns to a life of crime.

Dorothy Lamour, Lloyd Nolan, Edward Arnold, Charley Grapewin, Lionel Atwill, Marc Lawrence, Jonathan Hale, Russell Hicks, Fuzzy Knight, Charles Lane, Selmer Jackson, Anthony Caruso, Milburn Stone.

Brigham Young—Frontiersman (1940, 20th-Fox). *d:* Henry Hathaway; *p:* Kenneth MacGowan; *sc:* Lamar Trotti—*b/o* a story by Louis Bromfield.

JONATHAN KENT: Young Mormon who, with his family, joins the 20,000 Mormons who follow Brigham Young on the gruelling 1840s trek from Navuoo, Illinois, to find a new home in Utah.

Linda Darnell, Dean Jagger, Brian Donlevy, Jane Darwell, John Carradine, Mary Astor, Vincent Price, Jean Rogers, Willard Robertson, Moroni Olsen, Marc Lawrence, Fuzzy Knight, Tully Marshall.

The Mark of Zorro (1940, 20th-Fox). *d:* Rouben Mamoulian; *p:* Raymond Griffith; *sc:* John Tainton Foote (adaptation by Garrett Fort and Bess Meredyth)—*b/o* Johnston McCully's novel *The Curse of Capistrano.*

DON DIEGO VEGA (alias ZORRO): Son of a California aristocrat in the 1800s who acts the fop by day but at night is a swashbuckling masked bandit seeking to avenge evil.

Linda Darnell, Basil Rathbone, Gale Sondergaard, Eugene Pallette, J. Edward Bromberg, Montagu Love, Janet Beecher, Robert Lowery, Chris-Pin Martin, Pedro De Cordoba, Frank Puglia, Ralph Byrd, Michael (Ted) North, Fortunio Bonanova, Victor Kilian.

Blood and Sand (1941, 20th-Fox). *d:* Rouben Mamoulian; *p:* Darryl F. Zanuck; *sc:* Jo Swerling—*b/o* the novel *Sangre y Arena* by Vicente Blasco Ibanez.

JUAN GALLARDO: Naïve young Spanish bullfighter who rises from rags to riches but meets disaster when he forsakes his wife for a sultry society woman and grows careless in the ring.

Linda Darnell, Rita Hayworth, Nazimova, Anthony Quinn, J. Carrol Naish, John Carradine, Lynn Bari, Laird Cregar, George Reeves, Pedro De Cordoba, Fortunio Bonaova, Victor Kilian, Charles Stevens, Elena Verdugo, Monty Banks.

A Yank in the R.A.F. (1941, 20th-Fox). *d:* Henry King; *p:* Lou Edelman; *sc:* Darrell Ware and Karl Tunberg—*b/o* a story by Melville Crossman.

TIM BAKER: Cocky, happy-go-lucky Yank flyer who joins the R.A.F. in WWII so that he can be near his old flame, an American chorus girl in London.

Betty Grable, John Sutton, Reginald Gardiner, Donald Stuart, John Wilde, Ralph Byrd, Lester Matthews, Claude Allister, Fortunio Bonanova, Gladys Cooper, G. P. Huntley Jr., Kurt Kreuger.

Son of Fury (1942, 20th-Fox). *d:* John Cromwell; *p:* William Perlberg; *sc:* Philip Dunne—*b/o* the novel *Benjamin Blake* by Edison Marshall.

BENJAMIN BLAKE: Young eighteenth-century Englishman who—when his uncle steals his inheritance—flees England, finds a fortune in pearls on a South Seas island, and returns home to seek revenge.

Gene Tierney, George Sanders, Frances Farmer, Roddy McDowall, John Carradine, Elsa Lanchester, Harry Davenport, Kay Johnson, Dudley Digges, Halliwell Hobbes, Arthur Hohl, Robert Greig, Pedro De Cordoba, Mae Marsh.

This Above All (1942, 20th-Fox). *d:* Anatole Litvak; *p:* Darryl F. Zanuck; *sc:* R. C. Sheriff—*b/o* the novel by Eric Knight.

CLIVE BRIGGS: Disillusioned WWII British Army hero who turns deserter but then finds new courage and love with a patriotic young English noblewoman who has joined the WAAF.

Joan Fontaine, Thomas Mitchell, Henry Stephenson, Nigel Bruce, Gladys Cooper, Philip Merivale, Sara Allgood, Alexander Knox, Queenie Leonard, Melville Cooper, Arthur Shields, Miles Mander, Rhys Williams.

The Black Swan (1942, 20th-Fox). *d:* Henry King; *p:* Robert Bassler; *sc:* Ben Hecht and Seton I. Miller—*b/o* the novel by Rafael Sabatini.

JAMIE WARING: Swashbuckling ex-buccaneer who, when his friend Morgan the pirate is pardoned by the Crown and appointed governor of Jamaica, is enlisted to stop their former cutthroat shipmates from plundering English ships in the Spanish Main.

Maureen O'Hara, George Sanders, Laird Cregar, Thomas Mitchell, Anthony Quinn, George Zucco, Edward Ashley, Fortunio Bonanova, Arthur Shields, Clarence Muse, Willie Fung, Rondo Hatton.

Crash Dive (1943, 20th-Fox). *d:* Archie Mayo; *p:* Milton Sperling; *sc:* Jo Swerling—*b/o* a story by W. R. Burnett.

LT. WARD STEWART: WWII U.S. submarine executive officer who falls for a pretty schoolteacher, only to discover later that she's his skipper's fiancée.

Anne Baxter, Dana Andrews, James Gleason, Dame May Whitty, Henry (Harry) Morgan, Ben Carter, Frank Conroy, Minor Watson, Charles Tannen, Florence Lake, John Archer, Thurston Hall.

The Razor's Edge (1946, 20th-Fox). *d:* Edmund Goulding; *p:* Darryl F. Zanuck; *sc:* Lamar Trotti—*b/o* the novel by W. Somerset Maugham.

LARRY DARRELL: Ex–WWI flyer from Chicago who travels the globe in search of truth and spiritual peace, hoping to bring goodness into the lives of some of his troubled friends.

Gene Tierney, Anne Baxter, John Payne, Clifton Webb, Herbert Marshall, Lucile Watson, Frank Latimore, Elsa Lanchester, Fritz Kortner, Cecil Humphreys, Cobina Wright Sr.

Nightmare Alley (1947, 20th-Fox). *d:* Edmund Goulding; *p:* George Jessel; *sc:* Jules Furthman—*b/o* the novel by William Lindsay Gresham.

STAN CARLISLE: Unscrupulous carnival roustabout who becomes a phony big-time mind-reader and spiritualist but hits the skids, turns into an alcoholic hobo, and winds up back at the carney as a geek.

Joan Blondell, Coleen Gray, Helen Walker, Taylor Holmes, Ian Keith, Mike Mazurki, Julia Dean, James Flavin, Roy Roberts, James Burke, Leo Gray, Marjorie Wood, Harry Cheshire, Eddy Waller, George Chandler.

Captain from Castile (1947, 20th-Fox). *d:* Henry King; *p:* Lamar Trotti; *sc:* Lamar Trotti—*b/o* the novel by Samuel Shellabarger.

PEDRO de VARGAS: Young sixteenth-century Spanish nobleman who is jailed during the Inquisition but escapes to the New World, where he serves with Hernando Cortez during Cortez's conquest of Mexico.

Jean Peters, Cesar Romero, Lee J. Cobb, John Sutton, Thomas Gomez, Alan Mowbray, Roy Roberts, Marc Lawrence, George Zucco, Antonio Moreno, Jay Silverheels, Reed Hadley.

The Luck of the Irish (1948, 20th-Fox). *d:* Henry Koster; *p:* Fred Kohlmar; *sc:* Philip Dunne—*b/o* the novel by Guy Jones and Constance Jones.

STEPHEN FITZGERALD: Happy-go-lucky New York political reporter whose career and love life are complicated by a leprechaun he discovers while in Ireland.

Anne Baxter, Cecil Kellaway, Lee J. Cobb, James Todd, Jayne Meadows, J. M. Kerrigan, Phil Brown, Charles Irwin, Louise Lorimer, Harry Antrim, J. Farrell MacDonald.

That Wonderful Urge (1948, 20th-Fox). *d:* Robert B. Sinclair; *p:* Fred Kohlmar; *sc:* Jay Dratler—*b/o* a story by William R. Lipman and Frederick Stephani.

THOMAS JEFFERSON TYLER: Hot-shot news reporter who upsets a publicity-shy heiress by writing nasty stories about her, then finds himself the victim of unfavorable publicity when—to get even—she falsely announces to the press that they're married.

Gene Tierney, Reginald Gardiner, Arleen Whelan, Lucile Watson, Gene Lockhart, Lloyd Gough, Porter Hall, Richard Gaines, Taylor Holmes, Chill Wills, Hope Emerson, Frank Ferguson, Charles Arnt.

Prince of Foxes (1949, 20th-Fox). *d:* Henry King; *p:* Sol C. Siegel; *sc:* Milton Krims—*b/o* the novel by Samuel Shellabarger.

ANDREA ORSINI: Bold adventurer during the Italian Renaissance who runs into treachery and intrigue as he fights to stop the infamous Cesare Borgia's relentless quest for power.

Orson Welles, Wanda Hendrix, Everett Sloane, Marina Berti, Katina Paxinou, Felix Aylmer, Leslie Bradley, Joop van Hulzen, James Carney, Eduardo Ciannelli, Rena Lennart, Giuseppe Faeti.

The Black Rose (1950, 20th-Fox). *d:* Henry Hathaway; *p:* Louis D. Leighton; *sc:* Talbot Jennings—*b/o* the novel by Thomas B. Costain.

WALTER OF GURNIE: Thirteenth-century Saxon with a price on his head who flees England and finds adventure in the Orient, then—when he returns to England with some valuable Chinese inventions—is knighted by King Edward.

Orson Welles, Cecile Aubrey, Jack Hawkins, Finley Currie, Michael Rennie, Herbert Lom, Mary Clare, Bobby Blake, Alfonso Bedoya, James Robertson Justice, Torin Thatcher, Laurence Harvey.

An American Guerrilla in the Philippines (1950, 20th-Fox). *d:* Fritz Lang; *p:* Lamar Trotti; *sc:* Lamar Trotti—*b/o* the novel by Ira Wolfert.

ENS. CHUCK PALMER: WWII American PT boat officer who, when the U.S. surrenders at Bataan, forms a guerrilla band of Filipinos on the island of Leyte to fight the Japanese.

Micheline Presle, Tom Ewell, Bob Patten, Tommy Cook, Juan Torena, Jack Elam, Robert Barrat, Carleton Young, Maria Del Val, Eddie Infante, Orlando Martin, Sabu Camacho.

Rawhide (1951, 20th-Fox). *d:* Henry Hathaway; *p:* Samuel C. Engel; *sc:* Dudley Nichols.

TOM OWENS: Assistant stagecoach stationmaster in the 1880s who, with a young woman and her niece, is held prisoner by a band of outlaws at an off-the-beaten-path relay post.

Susan Hayward, Hugh Marlowe, Dean Jagger, Edgar Buchanan, Jack Elam, George Tobias, Jeff Corey, James Millican, Louis Jean Heydt, William Haade, Ken Tobey, Max Terhune, Walter Sande, Dick Curtis.

I'll Never Forget You (1951, 20th-Fox). *d:* Roy Baker; *p:* Sol C. Siegel; *sc:* Ranald MacDougall—*b/o* the play *Berkeley Square* by John L. Balderston.

PETER STANDISH: Modern-day nuclear physicist living in London who, when he's struck by lightning, is transported back in time to the eighteenth century and falls in love with a beautiful woman.

Ann Blyth, Michael Rennie, Dennis Price, Beatrice Campbell, Kathleen Byron, Raymond Huntley, Irene Browne, Robert Atkins, Felix Aylmer, Tom Gill.

Diplomatic Courier (1952, 20th-Fox). *d:* Henry Hathaway; *p:* Casey Robinson; *sc:* Casey Robinson and Liam O'Brien—*b/o* the novel *Sinister Errand* by Peter Cheyney.

MIKE KELLS: U.S. State Department courier who, while seeking to avenge a friend's death in Trieste, gets involved in Cold War espionage and intrigue with two beautiful spies.

Patricia Neal, Stephen McNally, Hildegarde Neff, Karl Malden, James Millican, Stefan Schnabel, Michael Ansara, Sig Arno, E. G. Marshall, Lee Marvin, Dabbs Greer, Carleton Young, Tom Powers, Charles Buchinski (Charles Bronson).

Pony Soldier (1952, 20th-Fox). *d:* Joseph M. Newman; *p:* Samuel G. Engel; *sc:* John C. Higgins—*b/o* a *Saturday Evening Post* story by Garnett Weston.

DUNCAN MacDONALD: Intrepid Royal Canadian Mountie in 1876 who is assigned to track down a tribe of hostile Cree Indians when they illegally cross into Montana to hunt buffalo and go on the warpath against the U.S. Cavalry.

Cameron Mitchell, Thomas Gomez, Penny Edwards, Robert Horton, Stuart Randall, Anthony Earl Numkena, Howard Petrie, Richard Shackleton, Frank DeKova, Chief Bright Fire, Richard Thunder-Sky.

The Mississippi Gambler (1953, Univ.). *d:* Rudolph Mate; *p:* Ted Richmond; *sc:* Seton I. Miller.

MARK FALLON: Nineteenth-century riverboat gambler—an expert at cards, women, and dueling—who opens a gambling house in New Orleans and has trouble with an arrogant young aristocrat and his headstrong Southern-belle sister.

Piper Laurie, Julia Adams, John McIntire, William Reynolds, Paul Cavanagh, John Baer, Ron Randell, Robert Warwick, Guy Williams, Ralph Dumke, Hugh Beaumont, King Donovan, Gwen Verdon, Dennis Weaver, George Hamilton.

King of the Khyber Rifles (1953, 20th-Fox). *d:* Henry King; *p:* Frank P. Rosenberg; *sc:* Ivan Goff and Ben Roberts—*b/o* the novel by Talbot Munday.

CAPT. ALAN KING: Half-caste British Army captain in India who commands a company of native soldiers known as the Khyber Riflemen during the Sepoy Mutiny of 1857.

Terry Moore, Michael Rennie, John Justin, Guy Rolfe, Richard Stapley, Murray Matheson, Frank DeKova, Argentina Brunetti, Frank Lackteen, John Farrow, Richard Peel, Gavin Muir.

The Long Gray Line (1955, Col.). *d:* John F. p: Robert Arthur; *sc:* Edward Hope—*b/o* the novel *Bringing Up the Brass* by Marty Maher and Nardi Reeder Campion.

MARTY MAHER: Irish immigrant who comes to West Point in 1903 to work as a waiter—and remains there for fifty years as assistant athletic director and friend of generations of "the long gray line" of cadets.

Maureen O'Hara, Robert Francis, Donald Crisp, Betsy Palmer, Ward Bond, Philip Carey, William Leslie, Harry Carey Jr., Patrick Wayne, Sean McClory, Peter Graves, Milburn Stone, Erin O'Brien Moore, Willis Bouchey, Martin Milner, Norman Van Brocklin.

Untamed (1955, 20th-Fox). *d:* Henry King; *p:* Bert E. Friedlob and William A. Bacher; *sc:* Talbot

Jennings, Frank Fenton, and Michael Blankfort (adaptation by Talbot Jennings and William A. Bacher)—*b/o* the novel by Helga Moray.

PAUL VAN RIEBECK: South African Boer leader in the 1850s who carries on a long-time on-again–off-again romance with an Irish colleen while fighting Zulus and helping to establish a Dutch Free State.

Susan Hayward, Richard Egan, John Justin, Agnes Moorehead, Rita Moreno, Hope Emerson, Brad Dexter, Henry O'Neill, Louis Mercier, Emmett Smith, Trude Wyler, Philip Van Zandt.

The Eddy Duchin Story (1956, Col.). *d:* George Sidney; *p:* Jerry Wald; *sc:* Samuel Taylor—*b/o* a story by Leo Katcher.

EDDY DUCHIN: Late-1920s pharmacist graduate from Boston who goes to New York to try to be a professional musician, succeeds in becoming a famous pianist-bandleader in the '30s and '40s, but is plagued by personal tragedies.

Kim Novak, Victoria Shaw, James Whitmore, Rex Thompson, Mickey Maga, Shepperd Strudwick, Frieda Inescort, Gloria Holden, Larry Keating, Kirk Alyn, Jack Albertson, Xavier Cugat.

Abandon Ship (1957, Col.). *d:* Richard Sale; *p:* John R. Sloan (Copa); *sc:* Richard Sale.

EXEC. OFFICER ALEC HOLMES: Luxury-liner officer who, when the ship sinks, winds up in command of an overcrowded lifeboat and has to decide which passengers must be thrown overboard so that the rest can survive.

Mai Zetterling, Lloyd Nolan, Stephen Boyd, Moira Lister, James Hayter, Moultrie Kelsall, Victor

Maddern, Gordon Jackson, Laurence Naismith, John Stratton, Eddie Byrne, Finlay Currie.

The Sun Also Rises (1957, 20th-Fox). *d:* Henry King; *p:* Darryl F. Zanuck (Darryl F. Zanuck); *sc:* Peter Viertel—*b/o* the novel by Ernest Hemingway.

JAKE BARNES: American newspaperman—impotent as a result of WWI injuries—who becomes involved with an ex-girlfriend, now a promiscuous lady of title, and with other "lost generation" expatriates in 1920s Paris and Spain.

Ava Gardner, Mel Ferrer, Errol Flynn, Eddie Albert, Gregory Ratoff, Juliette Greco, Marcel Dalio, Henry Daniell, Danik Patisson, Robert Evans, Carlos Muzquiz, Rebecca Iturbi.

Witness for the Prosecution (1957, UA). *d:* Billy Wilder; *p:* Arthur Hornblow Jr. (Theme/Edward Small); *sc:* Billy Wilder and Harry Kurnitz (adaptation by Larry Marcus)—*b/o* the novel and play by Agatha Christie.

LEONARD VOLE: Likeable drifter who, when he is charged with the murder of a middle-aged widow, is defended by a famed and colorful London barrister.

Marlene Dietrich, Charles Laughton, Elsa Lanchester, John Williams, Henry Daniell, Ian Wolfe, Una O'Connor, Torin Thatcher, Francis Compton, Norma Varden, Philip Tonge, Ruta Lee, J. Pat O'Malley.

• In addition, Tyrone Power appeared in the following feature film as the on-camera presenter of three short stories: *The Rising of the Moon* (1957, WB).

☆ ELVIS PRESLEY

Elvis Aron Presley

b: Jan. 8, 1935, Tupelo, Miss.
d: Aug. 16, 1977, Memphis, Tenn.

"What else is there?"

> Vince (Elvis Presley) to Peggy Van Alden (Judy Tyler) when she asks him if anything else interests him besides money in *Jailhouse Rock*, 1957.

Love Me Tender (1956, 20th-Fox). *d:* Robert D. Webb; *p:* David Weisbart; *sc:* Robert Buckner—*b/o* a story by Maurice Geraghty.

CLINT RENO: Young Southerner who, after he mistakenly thinks his Confederate officer's older brother has been killed in the Civil War, marries

the brother's sweetheart—then has to deal with the situation when the brother shows up.

Richard Egan, Debra Paget, Robert Middleton, William Campbell, Neville Brand, Mildred Dunnock, Bruce Bennett, James Drury, Russ Conway, Barry Coe, L. Q. Jones.

Loving You (1957, Para.). *d:* Hal Kanter; *p:* Hal B. Wallis (Hal Wallis Prod.); *sc:* Herbert Baker and Hal Kanter—*b/o* a story by Mary Agnes Thompson.

DEKE RIVERS: Small-town truck driver who, after he's signed up by a glamorous female press agent to be a vocalist with her ex-husband's country band, becomes an overnight singing idol.

Lizabeth Scott, Wendell Corey, Dolores Hart, James Gleason, Ralph Dumke, Paul Smith, Ken Becker, Jana Lund.

Jailhouse Rock (1957, MGM). *d:* Richard Thorpe; *p:* Pandro S. Berman; *sc:* Guy Trosper—*b/o* a story by Ned Young.

VINCE EVERETT: Young truck driver who is sent to prison for manslaughter, learns to play the guitar while serving time, and becomes a top rock star when he gets out.

Judy Tyler, Mickey Shaughnessy, Vaughn Taylor, Jennifer Holden, Dean Jones, Ann Neyland.

King Creole (1958, Para.). *d:* Michael Curtiz; *p:* Hal B. Wallis (Hal Wallis Prod.); *sc:* Herbert Baker and Michael Vincente Gazzo—*b/o* the novel *A Stone for Danny Fisher* by Harold Robbins.

DANNY FISHER: New Orleans busboy who becomes a hit as a singer in the King Creole nightclub but has big problems with a gangster and his mob.

Carolyn Jones, Dolores Hart, Dean Jagger, Liliane Montevecchi, Walter Matthau, Jan Shepard, Paul Stewart, Vic Morrow, Dick Winslow, Raymond Bailey, Ned Glass.

G.I. Blues (1960, Para.). *d:* Norman Taurog; *p:* Hal B. Wallis (Hal Wallis Prod.); *sc:* Edmund Beloin and Henry Garson.

TULSA McCAULEY: Guitar-playing tank gunner with the U.S. Army in West Germany who, to win a bet for his buddies, tries to melt the icy heart of a hard-to-get cabaret dancer.

Juliet Prowse, James Douglas, Robert Ivers, Leticia Roman, Sigrid Maier, Arch Johnson, Mickey Knox, Jeremy Slate, Ludwig Stossel, Dick Winslow.

Flaming Star (1960, 20th-Fox). *d:* Don Siegel; *p:* David Weisbart; *sc:* Clair Huffaker and Nunnally Johnson—*b/o* the novel *Flaming Lance* by Clair Huffaker.

PACER BURTON: Half-breed son of an 1870s Texas rancher father and a Kiowa Indian mother who, when his mother's people go on the warpath, must choose which side of the Kiowa–settler battle he is on.

Barbara Eden, Steve Forrest, Dolores Del Rio, John McIntire, Rudolpho Acosta, Karl Swenson, Ford Rainey, Richard Jaeckel, L. Q. Jones, Douglas Dick, Anne Benton, Perry Lopez, Sharon Bercutt.

Wild in the Country (1961, 20th-Fox). *d:* Philip Dunne; *p:* Jerry Wald; *sc:* Clifford Odets—*b/o* the novel *The Lost Country* by J. R. Salamanca.

GLENN TYLER: Rebellious back-country youth who gets into trouble with the law but is rehabilitated with the help of a pretty social worker who encourages him to become a writer.

Hope Lange, Tuesday Weld, Millie Perkins, Rafer Johnson, John Ireland, Gary Lockwood, William Mims, Raymond Greenleaf, Christina Crawford,

Charles Arnt, Alan Napier, Jason Robards Sr., Walter Baldwin.

Blue Hawaii (1961, Para.). *d:* Norman Taurog; *p:* Hal B. Wallis (Hal Wallis Prod.); *sc:* Hal Kanter—*b/o* the story "Beach Boy" by Alan Weiss.

CHAD GATES: Ex-G.I. who—when he comes back home to Hawaii—defies his parents by refusing to work in the family pineapple business and instead takes a job with a tourist agency where his girlfriend works.

Joan Blackman, Angela Lansbury, Nancy Walters, Roland Winters, John Archer, Howard McNear, Flora Hayes, Gregory Gay, Steve Brodie, Iris Adrian, Darlene Tompkins.

Follow That Dream (1962, UA). *d:* Gordon Douglas; *p:* David Weisbart (Mirisch); *sc:* Charles Lederer—*b/o* the novel *Pioneer, Go Home!* by Richard Powell.

TOBY KWIMPER: Eldest son of a Southern hillbilly family that, despite the protests of government officials, homesteads a piece of unclaimed land alongside a Florida highway and develops a thriving little community.

Arthur O'Connell, Anne Helm, Joanna Moore, Jack Kruschen, Simon Oakland, Herbert Rudley, Roland Winters, Howard McNear, Frank De Kova, Gavin Koon, Robert Koon, Pam Ogles.

Kid Galahad (1962, UA). *d:* Phil Karlson; *p:* David Weisbart (Mirisch); *sc:* William Fay—*b/o* a story by Francis Wallace.

WALTER GULICK (alias KID GALAHAD): Ex-G.I. who becomes a sparring partner at a fighter's camp, develops into a boxer when the camp's owner discovers that he has a knockout punch, then—despite the threats of gangsters—refuses to throw a championship fight and wins the title.

Gig Young, Lola Albright, Joan Blackman, Charles Bronson, Ned Glass, Robert Emhardt, David Lewis, Michael Dante, Judson Pratt.

Girls! Girls! Girls! (1962, Para.). *d:* Norman Taurog; *p:* Hal B. Wallis (Hal Wallis Prod.); *sc:* Edward Anhalt and Allan Weiss—*b/o* a story by Allan Weiss.

ROSS CARPENTER: Skipper of a charter fishing boat who takes a job singing in a nightclub in order to raise money to buy back, from a boat broker, a sailboat that he and his father built before the father died.

Stella Stevens, Jeremy Slate, Laurel Goodwin, Frank Puglia, Robert Strauss, Benson Fong, Nestor Paiva, Mary Treen, Richard Collier.

It Happened at the World's Fair (1963, MGM). *d:* Norman Taurog; *p:* Ted Richmond; *sc:* Si Rose and Seaman Jacobs.

MIKE EDWARDS: One of a pair of crop-duster pilots who experience a variety of adventures—

including getting involved with pretty women, babysitting a little Chinese girl, battling smugglers, and visiting the Seattle World's Fair.

Joan O'Brien, Gary Lockwood, Vicky Tiu, H. M. Wynant, Edith Atwater, Guy Raymond, Dorothy Green, Kam Tong, Yvonne Craig, Alan Soule, Kurt Russell.

Fun in Acapulco (1963, Para.). *d:* Richard Thorpe; *p:* Hal B. Wallis (Hal Wallis Prod.); *sc:* Allan Weiss.

MIKE WINDGREN: American trapeze artist who, when he goes to an Acapulco resort to be a lifeguard and an entertainer, gets involved with two beautiful women—one a bullfighter, the other the hotel's social director.

Ursula Andress, Elsa Cardenas, Paul Lukas, Larry Domasin, Alejandro Rey, Robert Carricart, Teri Hope, Howard McNear, Mary Treen.

Kissin' Cousins (1964, MGM). *d:* Gene Nelson; *p:* Sam Katzman; *sc:* Gerald Drayson Adams and Gene Nelson—*b/o* a story by Gerald Drayson Adams.

(Dual role) JODIE TATUM: Nephew of a Tennessee hillbilly moonshiner who, in order to protect the still, helps the uncle resist the U.S. Air Force's efforts to build a missile base on the uncle's property.

LT. JOSH MORGAN: Air Force officer who, when he's assigned to talk a hillbilly moonshiner into allowing the U.S.A.F. to build a missile base on the moonshiner's property, discovers that the moonshiner's nephew (Jodie) is not only a distant cousin but also his double.

Arthur O'Connell, Glenda Farrell, Jack Albertson, Pam Austin, Cynthia Pepper, Yvonne Craig, Donald Woods, Tommy Farrell, Beverly Powers, Robert Stone.

Viva Las Vegas (1964, MGM). *d:* George Sidney; *p:* Jack Cummings and George Sidney; *sc:* Sally Benson.

LUCKY JACKSON: Sports-car race driver who—along with his friend the Italian champion—goes to Las Vegas for the annual Grand Prix, where they both fall for a pretty young swimming instructor.

Ann-Margret, Cesare Danova, William Demarest, Nicky Blair, Jack Carter, Robert B. Williams, Roy Engel, Eddie Quillan.

Roustabout (1964, Para.). *d:* John Rich; *p:* Hal B. Wallis (Hal Wallis Prod.); *sc:* Anthony Lawrence and Allan Weiss—*b/o* a story by Allan Weiss.

CHARLIE ROGERS: Footloose, guitar-playing motorcyclist who, after he becomes a roustabout for a traveling carnival run by a middle-aged woman, packs in the customers when he starts singing in a honkytonk on the midway.

Barbara Stanwyck, Joan Freeman, Leif Erickson, Sue Ane Langdon, Pat Buttram, Joan Staley, Dabbs Greer, Steve Brodie, Norman Grabowski, Jack Albertson, Jane Dulo, Billy Barty, Raquel Welch.

Girl Happy (1965, MGM). *d:* Boris Sagal; *p:* Joe Pasternak (Euterpe); *sc:* Harvey Bullock and R. S. Allen.

RUSTY WELLS: Combo leader and pop singer who is hired by a Chicago nightclub owner to secretly keep an eye on his daughter, one of a group of college students living it up in Fort Lauderdale during Easter vacation.

Shelley Fabares, Harold J. Stone, Gary Crosby, Joby Baker, Nita Talbot, Mary Ann Mobley, Fabrizio Mioni, Jimmy Hawkins, Jackie Coogan, Peter Brooks, John Fiedler, Chris Noel, Alan Soule, Norman Grabowski, Milton Frome.

Tickle Me (1965, AA). *d:* Norman Taurog; *p:* Ben Schwalb; *sc:* Elwood Ullman and Edward Bernds.

LONNIE BEALE: Unemployed singing rodeo star who, after signing on as a wrangler at an all-girl dude ranch/health spa, finds himself helping a pretty physical-education instructor escape from villains looking for hidden treasure.

Jocelyn Lane, Julie Adams, Jack Mullaney, Merry Anders, Connie Gilchrist, Edward Faulkner, Bill Williams, Laurie Burton, John Dennis, Grady Sutton.

Harum Scarum (1965, MGM). *d:* Gene Nelson; *p:* Sam Katzman (Four Leaf); *sc:* Gerald Drayson Adams.

JOHNNY TYRONNE: American movie star who, when he's kidnapped while making a personal-appearance tour of the Middle East, becomes involved in an Arabian Nights–type adventure—including a plot to assassinate a king and a love affair with a beautiful princess.

Mary Ann Mobley, Fran Jeffries, Michael Ansara, Jay Novello, Philip Reed, Theo Marcuse, Billy Barty, Richard Reeves.

Paradise—Hawaiian Style (1966, Para.). *d:* Michael Moore; *p:* Hal B. Wallis (Hal Wallis Prod.); *sc:* Allan Weiss and Anthony Lawrence—*b/o* a story by Allan Weiss.

RICK RICHARDS: Out-of-a-job pilot who returns to Hawaii and starts a charter helicopter service with an old flying buddy while romancing assorted local cuties.

Suzanna Leigh, James Shigeta, Marianna Hill, Donna Butterworth, Irene Tsu, Linda Wong, Julie Parrish, Jan Shepard, John Doucette, Philip Ahn, Grady Sutton, Mary Treen.

Frankie and Johnny (1966, UA). *d:* Frederick de Cordova; *p:* Edward Small (Edward Small Prod.); *sc:* Alex Gottlieb—*b/o* a story by Nat Perrin.

JOHNNY: Mississippi showboat singer whose female partner, Frankie, is afraid to marry him because of his gambling and resents his involvement with a redhead who a gypsy fortune teller has predicted will bring him luck.

Donna Douglas, Nancy Kovack, Sue Ane Langdon, Anthony Eisley, Harry Morgan, Audrey Christie, Robert Strauss, Jerome Cowan.

Spinout (1966, MGM). *d:* Norman Taurog; *p:* Joe Pasternak (Euterpe); *sc:* Theodore J. Flicker and George Kirgo.

MIKE McCOY: Combo leader and singer who is chased by three marriage-minded women, one of whose millionaire father owns a racing car that the singer agrees to drive in the Santa Fe Road Race.

Shelley Fabares, Diane McBain, Deborah Walley, Dodie Marshall, Jack Mullaney, Will Hutchins, Warren Berlinger, Jimmy Hawkins, Carl Betz, Cecil Kellaway, Una Merkel.

Easy Come, Easy Go (1966, Para.). *d:* John Rich; *p:* Hal B. Wallis (Hal Wallis Prod.); *sc:* Allan Weiss and Anthony Lawrence.

TED JACKSON: Navy frogman who finds a treasure chest in the hull of an old sunken ship, outwits his adversaries who are also after the treasure, but then discovers that the coins are only copper, not gold.

Dodie Marshall, Pat Priest, Pat Harrington, Skip Ward, Sandy Kenyon, Frank McHugh, Elsa Lanchester, Diki Lerner.

Double Trouble (1967, MGM). *d:* Norman Taurog; *p:* Judd Bernard and Irwin Winkler; *sc:* Jo Heims—*b/o* a story by Marc Brandel.

GUY LAMBERT: American rock singer in London who, when he falls for a teen-age English heiress and winds up on a ship bound for Belgium, discovers that they've become targets for murder.

Annette Day, John Williams, Yvonne Romain, The Wiere Brothers, Chips Rafferty, Stanley Adams, Michael Murphy, Norman Rossington, John Alderson, Maurice Marsac, Leon Askin.

Clambake (1967, UA). *d:* Arthur Nadel; *p:* Jules Levy, Arthur Gardner, and Arnold Laven (Levy–Gardner–Laven); *sc:* Arthur Browne Jr.

SCOTT HEYWARD: Oil millionaire's son who—when he comes to Miami wanting to make good on his own—exchanges identities with a poor water-skiing instructor, falls for one of his students, and wins a big speed-boat race.

Shelley Fabares, Will Hutchins, Bill Bixby, Gary Merrill, James Gregory, Amanda Harley, Suzie Kaye, Angelique Pettyjohn, Hal Peary.

Stay Away, Joe (1968, MGM). *d:* Peter Tewksbury; *p:* Douglas Laurence; *sc:* Michael A. Hoey—*b/o* the novel by Dan Cushman.

JOE LIGHTCLOUD: Hell-raising half-breed rodeo champ who returns to the Navajo reservation to help his people, under a U.S. government program, prove that they can be responsible cattlemen.

Burgess Meredith, Joan Blondell, Katy Jurado, Thomas Gomez, Henry Jones, L. Q. Jones, Quentin Dean, Anne Seymour, Angus Duncan, Douglas Henderson.

Speedway (1968, MGM). *d:* Norman Taurog; *p:* Douglas Laurence; *sc:* Philip Shuken.

STEVE GRAYSON: High-living champion stock-car racer who—when he finds himself owing the IRS $145,000 in back taxes—wins the "Charlotte 600" race, wins the girl, and pays off Uncle Sam.

Nancy Sinatra, Bill Bixby, Gale Gordon, William Schallert, Victoria Meyerink, Carl Ballantine, Ross Hagen.

Live a Little, Love a Little (1968, MGM). *d:* Norman Taurog; *p:* Douglas Laurence; *sc:* Michael A. Hoey and Dan Greenburg—*b/o* the novel *Kiss My Firm but Pliant Lips* by Dan Greenburg.

GREG NOLAN: Los Angeles news photographer who, while being chased by an aggressive young woman, loses his job—but then winds up with *two* jobs as a commercial photographer, thus keeping him frantically hopping back and forth.

Michele Carey, Don Porter, Rudy Vallee, Dick Sargent, Sterling Holloway, Celeste Yarnall, Eddie Hodges, Joan Shawlee, Emily Banks, Merri Ashley, Morgan Windbell.

Charro! (1969, Nat. Gen.). *d:* Charles Marquis Warren; *p:* Charles Marquis Warren; *sc:* Charles Marquis Warren—*b/o* a story by Frederic Louis Fox.

JESS WADE: Reformed outlaw in the 1870s who, when he's captured by his former cohorts in a Mexican border town, is framed for the theft of Mexico's gold-and-silver Victory Gun—the weapon that fired the last shot against Emperor Maximilian and freed the country.

Ina Balin, Victor French, Barbara Werle, Solomon Sturges, Paul Brinegar, James Sikking, Harry Landers, Tony Young, Rodd Redwing, Lynn Kellogg.

Change of Habit (1969, Univ.). *d:* William Graham; *p:* Joe Connelly; *sc:* James Lee, S. S. Schweitzer, and Eric Bercovici—*b/o* a story by John Joseph and Richard Morris.

DR. JOHN CARPENTER: Head of a medical clinic in the ghetto who falls for one of his assistants who, unbeknownst to him, is a nun (dressed in plain clothes) assigned to get practical experience in the real world before taking her final vows.

Mary Tyler Moore, Barbara McNair, Jane Elliot, Leora Dana, Edward Asner, Robert Emhardt,

Regis Toomey, Ruth McDevitt, Richard Carlson, Nefti Millet, Bill Elliott.

The Trouble with Girls (1969, MGM). *d:* Peter Tewksbury; *p:* Lester Welch; *sc:* Arnold Peyser and Lois Peyser—*b/o* Day Keene and Dwight Babcock's novel *The Chatauqua*.

WALTER HALE: Manager of a 1920s traveling tent show who—when the show hits the small Midwestern town of Radford Center—gets into difficulties with women, unions, local talent, and a murder case.

Marlyn Mason, Vincent Price, John Carradine, Sheree North, Joyce Van Patten, Edward Andrews, Bill Zuckert, Dabney Coleman, Anthony Teague.

• In addition, Elvis Presley appeared as himself in the following feature-length films: *Elvis: That's the Way It Is* (1970, MGM—a documentary showing Elvis rehearsing and performing in Las Vegas) and *Elvis on Tour* (1972, MGM—a documentary showing Elvis performing in a series of concerts around the U.S.).

☆ RONALD REAGAN

Ronald Wilson Reagan

b: Feb. 6, 1911, Tampico, Ill.

"Where's the rest of me?"

Drake McHugh (Ronald Reagan)
discovering that his legs have been
amputated by Dr. Henry Gordon (Charles
Coburn) in *Kings Row,* 1941.

Love Is on the Air (1937, WB). *d:* Nick Grinde; *p:* Bryan Foy; *sc:* Morton Grant—*b/o* a story by Roy Chanslor.

ANDY McLEOD: Crusading small-town radio announcer who, when he puts the heat on local crooks, is demoted to kids' programming, but then winds up a hero by tricking the crooks into incriminating themselves over the air on an open mike.

Eddie Acuff, Robert Barrat, Raymond Hatton, Willard Parker, Spec O'Donnell, June Travis, Ben Welden, Addison Richards, Dickie Jones, William Hopper, Herbert Rawlinson, Harry Hayden.

Hollywood Hotel (1938, WB). *d:* Busby Berkeley; *p:* Hal B. Wallis; *sc:* Jerry Wald, Maurice Leo, and Richard Macaulay.

Unbilled "bit" as a radio announcer on the famous movie gossip columnist Louella Parsons' radio show entitled "Hollywood Hotel."

Dick Powell, Rosemary Lane, Lola Lane, Ted Healy, Johnnie Davis, Alan Mowbray, Frances Langford, Louella Parsons, Hugh Herbert, Glenda Farrell, Ken Niles, Allyn Joslyn, Edgar Kennedy, Curt Bois, Eddie Acuff, Mabel Todd, Jerry Cooper, Benny Goodman and His Orchestra.

Swing Your Lady (1938, WB). *d:* Ray Enright; *p:* Samuel Bischoff; *sc:* Joseph Schrank and Maurice Leo—*b/o* the play by Kenyon Nicholson and Charles Robinson.

JACK MILLER: Smooth-talking sports reporter who gets involved in a slick promoter's plan to match his big dimwitted wrestler against a female blacksmith in a small town in the Ozarks.

Humphrey Bogart, Frank McHugh, Louise Fazenda, Nat Pendleton, Penny Singleton, Allen Jenkins, Leon Weaver, Frank Weaver, Elvira Weaver, Daniel Boone Savage, Hugh O'Connell, Tommy Bupp, Sonny Bupp, Olin Howland.

Sergeant Murphy (1938, WB). *d:* B. Reeves Eason; *p:* Bryan Foy; *sc:* William Jacobs—*b/o* a story by Sy Bartlett.

PVT. DENNIS MURPHY: Enlisted man in the U.S. Cavalry who, when an Army jumping horse he's devoted to is judged unfit for service, smuggles the horse—named "Sergeant Murphy"—into England and enters him in the Grand National.

Mary Maguire, Donald Crisp, Ben Hendricks, William Davidson, David Newell, Emmett Vogan, Tracy Lane, Edmund Cobb, Sam McDaniels.

Accidents Will Happen (1938, WB). *d:* William Clemens; *p:* Bryan Foy; *sc:* George Bricker and Anthony Coldeway.

ERIC GREGG: Young insurance adjuster who, after he loses his job because of a fraudulent claims gang, sets up his own phony claims racket so that he can get evidence against the crooks and turn them over to the law.

Gloria Blondell, Dick Purcell, Sheila Bromley, Addison Richards, Hugh O'Connell, Janet Shaw, Spec O'Donnell, Kenneth Harlan, Max Hoffman Jr.

Cowboy from Brooklyn (1938, WB). *d:* Lloyd Bacon; *p:* Lou Edelman; *sc:* Earl Baldwin—*b/o* the play *Howdy, Stranger* by Louis Peletier Jr. and Robert Sloane.

PAT DUNN: One of two glib show-biz promoters who turn a city dude into a singing-cowboy radio star but run into problems when the dude—who's afraid of horses—has to make personal appearances at rodeos.

Dick Powell, Pat O'Brien, Priscilla Lane, Dick Foran, Ann Sheridan, Johnny Davis, Emma Dunn, Granville Bates, James Stephenson, Hobart Cavanaugh, Elisabeth Risdon, Harry Barris, Candy Candido.

Boy Meets Girl (1938, WB). *d:* Lloyd Bacon; *p:* George Abbott; *sc:* Sam Spewack and Bella Spewack—*b/o* their play.

Billed as "ANNOUNCER": Enthusiastic young radio announcer who MCs a gala movie premiere at the Carthay Circle Theater in Los Angeles.

James Cagney, Pat O'Brien, Marie Wilson, Ralph Bellamy, Frank McHugh, Dick Foran, Penny Singleton, Bert Hanlon, James Stephenson, Pierre Watkin, John Ridgely, Carole Landis, Curt Bois, Hal K. Dawson, Clem Bevans.

Girls on Probation (1938, WB). *d:* William McGann; *p:* Bryan Foy; *sc:* Crane Wilbur.

NEIL DILLON: Sympathetic lawyer who defends a young woman against a false theft charge, falls in love with her, and helps save her from a racketeer and his blackmailing girlfriend.

Jane Bryan, Anthony Averill, Sheila Bromley, Henry O'Neill, Elisabeth Risdon, Sig Rumann, Dorothy Peterson, Esther Dale, Susan Hayward, Arthur Hoyt, Joseph Crehan, Pierre Watkin.

Brother Rat (1938, WB). *d:* William Keighley; *p:* Robert Lord; *sc:* Richard Macaulay and Jerry Wald—*b/o* the play by John Monks Jr. and Fred F. Finklehoffe.

DAN CRAWFORD: One of three pals at Virginia Military Institute who run into all sorts of funny complications during the last few weeks before they finally manage to earn their diplomas.

Wayne Morris, Priscilla Lane, Eddie Albert, Jane Wyman, Jane Bryan, Johnny Davis, Henry O'Neill, William Tracy, Gordon Oliver, Jessie Busley, Louise Beavers, Isabel Jewell.

Going Places (1939, WB). *d:* Ray Enright; *p:* Hal B. Wallis; *sc:* Jerry Wald, Sig Herzig, and Maurice Leo—*b/o* Victor Mapes and William Collier Sr.'s play *The Hottentot.*

JACK WITHERING: Dashing son of a rich Maryland horse owner whose prize steed—named "Jeepers Creepers"—is able to win the big race only when it hears the groomsman singing the song "Jeepers Creepers."

Dick Powell, Anita Louise, Allen Jenkins, Walter Catlett, Harold Huber, Larry Williams, Thurston Hall, Minna Gombell, Joyce Compton, Robert Warwick, Louis Armstrong.

Secret Service of the Air (1939, WB). *d:* Noel Smith; *p:* Bryan Foy; *sc:* Raymond Schrock—*b/o* material provided by W. H. Moran.

LT. BRASS BANCROFT: Ex–Army Air Corps lieutenant and commercial pilot who joins the Secret Service and poses as a counterfeiter in order to infiltrate an airborne gang that smuggles aliens into the United States.

John Litel, Ila Rhodes, James Stephenson, Eddie Foy Jr., Rosella Towne, Larry Williams, John Ridgely, Anthony Averill, Bernard Nedell, Frank M. Thomas.

Dark Victory (1939, WB). *d:* Edmund Goulding; *p:* Hal B. Wallis and David Lewis; *sc:* Casey Robinson—*b/o* the play by George Emerson Brewer Jr., and Bertram Bloch.

ALEC HAMM: Wealthy, tippling young suitor of a spoiled Long Island socialite who remains a true friend to her after she has learned that she's dying of a brain tumor and has married her brain surgeon.

Bette Davis, George Brent, Humphrey Bogart, Geraldine Fitzgerald, Henry Travers, Cora Witherspoon, Dorothy Peterson, Virginia Brissac, Herbert Rawlinson, Leonard Mudie, Lottie Williams.

Code of the Secret Service (1939, WB). *d:* Noel Smith; *p:* Bryan Foy; *sc:* Lee Katz and Dean Franklin.

LT. BRASS BANCROFT: U.S. Secret Service agent whose assignment is to track down a gang of American counterfeiters operating in Mexico.

Rosella Towne, Eddie Foy Jr., Moroni Olsen, Edgar Edwards, Jack Mower, John Gallaudet, Joe King, Sol Gorss.

Naughty but Nice (1939, WB). *d:* Ray Enright; *p:* Sam Bischoff; *sc:* Jerry Wald and Richard Macauley.

ED CLARK: Sympathetic New York music publisher who helps a naïve small-town music professor who's come to New York to try to get his symphonic composition published.

Dick Powell, Gale Page, Ann Sheridan, Helen Broderick, Allen Jenkins, ZaSu Pitts, Maxie Rosenbloom, Jerry Colonna, Vera Lewis, Luis Alberni, Bill Davidson, Granville Bates, Halliwell Hobbes, Peter Lind Hayes.

Hell's Kitchen (1939, WB). *d:* Lewis Seiler and E. A. Dupont; *p:* Mark Hellinger and Bryan Foy; *sc:* Crane Wilbur and Fred Niblo Jr.

JIM: Dedicated social worker who, with his girlfriend and a rough ex-con, straightens out some tough kids in a city shelter for wayward boys and exposes the cruel, corrupt superintendent in charge.

Billy Halop, Bobby Jordan, Leo Gorcey, Huntz Hall, Gabriel Dell, Bernard Punsley, Frankie Burke, Margaret Lindsay, Stanley Fields, Grant Mitchell, Arthur Loft, Raymond Bailey, Clem Bevans.

Angels Wash Their Faces (1939, WB). *d:* Ray Enright; *p:* Robert Fellows; *sc:* Michael Fessier, Niven Busch, and Robert Buckner—*b/o* an idea by Jonathan Finn.

PAT REMSEN: District attorney's son who, with the help of a gang of reformed kids, gathers evidence against an arson ring and clears one of the kids who is falsely accused of being an arsonist.

Ann Sheridan, Billy Halop, Bonita Granville, Frankie Thomas, Bobby Jordan, Bernard Punsley, Leo Gorcey, Huntz Hall, Gabriel Dell, Henry O'Neill, Eduardo Ciannelli, Berton Churchill, Minor Watson, Margaret Hamilton, Jackie Searle, Grady Sutton, Marjorie Main.

Smashing the Money Ring (1939, WB). *d:* Terry Morse; *p:* Bryan Foy; *sc:* Anthony Coldeway and Raymond Schrock.

LT. BRASS BANCROFT: U.S. Secret Service agent who poses as a counterfeiter, has himself thrown into prison, and discovers that a counterfeiting gang inside the prison is printing phony bills on the prison press.

Margot Stevenson, Eddie Foy Jr., Joe Downing, Charles D. Brown, Elliott Sullivan, Don Douglas, Charles Wilson, Joe King, William Davidson, Dick Rich, John Hamilton.

Brother Rat and a Baby (1940, WB). *d:* Ray Enright; *p:* Robert Lord; *sc:* Jerry Wald and Richard Macaulay—*b/o* a story by Fred F. Finklehoffe and John Monks Jr.

DAN CRAWFORD: One of a pair of recent graduates of Virginia Military Institute who get involved in a number of humorous escapades as they devise schemes to get their classmate pal a coaching job at the school.

Wayne Morris, Priscilla Lane, Eddie Albert, Jane Wyman, Jane Bryan, Peter B. Good, Larry Williams, Arthur Treacher, Moroni Olsen, Paul Harvey, Berton Churchill, Mayo Methot, Ed Gargan.

An Angel from Texas (1940, WB). *d:* Ray Enright; *p:* Robert Fellows; *sc:* Fred Niblo Jr. and Bertram Millhauser—*b/o* George S. Kaufman's play *The Butter and Egg Man.*

MR. ALLEN: One of a duo of fast-talking show-biz producers who manage to convince a naïve young Texan—when he arrives in New York with $20,000 to invest in a hotel—that he should use it to back their show.

Eddie Albert, Wayne Morris, Rosemary Lane, Jane Wyman, Ruth Terry, John Litel, Hobart Cavanaugh, Ann Shoemaker, Tom Kennedy, Milburn Stone, Elliott Sullivan, Emmett Vogan.

Murder in the Air (1940, WB). *d:* Lewis Seiler; *p:* Bryan Foy; *sc:* Raymond Schrock.

BRASS BANCROFT: U.S. Secret Service agent who masquerades as a crewman on a U.S. Navy dirigible in order to prevent enemy agents from stealing the plans for a new death-ray device that's aboard.

John Litel, James Stephenson, Eddie Foy Jr., Lya Lys, Robert Warwick, Kenneth Harlan, Frank Wilcox, Dick Rich, Cliff Clark, Selmer Jackson, John Hamilton.

Knute Rockne—All American (1940, WB). *d:* Lloyd Bacon; *p:* Hal B. Wallis and Robert Fellows; *sc:* Robert Buckner—*b/o* material provided by Mrs. Knute Rockne.

GEORGE GIPP: Legendary All-American Notre Dame football halfback who, when he catches pneumonia in 1920 and is on his deathbed, tells famed coach Knute Rockne to ask the team, someday when the going is rough, to "win just one for the Gipper."

Pat O'Brien, Gale Page, Donald Crisp, Albert Basserman, John Litel, Henry O'Neill, Owen Davis Jr., John Qualen, Dorothy Tree, John Sheffield, Nick Lukats, Kane Richmond, William Marshall, William Byrne, John Ridgely.

Tugboat Annie Sails Again (1940, WB). *d:* Lewis Seiler; *p:* Bryan Foy; *sc:* Walter De Leon—*b/o* the character created by Norman Reilly Raine.

EDDIE KING: Sailor who, while falling for a wealthy young society woman, helps a gruff widowed skipper of a tugboat when she gets involved in towing a drydock from Washington State to Alaska.

Marjorie Rambeau, Jane Wyman, Alan Hale, Charles Halton, Clarence Kolb, Paul Hurst, Victor Kilian, Chill Wills, Harry Shannon, John Hamilton, Neil Reagan.

Santa Fe Trail (1940, WB). *d:* Michael Curtiz; *p:* Hal B. Wallis and Robert Fellows; *sc:* Robert Buckner.

GEORGE ARMSTRONG CUSTER: Young West Point graduate who, prior to the Civil War, is assigned to the Second U.S. Cavalry at Fort Leavenworth, Kansas—along with other West Point graduates—and later takes part in the bloody 1859 battle against radical abolitionist John Brown at Harpers Ferry, West Virginia.

Errol Flynn, Olivia de Havilland, Raymond Massey, Alan Hale, William Lundigan, Van Heflin, Gene Reynolds, Henry O'Neil, Guinn (Big Boy) Williams, Alan Baxter, John Litel, Moroni Olsen, David Bruce, Hobart Cavanaugh, Joseph Sawyer, Ward Bond, Suzanne Carnahan (Susan Peters).

The Bad Man (1941, MGM). *d:* Richard Thorpe; *p:* J. Walter Ruben; *sc:* Wells Root—*b/o* a story by Porter Emerson Browne.

GIL JONES: Young Westerner who, when he and his wheelchair-ridden uncle can't pay the mortgage on their ranch, is helped by a strutting, blustering Mexican bandit who owes him a favor.

Wallace Beery, Lionel Barrymore, Laraine Day, Henry Travers, Tom Conway, Chill Wills, Nydia Westman, Chris-Pin Martin, Charles Stevens.

Million Dollar Baby (1941, WB). *d:* Curtis Bernhardt; *p:* Hal B. Wallis and David Lewis; *sc:* Casey Robinson, Richard Macaulay, and Jerry Wald—*b/o* a story by Leonard Spigelgass.

PETER ROWAN: Struggling young concert pianist who, when his girlfriend inherits a million dollars, refuses to marry her because now she's rich—which prompts her to give the money to charity.

Priscilla Lane, Jeffrey Lynn, May Robson, Lee Patrick, Helen Westley, Walter Catlett, Richard Carle, George Barbier, John Qualen, Fay Helm, Nan Wynn, John Ridgely, Johnny Sheffield, James Burke.

Nine Lives Are Not Enough (1941, WB). *d:* A. Edward Sutherland; *p:* William Jacobs; *sc:* Fred Niblo Jr.—*b/o* the novel by Jerome Odlum.

MATT SAWYER: Breezy news reporter who, after causing his paper to be sued for libel in a murder case, is fired but with the help of his girlfriend and two friendly cops tracks down the murderers.

Joan Perry, James Gleason, Peter Whitney, Faye Emerson, Howard da Silva, Edward Brophy, Charles Drake, Vera Lewis, Ben Welden, Howard Hickman, John Ridgely, Cliff Clark, Joseph Crehan.

International Squadron (1941, WB). *d:* Lothar Mendes; *p:* Edmund Grainger; *sc:* Barry Trivers and Kenneth Gamet—*b/o* a play by Frank Wead.

JIMMY GRANT: Cocky American WWII pilot in an international RAF squadron who rubs his fellow flyers the wrong way, is blamed for the death of his American pilot friend, but atones for it by taking another flyer's place on a suicide bombing mission.

James Stephenson, Olympe Bradna, William Lundigan, Joan Perry, Julie Bishop, Tod Andrews, Cliff Edwards, John Ridgely, Reginald Denny, Selmer Jackson, Addison Richards, Holmes Herbert, Helmut Dantine.

Kings Row (1942, WB). *d:* Sam Wood; *p:* Hal B. Wallis; *sc:* Casey Robinson—*b/o* the novel by Henry Bellamann.

DRAKE McHUGH: Breezy, good-natured playboy in a turn-of-the-century small Midwestern town (Kings Row) who loses his inheritance, then gets a job as a railroad laborer, but—when he's hit by a train—loses both his legs through unnecessary amputation by a sadistic doctor.

Ann Sheridan, Robert Cummings, Charles Coburn,

Betty Field, Claude Rains, Judith Anderson, Nancy Coleman, Maria Ouspenskaya, Harry Davenport, Ernest Cossart, Minor Watson, Ludwig Stossel, Ann Todd, Scotty Beckett.

Juke Girl (1942, WB). *d:* Curtis Bernhardt; *p:* Jerry Wald and Jack Saper; *sc:* A. I. Bezzerides (adaptation by Kenneth Gamet)—*b/o* a story by Theodore Pratt.

STEVE TALBOT: Migratory fruit picker in Florida who runs into mob violence and murder when he joins a battle between angry farmers and workers and the owner of a monopolistic packing house.

Ann Sheridan, Richard Whorf, George Tobias, Gene Lockhart, Alan Hale, Betty Brewer, Howard da Silva, Willard Robinson, Faye Emerson, Willie Best, Fuzzy Knight, Spencer Charters, William Davidson, Frank Wilcox, William Haade.

Desperate Journey (1942, WB). *d:* Raoul Walsh; *p:* Hal B. Wallis; *sc:* Arthur T. Horman.

FLYING OFFICER JOHNNY HAMMOND: American crew member of a WWII RAF bomber who, when the plane is shot down over Germany, tries to make his way back to England as he and his fellow airmen are pursued by a relentless Nazi colonel and his troops.

Errol Flynn, Nancy Coleman, Raymond Massey, Alan Hale, Arthur Kennedy, Ronald Sinclair, Albert Basserman, Sig Rumann, Patrick O'Moore, Ilka Gruning, Elsa Basserman, Lester Matthews, Helmut Dantine, Hans Schumm, Douglas Walton.

This Is the Army (1943, WB). *d:* Michael Curtiz; *p:* Jack L. Warner and Hal B. Wallis; *sc:* Casey Robinson and Claude Binyon—*b/o* the play by Irving Berlin.

JOHNNY JONES: Broadway producer's son who—just like his father in WWI—goes into the U.S. Army in WWII and is put in charge of producing a big musical show.

George Murphy, Joan Leslie, George Tobias, Alan Hale, Charles Butterworth, Rosemary DeCamp, Dolores Costello, Una Merkel, Stanley Ridges, Ruth Donnelly, Dorothy Peterson, Kate Smith, Joe Louis, Francis Langford, Gertrude Niesen, Irving Berlin.

Stallion Road (1947, WB). *d:* James V. Kern; *p:* Alex Gottlieb; *sc:* Stephen Longstreet—*b/o* the novel by Stephen Longstreet.

LARRY HANRAHAN: Dedicated veterinarian who, while vying with a novelist friend for the affections of a pretty rancher, fights to stamp out an outbreak of anthrax.

Alexis Smith, Zachary Scott, Peggy Knudsen, Patti Brady, Harry Davenport, Frank Puglia, Ralph Byrd, Lloyd Corrigan, Mary Gordon, Dewey Robinson.

That Hagen Girl (1947, WB). *d:* Peter Godfrey; *p:*

Alex Gottlieb; *sc:* Charles Hoffman—*b/o* the novel by Edith Roberts.

TOM BATES: Ex–WWII hero and lawyer who, when a young woman becomes convinced that she's his illegitimate daughter, proves that she's not—but falls in love with her.

Shirley Temple, Rory Calhoun, Lois Maxwell, Dorothy Peterson, Charles Kemper, Conrad Janis, Penny Edwards, Jean Porter, Harry Davenport, Moroni Olsen, Frank Conroy, Douglas Kennedy, Kathryn Card.

The Voice of the Turtle (1947, WB). *d:* Irving Rapper; *p:* Charles Hoffman; *sc:* John Van Druten—*b/o* his play.

BILL PAGE: WWII U.S. Army sergeant who becomes involved in a weekend romance with a naïve young New York actress when—because he has no place to stay—she lets him share her apartment.

Eleanor Parker, Eve Arden, Wayne Morris, Kent Smith, John Emery, Erskine Sanford, John Holland, Nino Pepitone.

John Loves Mary (1949, WB). *d:* David Butler; *p:* Jerry Wald; *sc:* Phoebe Ephron and Henry Ephron—*b/o* the play by Norman Krasna.

JOHN LAWRENCE: Post–WWII Army sergeant who marries a young English woman to get her into the U.S. for an old Army buddy, then has to explain the situation to his fiancée and her parents.

Jack Carson, Patricia Neal, Wayne Morris, Edward Arnold, Virginia Field, Katherine Alexander, Paul Harvey, Ernest Cossart, Irving Bacon.

Night Unto Night (1949, WB). *d:* Don Siegel; *p:* Owen Crump; *sc:* Kathryn Scola—*b/o* the novel by Philip Wylie.

JOHN: Sensitive biochemist suffering from epilepsy who, when he rents a secluded beach house on the Florida coast, falls in love with the owner—a young widow haunted by the ghost of her dead husband.

Viveca Lindfors, Broderick Crawford, Rosemary DeCamp, Osa Massen, Art Baker, Craig Stevens, Ross Ford, Irving Bacon, Almira Sessions.

The Girl from Jones Beach (1949, WB). *d:* Peter Godfrey; *p:* Alex Gottlieb; *sc:* I. A. L. Diamond—*b/o* a story by Allen Boretz.

BOB RANDOLPH: Famous pin-up-girl artist who spots the "perfect" female model in a bathing suit at Jones Beach, learns that she's a teacher, and—posing as a Czech immigrant called Robert Venerik—enrolls in her citizenship class in order to get to know her better.

Virginia Mayo, Eddie Bracken, Dona Drake, Henry Travers, Lois Wilson, Florence Bates,

Jerome Cowan, Helen Westcott, Paul Harvey, Lloyd Corrigan, Myrna Dell, Buddy Roosevelt.

The Hasty Heart (1950, WB). *d:* Vincent Sherman; *p:* Howard Lindsay and Russel Crouse; *sc:* Ranald MacDougall—*b/o* the play by John Patrick.

YANK: Sympathetic American soldier—recovering from malaria in a British Army hospital in Burma—who, along with other patients, tries to become friends with a proud, stubborn, standoffish Scottish soldier who has only a few weeks to live.

Richard Todd, Patricia Neal, Anthony Nicholls, Howard Crawford, John Sherman, Ralph Michael, Alfred Bass, Orlando Martins.

Louisa (1950, Univ.). *d:* Alexander Hall; *p:* Robert Arthur; *sc:* Stanley Roberts.

HAL NORTON: Middle-aged architect who is flabbergasted when his senior-citizen mother becomes the romantic object of a tug-of-war between two elderly suitors—a mild-mannered grocer and the architect's business-tycoon boss.

Charles Coburn, Ruth Hussey, Edmund Gwenn, Spring Byington, Piper Laurie, Scotty Beckett, Connie Gilchrist, Willard Waterman, Martin Milner, Dave Willock.

Storm Warning (1951, WB). *d:* Stuart Heisler; *p:* Jerry Wald; *sc:* Daniel Fuchs and Richard Brooks.

BURT RAINEY: Southern district attorney who sets out to break up the local Ku Klux Klan chapter after a New York model—in town to visit her sister—accidentally witnesses a KKK murder and recognizes her sister's husband as one of the killers.

Ginger Rogers, Doris Day, Steve Cochran, Hugh Sanders, Lloyd Gough, Raymond Greenleaf, Ned Glass, Walter Baldwin, Stuart Randall, Sean McClory.

Bedtime for Bonzo (1951, Univ.). *d:* Frederick de Cordova; *p:* Michel Kraike; *sc:* Val Burton and Lou Breslow—*b/o* a story by Raphel David Blau and Ted Berkman.

PETER BOYD: Psychology professor who, in order to prove that environment is a more important factor than heredity in how a child turns out, takes a chimpanzee named Bonzo into his home and raises him as though he were human.

Diana Lynn, Walter Slezak, Jesse White, Lucille Barkley, Herbert Heyes, Herbert Vigran, Ed Gargan, Howard Banks, Ed Clark, Elizabeth Flournoy, Bonzo.

The Last Outpost (1951, Para.). *d:* Lewis R. Foster; *p:* William H. Pine and William C. Thomas (Pine–Thomas); *sc:* Geoffrey Homes, George Worthing Yates, and Winston Miller.

VANCE BRITTEN: Civil War Confederate cavalry officer who, while in Arizona trying to stop gold shipments to the North, teams up with Union soldiers—commanded by his brother—to fight off an attack by Apache Indians.

Rhonda Fleming, Bruce Bennett, Bill Williams, Peter Hanson, Noah Beery Jr., Hugh Beaumont, John Ridgely, Lloyd Corrigan, Charles Evans.

Hong Kong (1952, Para.). *d:* Lewis R. Foster; *p:* William H. Pine and William C. Thomas (Pine–Thomas); *sc:* Winston Miller—*b/o* a story by Lewis R. Foster.

JEFF WILLIAMS: Hardboiled WWII veteran in the Orient who plans to steal a valuable antique idol from a young orphaned Chinese boy but, after tangling with jewel thieves and murderers, decides to go straight.

Rhonda Fleming, Nigel Bruce, Lady May Lawton, Marvin Miller, Claude Allister, Danny Chang.

She's Working Her Way Through College (1952, WB). *d:* H. Bruce Humberstone; *p:* William Jacobs; *sc:* Peter Milne—*b/o* James Thurber and Elliott Nugent's play *The Male Animal.*

JOHN PALMER: Mild-mannered professor at a Midwestern college who gets into trouble with his wife and the school board when he refuses to expel a glamorous ex–burlesque queen enrolled in his writing class.

Virginia Mayo, Gene Nelson, Don Defore, Phyllis Thaxter, Patrice Wymore, Roland Winters, Raymond Greenleaf, Amanda Randolph, George Meander.

The Winning Team (1952, WB). *d:* Lewis Seiler; *p:* Bryan Foy; *sc:* Ted Sherdeman, Seeleg Lester, and Mervin Gerrard.

GROVER C. ALEXANDER: Nebraska telephone lineman who—after becoming a pre-WWI star pitcher for the Philadelphia Phillies—suffers an accident and has trouble with his vision, develops a drinking problem and leaves baseball, but then makes a sensational comeback in the 1920s with the St. Louis Cardinals.

Doris Day, Frank Lovejoy, Eve Miller, James Millican, Russ Tamblyn, Gordon Jones, Hugh Sanders, Frank Ferguson, Walter Baldwin, Dorothy Adams.

Tropic Zone (1953, Para.). *d:* Lewis R. Foster; *p:* William H. Pine and William C. Thomas (Pine–Thomas); *sc:* Lewis R. Foster—*b/o* a story by Tom Gill.

DAN McCLOUD: American adventurer in Central America who, after he's hired as foreman of a pretty woman's banana plantation, helps a group of owners fight a greedy shipping magnate who's out to take over their plantations.

Rhonda Fleming, Estelita, Noah Beery Jr., Grant Withers, John Wengraf, Argentina Brunetti, Rico Alanez, Maurice Jara, Pilar Del Rey.

Law and Order (1953, Univ.). *d:* Nathan Juran; *p:* John W. Rogers; *sc:* John Bagni, Owen Bagni, and D. D. Beauchamp—*b/o* a story by William R. Burnett.

FRAME JOHNSON: U.S. marshal who, after becoming famous by cleaning up Tombstone, Arizona, retires to another town—but when his brother is gunned down, pins on his badge again to help the citizens fight the crooked town boss and his gang.

Dorothy Malone, Alex Nicol, Preston Foster, Ruth Hampton, Russell Johnson, Barry Kelley, Chubby Jackson, Dennis Weaver, Jack Kelly, Tristram Coffin, Wally Cassell.

Prisoner of War (1954, MGM). *d:* Andrew Marton; *p:* Henry Berman; *sc:* Allen Rivkin.

WEB SLOANE: U.S. Army officer in the Korean War who volunteers to parachute behind enemy lines and become a prisoner so that he can get first-hand proof of the brutal treatment of Americans in North Korean POW camps.

Steve Forrest, Dewey Martin, Oscar Homolka, Robert Horton, Paul Stewart, Harry Morgan, Stephen Bekassy, Leonard Strong, Darryl Hickman.

Cattle Queen of Montana (1954, RKO). *d:* Allan Dwan; *p:* Benedict Borgeaus; *sc:* Robert Blees and Howard Estabrook—*b/o* a story by Thomas Blackburn.

FARRELL: Undercover Army officer who helps a female cattle rancher in Montana fight to save her land and cattle from outlaws and marauding Indians.

Barbara Stanwyck, Gene Evans, Lance Fuller, Anthony Caruso, Jack Elam, Yvette Dugay, Morris Ankrum, Chubby Johnson, Myron Healey, Rod Redwing, Paul Birch, Byron Foulger, Burt Mustin, Hugh Sanders.

Tennessee's Partner (1955, RKO). *d:* Allan Dwan; *p:* Benedict Borgeaus; *sc:* Milton Krims, D. D. Beauchamp, Graham Baker, and Teddi Sherman—based on a story by Bret Harte.

COWPOKE: Good-hearted cowboy pal of a slick gambler in a California gold-rush mining town who is gunned down while saving the gambler's life in a fight with claim jumpers.

John Payne, Rhonda Fleming, Coleen Gray, Anthony Caruso, Leo Gordon, Myron Healey, Morris Ankrum, Chubby Johnson, Joe Devlin, John Mansfield, Angie Dickinson.

Hellcats of the Navy (1957, Col.). *d:* Nathan Juran; *p:* Charles H. Schneer; *sc:* David Lang and Raymond Marcus—*b/o* the book by Charles A. Lockwood and Hans Christian Adamson.

CMDR. CASEY ABBOTT: WWII U.S. submarine commander who is assigned to find out why

Japanese mines in the Tsushima Strait are resistant to sonar detectors so that the minefields can be cleared and American subs can attack Japanese ships.

Nancy Davis (Nancy Reagan), Arthur Franz, Robert Arthur, William Leslie, William Phillips, Harry Lauter, Michael Garth, Joseph Turkel, Don Keefer, Selmer Jackson, Maurice Manson, Bing Russell.

The Killers (1964, Univ.). *d:* Don Siegel; *p:* Don Siegel (Revue Prod.); *sc:* Gene L. Coon—*b/o* the short story by Ernest Hemingway.

JACK BROWNING: Brutal crime boss who hires two hit men to track down and kill an ex–race-car driver who doublecrossed him years earlier in a million-dollar robbery.

Lee Marvin, John Cassavetes, Angie Dickinson, Clu Gulager, Claude Akins, Norman Fell, Virginia Christine, Don Haggerty, Kathleen O'Malley, Scott Hale.

• In addition, Ronald Reagan made a cameo/guest appearance in the following feature film: *It's a Great Feeling* (1949, WB).

☆ ROBERT REDFORD

Charles Robert Redford Jr.

b: Aug. 18, 1937, Santa Monica, Cal.

"What do we do now?"

> Bill McKay (Robert Redford) asking a revealing question of his campaign manager after winning a California election to the U.S. Senate in *The Candidate,* 1972.

War Hunt (1962, UA). *d:* Denis Sanders; *p:* Terry Sanders (T-D Enterprise); *sc:* Stanford Whitmore.

PVT. ROY LOOMIS: Sensitive young American soldier in the Korean War who befriends a Korean orphan boy and tries to save him from the bad influence of a mentally unbalanced G.I. who has begun to enjoy killing.

John Saxon, Charles Aidman, Sydney Pollack, Gavin MacLeod, Tommy Matsuda, Tom Skerritt, Tony Ray.

Situation Hopeless—But Not Serious (1965, Para.). *d:* Gottfried Reinhardt; *p:* Gottfried Reinhardt (Castle); *sc:* Silvia Reinhardt (adaptation by Jan Lustig)—*b/o* Robert Shaw's novel *The Hiding Place.*

HANK: One of a pair of American WWII airmen who, after being shot down over Germany in 1944 and taking refuge in the cellar of an eccentric German shopkeeper, are held prisoner for several years after the war is over—because the shopkeeper enjoys their company.

Alec Guinness, Michael Connors, Anita Hoefer, Mady Rahl, Paul Dahlke, Frank Wolff, John Briley, Elisabeth Von Molo, Carola Regnier.

Inside Daisy Clover (1965, WB). *d:* Robert Mulligan; *p:* Alan J. Pakula (Park Place); *sc:* Gavin Lambert—*b/o* the novel by Gavin Lambert.

WADE LEWIS: Handsome, mysterious screen idol who is briefly married to young new superstar Daisy Clover—until he deserts her because he's a homosexual.

Natalie Wood, Christopher Plummer, Roddy McDowall, Ruth Gordon, Katharine Bard, Betty Harford, Paul Hartman, John Hale, Harold Gould, Edna Holland, Peter Helm.

The Chase (1966, Col.). *d:* Arthur Penn; *p:* Sam Spiegel (Horizon); *sc:* Lillian Hellman—*b/o* the novel and play by Horton Foote.

BUBBER REEVES: Young Texan who, after escaping from the penitentiary where he's been serving time for a crime he didn't commit, heads for his hostile home town and finds that his wife is having an affair with the son of the town's most influential citizen.

Marlon Brando, Jane Fonda, E. G. Marshall, Angie Dickinson, Janice Rule, Miriam Hopkins, Martha Hyer, Robert Duvall, James Fox, Diana Hyland, Henry Hull, Jocelyn Brando, Paul Williams, Malcolm Atterbury, Nydia Westman, Bruce Cabot.

This Property Is Condemned (1966, Para.). *d:* Sydney Pollack; *p:* John Houseman (Seven Arts–Ray Stark); *sc:* Francis Ford Coppola, Fred Coe, and Edith Sommer—*b/o* a one-act play by Tennessee Williams.

OWEN LEGATE: Railroad efficiency expert who comes to a small Mississippi town on business but becomes involved with his landlady's amorous daughter.

Natalie Wood, Charles Bronson, Kate Reid, Mary Badham, Alan Baxter, Robert Blake, Dabney Coleman, Jon Provost, Quentin Sondergaard, Michael Steen, Bruce Watson.

Barefoot in the Park (1967, Para.). *d:* Gene Saks;

p: Hal Wallis (Hal B. Wallis Prod.); *sc:* Neil Simon—*b/o* his play.

PAUL BRATTER: Conservative young newlywed lawyer who runs into marital problems, as well as kooky neighbors, when he and his uninhibited wife move into a fifth-floor walk-up apartment in Greenwich Village.

Jane Fonda, Charles Boyer, Mildred Natwick, Herbert Edelman, James Stone, Ted Hartley, Mabel Albertson, Fritz Feld.

Butch Cassidy and the Sundance Kid (1969, 20th-Fox). *d:* George Roy Hill; *p:* John Foreman and Paul Monash (Campanile); *sc:* William Goldman.

THE SUNDANCE KID: Famed nineteenth-century gun-slinging outlaw who joins up with Butch Cassidy (leader of a Wyoming gang known as the Wild Bunch, or the Hole-in-the-Wall Gang) to rob trains—first in the Old West, and then in Bolivia, where they are finally ambushed.

Paul Newman, Katharine Ross, Strother Martin, Henry Jones, Jeff Corey, Cloris Leachman, Ted Cassidy, Kenneth Mars, Don Keefer, Charles Dierkop, Nelson Olmstead, Sam Elliott.

Downhill Racer (1969, Para.). *d:* Michael Ritchie; *p:* Richard Gregson (Wildwood); *sc:* James Salter—*b/o* Oakley Hall's novel *The Downhill Racers.*

DAVID CHAPPELLET: Aloof, arrogant Colorado farm boy who is obsessed with becoming the world's fastest skier—and gets his chance when he makes the U.S. Olympic ski team.

Gene Hackman, Camilla Sparv, Karl Michael Vogler, Jim McMullan, Christian Doermer, Kathleen Crowley, Dabney Coleman, Timothy Kirk, Walter Stroud, Rip McManus, Joe Jay Jalbert, Tom J. Kirk.

Tell Them Willie Boy Is Here (1969, Univ.). *d:* Abraham Polonsky; *p:* Philip A. Waxman; *sc:* Abraham Polonsky—*b/o* the novel *Willie Boy* by Harry Lawton.

CHRISTOPHER COOPER: Sheriff of a small California town in 1909 who hunts down a young Paiute Indian accused of murdering a white man.

Katharine Ross, Robert Blake, Susan Clark, Barry Sullivan, John Vernon, Charles Aidman, Charles McGraw, Shelly Novack, Robert Lipton.

Little Fauss and Big Halsy (1970, Para.). *d:* Sidney J. Furie; *p:* Albert S. Ruddy (Alfran/Furie); *sc:* Charles Eastman.

HALSY KNOX ("BIG HALSY"): Bragging, self-centered motorcycle racer who keeps taking advantage of his shy, gullible motorcycling pal—but in the end proves to be a loser.

Michael J. Pollard, Lauren Hutton, Noah Beery, Lucille Benson, Linda Gaye Scott, Ray Ballard, Shara St. John, Ben Archibek.

The Hot Rock (1972, 20th-Fox). *d:* Peter Yates; *p:* Hal Landers and Bobby Roberts; *sc:* William Goldman—*b/o* the novel by Donald E. Westlake.

JOHN ARCHIBALD DORTMUNDER: Inept small-time crook who—after he, his equally inept brother-in-law, and two other shady characters are hired by an African ambassador to steal a priceless diamond from the Brooklyn Museum—manages to goof up every step of the way.

George Segal, Ron Leibman, Paul Sand, Zero Mostel, Moses Gunn, William Redfield, Topo Swope, Charlotte Rae, Harry Bellaver.

The Candidate (1972, WB). *d:* Michael Ritchie; *p:* Walter Coblenz (Wildwood–Ritchie); *sc:* Jeremy Larner.

BILL McKAY: Dedicated young California lawyer who, after he's talked into running as the Democratic candidate for the U.S. Senate, finds himself sacrificing his idealism in order to win the election.

Peter Boyle, Don Porter, Allen Garfield, Karen Carlson, Quinn Redeker, Morgan Upton, Michael Lerner, Kenneth Tobey, Melvyn Douglas.

Jeremiah Johnson (1972, WB). *d:* Sydney Pollack; *p:* Joe Wizan; *sc:* John Milius and Edward Anhalt—*b/o* the novel *Mountain Man* by Vardis Fisher and the story "Crow Killer" by Raymond W. Thorp and Robert Bunker.

JEREMIAH JOHNSON: Ex–U.S. soldier of the Mexican War who—after he deserts civilization in the 1820s to be a "mountain man" in the Rockies—becomes a legendary hero as he learns to survive the harsh, wintry wilderness and carries on a bitter feud with the Crow Indians.

Will Geer, Stefan Gierasch, Allyn Ann McLerie, Charles Tyner, Delle Bolton, Josh Albee, Joaquin Martinez, Paul Benedict, Matt Clark, Richard Angarola, Jack Colvin.

The Way We Were (1973, Col.). *d:* Sydney Pollack; *p:* Ray Stark (Rastar); *sc:* Arthur Laurents—*b/o* his novel.

HUBBELL GARDINER: Handsome all-American college boy in the early 1940s who is briefly attracted to a politically active left-wing coed, then marries her after WWII, but—during his career as a Hollywood screenwriter—realizes that they are incompatible and divorces her.

Barbra Streisand, Bradford Dillman, Lois Chiles, Patrick O'Neal, Viveca Lindfors, Allyn Ann McLerie, Murray Hamilton, Herb Edelman, Diana Ewing, Marcia Mae Jones, Don Keefer, James Woods, Dan Seymour, Susie Blakely.

The Sting (1973, Univ.). *d:* George Roy Hill; *p:* Tony Bill, Michael Phillips, and Julia Phillips (R. Zanuck/D. Brown); *sc:* David S. Ward.

JOHNNY HOOKER*: Young con man in 1930s Chicago who—when an egotistical racketeer from New York causes the death of a friend of his—teams up with an "old pro" con man to get revenge by putting the "Big Con" on the racketeer.

Paul Newman, Robert Shaw, Charles Durning, Ray Walston, Sally Kirkland, Eileen Brennan, Robert Earl Jones, Harold Gould, John Heffernan, Dana Elcar, Jack Kehoe, Dimitra Arliss, Avon Long.

The Great Gatsby (1974, Para.). *d:* Jack Clayton; *p:* David Merrick (Newdon); *sc:* Francis Ford Coppola—*b/o* the novel by F. Scott Fitzgerald.

JAY GATSBY: Ex-bootlegger/racketeer in the 1920s who buys an opulent Long Island estate to be near a married society girl he once loved and lost—and now hopes to win back.

Mia Farrow, Bruce Dern, Karen Black, Scott Wilson, Sam Waterston, Lois Chiles, Howard Da Silva, Roberts Blossom, Edward Herrmann, Elliot Sullivan, Tom Ewell.

The Great Waldo Pepper (1975, Univ.). *d:* George Roy Hill; *p:* George Roy Hill; *sc:* William Goldman—*b/o* a story by George Roy Hill.

WALDO PEPPER: Ex-WWI barnstorming pilot in the 1920s who, when he winds up as a stunt flyer in a movie, stages a mock dogfight with a famous German ace he dreamed of fighting in the war but never had the chance.

Bo Svenson, Bo Brundin, Susan Sarandon, Geoffrey Lewis, Edward Herrmann, Philip Bruns, Roderick Cook, Kelly Jean Peters, Margot Kidder.

Three Days of the Condor (1975, Para.). *d:* Sydney Pollack; *p:* Stanley Schneider (Dino De Laurentiis/Wildwood); *sc:* Lorenzo Semple Jr. and David Rayfiel—*b/o* the novel *Six Days of the Condor* by James Grady.

JOE TURNER: C.I.A. reader-researcher for a cover operation in New York who—when his co-workers are all mysteriously murdered one afternoon, and he discovers secrets he's not supposed to know—suddenly finds that he's been targeted for assassination by killers working for another branch of the agency.

Faye Dunaway, Cliff Robertson, Max von Sydow, John Houseman, Addison Powell, Walter McGinn, Tina Chen, Michael Kane, Don McHenry, Michael Miller, Jess Osuna, Helen Stenborg.

All The President's Men (1976, WB). *d:* Alan J. Pakula; *p:* Walter Coblenz and Robert Redford (Wildwood); *sc:* William Goldman—*b/o* the book by Carl Bernstein and Bob Woodward.

BOB WOODWARD: One of a duo of *Washington Post* reporters who persevere in their investigative reporting of the June 17, 1972, break-in at the Democratic National Headquarters in the Watergate Hotel, and its subsequent far-reaching consequences.

Dustin Hoffman, Jack Warden, Martin Balsam, Hal Holbrook, Jason Robards, Jane Alexander, Meredith Baxter, Ned Beatty, Stephen Collins, Penny Fuller, Lindsay Ann Crouse, Polly Holliday, Frank Latimore, Neva Patterson.

A Bridge Too Far (1977, UA). *d:* Richard Attenborough; *p:* Joseph E. Levine, Richard P. Levine, Michael Stanley-Evans, and John Palmer (Joseph E. Levine); *sc:* William Goldman—*b/o* the book by Cornelius Ryan.

MAJ. JULIAN COOK: Heroic WWII battalion commander in the U.S. 82nd Airborne Division who, during British General Bernard Montgomery's 1944 Operation Market-Garden, leads his men across Holland's Waal River for the assault on the Nijmegen Bridge.

Dirk Bogarde, James Caan, Michael Caine, Sean Connery, Edward Fox, Elliott Gould, Gene Hackman, Anthony Hopkins, Hardy Kruger, Laurence Olivier, Ryan O'Neal, Maximillian Schell, Liv Ullman, Arthur Hill, Wolfgang Preiss, Paul Maxwell, Denholm Elliott, Donald Douglas, Jeremy Kemp.

The Electric Horseman (1979, Col./Univ.). *d:* Sydney Pollack; *p:* Ray Stark (Ray Stark/Wildwood); *sc:* Robert Garland—*b/o* a story by Paul Gaer, Robert Garland, and Shelly Burton.

NORMAN "SONNY" STEELE: Former champion rodeo cowboy who hits the bottle when he's reduced to doing breakfast-cereal commercials while dressed in an electrified cowboy suit, but who regains his self-respect when he kidnaps a once-great racehorse (that's being given tranquilizers) and returns it to a remote valley to run free.

Jane Fonda, Valerie Perrine, Willie Nelson, John Saxon, Nicolas Coster, Allan Arbus, Wilford Brimley, Will Hare, Timothy Scott, James B. Sikking, Quinn Redeker, Tasha Zemrus.

Brubaker (1980, 20th-Fox). *d:* Stuart Rosenberg; *p:* Ron Silverman; *sc:* W. D. Richter—*b/o* a story by W. D. Richter and Arthur Ross, suggested by a book by Thomas O. Murton and Joy Hyams.

HENRY BRUBAKER: Maverick crusader who, before he takes over as the reform-minded warden of a Southern prison farm, deliberately becomes an inmate so that he can experience the corrupt and brutal conditions that exist there.

Yaphet Kotto, Jane Alexander, Murray Hamilton, David Keith, Morgan Freeman, Matt Clark, Tim McIntire, Richard Ward, Jon Van Ness, Albert Salmi, Linda Haynes, Val Avery.

*Received an Academy Award nomination as Best Actor for this role.

The Natural (1984, Tri-Star Pictures). *d:* Barry Levinson; *p:* Mark Johnson (The Natural Movie Co.); *sc:* Roger Towne and Phil Dusenberry.

ROY HOBBS: Middle-aged rookie baseball player in 1939 who is signed by the down-and-out New York Knights baseball team and manages to turn the team's luck around.

Robert Duvall, Glenn Close, Kim Basinger, Wilford Brimley, Barbara Hershey, Robert Prosky, Richard Farnsworth.

☆ BURT REYNOLDS

Burton Leon Reynolds

b: Feb. 11, 1936, Waycross, Ga.

"You see any law around here? *We're* the law. What we decide is the way things are. So let's vote on it."

> Lewis (Burt Reynolds) telling his three camping companions how to decide what to do with the body of the hillbilly he has had to kill in *Deliverance*, 1972.

Angel Baby (1961, AA). *d:* Paul Wendkos; *p:* Thomas F. Woods; *sc:* Orin Borsten, Paul Mason, and Samuel Roeca—*b/o* the novel *Jenny Angel* by Elsie Oaks Barber.

HOKE ADAMS: Florida tough who bullies a young traveling evangelist and tries to force his attentions on a pretty young mute woman the evangelist has fallen in love with.

George Hamilton, Mercedes McCambridge, Salome Jens, Joan Blondell, Henry Jones, Roger Clark, Dudley Remus, Victoria Adams, Harry Swoger, Barbara Biggart, Davy Biladeau.

Armored Command (1961, AA). *d:* Byron Haskin; *p:* Ron W. Alcorn; *sc:* Ron W. Alcorn.

SKEE: Opportunistic U.S. Army private in a tank outfit who, during WWII's Battle of the Bulge, gets involved with a sexy German spy who's been wounded and left by the Nazis as part of a scheme to learn American plans.

Howard Keel, Tina Louise, Warner Anderson, Earl Holliman, Carleton Young, James Dobson, Marty Ingels, Clem Harvey, Maurice Marsac, Thomas A. Ryan, Peter Capell, Charles Nolte.

Operation C.I.A. (1965, AA). *d:* Christian Nyby; *p:* Peter J. Oppenheimer; *sc:* Bill S. Ballinger and Peer J. Oppenheimer—*b/o* a story by Peer J. Oppenheimer.

MARK ANDREWS: Two-fisted C.I.A. agent in Saigon who uncovers a misplaced secret message intended for the Allies that leads to a plot to assassinate the U.S. Ambassador.

Kieu Chinh, Danielle Aubry, John Hoyt, Cyril Collick, Victor Diaz, William Catching, Marsh Thompson, John Laughinghouse, Frank Estes.

Navajo Joe (1967, UA). *d:* Sergio Corbucci; *p:* Ermanno Donati and Luigi Carpentieri (Dino de Laurentiis); *sc:* Dean Craig and Fernando Di Leo—*b/o* a story by Ugo Pirro.

JOE: Steely-nerved Indian who, after being the lone survivor of a massacre, swears revenge against the bandit leader and gang responsible and eliminates them one by one.

Aldo Sanbrell, Nicoletta Machiavelli, Tanya Lopert, Fernando Rey, Franca Polesello, Lucia Modugno, Pierre Cressoy, Nino Imparato, Alvaro De Luna, Valeria Sabel, Mario Lanfranchi, Lucio Rosato, Simon Arriaga, Cris Huerta.

Shark! (1968, Excelsior). *d:* Samuel Fuller; *p:* Skip Steloff and Marc Cooper; *sc:* Samuel Fuller and John Kingsbridge—*b/o* Victor Channing's book *The Coral Are the Bones.*

CAINE: Rugged member of a group of adventurers diving for sunken treasure in the Red Sea who has to contend not only with vicious sharks but with a treacherous blonde as well.

Barry Sullivan, Arthur Kennedy, Silvia Pinal, Enrique Lucero, Charles Berriochoa, Manuel Alvarado, Emilia Suart.

Fade In (1968, Para.). *d:* Jud Taylor; *p:* Judd Bernard and Silvio Narizzano; *sc:* Jerry Ludwig.

ROB: Local cowboy Romeo who—when he meets a female film editor during the on-location shooting of a Western movie in the desert—is helped by her to get a job on the set and finds himself falling hard for her.

Barbara Loden, Patricia Casey, Noam Pitlik, James Hampton, Joseph Perry, Lawrence Heller, Robert Sorrells, Steve Ferry, George Savalas.

Impasse (1969, UA). *d:* Richard Benedict; *p:* Aubrey Schenck and Hal Klein; *sc:* John C. Higgins.

PAT MORRISON: Enterprising American adventurer who recruits four ex-soldiers to search for $3 million in gold that they buried on Corregidor during WWII in order to hide it from Japanese invaders.

Anne Francis, Lyle Bettger, Rodolfo Acosta, Jeff Corey, Clarke Gordon, Miko Mayama, Joanne Dalsass, Vic Diaz, Dely Atay-Atayan.

Sam Whiskey (1969, UA). *d:* Arnold Laven; *p:* Jules Levy, Arthur Gardner, and Arnold Laven (Brighton); *sc:* William Norton.

SAM WHISKEY: Itinerant gambler who is seduced and hired by a beautiful widow in Colorado to retrieve a fortune in gold bars (stolen by her late husband) from a sunken steamboat at the bottom of the Platte River.

Clint Walker, Ossie Davis, Angie Dickinson, Rick Davis, Del Reeves, William Schallert, Woodrow Parfrey, Anthony James, John Damler, Bob Adler, Chubby Johnson.

100 Rifles (1969, 20th-Fox). *d:* Tom Gries; *p:* Marvin Schwartz; *sc:* Clair Huffaker and Tom Gries—*b/o* Robert MacLeod's novel *The Californio*.

YAQUI JOE: Indian bank robber in Mexico who teams up with a black American lawman and a female Mexican revolutionary to transport 100 rifles to the Yaqui Indians for their battle against a tyrannical military governor.

Jim Brown, Raquel Welch, Fernando Lamas, Dan O'Herlihy, Hans Gudegast, Michael Forest, Aldo Sanbrell, Soledad Miranda, Alberto Dalbes.

Skullduggery (1970, Univ.). *d:* Gordon Douglas; *p:* Saul David; *sc:* Nelson Gidding.

DOUGLAS TEMPLE: Adventurer who—though he's searching for phosphor, a rare and valuable mineral used in color TV sets—joins a New Guinea scientific expedition that's searching for the missing link between man and ape.

Susan Clark, Roger C. Carmel, Paul Hubschmid, Chips Rafferty, Alexander Knox, Pat Suzuki, Edward Fox, Wilfrid Hyde-White, William Marshall, Rhys Williams, Mort Marshall, Michael St. Clair, Booker Bradshaw.

Fuzz (1972, UA). *d:* Richard A. Colla; *p:* Edward S. Feldman and Jack Farren (Filmways/Javelin); *sc:* Evan Hunter—*b/o* a novel by Ed McBain.

DET. STEVE CARELLA: Free-wheeling police detective in Boston's 87th precinct who, along with assorted fellow cops, tries to solve an extortion plot involving several murders.

Jack Weston, Tom Skerritt, Yul Brynner, Raquel Welch, James McEachin, Steve Ihnat, Stewart Moss, Dan Frazer, Bert Remsen, Peter Bonerz, Cal Bellini, Don Gordon, Charles Tyner, Gary Morgan, Neile Adams.

Deliverance (1972, WB). *d:* John Boorman; *p:* John Boorman (Elmer Enterprises); *sc:* James Dickey—*b/o* his novel.

LEWIS: One of four Atlanta businessmen whose weekend canoe trip down a dangerous river in the Georgia wilderness turns into a terror-filled battle

for survival when they run afoul of a pair of sadistic mountain men.

Jon Voight, Ned Beatty, Ronny Cox, Billy McKinney, Herbert Coward, James Dickey, Ed Ramey, Billy Redden, Seamon Glass, Randall Deal, Lewis Crone, Ken Keener, Johnny Popwell.

Everything You Always Wanted to Know About Sex (1972, UA). *d:* Woody Allen; *p:* Jack Brodsky and Charles H. Joffe; *sc:* Woody Allen—*b/o* the book by Dr. David Reuben.

Member of a mission control center that is trying to launch reluctant sperm. (This segment of the film is a science-fiction spoof.)

Woody Allen, John Carradine, Lou Jacobi, Louise Lasser, Anthony Quayle, Tony Randall, Lynn Redgrave, Gene Wilder, Jack Barry, Erin Fleming, Robert Q. Lewis, Heather MacRae, Pamela Mason.

Shamus (1973, Col.). *d:* Buzz Kulik; *p:* Robert M. Weitman; *sc:* Barry Beckerman.

McCOY: Brooklyn private eye who, when he's hired to recover some stolen diamonds, gets involved with a sexy woman, her ex–football-star brother, and a crooked Army officer who's illegally selling surplus military hardware.

Dyan Cannon, John Ryan, Joe Santos, Georgio Tozzi, Ron Weyand, Larry Block, Beeson Carroll, Kevin Conway, Kay Frye, John Glover.

White Lightning (1973, UA). *d:* Joseph Sargent; *p:* Arthur Gardner and Jules Levy (Levy–Gardner–Laven); *sc:* William Norton.

GATOR McKLUSKY: Southern bootlegger who is let out of prison when he volunteers to get the goods on a corrupt, sadistic sheriff who has murdered the bootlegger's kid brother.

Jennifer Billingsley, Ned Beatty, Bo Hopkins, Matt Clark, Louise Latham, Diane Ladd, R. G. Armstrong, Conlan Carter, Dabbs Greer, Lincoln Demyan, John Steadman.

The Man Who Loved Cat Dancing (1973, MGM). *d:* Richard C. Sarafian; *p:* Martin Poll and Eleanor Perry; *sc:* Eleanor Perry—*b/o* the novel by Marilyn Durham.

JAY GROBART: Ex–Union Army Civil War captain who, while pulling a train robbery, inadvertantly captures the runaway wife of a rancher, then falls in love with her.

Sarah Miles, Lee J. Cobb, Jack Warden, George Hamilton, Bo Hopkins, Robert Donner, Sandy Kevin, Larry Littlebird, Nancy Malone, Jay Silverheels, Jay Varela, Sutero Garcia Jr.

The Longest Yard (1974, Para.). *d:* Robert Aldrich; *p:* Albert S. Ruddy (Long Road); *sc:* Tracy Keenan Wynn—*b/o* a story by Albert S. Ruddy.

PAUL CREWE: Ex–pro quarterback in a Southern prison who is blackmailed by the warden into forming a football team of misfit convicts and playing the warden's team of prison guards in a bone-crunching game.

Eddie Albert, Ed Lauter, Michael Conrad, James Hampton, Harry Caesar, John Steadman, Charles Tyner, Mike Henry, Joe Kapp, Bernadette Peters, Pepper Martin, Ernie Wheelwright, Tony Cacciotti, Richard Kiel, Pervis Atkins, Dino Washington, Ray Nitschke, Jim Reynolds.

W.W. and the Dixie Dancekings (1975, 20th-Fox). *d:* John G. Avildsen; *p:* Steve Shagan and Stanley S. Canter; *sc:* Thomas Rickman.

W. W. BRIGHT: Good-ole-boy con artist in 1957 Nashville who, while pulling off a series of gas-station heists, ties up with a country-and-western musical group and convinces them that he can make them into Grand Ole Opry stars.

Conny Van Dyke, Jerry Reed, Ned Beatty, James Hampton, Don Williams, Richard Hurst, Art Carney, Sherman G. Lloyd, Bill McCutcheon, Mel Tillis, Fred Stuthman, Furry Lewis, Mort Marshall, Sherry Mathis, Nancy Andrews, Peg Murray.

At Long Last Love (1975, 20th-Fox). *d:* Peter Bogdanovich; *p:* Peter Bogdanovich; *sc:* Peter Bogdanovich.

MICHAEL OLIVER PRITCHARD III: Millionaire playboy in 1935 New York who gets involved in a romantic mix-up when he falls for a beautiful heiress, and his Latin gambler pal goes for a flashy Broadway musical star.

Cybill Shepherd, Madeline Kahn, Duilio del Prete, Eileen Brennan, John Hillerman, Mildred Natwick, M. Emmet Walsh, Artie Butler.

Hustle (1975, Para.). *d:* Robert Aldrich; *p:* Robert Aldrich (RoBurt); *sc:* Steve Shagan—*b/o* his novel *City of Angels*.

LT. PHIL GAINES: Hard-nosed Los Angeles cop who, while he tries to solve the case of a young girl whose body washes up on the beach, has problems dealing both with his profession and the beautiful jet-set call girl he loves.

Catherine Deneuve, Ben Johnson, Paul Winfield, Eileen Brennan, Eddie Albert, Ernest Borgnine, Catherine Bach, Jack Carter, Sharon Kelly, James Hampton, David Spielberg, Donald "Red" Barry.

Lucky Lady (1975, 20th-Fox). *d:* Stanley Donen; *p:* Michael Gruskoff (Grusskoff/Venture); *sc:* Willard Huyck and Gloria Katz.

WALKER: One of a pair of down-on-their-luck adventurers during the Prohibition era who, along with a Tijuana cabaret girl, become amateur rumrunners who smuggle booze by boat between Mexico and California.

Gene Hackman, Liza Minnelli, Geoffrey Lewis, John Hillerman, Robby Benson, Michael Hordean, Anthony Holland, John McLiam, Val Avery, Louis Guss, William H. Bassett, Duncan McLeod.

Gator (1976, UA). *d:* Burt Reynolds; *p:* Jules Levy and Arthur Gardner (Levy–Gardner–Laven); *sc:* William Norton.

GATOR McKLUSKY: Southern moonshiner who is coerced by the Feds into teaming up with an inept agent in order to get the goods on an old school buddy–turned–corrupt political boss.

Jack Weston, Lauren Hutton, Jerry Reed, Alice Ghostley, Dub Taylor, Mike Douglas, Burton Gilliam, William Engesser, John Steadman, Lori Futch, Stephanie Burchfield, Alex Hawkins.

Silent Movie (1976, 20th-Fox). *d:* Mel Brooks; *p:* Michael Hertzberg; *sc:* Mel Brooks, Ron Clark, Rudy De Luca, and Barry Levinson—*b/o* a story by Ron Clark.

(Appears as himself.) One of several top Hollywood stars whom a has-been Hollywood director tries to sign up to appear in a silent movie he plans to make.

Mel Brooks, Marty Feldman, Dom De Luise, Bernadette Peters, Sid Caesar, Harold Gould, Ron Carey, Fritz Feld, Harry Ritz, Charlie Callas, Henny Youngman, Anne Bancroft, James Caan, Marcel Marceau, Liza Minnelli, Paul Newman.

Nickelodeon (1976, Col.). *d:* Peter Bogdanovich; *p:* Irwin Winkler and Robert Chartoff (EMI/Chartoff–Winkler); *sc:* W. D. Richter and Peter Bogdanovich.

BUCK GREENWAY: Country bumpkin in 1910 who meets up with a young lawyer–turned–silent-movie director and winds up becoming a big cowboy movie star.

Ryan O'Neal, Tatum O'Neal, Brian Keith, Stella Stevens, John Ritter, Jane Hitchcock, Priscilla Pointer, Don Calfa, Mathew Anden, James Best, Harry Carey Jr., M. Emmet Walsh.

Smokey and the Bandit (1977, Univ.). *d:* Hal Needham; *p:* Robert L. Levy and Mort Engelberg (Rastar); *sc:* James Lee Barrett, Charles Shyer, and Alan Mandel—*b/o* a story by Hal Needham and Robert L. Levy.

BANDIT: High-flying, drag-racing trucker who, along with his sidekick, is offered $80,000 if he can drive to Texarkana, pick up an illegal load of beer, and return to Atlanta (an 1800-mile round trip) in twenty-eight hours.

Sally Field, Jackie Gleason, Jerry Reed, Mike Henry, Paul Williams, Pat McCormick, Alfie Wise, George Reynolds, Macon McCalman, Linda McClure, Susan McIver, Michael Mann, Lamar Jackson.

Semi-Tough (1977, UA). *d:* Michael Ritchie; *p:* David Merrick (David Merrick Prod.); *sc:* Walter Bernstein—*b/o* the novel by Dan Jenkins.

BILLY CLYDE PUCKETT: Star running back for the Miami Dolphins pro football team who—along with his pal, a star end involved in a phony consciousness movement—loves the daughter of the team's Texas oil millionaire owner.

Kris Kristofferson, Jill Clayburgh, Robert Preston, Bert Convy, Roger E. Mosley, Lotte Lenya, Richard Masur, Carl Weathers, Brian Dennehy.

The End (1978, Para.). *d:* Burt Reynolds; *p:* Hank Moonjean and Lawrence Gordon; *sc:* Jerry Belson.
SONNY LAWSON: Middle-aged real-estate salesman who, when his doctor tells him that he's dying of a fatal disease, tries committing suicide in various ways, but—after bungling each attempt—decides that he wants to live as long as possible.

Dom De Luise, Sally Field, Strother Martin, David Steinberg, Joanne Woodward, Norman Fell, Myrna Loy, Kristy McNichol, Pat O'Brien, Robby Benson, Carl Reiner, Louise Letourneau.

Hooper (1978, WB). *d:* Hal Needham; *p:* Hank Moonjean (Burt Reynolds/Lawrence Gordon); *sc:* Thomas Rickman and Bill Kerby—*b/o* a story by Walt Green and Walter S. Herndon.
SONNY HOOPER: World's best Hollywood movie stuntman—on top for twenty years—who insists on doing one last big stunt before retiring: a 450-foot jump in a jet-powered car over a collapsed bridge.

Jan-Michael Vincent, Sally Field, Brian Keith, John Marley, Robert Klein, James Best, Adam West, Alfie Wise, Terry Bradshaw, Norm Grabowski, George Furth, Jim Burk, Donald "Red" Barry.

Starting Over (1979, Para.). *d:* Alan J. Pakula; *p:* Alan J. Pakula and James L. Brooks; *sc:* James L. Brooks—*b/o* the novel by Dan Wakefield.
PHIL POTTER: Newly divorced writer who falls for a spinsterish Boston schoolteacher but has trouble getting over his feelings for his pop-songwriting ex-wife.

Jill Clayburgh, Candice Bergen, Charles Durning, Frances Sternhagen, Austin Pendleton, Mary Kay Place, MacIntyre Dixon, Jay Sanders, Richard Whiting, Alfie Wise, Wallace Shawn, Sturgis Warner.

Rough Cut (1980, Para.). *d:* Donald Siegel; *p:* David Merrick; *sc:* Francis Burns—*b/o* the novel *Touch the Lion's Paw* by Derek Lambert.
JACK RHODES: Retired gentleman jewel thief who falls for an English society woman who—unbeknownst to him—has been set up by Scotland Yard to help him pull a $30 million diamond heist so that the Yard can snare him.

Lesley-Anne Down, David Niven, Timothy West, Patrick Magee, Al Matthews, Susan Littler, Joss Ackland, Isobel Dean, Wolf Kahler, Ronald Hines, David Howey, Frank Mills, Roland Culver.

Smokey and the Bandit II (1980, Univ.). *d:* Hal Needham; *p:* Hank Moonjean; *sc:* Jerry Belson and Brock Yates—*b/o* a story by Michael Kane.
BANDIT: Hell-raising, drag-racing trucker who, along with his sidekick, is offered $400,000 to transport a pregnant elephant named Charlotte from Miami to Dallas.

Jackie Gleason, Jerry Reed, Dom De Luise, Sally Field, Paul Williams, Pat McCormick, David Huddleston, Mike Henry, John Anderson, Brenda Lee, The Statler Brothers, Mel Tillis.

The Cannonball Run (1981, 20th-Fox). *d:* Hal Needham; *p:* Raymond Chow and Albert S. Ruddy (Golden Harvest); *sc:* Brock Yates.
J. J. McCLURE: Free-wheeling car lover whose strategy to win a cross-country race from Connecticut to California (which allows any type of vehicle and any route) is to team up with a zany auto mechanic and a pretty ecologist and drive an ambulance.

Roger Moore, Farrah Fawcett, Dom De Luise, Dean Martin, Sammy Davis Jr., Jack Elam, Rick Aviles, Adrienne Barbeau, Warren Berlinger, Terry Bradshaw, Bert Convy, Jamie Farr, Peter Fonda, Bianca Jagger, Mel Tillis, Pat Henry, Jimmy "The Greek" Snyder, Alfie Wise.

Paternity (1981, Para.). *d:* David Steinberg; *p:* Jerry Tokofsky, Lawrence Gordon, and Hank Moonjean; *sc:* Charlie Peters.
BUDDY EVANS: Successful forty-four-year-old manager of New York's Madison Square Garden who, when he decides that he wants a child but not a wife, hires a waitress–music student to be a surrogate mother.

Beverly D'Angelo, Norman Fell, Paul Dooley, Elizabeth Ashley, Lauren Hutton, Juanita Moore, Peter Billingsley, Jacqueline Brookes, Linda Gillin, Mike Kellin, Victoria Young, Tony Di Benedetto.

Sharky's Machine (1982, WB). *d:* Burt Reynolds; *p:* Burt Reynolds and Hank Moonjean (Orion/Deliverance); *sc:* Gerald Di Pego—*b/o* the novel by William Diehl.
SHARKY: Atlanta cop who investigates the attempted murder of a beautiful $1000-a-night hooker and—while falling in love with her—discovers that she's been involved with a sadistic underworld czar and a corrupt politician.

Vittorio Gassman, Brian Keith, Charles Durning, Earl Holliman, Henry Silva, Bernie Casey, Richard Libertini, Rachel Ward, Darryl Hickman, Joseph Mascolo.

The Best Little Whorehouse in Texas (1982, Univ.). *d:* Colin Higgins; *p:* Thomas L. Miller, Edward K. Milkis, and Robert L. Boyett; *sc:* Larry L. King, Peter Masterson, and Colin Higgins—*b/o* the play by Larry L. King and Peter Masterson.

SHERIFF ED EARL DODD: Texas sheriff who, because he's in love with the busty madam of a bawdy house known as the Chicken Ranch, tries to save her business when a flamboyant TV reporter leads a crusade to close it.

Dolly Parton, Dom De Luise, Charles Durning, Jim Nabors, Robert Mandan, Lois Nettleton, Noah Beery, Raleigh Bond, Barry Corbin, Mary Jo Catlett, Howard K. Smith.

Best Friends (1982, WB). *d:* Norman Jewison; *p:* Norman Jewison and Patrick Palmer; *sc:* Valerie Curtin and Barry Levinson.

RICHARD BABSON: Hollywood screenwriter who, after finally marrying his screenwriter live-in of three years, has second thoughts—as does she—when they make an ill-advised trip back East and meet each other's families.

Goldie Hawn, Jessica Tandy, Barnard Hughes, Audra Lindley, Keenan Wynn, Ron Silver.

Stroker Ace (1983, Univ./WB). *d:* Hal Needham; *p:* Hank Moonjean (Walter Wood Prod.); *sc:* Hugh Wilson and Hal Needham—*b/o* the novel *Stand on It* by William Neely and Robert K. Ottum.

STROKER ACE: Woman-chasing, good-ol'-boy stock car racer from Texas who has a singing mechanic and whose sponsor—a fried-chicken king—makes him dress up in a chicken suit to hype his chain of restaurants.

Ned Beatty, Jim Nabors, Parker Stevenson, Loni Anderson, Cassandra Peterson.

The Man Who Loved Women (1983, Col.). *d:* Blake Edwards; *p:* Blake Edwards and Tony Adams; *sc:* Blake Edwards, Milton Wexler, and Geoffrey Edwards—*b/o* François Truffaut's 1977 film.

DAVID FOWLER: Famed Los Angeles sculptor who, when he seeks help from an attractive psychiatrist because his obsession with making love to beautiful women is adversely affecting both his work and his sexual potency, falls for her too.

Julie Andrews, Kim Basinger, Marilu Henner, Cynthia Sikes, Jennifer Edwards.

• In addition, Burt Reynolds made a cameo/guest appearance in the following feature film: *Smokey and the Bandit, Part 3* (1983, Univ.).

☆ EDWARD G. ROBINSON

Emanuel Goldenberg

b: Dec. 12, 1893, Bucharest, Rumania
d: Jan. 26, 1973, Los Angeles, Cal.

"Mother of Mercy, is this the end of Rico?"

Caesar Enrico "Rico" Bandello (Edward G. Robinson) as he dies in a hail of bullets in *Little Caesar*, 1930.

The Bright Shawl (1923, FN). *d:* John S. Robertson; *sc:* Edmund Goulding—*b/o* the novel by Joseph Hergesheimer.

DOMINGO ESCOBAR: Spanish aristocrat in Spanish-oppressed 1850s Cuba whose son, a Cuban patriot, is killed by a spy.

Richard Barthelmess, Dorothy Gish, Jetta Goudal, William Powell, Mary Astor, Andre de Beranger, Margaret Seddon, Anders Randolf, Luis Alberni, George Humbert.

The Hole in the Wall (1929, Para.). *d:* Robert Florey; *sc:* Pierre Collings—*b/o* the play by Fred Jackson.

"THE FOX": Gangster who falls for a female ex-con who is masquerading as a gypsy fortune teller in order to get revenge on the woman who wrongly sent her to prison.

Claudette Colbert, David Newell, Nelly Savage, Donald Meek, Alan Brooks, Louise Closser Hale, Marcia Kagno, George McQuarrie.

Night Ride (1929, Univ.). *d:* John Robertson; *sc:* Edward T. Lowe Jr.—*b/o* a story by Henry La Cossit.

TONY GAROTTA: Gangland leader who goes gunning for a reporter who's trying to pin a murder rap on him.

Joseph Schildkraut, Barbara Kent, Harry Stubbs, DeWitt Jennings, Ralph Welles, Hal Price, George Ovey.

A Lady to Love (1930, MGM). *d:* Victor Seastrom; *sc:* Sidney Howard—*b/o* his play *They Knew What They Wanted.*

TONY: Aging, crippled Italian grape-vineyard owner in California who sends a marriage proposal by mail to a young San Francisco waitress (who's never seen him) and gets her to marry him.

Vilma Banky, Robert Ames, Richard Carle, Lloyd Ingraham, Anderson Lawler, Gum Chin, Henry Armetta, George Davis.

Outside the Law (1930, Univ.). *d:* Tod Browning; *sc:* Tod Browning and Garrett Fort.

COBRA COLLINS: Gang leader who, when he learns that a rival crook plans to pull a $500,000 bank robbery, tries to cut himself in on the deal.

Mary Nolan, Owen Moore, Edwin Sturgis, John George, Delmar Watson, DeWitt Jennings, Rockliffe Fellowes.

East Is West (1930, Univ.). *d:* Monta Bell; *sc:* Winifred Eaton Reeve and Tom Reed—*b/o* the play by Samuel Shipman and John Hymer.

CHARLIE YONG: Egocentric half-caste Chinese—known as the "Chop Suey King" of San Francisco's Chinatown—who saves a young illegal-immigrant Chinese girl from being deported.

Lupe Velez, Lewis (Lew) Ayres, E. Allyn Warren, Tetsu Komai, Henry Kolker, Mary Forbes, Edgar Norton.

The Widow from Chicago (1930, WB). *d:* Edward Cline; *sc:* Earl Baldwin.

DOMINIC: New York racketeer and nightclub owner who hires a woman who's posing as a Chicago mobster's widow, then discovers that she's really the vengeance-seeking sister of one of his murder victims.

Alice White, Neil Hamilton, Frank McHugh, Lee Shumway, Brooks Benedict, John Elliott, Dorothy Mathews, Ann Cornwall, Harold Goodwin, Robert Homans, Al Hill.

Little Caesar (1931, WB). *d:* Mervyn LeRoy; *sc:* Francis E. Faragoh—*b/o* the novel by W. R. Burnett.

CESARE ENRICO BANDELLO (alias RICO): Small-time power-hungry hood and cold-blooded killer who rises to become the czar of gangland but ends up dying in the gutter after a shoot-out with police.

Douglas Fairbanks Jr., Glenda Farrell, Sidney Blackmer, Thomas Jackson, Ralph Ince, William Collier Jr., Maurice Black, Stanley Fields, George E. Stone.

Smart Money (1931, WB). *d:* Alfred E. Green; *sc:* Kubec Glasmon, John Bright, Lucien Hubbard, and Joseph Jackson—*b/o* Lucien Hubbard and Joseph Jackson's story "The Idol."

NICK (THE BARBER) VENIZELOS: Small-town barber with a penchant for gambling—and a weakness for blondes—who goes to the big city and becomes a successful big-time gambler but finally winds up behind bars.

James Cagney, Evalyn Knapp, Ralf Harolde, Noel Francis, Maurice Black, Boris Karloff, Morgan Wallace, Billy House, Paul Porcasi, Polly Walters, Ben Taggart, John Larkin, Allan Lane, Charles Lane.

Five Star Final (1931, WB). *d:* Mervyn LeRoy; *sc:* Byron Morgan (adaptation by Robert Lord)—*b/o* the play by Louis Weitzenkorn.

JOSEPH RANDALL: Cynical editor of a muck-raking New York tabloid who, after running a story that causes a double suicide, develops a conscience, tells off the publisher, and quits the paper.

H. B. Warner, Marion Marsh, Anthony Bushell, Frances Starr, Ona Munson, George E. Stone, Oscar Apfel, Purnell Pratt, Aline MacMahon, Boris Karloff, Robert Elliott, Gladys Lloyd.

The Hatchet Man (1932, WB). *d:* William A. Wellman; *sc:* J. Grubb Alexander—*b/o* Achmed Abdullah and David Belasco's play *The Honorable Mr. Wong.*

WONG LOW GET: Powerful figure in San Francisco's Chinatown who marries the young Chinese daughter of a friend he was forced to execute—years earlier—when he was the hatchet man of a Chinese secret society.

Loretta Young, Dudley Digges, Leslie Fenton, Edmund Breese, Tully Marshall, Noel N. Madison, J. Carrol Naish, Charles Middleton, Ralph Ince, Willie Fung, Anna Chang.

Two Seconds (1932, WB). *d:* Mervyn LeRoy; *sc:* Harvey Thew—*b/o* the play by Elliott Lester.

JOHN ALLEN: Construction worker who, during the two seconds it takes him to die in the electric chair, recalls the events leading up to his murdering his wife.

Preston Foster, Vivienne Osborne, J. Carrol Naish, Guy Kibbee, Frederick Burton, Edward McWade, Berton Churchill, William Janney, Lew Brice, Luana Walters.

Tiger Shark (1932, WB). *d:* Howard Hawks; *sc:* Wells Root—*b/o* the story "Tuna" by Houston Branch.

MIKE MASCARENA: Hook-handed tuna-boat captain (he lost a hand to a shark while saving his best friend's life) who later finds himself seeking revenge against the best friend when he discovers that his wife and the friend are in love.

Zita Johnson, Richard Arlen, Leila Bennett, Vince Barnett, J. Carrol Naish, William Ricciardi.

Silver Dollar (1932, WB). *d:* Alfred E. Green; *sc:* Carl Erickson and Harvey Thew—*b/o* the biography of H. A. W. Tabor by David Karsner.

YATES MARTIN: Kansas farmer in the 1800s who strikes it rich in Colorado, becomes a silver tycoon and a powerful politician who helps turn Denver from a mining camp into a thriving city, but finally winds up broke and alone.

Bebe Daniels, Aline MacMahon, Jobyna Howland, DeWitt Jennings, Robert Warwick, Russell Simpson, Harry Holman, Charles Middleton, Marjorie Gateson, Wade Boteler.

The Little Giant (1933, WB). *d:* Roy Del Ruth; *p:* Joseph Gershenson; *sc:* Robert Lord and Wilson

Mizner—*b/o* a story by Robert Lord.

JAMES FRANCIS "BUGS" AHEARN: Chicago bear baron who, after his bootlegging racket collapses, heads for California and tries to break into high society.

Helen Vinson, Mary Astor, Kenneth Thompson, Russell Hopton, Donald Dillaway, Berton Churchill, Selmer Jackson, Dewey Robinson, Adrian Morris, Bill Elliott.

I Loved a Woman (1933, WB). *d:* Alfred E. Green; *sc:* Charles Kenyon and Sidney Sutherland—*b/o* the book by David Karsner.

JOHN HAYDEN: Gentle art student who inherits his father's Chicago meat-packing business and becomes a ruthless beef baron but is ruined by his social-climbing wife and the ambitious opera singer he loves.

Kay Francis, Genevieve Tobin, J. Farrell MacDonald, Henry Kolker, Robert Barrat, Robert McWade, Henry O'Neill, E. J. Ratcliffe, Paul Porcasi.

Dark Hazard (1934, WB). *d:* Alfred E. Green; *sc:* Ralph Block and Brown Holmes—*b/o* the novel by William R. Burnett.

JIM "BUCK" TURNER: Born gambler who promises to quit betting when he gets married but finds, to his wife's dismay, that he can't stop—especially after he buys a racing dog named "Dark Hazard."

Genevieve Tobin, Glenda Farrell, Robert Barrat, Hobart Cavanaugh, George Meeker, Henry B. Walthall, Sidney Toler, Emma Dunn, Willard Robertson.

The Man with Two Faces (1934, WB). *d:* Archie Mayo; *sc:* Tom Reed and Niven Busch—*b/o* George S. Kaufman and Alexander Woollcott's play *The Dark Tower.*

DAMON WELLS: Famous New York actor who disguises himself as a mysterious French theatrical producer named Chautard, murders his sister's cruel husband, and gets away with it.

Mary Astor, Ricardo Cortez, Mae Clarke, Louis Calhern, John Eldredge, Arthur Byron, Henry O'Neill, David Landau, Arthur Aylesworth, Virginia Sale, Howard Hickman, Dick Winslow, Wade Boteler, Milton Kibbee, Joseph Crehan.

The Whole Town's Talking (1935, Col.). *d:* John Ford; *p:* Lester Cowan; *sc:* Jo Swerling and Robert Riskin—*b/o* the novel by William R. Burnett.

(Dual role) ARTHUR FERGUSON JONES: Meek hardware clerk who—because he's a look-alike for an escaped convict who is Public Enemy No. 1—gets involved in all sorts of trouble.

KILLER MANNION: Public Enemy No. 1 who breaks out of prison, discovers that there's a meek clerk who's his double, and poses as the clerk to mask his criminal activities.

Jean Arthur, Arthur Hohl, Wallace Ford, Arthur Byron, Donald Meek, Paul Harvey, Edward Brophy, Etienne Girardot, J. Farrell Macdonald, Robert Emmett O'Connor, John Wray, Joseph Sauers (Sawyer), Francis Ford, Lucille Ball.

Barbary Coast (1935, UA). *d:* Howard Hawks; *p:* Samuel Goldwyn (Samuel Goldwyn Prod.); *sc:* Ben Hecht and Charles MacArthur.

LOUIS CHAMALIS: Ruthless criminal boss of the Barbary Coast—during San Francisco's gold-rush days—who loses his gambling-hall-queen companion to a young prospector from the East and is finally done in by vigilantes.

Miriam Hopkins, Joel McCrea, Walter Brennan, Frank Craven, Brian Donlevy, Donald Meek, Harry Carey, J. M. Kerrigan, Wong Chung, Matt McHugh, David Niven, Edward Gargan, Herman Bing, Tom London.

Bullets or Ballots (1936, WB). *d:* William Keighley; *p:* Louis F. Edelman; *sc:* Seton I. Miller—*b/o* a story by Martin Mooney and Seton I. Miller.

JOHNNY BLAKE: Tough New York cop who gets himself kicked off the force as part of the police commissioner's plan for him to infiltrate a city-wide crime ring.

Joan Blondell, Barton MacLane, Humphrey Bogart, Frank McHugh, Richard Purcell, George E. Stone, Louise Beavers, Joseph Crehan, Henry O'Neill, Henry Kolker, Herbert Rawlinson, Frank Faylen.

Thunder in the City (1937, Col.). *d:* Marion Gering; *p:* Alexander Esway; *sc:* Robert Sherwood and Aben Kandel.

DAN ARMSTRONG: High-pressure American salesman who—when his conservative company sends him to London to learn the British soft-sell approach—helps a financially-strapped duke make some money and winds up marrying the duke's daughter.

Luli Deste, Nigel Bruce, Constance Collier, Ralph Richardson, Annie Esmond, Arthur Wontner, Cyril Raymond, Elliott Nugent, Roland Drew.

Kid Galahad (1937, WB). *d:* Michael Curtiz; *p:* Samuel Bischoff; *sc:* Seton I. Miller—*b/o* the novel by Francis Wallace.

NICK DONATI: Prize-fight manager who develops a naïve ex-bellboy into a championship contender but turns against him when the fighter falls for the manager's young sister.

Bette Davis, Humphrey Bogart, Wayne Morris, Jane Bryan, Harry Carey, Ben Welden, Joseph Crehan, Veda Ann Borg, Frank Faylen, Joyce Compton, Horace MacMahon, John Shelton.

The Last Gangster (1937, MGM). *d:* Edward Ludwig; *sc:* John Lee Mahin—*b/o* a story by William A. Wellman and Robert Carson.

JOE KROZAC: Aging former big-shot gangleader—released from Alcatraz after ten years—who finds that the world has changed when he makes a futile fight to regain his power, his ex-wife (now married to a newspaper editor), and his young son.

James Stewart, Rose Stradner, Lionel Stander, John Carradine, Sidney Blackmer, Edward Brophy, Alan Baxter, Grant Mitchell, Frank Conroy, Moroni Olson, Louise Beavers, Donald Barry, Horace MacMahon, Phillip Terry.

A Slight Case of Murder (1938, WB). *d:* Lloyd Bacon; *p:* Hal B. Wallis; *sc:* Earl Baldwin and Joseph Schrank—*b/o* the play by Damon Runyon and Howard Lindsay.

REMY MARCO: Big-shot beer baron and racketeer who—when the repeal of Prohibition ruins his bootlegging activities and he decides to go legit—finds that he's become the target of his former associates.

Jane Bryan, Willard Parker, Ruth Donnelly, Allen Jenkins, John Litel, Harold Huber, Edward Brophy, Paul Harvey, Bobby Jordan, Margaret Hamilton, George E. Stone, Betty Compson, Bert Roach.

The Amazing Dr. Clitterhouse (1938, WB). *d:* Anatole Litvak; *p:* Robert Lord; *sc:* John Wexley and John Huston—*b/o* the play by Barre Lyndon.

DR. CLITTERHOUSE: Prominent psychologist who, in order to study the criminal mind, joins a gang of safecrackers—and finds himself starting to like being a crook.

Claire Trevor, Humphrey Bogart, Allen Jenkins, Donald Crisp, Gale Page, Henry O'Neill, John Litel, Thurston Hall, Maxie Rosenbloom, Bert Hanlon, Curt Bois, Ward Bond, Vladimir Sokoloff, Irving Bacon.

I Am the Law (1938, Col.). *d:* Alexander Hall; *p:* Everett Riskin; *sc:* Jo Swerling—*b/o* magazine articles by Fred Allhoff.

JOHN LINDSAY: College law professor who, at the request of a civic leader, agrees to become a special prosecutor to help clean up the rackets that are running rampant in his city.

Barbara O'Neil, John Beal, Wendy Barrie, Otto Kruger, Marc Lawrence, Robert Middlemass, Charles Halton, Louis Jean Heydt, Emory Parnell, Theodore Von Eltz, Horace MacMahon, Lucien Littlefield, James Flavin.

Confessions of a Nazi Spy (1939, WB). *d:* Anatole Litvak; *p:* Robert Lord; *sc:* Milton Krims and John Wexley—*b/o* Leon G. Turrou's book *The Nazi Spy Conspiracy in America*.

ED RENARD: G-man who is assigned to investigate and break up a Nazi spy network in the U.S. just prior to the outbreak of WWII.

Francis Lederer, George Sanders, Paul Lukas, Henry O'Neill, Lya Lys, James Stephenson, Sig Rumann, Joe Sawyer, Ward Bond, Charles Trowbridge, John Ridgely, Selmer Jackson.

Blackmail (1939, MGM). *d:* H. C. Potter; *p:* John Considine Jr.; *sc:* David Hertz and William Ludwig—*b/o* the story by Endre Bohem and Dorothy Yost.

JOHN INGRAM: Innocent man who is sent to a chain gang, then escapes and becomes a successful oilwell firefighter but is blackmailed by the real criminal.

Ruth Hussey, Gene Lockhart, Bobs Watson, Guinn Williams, John Wray, Arthur Hohl, Esther Dale, Joseph Crehan, Victor Kilian, Willie Best, Robert Middlemass, Hal K. Dawson, Charles Middleton, Cy Kendall, Wade Boteler.

Dr. Erlich's Magic Bullet (1940, WB). *d:* William Dieterle; *p:* Hal B. Wallis and Wolfgang Reinhardt; *sc:* John Huston, Heinz Herald, and Norman Burnside—*b/o* a story by Norman Burnside.

DR. PAUL ERLICH: Famous nineteenth-century German microbe hunter who develops a formula called "606," the first cure for syphilis.

Ruth Gordon, Otto Kruger, Donald Crisp, Sig Rumann, Maria Ouspenskaya, Henry O'Neill, Harry Davenport, Montagu Love, Albert Basserman, Louis Jean Heydt, Donald Meek, Irving Bacon, Charles Halton, Louis Calhern, Paul Harvey.

Brother Orchid (1940, WB). *d:* Lloyd Bacon; *p:* Hal B. Wallis; *sc:* Earl Baldwin—*b/o* the *Collier's* magazine story by Richard Connell.

LITTLE JOHN SARTO: Former big-time racketeer who—when he's taken for a ride by his old gang—escapes and hides in a monastery, dons a monk's robe, and becomes a flower grower.

Ann Sothern, Humphrey Bogart, Donald Crisp, Ralph Bellamy, Allen Jenkins, Charles D. Brown, Cecil Kellaway, Richard Lane, Paul Guilfoyle, John Ridgely, Tom Tyler, Dick Wessel, Granville Bates, Tim Ryan.

A Dispatch from Reuters (1940, WB). *d:* William Dieterle; *p:* Hal B. Wallis; *sc:* Milton Krims—*b/o* a story by Valentine Williams and Wolfgang Wilhelm.

JULIUS REUTER: Owner of a carrier-pigeon message service in the 1830s who goes on to become, in 1858, the founder of Europe's first news service—the world-famous Reuters English news-gathering agency.

Edna Best, Eddie Albert, Albert Basserman, Nigel Bruce, Gene Lockhart, Montagu Love, Otto Kruger, James Stephenson, Walter Kingsford, David Bruce, Dickie Moore, Gilbert Emery, Robert Warwick, Pat O'Malley.

The Sea Wolf (1941, WB). *d:* Michael Curtiz; *p:* Henry Blanke; *sc:* Robert Rossen—*b/o* the novel by Jack London.

WOLF LARSEN: Sadistic, psychopathic sea captain of an eerie ship called the *Ghost* who likes to torment his crew, as well as two shipwreck survivors he's taken aboard and is holding captive.

John Garfield, Ida Lupino, Alexander Knox, Gene Lockhart, Barry Fitzgerald, Stanley Ridges, Francis McDonald, David Bruce, Howard da Silva, Frank Lackteen, Cliff Clark, Ernie Adams.

Manpower (1941, WB). *d:* Raoul Walsh; *p:* Mark Hellinger; *sc:* Richard Macaulay and Jerry Wald.

HANK McHENRY: High-tension lineman whose marriage to a clip-joint hostess leads to a clash with his linesman buddy, the one his wife really loves.

Marlene Dietrich, George Raft, Alan Hale, Frank McHugh, Eve Arden, Barton MacLane, Walter Catlett, Joyce Compton, Ward Bond, Cliff Clark, Ben Welden, Barbara Pepper, Faye Emerson.

Unholy Partners (1941, MGM). *d:* Mervyn LeRoy; *p:* Samuel Marx; *sc:* Earl Baldwin, Bartlett Cormack, and Lesser Samuels.

BRUCE COREY: Ex–WWI war correspondent in the Roaring '20s who, in order to become a tabloid editor, is forced to accept a rich racketeer as his partner but then decides to expose him in their own paper.

Laraine Day, Edward Arnold, Marsha Hunt, William T. Orr, Don Beddoe, Charles Dingle, Walter Kingsford, Charles Halton, Frank Faylen, William Benedict, Charles B. Smith, Emory Parnell, Jay Novello.

Larceny, Inc. (1942, WB). *d:* Lloyd Bacon; *p:* Hal B. Wallis; *sc:* Everett Freeman and Edwin Gilbert—*b/o* Laura Perelman and S. J. Perelman's play *The Night Before Christmas.*

PRESSURE MAXWELL: Small-time hood who, after being paroled from Sing Sing, intends to go straight—but winds up buying a luggage shop next to a bank so that he can dig a tunnel from the store's basement into the bank's vault.

Jane Wyman, Broderick Crawford, Jack Carson, Anthony Quinn, Edward Brophy, Harry Davenport, John Qualen, Grant Mitchell, Jack C. (Jackie) Gleason, Fortunio Bonanova, Andrew Tombes, Joseph Crehan, James Flavin, Charles Drake.

Tales of Manhattan (1942, 20th-Fox). *d:* Julien Duvivier; *p:* Boris Morros and S. P. Eagle (Sam Spiegel); *Original stories/sc:* Ben Hecht, Ferenc Molnar, Donald Ogden Stewart, Samuel Hoffenstein, Alan Campbell, Ladislas Fodor, Laslo Vadnay, Laszlo Gorog, Lamar Trotti, and Henry Blankfort.

BROWNE: Down-and-out lawyer in the Bowery who, when he's given a moth-eaten tail coat, wears it to his twenty-fifth-anniversary college dinner at the Waldorf Astoria.

Charles Boyer, Rita Hayworth, Thomas Mitchell, Ginger Rogers, Henry Fonda, Cesar Romero, Gail Patrick, Charles Laughton, Elsa Lanchester, George Sanders, James Gleason, Paul Robeson, Ethel Waters, Rochester (Eddie Anderson).

Destroyer (1943, Col.). *d:* William A. Seiter; *p:* Louis F. Edelman; *sc:* Frank Wead, Lewis Melzer, and Borden Chase—*b/o* a story by Frank Wead.

STEVE BOLESLAVSKI: Aging U.S. Navy veteran who—after rejoining the Navy as a petty officer on a WWII destroyer—clashes with a younger petty officer and rubs the crew the wrong way but winds up a hero during a sea battle with the Japanese.

Glenn Ford, Marguerite Chapman, Edgar Buchanan, Leo Gorcey, Regis Toomey, Ed Brophy, Pierre Watkin, Bobby Jordan, Virginia Sale, Addison Richards, Larry Parks, Lloyd Bridges, Charles McGraw.

Flesh and Fantasy (1943, Univ.). *d:* Julien Duvivier; *p:* Charles Boyer and Julien Duvivier; *sc:* Ernest Pascal, Samuel Hoffenstein, and Ellis St. Joseph—*b/o* the story "Lord Arthur Saville's Crime" by Oscar Wilde, and stories by Laslo Vadnay and Ellis St. Joseph.

MARSHALL TYLER: Rich lawyer in London who, when he's told by a fortune teller that he will commit a murder in the near future, fulfills the prediction by strangling the fortune teller.

Charles Boyer, Barbara Stanwyck, Betty Field, Robert Cummings, Thomas Mitchell, Charles Winninger, Anna Lee, Dame May Whitty, C. Aubrey Smith, Robert Benchley, June Lang, Peter Lawford.

Tampico (1944, 20th-Fox). *d:* Lothar Mendes; *p:* Robert Bassler; *sc:* Kenneth Gamet, Fred Niblo Jr., and Richard Macaulay—*b/o* a story by Ladislas Fodor.

CAPT. BART MANSON: WWII merchant-marine skipper who, when his tanker is torpedoed, suspects his newlywed wife of being a member of an Axis spy ring that preys on Allied tankers.

Lynn Bari, Victor McLaglen, Robert Bailey, Marc Lawrence, Mona Maris, Roy Roberts, Charles Lang, Ralph Byrd, Nestor Paiva, Antonio Moreno, Chris-Pin Martin, Trevor Bardette.

Mr. Winkle Goes to War (1944, Col.). *d:* Alfred E. Green; *p:* Jack Moss; *sc:* Waldo Salt, George Corey, and Louis Solomon—*b/o* the novel by Theodore Pratt.

WILBERT WINKLE: Meek, henpecked forty-four-year-old bank clerk who is drafted into the U.S.

Army during the early part of WWII and winds up a hero in the South Pacific.

Ruth Warrick, Ted Donaldson, Bob Haymes, Richard Lane, Robert Armstrong, Walter Baldwin, Art Smith, Ann Shoemaker, Jeff Donnell, Howard Freeman, James Flavin, Bob Mitchum, Hugh Beaumont.

Double Indemnity (1944, Para.). *d:* Billy Wilder; *p:* Joseph Sistrom; *sc:* Billy Wilder and Raymond Chandler—*b/o* the novel by James M. Cain.

BARTON KEYES: Insurance-company sleuth who suspects that the accidental death of a client with a double-indemnity insurance policy was really a case of murder by the man's wife and a fall-guy insurance man in love with her.

Fred MacMurray, Barbara Stanwyck, Porter Hall, Jean Heather, Tom Powers, Byron Barr (Gig Young), Richard Gaines, Fortunio Bonanova, Bess Flowers, Edmund Cobb, Clarence Muse.

The Woman in the Window (1945, RKO). *d:* Fritz Lang; *p:* Nunnally Johnson; *sc:* Nunnally Johnson—*b/o* the novel *Once Off Guard* by J. H. Wallis.

PROF. RICHARD WANLEY: Respectable psychology professor who, when his family goes on vacation, becomes involved with a beautiful woman and is forced to kill her famous financier lover in self-defense.

Raymond Massey, Joan Bennett, Edmond Breon, Dan Duryea, Dorothy Peterson, Spanky MacFarland, Arthur Space, Thomas E. Jackson, Arthur Loft, Bobbie Blake.

Our Vines Have Tender Grapes (1945, MGM). *d:* Roy Rowland; *p:* Robert Sisk; *sc:* Dalton Trumbo—*b/o* the novel *For Our Vines Have Tender Grapes* by George Victor Martin.

MARTINIUS JACOBSON: Kindly, understanding farmer who, with his wife and seven-year-old daughter, experiences the ups and downs of life in a small Norwegian community in southern Wisconsin.

Margaret O'Brien, James Craig, Agnes Moorehead, Jackie "Butch" Jenkins, Morris Carnovsky, Francis Gifford, Sara Haden, Louis Jean Heydt, Arthur Space, Charles Middleton, Arthur Hohl.

Scarlet Street (1946, Univ.). *d:* Fritz Lang; *p:* Walter Wanger (Diana); *sc:* Dudley Nichols—*b/o* the novel and play *La Chienne* by George de la Fouchardiere.

CHRISTOPHER CROSS: New York clothing-company cashier and amateur painter who gets involved with a crook's no-good girlfriend, murders her, and lets the crook—wrongly convicted of the murder—die in the electric chair.

Joan Bennett, Dan Duryea, Jess Barker, Margaret

Lindsay, Samuel S. Hinds, Vladimir Sokoloff, Russell Hicks, Cyrus W. Kendall, Edgar Dearing, Tom Daly, Clarence Muse, Will Wright, Syd Saylor, Dewey Robinson, Fritz Leiber.

Journey Together (1946, English Films). *d:* John Boulting; *p:* John Boulting—*b/o* a story by Terence Rattigan.

DEAN McWILLIAMS: Tough but understanding American flying instructor who trains WWII British RAF flyers at an American base in Arizona.

Sgt. Richard Attenborough, Aircraftsman Jack Watling, Flying Officer David Tomlison, Warrant Officer Sid Rider, Squadron Leader Stuart Latham, Patrick Waddington, Bessie Love.

The Stranger (1946, RKO). *d:* Orson Welles; *p:* S. P. Eagle (Sam Spiegel); *sc:* Anthony Veiller, John Huston, and Orson Welles—*b/o* a story by Victor Trivas and Decia Dunning.

WILSON: U.S. federal agent for the War Crimes Commission who tracks down an escaped Nazi war criminal who is living in a Connecticut college town as a respected professor.

Loretta Young, Orson Welles, Philip Merivale, Richard Long, Byron Keith, Billy House, Konstantin Shayne, Martha Wentworth, Isabel O'Madigan, Pietro Sasso.

The Red House (1947, UA). *d:* Delmer Daves; *p:* Sol Lesser (Sol Lesser Prod.); *sc:* Delmer Daves—*b/o* the novel by George Agnew Chamberlain.

PETE MORGAN: Moody, crippled farmer who harbors a grisly secret concerning the sinister red house in the woods near his farm—that years before, he murdered two people there.

Lon McCallister, Judith Anderson, Allene Roberts, Julie London, Rory Calhoun, Ona Munson, Harry Shannon, Arthur Space, Walter Sande, Pat Flaherty.

All My Sons (1948, Univ.). *d:* Irving Reis; *p:* Chester Erskine; *sc:* Chester Erskine—*b/o* the play by Arthur Miller.

JOE KELLER: Wealthy small-town manufacturer whose son is shattered when he learns that the father was guilty of selling defective airplane parts to the U.S. Army Air Force, which resulted in the death of several American WWII pilots.

Burt Lancaster, Mady Christians, Louisa Horton, Howard Duff, Frank Conroy, Lloyd Gough, Arlene Francis, Henry (Harry) Morgan, Charles Meredith, Elizabeth Fraser, Herbert Vigran, Harry Harvey.

Key Largo (1948, WB). *d:* John Huston; *p:* Jerry Wald; *sc:* Richard Brooks and John Huston—*b/o* the play by Maxwell Anderson.

JOHNNY ROCCO: Cruel gangster who takes over

a run-down hotel on a Florida key during a rough storm and holds several people captive.

Humphrey Bogart, Lauren Bacall, Lionel Barrymore, Claire Trevor, Thomas Gomez, Harry Lewis, John Rodney, Marc Lawrence, Dan Seymour, Monte Blue, William Haade, Jay Silverheels, Rodric Redwing.

Night Has a Thousand Eyes (1948, Para.). *d:* John Farrow; *p:* Endre Bohem; *sc:* Barry Lyndon and Jonathan Latimer—*b/o* the novel by Cornell Woolrich.

JOHN TRITON: Ex-vaudeville magician who discovers that he has the uncanny power to predict tragic events that will occur in the future—including his own death.

Gail Russell, John Lund, Virginia Bruce, William Demarest, Richard Webb, Jerome Cowan, Onslow Stevens, John Alexander, Louis Van Rooten, William Haade.

House of Strangers (1949, 20th-Fox). *d:* Joseph L. Mankiewicz; *p:* Sol C. Siegel; *sc:* Philip Yordan—*b/o* the novel by Jerome Weidman.

GINO MONETTI: Ruthless Italian-American financier in New York's "Little Italy" who, before he dies, asks his one loyal son to seek revenge against the other three sons, who stole the father's business.

Susan Hayward, Richard Conte, Luther Adler, Paul Valentine, Efrem Zimbalist Jr., Debra Paget, Hope Emerson, Esther Minciotti, Sid Tomack, Thomas Browne Henry, Herbert Vigran, Mushy Callahan.

My Daughter Joy [U.S. title: ***Operation X***] (1950, Col.). *d:* Gregory Ratoff; *p:* Gregory Ratoff and Phil Brandon; *sc:* Robert Thoeren and William Rose—*b/o* the novel *David Golder* by Irene Nemirowsky.

GEORGE CONSTANTIN: Ruthless, power-hungry Greek millionaire who, as part of his secret plan to rule the world (known as Operation X), intends to pressure his daughter into marrying the son of an African sultan.

Nora Swinburne, Peggy Cummins, Richard Greene, Finlay Currie, Gregory Ratoff, Ronald Adam, Walter Rilla, James Robertson Justice.

Actors and Sin (1952, UA). *d:* Ben Hecht and Lee Garmes; *p:* Ben Hecht; *sc:* Ben Hecht.

MAURICE TILLAYOU: Has-been Shakespearean actor and devoted father who—when his neurotic, fading-Broadway-star daughter commits suicide—tries to cover up her failure by making her death look like murder.

Marsha Hunt, Dan O'Herlihy, Rudolph Anders, Alice Key, Rick Roman, Eddie Albert, Alan Reed, Tracy Roberts, Paul Guilfoyle, Jody Gilbert.

Vice Squad (1953, UA). *d:* Arnold Laven; *p:* Jules

Levy and Arthur Gardner (Levy–Gardner); *sc:* Lawrence Roman—*b/o* the novel *Harness Bull* by Leslie T. White.

CAPTAIN BARNABY: Tough big-city captain of detectives who, with the help of a woman who owns a female escort service, tracks down two cop-killer bank robbers.

Paulette Goddard, K. T. Stevens, Porter Hall, Adam Williams, Edward Binns, Lee Van Cleef, Jay Adler, Joan Vohs, Dan Riss, Mary Ellen Kay.

Big Leaguer (1953, MGM). *d:* Robert Aldrich; *p:* Matthew Rapf; *sc:* Herbert Baker—*b/o* a story by John McNulty and Louis Morheim.

JOHN B. "HANS" LOBERT: Aging baseball player who becomes the head of the New York Giants' training camp in Florida and devotes himself to coaching a group of young rookies.

Vera-Ellen, Jeff Richards, Richard Jaeckel, William Campbell, Carl Hubbell, Paul Langton, Lalo Rios, Bill Crandall, Frank Ferguson, Robert Caldwell.

The Glass Web (1953, Univ.). *d:* Jack Arnold; *p:* Albert J. Cohen; *sc:* Robert Blees and Leonard Lee—*b/o* the novel by Max S. Ehrlich.

HENRY HAYES: Crime researcher for a weekly TV crime program who murders a blackmailing actress, then—when the unsolved case is used as the basis for one of the shows—tries to frame the scriptwriter.

John Forsythe, Marcia Henderson, Kathleen Hughes, Richard Denning, Hugh Sanders, Jack Kelly, Kathleen Freeman, Beverly Garland, Benny Rubin.

Black Tuesday (1954, UA). *d:* Hugo Fregonese; *p:* Robert Goldstein (Leonard Goldstein); *sc:* Sydney Boehm.

VINCENT CANELLI: Death-row convict who escapes and holds a group of people hostage while he tries to lay his hands on the stashed-away loot from a bank robbery.

Peter Graves, Jean Parker, Milburn Stone, Warren Stevens, Jack Kelly, Sylvia Findley, James Bell, Victor Perrin.

The Violent Men (1955, Col.). *d:* Rudolph Mate; *p:* Lewis J. Rackmil; *sc:* Harry Kleiner—*b/o* the novel by Donald Hamilton.

LEW WILKISON: Ruthless, crippled cattle baron who, while his grasping wife has an affair with his younger brother, tries to drive out the small ranchers and farmers from his valley.

Glenn Ford, Barbara Stanwyck, Dianne Foster, Brian Keith, May Wynn, Warner Anderson, Richard Jaeckel, Basil Ruysdael, James Westerfield, Jack Kelly, Willis Bouchey, Peter Hanson, Don C. Harvey.

Tight Spot (1955, Col.). *d:* Phil Karlson; *p:* Lewis J. Rachmil; *sc:* William Bowers—*b/o* the play *Dead Pigeon* by Lenard Kantor.

LLOYD HALLETT: U.S. Attorney who uses a big-time gangster's former moll as a decoy in order to trap the gangster and his crooked cop accomplice.

Ginger Rogers, Brian Keith, Lucy Marlow, Lorne Greene, Katherine Anderson, Allen Nourse, Peter Leeds, Doye O'Dell, Eve McVeagh, Helen Wallace, Frank Gerstle.

A Bullet for Joey (1955, UA). *d:* Lewis Allen; *p:* Samuel Bischoff and David Diamond; *sc:* Geoffrey Homes and A. I. Bezzerides—*b/o* a story by James Benson.

INSPECTOR RAOUL LEDUC: Canadian police inspector who battles an ex-gangster hired by Communist agents to kidnap a nuclear scientist.

George Raft, Audrey Totter, George Dolenz, Peter Hanson, Peter Van Eyck, Ralph Smiley, Joseph Vitale, Sally Blane, Bill Henry.

Illegal (1955, WB). *d:* Lewis Allen; *p:* Frank P. Rosenberg; *sc:* W. R. Burnett and James R. Webb—*b/o* Frank J. Collins's play *The Mouthpiece.*

VICTOR SCOTT: District attorney who—when he sends an innocent man to the electric chair—resigns and becomes a racketeer's lawyer, but then turns on him to save his ex-secretary from a murder rap.

Nina Foch, Hugh Marlowe, Robert Ellenstein, DeForest Kelly, Jay Adler, Edward Platt, Albert Dekker, Ellen Corby, Jayne Mansfield, Addison Richards, Howard St. John, Lawrence Dobkin, Jonathan Hale, Julie Bennett, Herb Vigran.

Hell on Frisco Bay (1956, WB). *d:* Frank Tuttle; *p:* George Bertholon; *sc:* Sydney Boehm and Martin Rackin—*b/o* a novel by William P. McGivern.

VICTOR AMATO: Big-shot gangster boss of the San Francisco docks who clashes with a hardboiled waterfront cop who's out of prison after being framed by the gangster.

Alan Ladd, Joanne Dru, William Demarest, Paul Stewart, Fay Wray, Perry Lopez, Nestor Paiva, Willis Bouchey, Peter Hanson, Anthony Caruso, Jayne Mansfield.

Nightmare (1956, UA). *d:* Maxwell Shane; *p:* William Thomas and Howard Pine (Pine–Thomas–Shane); *sc:* Maxwell Shane—*b/o* the novel by Cornell Woolrich.

RENE: New Orleans detective who discovers that his jazz-musician brother-in-law has committed murder under the influence of an evil hypnotist.

Kevin McCarthy, Connie Russell, Virginia Christine, Rhys Williams, Gage Clarke, Barry Atwater, Marian Carr, Billy May.

The Ten Commandments (1956, Para.). *d:* Cecil B. DeMille; *p:* Cecil B. DeMille; *sc:* Aeneas MacKenzie, Jesse L. Lasky Jr., Jack Gariss, and Fredric M. Frank—*b/o* the novels *Prince of Egypt* by Dorothy Clarke Wilson, *Pillar of Fire* by Rev. J. H. Ingraham, *On Eagle's Wings* by Rev. A. E. Southon, in accordance with the Holy Scripture.

DATHAN: Treacherous Hebrew overseer whose betrayal of Moses leads to Moses' being exiled to the desert by the Egyptian Prince Rameses.

Charlton Heston, Yul Brynner, Anne Baxter, Yvonne De Carlo, Debra Paget, John Derek, Sir Cedric Hardwicke, Nina Foch, Martha Scott, Judith Anderson, Vincent Price, John Carradine, H. B. Warner, Henry Wilcoxon, Woodrow Strode, Touch (Mike) Connors, Onslow Stevens, Clint Walker, Frankie Darro, Carl Switzer, Robert Vaughn.

A Hole in the Head (1959, UA). *d:* Frank Capra; *p:* Frank Capra and Frank Sinatra (Sincap); *sc:* Arnold Schulman—*b/o* his play.

TONY MANETTA: Officious New York clothing manufacturer who keeps financially bailing out his irresponsible forty-year-old younger brother, the owner of a run-down hotel in Miami Beach.

Frank Sinatra, Eleanor Parker, Eddie Hodges, Carolyn Jones, Thelma Ritter, Keenan Wynn, Joi Lansing, Jimmy Komack, Dub Taylor, Benny Rubin, Ruby Dandridge, B. S. Pully, Pupi Campo.

Seven Thieves (1960, 20th-Fox). *d:* Henry Hathaway; *p:* Sydney Boehm; *sc:* Sydney Boehm—*b/o* the novel *Lions at the Kill* by Max Catto.

THEO WILKINS: Aging American gangster who, hoping to pull off one last big heist, recruits six accomplices in a daring plot to rob the Monte Carlo gambling casino of four million francs.

Rod Steiger, Joan Collins, Eli Wallach, Michael Dante, Alexander Scourby, Berry Kroeger, Sebastian Cabot, Marcel Hillaire, John Berardino.

My Geisha (1961, Para.). *d:* Jack Cardiff; *p:* Steve Parker (Steve Parker); *sc:* Norman Krasna.

SAM LEWIS: Understanding movie producer who accompanies an American actress friend to Japan, where the actress disguises herself as a geisha and tries to get the lead in a film that her movie-director husband is shooting there.

Shirley MacLaine, Yves Montand, Bob Cummings, Yoko Tani, Tatsuo Saito, Tamae Kyokawa, Ichi Hayakawa, Alex Gerry, Taugundo Maki, Satoko Kuni.

Two Weeks in Another Town (1962, MGM). *d:* Vincente Minnelli; *p:* John Houseman; *sc:* Charles Schnee—*b/o* the novel by Irwin Shaw.

MAURICE KRUGER: Aging, once-great American film director who, while shooting an Italo-American film in Rome, is plagued by his fading ability, production complications, and personal problems.

Kirk Douglas, Cyd Charisse, George Hamilton, Dahlia Lavi, Claire Trevor, James Gregory, Rosanna Schiaffino, George Macready, Mino Doro, Eric Von Stroheim Jr., Leslie Uggams.

The Prize (1963, MGM). *d:* Mark Robson; *p:* Pandro S. Berman (Roxbury); *sc:* Ernest Lehman—*b/o* the novel by Irving Wallace.

(Dual role) DR. MAX STRATMAN: American physicist who goes to Stockholm to receive a Nobel Prize and is kidnapped as part of a Communist plot.

PROF. WALTHER STRATMAN: Traitorous twin brother of Max who, as part of the Communist plot, temporarily takes the kidnapped Max's place. (In reality, Walther is dead and an actor with a mask of Max is impersonating Walther impersonating Max.)

Paul Newman, Elke Sommer, Diane Baker, Micheline Presle, Gerard Oury, Sergio Fantoni, Kevin McCarthy, Leo G. Carroll, Don Dubbins, John Qualen, Karl Swenson, Lester Mathews, John Banner, Jerry Dunphy, Queenie Leonard.

Good Neighbor Sam (1964, Col.). *d:* David Swift; *p:* David Swift (David Swift Prod.); *sc:* James Fritzel, Everett Greenbaum, and David Swift—*b/o* the novel by Jack Finney.

SIMON NURDLINGER: Bible-quoting dairy owner who is a stickler about marital fidelity and so insists that his advertising account be handled by the straightest, most happily married account executive in his company's New York ad agency.

Jack Lemmon, Romy Schneider, Dorothy Provine, Michael (Mike) Connors, Edward Andrews, Louis Nye, Robert Q. Lewis, Joyce Jameson, Anne Seymour, Charles Lane, Tris Coffin, Neil Hamilton, The Hi-Lo's, Bernie Kopell, Dave Ketchum.

Robin and the 7 Hoods (1964, WB). *d:* Gordon Douglas; *p:* Frank Sinatra and Howard W. Koch (P-C Prod.); *sc:* David R. Schwartz.

BIG JIM (unbilled): The Number One mobster in 1928 Chicago, who is rubbed out by his gangland friends when they throw a birthday party for him.

Frank Sinatra, Dean Martin, Sammy Davis Jr., Bing Crosby, Peter Falk, Barbara Rush, Victor Buono, Hank Henry, Allen Jenkins, Jack LaRue, Phil Crosby, Phil Arnold, Hans Conried, Sig Rumann.

The Outrage (1964, MGM). *d:* Martin Ritt; *p:* A. Ronald Lubin (Harvest/February/Ritt/Kayos); *sc:* Michael Kanin—*b/o* the Japanese film *Rashomon;* from stories by Ryunosuke Akutagawa and the play *Rashomon* by Fay Kanin and Michael Kanin.

Billed as "CON MAN": Cynical con man in the nineteenth-century West who, after listening to various conflicting versions of a heinous crime that's been committed, doesn't believe any of them—because he knows that "truth" changes in the eye of the beholder.

Paul Newman, Laurence Harvey, Claire Bloom, William Shatner, Howard da Silva, Albert Salmi, Thomas Chalmers, Paul Fix.

Cheyenne Autumn (1964, WB). *d:* John Ford; *p:* Bernard Smith (Ford–Smith); *sc:* James R. Webb—*b/o* the novel by Mari Sandoz.

CARL SCHURZ: U.S. secretary of the interior in the 1870s who intercedes on behalf of the Cheyenne Indians to help them get from their Oklahoma reservation back to their old homeland in Wyoming.

Richard Widmark, Carroll Baker, Karl Malden, James Stewart, Sal Mineo, Dolores Del Rio, Ricardo Montalban, Gilbert Roland, Arthur Kennedy, Patrick Wayne, John Carradine, Victor Jory, Mike Mazurki, George O'Brien, Ben Johnson, Denver Pyle.

A Boy Ten Feet Tall (1965, Para.). *d:* Alexander Mackendrick; *p:* Hal Mason (Seven Arts–Bryanston); *sc:* Denis Cannan—*b/o* the novel *Sammy Going South* by W. H. Canaway.

COCKY WAINWRIGHT: Grizzled, warm-hearted diamond smuggler and big-game hunter who befriends a ten-year-old orphan boy who's traveling alone through Africa on a 5000-mile journey from Port Said to reach his aunt in Durban, South Africa.

Fergus McClelland, Constance Cummings, Harry H. Corbett, Paul Stassino, Zia Mohyeddin, Orlando Martins, John Turner, Zena Walker.

The Cincinnati Kid (1965, MGM). *d:* Norman Jewison; *p:* Martin Ransohoff and John Calley (Filmways); *sc:* Ring Lardner Jr. and Terry Southern—*b/o* the novel by Richard Jessup.

LANCEY HOWARD: Aging but suave and shrewd stud-poker champ in 1930s New Orleans who is challenged to a game by the Cincinnati Kid, a young itinerant card shark ready for the big time.

Steve McQueen, Ann-Margret, Karl Malden, Tuesday Weld, Joan Blondell, Rip Torn, Jack Weston, Cab Calloway, Jeff Corey, Karl Swenson, Ron Soble, Midge Ware, Dub Taylor, Olan Soule, Andy Albin.

The Blonde from Peking (1968, Para.). *d:* Nicolas Gessner; *sc:* Nicolas Gessner and Mark Behm (adaptation by Jacques Vilfrid)—*b/o* the novel by James Hadley Chase.

DOUGLAS: American C.I.A. chief who, along with Chinese and Russian agents, is after some errant Red Chinese missile data, a pretty blonde from Peking, and a priceless jewel called the Blue Grape Pearl.

Mireille Darc, Claudio Brook, Pascale Roberts, Françoise Brion, Joe Warfield, Giorgia Moll, Karl Studer, Tiny Young.

The Biggest Bundle of Them All (1968, MGM). *d:* Ken Annakin; *p:* Joseph Shaftel and Sy Stewart; *sc:* Sy Salkowitz—*b/o* a story by Joseph Shaftel.

PROFESSOR SAMUELS: Aging mastermind who is recruited to blueprint a $5 million platinum robbery in Italy by a deported American gangster and his inept gang of amateur criminals.

Robert Wagner, Raquel Welch, Godfrey Cambridge, Vittorio De Sica, Davy Kaye, Francesco Mule, Victor Spinetti, Yvonne Sanson, Mickey Knox, Femi Benussi, Carlo Croccolo.

Grand Slam (1968, Para.). *d:* Giuliano Montaldo; *p:* Harry Colombo and George Papi; *sc:* Mino Roli, Caminito, Marcello Fondato, Antonio De La Loma, and Marcello Coscia.

PROF. JAMES ANDERS: Mild-mannered retired schoolteacher in Rio de Janeiro who recruits a quartet of crooks to help him steal $10 million in diamonds and emeralds from a jewelry company near his former school.

Janet Leigh, Adolph Celi, Klaus Kinski, George Rigaud, Robert Hoffman, Riccardo Cucciolla, Jussara, Miguel Del Castillo.

It's Your Move [in U.S., shown only on TV] (1968, Kinesis Films). *d:* Robert Fiz; *p:* Franco Porro; *sc:* Robert Fiz, Massimilliano Capriccoli, Ennio De Concini, Jose G. Maesso, Leonardo Martin, and Juan Cesarabea.

MacDOWELL: Retired Englishman on the island of Majorca who plans a wild and complicated bank heist using look-alikes for four bank officials.

Terry-Thomas, Maria Grazia Buccella, Adolfo Celi, Manuel Zarzo, Jorge Rigaud, Rosella Como.

Operation St. Peter's (1968, Para.). *d:* Lucio Fulci; *p:* Turi Vasile; *sc:* Ennio De Concini, Adriano Baracco, Roberto Giovannini, and Lucio Fulci.

JOE VENTURA: Former big-time American gangster who, after some small-time crooks steal Michelangelo's famed sculpture The Pieta (worth $30 billion), buys it from them for $40 (and a large bowl of spaghetti) and plots to sell it back to the Vatican.

Lando Buzzanca, Heinz Ruhmann, Jean-Claude Brialy, Pinuccio Ardia, Dante Maggio, Marie-Christine Barclay, Uta Levka.

Never a Dull Moment (1968, Buena Vista). *d:* Jerry Paris; *p:* Ron Miller (Walt Disney Prod.); *sc:* A. J. Carothers—*b/o* the novel by John Godey.

LEO JOSEPH SMOOTH: Criminal art expert who mistakenly thinks that an actor who's played gangster parts is the hit man he's hired to help him steal a priceless painting from the New York Museum.

Dick Van Dyke, Dorothy Provine, Henry Silva, Joanna Moore, Tony Bill, Slim Pickens, Jack Elam, Ned Glass, Mickey Shaughnessy, Anthony Caruso, Dick Winslow, Jerry Paris.

Mackenna's Gold (1969, Col.). *d:* J. Lee Thompson; *p:* Carl Foreman and Dimitri Tiomkin (Highroad); *sc:* Carl Foreman—*b/o* the novel by Will Henry.

OLD ADAMS: Old blind prospector in the 1870s who goes along with a ruthless gang of bandits and greedy townspeople to search for treasure in the legendary Valley of Gold.

Gregory Peck, Omar Sharif, Telly Savalas, Keenan Wynn, Julie Newmar, Ted Cassidy, Lee J. Cobb, Raymond Massey, Burgess Meredith, Anthony Quayle, Eli Wallach, Eduardo Ciannelli, John Garfield Jr.

Song of Norway (1970, Cinerama). *d:* Andrew L. Stone; *p:* Andrew L. Stone and Virginia Stone (ABC–Stone); *sc:* Andrew L. Stone—suggested by a play by Milton Lazarus, Robert Wright, and George Forrest—from a play by Homer Curran.

KROGSTAD: Kindly old piano dealer in Norway who has dealings with the famous Norwegian composer Edvard Grieg and his wife, Nina.

Toralv Maurstad, Florence Henderson, Christina Schollin, Frank Poretta, Harry Secombe, Robert Morley, Elizabeth Larner, Oscar Homolka, Frederick Jaeger, Henry Gilbert, Richard Wordsworth.

Soylent Green (1973, MGM). *d:* Richard Fleischer; *p:* Walter Seltzer and Russell Thacher; *sc:* Stanley R. Greenberg—*b/o* the novel *Make Room! Make Room!* by Harry Harrison.

SOL ROTH: Disillusioned elderly philosopher in the year 2022 who nostalgically remembers life as it was in the good old days, despairs of living in polluted, overpopulated New York City (40 million people), and chooses legal euthanasia.

Charlton Heston, Leigh Taylor-Young, Chuck Connors, Joseph Cotten, Brock Peters, Paula Kelly, Stephen Young, Mike Henry, Whit Bissell, Jane Dulo, Dick Van Patten, Tim Herbert, Carlos Romero.

• In addition, Edward G. Robinson made cameo/guest appearances in the following feature films: *It's a Great Feeling* (1949, WB) and *Pepe* (1960, Col.).

☆ GINGER ROGERS

Virginia Katherine McMath

b: July 16, 1911, Independence, Mo.

"I guess rich people are only poor people with money."

Mary Gray (Ginger Rogers) in
Fifth Avenue Girl, 1939.

Young Man of Manhattan (1930, Para.). *d:* Monta Bell; *sc:* Robert Presnell—*b/o* a novel by Katherine Brush.
PUFF RANDOLPH: Wisecracking collegiate flapper who has a problem getting her sports-writer boyfriend to concentrate on her instead of on sporting events.
Claudette Colbert, Norman Foster, Charles Ruggles, Leslie Austin, H. Dudley Hawley, Tommy Reilly.

Queen High (1930, Para.). *d:* Fred Newmeyer; *p:* Lawrence Schwab and Frank Mandel; *sc:* Frank Mandel—*b/o* the play *A Pair of Sixes* by Edward H. Peple, adapted from the musical comedy by Lawrence Schwab, Lewis Gensler, and B. G. DeSylva.
POLLY ROCKWELL: Young woman who works for a garter business owned by two bickering partners.
Charles Ruggles, Frank Morgan, Stanley Smith, Helen Carrington, Rudy Cameron, Betty Garde, Nina Olivette, Tom Brown.

The Sap from Syracuse (1930, Para.). *d:* A. Edward Sutherland; *sc:* Gertrude Purcell—*b/o* the play by John Wray, Jack O'Donnell, and John Hayden.
ELLEN SAUNDERS: Young mining heiress on an ocean liner who is saved by an Erie Canal worker (who she mistakenly thinks is a prominent mining engineer) from crooks hired by her greedy guardian to get her out of the way.
Jack Oakie, Granville Bates, George Barbier, Sidney Riggs, Betty Starbuck, Verree Teasdale, J. Malcolm Dunn, Bernard Jukes.

Follow the Leader (1930, Para.). *d:* Norman Taurog; *sc:* Gertrude Purcell and Sid Silvers—*b/o* the play *Manhattan Mary* by William K. Wells, George White, Lew Brown, B. G. DeSylva, and Ray Henderson.
MARY BRENNAN: Young woman who, with the help of a waiter friend, gets her big chance in a show when she is picked to replace the star, who has been kidnapped.
Ed Wynn, Stanley Smith, Lou Holtz, Lida Kane, Ethel Merman, Bobby Watson, Holly Hall, Preston Foster, Jack La Rue, William Gargan.

Honor Among Lovers (1931, Para.). *d:* Dorothy Arzner; *sc:* Austin Parker and Gertrude Purcell—*b/o* a story by Austin Parker.
DORIS BLAKE: Pretty young woman who follows her reporter boyfriend nearly everywhere he goes.
Claudette Colbert, Fredric March, Monroe Owsley, Charles Ruggles, Pat O'Brien, Ralph Morgan, Leonard Carey, Charles Halton, Granville Bates.

The Tip Off (1931, RKO). *d:* Albert Rogell; *p:* Charles H. Rogers; *sc:* Earl Baldwin—*b/o* a story by George Kibbe Turner.
BABY FACE: Wisecracking young woman who, along with her prize-fighter boyfriend, helps an innocent radio technician when he unintentionally runs afoul of a gangster.
Eddie Quillan, Robert Armstrong, Joan Peers, Ralf Harolde, Charles Sellon, Ernie Adams, Frank Darien, Luis Alberni, Swanky Jones.

Suicide Fleet (1931, RKO). *d:* Albert Rogell; *p:* Charles R. Rogers; *sc:* Lew Lipton (with dialogue by F. McGrew Wills)—*b/o* the story "Mystery Ship" by Commander Herbert A. Jones.
SALLY: Perky salt-water-taffy concessionaire on the Coney Island midway during WWI who is romanced by three sailors involved with an American decoy ship that helps sink German subs.
William Boyd, Robert Armstrong, James Gleason, Harry Bannister, Frank Reicher, Ben Alexander, Hans Joby, James Pierce, Tom Keene.

Carnival Boat (1932, RKO). *d:* Albert Rogell; *p:* Harry Joe Brown; *sc:* James Seymour—*b/o* a story by Marion Jackson and Don Ryan.
HONEY: Carnival-boat entertainer who, when she falls for a young lumberjack, causes a falling out between him and his father, who wants the son to eventually take over the father's Northwoods logging camp.
William Boyd, Fred Kohler, Hobart Bosworth, Marie Prevost, Edgar Kennedy, Harry Sweet, Charles Sellon, Walter Percival, Eddie Chandler.

The Tenderfoot (1932, FN). *d:* Ray Enright; *sc:* Arthur Caesar, Monty Banks, and Earl Baldwin—*b/o* the story by Richard Carle, from George S. Kaufman's play *The Butter and Egg Man.*
RUTH: Secretary who, when her theatrical-producer boss tries to swindle a naïve Texas cowboy into investing in a Broadway show, saves the cowboy and falls for him too.
Joe E. Brown, Lew Cody, Vivien Oakland, Robert Greig, Spencer Charters, Ralph Ince, Walter Percival, George Chandler, John Larkin, Allan Lane, Richard Cramer.

The Thirteenth Guest (1932, Mono.). *d:* Albert Ray; *p:* M. H. Hoffman; *sc:* Frances Hyland and Arthur Hoerl (with dialogue by Armitage Trail)—*b/o* the novel by Armitage Trail.

MARIE MORGAN: One of thirteen people who, thirteen years after they were guests at a dinner party where the host mysteriously died, become the target of a murderer who apparently intends to kill them all.

Lyle Talbot, J. Farrell MacDonald, James Eagles, Eddie Phillips, Erville Alderson, Crauford Kent, Paul Hurst, William Davidson, Tom London, Alan Bridge, Tiny Sandford.

Hat Check Girl (1932, Fox). *d:* Sidney Lanfield; *sc:* Philip Klein and Barry Conners—*b/o* the novel by Rian James.

JESSIE KING: Wisecracking hat-check girl who, along with her hat-check girlfriend, gets involved with nightclubbers, bootleggers, blackmailers, and a millionaire playboy.

Sally Eilers, Ben Lyon, Monroe Owsley, Arthur Pierson, Noel Madison, Dewey Robinson, Purnell Pratt, Iris Meredith, Eddie "Rochester" Anderson, Snowflake (Fred Toones), Henry Armetta, Bert Roach, Joyce Compton.

You Said a Mouthful (1932, FN). *d:* Lloyd Bacon; *sc:* Robert Lord and Bolton Mallory—*b/o* a story by William B. Dover.

ALICE BRANDON: Young society woman who falls for a man who she believes is a famous Canadian swimmer, but who turns out to be a shipping clerk who has invented an unsinkable bathing suit.

Joe E. Brown, Preston Foster, Sheila Terry, Farina, Guinn Williams, Harry Gribbon, Oscar Apfel, Edwin Maxwell, Selmer Jackson, Arthur Byron.

Forty-Second Street (1933, WB). *d:* Lloyd Bacon; *p:* Hal B. Wallis; *sc:* James Seymour, Rian James, and Whitney Bolton—*b/o* the novel by Bradford Ropes.

ANN LOWELL: Wisecracking, society-conscious Broadway chorus girl—known as "Anytime Annie"—who affects an English accent, wears a monocle, and carries around a Pekinese.

Warner Baxter, Bebe Daniels, George Brent, Una Merkel, Ruby Keeler, Guy Kibbee, Dick Powell, George E. Stone, Ned Sparks, Allen Jenkins, Henry B. Walthall, Toby Wing, Jack La Rue, Louise Beavers, Dave O'Brien, Patricia Ellis, Charles Lane.

Broadway Bad (1933, Fox). *d:* Sidney Lanfied; *sc:* Arthur Kober and Maude Fulton—*b/o* a story by William Lipman and A. W. Pezet.

FLIP DALY: Good-hearted chorus girl who stands by a chorus-girl pal seeking a divorce and custody of her son.

Joan Blondell, Ricardo Cortez, Adrienne Ames, Allen Vincent, Phil Tead, Francis McDonald, Spencer Charters, Frederick Burton, Margaret Seddon, Donald Crisp, Harold Goodwin.

Gold Diggers of 1933 (1933, WB). *d:* Mervyn LeRoy; *p:* Jack L. Warner; *sc:* Erwin Gelsey and James Seymour (with dialogue by David Boehm and Ben Markson)—*b/o* Avery Hopwood's play *The Gold Diggers.*

FAY FORTUNE: Gold-digging chorus girl—one of several out-of-work actors, singers, and dancers who are helped by a millionaire composer who backs them in a Broadway musical.

Warren William, Joan Blondell, Aline MacMahon, Ruby Keeler, Dick Powell, Guy Kibbee, Ned Sparks, Sterling Holloway, Billy Barty, Snowflake (Fred Toones), Charles Lane, Hobart Cavanaugh.

Professional Sweetheart (1933, RKO). *d:* William A. Seiter; *p:* H. N. Swanson and Merian C. Cooper; *sc:* Maurine Watkins.

GLORY EDEN: Temperamental radio star who, as a publicity stunt, agrees to become engaged to one of her fan-mail correspondents—a hick from Kentucky.

Norman Foster, ZaSu Pitts, Frank McHugh, Allen Jenkins, Gregory Ratoff, Edgar Kennedy, Lucien Littlefield, Franklin Pangborn, Frank Darien, Betty Furness, Sterling Holloway.

A Shriek in the Night (1933, Allied). *d:* Albert Ray; *p:* M. H. Hoffman; *sc:* Frances Hyland—*b/o* a story by Kurt Kempler.

PATRICIA MORGAN: Newspaper reporter who, while trying to outscoop a rival reporter, helps solve a series of murders in an exclusive apartment building.

Lyle Talbot, Arthur Hoyt, Purnell Pratt, Harvey Clark, Lillian Harmer, Maurice Black, Clarence Wilson, Louise Beavers.

Don't Bet on Love (1933, Univ.). *d:* Murray Roth; *p:* Carl Laemmle; *sc:* Murray Roth and Howard Emmett Rogers—*b/o* a story by Murray Roth.

MOLLY GILBERT: Manicurist who loves a plumber who's lucky at the racetrack, then stands by him even though his luck runs out and he almost loses his business.

Lew Ayres, Charles Grapewin, Shirley Grey, Tom Dugan, Robert Emmett O'Connor, Lucille Gleason, Henry Armetta, Brooks Benedict, Eddie Kane, Craig Reynolds.

Sitting Pretty (1933, Para.). *d:* Harry Joe Brown; *p:* Charles R. Rogers; *sc:* Jack McGowan, S. J. Perelman, and Lou Breslow—*b/o* a story by Nina Wilcox Putnam.

DOROTHY: Pretty young lunch-wagon proprietress who joins a pair of eager young male songwriters as they hitchhike from New York to

Hollywood to seek fame and fortune in the movies.

Jack Oakie, Jack Haley, Thelma Todd, Gregory Ratoff, Lew Cody, Harry Revel, Mack Gordon, Hale Hamilton, William B. Davidson, Art Jarrett, Anne Nagel, Irving Bacon, Fuzzy Knight.

Flying Down to Rio (1933, RKO). *d:* Thornton Freeland; *p:* Louis Brock and Merian C. Cooper; *sc:* Cyril Hume, H. W. Hanemann, and Erwin Gelsey—*b/o* a story by Louis Brock, from a play by Anne Caldwell.

HONEY HALE: Singer-dancer with an American dance band that becomes successful when it flies to Rio de Janeiro to work at a large resort hotel.

Dolores Del Rio, Gene Raymond, Raul Roulien, Fred Astaire, Blanche Frederici, Walter Walker, Etta Moten, Roy D'Arcy, Maurice Black, Paul Porcasi, Franklin Pangborn, Eric Blore, Luis Alberni, Clarence Muse, Betty Furness.

Chance at Heaven (1933, RKO). *d:* William A. Seiter; *p:* Merian C. Cooper; *sc:* Julian Josephson and Sarah Y. Mason—*b/o* a story by Vina Delmar.

MARJE HARRIS: Young woman who loses her service-station boyfriend to a rich debutante but gets him back when the marriage fails.

Joel McCrea, Marian Nixon, Andy Devine, Virginia Hammond, Lucien Littlefield, Ann Shoemaker, George Meeker, Herman Bing, Betty Furness, Robert McWade.

Rafter Romance (1934, RKO). *d:* William A. Seiter; *p:* Alexander McKaig; *sc:* Sam Mintz and H. W. Haneman (adaptation by Glenn Tryon)—*b/o* a novel by John Wells.

MARY CARROLL: Day-shift working girl who—before she actually sees him—hates the artist–night watchman who shares her Greenwich Village attic apartment but falls for him after they finally meet each other.

Norman Foster, George Sidney, Robert Benchley, Laura Hope Crews, Guinn Williams, Ferike Boros, Sidney Miller.

Finishing School (1934, RKO). *d:* Wanda Tuchock and George Nicholls Jr.; *p:* Kenneth MacGowan; *sc:* Wanda Tuchock and Laird Doyle—*b/o* the play *These Days* by Katherine Clugston, from the story by David Hempstead.

CECELIA "PONY" FERRIS: Wisecracking, worldly good-time student in a private girls' school whose rich, naïve roommate finds herself pregnant.

Frances Dee, Billie Burke, Bruce Cabot, John Halliday, Beulah Bondi, Sara Haden, Marjorie Lytell, Adalyn Doyle, Dawn O'Day (Anne Shirley), Jack Norton.

Twenty Million Sweethearts (1934, WB). *d:* Ray Enright; *p:* Sam Bischoff; *sc:* Warren Duff and Harry Sauber—*b/o* a story by Paul Finder Moss and Jerry Wald.

PEGGY: Vivacious young radio actress who, when a singing waiter gets a chance to go on the radio, helps him overcome his mike fright and become a star.

Pat O'Brien, Dick Powell, The Four Mills Brothers, Ted Fiorito & His Band, Allen Jenkins, Grant Mitchell, Joseph Cawthorne, Henry O'Neill, Johnny Arthur, Gordon (Bill) Elliott, Sam Hayes, George Chandler.

Change of Heart (1934, Fox). *d:* John G. Blystone; *p:* Winfield Sheehan; *sc:* Sonya Levien and James Gleason (with additional dialogue by Samuel Hoffenstein)—*b/o* the novel *Manhattan Love Song* by Kathleen Norris.

MADGE ROUNTREE: One of four happy young California college graduates who fly to New York to seek careers and fortunes but find disharmony and problems along the way.

Janet Gaynor, Charles Farrell, James Dunn, Beryl Mercer, Gustav Von Seyffertitz, Theodore Von Eltz, Shirley Temple, Jane Darwell, Mischa Auer, Nick (Dick) Foran, Leonid Kinsky, Bess Flowers.

Upperworld (1934, WB). *d:* Roy Del Ruth; *p:* Robert Lord; *sc:* Ben Markson—*b/o* a story by Ben Hecht.

LILLY LINDER: Jazzy burlesque queen from the Bronx who gets involved with a wealthy married businessman, leading to blackmail and murder.

Warren William, Mary Astor, Theodore Newton, Andy Devine, Dickie Moore, J. Carrol Naish, Robert Barrat, Robert Greig, Willard Robertson, Mickey Rooney, John Qualen, Henry O'Neill, Sidney Toler.

The Gay Divorcee (1934, RKO). *d:* Mark Sandrich; *p:* Pandro S. Berman; *sc:* George Marion Jr., Dorothy Yost, and Edward Kaufman—*b/o* the musical comedy *Gay Divorce* by Dwight Taylor.

MIMI GLOSSOP: Young woman at a Brighton seaside resort who mistakenly thinks that a famous American hoofer making a play for her is the professional corespondent hired by her lawyer to help provide grounds for her divorce.

Fred Astaire, Alice Brady, Edward Everett Horton, Erik Rhodes, Eric Blore, Betty Grable, Charles Coleman, William Austin, Lillian Miles, Paul Porcasi, E. E. Clive.

Romance in Manhattan (1934, RKO). *d:* Stephen Roberts; *p:* Pandro S. Berman; *sc:* Jane Murfin and Edward Kaufman—*b/o* a story by Norman Krasna and Don Hartman.

SYLVIA DENNIS: Pretty chorus girl who helps a friendless Czech immigrant become a New York cab driver, then falls in love with him.

Francis Lederer, Arthur Hohl, Jimmy Butler, J. Farrell MacDonald, Oscar Apfel, Lillian Harmer, Reginald Barlow, Donald Meek, Sidney Toler, Harold Goodwin.

Roberta (1935, RKO). *d:* William A. Seiter; *p:* Pandro S. Berman; *sc:* Jane Murfin and Sam Mintz (with additional dialogue by Glenn Tryon and Allan Scott)—*b/o* the novel *Gowns by Roberta* by Alice Duer Miller and the Broadway musical *Roberta* by Jerome Kern and Otto Harbach.

LIZZIE GATZ (alias COUNTESS TANKA SCHARWENKA: Young Indiana woman in Paris who—while posing as a Polish countess—falls for an old sweetheart, an American bandleader whose pal has inherited the most fashionable dress salon in the city.

Irene Dunne, Fred Astaire, Randolph Scott, Helen Westley, Victor Varconi, Claire Dodd, Luis Alberni, Torben Meyer, Adrian Rosley, Johnny "Candy" Candido, Gene Sheldon, Lucille Ball, Virgina Reid (Lynne Carver).

Star of Midnight (1935, RKO). *d:* Stephen Roberts; *p:* Pandro S. Berman; *sc:* Howard J. Green, Anthony Veiller, and Edward Kaufman—*b/o* the novel *Star of Midnight* by Arthur Somers Roche.

DONNA MANTIN: Park Avenue society girl who, along with a suave lawyer-sleuth, gets involved in solving the disappearance of a theatrical leading lady and the mysterious murder of a gossip columnist.

William Powell, Paul Kelly, Gene Lockhart, Ralph Morgan, Leslie Fenton, J. Farrell MacDonald, Russell Hopton, Frank Reicher, Robert Emmett O'Connor, Francis McDonald, Paul Hurst.

Top Hat (1935, RKO). *d:* Mark Sandrich; *p:* Pandro S. Berman; *sc:* Dwight Taylor and Allan Scott (adaptation by Karl Nolti)—*b/o* Alexander Farago and Laszlo Aladar's play *The Girl Who Dared.*

DALE TREMONT: Pretty young woman in London who, though attracted to an American dancer who pursues her from London to Venice, mistakenly believes that he's the husband of her best friend.

Fred Astaire, Edward Everett Horton, Helen Broderick, Erik Rhodes, Eric Blore, Lucille Ball, Leonard Mudie, Donald Meek, Edgar Norton.

In Person (1935, RKO). *d:* William A. Seiter; *p:* Pandro S. Berman; *sc:* Allan Scott—*b/o* a novel by Samuel Hopkins Adams.

CAROL CORLISS (alias CLARA COLFAX): Glamorous movie star who, when she masquerades as an ugly duckling to get away from the public, joins a playboy in a retreat to the mountains and learns how to better cope with her life.

George Brent, Alan Mowbray, Grant Mitchell, Samuel S. Hinds, Spencer Charters, Lew Kelly, Lee Shumway, William B. Davidson, Tiny Jones, Bud Jamison.

Follow the Fleet (1936, RKO). *d:* Mark Sandrich; *p:* Pandro S. Berman; *sc:* Dwight Taylor—*b/o* the play *Shore Leave* by Hubert Osborne and Allan Scott.

SHERRY MARTIN: One of a pair of singing sisters who get involved with a couple of sailors who put on a musical benefit show on an old converted showboat.

Fred Astaire, Randolph Scott, Harriet Hilliard, Astrid Allwyn, Harry Beresford, Addison (Jack) Randall, Russell Hicks, Brooks Benedict, Lucille Ball, Betty Grable, Tony Martin, Frank Jenks, Doris Lloyd.

Swing Time (1936, RKO). *d:* George Stevens; *p:* Pandro S. Berman; *sc:* Howard Lindsay and Allan Scott—*b/o* a story by Erwin Gelsey.

PENELOPE "PENNY" CARROLL: Dancing teacher who falls for a New York hoofer-gambler as they go on to become a top-notch dance team.

Fred Astaire, Victor Moore, Helen Broderick, Eric Blore, Betty Furness, Georges Metaxa, Pierre Watkin, John Harrington, Edgar Dearing, Frank Jenks, Ralph Byrd.

Shall We Dance (1937, RKO). *d:* Mark Sandrich; *p:* Pandro S. Berman; *sc:* Allan Scott and Ernest Pagano (adaptation by P. J. Wolfson)—*b/o* the story "Watch Your Step" by Lee Loeb and Harold Buchman.

LINDA KEENE: Famous musical-comedy star who is mistakenly believed to be married to a reknowned ballet dancer, whereupon they both have difficulty in convincing people that they really aren't married.

Fred Astaire, Edward Everett Horton, Eric Blore, Jerome Cowan, Ketti Gallian, Harriet Hoctor, Ann Shoemaker, Ben Alexander, William Brisbane, Emma Young, Rolfe Sedan.

Stage Door (1937, RKO). *d:* Gregory La Cava; *p:* Pandro S. Berman; *sc:* Morrie Ryskind and Anthony Veiller—*b/o* the play by Edna Ferber and George S. Kaufman.

JEAN MAITLAND: Hardboiled singer and dancer who is one of several aspiring stage actresses who live in a New York theatrical boarding house and are competing for the lead in a Broadway play.

Katharine Hepburn, Adolphe Menjou, Gail Patrick, Constance Collier, Andrea Leeds, Samuel S. Hinds, Lucille Ball, Pierre Watkin, Franklin Pangborn, Grady Sutton, Jack Carson, Frank Reicher, Eve Arden, Ann Miller, Katherine Alexander, Ralph Forbes, Theodore Von Eltz, Frances Gifford.

Having Wonderful Time (1938, RKO). *d:* Alfred Santell; *p:* Pandro S. Berman; *sc:* Arthur Kober—*b/o* his play.

TEDDY SHAW: Bored New York office girl who goes on a summer vacation at Camp Kare-Free in the Catskill Mountains and finds romance with a young waiter who works there.

Douglas Fairbanks Jr., Peggy Conklin, Lucille Ball, Lee Bowman, Eve Arden, Red Skelton, Donald Meek, Jack Carson, Clarence H. Wilson, Allan Lane, Grady Sutton, Inez Courtney, Juanita Quigley.

Vivacious Lady (1938, RKO). *d:* George Stevens; *p:* Pandro S. Berman; *sc:* P. J. Wolfson and Ernest Pagano—*b/o* a story by I. A. R. Wylie.

FRANCES BRENT (alias FRANCEY LA ROCHE): New York nightclub singer who marries a shy botany professor, then has problems when he takes her back home to meet his horrified parents and break the news to his fiancée.

James Stewart, James Ellison, Charles Coburn, Beulah Bondi, Franklin Pangborn, Grady Sutton, Hattie McDaniel, Jack Carson, Willie Best, Frank M. Thomas, Spencer Charters, Maude Eburne.

Carefree (1938, RKO). *d:* Mark Sandrich; *p:* Pandro S. Berman; *sc:* Ernest Pagano and Allan Scott (adaptation by Dudley Nichols and Hagar Wilde)—*b/o* a story by Marian Ainslee and Guy Endore.

AMANDA COOPER: Radio singing star who, when she can't make up her mind whether to marry her lawyer fiancé, goes to a psychiatrist for help and winds up falling for him.

Fred Astaire, Ralph Bellamy, Luella Gear, Jack Carson, Clarence Kolb, Franklin Pangborn, Walter Kingsford, Kay Sutton, Hattie McDaniel, Richard Lane, James Finlayson.

The Story of Vernon and Irene Castle (1939, RKO). *d:* H. C. Potter; *p:* George Haight and Pandro S. Berman; *sc:* Richard Sherman (adaptation by Oscar Hammerstein II and Dorothy Yost)—*b/o* the books *My Husband* and *My Memories of Vernon Castle* by Irene Castle.

IRENE FOOTE CASTLE: Young dancer who marries vaudeville performer Vernon Castle, whereupon they become a world-famous dance team—which comes to an end when he's killed in WWI serving as a flying instructor in Texas.

Fred Astaire, Edna May Oliver, Walter Brennan, Lew Fields, Etienne Girardot, Janet Beecher, Rolfe Sedan, Leonid Kinsky, Douglas Walton, Frances Mercer, Victor Varconi, Donald MacBride, Dick Elliott, Marjorie Bell (Marge Champion).

Bachelor Mother (1939, RKO). *d:* Garson Kanin; *p:* B. G. DeSylva; *sc:* Norman Krasna—*b/o* a story by Felix Jackson.

POLLY PARRISH: Department-store sales clerk who finds an abandoned baby and is mistakenly thought to be its unwed mother—while the store owner's son is mistakenly suspected of being the father.

David Niven, Charles Coburn, Frank Albertson, E. E. Clive, Ferike Boros, Ernest Truex, Paul Stanton, June Wilkins, Frank M. Thomas, Irving Bacon, Reed Hadley, Chester Clute.

Fifth Avenue Girl (1939, RKO). *d:* Gregory La Cava; *p:* Gregory La Cava; *sc:* Allan Scott.

MARY GRAY: Unemployed woman who is hired by an unhappy New York business tycoon to pose as his gold-digging mistress in order to annoy and arouse his bored, selfish, money-hungry family.

Walter Connolly, Verree Teasdale, James Ellison, Tim Holt, Franklin Pangborn, Louis Calhern, Theodore Von Eltz, Alexander D'Arcy, Bess Flowers, Robert Emmett Keane.

Primrose Path (1940, RKO). *d:* Gregory La Cava; *p:* Gregory La Cava; *sc:* Allan Scott and Gregory La Cava—*b/o* the play by Robert Buckner and Walter Hart, from the novel *February Hill* by Victoria Lincoln.

ELLIE MAY ADAMS: Young woman from the wrong side of the tracks who marries a promising young garage mechanic but has trouble escaping from the influence of two former prostitutes—her mother and her grandmother.

Joel McCrea, Marjorie Rambeau, Henry Travers, Miles Mander, Queenie Vassar, Joan Carroll, Vivienne Osborne, Gene Morgan, Charles Lane, Nestor Paiva.

Lucky Partners (1940, RKO). *d:* Lewis Milestone; *p:* George Haight; *sc:* Allan Scott and John Van Druten—*b/o* the story "Bonne Chance" by Sacha Guitry.

JEAN NEWTON: Young bookstore clerk who wins a shared sweepstakes ticket with a handsome Greenwich Village artist, then—much to the chagrin of her insurance-salesman fiancé—embarks on a make-believe, platonic "honeymoon" with him.

Ronald Colman, Spring Byington, Jack Carson, Billy Gilbert, Hugh O'Connell, Harry Davenport, Leon Belasco, Olin Howland, Benny Rubin, Tom Dugan, Walter Kingsford, Lucille Gleason, Murray Alper.

Kitty Foyle (1940, RKO). *d:* Sam Wood; *p:* David Hempstead; *sc:* Dalton Trumbo (with additional dialogue by Donald Ogden Stewart)—*b/o* the novel by Christopher Morley.

KITTY FOYLE*: Hard-working white-collar sales clerk from a lower-middle-class family whose troubled love life includes a young Philadelphia

*Won the Academy Award as Best Actress for this role.

blueblood and a sincere young man from her own side of the tracks.

Dennis Morgan, James Craig, Eduardo Ciannelli, Ernest Cossart, Gladys Cooper, Mary Treen, Walter Kingsford, Cecil Cunningham, Florence Bates, Heather Angel.

Tom, Dick, and Harry (1941, RKO). *d:* Garson Kanin; *p:* Robert Sisk; *sc:* Paul Jarrico.

JANIE: Telephone switchboard operator who has trouble deciding which of her three suitors to choose—Tom, a down-to-earth auto salesman; Dick, a handsome millionaire; or Harry, an idealistic nonconformist.

George Murphy, Alan Marshal, Burgess Meredith, Joe Cunningham, Jane Seymour, Vicki Lester, Phil Silvers, Edna Holland, Netta Packer.

Roxie Hart (1942, 20th-Fox). *d:* William A. Wellman; *p:* Nunnally Johnson; *sc:* Nunnally Johnson—*b/o* the play *Chicago* by Maurine Watkins.

ROXIE HART: Gum-chewing, wisecracking dancer in Roaring '20s Chicago who confesses to a murder she didn't commit so that she can use the murder trial as a publicity stunt.

Adolphe Menjou, George Montgomery, Lynne Overman, Nigel Bruce, Phil Silvers, Sara Allgood, William Frawley, Spring Byington, Ted North, George Chandler, Iris Adrian.

Tales of Manhattan (1942, 20th-Fox). *d:* Julien Duvivier; *p:* Boris Morros and S. P. Eagle (Sam Spiegal); *Original Stories/sc:* Ben Hecht, Ferenc Molnar, Donald Ogden Stewart, Samuel Hoffenstein, Alan Campbell, Ladislas Fodor, Laslo Vadnay, Laszlo Gorog, Lamar Trotti, and Henry Blankfort.

DIANE: Young woman who suspects that her fiancé is cheating on her and who winds up falling for the fiancé's shy friend.

Charles Boyer, Rita Hayworth, Thomas Mitchell, Henry Fonda, Cesar Romero, Gail Patrick, Charles Laughton, Elsa Lanchester, Edward G. Robinson, George Sanders, James Gleason, Paul Robeson, Ethel Waters, Rochester (Eddie Anderson).

The Major and the Minor (1942, Para.). *d:* Billy Wilder; *p:* Arthur Hornblow Jr.; *sc:* Charles Brackett and Billy Wilder—*b/o* the play *Connie Goes Home* by Edward Childs Carpenter and the story "Sunny Goes Home" by Fannie Kilbourne.

SUSAN APPLEGATE: Financially strapped New York working girl who, when she disguises herself as a child to travel for half fare on a train back home to Iowa, meets a U.S. Army major who feels sorry for her—and suddenly finds herself at a boys' military school warding off the advances of teen-age cadets.

Ray Milland, Rita Johnson, Robert Benchley, Diana Lynn, Edward Fielding, Frankie Thomas, Charles Smith, Larry Nunn, Lela Rogers, Norma Varden, Will Wright.

Once Upon a Honeymoon (1942, RKO). *d:* Leo McCarey; *p:* Leo McCarey; *sc:* Sheridan Gibney—*b/o* a story by Leo McCarey.

KATIE O'HARA: Ex–Brooklyn burlesque queen during WWII who, after she marries a wealthy baron in Europe, discovers that he's one of Hitler's top-secret agents—and has to be rescued by an American radio correspondent.

Cary Grant, Walter Slezak, Albert Dekker, Albert Basserman, Ferike Boros, Harry Shannon, John Banner, Hans Conried, George Irving, Fred Niblo, Bert Roach, Johnny Dime.

Tender Comrade (1943, RKO). *d:* Edward Dmytryk; *p:* David Hempstead; *sc:* Dalton Trumbo.

JO: Defense-plant worker who, while her husband is away in the service during WWII, shares a house with three other women whose husbands are also in the service.

Robert Ryan, Ruth Hussey, Patricia Collinge, Mady Christians, Kim Hunter, Jane Darwell, Mary Forbes, Richard Martin, Patti Brill.

Lady in the Dark (1944, Para.). *d:* Mitchell Leisen; *p:* Mitchell Leisen; *sc:* Frances Goodrich and Albert Hackett—*b/o* the play by Moss Hart.

LIZA ELLIOTT: Editor of a swanky New York fashion magazine who, when she is torn between three men and suffers from headaches and frequent daydreams, seeks the help of a psychoanalyst.

Ray Milland, Warner Baxter, Jon Hall, Barry Sullivan, Mischa Auer, Phyllis Brooks, Don Loper, Fay Helm, Gail Russell, Harvey Stephens, Charles Smith.

I'll Be Seeing You (1944, UA). *d:* William Dieterle; *p:* Dore Schary (Vanguard/Selznick International); *sc:* Marion Parsonnet—*b/o* the radio drama *Double Furlough* by Charles Martin.

MARY MARSHALL: Woman in prison for manslaughter who, when she is allowed to go home on parole for the Christmas holidays, meets and falls in love with a shell-shocked WWII U.S. Army sergeant who's on a brief furlough from the hospital.

Joseph Cotten, Shirley Temple, Spring Byington, Tom Tully, Chill Wills, Kenny Bowers, Stanley Ridges, Walter Baldwin, Dorothy Stone.

Weekend at the Waldorf (1945, MGM). *d:* Robert Z. Leonard; *p:* Arthur Hornblow Jr.; *sc:* Sam Spewack and Bella Spewack (adaptation by Guy Bolton)—*b/o* the play *Grand Hotel* by Vicki Baum.

IRENE MALVERN: Successful but lonely film actress staying at New York's famed Waldorf-Astoria Hotel during WWII who, when she discovers a handsome war correspondent in her room, mistakenly thinks that he's a thief and undertakes to reform him.

Lana Turner, Walter Pidgeon, Van Johnson, Robert Benchley, Edward Arnold, Constance Collier, Leon Ames, Warner Anderson, Phyllis Thaxter, Keenan Wynn, Porter Hall, Samuel S. Hinds, George Zucco, Rosemary DeCamp, Irving Bacon.

Heartbeat (1946, RKO). *d:* Sam Wood; *p:* Robert Hakim and Raymond Hakim; *sc:* Hans Wilhelm, Max Kolpe, and Michel Duran (adaptation by Morris Ryskind—with additional dialogue by Roland Leigh)—*b/o* the French film *Battement de Coeur.*

ARLETTE: Destitute French waif who gets out of reform school and joins a school for pickpockets, then falls in love with her first important victim—a handsome French diplomat—and moves up into society.

Jean-Pierre Aumont, Adolphe Menjou, Basil Rathbone, Eduardo Ciannelli, Mikhail Rasumny, Melville Cooper, Mona Maris, Henry Stephenson.

Magnificent Doll (1946, Univ.). *d:* Frank Borzage; *p:* Jack H. Skirball and Bruce Manning (Hallmark); *sc:* Irving Stone.

DOLLY PAYNE: Eighteenth-century widow who is pursued by both the fiery Senator Aaron Burr and the gentle Congressman James Madison but finally marries Madison—who goes on to become the fourth president of the United States.

David Niven, Burgess Meredith, Horace (Stephen) McNally, Peggy Wood, Robert H. Barrat, Erville Alderson, Arthur Space, Joseph Crehan, Byron Foulger, Pierre Watkin.

It Had to Be You (1947, Col.). *d:* Don Hartman and Rudolph Mate; *p:* Don Hartman; *sc:* Norman Panama and Melvin Frank—*b/o* a story by Don Hartman and Allen Boretz.

VICTORIA STAFFORD: Young society woman who always backs out of marriage at the very last minute—until she finally finds her dream man, a handsome Indian fireman.

Cornel Wilde, Percy Waram, Spring Byington, Ron Randell, Thurston Hall, William Bevan, Frank Orth, Douglas Wood, Anna Q. Nilsson, Mary Forbes.

The Barkleys of Broadway (1949, MGM). *d:* Charles Walters; *p:* Arthur Freed; *sc:* Betty Comden and Adolph Green.

DINAH BARKLEY: Half of a bickering married musical-comedy team that breaks up when she decides to become a dramatic actress but that gets back together when the two both realize that they love and need each other.

Fred Astaire, Oscar Levant, Billie Burke, Gale

Robbins, Jacques Francois, George Zucco, Clinton Sundberg, Inez Cooper, Carol Brewster, Wilson Wood, Bess Flowers, Frank Ferguson, Hans Conried.

Perfect Strangers (1950, WB). *d:* Bretaigne Windust; *p:* Jerry Wald; *sc:* Edith Sommer (adaptation by George Oppenheimer)—*b/o* the play *Ladies and Gentlemen* by Ben Hecht and Charles MacArthur.

TERRY SCOTT: Los Angeles divorcée who, while serving on a sequestered jury during a murder trial, falls in love with an unhappily married fellow juror.

Dennis Morgan, Thelma Ritter, Margalo Gillmore, Anthony Ross, Howard Freeman, Alan Freed, Paul Ford, Harry Bellaver, George Chandler, Charles Meredith, Whit Bissell.

Storm Warning (1951, WB). *d:* Stuart Heisler; *p:* Jerry Wald; *sc:* Daniel Fuchs and Richard Brooks.

MARSHA MITCHELL: New York dress model who, when she stops in a small Southern town to visit her younger married sister—after first accidentally witnessing a murder by the Ku Klux Klan—recognizes her sister's husband as one of the killers.

Ronald Reagan, Doris Day, Steve Cochran, Hugh Sanders, Lloyd Gough, Raymond Greenleaf, Ned Glass, Walter Baldwin, Stuart Randall, Sean McClory.

The Groom Wore Spurs (1951, Univ.). *d:* Richard Whorf; *p:* Howard Welsch (Fidelity); *sc:* Robert Carson, Robert Libbott, and Frank Burt—*b/o* the story "Legal Bride" by Robert Carson.

ABIGAIL FURNIVAL: Lawyer who is hired to keep a rich Hollywood cowboy out of trouble and winds up marrying him.

Jack Carson, Joan Davis, Stanley Ridges, James Brown, John Litel, Victor Sen Yung, Mira McKinney, Kemp Niver, Franklyn Farnum, Ross Hunter.

We're Not Married (1952, 20th-Fox). *d:* Edmund Goulding; *p:* Nunnally Johnson; *sc:* Nunnally Johnson (adaptation by Dwight Taylor)—*b/o* a story by Gina Kaus and Jay Dratler.

RAMONA GLADWYN: Half of a married couple whose morning radio show runs into trouble when the sponsor and the couple learn that, through a mistake by a bumbling justice of the peace, they are one of five couples who were never legally married.

Fred Allen, Victor Moore, Marilyn Monroe, David Wayne, Eve Arden, Paul Douglas, Eddie Bracken, Mitzi Gaynor, Louis Calhern, Zsa Zsa Gabor, James Gleason, Paul Stewart, Jane Darwell, Tom Powers, Alan Bridge, Ralph Dumke, Lee Marvin, Marjorie Weaver, Selma Jackson.

Monkey Business (1952, 20th-Fox). *d:* Howard Hawks; *p:* Sol C. Siegel; *sc:* Ben Hecht, I. A. L. Diamond, and Charles Lederer—*b/o* a story by Harry Segall.

EDWINA FULTON: Wife whose absent-minded-professor husband develops a formula to make people grow younger, then chooses her and himself to be the "guinea pigs."

Cary Grant, Charles Coburn, Marilyn Monroe, Hugh Marlowe, Robert Cornthwaite, Larry Keating, Esther Dale, George Winslow, Kathleen Freeman, Olan Soule, Harry Carey Jr., Jerry Paris, Roger Moore, Dabbs Greer.

Dreamboat (1952, 20th-Fox). *d:* Claude Binyon; *p:* Sol C. Siegel; *sc:* Claude Binyon—*b/o* a story by John D. Weaver.

GLORIA MARLOWE: Ex–silent-movie queen who disrupts the life of her former matinee-idol co-star—now a distinguished but pompous college professor—when she becomes a television-show hostess and revives their old films on TV.

Clifton Webb, Anne Francis, Jeffrey Hunter, Elsa Lanchester, Fred Clark, Paul Harvey, Ray Collins, Helene Stanley, Richard Garrick, Jay Adler, Emory Parnell, Mary Treen.

Forever Female (1953, Para.). *d:* Irving Rapper; *p:* Pat Duggan; *sc:* Julius J. Epstein and Philip G. Epstein—*b/o* the play *Rosalind* by James M. Barrie.

BEATRICE PAGE: Aging New York stage actress who insists on trying to play a starring role for which she's too old, but who finally realizes she should step aside so that a promising young actress can have the part.

William Holden, Paul Douglas, Pat Crowley, James Gleason, Jesse White, Marjorie Rambeau, George Reeves, King Donovan, Vic Perrin, Marion Ross, Almira Sessions, Hyacinthe Railla.

Black Widow (1954, 20th-Fox). *d:* Nunnally Johnson; *p:* Nunnally Johnson; *sc:* Nunnally Johnson—*b/o* a story by Patrick Quentin.

LOTTIE: Phony, insolent Broadway stage star who is one of several show-business people who are suspects in the mysterious murder of an ambitious young actress.

Van Heflin, Gene Tierney, George Raft, Peggy Ann Garner, Reginald Gardiner, Otto Kruger, Cathleen Nesbitt, Skip Homeier, Hilda Simms, Mabel Albertson, Bea Benaderet.

Twist of Fate (1954, UA). *d:* David Miller; *p:* Maxwell Setton and John R. Sloan (British Lion); *sc:* Robert Westerby and Carl Nystron—*b/o* a story by Rip Van Ronkel and David Miller.

"JOHNNY" VICTOR: Former actress and rich man's mistress who, while becoming involved with a handsome young Frenchman on the Riviera,

discovers that her wealthy lover—whom she's been planning to marry—is a dangerous criminal.

Herbert Lom, Stanley Baker, Jacques Bergerac, Margaret Rawlings, Eddie Byrne, Coral Browne.

Tight Spot (1955, Col.). *d:* Phil Karlson; *p:* Lewis J. Rachmil; *sc:* William Bowers—*b/o* the play *Dead Pigeon* by Lenard Kantor.

SHERRY CONLEY: Former gangster's moll who finds herself on the spot when she's released from prison and used as a decoy by a U.S. Attorney to trap the gangster and his crooked cop accomplice.

Edward G. Robinson, Brian Keith, Lucy Marlow, Lorne Greene, Katherine Anderson, Allen Nourse, Peter Leeds, Doye O'Dell, Eve McVeagh, Helen Wallace, Frank Gerstle.

The First Traveling Saleslady (1956, RKO). *d:* Arthur Lubin; *p:* Arthur Lubin; *sc:* Stephen Longstreet and Devery Freeman.

ROSE GILRAY: New York corset designer in 1897 who, along with her secretary, heads out West—ostensibly to sell corsets—but in reality to secretly sell barbed wire to homesteaders.

Barry Nelson, Carol Channing, Brian Keith, James Arness, Clint Eastwood, Robert Simon, Frank Wilcox, John Eldredge, Edward Cassidy, Bill Hale, Kate Drain Lawson.

Teenage Rebel (1956, 20th-Fox). *d:* Edmund Goulding; *p:* Charles Brackett; *sc:* Walter Reisch and Edmund Goulding—*b/o* the play *A Roomful of Roses* by Edith Sommer.

NANCY FALLON: Wealthy California divorcée, now remarried, who runs into problems when she gets back custody of her teen-age daughter and tries to win her love.

Michael Rennie, Mildred Natwick, Rusty Swope, Lili Gentle, Louise Beavers, Irene Hervey, Betty Lou Keim, Warren Berlinger, Diane Jergens, Richard Collier.

Oh, Men! Oh, Women! (1957, 20th-Fox). *d:* Nunnally Johnson; *p:* Nunnally Johnson; *sc:* Nunnally Johnson—*b/o* the play by Edward Chodorov.

MILDRED TURNER: Bored wife of a Hollywood star who, when she begins to feel useless, seeks help from a psychiatrist (who, it turns out, has emotional problems too).

Dan Dailey, David Niven, Barbara Rush, Tony Randall, Natalie Schafer, Rachel Stephens, John Wengraf, Clancy Cooper, Franklin Pangborn, Franklyn Farnum.

Harlow (1965, Magna). *d:* Alex Segal; *p:* Bill Sargant and Lee Savin; *sc:* Karl Tunberg.

MAMA JEAN: Clinging mother of Jean Harlow—the famous 1930s blonde-bombshell screen star who began as a bit player in a Laurel and Hardy comedy, became one of Hollywood's brightest stars, but died unhappy and disillusioned at twenty-six.

Carol Lynley, Efrem Zimbalist Jr., Barry Sullivan, Hurd Hatfield, Lloyd Bochner, Hermione Baddeley, Audrey Totter, John Williams, Jack Kruschen, Michael Dante, Audrey Christie, Sonny Liston, Cliff Norton, Jim Plunkett.

Quick, Let's Get Married (1965, Golden Eagle). *d:* William Dieterle; *p:* William Marshall (William Marshall Prod./Kay Lewis Enterprises); *sc:* Allan Scott.

MADAME RINALDI: Bordello madam who helps a big-time thief locate an ancient buried treasure—which turns out to be under a religious statute.

Ray Milland, Barbara Eden, Walter Abel, Pippa Scott, Elliott Gould, Michael Ansara, Cecil Kellaway, Vinton Hayworth.

☆ FRANK SINATRA

Francis Albert Sinatra

b: Dec. 12, 1915, Hoboken, N.J.

". . . Prew, listen. Fatso done it, Prew. He liked to whack me in the gut. He asks me if it hurts, and I spit at him like always—only yesterday it was bad. He hit me. He hit me. He hit me. . . ."

> Angelo Maggio (Frank Sinatra)—as he's dying—warning Robert E. Lee Prewitt (Montgomery Clift) about the sadistic Sgt. "Fatso" Judson (Ernest Borgnine) in *From Here to Eternity*, 1953.

Higher and Higher (1943, RKO). *d:* Tim Whelan; *p:* Tim Whelan; *sc:* Jay Dratler and Ralph Spence (with additional dialogue by William Bowers and Howard Harris)—*b/o* the play by Gladys Hurlbut and Joshua Logan.

FRANK: Wealthy young man who gets involved with a scullery maid who he mistakenly believes is a rich debutante.

Michele Morgan, Jack Haley, Leon Errol, Marcy McGuire, Victor Borge, Mary Wickes, Elisabeth Risdon, Barbara Hale, Paul Hartman, Mel Torme, Dooley Wilson, Rex Evans, Dorothy Malone.

Step Lively (1944, RKO). *d:* Tim Whelan; *p:* Robert Fellows; *sc:* Warren Duff and Peter Milne—*b/o* the play *Room Service* by John Murray and Allen Boretz.

GLEN: Country bumpkin who goes to New York to be a playwright, gets involved with a free-wheeling, broke producer, and winds up as a singing star in a Broadway musical.

George Murphy, Adolphe Menjou, Gloria DeHaven, Walter Slezak, Eugene Pallette, Wally Brown, Alan Carney, Grant Mitchell, Anne Jeffreys, George Chandler, Dorothy Malone.

Anchors Aweigh (1945, MGM). *d:* George Sidney; *p:* Joe Pasternak; *sc:* Isobel Lennart—*b/o* a story by Natalie Marcin.

CLARENCE DOOLITTLE: Bashful sailor on shore leave in WWII Los Angeles who loses some of his shyness when he falls for a girl from Brooklyn.

Kathryn Grayson, Gene Kelly, Jose Iturbi, Dean Stockwell, Pamela Britton, Rags Ragland, Billy Gilbert, Henry O'Neill, Edgar Kennedy, Grady Sutton, Leon Ames, James Flavin, James Burke, Henry Armetta, Chester Clute, Ray Teal, Renie Riano, Garry Owen, Steve Brodie.

It Happened in Brooklyn (1947, MGM). *d:* Richard Whorf; *p:* Jack Cummings; *sc:* Isobel Lennart—*b/o* a story by John McGowan.

DANNY WEBSON MILLER: G.I. who returns home to Brooklyn, moves in with an old pal who is a high-school janitor, and tries to make it big in the music business.

Kathryn Grayson, Peter Lawford, Jimmy Durante, Gloria Grahame, Marcy McGuire, Aubrey Mather, William Haade, Lumsden Hare, Dick Wessel, Bruce Cowling.

The Miracle of the Bells (1948, RKO). *d:* Irving Pichel; *p:* Jesse L. Lasky and Walter MacEwen; *sc:* Ben Hecht and Quentin Reynolds (with additional material by DeWitt Bodeen)—*b/o* the novel by Russell Janney.

FATHER PAUL: Soft-spoken priest in a Pennsylvania coal-mining town where—when a young Hollywood actress is brought back home to be buried—a "miracle" takes place.

Fred MacMurray, Alida Valli, Lee J. Cobb, Frank Ferguson, Harold Vermilye, Charles Meredith, Philip Ahn, Frank Wilcox, Ray Teal, Syd Saylor, Ian Wolfe, George Chandler, Franklin Farnum, Snub Pollard.

The Kissing Bandit (1948, MGM). *d:* Laslo Benedek; *p:* Joe Pasternak; *sc:* Isobel Lennart and John Briard Harding.

RICARDO: Mild-mannered Boston business-school graduate who returns to Spanish California in the 1830s and finds that he's expected to take over the old gang of his late father, a romantic outlaw known as "The Kissing Bandit."

Kathryn Grayson, J. Carrol Naish, Mildred Natwick, Mikhail Rasumny, Billy Gilbert, Clinton Sundberg, Carleton Young, Vincente Gomez, Byron Foulger, Ricardo Montalban, Ann Miller, Cyd Charisse.

Take Me Out to the Ballgame (1949, MGM). *d:* Busby Berkeley; *p:* Arthur Freed; *sc:* Harry Tugend and George Wells—*b/o* a story by Gene Kelly and Stanley Donen.

DENNIS RYAN: One of a pair of vaudeville song-and-dance men who spend their summers as star baseball players on the Wolves baseball team and who, when the team gets a pretty new manager, both fall for her.

Esther Williams, Gene Kelly, Betty Garrett, Edward Arnold, Jules Munshin, Richard Lane, Tom Dugan, Murray Apler, Mack Gray, Douglas Fowley, James Burke, Gordon Jones, Henry Kulky, Dick Wessel, Pat Flaherty, Joi Lansing.

On the Town (1949, MGM). *d:* Gene Kelly and Stanley Donen; *p:* Arthur Freed; *sc:* Adolph Green and Betty Comden—from their musical play—*b/o* an idea by Jerome Robbins.

CHIP: Footloose sailor, one of a trio of gobs out for fun and girls on a twenty-four-hour shore leave in New York City, who falls for a female cab driver.

Gene Kelly, Betty Garrett, Ann Miller, Jules Munshin, Vera-Ellen, Florence Bates, Alice Pearce, George Meader.

Double Dynamite (1951, RKO). *d:* Irving Cummings; *p:* Irving Cummings Jr.; *sc:* Melville Shavelson (with additional dialogue by Harry Crane)—from a story by Leo Rosten—*b/o* a character created by Mannie Manheim.

JOHNNY DALTON: Bank clerk who saves a bookie's life, then—when the bookie makes a lot of money for him on a horse bet—is accused of embezzling the money from his bank.

Jane Russell, Groucho Marx, Don McGuire, Howard Freeman, Nestor Paiva, Frank Orth, Harry Hayden, Joe Devlin, Lou Nova, Ida Moore, Hal K. Dawson, George Chandler.

Meet Danny Wilson (1951, Univ.). *d:* Joseph Pevney; *p:* Leonard Goldstein; *sc:* Don McGuire.

DANNY WILSON: Chicago crooner who, when he promises a racketeer nightclub owner 50 percent of his future earnings, winds up a big star—but also in big trouble.

Shelley Winters, Alex Nicol, Raymond Burr, Tommy Farrell, Vaughn Taylor, Donald McBride, Jack Kruschen, Tom Dugan, Pat Flaherty, Tony Curtis.

From Here to Eternity (1953, Col.). *d:* Fred Zinnemann; *p:* Buddy Adler; *sc:* Daniel Taradash—*b/o* the novel by James Jones.

ANGELO MAGGIO*: Tough U.S. Army private at Schofield Barracks, Honolulu, in the summer of 1941 who, after he's thrown into the stockade and is brutally beaten, escapes but dies.

Burt Lancaster, Montgomery Clift, Deborah Kerr, Donna Reed, Philip Ober, Mickey Shaughnessy, Harry Bellaver, Ernest Borgnine, Jack Warden, Tim Ryan, Claude Akins, Robert Wilke, George Reeves, Don Dubbins, Willis Bouchey.

Suddenly (1954, UA). *d:* Lewis Allen; *p:* Robert Bassler (Libra); *sc:* Richard Sale.

JOHN BARON: Cold-blooded killer who is hired for $500,000 to assassinate the president of the United States in the small town of Suddenly, California.

Sterling Hayden, James Gleason, Nancy Gates, Willis Bouchey, Paul Frees, Christopher Dark, Charles Smith, Richard Collier.

Young at Heart (1955, WB). *d:* Gordon Douglas; *p:* Henry Blanke (Arwin); *sc:* Adaptation by Liam O'Brien from the screenplay *Four Daughters* by Julius J. Epstein and Lenore Coffee—*b/o* the *Cosmopolitan* magazine story "Sister Act" by Fannie Hurst.

BARNEY SLOAN: Moody, bitter piano player–arranger who finally gains faith in himself after he marries one of the three daughters of a small-town Connecticut music teacher.

Doris Day, Gig Young, Ethel Barrymore, Dorothy Malone, Robert Keith, Elisabeth Fraser, Alan Hale Jr., Lonny Chapman, Frank Ferguson, Barbara Pepper, Robin Raymond.

Not As a Stranger (1955, UA). *d:* Stanley Kramer; *p:* Stanley Kramer (Stanley Kramer Prod.); *sc:* Edna Anhalt and Edward Anhalt—*b/o* the novel by Morton Thompson.

DR. ALFRED BOONE: Easy-going but cynical young doctor who stands by his best friend, a serious, totally dedicated doctor with marital and professional problems.

Olivia de Havilland, Robert Mitchum, Gloria Grahame, Broderick Crawford, Charles Bickford, Myron McCormick, Lon Chaney Jr., Jesse White, Harry Morgan, Lee Marvin, Virginia Christine, Whit Bissell, Mae Clark.

The Tender Trap (1955, MGM). *d:* Charles Walters; *p:* Lawrence Weingarten; *sc:* Julius J.

---

*Won the Academy Award as Best Supporting Actor for this role.

Epstein—*b/o* the play by Max Shulman and Robert Paul Smith.

CHARLIE Y. READER: Swinging bachelor and New York theatrical agent who has a bevy of beauties on the string but finally is "tenderly trapped" into marriage.

Debbie Reynolds, David Wayne, Celeste Holm, Jarma Lewis, Lola Albright, Carolyn Jones, Howard St. John, Joey Faye, Tom Helmore, James Drury, Benny Rubin, Frank Sully, Dave White.

Guys and Dolls (1955, MGM). *d:* Joseph L. Mankiewicz; *p:* Samuel Goldwyn (Samuel Goldwyn Prod.); *sc:* Joseph L. Mankiewicz—from the musical play by Jo Swerling, Abe Burrows, and Frank Loesser—*b/o* Damon Runyon's story "The Idyll of Miss Sarah Brown."

NATHAN DETROIT: Colorful gambler who runs "the oldest established, permanent floating crap game in New York" and has been engaged to the same chorus girl for fourteen years.

Marlon Brando, Jean Simmons, Vivian Blaine, Robert Keith, Stubby Kaye, B. S. Pully, Johnny Silver, Sheldon Leonard, George E. Stone, Regis Toomey, Veda Ann Borg, Joe McTurk.

The Man with the Golden Arm (1955, UA). *d:* Otto Preminger; *p:* Otto Preminger (Carlyle); *sc:* Walter Newman and Lewis Meltzer—*b/o* the novel by Nelson Algren.

FRANKIE MACHINE*: Chicago card dealer who wants to become a jazz drummer but is having trouble kicking a drug habit and is plagued by a scheming, nagging wife.

Eleanor Parker, Kim Novak, Arnold Stang, Darren McGavin, Robert Strauss, John Conte, George E. Stone, George Mathews, Leonid Kinskey, Emile Meyer, Shorty Rogers, Shelly Manne, Will Wright, Joe McTurk.

Johnny Concho (1956, UA). *d:* Don McGuire; *p:* Frank Sinatra (Kent); *sc:* David P. Harmon and Don McGuire—*b/o* David P. Harmon's story "The Man Who Owned the Town."

JOHNNY CONCHO: Cowardly card cheat in 1875 Arizona who, when his older brother—a top gunman—is killed, runs from the killers but finally gains the courage to return and face them.

Keenan Wynn, William Conrad, Phyllis Kirk, Wallace Ford, Christopher Dark, Howard Petrie, Willis Bouchey, Robert Osterloh, Leo Gordon, Dorothy Adams, Jean Byron, Claude Akins, John Qualen.

High Society (1956, MGM). *d:* Charles Walters; *p:* Sol C. Siegel; *sc:* John Patrick—*b/o* Philip Barry's play *The Philadelphia Story.*

---

*Received an Academy Award nomination as Best Actor for this role.

MIKE CONNOR: Personable, brash magazine reporter who, while covering the upcoming wedding of a wealthy Newport, Connecticut, divorcée, has a one-night fling with her.

Bing Crosby, Grace Kelly, Celeste Holm, John Lund, Louis Calhern, Sidney Blackmer, Louis Armstrong, Margalo Gillmore, Lydia Reed, Gordon Richards, Richard Garrick, Hugh Boswell.

Around the World in 80 Days (1956, UA). *d:* Michael Anderson; *p:* Michael Todd (Michael Todd Prod.); *sc:* James Poe, John Farrow, and S. J. Perelman—*b/o* the novel by Jules Verne.

Billed as "PIANO PLAYER": Honkytonk piano player in a Barbary Coast saloon—one of many colorful characters encountered by the English gentleman Phileas Fogg in 1872 while he is winning his bet that he can journey around the world in eighty days.

David Niven, Cantinflas, Robert Newton, Shirley MacLaine, Charles Boyer, Joe E. Brown, Ronald Colman, Noel Coward, Andy Devine, Marlene Dietrich, Fernandel, Sir John Gielgud, Sir Cedric Hardwicke, Buster Keaton, Peter Lorre, Col. Tim McCoy, John Mills, Robert Morley, George Raft, Cesar Romero, Red Skelton.

The Pride and the Passion (1957, UA). *d:* Stanley Kramer; *p:* Stanley Kramer (Stanley Kramer Prod.); *sc:* Edna Anhalt and Edward Anhalt—*b/o* C. S. Forester's novel *The Gun.*

MIGUEL: Spanish guerrilla leader during the Napoleonic campaign in Spain who joins forces with a British naval captain to transport a huge 6000-pound cannon across difficult terrain in order to destroy a French-held fort.

Cary Grant, Sophia Loren, Theodore Bikel, John Wengraf, Jay Novello, Jose Nieto, Carlos Larranaga, Philip Van Zandt, Julian Ugarte.

The Joker Is Wild (1957, Para.). *d:* Charles Vidor; *p:* Samuel J. Briskin (A.M.B.L. Prod.); *sc:* Oscar Saul—*b/o* the book by Art Cohn.

JOE E. LEWIS: Young Chicago singer who, after his throat and vocal cords are slashed by mobsters, becomes a well-known nightclub comedian but has a problem with booze and gambling.

Mitzi Gaynor, Jeanne Crain, Eddie Albert, Beverly Garland, Jackie Coogan, Barry Kelley, Ted De Corsia, Hank Henry, Harold Huber, Ned Glass, Walter Woolf King, Sid Melton, Wally Brown, Don Beddoe, Mary Treen, Sophie Tucker.

Pal Joey (1957, Col.). *d:* George Sidney; *p:* Fred Kohlmar (Essex–Sidney); *sc:* Dorothy Kingsley—*b/o* the musical play by John O'Hara, Richard Rodgers, and Lorenz Hart.

JOEY EVANS: Fast-talking heel of a nightclub singer who, with the financial backing of a wealthy, widowed ex-stripper, hopes to build his own San Francisco nightclub.

Rita Hayworth, Kim Novak, Barbara Nichols, Bobby Sherwood, Hank Henry, Elizabeth Patterson, Frank Wilcox, Pierre Watkin, Frank Sully, John Hubbard, Hermes Pan, Gail Bonney.

Kings Go Forth (1958, UA). *d:* Delmer Daves; *p:* Frank Ross (Ross–Eton); *sc:* Merle Miller—*b/o* the novel by Joe David Brown.

LT. SAM LOGGINS: WWII American Army officer in 1944 southern France who, after falling in love with a beautiful American woman living in Nice, is stunned to learn that she's part Negro.

Tony Curtis, Natalie Wood, Leora Dana, Karl Swenson, Ann Codee, Edward Ryder, Jackie Berthe, Marie Isnard, Red Norvo, Pete Candoli.

Some Came Running (1958, MGM). *d:* Vincente Minnelli; *p:* Sol C. Siegel; *sc:* John Patrick and Arthur Sheekman—*b/o* the novel by James Jones.

DAVE HIRSH: Disillusioned ex-WWII G.I. who, when he returns to his hometown in Indiana and tries to become a successful writer, takes up with an easy-going gambler and a good-hearted prostitute.

Dean Martin, Shirley MacLaine, Martha Hyer, Arthur Kennedy, Nancy Gates, Leora Dana, Betty Lou Keim, Connie Gilchrist, Larry Gates, Don Haggerty, William Schallert, George E. Stone, Marion Ross.

A Hole in the Head (1959, UA). *d:* Frank Capra; *p:* Frank Capra and Frank Sinatra (Sincap); *sc:* Arnold Schulman—*b/o* his play.

TONY MANETTA: Ne'er-do-well widower who, with his eleven-year-old son, operates a fleabag hotel in Miami Beach but has to turn to his rich but frugal New York merchant brother for financial help to save the hotel.

Edward G. Robinson, Eleanor Parker, Eddie Hodges, Carolyn Jones, Thelma Ritter, Keenan Wynn, Joi Lansing, Jimmy Komack, Dub Taylor, Benny Rubin, Ruby Dandridge, B. S. Pully, Pupi Campo.

Never So Few (1959, MGM). *d:* John Sturges; *p:* Edmund Grainger (Canterbury); *sc:* Millard Kaufman—*b/o* the novel by Tom T. Chamales.

CAPT. TOM C. REYNOLDS: American leader of a band of G.I.s and guerrillas who, while fighting the Japanese in Burma during WWII, also have to contend with Chinese bandits.

Gina Lollobrigida, Peter Lawford, Steve McQueen, Richard Johnson, Paul Henreid, Brian Donlevy, Dean Jones, Charles Bronson, Philip Ahn, John Hoyt, Whit Bissell, Ross Elliott.

Can-Can (1960, 20th-Fox). *d:* Walter Lang; *p:* Jack Cummings (Suffolk–Cummings); *sc:* Dorothy Kingsley and Charles Lederer—*b/o* the musical play by Abe Burrows and Cole Porter.

FRANÇOIS DURNAIS: An 1890s Parisian lawyer who defends a pretty café owner's right to perform the daring "can-can" dance—even though it's forbidden by an old French law.

Shirley MacLaine, Maurice Chevalier, Louis Jourdan, Juliet Prowse, Marcel Dalio, Leon Belasco, Nestor Paiva, Ann Codee, Jonathan Kidd.

Ocean's Eleven (1960, WB). *d:* Lewis Milestone; *p:* Lewis Milestone (Dorchester); *sc:* Harry Brown and Charles Lederer—*b/o* a story by George Clayton Johnson and Jack Golden Russell.

DANNY OCEAN: Ex–WWII paratrooper who leads an eleven-man gang of ex-G.I.s in an attempt to simultaneously rob five Las Vegas casinos at midnight on New Year's Eve.

Dean Martin, Sammy Davis Jr., Peter Lawford, Angie Dickinson, Richard Conte, Cesar Romero, Patrice Wymore, Joey Bishop, Akim Tamiroff, Henry Silva, Ilka Chase, Buddy Lester, Richard Benedict, Red Skelton, George Raft, Shirley MacLaine, Norman Fell, Clem Harvey, George E. Stone, Hoot Gibson, Don "Red" Barry.

The Devil at 4 O'clock (1961, Col.). *d:* Mervyn LeRoy; *p:* Fred Kohlmar (LeRoy/Kohlmar); *sc:* Liam O'Brien—*b/o* the novel by Max Catto.

HARRY: One of three convicts on a French tropical island who help an aging priest evacuate a children's leper hospital when a volcano erupts.

Spencer Tracy, Kerwin Mathews, Jean-Pierre Aumont, Gregoire Aslan, Alexander Scourby, Barbara Luna, Cathy Lewis, Bernie Hamilton, Marcel Dalio, Louis Mercier.

Sergeants 3 (1962, UA). *d:* John Sturges; *p:* Frank Sinatra (Essex–Claude); *sc:* W. R. Burnett.

1st SGT. MIKE MERRY: One of a trio of colorful U.S. Cavalry sergeants in the Dakota Badlands during the 1870s who, with the help of a recently freed slave, prevent a planned massacre by Sioux Indians.

Dean Martin, Sammy Davis Jr., Peter Lawford, Joey Bishop, Henry Silva, Ruta Lee, Buddy Lester, Phillip Crosby, Dennis Crosby, Lindsay Crosby, Hank Henry, Richard Simmons, Mickey Finn, Rodd Redwing.

The Manchurian Candidate (1962, UA). *d:* John Frankenheimer; *p:* George Axelrod and John Frankenheimer (M.C. Prod.); *sc:* George Axelrod—*b/o* the novel by Richard Condon.

BENNETT MARCO: U.S. Army intelligence officer who is trying to prevent the assassination of a presidential nominee by a Korean War vet who was brainwashed and programmed by Chinese Communists while he was a POW.

Laurence Harvey, Janet Leigh, Angela Lansbury, Henry Silva, James Gregory, Leslie Parrish, John McGiver, Khigh Dhiegh, James Edwards, Madame Spivy, Barry Kelley, Lloyd Corrigan, Whit Bissell.

Come Blow Your Horn (1963, Para.). *d:* Bud Yorkin; *p:* Norman Lear and Bud Yorkin (Essex–Tandem); *sc:* Norman Lear—*b/o* the play by Neil Simon.

ALAN BAKER: Swinging New York bachelor who, when his younger brother moves into his apartment with him, is delighted—until the brother starts taking over his private stock of booze and women.

Lee J. Cobb, Molly Picon, Barbara Rush, Jill St. John, Tony Bill, Dan Blocker, Phyllis McGuire, Herbie Faye, Romo Vincent, Eddie Quillan, Grady Sutton, Dean Martin.

The List of Adrian Messenger (1963, Univ.). *d:* John Huston; *p:* Edward Lewis (Joel); *sc:* Anthony Veiller—*b/o* the novel by Philip MacDonald.

Played (in disguise) the part of a gypsy stableman—one of several characters involved in the mysterious case of a series of murders that a retired British Intelligence officer and Scotland Yard are trying to solve.

George C. Scott, Dana Wynter, Clive Brook, Gladys Cooper, Herbert Marshall, John Merivale, Marcel Dalio, John Huston, Bernard Fox, Tony Curtis, Kirk Douglas, Burt Lancaster, Robert Mitchum.

4 for Texas (1963, WB). *d:* Robert Aldrich; *p:* Robert Aldrich (Sam Co.); *sc:* Teddi Sherman and Robert Aldrich.

ZACK THOMAS: One of two 1870s Texas gamblers who try to outwit each other but finally join forces to fight a doublecrossing crooked banker and his hired gang of bandits.

Dean Martin, Anita Ekberg, Ursula Andress, Charles Bronson, Victor Buono, Nick Dennis, Richard Jaeckel, Mike Mazurki, Ellen Corby, Jack Elam, Jesslyn Fax, Fritz Feld, Percy Helton, Bob Steele, Grady Sutton, David Willock, Arthur Godfrey, The Three Stooges.

Robin and the 7 Hoods (1964, WB). *d:* Gordon Douglas; *p:* Frank Sinatra and Howard W. Koch (P-C Prod.); *sc:* David R. Schwartz.

ROBBO: Modern-day "Robin Hood" leader of a Prohibition-era Chicago gang that—while battling a rival mob for supremacy—fleeces the rich and gives to the poor, such as orphans.

Dean Martin, Sammy Davis Jr., Bing Crosby, Peter Falk, Barbara Rush, Victor Buono, Hank Henry, Allen Jenkins, Jack La Rue, Phil Crosby, Phil Arnold, Hans Conried, Sig Rumann, Edward G. Robinson.

None But the Brave (1965, WB). *d:* Frank Sinatra; *p:* Frank Sinatra (Artanis); *sc:* John Twist and Katsuya Susaki—*b/o* a story by Kikumaru Okuda.

CHIEF PHARMACIST'S MATE MALONEY: Whiskey-drinking medical member of a cracked-up American Navy plane's crew that makes a temporary truce with a stranded Japanese Army patrol on a small Pacific island.

Clint Walker, Tommy Sands, Brad Dexter, Tony Bill, Tatsuya Mihashi, Takeshi Kato, Sammy Jackson, Richard Bakalyan, Rafer Johnson, Jimmy Griffin, Christopher Dark, Phillip Crosby.

Von Ryan's Express (1965, 20th-Fox). *d:* Mark Robson; *p:* Saul David (P-R Prod.); *sc:* Wendell Mayes and Joseph Landon—*b/o* the novel by David Westheimer.

COL. JOSEPH L. RYAN: American Air Force officer in a WWII Italian POW camp who is accused by his British fellow prisoners of appeasing their captors—until he helps lead a daring escape in which a German freight train is taken over.

Trevor Howard, Raffaella Carra, Brad Dexter, Sergio Fantoni, John Leyton, Edward Mulhare, Wolfgang Preiss, James Brolin, Adolfo Celi, Richard Bakalyan, Mike Romanoff.

Marriage on the Rocks (1965, WB). *d:* Jack Donahue; *p:* William H. Daniels (A-C Prod.); *sc:* Cy Howard.

DAN EDWARDS: Ad-agency president who, when he goes to Mexico to celebrate his nineteenth wedding anniversary, winds up getting divorced by mistake—whereupon his wife marries his best friend by mistake.

Deborah Kerr, Dean Martin, Cesar Romero, Hermione Baddely, Tony Bill, John McGiver, Nancy Sinatra, Joi Lansing, Kathleen Freeman, DeForest Kelley, Byron Foulger, Parley Baer, Trini Lopez.

Cast a Giant Shadow (1966, UA). *d:* Melville Shavelson; *p:* Melville Shavelson and Michael Wayne (Mirisch/Llenroe/Batjac); *sc:* Melville Shavelson—*b/o* the biography of Col. David Marcus by Ted Berkman.

VINCE TALMADGE: New Jersey soldier-of-fortune pilot who, while fighting for Israel in 1949, loses his life bombing Egyptian tanks with seltzer bottles because there is no more ammunition.

Kirk Douglas, Yul Brynner, Senta Berger, John Wayne, Angie Dickinson, Luther Adler, Stathis Giallelis, James Donald, Gordon Jackson, Haym Topol, Gary Merrill, Jeremy Kemp, Sean Barrett, Frank Latimore.

Assault on a Queen (1966, Para.). *d:* Jack Donahue; *p:* William Goetz (Seven Arts/Sinatra); *sc:* Rod Serling—*b/o* the novel by Jack Finney.

MARK BRITTAIN: Ex–submarine officer who is one of a group that plans to hijack the *Queen Mary* on the high seas by using a reconverted German U-boat.

Virna Lisi, Tony Franciosa, Richard Conte, Alf Kjellin, Errol John, Murray Matheson, Reginald

Denny, John Warburton, Lester Matthews, Alan Baxter.

The Naked Runner (1967, WB). *d:* Sidney J. Furie; *p:* Brad Dexter (Sinatra Enterprises); *sc:* Stanley Mann—*b/o* the novel by Francis Clifford.

SAM LAKER: American businessman living in London who, when his young son is kidnapped, is tricked into a bizarre plot to assassinate a British spy who has defected behind the Iron Curtain.

Peter Vaughan, Derren Nesbitt, Nadia Gray, Toby Robbins, Inger Stratton, Cyril Luckham, Edward Fox, J. A. B. Dubin-Behrmann, Michael Newport.

Tony Rome (1967, 20th-Fox). *d:* Gordon Douglas; *p:* Aaron Rosenberg (Arcola–Millfield); *sc:* Richard L. Breen—*b/o* the novel *Miami Mayhem* by Marvin H. Albert.

TONY ROME: Tough Miami private eye who is hired by a millionaire to investigate why his daughter was found drunk and unconscious in a cheap motel.

Jill St. John, Richard Conte, Gena Rowlands, Simon Oakland, Jeffrey Lynn, Lloyd Bochner, Robert J. Wilke, Babe Hart, Rocky Graziano, Shecky Greene, Joe E. Ross, Michael Romanoff, Sue Lyon.

The Detective (1968, 20th-Fox). *d:* Gordon Douglas; *p:* Aaron Rosenberg (Arcola–Millfield); *sc:* Abby Mann—*b/o* the novel by Roderick Thorp.

JOE LELAND: Hard-bitten New York homicide detective who becomes disillusioned after he helps send an innocent man to the electric chair and when he discovers that his community and much of his own department are crooked.

Lee Remick, Ralph Meeker, Jack Klugman, Horace McMahon, Lloyd Bochner, Tony Musante, William Windom, Al Freeman Jr., Robert Duvall, Sugar Ray Robinson, Ranee Taylor, Jacqueline Bisset.

Lady in Cement (1968, 20th-Fox). *d:* Gordon Douglas; *p:* Aaron Rosenberg (Arcola–Millfield); *sc:* Marvin H. Albert and Jack Guss—*b/o* the novel by Marvin H. Albert.

TONY ROME: Miami shamus who, when he discovers a nude female corpse with her feet encased in cement, sets out to track down the killer.

Raquel Welch, Dan Blocker, Richard Conte, Martin Gabel, Lainie Kazan, Pat Henry, Steve Peck, Virginia Wood, Richard Deacon, Peter Hock, Alex Stevens.

Dirty Dingus Magee (1970, MGM). *d:* Burt Kennedy; *p:* Burt Kennedy; *sc:* Tom Waldman, Frank Waldman, and Joseph Heller—*b/o* David Markson's novel *The Ballad of Dingus Magee*

DINGUS MAGEE: Thieving cowboy in 1880s New Mexico who manages to get into hot water with practically everybody—including the sheriff, the Indians, and assorted amorous women.

George Kennedy, Anne Jackson, Lois Nettleton, Jack Elam, Michele Carey, John Dehner, Henry Jones, Harry Carey Jr., Paul Fix, Donald Barry, Mike Wagner.

Contract on Cherry Street (1977, Columbia TV [made for TV]). *d:* William A. Graham; *p:* Hugh Benson (Artanis/Columbia TV); *sc:* Edward Anhalt—*b/o* the novel by Phillip Rosenberg.

DET. FRANK HOVANNES: Angry New York police inspector who, after a buddy is killed, goes underground with his own men to fight the crime syndicate vigilante-style.

Martin Balsam, Jay Black, Verna Bloom, Joe DeSantis, Martin Gabel, Harry Guardino, Henry Silva, James Luisi, Michael Nouri.

The First Deadly Sin (1980, Filmways). *d:* Brian Hutton; *p:* George Pappas and Mark Shanker; *sc:* Mann Rubin—*b/o* the novel by Lawrence Sanders.

EDWARD DELANEY: New York police detective who, just weeks before retirement, sets out to trap a psycho who has killed eleven people in a series of murders committed with a mountain climber's ice hammer.

Faye Dunaway, David Dukes, George Coe, Brenda Vaccaro, Martin Gabel, Joe Spinnel, James Whitmore, Anthony Zerbe.

• In addition, Frank Sinatra made cameo/guest appearances in the following feature films: *Las Vegas Nights* (1941, Para.), *Ship Ahoy* (1942, MGM), *Reveille with Beverly* (1943, Col.), *Till the Clouds Roll By* (1946, MGM), *Meet Me in Las Vegas* (1956, MGM), *Pepe* (1960, Col.), *The Road to Hong Kong* (1962, UA), *The Oscar* (1966, Embassy), and *That's Entertainment* (1974, MGM—on-screen co-narrator).

☆ JAMES STEWART

James Maitland Stewart

b: May 20, 1908, Indiana, Pa.

"I suppose it'd been better if I'd never been born at all."

> George Bailey (James Stewart) to himself, though being observed by the angel Clarence (Henry Travers) in *It's a Wonderful Life*, 1946.

The Murder Man (1935, MGM). *d:* Tim Whelan; *p:* Harry Rapf; *sc:* Tim Whelan and John C. Higgins—*b/o* a story by Tim Whelan and Guy Bolton.

SHORTY: Young cub reporter whose veteran-reporter friend frames a crooked financier for a murder the veteran reporter actually committed himself.

Spencer Tracy, Virginia Bruce, Lionel Atwill, Harvey Stephens, Robert Barrat, William Collier Sr., Bobby Watson, William Demarest, Lucien Littlefield, George Chandler, Fuzzy Knight, Louise Henry, Robert Warwick.

Rose Marie (1936, MGM). *d:* W. S. Van Dyke; *p:* Hunt Stromberg; *sc:* Frances Goodrich, Albert Hackett, and Alice Duer Miller—*b/o* the play by Otto A. Harbach and Oscar Hammerstein II.

JOHN de FLOR: Canadian opera singer's brother who, after escaping from prison and killing a Royal Northwest Mounted Policeman, is pursued by his sister's Mountie sweetheart.

Jeanette MacDonald, Nelson Eddy, Reginald Owen, Allan Jones, Alan Mowbray, Gilda Gray, George Regas, Robert Greig, Lucien Littlefield, Una O'Connor, David Niven, Herman Bing.

Next Time We Love (1936, Univ.). *d:* Edward H. Griffith; *p:* Paul Kohner; *sc:* Melville Baker—*b/o* a story by Ursula Parrott.

CHRISTOPHER TYLER: Roving foreign correspondent who has marital troubles when his wife refuses to travel abroad with him because she wants to stay at home and further her Broadway acting career.

Margaret Sullavan, Ray Milland, Grant Mitchell, Robert McWade, Anna Demetrio, Ronnie Cosbey, Christian Rub.

Wife vs. Secretary (1936, MGM). *d:* Clarence Brown; *p:* Hunt Stromberg; *sc:* Norman Krasna, Alice Duer Miller, and John Lee Mahin—*b/o* the novel by Faith Baldwin.

DAVE: Young man who has problems with his girlfriend when she not only refuses to quit her private secretary's job and marry him but also is suspected of having an affair with her publisher boss.

Clark Gable, Jean Harlow, Myrna Loy, May Robson, George Barbier, Hobart Cavanaugh, Gilbert Emery, Marjorie Gateson, Gloria Holden, Tom Dugan.

Small Town Girl (1936, MGM). *d:* William A. Wellman; *p:* Hunt Stromberg; *sc:* John Lee Mahin and Edith Fitzgerald—*b/o* the novel by Ben Ames Williams.

ELMER: Small-town boy in Massachusetts who loses his small-town girlfriend to a handsome, wealthy playboy.

Janet Gaynor, Robert Taylor, Binnie Barnes, Lewis Stone, Andy Devine, Elizabeth Patterson, Frank Craven, Douglas Fowley, Isabel Jewell, Charley Grapewin, Nella Walker, Robert Greig, Edgar Kennedy, Willie Fung.

Speed (1936, MGM). *d:* Edwin L. Marin; *p:* Lucien Hubbard; *sc:* Michael Fessier—*b/o* a story by Milton Krims and Larry Bachman.

TERRY MARTIN: Young automobile test driver who helps develop a new high-speed carburetor and tries it out on the Indianapolis Speedway.

Una Merkel, Ted Healy, Wendy Barrie, Weldon Heyburn, Ralph Morgan, Patricia Wilder.

The Gorgeous Hussy (1936, MGM). *d:* Clarence Brown; *p:* Joseph L. Mankiewicz; *sc:* Ainsworth Morgan and Stephen Morehouse Avery—*b/o* the book by Samuel Hopkins Adams.

"ROWDY" DOW: One of several male admirers of the notorious Washington belle Peggy O'Neal (Eaton), a protégé and confidante of President Andrew Jackson's.

Joan Crawford, Robert Taylor, Lionel Barrymore, Melvyn Douglas, Franchot Tone, Louis Calhern, Alison Skipworth, Beulah Bondi, Melville Cooper, Sidney Toler, Gene Lockhart, Clara Blandick, Frank Conroy, Nydia Westman, Louise Beavers, Charles Trowbridge, Willard Robertson, Bert Roach, Ward Bond.

Born to Dance (1936, MGM). *d:* Roy Del Ruth; *p:* Jack Cummings; *sc:* Jack McGowan and Sid Silvers—*b/o* a story by Jack McGowan, Sid Silvers, and B. G. DeSylva.

TED BARKER: Bashful U.S. Navy non-com who falls for a dancer he meets in a Lonely Hearts Club before she goes on to become a Broadway star.

Eleanor Powell, Virginia Bruce, Una Merkel, Sid Silvers, Francis Langford, Raymond Walburn,

Alan Dinehart, Buddy Ebsen, Juanita Quigley, Reginald Gardiner.

After the Thin Man (1936, MGM). *d:* W. S. Van Dyke; *p:* Hunt Stromberg; *sc:* Frances Goodrich and Albert Hackett—*b/o* a story by Dashiell Hammett.

DAVID GRAHAM: Pleasant young man who is in love with a woman suspected of a San Francisco murder, but who—when famous sleuth Nick Charles gets on the case—turns out to be the murderer himself.

William Powell, Myrna Loy, Elissa Landi, Joseph Calleia, Jessie Ralph, Alan Marshall, Sam Levene, Dorothy McNulty, George Zucco, Paul Fix, Guy Usher, Robert E. O'Connor.

Seventh Heaven (1937, MGM). *d:* Henry King; *p:* Raymond Griffith; *sc:* Melville Baker—*b/o* the play by Austin Strong.

CHICO: Parisian sewer worker who falls in love with a pretty street urchin, goes off to fight in WWI and is blinded, but finally returns four years later to find her faithfully waiting for him.

Simone Simon, Jean Hersholt, Gregory Ratoff, Gale Sondergaard, J. Edward Bromberg, John Qualen, Victor Kilian, Thomas Beck, Sig Rumann, Mady Christians, Paul Porcasi, Irving Bacon.

The Last Gangster (1937, MGM). *d:* Edward Ludwig; *sc:* John Lee Mahin—*b/o* a story by William A. Wellman and Robert Carson.

PAUL NORTH: Newspaperman who, after he marries the ex-wife of a gangster sent to Alcatraz, finds that they are the object of revenge when the gangster is released after ten years on the Rock.

Edward G. Robinson, Rose Stradner, Lionel Stander, John Carradine, Sidney Blackmer, Edward Brophy, Alan Baxter, Grant Mitchell, Frank Conroy, Moroni Olson, Louise Beavers, Donald Barry, Horace MacMahon, Phillip Terry.

Navy Blue and Gold (1937, MGM). *d:* Sam Wood; *p:* Sam Zimbalist; *sc:* George Bruce—*b/o* his novel.

"TRUCK" CROSS: Young sailor who—after he wins an appointment to Annapolis—becomes a football star, along with his two best pals, then is unjustly suspended from school but gets reinstated in time to help win the big Army-Navy game.

Robert Young, Florence Rice, Billie Burke, Lionel Barrymore, Tom Brown, Samuel S. Hinds, Paul Kelly, Barnett Parker, Frank Albertson, Minor Watson, Robert Middlemass, Philip Terry, Stanley Morner (Dennis Morgan), Matt McHugh.

Of Human Hearts (1938, MGM). *d:* Clarence Brown; *p:* John Considine Jr.; *sc:* Bradbury Foote—*b/o* the novel *Benefits Forgot* by Honore Morrow.

JASON WILKINS: Ohio minister's son who gains distinction as a Union Army doctor in the Civil War but is reprimanded by President Lincoln because for two years he's neglected to write to his self-sacrificing mother.

Walter Huston, Gene Reynolds, Beulah Bondi, Guy Kibbee, Charles Coburn, John Carradine, Ann Rutherford, Charley Grapewin, Gene Lockhart, Clem Bevans, Sterling Holloway, Minor Watson, Robert McWade.

Vivacious Lady (1938, RKO). *d:* George Stevens; *p:* Pandro S. Berman; *sc:* P. J. Wolfson and Ernest Pagano—*b/o* a story by I. A. R. Wylie.

PETER MORGAN: Shy young botany professor who marries a New York nightclub singer, then has problems when he breaks the news to his conservative, dignified family and his fiancée.

Ginger Rogers, James Ellison, Charles Coburn, Beulah Bondi, Franklin Pangborn, Grady Sutton, Hattie McDaniel, Jack Carson, Willie Best, Frank M. Thomas, Spencer Charters, Maude Eburne.

Shopworn Angel (1938, MGM). *d:* H. C. Potter; *p:* Joseph L. Mankiewicz; *sc:* Waldo Salt—*b/o* the play *Private Pettigrew's Girl* by Dana Burnet.

PVT. BILL PETTIGREW: Naïve WWI Texas doughboy who marries a jaded New York actress on the eve he ships overseas but is killed in action shortly after.

Margaret Sullavan, Walter Pidgeon, Hattie McDaniel, Nat Pendleton, Alan Curtis, Sam Levene, Eleanor Lynn, Charles D. Brown.

You Can't Take It with You (1938, Col.). *d:* Frank Capra; *p:* Frank Capra; *sc:* Robert Riskin—*b/o* the play by George S. Kaufman and Moss Hart.

TONY KIRBY: Down-to-earth son of a rich, snobbish businessman who gets involved with a screwball family when he falls for one of the daughters.

Jean Arthur, Lionel Barrymore, Edward Arnold, Mischa Auer, Ann Miller, Spring Byington, Samuel S. Hinds, Donald Meek, H. B. Warner, Halliwell Hobbes, Dub Taylor, Eddie Anderson, Clarence Wilson, Charles Lane, Harry Davenport.

Made for Each Other (1939, UA). *d:* John Cromwell; *p:* David O. Selznick (Selznick International); *sc:* Jo Swerling.

JOHN MASON: Young New York attorney who marries a young Boston woman, then runs into problems with meddling in-laws, his job, money, and illness.

Carole Lombard, Charles Coburn, Lucile Watson, Eddie Quillan, Alma Kruger, Ruth Weston, Donald Briggs, Harry Davenport, Esther Dale, Louise Beavers, Ward Bond, Olin Howland.

Ice Follies of 1939 (1939, MGM). *d:* Reinhold Schunzel; *p:* Harry Rapf; *sc:* Leonard Praskins,

Florence Ryerson, and Edgar Allan Woolf—*b/o* a story by Leonard Praskins.

LARRY HALL: Ice Follies skater and producer—based in New York— who has marital problems after his wife becomes a Hollywood movie star, but who solves the situation by becoming a Hollywood film producer so that their careers are compatible.

Joan Crawford, Lew Ayres, Lewis Stone, Bess Ehrhardt, Lionel Stander, Charles D. Brown, Roy Shipstad, Eddie Shipstad, Oscar Johnson.

It's a Wonderful World (1939, MGM). *d:* W. S. Van Dyke II; *p:* Frank Davis; *sc:* Ben Hecht—*b/o* a story by Ben Hecht and Herman J. Mankiewicz.

GUY JOHNSON: Novice detective who, when he's falsely accused of being an accessory to murder, tracks down the killer with the help of a pretty woman who's a poet.

Claudette Colbert, Guy Kibbee, Nat Pendleton, Frances Drake, Edgar Kennedy, Ernest Truex, Richard Carle, Sidney Blackmer, Andy Clyde, Cecil Cunningham, Hans Conried, Grady Sutton.

Mr. Smith Goes to Washington (1939, Col.). *d:* Frank Capra; *p:* Frank Capra; *sc:* Sidney Buchman—*b/o* a story by Lewis R. Foster.

JEFFERSON SMITH*: Naïve, idealistic head of a group of boys' clubs who, though he's appointed to the U.S. Senate by machine politicians to be a patsy, fights corruption and stages a marathon one-man filibuster when he's falsely accused of misconduct.

Jean Arthur, Claude Rains, Edward Arnold, Guy Kibbee, Thomas Mitchell, Eugene Pallette, Beulah Bondi, H. B. Warner, Harry Carey, Astrid Allwyn, Ruth Donnelly, Grant Mitchell, Porter Hall, H. V. Kaltenborn, Pierre Watkin, Charles Lane, William Demarest, Dick Elliott.

Destry Rides Again (1939, Univ.). *d:* George Marshall; *p:* Joe Pasternak; *sc:* Felix Jackson, Henry Myers, and Gertrude Purcell—*b/o* the novel by Max Brand.

TOM DESTRY: Easy-going son of a famous lawman who, when he becomes deputy sheriff of the 1870s town of Bottle Neck, tangles with a hardboiled dance-hall girl from the Last Chance Saloon and tries to tame the town's badmen without a gun.

Marlene Dietrich, Charles Winninger, Mischa Auer, Brian Donlevy, Irene Hervey, Una Merkel, Allen Jenkins, Warren Hymer, Samuel S. Hinds, Jack Carson, Lillian Yarbo, Tom Fadden, Dickie Jones, Virginia Brissac, Joe King.

The Shop Around the Corner (1940, MGM). *d:* Ernst Lubitsch; *p:* Ernst Lubitsch; *sc:* Samson

Raphaelson—*b/o* the play by Nikolaus Laszlo.

ALFRED KRALIK: Clerk in a Budapest novelty shop who carries on an anonymous lonely-hearts correspondence with a young woman who, although neither of them knows it, works in the same shop he does.

Margaret Sullavan, Frank Morgan, Joseph Schildkraut, Sara Haden, Felix Bressart, William Tracy, Inez Courtney, Edwin Maxwell, Charles Halton, Charles Smith.

The Mortal Storm (1940, MGM). *d:* Frank Borzage; *sc:* Claudine West, Anderson Ellis, and George Froeschel—*b/o* the novel by Phyllis Bottome.

MARTIN BREITNER: Courageous young 1930s farmer in Hitler's Germany who refuses to join the Nazi Party and—along with his girlfriend, the daughter of a Jewish professor—tries to escape to Austria.

Margaret Sullavan, Robert Young, Frank Morgan, Robert Stack, Bonita Granville, Irene Rich, William T. Orr, Maria Ouspenskaya, Esther Dale, Gene Reynolds, Russell Hicks, Dan Dailey Jr., Granville Bates, Ward Bond.

No Time for Comedy (1940, WB). *d:* William Keighley; *p:* Jack L. Warner and Hal B. Wallis; *sc:* Julius J. Epstein and Philip G. Epstein—*b/o* the play by S. N. Behrman.

GAYLORD ESTERBROOK: Minnesota newspaper reporter who becomes a successful New York comedy playwright but flops when a conniving wealthy woman convinces him—much to the dismay of his actress wife—that he should write message dramas.

Rosalind Russell, Genevieve Tobin, Charles Ruggles, Allyn Joslyn, Clarence Kolb, Louise Beavers, J. M. Kerrigan, Lawrence Grossmith, Robert Greig, Frank Faylen, Ed Dearing.

The Philadelphia Story (1940, MGM). *d:* George Cukor; *p:* Joseph L. Mankiewicz; *sc:* Donald Ogden Stewart—*b/o* the play by Philip Barry.

MACAULEY "MIKE" CONNOR*: Magazine reporter who, while on an assignment to cover the upcoming second marriage of a wealthy young Philadelphia society woman, has a one-night fling with her.

Cary Grant, Katharine Hepburn, Ruth Hussey, John Howard, Roland Young, John Halliday, Mary Nash, Virginia Weidler, Henry Daniell, Lionel Pape, Rex Evans, Hilda Plowright, Lee Phelps, Hillary Brooke.

Come Live with Me (1941, MGM). *d:* Clarence Brown; *p:* Clarence Brown; *sc:* Patterson McNutt—*b/o* a story by Virginia Van Upp.

---

*Received an Academy Award nomination as Best Actor for this role.

---

*Won the Academy Award as Best Actor for this role.

BILL SMITH: Financially strapped young writer who agrees to marry, strictly on a business basis, a wealthy Austrian refugee to keep her from being deported—but winds up falling in love with her.

Hedy Lamarr, Ian Hunter, Verree Teasdale, Donald Meek, Barton MacLane, Edward Ashley, King Baggot, Frank Orth, Frank Faylen, Horace MacMahon.

Pot O'Gold (1941, UA). *d:* George Marshall; *p:* James Roosevelt; *sc:* Walter De Leon—*b/o* a story by Monte Brice, Andrew Bennison, and Harry Tugend.

JIMMY HASKEL: Harmonica-playing nephew of a music-hating food manufacturer who joins Horace Heidt's band, then talks the uncle into putting the band on a radio giveaway show sponsored by the uncle.

Paulette Goddard, Horace Heidt, Charles Winninger, Mary Gordon, Frank Melton, Jed Prouty, James Burke, Charlie Arnt, Donna Wood, Irving Bacon.

Ziegfeld Girl (1941, MGM). *d:* Robert Z. Leonard; *p:* Pandro S. Berman; *sc:* Marguerite Roberts and Sonya Levien—*b/o* a story by William Anthony McGuire.

GILBERT YOUNG: Young truck driver whose girlfriend, a beautiful elevator operator, becomes a star in the Ziegfeld Follies—but dies of a heart attack on the opening night of a new show.

Judy Garland, Hedy Lamarr, Lana Turner, Tony Martin, Jackie Cooper, Ian Hunter, Charles Winninger, Edward Everett Horton, Philip Dorn, Paul Kelly, Eve Arden, Dan Dailey Jr., Al Shean, Fay Holden, Felix Bressart, Rose Hobart.

It's a Wonderful Life (1947, RKO). *d:* Frank Capra; *p:* Frank Capra (Liberty); *sc:* Frances Goodrich, Albert Hackett, and Frank Capra—*b/o* Philip Van Doren Stern's short story "The Greatest Gift."

GEORGE BAILEY*: Businessman father in the small New England town of Bedford Falls who, on Christmas Eve, decides that his life has been a failure and contemplates suicide; but he's visited by guardian angel Clarence who shows him how different his family and Bedford Falls would have been if he'd never been born, and how worthwhile his life really has been.

Donna Reed, Lionel Barrymore, Thomas Mitchell, Henry Travers, Beulah Bondi, Frank Faylen, Ward Bond, Gloria Grahame, H. B. Warner, Frank Albertson, Todd Karnes, Samuel S. Hinds, Mary Treen, Sheldon Leonard, Danny Mummert, Larry Sims, Carl (Alfalfa) Switzer, Ray Walker.

---

*Received an Academy Award nomination as Best Actor for this role.

Magic Town (1947, RKO). *d:* William A. Wellman; *p:* Robert Riskin; *sc:* Robert Riskin—*b/o* a story by Robert Riskin and Joseph Krumgold.

RIP SMITH: Public-opinion pollster who, when he discovers a small town whose population's views exactly coincide with the U.S.A. population's views, makes the town famous but then sees it drastically change.

Jane Wyman, Kent Smith, Ned Sparks, Regis Toomey, Wallace Ford, Ann Doran, Ann Shoemaker, Donald Meek, Howard Freeman, Frank Fenton, Tom Kennedy, William Haade, Selmer Jackson, Richard Wessel.

Call Northside 777 (1948, 20th-Fox). *d:* Henry Hathaway; *p:* Otto Lang; *sc:* Jerome Cady and Jay Dratler—*b/o* a story by James P. McGuire.

NcNEAL: Chicago newspaper reporter who helps a scrubwoman prove that her son—in prison for the past eleven years for killing a policeman—is innocent and was wrongly imprisoned.

Richard Conte, Lee J. Cobb, Helen Walker, Howard Smith, Moroni Olsen, John McIntire, Paul Harvey, J. M. Kerrigan, Samuel S. Hinds, Addison Richards, Richard Rober, Eddie Dunn, Percy Helton, Charles Lane, E. G. Marshall.

On Our Merry Way (1948, UA). *d:* King Vidor and Leslie Fenton; *p:* Benedict Bogeaus and Burgess Meredith; *sc:* Laurence Stallings and Lou Breslow—*b/o* a story by Arch Oboler (original material for Stewart-Fonda sequence by John O'Hara).

SLIM: One of a pair of musicians who try to make a fast buck by fixing an amateur music contest at a California beach resort so that the local mayor's son wins.

Burgess Meredith, Paulette Goddard, Fred MacMurray, Hugh Herbert, Henry Fonda, Dorothy Lamour, Victor Moore, William Demarest, Charles D. Brown, Tom Fadden, Paul Hurst, Carl "Alfalfa" Switzer.

Rope (1948, WB). *d:* Alfred Hitchcock; *p:* Alfred Hitchcock (Transatlantic); *sc:* Arthur Laurents—*b/o* the play by Patrick Hamilton.

RUPERT CADELL: Professor who solves a case involving two of his ex-students, who killed a college friend for the thrill of it and to prove their super-intelligence by pulling off "the perfect crime."

John Dall, Farley Granger, Sir Cedric Hardwicke, Constance Collier, Douglas Dick, Edith Evanson, Dick Hogan, Joan Chandler.

You Gotta Stay Happy (1949, Univ.). *d:* H. C. Potter; *p:* Karl Tunberg; *sc:* Karl Tunberg—*b/o* a story by Robert Carson.

MARVIN PAYNE: Flyer/owner of a nearly bankrupt two-plane cargo airline who gets involved with a millionairess who has run away from her husband on their wedding night.

Joan Fontaine, Eddie Albert, Roland Young, Willard Parker, Percy Kilbride, Porter Hall, Marcy McGuire, William Bakewell, Paul Cavanagh, Halliwell Hobbes, Emory Parnell, Hal K. Dawson.

The Stratton Story (1949, MGM). *d:* Sam Wood; *p:* Jack Cummings; *sc:* Douglas Morrow and Guy Trosper—*b/o* a story by Douglas Morrow.

MONTY STRATTON: Famous Chicago White Sox pitcher who loses a leg because of a hunting accident but—with hope, courage, and the help of his wife—returns to baseball and greater success.

June Allyson, Frank Morgan, Agnes Moorehead, Bill Williams, Bruce Cowling, Cliff Clark, Robert Gist, Gene Bearden, Bill Dickey.

Malaya (1950, MGM). *d:* Richard Thorpe; *p:* Edwin Knopf; *sc:* Frank Fenton—*b/o* a story by Manchester Boddy.

JOHN ROYER: WWII American newspaper reporter who joins forces with an old-pro American smuggler to smuggle raw rubber out of Japanese-occupied Malaya for use by the U.S. armed forces.

Spencer Tracy, Valentina Cortesa, Sydney Greenstreet, John Hodiak, Lionel Barrymore, Gilbert Roland, Roland Winters, Richard Loo, Ian MacDonald, Lester Matthews, Charles Meredith, James Todd.

Winchester '73 (1950, Univ.). *d:* Anthony Mann; *p:* Aaron Rosenberg; *sc:* Robert L. Richards and Borden Chase—*b/o* a story by Stuart Lake.

LIN McADAM: Cowboy in 1873 who tracks down his father's killer and a prize Winchester '73 repeater rifle that the killer has stolen from him.

Shelley Winters, Dan Duryea, Stephen McNally, Millard Mitchell, Charles Drake, John McIntire, Will Geer, Jay C. Flippen, Rock Hudson, Steve Brodie, James Millican, Abner Biberman, Tony Curtis.

Broken Arrow (1950, 20th-Fox). *d:* Delmer Daves; *p:* Julian Blaustein; *sc:* Michael Blankfort—*b/o* the novel *Blood Brother* by Elliott Arnold.

TOM JEFFORDS: Civil War veteran and scout in 1870s Arizona who, while trying to make peace between the Apache leader Cochise and the white man, falls in love with a young Indian woman and marries her.

Jeff Chandler, Debra Paget, Basil Ruysdael, Will Geer, Joyce MacKenzie, Arthur Hunnicutt, Jay Silverheels, Iron Eyes Cody, John Doucette.

The Jackpot (1950, 20th-Fox). *d:* Walter Lang; *p:* Sam Engel; *sc:* Phoebe Ephron and Henry Ephron.

BILL LAWRENCE: Small-town department-store executive who wins a giant radio-quiz jackpot but finds that it leads to financial, marital, and other assorted problems.

Barbara Hale, James Gleason, Fred Clark, Alan Mowbray, Patricia Medina, Natalie Wood, Tommy Rettig, Lyle Talbot, Claude Stroud, Syd Saylor, John Qualen, Fritz Feld, Andrew Tombes.

Harvey (1950, Univ.). *d:* Henry Koster; *p:* John Beck; *sc:* Mary Chase and Oscar Brodney—*b/o* the play by Mary Chase.

ELWOOD P. DOWD*: Whimsical, tippling philosopher whose sister tries to have him committed when he acquires an imaginary companion: a six-foot invisible rabbit named Harvey.

Josephine Hull, Peggy Dow, Charles Drake, Cecil Kellaway, Jesse White, Wallace Ford, Nana Bryant, Clem Bevans, Ida Moore.

No Highway in the Sky (1951, 20th-Fox). *d:* Henry Koster; *p:* Louis D. Lighton; *sc:* R. C. Sherriff, Oscar Millard, and Alec Coppel—*b/o* the novel by Nevil Shute.

MR. HONEY: Eccentric, absent-minded engineer in Britain's Royal Aircraft Establishment who, during a transatlantic flight on a new type of British commercial aircraft, insists that his calculations show that the tail assembly is about to snap from metal fatigue.

Marlene Dietrich, Glynis Johns, Jack Hawkins, Ronald Squire, Janette Scott, Niall McGinnis, Elizabeth Allan, Kenneth More, David Hutcheson, Wilfrid Hyde-White.

The Greatest Show on Earth (1952, Para.). *d:* Cecil B. DeMille; *p:* Cecil B. DeMille; *sc:* Fredric M. Frank, Barre Lyndon, and Theodore St. John—*b/o* a story by Fredric M. Frank, Theodore St. John, and Frank Cavett.

BUTTONS: Circus clown who is never seen without his makeup—which serves to hide his true identity as a doctor wanted for the mercy killing of his wife.

Betty Hutton, Charlton Heston, Cornel Wilde, Dorothy Lamour, Gloria Grahame, Lyle Bettger, Henry Wilcoxon, Emmett Kelly, Lawrence Tierny, John Kellogg, John Ringling North, John Ridgely, Frank Wilcox, Julia Faye, Lane Chandler.

Bend of the River (1952, Univ.). *d:* Anthony Mann; *p:* Aaron Rosenberg; *sc:* Borden Chase—*b/o* the novel *Bend of the Snake* by William Gulick.

GLYN McLYNTOCK: Ex-outlaw who leads an 1840s wagon train to Oregon and clashes with a former sidekick who is hijacking settler's supplies.

Arthur Kennedy, Julia Adams, Rock Hudson, Lori Nelson, Jay C. Flippen, Stepin Fetchit, Henry

---

*Received an Academy Award nomination as Best Actor for this role.

(Harry) Morgan, Chubby Johnson, Howard Petrie, Frances Bavier, Jack Lambert, Royal Dano, Frank Ferguson.

Carbine Williams (1952, MGM). *d:* Richard Thorpe; *p:* Armand Deutsch; *sc:* Art Cohn.

MARSH WILLIAMS: Prohibition-era North Carolina metalworker and moonshiner who, when he's convicted of second-degree murder and sentenced to thirty years in prison, invents the famed WWII 30 M-1 carbine and is rewarded with a pardon after serving eight years.

Jean Hagen, Wendell Corey, Carl Benton Reid, Paul Stewart, Rhys Williams, James Arness, Porter Hall, Ralph Dumke, Leif Erickson, Howard Petrie, Dan Riss.

The Naked Spur (1953, MGM). *d:* Anthony Mann; *p:* William H. Wright; *sc:* Sam Rolfe and Harold Jack Bloom.

HOWARD KEMP: Bounty hunter in the Colorado Rockies who has to contend with a greedy old prospector and a dishonorably discharged Union soldier when the three of them capture an escaped killer with a $5000 price on his head.

Janet Leigh, Ralph Meeker, Robert Ryan, Millard Mitchell.

Thunder Bay (1953, Univ.). *d:* Anthony Mann; *p:* Aaron Rosenberg; *sc:* Gil Doud and John Michael Hayes—*b/o* a story by John Michael Hayes, from an idea by George W. George and George F. Slavin.

STEVE MARTIN: Oil wildcatter in Louisiana who is opposed by local shrimp fishermen who fear that the oil company's off-shore drilling will threaten their livelihood.

Joanne Dru, Gilbert Roland, Dan Duryea, Jay C. Flippen, Marcia Henderson, Robert Monet, Antonio Moreno, Henry (Harry) Morgan.

The Glenn Miller Story (1954, Univ.). *d:* Anthony Mann; *p:* Aaron Rosenberg; *sc:* Valentine Davies and Oscar Brodney.

GLENN MILLER: Trombone-playing big-band leader who creates a new sound during the 1930s–'40s swing era but loses his life in a plane crash over the English Channel while serving in the U.S. Army in WWII.

June Allyson, Charles Drake, George Tobias, Henry (Harry) Morgan, Frances Langford, Louis Armstrong, Gene Krupa, Ben Pollack, The Modernaires, Marion Ross, Irving Bacon, Barton MacLane, Sig Rumann, Phil Harris, James Bell.

Rear Window (1954, Para.). *d:* Alfred Hitchcock; *p:* Alfred Hitchcock; *sc:* John Michael Hayes—*b/o* the short story by Cornell Woolrich.

L. B. (JEFF) JEFFRIES: Magazine photographer—laid up in his Greenwich Village apartment with a broken leg—who takes to watching his neighbors through binoculars and witnesses a murder.

Grace Kelly, Wendell Corey, Thelma Ritter, Raymond Burr, Judith Evelyn, Ross Bagdasarian, Frank Cady, Jesslyn Fax, Bess Flowers, Rand Harper, Marla English.

The Far Country (1955, Univ.). *d:* Anthony Mann; *p:* Aaron Rosenberg; *sc:* Borden Chase.

JEFF WEBSTER: Straight-shooting cowpoke who, when he herds his steers by boat to Alaska to sell, tries to stay peaceful but is forced to use his guns when his sidekick is gunned down by cattle rustlers.

Ruth Roman, Corinne Calvet, Walter Brennan, John McIntire, Jay C. Flippen, Henry (Harry) Morgan, Steve Brodie, Royal Dano, Chubby Johnson, Eddy C. Waller.

Strategic Air Command (1955, Para.). *d:* Anthony Mann; *p:* Samuel J. Briskin; *sc:* Valentine Davies and Beirne Lay Jr.

ROBERT HOLLAND: St. Louis Cardinals' star third baseman and reserve lieutenant colonel who, at the peak of his career, is recalled to the 1950s peacetime U.S. Air Force to fly an SAC bomber.

June Allyson, Frank Lovejoy, Barry Sullivan, Alex Nicol, Bruce Bennett, Jay C. Flippen, James Millican, James Bell, Rosemary DeCamp, Henry (Harry) Morgan, Don Haggerty, Strother Martin.

The Man from Laramie (1955, Col.). *d:* Anthony Mann; *p:* William Goetz; *sc:* Philip Yordan and Frank Burt—*b/o* a story by Thomas T. Flynn.

WILL LOCKHART: Cowboy who rides from Laramie, Wyoming, to New Mexico to find the man responsible for selling automatic rifles to the Apaches who killed his cavalry-officer younger brother.

Arthur Kennedy, Donald Crisp, Cathy O'Donnell, Alex Nicol, Aline MacMahon, Wallace Ford, Jack Elam, James Millican, Frank de Kova, John War Eagle.

The Man Who Knew Too Much (1956, Para.). *d:* Alfred Hitchcock; *p:* Alfred Hitchcock; *sc:* John Michael Hayes and Angus MacPhail—*b/o* a story by Charles Bennett and D. B. Wyndham-Lewis.

BEN McKENNA: American surgeon on vacation in Morocco whose young son is kidnapped to prevent the surgeon and his wife from revealing what they've discovered about an assassination plot.

Doris Day, Brenda De Banzie, Bernard Miles, Ralph Truman, Daniel Gelin, Mognes Wieth, Alan Mowbray, Hillary Brooke, Carolyn Jones, Leo Gordon, Louis Mercier, Lewis Martin.

The Spirit of St. Louis (1957, WB). *d:* Billy Wilder; *p:* Leland Hayward; *sc:* Billy Wilder and Wendell Mayes (adaptation by Charles Lederer)—

b/o the 1953 Pulitzer Prize–winning book by Charles A. Lindbergh.

CHARLES A. LINDBERGH: Famed American aviator who in 1927 flies his monoplane—"The Spirit of St. Louis"—from New York to Paris on the first successful solo flight across the Atlantic Ocean.

Murray Hamilton, Patricia Smith, Bartlett Robinson, Robert Cornthwaite, Marc Connelly, Arthur Space, Dabbs Greer, Robert Burton, Erville Alderson, Sid Saylor, Ray Walker, Richard Deacon.

Night Passage (1957, Univ.). *d:* James Neilson; *p:* Aaron Rosenberg; *sc:* Borden Chase—*b/o* a story by Norman A. Fox.

GRANT McLAINE: Accordian-playing railroad troubleshooter who, when he's hired to protect the railroad from a gang of outlaws, discovers that his younger brother belongs to the gang.

Audie Murphy, Dan Duryea, Diane Foster, Elaine Stewart, Brandon de Wilde, Jay C. Flippen, Herbert Anderson, Robert J. Wilke, Hugh Beaumont, Jack Elam, Paul Fix, Olive Carey, James Flavin, Ellen Corby.

Vertigo (1958, Para.). *d:* Alfred Hitchcock; *p:* Alfred Hitchcock; *sc:* Alex Coppel and Samuel Taylor—*b/o* a story by Pierre Boileau and Thomas Narcejac.

JOHN "SCOTTIE" FERGUSON: Ex–San Francisco police detective with a fear of heights who—when he's hired to shadow a friend's wife—falls in love with her, suffers a nervous breakdown when she apparently falls to her death, then meets a girl who looks just like her.

Kim Novak, Barbara Bel Geddes, Tom Helmore, Henry Jones, Raymond Bailey, Ellen Corby, Konstantin Shayne, Lee Patrick.

Bell, Book and Candle (1958, Col.). *d:* Richard Quine; *p:* Julian Blaustein (Phoenix); *sc:* Daniel Taradash—*b/o* the play by John Van Druten.

SHEPHERD HENDERSON: New York publisher who unsuspectingly falls in love with a beautiful modern-day witch when she casts a spell over him.

Kim Novak, Jack Lemmon, Ernie Kovacs, Hermione Gingold, Elsa Lanchester, Janice Rule, Howard McNear, Gail Bonney, Wolfe Barzell, Monty Ash.

Anatomy of a Murder (1959, Col.). *d:* Otto Preminger; *p:* Otto Preminger (Carlyle); *sc:* Wendell Mayes—*b/o* the novel by Robert Traver.

PAUL BIEGLER*: Small-town Michigan lawyer who is hired to defend an Army lieutenant

---

*Received an Academy Award nomination as Best Actor for this role.

accused of murdering a bartender who beat and raped his (the officer's) wife.

Lee Remick, Ben Gazzara, Arthur O'Connell, Eve Arden, Kathryn Grant (Crosby), Joseph N. Welch, George C. Scott, Murray Hamilton, Orson Bean, Howard McNear, Jimmy Conlin, Don Ross, John Qualen, Duke Ellington.

The FBI Story (1959, WB). *d:* Mervyn LeRoy; *p:* Mervyn LeRoy; *sc:* Richard L. Breen and John Twist.

CHIP HARDESTY: Dedicated FBI agent who, from the 1920s through the 1950s, helps fight a wide variety of crimes.

Vera Miles, Murray Hamilton, Larry Pennell, Nick Adams, Diane Jergens, Parley Baer, Fay Roope, Ed Prentiss, Robert Gist, Ann Doran, Forrest Taylor.

The Mountain Road (1960, Col.). *d:* Daniel Mann; *p:* William Goetz; *sc:* Alfred Hayes—*b/o* the novel by Theodore White.

MAJOR BALDWIN: Emotionless U.S. Army officer in WWII China who learns compassion for his fellow men when he heads a demolition team assigned to destroy vital bridges, roads, and villages in order to stop Japanese troops from advancing.

Lisa Lu, Glenn Corbett, Henry (Harry) Morgan, Frank Silvera, James Best, Rudy Bond, Mike Kellin, Frank Maxwell, Alan Baxter.

Two Rode Together (1961, Col.). *d:* John Ford; *p:* Stan Sheptner; *sc:* Frank Nugent—*b/o* the novel by Will Cook.

GUTHRIE McCABE: Cynical 1880s Texas marshal who is hired to help a U.S. Cavalry lieutenant lead a wagon train on a mission to rescue white captives held by Commanche Indians for many years.

Richard Widmark, Shirley Jones, Linda Cristal, Andy Devine, John McIntire, Paul Birch, Willis Bouchey, Henry Brandon, Harry Carey Jr., Olive Carey, Mae Marsh, Ken Curtis, Anna Lee, Woody Strode, Ted Knight, Ford Rainey, John Qualen, O. Z. Whitehead.

The Man Who Shot Liberty Valance (1962, Para.). *d:* John Ford; *p:* Willis Goldbeck (John Ford Prods.); *sc:* James Warner Bellah and Willis Goldbeck—*b/o* the short story by Dorothy M. Johnson.

RANSE STODDARD: Young lawyer in the Old West who, after he becomes famous as the man who killed a notorious bad man, is elected to Congress—though in fact his rancher friend really did the killing.

John Wayne, Vera Miles, Lee Marvin, Edmond O'Brien, Andy Devine, Woody Strode, Ken Murray, John Qualen, Jeanette Nolan, Lee Van Cleef, Strother Martin, John Carradine, Willis

Bouchey, Denver Pyle, Robert F. Simon, Paul Birch.

Mr. Hobbs Takes a Vacation (1962, 20th-Fox). *d:* Henry Koster; *p:* Jery Wald; *sc:* Nunnally Johnson—*b/o* the novel by Edward Streeter.

ROGER HOBBS: Bemused head of a family whose members run into all kinds of problems when they take a summer vacation in a run-down cottage at the beach.

Maureen O'Hara, Fabian, John Saxon, Marie Wilson, Reginald Gardiner, Lauri Peters, Valerie Varda, Lili Gentle, John McGiver, Natalie Trundy, Minerva Urecal, Richard Collier.

How the West Was Won (1963, MGM/Cinerama). *d:* Henry Hathaway, John Ford, and George Marshall; *p:* Bernard Smith; *sc:* James R. Webb—*b/o* the series *How the West Was Won* in *Life* magazine.

LINUS RAWLINGS: Fur trapper in the 1830s who rescues a family from river pirates on the Ohio River, marries one of the daughters and settles down on a farm, but is later killed in action with the Union Army during the Civil War.

Carroll Baker, Lee J. Cobb, Henry Fonda, Carolyn Jones, Karl Malden, Gregory Peck, George Peppard, Robert Preston, Debbie Reynolds, Eli Wallach, John Wayne, Richard Widmark, Walter Brennan, David Brian, Andy Devine, Raymond Massey, Agnes Moorehead, Henry (Harry) Morgan, Thelma Ritter, Mickey Shaughnessy, Russ Tamblyn.

Take Her, She's Mine (1963, 20th-Fox). *d:* Henry Koster; *p:* Henry Koster; *sc:* Nunnally Johnson—*b/o* the play by Phoebe Ephron and Henry Ephron.

FRANK MICHAELSON: Harried lawyer father whose wild teen-age daughter gets involved with beatniks at college and, later, with a young French painter in Paris.

Sandra Dee, Audrey Meadows, Robert Morley, Philippe Forquet, John McGiver, Robert Denver, Monica Moran, Jenny Maxwell, Cynthia Pepper.

Cheyenne Autumn (1964, WB). *d:* John Ford; *p:* Bernard Smith (Ford–Smith); *sc:* James R. Webb—*b/o* the novel by Mari Sandoz.

WYATT EARP: Lawman/gambler who, when he's pressured into leading a posse against Cheyenne Indians trying to get from an Oklahoma reservation back to their Wyoming homeland, steers the posse the wrong way to avoid unnecessary bloodshed.

Richard Widmark, Carroll Baker, Karl Malden, Edward G. Robinson, Sal Mineo, Dolores Del Rio, Ricardo Montalban, Gilbert Roland, Arthur Kennedy, Patrick Wayne, John Carradine, Victor Jory, Mike Mazurki, George O'Brien, Ben Johnson, Denver Pyle.

Dear Brigitte (1965, 20th-Fox). *d:* Henry Koster; *p:* Henry Koster; *sc:* Hal Kanter—*b/o* the novel *Erasmus with Freckles* by John Haase.

ROBERT LEAF: Poetry professor at a California college whose eight-year-old son develops a crush on Brigitte Bardot, writes her fan letters, and finally gets to visit her in Paris—along with Dad.

Fabian, Glynis Johns, Cindy Carol, Billy Mumy, John Williams, Jack Kruschen, Howard Freeman, Alice Pearce, Jesse White, Ed Wynn, Brigitte Bardot.

Shenandoah (1965, Univ.). *d:* Andrew V. McLaglen; *p:* Robert Arthur; *sc:* James Lee Barrett.

CHARLIE ANDERSON: Virginia farmer who refuses to take sides in the Civil War until the youngest of his six sons is mistaken for a Confederate soldier and captured by Yankee troops.

Doug McClure, Glenn Corbett, Patrick Wayne, Rosemary Forsyth, Phillip Alford, Katharine Ross, Paul Fix, Denver Pyle, George Kennedy, Warren Oates, Strother Martin, Dabbs Greer, Harry Carey Jr., James Best, Tim McIntire, Bob Steele.

Flight of the Phoenix (1966, 20th-Fox). *d:* Robert Aldrich; *p:* Robert Aldrich (Associates and Aldrich); *sc:* Lukas Hellar—*b/o* the novel by Elleston Trevor.

FRANK TOWNS: Pilot of an old twin-engine plane that crashes in the Sahara, stranding an assorted group of male passengers who try to rebuild the plane in order to save themselves.

Richard Attenborough, Peter Finch, Hardy Kruger, Ernest Borgnine, Ian Bannen, Ronald Fraser, Christian Marquand, Dan Duryea, George Kennedy, Alex Montoya, Barrie Chase.

The Rare Breed (1966, Univ.). *d:* Andrew V. McLaglen; *p:* William Alland; *sc:* Ric Hardman.

SAM BURNETT: Cowhand in 1880s Kansas who helps the widow of a British cattle-breeder prove that her prize white-faced Hereford bull can be crossbred with traditional longhorn stock to begin a "rare breed."

Maureen O'Hara, Brian Keith, Juliet Mills, Don Galloway, David Brian, Jack Elam, Ben Johnson, Perry Lopez, Harry Carey Jr.

Firecreek (1968, WB–Seven Arts). *d:* Vincent McEveety; *p:* Philip Leacock; *sc:* Calvin Clements.

JOHNNY COBB: Mild-mannered farmer and part-time sheriff of a small town who finds himself face to face with a hardened outlaw leader and his gang of bad men from the Missouri range wars.

Henry Fonda, Inger Stevens, Gary Lockwood, Dean Jagger, Ed Begley, Jay C. Flippen, Jack Elam, James Best, Barbara Luna, John Qualen.

Bandolero! (1968, 20th-Fox). *d:* Andrew V. McLaglen; *p:* Robert L. Jacks; *sc:* James Lee Barrett—*b/o* a story by Stanley L. Hough.

MACE BISHOP: One of two outlaw brothers in Texas whose post–Civil War gang robs a bank, takes a rancher's widow hostage, and heads across the Mexican border with a sheriff's posse in pursuit.

Dean Martin, Raquel Welch, George Kennedy, Andrew Prine, Will Geer, Clint Ritchie, Denver Pyle, Sean McClory, Harry Carey Jr., Donald Barry, Guy Raymond, Jock Mahoney.

The Cheyenne Social Club (1970, Nat. Gen.). *d:* Gene Kelly; *p:* James Lee Barrett and Gene Kelly; *sc:* James Lee Barrett.

JOHN O'HANLAN: Drifting cowpoke in 1867 who inherits the "Cheyenne Social Club" and is delighted, along with his genial cowpoke pal, to discover that it's a high-class bawdy house.

Henry Fonda, Shirley Jones, Jackie Joseph, Sue Ane Langdon, Robert Middleton; Sharon De Bord, Elaine Devry, Jackie Russell, Dabbs Greer, Richard Collier, Arch Johnson.

Fools' Parade (1971, Col.). *d:* Andrew V. McLaglen; *p:* Andrew V. McLaglen; *sc:* James Lee Barrett—*b/o* the novel by Davis Grubb.

MATTIE APPLEYARD: Aging West Virginia convict who—when he's released from prison after forty years—has trouble cashing his $25,000 prison-earnings check and discovers that his ex-prison guard and the crooked bank president plan to kill him and keep the money for themselves.

George Kennedy, Strother Martin, Kurt Russell, William Windom, Mike Kellin, Anne Baxter, Kathy Cannon, David Huddleston, Robert Donner.

The Shootist (1976, Para.). *d:* Don Siegel; *p:* M. J. Frankovich and William Self (Dino De Laurentiis); *sc:* Miles Hood Swarthout and Scott Hale—*b/o* the novel by Glendon Swarthout.

DR. HOSTETLER: Sympathetic doctor in turn-of-the-century Carson City who, when an ailing legendary gunfighter comes to him, examines the man and tells him that he's dying of cancer.

John Wayne, Lauren Bacall, Ron Howard, Richard Boone, Hugh O'Brian, Bill McKinney, Harry Morgan, John Carradine, Sheree North, Richard Lane, Scatman Crothers, Gregg Palmer, Alfred Dennis, Dick Winslow, Melody Thomas, Kathleen O'Malley.

Airport 77 (1977, Univ.). *d:* Jerry Jameson; *p:* Jennings Lang and William Frye; *sc:* David Spector and Michael Scheff—inspired by the movie *Airport,* *b/o* the novel *Airport* by Arthur Hailey.

PHILLIP STEVENS: Wealthy art collector and owner of a 747 jet that—when it's hijacked while flying over the Bermuda Triangle with millions of dollars' worth of art treasures aboard—crashes and sinks into 100 feet of water, forcing a daring rescue attempt.

Jack Lemmon, Lee Grant, Brenda Vaccaro, George Kennedy, Joseph Cotten, Olivia de Havilland, Darren McGavin, Christopher Lee, Robert Foxworth, Robert Hooks, Monte Markham, James Booth.

The Big Sleep (1978, UA). *d:* Michael Winner; *p:* Elliott Kastner and Michael Winner; *sc:* Michael Winner—*b/o* the novel by Raymond Chandler.

GENERAL STERNWOOD: Wealthy gentleman living in London who calls tough private eye Philip Marlowe in on a case involving his two daughters, blackmail, and murder.

Robert Mitchum, Sarah Miles, Richard Boone, Candy Clark, Joan Collins, Edward Fox, John Mills, Oliver Reed, Harry Andrews.

The Magic of Lassie (1978, Lassie Productions). *d:* Don Chaffey; *p:* Bonita Granville Wrather and William Beaudine Jr.; *sc:* Jean Holloway, Robert B. Sherman, and Richard M. Sherman—*b/o* a story by Robert B. Sherman and Richard M. Sherman.

CLOVIS MITCHELL: Kindly vineyards owner who, along with his two grandchildren, outwits an evil rich man who tries to take their collie, Lassie, away from them because the grandfather won't sell him his vineyards.

Mickey Rooney, Alice Faye, Pernell Roberts, Stephanie Zimbalist, Michael Sharrett, Lane Davies, Mike Mazurki, Lassie.

• In addition, James Stewart made a cameo/guest appearance in the following feature film: *That's Entertainment* (1974, MGM—on-screen co-narrator).

☆ ELIZABETH TAYLOR

Elizabeth Rosemond Taylor

b: Feb. 27, 1932, London, England

"I'm loud and I'm vulgar and I wear the pants in the house because somebody's got to, but I am not a monster."

Martha (Elizabeth Taylor) in *Who's Afraid of Virginia Woolf?*, 1966.

There's One Born Every Minute (1942, Univ.). *d:* Harold Young; *p:* Ken Goldsmith; *sc:* Robert B. Hunt and Brenda Weisberg—*b/o* a story by Robert B. Hunt.
GLORIA TWINE: Bratty young daughter whose zany father, the owner of a pudding company, is elected mayor of a small town.
Hugh Herbert, Tom Brown, Peggy Moran, Guy Kibbee, Catherine Doucet, Edgar Kennedy, Gus Schilling, Charles Halton, Renie Riano, Carl "Alfalfa" Switzer.

Lassie Come Home (1943, MGM). *d:* Fred M. Wilcox; *p:* Samuel Marx; *sc:* Hugh Butler—*b/o* the novel by Eric Knight.
PRISCILLA: English nobleman's twelve-year-old granddaughter who, after her grandfather buys a beautiful collie named Lassie from a poor Yorkshire family, helps the dog escape from their Scottish estate so that it can make a remarkable 1000-mile trek back home to its beloved young master.
Roddy McDowall, Donald Crisp, Edmund Gwenn, Dame May Whitty, Nigel Bruce, Elsa Lanchester, J. Patrick O'Malley, Ben Webster, Arthur Shields, Alan Napier, Lassie.

Jane Eyre (1944, 20th-Fox). *d:* Robert Stevenson; *p:* William Goetz; *sc:* Aldous Huxley, Robert Stevenson, and John Houseman—*b/o* the novel by Charlotte Bronte.
HELEN: Tender young girl in an English orphanage who—after breaking the rules by sharing her food with her friend Jane Eyre—is forced to stand outside in the rain as punishment, catches pneumonia, and dies.
Orson Welles, Joan Fontaine, Margaret O'Brien, Peggy Ann Garner, John Sutton, Sara Allgood, Henry Daniell, Agnes Moorehead, Aubrey Mather, Hillary Brooke, Mae Marsh, John Abbott.

The White Cliffs of Dover (1944, MGM). *d:* Clarence Brown; *p:* Sidney Franklin; *sc:* Claudine West, Jan Lustig, and George Froeschel—*b/o* Alice Duer Miller's poem "The White Cliffs."
BETSY: Flirtatious ten-year-old country girl in

post-WWI England who has a crush on the young son of a courageous American woman and a dashing British nobleman.
Irene Dunne, Alan Marshal, Frank Morgan, Roddy McDowall, Dame May Whitty, C. Aubrey Smith, Gladys Cooper, Peter Lawford, Van Johnson, Norma Varden, June Lockhart, Tom Drake, Miles Mander, Lumsden Hare, Arthur Shields, Doris Lloyd.

National Velvet (1944, MGM). *d:* Clarence Brown; *p:* Pandro S. Berman; *sc:* Theodore Reeves and Helen Deutsch—*b/o* the novel by Enid Bagnold.
VELVET BROWN: Butcher's twelve-year-old daughter in Sussex, England, who—after winning a horse named "The Pye" in a raffle and doggedly helping a former teen-age jockey train it—disguises herself as a boy and rides the horse to come in first in the famed Grand National steeplechase.
Mickey Rooney, Donald Crisp, Anne Revere, Angela Lansbury, Juanita Quigley, Jackie "Butch" Jenkins, Reginald Owen, Terry Kilburn, Norma Varden, Arthur Shields, Aubrey Mather, Arthur Treacher, Billy Bevan.

Courage of Lassie (1946, MGM). *d:* Fred M. Wilcox; *p:* Robert Sisk; *sc:* Lionel Hauser.
KATHIE MERRICK: Young farm girl in Washington state who, after her collie is put into the U.S. Army during WWII and taught to kill, has to convert him with loving care into a kind animal again when he's discharged.
Frank Morgan, Tom Drake, Selena Royle, Harry Davenport, Moris Ankrum, George Cleveland, Minor Watson, Carl "Alfalfa" Switzer, Conrad Binyon, Lassie.

Cynthia (1947, MGM). *d:* Robert Z. Leonard; *p:* Edwin H. Knopf; *sc:* Harold Buchman and Charles Kaufman—*b/o* Vina Delmar's play *The Rich Full Life.*
CYNTHIA BISHOP: Lonely, sickly teen-age daughter of overprotective parents who has never had a date nor a normal teen-ager's life but changes things when she rebels and gets a boy to take her to the school prom.
George Murphy, S. Z. Sakall, Mary Astor, Gene Lockhart, Spring Byington, James Lydon, Scotty Beckett, Anna Q. Nilsson, Morris Ankrum, Kathleen Howard, Harlan Briggs, Will Wright.

Life with Father (1947, WB). *d:* Michael Curtiz; *p:* Robert Buckner; *sc:* Donald Ogden Stewart—*b/o* the play by Howard Lindsay and Russel Crouse.

MARY SKINNER: Pretty young girl in turn-of-the-century New York City who visits the family of an irascible, well-to-do businessman and becomes romantically involved with his eldest son.

William Powell, Irene Dunne, Edmund Gwen, ZaSu Pitts, James Lydon, Emma Dunn, Moroni Olsen, Elisabeth Risdon, Martin Milner, Monte Blue, Queenie Leonard, Clara Blandick, Arlene Dahl.

A Date with Judy (1948, MGM). *d:* Richard Thorpe; *p:* Joe Pasternak; *sc:* Dorothy Cooper and Dorothy Kingsley—*b/o* characters created by Aleen Leslie.

CAROL PRINGLE: Spoiled but good-hearted small-town teen-ager—neglected by her rich banker father—whose beauty and sophistication help her win when she competes with her best girlfriend for a handsome older man.

Wallace Beery, Jane Powell, Carmen Miranda, Xavier Cugat, Robert Stack, Selena Royle, Scotty Beckett, Leon Ames, George Cleveland, Lloyd Corrigan, Clinton Sundberg, Francis Pierlot.

Julia Misbehaves (1948, MGM). *d:* Jack Conway; *p:* Everett Riskin; *sc:* William Ludwig, Harry Ruskin, and Arthur Wimperis (adaptation by Gina Kaus and Monckton Hoffe)—*b/o* Margery Sharp's novel *The Nutmeg Tree.*

SUSAN PACKETT: Eighteen-year-old woman who, when she's slated to marry a man she doesn't really love, is visited by her estranged, divorced actress mother, who manages to guide her into eloping with the young artist she does love.

Greer Garson, Walter Pidgeon, Peter Lawford, Cesar Romero, Lucile Watson, Nigel Bruce, Mary Boland, Reginald Owen, Ian Wolfe, Fritz Feld, Marcelle Corday, Veda Ann Borg, Aubrey Mather, Henry Stephenson.

Little Women (1949, MGM). *d:* Mervyn LeRoy; *p:* Mervyn LeRoy; *sc:* Andrew Solt, Sarah Y. Mason, and Victor Heerman—*b/o* the novel by Louisa May Alcott.

AMY MARCH: Spoiled, flighty young girl—one of four sisters growing up in Concord, Massachusetts, during the Civil War—who marries the rejected suitor (Laurie) of her older sister, Jo.

June Allyson, Peter Lawford, Margaret O'Brien, Janet Leigh, Rossano Brazzi, Mary Astor, Lucile Watson, Sir C. Aubrey Smith, Elizabeth Patterson, Leon Ames, Harry Davenport, Richard Stapley.

Conspirator (1950, MGM). *d:* Victor Saville; *p:* Arthur Hornblow Jr.; *sc:* Sally Benson and Gerard Fairlie—*b/o* a novel by Humphrey Slater.

MELINDA GREYTON: Beautiful young American debutante in London who marries a handsome British Army major, then discovers that he's a Communist secretly spying for the Soviets.

Robert Taylor, Robert Flemyng, Harold Warrender, Honor Blackman, Marjorie Fielding, Thora Hird, Wilfred Hyde-White, Marie Ney, Cicely Paget Bowman, Cyril Smith.

The Big Hangover (1950, MGM). *d:* Norman Krasna; *p:* Norman Krasna; *sc:* Norman Krasna.

MARY BELNEY: Boss's daughter who plays amateur psychiatrist in order to help her lawyer boyfriend overcome a most unusual problem: an allergy to alcohol, such that even one whiff makes him intoxicated.

Van Johnson, Percy Waram, Fay Holden, Leon Ames, Edgar Buchanan, Selena Royle, Gene Lockhart, Rosemary DeCamp, Phillip Ahn, Gordon Richards, Matt Moore, Pierre Watkin, Russell Hicks.

Father of the Bride (1950, MGM). *d:* Vincente Minnelli; *p:* Pandro S. Berman; *sc:* Frances Goodrich and Albert Hackett—*b/o* the novel by Edward Streeter.

KAY BANKS: Suburban lawyer's daughter who announces her engagement and plans for a formal wedding, then complicates her parents' hectic preparations by threatening not to go through with the ceremony but finally is happily married.

Spencer Tracy, Joan Bennett, Don Taylor, Billie Burke, Leo G. Carroll, Moroni Olsen, Melville Cooper, Russ Tamblyn, Tom Irish, Paul Harvey, Taylor Holmes, Frank Orth, Willard Waterman.

Father's Little Dividend (1951, MGM). *d:* Vincente Minnelli; *p:* Pandro S. Berman; *sc:* Frances Goodrich and Albert Hackett—*b/o* characters created by Edward Streeter.

KAY BANKS DUNSTAN: Young married daughter of a suburban lawyer who shatters his peace and quiet when she announces that he's going to become a grandfather.

Spencer Tracy, Joan Bennett, Don Taylor, Billie Burke, Moroni Olsen, Marietta Canty, Russ Tamblyn, Tom Irish, Richard Rober, Hayden Rorke, Paul Harvey.

A Place in the Sun (1951, Para.). *d:* George Stevens; *p:* George Stevens; *sc:* Michael Wilson and Harry Brown—*b/o* the novel *An American Tragedy* by Theodore Dreiser.

ANGELA VICKERS: Beautiful society girl whose love affair with a young factory worker ends in tragedy when he's convicted and executed for causing the drowning of a poor young factory woman he has made pregnant.

Montgomery Clift, Shelley Winters, Anne Revere, Raymond Burr, Keefe Brasselle, Shepperd Strudwick, Frieda Inescort, Ian Wolfe, Fred Clark, Walter Sande, John Ridgely, Ted de Corsia, Paul Frees, Kathleen Freeman.

Love is Better Than Ever (1952, MGM). d: Stanley Donen; p: William H. Wright; sc: Ruth Brooks Flippen.

ANASTASIA MACABOY: Pretty dance teacher from New Haven, Connecticut, who comes to a New York City dance convention, falls for a Broadway agent who's a dyed-in-the wool bachelor, and manages to get him to the altar.

Larry Parks, Josephine Hutchinson, Tom Tully, Ann Doran, Elinor Donohue, Kathleen Freeman, Doreen McCann, Alex Gerry, Dick Wessel.

Ivanhoe (1952, MGM). d: Richard Thorpe; p: Pandro S. Berman; sc: Noel Langley (adaptation by Aeneas MacKenzie)—b/o the novel by Sir Walter Scott.

REBECCA: Beautiful Jewish woman in Saxon-Norman England during the Middle Ages who competes for the affections of the chivalrous Saxon knight Ivanhoe but sacrifices her love for him in favor of his betrothed, the fair Saxon Lady Rowena.

Robert Taylor, Joan Fontaine, George Sanders, Emlyn Williams, Robert Douglas, Finlay Currie, Felix Aylmer, Guy Rolfe, Basil Sydney, Patrick Holt, Roderick Lovell, Sebastian Cabot.

The Girl Who Had Everything (1953, MGM). d: Richard Thorpe; p: Armand Deutsch; sc: Art Cohn—b/o the novel *A Free Soul* by Adela Rogers St. John and the subsequent play by Willard Mack.

JEAN LATIMER: Daughter of a big-time criminal lawyer who becomes infatuated with one of her father's crooked clients—a suave gambling-syndicate boss—and almost ruins her life.

Fernando Lamas, William Powell, Gig Young, James Whitmore, Robert Burton, William Walker.

Rhapsody (1954, MGM). d: Charles Vidor; p: Lawrence Weingarten; sc: Fay Kanin and Michael Kanin (adaptation by Ruth Goetz and Augustus Goetz)—b/o the novel *Maurice Guest* by Henry Handel Richardson.

LOUISE DURANT: Beautiful heiress who, while still carrying the torch for her ex-fiancé, a violinist, marries an aspiring concert pianist and almost ruins his career but finally realizes that she loves him and helps him become a success.

Vittorio Gassman, John Ericson, Louis Calhern, Michael Chekhov, Barbara Bates, Richard Hageman, Richard Lupino, Celia Lovsky, Stuart Whitman, Madge Blake, Jack Raine, Brigit Nielsen, Jacqueline Duval, Norma Nevens.

Elephant Walk (1954, Para.). d: William Dieterle; p: Irving Asher; sc: John Lee Mahin—b/o the novel by Robert Standish.

RUTH WILEY: Young English bride of a Ceylon tea-plantation owner who has to cope with her husband's obsessive devotion to the memory of his dead father, her romance with the plantation's

overseer, a cholera epidemic, and an elephant stampede.

Dana Andrews, Peter Finch, Abraham Sofaer, Abner Biberman, Noel Drayton, Rosalind Ivan, Barry Bernard, Philip Tonge, Edward Ashley, Leo Britt, Mylee Haulani.

Beau Brummell (1954, MGM). d: Curtis Bernhardt; p: Sam Zimbalist; sc: Karl Tunberg—b/o the play by Clyde Fitch.

LADY PATRICIA: Beautiful eighteenth-century English noblewoman who must choose between the famed Regency dandy Beau Brummell and a stolid young court politician—and opts for the latter.

Stewart Granger, Peter Ustinov, Robert Morley, James Donald, James Hayter, Rosemary Harris, Paul Rogers, Noel Willman, Peter Dyneley, Charles Carson, Ernest Clark, Desmond Roberts, David Horne.

The Last Time I Saw Paris (1954, MGM). d: Richard Brooks; p: Jack Cummings; sc: Julius J. Epstein, Philip G. Epstein, and Richard Brooks—b/o the story "Babylon Revisited" by F. Scott Fitzgerald.

HELEN ELLSWIRTH: Pleasure-loving young American woman in post-WWII Paris whose marriage to an American writer has a carefree, happy beginning but—when she becomes bored with Parisian social life and he takes to the bottle because he's failing as a writer—starts falling apart and finally ends in tragedy when she dies of pneumonia.

Van Johnson, Walter Pidgeon, Donna Reed, Eva Gabor, Kurt Kasznar, George Dolenz, Roger Moore, Sandy Descher, Celia Lovsky, Peter Leeds, John Doucette, Odette.

Giant (1956, WB). d: George Stevens; p: George Stevens and Henry Ginsberg; sc: Fred Guiol and Ivan Moffat—b/o the novel by Edna Ferber.

LESLIE LYNNTON BENEDICT: Strong-willed young woman from Maryland whose adjustment to life on a Texas ranch, after she marries a wealthy Texas cattleman, is interwoven with problems of Mexican workers and an ambitious young ranch hand who becomes an oil tycoon.

Rock Hudson, James Dean, Carroll Baker, Jane Withers, Chill Wills, Mercedes McCambridge, Sal Mineo, Dennis Hopper, Judith Evelyn, Paul Fix, Rod Taylor, Earl Holliman, Robert Nichols, Alexander Scourby, Fran Bennett.

Raintree County (1957, MGM). d: Edward Dmytryk; p: David Lewis; sc: Millard Kaufman—b/o the novel by Ross Lockridge Jr.

SUSANNA DRAKE*: Civil War–era southern

---

*Received an Academy Award nomination as Best Actress for this role.

belle who traps an idealistic Raintree County, Indiana, schoolteacher into marriage with the lie that she's pregnant, then begins to show signs of the insanity from which her mother died.

Montgomery Clift, Eva Marie Saint, Nigel Patrick, Lee Marvin, Rod Taylor, Agnes Moorehead, Walter Abel, Tom Drake, Russell Collins, DeForest Kelley, Gardner McKay.

Cat on a Hot Tin Roof (1958, MGM). *d:* Richard Brooks; *p:* Lawrence Weingarten (Avon); *sc:* Richard Brooks and James Poe—*b/o* the play by Tennessee Williams.

MAGGIE POLLITT*: Beautiful, lusty wife—living on a Mississippi plantation—whose neurotic husband broods about his younger days as a football hero and has grown to like booze better than her.

Paul Newman, Burl Ives, Jack Carson, Judith Anderson, Madeleine Sherwood, Larry Gates, Vaughn Taylor, Patty Ann Gerrity, Rusty Stevens, Hugh Corcoran, Deborah Miller, Brian Corcoran, Vince Townsend Jr., Zelda Cleaver.

Suddenly, Last Summer (1959, Col.). *d:* Joseph L. Mankiewicz; *p:* Sam Spiegel (Horizon); *sc:* Gore Vidal and Tennessee Williams—*b/o* the play by Tennessee Williams.

CATHERINE HOLLY*: Young woman who is committed to an insane asylum by her domineering New Orleans aunt in a desperate attempt to keep her from revealing the grisly details of the death of the aunt's homosexual son in North Africa.

Katharine Hepburn, Montgomery Clift, Albert Dekker, Mercedes McCambridge, Gary Raymond, Mavis Villiers, Patricia Marmont, Joan Young, Maria Britneva.

Scent of Mystery (1960, A Michael Todd Jr. Release). *d:* Jack Cardiff; *p:* Michael Todd Jr.; *sc:* William Roos—*b/o* an original story by Kelley Roos.

THE REAL SALLY KENNEDY: A missing American heiress in Spain who is finally found.

Denholm Elliott, Peter Lorre, Beverly Bentley, Paul Lukas, Liam Redmond, Leo McKern, Peter Arne, Diana Dors, Mary Laura Wood, Judith Furse, Maurice Marsac.

Butterfield 8 (1960, MGM). *d:* Daniel Mann; *p:* Pandro S. Berman; *sc:* Charles Schnee and John Michael Hayes—*b/o* the novel by John O'Hara.

GLORIA WANDROUS†: Beautiful Manhattan part-time model, part-time call girl whose turbulent love affair with a married socialite ends tragically when she loses her life in an automobile crash.

Laurence Harvey, Eddie Fisher, Dina Merrill, Mildred Dunnock, Betty Field, Jeffery Lynn, Kay Medford, Susan Oliver, George Voskovec.

Cleopatra (1963, 20th-Fox). *d:* Joseph L. Mankiewicz; *p:* Walter Wanger; *sc:* Joseph L. Mankiewicz, Ranald MacDougall, and Sidney Buchman—*b/o* histories by Plutarch, Suetonius, and Appian, and *The Life and Times of Cleopatra* by C. M. Franzero.

CLEOPATRA: Legendary Egyptian Queen of the Nile who takes up with Julius Caesar when he arrives as the conqueror of Egypt, turns her attention to Mark Antony after Caesar's death, and finally winds up—along with Antony—committing suicide.

Richard Burton, Rex Harrison, Pamela Brown, George Cole, Hume Cronyn, Cesare Danova, Kenneth Haigh, Roddy McDowall, Martin Landau, Andrew Keir, John Hoyt, Carroll O'Connor, Jean Marsh.

The V.I.P.s (1963, MGM). *d:* Anthony Asquith; *p:* Anatole de Grunwald; *sc:* Terence Rattigan.

FRANCES ANDROS: Millionaire shipping magnate's wife who is about to fly away with a handsome French playboy but realizes that her husband—when he threatens to kill himself—needs her, and stays with him.

Richard Burton, Louis Jourdan, Elsa Martinelli, Margaret Rutherford, Maggie Smith, Rod Taylor, Linda Christian, Orson Welles, Robert Coote, David Frost, Stringer Davis.

The Sandpiper (1965, MGM). *d:* Vincente Minnelli; *p:* Martin Ransohoff and John Calley (Filmways); *sc:* Dalton Trumbo and Michael Wilson (adaptation by Irene Kamp and Louis Kamp)—*b/o* a story by Martin Ransohoff.

LAURA REYNOLDS: Liberated beatnik artist who lives in a California beach shack with her young illegitimate son and has a love affair with the headmaster of the boy's school, a married Episcopalian minister.

Richard Burton, Eva Marie Saint, Charles Bronson, Robert Webber, James Edwards, Tom Drake, Doug Henderson, Morgan Mason.

Who's Afraid of Virginia Woolf? (1966, WB). *d:* Mike Nichols; *p:* Ernest Lehman; *sc:* Ernest Lehman—*b/o* the play by Edward Albee.

MARTHA*: Dowdy, bitchy, foul-mouthed wife who has an all-night shouting match with her henpecked college-professor husband when a young academic couple visits their home one Saturday night.

Richard Burton, George Segal, Sandy Dennis.

---

*Received an Academy Award nomination as Best Actress for this role.

†Won the Academy Award as Best Actress for this role.

---

*Won the Academy Award as Best Actress for this role.

The Taming of the Shrew (1967, Col.). *d:* Franco Zeffirelli; *p:* Richard McWhorter, Richard Burton, Elizabeth Taylor, and Franco Zeffirelli (Royal/FAI); *sc:* Paul Dehn, Suso Cecchi D'Amico, and Franco Zeffirelli—*b/o* the play by William Shakespeare.

KATHARINA (KATE): Fiery shrew in fourteenth-century Padua, Italy, who is wooed and finally tamed by a robust and wily suitor from Verona.

Richard Burton, Cyril Cusack, Michael Hordern, Michael York, Natasha Pyne, Victor Spinetti, Alfred Lynch, Alan Webb.

Doctor Faustus (1967, Col.). *d:* Richard Burton and Nevill Coghill; *p:* Richard Burton and Richard McWhorter (Oxford/Nassau/Venfilms); *sc:* Nevill Coghill—*b/o* Christopher Marlowe's play *The Tragicall History of Doctor Faustus*.

HELEN OF TROY: Historical woman's spirit who—after a sixteenth-century scholar sells his soul to the Devil in exchange for youth and pleasure—escorts him into the fires of Hell.

Richard Burton, Andreas Teuber, Elizabeth O'Donovan, Ian Marter, Jeremy Eccles, David McIntosh, Richard Harrison.

Reflections in a Golden Eye (1967, WB–Seven Arts). *d:* John Huston; *p:* Ray Stark (Huston–Stark); *sc:* Chapman Mortimer and Gladys Hill—*b/o* the novel by Carson McCullers.

LEONORA PENDERTON: Frustrated, amoral wife at a peacetime Georgia Army camp who is having an affair with a lieutenant colonel while her husband, a major, is obsessed with a young private who rides horseback naked through the woods.

Marlon Brando, Brian Keith, Julie Harris, Zorro David, Gordon Mitchell, Irvin Dugan, Fay Sparks, Robert Forster.

The Comedians (1967, MGM). *d:* Peter Glenville; *p:* Peter Glenville (Maximilian/Trianon); *sc:* Graham Greene—*b/o* his novel.

MARTHA PINEDA: German-born wife of a South American diplomat in dictator-controlled Haiti who—against a backdrop of political intrigue and a native rebellion—has an affair with the English owner of a seedy hotel.

Richard Burton, Alec Guiness, Peter Ustinov, Paul Ford, Lillian Gish, Raymond St. Jacques, Zaeks Mokae, Roscoe Lee Browne, James Earl Jones, Cicely Tyson.

Boom! (1968, Univ.). *d:* Joseph Losey; *p:* John Heyman and Norman Priggen (World Film/Moon Lake); *sc:* Tennessee Williams—*b/o* his short story *Man Bring This Up the Road* and his play *The Milk Train Doesn't Stop Here Anymore*.

FLORA "SISSY" GOFORTH: Ex-burlesque queen and now the world's richest woman who—while dying of tuberculosis on her own private

Mediterranean volcanic island—plans to take as her lover a wandering poet who is really an angel of death.

Richard Burton, Noel Coward, Joanna Shimkus, Michael Dunn, Romolo Valli, Fernando Piazza, Veronica Wells.

Secret Ceremony (1968, Univ.). *d:* Joseph Losey; *p:* John Heyman and Norman Priggen (World Films/Paul M. Heller); *sc:* George Tabori—*b/o* a short story by Marco Denevi.

LEONORA: Fading, middle-aged prostitute who—when a wealthy, mentally unbalanced young woman insists that the prostitute is her dead mother—goes to live in the woman's London townhouse and becomes entangled in a bizarre triangle with the woman and her professor stepfather.

Mia Farrow, Robert Mitchum, Pamela Brown, Peggy Ashcroft.

The Only Game in Town (1970, 20th-Fox). *d:* George Stevens; *p:* Fred Kohlmar (George Stevens–Fred Kohlmar); *sc:* Frank D. Gilroy—*b/o* his Broadway play.

FRAN WALKER: Starting-to-age Las Vegas chorus girl who, while waiting in vain for her married lover to get a divorce, falls for a smooth-talking piano player who has a compulsive gambling problem.

Warren Beatty, Charles Braswell, Hank Henry, Olga Valery.

Under Milk Wood (1971, Rank [released in the U.S. in 1973 by Altura]). *d:* Andrew Sinclair; *p:* Hugh French and Jules Buck (Timon); *sc:* Andrew Sinclair—*b/o* the radio play by Dylan Thomas.

ROSIE PROBERT: Town trollop in the Welsh village of Llaneggub.

Richard Burton, Peter O'Toole, Glynis Johns, Vivien Merchant, Sian Phillips, Victor Spinetti.

X Y & Zee (1972, Col.). *d:* Brian G. Hutton; *p:* Jay Kanter and Alan Ladd Jr. (Zee/Kastner–Ladd–Kanter); *sc:* Edna O'Brien.

ZEE BLAKELEY: Shrewish London wife who, when her British architect husband starts sleeping with an attractive young widow, stops at nothing to get him back—including initiating an affair of her own with the widow.

Michael Caine, Susannah York, Margaret Leighton, John Standing, Mary Larkin, Michael Cashman.

Hammersmith Is Out (1972, Cinerama). *d:* Peter Ustinov; *p:* Alex Lucas (J. Cornelius Crean Films); *sc:* Stanford Whitmore.

JIMMIE JEAN JACKSON: Voluptuous blonde waitress in a Southern roadside diner who becomes the companion of a hillbilly male nurse who has helped a homicidal maniac escape from a mental institution in return for a promise of wealth and power.

Richard Burton, Beau Bridges, Peter Ustinov, Leon Ames, Leon Askin, John Schuck, George Raft, Anthony Holland, Marjorie Eaton, Lisa Jak.

Divorce His—Divorce Hers (1973, ABC-TV [Made for TV]). *d:* Waris Hussein; *p:* John Heyman (General Continental/Harlech TV); *sc:* John Hopkins.

JANE REYNOLDS: Distraught wife whose eighteen-year marriage is crumbling because of quarrels, separations, and adultery.

Richard Burton, Carrie Nye, Barry Foster, Gabriele Ferzetti, Thomas Baptiste, Ronald Radd, Marietta Schupp.

Night Watch (1973, Avco Embassy). *d:* Brian G. Hutton; *p:* Martin Poll, George W. George, and Bernard S. Straus (Joseph E. Levine/Burt); *sc:* Tony Williamson (with additional dialogue by Evan Jones)—*b/o* the play by Lucille Fletcher.

ELLEN WHEELER: Wife in England who is suspected of losing her sanity when she insists that she's witnessed a murder and seen dead bodies, but who is really laying the groundwork for murdering her straying husband and her cheating best friend.

Laurence Harvey, Billie Whitelaw, Robert Lang, Tony Britton, Bill Dean, Michael Danvers-Walker, Rosario Serrano, Pauline Jameson.

Ash Wednesday (1973, Para.). *d:* Larry Peerce; *p:* Dominick Dunne (Sagittarius); *sc:* Jean-Claude Tramont.

BARBARA SAWYER: Gone-to-seed woman in her fifties who undergoes extensive cosmetic surgery in Europe in a desperate attempt to win back the love of her husband.

Henry Fonda, Helmut Berger, Keith Baxter, Maurice Teynac, Margaret Blye, Monique Van Vooren, Kathy Van Lypps, Andrea Esterhazy, Jill Pratt.

The Driver's Seat (1974, Avco Embassy). *d:* Giuseppe Patroni Griffi; *p:* Franco Rossellini (Rizzoli); *sc:* Raffaele La Capria and Giuseppe Patroni Griffi—*b/o* Muriel Spark's novella *The Driver's Seat.*

LISE: Mentally disturbed spinster who experiences a series of bizarre encounters as she searches for someone to murder her.

Ian Bannen, Guido Mannari, Mona Washbourne, Maxence Mailfort.

The Blue Bird (1976, 20th-Fox). *d:* George Cukor; *p:* Edward Lewis and Paul Maslansky; *sc:* Hugh Whitemore and Alfred Hayes—*b/o* the play by Maurice Maeterlinck.

Plays four roles: QUEEN OF LIGHT, MOTHER, MATERNAL LOVE, and WITCH—some of the many symbolic fairy-tale characters who become involved with Mytyl and Tyltyl, two Russian peasant children who are sent by the fairy Berylune to search for the Bluebird of Happiness but finally discover that it's in their own back yard.

Jane Fonda, Ava Gardner, Cicely Tyson, Robert Morley, Harry Andrews, Todd Lookinland, Patsy Kensit, Will Geer, Mona Washbourne, George Cole, Richard Pearson, Oleg Popov, Nadejda Pavlova.

A Little Night Music (1977, New World Pictures). *d:* Harold Prince; *p:* Elliott Kastner (S & T Prod.); *sc:* Hugh Wheeler—*b/o* Hugh Wheeler's and Stephen Sondheim's musical play, suggested by Ingmar Bergman's film *Smiles of a Summer Night.*

DESIREE ARMFELDT: Seductive, worldly turn-of-the-century actress who is one of a small group of mismatched lovers who—while spending a summer weekend at her mother's country estate—finally all end up with the right partners.

Diana Rigg, Len Cariou, Lesley-Anne Down, Hermione Gingold, Lawrence Guittard, Christopher Guard, Chloe Franks, Heinz Marecek, Lesley Dunlop, Jonathan Tunick, Hubert Tscheppe.

The Mirror Crack'd (1980, EMI/Associated Film). *d:* Guy Hamilton; *p:* John Brabourne and Richard Goodwin; *sc:* Jonathan Hales and Barry Sandler—*b/o* the novel by Agatha Christie.

MARINA RUDD: Fading movie star who, while making a comeback in an American film being shot in 1950s England, becomes one of several persons suspected by the English sleuth Miss Jane Marple of fatally poisoning a young woman at a cocktail party.

Angela Lansbury, Wendy Morgan, Margaret Courtenay, Charles Gray, Maureen Bennett, Carolyn Pickles, Richard Pearson, Thick Wilson, Geraldine Chaplin, Tony Curtis, Edward Fox, Rock Hudson, Kim Novak, Marella Oppenheim.

• In addition, Elizabeth Taylor made cameo/guest appearances in the following feature films: *Callaway Went Thataway* (1951, MGM), *What's New Pussycat?* (UA, 1965), *Anne of the Thousand Days* (Univ., 1969), *That's Entertainment* (1974, MGM/UA—as on-screen co-narrator), and *Winter Kills* (Avco Embassy, 1979).

☆ ROBERT TAYLOR

Spangler Arlington Brugh

b: Aug. 5, 1911, Filley, Neb.
d: June 8, 1969, Los Angeles, Cal.

"Come on, you bastards, I'm here! I'll *always* be here!"

Sgt. Bill Dane (Robert Taylor) shouting wildly while blazing away with a machine gun at Japanese soldiers as they overrun his position in *Bataan*, 1943.

Handy Andy (1934, Fox). *d:* David Butler; *p:* Sol M. Wurtzel; *sc:* William Counselman and Henry Johnson (adaptation by Kubec Glasmon)—*b/o* the play *Merry Andrew* by Lewis Beach.
LLOYD BURMEISTER: Likeable young man who wins the hand of a pretty young woman with the help of her friendly small-town-druggist father.
Will Rogers, Peggy Wood, Conchita Montenegro, Mary Carlisle, Roger Imhof, Paul Harvey, Grace Goodall, Frank Melton, Jessie Pringle.

There's Always Tomorrow (1934, Univ.). *d:* Edward Sloman; *p:* William Hurlburt; *sc: b/o* the novel by Ursula Parrott.
ARTHUR WHITE: Eldest of five grown children who all selfishly neglect their kind and gentle father.
Frank Morgan, Binnie Barnes, Lois Wilson, Louise Latimer, Elizabeth Young, Alan Hale, Maurice Murphy, Dick Winslow, Helen Parrish, Margaret Hamilton.

A Wicked Woman (1934, MGM). *d:* Charles Brabin; *p:* Harry Rapf; *sc:* Florence Ryerson and Zelda Sears—*b/o* the novel by Anne Austin.
BILL RENTON: Heel who gets involved with a nice young woman, brings her unhappiness, and is responsible for a serious injury that befalls her brother.
Mady Christians, Jean Parker, Charles Bickford, Betty Furness, William Henry, Jackie Searle, Paul Harvey, Zelda Sears, Sterling Holloway, Dewitt Jennings.

Society Doctor (1935, MGM). *d:* George B. Seitz; *p:* Lucien Hubbard; *sc:* Michael Fessier and Samuel Marx—*b/o* Theodore Reeves's novel *The Harbor.*
DR. ELLIS: Handsome young doctor who competes with his doctor friend for the affections of a pretty nurse and who helps operate on the friend when he's wounded by a gangster.
Chester Morris, Virginia Bruce, Billie Burke, Raymond Walburn, Henry Kolker, William Henry, Mary Jo Mathews, Robert McWade.

Times Square Lady (1935, MGM). *d:* George B. Seitz; *p:* Lucien Hubbard; *sc:* Albert Cohen and Robert Shannon.
STEVE: Nightclub operator who is hired by a crooked lawyer to fleece a rich young woman out of her inheritance but instead falls in love with her.
Virginia Bruce, Helen Twelvetrees, Isabel Jewell, Nat Pendleton, Pinky Tomlin, Henry Kolker, Raymond Hatton, Jack La Rue, Robert Elliott, Russell Hopton, Fred Kohler.

West Point of the Air (1935, MGM). *d:* Richard Rosson; *p:* Monta Bell; *sc:* James K. McGuinness and John Monk Saunders (adaptation by Frank Wead and Arthur J. Beckhard).
JASKERELLI: One of several young pre-WWII U.S. Army air cadets who are training at Randolph Field in Texas.
Wallace Beery, Robert Young, Maureen O'Sullivan, Lewis Stone, James Gleason, Rosalind Russell, Russell Hardie, Henry Wadsworth, Robert Livingston, Frank Conroy.

Murder in the Fleet (1935, MGM). *d:* Edward Sedgwick; *p:* Lucien Hubbard; *sc:* Edward Sedgwick (adaptation by Frank Wead and Joe Sherman).
LT. TOM RANDOLPH: Young U.S. Naval officer who fights sabotage and solves a series of murders aboard a U.S. battle cruiser that's equipped with a revolutionary new firing device.
Jean Parker, Ted Healy, Una Merkel, Nat Pendleton, Jean Hersholt, Arthur Byron, Raymond Hatton, Donald Cook, Mischa Auer, Tom Dugan, Ward Bond, Richard Tucker.

Broadway Melody of 1936 (1935, MGM). *d:* Roy Del Ruth; *p:* John W. Considine Jr.; *sc:* Jack McGowan and Sid Silvers (with additional dialogue by Harry Conn)—*b/o* a story by Moss Hart.
BOB GORDON: Broadway producer who is tricked by a feuding Winchell-type gossip columnist into signing up a small-town would-be singer/dancer who's masquerading as a famous Parisian musical star.
Jack Benny, Eleanor Powell, June Knight, Una Merkel, Buddy Ebsen, Vilma Ebsen, Sid Silvers, Frances Langford, Paul Harvey, Bernadene Hayes, Lee Phelps, Eddie Tamblyn.

Magnificent Obsession (1935, Univ.). *d:* John M. Stahl; *p:* John M. Stahl; *sc:* George O'Neill, Sarah Y. Mason, and Victor Heerman—*b/o* the novel by Lloyd C. Douglas.
BOBBY MERRICK: Drunken playboy who, after a woman is blinded in an auto accident he caused,

reforms and studies to become a surgeon so that he can restore the woman's eyesight.

Irene Dunne, Charles Butterworth, Betty Furness, Sara Haden, Ralph Morgan, Henry Armetta, Gilbert Emery, Arthur Hoyt, Inez Courtney, Beryl Mercer, Cora Sue Collins, Arthur Treacher, Frank Reicher, Purnell Pratt, Lucien Littlefield, Theodore Von Eltz.

Small Town Girl (1936, MGM). *d:* William A. Wellman; *p:* Hunt Stromberg; *sc:* John Lee Mahin and Edith Fitzgerald—*b/o* the novel by Ben Ames Williams.

BOB DAKIN: Rich playboy who goes on a drunken spree, wakes up to find himself married to a small-town girl, and—although devastated at first—finally falls in love with her.

Janet Gaynor, Binnie Barnes, Lewis Stone, Andy Devine, Elizabeth Patterson, Frank Craven, James Stewart, Douglas Fowley, Isabel Jewell, Charley Grapewin, Nella Walker, Robert Greig, Edgar Kennedy, Willie Fung.

Private Number (1936, 20th-Fox). *d:* Roy Del Ruth; *p:* Darryl F. Zanuck and Raymond Griffith; *sc:* Gene Markey and William Conselman—*b/o* the play *Common Clay* by Cleves Kinkead.

RICHARD WINFIELD: Wealthy college boy whose socially conscious family is horrified when they discover that he has married the family's pretty housekeeper.

Loretta Young, Patsy Kelly, Basil Rathbone, Marjorie Gateson, Paul Harvey, Joe Lewis, Jane Darwell, Monroe Owsley, George Irving, John Miljan, Jack Pennick.

His Brother's Wife (1936, MGM). *d:* W. S. Van Dyke II; *p:* Lawrence Weingarten; *sc:* Leon Gordon and John Meehan—*b/o* a story by George Auerbach.

CHRIS: Dedicated young scientist who—when he's forced to forsake a young woman he loves and she marries his brother for spite—goes to the South American jungles, where he develops a cure for spotted fever.

Barbara Stanwyck, Jean Hersholt, Joseph Calleia, John Eldredge, Samuel S. Hinds, Phyllis Clare, Leonard Mudie, Jed Prouty, Pedro de Cordoba, Edgar Edwards.

The Gorgeous Hussy (1936, MGM). *d:* Clarence Brown; *p:* Joseph L. Mankiewicz; *sc:* Ainsworth Morgan and Stephen Morehouse Avery—*b/o* the book by Samuel Hopkins Adams.

BOW TIMBERLAKE: Handsome Navy lieutenant who is briefly married to the notorious Washington belle Peggy O'Neal (Eaton), a protégée and confidante of President Andrew Jackson's.

Joan Crawford, Lionel Barrymore, Melvyn Douglas, James Stewart, Franchot Tone, Louis Calhern, Alison Skipworth, Beulah Bondi, Melville Cooper, Sidney Toler, Gene Lockhart, Clara Blandick, Frank Conroy, Nydia Westman, Louise Beavers, Charles Trowbridge, Willard Robertson, Bert Roach, Ward Bond.

Camille (1937, MGM). *d:* George Cukor; *p:* Irving Thalberg and Bernard Hyman; *sc:* Zoe Akins, Frances Marion, and James Hilton—*b/o* the novel and play *La Dame aux Camélias* by Alexandre Dumas.

ARMAND DUVAL: Boyish young Frenchman in the nineteenth century who has a tragic love affair with a cynical Parisian courtesan afflicted with a fatal illness.

Greta Garbo, Lionel Barrymore, Elizabeth Allan, Jessie Ralph, Henry Daniell, Lenore Ulric, Laura Hope Crews, Russell Hardie, E. E. Clive, Douglas Walton, Joan Brodel (Joan Leslie), Fritz Leiber Jr., Edwin Maxwell.

Personal Property (1937, MGM). *d:* W. S. Van Dyke II; *p:* John W. Considine Jr.; *sc:* Hugh Mills and Ernest Vajda—*b/o* H. M. Harwood's play *The Man in Possession.*

RAYMOND DABNEY: Irresponsible playboy in England who, after his family disowns him, is sent as a bailiff to keep an eye on the house and furniture of a financially strapped American widow and ends up falling in love with her.

Jean Harlow, Reginald Owen, Una O'Connor, Henrietta Crosman, E. E. Clive, Cora Witherspoon, Marla Shelton, Forrester Harvey, Lionel Braham, Barnett Parker.

This Is My Affair (1937, 20th-Fox). *d:* William A. Seiter; *p:* Kenneth MacGowan; *sc:* Allen Rivkin and Lamar Trotti.

LT. RICHARD PERRY: U.S. Navy officer who is secretly ordered by President William McKinley to become an undercover agent and join a gang of bank robbers but—when McKinley is suddenly assassinated—is captured and sentenced to hang.

Barbara Stanwyck, Victor McLaglen, Brian Donlevy, Sidney Blackmer, John Carradine, Alan Dinehart, Douglas Fowley, Robert McWade, Frank Conroy, Sig Rumann, Marjorie Weaver, Willard Robertson, Paul Hurst, Douglas Wood.

Broadway Melody of 1938 (1937, MGM). *d:* Roy Del Ruth; *p:* Jack Cummings; *sc:* Jack McGowan—*b/o* a story by Jack McGowan and Sid Silvers.

STEVE RALEIGH: Broadway producer who needs cash for his new musical—and gets it when his singer-dancer girlfriend enters her racehorse in the Saratoga Steeplechase and it wins.

Eleanor Powell, George Murphy, Binnie Barnes, Buddy Ebsen, Sophie Tucker, Judy Garland, Charles Igor Gorin, Raymond Walburn, Robert Benchley, Willie Howard, Charley Grapewin, Robert Wildhack, Billy Gilbert, Barnett Parker, Helen Troy.

A Yank at Oxford (1938, MGM). *d:* Jack Conway; *p:* Michael Balcon; *sc:* Malcolm Stuart Boylan, Walter Ferris, and George Oppenheimer—*b/o* a story by Leon Gordon, Sidney Gilliatt, and Michael Hogan (from an idea by John Monk Saunders).

LEE SHERIDAN: Cocky American track and rowing star who, after winning a scholarship to Oxford University, rubs the English students the wrong way—but eventually earns their respect.

Lionel Barrymore, Maureen O'Sullivan, Vivien Leigh, Edmund Gwenn, Griffith Jones, Edward Rigby, Claude Gillingwater, Tully Marshall, Walter Kingsford, Robert Coote, Peter Croft, Edmund Breon.

Three Comrades (1938, MGM). *d:* Frank Borzage; *p:* Joseph L. Mankiewicz; *sc:* F. Scott Fitzgerald and Edward E. Paramore—*b/o* the novel by Erich Maria Remarque.

ERICH LOHKAMP: One of three ex–German soldiers—owners of an auto-repair shop—who find life difficult in post-WWI Germany but get a little happiness from their love for a high-spirited young woman who's dying from tuberculosis.

Margaret Sullavan, Franchot Tone, Robert Young, Guy Kibbee, Lionel Atwill, Henry Hull, George Zucco, Charley Grapewin, Monty Woolley, Spencer Charters, Sarah Padden, Esther Muir, Henry Brandon, George Chandler, William Haade, Marjorie Main.

The Crowd Roars (1938, MGM). *d:* Richard Thorpe; *p:* Sam Zimbalist; *sc:* Thomas Lennon, George Bruce, and George Oppenheimer—*b/o* a story by George Bruce.

TOMMY "KILLER" McCOY: Young boxer from the slums who—as he rises in the fight game—accidentally kills an old friend in the ring, gets tied in with crooks, and takes a beating to save his girlfriend from being kidnapped by them.

Edward Arnold, Frank Morgan, Maureen O'Sullivan, William Gargan, Lionel Stander, Jane Wyman, Nat Pendleton, Charles D. Brown, Gene Reynolds, Donald Barry, Donald Douglas, Isabel Jewell, J. Farrell MacDonald.

Stand Up and Fight (1939, MGM). *d:* W. S. Van Dyke II; *p:* Mervyn LeRoy; *sc:* James M. Cain, Jane Murfin, and Harvey Ferguson—*b/o* a story by Forbes Parkhill.

BLAKE CANTRELL: Maryland aristocrat during the Civil War era who, after going broke and losing his plantation, joins the railroad in its fight against a stage-coach line that is being used to transport stolen slaves.

Wallace Beery, Florence Rice, Helen Broderick, Charles Bickford, Barton MacLane, Charley Grapewin, John Qualen, Cy Kendall, Selmer Jackson, Robert Middlemass, Jonathan Hale.

Lucky Night (1939, MGM). *d:* Norman Taurog; *p:* Louis D. Lighton; *sc:* Vincent Lawrence and Grover Jones—*b/o* a story by Oliver Claxton.

BILL OVERTON: Broke, jobless young man who meets a broke, jobless young woman on a park bench and marries her—then discovers that she's really the wealthy daughter of a steel tycoon.

Myrna Loy, Joseph Allen, Henry O'Neill, Douglas Fowley, Bernard Nedell, Charles Lane, Bernadene Hayes, Gladys Blake, Marjorie Main, Edward Gargan, Irving Bacon, Oscar O'Shea.

Lady of the Tropics (1939, MGM). *d:* Jack Conway; *p:* Sam Zimbalist; *sc:* Ben Hecht.

BILL CAREY: American playboy in Saigon whose marriage to a beautiful half-caste girl ends in tragedy when her rich and powerful former admirer prevents her from getting a passport.

Hedy Lamarr, Joseph Schildkraut, Gloria Franklin, Ernest Cossart, Mary Taylor, Charles Trowbridge, Frederick Worlock, Paul Porcasi, Margaret Padula, Cecil Cunningham, Natalie Moorhead.

Remember? (1939, MGM). *d:* Norman Z. McLeod; *p:* Milton Bren; *sc:* Corey Ford and Norman Z. McLeod.

JEFF HOLLAND: Busy young businessman who elopes with his best friend's bride-to-be, loses her because he neglects her for his work, but—when the friend slips them both a potion that makes them lose their memories—falls in love with her again.

Greer Garson, Lew Ayres, Billie Burke, Reginald Owen, George Barbier, Henry Travers, Richard Carle, Laura Hope Crews, Sara Haden, Sig Ruman, Halliwell Hobbes, Paul Hurst.

Flight Command (1940, MGM). *d:* Frank Borzage; *p:* J. Walter Ruben; *sc:* Wells Root and Commander Harvey Haislip—*b/o* the story by Commander Harvey Haislip and John Sutherland.

ENS. ALAN DRAKE: Cocky U.S. Navy flyer, fresh out of Pensacola, who—when he's assigned to the elite Hellcats Squadron at San Diego's Naval Air Station—is resented by the veteran flyers but finally wins them over.

Ruth Hussey, Walter Pidgeon, Paul Kelly, Shepperd Strudwick, Red Skelton, Nat Pendleton, Dick Purcell, William Tannen, Addison Richards, Donald Douglas, Pat Flaherty, Marsha Hunt.

Waterloo Bridge (1940, MGM). *d:* Mervyn LeRoy; *p:* Sidney Franklin; *sc:* S. N. Behrman, Hans Rameau, and George Froeschel—*b/o* the play by Robert E. Sherwood.

ROY CRONIN: WWI British Army officer who falls in love with a London ballerina who becomes a prostitute after she mistakenly thinks that the officer has been killed in action.

Vivien Leigh, Lucile Watson, Virginia Field, Maria Ouspenskaya, C. Aubrey Smith, Janet Shaw, Janet Waldo, Steffi Duna, Virginia Carroll, Leda Nicova, Leo G. Carroll.

Escape (1940, MGM). *d:* Mervyn LeRoy; *p:* Mervyn LeRoy; *sc:* Arch Oboler and Marguerite Roberts—*b/o* the novel by Ethel Vance.

MARK PREYSING: American doctor who is helped by a widowed American-born countess living in Germany when he goes there to try to rescue his mother—a once-famous German actress—from a pre-WWII concentration camp.

Norma Shearer, Conrad Veidt, Alla Nazimova, Felix Bressart, Albert Bassermann, Philip Dorn, Bonita Granville, Edgar Barrier, Elsa Basserman, Blanche Yurka, Lisa Golm.

Billy the Kid (1941, MGM). *d:* David Miller; *p:* Irving Asher; *sc:* Gene Fowler—*b/o* a story by Howard Emmett Rogers and Bradbury Foote, suggested by Walter Noble Barnes's book *The Saga of Billy the Kid.*

WILLIAM BONNEY (alias BILLY THE KID): Notorious young outlaw of the old Southwest who tries to reform but reverts to his old ways when he seeks revenge against a gang that killed a kindly rancher friend of his.

Brian Donlevy, Ian Hunter, Mary Howard, Gene Lockhart, Henry O'Neill, Frank Puglia, Cy Kendall, Connie Gilchrist, Chill Wills, Guinn Williams, Lon Chaney Jr., Dick Curtis, Eddie Dunn, Grant Withers, Joe Yule, Kermit Maynard, Slim Whitaker, Ray Teal, Tom London.

When Ladies Meet (1941, MGM). *d:* Robert Z. Leonard; *p:* Robert Z. Leonard and Orville O. Dull; *sc:* S. K. Lauren and Anita Loos—*b/o* the play by Rachel Crothers.

JIMMY LEE: Playboy newspaperman who—as part of his plan to win a novelist away from the married publisher she loves—sets up a weekend meeting at a country house between the unsuspecting novelist and the publisher's wife.

Joan Crawford, Greer Garson, Herbert Marshall, Spring Byington, Rafael Storm, Mona Barrie.

Johnny Eager (1942, MGM). *d:* Mervyn LeRoy; *p:* John W. Considine; *sc:* John Lee Mahin and James Edward Grant—*b/o* a story by James Edward Grant.

JOHNNY EAGER: Unscrupulous, egotistical racketeer who tries to frame the D.A.'s daughter with a fake murder she believes she's committed but changes his mind when he falls in love with her.

Lana Turner, Edward Arnold, Van Heflin, Robert Sterling, Patricia Dane, Glenda Farrell, Henry O'Neill, Diana Lewis, Barry Nelson, Charles Dingle, Paul Stewart, Cy Kendall, Don Costello, Connie Gilchrist.

Her Cardboard Lover (1942, MGM). *d:* George Cukor; *p:* J. Walter Ruben; *sc:* Jacques Deval, John Collier, Anthony Veiller, and William H. Wright—*b/o* the play by Jacques Deval.

TERRY TRINDALE: Handsome but broke young songwriter who is hired by a wealthy woman to pose as her secretary and "lover" in order to hold at bay the "wolf" she thinks she loves.

Norma Shearer, George Sanders, Frank McHugh, Elizabeth Patterson, Chill Wills.

Stand by for Action (1943, MGM). *d:* Robert Z. Leonard; *p:* Robert Z. Leonard and Orville O. Dull; *sc:* George Bruce, John L. Balderston, and Herman J. Mankiewicz—*b/o* a story by Captain Harvey Haislip and R. C. Sherriff (from the story "A Cargo of Innocence" by Lawrence Kirk).

LT. GREGG MASTERSON: Spoiled Harvard graduate and U.S. Naval Reserve officer who, when he's called up to serve on a WWII destroyer, learns—under Japanese fire—to respect his superiors and the Navy.

Charles Laughton, Brian Donlevy, Walter Brennan, Marilyn Maxwell, Henry O'Neill, Chill Wills, Douglas Dumbrille, Richard Quine, Douglas Fowley, Tim Ryan, Dick Simmons, Byron Foulger, Hobart Cavanaugh, Inez Cooper, Ben Welden.

Bataan (1943, MGM). *d:* Tay Garnett; *p:* Irving Starr; *sc:* Robert D. Andrews—based partly on the 1934 film *The Lost Patrol.*

SGT. BILL DANE: Tough U.S. infantry sergeant who's in charge of a WWII "suicide" squad: thirteen men who die, one by one, as they hold a vital bridge against Japanese attacks in order to protect the 1942 American retreat down the Bataan peninsula in the Philippines.

George Murphy, Thomas Mitchell, Lloyd Nolan, Lee Bowman, Robert Walker, Desi Arnaz, Barry Nelson, Phillip Terry, Roque Espiritu, Kenneth Spencer, J. Alex Hauei, Tom Dugan, Donald Curtis, Lynne Carver.

Song of Russia (1944, MGM). *d:* Gregory Ratoff; *p:* Joseph Pasternak; *sc:* Paul Jarrico and Richard Collins—*b/o* a story by Leo Mittler, Victor Trivas, and Guy Endore.

JOHN MEREDITH: American symphony conductor in Russia who, when Germany invades Russia during WWII, is faced with his young Russian pianist wife's patriotic desire to return to her native village to fight the Nazis alongside her people.

Susan Peters, John Hodiak, Robert Benchley, Felix Bressart, Michael Chekhov, Darryl Hickman, Jacqueline White.

Undercurrent (1946, MGM). *d:* Vincente Minnelli; *p:* Pandro S. Berman; *sc:* Edward Chodorov—*b/o* a story by Thelma Strabel.

ALAN GARROWAY: Handsome, mysterious industrialist whose new bride—a college professor's daughter—slowly comes to the horrifying realization that he's a psychopathic murderer.

Katharine Hepburn, Robert Mitchum, Edmund Gwenn, Marjorie Main, Jayne Meadows, Clinton Sundberg, Leigh Whipper, Dan Tobin, Charles Trowbridge, James Westerfield, Betty Blythe, Bess Flowers.

The High Wall (1947, MGM). *d:* Curtis Bernhardt; *p:* Robert Lord; *sc:* Sidney Boehm and Lester Cole—*b/o* a story and play by Alan R. Clark and Bradbury Foote.

STEVEN KENET: Former WWII bomber pilot who, after finding himself in a mental hospital when he's accused of killing his wife, escapes and—with the help of his female psychiatrist—sets out to prove his innocence.

Audrey Totter, Herbert Marshall, Dorothy Patrick, H. B. Warner, Warner Anderson, Moroni Olsen, John Ridgely, Morris Ankrum, Elizabeth Risdon, Vince Barnett.

The Bribe (1949, MGM). *d:* Robert Z. Leonard; *p:* Pandro S. Berman; *sc:* Marguerite Roberts—*b/o* a short story by Frederick Nebel.

RIGBY: U.S. government agent who, when he's sent to the Caribbean to track down smugglers, falls for a sexy café singer who's married to one of the crooks.

Ava Gardner, Charles Laughton, Vincent Price, John Hodiak, Samuel S. Hinds, John Hoyt, Tito Renaldo, Martin Garralaga.

Ambush (1950, MGM). *d:* Sam Wood; *p:* Armand Deutsch; *sc:* Marguerite Roberts—*b/o* a story by Luke Short.

WARD KINSMAN: Civilian scout for the U.S. Cavalry who leads a posse to capture an Apache Indian chief who's holding a white woman hostage.

John Hodiak, Arlene Dahl, Don Taylor, Jean Hagen, Bruce Cowling, Leon Ames, John McIntire, Charles Stevens, Chief Thundercloud, Ray Teal, Robin Short.

Conspirator (1950, MGM). *d:* Victor Saville; *p:* Arthur Hornblow Jr.; *sc:* Sally Benson and Gerard Fairlie—*b/o* a novel by Humphrey Slater.

MICHAEL CURRAGH: British Army major who, unbeknownst to the beautiful young American woman he marries, is a Communist secretly spying for the Soviets.

Elizabeth Taylor, Robert Flemyng, Harold Warrender, Honor Blackman, Marjorie Fielding, Thora Hird, Wilfred Hyde-White, Marie Ney, Cicely Paget Bowman, Cyril Smith.

The Devil's Doorway (1950, MGM). *d:* Anthony Mann; *p:* Nicholas Nayfack; *sc:* Guy Trosper.

LANCE POOLE: Shoshone Indian who, after winning the Medal of Honor fighting with Union forces at Gettysburg, returns to his home in Wyoming and fights to right injustices done to him and his people by whites.

Louis Calhern, Paula Raymond, Marshall Thompson, James Mitchell, Edgar Buchanan, Rhys Williams, Spring Byington, James Millican, Bruce Cowling, Fritz Leiber, Harry Antrim, Chief John Big Tree.

Quo Vadis? (1951, MGM). *d:* Mervyn LeRoy; *p:* Sam Zimbalist; *sc:* John Lee Mahin, S. N. Behrman, and Sonya Levien—*b/o* the novel by Henryk Sienkiewicz.

MARCUS VINICIUS: Aristocratic Roman Legion commander who falls in love with a persecuted young Christian woman and incurs the disfavor of the corrupt and insane Emperor Nero.

Deborah Kerr, Leo Genn, Peter Ustinov, Patricia Laffan, Finlay Currie, Buddy Baer, Felix Aylmer, Nora Swinburne, Ralph Truman, Peter Miles, Geoffrey Dunn, Rosalie Crutchley.

Westward the Women (1951, MGM). *d:* William A. Wellman; *p:* Dore Schary; *sc:* Charles Schnee—*b/o* a story by Frank Capra.

BUCK: Tough wagonmaster in the 1850s who leads a wagon train with 140 women on a rugged trip West from Chicago to California to meet their mail-order husbands.

Denise Darcel, Henry Nakamura, Lenore Lonergan, Marilyn Erskine, Hope Emerson, Julie Bishop, John McIntire, Renata Vanni, Beverly Dennis.

Ivanhoe (1952, MGM). *d:* Richard Thorpe; *p:* Pandro S. Berman; *sc:* Noel Langley (adaptation by Aeneas MacKenzie)—*b/o* the novel by Sir Walter Scott.

IVANHOE: Chivalrous Saxon knight of the Middle Ages who fights to save the English throne for King Richard when the monarch is captured and held prisoner on his way back from the Crusades.

Elizabeth Taylor, Joan Fontaine, George Sanders, Emlyn Williams, Robert Douglas, Finlay Currie, Felix Aylmer, Guy Rolfe, Basil Sydney, Patrick Holt, Roderick Lovell, Sebastian Cabot.

Above and Beyond (1953, MGM). *d:* Melvin Frank and Norman Panama; *p:* Melvin Frank and Norman Panama; *sc:* Beirne Lay Jr., Melvin Frank, and Norman Panama—*b/o* a story by Beirne Lay Jr.

COL. PAUL TIBBETS: U.S. Army Air Force officer who pilots the *Enola Gay*, the B-29 plane that drops the atomic bomb on Hiroshima on August 6, 1945.

Eleanor Parker, James Whitmore, Larry Keating, Larry Gates, Marilyn Erskine, Stephen Dunne,

Robert Burton, Hayden Rorke, Larry Dobkin, Jeff Richards, Dick Simmons, Jim Backus, Dabbs Greer, John W. Baer, Robert Fuller.

Ride Vaquero! (1953, MGM). *d:* John Farrow; *p:* Stephen Ames; *sc:* Frank Fenton.

RIO: Quiet but deadly sidekick of a vicious Mexican outlaw whose gang terrorizes and tries to drive out a young settler and his wife who are attempting to build a ranch in post–Civil War Texas.

Ava Gardner, Howard Keel, Anthony Quinn, Kurt Kasznar, Ted de Corsia, Jack Elam, Walter Baldwin, Joe Dominguez, Frank McGrath, Charles Stevens, Rex Lease, Tom Greenway.

All the Brothers Were Valiant (1953, MGM). *d:* Richard Thorpe; *p:* Pandro S. Berman; *sc:* Harry Brown—*b/o* the story by Ben Ames Williams.

JOEL SHORE: New England whaling captain who clashes with his whaling-captain brother over a treasure of pearls and a pretty young woman.

Stewart Granger, Ann Blyth, Betta St. John, Keenan Wynn, James Whitmore, Kurt Kasznar, Lewis Stone, Robert Burton, Peter Whitney, John Lupton, James Bell, Leo Gordon, Michael Pate, Frank de Kova.

Knights of the Round Table (1954, MGM). *d:* Richard Thorpe; *p:* Pandro S. Berman; *sc:* Talbot Jennings, Jan Lustig, and Noel Langley—*b/o Le Morte d' Arthur* by Sir Thomas Malory.

SIR LANCELOT: Heroic knight of King Arthur's Round Table in seventh-century England who, though loyal to King Arthur, falls in love with Queen Guinevere.

Ava Gardner, Mel Ferrer, Anne Crawford, Stanley Baker, Felix Aylmer, Maureen Swanson, Gabriel Woolf, Anthony Forwood, Robert Urquhart, Niall MacGinnis.

Valley of the Kings (1954, MGM). *d:* Robert Pirosh; *sc:* Robert Pirosh and Karl Tunberg—suggested by historical data in *Gods, Graves and Scholars* by C. W. Ceram.

MARK BRANDON: Archaeologist in 1900 who has to fight grave robbers and other obstacles in Egypt while aiding a married couple in their search for the tomb of an Eighteenth Dynasty pharaoh named Ra-Hotep.

Eleanor Parker, Carlos Thompson, Kurt Kasznar, Victor Jory, Leon Askin, Aldo Silvani, Samia Gamal.

Rogue Cop (1954, MGM). *d:* Roy Rowland; *p:* Nicholas Nayfack; *sc:* Sidney Boehm—*b/o* the novel by William P. McGivern.

CHRISTOPHER KELVANEY: Police detective on the take who goes straight and seeks revenge against the mob when they kill his younger brother, an honest cop.

Janet Leigh, George Raft, Steve Forrest, Anne Francis, Robert Ellenstein, Robert F. Simon, Anthony Ross, Alan Hale Jr., Peter Brocco, Vince Edwards, Olive Carey, Roy Barcroft, Dale Van Sickel, Ray Teal.

Many Rivers to Cross (1955, MGM). *d:* Roy Rowland; *p:* Jack Cummings; *sc:* Harry Brown and Guy Trosper—*b/o* a story by Steve Frazee.

BUSHROD GENTRY: Marriage-shy trapper and adventurer in 1798 Kentucky who is pursued by an aggressive, sharp-shooting frontier woman determined to drag him to the altar.

Eleanor Parker, Victor McLaglen, Jeff Richards, Russ Tamblyn, James Arness, Alan Hale Jr., John Hudson, Rhys Williams, Josephine Hutchinson, Sig Ruman, Rosemary DeCamp, Russell Johnson, Ralph Moody.

Quentin Durward (1955, MGM). *d:* Richard Thorpe; *p:* Pandro S. Berman; *sc:* Robert Ardrey (adaptation by George Froeschel)—*b/o* the novel by Sir Walter Scott.

QUENTIN DURWARD: Dashing fifteenth-century Scottish adventurer who—when he's sent to King Louis XI's France by his aging lord uncle to woo a young French countess on the uncle's behalf—falls in love with her himself.

Kay Kendall, Robert Morley, George Cole, Alex Clunes, Ducan Lamont, Laya Raki, Marius Goring, Wilfrid Hyde-White, Eric Pohlmann, Harcourt Williams.

The Last Hunt (1956, MGM). *d:* Richard Brooks; *p:* Dore Schary; *sc:* Richard Brooks—*b/o* the novel by Milton Lott.

CHARLES GILSON: Sadistic 1880s buffalo hunter in the Dakotas who clashes with his hunting partner while proving that he likes killing people as much as he enjoys killing buffalo.

Stewart Granger, Lloyd Nolan, Debra Paget, Russ Tamblyn, Constance Ford, Joe De Santis, Ainslie Pryor, Ralph Moody, Fred Graham, Ed Lonehill.

D-Day the Sixth of June (1956, 20th-Fox). *d:* Henry Koster; *p:* Charles Brackett; *sc:* Ivan Moffat and Harry Brown—*b/o* the novel by Lionel Shapiro.

BRAD PARKER: WWII American infantry captain who hits the Normandy beaches on D-Day in 1944, along with a British colonel with whose girlfriend he has been having an affair.

Richard Todd, Dana Wynter, Edmond O'Brien, John Williams, Jerry Paris, Robert Gist, Ross Elliott, Alex Finlayson, Dabbs Greer, Geoffrey Steele, Damien O'Flynn, Queenie Leonard, Parley Baer.

The Power and the Prize (1956, MGM). *d:* Henry Koster; *p:* Nicholas Nayfack; *sc:* Robert Ardrey—*b/o* the novel by Howard Swiggett.

CLIFF BARTON: Ambitious executive—picked by

a ruthless tycoon to be his successor—who, after he falls in love with a German refugee, changes his values and refuses to go along with the tycoon's unethical practices.

Elisabeth Mueller, Burl Ives, Charles Coburn, Sir Cedric Hardwicke, Mary Astor, Nicola Michaels, Cameron Prud'homme, Richard Erdman, Ben Wright, Jack Raine, Tom Browne Henry, Richard Deacon.

Tip on a Dead Jockey (1957, MGM). *d:* Richard Thorpe; *p:* Edwin H. Knopf; *sc:* Charles Lederer—*b/o* a story in *The New Yorker* magazine by Irwin Shaw.

LLOYD TREDMAN: Emotionally troubled ex-WWII pilot who tries to help an old war buddy in need of money and gets involved with a smuggling syndicate in Madrid.

Dorothy Malone, Gia Scala, Martin Gabel, Marcel Dalio, Jack Lord, Joyce Jameson.

Saddle the Wind (1958, MGM). *d:* Robert Parrish; *p:* Armand Deutsch; *sc:* Rod Serling—*b/o* a story by Thomas Thompson.

STEVE SINCLAIR: Reformed gunslinger-turned-rancher who is forced into a showdown with his reckless, trigger-happy younger brother.

Julie London, John Cassavetes, Donald Crisp, Charles McGraw, Royal Dano, Richard Erdman, Douglas Spencer, Ray Teal.

The Law and Jake Wade (1958, MGM). *d:* John Sturges; *p:* William Hawks; *sc:* William Bowers—*b/o* the novel by Marvin H. Albert.

JAKE WADE: Reformed outlaw-turned-marshal in a New Mexico town who helps an old outlaw crony break out of jail but then is forced to lead him to buried loot in a deserted ghost town.

Richard Widmark, Patricia Owens, Robert Middleton, Henry Silva, DeForest Kelley, Burt Douglas, Eddie Firestone.

Party Girl (1958, MGM). *d:* Nicholas Ray; *p:* Joe Pasternak (Euterpe); *sc:* George Wells—*b/o* a story by Leo Katcher.

THOMAS FARRELL: Rich, crooked lawyer in early 1930s Chicago who falls in love with a show girl, then runs into trouble when he tries to break his ties with the mob.

Cyd Charisse, Lee J. Cobb, John Ireland, Kent Smith, Claire Kelly, Corey Allen, Lewis Charles, David Opatoshu, Patrick McVey, Myrna Hansen.

The Hangman (1959, Para.). *d:* Michael Curtiz; *p:* Frank Freeman Jr.; *sc:* Dudley Nichols—*b/o* a story by Luke Short.

MacKENZIE BOVARD: U.S. deputy marshal who finds himself being thwarted by the people of an 1870s Southwest town when he tries to track down a respected citizen wanted for murder.

Fess Parker, Tina Louise, Jack Lord, Shirley Harmer, Gene Evans, Mickey Shaughnessy, James Westerfield, Mabel Albertson, Lucille Curtis.

The House of the Seven Hawks (1959, MGM). *d:* Richard Thorpe; *p:* David Rose; *sc:* Jo Eisinger—*b/o* Victor Canning's novel *The House of the Seven Flies.*

JOHN NORDLEY: American charter-boat skipper who gets involved with international thieves, two beautiful women, the Dutch police, and a long-lost treasure of diamonds that were stolen by the Nazis and hidden in Holland.

Nicole Maurey, Linda Christian, Donald Wolfit, David Kossoff, Gerard Heinz, Eric Pohlmann, Philo Hauser, Paul Hardmuth, Lily Kann, Richard Shaw, Peter Welch.

Killers of Kilimanjaro (1960, Col.). *d:* Richard Thorpe; *p:* Irving Allen and Albert R. Broccoli (Warwick); *sc:* John Gilling and Earl Felton—*b/o* the book *African Bush Adventures* by J. A. Hunter and Daniel P. Mannix.

ADAMSON: American engineer who, while involved in building the first East African railway, helps a young English woman search for her father and fiancé, who have disappeared in the interior.

Anthony Newley, Anne Aubrey, Gregoire Aslan, Allan Cuthbertson, Martin Benson, Orlando Martins, Donald Pleasance, Earl Cameron, Harry Baird.

Miracle of the White Stallions (1963, Buena Vista). *d:* Arthur Hiller; *p:* Walt Disney (Walt Disney Prod.); *sc:* A. J. Carothers—*b/o* Colonel Alois Podhajsky's book *The Dancing White Horses of Vienna.*

COL. ALOIS PODHAJSKY: Austrian owner of Vienna's Spanish Riding School who engineers the rescue of the school's valuable Lippizaner horses during the closing days of WWII.

Lilli Palmer, Curt Jurgens, Eddie Albert, James Franciscus, John Larch, Brigitte Horney, Philip Abbott, Douglas Fowley, Fritz Wepper, Philo Hauser.

Cattle King (1963, MGM). *d:* Tay Garnett; *p:* Nat Holt (Missouri); *sc:* Thomas Thompson.

SAM BRASSFIELD: Wyoming rancher in 1883 who fights an unscrupulous cattle speculator when he tries to encroach on his fenced-in, controlled grazing land.

Joan Caulfield, Robert Loggia, Robert Middleton, Larry Gates, Malcolm Atterbury, William Windom, Virginia Christine, Ray Teal, Richard Devon, John Mitchum.

A House Is Not a Home (1964, Para.). *d:* Russell Rouse; *p:* Joseph E. Levine and Clarence Greene

(Embassy); *sc:* Russell Rouse and Clarence Greene—*b/o* the book by Polly Adler.

FRANK COSTIGAN: Racketeer who starts the career of Polly Adler, a notorious Broadway bordello madam of the 1920s.

Shelley Winters, Cesar Romero, Ralph Taeger, Kaye Ballard, Broderick Crawford, Mickey Shaughnessy, Meri Welles, Jesse White, Connie Gilchrist, Lewis Charles, J. Pat O'Malley, Hayden Rorke, Benny Rubin, Tom D'Andrea, Gee Gee Galligan, Raquel Welch.

The Night Walker (1965, Univ.). *d:* William Castle; *p:* William Castle and Dona Holloway (William Castle Prod.); *sc:* Robert Bloch.

BARRY MORLAND: Supposedly respectable lawyer who devises a bizarre plot to terrorize a wealthy female client in order to get his hands on her money.

Barbara Stanwyck, Lloyd Bochner, Hayden Rorke, Judith Meredith, Rochelle Hudson, Marjorie Bennett, Jess Barker, Pauelle Clark, Tetsu Komai.

Johnny Tiger (1966, Univ.). *d:* Paul Wendkos; *p:* R. John Hugh (Nova–Hugh); *sc:* R. John Hugh and Paul Crabtree—*b/o* a story by R. John Hugh.

GEORGE DEAN: Widowed professor who, with his three children, goes to an Indian reservation in Florida to teach underprivileged Seminole children.

Geraldine Brooks, Chad Everett, Brenda Scott, Marc Lawrence, Ford Rainey, Carol Seflinger, Steven Wheeler, Pamela Melendez, Deanna Lund.

Savage Pampas (1967, Comet). *d:* Hugo Fregonese; *p:* Jaime Prades (Jaime Prades–Dasa–Samuel Bronston); *sc:* Hugo Fregonese and John Melson—*b/o* the novel *Pampa Barbera* by Homero Manzi and Ulises Petit De Murat.

CAPTAIN MARTIN: Rugged commanding officer of an Army outpost in Argentina during the 1800s who fights a gang of renegade deserters and hostile Indians.

Ron Randell, Marc Lawrence, Ty Hardin, Rosenda Monteros, Felicia Roc, Angel Del Pozo, Mario Lozano, Enrique Avila, Laura Granados, Milo Quesada.

The Glass Sphinx (1968, AIP). *d:* Luigi Scattini and Kamel El Sheikh; *p:* Fulvio Lucisano; *sc:* Adriano Bolzoni and Louis M. Heyward—*b/o* a story by Adriano Bolzoni and Adalberto Albertini.

PROF. KARL NICHOLS: Famous archaeologist who digs in Egypt for the ancient tomb of King Aposis, which contains the legendary Glass Sphinx—an artifact said to contain an elixir that prolongs life.

Anita Ekberg, Gianna Serra, Jack Stuart, Del Pozo, Ahmed Kamis, Remo De Angelis, José Truchado.

Where Angels Go—Trouble Follows (1968, Col.). *d:* James Neilson; *p:* William Frye; *sc:* Blanche Hanalis—*b/o* characters created by Jane Trahey.

MR. FARRIDAY: Friendly rancher who helps some nuns and their convent schoolgirls when they travel from Pennsylvania to a youth rally in California.

Rosalind Russell, Stella Stevens, Binnie Barnes, Mary Wickes, Dolores Sutton, Susan Saint James, Barbara Hunter, Milton Berle, Arthur Godfrey, Van Johnson, William Lundigan.

The Day the Hotline Got Hot (1968, Commonwealth United–AIP). *d:* Etienne Perier; *p:* Francisco Balcazar (International/Cinematografias Balcazar); *sc:* Paul Jarrico, Dominique Fabre, and M. Trueblood.

ANDERSON: C.I.A. chief who vies with the head of the Russian secret police when secret agents foul up the Washington–Moscow hot line and cause an international crisis.

Charles Boyer, George Chakiris, Marie Dubois, Gerard Tichy, Marta Gram, Maurice de Canonge, Gustavo Rey.

· In addition, Robert Taylor made cameo/guest appearances in the following feature films: *The Youngest Profession* (1943, MGM) and *I Love Melvin* (1953, MGM).

☆ SPENCER TRACY

Spencer Bonaventure Tracy

b: April 5, 1900, Milwaukee, Wis.
d: June 11, 1967, Los Angeles, Cal.

"Not much meat on her, but what's there is cherce."

> Mike Conovan (Spencer Tracy) referring to
> Pat Pemberton (Katharine Hepburn) in
> *Pat and Mike, 1952.*

Up the River (1930, Fox). *d:* John Ford; *p:* William Collier Sr.; *sc:* Maurine Watkins.
SAINT LOUIS: Hardboiled but likeable crook who—after he and his sidekick escape from prison to save a friend from a blackmail scheme—returns to play in the big prison baseball game.
Claire Luce, Warren Hymer, Humphrey Bogart, Joan Marie Lawes, William Collier Sr., George MacFarlane, Robert E. O'Connor, Gaylord Pendleton, Goodee Montgomery, Noel Francis.

Quick Millions (1931, Fox). *d:* Rowland Brown; *sc:* Courtney Terrett and Rowland Brown.
DANIEL J. "BUGS" RAYMOND: Ambitious truck driver who becomes a ruthless racketeer, then tries to marry a society debutante, but winds up being "taken for a ride" by his own gang.
Marguerite Churchill, Sally Eilers, Robert Burns, John Wray, Warner Richmond, George Raft, John Swor.

Six Cylinder Love (1931, Fox). *d:* Thornton Freeland; *sc:* William Conselman and Norman Houston—*b/o* a play by William Anthony McGuire.
WILLIAM DONROY: Slick, high-pressure auto salesman who, when a middle-aged couple go broke because of an expensive car he sold them, agrees to help them unload it on another unsuspecting couple.
Edward Everett Horton, Sidney Fox, William Collier Sr., Una Merkel, Lorin Raker, William Holden, Ruth Warren, Bert Roach, El Brendel.

Goldie (1931, Fox). *d:* Benjamin Stoloff; *sc:* Gene Towne and Paul Perez.
BILL: Dame-chasing merchant seaman who, when his sailor pal falls for a sexy carnival high-diver in Calais, tries to warn him that she's a gold digger he knew back in Brooklyn.
Warren Hymer, Jean Harlow, Jesse DeVorska, Leila Karnelly, Ivan Linow, Lina Basquette, Eleanor Hunt, Maria Alba, Eddie Kane.

She Wanted a Millionaire (1932, Fox). *d:* John Blystone; *sc:* William A. McGuire—*b/o* a story by Sonya Levien.
WILLIAM KELLEY: Breezy young newspaperman who is in love with an Atlantic City beauty-contest winner who makes the mistake of marrying a sadistic millionaire.
Joan Bennett, Una Merkel, James Kirkwood, Dorothy Peterson, Douglas Cosgrove, Donald Dillaway, Lucille LaVerne, Tetsu Komai.

Sky Devils (1932, UA). *d:* Edward Sutherland; *p:* Howard Hughes (Caddo); *sc:* Joseph Moncure March and Edward Sutherland (with additional dialogue by Robert Benchley, James Starr, Carroll Graham, and Garrett Graham).
WILKIE: Cocky lifeguard who is reluctantly drafted during WWI, battles his harboiled sergeant over a woman, and winds up a hero when he and his buddy accidentally blow up a German ammo dump.
William "Stage" Boyd, George Cooper, Ann Dvorak, Billy Bevan, Yola D'Avril, Forrester Harvey, William B. Davidson, Jerry Miley.

Disorderly Conduct (1932, Fox). *d:* John W. Considine Jr.; *sc:* William Anthony McGuire.
DICK FAY: Motorcycle cop who, after clashing with his captain and a crooked politician's daughter, is demoted and gets involved with gangsters—but reforms when a bullet meant for him accidentally kills his nephew.
Sally Eilers, El Brendel, Ralph Bellamy, Ralph Morgan, Frank Conroy, Dickie Moore, Alan Dinehart, Nora Lane, Charles Grapewin, James Todd, Sally Blane.

Young America (1932, Fox). *d:* Frank Borzage; *sc:* William Conselman—*b/o* a play by John Frederick Ballard.
JACK DORAY: Small-town druggist who, when a young boy breaks into his store, demands that he be punished—but changes his mind when the youth risks his life to apprehend crooks who have robbed the store.
Doris Kenyon, Tommy Conlon, Ralph Bellamy, Beryl Mercer, Sarah Padden, Robert Homans, Raymond Borzage, Dawn O'Day (Anne Shirley), Louise Beavers, Spec O'Donnell, William Pawley.

Society Girl (1932, Fox). *d:* Sidney Lanfield; *sc:* Elmer Harris—*b/o* a play by John Larkin Jr.
BRISCOE: Prize-fight manager whose promising young fighter falls for a fickle debutante and, as a result, loses a big fight.
James Dunn, Peggy Shannon, Walter Byron, Bert Hanlon, Marjorie Gateson, Eula Guy Todd.

Painted Woman (1932, Fox). *d:* John Blystone; *sc:*
Guy Bolton and Leon Gordon—*b/o* a play by
Alfred C. Kennedy.

TOM BRIAN: Two-fisted ex-marine in the pearl-
diving business in the South Seas whose newlywed
wife—an ex–Singapore nightclub entertainer—is
accused of murdering a sea captain with whom
she formerly was involved.

Peggy Shannon, William "Stage" Boyd, Irving
Pichel, Laska Winter, Paul Porcasi, Stanley
Fields, Wade Boteler, Jack Kennedy, Dewey
Robinson.

Me and My Gal (1932, Fox). *d:* Raoul Walsh; *sc:*
Arthur Kober—*b/o* a story by Barry Connors and
Philip Klein.

DAN: Happy-go-lucky New York waterfront cop
who falls for a waitress, rescues her sister and
father from a gangster, and uses the reward
money for a Bermuda honeymoon.

Joan Bennett, Marion Burns, George Walsh, J.
Farrell MacDonald, Noel Madison, Henry B.
Walthall, Bert Hanlon, Adrian Morris, George
Chandler.

20,000 Years in Sing Sing (1932, WB). *d:* Michael
Curtiz; *p:* Robert Lord; *sc:* Courtenay Terrett,
Robert Lord, Wilson Mizner, and Brown Holmes—
b/o the book by Warden Lewis E. Lawes.

TOM CONNORS: Tough gangster who is granted
a twenty-four-hour "honor system" leave from
Sing Sing to visit his seriously injured girlfriend,
then takes the blame when she shoots the crooked
lawyer who injured her, and returns to prison to
face the electric chair for murder.

Bette Davis, Lyle Talbot, Arthur Byron, Grant
Mitchell, Warren Hymer, Louis Calhern, Sheila
Terry, Spencer Charters, Nella Walker, Harold
Huber, Arthur Hoyt, Clarence Wilson.

Face in the Sky (1933, Fox). *d:* Harry Lachman;
sc: Humphrey Pearson—*b/o* a story by Myles
Connolly.

JOE BUCK: Wandering sign painter who falls for
a New England farm girl, then loses her, but wins
her back when he paints her face on a huge sign
atop a New York skyscraper.

Marian Nixon, Stuart Erwin, Sam Hardy, Sara
Padden, Frank McGlynn Jr., Russell Simpson,
Lila Lee, Guy Usher.

Shanghai Madness (1933, Fox). *d:* John Blystone;
sc: Austin Parker (adaptation by Gordon
Wellesley)—*b/o* a story by Frederick Hazlitt
Brennan.

PAT JACKSON: U.S. Navy lieutenant in 1920s
China who, after he's court-martialed and
discharged from the service for attacking Chinese
Communists, becomes a riverboat gunrunner for a
Mandarin.

Fay Wray, Ralph Morgan, Eugene Pallette,
Herbert Mundin, Reginald Mason, Arthur Hoyt,
Albert Conti, Maude Eburne, William von
Brincken.

The Power and the Glory (1933, Fox). *d:*
William K. Howard; *p:* Jesse L. Lasky; *sc:* Preston
Sturges.

TOM GARNER: Railroad-track walker who, after
working his way up to the presidency of the
Chicago and Southwestern Railway, lets the
"power and glory" go to his head and winds up
destroying both his wife and himself.

Colleen Moore, Ralph Morgan, Helen Vinson,
Clifford Jones, Henry Kolker, Sarah Padden, Billy
O'Brien, Cullen Johnston, J. Farrell MacDonald.

The Mad Game (1933, Fox). *d:* Irving Cummings;
p: Sol Wurtzel; *sc:* William Conselman and Henry
Johnson.

EDWARD CARSON: Imprisoned Prohibition-era
bootlegger who, when his old mob kidnaps a
young couple, gets the warden to release him long
enough to rescue the couple and capture the
kidnappers.

Claire Trevor, Ralph Morgan, Harold Lolly, Mary
Mason, J. Carrol Naish, John Miljan, Matt
McHugh, Kathleen Burke, Willard Robertson,
Paul Fix.

A Man's Castle (1933, Col.). *d:* Frank Borzage; *sc:*
Jo Swerling—*b/o* a play by Lawrence Hazard.

BILL: Young odd-jobs man during the 1930s
Depression who encounters a homeless, hungry
young woman and takes her to live in his shack
in a shanty town on the banks of the East River.

Loretta Young, Glenda Farrell, Walter Connolly,
Arthur Hohl, Marjorie Rambeau, Dickie Moore,
Helen Eddy, Harvey Clark, Robert Grey, Kendall
McComas.

Looking for Trouble (1934, UA). *d:* William
Wellman; *p:* Darryl F. Zanuck (20th Century); *sc:*
Leonard Praskins and Elmer Harris—*b/o* a story
by J. R. Bren.

JOE GRAHAM: Ace troubleshooter and lineman
for the Los Angeles telephone company who, after
his girlfriend is accused of murdering her crooked
boss, gets a last-minute confession from the real
murderess when she's fatally injured in an
earthquake.

Jack Oakie, Constance Cummings, Arline Judge,
Judith Wood, Morgan Conway, Paul Harvey,
Joseph Sauers, Franklin Ardell, Robert Homans.

The Show-Off (1934, MGM). *d:* Charles F.
Reisner; *p:* Lucien Hubbard; *sc:* Herman J.
Mankiewicz—*b/o* the play by George Kelly.

AUBREY PIPER: Loud-mouthed, bragging
railroad clerk who is kicked out by his wife when
he loses his job but—after one of his wild schemes

accidentally makes money for the railroad—gets both his job and his wife back.

Madge Evans, Lois Wilson, Grant Mitchell, Clara Blandick, Claude Gillingwater, Henry Wadsworth, Alan Edward, Richard Tucker.

Bottoms Up (1934, Fox). *d:* David Butler; *p:* B. G. DeSylva; *sc:* B. G. DeSylva, David Butler, and Sid Silvers.

SMOOTHE KING: Fast-talking Hollywood promoter who passes off a beauty-contest winner as British nobility and makes a movie star of her but loses her love to a handsome matinee idol.

John Boles, Pat Paterson, Herbert Mundin, Sid Silvers, Harry Green, Thelma Todd, Robert Emmett O'Connor, Del Henderson, Susanne Kaaren, Douglas Wood.

Now I'll Tell (1934, Fox). *d:* Edwin Burke; *p:* Winfield Sheehan; *sc:* Edwin Burke—*b/o* the book by Mrs. Arnold Rothstein.

MURRAY GOLDEN: Big-time 1920s gambler whose lust for wealth and power gets him into trouble with mobsters, causes him to lose his wife, and finally destroys him.

Helen Twelvetrees, Alice Faye, Robert Gleckler, Hobart Cavanaugh, Henry O'Neill, G. P. Huntley Jr., Shirley Temple, Frank Marlowe, Clarence Wilson, Barbara Weeks, Vince Barnett, Jim Donlon.

Marie Galante (1934, Fox). *d:* Henry King; *p:* Winfield Sheehan; *sc:* Reginald Berkeley—*b/o* a novel and play by Jacques Deval.

CRAWBETT: American intelligence officer, posing as a scientist, who gets involved with a café singer in the Panama Canal zone while trying to prevent a counterspy plot to sabotage the Canal.

Ketti Gallian, Ned Sparks, Helen Morgan, Sigfried Rumann, Leslie Fenton, Arthur Byron, Robert Lorraine, Jay C. Flippen, Frank Darien, Stepin Fetchit.

It's a Small World (1935, Fox). *d:* Irving Cummings; *p:* Edward Butcher; *sc:* Samuel Hellman and Gladys Lehman—*b/o* the story "Highway Robbery" by Albert Treynor.

BILL SHEVLIN: Young lawyer who, after colliding with a dizzy debutante in an auto accident and being arrested for disturbing the peace, falls for her during a trial held by a zany judge trying to promote a romance between them.

Wendy Barrie, Raymond Walburn, Virginia Sale, Astrid Allwyn, Irving Bacon, Charles Seldon, Nick Foran, Belle Daube, Frank McGlynn Sr., Frank McGlynn Jr., Edwin Brady.

Murder Man (1935, MGM). *d:* Tim Whelan; *p:* Harry Rapf; *sc:* Tim Whelan and John C. Higgins—*b/o* a story by Tim Whelan and Guy Bolton.

STEVE GRAY: Newspaper reporter who kills a crooked stockbroker responsible for his wife's suicide, then frames the dead man's partner on a murder rap but finally confesses in order to keep the wrongly convicted man from going to the chair.

Virginia Bruce, Lionel Atwill, Harvey Stephens, Robert Barrat, James Stewart, William Collier Sr., Bobby Watson, William Demarest, Lucien Littlefield, George Chandler, Fuzzy Knight, Louise Henry, Robert Warwick.

Dante's Inferno (1935, Fox). *d:* Harry Lachman; *p:* Sol M. Wurtzel; *sc:* Philip Klein and Robert M. Yost—*b/o* a story by Cyrus Wood.

JIM CARTER: Ex–steamship stoker who becomes a carnival barker, then makes a fortune buying up amusement piers, but suffers a downfall when his ruthless and unscrupulous methods backfire.

Claire Trevor, Henry B. Walthall, Scotty Beckett, Alan Dinehart, Joe Brown, Nella Walker, Richard Tucker, Don Ameche, Rita Cansino (Rita Hayworth), Warren Hymer, Willard Robertson, Barbara Pepper.

Whipsaw (1935, MGM). *d:* Sam Wood; *p:* Harry Rapf; *sc:* Howard E. Rogers—*b/o* a story by James E. Grant.

ROSS McBRIDE: G-man who pretends to be a crook while romancing a jewel thief in hopes that she'll lead him to the rest of the gang.

Myrna Loy, Harvey Stephens, William Harrigan, Clay Clement, Robert Gleckler, Robert Warwick, Halliwell Hobbes, Wade Boteler, Don Rowan, John Qualen, Irene Franklin.

Riffraff (1936, MGM). *d:* J. Walter Ruben; *p:* Irving Thalberg; *sc:* Frances Marion, H. W. Hanemann, and Anita Loos—*b/o* a story by Frances Marion.

DUTCH: Tough California tuna fisherman who marries a cannery worker who gets into trouble with the law and goes to prison, where she gives birth to his baby.

Jean Harlow, Una Merkel, Joseph Calleia, Victor Kilian, Mickey Rooney, J. Farrell MacDonald, Roger Imhof, Juanita Quigley, Paul Hurst, Vince Barnett, Arthur Housman, Wade Boteler, George Givot.

Fury (1936, MGM). *d:* Fritz Lang; *p:* Joseph L. Mankiewicz; *sc:* Bartlett Cormack and Fritz Lang—*b/o* a story by Norman Krasna.

JOE WILSON: Young man mistakenly arrested for kidnapping who, when a lynch mob burns the jail, secretly escapes but lets the town think he was killed so that members of the mob will be charged with murder.

Sylvia Sidney, Walter Abel, Bruce Cabot, Edward Ellis, Walter Brennan, George Walcott, Frank

Albertson, Arthur Stone, Morgan Wallace, George Chandler, Roger Gray, Edwin Maxwell, Howard Hickman, Jonathan Hale, Esther Dale.

San Francisco (1936, MGM). *d:* W. S. Van Dyke; *p:* John Emerson and Bernard H. Hyman; *sc:* Anita Loos—*b/o* a story by Robert Hopkins.
FATHER TIM MULLIN*: Rugged chaplain of a Barbary Coast mission—at the time of the 1906 San Francisco earthquake—who tries to protect a small-town minister's daughter–turned–café singer from being exploited by an opportunistic saloon owner.
Clark Gable, Jeanette MacDonald, Jack Holt, Jessie Ralph, Ted Healy, Shirley Ross, Harold Huber, Al Shean, Kenneth Harlan, Roger Imhof, Russell Simpson, Bert Roach, Warren Hymer, Edgar Kennedy.

Libeled Lady (1936, MGM). *d:* Jack Conway; *p:* Lawrence Weingarten; *sc:* Maurine Watkins, Howard Emmett Rogers, and George Oppenheimer—*b/o* a story by Wallace Sullivan.
HAGGERTY: Conniving newspaper editor who talks his tough blonde fiancée into marrying a financially strapped lawyer as part of a blackmail scheme to keep a hot-headed heiress from suing the paper for libel.
Jean Harlow, William Powell, Myrna Loy, Walter Connolly, Charley Grapewin, Cora Witherspoon, E. E. Clive, Charles Trowbridge, Spencer Charters, George Chandler, William Benedict, Hal K. Dawson, William Newell.

They Gave Him a Gun (1937, MGM). *d:* W. S. Van Dyke; *p:* Harry Rapf; *sc:* Cyril Hume, Richard Maibaum, and Maurice Rapf—*b/o* a book by William Joyce Cowen.
FRED WILLIS: Good-natured WWI doughboy who, after the Armistice, becomes the law-abiding owner of a circus, but whose young Army buddy—hardened by guns and war—turns to a life of crime.
Gladys George, Franchot Tone, Edgar Dearing, Mary Lou Treen, Cliff Edwards, Charles Trowbridge, Joseph Sawyer, George Chandler, Gavin Gordon, Ernest Whitman, Nita Pike, Joan Woodbury.

Captains Courageous (1937, MGM). *d:* Victor Fleming; *p:* Louis D. Lighton; *sc:* John Lee Mahin, Marc Connelly, and Dale Van Every—*b/o* the novel by Rudyard Kipling.
MANUEL†: Happy-go-lucky Portuguese fisherman on a fishing schooner who—when a spoiled, rich twelve-year-old boy falls off an ocean liner—hauls

him aboard, teaches him warmth and kindness, and changes the boy's life—but loses his own.
Freddie Bartholomew, Lionel Barrymore, Melvyn Douglas, Charles Grapewin, Mickey Rooney, John Carradine, Oscar O'Shea, Jack La Rue, Walter Kingsford, Donald Briggs.

Big City (1937, MGM). *d:* Frank Borzage; *p:* Norman Krasna; *sc:* Dore Schary and Hugo Butler—*b/o* a story by Norman Krasna.
JOE BENTON: Big-city cab driver who, with his immigrant wife and some friendly prize fighters, battles crooked taxi hoodlums trying to force independent cabbies like him out of business.
Luise Rainer, Charley Grapewin, Janet Beecher, Eddie Quillan, Victor Varconi, Oscar O'Shea, Helen Troy.

Mannequin (1938, MGM). *d:* Frank Borzage; *p:* Joseph L. Mankiewicz; *sc:* Lawrence Hazard—*b/o* a story by Katharine Brush.
JOHN HENNESSEY: Self-made shipping magnate who marries a slum girl–turned–model from his old neighborhood, then encounters trouble from her small-time-crook ex-husband.
Joan Crawford, Alan Curtis, Ralph Morgan, Mary Phillips, Oscar O'Shea, Elizabeth Risdon, Leo Gorcey, George Chandler, Bert Roach, Marie Blake, Matt McHugh, Paul Fix, Helen Troy, Phillip Terry.

Test Pilot (1938, MGM). *d:* Victor Fleming; *p:* Louis D. Lighton; *sc:* Vincent Lawrence and Waldemar Young—*b/o* on a story by Frank Wead.
GUNNER: Loyal, understanding airplane mechanic who watches over and tries to protect his best friend—an egotistical daredevil test pilot—but loses his own life in a crash while they're testing a bomber for the Army.
Clark Gable, Myrna Loy, Lionel Barrymore, Samuel S. Hinds, Marjorie Main, Ted Pearson, Gloria Holden, Louis J. Heydt, Virginia Grey, Priscilla Lawson, Claudia Coleman, Arthur Aylesworth.

Boys Town (1938, MGM). *d:* Norman Taurog; *p:* John W. Considine Jr.; *sc:* John Meehan and Dore Schary—*b/o* a story by Dore Schary and Eleanor Griffin.
FATHER EDWARD J. FLANAGAN*: Dedicated Catholic priest who—after a condemned convict tells him that if he had been helped as a child he might not have become a murderer—establishes Boys Town, a school and community in Nebraska for homeless boys.
Mickey Rooney, Henry Hull, Leslie Fenton, Addison Richards, Edward Norris, Gene Reynolds, Minor Watson, Victor Kilian, Jonathan Hale,

---

*Received an Academy Award nomination as Best Actor for this role.

†Won the Academy Award as Best Actor for this role.

---

*Won the Academy Award as Best Actor for this role.

Bobs Watson, Frankie Thomas, Jimmy Butler, Sidney Miller.

Stanley and Livingstone (1939, 20th-Fox). *d:* Henry King; *p:* Darryl F. Zanuck and Kenneth Macgowan; *sc:* Philip Dunne and Julien Josephson—*b/o* research material and a story outline by Hal Long and Sam Hellman.

HENRY M. STANLEY: New York newspaper reporter who, after he's assigned by his editor to search for the lost Victorian missionary Dr. David Livingstone, finds him working among the natives in an isolated African village.

Nancy Kelly, Richard Greene, Walter Brennan, Charles Coburn, Sir Cedric Hardwicke, Henry Hull, Henry Travers, Miles Mander, Holmes Herbert, Brandon Hurst, Paul Harvey, Russell Hicks, Joseph Crehan, Robert Middlemass.

I Take This Woman (1940, MGM). *d:* W. S. Van Dyke; *p:* Bernard H. Hyman; *sc:* James Kevin McGuinness—*b/o* a story by Charles MacArthur.

KARL DECKER: Dedicated doctor who—when he marries a selfish café-society playgirl—reluctantly gives up his tenement-district clinic to become a physician for the rich, then breaks up with her, but finally gets both her and the clinic back.

Hedy Lamarr, Verree Teasdale, Kent Taylor, Laraine Day, Mona Barrie, Jack Carson, Paul Cavanagh, Louis Calhern, Marjorie Main, Frances Drake, George E. Stone, Willie Best, Don Castle, Reed Hadley.

Northwest Passage (1940, MGM). *d:* King Vidor; *p:* Hunt Stromberg; *sc:* Laurence Stallings and Talbot Jennings—*b/o* the novel by Kenneth Rogers.

MAJ. ROBERT ROGERS: Rugged leader of Rogers' Rangers who, in 1759 during the French and Indian Wars, takes his men on a strenuous and perilous expedition to wipe out a village of marauding Indians.

Robert Young, Walter Brennan, Ruth Hussey, Nat Pendleton, Robert Barrat, Lumsden Hare, Donald McBride, Isabel Jewell, Addison Richards, Hugh Sothern, Regis Toomey, Montagu Love, Lester Matthews, Truman Bradley.

Edison, the Man (1940, MGM). *d:* Clarence Brown; *p:* John W. Considine Jr.; *sc:* Talbot Jennings and Bradbury Foote—*b/o* a story by Dore Schary and Hugo Butler.

THOMAS ALVA EDISON: Penniless young man who comes to New York from Boston, struggles for years in poverty, and finally becomes America's most famous inventor when he develops such miraculous devices as the electric light and the phonograph.

Rita Johnson, Lynne Overman, Charles Coburn, Gene Lockhart, Henry Travers, Felix Bressart, Peter Godfrey, Byron Foulger, Arthur Aylesworth,

Gene Reynolds, Addison Richards, Grant Mitchell, Paul Hurst, Jay Ward, Ann Gillis.

Boom Town (1940, MGM). *d:* Jack Conway; *p:* Sam Zimbalist; *sc:* John Lee Mahin—*b/o* a short story by James Edward Grant.

"SQUARE JOHN" SAND: One of a pair of rugged oil wildcatters who become partners, argue and break up, then alternately make and lose millions of dollars but finally become partners again.

Clark Gable, Claudette Colbert, Hedy Lamarr, Frank Morgan, Lionel Atwill, Chill Wills, Marion Martin, Minna Gombell, Joe Yule, Richard Lane, George Lessey, Sara Haden, Frank Orth, Frank McGlynn Sr., Curt Bois.

Men of Boys Town (1941, MGM). *d:* Norman Taurog; *p:* John W. Considine Jr.; *sc:* James K. McGuinness.

FATHER EDWARD J. FLANAGAN: Dedicated founder of Boys Town (the Nebraska community for homeless boys) who, along with his junior mayor, battles juvenile delinquency and exposes the brutal conditions in a reform school.

Mickey Rooney, Bobs Watson, Larry Nunn, Darryl Hickman, Henry O'Neill, Mary Nash, Lee J. Cobb, Sidney Miller, Addison Richards, Lloyd Corrigan, Robert Emmett Keane, Arthur Hohl, Ben Welden, Anne Revere, George Lessey.

Dr. Jekyll and Mr. Hyde (1941, MGM). *d:* Victor Fleming; *p:* Victor Fleming; *sc:* John Lee Mahin—*b/o* the story by Robert Louis Stevenson.

DR. HARRY JEKYLL/MR. HYDE: Respectable doctor in Victorian London who discovers a formula that separates the good and the evil in his soul—and when the evil takes over, it turns him into a sadistic fiend known as Mr. Hyde.

Ingrid Bergman, Lana Turner, Ian Hunter, Donald Crisp, Barton MacLane, C. Aubrey Smith, Sara Allgood, Peter Godfrey, William Tannen, Billy Bevan, Forrester Harvey, Lumsden Hare.

Woman of the Year (1942, MGM). *d:* George Stevens; *p:* Joseph L. Mankiewicz; *sc:* Ring Lardner Jr. and Michael Kanin.

SAM CRAIG: New York sports reporter who marries a famous, intellectual female political columnist and discovers that they both have definite and different ideas about life and marriage.

Katharine Hepburn, Fay Bainter, Reginald Owen, Minor Watson, William Bendix, Gladys Blake, Dan Tobin, Roscoe Karns, Ludwig Stossel, Sara Haden, Jimmy Coslin, Ben Lessy, Ray Teal, Joe Yule.

Tortilla Flat (1942, MGM). *d:* Victor Fleming; *p:* Sam Zimbalist; *sc:* John Lee Mahin and Benjamin Glazer—*b/o* the novel by John Steinbeck.

PILON: Leader of a group of poor Mexican

peasants in a small Southern California fishing community who vies with a young friend for the hand of the village beauty.

Hedy Lamarr, John Garfield, Frank Morgan, Akim Tamiroff, Sheldon Leonard, John Qualen, Donald Meek, Connie Gilchrist, Allen Jenkins, Henry O'Neill, Betty Wells, Harry Burns.

Keeper of the Flame (1942, MGM). *d:* George Cukor; *p:* Victor Saville; *sc:* Donald Ogden Stewart—*b/o* a novel by I. A. R. Wylie.

STEVEN O'MALLEY: Reporter who, when he visits the widow of a recently deceased American national hero in order to write a favorable article, digs deeper into the story and forces the widow to reveal that the husband was really a traitorous Fascist.

Katharine Hepburn, Richard Whorf, Margaret Wycherly, Donald Meek, Horace (Stephen) McNally, Audrey Christie, Frank Craven, Forrest Tucker, Percy Kilbride, Howard da Silva, Darryl Hickman, William Newell, Rex Evans, Blanche Yurka.

A Guy Named Joe (1943, MGM). *d:* Victor Fleming; *p:* Everett Riskin; *sc:* Dalton Trumbo—*b/o* a story by Chandler Sprague, David Boehm, and Frederick H. Brennan.

PETE SANDIDGE: Courageous but reckless WWII U.S. Army combat pilot who, after he's killed when he crashes his plane into an enemy aircraft carrier, goes to Heaven but is assigned to return to Earth—unseen and unheard by mortals—to help a neophyte pilot learn to fly.

Irene Dunne, Van Johnson, Ward Bond, James Gleason, Lionel Barrymore, Barry Nelson, Harry O'Neill, Don Defore, Charles Smith, Addison Richards, Esther Williams.

The Seventh Cross (1944, MGM). *d:* Fred Zinnemann; *p:* Pandro S. Berman; *sc:* Helen Deutsch—*b/o* a book by Anna Seghers.

GEORGE HEISLER: Anti-Nazi German escapee from a 1936 German concentration camp who, although his six fellow escapees are caught and crucified on six crosses at the camp, manages to reach safety in Holland—leaving the seventh cross empty.

Signe Hasso, Hume Cronyn, Jessica Tandy, Agnes Moorehead, Herbert Rudley, Felix Bressart, Ray Collins, George Macready, Paul Guilfoyle, Steven Geray, Kurt Katch, Konstantin Shayne, John Wengraf, George Zucco.

Thirty Seconds Over Tokyo (1944, MGM). *d:* Mervyn LeRoy; *p:* Sam Zimbalist; *sc:* Dalton Trumbo—*b/o* the book by Ted W. Lawson and Robert Considine.

LT. COL. JAMES H. DOOLITTLE: Famous American flyer who leads a flight of sixteen B-25 U.S. bombers from the deck of the "*Shangri-La*"

(the code name for the WWII aircraft carrier *Hornet*) in April 1942 on the first raid against mainland Japan.

Van Johnson, Robert Walker, Phyllis Thaxter, Scott McKay, Don Defore, Robert Mitchum, Horace (Stephen) McNally, Donald Curtis, Louis J. Heydt, William Phillips, Paul Langton, Leon Ames.

Without Love (1945, MGM). *d:* Harold S. Bucquet; *p:* Lawrence A. Weingarten; *sc:* Donald Ogden Stewart—*b/o* a play by Philip Barry.

PAT JAMIESON: Scientist in WWII Washington, D.C., who, when he rents the home of an attractive widow in order to conduct secret government experiments, enters into a platonic marriage with her—but fails to keep it platonic.

Katharine Hepburn, Lucille Ball, Keenan Wynn, Carl Esmond, Patricia Morison, Felix Bressart, Gloria Grahame, George Chandler, Clancy Cooper, Charles Arnt, Eddie Acuff, Clarence Muse, Garry Owen, William Newell, James Flavin.

The Sea of Grass (1947, MGM). *d:* Elia Kazan; *p:* Pandro S. Berman; *sc:* Marguerite Roberts and Vincent Lawrence—*b/o* the novel by Conrad Richter.

COL. JAMES BREWTON: Ruthless New Mexico cattle baron in the 1880s whose hatred of homesteaders and his obsession with his land drives his wife into the arms of his bitter lawyer enemy.

Katharine Hepburn, Melvyn Douglas, Phyllis Thaxter, Robert Walker, Edgar Buchanan, Harry Carey, William Phillips, James Bell, Robert Barrat, Charles Trowbridge, Russell Hicks, Robert Armstrong, Trevor Bardette, Morris Ankrum.

Cass Timberlane (1947, MGM). *d:* George Sidney; *p:* Arthur Hornblow Jr.; *sc:* Donald Ogden Stewart and Sonya Levien—*b/o* the novel by Sinclair Lewis.

CASS TIMBERLANE: Middle-aged Midwestern judge who, when he marries a beautiful young woman from the wrong side of the tracks, has trouble keeping up with her youthful ideas and suspects her of infidelity—but finally comes to a happy understanding with her.

Lana Turner, Zachary Scott, Tom Drake, Mary Astor, Albert Dekker, Margaret Lindsay, Rose Hobart, John Litel, Mona Barrie, Josephine Hutchinson, Selena Royle, Frank Wilcox, Cameron Mitchell, Howard Freeman, Cliff Clark.

State of the Union (1948, MGM). *d:* Frank Capra; *p:* Frank Capra (Liberty Films); *sc:* Anthony Veiller and Myles Connolly—*b/o* the play by Howard Lindsay and Russel Crouse.

GRANT MATTHEWS: Honest businessman who—after being persuaded to run as the Republican candidate for president—rebels against the shady politicians guiding him and, with the help of his estranged wife, retains his integrity.

Katharine Hepburn, Van Johnson, Angela Lansbury, Adolphe Menjou, Lewis Stone, Howard Smith, Raymond Walburn, Charles Dingle, Pierre Watkin, Margaret Hamilton, Irving Bacon, Carl Switzer, Tom Fadden, Charles Lane, Art Baker, Arthur O'Connell.

Edward, My Son (1949, MGM). *d:* George Cukor; *p:* Edwin C. Knopf; *sc:* Donald Ogden Stewart—*b/o* a play by Robert Morley and Noel Langley.

ARNOLD BOULT: Unscrupulous businessman who—obsessed with giving his only son every advantage—claws and cheats his way upward in the business world as he destroys friends, his alcoholic wife, and finally even his son and himself.

Deborah Kerr, Ian Hunter, Leueen MacGrath, James Donald, Mervyn Johns, Felix Aylmer, Walter Fitzgerald, Tilsa Page, Ernest Jay, Colin Gordon, Clement McCallin.

Adam's Rib (1949, MGM). *d:* George Cukor; *p:* Lawrence Weingarten; *sc:* Garson Kanin and Ruth Gordon.

ADAM BONNER: District attorney who runs into a marital hassle when he and his feminist lawyer wife wind up in court on opposing sides in the trial of a woman who shot her husband.

Katharine Hepburn, Judy Holliday, Tom Ewell, David Wayne, Jean Hagen, Hope Emerson, Clarence Kolb, Polly Moran, Will Wright, Marvin Kaplan, Ray Walker, Tommy Noonan, Anna Q. Nilsson.

Malaya (1950, MGM). *d:* Richard Thorpe; *p:* Edwin Knopf; *sc:* Frank Fenton—*b/o* a story by Manchester Boddy.

CARNAHAN: American adventurer who is released from prison during WWII so that he can take part in a scheme, concocted by an American newspaper reporter, to smuggle badly needed raw rubber out of Japanese-occupied Malaya for the Allies.

James Stewart, Valentina Cortesa, Sydney Greenstreet, John Hodiak, Lionel Barrymore, Gilbert Roland, Roland Winters, Richard Loo, Ian MacDonald, Lester Matthews, Charles Meredith, James Todd.

Father of the Bride (1950, MGM). *d:* Vincente Minnelli; *p:* Pandro S. Berman; *sc:* Frances Goodrich and Albert Hackett—*b/o* the novel by Edward Streeter.

STANLEY T. BANKS*: Suburban lawyer who, after his only daughter announces her engagement and plans for a formal wedding, has to contend with the cost and chaos of the preparations, the ceremony, and the reception—but emerges happy for his daughter.

Joan Bennett, Elizabeth Taylor, Don Taylor, Billie Burke, Leo G. Carroll, Moroni Olsen, Melville Cooper, Russ Tamblyn, Tom Irish, Paul Harvey, Taylor Holmes, Frank Orth, Willard Waterman.

Father's Little Dividend (1951, MGM). *d:* Vincente Minnelli; *p:* Pandro S. Berman; *sc:* Frances Goodrich and Albert Hackett—*b/o* characters created by Edward Streeter.

STANLEY T. BANKS: Suburban lawyer who, when his daughter and son-in-law announce that they are expecting a baby, is apprehensive but manages to cope with the adjustments and problems involved.

Joan Bennett, Elizabeth Taylor, Don Taylor, Billie Burke, Moroni Olsen, Marietta Canty, Russ Tamblyn, Tom Irish, Richard Rober, Hayden Rorke, Paul Harvey.

The People Against O'Hara (1951, MGM). *d:* John Sturges; *p:* William H. Wright; *sc:* John Monks Jr.—*b/o* the novel by Eleazar Lipsky.

JAMES P. CURTAYNE: Once-brilliant criminal lawyer who—while trying to make a comeback—loses a murder case because of his drinking, but then sets out to trap the real killer and exonerate his innocent client.

Diana Lynn, Pat O'Brien, John Hodiak, James Arness, Eduardo Ciannelli, Richard Anderson, Jay C. Flippen, Regis Toomey, William Campbell, Ann Doran, Henry O'Neill, Arthur Shields, Emile Meyer, Frank Ferguson, Lee Phelps, Charles Buchinski (Bronson), Mae Clarke, Jack Kruschen.

Pat and Mike (1952, MGM). *d:* George Cukor; *p:* Lawrence Weingarten; *sc:* Ruth Gordon and Garson Kanin.

MIKE CONOVAN: Fast-talking sports promoter who signs up a female physical-education teacher and, while helping her become a top all-around pro athlete, falls in love with her.

Katharine Hepburn, Aldo Ray, William Ching, Sammy White, George Mathews, Charles Buchinski (Bronson), Jim Backus, Chuck Connors, Carl Switzer, Frankie Darro, Mae Clarke, Tom Harmon, Babe Didrikson Zaharias, Gussie Moran, Don Budge, Alice Marble, Frank Parker.

Plymouth Adventure (1952, MGM). *d:* Clarence Brown; *p:* Dore Schary; *sc:* Helen Deutsch—*b/o* a novel by Ernest Gabler.

CAPTAIN JONES: Captain of the ship *Mayflower* who dislikes his passengers—a group of seventeenth-century Pilgrims bound from England to the New World—but later has a change of heart and helps their newly founded colony of Plymouth, Massachusetts, survive.

---

*Received an Academy Award nomination as Best Actor for this role.

Gene Tierney, Van Johnson, Leo Genn, Lloyd Bridges, Dawn Addams, Barry Jones, Noel Drayton, John Dehner, Tommy Ivo, Lowell Gilmore.

The Actress (1953, MGM). *d:* George Cukor; *p:* Lawrence Weingarten; *sc:* Ruth Gordon—*b/o* her play *Years Ago*.

CLINTON JONES: Gruff but good-hearted ex-sea captain in pre-WWI Massachusetts who tries to keep his young daughter from becoming an actress but finally lets her go with his blessing to New York to pursue her career.

Jean Simmons, Teresa Wright, Anthony Perkins, Ian Wolfe, Kay Williams, Mary Wickes, Norma Jean Nilsson, Dawn Bender.

Broken Lance (1954, 20th-Fox). *d:* Edward Dmytryk; *p:* Sol C. Siegel; *sc:* Richard Murphy—*b/o* a story by Philip Yordan.

MATT DEVEREAUX: Ruthless cattle baron who is hated by and feuds with the three ranch-hand sons of his first wife but is helped and loved by the half-breed son of his second wife, a Comanche Indian.

Robert Wagner, Jean Peters, Richard Widmark, Katy Jurado, Hugh O'Brian, Eduard Franz, Earl Holliman, E. G. Marshall, Carl Benton Reid, Philip Ober, Robert Burton, Edmund Cobb, Russell Simpson, King Donovan, George Stone.

Bad Day at Black Rock (1955, MGM). *d:* John Sturges; *p:* Dore Schary; *sc:* Millard Kaufman—*b/o* a story by Howard Breslin.

JOHN J. MACREEDY*: One-armed stranger who, when he gets off a train at a tiny Southwestern desert town in post-WWII 1945 to give a Japanese-American war hero's posthumous medal to his father, runs into hostile townspeople trying to cover up the father's murder.

Robert Ryan, Anne Francis, Dean Jagger, Walter Brennan, John Ericson, Ernest Borgnine, Lee Marvin, Russell Collins, Walter Sande.

The Mountain (1956, Para.). *d:* Edward Dmytryk; *p:* Edward Dmytryk; *sc:* Ranald MacDougall—*b/o* the novel by Henri Troyat.

ZACHARY TELLER: Retired mountain guide who, when his unscrupulous younger brother sets out to climb a rugged French Alpine peak in order to loot a crashed airliner, reluctantly goes along to protect him.

Robert Wagner, Claire Trevor, William Demarest, Barbara Darrow, E. G. Marshall, Anna Kashfi, Richard Arlen, Harry Townes, Stacy Harris.

Desk Set (1957, 20th-Fox). *d:* Walter Lang; *p:* Henry Ephron; *sc:* Phoebe Ephron and Henry Ephron—*b/o* a play by William Marchant.

RICHARD SUMNER: Efficiency expert who—when he's hired by a TV network to evaluate its reference and research department—clashes with the department head and her co-workers, who mistakenly suspect that he wants to replace them with a giant computer.

Katharine Hepburn, Gig Young, Joan Blondell, Dina Merrill, Sue Randall, Neva Patterson, Harry Ellerbe, Nicholas Jay, Diane Jergens, Merry Anders, Ida Moore, Rachel Stephens, Sammy Ogg.

The Old Man and the Sea (1958, WB). *d:* John Sturges; *p:* Leland Hayward; *sc:* Peter Viertel—*b/o* the novel by Ernest Hemingway.

THE OLD MAN*: Aging Cuban fisherman who, after failing to catch even one fish in nearly three months, perseveres and finally lands a huge marlin—only to have it devoured by sharks before he can tow it to shore.

Felipe Pazes, Harry Bellaver, Donald Diamond, Don Blackman, Joey Ray, Richard Alameda, Tony Rosa, Carlos Rivera, Robert Alderette, Mauritz Hugo.

The Last Hurrah (1958, Col.). *d:* John Ford; *p:* John Ford; *sc:* Frank Nugent—*b/o* the novel by Edwin O'Connor.

FRANK SKEFFINGTON: Aging Irish-American political boss of a New England city whose fifth mayoral campaign, which he confidently believes he'll win, unexpectedly turns out to be his "last hurrah."

Jeffrey Hunter, Dianne Foster, Pat O'Brien, Basil Rathbone, Donald Crisp, James Gleason, Edward Brophy, John Carradine, Willis Bouchey, Basil Ruysdael, Ricardo Cortez, Wallace Ford, Frank McHugh, Carleton Young, Frank Albertson, Bob Sweeney, Anna Lee, Ken Curtis, Jane Darwell, Helen Westcott, James Flavin, Frank Sully.

Inherit the Wind (1960, UA). *d:* Stanley Kramer; *p:* Stanley Kramer (Lomitas); *sc:* Nathan Douglas and Harold Smith—*b/o* the play by Jerome Lawrence and Robert E. Lee.

HENRY DRUMMOND*: Famous Chicago lawyer who comes to Tennessee in 1925 to defend a young biology teacher being prosecuted by a Bible-thumping politician for teaching Darwin's Theory of Evolution in violation of state law.

Fredric March, Gene Kelly, Florence Eldridge, Dick York, Donna Anderson, Harry Morgan, Elliott Reid, Claude Akins, Paul Hartman, Jimmy Boyd, Noah Beery Jr., Ray Teal, Norman Fell, Hope Summers.

The Devil at Four O'clock (1961, Col.). *d:* Mervyn LeRoy; *p:* Fred Kohlmar (LeRoy/

---

*Received an Academy Award nomination as Best Actor for this role.

*Received an Academy Award nomination as Best Actor for this role.

Kohlmar); *sc:* Liam O'Brien—*b/o* the novel by Max Catto.

FATHER MATTHEW DOONON: Aging priest on a French island in the South Pacific who, with the help of three convicts, saves a colony of leper children from a volcanic eruption.

Frank Sinatra, Kerwin Mathews, Jean-Pierre Aumont, Gregoire Aslan, Alexander Scourby, Barbara Luna, Cathy Lewis, Bernie Hamilton, Marcel Dalio, Louis Mercier.

Judgement at Nuremberg (1961, UA). *d:* Stanley Kramer; *p:* Stanley Kramer (Roxlom); *sc:* Abby Mann—*b/o* his TV play.

JUDGE DAN HAYWOOD*: Retired American judge from Maine who is sent to Germany to preside over the 1948 Nazi War Crimes Trials in an American court in Nuremberg, where four former Nazis are charged with crimes against humanity.

Burt Lancaster, Richard Widmark, Marlene Dietrich, Maximilian Schell, Judy Garland, Montgomery Clift, William Shatner, Edward Binns, Kenneth MacKenna, Werner Klemperer, Alan Baxter, Ray Teal, Virginia Christine, Karl Swenson, Sheila Bromley.

*Received an Academy Award nomination as Best Actor for this role.

It's a Mad, Mad, Mad, Mad World (1963, UA). *d:* Stanley Kramer; *p:* Stanley Kramer (Stanley Kramer Prod.); *sc:* William Rose and Tania Rose.

CAPTAIN C. G. CULPEPER: Cynical police captain who, with larceny in mind, keeps an eye on a group of assorted California characters trying frantically to beat one another in finding $350,000 worth of buried stolen loot.

Milton Berle, Sid Caesar, Buddy Hackett, Ethel Merman, Mickey Rooney, Dick Shawn, Phil Silvers, Terry-Thomas, Jonathan Winters, Edie Adams, Jimmy Durante, Dorothy Provine, Eddie Anderson, Ben Blue, William Demarest, Peter Falk, Paul Ford, Buster Keaton, Don Knotts, Joe E. Brown, Andy Devine, Sterling Holloway.

Guess Who's Coming to Dinner (1967, Col.). *d:* Stanley Kramer; *p:* Stanley Kramer (Stanley Kramer Prod.); *sc:* William Rose.

MATT DRAYTON*: Wealthy, crusading San Francisco newspaper publisher who, along with his wife, faces a test of his liberal beliefs when their daughter brings home a black doctor and announces that she's going to marry him.

Katharine Hepburn, Sidney Poitier, Katharine Houghton, Cecil Kellaway, Beah Richards, Roy E. Glenn Sr., Isabel Sanford, Virginia Christine, Alexandra Hay, Grace Gaynor, Skip Martin.

*Received an Academy Award nomination as Best Actor for this role.

☆ JOHN WAYNE

Marion Michael Morrison

b: May 26, 1907, Winterset, Iowa
d: June 11, 1979, Los Angeles, Cal.

"I haven't lost my temper in forty years. But, pilgrim, someone ought to belt you in the mouth. But I won't. I won't. The *hell* I won't!"

> George Washington McLintock
> (John Wayne) changing his mind about not
> belting Jones (Leo Gordon)
> in *McLintock!*, 1963.

The Drop Kick (1927, FN). *d:* Millard Webb; *sc:* Winifred Dunn—*b/o* the story "Glitter" by Katharine Brush.

One of the players on the football team from the University of Southern California in a drama about a young football star who wins the big game with a drop kick.

Richard Barthelmess, Barbara Kent, Dorothy Reiver, James Bradbury Jr., Brooks Benedict, Hedda Hopper.

Mother Machree (1928, Fox). *d:* John Ford; *sc:* Gertrude Orr—*b/o* a story by Rita Johnson Young.

An unbilled extra in a tale of an Irish mother in America who gives up her son but, years later, is reconciled with him.

Belle Bennett, Neil Hamilton, Victor McLaglen, Ted McNamara, Ethel Clayton, Constance Howard, William Platt, Philippe De Lacy.

Hangman's House (1928, Fox). *d:* John Ford; *sc:* Marion Orth (adaptation by Philip Klein and titles by Malcolm Stuart Boylan)—*b/o* a story by Donn Byrne.

Billed as "HORSE RACE SPECTATOR": An onlooker at a horse race in Ireland who breaks through a fence along with other spectators to gather around the winning horse.

Victor McLaglen, June Collyer, Hobart Bosworth, Larry Kent, Earle Fox, Eric Mayne, Belle Stoddard.

Salute (1929, Fox). *d:* John Ford and David Butler; *sc:* John Stone (with dialogue by James K. McGuinness)—*b/o* a story by Tristram Tupper.

Billed as "FOOTBALL PLAYER": Annapolis midshipman who plays on the Navy football team against West Point in a tale about two brothers, one who goes to West Point and one who goes to Annapolis.

George O'Brien, Helen Chandler, Stepin Fetchit, William Janney, Frank Albertson, Joyce Compton, Lumsden Hare, David Butler, Rex Bell, John Breeden, Ward Bond.

Words and Music (1929, Fox). *d:* James Tinling; *p:* Chandler Sprague; *sc:* Andrew Bennison—*b/o* a story by Frederick Hazlitt Brennan and Jack McEdward.

Billed (under the name of Duke Morrison) as PETE DONAHUE: One of two college-student rivals who compete for the campus belle and the $1500 being offered for the best musical-comedy number written by a student.

Lois Moran, David Percy, Helen Twelvetrees, William Orlamond, Elizabeth Patterson, Frank Albertson, Tom Patricola, Bubbles Crowell, Ward Bond.

Men without Women (1930, Fox). *d:* John Ford; *p:* James K. McGuinness; *sc:* Dudley Nichols—*b/o* a story by John Ford and James K. McGuiness.

Young sailor in the tale of a damaged submarine that is trapped on the ocean floor with fourteen men aboard.

Kenneth MacKenna, Frank Albertson, Paul Page, Pat Somerset, Walter McGrail, Stuart Erwin, Warren Hymer, J. Farrell McDonald, Roy Stewart, Warner Richmond, Harry Tenbrook, Ben Hendricks Jr., Robert Parrish.

Rough Romance (1930, Fox). *d:* A. F. Erickson; *sc:* Elliott Lester (with dialogue by Donald Davis)—*b/o* a story by Kenneth B. Clarke.

Character briefly involved in a tale of two feuding outdoorsmen in Oregon.

George O'Brien, Helen Chandler, Antonio Moreno, Noel Francis, Eddie Borden, Harry Cording, Roy Stewart.

Cheer Up and Smile (1930, Fox). *d:* Sidney Lanfield; *p:* Al Rockett; *sc:* Howard J. Green—*b/o* a story by Richard Connell.

Character briefly involved in a college-campus story in which a vamp tries to steal another girl's boyfriend.

Arthur Lake, Dixie Lee, Olga Baclanova, Whispering Jack Smith, Johnny Arthur, Charles Judels, John Darrow, Sumner Getchell, Franklin Pangborn, Buddy Messinger.

The Big Trail (1930, Fox). *d:* Raoul Walsh; *sc:* Jack Peabody, Marie Boyle, and Florence Postal—*b/o* a story by Hal G. Evarts.

BRECK COLEMAN: Young pioneer scout who battles rainstorms, blizzards, desert heat, and Indians as he leads a wagon train westward from Missouri to Oregon.

Marguerite Churchill, El Brendel, Tully Marshall, Tyrone Power Sr., David Rollins, Frederick Burton, Russ Powell, Ward Bond, Marcia Harris, Andy Shufford, Helen Parrish.

Girls Demand Excitement (1931, Fox). *d:* Seymour Felix; *sc:* Harlan Thompson.

PETER BROOKS: College boy who is the leader of a male movement to end the co-ed system at his school but changes his mind when he falls for one of the coeds.

Virginia Cherrill, Marguerite Churchill, Helen Jerome Eddy, William Janney, Eddie Nugent, Terrance Ray, Marion Byron, Martha Sleeper, Addie McPhail, Ray Cooke.

Three Girls Lost (1931, Fox). *d:* Sidney Lanfield; *sc:* Bradley King—*b/o* a story by Robert D. Andrews.

GORDON WALES: Young Chicago architect who is wrongly accused of murdering a gold digger but is cleared and finds happiness with her "nice girl" roommate.

Loretta Young, Lew Cody, Joyce Compton, Joan Marsh, Katherine Clare Ward, Paul Fix, Bert Roach.

Men Are Like That (1931, Col.). *d:* George B. Seitz; *sc:* Robert Riskin and Dorothy Howell—*b/o* the play *Arizona* by Augustus Thomas.

LT. BOB DENTON: West Point cadet who, when he graduates, breaks off with his girlfriend, then winds up at an Army post in Arizona and finds that she has married his commanding officer.

Laura LaPlante, June Clyde, Forrest Stanley, Nena Quartaro, Susan Fleming, Loretta Sayers, Hugh Cummings.

Range Feud (1931, Col.). *d:* D. Ross Lederman; *sc:* Milton Krims.

CLINT TURNER: Rancher's son who is falsely accused of killing a rival rancher but is saved from the gallows when the sheriff—his foster brother—exposes the real murderer.

Buck Jones, Susan Fleming, Ed Le Saint, William Walling, Wallace MacDonald, Harry Woods.

Maker of Men (1931, Col.). *d:* Edward Sedgwick; *sc:* Howard J. Green and Edward Sedgwick.

DUSTY: College football player who, along with his coach, believes that the coach's sensitive son is a coward—until the son proves otherwise in a big game.

Jack Holt, Richard Cromwell, Joan Marsh, Robert Alden, Walter Catlett, Natalie Moorhead, Ethel Wales, Richard Tucker, Mike McKay.

Haunted Gold (1932, WB). *d:* Mack V. Wright; *p:* Leon Schlesinger; *sc:* Adele Buffington.

JOHN MASON: Young Westerner who helps outwit a gang of outlaws in a ghost town for possession of an abandoned gold mine.

Sheila Terry, Erville Alderson, Harry Woods, Otto Hoffman, Martha Mattox, Blue Washington.

Texas Cyclone (1932, Col.). *d:* D. Ross Lederman; *sc—b/o* a story by William Colt MacDonald.

STEVE PICKETT: Young cowpoke whose cowboy pal (as they both battle rustlers in a Texas town) turns out to be a rancher with amnesia who disappeared from the town five years before.

Tim McCoy, Shirley Grey, Wheeler Oakman, Wallace MacDonald, Harry Cording, Vernon Dent, Walter Brennan, Mary Gordon.

Lady and Gent (1932, Para.). *d:* Stephen Roberts; *sc:* Grover Jones and William Slavens McNutt.

BUZZ KINNEY: Former college student–turned–boxer who K.O.s an overconfident veteran fighter but finally winds up as a broken-nosed, cauliflower-eared has-been.

George Bancroft, Wynne Gibson, Charles Starrett, James Gleason, Joyce Compton, Frank McGlynn, Charles Grapewin, Sid Saylor, Tom Kennedy.

Two-Fisted Law (1932, Col.). *d:* D. Ross Lederman; *sc:* Kurt Kempler—*b/o* a story by William Colt MacDonald.

DUKE: Cowboy whose boss is cheated out of his ranch by a crooked cattleman but finally brings the villain to justice.

Tim McCoy, Alice Day, Wheeler Oakman, Tully Marshall, Wallace MacDonald, Walter Brennan, Richard Alexander.

Ride Him, Cowboy (1932, WB). *d:* Fred Allen; *sc:* Scott Mason—*b/o* the story by Kenneth Perkins.

JOHN DRURY: Cowboy who—after saving an innocent horse named Duke from being shot for killing a rancher—trains the horse to help him track down the real killer, a bandit called "The Hawk."

Ruth Hall, Henry B. Walthall, Harry Gribbon, Otis Harlan, Charles Sellon, Frank Hagney, Duke the Devil Horse.

The Big Stampede (1932, WB). *d:* Tenny Wright; *p:* Leon Schlesinger; *sc:* Kurt Kempler—*b/o* a story by Marion Jackson.

JOHN STEELE: Deputy sheriff in New Mexico who, along with a bandit he hires as a helper, battles an evil cattle baron and his gang of rustlers.

Noah Beery, Mae Madison, Luis Alberni, Berton Churchill, Paul Hurst, Hank Bell, Lafe McKee, Duke the Miracle Horse.

The Telegraph Trail (1933, WB). *d:* Tenny Wright; *p:* Leon Schlesinger; *sc:* Kurt Kempler.

JOHN TRENT: U.S. Army scout who, when Indians kill his telegraph-lineman friend, volunteers to help complete the stringing of the first telegraph line across the western plains.

Marceline Day, Frank McHuch, Otis Harlan, Yakima Canutt, Albert J. Smith, Clarence Gelbert, Lafe McKee, Slim Whitaker, Duke the Miracle Horse.

Central Airport (1933, WB). *d:* William A. Wellman; *sc:* Rian James and James Seymour—*b/o* a story by Jack Moffitt.

One of the men on an airplane that crash-lands in the ocean.

Richard Barthlemess, Sally Eilers, Tom Brown, Glenda Farrell, Harold Huber, Grant Mitchell, James Murray, Claire McDowell, Willard Robertson.

His Private Secretary (1933, Showmen's Pictures). *d:* Philip H. Whitman; *sc:* John Francis Natteford—*b/o* a story by Lew Collins.

DICK WALLACE: Millionaire's woman-chasing playboy son who has a falling out with his father but—after he falls for a minister's granddaughter—reforms and makes up with the father.

Evelyn Knapp, Alec B. Francis, Natalie Kingston, Arthur Hoyt, Al St. John, Michey Rentschler, Patrick Cunning.

Somewhere in Sonora (1933, WB). *d:* Mack V. Wright; *p:* Leon Schlesinger; *sc:* Joe Roach—*b/o* the novel *Somewhere South in Sonora* by Will Levington Comfort.

JOHN BISHOP: Young cowboy who goes to Sonora to search for a friend's son who has been forced to join a gang of robbers.

Shirley Palmer, Henry B. Walthall, Paul Fix, Ann Fay, Billy Franey, Ralph Lewis, Frank Rice, J. P. McGowan.

The Life of Jimmy Dolan (1933, WB). *d:* Archie Mayo; *sc:* Bertram Milhauser and Beulah Marie Dix (with dialogue by Erwin Gelsey and David Boehm).

SMITH: Confident young boxer who is knocked out in a prize fight.

Douglas Fairbanks Jr., Loretta Young, Aline MacMahon, Guy Kibbee, Fifi D'Orsay, Shirley Grey, Lyle Talbot, Farina, Harold Huber, George Meeker, David Durand, Dawn O'Day (Anne Shirley), Mickey Rooney.

Baby Face (1933, WB). *d:* Alfred E. Green; *p:* Ray

Griffith; *sc:* Gene Markey, Kathryn Scola, and Mark Canfield (Darryl F. Zanuck).

JIMMY McCOY: Young banker who, after helping a speakeasy owner's daughter get a job and a promotion, gets the brush-off when she becomes the bank president's mistress.

Barbara Stanwyck, George Brent, Donald Cook, Arthur Hohl, Henry Kolker, James Murray, Robert Barrat, Margaret Lindsay, Douglas Dumbrille, Nat Pendleton, Harry Gribbon.

The Man from Monterey (1933, WB). *d:* Mack V. Wright; *p:* Leon Schlesinger; *sc:* Leslie Mason.

CAPT. JOHN HOLMES: Young U.S. Army captain who's sent on a mission to Monterey to prevent Mexican landholders from being swindled out of their property by crooks.

Ruth Hall, Nina Quartaro, Luis Alberni, Francis Ford, Donald Reed, Lillian Leighton, Lafe McKee, Duke the Devil Horse.

Riders of Destiny (1933, Mono.). *d:* Robert N. Bradbury; *p:* Paul Malvern; *sc:* Robert N. Bradbury.

SANDY SAUNDERS ("SINGIN' SANDY"): Undercover Secret Service agent who, when he's assigned to help some ranchers get water rights, tangles with the gang leader who controls the water supply for the entire valley.

Cecelia Parker, George "Gabby" Hayes, Forrest Taylor, Al St. John, Heinie Conklin, Earl Dwire, Lafe McKee.

College Coach (1933, WB). *d:* William A. Wellman; *sc:* Niven Busch and Manuel Seff.

Character "bit" in a story about a ruthless football coach and a know-it-all star player.

Pat O'Brien, Ann Dvorak, Dick Powell, Hugh Herbert, Lyle Talbot, Arthur Byron, Guinn Williams, Nat Pendleton, Donald Meek, Berton Churchill, Herman Bing, Ward Bond.

Sagebrush Trail (1933, Mono.). *d:* Armand Schaefer; *p:* Paul Malvern; *sc:* Lindsley Parsons.

JOHN BRANT: Young man who, after being wrongly imprisoned on a murder charge, escapes and heads out West to look for the real killer—who winds up becoming his friend and saving his life.

Nancy Shubert, Lane Chandler, Yakima Canutt, Wally Wales, Art Mix, Robert Burns, Earl Dwire.

The Lucky Texan (1934, Mono.). *d:* Robert N. Bradbury; *p:* Paul Malvern; *sc:* Robert N. Bradbury.

JERRY MASON: Young Westerner who, when his grizzled gold-prospecting partner is accused of robbery and murder, proves that the real culprit is the local sheriff's son.

Barbara Sheldon, George "Gabby" Hayes, Lloyd

Whitlock, Yakima Canutt, Earl Dwire, Edward Parker.

West of the Divide (1934, Mono.). *d:* Robert N. Bradbury; *p:* Paul Malvern; *sc:* Robert N. Bradbury.

TED HAYDEN: Rough-and-tough cowboy who goes back to his home town to track down his father's killer and to search for his missing younger brother.

Virginia Brown Faire, Lloyd Whitlock, Yakima Canutt, George "Gabby" Hayes, Earl Dwire, Lafe McKee.

Blue Steel (1934, Mono.). *d:* Robert N. Brabury; *p:* Paul Malvern; *sc:* Robert N. Bradbury.

JOHN CARRUTHERS: Undercover U.S. marshal who helps a group of citizens stand up against a gang of outlaws who are trying to drive them out of town so they can claim the gold that's in the ground.

Eleanor Hunt, George "Gabby" Hayes, Ed Peil, Yakima Canutt, George Cleveland, George Nash, Lafe McKee, Hank Bell.

The Man from Utah (1934, Mono.). *d:* Robert N. Bradbury; *p:* Paul Malvern; *sc:* Lindsley Parsons.

JOHN WESTON: Undercover deputy sheriff who, in order to get the goods on a gang of crooks who have made a racket out of a rodeo, enters the rodeo himself.

Polly Ann Young, George "Gabby" Hayes, Yakima Canutt, Ed Peil, Anita Campillo, George Cleveland, Lafe McKee.

Randy Rides Alone (1934, Mono.). *d:* Harry Fraser; *p:* Paul Malvern; *sc:* Lindsley Parsons.

RANDY BOWERS: Young cowboy who, in order to get evidence, joins a gang of crooks who have been robbing the local express office and brings them all to justice.

Alberta Vaughn, George "Gabby" Hayes, Earl Dwire, Yakima Canutt, Tex Phelps, Arthur Ortega.

The Star Packer (1934, Mono.). *d:* Robert N. Bradbury; *p:* Paul Malvern; *sc:* Robert N. Bradbury.

JOHN TRAVERS: U.S. marshal who swears in a group of ranchers as deputies and cleans up a gang—headed by "The Shadow"—that has been terrorizing the ranchers.

Verna Hillie, George "Gabby" Hayes, Yakima Canutt, Earl Dwire, George Cleveland, Arthur Ortega, Edward Parker.

The Trail Beyond (1934, Mono.). *d:* Robert N. Bradbury; *p:* Paul Malvern; *sc:* Lindsley Parsons— *b/o* James Oliver Curwood's novel *The Wolf Hunters.*

ROD DREW: Young cowboy who, when he hits the trail in the Northwest to search for a missing young woman and a gold mine, outsmarts the gang that has kidnapped the woman and takes over the mine.

Verna Hillie, Noah Beery, Iris Lancaster, Noah Beery Jr., Robert Frazer, Earl Dwire, Edward Parker.

The Lawless Frontier (1934, Mono.). *d:* Robert N. Bradbury; *p:* Paul Malvern; *sc:* Robert N. Bradbury.

JOHN TOBIN: Cowboy who, along with his old-timer sidekick, tracks down the notorious Mexican bandit who killed his parents.

Sheila Terry, George "Gabby" Hayes, Earl Dwire, Yakima Canutt, Jack Rockwell, Gordon D. Woods.

'Neath Arizona Skies (1934, Mono.). *d:* Harry Fraser; *p:* Paul Malvern; *sc:* B. R. Tuttle.

CHRIS MORRELL: Cowboy who saves a little Indian girl who's an oil heiress when a band of outlaws kidnap her and try to kill her father.

Sheila Terry, Jay Wilsey, Yakima Canutt, Jack Rockwell, Shirley Ricketts, George "Gabby" Hayes.

Texas Terror (1935, Mono.). *d:* Robert N. Bradbury; *p:* Paul Malvern; *sc:* Robert N. Bradbury.

JOHN HIGGINS: Government agent in Texas who, when he believes he's accidentally killed his best friend in a shoot-out with outlaws, becomes a lonely prospector but later discovers the real killer and starts a new life.

Lucille Browne, LeRoy Mason, George "Gabby" Hayes, Buffalo Bill Jr., Bert Dillard, Lloyd Ingraham.

Rainbow Valley (1935, Mono.). *d:* Robert N. Bradbury; *p:* Paul Malvern; *sc:* Lindsley Parsons.

JOHN MARTIN: Undercover agent who deliberately goes to prison so that he can become friendly with a fellow convict and get the necessary evidence to break up a gang of crooks.

Lucille Browne, LeRoy Mason, George "Gabby" Hayes, Buffalo Bill Jr., Bert Dillard, Lloyd Ingraham, Art Dillard, Frank Ball.

The Desert Trail (1935, Mono.). *d:* Cullen Lewis; *p:* Paul Malvern; *sc:* Lindsley Parsons.

JOHN SCOTT: Star rodeo performer who, when he and his gambler pal are wrongly accused of a hold-up, tracks down the two culprits who are really guilty.

Mary Kornman, Paul Fix, Edward Chandler, Lafe McKee, Henry Hall, Al Ferguson, Carmen LaRoux.

The Dawn Rider (1935, Mono.). *d:* Robert N. Bradbury; *p:* Paul Malvern; *sc:* Robert N. Bradbury *b/o* a story by Lloyd Nosler.

JOHN MASON: Young Westerner who, when his father is gunned down by a bandit in an express-office holdup, vows revenge—then discovers that the bandit is his girlfriend's brother.

Marion Burns, Yakima Canutt, Reed Howes, Denny Meadows, Bert Dillard, Jack Jones.

Paradise Canyon (1935, Mono.). *d:* Carl Pierson; *p:* Paul Malvern; *sc:* Lindsley Parsons and Robert Emmett—*b/o* a story by Lindsley Parsons.

JOHN WYATT: U.S. government undercover agent who joins Dr. Carter's traveling medicine show as part of a plan to break up a gang of counterfeiters near the Mexican border.

Marion Burns, Earl Hodgins, Yakima Canutt, Reed Howes, Perry Murdock, Gino Corrado, Gordon Clifford.

Westward Ho (1935, Rep.). *d:* Robert N. Bradbury; *p:* Paul Malvern; *sc:* Lindsley Parsons, Harry Friedman, and Robert Emmett—*b/o* a story by Lindsley Parsons.

JOHN WYATT: Vigilante leader who, as he battles the outlaws responsible for killing his parents when he was a child, discovers that his long-lost brother is now a member of the gang.

Sheila Manners, Frank McGlynn Jr., Jack Curtis, Yakima Canutt, Mary McLaren, Dickie Jones, Hank Bell.

The New Frontier (1935, Rep.). *d:* Carl Pierson; *p:* Paul Malvern; *sc:* Robert Emmett.

JOHN DAWSON: Cowboy who is helped by a group of friendly bad men in avenging the murder of his sheriff father by an evil saloon owner and his gang.

Muriel Evans, Mary McLaren, Murdock MacQuarrie, Warner Richmond, Sam Flint, Earl Dwire, Alfred Bridge.

The Lawless Range (1935, Rep.). *d:* Robert N. Bradbury; *p:* Trem Carr; *sc:* Lindsley Parsons.

JOHN MIDDLETON: Undercover agent whose mission is to stop a ruthless banker from driving out the inhabitants of a valley and getting control of some gold mines there.

Sheila Manners, Earl Dwire, Frank McGlynn Jr., Jack Curtis, Yakima Canutt, Wally Howe.

The Oregon Trail (1936, Rep.). *d:* Scott Pembroke; *p:* Paul Malvern; *sc:* Lindsley Parsons and Robert Emmett.

CAPT. JOHN DELMONT: U.S. Army officer who, with the help of some Mexican friends, pursues and captures a band of renegades who were responsible for the death of his father.

Ann Rutherford, Yakima Canutt, E. H. Calvert, Fern Emmett, Gino Corrado, Marian Farrell, Frank Rice, Joe Girard, Harry Harvey.

The Lawless Nineties (1936, Rep.). *d:* Joseph

Kane; *p:* Paul Malvern; *sc:* Joseph Poland—*b/o* a story by Joseph Poland and Scott Pembroke.

JOHN TIPTON: Undercover government agent who is sent from Washington to Wyoming to foil a ruthless gang of terrorists who are trying to rig the 1890 Wyoming Statehood elections.

Ann Rutherford, Lane Chandler, Harry Woods, Snowflake, George "Gabby" Hayes, Etta McDaniel, Charles King, Sam Flint, Al Taylor, Cliff Lyons.

King of the Pecos (1936, Rep.). *d:* Joseph Kane; *p:* Paul Malvern; *sc:* Bernard McConville, Dorell McGowan, and Stuart McGowan—*b/o* a story by Bernard McConville.

JOHN CLAYBORN: Young lawyer in 1870s Texas who seeks revenge against a greedy cattle baron for the murder of his homesteader parents when he was a boy.

Muriel Evans, Cy Kendall, Jack Clifford, Frank Glendon, Herbert Heywood, Arthur Aylesworth, John Beck, Mary McLaren, Bradley Metcalfe Jr., Yakima Canutt.

The Lonely Trail (1936, Rep.). *d:* Joseph Kane; *p:* Nat Levine; *sc:* Bernard McConville and Jack Natteford—*b/o* a story by Bernard McConville.

JOHN: Ex–Union soldier who, when he becomes a ranch owner in Texas during Reconstruction days, is enlisted by the governor to rid the state of plundering carpet-baggers.

Ann Rutherford, Cy Kendall, Snowflake, Etta McDaniel, Bob Kortman, Sam Flint, Yakima Canutt, Bob Burns, Lloyd Ingraham.

Winds of the Wasteland (1936, Rep.). *d:* Mack V. Wright; *p:* Nat Levine; *sc:* Joseph Poland.

JOHN BLAIR: One of a pair of out-of-work Pony Express riders who buy a stagecoach line and win a lucrative government mail contract by beating a rival stage-coach company in a mail-hauling race to Sacramento.

Phyllis Fraser, Yakima Canutt, Lane Chandler, Sam Flint, Lew Kelly, Bob Kortman, Douglas Cosgrove, W. M. McCormick.

The Sea Spoilers (1936, Univ.). *d:* Frank Strayer; *p:* Trem Carr; *sc:* George Waggner—*b/o* a story by Dorrell McGowan and Stuart E. McGowan.

BOB RANDALL: Rough skipper of a U.S. Coast Guard cutter who is replaced by an inefficient younger man but takes over again to capture a band of seal poachers and smugglers who have kidnapped his girlfriend.

Nan Grey, Fuzzy Knight, William Bakewell, Russell Hicks, George Irving, Lotus Long, Harry Worth, Cy Kendall.

Conflict (1936, Univ.). *d:* David Howard; *p:* Trem Carr; *sc:* Charles A. Logue and Walter Weems—*b/o* Jack London's novel *The Abysmal Brute.*

PAT: Turn-of-the-century lumberjack who stages rigged prize fights in small towns but—when he falls for a pretty reporter—goes straight.

Jean Rogers, Tommy Bupp, Eddie Borden, Ward Bond, Harry Woods, Frank Sheridan, Bryant Washburn, Frank Hagney.

California Straight Ahead (1937, Univ.). *d:* Arthur Lubin; *p:* Trem Carr; *sc:* Scott Darling—*b/o* a story by Herman Boxer.

BIFF SMITH: Bus driver who, when he becomes traffic manager of a big trucking company, leads a convoy of trucks cross-country in a race against a special freight train to deliver vital aviation parts to the West Coast.

Louise Latimer, Robert McWade, Tully Marshall, Theodore Von Eltz, LeRoy Mason, Grace Goodall.

I Cover the War (1937, Univ.). *d:* Arthur Lubin; *p:* Trem Carr; *sc:* George Waggner.

BOB ADAMS: Ace newsreel cameraman who, when he's sent to Samari in North Africa to cover an uprising against the British, clashes with an Arab rebel leader and saves a whole company of British lancers.

Gwen Gaze, Don Barclay, James Bush, Pat Somerset, Charles Brokaw, Arthur Aylesworth, Earl Hodgins, Jack Mack, Frank Lackteen.

Idol of the Crowds (1937, Univ.). *d:* Arthur Lubin; *p:* Paul Malvern; *sc:* George Waggner and Harold Buckley—*b/o* a story by George Waggner.

JOHNNY HANSON: Pro hockey player who, when he's offered a bribe to throw a championship game, pretends to play along with the crooks but then foils them by leading his team to victory.

Sheila Bromley, Billy Burrud, Russell Hopton, Charles Brokaw, Virginia Brissac, Clem Bevans, George Lloyd.

Adventure's End (1937, Univ.). *d:* Arthur Lubin; *p:* Trem Carr; *sc:* Ben Grauman Kohn, Scott Darling, and Sid Sutherland—*b/o* a story by Ben Ames Williams.

DUKE SLADE: Pearl diver in the Pacific who—when he's pursued by unfriendly natives—seeks safety on a whaler, marries the captain's daughter, and helps put down a mutiny by the crew.

Diana Gibson, Moroni Olsen, Montagu Love, Ben Carter, Maurice Black, George Cleveland, Glenn Strange, Britt Wood.

Born to the West (1937, Para.). *d:* Charles Barton; *sc:* Stuart Anthony and Robert Yost—*b/o* on the novel by Zane Grey.

DARE RUDD: Wandering cowpoke who, when he leads a cattle drive for his ranch-owner cousin, loses the cattle money in a crooked poker game with rustlers but—with his cousin's help—gets back the money and routs the rustlers.

Marsha Hunt, John Mack Brown, John Patterson, Monte Blue, Lucien Littlefield, Alan Ladd, James Craig, Nick Lukats.

Pals of the Saddle (1938, Rep.). *d:* George Sherman; *p:* William Berke; *sc:* Stanley Roberts and Betty Burbridge—*b/o* characters created by William Colt MacDonald.

STONY BROOKE: One of a trio of wandering cowboys known as "The Three Mesquiteers" who help a female government agent trap spies who are smuggling a chemical—used in making poison gas—across the border into Mexico.

Ray Corrigan, Max Terhune, Doreen McKay, Frank Milan, Jack Kirk, Ted Adams, Harry Depp.

Overland Stage Raiders (1938, Rep.). *d:* George Sherman; *p:* William Berke; *sc:* Luci Ward—*b/o* a story by Bernard McConville and Edmond Kelso and characters created by William Colt MacDonald.

STONY BROOKE: One of three cowpokes known as "The Three Mesquiteers" who—when they buy an interest in the airport of an isolated gold-mining town and start shipping gold by plane—find themselves battling a gang of hijackers.

Louise Brooks, Ray Corrigan, Max Terhune, Fern Emmett, Frank LaRue, Anthony Marsh, Gordon Hart.

Santa Fe Stampede (1938, Rep.). *d:* George Sherman; *p:* William Berke; *sc:* Luci Ward and Betty Burbridge—*b/o* a story by Luci Ward and characters created by William Colt MacDonald.

STONY BROOKE: Stalwart cowboy—one of a trio known as "The Three Mesquiteers"—who is wrongly jailed for the killing of a gold miner but is cleared when The Mesquiteers prove that the crooked mayor is the real culprit.

June Martel, Ray Corrigan, Max Terhune, William Farnum, LeRoy Mason, Martin Spellman, Tom London.

Red River Range (1938, Rep.). *d:* George Sherman; *p:* William Berke; *sc:* Stanley Roberts, Betty Burbridge, and Luci Ward—*b/o* a story by Luci Ward and characters created by William Colt MacDonald.

STONY BROOKE: Good-guy cowboy—one of a trio known as "The Three Mesquiteers"—who poses as an escaped convict and joins a gang of cattle rustlers in order to get the goods on them.

Ray Corrigan, Max Terhune, Polly Moran, Kirby Grant, William Royle, Perry Ivins, Stanley Blystone, Lenore Bushman, Roger Williams, Olin Francis.

Stagecoach (1939, UA). *d:* John Ford; *p:* Walter Wanger (Walter Wanger Prod.); *sc:* Dudley Nichols—*b/o* the short story "Stage to Lordsburg" by Ernest Haycox.

THE RINGO KID: Young Westerner who—after escaping from jail—boards a crowded stagecoach that's heading through hostile Apache territory for Lordsburg, New Mexico, where he plans to settle the score with the Plummer boys, desperadoes who murdered his father and brother.

Claire Trevor, Thomas Mitchell, John Carradine, Andy Devine, Louise Platt, George Bancroft, Berton Churchill, Donald Meek, Tim Holt, Tom Tyler, Elvira Rios, Francis Ford, Marga Ann Deighton, Kent Odell, Yakima Canutt, Chief Big Tree, Florence Lake.

The Night Riders (1939, Rep.). *d:* George Sherman; *p:* William Berke; *sc:* Betty Burbridge and Stanley Roberts—*b/o* characters created by William Colt MacDonald.

STONY BROOKE: One of a trio of cowboys known as "The Three Mesquiteers" who put on capes and masks and rob the tax collector to pay back money to oppressed farmers being bilked by a corrupt gambler who has gained control of their area.

Ray Corrigan, Max Terhune, Doreen McKay, Ruth Rogers, Tom Tyler, Kermit Maynard, George Douglas.

Three Texas Steers (1939, Rep.). *d:* George Sherman; *p:* William Berke; *sc:* Betty Burbridge and Stanley Roberts—*b/o* characters created by William Colt MacDonald.

STONY BROOKE: One of three cowboys known as "The Three Mesquiteers" who—when a young woman is in danger of losing the ranch and circus she's inherited—pay off her mortgage by entering her circus horse in a trotting race and winning.

Carole Landis, Ray Corrigan, Ralph Graves, Max Terhune, Colette Lyons, Roscoe Ates, Lew Kelly, David Sharpe.

Wyoming Outlaw (1939, Rep.). *d:* George Sherman; *p:* William Berke; *sc:* Betty Burbridge and Jack Natteford—*b/o* a story by Jack Natteford and characters created by William Colt MacDonald.

STONY BROOKE: One of a trio of cowhands called "The Three Mesquiteers" who expose a corrupt local politician who's selling state and federal road-work jobs to financially strapped ranchers and farmers.

Adele Pearce (Pamela Blake), Ray Corrigan, Donald Barry, Raymond Hatton, LeRoy Mason, Yakima Canutt, Charles Middleton, Elmo Lincoln, David Sharpe.

New Frontier (1939, Rep.). *d:* George Sherman; *p:* William Berke; *sc:* Betty Burbridge and Luci Ward—*b/o* characters created by William Colt MacDonald.

STONY BROOKE: One of three cowboys known as "The Three Mesquiteers" who, after they mistakenly give a group of settlers bad advice about a land deal with some scheming land grabbers, make up for it by outsmarting the crooks.

Ray Corrigan, Raymond Hatton, Phyllis Isley (Jennifer Jones), Eddy Waller, Sammy McKim, LeRoy Mason, Harrison Greene, Dave O'Brien, Jack Ingram, Bud Osborne.

Allegheny Uprising (1939, RKO). *d:* William A. Seiter; *p:* P. J. Wolfson; *sc:* P. J. Wolfson—*b/o* Neil Swanson's story "The First Rebel."
JIM SMITH: Young leader of a handful of Pennsylvania frontiersmen in 1759 who battle a crooked trader and British soldiers in order to stop the sale of guns and rum to the Indians.
Claire Trevor, George Sanders, Brian Donlevy, Wilfrid Lawson, Robert Barrat, John F. Hamilton, Moroni Olsen, Eddie Quillan, Chill Wills, Ian Wolfe, Wallis Clark, Monte Montague, Eddy Waller, Olaf Hytten, Clay Clement.

The Dark Command (1940, Rep.). *d:* Raoul Walsh; *p:* Sol C. Siegel; *sc:* Grover Jones, Lionel Houser, and F. Hugh Herbert (adaptation by Jan Fortune)—*b/o* the novel by W. R. Burnett.
BOB SETON: Federal marshal in pre–Civil War Kansas who clashes with an ex–schoolteacher–turned–guerrilla leader named Cantrell and finally kills him when Cantrell and his men murder women and children during the burning and sacking of the town of Lawrence.
Claire Trevor, Walter Pidgeon, Roy Rogers, George "Gabby" Hayes, Porter Hall, Marjorie Main, Raymond Walburn, Joseph Sawyer, J. Farrell MacDonald, Harry Woods, Al Bridge, Glenn Strange, Ernie S. Adams, Hal Taliaferro, Yakima Canutt.

Three Faces West (1940, Rep.). *d:* Bernard Vorhaus; *p:* Sol C. Siegel; *sc:* F. Hugh Herbert, Joseph Moncure March, and Samuel Ornitz.
JOHN PHILLIPS: Young North Dakota farmer during the Dust Bowl days who leads a group of fellow farmers and friends on a trek to Oregon, where the land is more farmable.
Sigrid Gurie, Charles Coburn, Spencer Charters, Helen MacKellar, Roland Varno, Sonny Bupp, Wade Boteler, Trevor Bardette, Russell Simpson, Charles Waldron, Wendell Niles.

The Long Voyage Home (1940, UA). *d:* John Ford; *p:* Walter Wanger (Walter Wanger Prod.); *sc:* Dudley Nichols—*b/o* the play by Eugene O'Neill.
OLE OLSEN: Naïve, good-natured Swedish merchant seaman who, when his hitch is up and he plans to return to his home and family, almost gets Shanghaied but is saved by his shipmates.

Thomas Mitchell, Ian Hunter, Barry Fitzgerald, Wilfrid Lawson, Mildred Natwick, John Qualen, Ward Bond, Arthur Shields, Joseph Sawyer, Douglas Walton, Billy Bevan, Cyril McLaglen.

Seven Sinners (1940, Univ.). *d:* Tay Garnett; *p:* Joe Pasternak; *sc:* John Meehan and Harry Tugend—*b/o* a story by Ladislas Fodor and Laslo Vadnay.
LT. BRUCE WHITNEY: Handsome American officer at a South Seas Island Naval base whose affair with a honkytonk singer from Tony's 7 Sinners Café threatens to ruin his career—until she gives him up just as he's about to quit the Navy for her.
Marlene Dietrich, Broderick Crawford, Mischa Auer, Albert Dekker, Billy Gilbert, Anna Lee, Oscar Homolka, Samuel S. Hinds, Reginald Denny, Vince Barnett, Herbert Rawlinson, James Craig, William Bakewell, Antonio Moreno, Russell Hicks.

A Man Betrayed (1941, Rep.). *d:* John H. Auer; *p:* Armand Schaefer; *sc:* Isabel Dawn (adaptation by Tom Kilpatrick)—*b/o* a story by Jack Moffitt.
LYNN HOLLISTER: Small-town lawyer who, when he comes to the city to investigate the death of a friend, falls for a pretty young woman but crusades against her political-boss father and proves that he's a crook.
Frances Dee, Edward Ellis, Wallace Ford, Ward Bond, Harold Huber, Alexander Granach, Barnett Parker, Ed Stanley, Tim Ryan, Harry Hayden, Russell Hicks, Pierre Watkin, Ferris Taylor.

Lady from Louisiana (1941, Rep.). *d:* Bernard Vorhaus; *p:* Bernard Vorhaus; *sc:* Vera Caspary, Michael Hogan, and Guy Endore—*b/o* a story by Edward James and Francis Faragoh.
JOHN REYNOLDS: Young attorney who falls in love with a Southern belle aboard a Mississippi river boat, then learns that her father runs the New Orleans lottery racket that he's been hired to break up.
Ona Munson, Ray Middleton, Henry Stephenson, Helen Westley, Jack Pennick, Dorothy Dandridge, Shimen Ruskin, Jacqueline Dalya, Maurice Costello.

The Shepherd of the Hills (1941, Para.). *d:* Henry Hathaway; *p:* Jack Moss; *sc:* Grover Jones and Stuart Anthony—from a story by Harold Bell Wright, *b/o* his novel.
YOUNG MATT MATTHEWS: Hot-headed Ozark mountaineer who—when the father he's never seen returns to the region—vows to kill him because he believes that the father deserted the mother, causing her early death.
Betty Field, Harry Carey, Beulah Bondi, James Barton, Samuel S. Hinds, Marjorie Main, Ward

Bond, Marc Lawrence, John Qualen, Fuzzy Knight, Tom Fadden.

Lady for a Night (1941, Rep.). *d:* Leigh Jason; *p:* Albert J. Cohen; *sc:* Isabel Dawn and Boyce DeGaw—*b/o* a story by Garrett Fort.
JACK MORGAN: Dashing gambler in 1880s Memphis who keeps on loving the owner of a Mississippi River gambling boat, even when she marries a no-good aristocrat for social position and is accused of murdering him.
Joan Blondell, Ray Middleton, Philip Merivale, Blanche Yurba, Edith Barrett, Leonid Kinsky, Hattie Noel, Montagu Love, Carmel Myers, Dewey Robinson.

Reap the Wild Wind (1942, Para.). *d:* Cecil B. DeMille; *p:* Cecil B. DeMille; *sc:* Alan LeMay, Charles Bennett, and Jesse Lasky Jr.—*b/o* a story by Thelma Strabel.
CAPT. JACK STUART: Lusty 1840s sea captain who vies with a suave sea lawyer for the hand of the pretty owner of a salvage schooner but—when he falls in with pirate shipwreckers off the Florida keys—loses not only her but his life.
Ray Milland, Paulette Goddard, Raymond Massey, Robert Preston, Susan Hayward, Lynne Overman, Walter Hampden, Louise Beavers, Hedda Hopper, Monte Blue, Charles Bickford, Barbara Britton, Milburn Stone.

The Spoilers (1942, Univ.). *d:* Ray Enright; *p:* Frank Lloyd; *sc:* Lawrence Hazard and Tom Reed—*b/o* the novel by Rex Beach.
ROY GLENNISTER: One of two rugged adventurers during the turn-of-the-century Alaska gold rush whose battle over valuable land rights and the affections of a saloon entertainer culminates in a marathon fistfight.
Marlene Dietrich, Randolph Scott, Margaret Lindsay, Harry Carey, Richard Barthelmess, George Cleveland, Samuel S. Hinds, Russell Simpson, William Farnum, Jack Norton, Charles Halton, Bud Osborne, Robert W. Service.

In Old California (1942, Rep.). *d:* William McGann; *p:* Robert North; *sc:* Gertrude Purcell and Frances Hyland—*b/o* a story by J. Robert Bren and Gladys Atwater.
TOM CRAIG: Two-fisted Bostonian who—when he heads for California during the early gold-rush days and sets up a pharmacy—becomes involved with a glamorous dance-hall singer and clashes with her fiancé, the crooked political boss of Sacramento.
Binnie Barnes, Albert Dekker, Helen Parrish, Patsy Kelly, Edgar Kennedy, Dick Purcell, Harry Shannon, Charles Halton, Emmett Lynn, Bob McKenzie, Milt Kibbee, Paul Sutton, Anne O'Neal.

Flying Tigers (1942, Rep.). *d:* David Miller; *p:* Edmund Grainger; *sc:* Kenneth Gamet and Barry Trivers—*b/o* a story by Kenneth Gamet.
JIM GORDON: American squadron leader with the famous Flying Tigers in WWII China who vies with his reckless, egotistical pal for the affections of a pretty Red Cross worker as they battle Japanese invaders.
John Carroll, Anna Lee, Paul Kelly, Gordon Jones, Mae Clarke, Addison Richards, Edmund MacDonald, Bill Shirley, Tom Neal, James Dodd, Gregg Barton, John James, Chester Gan, David Bruce.

Reunion in France (1942, MGM). *d:* Jules Dassin; *p:* Joseph L. Mankiewicz; *sc:* Jan Lustig, Martin Borowsky, and Marc Connelly—*b/o* a story by Ladislas Bus-Fekete.
PAT TALBOT: Downed American RAF pilot in WWII who, after breaking out of a POW camp and heading for Nazi-occupied Paris, is helped by a glamorous former dress designer to escape back to England.
Joan Crawford, Philip Dorn, Reginald Owen, Albert Basserman, John Carradine, Ann Ayars, Moroni Olsen, J. Edward Bromberg, Henry Daniell, Howard Da Silva, Charles Arnt, Morris Ankrum, Ava Gardner.

Pittsburgh (1942, Univ.). *d:* Lewis Seiler; *p:* Charles K. Feldman; *sc:* Kenneth Gamet and Tom Reed (with additional dialogue by John Twist)—*b/o* a story by George Owen and Tom Reed.
CHARLES "PITTSBURGH" MARKHAM: Ambitious Pittsburgh coal miner who, after working his way up to becoming head of his own corporation and marrying a steel magnate's daughter, loses everything—but then gains a little humility and winds up on top again.
Marlene Dietrich, Randolph Scott, Frank Craven, Louise Allbritton, Shemp Howard, Thomas Gomez, Samuel S. Hinds, Paul Fix, William Haade, Douglas Fowley, Hobart Cavanaugh, Wade Boteler.

A Lady Takes a Chance (1943, RKO). *d:* William A. Seiter; *p:* Frank Ross; *sc:* Robert Ardrey—*b/o* a story by Jo Swerling.
DUKE HUDKINS: Easy-going rodeo rider in Oregon who likes horses better than women but changes his mind when he gets involved with a New York working girl who comes out West on a bus tour.
Jean Arthur, Charles Winninger, Phil Silvers, Mary Field, Don Costello, John Philliber, Grady Sutton, Grant Withers, Hans Conried, Peggy Carroll.

War of the Wildcats (1943, Rep.). *d:* Albert S. Rogell; *p:* Robert North; *sc:* Ethel Hill and

Eleanore Griffith (adaptation by Thomson Burtis)—*b/o* a story by Thomson Burtis.

DAN SOMERS: Ex-cowpuncher and friend of the Indians who, during the 1906 oil boom in Oklahoma, fights a ruthless oil tycoon for the rights to Indian oil lands and the hand of a pretty schoolteacher-turned-author.

Martha Scott, Albert Dekker, George "Gabby" Hayes, Marjorie Rambeau, Dale Evans, Grant Withers, Sidney Blackmer, Paul Fix, Cecil Cunningham, Irving Bacon, Anne O'Neal.

The Fighting Seabees (1944, Rep.). *d:* Howard Lydecker and Edward Ludwig; *p:* Albert J. Cohen; *sc:* Borden Chase and Aeneas MacKenzie—*b/o* a story by Borden Chase.

WEDGE DONOVAN: Tough, hot-headed construction foreman during WWII who, when his civilian workers keep getting killed by Japanese in the Pacific, joins forces with a Navy officer to get Washington to form a special Navy branch of trained, armed construction workers called the Seabees.

Susan Hayward, Dennis O'Keefe, William Frawley, Addison Richards, Leonid Kinsky, Paul Fix, J. M. Kerrigan, Ben Welden, Grant Withers, Duncan Renaldo.

Tall in the Saddle (1944, RKO). *d:* Edwin L. Marin; *p:* Robert Fellows; *sc:* Michael Hogan and Paul J. Fix—*b/o* a story by Gordon Ray Young.

ROCKLIN: Woman-hating cowpuncher who, when he arrives at a ranch to take over as foreman, finds that the man who hired him has been murdered and that his new bosses are a pretty young woman and her spinster aunt.

Ella Raines, Ward Bond, George "Gabby" Hayes, Audrey Long, Elisabeth Risdon, Don Douglas, Paul Fix, Russell Wade, Emory Parnell, Raymond Hatton, Harry Woods, Wheaton Chambers, Frank Puglia, Cy Kendall, Frank Orth, George Chandler, Clem Bevans.

Flame of the Barbary Coast (1945, Rep.). *d:* Joseph Kane; *p:* Joseph Kane; *sc:* Borden Chase—*b/o* a story by Prescott Chaplin.

DUKE FERGUS: Montana cattleman in San Francisco who falls for a Barbary Coast saloon singer, then wins a bundle and opens his own gambling place, only to have it destroyed in the 1906 San Francisco earthquake.

Ann Dvorak, Joseph Schildkraut, William Frawley, Virginia Grey, Russell Hicks, Jack Norton, Paul Fix, Eve Lynne, Marc Lawrence, Butterfly McQueen, Rex Lease, Hank Bell, Emmett Vogan.

Back to Bataan (1945, RKO). *d:* Edward Dmytryk; *p:* Robert Fellows; *sc:* Ben Barzman and Richard Landau—*b/o* a story by Aeneas MacKenzie and William Gordon.

COL. JOSEPH MADDEN: WWII American colonel who, when Bataan falls to the Japanese, stays in the Philippines to organize guerrilla resistance among stranded U.S. and Filipino troops and Filipino freedom fighters.

Anthony Quinn, Beulah Bondi, Fely Franquelli, Leonard Strong, Richard Loo, Philip Ahn, Lawrence Tierney, Paul Fix, Abner Biberman, Vladimir Sokoloff, J. Alex Havier.

Dakota (1945, Rep.). *d:* Joseph Kane; *p:* Joseph Kane; *sc:* Lawrence Hazard (adaptation by Howard Estabrook)—*b/o* a story by Carl Foreman.

JOHN DEVLIN: Ex-soldier who, after he elopes with a railroad tycoon's daughter and settles in North Dakota, gets involved in a battle between local wheat farmers and crooks trying to grab their land.

Vera Hruba Ralston, Walter Brennan, Ward Bond, Ona Munson, Hugo Haas, Mike Mazurki, Olive Blakeney, Paul Fix, Nicodemus Stewart, Grant Withers, Jack LaRue, Bobby (Robert) Blake, Robert Barrat.

They Were Expendable (1945, MGM). *d:* John Ford; *p:* John Ford; *sc:* Lt. Commander Frank Wead—*b/o* the book by William L. White.

LT. (j.g.) RUSTY RYAN: WWII skipper of a U.S. motor torpedo boat who, during the Japanese invasion of the Philippines, falls in love with a Navy nurse while he and his squadron mates prove that PT boats can sink Japanese ships.

Robert Mongomery, Donna Reed, Jack Holt, Ward Bond, Marshall Thompson, Paul Langton, Leon Ames, Donald Curtis, Cameron Mitchell, Jeff York, Murray Alper, Jack Pennick, Charles Trowbridge, Robert Barrat, Bruce Kellog, Tim Murdock, Louis Jean Heydt, Russell Simpson, Tom Tyler.

Without Reservations (1946, RKO). *d:* Mervyn LeRoy; *p:* Jesse L. Lasky; *sc:* Andrew Solt—*b/o* a novel by Jane Allen and Mae Livingston.

CAPT. RUSTY THOMAS: U.S. Marine flyer who, while on a Hollywood-bound train, becomes involved with a famous novelist who thinks he would be the ideal man to play the hero in the movie version of her new best-seller.

Claudette Colbert, Don Defore, Anne Triola, Phil Brown, Frank Puglia, Dona Drake, Thurston Hall, Fernando Alvarado, Charles Arnt, Louella Parsons, Cary Grant.

Angel and the Badman (1947, Rep.). *d:* James Edward Grant; *p:* John Wayne; *sc:* James Edward Grant.

QUIRT EVANS: Notorious gunslinger who has vowed to kill his foster father's murderer but gives up his gun when he falls in love with a pretty young Quaker woman.

Gail Russell, Harry Carey, Bruce Cabot, Irene Rich, Lee Dixon, Tom Powers, John Halloran, Stephen Grant, Joan Barton, Paul Hurst, Craig Woods, Marshall Reed, Hank Worden, Pat Flaherty.

Tycoon (1947, RKO). *d:* Richard Wallace; *p:* Stephen Ames; *sc:* Borden Chase and John Twist—*b/o* the novel by C. E. Scoggins.

JOHNNY MUNROE: American construction engineer who, after he's hired by a South American tycoon to build a tunnel through the Andes to form a railroad link with some mines, runs into problems when he marries the tycoon's daughter against the tycoon's wishes.

Laraine Day, Sir Cedric Hardwicke, Judith Anderson, James Gleason, Anthony Quinn, Grant Withers, Paul Fix, Fernando Alvarado, Harry Woods, Michael Harvey, Charles Trowbridge.

Fort Apache (1948, RKO). *d:* John Ford; *p:* John Ford and Merian C. Cooper (Argosy); *sc:* Frank S. Nugent—*b/o* the *Saturday Evening Post* story "Massacre" by James Warner Bellah.

CAPT. KIRBY YORK: Veteran captain in the U.S. Cavalry at Fort Apache, Arizona, who—when a stubborn, glory-seeking lieutenant colonel takes over as post commander—is unable to stop him from leading his outnumbered troops to certain slaughter in a battle against Apaches led by Cochise.

Henry Fonda, Shirley Temple, Pedro Armendariz, Ward Bond, Irene Rich, John Agar, George O'Brien, Anna Lee, Victor McLaglen, Dick Foran, Jack Pennick, Guy Kibbee, Grant Withers, Mae Marsh, Movita, Mary Gordon, Francis Ford, Frank Ferguson.

Red River (1948, UA). *d:* Howard Hawks; *p:* Howard Hawks (Monterey); *sc:* Borden Chase and Charles Schnee—*b/o* Borden Chase's *Saturday Evening Post* story "The Chisholm Trail."

THOMAS (TOM) DUNSON: Rugged cattleman leader of a Chisholm Trail cattle drive who, after he's left behind by his foster son and others when they rebel at his hard-bitten ways and take the herd, finally catches up with them in Abilene, Kansas, for a showdown.

Montgomery Clift, Joanne Dru, Walter Brennan, Coleen Gray, John Ireland, Noah Beery Jr., Chief Yowlachie, Harry Carey Sr., Harry Carey Jr., Paul Fix, Hank Worden, Hal Taliaferro, Glenn Strange, Tom Tyler, Lane Chandler, Lee Phelps, Shelley Winters.

Three Godfathers (1948, MGM). *d:* John Ford; *p:* John Ford and Merian C. Cooper (Argosy); *sc:* Laurence Stallings and Frank S. Nugent—*b/o* a story by Peter B. Kyne.

ROBERT MARMADUKE "BOB" HIGHTOWER: Tough but soft-hearted bank robber who, after he

and his two sidekicks encounter a dying woman in the Arizona desert and promise to save her newborn baby, finally staggers into the town of New Jerusalem, Arizona, on Christmas Eve with the baby in his arms.

Pedro Armendariz, Harry Carey Jr., Ward Bond, Mae Marsh, Mildred Natwick, Jane Darwell, Guy Kibbee, Dorothy Ford, Ben Johnson, Charles Halton, Hank Worden, Jack Pennick, Fred Libby, Michael Dugan, Don Summers.

Wake of the Red Witch (1948, Rep.). *d:* Edward Ludwig; *p:* Edmund Grainger; *sc:* Harry Brown and Kenneth Gamet—*b/o* the novel by Garland Roark.

CAPTAIN RALLS: Hell-raising adventurer and sea captain whose bitter feud with a ruthless East Indies trader ends in their losing $5,000,000 of gold bullion and the woman they both love.

Gail Russell, Gig Young, Adele Mara, Luther Adler, Eduard Franz, Grant Withers, Henry Daniell, Paul Fix, Dennis Hoey, Jeff Corey, Erskine Sanford, Henry Brandon, Myron Healey, Duke Kahanamoku.

She Wore a Yellow Ribbon (1949, RKO). *d:* John Ford; *p:* John Ford and Merian C. Cooper (Argosy); *sc:* Frank S. Nugent and Laurence Stallings—*b/o* a *Saturday Evening Post* story by James Warner Bellah.

CAPT. NATHAN BRITTLES: Veteran U.S. Cavalry officer on the Western frontier who, with only hours to go until his retirement to civilian life, insists on leading a bold raid against hostile Indians.

Joanne Dru, John Agar, Ben Johnson, Harry Carey Jr., Victor McLaglen, Mildred Natwick, George O'Brien, Arthur Shields, Harry Woods, Chief Big Tree, Tom Tyler, Jack Pennick.

The Fighting Kentuckian (1949, Rep.). *d:* George Waggner; *p:* John Wayne; *sc:* George Waggner.

JOHN BREEN: Rough-and-ready Kentucky rifleman in 1818 Alabama who, while foiling a plot by crooks trying to steal land from French exiles who've settled there, falls for a French general's aristocratic daughter.

Vera Ralston, Philip Dorn, Oliver Hardy, Marie Windsor, John Howard, Hugo Haas, Grant Withers, Odette Myrtil, Paul Fix, Mae Marsh, Jack Pennick, Mickey Simpson.

Sands of Iwo Jima (1949, Rep.). *d:* Allan Dwan; *p:* Edmund Grainger; *sc:* Harry Brown and James Edward Grant—*b/o* a story by Harry Brown.

SGT. JOHN M. STRYKER*: Battle-hardened WWII U.S. Marine sergeant who, after incurring the hatred of recruits he trains in New Zealand,

---

*Won the Academy Award as Best Actor for this role.

wins their respect when they go into combat with him at Tarawa and Iwo Jima (where he's killed by a Japanese sniper).

John Agar, Adele Mara, Forrest Tucker, Wally Cassell, James Brown, Richard Webb, Arthur Franz, Julie Bishop, Richard Jaeckel, John McGuire, Martin Milner.

Rio Grande (1950, Rep.). *d:* John Ford; *p:* John Ford and Merian C. Cooper (Argosy); *sc:* James Kevin McGuinness—*b/o* the *Saturday Evening Post* story "Mission with No Record" by James Warner Bellah.

LT. COL. KIRBY YORKE: Tough U.S. Cavalry commander in the 1880s who, after his enlisted-man son is assigned to his command and his estranged wife shows up at the fort, is ordered to cross the Rio Grande into Mexico to punish marauding Apaches who are hiding out there.

Maureen O'Hara, Ben Johnson, J. Carrol Naish, Victor McLaglen, Chill Wills, Harry Carey Jr., Claude Jarman Jr., Grant Withers.

Operation Pacific (1951, WB). *d:* George Waggner; *p:* Louis F. Edelman; *sc:* George Waggner.

"DUKE" GIFFORD: WWII U.S. submarine executive officer who incurs the hatred of his skipper's younger brother Navy flyer when he has to submerge the sub, leaving the wounded skipper topside to die.

Patricia Neal, Ward Bond, Scott Forbes, Philip Carey, Paul Picerni, William Campbell, Martin Milner, Cliff Clark, Jack Pennick, Virginia Brissac, Lewis Martin.

Flying Leathernecks (1951, RKO). *d:* Nicholas Ray; *p:* Edmund Grainger; *sc:* James Edward Grant—*b/o* a story by Kenneth Gamet.

MAJ. DAN KIRBY: Tough disciplinarian commander of a WWII U.S. Marine fighter squadron on Guadalcanal who is disliked by his men and executive officer until they finally realize in combat that his kind of discipline pays off.

Robert Ryan, Don Taylor, Janis Carter, Jay C. Flippen, William Harrigan, James Bell, Barry Kelley, Maurice Jara, Adam Williams, James Dobson, Carleton Young, Dick Wessell.

The Quiet Man (1952, Rep.). *d:* John Ford; *p:* John Ford and Merian C. Cooper (Argosy); *sc:* Frank S. Nugent—*b/o* the story "Green Rushes" by Maurice Walsh.

SEAN THORNTON: Irish-American boxer who—after accidentally killing a man in the ring—returns to his native village in Ireland, marries a strong-willed local beauty, and is forced into a marathon fistfight when her bullying brother refuses to pay her dowry.

Maureen O'Hara, Barry Fitzgerald, Ward Bond, Victor McLaglen, Mildred Natwick, Francis Ford, Arthur Shields, Sean McClory, Ken Curtis, Mae Marsh, Paddy O'Donnell, Patrick Wayne, Michael Wayne.

Big Jim McLain (1952, WB). *d:* Edward Ludwig; *p:* Robert Fellows (Wayne–Fellows); *sc:* James Edward Grant, Richard English, and Eric Taylor—*b/o* a story by Richard English.

BIG JIM McLAIN: Special agent for the House Committee on Un-American Activities who helps smash an international Communist spy ring that's headquartered in Hawaii.

Nancy Olson, James Arness, Alan Napier, Gayne Whitman, Hans Conried, Veda Ann Borg, Hal Baylor, Robert Keys, John Hubbard, Sarah Padden, Dan Liu.

Trouble Along the Way (1953, WB). *d:* Michael Curtiz; *p:* Melville Shavelson; *sc:* Melville Shavelson and Jack Rose—*b/o* a story by Douglas Morrow and Robert Hardy Andrews.

STEVE ALOYSIUS WILLIAMS: Down-and-out former big-time football coach who, in order to keep custody of his young daughter, lets himself be talked into taking a job as coach at a small, financially troubled Catholic college.

Donna Reed, Charles Coburn, Tom Tully, Marie Windsor, Sherry Jackson, Tom Helmore, Dabbs Greer, Leif Erickson, Douglas Spencer, Chuck Connors, Murray Alper, Ned Glass, James Flavin.

Island in the Sky (1953, WB). *d:* William A. Wellman; *p:* Robert Fellows (Wayne–Fellows); *sc:* Ernest K. Gann—*b/o* his novel.

CAPT. DOOLEY: Veteran Army Transport Command pilot during WWII who, when his C-47 is forced down in 40°-below-zero weather over the frozen wastes north of Labrador, struggles to keep his crew together and alive until search planes can rescue them.

Lloyd Nolan, Walter Abel, James Arness, Andy Devine, Allyn Joslyn, James Lydon, Harry Carey Jr., Hal Baylor, Sean McClory, Gordon Jones, Regis Toomey, Paul Fix, Bob Steele, Darryl Hickman, Touch (Mike) Connors, Carl Switzer.

Hondo (1953, WB). *d:* John Farrow; *p:* Robert Fellows (Wayne–Fellows); *sc:* James Edward Grant—*b/o* Louis L'Amour's story "The Gift of Cochise."

HONDO LANE: Ex-gunfighter and U.S. Cavalry dispatch rider in the Southwest of 1874 who stops at an isolated ranch to defend a lonely woman and her small son against the Apaches.

Geraldine Page, Ward Bond, Michael Pate, Lee Aaker, James Arness, Rodolfo Acosta, Leo Gordon, Tom Irish, Paul Fix, Rayford Barnes.

The High and the Mighty (1954, WB). *d:*

William A. Wellman; *p:* Robert Fellows (Wayne–Fellows); *sc:* Ernest K. Gann—*b/o* his novel.

DAN ROMAN: Aging co-pilot of a passenger flight from Honolulu to San Francisco who, when the plane is damaged over the middle of the Pacific and the younger co-pilot panics, takes over and stubbornly insists that there's a chance of reaching San Francisco safely.

Claire Trevor, Laraine Day, Robert Stack, Jan Sterling, Phil Harris, Robert Newton, David Brian, Paul Kelly, Sidney Blackmer, Julie Bishop, John Howard, John Qualen, Paul Fix, Douglas Fowley, Regis Toomey, Carl Switzer, William DeWolf Hopper.

The Sea Chase (1955, WB). *d:* John Farrow; *p:* John Farrow; *sc:* James Warner Bellah and John Twist—*b/o* the novel by Andrew Geer.

CAPT. KARL EHRLICH: WWII German skipper of an outlaw freighter who tries to make it from Sydney harbor back to Germany but is tracked down and sunk by a British warship.

Lana Turner, David Farrar, Lyle Bettger, Tab Hunter, James Arness, Richard Davalos, John Qualen, Paul Fix, Lowell Gilmore, Luis Van Rooten, Peter Whitney, Claude Akins, John Doucette.

Blood Alley (1955, WB). *d:* William A. Wellman; *sc:* A. S. Fleischman—*b/o* the novel *Blood Alley* by A. S. Fleischman.

WILDER: American merchant-marine captain who helps an entire village escape from Red China to freedom in Hong Kong by taking them on a paddle-wheel ferry boat down the Communist-patrolled Formosa Straits—a 300-mile stretch called "Blood Alley."

Lauren Bacall, Paul Fix, Joy Kim, Berry Kroeger, Mike Mazurki, Anita Ekberg, Henry Nakamura, W. T. Chang, George Chan, Victor Sen Yung.

The Conqueror (1956, RKO). *d:* Dick Powell; *p:* Dick Powell; *sc:* Oscar Millard.

TEMUJIN: Twelfth- and thirteenth-century Mongol warrior who—after capturing the daughter of a Tartar ruler and making her his wife—becomes the ruler of all the Mongols and, under his new name of Genghis Khan, gains fame as one of history's greatest conquerors.

Susan Hayward, Pedro Armendariz, Agnes Moorehead, Thomas Gomez, John Hoyt, William Conrad, Ted de Corsia, Lee Van Cleef, Richard Loo, George E. Stone, Phil Arnold.

The Searchers (1956, WB). *d:* John Ford; *p:* Merian C. Cooper and C. V. Whitney (C. V. Whitney Prod.); *sc:* Frank S. Nugent—*b/o* the novel by Alan LeMay.

ETHAN EDWARDS: Texas Civil War veteran who, with his young ward, relentlessly searches for five years for his niece, who was kidnapped by Commanches when they killed his brother and sister-in-law.

Jeffrey Hunter, Vera Miles, Ward Bond, Natalie Wood, John Qualen, Olive Carey, Henry Brandon, Ken Curtis, Harry Carey Jr., Antonio Moreno, Hank Worden, Pippa Scott, Pat Wayne, Jack Pennick.

The Wings of Eagles (1957, MGM). *d:* John Ford; *p:* Charles Schnee; *sc:* Frank Fenton and William Wister Haines—*b/o* the life and writings of Commander Frank W. "Spig" Wead.

FRANK W. "SPIG" WEAD: Barnstorming Navy flyer who helps build up U.S. Navy air power in the 1920s, then becomes a Hollywood screenwriter after he's crippled in an accident, but is taken back by the Navy as an instructor in WWII.

Dan Dailey, Maureen O'Hara, Ward Bond, Ken Curtis, Edmund Lowe, Kenneth Tobey, Sig Ruman, Henry O'Neill, Louis Jean Heydt, Tige Andrews, William Tracy, Jack Pennick, Bill Henry, Charles Trowbridge, Mae Marsh, Olive Carey.

Jet Pilot (1957, Univ.). *d:* Josef von Sternberg; *p:* Jules Furthman (Howard Hughes/RKO); *sc:* Jules Furthman.

COLONEL SHANNON: American flyer who, when a female Russian pilot lands at a U.S. Air Force base in Alaska, is assigned to try to get information out of her—and winds up marrying her.

Janet Leigh, Jay C. Flippen, Paul Fix, Richard Rober, Roland Winters, Hans Conried, Ivan Triesault, John Bishop, Perdita Chandler, Joyce Compton, Denver Pyle.

Legend of the Lost (1957, UA). *d:* Henry Hathaway; *p:* Henry Hathaway; (Batjac/Haggiag/Dear); *sc:* Robert Presnell Jr. and Ben Hecht.

JOE JANUARY: Cynical American adventurer who, along with a famous archeologist's son and a seductive slave girl, searches for treasure and a lost city in the Sahara.

Sophia Loren, Rossano Brazzi, Kurt Kasznar, Sonia Moser, Angela Portaluri, Ibrahim El Hadish.

The Barbarian and the Geisha (1958, 20th-Fox). *d:* John Huston; *p:* Eugene Frenke; *sc:* Charles Grayson—*b/o* a story by Ellis St. Joseph.

TOWNSEND HARRIS: Dedicated American who, when he's sent to Japan in 1856 by President Franklin Pierce to be the first U.S. Consul-General, overcomes Japanese opposition and helps open trade between the two countries.

Eiko Ando, Sam Jaffe, So Yamamura, Norman Thomson, James Robbins, Morita, Kodaya Ichikawa, Hiroshi Yamato, Tokujiro Iketaniuchi, Fuji Kasai, Takeshi Kumagai.

Rio Bravo (1959, WB). *d:* Howard Hawks; *p:* Howard Hawks (Armada); *sc:* Jules Furthman and Leigh Brackett—*b/o* a short story by B. H. McCampbell.

JOHN T. CHANCE: Rugged sheriff who—when a powerful rancher's gunmen try to get the rancher's killer brother out of jail—fights them off with the help of an alcoholic ex-deputy, a gimpy old jailkeeper, a quiet young gunhand, and a sexy saloon girl.

Dean Martin, Ricky Nelson, Angie Dickinson, Walter Brennan, Ward Bond, John Russell, Pedro Gonzalez-Gonzalez, Claude Akins, Malcolm Atterbury, Harry Carey Jr., Bob Steele, Bing Russell, Myron Healey.

The Horse Soldiers (1959, UA). *d:* John Ford; *p:* John Lee Mahin and Martin Rackin (Mahin–Rackin/Mirisch); *sc:* John Lee Mahin and Martin Rackin—*b/o* the novel by Harold Sinclair.

COL. JOHN MARLOWE: Tough Union cavalry Civil War officer who repeatedly clashes with his humanitarian medical officer and falls for a fiery Southern belle as he leads his brigade deep into Confederate territory to destroy a railroad supply center in Mississippi.

William Holden, Constance Towers, Althea Gibson, Hoot Gibson, Anna Lee, Russell Simpson, Basil Ruysdael, Denver Pyle, Strother Martin, Hank Worden, Walter Reed, Jack Pennick.

The Alamo (1960, UA). *d:* John Wayne; *p:* John Wayne (Batjac); *sc:* James Edward Grant.

COL. DAVY CROCKETT: Celebrated American frontiersman, politician, and humorist from Tennessee who is one of the outnumbered heroic defenders killed during the seige of The Alamo in 1836 Texas by General Santa Anna and his 7000 Mexican troops.

Richard Widmark, Laurence Harvey, Richard Boone, Frankie Avalon, Patrick Wayne, Linda Cristal, Chill Wills, Joseph Calleia, Ken Curtis, Veda Ann Borg, John Dierkes, Denver Pyle, Hank Worden, Guinn Williams, Olive Carey.

North to Alaska (1960, 20th-Fox). *d:* Henry Hathaway; *p:* Henry Hathaway; *sc:* John Lee Mahin, Martin Rackin, and Claude Binyon—*b/o* the play *Birthday Gift* by Laszlo Fodor (from an idea by John Kafka).

SAM McCORD: Woman-hating prospector in 1900 Alaska who, when he goes to Seattle to bring back his partner's fiancée but discovers that she's married someone else, brings back a dance-hall girl as a substitute and falls for her himself.

Stewart Granger, Ernie Kovacs, Fabian, Capucine, Mickey Shaughnessy, Karl Swenson, Joe Sawyer, Kathleen Freeman, John Qualen, Douglas Dick, Richard Deacon, Richard Collier.

The Comancheros (1961, 20th-Fox). *d:* Michael Curtiz; *p:* George Sherman; *sc:* James Edward Grant and Clair Huffaker—*b/o* the novel by Paul I. Wellman.

JAKE CUTTER: Hard-nosed Texas Ranger in 1843 who teams up with his gambler prisoner to infiltrate and break up the Comancheros, a gang of white renegades supplying guns and liquor to the Comanche Indians.

Stuart Whitman, Ina Balin, Nehemiah Persoff, Lee Marvin, Michael Ansara, Pat Wayne, Bruce Cabot, Joan O'Brien, Jack Elam, Edgar Buchanan, Guinn "Big Boy" Williams, Henry Daniell, John Dierkes, Bob Steele, Luisa Triana.

The Man Who Shot Liberty Valance (1962, Para.). *d:* John Ford; *p:* Willis Goldbeck (John Ford Prods.); *sc:* James Warner Bellah and Willis Goldbeck—*b/o* the short story by Dorothy M. Johnson.

TOM DONIPHON: Good-natured but tough rancher whose idealistic young lawyer friend becomes famous as the man who killed a notorious bad man and is elected to Congress—though in fact the rancher did the killing.

James Stewart, Vera Miles, Lee Marvin, Edmond O'Brien, Andy Devine, Woody Strode, Ken Murray, John Qualen, Jeanette Nolan, Lee Van Cleef, Strother Martin, John Carradine, Willis Bouchey, Denver Pyle, Robert F. Simon, Paul Birch.

Hatari! (1962, Para.). *d:* Howard Hawks; *p:* Howard Hawks (Malabar); *sc:* Leigh Brackett—*b/o* a story by Harry Kurnitz.

SEAN MERCER: Irish-American leader of a bunch of big-game trappers in Tanganyika who, while he's rounding up wild animals for sale to zoos, falls for a pretty photographer who's joined the group.

Hardy Kruger, Elsa Martinelli, Red Buttons, Gerard Blain, Michele Girardon, Bruce Cabot, Valentin De Vargas, Eduard Franz, Queenie Leonard.

The Longest Day (1962, 20th-Fox). *d:* Ken Annakin, Andrew Martin, and Bernhard Wicki; *sc:* Cornelius Ryan (additional material by Romain Gary, James Jones, David Pursall, and Jack Seddon)—*b/o* the book by Cornelius Ryan.

LT. COL. BENJAMIN VANDERVOOT: WWII American paratrooper in the 82nd Airborne Division who—on D-Day, June 6, 1944—breaks his ankle in a drop on Ste. Mere Eglise but keeps on fighting, helping to make the ancient French town the first to be liberated by the Allies.

Robert Mitchum, Henry Fonda, Robert Ryan, Rod Steiger, Robert Wagner, Richard Beymer, Mel Ferrer, Jeffrey Hunter, Paul Anka, Sal Mineo, Roddy McDowall, Stuart Whitman, Eddie Albert,

Edmond O'Brien, Fabian, Red Buttons, Tom Tryon, Alexander Knox, Tommy Sands, Ray Danton, Steve Forrest, Richard Burton, Kenneth More, Peter Lawford, Richard Todd, Sean Connery, Curt Jurgens, Peter Van Eyck, Gert Froebe, Hans Christian Blech.

How the West Was Won (1962, MGM/Cinerama). *d:* Henry Hathaway, John Ford, and George Marshall; *p:* Bernard Smith; *sc:* James R. Webb—*b/o* the series *How the West Was Won* in *Life* magazine.

GEN. WILLIAM TECUMSEH SHERMAN: Famed Civil War Union Army general who, after the bloody defeat of the North at Shiloh, meets with General Ulysses S. Grant in a clearing in the woods to discuss the course of the war.

Carroll Baker, Lee J. Cobb, Henry Fonda, Carolyn Jones, Karl Malden, Gregory Peck, George Peppard, Robert Preston, Debbie Reynolds, James Stewart, Eli Wallach, Richard Widmark, Walter Brennan, David Brian, Andy Devine, Raymond Massey, Agnes Moorehead, Henry (Harry) Morgan, Thelma Ritter, Mickey Shaughnessy, Russ Tamblyn.

Donovan's Reef (1963, Para.). *d:* John Ford; *p:* John Ford (John Ford Prods.); *sc:* Frank Nugent and James Edward Grant—*b/o* a story by Edmund Beloin.

MICHAEL PATRICK DONOVAN: Ex-WWII Navy man and owner of a bar called "Donovan's Reef" on a South Pacific isle who tangles with a stuffy young woman from Boston when she arrives on the island in search of her father.

Lee Marvin, Jack Warden, Elizabeth Allen, Cesar Romero, Dorothy Lamour, Mike Mazurki, Marcel Dalio, Edgar Buchanan, Patrick Wayne, Dick Foran, Mae Marsh.

McLintock! (1963, UA). *d:* Andrew V. McLaglen; *p:* Michael Wayne (Batjac); *sc:* James Edward Grant.

GEORGE WASHINGTON McLINTOCK: Rough-and-tumble cattle baron who has no trouble controlling the town of McLintock but finds his hands full when he tries to win back his estranged headstrong wife.

Maureen O'Hara, Patrick Wayne, Stefanie Powers, Yvonne De Carlo, Jack Kruschen, Chill Wills, Jerry Van Dyke, Edgar Buchanan, Bruce Cabot, Strother Martin, Gordon Jones, Robert Lowery, H. W. Gim, Hal Needham, Bob Steele.

Circus World (1964, Para.). *d:* Henry Hathaway; *p:* Samuel Bronston (Bronston/Midway); *sc:* Ben Hecht, Julian Halevy, and James Edward Grant—*b/o* a story by Philip Yordan and Nicholas Ray.

MATT MASTERS: American owner of a Wild West Show and Circus who, when he tours Europe in search of an aerialist he loved fifteen years before and whose daughter he has raised as his

own, finds her and reunites the two in an aerial act with the show.

Claudia Cardinale, Rita Hayworth, Lloyd Nolan, Richard Conte, John Smith, Henri Dantes, Wanda Rotha, Kay Walsh, Margaret MacGrath, Katharine Kath, Moustache.

The Greatest Story Ever Told (1965, UA). *d:* George Stevens; *p:* George Stevens (George Stevens); *sc:* James Lee Barrett and George Stevens, in creative association with Carl Sandburg—*b/o* Books of the Old and New Testaments, other ancient writings, the book by Fulton Oursler, and writings by Henry Denker.

Billed as "THE CENTURION": A Roman military officer who leads Jesus Christ to the crucifixion at Calvary.

Max von Sydow, Dorothy McGuire, Robert Loggia, Charlton Heston, Robert Blake, Jamie Farr, David McCallum, Roddy McDowall, Sidney Poitier, Carroll Baker, Pat Boone, Van Heflin, Sal Mineo, Shelley Winters, Ed Wynn, Telly Savalas, Angela Lansbury, Joseph Schildkraut, Jose Ferrer, Claude Rains, Richard Conte.

In Harm's Way (1965, Para.). *d:* Otto Preminger; *p:* Otto Preminger (Sigma); *sc:* Wendell Mayes—*b/o* the novel by James Bassett.

CAPT. ROCKWELL "THE ROCK" TORREY: U.S. Navy career officer who, right after Pearl Harbor, is beached on a technicality, then—while he clashes with his young Navy-officer son and falls for a Navy nurse—is given command of a secret operation to capture strategic Japanese-held islands.

Kirk Douglas, Patricia Neal, Tom Tryon, Paula Prentiss, Brandon De Wilde, Jill Haworth, Dana Andrews, Stanley Holloway, Burgess Meredith, Franchot Tone, Henry Fonda, Patrick O'Neal, Carroll O'Connor, Slim Pickens, James Mitchum, George Kennedy, Bruce Cabot, Hugh O'Brian, Tod Andrews, Larry Hagman, Christopher George.

The Sons of Katie Elder (1965, Para.). *d:* Henry Hathaway; *p:* Hal B. Wallis (Hal Wallis Prod.); *sc:* William H. Wright, Allan Weiss, and Harry Essex—*b/o* a story by Talbot Jennings.

JOHN ELDER: Oldest of four hell-raising sons who, when they return to a Texas town for their mother's funeral, determine to find out what happened to her and their ranch and to learn who killed their father some years earlier.

Dean Martin, Martha Hyer, Michael Anderson Jr., Earl Holliman, Jeremy Slate, James Gregory, Paul Fix, George Kennedy, Dennis Hopper, John Litel, Strother Martin, Rhys Williams, John Qualen, Percy Helton, Rodolfo Acosta, James Westerfield.

Cast a Giant Shadow (1966, UA). *d:* Melville Shavelson; *p:* Melville Shavelson and Michael

Wayne (Mirisch/Llenroc/Batjac); sc: Melville Shavelson—b/o the biography of Col. David Marcus by Ted Berkman.

GEN. MIKE RANDOLPH: American general who unofficially supports the sending of an American-Jewish ex–U.S. Army colonel to Israel to face Arab attacks when Israel becomes a state in 1947.

Kirk Douglas, Yul Brynner, Senta Berger, Frank Sinatra, Angie Dickinson, Luther Adler, Stathis Giallelis, James Donald, Gordon Jackson, Haym Topol, Gary Merrill, Jeremy Kemp, Sean Barrett, Frank Latimore.

The War Wagon (1967, Univ.). *d:* Burt Kennedy; *p:* Marvin Schwartz (Batjac/Marvin Schwartz); *sc:* Clair Huffaker—*b/o* his novel *Badman.*

TAW JACKSON: Rancher who, when he gets out of prison after being framed by a powerful crook, joins forces with four confederates to steal a half-million dollars' worth of gold that the crook is shipping in an armor-plated stagecoach called the War Wagon.

Kirk Douglas, Howard Keel, Robert Walker, Keenan Wynn, Bruce Cabot, Gene Evans, Joanna Barnes, Bruce Dern, Sheb Wooley, Frank McGrath, Hal Needham.

El Dorado (1967, Para.). *d:* Howard Hawks; *p:* Howard Hawks (Laurel); *sc:* Leigh Brackett—*b/o* Harry Brown's novel *The Stars in Their Courses.*

COLE THORNTON: Wandering gunslinger who, along with an old-timer deputy, a young knife-throwing gambler, and a sexy saloon girl, joins forces with his whiskey-soaked sheriff pal in routing a villainous land baron and his gang.

Robert Mitchum, James Caan, Charlene Holt, Michele Carey, Arthur Hunnicutt, R. G. Armstrong, Edward Asner, Paul Fix, Johnny Crawford, Christopher George, Robert Rothwell, Adam Roarke, Charles Courtney, Robert Donner, William Henry, John Mitchum, Jim Davis.

The Green Berets (1968, WB–Seven Arts). *d:* John Wayne and Ray Kellogg; *p:* Michael Wayne (Batjac); *sc:* James Lee Barrett—*b/o* the novel by Robin Moore.

COL. MICHAEL KIRBY: Rugged U.S. Army career officer in 1963 who leads a group of Green Berets (U.S. Special Forces troops trained for guerrilla warfare in Vietnam) into Viet Cong territory to complete construction of a vital strike camp.

David Janssen, Jim Hutton, Aldo Ray, Raymond St. Jacques, Bruce Cabot, Jack Soo, George Takei, Patrick Wayne, Irene Tsu, Edward Faulkner, Jason Evers, Mike Henry, Craig Jue, Luke Askew.

Hellfighters (1968, Univ.). *d:* Andrew V. McLaglen; *p:* Robert Arthur; *sc:* Clair Huffaker.

CHANCE BUCKMAN: Rough-and-ready oil-well firefighter who battles fires all over the world—

but also has a few domestic fires to put out when his estranged wife shows up and his daughter marries his young firefighter sidekick.

Katharine Ross, Vera Miles, Jim Hutton, Jay C. Flippen, Bruce Cabot, Edward Faulkner, Barbara Stuart, Edmund Hashim, Valentin De Vargas, Pedro Gonzales Gonzales.

True Grit (1969, Para.). *d:* Henry Hathaway; *p:* Hal B. Wallis (Hal Wallis Prod.); *sc:* Marguerite Roberts—*b/o* the novel by Charles Portis.

REUBEN J. "ROOSTER" COGBURN*: Hardboiled, whiskey-drinking, one-eyed deputy U.S. marshal in the Old West who is hired by a plucky teen-age girl to help her track down her father's killer.

Glen Campbell, Kim Darby, Jeremy Slate, Robert Duvall, Dennis Hopper, Alfred Ryder, Strother Martin, Jeff Corey, Ron Soble, John Fiedler, James Westerfield, John Doucette, Donald Woods, Edith Atwater, Myron Healey, Hank Worden.

The Undefeated (1969, 20th-Fox). *d:* Andrew V. McLaglen; *p:* Robert L. Jacks; *sc:* James Lee Barrett—*b/o* a story by Stanley L. Hough.

COL. JOHN HENRY THOMAS: Civil War Union colonel who after the war ends leads his men south of the border to sell horses to Mexico's Emperor Maximilian, meets up with a former Confederate colonel enemy, and joins forces with him against Mexican bandidos and Juaristas opposed to Maximilian.

Rock Hudson, Antonio Aguilar, Roman Gabriel, Marian McCargo, Lee Meriwether, Merlin Olsen, Bruce Cabot, Michael Vincent, Ben Johnson, Harry Carey Jr., Paul Fix, Royal Dano, Richard Mulligan, John Agar, Dub Taylor.

Chisum (1970, WB). *d:* Andrew V. McLaglen; *p:* Michael A. Wayne and Andrew J. Fenady (Batjac); *sc:* Andrew J. Fenady.

JOHN SIMPSON CHISUM: Cigar-puffing cattle king in 1870s New Mexico who gets a helping hand from Billy the Kid and Sheriff Pat Garrett as he fights corrupt, land-grabbing law officials during the bloody Lincoln County cattle war.

Forrest Tucker, Christopher George, Ben Johnson, Glenn Corbett, Andrew Prine, Bruce Cabot, Geoffrey Deuel, Patric Knowles, Richard Jaeckel, Lynda Day, John Agar, Ray Teal, Ron Soble, Glenn Langan, William Bryant, John Mitchum, Alan Baxter, Christopher Mitchum.

Rio Lobo (1970, Cinema Center). *d:* Howard Hawks; *p:* Howard Hawks (Malabar); *sc:* Burton Wohl and Leigh Brackett—*b/o* a story by Burton Wohl.

---

*Won the Academy Award as Best Actor for this role.

CORD McNALLY: Ex–Civil War Union colonel who, together with two ex–Confederate soldiers, catches up with a wartime informer and saves a Texas town from land-grabbing crooks.

Jorge Rivero, Jennifer O'Neill, Jack Elam, Victor French, Chris Mitchum, Susana Dosamantes, Mike Henry, David Huddleston, Bill Williams, Edward Faulkner, Jim Davis, George Plimpton, Bob Steele, Hank Worden.

Big Jake (1971, Nat. Gen./Cinema Center). *d:* George Sherman; *p:* Michael A. Wayne (Batjac); *sc:* Harry Julian Fink and R. M. Fink.

JACOB (JAKE) McCANDLES: Texas cattleman in 1909—estranged from his family for fifteen years—who sets out with two of his sons, an old Indian friend, and his dog to get back his kidnapped grandson.

Richard Boone, Maureen O'Hara, Patrick Wayne, Chris Mitchum, Bobby Vinton, Bruce Cabot, Glenn Corbett, Harry Carey Jr., John Doucette, Jim Davis, John Agar, Jim Burke, Hank Worden, Bernard Fox.

The Cowboys (1972, WB). *d:* Mark Rydell; *p:* Mark Rydell (Sanford); *sc:* Irving Ravetch, Harriet Frank Jr., and William Dale Jennings—*b/o* the novel by William Dale Jennings.

WIL ANDERSON: Aging rancher in the Old West of the 1870s who makes a big cattle drive with the help of eleven young boys who, when he's shot in the back by a cowardly bad man, avenge his death and finish the drive.

Roscoe Lee Browne, Bruce Dern, A. Martinez, Alfred Barker Jr., Nicolas Beauvy, Steve Benedict, Robert Carradine, Colleen Dewhurst, Slim Pickens, Sarah Cunningham, Charles Tyner, Dick Farnsworth.

The Train Robbers (1973, WB). *d:* Burt Kennedy; *p:* Michael A. Wayne (Batjac); *sc:* Burt Kennedy.

LANE: Gunslinger who, after agreeing to help a voluptuous widow clear her family name (for the sake of her son) by recovering and returning the gold her late husband stole, discovers that she's really a con woman with no son and no late husband.

Ann-Margret, Rod Taylor, Ben Johnson, Chris George, Bobby Vinton, Jerry Gatlin, Ricardo Montalban.

Cahill, United States Marshal (1973, WB). *d:* Andrew V. McLaglen; *p:* Michael A. Wayne (Batjac); *sc:* Harry Julian Fink and Rita M. Fink—*b/o* a story by Barney Slater.

J. D. CAHILL: Veteran lawman in the West who faces danger and disillusionment when he goes after a gang of bank robbers and discovers that his two neglected teenage sons are mixed up with them.

George Kennedy, Gary Grimes, Neville Brand, Clay O'Brien, Marie Windsor, Morgan Paull, Royal Dano, Denver Pyle, Jackie Coogan, Harry Carey Jr., Paul Fix, Pepper Martin, Hank Worden.

McQ (1974, WB). *d:* John Sturges; *p:* Jules Levy, Arthur Gardner, and Lawrence Roman (Batjac/Levy–Gardner); *sc:* Lawrence Roman.

DET. LT. LON McQ: Tough Seattle police detective who, when his cop buddy is murdered, quits the force to trace down the killer and expose corruption and drug dealing within the police department.

Eddie Albert, Diana Muldaur, Colleen Dewhurst, Clu Gulager, David Huddleston, Jim Watkins, Al Lettieri, Julie Adams, Roger E. Mosley, William Bryant, Dick Friel, Fred Waugh.

Brannigan (1975, UA). *d:* Douglas Hickox; *p:* Jules Levy and Arthur Gardner (Wellborn); *sc:* Christopher Trumbo, Michael Butler, William P. McGivern, and William Norton—*b/o* a story by Christopher Trumbo and Michael Butler.

BRANNIGAN: Tough Irish-American cop from Chicago who, when he's sent to London to escort a drug trafficker who's being extradited, learns that the crook has been kidnapped for ransom and clashes with a Scotland Yard commander over how to handle the case.

Richard Attenborough, Mel Ferrer, Judy Geeson, John Vernon, Daniel Pilon, James Booth, John Stride, Anthony Booth, Del Henney, Don Henderson, Ralph Meeker.

Rooster Cogburn (1975, Univ.). *d:* Stuart Millar; *p:* Hal B. Wallis (Hal Wallis Prod.); *sc:* Martin Julien—*b/o* the "Rooster Cogburn" character created by Charles H. Portis in his novel *True Grit*.

REUBEN J. "ROOSTER" COGBURN: Hard-drinking, hard-fighting, one-eyed U.S. marshal in the Old West who joins up with a Bible-thumping spinster to go after the gang of outlaws who murdered her minister father.

Katharine Hepburn, Anthony Zerbe, Richard Jordan, John McIntire, Strother Martin, Paul Koslo, Jack Colvin, Jon Lormer, Richard Romancito, Lane Smith, Tommy Lee.

The Shootist (1976, Para.). *d:* Don Siegel; *p:* M. J. Frankovich and William Self (Dino De Laurentiis); *sc:* Miles Hood Swarthout and Scott Hale—*b/o* the novel by Glendon Swarthout.

JOHN BERNARD (J.B.) BOOKS: Aging legendary gunfighter in 1901 who, when a Carson City doctor tells him he's dying of cancer, tries to die in peace but finally decides to go out with his guns blazing as he eliminates some of the town's bad men.

Lauren Bacall, Ron Howard, James Stewart, Richard Boone, Hugh O'Brian, Bill McKinney, Harry Morgan, John Carradine, Sheree North, Richard Lenz, Scatman Crothers, Gregg Palmer, Alfred Dennis, Dick Winslow, Melody Thomas, Kathleen O'Malley.

· In addition, John Wayne made cameo/guest appearances in the following feature films: *I Married a Woman* (1958, WB) and *Cancel My Reservation* (1972, WB). He also starred in the following serials: *Shadow of the Eagle* (1932, Mascot—as CRAIG McCOY), *The Hurricane Express* (1932, Mascot—as LARRY BAKER), and *The Three Musketeers* (1933, Mascot—as TOM WAYNE).

☆ MAE WEST

b: Aug. 17, 1892, Brooklyn, N.Y.
d: Nov. 23, 1980, Los Angeles, Cal.

"Beulah, peel me a grape."

Tira (Mae West) to her maid, Beulah Thorndyke (Gertrude Howard), in *I'm No Angel*, 1933.

Night After Night (1932, Para.). *d:* Archie Mayo; *p:* William LeBaron; *sc:* Vincent Lawrence (with additional dialogue by Mae West)—*b/o* the story "Single Night" by Louis Bromfield.

MAUDIE TRIPLETT: Worldly owner of a string of beauty parlors who frequents a swank speakeasy owned by an ex-pugilist who's an old flame of hers.

George Raft, Constance Cummings, Wynne Gibson, Alison Skipworth, Roscoe Karns, Louis Calhern, Tom Kennedy, Gordon (Bill) Elliott.

She Done Him Wrong (1933, Para.). *d:* Lowell Sherman; *p:* William LeBaron; *sc:* Harvey Thew and John Bright—*b/o* the play *Diamond Lil* by Mae West.

LADY LOU: Shady lady Bowery saloon keeper during the Gay Nineties who falls for a handsome Salvation Army worker, unaware that he's a Federal undercover agent assigned to get the goods on her.

Cary Grant, Gilbert Roland, Noah Beery Sr., Rafaela Ottiano, David Landau, Rochelle Hudson, Owen Moore, Fuzzy Knight, Dewey Robinson, Tom Kennedy, Wade Boteler, Louise Beavers.

I'm No Angel (1933, Para.). *d:* Wesley Ruggles; *p:* William LeBaron; *sc:* Mae West (with continuity by Harlan Thompson and story suggestions by Lowell Brentano).

TIRA: Shapely circus dancer and lion tamer who manages to crash society when she sues a handsome, rich playboy for breach of promise and finally gets him to the altar.

Cary Grant, Edward Arnold, Ralf Harolde, Russell Hopton, Gertrude Michael, Kent Taylor, Dorothy Peterson, Gregory Ratoff, Gertrude Howard, William Davidson, Irving Pichel, Nat Pendleton.

Belle of the Nineties (1934, Para.). *d:* Leo McCarey; *p:* William LeBaron; *sc:* Mae West.

RUBY CARTER: St. Louis saloon entertainer in the Gay Nineties who heads for New Orleans and gathers a flock of male admirers but winds up with a prize fighter known as "The Tiger Kid."

Roger Pryor, John Mack Brown, John Miljan, Katherine De Mille, Harry Woods, Edward Gargan, Warren Hymer, Benny Baker, Fuzzy Knight, Mike Mazurki, Gene Austin.

Goin' to Town (1935, Para.). *d:* Alexander Hall; *p:* William LeBaron; *sc:* Mae West—*b/o* a story by Marion Morgan and George B. Dowell.

CLEO BORDEN: Curvaceous dance-hall girl in the Old West who becomes a cattle queen, gets involved with oil wells and a handsome English geologist, and crashes the swanky set.

Paul Cavanagh, Gilbert Emery, Marjorie Gateson, Ivan Lebedeff, Fred Kohler Sr., Grant Withers, Luis Alberni, Paul Harvey, Tom London, Syd Saylor, Irving Bacon, Bert Roach, Francis Ford, Dewey Robinson.

Klondike Annie (1936, Para.). *d:* Raoul Walsh; *p:* William LeBaron; *sc:* Mae West (with material suggested by Frank Mitchell Dazey)—*b/o* a story by Mae West (with story ingredients by Marion Morgan and George B. Dowell).

ROSE CARLTON (alias "THE FRISCO DOLL"): Gay Nineties Barbary Coast torch singer who takes it on the lam from the law for a murder rap, heads for the Yukon, and arrives at a Klondike mission disguised as an evangelist named Sister Annie.

Victor McLaglen, Phillip Reed, Helen Jerome Eddy, Harry Beresford, Lucille Webster Gleason, Conway Tearle, Soo Yong, Gene Austin, James Burke.

Go West, Young Man (1936, Para.). *d:* Henry Hathaway; *p:* Emanuel Cohen; *sc:* Mae West—*b/o* the play by Lawrence Riley.

MAVIS ARDEN: Hollywood movie queen who, when she is stranded in a small Pennsylvania town while making a personal appearance, livens things up by passing the time with a handsome farm boy.

Warren William, Randolph Scott, Alice Brady, Elizabeth Patterson, Lyle Talbot, Isabel Jewell, Etienne Girardot, Jack LaRue, Xavier Cugat, Eddie Dunn, Dick Elliott.

Every Day's a Holiday (1938, Para.). *d:* A. Edward Sutherland; *p:* Emanuel Cohen; *sc:* Mae West.

PEACHES O'DAY: Gay Nineties con woman who sells the Brooklyn Bridge to a sucker and is kicked out of New York but returns to help expose a crooked police chief.

Edmund Lowe, Charles Butterworth, Charles Winninger, Walter Catlett, Lloyd Nolan, Louis Armstrong, Herman Bing, Roger Imhoff, Chester Conklin, Lucien Prival, Adrian Morris, Francis McDonald, Irving Bacon, Dick Elliott, Johnny Arthur.

My Little Chickadee (1940, Univ.). *d:* Edward Cline; *p:* Lester Cowan; *sc:* Mae West and W. C. Fields.

FLOWER BELLE LEE: Shady lady in the Old West who fakes a marriage to a card-cheating con man, but whose real heartthrob is a mysterious masked bandit.

W. C. Fields, Joseph Calleia, Dick Foran, Margaret Hamilton, James Conlin, Gene Austin, Fuzzy Knight, Ruth Donnelly, Donald Meek, Jackie Searle, Billy Benedict, Hank Bell, Lane Chandler.

The Heat's On (1943, Col.). *d:* Gregory Ratoff; *p:* Gregory Ratoff; *sc:* Fitzroy Davis, George S. George, and Fred Schiller—*b/o* a story by Boris Ingster and Lou Breslow.

FAY LAWRENCE: Musical-comedy star who, while she's seeking financial backing from an elderly gentleman whose sister runs the Legion of Purity, gets caught in the middle of the schemes and dirty tricks of two rival producers.

Victor Moore, William Gaxton, Xavier Cugat, Hazel Scott, Lester Allan, Allen Dinehart, Mary Roche, Lloyd Bridges, Almira Sessions, Sam Ash.

Myra Breckinridge (1970, 20th-Fox). *d:* Michael Sarne; *p:* Robert Fryer; *sc:* Michael Sarne and David Giler—*b/o* the novel by Gore Vidal.

LETITIA VAN ALLEN: Man-hungry Hollywood talent agent who requires sexual favors from her virile young male clients.

John Huston, Raquel Welch, Rex Reed, Farrah Fawcett, Roger C. Carmel, Roger Herren, Jim Backus, John Carradine, Andy Devine, Grady Sutton, Kathleen Freeman, Tom Selleck, William Hopper, Michael Sarne.

Sextette (1978, Crown International). *d:* Ken Hughes; *p:* Robert Sullivan and Daniel Briggs; *sc:* Herbert Baker—*b/o* the play by Mae West.

MARLO MANNERS: Aging movie sex goddess who marries a young man in his early thirties—her sixth husband—and spends her wedding night in a wild hotel where assorted characters keep popping in and out of one another's suites.

Timothy Dalton, Dom De Luise, Tony Curtis, Ringo Starr, George Hamilton, Alice Cooper, Keith Allison, Rona Barrett, Keith Moon, Regis Philbin, Walter Pidgeon, Harry Weiss, George Raft, Gil Stratton.

And Speaking of Characters' Names, How About ...

J. PINKERTON SNOOPINGTON: Franklin Pangborn in *The Bank Dick* (1940).

FILTHY McNASTY: Al Hill in *The Bank Dick* (1940).

A. PISMO CLAM: Jack Norton in *The Bank Dick* (1940).

MIGG TWEENY: Jack Oakie in *Million Dollar Legs* (1932).

LITTLETON LOONEY: Jack Oakie in *The Sap from Syracuse* (1930).

J. PINKHAM WHINNY: Charlie Ruggles in *Six of a Kind* (1934).

ELSIE MAE ADELE BRUNCH SOUSE: Evelyn Del Rio in *The Bank Dick* (1940).

VAN REIGBLE VAN PELTER VAN DOON III: Charles Winninger in *Every Day's a Holiday* (1938).

TITUS QUEASLEY: Will Wright in *Alias Jesse James* (1959).

LESLIE McWHINNEY: Stuart Erwin in *The Big Broadcast* (1932).

EGBERT AND EFFIE FLOUD: Charlie Ruggles and Mary Boland in *Ruggles of Red Gap* (1935).

ACHILLES BOMBANASSA: Jerry Colonna in *Road to Singapore* (1940).

ALARDYCE T. MERRIWEATHER: Martin Balsam in *Little Big Man* (1970).

HERBERT TERWILLIGER VAN DYCK: Elisha Cook Jr. in *Pigskin Parade* (1936).

MUZZY VAN HOSSMERE: Carol Channing in *Thoroughly Modern Millie* (1967).

LILI VON SHTUPP: Madeline Kahn in *Blazing Saddles* (1974).

HEDLEY LAMARR: Harvey Korman in *Blazing Saddles* (1974).

JASPER BLUBBER: John Houseman in *The Cheap Detective* (1978).

MAXIMILLIAN MEEN: Peter Falk in *The Great Race* (1965).

PICKLE BIXBY: Andy Devine in *In Old Chicago* (1938).

TENNESSEE STEINMETZ: Buddy Hackett in *The Love Bug* (1969).

DOM BELL: Dom De Luise in *Silent Movie* (1976).

SOURPUSS SMITHERS: J. Farrell MacDonald in *Meet John Doe* (1940).

ASTHMA ANDERSON: Ralph Peters in *Ball of Fire* (1941).

DOUGLAS FAIRBANKS ROSENBLOOM: Bobby Jordan in *A Slight Case of Murder* (1938).

COL. BAT GUANO: Keenan Wynn in *Dr. Strangelove* (1964).

GEN. JACK D. RIPPER: Sterling Hayden in *Dr. Strangelove* (1964).

JESSICA MARBLES: Elsa Lanchester in *Murder by Death* (1976).

BRUNHILDE ESTERHAZY: Betty Garrett in *On the Town* (1949).

TRIXIE DELIGHT: Madeline Kahn in *Paper Moon* (1973).

JUNE JANUARY: Judy Harriet in *Say One for Me* (1959).

SEARS SWIGGLES: Spencer Ross in *Sleeper* (1973).

SPIT: Leo Gorcey in *Dead End* (1937).

JAWS: Richard Kiel in *The Spy Who Loved Me* (1977).

ANIMAL: Robert Strauss in *Stalag 17* (1953).

TOMATOES: Jack La Rue in *Robin and the 7 Hoods* (1964).

VERMIN: Allen Jenkins in *Robin and the 7 Hoods* (1964).

SNAKE EYES: John Larkin in *Smart Money* (1931).

THE LAMB: Wee Willie (William) Davis in *Reap the Wild Wind* (1942).

NICK NACK: Herve Villechaize in *The Man with the Golden Arm* (1955).

ODDJOB: Harold Sakata in *Goldfinger* (1964).

GOLD HAT: Alfonso Bedoya in *The Treasure of the Sierra Madre* (1948).

PEACH LIPS: Amanda Blake in *Lili* (1953).

PLENTY O'TOOLE: Lana Wood in *Diamonds Are Forever* (1971).

PUSSY GALORE: Honor Blackman in *Goldfinger* (1964).

KISSY SUZUKI: Mia Hama in *You Only Live Twice* (1967).

LOVEY KRAVEZIT: Beverly Adams in *The Silencers* (1966).

MISS GOODTHIGHS: Jacky (Jacqueline) Bisset in *Casino Royale* (1967).

OCTOPUSSY: Maud Adams in *Octopussy* (1983).

Bibliography

American Film Institute. *Catalog of Motion Pictures Produced in the United States. Feature Films, 1921–1930. Feature Films, 1961–1970.* New York: Bowker, 1971–

Aros, Andrew A. *An Actor Guide to the Talkies, 1964–1974.* Metuchen, N.J.: Scarecrow Press, 1977 (as conceived by Richard B. Dimmitt).

———. *A Title Guide to the Talkies, 1964–1974.* Metuchen, N.J.: Scarecrow Press, 1977 (as conceived by Richard B. Dimmitt).

Baer, D. Richard (ed.). *The Film Buff's Checklist of Motion Pictures, 1912–1979.* Hollywood, Cal.: Hollywood Film Archive, 1978.

Braithwaite, Bruce. *The Films of Marlon Brando.* New York: Confucian Press and Beaufort Books, 1982.

Brown, Jay A., and the editors of *Consumer Guide. Rating the Movies.* New York: Beekman House, 1982.

Catalog of Copyright Entries, Cumulative series. Motion Pictures, 1912–1939. Washington, D.C.: Copyright Office, Library of Congress, 1951.

Catalog of Copyright Entries, Cumulative series. Motion Pictures, 1940–1949. Washington, D.C.: Copyright Office, Library of Congress, 1953.

Catalog of Copyright Entries, Cumulative series. Motion Pictures, 1950–1959. Washington, D.C.: Copyright Office, Library of Congress, 1963.

Catalog of Copyright Entries, Cumulative series. Motion Pictures, 1960–1969. Washington, D.C.: Copyright Office, Library of Congress, 1971.

Catalog of Copyright Entries: Motion Pictures. Washington, D.C.: Copyright Office, Library of Congress. Semi-annual.

Crist, Judith. *TV Guide to the Movies.* New York: Popular Library, 1974.

d'Arcy, Susan. *The Films of Elizabeth Taylor.* New York: Confucian Press and Beaufort Books, 1982.

———. *A Title Guide to the Talkies: A Comprehensive Listing of 16,000 Feature-length Films from October 1926 until December 1963.* Metuchen, N.J.: Scarecrow Press, 1965.

Dimmitt, Richard B. *An Actor Guide to the Talkies: A Comprehensive Listing of 8,000 Feature-length Films from January 1949 until December 1964.* Metuchen, N.J.: Scarecrow Press, 1967.

Eames, John Douglas. *The MGM Story: The Complete History of Over Fifty Roaring Years.* New York: Crown Publishers, 1975.

Eyles, Allen. *The Marx Brothers: Their World of Comedy.* London: Tantivy Press, 1966 (in association with A. Zwemmer Limited, London, and A. S. Barnes & Co., New Jersey).

———. *John Wayne* (memorial edition). South Brunswick and New York: A. S. Barnes & Co., London: Tantivy Press, 1976, 1979.

Film Daily Year Book of Motion Pictures. New York: 1918–1970.

Filmfacts. Los Angeles: University of Southern California, 1958– (semi-monthly).

Films in Review. New York: National Board of Review of Motion Pictures, 1950– (monthly; bi-monthly in summer).

The Films of ——— series. (A continuing series of pictorial biography/filmography books on individual film stars.) Secaucus, N.J.: Citadel Press.

Fitzgerald, Michael. *Universal Pictures: A Panoramic History in Words, Pictures and Filmographies.* New Rochelle, N.Y.: Arlington House, 1977.

Frank, Alan. *Sinatra.* New York: Leon Amiel Publisher, 1978.

Gifford, Denis (ed.). *The British Film Catalog, 1895–1970: A Reference Guide.* New York: McGraw-Hill, 1973.

Goldstein, Norm, and the Associated Press. *Henry Fonda: A Celebration of the Life and Work of One of America's Most Beloved Actors.* New York: Holt, Rinehart and Winston, 1982.

Green, Stanley, and Burt Goldblatt. *Starring Fred Astaire.* New York: Dodd, Mead & Co., 1973.

317

Griffith, Richard, and Arthur Mayer. *The Movies.* New York: Simon and Schuster, 1983.

Halliwell, Leslie. *The Filmgoer's Book of Quotes.* New Rochelle, N.Y.: Arlington House, 1974.

———. *The Filmgoer's Companion.* 7th ed. New York: Charles Scribner's Sons, 1983.

———. *Halliwell's Film Guide.* 4th ed. New York: Charles Scribner's Sons, 1983.

Haun, Harry. *The Movie Quote Book.* New York: Harper & Row, 1983.

Herman, Gary, and David Downing. *Jane Fonda: All-American Anti-Heroine.* New York: Quick Fox, 1980.

Hirschhorn, Clive. *The Universal Story.* New York: Crown Publishers, 1983.

Hirschhorn, Clive (ed.). *The Warner Bros. Story: The Complete History of Hollywood's Greatest Studio.* New York: Crown Publishers, 1979.

Hope, Bob, and Bob Thomas. *The Road to Hollywood: My 40-Year Love Affair with the Movies.* Garden City, N.Y.: Doubleday & Co., 1977.

Hurwood, Bernhardt J. *Burt Reynolds.* New York: Quick Fox, 1979.

International Film Guide, ed. Peter Cowie. New York: A. S. Barnes Co., 1964— (annual).

International Motion Picture Almanac. New York: Quigley Publications, 1929— (annual).

Jensen, Paul M. *Boris Karloff and His Films.* South Brunswick: A. S. Barnes, 1974.

Jewell, Richard B. *The RKO Story,* ed. Vernon Harbin. New York: Arlington House, 1982.

Johnstone, Iain. *The Man with No Name: A Biography of Clint Eastwood.* New York: Morrow Quill, 1981.

Kael, Pauline. *5001 Nights at the Movies.* New York: Holt, Rinehart and Winston, 1982.

Katz, Ephraim. *The Film Encyclopedia.* New York: G. P. Putnam's Sons, 1979.

Lichter, Paul. *Elvis in Hollywood.* New York: Simon and Schuster, 1975.

Maltin, Leonard (ed.). *TV Movies* (1983–84 edition). New York: A Signet Book/New American Library, 1982.

Marill, Alvin H. *Movies Made for TV.* Westport, Conn.: Arlington House, 1980.

McClure, Arthur F., Ken D. Jones, and Alfred E. Twomey. *The Films of James Stewart.* New York: Castle Books (published by arrangement with A. S. Barnes), 1970.

Michael, Paul (ed.). *The American Movies Reference Book: The Sound Era.* Englewood Cliffs, N.J.: Prentice-Hall, Inc., 1969.

———, and James Robert Parish (eds.). *The Great American Movie Book.* Englewood Cliffs, N.J.: Prentice-Hall, Inc., 1980.

Morley, Sheridan. *Marlene Dietrich.* New York: McGraw-Hill Book Co., 1977.

The New York Times Film Reviews. New York: Arno Press, 1913— (continuing volumes).

Parish, James Robert, and Alvin H. Marill. *The Cinema of Edward G. Robinson.* Cranbury, N.J.: A. S. Barnes and Co., 1972.

Pickard, R. A. E. *Dictionary of 1,000 Best Films.* New York: Association Press, 1971.

Pyramid Illustrated History of the Movies series. (A series of pictorial biography/filmography books on individual film stars.) New York: Pyramid Publications.

Sadoul, Georges. *Dictionary of Films.* Berkeley: University of California Press, 1972.

Scheuer, Steven H. (ed.). *Movies on TV* (1984–85 edition). New York: Bantam Books, 1983.

Schickel, Richard. *Cary Grant: A Celebration.* Boston: Little, Brown and Co., 1983.

Screen World, ed. John Willis. New York: Crown, 1949— (annual).

Sennett, Ted (ed.). *The Movie Buff's Book.* New York: Bonanza Books, 1975.

Shale, Richard (comp.). *Academy Awards: An Ungar Reference Index.* 2nd edition. New York: Frederick Ungar Publishing Co., 1983.

Shipman, David. *The Great Movie Stars: The Golden Years.* New York: Hill & Wang, 1981.

Simonet, Thomas, with the editors of the Associated Press. *Oscar: A Pictorial History of the Academy Awards.* Chicago: Contemporary Books, 1983.

Smith, John M., and Tim Cawkwell (eds.). *The World Encyclopedia of the Film.* New York: World Publishing, 1972.

Thomas, Tony, and Aubrey Solomon. *The Films of 20th Century–Fox.* Secaucus, N.J.: Citadel Press, 1979.

Trigg, Harry D., and Yolanda L. Trigg. *The Compleat Motion Picture Quiz Book.* Garden City, N.Y.: Doubleday, 1975.

———. *Son of the Compleat Motion Picture Quiz Book.* Garden City, N.Y.: Doubleday, 1977.

TV Feature Film Source Book. New York: Broadcast Information Bureau, Inc. (annual).

Variety. New York: Variety, Inc., 1905— (weekly film reviews).

Vermilye, Jerry. *Burt Lancaster: A Pictorial History of His Films.* New York: Falcon Enterprises, 1971.

Weaver, John T. (comp.). *Forty Years of Screen Credits, 1929–1969.* Metuchen, N.J.: Scarecrow Press, 1970 (2 vols.).

———. *Twenty Years of Silents, 1908–1928.* Metuchen, N.J.: Scarecrow Press, 1971.

Index

75¢